"No other guide has as much to offer . . . these books are a pleasure to read."

Gene Shalit on the *Today Show*

★ ★ ★ ★ ★ (5 star rating) "Crisply written and remarkably personable. Cleverly organized so you can pluck out the minutest fact in a moment. Satisfyingly thorough."

Réalités

"The information they offer is up-to-date, crisply presented but far from exhaustive, the judgments knowledgeable but not opinionated."

New York Times

"The individual volumes are compact, the prose succinct, and the coverage up-to-date and knowledgeable . . . The format is portable and the index admirably detailed."

John Barkham Syndicate

"They contain an amount of information that is truly staggering, besides being surprisingly current."

Detroit News

"These guides address themselves to the needs of the modern traveler demanding precise, qualitative information . . . Up-beat, slick, and well-put-together."

Dallas Morning News

". . . Attractive to look at, refreshingly easy to read, and generously packed with information."

Miami Herald

"These guides are as good as any published, and much better than most."

Louisville (Kentucky) *Times*

Stephen Birnbaum Travel Guides

Canada
Caribbean, Bermuda, and the Bahamas
Disneyland
Europe
Europe for Business Travelers
Florida for Free
France
Great Britain
Hawaii
Ireland
Italy
Mexico
South America
Spain and Portugal
United States
USA for Business Travelers
Walt Disney World

CONTRIBUTING EDITORS

Jeremy Addis
Tom Barrington
Isabel Bass
Cathy Beason
Susan Braybrooke
Karen Cure
Jeff Davidson
James Davie
Frank Dawes
Michael Dervan
Robin Dewhurst
Bonnie Dudley Edwards
Owen Edwards
Roger Edwards
R. D. Eno
Ronald Faux
Trevor Fishlock
Bryn Frank
Emily Greenspan
Ida Grehan
Susan Grossman
David Hanly
Ben Harte
David Hoyle
Paul Hughes
Peter Johnston
John B. Keane
Michael Leech
Nancy Lyon
Carole Martin
Robin Mead
Ann Millman
Daphne Pochin Mould
Ann Nugent
David Owen
Alan Reeve-Jones
Allan Rokach
Peter Rubie
Anne-Marie Sheehan
George Stacpoole
Gillian Thomas
Kathy Wade
Paul Wade
Marcia Wallace
Leslie Westbrook
Sean White
David Wickers
Diane Wood
Carol Wright
Kristin Zimmerman

COVER
Robert Anthony

SYMBOLS
Gloria McKeown

MAP
Andrew Mudryk

A Stephen Birnbaum Travel Guide

Birnbaum's GREAT BRITAIN 1990

Stephen Birnbaum
Alexandra Mayes Birnbaum
EDITORS

Lois Spritzer
EXECUTIVE EDITOR

Laura Brengelman
Managing Editor

Kristin Moehlmann
John Storch
Senior Editors

Catherine J. Langevin
Julie Quick
Associate Editors

Stephen Coleman
Assistant Editor

HOUGHTON MIFFLIN COMPANY / BOSTON 1989

For Grace and Herbert Mayes, who set the standards and style

This book is published by special arrangement
with Eric Lasher and Maureen Lasher.

ISBN: 0-395-51148-8
ISSN: 0749-2561 (Stephen Birnbaum Travel Guides)
ISSN: 0896-8683 (Great Britain)

Printed in the United States of America

WP 10 9 8 7 6 5 4 3 2 1

Contents

GETTING READY TO GO

All the practical travel data you need to plan your vacation down to the final detail.

When and How to Go

Preparing

On the Road

Sources and Resources

PERSPECTIVES

A cultural and historical survey of Britain's past and present, its people, politics, and heritage.

THE CITIES

Thorough, qualitative guides to each of the 21 cities most often visited by vacationers and businesspeople. Each section, a comprehensive report of the city's most appealing attractions and amenities, is designed to be used on the spot. Directions and recommendations are immediately accessible because each city guide is presented in consistent form.

DIVERSIONS

A selective guide to more than 15 active and cerebral vacations, including the places to pursue them where the quality of experience is likely to be highest.

For the Body

For the Mind

For the Experience

DIRECTIONS

The most spectacular routes and roads; most arresting natural wonders; and most magnificent castles, manor houses, and gardens — all organized into 19 specific driving tours.

A Word from the Editor

This guide to Great Britain was the initial volume of an entirely new phase in our travel guide series. Whereas our first half-dozen guides covered rather broad geographic areas, this in-depth examination of Great Britain was our first guide to treat the world's most popular travel destinations in considerably greater detail than is possible in an "area" book. Our guidebooks to France, Italy, and Spain and Portugal have continued this direction.

Such treatment in depth only reflects an increasingly obvious trend among travelers — the frequent return to favorite foreign travel spots. Once upon a time, even dedicated travelers would visit distant parts of the world no more than once in a lifetime — usually as part of that fabled old Grand Tour. But greater numbers of would-be sojourners are now availing themselves of the increasingly easy opportunity to visit favored parts of the world over and over again.

So where once it was routine to say that you'd "seen" a particular country after a very superficial, once-over-lightly encounter, the more perceptive travelers of today recognize that it's entirely possible to have only skimmed the surface of a specific travel destination even after having visited that place more than a dozen times. Similarly, repeated visits to a single site permit true exploration of special interests, whether they be sporting, artistic, or intellectual in nature. Multiple visits also allow an ongoing relationship with foreign citizens sharing similar interests, and an opportunity to discover and appreciate different perspectives on a single field of endeavor.

For those of us who spent the last several years working out the special system under which we present information in this series, the luxury of being able to devote nearly as much space as we like to just a trio of countries is as close to guidebook heaven as any of us expects to come. But clearly, this is not the first guide to what were once called the British Isles — one suspects that guides of one sort or another have existed at least since Caesar's legions crossed the English Channel. Guides to Great Britain have existed literally for centuries, so a traveler might logically ask why a new one is necessary at this particular moment.

Our answer is that the nature of travel to Great Britain, and the travelers who now routinely make the trip, have changed dramatically of late. For 2,000 years or so, travel to and through Britain was an extremely elaborate undertaking, one that required extensive advance planning. Even as recently as the 1950s, a person who had actually been to England, Scotland, or Wales could dine out on his or her experiences for years, since such adventures were quite extraordinary and usually the province of the privileged alone.

With the advent of jet air travel in the late 1950s, however, and of increased-capacity, wide-body aircraft during the 1960s, travel to and around once distant lands became extremely common. In fact, in more than two decades of nearly unending inflation, airfares may be the only commodity in the world that has actually gone down in price. And as a result, international travel is now well within the budgets of mere mortals.

Attitudes, as well as costs, have changed significantly in the last couple of decades. Beginning with the so-called flower children of the 1960s, international travel lost much of its aura of mystery. Whereas their parents might have chosen a superficial sampling of London, these young people, motivated as much by wildly inexpensive "youth fares" as by the inclination to see the world, simply picked up and settled in various parts of Europe for an indefinite stay. While living as inexpensively as possible, they usually adopted with great gusto the local lifestyle and generally immersed themselves in things European.

Thus began an explosion of travel to and in Great Britain. And over the years, the development of inexpensive charter flights and packages fueled and sharpened the new American interest in and appetite for more extensive exploration.

Now, as we enter the 1990s, those same flower children who were in the forefront of the modern travel revolution have undeniably aged. While it may be impolite to point out that they are probably well into their untrustworthy 30s (and some their 40s), their original zeal for travel remains undiminished. For them it's hardly news that the way to get to Dover is to head toward Canterbury, make a right, and then wait for white cliffs to appear. Such experienced and knowledgeable travelers have decided precisely where they want to go and are more often searching for ideas and insights to expand their already sophisticated travel consciousness. And — reverting to their youthful instincts and habits — they are after a deeper understanding and fuller assimilation of the British milieu. Typically, they visit single countries (or even cities) several times and may actually do so more than once in a single year.

Obviously, any new guidebook to Great Britain must keep pace with and answer the real needs of today's travelers. That's why we've tried to create a guide that's specifically organized, written, and edited for this more demanding modern audience, one for whom qualitative information is infinitely more desirable than mere quantities of unappraised data. We think that this book and the other guides in our series represent a new generation of travel guides, one that is especially responsive to modern needs and interests.

For years, dating back as far as Herr Baedeker, travel guides have tended to be encyclopedic, seemingly much more concerned with demonstrating expertise in geography and history than in any analysis of the sorts of things that more frequently concern a typical tourist. But today, when it is hardly necessary to tell a traveler where London is located, it's hard to justify devoting endless pages to historical perspectives. As suggested earlier, it's not impossible that the guidebook reader may have been to Great Britain nearly as often as the guidebook editor, so it becomes the responsibility of that editor to provide new perceptions and to suggest new directions to make the guide genuinely valuable.

That's exactly what we've tried to do in our series. I think you'll notice a different, more contemporary tone to the text, as well as an organization and focus that are distinctive and more functional. And even a random examination of what follows will demonstrate a substantial departure from the standard guidebook orientation, for we've not only attempted to provide information of a different sort but we've also tried to present it in a context that makes it particularly accessible.

Needless to say, it's difficult to decide precisely what to include in a guidebook of this size — and what to omit. Early on, we realized that giving up the encyclopedic approach precluded the inclusion of every single route and restaurant, which actually helped define our overall editorial focus. Similarly, when we discussed the possibility of presenting certain information in other than strict geographical order, we found that the new format enabled us to arrange data in a way that we feel best answers the questions travelers typically ask.

Large numbers of specific questions have provided the real editorial skeleton for this book. The volume of mail I regularly receive seems to emphasize that modern travelers want very precise information, so we've tried to address these needs and have organized our material in the most responsive way possible. Readers who want to know the best restaurants in Cardiff or the best golf courses in Scotland will have no trouble whatever finding that data in this guide.

Travel guides are, understandably, reflections of personal taste, and putting one's name on a title page obviously puts one's preferences on the line. But I think I ought to amplify just what "personal" means. I do not believe in the sort of personal guidebook that's a palpable misrepresentation on its face. It is, for example, hardly possible for any single travel writer to visit thousands of restaurants (and nearly as many hotels) in any given year and provide accurate appraisals of each one. And even if it were possible for one human being to survive such an itinerary, it would of necessity have to be done at a dead sprint and the perceptions derived therefrom would probably be less valid than those of any other intelligent individual visiting the same establishments. It is, therefore, impossible (especially in an annually revised and updated guidebook *series* such as we offer) to have only one person provide all the data on the entire world.

I also happen to think that such individual orientation is of substantially less value to readers. Visiting a single hotel for just one night or eating one hasty meal in a given restaurant hardly equips anyone to provide appraisals that are of more than passing interest. No amount of doggedly alliterative or oppressively onomatopoeic text can camouflage a technique that is specious on its face. We have therefore chosen what I like to describe as the "thee and me" approach to restaurant and hotel evaluation and, to a somewhat more limited degree, to the sites and sights we have included in the other sections of our text. What this really reflects is personal sampling tempered by intelligent counsel from informed local sources, and these additional friends-of-the-editor are almost always residents of the city and/or area about which they have been consulted.

Despite the presence of several editors, a considerable number of writers and researchers, and numerous insightful local correspondents, very precise editing and tailoring keep our text fiercely subjective. So what follows is purposely designed to be the gospel according to Birnbaum, and it represents as much of my own taste and insight as is humanly possible. It is probable, therefore, that if you like your cities genteel and your mountainsides uncrowded, prefer small hotels with personality to huge high-rise anonymities, and can't tolerate fresh fish that's been relentlessly overcooked, we're likely to have a long and meaningful relationship. Readers with dissimilar tastes may be less enraptured.

I also should point out something about the person to whom this guidebook is directed. Above all, he or she is a "visitor." This means that such elements as restaurants have been specifically picked to provide the visitor with a representative, enlightening, stimulating, and above all, pleasant experience. Since so many extraneous considerations can affect the reception and service accorded a regular restaurant patron, our choices can in no way be construed as a definitive guide to resident dining. We think we've listed all the best places, in various price ranges, but they were chosen with a visitor's viewpoint in mind.

Other evidence of how we've tried to tailor our text to reflect changing travel habits is most apparent in the section we call DIVERSIONS. Where once it was common for travelers to spend a foreign visit nailed to a single spot, the emphasis today is more likely to be directed toward pursuing some active enterprise or special interest while seeing the surrounding countryside. So we've selected every activity we could reasonably evaluate and organized the material in a way that is especially accessible to activists of either an athletic or cerebral bent. It is no longer necessary, therefore, to wade through a pound or two of extraneous prose just to find the very best crafts shop or the quaintest country inn within a reasonable radius of your destination.

If there is a single thing that best characterizes the revolution in and evolution of current holiday habits, it is that most travelers now consider travel a right rather than a privilege. Travel today translates as the enthusiastic desire to sample all of the world's opportunities, to find that elusive quality of experience that is not only enriching but comfortable. For that reason, we've tried to make what follows not only helpful and enlightening but the sort of welcome companion of which every traveler dreams.

Finally, I should point out that every good travel guide is a living enterprise; that is, no part of this text is cast in bronze. In our annual revisions, we refine, expand, and further hone all our material to serve your travel needs even better. To this end, no contribution is of greater value to us than your personal reaction to what we have written, as well as information reflecting your own experiences while using the book. We earnestly and enthusiastically solicit your comments on this book and your opinions and perceptions about places you have recently visited. In this way, we will be able to provide the most current information — including the actual experiences of the travel public — and to make those experiences more readily available to others. So please write to us at 60 E. 42nd St., New York, NY 10165.

We sincerely hope to hear from you.

STEPHEN BIRNBAUM

How to Use This Guide

A great deal of care has gone into the organization of this guidebook, and we believe it represents a real breakthrough in the presentation of travel material. Our aim has been to create a new, more modern generation of travel books and to make this guide the most useful and practical travel tool available today.

Our text is divided into five basic sections, in order to best present information on every possible aspect of a vacation in Britain. This organization itself should alert you to the vast and varied opportunities available as well as indicating all the specific, detailed data necessary to plan a trip. You won't find much of the conventional "quaint villages and beautiful scenery" text in this guide; we've chosen instead to use the available space for more useful and practical information. Prospective itineraries tend to speak for themselves, and with so many diverse travel opportunities, we feel our main job is to explain them and to provide the basic information — how, when, where, how much, and what's best — to allow you to make the most intelligent choices possible.

What follows is a brief summary of the five sections of this book and what you can expect to find in each. We believe that you will find both your travel planning and en route enjoyment enhanced by having this book at your side.

GETTING READY TO GO

This compendium of practical travel facts is a sort of know-it-all companion that provides all the precise information necessary to go about creating a trip. There are entries on more than 30 separate topics, including how to travel, what preparations to make before leaving, what to expect in the different countries, what the trip is likely to cost, and how to avoid problems. The individual entries are specific, realistic, and cost-oriented.

We expect that you will use this section most in the course of planning your trip, for its ideas and suggestions are intended to facilitate the often confusing planning period. Entries are intentionally concise in an effort to get directly to the meat of the matter. This information is further augmented by extensive lists of sources for more specialized information and some suggestions for obtaining travel information on your own.

PERSPECTIVES

Any visit to an unfamiliar destination is enhanced and enriched by understanding the cultural and historical heritage of that area. We have therefore provided just such an introduction to Great Britain, its past and present, people, architecture, literature, music and dance, and food and drink.

THE CITIES

Individual reports on the 20 cities most visited by tourists and businesspeople have been researched primarily by professional journalists on their own turf. Useful at the planning stage, THE CITIES is really designed to be taken along and used on the spot. Each report offers a short-stay guide to its city within a consistent format: an essay, introducing the city as a historic entity and a contemporary place to live; *At-a-Glance,* a site-by-site survey of the most important (and sometimes most eclectic) sights to see and things to do; *Sources and Resources,* a concise listing of pertinent tourist information, meant to answer a myriad of potentially pressing questions as they arise — from the address of the tourist office to where to find the best night spot, see a show, play golf, or get a taxi; and *Best in Town,* our cost-and-quality choices of the best places to eat and sleep on a variety of budgets.

DIVERSIONS

This very selective guide is designed to help travelers find the very best places in which to pursue a wide range of physical and cerebral activities without having to wade through endless pages of unrelated text. With a list of more than 15 theme vacations — for the body, the mind, and the experience — DIVERSIONS provides a guide to the special places where the quality of experience is likely to be highest. Whether you seek golf courses or fishing boats, luxurious hotels or atmospheric pubs, each entry is the equivalent of a comprehensive checklist of the absolute best in Britain.

DIRECTIONS

Here are 15 itineraries that range all across the countryside, along the most beautiful routes and roads, past the most spectacular natural wonders, through the most historic cities and countryside. DIRECTIONS is the only section of this book to be organized geographically, and its itineraries cover the touring highlights of England, Scotland, and Wales in short, independent journeys of 3 to 5 days' duration. Itineraries within each country can be connected for longer trips or used individually for short, intensive explorations.

Each entry includes a guide to sightseeing highlights; a cost-and-quality guide to accommodations and food along the road (small inns, castle hotels, hospitable farms, country and off-the-main-road discoveries); and suggestions for activities.

Although each section of the book has a distinct format and a special function, they have all been designed to be used together to provide a complete package of travel information. To use this book to full advantage, take a few minutes to read the table of contents and random entries in each section to get an idea of how it all fits together.

Pick and choose information from the different sections. Assume, for example, that you have always wanted to take that typically English vacation, a walking tour through rural England, but you never really knew how to organize it or where to go. Turn first to the hiking section of GETTING READY TO GO, as well as the chapters on planning a trip, accommodations, and climate and clothes. These short, informative entries provide plenty of practical information. But where to go? Turn next to DIRECTIONS. Perhaps you choose to walk the 100-odd-mile Cotswold Way. Your trip will certainly begin and end in London, and for a complete rundown on that fabulous city, you should read the London chapter of THE CITIES. Finally, turn to DIVERSIONS to peruse the chapters on sports, hotels, antiques, and other activities in which you are interested to make sure you don't miss anything in the neighborhood.

In other words, the sections of this book are building blocks to help you put together the best possible trip. Use them selectively as a tool, a source of ideas, a reference work for accurate facts, and a guide to the best buys, the most exciting sights, the most pleasant accommodations, the tastiest food — the best travel experiences that you can have.

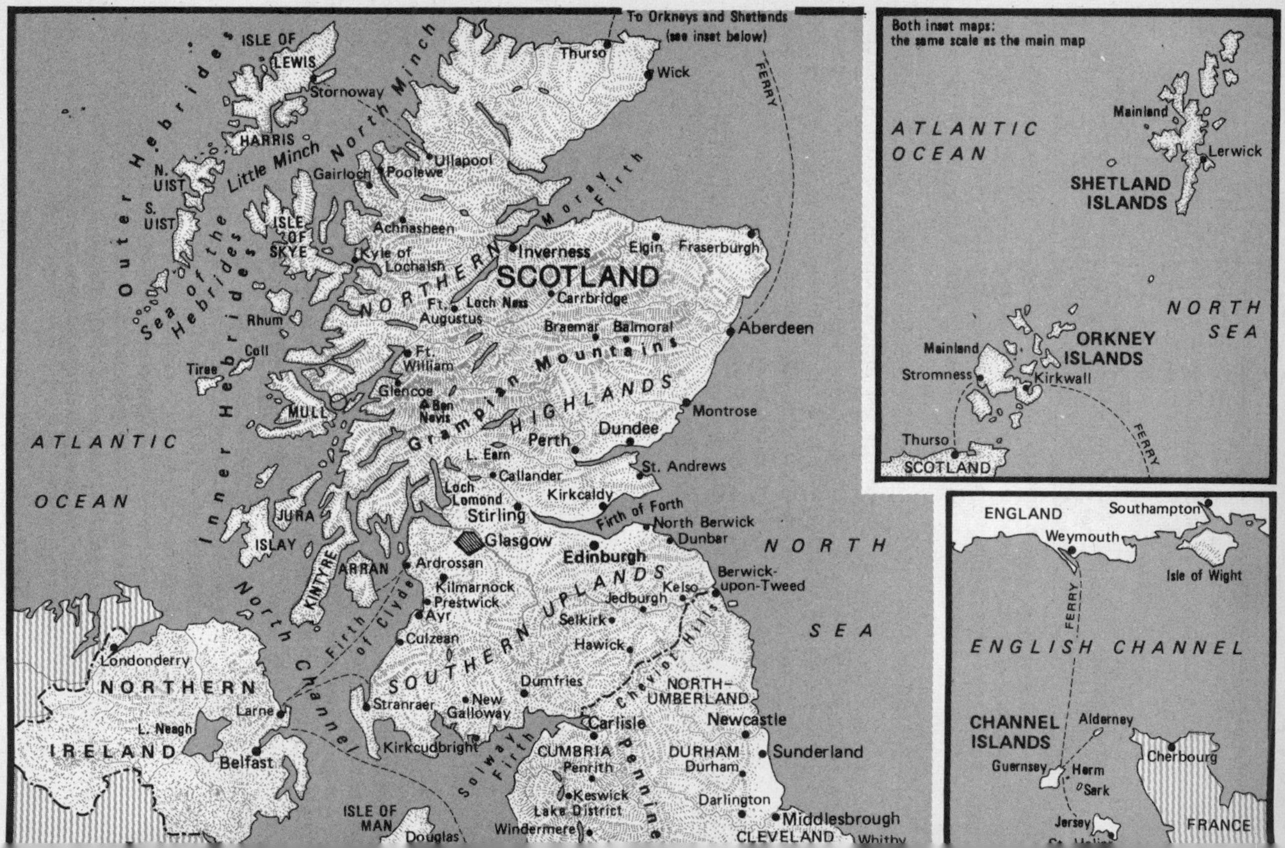

To Orkneys and Shetlands (see inset below)
FERRY
ISLE OF LEWIS
Stornoway
HARRIS
N. UIST
S. UIST
Outer Hebrides
Little Minch
North Minch
Sea of the Hebrides
Inner Hebrides
ISLE OF SKYE
Rhum
Coll
Tiree
MULL
JURA
ISLAY
KINTYRE
ARRAN
Thurso
Wick
Ullapool
Gairloch
Poolewe
Achnasheen
Kyle of Lochalsh
Moray Firth
Inverness
Elgin
Fraserburgh
SCOTLAND
NORTHERN
Ft. Augustus
Loch Ness
Carrbridge
Braemar
Balmoral
Aberdeen
Ft. William
Glencoe
Ben Nevis
Grampian Mountains
HIGHLANDS
Montrose
Perth
Dundee
L. Earn
Callander
St. Andrews
Loch Lomond
Kirkcaldy
Stirling
Firth of Forth
North Berwick
Dunbar
Glasgow
Edinburgh
ATLANTIC OCEAN
NORTH SEA
Ardrossan
Kilmarnock
Prestwick
Ayr
Culzean
SOUTHERN UPLANDS
Kelso
Berwick-upon-Tweed
Jedburgh
Selkirk
Hawick
Cheviot Hills
Firth of Clyde
North Channel
Dumfries
Stranraer
New Galloway
Kirkcudbright
Solway Firth
NORTH-UMBERLAND
Newcastle
Sunderland
Carlisle
CUMBRIA
Penrith
Keswick
Lake District
Windermere
Pennines
DURHAM
Durham
Darlington
Middlesbrough
CLEVELAND
Whitby
Londonderry
NORTHERN IRELAND
L. Neagh
Larne
Belfast
ISLE OF MAN
Douglas
Both inset maps:
the same scale as the main map
ATLANTIC OCEAN
Mainland
Lerwick
SHETLAND ISLANDS
NORTH SEA
ORKNEY ISLANDS
Mainland
Stromness
Kirkwall
FERRY
Thurso
SCOTLAND
ENGLAND
Southampton
Weymouth
Isle of Wight
FERRY
ENGLISH CHANNEL
CHANNEL ISLANDS
Alderney
Guernsey
Herm
Sark
Jersey
Cherbourg
FRANCE

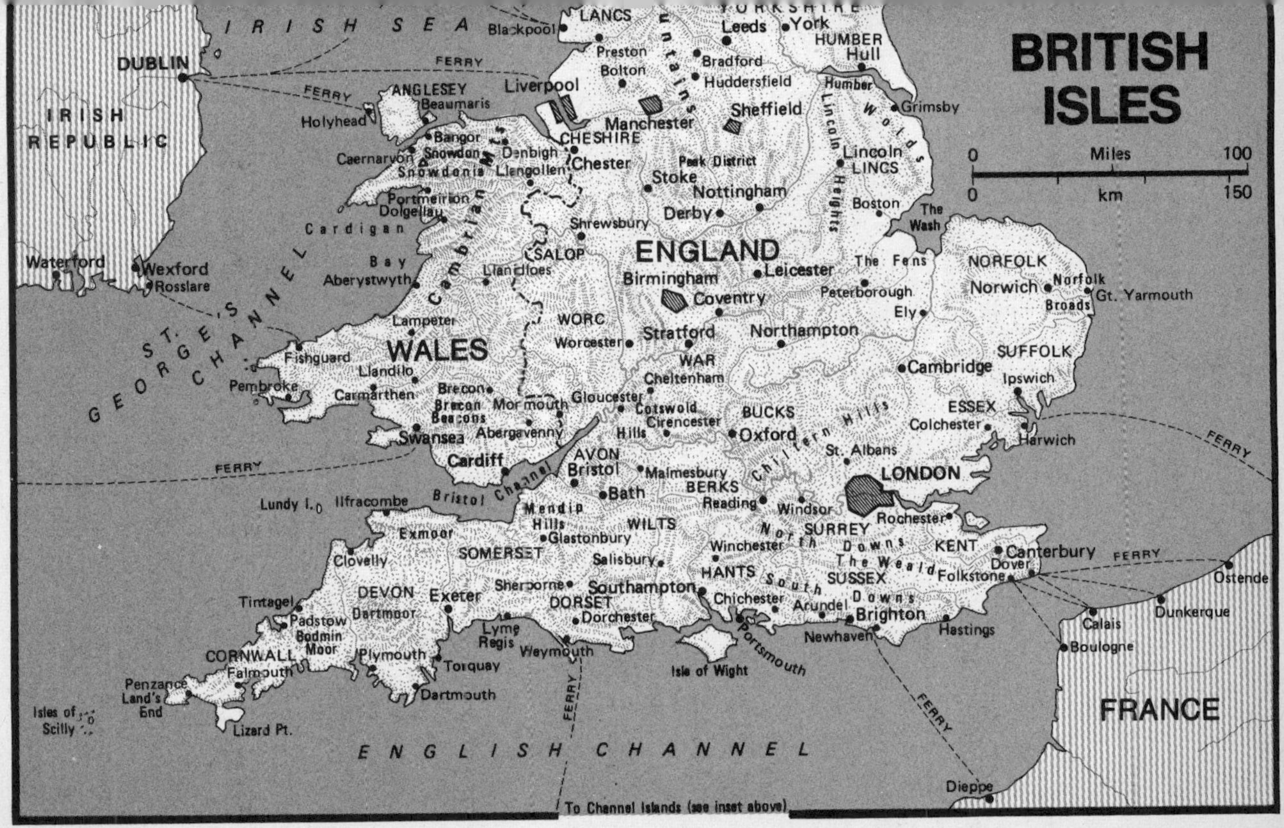
BRITISH
ISLES
Miles
0
100
km
0
150
IRISH SEA
ST. GEORGE'S CHANNEL
ENGLISH CHANNEL
Bristol Channel
Cardigan Bay
IRISH REPUBLIC
DUBLIN
Waterford
Wexford
Rosslare
FERRY
ANGLESEY
Beaumaris
Holyhead
Bangor
Caernarvon
Snowdon
Snowdonia
Denbigh
Llangollen
Portmeirion
Dolgellau
Aberystwyth
Cambrian Mts
Llanidloes
Lampeter
WALES
Fishguard
Llandilo
Pembroke
Carmarthen
Brecon
Brecon Beacons
Monmouth
Abergavenny
Swansea
Cardiff
Blackpool
LANCS
Preston
Bolton
Liverpool
Manchester
CHESHIRE
Chester
YORKSHIRE
Leeds
York
Bradford
Huddersfield
Sheffield
HUMBER
Hull
Humber
Grimsby
Wolds
Lincoln Heights
Lincoln
LINCS
Boston
The Wash
Peak District
Stoke
Nottingham
Derby
Shrewsbury
SALOP
ENGLAND
Leicester
Birmingham
Coventry
The Fens
Peterborough
Ely
NORFOLK
Norwich
Norfolk Broads
Gt. Yarmouth
WORC
Worcester
Stratford
WAR
Northampton
SUFFOLK
Cambridge
Ipswich
Cheltenham
Gloucester
Cotswold Hills
Cirencester
BUCKS
Oxford
Chiltern Hills
ESSEX
Colchester
Harwich
St. Albans
LONDON
AVON
Bristol
Malmesbury
Bath
BERKS
Reading
Windsor
Rochester
Lundy I.
Ilfracombe
Mendip Hills
Glastonbury
WILTS
North Downs
SURREY
KENT
Canterbury
Dover
Folkstone
Exmoor
Clovelly
SOMERSET
Salisbury
Winchester
The Weald
HANTS
South Downs
SUSSEX
Sherborne
Southampton
DORSET
Dorchester
Chichester
Arundel
Brighton
Hastings
Newhaven
Tintagel
DEVON
Dartmoor
Exeter
Padstow
Bodmin Moor
Lyme Regis
Weymouth
Portsmouth
Isle of Wight
CORNWALL
Falmouth
Plymouth
Torquay
Dartmouth
Penzance
Land's End
Isles of Scilly
Lizard Pt.
To Channel Islands (see inset above)
FRANCE
Ostende
Dunkerque
Calais
Boulogne
Dieppe

GETTING READY TO GO

When and How to Go

What's Where

Great Britain — principally the countries of England, Scotland, and Wales — lies in the North Atlantic immediately off the northwest coast of France, separated from the Continent by the English Channel, the Strait of Dover, and the North Sea. Dover, on the southeastern tip of England, and Calais, in the northwestern corner of France, are only 25 miles from each other. Included in the scattering of tiny islands nearby that are part of Great Britain are the Channel Islands, the Isle of Man, and the Orkneys, Hebrides, and Shetlands off the coast of Scotland.

These three countries (together with Northern Ireland, covered in *Birnbaum's Ireland*) are the major entities that compose the United Kingdom, which covers a total of some 94,000 square miles and has a population of 56 million. Physically, England dominates its island, covering well over half the area that extends from the southern coast along the English Channel to Newcastle and the Border Country at the edge of the Scottish Lowlands. Wales abuts England on the west, projecting into St. George's Channel, which separates it from Ireland. Scotland forms the northern third of the island.

ENGLAND

Broadly speaking, England is rather flat in the south and east and mountainous in the north and west. Like all generalizations, however, this one has a striking exception — the southwestern peninsula, which is dominated by two large, wild moorlands, Dartmoor and Exmoor. The more southerly, Dartmoor, is a granite-based, desolately beautiful region of rugged hills and bogs; the gentler Exmoor is a heather-clad plateau creased by deep valleys cradling tiny, whitewashed villages.

The south and east of England are low-lying lands crossed by ranges of rolling hills and gently sculpted by slow-moving rivers. The highlands here are paradoxically called "the Downs." Much of the area is now "Londonized," but it's still possible to find delightfully rural and provincial towns.

To the north, the lowlands merge imperceptibly with the midlands, a mining and manufacturing region centered in Birmingham. The landscape, although often marred by industry, is subtly attractive, especially around the Derbyshire hills and the Peak National Park. The midlands slope away to East Anglia, a large tract of flat and beautifully still countryside whose citizens retain a strong regional identity. At the coast the land slips quietly into the North Sea; here, there are many deserted beaches, peaceful wildlife reserves, and the famous Norfolk Broads, haunt of farmers and fishermen.

The great backbone of England is the Pennine chain, a mountain range that runs north from South Yorkshire to Scotland. Although surrounded on three sides by heavily populated cities, the Pennines remain remarkably wild. To the west is the Lake District, where volcanic rocks and glaciation have combined to produce a stunning landscape of mountains, woods, and lakes. England's highest mountain, Scafell Pike (3,210 feet), dominates this region, loved by hikers and campers. In the east, the North York Moors, cut by fast-flowing rivers into a patchwork of dales, reach northward to a very secluded corner of England, Northumberland. No industry has ever penetrated here, or large town ever grown up. Even the roads hesitate; only river valleys like Coquetdale penetrate the heart of this wild region.

SCOTLAND

Emerging without fuss from northern England, the Lowlands of Scotland are a region of broad valleys and rounded green hills, quite unlike the stereotypical image of wild Scotland, but no less beautiful. Farther north, however, above the Highland Boundary Fault, that wilder Scotland begins; here are the towering mountains, cascading waterfalls, and deep forests. The fault runs right through Loch Lomond, Britain's largest stretch of inland water, which is dotted with tiny islands. In the east are the Trossachs ("the Bristly Country"), an uncivilized thicket of birch, oak, and heather crowding Lochs Katrine, Archay, and Venachar. This is the heart of the romantic region immortalized by Sir Walter Scott in his long poem "The Lady of the Lake."

Farther north are the Highlands proper, running from Fort William, in the southwest, up the coast to Cape Wrath, at the northern tip of the country, and to the Highlands capital, Inverness. The mountains here are often snowcapped in summer, and the rivers have sliced through the harsh slopes to feed dense pine forests. In the far west the Atlantic has taken charge and carved long, rugged fingers from the land, leaving sea-filled valleys between them. Off that remote coast are the Hebrides — a group of rocky islands flung into the ocean. Largest and perhaps best of all is Skye, "the Faery Isle," a volcanic wonderland softened by rivers and mists, still serenely remote from the present century and breathtakingly beautiful.

WALES

Wales is ringed with huge castles, reminders of those days when its people were kept under strict control by their nervous English neighbors. The need for caution has gone, but the sense of difference between the two countries persists and is reflected by the striking change of scenery as you cross from the green and gentle hills and valleys of England to the rugged mountains of Wales.

The Brecon Beacons in the south and center are the heart of wild Wales. Their highest point, Pen-y-Fan, is 2,906 feet above sea level, and the roads give up long before reaching its heights. But pony trails abound, and it's very easy to forget civilization as you trot along past slate outcroppings and thundering waterfalls. The Pembrokeshire coast in southwestern Wales is considered the most spectacular in all Britain. Here, the mountains rush headlong into the sea, only sometimes softened by sandy bays and quiet creeks. The industrial towns of Port Talbot, Swansea, and Cardiff are located along the southern coast. The people there make their living refining and shipping the coal and iron ore carved from mines in the steep and isolated valleys of South Wales.

Wales is at its most dramatic, however, in the far northwest. Here, its highest mountains, the Snowdon Massif (3,560 feet at the highest peak), look down over range upon range of slate-brown mountains and valleys, rushing rivers, and huge lakes. The drive from Barmouth on the coast inland to Dolgellau follows the Maddach Estuary, with the Cader Idris mountains towering above you. This experience will banish forever any misconceptions you may have of Britain's (especially Wales's) countryside being flat and tame. But to experience the full beauty of Snowdonia, you must leave the car and walk or climb in the mountains themselves.

When to Go

The decision of exactly when to travel may be imposed by the requirements of a rigid schedule; more likely there will be some choice, and the decision will be made on the basis of precisely what you want to see and do, what activities or events you'd like to attend, and what suits your mood.

There really isn't a "best" time to visit Great Britain. For North Americans as well as Europeans, the period from mid-May to mid-September has long been — and remains — the peak travel period, traditionally the most popular vacation time. As far as weather is concerned, Great Britain is at its best then: cooler and more comfortable than many other less temperate destinations on the Continent, where heat waves are inevitable. It is important to emphasize, however, that Britain is hardly a single-season destination; more and more vacationers who have a choice are enjoying the substantial advantages of off-season travel. Though many of the lesser tourist attractions may close for the winter — around December through Easter in rural areas — the major ones remain open and tend to be less crowded, as are the cities. During the off-season, British life proceeds at its most natural pace, and a lively social and cultural season flourishes. What's more, travel is generally less expensive.

For some, the most convincing argument in favor of off-season travel is the economic one. Airfares drop and hotel rates go down in the late fall, winter, and spring. Relatively inexpensive package tours become available, and the independent traveler can go farther on less, too. Europe is not like the Caribbean, where high season and low season are precisely defined and rates drop automatically on a particular date. But many British hotels reduce rates during the off-season, and savings can be as much as 20%, unless high-season rates prevail because of an important local event — such as the *Chelsea Flower Show* in London and the *Edinburgh International Festival.* Particularly in the larger cities, major trade shows or conferences held at the time of your visit are also sure to affect the availability of discounts. Although many smaller guesthouses and bed-and-breakfast establishments may close off-season in response to reduced demand, there are still plenty of alternatives, and cut-rate "minibreak" packages for stays of more than 1 night, especially over weekends (when business travelers traditionally go home), are more common.

It should be noted that what the travel industry refers to as shoulder seasons — the 1½ to 2 months preceding and following the peak summer months — are often sought out because they offer reasonably good weather and smaller crowds. But be warned that high-season prices can still prevail for many popular destinations during these periods.

CLIMATE: Most people prefer traveling when the weather is most likely to be fair. To the extent that it is mild, with no beastly hot summers or bone-chilling winters, the weather in Great Britain makes it a multi-seasonal destination. Warm currents from the Gulf Stream soften extremes of temperature and even provide the surprising touch of palm trees in western Scottish gardens.

The climate is hardly perfect, however, and has been a topic of conversation among the British for centuries. For one thing, visitors probably won't come home with a suntan, even in summer. There is a reason for those renowned peaches-and-cream complexions: moisture, meaning frequently overcast skies or even rain. Beautiful mornings often turn into dreary afternoons and vice versa. Because of westerly winds off the Atlantic, there is heavier rainfall in the west than in the east, but because of the island's relatively small size, it has fairly uniform temperatures throughout. Summers are cool and winters are mild. Remember, too, that although winters are not the marrow-freezing scourges of the northern US and Canada, they are damp, and central heating is usually inadequate by North American standards. Mid-October through mid-March is admittedly not an ideal time for touring the British countryside, though it may be suitable for those with special outdoor interests, such as fishing and hunting in Scotland. (*Please note that although temperatures in Great Britain are currently recorded on both the Fahrenheit and Celsius scales, as part of the metric conversion process, for purposes of clarity we shall discuss climate and temperature using the more familiar Fahrenheit scale.*)

London is very much a city of the temperate zone. With occasional exceptions, summers tend to be moderately warm, with few days above 75F, and winters moderately cold, with few days dropping below 30F. Spring and autumn tend to be comfortable, requiring little more than a sweater or light overcoat. Umbrellas or raincoats are necessary, but legends about London's incessant rain are exaggerations. London has less rainfall than Rome, which is known as a sunny city. London simply spreads its rain over more days: not hard, driving rains, but showers.

Though changeability is typical of British weather, it is safe to say that the farther north and west you go from the heart of England, the wetter it gets. This is because winds moving from west to east drop their rain over Britain's mountainous backbone and proceed over the rest of the country a good deal drier. In Edinburgh, a day with no rain is a rarity, even in summer. Mists are not unknown either, and when the wind blows, put millstones in your shoes. On the other hand, temperatures usually don't go below freezing in winter or over 70F in summer. A mackintosh (with a zip-in lining) that fits over everything you own is a recommended survival kit. In the Scottish Highlands and islands, chances for good weather are best from May through September. Cloudy days are a matter of course, but this doesn't mean the sun never shines. Days get very long in the summer, and there is daylight well into the June night in northernmost areas.

The chart below lists seasonal temperature ranges for specific cities at different times of the year to help in planning.

AVERAGE TEMPERATURES (in °F)

	January	*April*	*July*	*October*
Aberdeen, Scot.	36–43	40–49	52–63	43–54
Bath, Eng.	38–49	40–54	54–67	41–52
Brighton, Eng.	43–49	43–56	58–65	47–52
Bristol, Eng.	40–47	38–56	54–67	45–58
Cambridge, Eng.	34–43	40–58	54–72	43–59
Cardiff, Wales	36–45	41–56	54–68	47–58
Chester, Eng.	38–45	40–54	54–68	45–58
Dover, Eng.	36–45	43–54	58–68	49–59
Edinburgh, Scot.	34–43	40–52	52–65	45–54
Glasgow, Scot.	34–41	40–54	52–67	43–56
Inverness, Scot.	34–43	38–50	52–63	43–54
Liverpool, Eng.	36–45	41–52	56–67	47–56
London, Eng.	36–45	40–56	56–72	45–58
Manchester, Eng.	36–43	41–56	56–70	45–58
Oxford, Eng.	34–45	41–58	54–72	45–58
Stratford-upon-Avon, Eng.	36–47	41–56	52–76	43–59
York, Eng.	36–47	41–54	58–72	43–56

SPECIAL EVENTS: Many travelers want to time a trip to coincide with a special event. The highlight of a sports lover's trip may be attendance at the British championship of his or her game. For a music lover, a concert in a great cathedral may be a thrilling experience and much more memorable than seeing the same church on a sightseeing itinerary. A folklore festival can bring nearly forgotten traditions alive or underscore their continuing significance in modern life.

In Great Britain, the calendar of such events is a busy one from spring through fall, but there is still much happening in winter. In London, the cultural season proceeds at a pace that few other cities can match. Museums and galleries mount special exhibitions; ballet and opera take place at *Covent Garden* and the *Coliseum;* concerts are held at the *Royal Festival Hall, Royal Albert Hall,* and *Queen Elizabeth Hall;* and the theater is everywhere. Other cities and towns, whatever their size, promote their own smaller cultural programs. Winter is also the height of the soccer and rugby season throughout the island, and curling and other winter sports are under way in Scotland. The grouse-hunting season in the Highlands opens in mid-August and runs to mid-December.

The events below are the major ones, listed according to the months in which they usually occur. Since there can be variations from year to year, check with the British Tourist Authority for the exact dates of anything you don't want to miss and for current schedules of fairs, festivals, and other events. It is also possible to book tickets in advance for many of the major festivals through several agents in the US (see "Theater and Special Event Tickets," *Sources and Resources*).

February

Crufts Dog Show: Over 8,000 canine entries, representing over 100 breeds, compete for the "Best of Show" title. London.

March

Oxford vs. Cambridge Boat Race: Since 1829 and Cambridge is ahead. The big event in intercollegiate rowing takes place on the Thames between Putney and Mortlake and can be viewed from the towpath. London.

April

Shakespeare Theatre Season: Shakespeare's plays performed in the town of his birth by the outstanding cast of the *Royal Shakespeare Company.* Season runs until January. Stratford-upon-Avon.

Grand National Steeplechase: Britain's most famous jumping race, with all Britain betting on the outcome. *Aintree Racecourse,* Liverpool.

Whitbread Badminton Horse Trials: Major event on the equestrian calendar: dressage, cross-country, and show jumping. Badminton.

London Marathon: A marathon run through the streets of London, including historic areas.

May

Chichester Festival Theatre Season: Drama festival with 4 plays running for 5 months at the modern *Festival Theatre.* After London, a good place to catch top-flight British productions. Chichester.

Pitlochry Festival Theatre Season: Five months of summer theater in a Scottish Highlands resort. Pitlochry.

Brighton International Festival: Music and theater plus fringe events and fireworks in this seaside resort. Some performances in the *Royal Pavilion.* Brighton.

Chelsea Flower Show: Acres of flowers, shrubs, trees, and flower arrangements on the grounds of the Royal Hospital. London.

Bath International Festival: Two weeks of choral and chamber music, art and film shows, lectures, garden and walking tours, throughout the lovely Georgian town. Bath.

Glyndebourne Festival Opera: Over 2 months of first-rate opera. At intermission, festival-goers in formal dress dine in the restaurant or picnic on the lawn. Near Lewes, East Sussex.

June

The Derby: The world's most famous horse race, run since 1780, when Lord Derby didn't make the winner's circle but did win the toss of a coin that gave his name to the event. *Epsom Racecourse,* Epsom, Surrey.

Robert Burns Festival: An annual celebration of Scotland's national bard, including drama, music, competitions, and other events. Ayr.

Aldeburgh Festival: A 2-week music festival founded by composer Benjamin Britten. Concerts — the emphasis is on new works — take place in churches, houses, and in the *Snape Maltings Concert Hall.* Aldeburgh.

Greenwich Festival: Wide-ranging arts festival with music, drama, films, and exhibitions. Greenwich, London.

York Mystery Plays and Festival of the Arts: Re-creation of 14th-century mystery plays by 200 citizens of York. Held every 4 years (the next one is in 1992), it takes place over 3 weeks and includes an arts festival with symphony and chamber concerts, choral music, and ballet. York.

Trooping the Colour: The queen's official birthday parade and the pageantry of royal Britain at its best; from Buckingham Palace to Horse Guards Parade and back. London.

Royal Ascot: Part of the London season, the June meeting at *Ascot Racecourse* is attended by the queen, members of the royal family, and high society in hats. Ascot.

Wimbledon Lawn Tennis Championships: The world's most prestigious tennis tournament and another part of the London season — there's a royal box at Centre Court — lasting 2 full weeks. *All-England Lawn Tennis and Croquet Club,* London.

July

Henley Royal Regatta: The international rowing regatta is watched from grandstands or from boats moored to the riverbank; another fashionable gathering on the London social calendar. Henley-on-Thames.

City of London Festival: Orchestral, choral, and chamber concerts, as well as arts events, in St. Paul's Cathedral, the Mansion House, the Guildhall, the Tower of London, and other spots within the square-mile City of London. London.

Llangollen International Musical Eisteddfod: An extremely popular festival of choral and folk music and dancing that draws more than 10,000 competitors from over 30 countries yearly to a small town in Wales. *Eisteddfod* is the Welsh word for "session," and this one is 5 days of song in foreign tongues and colorful national costumes. Llangollen.

British Grand Prix: Top British motor race. Held in even-numbered years at *Brands Hatch,* near Dartford, and in odd-numbered years at *Silverstone,* near Towcester.

British Open Golf Championship: One of golf's great moments. First held in 1860, it now moves annually from course to prestigious course in England and the sport's ancestral home in Scotland.

August

Royal National Eisteddfod of Wales: A celebration of the Welsh language and culture and the chance to hear some of those famous Welsh choirs; arts and crafts contests and the "chairing of the bard" ceremony. Site alternates yearly between North and South Wales.

Cowes Week: International sailing festival at the headquarters of British yachting. Cowes, Isle of Wight.

Three Choirs Festival: Founded in the early 18th century and considered Europe's oldest continuing music festival — in this case, choral music. Held annually in rotation in the three cathedral cities of Gloucester, Worcester, and Hereford.

Edinburgh International Festival: Several festivals crammed into one 3-week extravaganza: the main music and drama festival with performing artists of world renown; the *Festival Fringe,* shoestring to big-time productions by amateurs and professionals who come at their own expense; the *Military Tattoo,* a nightly concert spectacle of pipe bands and kilted regiments on the esplanade of Edinburgh Castle; the *Film Festival;* the *Jazz Festival;* the *Book Festival.* Edinburgh.

September

Farnborough Air Show: Biennial aerospace exhibition and display of flying held in even-numbered years. Farnborough.

Braemar Royal Highland Gathering: Best known of the Scottish Highland gatherings takes place near Balmoral Castle under the patronage of the queen; piping, dancing, and Highland games such as "putting the stone" and "tossing the caber." Braemar.

October

Horse of the Year Show: A major show-jumping event. Wembley, London.

Swansea Festival Fringe: A multimedia arts festival comprising exhibitions, poetry, theater, cabaret and music. Swansea, West Glamorgan.

State Opening of Parliament: The queen rides in the Irish State Coach from Buckingham Palace to the Houses of Parliament; the ceremony inside is closed to the public, but the procession can be viewed en route. (It is sometimes held at the beginning of November.) London.

November

London to Brighton Veteran Car Run. Antique cars leave Hyde Park Corner, London, and drive to Brighton to celebrate the turn-of-the-century day on which a law requiring cars to be preceded by a man waving a red flag was dropped from the books.

Lord Mayor's Procession: Colorful parade of the newly elected lord mayor, who rides from the Guildhall to the Royal Courts of Justice in an antique, horse-drawn carriage attended by costumed bodyguards. London.

Traveling by Plane

The air space between North America and Europe is the most heavily trafficked in the world. It is served by dozens of airlines, almost all of which sell seats at a variety of prices under widely different terms. You probably will spend more for your airfare than for any other single item in your travel budget. In order to take advantage of the low fares offered by both scheduled airlines and charter companies, you should know what kinds of flights are available, the rules and regulations pertaining to air travel, and the options for special packages.

SCHEDULED FLIGHTS: Among the dozens of airlines serving Europe from the United States, those offering regularly scheduled flights to Great Britain, many on a daily basis, are Aer Lingus, Air France, Air India, Air New Zealand International,

Alitalia, American, British Airways, Continental, Delta, El Al, Kuwait Airways, Icelandair, Northwest, Pan American, TWA, and Virgin Atlantic.

Gateways – At present, direct flights to Great Britain depart from Anchorage, Atlanta, Boston, Charlotte, Chicago, Cincinnati, Dallas/Ft. Worth, Denver, Detroit, Honolulu, Houston, Los Angeles, Miami, Minneapolis/St. Paul, Newark, New York, Orlando, Philadelphia, Pittsburgh, St. Louis, San Diego, San Francisco, Seattle, Tampa, and Washington, DC. As defined here, a direct flight is one requiring no change of plane between the starting and terminating cities, though the flight may not necessarily be nonstop. Airlines also consider flights involving a change of plane as direct flights as long as the flight number remains the same. With direct flights thus defined, many more US cities serve as gateways to Britain. Scheduled flights from the US land at London's Heathrow and Gatwick airports, at Manchester Airport, and at Glasgow's Prestwick Airport.

Tickets – When traveling on one of the many regularly scheduled flights, a full-fare ticket provides maximum travel flexibility (although at considerable expense), because tickets are sold on an open reservation system. This means that there are no advance booking requirements — a prospective passenger can buy a ticket for a flight right up to the minute of takeoff, if seats are available. If your ticket is for a round trip, you can make the return reservation any time you wish — months before you leave or the day before you return. Assuming your passport and other paperwork required for stays in Great Britain of longer than 3 months are in order, you can remain at your destination for as long as you like. (Tickets are generally good for a year and can be renewed if not used.) You can also cancel your flight at any time without penalty. However, while it is true that this category of ticket can be purchased at the last minute, it is advisable to reserve well in advance during popular travel periods and around holiday times.

No matter what kind of ticket you buy, it is wise to reconfirm that you will be using your return reservations. If you do not call the airline to let them know you will be using the return leg of your reservation, they (or their computer) may assume you are not coming and automatically cancel your seat. Some airlines no longer require reconfirmations; others recommend that you confirm your return flight 48 or 72 hours in advance. Although policies vary from carrier to carrier, reconfirmation is advisable for *all* international flights.

Fares – Airfares are changing so rapidly that even experts find it difficult to keep up with them. This volatile situation is due to a number of factors, including airline deregulation, high labor costs, and vastly increased competition. Before the Airline Deregulation Act of 1978, US airlines had no choice but to set their rates and routes within the guidelines of the Civil Aeronautics Board (CAB), and they could compete for passengers only by offering better service than their competitors. With the loosening of controls (and the elimination of the CAB), airlines are now engaged in a far more intense competition relating to price and schedule, which has opened the door to a wide range of discount fares and promotional offers. Intensifying the competitive atmosphere has been the creation of several new carriers offering fewer frills and far lower prices. These carriers seem to appear and disappear with dismaying regularity. They have, however, served to drive down fares and make older, more entrenched carriers aware that they are in a genuine competition for travelers' dollars.

Perhaps the most common misconception about fares on scheduled airlines is that the cost of the ticket determines how much service will be provided on the flight. This is true only to a certain extent. A far more realistic rule of thumb is that the less you pay for your ticket, the more restrictions and qualifications you're likely to be subject to before getting on the plane (as well as after you get off). These qualifying aspects relate to the months in which you travel, how far in advance you purchase your ticket, the minimum and maximum amount of time you may or must remain abroad, your willingness to make up your mind concerning a return date at the time of booking — and your ability to stick to that decision. It is not uncommon for passengers sitting side by side on the same wide-body jet to have paid fares varying by hundreds of dollars, and all too often the traveler paying more would have been equally willing to accept the terms regulating the far less expensive ticket. The ticket you buy will fall into one of several fare categories currently being offered by scheduled carriers flying between the US and Great Britain.

In general, the great variety of fares can be reduced to three basic categories: first class, business or executive class, and tourist, also called economy or coach. In addition, Advance Purchase Excursion (APEX) and "Eurosaver" fares offer savings with certain restrictions.

In a class by itself is the *Concorde,* the supersonic jet developed jointly by France and Great Britain, which cruises at a speed of 1,350 miles an hour (twice the speed of sound) and makes transatlantic crossings in half the time of conventional, subsonic jets. British Airways flies from Miami, Washington, DC, and New York to London. Additionally, at the time of this writing, British Airways was negotiating with Enterprise Airlines to bring Boston passengers to New York for the *Concorde* service. Service is "single" class (with champagne and caviar all the way), and the fare is expensive, about 20% more than a first class ticket on a subsonic aircraft. Some discounts have been offered, but time is the real gift of the *Concorde.*

A first class ticket is your admission to the special section of the aircraft with larger seats, more legroom, sleeperette seating on some wide-body aircraft, better food (or more elaborately served food, in any case), free drinks and headsets for movies and music channels, and, above all, personal attention. First class fares are about double those of full-fare economy, although both first class passengers and people paying economy fares are entitled to reserve seats and are sold tickets on an open reservation system. If you're planning to visit other countries besides Great Britain, you may stop in any number of cities en route to your most distant destination, provided that certain set, but generous, maximum mileage limits are respected.

Note: In March 1989, British Airways introduced its newly redesigned first class service, which cost about $40 million. At press time, it was still trying out individual videocassette players for first class passengers, giving each passenger choices from a video library of 50 films.

Not too long ago, there were only two classes of air travel, first class and all the rest, usually called economy or tourist. But because passengers paying full economy fares traveled in the same compartment as passengers flying for considerably less on various promotional or discount fares, the airlines introduced special services to compensate those paying the full price. Thus, business class came into being, one of the most successful recent airline innovations. At first, business class passengers were merely curtained off from the other economy passengers. Now a separate cabin, or cabins, usually toward the front of the plane, is the norm. While standards of comfort and service are not as high as in first class, they represent a considerable improvement over conditions in the rear of the plane, with roomier seats, more leg and shoulder space between passengers, and fewer seats abreast. Free liquor and headphones, a choice of meal entrées, and a separate counter for speedier check-in are other inducements. As in first class, you travel on any scheduled flight you wish, you may buy a one-way or round-trip ticket, and the ticket is valid for a year. There are no minimum or maximum stay requirements, no advance booking requirements, and no cancellation penalties, and the fare allows the same unlimited free stopover privileges as first class. Airlines have their own names for their business class service — such as Club World on British Airways, Clipper Class on Pan American, and Ambassador Class on TWA.

The terms of the coach or economy fare may vary slightly from airline to airline, and, in fact, from time to time airlines may be selling more than one type of economy fare.

Economy fares sell for substantially less than business fares, the savings effected by limited frills and stopovers. Coach or economy passengers sit more snugly, as many as 10 in a single row on a wide-body jet, behind the first class and business class sections, and receive standard meal service. Alcoholic drinks are not free, nor are the headsets (except on British Airways, which does offer these services free of charge). If there are two economy fares on the books, one (often called "regular economy") may still offer unlimited stopovers. The other, less expensive (often called "special economy"), may limit stopovers to one or two, with a charge (typically $25) for each one. Like first class passengers, however, passengers paying the full coach fare are subject to none of the restrictions that are usually attached to less expensive discount fares. There are no advance booking requirements, no minimum stay requirements, and no cancellation penalties. Tickets are sold on an open reservation system: They can be bought for a flight up to the minute of takeoff, if seats are available, and if the ticket is round-trip, the return reservation can be made at any time — months before you leave or the day before you return. Both first class and coach tickets are generally good for a year, after which they can be renewed if not used, and if you ultimately decide not to fly at all, your money will be refunded. The cost of economy and business class tickets does not vary much in the course of the year between the US and Great Britain, though on some transatlantic routes they vary in price from a basic (low-season) price in effect most of the year to a peak (high-season) price in summer.

Excursion and other discount fares are the airlines' equivalent of a special sale, and usually apply to round-trip bookings. These fares generally differ according to the season and the number of travel days permitted. They are only a bit less flexible than economy tickets and are, therefore, useful for both business travelers and tourists. Most round-trip excursion tickets include strict minimum and maximum stay requirements and reservations can be changed only within the prescribed time limits, so don't count on extending a ticket beyond the prescribed time of return or staying less time than required. Different airlines may have different regulations concerning the number of stopovers permitted, and sometimes excursion fares are less expensive during midweek. Needless to say, these reduced-rate seats are most limited at busy times such as holidays, when full-fare coach seats sell more quickly than usual. Passengers fortunate enough to get a discount or excursion fare ticket sit with the coach passengers and, for all intents and purposes, are indistinguishable from them. They receive all the same basic services, even though they have paid anywhere between 30% and 55% less for the trip. Obviously, it's wise to make plans early enough to qualify for the least expensive transportation.

These discount or excursion fares may masquerade under a variety of names and may vary from city to city, but they invariably have strings attached. In the past, some excursion fares to Great Britain came unencumbered by advance booking requirements and cancellation penalties, permitted one stopover (but not a free one) in each direction, and had "open jaws," meaning that you could fly to one city and depart from another, arranging and paying for your own transportation between the two. Excursion fares of this type do not, at present, exist on flights between the US and Great Britain, but a newer and less expensive type of excursion, the APEX, or Advance Purchase Excursion, does. As with traditional excursion fares, passengers sit with and receive the same basic services as coach or economy passengers, even though they may have paid up to 50% less for their seats. In return, they are subject to certain restrictions. The ticket is usually good for a minimum of 7 days abroad and a maximum, currently, in the case of tickets to Great Britain, of 3 months; as its name implies, it must be "ticketed" or paid for in its entirety 21 days before departure. The drawback to the APEX is that it penalizes travelers who change their minds — and travel plans. The return reservation must be made at the time of the original ticketing, and if for some reason you change your schedule while abroad, you pay a penalty of $100 or 10% of the ticket value, whichever is greater, as long as you travel within the validity period of your ticket. But, if you change your return to a date less than the minimum stay or more than the maximum stay, the difference between the round-trip APEX fare and the full round-trip coach rate will have to be paid. There is also a penalty of $125 or more for canceling or changing a reservation *before* travel begins — check the specific penalty in effect when you purchase your ticket — so careful planning is imperative. No stopovers are allowed, but it is possible to create an open-jaw effect by buying an APEX on a split-ticket basis, e.g., flying to London and returning from Glasgow (or some other city). The total price would be half the price of an APEX to London plus half the price of an APEX to Glasgow. APEX tickets to Great Britain are sold at basic and peak rates (peak season is around May through September) and may include surcharges for weekend flights.

There is also a Winter or Super APEX, which may go under different names for different carriers. Similar to the regular APEX fare, it costs slightly less, but is more restrictive. It is available only for off-peak winter travel and is limited to a stay of between 7 and 21 days. Advance purchase is still required (currently, 30 days prior to travel), and ticketing must be completed within 48 hours of reservation. The fare is nonrefundable except in cases of death or hospitalization.

Another type of fare that is sometimes available is the youth fare. At present, most airlines flying to Great Britain are using a form of APEX fare as a youth fare for those through age 24. The maximum stay is extended to a year, and the return booking must be left open. Seats can be reserved no more than 3 days before departure, and tickets must be purchased when the reservation is made. The return is booked from Great Britain in the same manner, no more than 3 days before flight time. There is no cancellation penalty, but the fare is subject to availability, so it may be difficult to book a return during peak travel periods.

Standby fares, at one time the rock-bottom tickets to Europe, have become elusive, but bargain hunters should not hesitate to ask if such fares exist. While the definition of standby varies from airline to airline, it generally means that you make yourself available to buy a ticket for a flight (usually no sooner than the day of departure), then literally stand by on the chance that a seat will be free. Once aboard, however, you have the same meal service and frills (or lack of them) enjoyed by others in the economy compartment.

Something else to check is the possibility of qualifying for a GIT (group inclusive travel) fare. The requirements vary as to number of travel days, number of stopovers permitted, and number of passengers required for a group. (The last can be as few as two full fares.) The group fare always requires that a specified dollar amount of ground arrangements be purchased, in advance, along with the ticket. The required number of participants varies, the required time abroad varies, and the actual fares also vary, but the cost will be spelled out in brochures distributed by the tour operators handling the ground arrangements. In the past, GIT fares typically were among the least expensive in the fare schedules of the established carriers, and, although very attractive group fares may still appear from time to time, with the advent of discount fares, group fares have all but disappeared from some air routes or their price tags have become the equivalent of the other discount fares. Travelers perusing brochures on group package tours to Great Britain will find that, in almost all cases, the applicable airfare given as a sample (to be added to the price of the land package to obtain the total tour price) is an APEX fare, the same discount fare available to the independent traveler.

Travelers looking for the least expensive possible airfares should, finally, scan the travel pages of their local newspapers for announcements of special promotional fares. Most major airlines offer their most attractive special fares to encourage travel in slow seasons and to inaugurate and publicize new routes. Even if none of the above conditions apply, prospective passengers can be fairly sure that the number of discount seats per flight at the lowest price is strictly limited or that the fare offering includes a set expiration date — which means it's absolutely necessary to move fast to enjoy the lowest possible price. Unfortunately, special offers come and go quickly and may not be available precisely when you want to travel.

The leading carriers now also offer a bonus system to frequent travelers. After the first 10,000 miles, for example, you might receive a first class ticket for the coach fare; after another 10,000 miles you might receive a discount on your next ticket purchase. The value of the bonuses continues to increase as you log more miles.

Given the frequency with which the airfare picture changes, it is more than possible that by the time you are ready to fly, the foregoing discussion may be somewhat out of date. That's why it is always wise to comparison shop, and to do a good job of it, it's necessary to read the business and travel sections of your newspaper regularly and to call the airlines that serve your destination from your most convenient gateway. The potential savings are well worth the effort.

Ask about discount or promotional fares and about any conditions that might restrict booking, payment, cancellation, and changes in plans. Check the prices from other cities. A special rate may be offered in a nearby city but not in yours, and it may be enough of a bargain to warrant your leaving from that city. If you have a flexible schedule, investigate standby fares. But remember that, depending on your departure point, they may not work out to be the rock-bottom price. Ask if there is a difference in price for midweek travel versus weekend travel, or if there is a further discount for traveling early in the morning or late at night. Also be sure to investigate package deals, which are offered by virtually every airline. They may include a car rental, accommodations, and/or dining or sightseeing features in addition to the basic airfare, and the combined cost of packaged elements is usually considerably less than the cost of the exact same elements when purchased separately.

When you're satisfied that you've found the lowest possible price for which you can conveniently qualify (you may have to call the airline more than once, because different clerks have been known to quote different prices), make your booking. Then, to protect yourself against fare increases, purchase and pay for your ticket as soon as possible after you've received a confirmed reservation. Airlines will generally honor their tickets, even if the operative price at the time of your flight is higher than the price you paid; if fares go up between the time you *reserve* a flight and the time you *pay* for it, you likely will be out of luck. Finally, with excursion or discount fares, it is important to remember that when a reservation clerk says that you must purchase a ticket by a specific date, this is an absolute deadline. Miss the deadline and the airline may automatically cancel your reservation without telling you.

If you don't have the time and patience to investigate personally all possible air departures and connections for a proposed trip, remember that a travel agent can be of inestimable help. A good agent should have all the information on which flights go where and when and which categories of tickets are available on each. Most have computerized reservation links with the major carriers, so a seat can be reserved and confirmed in minutes. An increasing number of agents also possess fare-comparison computer programs, so they are often very reliable sources of detailed competitive price data. (For more information, see *How to Use a Travel Agent.*)

Low-Fare Airlines – In today's economic climate, increasingly, the stimulus for special fares is the appearance of airlines associated with bargain rates. These tend to be smaller carriers that can offer more for less because of lower overhead, uncomplicated route networks, and other limitations in their service. On these airlines, all seats on any given flight generally sell for the same price, which is somewhat below the lowest discount fare offered by the larger, more established airlines, even after they cut their fares in response. This gap, too, may disappear in the future, but it is important to note that tickets offered by the smaller airlines specializing in low-cost travel frequently are not subject to the same restrictions as the lowest-priced ticket offered by the more established carriers. They may not require advance purchase or minimum and maximum stays, may involve no cancellation penalties, may be available one-way or round-trip, and may, for all intents and purposes, resemble the competition's high-priced full-fare coach. But never assume this until you know it's so.

London has always been a favorite destination for low-fare airlines. Sadly, more than one of the carriers that flew that route are no longer in existence. At press time, the only airline offering a relatively low fare was Virgin Atlantic (phone: 212-242-1330 in New York City; 800-862-8621 elsewhere in the US), which flies from Newark to London's Gatwick Airport daily year-round and from Miami to Gatwick at least four times a week. The airline sells tickets in several fare categories, including business or "upper" class, economy, APEX, and a nonrefundable variation on standby called the Late Saver fare, which must be purchased not more than 7 days prior to travel. At the time of this writing, the Late Saver fare to London was $199 one-way in off-season, rising to $289 one-way during the summer.

In a class by itself is Icelandair (formerly Icelandic), which has always been a scheduled airline and has long been known as a good source of low-cost flights to Europe (it flies from New York, Boston, Baltimore/Washington, Orlando, and Chicago via Reykjavik, Iceland, to Glasgow and London). The airline sells tickets in a variety of categories, from unrestricted economy fares to a sort of standby "3 days before" fare (which functions just like the youth fares described above but has no age requirement). For reservations and tickets, contact a travel agent or Icelandair (phone: 212-967-8888 in New York City; 800-223-5500 elsewhere in the US).

Intra-European Fares – The cost of the round trip across the Atlantic is not the only expense to be considered. Flights between European cities, when booked in Europe, can be quite expensive. Great Britain has been a leader in pushing for liberalization of intra-European airfares, however, and a great variety of bargain fares are available out of London, especially to Amsterdam and Dublin, and to a lesser extent to Belgium, Luxembourg, West Germany, and Switzerland. Less impressive discounted transatlantic and intra-European airfare packages between other countries may also be offered.

Recent Common Market moves toward airline deregulation are expected to lead gradually to a greater variety of budget fares. In the meantime, however, the high cost of European fares can be avoided by careful use of stopover rights on the higher-priced transatlantic tickets — first class, business class, and full-fare economy. If your ticket doesn't allow stopovers, ask about excursion fares such as PEX, Super PEX — the same as APEX and Super APEX, but without the advance purchase rules and therefore more expensive — APEX for round trips, and Eurobudget for one-way trips. If the restrictions that govern them allow you to use them (frequently the minimum stay requirement means staying over for at least one Saturday night), you may save as much as 35% to 50% off full-fare economy. Note that these fares, which once could be bought only after arrival in Europe, are now sold in the US and can be bought before departure.

Still another recourse is the London bucket shop (see "Bucket Shops," below), a flourishing industry given the British government's pro-consumer stance on airline competition. The majority of London bucket shops (discount travel agencies selling air tickets for less than the amount at which the airlines themselves would sell them) specialize in long-haul routes to the Middle East, Asia, Australia, Africa, and Latin America, rather than in flights within Britain or to other European countries. But many of the long-haul flights make interim stops in Europe, and discounted tickets for the intra-European segments are sometimes available. Bucket shops can be found most easily in London's Sunday newspapers: *The Sunday Times, The Sunday Express, The Observer,* and *The Sunday Telegraph* are best. *Time Out,* a weekly magazine with information on what's going on in London, also features discount air travel information. Although there is no longer anything shady about bucket shops (even some British travel agency chains deal in discounted tickets), it is always wise to be wary. Visit the premises in person, if possible. If you are quoted a price that is dramatically lower than that of other local bucket shop offerings to the same city, consider the possibility that the ticket may be stolen and may not be honored by the airline. A reputable bucket shop should allow you to pay a deposit; don't pay in full until you have checked with the carrier that a confirmed reservation exists in your name and until the ticket is in hand.

It is not easy to inform yourself about stopover possibilities by talking to most airline reservations clerks. More than likely, an inquiry concerning any projected trip will prompt the reply that a particular route is nonstop aboard the carrier in question, thereby precluding stopovers completely, or that the carrier does not fly to all the places you want to visit. It may take additional inquiries, perhaps with the aid of a travel agent, to determine the full range of options regarding stopover privileges. Travelers might be able to squeeze in visits to Dublin and Belfast on a first class ticket to Edinburgh, for instance; Paris and Nice can be visited on a ticket to London; and London might be only the first of many free European stopovers possible on a one-way or round-trip ticket to Eastern Europe or points beyond. The airline that flies you on the first leg of your trip across the Atlantic issues the ticket, though you may have to use several different airlines in order to complete your journey. First class tickets are valid for a full year, so there's no rush.

Taxes and Other Fees – Travelers who have shopped for the best possible flight at the lowest possible price should be warned that a number of extras will be added to that price and collected by the airline or travel agent who issues the ticket. In addition to the $3 International Air Transportation Tax — a tax paid by all passengers flying from the US to a foreign destination — there is now a $10 US Federal Inspection Fee levied on all air and cruise passengers who arrive in the US from outside North America (those arriving from Canada, Mexico, the Caribbean, and US territories are exempt). Payable at the time a round-trip or incoming ticket is purchased, it combines a $5 customs inspection fee and a $5 immigration inspection fee, both instituted in 1986 to finance additional inspectors to reduce delays at gateways.

Still another fee is charged by some airlines to cover more stringent security procedures, prompted by recent terrorist incidents. The 8% federal US Transportation Tax, which applies to travel within the US, is already included in advertised fares and in the prices quoted by reservations clerks. It does not apply to passengers flying between US cities en route to a foreign destination unless the trip includes a stopover of more than 12 hours at a US point. Someone flying from Los Angeles to New York and stopping in New York for more than 12 hours before boarding a flight to Europe, for instance, would pay the 8% tax on the domestic portion of the trip.

Reservations – Those who don't have the time and patience to investigate personally all possible air departures and connections for a proposed trip should consult a travel agent. When making reservations through a travel agent, ask the agent to give the airline your home phone number, as well as a daytime business number. All too often the agent uses the agency number as the official contact for changes in flight plans. During the winter, especially, weather conditions hundreds or even thousands of miles away can wreak havoc with flight schedules. Aircraft are constantly in use, and a plane delayed in the Orient or on the West Coast can miss its flight from the East Coast the next morning. The airlines are fairly reliable about getting this sort of information to passengers if they can reach them; diligence does little good at 6 PM if the airline has only the agency or an office number.

If you look at the back of your ticket, you'll see the need for reconfirmation of return flights stated explicitly. Some (though increasingly fewer) return reservations from international destinations are automatically canceled after a required reconfirmation period (typically 72 hours) has passed — even if you have a confirmed, fully paid ticket in hand. Reconfirmation is not required on domestic flights, but it is still a good idea, allowing you to make sure in plenty of time that the airline did not slip up in entering your original reservation, or in registering any changes you may have made since, and that it has your seat reservation request in the computer. Every travel agent or airline ticket office should give each passenger a reminder to reconfirm flights, but this seldom happens, so the responsibility rests with the traveler. Don't be lulled into a false sense of security by the "OK" on your ticket next to the number and time of the return flight. That only means that a reservation has been entered; a reconfirmation may still be necessary.

If you plan not to take a reserved flight, by all means inform the airline of your cancellation. Because the problem of "no-shows" is a consistently annoying one for airlines, they are allowed to overbook flights, a practice that often contributes to the threat of denied boarding for a certain number of passengers (see *Getting Bumped,* below). Let the airline know you're not coming and you'll spare everyone some confusion. Bear in mind that only certain kinds of tickets allow the luxury of last-minute changes in flight plans — those sold on an open reservation system (first class and full-fare coach) — while excursions and other discount fares are often restricted in some way. Even first class and coach passengers should remember that if they do not show up for a flight that is the first of several connecting ones, the airline will cancel all of their reservations unless informed not to do so.

Seating – For most types of tickets, airline seats are usually assigned on a first-come, first-served basis at check-in, although some airlines make it possible to reserve a seat at the time of ticket purchase. Always check in early for your flight, even with advance seat assignments.

Most airlines furnish seating charts, which make choosing a seat much easier, but in general, there are a few basics to consider. You must decide first whether you prefer the smoking or non-smoking section and a window, aisle, or middle seat.

The amount of legroom provided (as well as chest room, especially when the seat in front of you is in a reclining position) is determined by something called "pitch," a measure of the distance between the back of the seat in front of you and the front of your seat. The amount of pitch is a matter of airline policy, not the type of plane you fly. First class and business class seats have the greatest pitch, a fact that figures prominently in airline advertising. In economy class or coach, the standard pitch ranges from 33 to as little as 31 inches — downright cramped. The number of seats abreast, another factor determining comfort, depends on a combination of airline policy and airplane dimensions. First and business classes have the fewest seats per row. Economy generally has 9 seats per row on a DC-10 or an L-1011, making either one slightly more comfortable than a 747, on which there are normally 10 seats per row. Charter flights on DC-10s and L-1011s, however, often have 10 seats per row and can be noticeably more cramped than 747 charters, on which the seating normally remains at 10 per row.

Airline representatives claim that most aircraft are more stable toward the front and midsection, while seats farthest away from the engines are quietest. Passengers who have long legs and are traveling on a wide-body aircraft might request a seat directly behind a door or emergency exit, since these seats often have greater than average pitch, or a seat in the first row of a given section, since these seats have extra legroom. It is often impossible, however, to see the movie from these seats, which are directly behind the plane's exits. Be aware that the first row of the economy section (called "bulkhead" seats) on a conventional aircraft (not a wide-body) does *not* offer extra legroom, since the fixed partition will not permit passengers to slide their feet under it, and that watching a movie from this first row seat can be difficult and uncomfortable. A window seat protects you from aisle traffic and clumsy serving carts and also allows you a view, while an aisle seat enables you to get up and stretch your legs without disturbing anyone. Middle seats are the least desirable, and seats in the last row are the most undesirable of all, since they seldom recline fully. If you wish to avoid children on your flight, remember that families generally do not sit in smoking areas. Once in the air, if you find that you are sitting in an especially noisy section, you are usually free to move to any unoccupied seat — if there is one.

If you have a weight problem, you may face the prospect of a long flight with special trepidation. Center seats in the alignments of wide-body 747s, L-1011s, and DC-10s are about 1½ inches wider than those on either side, so larger travelers tend to be more comfortable there.

Simply reserving an airline seat in advance, however, may actually guarantee very little. Most airlines require that passengers arrive at the departure gate at least 30 minutes (sometimes more) ahead of time to hold a seat reservation. United, for example, cancels seat assignments and may not honor reservations of passengers not checked in 20 minutes before the scheduled flight time for flights within the US (except Hawaii), 30 minutes before flights to and from Hawaii, Canada, and Mexico, and 45 minutes to and from all other international destinations. As this is only one airline's policy, it pays to read the fine print on the back of your ticket carefully and plan ahead.

A far better strategy is to visit an airline ticket office (or one of a select group of travel agents) to secure an actual boarding pass for your specific flight. Once it has been issued, airline computers show you as checked in, and you effectively own the seat you have selected (although some carriers may not honor boarding passes of passengers arriving at the gate less than 10 minutes before departure). This is also good — but not foolproof — insurance against getting bumped from an overbooked flight and is, therefore, an especially valuable tactic at peak holiday travel times.

Smoking – The US government has adopted minimum standards to ensure that non-smokers will not be "unreasonably burdened" by passengers who smoke. For a wallet-size guide that notes in detail the rights of non-smokers, send a stamped, self-addressed envelope to ASH (Action on Smoking and Health), Airline Card, 2013 H St. NW, Washington, DC 20006 (phone: 202-659-4310). The US Department of Transportation has determined that non-smoking sections must be enlarged to accommodate all passengers who wish to sit in such a section. According to a recently added proviso, however, the airline does not have to shift seating to accommodate non-smokers who arrive late for the flight or travelers flying standby, and in general not all airlines can guarantee a seat in the non-smoking section on international flights. Check with the airline. Cigar and pipe smoking are prohibited on all flights, even in the smoking sections. These rules apply only to domestic flights and to flights by US carriers departing from or returning to the US. They do not apply to flights by foreign carriers into or out of the US.

Flying with Children – On longer flights, the bulkhead seats are usually reserved for families traveling with small children. As a general rule, an infant under 2 years of age (and not occupying a seat) flies to Europe at 10% of whatever fare the accompanying adult is paying. A second infant without a second adult pays the fare applicable to children age 2 through 11. In most cases this amounts to 50% of an adult economy fare and two-thirds of an adult APEX fare.

Most airlines have complimentary bassinets. Ask about obtaining one when you make your reservation, and when checking in, request a bulkhead or other seat that has enough room in front to use it. On some planes they hook into a bulkhead wall; on others they are placed on the floor in front of you. Even if you do use a bassinet, babies must be held during takeoff and landing. (For more information on flying with children, see *Hints for Traveling with Children.*)

Meals – If you have specific dietary requirements (vegetarian, kosher, low calorie, low sodium, and so on), make sure to let the airlines know well before departure time.

There is no extra charge for this option. It is, however, advisable to request special meals when you make your reservations — check-in time is too late. It's also wise to reconfirm that your request for a special meal has made its way into the airline's computer — the time to do this is 24 hours before departure.

Getting Bumped – A special air travel problem is the possibility that an airline will accept more reservations (and sell more tickets) than there are seats on a given flight. This is entirely legal and is done to make up for "no-shows," passengers who don't show up for a flight for which they have made reservations and bought tickets. If the airline has oversold the flight and everyone does show up, there simply aren't enough seats. When this happens, the airline is subject to stringent rules designed to protect travelers.

In such cases, the airline first seeks ticketholders willing to give up their seats voluntarily in return for a negotiable sum of money or some other inducement, such as an offer of upgraded seating on the next flight or a voucher for a free trip at some other time. If there are not enough volunteers, the airline may bump passengers against their wishes. Anyone inconvenienced in this way, however, is entitled to an explanation of the criteria used to determine who does and does not get on the flight, as well as to compensation if the resulting delay exceeds certain limits. If the airline can put the bumped passengers on an alternate flight that gets them to their destination within 1 hour of their originally scheduled arrival time, no compensation is owed. If the delay is more than an hour — but less than 2 hours on a domestic US flight — they must be paid denied-boarding compensation equivalent to the one-way fare to their destination (but not more than $200). If the delay is more than 2 hours beyond the original arrival time on a domestic flight or more than 4 hours on an international flight, the compensation must be doubled (not more than $400). The airline may also offer bumped travelers a voucher for a free flight instead of the denied-boarding compensation. The passenger can choose either the money or the voucher, the dollar value of which may be no less than the monetary compensation to which the passenger would be entitled. The voucher is not a substitute for the bumped passenger's original ticket; the airline continues to honor that as well. Keep in mind that the above regulations and policies are only for flights leaving the US, and do *not* apply to charters or inbound flights from Great Britain, even on US carriers.

In Great Britain, each airline is free to determine what compensation it will pay to passengers who are bumped because of overbooking. However, they are required to spell out their policies on the airline ticket. Some European airline policies are similar to the US policy. Passengers involuntarily bumped are paid twice the price of a one-way ticket (up to $400) if they reach their destination 4 or more hours late. However, don't assume all carriers will be as generous.

To protect yourself as best you can against getting bumped, arrive at the airport early, allowing plenty of time to check in and get to the gate. If the flight is oversold, ask immediately for the written statement explaining the airline's policy on denied-boarding compensation and its boarding priorities. If the airline refuses to give you this information, or if you feel it has not handled the situation properly, file a complaint with both the airline and the appropriate government agency (see *Consumer Protection,* below).

Delays and Cancellations – The above compensation rules also do not apply if the flight is canceled or delayed, or if a smaller aircraft is substituted due to mechanical problems. Each airline has its own policy for assisting passengers whose flights are delayed or canceled or who must wait for another flight because their original one was overbooked. Most airline personnel will make new travel arrangements if necessary. If the delay is longer than 4 hours, the airline may pay for a phone call or telegram, a meal, and in some cases a hotel room and transportation to it.

The deregulation of US airlines has meant that travelers must find out for themselves what they are entitled to receive. A useful booklet, *Fly Rights, A Guide to Air Travel in the US,* is available for $1 from the Superintendent of Documents, US Government Printing Office, Washington, DC 20402-9325 (phone: 202-783-3238). When ordering, specify the stock number of this publication, 050-000-00513-5, and allow 3 to 4 weeks for delivery.

■ **Caution:** If you are bumped or miss a flight, be sure to ask the airline to notify other airlines on which you have reservations or connecting flights. When your name is taken off the passenger list of your initial flight, the computer automatically cancels all of your reservations unless *you* take steps to preserve them.

Baggage – Travelers from the US face two different kinds of rules. When you fly in on a US airline or on a major international carrier, US baggage regulations will be in effect. Though airline baggage allowances vary slightly, in general all passengers are allowed to carry on board, without charge, one piece of luggage that will fit easily under a seat of the plane or in an overhead bin and whose combined dimensions (length, width, and depth) do not exceed 45 inches. Most airlines will allow you to check this bag in the hold if you prefer not to carry it with you, but a few require that it be carried on and stowed in the cabin. A reasonable amount of reading material, camera equipment, and a handbag are also allowed. In addition, all passengers are allowed to check two bags in the cargo hold: one usually not to exceed 62 inches in combined dimensions, the other not to exceed 55 inches. No single bag may weigh more than 70 pounds. Note, however, that this weight restriction may vary on some European airlines, ranging from as much as 88 pounds permitted for first class passengers to as little as 50 pounds for economy class — so check with the specific carrier in advance.

Charges for additional, oversize, or overweight bags are usually made at a flat rate; the actual dollar amount varying from carrier to carrier. If you plan to travel with a bike, golf clubs, or other sports gear, be sure to check with the airline beforehand. Most have procedures for handling such baggage, but you will probably have to pay for transport regardless of how much other baggage you have checked.

Airline policies regarding baggage allowances for children vary and are usually based on the percentage of full adult fare paid. Children paying 50% or more of an adult fare on most US carriers are entitled to the same baggage allowance as a full-fare passenger, whereas infants traveling at 10% of an adult fare are entitled to only one piece of baggage, the combined dimensions of which may not exceed 45 inches — 39 inches on TWA. Particularly for international carriers, it's wise to check ahead — for instance, often there is no luggage allowance for a child traveling on an adult's lap or in a bassinet. (For more information, see *Hints for Traveling with Children.*)

On European local or trunk carriers, in general, baggage allowances follow the same guidelines as those of major carriers. However, especially on regional and local airlines, luggage may be subject to the old weight determination, under which each economy or discount passenger is allowed only a total of 44 pounds of luggage without additional charge. First class and business passengers are allowed a total of 66 pounds.

To reduce the chances of your luggage going astray, remove all airline tags from previous trips, label each bag inside and out — with your business address rather than your home address on the outside, to prevent thieves from knowing whose house might be unguarded. Lock everything and double-check the tag that the airline attaches to make sure that it is coded for your destination: HTH for Heathrow in London, for instance. If your bags are not in the baggage claim area after your flight, or if they're damaged, report the problem to airline personnel immediately. Keep in mind that policies regarding the specific time limit in which you have to make your claim vary from carrier to carrier. Fill out a report form on your lost or damaged luggage and keep a copy of it and your claim check. If you must surrender the check to claim a damaged bag, get a receipt for it to prove that you did, indeed, check your baggage on the flight.

If luggage is missing, be sure to give the airline your destination and/or a telephone number where you can be reached. Also take the name and number of the person in charge of recovering lost luggage. Most airlines have emergency funds for passengers stranded away from home without their luggage, but if it turns out your bags are truly lost and not simply delayed, do not then and there sign any paper indicating you'll accept an offered settlement. Since the airline is responsible for the value of your bags within certain statutory limits ($1,250 for a lost bag on a domestic flight; $9.07 per pound on an international flight), you should take some time to assess the extent of your loss (see *Insurance,* in this section). It's a good idea to keep records indicating the value of the contents of your luggage. An alternative is to take a Polaroid picture of the most valuable of your packed items just after putting them in your suitcase.

Considering the increased incidence of damage to baggage, it's now more than ever a good idea to keep the sales slips that confirm how much you paid for your bags. These are invaluable in establishing the value of damaged baggage and eliminate any arguments. A better way to protect your precious baggage from the luggage-eating conveyers is to try to carry your gear on board wherever possible.

Be aware that airport security is increasingly an issue all over Europe, and the British take it very seriously. Heavily armed police patrol the airports, and unattended luggage of any description may be confiscated and even destroyed. Passengers checking in at an airport may undergo at least two separate inspections of their tickets, passports, and luggage by courteous but serious airline personnel — who ask passengers if their baggage has been out of their possession between packing and the airport or if they have been given gifts or other items to transport — before checked items are accepted into the baggage-handling system. In other words, do not agree to take anything on board for a stranger.

Airline Clubs – US carriers often have clubs for travelers who pay for membership. These are not solely for first class passengers. Membership (which, by law, now requires a fee) entitles the traveler to use the private lounges at airports along their route, to refreshments served in those lounges, and to check-cashing privileges at most of their counters. Extras include special telephone numbers for individual reservations, embossed luggage tags, and a membership card for identification. Two airlines that offer membership in such clubs are: Pan American — the *Clipper Club,* single yearly membership $150, spouse an additional $45, 3-year and lifetime memberships also available; and Delta — the *Crown Room,* single yearly membership $125, 3-year memberships also available. However, these companies do not have club facilities in all airports. Lounge privileges are also offered to first class passengers, and other airlines also offer a variety of special club and lounge facilities in many airports.

CHARTER FLIGHTS: By booking a block of seats on a specially arranged flight, charter operators offer travelers air transportation, often coupled with a hotel room, meals, and other travel services, for a substantial reduction over the full coach or economy fare.

Charters were once the best bargain around, but this is no longer necessarily the case. As a result, charter flights have been discontinued in many areas, but to some popular vacation spots, they can still be a good buy. They are especially attractive to people in smaller cities or out-of-the-way places, because they frequently take off from nearby airports, saving travelers the inconvenience and expense of getting to a major gateway. Where demand persists, charter operators will continue to rent planes or seats from scheduled airlines (or from special charter airlines) and offer flights to the public directly through advertisements or travel agents. You buy the ticket from the operator or the agent, not from the airline owning the plane. With the advent of APEX and various promotional fares on the major airlines and the appearance of low-fare airlines, however, charter flights lost some of their budget-conscious clientele and suffered some lean years, especially on highly competitive routes with a choice of other bargains. At the same time, many of the larger companies running charter programs began to offer both charter flights and discounted scheduled flights (see below). Nevertheless, among the current offerings, charter flights to European cities are common, a sign that they still represent a good value.

Charter travel once required that an individual be a member of a club or other "affinity" group whose main purpose was not travel. But since the approval of "public charters" years ago, operators have had some of the flexibility of scheduled airlines, making charters more competitive. Public charters are open to anyone, whether belonging to a group or not, and have no advance booking requirements or minimum stay requirements. One-way arrangements are permitted, though charters are almost always round-trip, and it is unlikely that you would be sold a one-way seat on a round-trip flight. Operators can offer air-only charters, selling transportation alone, or they can offer charter packages — the flight plus a combination of land arrangements such as accommodations, meals, tours, or car rental.

From the consumer's standpoint, charters differ from scheduled airlines in two main respects: you generally need to book and pay in advance, and you can't change the itinerary or the departure and return dates once you've booked the flight. In practice, however, these restrictions don't always apply. For instance, it's possible to book a one-way charter in the US, giving you more flexibility in scheduling your return. However, note that American regulations pertaining to charters may be more permissive than the charter laws of other countries. For example, if you want to book a one-way foreign charter back to the US, you may find advance booking rules in force.

Some things to keep in mind about the charter game:

1. It cannot be repeated often enough that if you are forced to cancel your trip, you can lose much (and possibly all) of your money unless you have cancellation insurance, which is a *must* (see *Insurance*). Frequently, if the cancellation is well in advance (often 6 weeks or more), you may forfeit only a $25 or $50 penalty. If you cancel only 2 or 3 weeks before the flight, there may be no refund at all unless you or the operator can supply a substitute passenger.
2. Charter flights may be canceled by the operator up to 10 days before departure for any reason, usually underbooking. Your money is returned in this event, but there may be too little time to make new arrangements.
3. Most charters have little of the flexibility of regularly scheduled flights regarding refunds and the changing of flight dates; if you book a return flight, you must be on it or lose your money.
4. Charter operators are permitted to assess a surcharge, if fuel or other costs warrant it, of up to 10% of the airfare up to 10 days before departure.
5. Because of the economics of charter flights, your plane almost always will be full, so you will be crowded, though not necessarily uncomfortable.

The saving provided by charters varies, depending on their point of departure in the US and on the countries to which they are headed (some governments do not allow charters to land at all; others allow them to undercut scheduled fares by a wide margin). As a rule, a charter to any given destination can cost anywhere from $50 to $200 less than an APEX fare on a major carrier, with West Coast charters realizing a greater saving than those on the East Coast.

Bookings – If you do take a charter, read the contract's fine print carefully and pay particular attention to the following:

1. Instructions concerning the payment of the deposit and its balance and to whom the check is to be made payable. Ordinarily, checks are made out to an escrow account, which means the charter company can't spend your money until your flight has safely returned. This provides some protection for you. To ensure the

safe handling of your money, make out your check to the escrow account, the number of which must appear by law on the brochure, though all too often it is on the back in fine print. Write the details of the charter, including the destination and dates, on the face of the check; on the back, print "For Deposit Only." Your travel agent may prefer that you make out your check to the agency, saying that it will then pay the tour operator the fee minus commission. It is perfectly legal to write the check as we suggest, however, and if your agent objects too vociferously (he or she should trust the tour operator to send the proper commission), consider taking your business elsewhere. If you don't make your check out to the escrow account, you lose the protection of escrow should the trip be canceled. Furthermore, recent bankruptcies in the travel industry have served to point out that even the protection of escrow may not be enough to safeguard a traveler's investment. More and more, insurance is becoming a necessity (see *Insurance*). The charter company should be bonded (usually by an insurance company), and if you want to file a claim against it, the claim should be sent to the bonding agent. The contract will set a time limit within which a claim must be filed.

2. Note specific stipulations and penalties for cancellations. Most charters allow you to cancel up to 45 days in advance, but some cancellation dates are 50 to 60 days before departure.
3. Stipulations regarding cancellation and major changes made by the charterer. US rules say that charter flights may not be canceled within 10 days of departure except when circumstances — such as natural disasters or political upheavals — make it physically impossible to fly. Charterers may make "major changes," however, such as in the date or place of departure or return, but you are entitled to cancel and receive a refund if you don't wish to accept these changes. A price increase of more than 10% at any time up to 10 days before departure is considered a major change; no price increase at all is allowed during the 10 days immediately before departure.

DISCOUNTS ON SCHEDULED FLIGHTS: The APEX fare is an example of a promotional fare offered on regularly scheduled transatlantic flights by most major airlines. Promotional fares are often called discount fares because they cost less than what used to be the standard airline fare — full-fare economy. Nevertheless, they cost the traveler the same whether they are bought through a travel agent or directly from the airline. Tickets that cost less if bought from some outlet other than the airline do exist, however. While it is likely that the vast majority of travelers flying to Europe in the near future will be doing so on a promotional fare or charter rather than on a "discount" air ticket of this sort, it is still a good idea for cost-conscious consumers to be aware of the latest developments in the budget airfare scene. Note that the following discussion makes clear distinctions among the types of discounts available based on how they reach the consumer; in actual practice, the distinctions are not nearly so precise. One organization may operate part of its business in one fashion and the remainder in another; a second organization may operate all of its business in the same fashion, but outsiders — and sometimes the organization itself — would have difficulty classifying it.

Net Fare Sources – The newest notion for reducing the costs of travel services comes from travel agents who offer individual travelers "net" fares. Defined simply, a net fare is the bare minimum amount at which an airline or tour operator will carry a prospective traveler. It doesn't include the amount that would normally be paid to the travel agent as a commission. Traditionally, such commissions amount to about 10% on domestic fares and from 8% to 20% on international tickets — not counting significant additions to these levels that are payable retroactively when agents sell more than a specific volume of tickets or trips for a single supplier. At press time, at least one travel agency in the US was offering travelers the opportunity to purchase tickets and/or tours for a net price. Instead of making its money from individual commissions, this agency assesses a fixed fee that may or may not be a bargain for travelers; it requires a little arithmetic to determine whether to use the services of a net travel agent or those of one who accepts conventional commissions.

McTravel Travel Services (130 S. Jefferson, Chicago, IL 60606-3691; phone: 800-333-3335 in the US except Illinois; 312-876-1116 in Illinois and Canada) is a formula fee-based agency that rebates its ordinary agency commission to the customer. For domestic flights, an agent will find the lowest retail ticket price, then rebate 8% of that price minus an $8 ticket-writing charge. The rebate percentage for international flights varies from 8% to 20%, depending on the airline selected, and the ticket-writing fee is $20. *McTravel* will rebate on all tickets including max savers, super savers, and senior citizen passes. Available 7 days a week, reservations should be made far enough in advance to allow the tickets to be sent by first class mail, since extra charges accrue for special handling, as they do for reservations that require any significant amount of research. It's possible to economize further by making your own airline reservation, then asking *McTravel* only to write/issue your ticket. For travelers outside the Chicago area, business may be transacted by phone and purchases charged to a credit card.

One of the potential drawbacks of buying from agencies selling travel services at net fares is that your options may be limited. *McTravel Travel Services* recently lost a court battle with American Airlines, which refused to do business with the discounter. A US District Court in Chicago ruled in the airline's favor, and other carriers are expected to follow suit.

Consolidators and Bucket Shops – Other vendors of travel services can afford to sell tickets to their customers at an even greater discount because the airline has sold the tickets to them at a substantial discount, a practice in which many airlines indulge, albeit discreetly, preferring that the general public not know they are undercutting their own "list" prices. Airlines anticipating a slow season on a particular route sometimes sell off a certain portion of their capacity at a very great discount to a wholesaler, or consolidator. The wholesaler is sometimes a charter operator who resells the seats to the public as though they were charter seats, which is why prospective travelers perusing the brochures of charter operators with large programs frequently see a number of flights designated as "scheduled service." As often as not, however, the consolidator, in turn, sells the seats to an agency specializing in discounting. Airlines can also sell seats directly to such an agency, which thus acts as its own consolidator. The airline offers the seats either at a net wholesale price, but without the volume-purchase requirement that would be difficult for a retail travel agency to fulfill, or at the standard price, but with a commission override large enough (as high as 50%) to allow both a profit and a price reduction to the public.

Travel agencies specializing in discounting were once known as "bucket shops," a term fraught with connotations of unreliability. But in today's highly competitive travel marketplace, more and more conventional travel agencies are selling consolidator-supplied tickets, and the old bucket shops are becoming more respectable, too. Agencies that specialize in discounted tickets are located in most large cities and can be found by studying the smaller ads in the travel sections of the Sunday newspapers. They deal largely in transatlantic and other international tickets, and on the whole do not offer notable reductions on domestic travel (if they sell domestic tickets at all).

Before buying a discounted ticket, whether from a bucket shop or a conventional, full-service travel agency, keep the following considerations in mind: To be in a position to judge the amount of money you'll be saving, first find out the "list" prices of tickets to your destination by calling the major airlines serving the route. Then, do some comparison shopping among agencies, always bearing in mind that the lowest-priced ticket may not provide the most convenient or most comfortable flight (bargain prices are usually available on an airline's less popular routes, so your routing might be roundabout or you may be required to endure a long layover along the way). Also bear in mind that a ticket that may not differ much in price from that available directly from the airline may, however, allow the circumvention of booking restrictions, such as the advance-purchase requirement. If your plans are less than final, be sure to find out about any other restrictions, such as penalties for canceling a flight or changing a reservation. Most discount tickets are non-endorsable, meaning they can be used only on the airline that issued them, and they are usually marked "nonrefundable" to prevent their being cashed in for a list price refund. (A refund of the price paid for the ticket is often possible, but it is obtained through the outlet from which it was purchased rather than from the airline.)

A great many bucket shops are small businesses operating on a thin margin, so it's a good idea to check the local Better Business Bureau for any complaints registered against the one with which you're dealing before parting with any money. If you still do not feel reassured, consider buying discounted tickets only through a conventional travel agency, which can be expected to have found its own reliable source of consolidator tickets — some of the largest consolidators, in fact, sell only to travel agencies.

A few bucket shops require payment in cash or by certified check or money order, but if credit cards are accepted, use that option, which allows purchasers to protest charges if they do not receive what they paid for. Note, however, if buying from a charter operator selling both scheduled and charter flights, that the scheduled seats are not protected by the regulations — including the use of escrow accounts — governing the charter seats. Well-established charter operators, nevertheless, may extend the same protections to their scheduled flights, and when this is the case, consumers should be sure that the payment option selected directs their money into the escrow account.

■ **Note:** Although rebating and discounting are becoming increasingly common, there is some legal ambiguity concerning them. Strictly speaking, it is legal to discount domestic tickets but not to discount international tickets. On the other hand, the law that prohibits discounting, the Federal Aviation Act of 1958, is consistently ignored these days, in part because consumers benefit from the practice and in part because many illegal arrangements are indistinguishable from legal ones. Since the line separating the two is so fine that even the authorities can't always tell the difference, it is unlikely that most consumers would be able to do so, and, in fact, it is not illegal to *buy* a discounted ticket. If the issue of legality bothers you, ask the agency whether any ticket you're about to buy would be permissible under the above-mentioned act.

Other Discount Travel Sources – An excellent source of information on economical travel opportunities is the *Consumer Reports Travel Letter,* published monthly by Consumers Union. It keeps abreast of the scene on a wide variety of fronts, including package tours, rental cars, insurance, and more, but it is especially helpful for its comprehensive coverage of airfares, offering guidance on all the options from scheduled flights on major or low-fare airlines to charters and discount sources. For a year's subscription, send $37 to Consumer Reports Travel Letter, PO Box 2886, Boulder, CO 80322 (phone: 800-525-0643). Another source is *Travel Smart,* a monthly newsletter offering information on a wide variety of trips with additional discount travel services available to subscribers. For a year's subscription, send $37 to Communications House, 40 Beechdale Rd., Dobbs Ferry, NY 10522 (phone: 914-693-8300 in New York; 800-327-3633 elsewhere in the US).

Still another way to take advantage of bargain airfares is open to those who have a flexible schedule. A number of organizations, usually set up as last-minute travel clubs and functioning on a membership basis, routinely keep in touch with travel suppliers to help them dispose of unsold inventory at discounts of between 15% and 60%. A great deal of the inventory consists of complete tour packages and cruises, but some clubs offer air-only charter seats and, occasionally, seats on scheduled flights. Members pay an annual fee and receive the toll-free number of a telephone hotline to call for information on imminent trips. In some cases, they also receive periodic mailings with information on upcoming trips for which there is more advance notice. Despite the suggestive names of the clubs providing these services, last-minute travel does not necessarily mean than you cannot make plans until literally the last minute. Trips can be announced as little as a few days or as much as 2 months before departure, but the average is from 1 to 4 weeks. It does mean that your choice at any given time is limited to what is offered, and, if your heart is set on a particular destination, you might not find what you want, no matter how attractive the bargains. Among these organizations are the following:

Discount Club of America, 61-33 Woodhaven Blvd., Rego Park, NY 11374 (phone: 718-335-9612 or 800-321-9587). Annual fee: $39.

Discount Travel International, Ives Building, 114 Forrest Ave., Suite 205, Narberth, PA 19072 (phone: 215-668-2182 in Pennsylvania; 800-824-4000 elsewhere in the US). Annual fee: $45 per household.

Encore Short Notice, 4501 Forbes Blvd., Lanham, MD 20706 (phone: 301-459-8020 or 800-638-0930 for customer service). Annual fee: $36 per family.

Last-Minute Travel Club, 132 Brookline Ave., Boston, MA 02215 (phone: 617-267-9800 or 800-LAST-MIN). Annual fee: $30 per person; $35 per couple or family.

Moment's Notice, 40 E. 49th St., New York, NY 10017 (phone: 212-486-0503). Annual fee: $45 per family.

On Call to Travel, 14335 SW Allen Blvd., Suite 209, Beaverton, OR 97005 (phone: 503-643-7212, members may call collect). Annual fee: $39 per family, first year; $29 yearly thereafter.

Spur-of-the-Moment Tours and Cruises, 10780 Jefferson Blvd., Culver City, CA 90230 (phone: 213-839-2418 in California; 800-343-1991 elsewhere in the US). No fee.

Stand Buys Limited, 311 W. Superior St., Suite 414, Chicago, IL 60610 (phone: 800-331-0257 for membership information; 800-848-8402 for customer service; 800-433-9383 for reservations). Annual fee: $45 per family.

Worldwide Discount Travel Club, 1674 Meridian Ave., Miami Beach, FL 33139 (phone: 305-534-2082). Annual fee: $40 per person; $50 per family.

Generic Air Travel – Organizations that apply the same flexible-schedule idea to air travel only and sell tickets at literally the last minute also exist. Their service is sometimes known as "generic" air travel, and it operates somewhat like an ordinary airline standby service except that the organizations running it offer seats on not one but several scheduled and charter airlines.

One pioneer of generic flights is *Airhitch* (2901 Broadway, Suite 100, New York, NY 10025; phone: 212-864-2000), which arranges flights to Europe from various US cities at very low prices ($160 or less one way from the East Coast in 1989, $269 or less from the West Coast, and $229 or less from other points). Precise destinations are not guaranteed, however. Prospective travelers register by paying a fee (applicable toward the fare) and stipulate a range of acceptable departure dates and their preferred destination, as well as alternatives. The Wednesday before the date range begins, they are notified of at least two flights that will be available during the time period, agree on an assignment, and remit the balance of the fare to the company. If they do not accept any of the suggested flights, they lose their deposit; if, through no fault of their own, they do not ultimately get on any agreed-on flight, all of their money is refunded. Return flights are arranged the same way. *Airhitch* cautions that, given the number of variables attached to the flights, they are suitable only for travelers willing to accept approximate destinations, although the time period will be the one specified and, for a majority of travelers, the place of arrival, too. Another of the company's programs, the Target program, offers greater certainty regarding destinations, but for higher prices.

BARTERED TRAVEL SOURCES: Say a company buys advertising space in a newspaper for a hotel. As a payment, the hotel gives the company a number of hotel rooms in lieu of cash. This is barter, a common means of exchange among hotels, airlines, car rental companies, cruise lines, tour operators, restaurants, and other service companies. When a bartering company finds itself with excess hotel rooms (or empty airline seats or cruise ship cabin space, and so on) and offers them to the public, considerable savings can be had.

Bartered-travel clubs can often offer discounts of up to 50% to members, who pay an annual fee (approximately $50 at press time) that entitles them to select the flights, cruises, hotels, that the company obtained by barter. Members usually present a voucher, club credit card, or scrip (a dollar-denomination voucher negotiable only for the bartered product) to the hotel, which in turn subtracts the dollar amount from the bartering company's account.

Selling bartered travel is a perfectly legitimate means of retailing. One advantage to club members is that they don't have to wait until the last minute to obtain room or flight reservations. However, hotel rooms and airline seats are usually offered to members on a space-available basis. Ticket vouchers are good only for a particular hotel and cannot be used at other hotels. The same goes for car rentals, cruises, package tours, and restaurants. The following clubs offer bartered travel at a discount to members:

IGT (*In Good Taste*) *Services,* 22 E. 29th St., New York, NY 10016 (phone: 212-725-9600 or 800-444-8872). The annual membership fee of $48 includes $25 credit toward future charges.

The Travel Guild, 18210 Redmond Way, Redmond, WA 98052 (phone: 206-885-1213). Annual membership fee is $48.

Travel World Leisure Club, 225 W. 34th St., Suite 2203, New York, NY 10122 (phone: 212-239-4855 or 800-444 TWLC). Annual membership fee: $50 per family.

CONSUMER PROTECTION: Consumers who feel that they have not been dealt with fairly by an airline should make their complaints known. Begin with the customer service representative at the airport where the problem occurs. If he or she cannot resolve your complaint to your satisfaction, write to the airline's consumer office. In a businesslike, typed letter, explain what reservations you held, what happened, the names of the employees involved, and how you expect the airline to remedy the situation. Send copies (never the originals) of the tickets, receipts, and other documents that back your claims. Ideally, all correspondence should be sent via certified mail, return receipt requested. This provides proof that your complaint was received.

If you still receive no satisfaction and your complaint is against a US carrier, contact the US Department of Transportation. Passengers with consumer complaints — lost baggage, compensation for getting bumped, smoking and non-smoking rules, deceptive practices by an airline, charter regulations — should write to the Consumer Affairs Division, Room 10405, US Department of Transportation, 400 Seventh St. SW, Washington, DC 20590, or call the office at 202-366-2220. DOT personnel stress, however, that consumers should initially direct their complaints to the airline that provoked them.

Travelers with an unresolved complaint involving a British airline can also contact the US Department of Transportation. DOT personnel will do what they can to help resolve all such complaints, although their influence may be limited. If the problem is with a domestic flight in Great Britain, the only other recourse is to write to the customer relations department of the particular airline, as Great Britain has no central office handling these complaints.

The Department of Transportation's consumer booklet, *Fly Rights, A Guide to Air Travel in the US,* is a good introduction to regulations governing the airlines. To receive a copy, send $1 to the Superintendent of Documents, US Government Printing Office, Washington, DC 20402-9325 (phone: 202-783-3238), specify its stock number, 050-000-00513-5, and allow 3 to 4 weeks for delivery.

To avoid more serious problems, *always* choose charter flights and tour packages with care. When you consider a charter, ask your travel agent who runs it and carefully check out the company. The Better Business Bureau in the company's home city can report on how many complaints, if any, have been lodged against it in the past. As emphasized above, protect yourself with trip cancellation and interruption insurance, which can help safeguard your investment if you or a traveling companion is unable to make the trip and must cancel too late to receive a full refund from the company providing your travel services. (This is advisable whether you're buying a charter flight alone or a tour package for which the airfare is provided by charter or scheduled flight.) Some travel insurance policies have an additional feature, covering the possibility of default or bankruptcy on the part of the tour operator or airline, charter or scheduled.

Should this type of coverage not be available to you (state insurance regulations vary, there is a wide difference in price, and so on), your best bet is to pay for airline tickets and tour packages with a credit card. The federal Fair Credit Billing Act permits purchasers to refuse payment for credit card charges where services have not been delivered, so the onus of dealing with the receiver for a bankrupt airline falls on the credit card company. Do not rely on another airline to honor the ticket you're holding, since the days when virtually all major carriers subscribed to a default protection program that bound them to do so are long gone. Some airlines may voluntarily step forward to accommodate the stranded passengers of a fellow carrier, but this is now an entirely altruistic act.

ON ARRIVAL: Heathrow, Britain's main international airport, is 15 miles from central London, and the trip into town can easily be made on the London underground (subway) from the airport itself. There are two Heathrow underground stations, one serving Terminal 4 and the other serving Terminals 1, 2, and 3. Piccadilly Line tube trains leave every few minutes, depending on the time of day, and operate between 5:00 AM and 11:40 PM from Heathrow to London, Mondays through Saturdays, 5:50 AM to 11:40 PM Sundays. Stops are convenient to most of London's main hotel areas, and the line feeds into the rest of the underground network. The fare to any central-zone station, such as Piccadilly Circus (about a 45-minute trip), is £1.70 (about $2.55).

London Regional Transport's two express *Airbus* services connect Heathrow with Victoria Station (A1) and with Euston Station (A2), as well as major hotel areas, for £3 (about $4.50) — journey time is anywhere from 50 minutes to 1½ hours. US currency is accepted on *Airbuses.* Heathrow *Flightline 767* buses also connect Heathrow with Victoria Coach Station; overall journey time is 50 to 60 minutes and the fare is £4 (about $6). Taxi fare from Heathrow to central London is approximately £27 (about $40.50).

Gatwick Airport, 29 miles from central London, is not linked to the underground, but it does have its own rail station. Gatwick express trains, for which tickets can be purchased from *BritRail Travel International* offices in the US, leave for Victoria Station every 15 minutes during the day and once an hour through the night. The trip takes 30 minutes (40 minutes at night) and costs £5 (about $7.50). Gatwick *Flightline 777* buses make the trip from the airport to Victoria Coach Station in approximately 70 minutes; fare is £3 (about $4.50). Taxi fare from Gatwick to central London is £27 to £30 (about $40.50 to $45).

Flights from the US also serve Manchester and Glasgow. Manchester Airport is 10 miles from central Manchester; express buses leave the International Arrivals Terminal for the Chorlton Street Bus Station and Victoria and Piccadilly rail stations every half hour between 6:20 AM and 7:20 PM, then hourly until 10:27 PM. Fare for the approximately 30-minute trip is £1.20 (about $2) on *Airport Express* buses, £1.10 (about $1.65) on *Route 44* and *Route 100* buses. Glasgow's Prestwick Airport is 32 miles from the center of the city, reached by train (a courtesy bus shuttles between the airport and Prestwick railway station); travel time is about an hour and the fare is £2.50. There is bus service to Buchanan Street Bus Station in central Glasgow; travel time is about 1¼ hours and the fare is £3 (about $4.50) or, via *Citylink bus,* £1.50 (about $2.25). Taxi fare is approximately £24 (about $36).

British Airways, British Midland, and several other domestic airlines have scheduled flights to major cities and islands. (British Airways runs many shuttle flights daily between London and Manchester, Glasgow, and Edinburgh.) Air service between London and Dublin is provided by British Airways, Aer Lingus, Virgin Atlantic, Britain's Dan-Air Services, and Ireland's Ryanair; the same and other airlines also connect other British and Irish cities. British Airways and British Midland both have daily flights between London and Belfast, Northern Ireland. Service to Scotland and the Shetland, Orkney, and Hebrides islands, Inverness, Channel Islands, as well as Londonderry and Belfast in Northern Ireland, is provided by Logainair out of Glasgow, Edinburgh, and Manchester. Another domestic carrier, Brymon Airways, serves Aberdeen, Scotland; Cork, Ireland; the islands of Jersey, Guernsey, and Scilly; and much of southwest Britain.

Traveling by Ship

Alas, the days when steamships reigned as the primary means of transatlantic transportation are gone, when Italy, France, Sweden, Germany, Norway, the Netherlands, and England — and the US — had fleets of passenger liners that offered week-plus trips across the North Atlantic. Only one ship (*Cunard*'s *Queen Elizabeth 2*) continues to offer this kind of service between the US and Europe with any degree of regularity, others make the trip at most a few times a year. At the same time, the possibility of booking passage to Europe on a cargo ship is becoming less practical. Fewer and fewer travelers, therefore, set foot on European soil with sea legs developed during an ocean voyage. But due to the growing popularity of trips on the inland waterways of Europe, more and more travelers — particularly repeat travelers — are climbing aboard some kind of waterborne conveyance once they've arrived in Europe and are seeing the country from the banks of a river or the towpath of a canal.

CABINS: The most important factor in determining the price of a cruise is the cabin. Cabin prices are set according to size and location. The size can vary considerably on older ships, less so on newer or more recently modernized ones, and may be entirely uniform on the very newest vessels.

Shipboard accommodations have the same pricing pattern as hotels. Suites, which consist of a sitting room–bedroom combination and occasionally a private small deck that could be compared to a patio, cost the most. Prices for other cabins (interchangeably called staterooms) are usually more expensive on the upper passenger decks, less expensive on lower decks. The outside cabins with portholes facing the water cost more than inside cabins without views and are generally preferred. If the cabin has a bathtub instead of a shower, the price will probably be higher. As in all forms of travel, accommodations are more expensive for single travelers. If you are traveling on your own but want to share a double cabin to reduce the cost, some ship lines will attempt to find someone of the same sex willing to share quarters (see *Hints for Single Travelers*).

FACILITIES AND ACTIVITIES: You may not use your cabin very much. Organized shipboard activities are geared to keep you busy. A standard schedule might consist of swimming, sunbathing, and numerous other outdoor recreations. Evenings are devoted to leisurely dining, lounge shows or movies, bingo and other organized games, gambling, dancing, and a midnight buffet. Your cruise fare includes all of these activities — except the cost of drinks.

All cruise ships have at least one major social lounge, a main dining room, several bars, an entertainment room that may double as a discotheque for late dancing, an exercise room, indoor games facilities, at least one pool, and shopping facilities that can range from a single boutique to an arcade. Still others have gambling casinos and/or slot machines, card rooms, libraries, children's recreation centers, indoor pools (as well as one or more on open decks), separate movie theaters, and private meeting rooms. Open deck space should be ample, because this is where most passengers spend their days at sea.

Usually there is a social director and staff to organize and coordinate activities. Evening entertainment is provided by professionals. Movies are mostly first-run and drinks are moderate in price (or should be) because a ship is exempt from local taxes when at sea.

To prepare for possible illnesses, travelers should get a prescription from their doctors for pills or stomach pacifiers to counteract motion sickness. All ships with more than 12 passengers have a doctor on board and facilities for handling sickness or medical emergencies.

MEALS: All meals on board are usually included in the basic price of a cruise; the meals are usually abundant and quite palatable. Evening meals are taken in the main dining room, where tables are assigned according to passengers' preferences. Tables usually accommodate from two to ten; specify your preference when you book your cruise. If there are two sittings, you can also specify which one you want at the time you book or, at the latest, when you board the ship. Later sittings are usually more leisurely. Breakfast is frequently available in your cabin as well as in the main dining room. For lunch, many people prefer the buffet on deck, usually at or near the pool, but again, the main dining room is available.

DRESS: Most people pack too much for a cruise on the assumption that daytime wear should be chic and every night is a big event. Comfort is a more realistic criterion.

Daytime wear on most ships is decidedly casual. For warm-weather cruises, women can wear a coverup over a bathing suit through breakfast, swimming, sunbathing and deck activities, lunch, and early cocktails without any change; for men, shorts (with swim trunks underneath) and a casual shirt are appropriate on deck or in any public room. (Bare feet and swimsuits are usually inappropriate in the dining room.) In cooler seasons, casual, comfortable clothes, including a variety of layers to allow for changes in the weather, are appropriate for all daytime activities. (For further information on choosing and packing a basic wardrobe, see *How to Pack,* in this section.)

Evening wear for most cruises is dressy-casual. Formal wear is probably not necessary on 1-week cruises, optional on longer ones. There aren't many nights when it's expected. Most ships have a captain's cocktail party the first or second night out and a farewell dinner near the end of the cruise. Women should feel comfortable in hostess gowns, cocktail dresses, or stylish slacks. (To feel completely secure, you may want to pack one very dressy item.) Jackets and ties are always preferred for men in the evening, but a long-sleeve, open-neck shirt with ascot or scarf is usually an acceptable substitute.

TIPS: Tips are a strictly personal expense, and you *are* expected to tip — in particular, your cabin and dining room stewards. Allow $2.50 a day for each steward (more if you wish) and additional sums for very good service. (*Note:* Tips should be paid by each individual in a cabin, whether there are one, two, or more.) Others who may merit tips are the deck steward who sets up your chair at the pool or elsewhere, the wine steward in the dining room, porters who handle your luggage (tip them individually at the time they assist you), and any others who provide you with personal service. On some ships you can charge your bar tab to your cabin; throw in the tip when you pay it at the end of the cruise. Smart travelers tip twice during the trip: about midway through the cruise and at the end; even wiser travelers tip a bit at the start of the trip to ensure better service throughout. In all, expect to distribute about 15% of your total fare in tips. Although some cruise lines do have a no-tipping policy and you are not penalized by the crew for not tipping, naturally, you aren't penalized for tipping, either. If you can restrain yourself, it is better not to tip on those few ships that discourage it. However, never make the mistake of not tipping on the majority of ships, where it is a common, expected practice.

SHIP SANITATION: The US Public Health Service (PHS) currently inspects all passenger vessels calling at US ports, so very precise information is available on which ships meet PHS requirements and which do not. The further requirement that ships immediately report illness that occurs on board adds to the available data.

So the problem for prospective cruise passengers is to determine whether the ship on which they plan to sail has met the official sanitary standard. US regulations require the PHS to publish actual grades for the ships inspected — rather than the old pass or fail designation — so it's now easy to determine any cruise ship's status. Nearly 4,000 travel agents, public health organizations, and doctors receive a copy of each monthly ship sanitation summary, though a random sampling of travel agents indicated that few had any idea what this ship inspection program is all about. Again, the best advice is to deal with a travel agent who specializes in cruise ships and bookings, for he or she is most likely to have the latest information on the sanitary conditions of all cruise ships. To receive a copy of the most recent summary or a particular inspection report, write to Tom Hunt, Public Health Service, 1015 N. America Way, Room 107, Miami, FL 33132, or call 305-536-4307.

TRANSATLANTIC CROSSINGS: For seagoing enthusiasts, *Cunard*'s *Queen Elizabeth 2* is one of the largest and most comfortable vessels afloat, and it has recently undergone a complete overhaul and refurbishing, from a replacement of its engines to a revitalization and redecoration of passenger quarters. Each year, in addition to a full calendar of Caribbean, Bermudian, and European cruises, plus a round-the-world cruise, the *QE2* schedules approximately a dozen round-trip transatlantic crossings between June and, usually, December.

The *QE2* normally sets its course from New York to Southampton, England (a 5-day trip), and then directly back to the US, although on a few of the crossings it proceeds from Southampton to Cherbourg, France, or to another European port before turning back across the Atlantic. (Similarly, on some crossings the ship calls at various US East Coast ports in addition to New York, thus giving passengers a choice of where to embark or disembark.)

Transatlantic crossings, however, do not come at bargain prices. Last year, the one-way, per-person cost of passage from New York to either Southampton or Cherbourg ranged from $1,330 (for the least expensive, two-per-cabin, transatlantic class accommodations at the end of the season) to $8,415 (for one of the grandest travel experiences imaginable). *Cunard* brings a voyage aboard a luxury liner within reach of the less affluent traveler, however, by offering an air/sea package in conjunction with British Airways. The one-way ticket to Europe by sea includes an allowance toward return economy class airfare from London to any of 57 North American cities — a free flight home, in essence — provided certain length-of-stay restrictions are respected. The allowance can be applied to an upgraded air ticket if desired, and if you want to splurge, you can even fly home on a specially reserved British Airways supersonic *Concorde,* provided you make up the difference between the allowance and the *Concorde* fare (the shortfall at press time was $995). *Cunard* also offers various European tour packages that can be added to the basic air/sea offer. One such tour offered in 1989, the 17-day "Shamrock," spent 5 full days in Ireland and the balance of its itinerary in England, Scotland, and Wales.

Cunard is now also offering a particularly economical round-trip air/sea option for travelers with a flexible schedule. Special "standby" fares are available on some transatlantic crossings between the US and London (20 sailings were offered between April and December 1989) and include airfare on British Airways to a number of US gateways. The package cost (at press time, $999 to $1,099 — depending on dates of travel) includes a berth in a double-occupancy "minimum" room on either the *QE2* or *Cunard*'s *Vistafjord* and a one-way British Airways economy class ticket to or from London and New York, Boston, Philadelphia, Miami, Chicago, Detroit, or Washington, DC. For an additional $100, passengers may fly to or from other British Airways US gateways, including Anchorage, Atlanta, Houston, Los Angeles, Pittsburgh, San Diego, San Francisco, and Seattle. Although this fare is offered strictly on a space-available basis, confirmations are provided 3 weeks prior to sailing. To qualify for this fare, travelers must submit a written application and a $100 deposit to a travel agent or *Cunard;* full payment is due upon confirmation. For information, check with your travel agent or contact Cunard, 555 Fifth Ave., New York, NY 10017 (phone: 212-661-7777, 800-221-4770, or 800-5-CUNARD).

Another interesting transatlantic crossing opportunity for those who have the time is what the industry calls a positioning cruise. This is the sailing of a US- or Caribbean-based vessel from its winter berth to the city in Europe from which it will be offering summer cruise programs. Eastbound positioning cruises take place in the spring; westbound cruises return in the fall. Since ships do not make the return trip until they need to position themselves for the next cruise season, most lines offering these cruises have some air/sea arrangement that allows passengers to fly home economically — though the cruises themselves are not inexpensive.

Among the ships that have been offering positioning cruises for a number of years are *Cunard*'s *Vistafjord* and ships of the *Royal Viking Line* and *Royal Cruise Line.* Itineraries and ports of call vary from year to year. Typically, the ships sail from Florida or from San Juan, Puerto Rico, and cross the Atlantic to any one of a number of European ports where the trip may be broken — Lisbon, Málaga, Barcelona, Genoa, Venice, Piraeus, Cherbourg, Le Havre, Southampton — before proceeding to cruise European waters (i.e., the Mediterranean, the Baltic Sea, the Black Sea, through the Norwegian fjords). Passengers can elect to stay aboard for the basic transatlantic segment alone or for both the crossing and the subsequent European cruise.

Anyone intent on taking a positioning cruise should note that the nearest point of disembarkation or embarkation is usually Southampton, England. In 1989, for instance, while none of the above ships made an eastbound positioning cruise this far north in the Atlantic, two of them made westbound cruises from Southampton to New York. The *Royal Viking Line*'s *Royal Viking Sky* made a 21-day leisure trip, calling at Scotland and various ports in Scandinavia and Canada as well as at Boston and Nantucket en route. This year, *Royal Viking* is offering a 12-day cruise from London to New York, sailing in August via Horta in the Portuguese Azores. Prices for the cruise range from $2,620 to $7,920. In 1990, the *Royal Viking Sun* will also be making a 14-day cruise from Copenhagen to London, with other ports of call including Norway, Iceland, and Scotland. (Prices range from $4,740 to $30,610.) The *Royal Cruise Line*'s *Crown Odyssey* is scheduled to make a 9-day direct trip in August from Southampton to New York called the "Great Transatlantic High Society Cruise;" fares range from $2,728 to $6,408. *Royal Cruise Line* also offers, during the summer, tours of Scandinavia for an 8- to 13-day cruise leaving round-trip from London; fares range from $3,498 to $9,248. In May, the *Crown Odyssey* will make a 12-day cruise called

"Great Capitals of Europe," sailing from Venice and ending in Southampton; fares range from $3,598 to $9,198. For all of these offerings, book well in advance in order to qualify for substantial "early bird" discounts.

For information, ask your travel agent or contact the following cruise lines directly: Cunard, 555 Fifth Ave., New York, NY 10017 (phone: 212-661-7777, 800-221-4770, or 800-5 CUNARD), Royal Viking Line, 95 Merrick, Coral Gables, FL 33134 (phone: 305-447-9660 or 800-634-8000); Royal Cruise Line, One Maritime Plaza, Suite 1400, San Francisco, CA 94111 (phone: 415-956-7200).

FREIGHTERS: These are cargo ships that also take a limited number of passengers (usually about 12) in reasonably comfortable accommodations. The idea of traveling by freighter has long appealed to romantic souls, but there are a number of drawbacks to keep in mind before casting off. Once upon a time, a major advantage of freighter travel was its low cost, but this is no longer the case. Though freighters are usually less expensive than cruise ships, the difference is not as great as it once was, and excursion airfares are certainly even less expensive. Accommodations and recreational facilities vary, but freighters were not designed to amuse passengers, so it is important to appreciate the idea of freighter travel itself. Schedules are erratic, and travelers must fit their timetable to that of the ship. Passengers have found themselves waiting as much as a month for a promised sailing, and because freighters follow their cargo commitments, it is possible that a scheduled port could be omitted at the last minute or a new one added.

Anyone contemplating taking a freighter from a US port across the Atlantic should be aware that at press time, only a few freighter lines were carrying passengers on such crossings. Once a week, *Polish Ocean Lines* freighters accommodate 6 passengers in 3 double cabins on voyages of approximately 8 to 10 days from Port Newark, New Jersey, to Le Havre (a bit less than 6 hours by ferry from Portsmouth, near Southampton), and Rotterdam (an overnight ferry ride from Hull, in Yorkshire). The one-way fare from Newark was $788 per person in 1989, and passengers could also board in Baltimore, Maryland, or Wilmington, North Carolina, for an additional $150; round-trip fares were simply double the one-way fares. For information, contact *Gdynia America Line,* the general agent for *Polish Ocean Lines,* at 39 Broadway, 14th Floor, New York, NY 10006 (phone: 212-952-1280).

Mineral Shipping also sails to Rotterdam (again, you can take an overnight ferry to Britain) from Savannah, Georgia, taking several weeks; the one-way fare is $850. The round trip takes 33 days and costs $1,900. It also sails from Savannah to Rotterdam via Jamaica; the one-way ticket is $1,000. The ships sail up to twice monthly year-round and can carry up to 12 passengers. Contact the general agent *Freighter World Cruises* (address below).

Container Ships Reederi, departing approximately every 2 weeks and with a capacity of 6 to 9 passengers, sails from Long Beach, California, via the Panama Canal to Le Havre, Rotterdam, and Felixstowe in Britain (northeast of London), taking 23 to 24 days to make the trip. The one-way, per-person fare is $1,975 to $2,110. For information, contact the line's general agent, *Freighter World Cruises* (address below). Another line, *Lykes Lines,* sails to Felixstowe and Rotterdam from New Orleans, with a capacity of up to 8 passengers. The trip lasts 12 to 13 days, and ships leave every 8 days year-round; a one-way ticket costs $1,400. Contact *Lykes Lines,* 300 Poydres, New Orleans, LA 70130 (phone: 504-523-6611).

Last, *Mediterranean Shipping Co.* sails from Baltimore, Boston, New York, and Norfolk to Antwerp, Hamburg, Felixstowe, and Le Havre, taking 28 days for the trip. The ships can carry 12 passengers and leave weekly year-round. Prices vary, based on departure point and destination, but on average the one-way fare runs between $1,200 and $1,800. Contact *Mediterranean Shipping Co.,* 96 Morton St., New York, NY 10014 (phone: 212-691-3760).

Specialists dealing only (or largely) in freighter travel exist to help prospective passengers arrange trips. They provide information, schedules, and, when you're ready to sail, booking services. Among them are the following:

Freighter World Cruises: A travel agency specializing in freighters. Publishes *Freighter Space Advisory,* a twice-monthly newsletter listing space available on sailings worldwide ($27 a year, $25 of which can be credited to the cost of a cruise), and acts as general agent for several freighter lines. 180 S. Lake Ave., Suite 335, Pasadena, CA 91101 (phone: 818-449-3106).

Pearl's Freighter Tips: Pearl Hoffman, an experienced hand in freighter travel, finds sailings for her customers and sends them off with all kinds of information and advice. 175 Great Neck Rd., Suite 306, Great Neck, NY 11021 (phone: 516-487-8351).

TravLTips Cruise and Freighter Travel Association: A freighter travel agency and club ($15 a year) whose members receive the bi-monthly *TravLTips* magazine of cruise and freighter travel. PO Box 188, Flushing, NY 11358 (phone: 718-939-2400).

INLAND WATERWAYS: Cruising the canals and rivers of Europe is becoming more and more popular, probably in reaction to the speed of jet travel and the normal rush to do as much as possible as quickly as possible. A cabin cruiser or converted barge averages only about 5 miles an hour, covering in a week of slow floating the same distance a car would travel in a few hours of determined driving. Passengers see only a small section of countryside, but they see it in depth and with an intimacy simply impossible any other way.

Great Britain's waterways are ideal for cruising, including the river Thames. Navigable for 125 miles, a favorite itinerary is to follow it past such venerable sights as Runnymede, where the Magna Carta was signed, Hampton Court, Windsor Castle, Cliveden House, the summer resort of Henley-on-Thames, the town of Abingdon, and Oxford University. Another itinerary follows the quiet flow of the river Avon from Stratford-upon-Avon to Tewkesbury, where it joins England's longest river, the Severn. Also popular are the rivers, lakes, and interconnecting waterways of the Norfolk Broads in East Anglia; the quiet, less trafficked Fens, just west of the Broads; and in the midlands, several hundred miles of old narrow canals that were crucial to the development of the Industrial Revolution. Here, only traditional narrowboats — from 30 to 70 feet long but never more than 6 feet 10 inches in the beam — can navigate, because the canals, some as narrow as 20 feet, have locks a uniform 7 feet wide.

There are two ways to cruise the inland waterways: by renting your own self-drive boat or by booking aboard a hotel boat. If you choose to skipper your own diesel-powered cruiser, you will be shown how to handle the craft and told whom to call if you break down. But once you cast off, you and your party — the boats sleep from 2 to 10 people — will be on your own. You help lock-keepers operate the few gates on the Severn or the Avon, and operate untended locks on the Grand Canal yourself. You can do your own cooking (village markets and farms that sell produce directly are a good source of fresh food and local delicacies) or eat at pubs and restaurants along the way. The cost of the rental can vary considerably depending on the size of the boat, the season, and the area. A boat sleeping two comfortably can cost from $550 to $650 per week in spring or fall and jump to $1,100-$1,800 per week at the height of the summer; an eight-berth boat can range from $1,000 to $8,000 per week. The average rental, however, sleeping four, works out to about $175 per person per week during the low season and $300 per person per week in the high season. Fuel is not included.

The alternative is to cruise on a hotel boat — often a converted barge. These can carry anywhere from 6 to 24 guests, occasionally even more, as well as the crew. You can charter the boat and have it all to yourself or join other guests aboard. Cruises usually last from 3 days to a week; accommodations can be simple or quite luxurious, and most meals are usually included. When reading the brochure, note the boat's facilities (most cabins have private washbasins, showers, and toilets, but bathrooms can also be separate and shared), as well as the itinerary and any special features, such as sightseeing excursions, that may be offered. Many cruises have a special emphasis, such as food or visiting historic spots. Prices can range from $480 per person, double occupancy, to a high of $1,690.

The travel firms listed below, including the operators of hotel-boat cruises and representatives of self-drive boat suppliers, can provide information or arrange your whole holiday afloat.

Abercrombie & Kent/Continental Waterways: Runs hotel-boat cruises, including Barging Through Great Britain. 1420 Kensington Rd., Suite 103, Oak Brook, IL 60521 (phone: 312-954-2944 in Illinois; 800-323-7308 elsewhere in the US).

Bargain Boating, Morgantown Travel Service: Books self-skippered boats. 127 High St., PO Box 757, Morgantown, WV 26507-0757 (phone: 304-292-8471).

Blakes Vacations: Books self-skippered boats. 4939 Dempster St., Skokie, IL 60077 (phone: 312-539-1010 in Illinois; 800-628-8118 elsewhere in the US).

Floating Through Europe: Operates hotel-boat cruises, including trips on the Severn through Stratford-upon-Avon, and the Cotswolds. 271 Madison Ave., New York, NY 10016 (phone: 212-685-5600 or 800-221-3140).

Horizon Cruises: Books hotel-boat cruises. 16000 Ventura Blvd., Encino, CA 91436 (phone: 818-906-8086 or 800-252-2103 in California; 800-421-0454 elsewhere in the US).

Skipper Travel Services: Books self-skippered boats and hotel-boat cruises. 210 California Ave., PO Box 60309, Palo Alto, CA 94306 (phone: 415-321-5658).

■ **A final note on picking a cruise:** A "cruise-only" travel agency can better help you choose a cruise ship and itinerary than a travel agency that does not specialize in cruises. Cruise-only agents are best equipped to tell you about a particular ship's "personality," the kind of person with whom you'll likely be traveling on a particular ship, what dress is acceptable (it varies from ship to ship), and much more. At press time, there were over 275 agencies across the country that belonged to the *National Association of Cruise Only Agencies* (*NACOA*). For a list of these agencies in a particular state (requests are limited to three states), send a self-addressed, stamped envelope to NACOA, PO Box 7209, Freeport, NY 11520, or call 816-795-7372.

FERRIES: Numerous ferries link Great Britain with Ireland and the rest of Europe. Nearly all of them carry both passengers and cars — travelers simply drive on and off in most cases — and most of the routes are in service year-round. Many operators offer reduced rates for round-trip excursions, midweek travel, or off-season travel. Space for cars should be booked as early as possible, especially during the high season, even though most lines schedule more frequent departures during the summer. Note that long journeys, of 8 to 10 hours or more, tend to be scheduled overnight.

Among the ferries to Great Britain is the fleet of *Sealink* ships, jointly operated by British, Dutch, and French partners. *Sealink* connects Hoek van Holland (Netherlands; the "Hook of Holland"), with Harwich; and the French port of Calais with Dover, Boulogne with Folkstone, Dieppe with Newhaven, and Cherbourg with Portsmouth and Weymouth.

Other ferry services to Great Britain operate from Bergen and Stavanger (Norway) to Newcastle, from Bergen to Lerwick, and from Kristiansand and Oslo to Harwich; from Göteborg (Sweden) and Esbjerg (Denmark) to Newcastle and Harwich; from Hamburg (West Germany) to Harwich; from Scheveningen (Netherlands) to Great Yarmouth, from Rotterdam to Hull, and from Vlissingen to Sheerness; and from

Zeebrugge (Belgium) to Hull, Felixstowe, and Dover, and from Ostend to Dover. Ferries from French ports operate from Dunkerque to Ramsgate, from Calais and Boulogne to Dover, from Le Havre, Ouistreham, and Cherbourg to Portsmouth, from St. Malo to Portsmouth and the Channel Islands, and from Roscoff to Plymouth. There is even a ferry from Santander, Spain, to Plymouth.

Hoverspeed hovercraft carry both cars and passengers on a cushion of air across the Channel between Calais or Boulogne and Dover. Service is daily year-round, but since hovercraft travel a few feet above the surface of the water, they can be obstructed by waves and are grounded when the Channel is rough. When the weather is good, however, they make the crossing in about 35 minutes (compared to the ferry's 1¼ to 1¾ hours). Passengers-only *Jetfoil* service, also daily, connects Dover with Ostend in approximately 1¾ hours (3¾ to 4 hours by ferry).

Ferries between Great Britain and Ireland include the daily, year-round *Sealink* services from Holyhead, Wales, to Dún Laoghaire, and the joint *Sealink–B & I Line* services, also daily year-round, from Fishguard, Wales, to Rosslare Harbour. Both trips take about 3½ hours. Other ferry lines make daily trips from Holyhead to Dublin directly (3½ hours) and from Liverpool to Dún Laoghaire (8 to 9 hours). Ferry services to Northern Ireland connect Liverpool to Belfast in 9 hours, and the Scottish port of Cairnryan to Larne in 2 to 2¼ hours. The *Sealink* ferry travels between Stranraer, Scotland, and Larne in 2¼ hours.

Scheduled car/passenger ferries travel from various mainland ports to the Orkney and Shetland islands, the Inner and Outer Hebrides, the Isle of Man, and the Isles of Scilly. *Sealink* ferries connect the mainland to the Channel Islands and the Isle of Wight.

Arrivals and departures of most ferries, *Hoverspeed* hovercraft, and the *Jetfoil* are well served by connecting passenger trains or buses, and it is possible to buy through tickets from London that include the ferry portion of the trip to cities such as Dublin, Amsterdam, Brussels, and Paris. The London to Paris route on through services by train/hovercraft/train takes an average of 5½ hours; London to Brussels by train/ship/train, an average of 7½ hours, or by train/Jetfoil/train, 5½ hours; London to Dublin by train/ship/bus, from 9½ to 10¼ hours.

For information on *B & I Line* services, contact *Lynott Tours* (350 Fifth Ave., Suite 2619, New York, NY 10118; phone: 212-760-0101 or 800-537-7575 in New York State; 800-221-2474 elsewhere in the US). For *Sealink* schedules and prices, contact *BritRail Travel International* or other *BritRail* offices in the US (see *Touring by Rail* for addresses). For information on other ferry services, contact the British Tourist Authority (see *Tourist Information Offices* for addresses). Other sources of information are the *International Cruise Centre* (250 Old Country Rd., Mineola, NY 11501; phone: 800-221-3254) and the *P & O European Ferries Center* (PO Box A, Saltillo, PA 17253; phone: 814-448-3945 or 800-458-3606); both are US representatives of several European ferry lines.

Touring by Train

Perhaps the most economical, and often the most satisfying, way to see a lot of a foreign country in a relatively short time is by rail. It is certainly the quickest way to travel between two city centers up to 300 miles apart (beyond that, a flight would be quicker, even counting commuting time from airport to city center). But time isn't always the only consideration. Traveling by train is a way to keep moving and to keep seeing at the same time, and with the special discounts available to visitors, it can be an almost irresistible bargain.

TRAINS AND FARES: While North Americans have been raised to depend on their cars, Europeans have long been able to depend on public transportation. In fact, the novel idea of carrying passengers by rail occurred to the British first, and in 1825 train travel was born. Today, *British Rail,* the national railroad company — known outside Great Britain as *BritRail* and represented in the US by *BritRail Travel International* (addresses below) — operates no fewer than 15,000 trains a day, a number exceeded only by the West Germans. As an example of today's service, consider the *Flying Scotsman,* one of the most famous British trains since the middle of the 19th century. Originally, it did not truly fly, but today it is one of *British Rail*'s high-speed *InterCity 125* trains on the London-Edinburgh route, making the 393-mile journey in a mere 4 hours and 23 minutes. Other *InterCity 125* trains, so called because they operate at speeds up to 125 mph for long stretches of track, lead from London to Bath and Bristol, to Cardiff and Swansea, to Exeter, Plymouth, and Penzance, and to Birmingham, Manchester, and Sheffield, among other routes. The rest of *British Rail*'s *InterCity* services are fast and frequent, connecting cities and major towns without many intermediate stops. Counting local and suburban lines as well, there are few places in England, Scotland, and Wales that can't be reached by rail.

Fares on British trains are based not only on the distance traveled but also on the quality of accommodations the passenger chooses. All *InterCity* services have first class and economy class (standard class) cars, although trains on many local routes, especially rural ones, may have one class only, corresponding to economy. Traditionally, seating is arranged in compartments, with three or four passengers on one side facing a like number on the other side, but on most trains, compartments have been replaced by an open central-aisle design, though a few older cars still remain. In general, seats in first class are two abreast facing two more abreast across a table. On the other side of the aisle, two single seats face each other across a smaller table. The seats are wider than those in economy. Economy class seats are also arranged around tables, but there are two abreast on both sides of the aisle. For the extra comfort it provides, first class travel costs roughly 50% more than economy class travel, and because of this, it is generally less crowded. But anyone electing to travel economy — as most British do — can count on service that compares favorably with that found anywhere in North America.

Round-trip tickets (called "return" tickets in Great Britain) generally cost twice as much as one-way ("single") tickets. There are ways to economize, however, if you travel when most Britons are hard at work and not riding the rails. Blue Saver Tickets (which are "day return" tickets that do not have to be used the same day) afford a substantial saving on a day's outing if you depart after the morning rush hour and return after the evening rush has subsided. White Saver Tickets (or "weekend returns") save money if you leave on a Friday, Saturday, or Sunday and return on the Saturday, Sunday, or Monday of the same weekend. On weekends on some trains, for an additional £2 to £3 (approximately $3 to $4.50) you can upgrade your economy class ticket to a first class ticket. Other discounted tickets are also available — when buying your ticket ask about current offerings. To save even more, consider buying one of the variety of rail passes allowing unlimited travel within a set time period. Some are meant for foreign tourists only and must be bought before you go (see below).

Most *InterCity* trains have either a restaurant car, where a full lunch or dinner costs about £7 to £12 ($10.50 to $18), excluding wine and tip, or a buffet car offering simpler, less expensive snacks and drinks, including alcoholic ones. If you're sure you will want to eat en route, however, it's a good idea to inquire beforehand exactly what meal service is offered on the train you'll be taking. Seats in the dining car should be reserved either before boarding or very early in the trip through the steward.

Sleeping cars are found on night trains to Scotland, the north and west of England, and Wales. The sleeper supplement is a standard £20 or £22 (about $30 and $33) addition to the price of a economy or first class ticket respectively, even if you're traveling on a discounted ticket. You will have a single compartment to yourself in first class (couples share connecting single compartments); in economy class you'll share double accommodations, one on the top bunk, the other below. The lone traveler is usually paired with a stranger of the same sex, but may occasionally have a compartment all alone. In either first or economy class, there is a washbasin in the compartment, and a morning wake-up is provided by the attendant, who leaves hot coffee or tea and biscuits at the door, free of charge. As a matter of course, you'll be awakened a half hour before your stop, but if that is not enough time, tell the attendant the night before what time you want to get up. Passengers traveling to the end of the line may stay in their bunks until 7 or 7:30 AM, even if the train is scheduled to arrive earlier.

Naturally, it is best to travel light enough to keep your suitcase with you on the overhead rack, but if you have quite a bit of luggage, it can be loaded onto the baggage car found on nearly every train (although occasionally, particularly on rural routes, there may not be enough room for all baggage and yours may arrive on a later train). No claim ticket is issued, so label your bags inside and out. If you are getting off at an intermediate station, make your way to the baggage car as you approach your stop and supervise the unloading yourself. It is not the attendant's responsibility to do it for you even if you have printed your destination conspicuously on the bag. Most stations have porters or self-service carts, though you may find either or both in short supply when you need one. Baggage can be checked overnight at the Left Luggage facilities in most stations or in 24-hour lockers in some.

Both first and economy class seats on most *InterCity 125* trains can be reserved in advance, either before leaving home or after arriving in Great Britain. Reservations may reduce flexibility, but they are advisable during the summer on certain popular routes, such as London-Edinburgh, London-Glasgow, London-Manchester, and London to points southwest. Sleeper reservations are necessary and should be made as far in advance as possible. Reservations can be made through travel agents or *BritRail Travel International* offices in North America (addresses below) or, in Great Britain, at *British Rail* Travel Centres set up to help passengers with bookings and information on all services offered by *British Rail.* The British Travel Centre at 12 Regent Street in London (a joint effort of *British Rail,* the British Tourist Authority, and American Express) is open daily and offers the broadest services; others are at most of London's main railway stations, at Heathrow and Gatwick airports, and at railway stations in many other cities.

The multiplicity of London's train stations requires an explanation. There are 11 principal stations, each the starting point for trains to a particular region, with occasional overlapping of routes. Those the tourist is most likely to encounter include King's Cross, the departure point for northeast England and eastern Scotland including Edinburgh; St. Pancras, for trains going north from London as far as Sheffield; Euston, serving the midlands, North Wales including Holyhead, and ferries for Dún Laoghaire, Ireland, northwest England, and western Scotland including Glasgow; Paddington, for the West Country and South Wales including Fishguard and ferries to Rosslare, Ireland; Victoria, for Gatwick Airport and, along with Charing Cross Station, for southeast England including Dover and ferries to France; and Liverpool Street Station, for departures to East Anglia and Harwich for ferries to the Continent and to Scandinavia. Though stations are connected via London's underground or "tube" (subway) system, allowing passengers to avoid busy streets while transferring from one to the other, you should still leave plenty of time to make the change. Note also, for your travels in other parts of Britain, that London is not the only city with more than one station.

Drivers should be aware of *British Rail*'s car-carrying trains, called *Motorails,* operating principally between London and Scotland and between London and the West

Country. *Motorail* allows car owners to take to the rails for long distances while their cars travel with them on a flatcar. Book well in advance for this, especially in the summer. Another service for motorists is the *Rail-Drive* booth, found in some 100 rail stations throughout Great Britain, operated by *Hertz.* Passengers can reserve a car before boarding the train and find it waiting for them at the station of their destination. Special rates apply for holders of the *BritRail* Pass, and *BritRail-Drive* packages can be arranged through *BritRail Travel International* offices in North America before leaving home.

Passenger and car-carrying ferries cross the Channel and the North Sea to continental Europe and the Irish Sea to Ireland, and travelers can buy through tickets from London to cities such as Paris, Brussels, Amsterdam, and Dublin, without making separate arrangements for the sea portion of the journey. Travel is by rail to the water, where the ship waits, equipped or not with sleeping cabins depending on the length of the trip. Passengers walk to the ship and, on the other shore, board a waiting train to complete the journey. Also available are through tickets from London to Paris using *Hoverspeed* hovercraft rather than the ship. These skim across the surface of the water with their cargo of passengers and autos, crossing the Channel from Dover to Boulogne or Calais in about 35 minutes (versus 1¼ to 1¾ hours by ship). Similarly, passengers-only *Jetfoil* service can be used on the trip from London to cities in Belgium and the Netherlands and to Luxembourg.

EXCURSIONS AND TOURS: *British Rail* offers a series of all-inclusive escorted tours out of London that combine fast rail travel with more leisurely sightseeing by bus. Known as Britainshrinkers and available only from April through October, they can be either day trips or overnighters. The Britainshrinker to Stratford-upon-Avon, for example, leaves London's Euston Station at 8:10 AM on Wednesdays (also Mondays and Fridays at the peak of the season) and includes a morning visit to Warwick Castle and afternoon visits to the home of Shakespeare's wife, Anne Hathaway, as well as to his own birthplace. After a stop at the cathedral in Coventry, participants arrive back in London at 6:21 PM. There are 8 other 1-day itineraries, 2 overnight tours of 2 and 3 days' duration (accommodations are in better hotels), plus "The Great Britain Express," a 6-day itinerary that crosses England from London to Plymouth, then moves all the way up to Edinburgh and back to London. Britainshrinkers can be booked through *BritRail Travel International* offices in North America or at the *British Rail* Travel Centres in London stations.

Other tour operators offer package tours using trains as a means of transport, as a hotel on some or all nights, and, since vintage rail coaches are usually involved, as attractions in themselves. For sources of a few of these tours geared to lovers of old trains as well as of scenery, see the discussion of the *Royal Scotsman, Flying Scotsman,* and *Venice Simplon–Orient Express* programs in *Package Tours.* Note that the British Pullman portion of the latter also makes day trips out of London to such popular destinations as Bath and Bristol, Folkestone, Beaulieu, Broadlands, Bournemouth, Hever Castle and Penshurst Place, Arundel Castle, and others.

PASSES: Rail passes are offered by the national railroad companies of most European countries. They allow unlimited train travel within a set time period, and they can save you a considerable amount of money as well as time. The only requirement is validation of the pass by an information clerk on the day of your first trip; for subsequent trips, there is no need to stand in line — and lines can be very long in the peak travel season. These passes are generally meant for foreign tourists only and thus must often be bought before departure.

The Eurailpass, the first and best known of all rail passes, is not valid in Great Britain. Britain, however, has its own rail passes, of which the *BritRail* Pass is the most extensive. It offers unlimited travel throughout England, Wales, Scotland, and Northern Ireland and is issued for either first or economy class travel for periods of 8, 15, or 22 days or for 1 month, with children from 5 through 15 years traveling at half fare in each of the eight categories. The *BritRail* Youth Pass, for those 16 through 25, allows unlimited travel in economy accommodations, and the *BritRail* Senior Citizen Pass allows anyone age 60 or over to travel in first class at reduced rates. All these passes must be bought before going abroad, either from a travel agent or through *BritRail Travel International* offices in North America. *BritRail* suggests that travelers apply for the passes at least 3 weeks prior to departure. *BritRail* also offers a new service this year, the *BritRail* Flexipass. Travelers decide how long they want to travel, then choose the pass that fits their plans. When they arrive in Britain, they can use any of *British Rail*'s 15,000 daily trains, including the *InterCity* high-speed trains. The pass's period of validity does not commence until the traveler first uses it. Travelers can purchase the Flexipass through a travel agent when they book their trip or at the outlets mentioned above. Prices range from first class (gold), for use on any 4 days out of 8 for $210 per person, to economy (silver) for $149; $310 (gold) per person or $219 (silver) for use on any 8 out of 15 days; additional discounts are available for seniors and children.

There is no doubt that the *BritRail* Pass is a bargain. At press time, the cost of an 8-day adult economy pass was $179, just $5 more than the cost of one round-trip fare between London and Edinburgh. However, some other passes are worth investigating if you plan to thoroughly explore a limited region. The Scottish Highlands and Islands Travelpass, for instance, provides 7 or 14 days of unlimited train and bus travel in the Scottish Highlands plus ferry service to the larger Scottish islands, and includes round-trip transportation between either Aberdeen, Glasgow or Edinburgh and the Highlands area. It is valid only from March through October and costs more at the height of the season (June through September) than in March, April, May, or October. The 1989 price for a 7-day off-season pass was just $60; peak season, $95. The pass can be bought either before you go, through *Scots-American Travel Advisors* (26 Ruger Dr., Harrington Park, NJ 07640; phone: 201-768-5505 or 800-247-7268) or in Great Britain, from *British Rail, Scottish Bus Group,* and *Scottish Citylink Coaches* offices, at the Scottish Centre in London, or by writing to *Hi-Line* (Dingwall, Ross-Shire IV15 9SL, Scotland). The Highlands and Islands Travelpass also includes a Scotpass, which includes a card and handbook that gives 10% to 50% discounts on accommodations, meals, and visitor attractions. Other rail passes — among them the Freedom of Scotland ticket, the North and Mid-Wales Explorer (for train and bus), and regional Railrovers — are designed primarily for British citizens who cannot take advantage of the *BritRail* Pass. They are sold locally and limited to the selected region, often on a seasonal basis. For rail buffs, there is even the Great Little Trains of Wales–Wanderer Ticket, good for as many scenic trips as desired on the eight quaint, restored, narrow-gauge steam railways of Wales. Tickets are issued for 4 or 8 consecutive days of travel (valid from March through September) and can be bought at any of the railways at the time of your first trip, though you can write ahead for details, timetables, or the ticket to *Brecon Mountain Railway* (Pant Station, Merthyr Tydfil, Mid Glamorgan CF48 2UP, Wales).

FURTHER INFORMATION: *BritRail Travel International* offices in North America provide information on all *British Rail* services, make reservations, sell tickets and rail passes, and distribute a free catalogue, *Go BritRail.* Addresses are 630 Third Ave., New York, NY 10017 (phone: 212-599-5400); 800 S. Hope St., Suite 603, Los Angeles, CA 90017-4697 (phone: 213-624-8787); Cedar Maple Plaza, Suite 210, 2305 Cedar Springs, Dallas, TX 75201 (phone: 214-748-0860); 94 Cumberland St., Toronto, Ont., Canada M5R 1A3 (phone: 416-929-3333); and 409 Granville St., Vancouver, BC V6C 1T2, Canada (phone: 604-683-6896). *BritRail*'s *Travel Times,* a booklet that summarizes the main *InterCity* train services between major tourist centers in England, Wales, and Scotland, is available free from these offices.

Serious rail travelers may want to stop at a travel bookstore for a copy of George

Ferguson's *Britain by BritRail* ($10.95), which discusses train travel in Britain in detail, gives travel tips, and describes numerous excursions out of London and Edinburgh. The *ABC Rail Guide* ($10.75) lists nearly all the rail services in Britain, ferries and cross-Channel services included, and is available from the *British Travel Bookshop* (40 W. 57th St., New York, NY 10019; phone: 212-765-0898; add $3 for postage and handling for either of the above books). Comparable books for those traveling by train beyond Britain are the *Eurail Guide* ($12.95), by Kathryn Saltzman Turpin and Marvin Saltzman, and the *Thomas Cook European Timetable* ($16.95). The former, available in most travel bookstores, discusses routes, rates, and all the ins and outs of special rail deals around the world, and it contains information on Great Britain. The latter, the most revered and most accurate compendium of European railway timetables, also includes information on Great Britain. Issued monthly, it is available in a few travel bookstores or from the Forsyth Travel Library, PO Box 2975, Shawnee Mission, KS 66201-1375 (add $3 for airmail postage; Kansas residents add 5½% sales tax). You can order by phone and pay by credit card by calling 913-384-0496 or 800-367-7984.

Touring by Bus

Going from place to place by bus may not be the fastest way to get from here to there, but that may be the only drawback to bus travel. A persuasive argument in its favor is its cost: Short of walking, traveling by bus is the least expensive way to cover a long distance. On average, a bus ticket between two cities in Great Britain costs about two-thirds of the corresponding train fare. For this amount, it is possible to travel comfortably, if not always speedily, and at the same time enjoy an equally scenic view. The bus trip from London to Edinburgh, for instance, takes 9 or 10 hours, and you could cover the same territory in 4½ to 4¾ hours on a high-speed train, but since high-speed trains do not operate everywhere, the time difference on most routes is not as extreme. Buses also reach outposts remote from the railroad tracks, for those so inclined. While train service in Great Britain is somewhat limited to major travel routes, a map of the bus routes is not much different from a road map: If the way is paved, it's certain that a bus — some bus — is assigned to travel it. The network of express buses (called "coaches") — those traveling long distances with few stops en route — is only slightly less extensive. Because of this, Great Britain is particularly well suited to bus travel.

BOOKING: Reservations are not normally necessary on most bus routes, which work on established and published schedules. In rural areas in particular, the bus is the main form of transport for residents. Tickets are usually bought on the bus and are valid only for that day and that ride.

SERVICES: Buses are not equipped for food service, and few trips are long enough to necessitate meal stops. If you plan to spend some time traveling around Great Britain by bus, you may want to pick up something to eat en route, though you're probably better off waiting until you reach a stop in a town or city where you can eat more comfortably at a pub or restaurant.

FOR COMFORTABLE TRAVEL: Dress casually in loose-fitting clothes. Be sure you have a sweater or jacket (even in the summer), and a raincoat or umbrella for when you disembark is a year-long must. Passengers are allowed to listen to radios or cassette players, but must use earphones. Choose a seat in the front near the driver for the best view, in the middle between the front and rear wheels for the smoothest ride. Smoking is not allowed, even upstairs in the doubledecker buses that serve major cities such as London and Edinburgh.

It should be noted that to the British, only the bus that takes you from stop to stop in town is known as a bus; the vehicle that takes you from city to city (or on a tour) is called a coach. Express coach service throughout Great Britain is operated jointly by *National Express,* serving England and Wales, and by *Scottish Citylink Coaches,* part of the *Scottish Bus Group.* Together, they carry passengers to more than 1,500 destinations, about 200 of which benefit from even faster *Rapide* service. *Rapide* buses, some of them doubledeckers, cost a bit more than the other expresses (a pound or two extra each way); in return, they provide guaranteed seating plus a hostess, refreshments, and washroom facilities on board.

National Express and *Scottish Citylink Coaches* offer a number of discounts on their already quite economical fares. If you are buying a round-trip ticket, for instance, always ask about the savings possible by traveling on off-peak days or returning on the same day — such a round-trip ticket may cost no more than a one-way ticket to the same destination. And if you're planning to use the bus regularly, consider buying one of the bus passes or other discount tickets or cards discussed below. Remember that children aged 5 through 16 receive a reduction of one-third off normal fares, as do people over 60. For each paying adult, one child under 5 travels free.

London's main bus depot is the Victoria Coach Station on Buckingham Palace Road. The *National Express* information office in the station and the new Coach Travel Centre at 13 Lower Regent Street (phone for both: 01-730-0202) supply information and timetables and handle bookings. If leaving from London during peak travel periods, it is advisable to book well in advance.

BUS PASSES: Several bus passes and other discount tickets and cards make the bus even more of a bargain. None of these has to be bought before leaving the US, but most of them can be bought here and it's a good idea to investigate them while planning your trip.

The Britexpress Card costs $18 and allows the bearer a one-third discount off one-way and round-trip fares for any number of trips taken during a 30-day period over the entire *National Express* and *Scottish Citylink* networks and on selected services of other companies. Meant for overseas visitors only, it is not available for seniors or children, as other discounts are available for these groups; the card can be bought through a travel agent before you go or directly from *National Express*'s US agent, *Worldwide Marketing Associates* (909 W. Vista Way, Vista, CA 92083; phone: 800-621-3405 for information on the card; 619-758-0462 for information on timetables and fares). It can be bought in Britain, showing a passport as ID, at *National Express/Green Line* information centers at Heathrow and Gatwick airports, at the *National Express* office in Victoria Coach Station, at the *National Express* Coach Travel Centre in Lower Regent Street, and at the Glasgow and Edinburgh bus stations.

The Tourist Trail offers unlimited travel on all buses on 3, 5, 8, 15, 22, or 30 consecutive days. In 1989, the prices ranged from $68 for 3 days to $257 for 30 days, with reduced rates for seniors and children. It can be bought in the US or Great Britain from the same sources listed for the Britexpress Card (see above.)

Not strictly for buses, the Scottish Highlands and Islands Travelpass allows unlimited travel for a specified period of time by bus and rail in the Highlands area of Scotland, on ferry services to the Scottish islands, and on transportation to the Highlands and islands area from Glasgow or Edinburgh. It is good, too, for travel on the post buses that in some rural areas of Scotland carry mail and the occasional passenger. The Travelpass, valid from March through October, is issued for either 7 or 14 days and can be bought in the US from *Scots-American Travel Advisors* offices (see above) or in Great Britain from *British Rail* offices, *Scottish Bus Group* and *Scottish Citylink Coaches* offices, the Scottish Centre in London, or by writing to *Hi-Line* (Dingwall, Ross-shire IV15 9SL, Scotland).

Though bus timetables can be picked up overseas, it may be useful to have them on hand to help you plan before you go. The *National Express Coach Guide* comes out twice yearly, in April and October (summer and winter schedules, including *Scottish Citylink* services), and costs £7 (about $10.50) by sea mail and £10 airmail (about $15). Write to National Express Ltd., Projects Office, 4 Vicarage Rd., Edgbaston, Birmingham B15 3ES (phone: 02145-61122). *Note:* US currency is not accepted; you must use an international money order.

Many city bus lines have their own tourist discount schemes that are good for anyone who expects to move around town a lot. Not only do they save money, they also spare the bearer the bother of digging in pockets and handbags for small change. *London Regional Transport* (a separate entity from *British Rail*), which runs the city's buses and underground (subway) trains, offers several such passes, but the main one is the London Visitor Travelcard for 3, 4, or 7 days of unlimited travel by bus and the underground within Greater London. (*Note:* There is also a 1-day pass, which is not available in the US.) Trips by underground between Heathrow Airport and central London are included, as are discount coupons for some of the city's top attractions. Buy the pass from *BritRail Travel International* before you go; if you buy it in London, you'll need a passport-size photo and you won't receive the discount coupons.

Another pass is the One-day Off Peak Travelcard, good for unlimited bus and underground travel within a specified zone and available from *London Regional Transport* travel information centers and almost any underground or bus station. The Golden Rover Ticket — valid for a day, a weekend, or 7 consecutive days of travel in the countryside around London on *Green Line Coaches* and *London Country Buses, Kentish Bus and Coach, Country Rider,* and *Herts Rider* — can be bought from the bus driver. Other cities also have bus bargains, so if you're interested, always ask before you buy — there's bound to be something available. If you don't use one of the unlimited travel tickets, remember that flat fares are not the rule in London (with the exception of *Red Arrow* buses); the rate varies with the distance traveled, and a conductor on board will tell you how much you owe. Remember, also, always to "queue up" at the bus stop.

Touring by Car

After mastering the trick of keeping to the left side of the road, a visitor will quickly find Great Britain ideally suited for driving tours. Distances between major cities are reasonable, and the historical and cultural density is such that the flexibility of a car can be used to maximum advantage; a visitor can cover large amounts of territory visiting major sites or spend the same amount of time motoring from village to village. (See DIRECTIONS for our choices of the most interesting routes.) Travelers who wish to cover the island from end to end can count on a good system of highways to help them make time, while those exploring only one region will find that the secondary and even lesser roads are generally well surfaced and in good condition. Either way, there is plenty of satisfying scenery en route.

But driving isn't an inexpensive way to travel. Gas prices are higher in Great Britain than in North America, and car rentals are seldom available at bargain rates. Keep in mind, however, that driving becomes more economical with more passengers. Because the price of getting wheels abroad will be more than an incidental expense, it is important to investigate every alternative before making a final choice. Many travelers find this expense amply justified when considering that rather than just the means to an end, a well-planned driving route can be an important part of the adventure.

Before setting out, make certain that everything you need is in order. Read about the places you intend to visit and study relevant maps. If at all possible, discuss your trip with someone who has already driven the route to find out about road conditions and available services. If you can't speak to someone personally, try to read about others' experiences. The British Tourist Authority offices in the US (see *Tourist Information Offices* for addresses) can be a good source of travel information, although when requesting brochures and maps be sure to specify the areas you're planning to visit. (Also see *Maps,* below.)

DRIVING: A valid driver's license from their state of residence enables US citizens to drive in Great Britain for up to 12 months. Liability insurance is also required and is a standard part of any car rental contract. (To be sure of having the appropriate coverage, let the rental staff know in advance about the national borders you plan to cross.) If buying a car and using it abroad, the driver must carry an International Insurance Certificate, known as a Green Card. Your insurance carrier can arrange for a special policy to cover you in Europe, and will automatically issue your Green Card.

The British drive on the left-hand side of the road and pass (or "overtake," as they say) on the right. For this reason, the steering wheel is on the right-hand side of the car and shifting in a car with manual transmission is done with the left hand. The change is confusing at first, but it is possible to adjust in enough time to enjoy the trip. Seat belts are compulsory for the driver and front seat passenger — the fine can be as much as £200 (about $300) if you're stopped by a policeman for not wearing one — and children under 12 must travel in the back seat.

European countries are most zealous in prosecuting offenders of driving laws, especially in the matter of drinking and driving. The British routinely administer sobriety tests and are rigorous in imposing heavy fines and jail sentences. If you've been drinking, do as the natives do and walk home, take a cab, or make sure that a licensed member in your party sticks strictly to soft drinks.

In Great Britain, unlike the rest of Europe, distances are generally measured in miles and are registered as such on the speedometer. British speed limits are 70 mph on motorways (expressways) and dual carriageways (four-lane highways), 60 mph on single carriageways (two-lane highways), and 30 mph in towns or built-up areas — unless other limits are posted. Note, however, as the British are moving toward the metric system, highway signs may be written in several styles: in black and white for miles; in green and white for kilometers; or in miles and kilometers (1 mile equals 1.6 kilometers; 1 kilometer equals .62 mile). And as speed limits may also be in kilometers per hour, think twice before hitting the gas when you see a speed limit of 100 kmh (which means 62 mph).

Pictorial direction signs are standardized according to the International Roadsign System and their meanings are indicated by their shapes — triangular signs mean danger; circular signs give instructions; and rectangular signs are informative. Watch out for "zebra" crossings — black and white stripes painted across the roadway with an edging of white zigzag lines. Any pedestrian who has stepped onto the crossing has the right of way. Also watch out for "pelican" crossings, where stoplights have a pedestrian-activated flashing amber phase in addition to red, green, and steady amber. When the amber is flashing, you must give the right of way to any pedestrian on the crossing, but you may drive on when the crossing is clear.

Driving in British cities can be tricky, since many of them do not have street signs at convenient corners but identify their byways with plaques attached to the walls of corner buildings. These are often difficult to spot until you've passed them, and since most streets don't run parallel to one another, taking the next turn can lead you astray. Fortunately, most British cities and towns post numerous signs leading to the center of the city, and plotting a course to your destination from there may be far easier. Look for the signs that read TOWN CENTRE.

Pay particular attention to parking signs in large British cities, especially those indicating "control zones," where an unattended parked car presents a serious security risk. If you park in a restricted zone, unlike in the US (where you chance only a ticket or being towed), you may return to find that the trunk and doors have been blown off by overly cautious security forces. More likely, however, you'll return to find one of the car's wheels "clamped," a procedure that renders your auto inoperable and involves a tedious (and costly) process to get it freed.

Traffic congestion is at its worst on main roads, particularly those radiating from major cities. Look for signs pointing out detours or alternate routes to popular holiday destinations. Service stations, information points, and tourist offices distribute free maps of these routes, which may be the long way around but will probably get you to your goal faster in the end.

MAPS: Excellent road maps are published by Britain's two main automobile clubs, the *Automobile Association,* or *AA* (Farnum House, Basing View, Basingstoke, Hampshire RG21 2EA; phone: 0256-20123), and the *Royal Automobile Club,* or *RAC* (49 Pall Mall, London SW1Y 5JG; phone: 01-839-7050). Both have more than one series available — national, regional, local, and town maps in varying scales. The *AA Touring Map* ($5.95) is available directly from the *AA* or from the *British Travel Bookshop* (40 W. 57th St., New York, NY 10019 (phone: 212-765-0898; add $2.50 for postage and handling). The *AA* will also provide members with suggested routes between destinations that vary from scenic to the most direct.

The *Automobile Association of America* (*AAA*) is another source of travel information, and members can also take advantage of the publications offered by the *AA,* with whom the *AAA* has a reciprocal agreement. The *AAA* also publishes a map of Great Britain and Ireland, available from the travel departments in most *AAA* offices, and can also give members its 600-page *Travel Guide to Europe* (price varies from branch to branch) and 64-page *Motoring Europe* ($5.95); both are available through local *AAA* offices. Another invaluable guide, *Euroad: The Complete Guide to Motoring in Europe,* is available for $7.80, including postage and handling, from VLE Limited, PO Box 547, Tenafly, NJ 07670 (phone: 201-567-5536).

Also very good are the Michelin guides, on a scale of 6.30 miles to 1 inch. They cover the whole island, outline particularly scenic routes in green, and include inset maps showing the main roads into and out of large cities. Michelin maps are readily available in bookstores and map shops around the US and also from the company's US headquarters, Michelin Guides and Maps, PO Box 3305, Spartanburg, SC 29304-3305 (phone: 803-599-0850).

The British Tourist Authority distributes a less detailed, free map of Great Britain (scale 12 miles to 1 inch) published by the Ordnance Survey, the official government cartographer. It, too, covers Great Britain and outlines scenic routes in green; in addition, it includes city center maps. If stocks in the US are exhausted, look for it at tourist offices and some bookstores and newsstands in Great Britain.

Other maps are published by John Bartholomew & Son Ltd., a Scottish company whose motoring maps are stocked in many bookstores and map shops around the US. A catalogue of the full line can be obtained by writing to the company at 12 Duncan St., Edinburgh, Scotland EH9 1TA. In the US, it is represented by Hammond, Inc., 515 Valley St., Maplewood, NJ 07040 (phone: 201-763-6000).

AUTOMOBILE CLUBS: Many European automobile clubs offer emergency assistance to any breakdown victim, whether a club member or not; however, only members of these clubs or affiliated clubs may have access to certain information services and discounts on or reimbursements for towing and repair services.

The main British automobile clubs are the *Automobile Association* (*AA*), Farnum House, Basing View, Basingstoke, Hampshire RG21 2EA (phone: 0256-20123), and the *Royal Automobile Club* (*RAC*), 49 Pall Mall, London SW1Y 5JG (phone: 01-839-7050). Due to a reciprocal agreement, AAA members are automatically granted a temporary membership in the *AA* in Great Britain — giving them access to information and emergency rescue services. A temporary membership in one of the British clubs

— giving visitors access to their emergency rescue services — is also usually a part of the standard car rental contract.

To signal for help, pull over to the side of the road and raise your hood. Motor patrols usually drive small cars painted a uniform color. Both the *AA* and the *RAC* patrol major routes and maintain emergency phones (yellow call boxes for the *AA,* blue for the *RAC*) for stranded travelers to dial for roadside assistance. Bear in mind that on secondary or very rural routes, these boxes may be few and far between.

Aside from these options, a driver in distress will have to contact the nearest service center by pay phone. Car rental companies also provide for breakdowns, emergency service, and assistance; ask for a number to call when you pick up the vehicle.

GASOLINE – Called "petrol" in Great Britain, gasoline is sold either by the liter (approximately 4 to a gallon) or by the British or "imperial" gallon, which is 20% larger than the American gallon. An imperial gallon equals 1.2 US gallons; or 1 imperial gallon equals 4.5 liters and 1 US gallon equals 3.8 liters. In Great Britain, three grades are available: 4-star equals 97 octane; 3-star equals 94 octane; 2-star equals 90 octane.

Gas prices everywhere rise and fall depending on the world supply of oil, and an American traveling overseas is further affected by the prevailing rate of exchange, so it is difficult to say precisely what fuel will cost when you travel. It is not difficult to predict, however, that fuel will cost substantially more than in the US, so check the current price before you go and budget accordingly. Remember that, depending on where you're driving, unleaded fuel may be difficult to find. At least until all European gas stations sell unleaded, your best bet is to rent a car that takes leaded gasoline.

Rental cars are usually delivered with a full tank of gas. Remember to fill the tank before you return the car or you will have to pay to refill the tank, and gasoline at the car rental company's pump is always much more expensive than gas at a service station. This policy may vary for smaller regional companies; ask when picking up the vehicle.

Considering gas prices in Europe relative to US prices at the time of this writing, gas economy is of particular concern. The prudent traveler should begin by doing some preliminary research, planning an itinerary, and making as many reservations as possible in advance, in order to not waste gas figuring out where to go, stay, or eat. Drive early in the day, when there is less traffic. Then leave your car at the hotel and use local transportation within cities.

Although it may be as dangerous to drive at a speed much below the posted limit as it is to drive above it (particularly on motorways — expressways where the speed limit is 70 mph), at 55 mph (89 kmh) a car gets 25% better mileage than at 70 mph (112 kmh). The number of miles per liter or gallon is also increased by driving smoothly. Accelerate gently, anticipate stops, get into high gear quickly, and maintain a steady speed.

RENTING A CAR: Although there are other options, such as leasing or outright purchase, most people who want to drive in Europe simply rent a car through a travel agent or international rental firm before they go or, once they are in Europe, from a local company. Another possibility, also arranged before departure, is to rent the car as part of a larger package. Arrangements of this sort used to be called fly-drive packages, but increasingly you'll also find them described in tour brochures as self-drive, go-as-you-please, or car tours.

Renting is not inexpensive, but it is possible to economize by determining your own needs and then shopping around among the car rental companies until you find the best deal. Keep in mind that rates vary considerably, not only from city to city, but also from location to location within the same city. It might be less expensive to rent a car in the center of a city rather than at the airport. Usually, local companies are less expensive than the national giants. Ask about special rates or promotional deals, such as weekend or weekly rates, bonus coupons for airline tickets, or 24-hour rates that include gas and unlimited mileage.

Requirements – Whether you decide to rent a car in advance from a US rental company with British branches or from a British company, you should know that renting a car is rarely as simple as signing on the dotted line and roaring off into the night. If you are renting for personal use, you must have a valid driver's license and will have to convince the renting agency that (1) you are personally credit-worthy; and (2) you will bring the car back at the stated time. This will be easy if you have a major credit card; all large agencies and most local companies accept credit cards in lieu of a cash deposit, as well as in payment of your final bill. If you prefer to pay in cash, leave your credit card imprint as a "deposit," then pay your bill in cash when you return the car.

If you don't have a major credit card, renting a car for personal use becomes more complicated. If you are planning to rent from an international agency with an office near your home, the best thing is to call the renting company several days in advance and give it your name, home address, and information on your business or employer; the agency then runs its own credit check on you. This can be time consuming, so you should try to have it done before you leave home. If you are paying in cash and renting a car in Great Britain, it is best to make arrangements in advance — otherwise you must bring along a letter of employment and go to the agency during business hours (don't forget to take into account the time difference) so it can call your employer for verification.

In addition to paying the rental fee up front, you will also have to leave a hefty deposit when you pick up the car — either a substantial flat fee or a percentage of the total rental cost. (Each company has a different policy; look around for the best deal.) If you return the car on time, the full deposit will be refunded, otherwise additional charges will be deducted and any unused portion of the deposit will be refunded.

If you are planning to rent a car once in Great Britain, *Avis, Hertz,* and other US rental companies *will* usually rent to travelers paying in cash and leaving either a credit card imprint or a substantial amount of cash as a deposit. This is not necessarily standard policy, however, as *Budget,* some other international chains, and many British companies *will not* rent to an individual without a credit card. In this case, you will have to call around to find a company that does.

Also keep in mind that the minimum age at which the British may drive a car is 17 years, but the minimum age to rent a car varies with the company supplying it. Many firms have a minimum age requirement of 21 years, and some raise that to 23 or 25 for some sizes of cars. The upper age limit at many companies is between 69 and 75; others have no upper limit or may make drivers above a certain age subject to special conditions.

No matter which firm you choose, the first factor influencing cost is, naturally, the type and size of car. Rentals are based on a tiered price system, with different sizes of cars — variations of budget, economy, regular, and luxury — often listed as A (the smallest and least expensive) through F, G, or H, and sometimes even higher. The typical A car available in Great Britain is a two-door subcompact or compact, often a hatchback, seating two or three adults (such as a small Ford, Fiat, or Renault), while the typical F, G, or H luxury car is a four-door sedan seating four or five adults (such as a Mercedes or BMW). The larger the car, the more it costs to rent in the first place and the more gas it consumes, but for some people the greater comfort and extra luggage space of a larger car (in which bags can be safely locked out of sight) may make it worth the additional expense, especially on a long trip. Be warned, too, that relatively few European cars have automatic transmissions, and those that do are more likely to be in the F group than the A group. Cars with automatic shift must be specifically requested at the time of booking, and, again, they cost more (anywhere from $5 to $10 a day more than the same model with standard shift) and they consume more gas.

Electing to pay for collision damage waiver (CDW) protection will add considerably to the cost of renting a car. The renter may be responsible for the full value of the vehicle being rented, but you can dispense with the possible obligation to pay even this amount by buying the offered waiver at a cost of about $10 a day. Before deciding, however, check with your own insurance agent and determine whether your personal auto policy covers rented vehicles; if it does, you probably won't need the waiver. Be aware, too, that increasing numbers of so-called premium credit cards — gold or platinum American Express cards, gold Visa and MasterCards — automatically cover CDW if the car rental is charged to that credit card. However, the specific terms of such coverage differ sharply among the credit card companies — whose policies may further vary depending on whether rentals are transacted in the US or abroad — so check with the credit card company for information on the amount of coverage provided (also see *Credit and Currency,* in this section). Considering that repair costs for a rental car have become a real headache of late, and car rental companies are getting away with steep fees (up to the full retail price of the car) for damage to their property — if you are not otherwise covered, it is wise to pay for the insurance offered by the rental company rather than risk traveling without any.

Overseas, the amount renters may be liable for should damage occur has not risen to the heights it has in the US. Some British car rental agreements include collision damage coverage. In this case, the CDW supplement frees the renter from liability for the deductible amount, which in Great Britain typically ranges from $2,200 to $4,500 at present, but can be more for some luxury car groups. The cost of waiving this liability (as with the full liability waiver) — generally $12 to $18 a day, but several dollars more for luxury cars — is far from negligible, however. Drivers who rent cars in the US are often able to decline the CDW because many personal car insurance policies (subject to their own deductibles) extend to rental cars; unfortunately, such coverage does not usually extend to cars rented outside the US and Canada. Similarly, CDW coverage provided by some credit cards if the rental is charged to the card may be limited to cars rented in the US or Canada.

Additional costs include dropoff charges or one-way service fees. The lowest price quoted by any given company may apply only to a car that is returned to the same location from which it was rented. A slightly higher rate may be charged if the car is to be returned to a different city in the same country, and a considerably higher rate may prevail if the rental begins in one country and ends in another. Few companies allow a car rented in Great Britain to be taken out of the country, and where this option does exist, a stiff dropoff fee may be required to return it to a location in the Irish Republic or Northern Ireland and an even stiffer one to leave it in continental Europe.

A further consideration: Don't forget that car rentals are subject to Value Added Tax (VAT). This tax is rarely included in the rental price quoted, but it must always be paid, whether you prepay it in the US or pay it when you drop off the car in Britain. In general, in Europe the tax on one-way rentals is determined by the country in which the car has been rented. However, some agencies that do not maintain their own fleets use a contractor, whose country of registration determines the rate of taxation. An example is *Kemwel Car Rental Europe,* whose one-way rentals from all countries except Germany, Italy, and Sweden are taxed at the Danish rate, 22%.

Kemwel's special programs offer savings to the client and allow travel agents to earn commissions on CDW fees and on the VAT. The new SuperSaver Plus and UniSaver Plus tariffs offer inclusive rentals in 24 countries throughout Europe and the Middle East. These programs offer full insurance coverage (with a $100 deductible) and all European VATs, plus unlimited mileage. Rates range from $79 up and are available in some 35 cities across Europe. Bookings must be reserved and paid for at least 7 days before delivery of the car, and the vehicle must be returned to the *Kemwel* station from which it was originally rented (for address, see below).

Finally, currency fluctuation is another factor to consider. Most brochures quote rental prices in dollars, but these amounts are frequently only guides; that is, they represent the prevailing rate of exchange at the time the brochure was printed. The rate may be very different when you call to make a reservation and different again when the time comes to pay the bill (when the amount owed may be paid in cash in foreign currency or as a charge to a credit card, which is recalculated at still a later date's rate of exchange). Some companies guarantee rates in dollars (often for a slight surcharge), but this is an advantage only when the value of the dollar is steadily declining overseas. If the dollar is growing stronger overseas, you may be better off with rates in the local currency.

Renting from the US – The British Tourist Authority has a supply of the rate brochures of numerous car rental companies, many of which have US representatives through whom arrangements can be made directly. Travel agents can arrange foreign rentals for clients, but it is just as easy to do it yourself by calling the international divisions of such familiar car rental firms as *National* (known in Great Britain as *Murray's Rent a Car* and throughout Europe as *Europcar;* phone: 800-CAR-EUROPE), *Hertz* (phone: 800-654-3001), *Avis* (phone: 800-331-1084), *Budget* (phone: 800-527-0700), or *Dollar Rent a Car* (known in Europe as *EuroDollar;* phone: 800-421-6868). Other firms include *Swan National British Car Rental,* whose US office is at 1133 Broadway, New York, NY 10010-7988 (phone: 212-929-0920 in New York; 800-999-8808 elsewhere in the US); *Town and Country Car Rental/ITS,* 3332 NE 33rd St., Ft. Lauderdale, FL 33308 (phone: 305-566-7111 or 800-248-4350 in Florida; 800-521-0643 elsewhere in the US); and *Guy Salmon Car Rentals,* 2809 Boston St., Suite 440, Baltimore, MD 21224 (phone: 301-563-6337).

All of these companies publish directories listing their foreign locations, and all quote weekly flat rates based on unlimited mileage with the renter paying for gas. Some also offer time and mileage rates (i.e., a basic per-day or per-week charge, plus a charge for each mile, or kilometer, driven), which are generally only to the advantage of those who plan to do very little driving — the basic time and mileage charge for a given period of time is lower than the unlimited mileage charge for a comparable period, but the miles add up more quickly than most people expect.

It is also possible to rent a car before you go by contacting any of a number of smaller or less well known US companies that do not operate worldwide but specialize in European auto travel, including leasing and car purchase in addition to car rental, or are actually tour operators with a well-established European car rental program. These firms, whose names and addresses are listed below, act as agents for a variety of European suppliers, offer unlimited mileage almost exclusively, and frequently manage to undersell their larger competitors by a significant margin.

Comparison shopping is always necessary, however, because the company that has the least expensive rentals in one country may not have the least expensive in another, and even the international giants offer discount plans whose conditions are easy for most travelers to fulfill. For instance, *National* offers discounts of anywhere from 15% to 30% off its usual rates according to the size and length of the car, provided that the car is reserved a certain number of days before departure (usually 7, but it can be less), is rented for a minimum period (5 days or, usually, a week), and, in most cases, is returned to the same location that supplied it or to another in the same country. Similar discount plans include *Hertz*'s Affordable Europe and *Avis*'s Supervalue Rates Europe. (*Note: Avis* also offers an "On call service," which gives tourist information to travelers while they are in Europe. It covers Great Britain, Switzerland, Belgium, France, Germany, Holland, and Italy. Each country has a different toll-free number, and the numbers are given to you when you rent from *Avis.* In Great Britain, dial 100 and ask the operator for "Free Phone Avis On Call.")

There are legitimate bargains in car rentals if you shop for them. Call all the familiar car rental names whose toll-free numbers are given at the beginning of this section (don't forget to ask about their special discount plans), then call the smaller companies listed below. In the recent past, the latter have tended to offer significantly lower rates, but it always pays to compare. Begin your shopping early, because the best deals may be booked to capacity quickly and may require payment 14 to 21 days or more before picking up the car.

Auto Europe, PO Box 1097, Camden, ME 04843 (phone: 207-236-8235; 800-223-5555; 800-458-9503 in Canada).

Cortell International, 17310 Red Hill Ave., Irvine, CA 92714 (phone: 800-228-2535).

Europe by Car, 1 Rockefeller Plaza, New York, NY 10020 (phone: 212-581-3040 or 800-223-1516), or 9000 Sunset Blvd., Los Angeles, CA 90069 (phone: 213-272-0424 or 800-252-9401).

Foremost Euro-Car, 5430 Van Nuys Blvd., Van Nuys, CA 91401 (phone: 818-786-1960 or 800-272-3299 in California; 800-423-3111 elsewhere in the US).

Kemwel Group, 106 Calvert St., Harrison, NY 10528 (phone: 800-627-0678 or 918-835-5555).

Another economical option is *Wheels International Rent-a-Car.* This company contracts with other car rental agencies worldwide to rent available portions of their fleets at a flat discounted rate. Rentals are for a minimum of 3 days, and full payment must be made in advance. Numerous dropoff alternatives are also available at a minimal additional charge. For information, contact Wheels International Rent-a-Car, Suite 308, 1682 W. 7th Ave., Vancouver, BC V6J 4S6, Canada (phone: 604-731-0441 or 800-663-8888 in the US).

Fly/Drive – Airlines, charter companies, car rental companies, and tour operators have been offering fly/drive packages for years, and even though the basic components of the package have changed somewhat — return airfare, a car waiting at the airport, and perhaps a night's lodging in the gateway city all for one inclusive price used to be the rule — the idea remains the same. You rent a car *here* for use *there* by booking it along with other arrangements. These days, the very minimum arrangement possible is the result of a tie-in between a car rental company and an airline that entitles customers to a rental car for less than the company's usual rates provided they show proof of having booked a flight on that airline.

Slightly more elaborate fly/drive packages are listed under various names (go-as-you-please, self-drive, or, simply, car tours) in the independent vacations sections of tour catalogues. Their most common ingredients are the rental car plus some sort of hotel voucher plan, with the applicable airfare listed separately. You set off on your trip with a block of prepaid accommodations vouchers, a list of hotels that accept them (usually members of a hotel chain or association), and a reservation for the first night's stay, after which the staff of each hotel books the next one for you or you make your own reservations. Naturally, the greater the number of establishments participating in the scheme, the more freedom you have to range at will during the day's driving and still be near a place to stay for the night.

The cost of these combination packages generally vary according to the size of the car and the quality of the hotels; there is usually a charge if the car is picked up in one city and dropped off in another. Most packages are offered at several price levels, ranging from a standard plan covering stays in hotels to a budget plan using accommodations such as bed-and-breakfast houses or farmhouses. Both *Hertz*'s Affordable Europe hotel program (discounts only for travelers who rent through *Holiday Inns*) and *Kemwel*'s Freewheeler self-drive packages provide a choice of vouchers at three different price levels in Great Britain (two levels feature hotels; the other, guesthouses and farmhouses), applicable to stays at about 1,800 participating properties. There are five price levels in the *Avis* Go-As-You-Please voucher system and about 450 participating British hotels.

Most airlines also offer special rental car rates, available when you book their flights, often with a flexible hotel voucher program. For instance, British Airways has a special deal for its passengers with *Europcar* (*Murray's Rent-a-Car* in Great Britain). Travelers can arrange car rentals before they leave, and because British Airways buys in bulk, it offers very competitive prices. For further information on similar packages from other carriers, check with the airline or your travel agent.

Less flexible car tours provide a rental car, a hotel plan, and a set itinerary that permits no deviation because the hotels are all reserved in advance. The deluxe car tours packaged by *AutoVenture* (425 Pike St., Suite 502, Seattle, WA 98101; phone: 206-624-6033), whose tours come in either self-drive or chauffeured versions, are of this type. *Avis* offers less deluxe car tours with its Personally Yours program. You must book 2 weeks in advance to receive this planned itinerary service. For information on other packagers of car tours, see *Package Tours,* in this section.

Local Rentals – It has long been common wisdom that the least expensive way to rent a car is to make arrangements in Europe. This is less true today than it used to be. Many medium to large European car rental companies have become the overseas suppliers of stateside companies, such as those mentioned previously, and often the stateside agency, by dint of sheer volume, has been able to negotiate more favorable rates for its US customers than the European firm offers its own. Lower rates may be found by searching out small, strictly local rental companies overseas, whether at less than prime addresses in major cities or in more remote areas. To find them, however, you must be willing to invest a sufficient amount of vacation time comparing prices on the scene. You must also be prepared to return the car to the location that rented it; dropoff possibilities are likely to be limited. The brochures of some of the smaller car rental companies, available from the British Tourist Authority (which also puts out a booklet, *Vehicle Hire*), can serve as a useful basis for comparison. Overseas, the local yellow pages is a good place to begin.

If you intend to rent a car only occasionally, relying mainly on other means of transportation, bear in mind that *Hertz* operates *Rail-Drive* booths in 100 British railroad stations, in addition to its 100-plus other locations (including 11 at airports). A car can be reserved before you board the train and it will be waiting at your destination. A special *BritRail-Drive* package, which combines unlimited train travel with car rental for 4 or 8 days, is sold by *BritRail Travel International* offices in the US. (For further information on rail-and-drive packages, see *Touring by Train.*)

LEASING: Anyone planning to be in Europe for 3 weeks or more should compare the cost of renting a car with the cost of leasing one for the same period. While the money saved by leasing for a 23-day (the minimum) or 30-day period may not be great, the savings on a long-term lease — 45, 60, 90 days, or more — amounts to hundreds, even thousands, of dollars. Part of the savings is due to the fact that leased cars are exempt from the stiff taxes applicable to rental cars. In addition, leasing plans provide collision insurance with no deductible amount, so there is no need to add the daily cost of a collision damage waiver, an option offered by rental companies. A further advantage of a car lease — actually a financed purchase/repurchase plan — is that you reserve your car by specific make and model rather than by group only and it is delivered to you fresh from the factory.

Unfortunately, leasing as described above is offered only in Belgium and France, and the saving it permits can be realized to the fullest only if the cars are picked up and returned in those countries. While leased cars can be delivered to other countries, the charge for this service can be very high ($325 or even more in the case of delivery to London), and on top of this must be added an identical return charge. If you don't intend to keep the car very long, the two charges can nullify the amount saved by leasing rather than renting, so you will have to do some arithmetic. It is possible to lease a car in countries other than Belgium or France, but most of the plans offered are best described as long-term rentals at preferential rates. They differ from true leasing in that you will pay tax and collision damage waiver protection (though it may be included in the quoted price), and the cars are usually late-model used cars rather than brand-new.

One of the major car leasing companies is *Renault,* offering leases of new cars for 23 days to 6 months. The cars are exempt from tax, all insurance is included, and there is no mileage charge. There is no pickup or dropoff charge for some locations in France; charges for other locations throughout Europe (including London) range from $85 to $350 and up (each way). For further information and reservations, ask your travel agent or contact Renault USA, 650 First Ave., New York, NY 10016 (phone: 212-532-1221 in New York State; 800-221-1052 elsewhere in the US). Some of the car rental firms listed above — *Auto-Europe, Europe by Car, Foremost Euro-Car,* and *Kemwel* — also arrange European car leases.

BUYING A CAR: If your plans include both buying a new car of European make and a driving tour of Europe, it's possible to combine the two ventures and save some money on each. By buying the car abroad and using it during your vacation, you pay quite a bit less for it than the US dealer would charge and at the same time avoid the expense of renting a car. There are two basic ways to achieve this desired end, but one, factory delivery, is far simpler than the other, direct import.

Factory delivery means that you place an order for a car in the US, then pick it up in Europe, often literally at the factory gate. It also means that your new car is built to American specifications, complying with all US emission and safety standards. Therefore, only cars made by companies who have established a formal program for sales to American customers can be bought at the factory. At present, the list includes Audi, BMW, Jaguar, Mercedes, Peugeot, Porsche, Renault, Saab, Volkswagen, and Volvo, among others (whose manufacturers generally restrict their offerings to those models they ordinarily export to the US). The factory delivery price, in US dollars, usually runs about 5% to 15% below the sticker price of the same model at a US dealership and includes the cost of shipping the car home. All contracts except BMW's include US customs duty, but the cost of the incidentals, and the insurance necessary for driving the car around Europe, is extra except for BMW's plan.

One of the few disadvantages of factory delivery is that car manufacturers make only a limited number of cars available each year, and for certain popular models you may have to get in line early in the season. Another is that you must take your trip when the car is ready, not when you are, although you will usually have 8 to 10 weeks' notice. The actual place of delivery can vary; it is more economical to pick up the car at the factory, but it can be delivered elsewhere for an extra charge.

Cars for factory delivery can usually be ordered either through one of the manufacturer's authorized US dealers or through companies — *Europe by Car, Foremost Euro-Car,* and *Kemwel,* among them — that specialize in such transactions. For example, Jaguars must be ordered through a US dealer and picked up at the factory in Coventry, England, although they can be dropped off for shipment home in any number of European cities. For information, write to Jaguar Cars, 600 Willow Tree Rd., Leonia, NJ 07605 (phone: 201-592-5200).

Occasionally an auto manufacturer offers a free or discounted airfare in connection with a European delivery program. Mercedes-Benz has a 1990 program offering a discounted plane ticket to Stuttgart ($1,070 for two coach seats or one business class seat), where the buyer picks up the new car, and a return ticket from other cities, including London. For details, contact Mercedes-Benz of North America, 1 Mercedes Dr., Montvale, NJ 07645 (phone: 800-458-8202).

The other way to buy a car abroad, direct import, is sometimes referred to as "gray market" buying. It is perfectly legal, but not hassle-free. Direct import means that you buy abroad a car that was meant for use abroad, not one built according to US specifications. It can be new or used and may even include — in Great Britain — a steering wheel on the right side of the front seat. The main drawback to direct import is that the process of modification to bring the car into compliance with US standards is expensive and time-consuming; it typically costs about $7,000 in parts and labor and takes from 2 to 6 months. In addition, the same shipping, insurance, and miscellaneous expenses (another $2,000 to $5,000, according to estimates) that would be included in the factory delivery price must be added to the purchase price of the car, and the considerable burden of shepherding it on its journey from showroom to backyard garage is usually borne by the purchaser. Direct import dealers do exist (they are not the same as your local, factory-authorized foreign car dealer, with whom you are now in competition), but even if you use one, you still need to do a great deal of paperwork yourself.

Once upon a time, the main advantage of the direct import method — besides the fact that it can be used for makes and models not available on factory delivery programs — was that much more money could be saved importing an expensive car. Given today's exchange rates, however, the method's potential greater gain is harder to realize and must be weighed against its greater difficulties. Still, if direct importing interests you, you can obtain a list of those makes and models approved for conversion in this country, and of the converters licensed to bring them up to US standards, by writing to the Environmental Protection Agency, Manufacturers' Operations Division, EN-340-F, Investigations/Imports Section, 401 M St. SW, Washington, DC 20460.

The regularly revised *Handbook of Vehicle Importation* ($22.95), published by the *Automobile Importers Compliance Association* (*AICA*), a trade group of direct importers, modifiers, and others involved in the process, is an invaluable resource for getting a grip on what lies ahead. Order it from AICA, 12030 Sunrise Valley Dr., Suite 201, Reston, VA 22091 (phone: 703-476-1100). If you have special problems getting your car into the US, you might contact Daniel Kokal, a regulatory consultant with Techlaw (14500 Avion Pkwy., Suite 300, Chantilly, VA 22021; phone: 703-818-1000).

Package Tours

If the mere thought of buying a package for travel to and through Europe conjures up visions of a race through ten countries in as many days in lockstep with a horde of frazzled fellow travelers, remember that packages have come a long way. For one thing, not all packages are necessarily escorted tours, and the one you buy does not have to include any organized touring at all — nor will it necessarily include traveling companions. If it does, however, you'll find that people of all sorts — many just like yourself — are taking advantage of packages today because they are economical and convenient, save you an immense amount of planning time, and exist in such variety that it's virtually impossible not to find one that fits at least the majority of your preferences. Given the high cost of travel these days, packages have emerged as a good buy.

Aside from the cost-saving advantages of package arrangements, Great Britain itself is ideally suited to package travel. The reason is that, essentially, Great Britain is a see-and-do destination as distinct from, say, the Caribbean, where most visitors go to a single island for a week or two and unpack everything until they're ready to return home. To be sure, many visitors do seek out a single city or area for a concentrated visit, booking themselves into a hotel, apartment, home, country inn, or farm that serves as a base from which they make regional tours and visits. But the bulk of North American travelers want to explore as much of the British Isles as possible within the restrictions of time and travel funds available. Hence the popularity — and practicality — of package tours.

There are hundreds of package programs on the market today. In the US, numerous packages to Great Britain are offered by tour operators or wholesalers, some retail travel agencies, airlines, charter companies, hotels, and even special interest organizations, and what goes into them depends on who is organizing them. The most common type, assembled by tour wholesalers and sold through travel agents, can run the gamut from deluxe everything to simple tourist class amenities or even bare necessities. Fly/drive and fly/cruise packages are usually the joint planning efforts of airlines and, respectively, car rental organizations and cruise line operators. Charter flight programs may range from little more than airfare and a minimum of ground arrangements to full-scale tours or vacations. There are also hotel packages organized by hotel chains or associations of independent hotels and applicable to stays at any combination of member establishments; resort packages covering arrangements at a specific hotel; and special interest tours, which can be once-only programs organized by particular groups through a retail agency or regular offerings packaged by a tour operator. They can feature food, music or theater festivals, a particular sporting activity or event, a commemorative occasion, and even scientific exploration.

In essence, a package is a combination of travel services that can be purchased as a single booking. It may include any or all of the following: transatlantic transportation, local transportation (and/or car rentals), accommodations, some or all meals, sightseeing, entertainment, transfers to and from the hotel at each destination, taxes, tips, escort service, and a variety of incidental features that might be offered as options at additional cost. In other words, a package can be any combination from a fully escorted tour offered at an all-inclusive price to a simple fly/drive booking allowing you to function totally on your own. Its principal advantage is that it saves money: The cost of the combined arrangements invariably is well below the price of all the elements bought separately, and (particularly if transportation is provided by charter or discount flight) it could even be less than a round-trip economy airline ticket on a regularly scheduled flight. A package tour provides more than economy and convenience: It releases the traveler from having to make separate arrangements for each section of the tour.

Lower prices are provided by package travel as a result of high-volume commerce. The tour packager negotiates for services in wholesale quantities — blocks of airline seats or hotel rooms, group meals, dozens of rental cars, busloads of ground transportation, and so on — and they are made available at a lower per-person price because of these large quantities used in a given time period. Most packages, however, are subject to restrictions governing the duration of the trip and require total payment by a given time before departure.

Tour programs generally can be divided into two categories — escorted and independent — depending on the arrangements offered. An escorted tour means that a guide will accompany the group from the beginning of the tour through to return. On independent tours, you generally have a choice of hotels, meal plans, and sightseeing trips in each city as well as a variety of special excursions. The independent plan is for people who do not want a set itinerary but who prefer confirmed reservations. Whichever plan you choose, always bring along full contact information for your tour operator in case problems arise, although US tour operators may have British affiliates who can give additional assistance or make other arrangements on the spot.

To determine whether a package — or, more specifically, which package — fits your plans, start by evaluating your interests and needs, deciding how much and what you want to spend, see, and do. Gather whatever package tour information is available for your time schedule. Be sure that you read the brochure *carefully* to determine precisely what is included. Keep in mind that travel brochures are written to entice you into signing up for a package tour. Often the language is deceptive and devious. For example, a brochure may quote the lowest prices for a package tour based on facilities that are unavailable during the off-season, undesirable at any season, or just plain nonexistent. Information such as "breakfast included" or taxes (which can add up) are important items. Note, too, that the prices quoted are almost always based on double occupancy: The rate listed is for each of two people sharing a double room. If you travel alone, the supplement for single accommodations can raise the price considerably (see *Hints for Single Travelers,* in this section).

Increasingly, in this age of rapidly rising airfares, the brochure will *not* include the price of the airline ticket in the price of the package, though sample applicable fares from various gateway cities will usually be listed separately as extras to be added to the price of the ground arrangements. Before doing this, get the latest fares from the airline, because the samples will invariably be out of date by the time you read them. If the brochure gives more than one category of sample fares per gateway city — such as an individual tour-basing fare, a group fare, an excursion or other discount ticket, or, in the case of flights to Great Britain, an APEX, winter or Super APEX, PEX, or Super PEX — your travel agent or airline tour desk will be able to tell you which one applies to the package you choose, depending on when you travel, how far in advance you book, and other factors. (An individual tour-basing fare is a fare computed as part of a package that includes land arrangements, thereby entitling a carrier to reduce the air portion to almost the absolute minimum. Though it always represents a saving over full-fare coach or economy, lately it has not been as inexpensive as the excursion and other discount fares that are also available to individuals. The group fare is usually the least expensive fare, and it is the tour operator, not you, who makes up the group.) When the brochure does include round-trip transportation in the package price, don't forget to add the cost of round-trip transportation from your home to the departure city to come up with the total cost of the package.

Finally, read the general information regarding terms and conditions and the responsibility clause (usually in fine print at the end of the descriptive literature) to determine the precise elements for which the tour operator is — and is not — liable. Here the tour operator frequently expresses the right to change services or schedules as long as equivalent arrangements are offered. This clause also absolves the operator of responsibility for circumstances beyond human control, such as floods or avalanches, or injury to you or your property. In reading, ask the following questions:

1. Does the tour include airfare or other transportation, sightseeing, meals, transfers, taxes, baggage handling, tips, and any other services? Do you want all these services?
2. If the brochure indicates that "some meals" are included, does this mean a welcoming and farewell dinner, two breakfasts, or every evening meal?
3. What classes of hotels are offered? If you will be traveling alone, what is the single supplement?
4. Does the tour itinerary or price vary according to the season?
5. Are the prices guaranteed; that is, if costs increase between the time you book and the time you depart, can surcharges unilaterally be added?
6. Do you get a full refund if you cancel? If not, be sure to obtain cancellation insurance.
7. Can the operator cancel if too few people join?

One of the consumer's biggest problems is finding enough information to judge the reliability of a tour packager, since individuals seldom have direct contact with the firm putting the package together. Usually, a retail travel agent intervenes between customer and tour operator, and much depends on his or her candor and cooperation. So ask a number of questions about the tour you are considering. For example: Has the agent ever used the package provided by this tour operator? How long has the tour operator been in business? Is the tour operator a member of the *United States Tour Operators Association* (*USTOA*)? (The *USTOA* provides a list of its members upon request and also offers a useful brochure, *How to Select a Package Tour;* contact the USTOA, 211 E. 51st St., Suite 12B, New York, NY 10022; phone: 212-944-5727. Also check the Better Business Bureau in your area to see if any complaints have been filed against the operator.) Which and how many companies are involved in the package? If air travel is by charter flight, is there an escrow account in which deposits will be held; if so, what is the name of the bank?

This last question is very important. US law requires that tour operators deposit every charter passenger's deposit and subsequent payment in a proper escrow account. Money paid into such an account cannot legally be used except to pay for the costs of a particular package or as a refund if the trip is canceled. To ensure the safe handling of your money, make your check payable to the escrow account — by law, the name of the depository bank appears in the operator-participant contract and is usually found in that mass of minuscule type on the back of the brochure. Write the details of the charter, including the destination and dates, on the face of the check; on the back, print "For Deposit Only." Your travel agent may prefer that you make your check out to the agency, saying that it will then pay the tour operator the fee minus commission. But it is perfectly legal to write your check as we suggest, and if your agent objects too strongly (the agent should have sufficient faith in the tour operator to trust him to send the proper commission), consider taking your business elsewhere. If you don't make your check out to the escrow account, you lose the protection of escrow should the trip be canceled or the tour operator or travel agent fail. Furthermore, recent bankruptcies in the travel industry have served to point out that even the protection of escrow may not be enough to safeguard your investment. Increasingly, insurance is becoming a necessity (see *Insurance*), and payment by credit card has become popular since it offers some additional safeguards if the tour operator defaults.

SAMPLE PACKAGES TO GREAT BRITAIN: There are so many packages available to Great Britain that it's probably safe to say that just about any arrangement anyone might want is available for as long as it is wanted, whether it's to hit the highlights from the English Channel to the Scottish Highlands, to explore a selected region in depth, or to visit only London. The keynote is flexibility. Nevertheless, those travelers seeking the maximum in structure will find that the classic sightseeing tour by motorcoach, fully escorted and all-inclusive (or nearly), has withstood the test of time and is still well represented among the programs of the major tour operators. Typically, these tours last from 1 to 2 weeks if they are visiting Great Britain exclusively, and they may last as long as 3 to 4 weeks if they combine Britain with Northern Ireland, a common arrangement.

Hotel accommodations in these packages are usually characterized as first class or better, with a private bath or shower in all rooms, although more than a few tour packagers offer less expensive alternatives by providing more modest lodgings. Breakfast daily is almost always included, whereas the number of lunches and dinners may vary considerably, and meals include wine only when the tour literature clearly states so. Also included are transfers between airport and hotel, baggage handling, tips to maids and waiters, local transportation, sightseeing excursions and admission fees, as well as any featured evening entertainment — almost everything, in fact, except round-trip airfare between the US and Great Britain (which is generally shown separately); personal expenses for laundry, incidentals, and souvenirs; and tips to the motorcoach driver and to the tour escort, who remains with the group from beginning to end.

An equally common type of package available to Great Britain is the car tour or fly/drive arrangement, often described in brochures as a self-drive or go-as-you-please tour. Usually included are the use of a rented car and a block of as many prepaid hotel vouchers as needed for the length of the stay (the packages are typically 4 or 7 days long, extendable by individual extra days), along with a list of participating hotels at which the vouchers are accepted. In most cases, only the first night's accommodation will be reserved; from then on, travelers book their rooms one stop ahead as they drive from place to place (the option of booking them all before departure — for a fee — is occasionally available). Most operators offering these packages have two versions, a standard version covering overnights at hotels and a budget version covering overnights in simple bed-and-breakfast houses and farmhouses. *CIE Tours International* (122 E. 42nd St., New York, NY 10168; phone: 212-972-5600 in New York City; 800-CIE-TOUR elsewhere in the US), for example, offers both versions, with the added twist that those choosing the town and country home/farmhouse plan may upgrade their accommodations to a hotel when they choose by paying a supplement directly to the hotel, and those choosing the hotel plan may spend the night in a farmhouse or other home and receive a home-cooked dinner at no extra charge. Other operators, such as *Brendan Tours* (15137 Califa St., Van Nuys, CA 91411; phone: 818-785-9696 or 800-421-8446), *Brian Moore International Tours* (116 Main St., Medway, MA 02053; phone: 800-982-2299), *Celtic International Tours* (161 Central Ave., Albany, NY 12206; phone: 518-463-5511 or 800-833-4373), and *Lismore Tours* (106 E. 31st St., New York, NY 10016; phone: 212-685-0100 in New York State; 800-547-6673 elsewhere in the US), also have self-drive tours in both versions, while *Lynott Tours* (350 Fifth Ave., Suite 2619, New York, NY 10118; phone: 800-537-7575 in New York, or 800-221 2474 elsewhere in the US) offers three versions.

British Airways Holidays (phone: 800-AIRWAYS), a subsidiary of British Airways, offers a variety of fly/drive and fly/rail packages, including a choice of mix-and-match independent holiday options ranging from bed-and-breakfast establishments to deluxe accommodations. Two particularly attractive packages are: the London Plus package, which includes a minimum stay of 3 days in London in combination with a 3-day stay in a number of European cities, airport transfers between cities, accommodations, and a half-day or more of touring in each city; and the Four City Classic package, which includes 3 days in London and 3 days each in Venice, Florence, and Rome, and air and rail transportation between the cities. Extended-stay options are available for both packages. Note that although these packages may be bought in conjunction with a transatlantic ticket, this airfare is not included in the basic package price. Other airlines also offer a variety of fly/drive packages.

Another type of arrangement is more restrictive in that the tour packager supplies an itinerary that is followed day by day, with a specific hotel to be reached each night. Often these plans are more deluxe as well. The 9- to 14-day British itineraries in the "Country Houses of Britain & Ireland" program designed by *Abercrombie & Kent International* (1420 Kensington Rd., Oak Brook, IL 60521; phone: 312-954-2944 in Illinois; 800-323-7308 elsewhere in the US) feature stays in hotels that are converted manor houses, castles, and other stately homes. The four 5- to 14-night British itineraries packaged by *AutoVenture* are similarly deluxe. In addition, the itineraries of both packagers can be bought in either a self-drive or a chauffeured version. Car tours with reserved but more economical lodgings are available from *Avis;* custom itineraries throughout Great Britain are also available.

As one of the world's greatest cities, London is by itself of interest to visitors, and many tour operators have packaged it that way. Basically, the city package — no matter what the city — includes transfers between airport and hotel, a choice of hotel accommodations (with breakfast) in several price ranges, plus any number of other features that you may not need or want but would lose valuable time arranging if you did. Among these are one or two half-day guided tours of the city; passes for unlimited travel by subway or bus; discount cards for shops, museums, and restaurants; temporary membership in and admission to clubs, casinos, and discotheques; and car rental for some or all of your stay — usually a week, although 4-day and even 14-day packages are available, and most packages can be extended by extra days. *American Express Vacations* has a 4-day package to London with some, but not all, of the above features; contact the nearest office of *American Express Vacations* for information.

With the addition of theater tickets, the basic London package turns into a show tour, one of the most popular city programs. *British Airways Holidays'* (phone: 800-AIR-WAYS) 6-night "London Showtime" package, for instance, includes hotel accommodations, 7 days of unlimited subway and bus travel, tickets to three plays or musicals, dinner at a theme restaurant, and other features. *TWA Getaway Tours* (phone: 800-GETAWAY) "London Theater Week" includes tickets to only two plays or musicals, but provides discounts at shops, restaurants, pubs, and other attractions among its features. *Pan Am Holidays* (phone: 800-843-8687) and *American Express Vacations* have similar London show tours (contact the nearest office), while *Edwards & Edwards* (1 Times Sq. Plaza, 20th Floor, New York, NY 10036; phone: 212-944-0290 in New York State; 800-223-6108 elsewhere in the US) offers a 7-night "Week on the British Aisle" (three tickets), to which the theatergoer can add an overnight theater tour to Stratford-upon-Avon and/or a 2-night tour to Edinburgh. The same company also packages 3- and 5-night London show tours.

A staple among special-interest packages to Great Britain is the golf tour. The main ingredient is a chance to play at some of the oldest and best courses in the world: *St. Andrews, Turnberry, Gleneagles, Troon,* and *Carnoustie* in Scotland, as well as at other courses in England and Wales. A fly/drive arrangement is usually involved, with rental car, hotel accommodations for a week or two, often one dinner per day, and some greens fees included. There are packages allowing you to spend an entire week at one course, to play at a choice of courses, to combine a golfing holiday in Britain with a visit to Irish courses, and both to play golf and attend the British Open when it's held. *BTH Holidays* (245 Fifth Ave., New York, NY 10016; phone: 212-684-1820, 800-221-1074; in Canada, 800-344-4034), *InterGolf* (PO Box 819, Champlain, NY 12919, or 4150 St. Catherine St. W., Suite 390, Montreal H3Z 2G1, Canada; phone: 514-933-2772), and *Scottish Golf Holidays* (9403 Kenwood Rd., Suite A205, Cincinnati, OH 45242; phone: 513-984-0414 in Ohio; 800-284-8884 elsewhere in the US) all have self-drive golf packages and tours by escorted motorcoach, and the latter includes escorted sightseeing itineraries for non-golfers in the group. *Golf Intercontinental* (19 W. 34th St., New York, NY 10001; phone: 212-239-3880 in New York State; 800-223-6114 elsewhere in the US) offers a "Gimme Scotland" tour for serious golfers only. *Perry Golf* (5584 Chamblee Dunwoody Rd., Atlanta, GA 30338; phone: 404-394-5400 or 800-344-5257) offers a basic 6-night "Classic Scotland" self-drive package that can be combined with a selection of 3-night "modular tours" to courses elsewhere in Scotland or in Ireland. Tours to the British Open for professional golfers are packaged by *Golf Links International* (1675 Palm Beach Lakes Blvd., Suite 107, Forum III, W. Palm Beach, FL 33401; phone: 305-471-5525 in Florida; 800-541-6898 elsewhere in the US), *Scottish Golf Holidays, Golf Intercontinental, Perry Golf,* and others. Information about many more golf packages can be obtained from a travel agent or the British Tourist Authority.

Among sports-oriented packages for spectators are the seven Wimbledon tennis packages run by *Keith Prowse & Co. Ltd.* (200 Galleria Pkwy., Suite 720, Atlanta, GA 30339; phone: 404-980-1783 in Georgia; 800-669-8687 elsewhere in the US). The most popular packages include seats for 4 days of play on the center and #1 courts and tickets to either the men's final and ladies' semifinals or the ladies' final and men's semifinals. Also for spectators are the *Keith Prowse & Co.* packages to the Derby at *Epsom Downs* and to *Royal Ascot.*

For enthusiasts of other outdoor activities, there are packages focused around — and guaranteeing entrance in — London's spring marathon, the world's largest. Both *Keith Prowse & Co. Ltd.* (address above) and *Marathon Tours* (108 Main St., Boston, MA 02129; phone: 617-242-7845) offer these. Horseback riding holidays are the province of *FITS Equestrian* (2011 Alamo Pintado Rd., Solvang, CA 93463; phone: 805-688-9494). The choices — but not for beginners — include 8 days of riding through the Scottish Highlands (nights are spent in village inns along the way) and 6 days of riding the hills and wild moors of England's Exmoor Forest (nights are in manor houses). *Fishing International* (Hilltop Estate, 4010 Montecito Ave., Santa Rosa, CA 95404; phone: 707-542-4242) also visits Scotland, on short 2- and 3-day salmon and trout fishing programs that take place on private estates.

A variety of biking packages and hiking trips through rural Britain are other possibilities. For more information, see *Camping and Caravanning, Biking, and Hiking.* Still another possibility and an increasingly popular one: an inland waterway trip on a canal boat or river barge. Many travelers simply rent their own boat, but if you prefer to let someone else do the driving (as well as the cooking), book aboard a hotel-boat cruise. *Floating through Europe* (271 Madison Ave., New York, NY 10016; phone: 212-685-5600 in New York State; 800-221-3140 elsewhere in the US) operates a pair of hotel wideboats on the Avon (trips are a week long); other cruises are discussed in *Traveling by Ship* in this section and *Wonderful Waterways and Coastal Cruises* in DIVERSIONS.

Deluxe trips aboard a hotel on wheels — i.e., a historic train — are also possible. Those interested should investigate the "Royal Scotsman" tours available through *Abercrombie & Kent International* (address above) and *Frontiers International* (PO Box 161, Pearce Mill Rd., Wexford, PA 15090; phone: 412-935-1577 in Pennsylvania; 800-245-1950 elsewhere in the US). The train is made up of restored carriages of the Victorian and Edwardian periods and carries guests on a 6-day itinerary (sometimes offered in 3- and 4-day portions) through the Scottish Highlands. See the "Flying Scotsman" tours offered by *Capricorn Leisure Tours* (15 Penn Plaza, 415 Seventh Ave., New York, NY 10001; phone: 212-967-2441 or 800-426-6544). Still another revival, the plush *Venice Simplon–Orient Express,* leaves London on deluxe 2-day excursions to Venice once or twice weekly from the end of February to mid-November and adds a second route, from London to Vienna, in July and August. Although it spends only a brief time on British soil during these excursions, the *Venice Simplon–Orient Express* is actually two trains — the British Pullman and the continental train — and when the British portion is available, it makes day trips to various destinations in England. In 1989, it also made a 4-day tour of Wales (affording, among other diversions, a chance to ride a few of Wales's picturesque narrow-gauge steam railways). For information, contact Venice Simplon–Orient Express, Suite 2565, 1 World Trade Ctr., New York, NY 10048 (phone: 212-938-6830 in New York State; 800-524-2420 elsewhere in the US).

The American fascination with British upper class life has prompted a number of special-interest packages. In addition to its car tours, *Abercrombie & Kent International* (address above) has 5- and 11-night "Country House Pursuit" packages that take groups of no more than 12 people on a tour of the English countryside, stopping for lunch and spending the night at stately private homes along the way — something like a traveling house party. The gardens that typically surround stately homes are the focus of various packages, including "English Spring Flowers," available through *The British Connection* (2490 Black Rock Turnpike, Suite 240, Fairfield, CT 06430; phone: 203-254-7221 in Connecticut; 800-727-2771 elsewhere in the US). The tour is run only once a year, timed to coincide with the *Chelsea Flower Show* in May. *The British Connection* also markets the 3- and 4-day tours packaged by *Prospect Art Tours,* a British tour operator. Two tour series, "Country Houses" and "Historic Gardens," focus on the houses or gardens of a well-defined area — "Houses of East Anglia," for instance, or "Gardens of Gloucestershire" — providing in-depth coverage.

Other special-interest packages include music and opera tours, the specialty of *Dailey-Thorp, Inc.* (315 W. 57th St., New York, NY 10019; phone: 212-307-1555). Its catalogue regularly includes an "English Festivals Revisited" package in late spring or early summer; opera in London and visits to the Edinburgh and Glyndebourne festivals are generally combined with events in other countries. For those who are serious about food, *Travel Concepts* (373 Commonwealth Ave., Suite 601, Boston, MA 02115-1815; phone: 617-266-8450) offers "The English Experience," featuring cooking demonstrations by some of England's leading chefs and behind-the-scenes visits to an ale brewery, a cheese shop, and a dairy, not to mention some out-of-the-ordinary meals. Mystery tours are gaining in popularity. The "Rendezvous with Murder" package run by *ICTS/InterContinental Travel Systems* (805 22nd St., San Diego, CA 92102; phone: 619-233-5851 or 800-457-9515 in California; 800-428-7462 elsewhere in the US) spends 11 days meeting authors and visiting sites associated with famous British mystery novels; a "murder weekend," with a crime to be solved by participants, is included. Christmas packages are a good way to avoid the disappointment of discovering a country virtually shut down for the holidays, and *ICTS* offers one of the best: "The Twelve Days of Christmas" begins with a variety of English Christmas festivities and spends New Year's in Scotland enjoying that most exuberant of Scottish celebrations, the *Hogmanay.*

PACKAGES BOOKED IN BRITAIN: For years, experienced travelers have known that some of the least expensive tours to and through Europe could be booked abroad and that British tour operators offered most of the best deals. Not long ago, for less than half the price of a scheduled air ticket from London to Athens and back, the smart shopper was able to pick up the flight plus a week's worth of adequate, if Spartan, accommodations and even some meals. Then the expenses of British packagers began to rise with inflation and the bargains became less enticing. But many British operators continue to cater to the budget end of the market, and they still manage to put together a good deal (which becomes even more attractive to Americans when the exchange rate is favorable). If your interest is a tour of Great Britain, note that most of these companies, with their local clientele in mind, tend to specialize in tours from London to the Continent, and the assortment of budget tours of their own country is less broad. A number offer a selection of 3- or 4-day mini-tours covering a limited area of Britain which make a welcome excursion in the midst of an otherwise independent stay in London.

The following are some of Britain's major high-volume or economy-minded tour operators. Some have become familiar names in this country because they maintain US offices and market some or all of the tour offerings in their British catalogues directly to the American public — i.e., booking one of their packages is no different from booking the package of an American tour operator. Almost all of the rest have at least a representative in the US to handle American bookings. Note that most of these offices or representatives prefer to deal with travel agents rather than individuals. Note also that because of the extra costs involved in making arrangements from this end, packages booked here can run 5% to 15% more than if booked in Britain; and if you attempt to book through the British office by mail, your request will most likely be referred to the US representative. Clearly, you will save money by waiting until you are in England to book, but there's a chance that the package you want will not be available at the last minute.

Cosmos: In 1989, this firm specializing in low-cost motorcoach tours of Europe offered 43 tour series, of which 8 were tours of Great Britain and/or Ireland. Breakfast daily and slightly more than half the dinners were included, and almost all rooms had private facilities, although not all had toilets. *Cosmos* matches singles wishing to share a room to avoid the single supplement. For information, contact Cosmos, 95-25 Queens Blvd., 3rd Floor, Rego Park, NY

11374 (phone: 818-449-2019; 800-221-0090 from the eastern US; 800-556-5454 from the western US, including Alaska and Hawaii). Bookings must be made through a travel agent. The London office is at 180 Vauxhall Bridge Rd., London SW1V 1ED (phone: 834-7412).

Eurobout: Smaller than *Cosmos* and less of a bargain specialist, *Eurobout* offered 9 economical tours of Europe and 7 of Great Britain in 1989. A full breakfast daily and all dinners were included on the British tours; continental breakfast and some dinners on the European tours; hotel rooms came with private facilities. For information, contact the company's US representatives: *Fourways Travel Ltd.* (1324 Boston Post Rd., Milford, CT 06460; phone: 203-878-8854 in Connecticut; 800-223-7872 elsewhere in the US) and *Solrep Inc.* (2524 Nottingham, Houston, TX 77005; phone: 713-529-5547 in Texas; 800-231-0985 elsewhere in the US). Bookings are made through travel agents. The London office is at 27 Cockspur St., 4th Floor, London SW1Y 5BN (phone: 930-1722).

Frames Rickards: Mini-tours (3 and 4 days long) of England, Scotland, and Wales are among the reasonably priced coach tours of Europe offered. The budget-oriented company provides rooms with private facilities on all tours; breakfast and dinner daily on the tours of Britain. *Frames Rickards'* US agent, *Trophy Tours* (1819 Glenville Dr., Suite 124, Richardson, TX 75081; phone: 800-527-2473), prefers booking through travel agents. The London office is at 11 Herbrand St., London WC1N 1EX (phone: 837-3111).

Glenton Tours: This long-established company is a specialist in first class but relatively inexpensive motorcoach tours of Great Britain (over 50 itineraries). Most prices are based on accommodations with private bath. It prefers booking through agents; the US representative is *European Travel Management* (191 Post Rd. W., Westport, CT 06880; phone: 203-454-0090 in Connecticut; 800-992-7700 elsewhere in the US). Headquarters is at 114 Peckham Rye, London SE15 4JE (phone: 639-9777).

Globus-Gateway: In 1989, *Globus-Gateway* offered 20 motorcoach tours of Great Britain and/or Ireland, with hundreds of departure dates, in addition to over 100 tours elsewhere in Europe. Breakfast and, except in major cities, dinner daily are included in the price of most tours, and all accommodations have private baths. Independent city tours of London are among the standard offerings. Bookings through travel agents only. *Globus-Gateway*'s US and London addresses and phone numbers are the same as those of *Cosmos* (see above).

Insight: It's known less as a budget company than as a tour operator offering value for money. In addition to 37 longer tours (from a week to 37 days) of Great Britain and/or Ireland, Europe, and the Middle East, the *Insight* catalogue includes a series of 2- to 5-day mini-tours of Britain. All hotel rooms come with private bath or shower; breakfast daily and most dinners are included. The US office, *Insight International Tours* (17310 Redhill Ave., Suite 330, Irvine, CA 92714; phone: 714-261-5373 or 800-792-7209 in California; 800-582-8380 elsewhere in the US), takes bookings from travel agents only. In London, the Insight Reception Centre is at 25A Cockspur St., Trafalgar Sq., London SW1Y 5BY (phone: 930-7444).

Thomson Holidays: Great Britain's largest tour operator owns its own airline, Britannia Airways, and its coach tours travel from home turf to Europe and venture as far afield as the Himalayas. *Thomson* is also known for a broad selection of Mediterranean holiday packages that include round-trip airfare (from Britain) and a week or two or more of villa or apartment rental. Write to Thomson Holidays, Greater London House, Hampstead Rd., London NW1 7SD (phone: 01-387-9321), for information; bookings may be made through *Portland Holidays* (phone: 01-388-5111) or travel agencies in Britain.

Trafalgar Tours: This agency offered an extensive selection of first class tours on the Continent in 1989 as well as 15 tours of Great Britain and/or Ireland, plus a group of budget-conscious CostSaver tours on which savings were realized by scheduling a number of nights in good or select tourist class hotels. Bookings are made through travel agents, but you can contact *Trafalgar Tours* directly (21 E. 26th St., New York, NY 10010; phone: 212-689-8977 in New York City; 800-854-0103 elsewhere in the US) for information. The office in London is at 15 Grosvenor Pl., London SW1X 7HH (phone: 235-7090).

Another British tour operator to investigate is *Thomas Cook,* the best known of them all. Its name is practically synonymous with the Grand Tour of Europe, but *Cook*'s tours span the world, with itineraries ranging from deluxe to moderate, including some of the budget variety as well. You can book a tour directly through any of its offices in major North American cities or through any travel agency. *Thomas Cook*'s headquarters are at 45 Berkeley St., Piccadilly, London W1A 1EB (phone: 499-4000).

Camping and Caravanning, Hiking and Biking

CAMPING AND CARAVANNING: Great Britain welcomes campers, alone or with a group, with tents or in recreational vehicles — generally known in Britain as "caravans," a term that technicaly refers to towable campers as opposed to fully motorized vehicles (known as "minibuses" or "minivans"). Camping is probably the best way to enjoy the British countryside. And, fortunately, campgrounds are plentiful.

Where to Camp – Most British campgrounds are open from Easter through October, but they fill quickly at the height of the summer season, so it's a good idea to arrive early in the day if a "pitch" has not been reserved in advance. Caravanning is extremely popular with European vacationers, and many parks cater more to the caravanner than to the tent dweller. Neither campers nor caravanners are restricted to the official sites. However, using private property means first obtaining permission of the landowner or tenant — as well as assuming the responsibility of leaving the land exactly as it was found in return for the hospitality. When in difficulty, remember that tourist information offices throughout Great Britain will gladly direct visitors to sites in the areas they serve.

Sites for camping and caravanning in Great Britain are generally well marked. Still, it's best to have a map or check the information available in one of numerous comprehensive guidebooks (see below). It's not always easy to find camping facilities open before June or after September, so a guide that gives this information comes in particularly handy off-season. Directors of campgrounds often have a great deal of information about their region, and some will even arrange local tours or recommend the best restaurants, shops, or attractions in the area. Campgrounds also provide the atmosphere and opportunity to meet other travelers and exchange useful information. Too much so, sometimes — the popularlity of British campgrounds causes them to be quite crowded during the summer, and campsites are frequently so close together that any attempt at privacy or getting away from it all is sabotaged.

In the US, camping maps, brochures, and lists of sites are distributed by the tourist authority offices, and a variety of useful publications are also available from American and British automobile clubs and other associations. The British Tourist Authority publishes *Caravan & Camping Parks,* a free guide to sites in England, Scotland, and Wales, with the directions to, charges for, and facilities of each. The comprehensive guide *Camping and Caravanning in Britain* ($11.75), published by the *Automobile Association of Great Britain* (*AA*), lists about 1,000 campsites inspected and rated by the *AA* and provides other information of interest to campers. The *AA* also publishes a broader guide, *Camping and Caravanning in Europe* ($14.95), listing over 4,000 sites throughout Europe. Both are available from the *AA* (Farnum House, Basingstoke, Hampshire RG21 2EA, England; phone: 0256-20123); and from the *British Travel Bookshop* (40 W. 57th St., New York, NY 10019; phone: 212-765-0898; when ordering, add a $3 handling charge), as well as from other travel bookstores.

The French international camping organization *Fédération Internationale de Camping et Caravaning* issues a pass, called a *carnet.* Available in the US from the *National Campers and Hikers Association* (4804 Transit Rd., Bldg. 2, Depew, NY 14043; phone: 716-668-6242) for $23, which includes membership in the organization, the *carnet* entitles the bearer to information on and moderate discounts at many campgrounds throughout Europe. The *carnet* is not necessary for camping in Great Britain, but it does open the gates to the sites operated exclusively for members by another major group, the *Camping and Caravanning Club Ltd. of Great Britain and Ireland* (11 Lower Grosvenor Pl., London SW1 WOEY; phone: 01-828-1012). The club publishes a free annual guide to its own and other British sites and provides information and assistance to members, foreign visitors with the *carnet,* and foreign visitors without a *carnet* who become temporary members. Another group that honors the *carnet* is the *Caravan Club Ltd.* (9 East Grinstead House, London Rd., East Grinstead, West Sussex RH19 1UA), which publishes a guide to its sites plus over 3,5000 farm sites. Additionally, almost all local tourist offices provide brochures about camping in the area, but you will probably have to request them.

Necessities – For outdoor camping, necessities include a tent with flyscreens (the lighter and easier to carry and assemble the better), a sleeping bag, a foam pad or air mattress, a waterproof ground cloth, first-aid kit (including sunscreen and insect repellent), sewing and toilet kits, backpack stove (building fires is prohibited in many areas), fuel for the stove, matches, nested cooking pots and utensils, a canteen, three-quarter ax (well sharpened and sheath-protected), jackknife, and flashlight with an extra set of batteries.

Keep food simple. Unless backpacking deep into the wilderness — there is wilderness in Great Britain, but you can't get *too* many days away from civilization — you will probably be close enough to a store to stock up on perishables; staples such as sugar, coffee, and powdered milk can be carried along. Dehydrated food has become quite popular among both hikers and campers, but it can be quite expensive. An economical option for the more enterprising camper is to dry a variety of food at home; camping supply stores and bookstores carry cookbooks covering this simple process. Keep in mind, particularly in wilderness areas, that accessible food will lure scavenging wildlife that may invade tents and vehicles.

Recreational Vehicle Rentals – Recreational vehicles (RVs, known in Great Britain as "caravans") will appeal most to the kind of person who prefers the flexibility of accommodation — there are countless campgrounds throughout Great Britain, and many provide RV hookups — and enjoys camping with a little extra comfort. An RV undoubtably saves a traveler a great deal of money on accommodations and, if cooking appliances are part of the unit, on food as well. However, it is important to remember that renting an RV is a major expense; also, any kind of RV increases gas consumption considerably. Reservations should be made well in advance, as the supply of RVs is limited and the demand great.

Although the term recreational vehicle is applied to all manner of camping vehicles, whether towed or self-propelled, generally the models available for rent in Great Britain are either towable campers ("caravans") or motorized RVs. The motorized models are either "minivans" or "minibuses" — vans customized in various ways for camping, often including elevated roofs — or larger, coach-type, fully equipped homes on wheels. Although most motorized models have standard shift, occasionally automatic shift vehicles may be available for an additional charge. Towed vehicles can be hired overseas but are not usually offered by US companies.

Those who plan to caravan all over Europe should make sure that whatever vehicle they drive is equipped to deal with the electrical and gas standards of all the countries on their itinerary. There are differences, for instance, between the bottled gas supplied in Great Britain and that available on the Continent. You should have either a sufficient supply of the type the camper requires or equipment that can use either. When towing a camper, note that nothing towed is automatically covered by the liability insurance of the primary vehicle, and the driver's Green Card must carry a specific endorsement for the towed vehicle.

Whether driving a camper or towing, it is essential to have some idea of the terrain en route. Not only are numerous mountain passes closed in winter, but grades are often too steep for certain vehicles to negotiate and some roads are off limits to towed caravans. The *AA* guides described above have detailed information on the main passes and tunnels, as do tourist offices.

Rentals of recreational vehicles can be arranged from the US through several companies, including the following:

Auto-Europe, PO Box 1097, Camden, ME 04843 (phone: 207-236-8235 or 800-223-5555).
Connex, 983 Main St., Peekskill, NY 10566 (phone: 800-333-3949).
Cortell International, 17310 Red Hill Ave., Irvine, CA 92714 (phone: 800-228-2535).
Europe by Car, 1 Rockefeller Plaza, New York, NY 10020, or 9000 Sunset Blvd., Los Angeles, CA 90069 (phone: 212-581-3040 in New York State; 800-272-0424 in California; 800-223-1516 elsewhere in the US).
Kemwel Group, 106 Calvert St., Harrison, NY 10528 (phone: 914-835-5555 or 800-678-0678).

Another particularly economical option is *Wheels International Rent-a-Car* (Suite 308, 1682 W. 7th Ave., Vancouver BC V6J 4S6, Canada; phone: 604-731-0441 or 800-663-8888 in the US). Through contracts with other rental agencies, this company arranges car, minibus, and minivan rentals at a variety of locations in Great Britain, depending on availability, at a flat discount rate. Full payment must be made in advance; dropoff alternatives are also available for an additional charge.

RV rentals are also available from a number of companies in Europe. Among them is *Autotours* (address below). For other rental sources, ask at local car rental companies and national tourist board offices.

A complimentary packet of information on how to operate, maintain, choose, and use an RV is available from the *Recreational Vehicle Industry Association* (PO Box 2999, Reston, VA 22090; phone 703-620-6003). You might also want to subscribe to *Trailer Life,* published by TL Enterprises, 29901 Agoura Rd., Agoura, CA (phone: 818-991-4980); a 1-year subscription costs $11.98. For further information on how to operate, choose, and use an RV, see Richard A. Wolters's *Living on Wheels* (Dutton; currently out of print; check your library).

ORGANIZED TRIPS – A packaged camping tour abroad is a good way to have your cake and eat it too. The problems of advance planning and day-to-day organizing are left to someone else, yet you still reap the savings that shoestring travel affords. Be aware, however, that these packages are usually geared to the young, with ages 18 to 35 as common limits. Transfer from place to place is by bus or van (as on other sightseeing tours), overnights are in tents, and meal arrangements vary. Often there is a food fund that covers meals in restaurants or in the camp; sometimes there is a chef, and sometimes the cooking is done by the participants themselves.

The *Specialty Travel Index* is a directory to special-interest travel and is an invaluable resource. Listings include tour operators specializing in camping, not to mention myriad other interests that combine nicely with a camping trip, such as biking, ballooning, diving, horseback riding, canoeing, motorcycling, and river rafting. It costs $5 per copy, $8 for a year's subscription of two issues. Write to *Specialty Travel Index,* 305 San Anselmo Ave., Suite 217, San Anselmo, CA 94960 (phone: 415-459-4900).

Among such packages are the camping tours offered by *Autotours,* which range from 3 to 10 weeks; a variety of itineraries are available. For information, contact Autotours, 20 Craven Terr., London W2 (phone: 258-0272). *Camping Tours of Europe* (2 Guilles La., Woodbury, NY 11797; phone: 516-496-7400) also markets the camping tours of British tour operators.

HIKING: If you would rather eliminate all the gear and planning and take to the outdoors unencumbered, park the car and go for a day's hike. Trails abound in Great Britain, and the British Tourist Authority distributes a number of information sheets on walking routes and mountaineering. One particularly useful publication is *Walking,* which describes national parks, long-distance footpaths, and other walking areas in England, Scotland, and Wales. There are several other sources of information for those intent on getting about on their own steam.

Mountaineering and hiking clubs clubs are a particularly good source of trail information for the average hiker. The *Ramblers Association* (1-5 Wandsworth Rd., London SW8 2XX; phone: 01-582-6878) publishes a yearbook that discusses accommodations for hikers and walkers and a magazine, *The Rambler,* that is only available to members. The *British Mountaineering Council* (Crawford House, Precinct Centre, Booth St. E., Manchester M13 9RZ) furnishes advice on mountaineering and rock climbing and a list of qualified guides.

For those who are hiking on their own, without benefit of a guide or group, a map of the trail is a must. Ordnance Survey maps of the Landranger series, on the scale of 1¼ inches to 1 mile (1:50,000), cover the whole of Great Britain; and the *Outdoor Leisure* series, ideal at 2½ inches to 1 mile (1.25,000), includes all of the more popular areas. The *British Travel Bookshop* (40 W. 57th St., New York, NY 10019; phone: 212-765-0898) carries a very limited selection of the maps; more are available by mail from *Stanfords* (12-14 Long Acre, Covent Garden, London WC2E 9LP; phone: 01-836-1321) and from *Hatchard's* (187 Piccadilly, London W1; phone: 01-437-3924).

A British company that specializes in maps and other publications for hikers and climbers is the *Robertson MacCarta Shop* (122 King's Cross Rd., London WC1X 9DS; phone: 01-278-8278). A useful set of guidebooks is the *Walking Through* series, which covers ten European cities (including London) and is available from VLE Limited (PO Box 547, Tenafly, NJ 07670; phone: 201-567-5536) for $3 each, or $2.50 each if ordering two or more.

To make outings safe and pleasant, find out in advance about the trails you plan to hike and be realistic about your own physical limitations. For instance, Britain's Pennine Way, one of the country's official long-distance footpaths and its roughest, meanders 270 lonely miles up the backbone of England to the Scottish border. Even those following only portions of this route should be aware that it is recommended only for experienced hikers equipped with maps and compass to steer them through remote moorland and probable bad weather. Choose an easy route if you are out of shape. Stick to defined trails unless you are an experience hiker or know the area well. Whether heading out for a short jaunt or a longer trek, particularly in more remote areas, let someone know where you are going and when you expect to be back. If the hike is impromptu, leave a note on your car.

All you need to set out are a pair of sturdy shoes and socks; jeans or long pants to keep branches, nettles, and bugs off your legs; a canteen of water; a hat to protect you from the sun; and, if you like, a picnic lunch. It is a good idea to dress in layers, so that you can add or remove clothing according to the elevation and weather. Make sure, too, to wear clothes with pockets or bring a pack to keep your hands free. Some useful and important pocket or pack stuffers include trail mix, a jackknife, first-aid kit, map, compass, and sunglasses. You may also want to tuck in a lightweight waterproof poncho (available in camping supply stores) in case of unexpected showers. In areas where snakes are common, include a snakebite kit.

Those who prefer to travel as part of an organized group should refer to the January/ February issue of *Sierra* magazine for the *Sierra Club*'s annual list of foreign outings. Some trips are backpacking trips, moving to a new camp each day; others make day hikes from a base camp. Overnights can be in small hotels, inns, bed-and-breakfast farmhouses, guesthouses, or campgrounds. Different trips are offered each year; variations in 1989 included a combined hiking and biking trip to Great Britain. For information, contact the Sierra Club Outing Department, 730 Polk St., San Francisco, CA 94109 (phone: 415-776-2211). *American Youth Hostels* also sponsors foreign hiking trips, though fewer than its foreign biking trips. Trips usually range from around 15 to 52 days. As with the *Sierra Club,* the itineraries offered vary from year to year, usually ranging from 15 to 52 days; Great Britain has been included among the destinations offered in recent years (address below; see *Hints for Single Travelers* for membership information).

Mountain Travel, a company specializing in adventure trips around the world, offers a great variety of trips ranging from easy walks that can be taken by anyone in good health to those that require basic or advanced mountaineering experience. Among the 1989 offerings were 11-day walking tours of Great Britain. Itineraries were graded according to difficulty, travel between areas of interest was by minibus, and accommodations were in small hotels and guesthouses. Note that *Mountain Travel* also designs special itineraries for independent travelers. Contact Mountain Travel, 6420 Fairmont Ave., El Cerrito, CA 94530 (phone: 415-527-8100 in California; 800-227-2384 elsewhere in the US). A variety of both hiking and biking tours emphasizing easy exercise and the finest in dining and accommodations is offered by *Butterfield & Robinson,* and *Country Cycling Tours* also offers several walking tours (see "Biking," below).

BIKING: For young or energetic travelers, a bicycle offers a marvelous way of seeing a country, especially where the terrain is conducive to easy cycling, as it is in most parts of Great Britain, a popular European biking destination. Much of the country is rural and, except for the environs of industrial cities, nearly traffic-free. Secondary roads are almost everywhere, threaded neatly through picturesque stretches of countryside. The landscape tends to be flat to rolling in the middle of the island, hilly on the coast, and scenic throughout. Biking does have its drawbacks: Little baggage can be carried, travel is slow, and cyclists are exposed to the elements, which in Great Britain, for most of the year, means a mild climate with cool evenings — and the ever-present possibility of showers. However, should a cyclist need rest or refuge from the weather, there is always a welcoming pub or comfortable bed-and-breakfast establishment around the next bend.

Road Safety – While the car may be the bane of cyclists — although British motorists are generally courteous and well accustomed to cyclists — those on bicycles who do not follow the rules of the road strike terror into the hearts of drivers. Follow the same rules and regulations as drivers. Stay to the left side of the road. Ride no more than two abreast — single file where traffic is heavy. Keep three bicycle lengths behind the cycle in front of you. Stay alert to sand, gravel, potholes, and wet or oily surfaces, all of which can make you lose control. Wear bright clothes and use lights or wear reflective material at dusk or at night, and, above all, even though British cyclists often don't, always wear a helmet.

Choosing, Renting, and Buying a Bike – Although many enthusiasts choose to take along their own bikes, bicycles are available for rent throughout Great Britain, although, particularly in rural areas, it may pay to check ahead. For details on rentals in British cities, see *Sources and Resources* in THE CITIES. Also, the British Tourist Authority publishes a brochure, *Britain Cycling,* that lists 25 rental outlets in various areas.

As an alternative to renting, you might consider buying a bicycle in Great Britain, often for less than what you might pay in the US; however, the bicycle may take some getting used to — seats especially need breaking in at first — and if you bring it home, it will be subject to an import duty by US Customs if its price (or the total of purchases in Great Britain) exceeds $400. When evaluating this cost, take into account additional charges for shipping. Those planning to buy a bicycle, be it in the US or Great Britain, should consider a good-quality, lightweight touring bike that has the all-important low gears for climbing hills and riding against the wind. A European bicycle purchased in the US should have proof-of-purchase papers to avoid potential customs problems.

A bicycle is the correct size for you if you can straddle its center bar with feet flat on the ground and still have an inch or so between your crotch and the bar. (Nowadays, because women's old-fashioned barless bikes are not as strong as men's, most women use men's bicycles.) The seat height is right if your leg is just short of completely extended when the pedal is at the bottom of its arc.

To be completely comfortable, divide your weight; put about 50% on your saddle and about 25% on your arms and legs. To stop sliding in your seat and for better support, set your saddle level. A firm saddle is better than a soft springy one for a long ride. Experienced cyclists keep the tires fully inflated (pressure requirements vary widely, but are always imprinted on the side of the tire; stay within 5 pounds of the recommended pressure). Do not use top, or tenth, gear all the way; for most riding the middle gears are best. On long rides remember that until you are very fit, short efforts with rests in between are better than one long haul, and pedal at an even pace.

The happiest biker in a foreign country is the one who arrives best prepared. Bring saddlebags, a handlebar bag, a tool kit that contains a bike wrench, screwdriver, pliers, tire repair kit, cycle oil, and work gloves, a bike repair book, a helmet (a rarity among British cyclists), a rain suit, a water bottle, a flashlight with an extra set of batteries, a small first-aid kit, and muscles that have been limbered up in advance.

Even the smallest towns usually have a bike shop, so it's not difficult to replace or add to gear; however, because tires and tubes are sized to metric dimensions in some parts of Great Britain, when riding your own bike, bring extras from home. Seasoned bikers swear that the second day of any trip is always the worst, so keep this in mind and be ready to meet the mental and physical challenges ahead.

Airlines going from the US (or elsewhere) to Great Britain generally allow bicycles to be checked as baggage and require that the pedals be removed, handlebars be turned sideways, and the bike be in a shipping carton, which some airlines provide, subject to availability — call ahead to make sure. If buying a shipping carton from a bicycle shop, check the airline's specifications and also ask about storing the carton at the destination airport so that you can use it again for the return flight. Although some airlines charge only a nominal fee, if the traveler has already checked two pieces of baggage, there may be an excess baggage charge of $70 to $80 for the bicycle. As regulations vary from carrier to carrier, be sure to call well before departure to find out your airline's requirements.

When the going gets rough, remember that arduous parts of the journey can be avoided by loading your bicycle on the luggage van of a train. Bicycles are generally transported free on British trains, except on *InterCity 125* routes, which have special arrangements for bicycles in the guard's van. There's a £3 (about $4.50) charge on weekdays and during rush hours on other routes, when there will be a supplemental charge of £1.25 to £3 ($2 to $4.50). Bicycle transportation is also available on *Motorail* car-carrying services and boat trains to the Continent. It's a good idea to check with the station the day before departure.

A good book to help you plan a trip is *Bicycle Touring in Europe,* by Karen and Gary Hawkins (Pantheon Books; $8.95). It offers information on buying and equipping a touring bike, useful clothing and supplies, and helpful techniques for the long-distance biker; it also contains tours of Wales, southern England, and the Scottish Highlands. Another good general book is *Europe by Bike,* by Karen and Terry Whitehill (Mountaineers Books; $10.95), which outlines a tour covering the length of England from Canterbury to York. *Cyclist's Britain,* produced by a cycling group in England, outlines several tours of England, Scotland, and Wales; it is available in the US (for $14.95 plus $2.50 postage and handling) through Hunter Publishing, 300 Raritan Center Pkwy., Edison, NJ 08818 (phone: 201-225-1900). The British Tourist Authority's booklet *Cycling* provides information on various aspects of biking in Britain and also describes several routes.

Also useful as a planning aid is *Information and Equipment,* the free store catalogue of the *Metropolitan New York Council of American Youth Hostels* (AYH; 75 Spring St., New York, NY 10012; phone: 212-431-7100). It provides information on equipment and has an excellent bibliography of paperbacks and maps for cyclists, campers, hikers, and travelers touring on skis. The *International Youth Hostel Handbook, Volume One: Europe and the Mediterranean* ($8.95 plus $2 for postage) is a guide to all the hostels of Europe to which members of *AYH* have access; a map of their locations is included. (For more information on *American Youth Hostels* see below; for information on joining, see *Hints for Single Travelers.*)

Good maps will infinitely improve a biking tour, and detailed maps show the scenic byways as well as the route that goes around the mountain, not up it. Such maps are available from a number of sources, but those of the Bartholomew *National* series (on a scale of 1:100,000 — 1 centimeter of map equals 100,000 centimeters or 1 kilometer or approximately 1.6 miles of road) or *GT* series (1:253,440 — 1 centimeter of map equals approximately 2.5 kilometers or 4 miles of road) are particularly useful for Great Britain. If unavailable locally, they can be ordered from John Bartholomew & Son Ltd., 12 Duncan St., Edinburgh EH9 1TA, Scotland. Michelin maps (on a scale of 1:200,000), with detailed and clear road references, can be ordered from Michelin Guides and Maps (PO Box 3305, Spartanburg, SC 29304-3305; phone: 803-599-0850) and are also readily available throughout Great Britain. Ordnance Survey maps are also quite good (see "Hiking," above).

Tours – A number of organizations offer bike tours in Great Britain. Linking up with a bike tour is more expensive than traveling alone, but with experienced leaders, an organized tour often becomes an educational as well as a very social experience that may lead to long-term friendships.

One of the attractions of a bike tour is that shipment of equipment — the bike — is handled by organizers, and the shipping fee is included in the total tour package. Travelers simply deliver the bike to the airport, already disassembled and boxed; shipping boxes can be obtained from most bicycle shops with little difficulty. Independent bikers must make their own arrangements with the airline, and there are no standard procedures (see above). Although some tour organizers will rent bikes, most prefer that participants bring a bike with which they are already familiar. Another attraction of *some* tours is the existence of a "sag wagon," which carries extra luggage, fatigued cyclists, and their bikes, too, when pedaling another mile is impossible.

Most bike tours are scheduled from May to October, last 1 or 2 weeks, are limited to 20 or 25 people, and provide lodging in inns or hotels, though some use hostels or even tents. Tours vary considerably in style and ambience, so request brochures from several operators in order to make the best decision. When contacting groups, be sure to ask about the maximum number of people on the trip, the maximum number of miles to be traveled each day, and the degree of difficulty of the biking; these details should determine which tour you join and can greatly affect your enjoyment of the experience. Planning ahead is essential because trips often fill up 6 months or more in advance.

Among the companies specializing in biking tours to Europe are the following:

Baumeler Tours, 10 Grand Ave., Rockville Centre, NY 11570-9861 (phone: 516-766-6160 collect in New York State; 800-6ABROAD nationwide). Specializes in arranging biking tours, both independent and escorted.

Butterfield & Robinson, 70 Bond St., Suite 300, Toronto M5B 1X3, Canada (phone: 416-864-1354). Offers a number of first class, sophisticated bike trips. Bikes are provided, though you can take your own, and there are many departure dates for each itinerary. This company also offers trips to anyone age 17 or older; tours are rated at four levels of difficulty.

Country Cycling Tours, 140 W. 83rd St., New York, NY 10024 (phone: 212-874-5151). Offers a variety of 14-day itineraries to England. (Hiking tours are also available.)

Gerhard's Bicycle Odysseys, 4949 SW Macadam, Portland, OR 97201 (phone: 503-223-2402). Offers a variety of 2-week itineraries in Europe.

Wilderness Travel, 801 Allston Way, Berkeley, CA 94710 (phone: 415-548-0420 or 800-247-6700). An adventure packager, known for expeditions in the wild, also offers bicycle trips with sag wagons a standard feature.

Hundreds of other organizations sponsoring biking tours have sprung up in response to an explosion of interest. Among them are *Euro-bike Tours,* PO Box 40, De Kalb, IL 60115 (phone: 815-758-8851), and *Open Roads,* 1601 Summit Dr., Haymarket, VA 22069 (phone: 703-754-4152 or 800-333-2453). The *Sierra Club* also occasionally includes a bike tour in its group of European offerings. For news about upcoming free-wheeling events, contact the club's Outing Department (address above).

The *Cyclists Touring Club* (*CTC*), Britain's largest cycling association, not only runs organized tours but also has a number of planned routes available in pamphlet form for bikers on their own. The club helps members plan their own tours and publishes a yearly handbook as well as magazines. For information on joining, write to the *CTC* at Cotterell House, 69 Meadrow, Godalming, Surrey GU7 3HS, England (phone: 04868-7217).

The *American Youth Hostels* (*AYH*) and its local chapters or councils also offer a variety of packages. You don't have to be a youngster to take an *AYH* trip; membership is open to all ages, and the catalogue includes a group of trips for adults only. *AYH* tours are for small groups of 9 or 10 participants and tend to be longer than average (up to 5 weeks). Departures are geared to various age groups and levels of skill and frequently feature accommodations in hostels — along with hotels for adult groups and campgrounds for younger groups.

The *Metropolitan New York Council of American Youth Hostels,* an *AYH* affiliate with a particularly broad tour program, offered a 16-day bicycle trip to Great Britain in 1989. It was geared to teenagers and provided overnight accommodations at hostels and campsites. This chapter is also a good source of camping, hiking, and cycling equipment. The 1989 summer program of the national organization included a 16-day tour of England with accommodations in hostels; versions of the tour were geared to adults 18 and up, to teenagers 15 to 18 only, and to mixed ages. Another itinerary featured 22 days of cycling through England, France, and Belgium. For information contact your local council, the national organization (PO Box 37613, Washington, DC

20013-7613; phone: 202-783-6161), or the Metropolitan New York Council of the American Youth Hostels (75 Spring St., New York, NY 10012; phone: 212-431-7100).

The *International Bicycle Touring Society* (*IBTS*) is another non-profit organization that regularly sponsors low-cost bicycle tours around the US and Canada and overseas led by member volunteers. Tours to England and Scotland were among the foreign itineraries on its 1989 program. Participants must be over 21. A sag wagon accompanies the group, accommodations are in inns and hotels, and some meals are included. For information, send $2 plus a 39¢ self-addressed, stamped envelope to IBTS, PO Box 6979, San Diego, CA 92106-0979 (phone: 619-226-TOUR).

The *League of American Wheelmen* (6707 Whitestone Rd., Suite 209, Baltimore, MD 21207; phone: 301-944-3399) publishes *Tourfinder,* a list of organizations, non-profit and commercial, that sponsor bicycle tours of the US and abroad; the list is free with membership ($22 individual, $27 family) and can be obtained by non-members who send $4. The *League* can also put you in touch with biking groups in your area.

Preparing

Calculating Costs

$ After years of living relatively high on the hog, travel from North America to Europe dropped off precipitously in 1987 in response, among other considerations, to the relative weakness of the US dollar on the Continent. Many Americans who had enjoyed bargain prices in Europe found that the recent disadvantageous exchange rates really put a crimp in their travel planning. But although the halcyon days of dollar domination seem over for the present, discount fares and the availability of charter flights can greatly reduce the cost of a European vacation; package tours can even further reduce the price. Great Britain has always been one of the most popular European countries for both the first-time and the seasoned traveler, and it is certainly one where the competition for American visitors works to inspire surprisingly affordable travel opportunities. Nevertheless, most travelers still have to plan carefully before they go, and prudent marshaling of funds is still necessary.

Although a little more expensive than the least expensive Mediterranean countries, Great Britain is not among the costliest countries in Europe. The British Tourist Authority, which promotes travel to the United Kingdom, has been very successfully campaigning to call the attention of potential visitors to the low-cost options available for almost every entry in the traveler's budget. Some publications stress this theme, among them its *Britain: Bed & Breakfast* brochure, an introduction to a most reasonable and pleasant way to bring down the cost of housing for the tourist in Great Britain.

Estimating the cost of travel in Britain depends on the mode of transportation, the part of the country, the length of your stay, and, in some cases, the time of year you plan to travel. In addition to the basics of transportation, hotels, meals, and sightseeing, you have to take into account seasonal price changes that apply on certain air routings and at popular vacation destinations, as well as inflation, price fluctuations, and the vagaries of currency exchange. So, while the guidelines in this book will remain useful, costs for both facilities and services may have changed somewhat in the months since publication.

DETERMINING A BUDGET: A realistic appraisal of your travel expenses is the most crucial bit of planning you will undertake before any trip. It is also, unfortunately, one for which it is most difficult to give precise, practical advice. Travel styles are intensely personal, and personal taste determines cost to a great extent. Will you stay in a hotel every night and eat every meal in a restaurant, or are you planning to do some camping and picnicking, thus reducing your daily expenses? Base your calculations on your own travel style and estimate expenses from that. If published figures on the cost of travel were always taken as gospel, many trips would not be taken. But in reality, it's possible to economize. On the other hand, don't be lulled into feeling that it is not necessary to do some arithmetic before you go. No matter how generous your travel budget, without careful planning beforehand — and strict accounting along the way — you will spend more than you anticipated.

When calculating costs, start with the basics — transportation, accommodations, and food. However, don't forget such extras as local transportation, sightseeing, shopping, and miscellaneous items such as laundry, taxes, and tips. And keep in mind, particularly when calculating the basic expenses, that costs vary according to fluctuations in the exchange rate — that is, how much of a given foreign currency the dollar will buy. Package programs can lessen the price of a vacation in Great Britain, because the group rates obtained by the tour packager are usually lower than the tariffs charged to someone traveling independently, that is, paying for each element — airfare, hotel, meals, car rental — separately.

Other expenses, such as the cost of local sightseeing tours, will vary from city to city. Official tourist information offices are plentiful throughout Great Britain, and most of the better hotels have someone at the front desk to provide a rundown on the cost of local tours and full-day excursions in and out of the city. Special discount passes that provide tourists with unlimited travel by the day or the week on regular city transportation are available in many large cities. The British Tourist Authority publishes an information sheet, *Tourist Tickets and Discount Cards,* that lists many transportation and admission discounts. Often, there is no admission charge, or a nominal one, for major museums.

If you spend every night in a moderately priced hotel and eat every meal in a moderately priced restaurant, you can expect to spend around $200 for two people per day. This figure does not include transportation costs, but it does include accommodations (based on two people sharing a room), three meals, some sightseeing, and other modest entertainment. The accommodations take into consideration the differences between relatively inexpensive lodgings in rural areas (about $40 to $50 per night for two) and moderate hotels in urban areas (about $80 to $100 per night for two). Meals are all calculated for inexpensive restaurants, and the entertainment normally includes one sightseeing tour and admission to one museum or historic site. These figures are based on averages compiled by travel sources across the country.

You should be able to use these averages to forecast a reasonably accurate picture of your daily travel costs, based on exactly how you want to travel. Savings on the daily allowance can occur while motoring in rural areas; budgeting families can take advantage of inexpensive accommodations throughout the country. Campgrounds are located throughout Great Britain and are a particularly inexpensive way to see the countryside.

Picnicking is another excellent way to cut costs, and Great Britain abounds with well-groomed parks and idyllic pastoral settings. A stop at a market can provide a feast of delicacies at a surprisingly low price when compared to the cost of a restaurant lunch.

In planning your budget, it is also wise to allow a realistic amount for both entertainment and recreation. Are you planning to spend time sightseeing and going to museums? Is daily golf or tennis a part of your plan? Will your children be disappointed if they don't take a boat ride on the Thames or take a trip in search of the Loch Ness monster? If so, charges for these attractions and recreations must be taken into account.

If at any point in the planning process it appears impossible to estimate expenses, consider this suggestion: The easiest way to put a ceiling on the price of all these elements is to consider buying a package tour. A totally planned and escorted one, with almost all transportation, rooms, meals, sightseeing, local travel, tips, and a dinner show or two included and prepaid, allows you to know beforehand almost exactly what the trip will cost, and the only surprise will be the one you spring on yourself by succumbing to some irresistible, expensive souvenir.

The various types of packages available are discussed in *Package Tours,* in this section, but a few points bear repeating here. Not all packages are package *tours.* There are loosely organized arrangements that include nothing more than transatlantic transportation, a stay at a hotel, transfers between hotel and airport, baggage handling, taxes, and tips, which leave the entire matter of how you spend your time and where you eat your meals — and with whom — up to you. Equally common are the hotel-plus-car packages, which take care of accommodations and local transportation. On such independent or hosted "tours," there may be a tour company representative or affiliated British travel agent available at a local office to answer questions, or a host may be stationed at a desk in the hotel to arrange optional excursions, but you will never have to travel in a group unless you wish to. More and more, even experienced travelers are being won over by the idea of packaged travel, not only for the convenience and the planning time saved, but above all for the money saved. Whatever elements you include in your package, the organizer has gotten them for you wholesale — and they are prepaid, thus eliminating the dismal prospect of returning to your hotel each night to subtract the day's disbursements from your remaining cash.

The possibility of prepaying certain elements of your trip is an important point to consider even if you intend to be strictly independent, with arrangements entirely of your own making, all bought separately. You may not be able to match the price of the wholesale tour package, but at least you will have introduced an element of predictability into your accounting, thus reducing the risk that some budget-busting expense along the way might put a damper on the rest of your plans. With the independent traveler in mind, what follows are some suggestions of how to pin down the cost of a trip beforehand; but there are two more variables that will influence the cost of your holiday whether you buy a package or do it all yourself. One is timing. If you are willing to travel during the less trafficked, off-season months, when airfares are lower, you'll find many hotels' rates lower also. Keep in mind those periods between the traditional high and low seasons generally referred to as the shoulder months (approximately late March to mid-May and late September to mid-November). Costs are only a little lower than in high season, and although the weather may not be as predictable, you won't be bucking the crowds that in peak months can force a traveler without a hotel reservation into the most expensive hostelry in town. Don't forget, however, to find out what is going on in any place you plan to spend a good deal of your vacation. The availability and possible economy gained by off-season travel are negated if a major conference or other special event is scheduled when you plan to visit.

Another factor influencing the cost of your trip is whether you will be traveling alone or as a couple. The prices quoted for package tours are almost always based on double occupancy of hotel rooms, and the surcharge — or single supplement — for a room by yourself can be quite hefty. When shopping for a hotel room, you'll find that there are many more double rooms than singles. Don't expect a discount if you occupy a double room as a single, and don't expect single rooms to cost less than two-thirds the price of doubles.

Those who want to travel independently but also want to eliminate the element of surprise from their accommodations budgets can take advantage of the hotel voucher schemes that frequently come as part of a fly/drive package. Travelers receive a block of prepaid vouchers and a list of hotels that accept them as total payment for a night's stay, and for those who may want to upgrade their lodgings from time to time, there is often another set of hotels that accept the same vouchers with payment of a supplement.

In Britain, slightly lower hotel rates can be expected off-season — January through March. Many hotels offer "mini-break" packages, that is, a discount for a stay of 2 or more nights, usually over a weekend; though these discounts may be in effect any time of the year, they are most common when demand is low. (For a discussion of the range and variety of places to stay in Britain, see *Accommodations.*)

TRANSPORTATION: In earlier sections of GETTING READY TO GO, we have discussed the comparative costs of different modes of transportation and the myriad special rates available through package tours, charter flights, train passes, car rental packages, and other budget deals. See each of the relevant sections for specific information. Transportation is likely to represent the largest item in your travel budget, but the encouraging aspect of this is that you will be able to determine most of these costs before you leave. Most fares will have to be paid in advance, particularly if you take advantage of charter air travel or other special deals.

Airfare is really the easiest cost to pin down, though the range and variety of available flights may be confusing initially. The possibilities are outlined fully in *Traveling by Plane,* in this section. Essentially, you can choose from various types of tickets on scheduled flights, ranging in expense from the luxury of the *Concorde* and first class fares to APEX, discount, and standby tickets or charters.

The most important factors in determining which mode of transportation to choose in traveling about Great Britain are the amount of traveling you plan to do and the length of time you will be abroad. If you intend to move about a great deal among cities, a pass allowing unlimited train or bus travel is likely to be the most economical approach. For more information on economical rail and bus options, see *Touring by Train* and *Touring by Bus.*

If you want to drive through the countryside, you should look carefully into fly/drive arrangements versus straight rentals and compare the rates offered by some of the smaller US firms specializing in car travel in Europe with the rates offered by the large, familiar names in car rental. The latter all have discount plans provided the car is booked a certain number of days before departure and the rental is for a minimum period of time (see *Touring by Car*). Always look for the flat rate based on unlimited mileage — usually the best deal. Also, when estimating driving costs, don't forget that the price of gas in Europe averages more than double the price you're used to in the US, so be sure to take this substantial expense into account.

FOOD: Meals are more difficult to estimate. If you stay in an apartment or are camping out, you will be able to prepare some meals yourself. Depending on where you're staying, groceries can be more expensive than they are at home, but they will certainly be less expensive than eating out. Restaurant dining — particularly in the better establishments of major tourist cities — is going to hit your purse, wallet, or credit card hardest.

Independent travelers who take all of their meals out should allow roughly $35 to $60 a day for food. This amount includes breakfast, because increasingly the standard breakfast included in the price of accommodations — although in many areas it is posted separately from the price of the room — is continental (coffee and rolls), though there is an extra charge for a full British breakfast (bacon and eggs, sausage, and toast); this should also cover taxes and the service charge and perhaps a carafe of table wine at dinner — but you won't be splurging. This estimate is based on a fixed menu (at a fixed price) in a moderate, neither-scrimp-nor-splurge restaurant, which can at least include a tasty and occasionally imaginative food selection, but no cocktails before dinner. If ordering an à la carte dinner and the pick of the wine list in one of the major cities, be prepared for the tab to rise much higher, and if you're addicted to *haute gastronomie,* the sky is the limit.

All of this is no reason to forgo your trip, however — remember, it's *dining* that is going to hit your wallet hard. Those who are up to a steady diet of fast food can get by on a lot less. And there is some relief out in the countryside, where the breakfast that comes with the bed in the typical bed-and-breakfast establishments and small inns can still be a filling one, apt to hold most folks straight through midday, though even travelers on a severe budget are advised not to skip lunch. Pub lunches in general are becoming more and more imaginative everywhere, and they're among the best food buys encountered. Picnic lunches, with ingredients purchased at shops and markets along the route, are less expensive (and more fun) still. Finish off the day with a carefully chosen meal in a bistro or inn and you will sacrifice nothing in experience and hold the cost down. Our restaurant selections, chosen to give the best value for money — whether expensive or dirt cheap — are listed in the *Best in Town* sections of THE CITIES and in the *Eating Out* sections of each tour route in DIRECTIONS.

ACCOMMODATIONS: There is a wide range of choice and a substantial difference in degrees of luxury provided among the expensive, moderate, and inexpensive hotels. Although room costs in Great Britain cover a very broad spectrum, for purposes of making an estimate, expect to pay in Great Britain about what you would pay in a major American city for equivalent accommodations. And figure on the high side if you've visiting major tourist centers during high season.

Most expensive — as high as $300 to $500 for a double room — will be the "palace" hotels of London or Edinburgh. Rates at international hotels with a full complement of business services also tend toward the top of the scale. Generally, the member hotels of international chains in any given city are priced roughly the same. In the larger cities (such as Manchester or Bristol), this ranges from around $150 up, although similar hotels elsewhere range from about $60 to $80 for a double. There is a big jump from these international class hotels to those in the moderate category in the same city, and prices will be from $20 to as much as $50 less per night.

There is no sacred edict stating that travelers must put up at deluxe hotels, and, in fact, you might be missing a good deal of the European experience by insisting on international standards and skipping over the great small hotels. Especially in Great Britain, hotels in the first class range usually are available at about one third less than their deluxe counterparts. Second class hotels offer clean, comfortable accommodations and are often thoroughly charming, and in the even more inexpensive range are hotels that many will find perfectly adequate. In rural areas, there are family-run hotels and inns and bed-and-breakfast establishments that are being used more and more by tourists. Budget accommodations designed to offer basic (but acceptable) lodging at especially economical prices — a double room may cost as little as $30 to $40 — do exist, and, recognizing the need, travel agents, tour packagers, airlines, and tourist offices are doing what they can to make their whereabouts known. Budget accommodations in central cities also exist, and the British Tourist Authority's recently expanded *London Budget Hotels* lists double room accommodations ranging from under £55 (about $85) per person per night.

Bed-and-breakfast establishments (known as B&Bs), where the night can be spent in surroundings that may be homey or Spartan, are almost always clean and adequate. B&Bs average about $20 per person per night in Britain, though in London, as in other large cities, space is at a premium, and few private homes have the spare room to rent to passing strangers.

There are other options for less expensive accommodations for anyone staying for an extended period of time in one place. One is renting an apartment, called a "holiday let" or "self-catering holiday" in Great Britain. These are available in most cities and can be arranged through travel agents. The other is a home exchange, in which you and a British family exchange houses for an agreed-upon period of time. Both are discussed in *Accommodations.*

LOCAL TAXES AND SERVICE CHARGES: A sales tax or VAT (Value Added Tax) is added to both goods and services in many European countries. The rate ranges from lows of 5.5% and 7% on food to a high of 33.33% on luxury articles. The VAT is buried in the prices charged for hotel rooms and restaurant meals, so you won't even notice it. It is also included in the amount shown on the price tag of purchased goods. There is no escaping the tax on services, but for foreigners, the tax on purchases, typically 18.6%, can frequently be reimbursed.

In Great Britain, the standard rate is 15%, whether on room accommodations or on purchased goods. All advertised prices must include the VAT. However, tourists can avoid the VAT on purchases by having the goods sent directly to their home address — if the store is willing to do so. In addition, many stores have long had a "retail export scheme" whereby you pay the tax, have a VAT relief form validated by a customs clerk as you leave the country, mail the form to the store, and receive a check in pounds in return. Under a newer tax-free shopping scheme, forms are mailed to a central address and a check in dollars or pounds is issued within 5 working days. For a full discussion of VAT refunds, see *Shopping*.

A service charge of, usually, 12% to 15% is almost universal on restaurant and hotel bills. Nevertheless, there are still many situations not covered by the service charge or where an additional gratuity is appropriate. For more on these, see *Tipping*.

■ **A note on our hotel/restaurant cost categories:** There are a great many moderate and inexpensive hotels and restaurants that we have not included in this book. Our *Checking In* and *Eating Out* listings include only those places we think are best in their price range. We have rated our listings by general price categories: expensive, moderate, and inexpensive. The introductory paragraph of each list explains just what those categories mean in the context of local prices.

Planning a Trip

123 Travelers fall into two categories: those who make lists and those who do not. Some people prefer to plot the course of their trip to the finest detail, with contingency plans and alternatives at the ready. For others, the joy of a voyage is its spontaneity; exhaustive planning only lessens the thrill of anticipation and the sense of freedom.

However, for most travelers, any week-plus trip to Great Britain can be too expensive for an "I'll take my chances" type of vacation. Even perennial gypsies and anarchistic wanderers have to take into account the logistics of getting around, and even with minimal baggage, they need to think about packing. Hence at least some planning is crucial. This is not to suggest that you work out your itinerary in minute detail before you go; however, you still have to decide certain basics at the very start: where to go, what to do, and how much to spend. These decisions require a certain amount of consideration. So before rigorously planning specific travel details, you might want to establish your general objectives:

1. How much time will you have for the entire trip, and how much of it are you willing to spend getting where you're going?
2. What interests and/or activities do you want to pursue while on vacation? Do you want to visit one, a few, or several different places?
3. At what time of year do you want to go?
4. What kind of geography or climate would you prefer?
5. Do you want peace and privacy or lots of action and company?
6. How much money can you spend for the entire vacation?

Obviously, your answers will be determined by your personal tastes and lifestyle. These will condition the degree of comfort you require; whether you select a tour or opt for total independence; and how much responsibility you want to take for your own arrangements (or whether you want everything done for you, with the kinds of services provided in a comprehensive package trip).

With firm answers to these major questions, start reviewing literature on the areas in which you're most interested. Good sources of information are airlines, hotel representatives, and travel agents who specialize in planning and arrange trips (see *How to Use a Travel Agent,* in this section). The British Tourist Authority has four offices in the US (see *Tourist Information Offices* for addresses). Stop in or write to any of these branches — all are ready resources for brochures, maps, and other information on British cities and the countryside. (Note that although the British Tourist Authority no longer promotes tourism to Northern Ireland, many of its publications do include useful information on the country.) Also consult general travel sources such as books and guidebooks. Up-to-date travel information on Britain is plentiful, and you should be able to accumulate everything you want to know, not only about the places you plan to visit, but also about the relevant tour and package options (see *Package Tours*). And if you're visiting Great Britain for the first time, make a special effort to read up on the cuisine, history, and culture. A good place to begin is PERSPECTIVES, but if you're planning an extended stay in a particular city or region, you'll probably want to do some more extensive reading.

You can now make almost all of your own travel arrangements if you have time to follow through with hotels, airlines, tour operators, and so on. But you'll probably save considerable time and energy if you have a travel agent do it for you. The agent also should be able to advise you of alternative arrangements of which you may not be aware. Only rarely will an agent's services cost a traveler any money, and they may even save you some (see *How to Use a Travel Agent*). Well before departure (depending on how far in advance you make your reservations), the agent will deliver a packet that includes all your tickets and hotel confirmations and often a day-by-day outline of where you'll be when, along with a detailed list of whatever flights you're taking.

Make plans early. During the summer season and on American holidays, make hotel reservations at least a month in advance in all major cities. If you are flying at these times and hope to take advantage of the considerable savings offered through discount fares or charter programs, purchase tickets as far ahead as possible. The more specific your requirements, the earlier you should book. Many hotels require deposits before they will guarantee reservations. Be sure you have a receipt for any deposit.

Before your departure, find out what the weather will be like at your destination. Consult *When to Go* for a chart of average temperatures in various British cities and *How to Pack* for further details on the climate and what clothes to take. See THE CITIES for information on special events that may occur during your stay as well as for other essential information on local resources, transportation, and so on.

While making vacation arrangements is fun and exciting, don't forget to prepare for your absence from home. Before you leave, attend to these household matters:

1. Arrange for your mail to be forwarded, held by the post office until you return, or picked up daily at your house. Someone should check your door occasionally to pick up any unexpected deliveries. Piles of mail or packages tell thieves that no one is home.
2. Cancel all deliveries (newspapers, milk, and so on).
3. Arrange for the lawn to be mowed and plants watered at regular intervals.
4. Arrange for the care of pets.
5. Etch your social security number in a prominent place on all appliances (television sets, radios, cameras, kitchen appliances). This considerably reduces their appeal to thieves and facilitates identification.
6. Leave a house key and your itinerary with a relative or friend. Notify the police, the building manager, or a neighbor that you are leaving and tell them who has your key and itinerary.
7. Empty the refrigerator and lower the thermostat.
8. Immediately before leaving, check that all doors, windows, and garage doors are securely locked.

To discourage thieves further, it is wise to set up several variable timers around the house so that lights and even the television set or a radio go on and off several times in different rooms each night.

Make a list of any valuable items you are carrying with you, including credit card numbers and the serial numbers of your traveler's checks. Put copies in your purse or pocket and leave other copies at home. Put a label with your name and home address on the inside of your luggage to facilitate identification in case of loss. Put your name and business address — *but never your home address* — on a label on the outside of your luggage.

Review your travel documents. If you are traveling by air, check to see that your ticket has been filled in correctly. The left side of the ticket should have a list of each stop you will make (even if you are only stopping to change planes), beginning with your departure point. Be sure that the list is correct, and count the number of carbons to see that you have one for each plane you will take. If you have confirmed reservations, be sure that the column marked "Status" says "OK" beside each flight. Have in hand vouchers or proof of payment for any reservation for which you've paid in advance; this includes hotels, transfers to and from the airport, sightseeing tours, car rentals, and special events.

If you are traveling by car, bring your driver's license, proof of insurance, maps, guidebooks, flashlight, an extra set of batteries, first-aid kit, and sunglasses. You may also want to pick up an emergency flasher and a container of water for the radiator.

If you are traveling by plane, call to reconfirm your flight 72 hours before departure, both going and returning. However, this will not prevent you from getting bumped in case the flight is overbooked; see *Traveling by Plane.*

Finally, you should always bear in mind that despite the most careful plans, things do not always occur on schedule. If you maintain a flexible attitude at all times, shrug cheerfully in the face of postponements and cancellations, you will enjoy yourself a lot more.

How to Use a Travel Agent

T.A. A reliable travel agent remains your best source of service and information for planning a trip abroad, whether you have prepared a specific itinerary and require an agent only to make reservations or need extensive help in sorting through the maze of airfares, tour offerings, hotel packages, and the scores of other arrangements that may be involved in a trip to the British Isles.

You should know what you want from a travel agent so that you can evaluate what you are getting. It is perfectly reasonable to expect your agent to be a thoroughly knowledgeable travel specialist, with information about your destination and, even more crucial, a command of current airfares, ground arrangements, and other wrinkles in the travel scene. Most agents work through computer reservations systems (CRS) to assess the availability and rates of flights, hotels, and car rental firms, and can book reservations through the CRS. Despite reports of "computer bias," in which a computer may favor one airline over another, the CRS should provide agents with the entire spectrum of flights to a destination and the complete range of fares in considerably less time than it takes to telephone the airlines individually — and at no extra charge to the client.

To make the most intelligent use of a travel agent's time and expertise, you should know something of the economics of the industry. As a client, traditionally you pay nothing for the agent's services; with few exceptions, it's all free, from hotel bookings to advice on package tours. Any money the travel agent makes on the time spent arranging your itinerary — booking hotels, resorts, or flights or suggesting activities — comes from commissions paid by the suppliers of these services — the airlines, hotels, and so on. These commissions generally run from 8% to 20% of the total cost of the service, although suppliers often reward agencies that sell their services in volume with an increased commission, called an override.

Among the few exceptions to the general rule of free service by a travel agency are the agencies beginning to practice *net pricing*. In essence, such agencies return all of their commissions and overrides to their customers and make their income instead by charging a flat fee per transaction (thus adding a charge after a reduction has been made). Sometimes the rebate from the agent arrives later, in the form of a check. Net pricing, however, has become rather controversial since a major airline refused to do business with a leading proponent of net pricing and the courts supported this action (see *Net Fare Sources*).

Net fares and fees are a very recent and not widespread practice, but even a conventional travel agent may sometimes charge a fee for such special services as long-distance telephone or cable costs incurred in making a booking, for reserving a room in a place that does not pay a commission (such as a small, out-of-the-way hotel), or for special attention such as planning a highly personal itinerary. A fee may also be assessed in instances of deeply discounted airfares. In most instances, however, you'll find that travel agents make their time and experience available to you at no charge, and you do not pay more for an airline ticket, package tour, or other product bought from a travel agent than you would for the same product bought directly from the supplier.

This commission system implies two things about your relationship with an agent:

1. You will get better service if you arrive at the agent's desk with your basic itinerary already planned. Know roughly where you want to go, what you want to do, and how much you want to spend. Use the agent to make bookings (which pay commissions) and to advise you on facilities, activities, and alternatives within the limits of your basic itinerary. You get the best service when you are requesting commissionable items. Since there are few commissions on camping or driving-camping tours, an agent is unlikely to be very enthusiastic about helping to plan one. (If you have this type of trip in mind, see *Camping and Caravanning, Hiking and Biking* for other sources of information on campgrounds throughout Britain.) The more vague your plans, the less direction you can expect from most agents. If you walk into an agency and say, "I have 2 weeks in June; what shall I do?" you will most likely walk out with nothing more than a handful of brochures. So do a little preliminary homework.
2. Be wary. There is always the danger that an incompetent or unethical agent will send you to a place offering the best commissions rather than the best facilities for your purposes. The only way to be sure you are getting the best service is to pick a good, reliable travel agent, one who knows where to go for information if he or she is unfamiliar with an area — although most agents are familiar with major destinations throughout Great Britain.

You should choose a travel agent with the same care with which you would choose a doctor or lawyer. You will be spending a good deal of money on the basis of the agent's judgment, so you have a right to expect that judgment to be mature, informed, and interested. At the moment, unfortunately, there aren't many standards within the travel agent industry to help you gauge competence, and the quality of individual agents varies enormously. At present, only seven states have registration, licensing, or other form of travel agent–related legislation on their books. Rhode Island licenses travel agents; Florida, Hawaii, and Ohio register them; and California, Illinois, and Washington have laws governing the sale of transportation or related services. While state licensing cannot absolutely guarantee competence, it can at least ensure that an agent has met some minimum requirements.

Perhaps the best-prepared agents are those who have completed the CTC Travel Management program offered by the *Institute of Certified Travel Agents* and carry the initials CTC (Certified Travel Counselor) after their names. This indicates a relatively high level of expertise. For a free list of CTCs in your area, send a self-addressed, stamped #10 envelope to ICTA, 148 Linden St., Box 82-56, Wellesley, MA 02181 (phone: 617-237-0280).

An agent's membership in the *American Society of Travel Agents* (*ASTA*) can be a useful guideline in selecting a travel agent. But keep in mind that *ASTA* is an industry organization, requiring only that its members be licensed in those states where required; be accredited to represent the suppliers whose products they sell, including airline and cruise tickets; and be adherents to its Principles of Professional Conduct and Ethics code. *ASTA* does not guarantee the competence, ethics, or financial soundness of its members, but it does offer some recourse if you feel you have been dealt with unfairly. Complaints may be registered with ASTA, Consumer Affairs Dept., PO Box 23992, Washington, DC 20026-3992 (phone: 703-739-2782). First try to resolve the complaint directly with the supplier. For a list of *ASTA* members in your area, send a self-addressed, stamped #10 envelope to ASTA, Public Relations Dept., at the address above. There is also the *Association of Retail Travel Agents* (*ARTA*), a smaller but highly respected trade organization similar to *ASTA*. Its member agencies and agents similarly agree to abide by a Code of Ethics, and complaints about a member can be made to ARTA's Grievance Committee, 25 S. Riverside Ave., Croton-on-Hudson, NY 10520 (phone: 914-271-HELP).

Agencies listed with the *National Association of Cruise Only Agencies* (*NACOA*) have demonstrated professionalism in the selling of cruises. For a list of cruise-only agencies in your state (requests are limited to three states), send a self-addressed, stamped envelope to NACOA, PO Box 7209, Freeport, NY 11520. Agencies that belong to a travel consortium, such as *Associated Travel Nationwide* and *Travel Trust International,* have access to preferred rates, as do the huge networks of *American Express* and *Ask Mr. Foster* travel agencies.

A number of banks own travel agencies, too. These provide the same services as other accredited commercial travel bureaus. Anyone can become a client, not only the bank's customers. You can find out more about these agencies, which belong to the *Association of Bank Travel Bureaus,* by inquiring at your bank or looking in the yellow pages.

Perhaps the best way to find a travel agent is by word of mouth. If the agent (or agency) has done a good job for your friends over a period of time, it probably indicates a certain level of commitment and competence. Always ask not only for the name of the company but for the name of the specific agent with whom your friends dealt, for it is that individual who will serve you, and quality can vary widely within a single agency. There are some superb travel agents in the business, and they can greatly facilitate vacation or business arrangements.

Once you've made an initial selection from those recommended, be entirely frank and candid with the agent. Budget considerations rank at the top of the candor list, and there's no sense in wasting the agent's (or your) time poring over itineraries that you know you can't afford. Similarly, if you like a fair degree of comfort, that fact should not be kept secret from your travel agent, who may assume wrongly that you wish to travel on a tight budget.

Entry Requirements and Documents

A valid US passport is the only document a US citizen needs to enter Great Britain, and that same passport is also needed to reenter the US. No visas are necessary. As a general rule, possession of a US passport entitles the bearer to remain as a tourist for up to 3 months; study, residency, or work requires completely different documents, and considerably more laborious procedures are involved. However, immigration officers in London airports *may* want to see that you have sufficient funds for your trip (for example, traveler's checks, credit cards, etc.) and a return ticket to the US.

Vaccination certificates are required only if the traveler is entering from an area of contagion as defined by the World Health Organization. Because smallpox is considered eradicated from the world, only a few countries continue to require visitors to have a smallpox vaccination certificate. You will certainly not need one to travel to Britain or to return to the US.

US passports are now valid for 10 years from the date of issue (5 years for those under age 18). The expired passport itself is not renewable but must be turned in along with your application for a new and valid one (you will get it back, voided, when you receive the new one). Delivery can take as little as 2 weeks or as long as a month, and anyone applying for a passport for the first time should allow at least 4 weeks for delivery — even 6 weeks during the high season, from approximately mid-March to mid-September.

Normal passports contain 24 pages, but frequent travelers can request a 48-page passport at no extra cost. Every individual, regardless of age, must have his or her own passport. Family passports are no longer issued.

Passport renewal can be done by mail, but anyone applying for the first time or anyone under 18 renewing a passport must do so in person at one of the following places:

1. The State Department passport agencies in Boston, Chicago, Honolulu, Houston, Los Angeles, Miami, New Orleans, New York City, Philadelphia, San Francisco, Seattle, Stamford, CT, and Washington, DC.
2. A federal or state courthouse.
3. Any of the 1,000 post offices across the country with designated acceptance facilities.

Application blanks are available at all these offices and must be presented with the following:

1. Proof of US citizenship. This can be a previous passport or one in which you were included. If you are applying for your first passport and you were born in the United States, your official birth certificate is the required proof. If you were born abroad, a Certificate of Naturalization, a Certificate of Citizenship, a Report of Birth Abroad of a Citizen of the United States, or a Certification of Birth is necessary.
2. Two 2-by-2-inch, front-view photographs in color or black and white, with a light, plain background, taken within the previous 6 months. These must be taken by a photographer rather than by a machine.
3. A check or a money order for the $35 passport fee ($20 for travelers under 18) and the $7 execution fee (not required if you are applying for a passport in person at one of the State Department passport agencies or if you are renewing a passport). *Note:* Your best bet is to bring the exact amount; you should have a separate check or money order for each passport. No cash is accepted.
4. Proof of identity. Again, this can be a previous passport, a Certificate of Naturalization or of Citizenship, a driver's license, or a government ID card with a physical description or a photograph. Failing any of these, you should be accompanied by a friend of at least 2 years' standing who will testify to your identity. Credit cards or social security cards do not suffice as proof of identity — but note that since 1988, US citizens *must* supply their social security numbers.

Passports can be renewed by mail on forms obtained at designated locations only if the expired passport was issued no more than 12 years before the date of application for renewal and if it was not issued before the applicant's 16th birthday. Send the completed form with the expired passport, two photos (signed in the center of the back), and $35 (no execution fee required) to the nearest passport agency office.

- **Should you lose your passport abroad:** Report the loss to the nearest US consulate immediately. You can get a 3-month temporary passport directly from the consulate, but you must fill out a "loss of passport" form and follow the same application procedure — and pay the same fees — as you did for the original. It's likely to speed things up if you have a record of your passport number and the place and date of its issue.

- **If you need an emergency passport:** Although a passport application normally takes several weeks to process, it is possible to be issued a passport in a matter of hours. Go directly to your nearest passport office — there is no way, however, to avoid waiting in line — and explain the nature of the emergency, usually as serious as a death in the family: a ticket in hand for a flight the following day will suffice. Should the emergency occur outside business hours, all is not lost. There's a 24-hour telephone number in Washington, DC (phone: 202-634-3600), that can put you in touch with a State Department duty officer who may be able to expedite your application.

DUTY AND CUSTOMS: As a general rule, the requirements for bringing the majority of items into Britain is that they must be in quantities small enough not to imply commercial import.

In Great Britain, no duty is imposed on quantities of up to 2 liters of wine, 2 liters of alcohol under 38.8 proof, 1 liter above 38.8 proof, 200 cigarettes, 100 cigars, 50 grams of perfume, a quarter of a liter of cologne, and on items designated as gifts valued at less than approximately $50 per item; for children under 15 years old, the limit is about $25 per item.

If you are bringing along a computer or other electronic equipment for your own use, which you will be taking back to the US, you should register the item with the US Customs Service in order to avoid being asked to pay duties both entering and returning from Britain. For information on this procedure, as well as for a variety of helpful pamphlets on customs regulations, contact the local office of the US Customs Service or the central office, PO Box 7407, Washington, DC 20044 (phone: 202-566-8195). Additional information regarding customs regulations is available from the British Tourist Authority. See *Tourist Information Offices* in this section for addresses of offices in the US.

- **One rule to follow:** When passing through customs, it is illegal not to declare dutiable items — penalties range from stiff fines and seizure of the goods to prison — so don't try to sneak anything through, it just isn't worth it.

Insurance

It is unfortunate that most decisions to buy travel insurance are impulsive and are usually made without any real consideration of the traveler's existing policies. Too often the result is the purchase of needlessly expensive short-term policies that duplicate existing coverage and reinforce the tendency to buy coverage on a trip-by-trip basis rather than to work out a total and continuing travel insurance package that might well be more effective and economical.

Therefore, the first person with whom you should discuss travel insurance is your own insurance broker, not a travel agent or the clerk behind the airport insurance counter. You may well discover that the insurance you already carry — homeowner's policies and/or accident, health, and life insurance — protects you adequately while you travel and that your real needs are in the more mundane areas of excess value insurance for baggage or trip cancellation insurance.

TYPES OF INSURANCE: To make insurance decisions intelligently, however, you should first understand the basic categories of travel insurance and what they are designed to cover. Then you can decide what you should have in the broader context of your personal insurance needs, and you can choose the most economical way of getting the desired protection: through riders on existing policies; with one-time short-term policies; through a special program put together for the frequent traveler; through coverage that's part of a travel club's benefits; or with a combination policy sold by insurance companies through brokers, automobile clubs, tour operators, and travel agents.

There are seven basic categories of travel insurance:

1. Baggage and personal effects insurance
2. Personal accident and sickness insurance
3. Trip cancellation and interruption insurance
4. Default and/or bankruptcy insurance
5. Flight insurance (to cover death or injury)
6. Automobile insurance (for driving your own or a rented car)
7. Combination policies

Baggage and Personal Effects Insurance – Ask your agent if baggage and personal effects are included in your current homeowner's policy or if you will need a special rider to cover you for the duration of a trip. The object is to protect your bags and their contents in case of damage or theft at any time during your travels, not just while you're in flight and covered by the airline's policy. Furthermore, only limited protection is provided by the airline. Baggage liability varies from carrier to carrier, but generally speaking, for domestic flights, luggage is generally insured to $1,250 — that's per passenger, not per bag. For most international flights, including domestic portions of international flights, the airline's liability limit is approximately $9.07 per pound or $20 per kilo (which comes to about $360 per 40-pound suitcase) for checked baggage, and up to $400 per passenger for unchecked baggage. These limits should be specified on your airline ticket, but to be awarded the specified amount, you'll have to provide an itemized list of lost property, and if you're including new and/or expensive items, be prepared for a request that you back up your claim with sales receipts or other proof of purchase.

If you are carrying goods worth more than the maximum protection offered by the airline, bus, or train company, you should consider excess value insurance. Additional coverage is available from the airlines at an average, currently, of $1 per $100 worth of coverage. This insurance can be purchased at the airline counter when you check in, though you should arrive early to fill out the necessary forms and to avoid holding up other passengers checking in. Major credit card companies, including American Express and Diners Club, also provide coverage for lost or delayed baggage. In some cases, you must enroll in advance to qualify. Check your membership brochure or contact the credit card company for details (see phone numbers listed in *Credit and Currency*). Excess value insurance is also included in certain of the combination travel insurance policies discussed below.

■ **A note of warning:** Be sure to read the fine print of any excess value insurance policy; there are often specific exclusions, such as cash, tickets, furs, gold and silver objects, art, and antiques. And remember that insurance companies ordinarily will pay only the depreciated value of the goods rather than their replacement value. The best way to protect the items you're carrying in your luggage is to take photos of your valuables, and keep a record of the serial numbers of such items as cameras, typewriters, radios, and so on. This will establish that you do, indeed, own the objects. If your luggage disappears en route or is damaged, deal with the situation immediately, at the airport or bus station. If an airline loses your luggage, you will be asked to fill out a Property Irregularity Report before you leave the airport. If your property disappears at other transportation centers, tell the local company, but also report it to the police (since the insurance company will check with the police when processing the claim). When traveling by train, if you are sending excess luggage as registered baggage, remember that in many countries not all trains have provisions for extra cargo; if your baggage has not been checked on your train, it may not be lost, just on the next train!

Personal Accident and Sickness Insurance – This covers you in case of illness during your trip or death in an accident. Most policies insure you for hospital and doctors' expenses, lost income, and so on. In most cases it is a standard part of existing health insurance policies, though you should check with your broker to be sure that your policy will pay for any medical expenses incurred abroad. If not, take out a separate vacation accident policy or an entire vacation insurance policy that includes health and life coverage.

Trip Cancellation and Interruption Insurance – Although modern public charters have eliminated many of the old advance booking requirements, most charter and package tour passengers still pay for their travel well before departure. The disappointment of having to miss a vacation because of illness or any other reason pales before the awful prospect that not all (and sometimes none) of the money paid in advance might be returned. So cancellation insurance for any package tour is a must. Although cancellation penalties vary (they are listed in the fine print in every tour brochure, and before you purchase a package tour you should know exactly what they are), rarely will a passenger get more than 50% of this money back if forced to cancel within a few weeks of leaving. Therefore, if you book a package tour or charter flight, you should have trip cancellation insurance to guarantee full reimbursement or refund should you, a traveling companion, or a member of your immediate family get sick, forcing you to cancel your trip or *return home early.* The key here is *not* to buy just enough insurance to guarantee full reimbursement for the cost of the package or charter in case of cancellation. The proper amount of coverage should be sufficient to reimburse you for the cost of having to catch up with a tour after its departure or having to travel home at the full economy airfare if you have to forgo the return flight of your charter. There is usually quite a discrepancy between a charter airfare and the amount necessary to travel the same distance on a regularly scheduled flight at full economy fare.

Trip cancellation insurance is available from travel agents and tour operators in two forms: as part of a short-term, all-purpose travel insurance package (sold by the travel agent); or as specific cancellation insurance designed by the tour operator for a specific charter tour. Generally, tour operators' policies are less expensive, but also less inclusive. Cancellation insurance is also available directly from insurance companies or their agents as part of a short-term, all-inclusive travel insurance policy.

Before you decide which policy you want, read each one carefully. (Either can be purchased from a travel agent when you book the charter or package tour.) Be certain that the policy you select includes enough coverage to pay your fare from the farthest destination on your itinerary should you have to miss the charter flight. Also, be sure to check the fine print for stipulations concerning "family members" and "pre-existing medical conditions," as well as allowance for living expenses if you must delay your return due to bodily injury or illness.

Default and/or Bankruptcy Insurance – Although trip cancellation insurance usually protects you if you are unable to complete — or depart on — your trip, a fairly recent innovation is coverage in the event of default and/or bankruptcy on the part of the tour operator, airline, or other travel supplier. In some travel insurance packages, this contingency is included in the trip cancellation portion of the coverage; in others, it is a separate feature. Either way, it is becoming increasingly important. Whereas sophisticated travelers have long known to beware of the possibility of default or bankruptcy when buying a charter flight or tour package, in recent years more than a few respected scheduled airlines have unexpectedly revealed their shaky financial condition, sometimes leaving hordes of stranded ticketholders in their wake. Moreover, the value of escrow protection of a charter passenger's funds has lately been unreliable. While default/bankruptcy insurance will not ordinarily result in reimbursement in time to pay for new arrangements, it can ensure that you will eventually get your money back, and even independent travelers buying no more than an airplane ticket may want to consider it.

Should this type of coverage be unavailable to you (state insurance regulations vary, there is a wide variation in price, and so on), the best bet is to pay for airline tickets and tour packages with a credit card. The federal Fair Credit Billing Act permits purchasers to refuse payment for credit card charges where services have not been delivered, so the potential onus of dealing with a receiver for a bankrupt airline falls on the credit card company. Do not assume that another airline will automatically honor the ticket you're holding on a bankrupt airline, since the days when virtually all major carriers subscribed to a default protection program are long gone. Some airlines may voluntarily step forward to accommodate stranded passengers, but this is now an entirely altruistic act.

Flight Insurance – US airlines have carefully established limits of liability for the death or injury of passengers. For international flights, they are printed right on the ticket: a maximum of $75,000 in case of death or injury. For domestic flights in the US, the limitation is established by state law, with a few states setting unlimited liability. But remember, these limits of liability are not the same thing as insurance policies; they merely state the *maximum* an airline will pay in the case of death or injury, and every penny of that is usually subject to a legal battle.

This may make you feel that you are not adequately protected, but before you buy last-minute flight insurance from an airport vending machine, consider the purchase in light of your total existing insurance coverage. A careful review of your current policies may reveal that you are already amply covered for accidental death, sometimes up to three times the amount provided for by the flight insurance you're buying in the airport.

Be aware that airport insurance, the kind typically bought at a counter or from a vending machine, is among the most expensive forms of life insurance available, and that even within a single airport, rates for roughly the same coverage vary widely. Often policies sold in vending machines are more expensive than those sold over the counter, even when they are with the same national company.

If you buy your plane ticket with an American Express, Carte Blanche, or Diners Club credit card, you are automatically issued life and accident insurance at no extra cost. American Express automatically provides $100,000 in insurance, Carte Blanche provides $150,000, and Diners Club, $350,000. Additional coverage can be obtained at extremely reasonable prices, but a cardholder must sign up for it in advance. With American Express, $4 per ticket buys an additional $250,000 worth of flight insurance; $6.50 buys $500,000 worth; and $13 provides an added $1 million worth of coverage. Carte Blanche and Diners Club each offer an additional $250,000 worth of insurance for $4; $500,000 for $6.50. Both also provide $1,250 free insurance — over and above what the airline will pay — for checked and carry-on baggage that's lost or damaged. American Express provides $500 coverage for checked baggage; $1,250 for carry-ons.

Automobile Insurance – Public liability and property damage (third-party) insurance is compulsory in Europe, and whether you drive your own car or a rental you must carry insurance. Car rentals in Great Britain usually include public liability, property damage, fire, and theft coverage and, sometimes (depending on the rental company), collision damage coverage with a deductible. In your car rental contract, you'll see that for about $11 to $12 a day, you may buy optional collision damage waiver (CDW) protection. If partial coverage with a deductible is included in the rental contract, CDW will cover the deductible in the event of an accident. If the contract does not include collision damage coverage, you may be liable for as much as the full retail cost of the car, and CDW relieves you of all responsibility for any damage to the rental car. Before agreeing to this coverage, however, check your auto insurance policy. It may very well cover your entire liability exposure without any additional cost, or you may automatically be covered by the credit card company (American Express, or premium cards from Visa or MasterCard) to which you are charging the cost of your rental.

Your rental contract (with the appropriate insurance box ticked off) as well as proof of your personal insurance policy, if applicable, are required as proof of insurance. If you will be driving your own car in Europe, you must carry an International Insurance Certificate (called a Green Card), available through insurance brokers in the US.

Combination Packages – Short-term insurance policies, which may include any combination or all of the types of insurance discussed above, are available through retail insurance agencies, automobile clubs, and many travel agents. These combination policies are designed to cover you for the duration of a single trip.

Two examples of standard combination policies, providing comprehensive coverage for travelers, are offered by *Wallach & Co.* The first, *HealthCare Global,* is available to men and women up to age 84. The medical insurance, which may be purchased for periods of 10 to 180 days, provides $25,000 medical insurance and $50,000 accidental-death benefit. The cost for 10 days is $25; for 75 days and more, it is $1 a day. Combination policies may include additional accidental-death coverage and baggage and trip cancellation insurance options. For $3 per day (minimum 10 days, maximum 90 days), another program, *HealthCare Abroad,* offers significantly better coverage in terms of dollar limits, although the age limit is 75. Its basic policy includes $100,000 medical insurance and $25,000 accidental-death benefit. As in the first policy, trip cancellation and baggage insurance are also available. For further information, write to Wallach & Co., 243 Church St. NW, Vienna, VA 22180 (phone: 703-281-9500 in Virginia, 800-237-6615 elsewhere in the US).

Other policies of this type include the following:

Access America International: A subsidiary of the Blue Cross/Blue Shield plans of New York and Washington, DC, now available nationwide. Contact *Access America,* 600 Third Ave., PO Box 807, New York, NY 10163 (phone: 212-490-5345 or 800-284-8300).

Carefree: Underwritten by The Hartford. Contact Carefree Travel Insurance, Arm Coverage, PO Box 247, Providence, RI 02901 (phone: 800-645-2424).

Near: Part of a benefits package offered by a travel service organization. An added feature is coverage for lost or stolen airline tickets. Contact Near Inc., 1900 N. MacArthur Blvd., Suite 210, Oklahoma City, OK 73127 (phone: 405-949-2500 or 800-654-6700).

Tele-Trip: Underwritten by the Mutual of Omaha Companies. Contact Tele-Trip Co., PO Box 31685, 3201 Farnam St., Omaha, NE 68131 (phone: 402-345-2400 in Nebraska; 800-228-9792 elsewhere in the US).

Travel Assistance International: Underwritten by Europe Assistance Worldwide Services. Contact Travel Assistance International, 1333 F St. NW, Suite 300,

Washington, DC 20005 (phone: 202-347-2025 in Washington; 800-821-2828 elsewhere in the US).

Travel Guard International: Endorsed by the *American Society of Travel Agents* (*ASTA*), underwritten by the Insurance Company of North America, it is available through authorized travel agents; or contact Travel Guard International, 1100 Centerpoint Dr., Stevens Point, WI 54481 (phone: 715-345-0505 in Wisconsin; 800-826-1300 elsewhere in the US).

Travel Insurance PAK: Underwritten by The Travelers. Contact The Travelers Companies, Ticket and Travel Plans, One Tower Sq., Hartford, CT 06183-5040 (phone: 203-277-2319 in Connecticut; 800-243-3174 elsewhere in the US).

WorldCare Travel Assistance Association: Contact this organization at 605 Market St., Suite 1300, San Francisco, CA 94105 (phone: 415-541-4991 or 800-666-4993).

How to Pack

No one can provide a completely foolproof list of precisely what to pack, so it's best to let common sense, space, and comfort guide you. Keep one maxim in mind: Less is more. You simply won't need as much clothing as you think, and though there is nothing more frustrating than arriving at your destination without just the item that in its absence becomes crucial, you are far more likely to need a forgotten accessory — or a needle and thread or scissors — than a particular piece of clothing.

As with almost anything relating to travel, a little planning can go a long way. There are specific things to consider before you open the first drawer or fold the first pair of underwear:

1. Where are you going (city, country, or both)?
2. How many total days will you be gone?
3. What's the average temperature likely to be during your stay?

The goal is to remain perfectly comfortable, neat, clean, and adequately fashionable wherever you go, but actually to pack as little as possible. The main obstacle to achieving this end is habit: Most of us wake up each morning with an entire wardrobe in our closets, and we assume that our suitcase should offer the same variety and selection. Not so — only our anxiety about being caught short makes us treat a suitcase like a mobile closet. This worry can be eliminated by learning to travel light and by following two firm packing principles:

1. Organize your travel wardrobe around a single color — blue or brown, for example — that allows you to mix, match, and layer clothes. Holding firm to one color scheme will make it easy to eliminate items of clothing that don't harmonize; and by picking clothes for their adaptability and compatibility with your basic color, you will put together the widest selection with the fewest pieces of clothing.
2. Use laundries to renew your wardrobe. Never overpack to ensure a supply of fresh clothing — shirts, blouses, underwear — for each day of a long trip. Businesspeople routinely use hotel laundries to wash and clean clothes. If these are too expensive, there are local, self-service laundries, called "launderettes," in most towns of any size.

CLIMATE AND CLOTHES: Exactly what you pack will be a function of where you are going and when, and the kinds of things you intend to do. As a first step, however, find out about the general weather conditions — temperature, rainfall, seasonal variations — at your destination, as a few degrees can make all the difference between being comfortably attired and very real suffering.

Although Britain is farther north than most of the US — London, sitting astride latitude 51°30', is a bit north of Quebec's Gaspé Peninsula — the climate is generally much milder. The Gulf Stream, which warms the coasts, brings moderate temperatures year-round, with few sub-zero winters or blisteringly hot summers. Winter temperatures rarely dip below 40F, and summer temperatures usually rise no higher than 70F. The stereotype about British weather being wet is true: It rains often throughout the year, and even on fairly clear days, the air feels damp. Generally speaking, a typical fall wardrobe in the northern tier of the US will probably have everything that's needed for the trip. However, anyone going to Great Britain from the late fall through the early spring should take into account that while central heating is prevalent, interiors are not usually as warm as they would be in the US. Thus, although there is no need to prepare for sub-zero winters outdoors, most people will probably feel more comfortable wearing heavier clothing indoors than they might at home, for instance, sweaters rather than lightweight shirts and blouses.

More information about the climate in Great Britain, along with a chart of average low and high temperatures for specific cities, is given in *When to Go,* in this section; other sources of information are airlines and travel agents.

Keeping temperature and climate in mind, consider the problem of luggage. Plan on one suitcase per person (and in a pinch, remember that it's always easier to carry two small suitcases than to schlepp one roughly the size of the *QE2*). Standard 26- to 28-inch suitcases can be made to work for 1 week or 1 month, and unless you are going for no more than a weekend, never cram wardrobes for two people into one suitcase.

FASHION: On the whole, Great Britain is no more formal than North America, so be guided by your own taste. The lucky individual attending an opening night at London's *Covent Garden* opera house should be wearing formal attire (though European students have been attending the opera in blue jeans for years, so don't make yourself crazy), but otherwise a blazer or sport jacket, trousers, and tie will get a man into the finest restaurants anywhere, and sometimes even the tie is not *de rigueur.* For women, a dress or, depending on the season, a suit will do in the same situations. Other diners may be more formally dressed, but you won't be turned away or made to feel self-conscious if you do not match them. By the same token, you won't feel you've overdone it if you choose to turn an evening at an elegant restaurant into something special and dress accordingly.

If you are planning to be on the move — either in a car, bus, train, or plane — consider loose-fitting clothes that do not wrinkle, although the recent trend toward fabrics with a wrinkled look is a boon to travelers. Despite the tendency of designers to use more and more 100% natural fabrics, synthetics are immensely practical for a trip, and they have improved immeasurably in appearance lately. As a general rule, clothes in pure cotton and linen are perishable and hard to keep up and should be left behind. Lightweight wools, manmade fabrics such as jerseys and knits, and drip-dry fabrics travel best (although in very hot weather, cotton clothing may be the most comfortable), and prints look fresher longer than solids.

Women should figure on a maximum of five daytime and three late afternoon–evening changes. Whether you are going to be gone for a week or a month, this number should be enough. Again, before packing, lay out every piece of clothing you think you might want to take. Select clothing on the basis of what can serve several functions and accessorize everything beforehand so you know exactly what you will be wearing with what. Eliminate items that don't mix or match with your color scheme. If you can't wear it in at least two distinct incarnations, leave it home.

Men will find that color coordination is crucial. Solid colors coordinate best, and a sport jacket that goes with a pair of pants from a suit and several pairs of slacks provides added options. Hanging bags are best for suits and jackets, and shirts should be chosen that can be used for both day and evening wear.

Pack clothes that have a lot of pockets for traveler's checks, documents, and tickets. If your bag gets lost or stolen, you will retain possession of the essentials. Men who prefer to keep their pockets free of coins, papers, and keys might consider a shoulder bag, useful for carrying camera equipment as well as daily necessities. It is a good idea to wear loose-fitting clothes that can be rinsed in Woolite or a similar cold-water detergent and hung to drip dry. And be sure to have comfortable shoes. Pack lightweight sandals for beach and evening wear. It is permissible to wear your most comfortable shoes almost everywhere.

A versatile item of clothing that travelers will find indispensable is a raincoat, preferably one with a zip-out lining and a hood. The removable lining allows you to adapt to temperature changes, and the hood is better suited (and less cumbersome) than an umbrella for fine, misty rain, although a practical alternative is a rain hat that can be rolled up in a pocket or carry-on bag. Other useful apparel includes a warm wool sweater or jacket, even in summer (tweeds are worn year-round), and, even on warmer days, it will be welcome for exploring castles, for example.

Finally, prepare for changes in the weather or for atypical temperatures; for instance, if you're going on a day's outing in the mountains, where it is cooler, dress in layers, which means a shirt on top of a T-shirt or lightweight turtleneck, with a sweater or two on top of both, topped by a jacket or windbreaker over all. As the weather changes, you can add or remove clothes as required, and layering adapts well to the ruling principle of dressing according to a single color scheme. Individual items in layers can mix and match, be used together or independently. And finally — since the best touring of castles, churches, and countryside is on foot — pack a comfortable pair of walking shoes.

Your carry-on luggage should contain a survival kit with the basic things you will need in case your luggage gets lost or stolen: a toothbrush, toothpaste, medication, a sweater, nightclothes, and a change of underwear. With all of your essential items at hand at all times, you will be prepared for any unexpected occurrence that separates you from your suitcase. If you have many 1- or 2-night stops, you can live out of your survival case without having to unpack completely at each hotel.

Sundries – If you are traveling in the heat of summer and will be spending a lot of time outdoors, particularly along the coast, pack special items so that you won't spend your entire vacation horizontal in a hotel room (or hospital) because of sunburn. Be sure to take a sun hat (to protect hair as well as skin), sunscreen, and tanning lotion, which is available in graduated degrees of sunblock corresponding to the level of your skin's sensitivity. (The quantity of sunscreen is indicated by number: The higher the number, the greater the protection.) A good moisturizer is necessary to help keep your skin from drying out and peeling. The best advice is to take the sun's rays in small doses — no more than 20 minutes at a stretch — increasing your sunbathing time as your vacation progresses.

PACKING: The basic idea of packing is to get everything into the suitcase and out again with as few wrinkles as possible. Simple, casual clothes — shirts, jeans and slacks, permanent press skirts — can be rolled into neat, tight sausages that keep other suitcase items in place and leave the clothes themselves amazingly unwrinkled. The rolled clothes can be retrieved, shaken out, and hung up at your destination. However, for items that are too bulky or delicate for even careful rolling, a suitcase should be packed with the heaviest items on the bottom, toward the hinges, so that they will not wrinkle more perishable clothes. Candidates for the bottom layer include shoes (stuff them with small items to save space), a toilet kit, handbags (stuff them to help keep their shape), and an alarm clock. Fill out this layer with things that will not wrinkle or will not matter if they do, such as sweaters, socks, a bathing suit, gloves, and underwear.

If you get this first, heavy layer as smooth as possible with the fill-ins, you will have a shelf for the next layer, or the most easily wrinkled items, like slacks, jackets, shirts, dresses, and skirts. These should be buttoned and zipped and laid along the whole length of the suitcase with as little folding as possible. When you do need to make a fold, do it on a crease (as with pants), along a seam in the fabric, or where it will not show, such as shirttails. Alternate each piece of clothing, using one side of the suitcase, then the other, to make the layers as flat as possible. Make the layers even and the total contents of your bag as full and firm as possible to keep things from shifting around during transit. On the top layer put the things you will want at once: nightclothes, an umbrella or raincoat, and a sweater.

With men's two-suiter suitcases, follow the same procedure. Then place jackets on hangers, straighten them out, and leave them unbuttoned. If they are too wide for the suitcase, fold them lengthwise down the middle, straighten the shoulders, and fold the sleeves in along the seam.

While packing, it is a good idea to separate each layer of clothes with plastic cleaning bags, which will help preserve pressed clothes while they are in the suitcase. Unpack your bags as soon as you get to your hotel. Nothing so thoroughly destroys freshly cleaned and pressed clothes as sitting for days in a suitcase. Finally, if something is badly wrinkled and can't be professionally pressed before you must wear it, hang it overnight in a bathroom where the bathtub has been filled with very hot water; keep the bathroom door closed so the room becomes something of a steamroom. It really works miracles.

SOME FINAL PACKING HINTS: Some travelers like to have at hand a small bag with the basics for an overnight stay, particularly if they are flying. Always keep necessary medicine, valuable jewelry, and travel or business documents in your purse, briefcase, or carry-on bag, not in the luggage you will check. Tuck a bathing suit into your handbag, too; in case of lost baggage, it's frustrating to be without one. And whether in your overnight bag or checked luggage, cosmetics and any liquids should be packed in plastic bottles or at least wrapped in plastic bags and tied.

Golf clubs may be checked through as luggage (most airlines are accustomed to handling them), but tennis rackets should be carried onto the plane. Some airlines require that bicycles be partially dismantled and packaged (see *Camping and Caravanning, Hiking and Biking*). Check with the airline before departure to see if there is a specific regulation regarding any special equipment or sporting gear you plan to take.

LUGGAGE: If you already own serviceable luggage, do not feel compelled to buy new bags. If, however, you have been looking for an excuse to throw out that old suitcase that saw you through 4 years of college and innumerable weekends, this trip to Great Britain can be the perfect occasion.

Luggage falls into three categories — hard, soft-sided, and soft — and each has advantages and disadvantages. Hard suitcases have a rigid frame and sides. They provide the most protection from the depredations of rough handling, but they are also the heaviest. Wheels and pull straps are available to rectify this problem, but they should be removed before the luggage is turned over at check-in or they may well be wrenched off in transit. In addition, hard bags will sometimes pop open, even when locked, so a strap around the suitcase is advised.

Soft-sided suitcases have a rigid frame that has been covered with leather, fabric, or a synthetic material. The weight of the suitcase is greatly reduced, but many of the materials used as coverings (except leather, which is also the heaviest) are vulnerable to rips and tears from conveyor machinery. Not surprisingly, the materials that wear better are generally found on more expensive luggage.

The third category, seen more and more frequently, is soft luggage. Lacking any rigid structural element, it comes in a wide variety of shapes and sizes and is easy to carry, especially since it often has a shoulder strap. Most carry-on bags are of this type because they can be squeezed under the plane seat. They are even more vulnerable to damage on conveyor equipment than soft-sided bags, and, as the weak point on these bags is the zipper, be sure to tie some cord or put several straps around the bag for extra insurance. Also be prepared to find a brand-new set of wrinkles pressed into everything that was carefully ironed before packing.

Whatever type of luggage you choose, remember that it should last for many years. Shop carefully, but be prepared to make a sizable investment.

It is always a good idea to add an empty, flattened airline bag or similar piece of luggage to your suitcase; you'll find it indispensable as a beach bag. Keep in mind, too, that you're likely to do some shopping, and save room for those items.

For more information on packing and luggage, send your request with a #10 stamped, self-addressed envelope to Samsonite Travel Advisory Service (PO Box 39609, Dept. 80, Denver, CO 80239) for its free booklet, *Getting a Handle on Luggage.*

Hints for Handicapped Travelers

From 35 to 50 million people in the US alone have some sort of disability, and at least half this number are physically handicapped. Like everyone else today, they — and the uncounted disabled millions around the world — are on the move. More than ever before, they are demanding facilities they can use comfortably, and they are being heard. The disabled traveler will find that services for the handicapped have considerably improved over the last few years, both in the US and abroad, and though accessibility is far from universal, it is being brought up to more acceptable standards every day.

PLANNING: Good planning is essential: Collect as much information as you can about your specific disability and about facilities for the disabled in the area you're visiting, make your travel arrangements well in advance, and specify to all services involved the exact nature of your condition or restricted mobility, as your trip will be much more comfortable if you know that there are accommodations and facilities to suit your needs. The best way to find out if your intended destination can accommodate a handicapped traveler is to write or phone the local tourist association or hotel and ask specific questions. If you require a corridor of a certain width to maneuver a wheelchair or if you need handles on the bathroom wall for support, ask the hotel manager. A travel agent or the local chapter or national office of the organization that deals with your particular disability — for example, the American Foundation for the Blind or the American Heart Association — will supply the most up-to-date information on the subject. The following sources offer general information on access:

Access in London (London: Robert Nicholson Publications; $4.95), a detailed accessibility guide to London sites and accommodations, is available at the *British Travel Bookshop,* 40 W. 57th St., New York, NY 10019 (phone: 212-765-0898).

Access to the World, by Louise Weiss, offers sound tips for the disabled traveler abroad. Published by Facts on File (460 Park Ave. S., New York, NY 10016; phone: 212-683-2244), it costs $16.95, and can be ordered by phone with a credit card. Henry Holt also now publishes Weiss's excellent book in paperback; check with your bookstore.

Access Travel: A Guide to the Accessibility of Airport Terminals, published by the Airport Operators Council International, provides information on more than

200 airports worldwide with ratings according to 70 features, including accessibility to bathrooms, corridor width, and parking spaces. For a free copy, write to the Consumer Information Center, Access America, Dept. 571T, Pueblo, CO 81009, or call 202-293-8500 and ask for "Item 571T — Access Travel." To help travel agents plan trips for the handicapped, this material is reprinted with additional information on tourist boards, city information offices, and tour operators specializing in travel for the handicapped (see "Tours," below) in the North American edition of the *Official Airline Guides Travel Planner,* issued quarterly by Official Airline Guides, 2000 Clearwater Dr., Oak Brook, IL 60521 (phone: 312-574-6000).

Air Transportation of Handicapped Persons, a booklet published by the US Department of Transportation, will be sent free upon written request. Ask for "Free Advisory Circular #AC-120-32" from the Distribution Unit, US Dept. of Transportation, Publications Section, M-443-2, Washington, DC 20590.

Handicapped Travel Newsletter, edited by wheelchair-bound Vietnam veteran Michael Quigley, who, undaunted, has traveled to 82 countries around the world and writes regular columns for travel magazines. Issued every 2 months (plus special issues), it is regarded as one of the finest sources of information for the disabled traveler. A subscription is $10 per year; write to Handicapped Travel Newsletter, PO Box 269, Athens, TX 75751.

Information for Individuals with Disabilities (*ICID*), Fort Point Pl., 1st Floor, 27-43 Wormwood St., Boston, MA 02210 (phone: 617-727-5440/1 or 800-462-5015 in Massachusetts only); both voice and TDD (telecommunications device for the deaf). *ICID* provides information and referral services on disability-related issues and will help you research your trip. The center publishes fact sheets on vacation planning, tour operators, travel agents, and travel resources.

The Itinerary is a travel magazine for people with disabilities. Published bimonthly, it includes information on accessibility, lists of tours, news of adaptive devices, travel aids, and special services as well as numerous general travel hints. A subscription is $10 a year; write to The Itinerary, PO Box 1084, Bayonne, NJ 07002-1084 (phone: 201-858-3400).

A List of Guidebooks for Handicapped Travelers is a free list of useful publications for the disabled, compiled by the President's Committee on Employment of People with Disabilities, 1111 20th St. NW, Suite 636, Vanguard Bldg., Washington, DC 20036 (published September 1975).

Mobility International/USA (*MIUSA*), the US branch of *Mobility International,* a non-profit British organization with affiliates in some 35 countries, offers advice and assistance to disabled travelers — including information on accommodations, access guides, and study tours. Its head office is *Mobility International Headquarters* (228 Borough High St., London SE1 1JX; phone: 01-403-5688). Among its publications are a quarterly newsletter and a comprehensive sourcebook, *World of Options, A Guide to International Education Exchange, Community Service, and Travel for Persons with Disabilities.* Individual membership is $20 a year; subscription to the newsletter alone is $10 annually. For more information, contact MIUSA, PO Box 3551, Eugene, OR 97403; phone: 503-343-1284, voice and TTD (telecommunications device for the deaf).

National Rehabilitation Information Center, 8455 Colesville Rd., Suite 935, Silver Spring, MD 20910 (phone: 301-588-9284), is a general information and referral service.

Paralyzed Veterans of America (*PVA*) is a national organization that offers information and advocacy services for veterans with spinal cord injuries. *PVA* also sponsors *Access to the Skies,* a program that coordinates the efforts of the national and international air travel industry in providing airport and airplane access for the handicapped. Members also receive several helpful publications as well as regular notification of conferences on subjects of interest to the handicapped traveler. For information, contact PVA/ATTS Program, 801 18th St. NW, Washington, DC 20006 (phone: 202-USA-1300).

Royal Association for Disability and Rehabilitation (*RADAR*), 25 Mortimer St., London W1N 8AB (phone: 011-44-1-637-5400), offers a number of publications for the handicapped, including a comprehensive guide, *Holidays and Travel Abroad for the Disabled,* which provides helpful advice to the disabled traveler abroad. Available by writing to *RADAR,* the price, including airmail postage, is £3 (about $4.50); *RADAR* requires payment in pounds sterling, so this should be sent via an international money order (available at the post office).

Society for the Advancement of Travel for the Handicapped (*SATH*), 26 Court St., Penthouse, Brooklyn, NY 11242 (phone: 718-858-5483). To keep abreast of developments in travel for the handicapped as they occur, you may want to join *SATH,* a non-profit organization whose members include travel agents, tour operators, and other travel suppliers, as well as consumers. Membership costs $40 ($25 for students and travelers 65 and older), and the fee is tax deductible. *SATH* publishes a quarterly newsletter, an excellent booklet, *Travel Tips for the Handicapped,* and provides information on travel agents and tour operators in the US and overseas who have experience (or an interest) in travel for the handicapped. *SATH* also offers a free 48-page guide, *The United States Welcomes Handicapped Visitors,* that covers domestic transportation and accommodations, as well as travel insurance, customs regulations, and other useful hints for the handicapped traveler abroad. Send a self-addressed #10 envelope to *SATH* at the address above, and include $1 for postage.

TravelAbility, by Lois Reamy, is a vast database with information on locating tours for the handicapped, coping with public transport, and finding accommodations, special equipment, and travel agents, and includes a helpful step-by-step planning guide. Although geared mainly to travel in the US, it is full of information useful to handicapped travelers anywhere. Previously published by Macmillan, *TravelAbility* is currently out of print but may be available at your library.

Travel Information Service at Moss Rehabilitation Hospital is designed to help physically handicapped people plan trips. It cannot make travel arrangements, but, for a nominal fee per package, it will supply information from its files on as many as three cities, countries, or special interests. Write to the Travel Information Service, Moss Rehabilitation Hospital, 12th St. and Tabor Rd., Philadelphia, PA 19141 (phone: 215-456-9600).

Other good sources of information are the English, Scottish, and Welsh tourist authorities, and the British Tourist Authority both in the US and Great Britain (see *Tourist Information Offices.*

For accommodations slanted to the disabled traveler, visitors to London should try the *Ramada* hotel (Berners St., London W1A 3BE; phone: 01-636-1629) and the *London Tara* hotel (Scarsdale Pl., Wrights Lane, Kensington, London W8 5SR), which offers discounts for disabled travelers booking through the charity-registered *Visitors Club* (10 Gloucester Dr., Finsbury Park, London N4 2LP; phone: 01-800-8696) if the booking is made well in advance. *John Grooms* (10 Gloucester Dr., Finsbury Park, London N4 2LP; phone: 01-802-7272) offers apartments ("flats") that are fully accessible to wheelchair users and sleep up to 6 people. The rents are from £122 to £135 (about $183 to $210) per week. They also have bungalows from £62 to £194 ($93 to $290) per week; chalets from £62 to £144 ($93 to $220); and caravans (fully motorized RVs or towed campers) from £62 to £139 ($93 to $212). (*Note:* Although the *Visitors Club* and *John Grooms* share the same mailing address, they are separate organizations.)

For accommodations elsewhere in Great Britain, try *Swallow* hotels (Seaburn Terr., Sunderland, Tyne and Wear SR6 8BB; phone: 091-529-4545; in the US call Thomas McFerran at 800-444-1545), with some 35 properties. Also worth mentioning is the *Alison Park* hotel (3 Temple Rd., Buxton, Derbyshire SK17 9BA; phone: 0298-22473), an ideal base for touring the Peak District. For self-contained holiday cottage rental, try *Cressbrook Hcll Cottages* (Cressbrook, Derbyshire SK17 8SY; phone: 0298-871289), also in the Peak District near Buxton. *Country Holidays* (Spring Mill, Stonybank Rd., Earby (near Colne), Lancashire, BB8 6RW; phone: 0282-445340), with 4,000 rental properties stretching from the Scottish Highlands to Land's End in Cornwall, also offers a free brochure for disabled travelers covering facilities available in England.

Other examples of services for the handicapped in Great Britain include: *Triscope* (63 Esmond Rd., London W4 1JE; phone: 01-994-9294), a telephone-based information and referral service (not a booking agent) that can help with transportation options for specific journeys either in London or throughout the rest of the country, which may also be able to recommend outlets leasing small family vehicles adapted to take a wheelchair. *Carelink* and *Airbus* are weekday minibus services adapted to take wheelchairs that connect with main *BritRail* stations and Heathrow Airport; for information, contact London Regional Transport Unit for Disabled Passengers, 55 Broadway, London SW1H 0BD (phone: 01-227-3312). *Artsline* (5 Crowndale Rd., London NW1 1TU; phone: 01-388-2227) offers free telephone advice on disabled access, programs, and facilities at London theaters and art venues (it does not make bookings); a monthly magazine and cassette tape are also available. And for general information, there's *Holiday Care Service* (2 Old Bank Chambers, Station Rd., Horley, Surrey RH6 9HW; phone: 0293-774535), a first-rate, free advisory service on accommodations, transportation, and holiday packages throughout Europe for disabled visitors.

Regularly revised hotel and restaurant guides using the symbol of access (person in a wheelchair — see the symbol at the beginning of this chapter) to point out accommodations suitable for wheelchair-bound guests include *Egon Ronay's Lucas Guide* and the *Michelin Red Guide to Great Britain and Ireland,* both of which sell for $17.95 in general and travel bookstores.

The *Canadian Rehabilitation Council for the Disabled* publishes two useful books by Cinnie Noble. The first, *Handi-Travel: A Resource Book for Disabled and Elderly Travelers* ($14.45 Canadian or $12.95 US postpaid), is a comprehensive travel guide full of practical tips for those with disabilities affecting mobility, hearing, or sight. The *Handicapped Traveler* ($12.95, plus $2 for shipping and handling, 50¢ each additional copy), though written for travel agents, also provides a wealth of useful information for the disabled traveler. To order these books, and for other useful information, contact the Canadian Rehabilitation Council for the Disabled, 1 Yonge St., Suite 2110, Toronto, Ont. M5E 1E5, Canada (phone: 416-862-0340).

A few more basic resources to look for are *Travel for the Disabled* by Helen Hecker ($9.95) and, by the same author, *The Directory of Travel Agencies for the Disabled* ($12.95). *Wheelchair Vagabond* by John G. Nelson is another useful guidebook for travelers confined to a wheelchair (softcover, $9.95; hardcover, $14.95). All three are published by Twin Peaks Press, PO Box 129, Vancouver, WA 98666; to order call 800-637-CALM. Additionally, *The Physically Disabled Traveler's Guide,* by Rod W. Durgin and Norene Lindsay, is helpful and informative. Available from Resource Directories (3361 Executive Pkwy., Suite 302, Toledo, OH 43606; phone: 419-536-5353) for $9.95, plus $2 for postage and handling.

Also check the library for Mary Meister Walzer's *A Travel Guide for the Disabled: Western Europe* (Van Nostrand Reinhold), which gives access ratings to a fair number of hotels along with information on the accessibility of some sightseeing attractions, restaurants, theaters, stores, and more.

It should be noted that almost all of the material published with disabled travelers in mind deals with the wheelchair-bound traveler, for whom architectural barriers are of prime concern. For travelers with diabetes, a pamphlet entitled *Ticket to Safe Travel* is available for 50¢ from the New York Diabetes Association, 505 Eighth Ave., 21st Floor, New York, NY 10018 (phone: 212-947-9707). Another, *Travel for the Patient with Chronic Obstructive Pulmonary Disease,* is available for $2 from Dr. Harold Silver, 1601 18th St. NW, Washington, DC 20009 (phone: 202-667-0134). For blind travelers, *Seeing Eye Dogs as Air Travelers* can be obtained free from the Seeing Eye, Box 375, Washington Valley Rd., Morristown, NJ 07960 (phone: 201-539-4425).

Travelers who depend on Seeing Eye dogs should check with the airline they plan to fly and the authorities of the countries they plan to visit well before they leave. In general, the rules that apply to bringing any dog into the country apply without exception to Seeing Eye dogs. The British Isles very strictly enforce the antirabies laws. Any dogs brought into England, Scotland, Wales, or Northern Ireland must spend 6 months in quarantine — and Seeing Eye dogs are not exempt. Since it is not practical to bring a dog for a short stay, blind people should plan to travel with companions.

PLANE: Advise the airline that you are handicapped when you book your flight. The Federal Aviation Administration (FAA) has ruled that US airlines must accept disabled and handicapped passengers as long as the airline has advance notice and the passenger represents no insurmountable problem in the emergency evacuation procedures. As a matter of course, US airlines were pretty good about helping handicapped passengers even before the ruling, although each airline has somewhat different procedures. European airlines are also generally good about accommodating the disabled traveler, but, again, policies vary with the carrier. Ask for details when you book your flight.

Disabled passengers should always make reservations well in advance and should give the airline all the relevant details of their condition at that time. These include information on mobility, toilet and special oxygen needs, and requirements for airline-supplied equipment, such as a wheelchair or portable oxygen. Be sure that the person you speak to understands fully the degree of your disability — the more details provided, the more effectively the airline can help you. On the day before the flight, call back to make sure that all arrangements have been taken care of, and on the day of the flight, arrive early so that you can board before the rest of the passengers. Carry a medical certificate with you, stating your specific disability or the need to carry particular medicine. (Some airlines require the certificate; you should find out the regulations of the airline you'll be flying well beforehand.)

Because most airports have jetways (corridors connecting the terminal with the door of the plane), a disabled passenger can usually be taken as far as the plane, and sometimes right onto it, in a wheelchair. If not, a narrow boarding chair may be used to take you to your seat. Your own wheelchair, which will be folded and put in the baggage compartment, should be tagged as escort luggage to assure that it's available at planeside upon landing rather than in the baggage claim area. Travel is not quite as simple if your wheelchair is battery-operated: Unless it has non-spillable batteries, it might not be accepted on board; you will have to check with the airline ahead of time to find out how the batteries and the chair should be packaged for the flight. Usually people in wheelchairs are asked to wait until other passengers have disembarked. If you are making a tight connection, be sure to tell the attendant.

Passengers who use oxygen may not use their personal supply in the cabin, though it may be carried on the plane as cargo when properly packed and labeled. If you will need oxygen during the flight, the airline will supply it to you (there is a charge) provided you have given advance notice — 24 hours to a few days, depending on the carrier.

Several airlines now have booklets describing procedures for accommodating the handicapped on their flights and including other general information for the disabled air traveler. For example, United Airlines has a list of travel tips for the handicapped;

contact United Airlines, Consumer Affairs Dept., PO Box 66100, Chicago, IL 60666 (phone: 312-952-6796).

Useful information on every stage of air travel, from planning to arrival, is provided in the booklet *Incapacitated Passengers Air Travel Guide.* To receive a free copy, write to Senior Manager, Passenger Services, International Air Transport Association, 2000 Peel St., Montreal, Que. H3A 2R4, Canada (phone: 514-844-6311). The *Directory of Airline Facilities for Disabled People,* available for 60 pence (about 90 ¢) and published by an English organization called *Access to the Skies* in conjunction with the *Royal Association for Disability and Rehabilitation,* gives details about booking procedures, seat allocation, escorts, access for wheelchairs, etc., for every major airline. Contact Access to the Skies, 25 Mortimer St., London W1 8AB. For an access guide to over 200 airports worldwide, write for *Access Travel: A Guide to the Accessibility of Airport Terminals,* published by the Airport Operators Council International (see listing above). *Air Transportation of Handicapped Persons* is another useful booklet and explains the general guidelines that govern air carrier policies. It is also available free upon written request. Ask for "Free Advisory Circular #AC-120-32" from the Distribution Unit, US Dept. of Transportation, Publications Section, M-443-2, Washington, DC 20590; for speedy service, enclose a self-addressed mailing label.

SHIP: *Cunard's Queen Elizabeth 2* is considered the best-equipped ship for the handicapped — all but the top deck is accessible. The *QE2* crosses the Atlantic regularly from June through December between New York and its home port of Southampton, England. For further information on the *QE2* and alternative travel by boat on Britain's inland waterways, see *Traveling by Ship.*

GROUND TRANSPORTATION: Perhaps the simplest solution to getting around is to travel with an able-bodied companion who can drive. If you are accustomed to driving your own hand-controlled car and are determined to rent one, you may have to do some extensive research, as it is difficult in Europe to find rental cars with hand controls. If agencies do provide hand-control cars, they are apt to be few and in high demand. One company that does supply them is *Kenning Car Hire Ltd.* (477-479 Green Lanes, Palmers Green, London N13). Its US representative is *All England Car Rentals* (PO Box 1511, Room 603, Mineola, NY 11501; phone: 516-747-1841 or 800-241-3228). Reserve at least 3 weeks in advance. The best general advice is to contact the major car rental agencies listed in *Traveling by Car* well before your departure, but be forewarned, you may still be out of luck. The *American Automobile Association* (*AAA*) publishes the booklet *The Handicapped Driver's Mobility Guide,* available free to members and for 95¢ to non-members. Send a stamped, self-addressed, 6-by-9-inch envelope to AAA Traffic Safety Department, 8111 Gatehouse Rd., Room 603, Falls Church, VA 22047.

Another quite expensive option is to hire a chauffeured auto. Other alternatives include taking taxis or using local public transportation; however, your mobility may be limited in rural areas.

BUS AND TRAIN: In addition to networks in metropolitan areas, just about anywhere a paved road leads to a town or village there is likely to be a British bus route, although the frequency and accessibility of buses for handicapped travelers varies widely. Bus travel in Great Britain is not recommended for travelers who are totally wheelchair-bound unless they have someone along who can lift them on and off or they are members of a group tour designed for the handicapped and are using a specially outfitted bus. If you have some mobility, however, you'll find local personnel usually quite happy to help you board and exit.

Handicapped travelers with some mobility can make do on short train trips, and the major stations have restroom facilities for the handicapped. Train travel for the wheelchair-bound is becoming more feasible in Britain. Many newer trains have removable seats in first class that can accommodate a wheelchair up to 24½ inches wide. The number of destinations (London to Liverpool, Manchester, Glasgow, Edinburgh, Bristol, the west of England, and South Wales among them) is still limited, and lavatories on even these trains are still not accessible, though most trips are not long; major stations, however, have restroom facilities for the handicapped. On other trains, passengers can arrange to travel in the guard's van (baggage car). Wheelchair passengers travel at one-third off the applicable standard fare (unless they occupy a normal seat), and arrangements, either to ride in the guard's van or to have seats removed, or for an escort at stations, must be made through the area manager in advance. *British Rail: A Guide for Disabled People,* an access guide to railway stations, is available through *RADAR* (address above). For more information on British trains, contact *BritRail Travel International* offices in the US; also see *Touring by Bus* and *Touring by Train* elsewhere in this section.

TOURS: Programs designed for the physically impaired are run by specialists who have researched hotels, restaurants, and places of interest to be sure they present no insurmountable obstacles. The following travel agencies and tour operators specialize in making group and individual arrangements for travelers with physical or other disabilities. All of them have experience in travel to Europe. Because of the requirements of handicapped travel, however, the same packages may not be offered regularly.

Access: The Foundation for Accessibility by the Disabled, PO Box 356, Malvern, NY 11565 (phone: 516-887-568). Travelers' referral service that acts as an intermediary with tour operators and agents worldwide. Also provides information on accessibility at various locations.

Accessible Tours/Directions Unlimited, 720 N. Bedford Rd., Bedford Hills, NY 10507 (phone: 914-241-1700 in New York State; 800-533-5343 elsewhere in the US). Arranges group or individual tours for disabled persons traveling with able-bodied friends or family members. Accepts the unaccompanied traveler if completely self-sufficient.

Evergreen Travel Service/Wings on Wheels Tours, 19595L 44th Ave. W., Lynnwood, WA 98036 (phone: 206-776-1184; 800-562-9298 in Washington State; 800-435-2288 elsewhere in the US). The oldest company in the world offering worldwide tours and cruises for the disabled (Wings on Wheels) and sight impaired/blind (White Cane Tours). Most programs are first class or deluxe, and include escort by the owner or his family.

Flying Wheels Travel, 143 W. Bridge St., Box 382, Owatonna, MN 55060 (phone: 507-451-5005 or 800-533-0363). Handles both tours and individual arrangements.

Gillmour Travel Services, Gillmour House, Blennerhasset, Carlisle CA5 3RE (phone: Aspatria 21553). A British company offering both set itineraries and custom tours for the physically as well as the mentally disabled. Arrangements can be made for a sign-language interpreter.

The Guided Tour, 555 Ashbourne Rd., Elkins Park, PA 19117 (phone: 215-782-1370). Arranges tours for people with developmental and learning disabilities, and sponsors separate tours for members of the same population who are also physically disabled or who simply need a slower pace.

Handi-Travel, First National Travel Corporation, 300 John St., Thorn Hill, Ont. L3T 5W4, Canada (phone: 416-731-4714). Handles tours and travel arrangements.

InterpreTours, Ask Mr. Foster Travel Service, 16660 Ventura Blvd., Encino, CA 91436 (phone: 818-788-4118 for voice; 818-788-5328 for TDD, telecommunications device for the deaf). Arranges independent travel, cruises, and tours for the deaf, with an interpreter as tour guide.

Mobility Tours, 84 E. 10th St., 2nd Floor, New York, NY 10003 (phone: 212-353-

0240). Associated with *SATH*, this agency arranges tours for both physically and developmentally disabled people.

Sprout, 204 W. 20th St., New York, NY 10011 (phone: 212-431-1265). Arranges travel programs for mildly and moderately disabled adults, 18 years of age and over.

Travel Horizons Unlimited, 11 E. 44th St., New York, NY 10017 (phone: 212-687-5121). Travel agent and registered nurse Mary Ann Hamm designs trips for individual travelers requiring all types of kidney dialysis and handles arrangements for the dialysis.

Whole Person Tours, PO Box 1084, Bayonne, NJ 07002-1084 (phone: 201-858-3400). Handicapped owner Bob Zywicki travels the world with his wheelchair, and offers a lineup of escorted tours (many by himself) for the disabled. A catalogue of foreign and domestic programs designed for travelers with disabilities is available for $2. *Whole Person Tours* also publishes *The Itinerary*, a bimonthly newsletter for disabled travelers (a 1-year subscription costs $10).

A special guiding service is offered by Oxford historian William Forrester, who became London's first fully qualified and registered guide in a wheelchair. He escorts travelers for entire holidays, or just helps in planning an independent tour suited to each traveler's particular interests and mobility. Contact William Forrester, 1 Belvedere Close, Manor Rd., Guildford, Surrey GU2 6NP (phone: 0483-575401).

Hints for Single Travelers

Just about the last trip in human history on which the participants were neatly paired was the voyage of Noah's Ark. Ever since, passenger lists and tour groups have reflected the same kind of asymmetry that occurs in real life, as countless individuals set forth to see the world unaccompanied (or unencumbered, depending on your outlook) by spouse, lover, friend, or relative.

There are some things to be said for traveling alone. There is the pleasure of privacy, though a solitary traveler must be self-reliant, independent, and responsible. Unfortunately, traveling alone can also turn a traveler into a second class citizen.

The truth is that the travel industry is not very fair to people who vacation by themselves. People traveling alone almost invariably end up paying more than individuals traveling in pairs. Most travel bargains, including package tours, accommodations, resort packages, and cruises, are based on *double occupancy*. This means that the per-person price is offered on the basis of two people traveling together and sharing a double room (which means they will each spend a good deal more on meals and extras). The single traveler will have to pay a surcharge, called a single supplement, for exactly the same package. In extreme cases, this can add as much as 30% to 55% to the basic per-person rate. As far as the travel industry is concerned, single travel has not yet come into its own.

Don't despair, however. Throughout Europe, there are scores of smaller hotels and other hostelries where, in addition to a more cozy atmosphere, prices are still quite reasonable for the single traveler. There are, after all, countless thousands of individuals who *do* travel alone. Inevitably, their greatest obstacle is the single supplement charge, which prevents them from cashing in on travel bargains available to anyone traveling as part of a pair.

The obvious, most effective alternative is to find a traveling companion. Even special "singles' tours" that promise no supplements are based on people sharing double rooms. Perhaps the most recent innovation along these lines is the creation of organizations that "introduce" the single traveler to other single travelers, somewhat like a dating service. If you are interested in finding another single traveler to help share the cost, consider contacting the agencies listed below. Some charge fees, others are free, but the basic service offered by all is the same: to match the unattached person with a compatible travel mate. Among the better established of these agencies are the following:

Contiki Holidays: Operates European tours for people age 18 to 35. Many of the destinations are British. 1432 E. Katella Ave., Anaheim, CA 92805 (phone: 714-937-0611).

Cosmos: This agency, specializing in budget motorcoach tours of Europe, offers a guaranteed-share plan whereby singles who wish to share rooms (and avoid paying the single supplement) are matched by the tour escort with like-minded individuals of the same sex and charged the basic tour price. Those wishing to stay on their own pay a single supplement. Contact *Cosmos* at one of its three North American branches: 95-25 Queens Blvd., Rego Park, NY 11374 (phone: 800-221-0090 from the eastern US); 150 S. Los Robles Ave., Pasadena, CA 91101 (phone: 818-449-0919 or 800-556-5454 from the western US); 1801 Eglinton Ave. W., Suite 104, Toronto, Ont. M6E 2H8, Canada (phone: 416-787-1281).

Grand Circle Travel: Arranges escorted cruise/air packages for "mature" travelers, including singles. Membership, which is automatic when you book a trip through *Grand Circle,* includes a free subscription to its quarterly magazine, discount certificates on future trips, and other extras. 347 Congress St., Boston, MA 02210 (phone: 617-350-7500 in Boston; 800-221-2610 elsewhere in the US).

Jane's International: This service puts potential traveling companions in touch with one another — no age limit, no fee. 2603 Bath Ave., Brooklyn, NY 11214 (phone: 718-266-2045).

Saga International Holidays: An organization for seniors over 60, including singles. Members receive the club magazine, which includes a classified section aimed at helping lone travelers find suitable travelling companions. A 3-year membership costs $5. 120 Boylston St., Boston MA 02116 (phone: 617-451-6808 or one of the following nationwide toll-free numbers: for reservations, 800-343-0273; for customer service, 800-441-6662; for brochure requests, 800-248-2234).

Singleworld, which organizes its own packages and also books singles on the cruises and tours of other operators, arranges shared accommodations if requested, charging a one-time surcharge that is much less than the single supplement would be. *Singleworld* is actually a club joined through travel agents for a yearly fee of $20, paid at the time of booking. About two-thirds of this agency's clientele are under 35, and about half this number are women, but *Singleworld* organizes tours and cruises with departures categorized by age group. 401 Theodore Fremd Ave., Rye, NY 10580 (phone: 914-967-3334 or 800-223-6490 in the continental US).

Travel Companion Exchange: Every 8 weeks this group publishes a directory of singles looking for travel companions and provides members with full-page profiles of likely partners. Members fill out a lengthy questionnaire to establish a personal profile and write a small listing, much like an ad in a personal column. This listing is circulated to other members, who can request a copy of the complete questionnaire and then go on to make contact to plan a joint vacation. It is wise to join as far ahead of your vacation as possible so that there's enough time to determine the suitability of prospective traveling companions. Membership fees range from $3 to $11 per month (with a 6-month minimum enrollment), depending on the level of service required. PO Box 833, Amityville, NY 11701 (phone: 516-454-0880).

Travel Mates International: Will search for and arrange shares on existing package tours for men and women of any age. The agency will also organize group tours for its own clients. Annual membership fee is $15. 49 W. 44th St., New York, NY 10036 (phone: 212-221-6565).

A special guidebook for solo travelers, prepared by Eleanor Adams Baxel, offers information on how to avoid paying supplementary charges, how to pick the right travel agent, how to calculate costs, and much more. Entitled *A Guide for Solo Travel Abroad* (Berkshire Traveller Press), it's out of print but may be available in your library.

WOMEN AND STUDENTS: Two specific groups of single travelers deserve special mention: women and students. Countless women travel by themselves in Europe, and such an adventure need not be feared. You will generally find people courteous and welcoming, but remember that crime is a worldwide problem. (In fact, most European cities are generally regarded as safer than American cities — for everyone, including single women.) Keep a careful eye on your belongings while on the beach or lounging in a park; lock your car and hotel doors; deposit your valuables in the hotel's safe; and don't hitchhike.

One lingering inhibition many female travelers still harbor is that of eating alone in public places. The trick here is to relax and enjoy your meal and surroundings; while you may run across the occasional unenlightened waiter, dining solo is no longer uncommon. A book offering lively, helpful advice on female solo travel is *The Traveling Woman,* by Dena Kaye. Though out of print, it may be found in your library.

A large number of single travelers, needless to say, are students. Travel *is* education. Travel broadens a person's knowledge and deepens his or her perception of the world in a way no media or "armchair" experience ever could. In addition, to study a country's language, art, culture, or history in one of its own schools is to enjoy the highest form of liberal education.

There are many benefits for students abroad, and the way to begin to discover them is to consult the *Council on International Educational Exchange* (*CIEE*), 205 E. 42nd St., New York, NY 10017 (phone: 212-661-1414), and 312 Sutter St., San Francisco, CA 94108 (phone: 415-421-3473). This organization, which administers a variety of work, study, and travel programs for students, is the US sponsor of the International Student Identity Card (ISIC). Reductions on trains, airfare, and entry fees to most museums and other exhibitions are only some of the advantages of the card. To apply for it, write to *CIEE* at one of the above addresses and mark the letter "Attn. Student ID." Application requires a $10 fee, a passport-size photograph, and proof that you are a matriculating student (this means either a transcript or a letter or bill from the registrar with the school's official seal; high school and junior high school students can use their report cards). There is no maximum age limit, but you must be at least 12 years old. The *ID Discount Guide,* which gives details of the discounts country by country, is free with membership. Another card of value in Britain and also available through *CIEE* is the Federation of International Youth Travel Organizations (FIYTO) card. This provides many of the benefits of the ISIC card and will give you entrée (that is, a discount) to certain "youth hotels" throughout Britain. Cardholders, in this case, need not be students, merely under age 26. To apply, send $10 with a passport-size photo and proof of birth date.

CIEE also sponsors charter flights to Europe that are open to students and non-students of any age. Flights between New York and London (with budget-priced add-ons available from Seattle, San Francisco, Los Angeles, San Diego, Las Vegas, Salt Lake City, Denver, St. Louis, El Paso, Minneapolis, and 10 other US cities) leave daily except Fridays from JFK or Newark Airport in high season, returning on Sunday, Monday, Wednesday, and Thursday. Regularly scheduled direct flights are also offered from Boston to Brussels and Paris (both ferry or Hovercraft rides from Great Britain) and from Chicago to Brussels.

Another company that specializes in travel for 18- to 30-year-olds is *STI,* 8619 Reseda Blvd., Suite 103, Northridge, CA 91324 (phone: 800-637-7687 in California; 800-225-2780 elsewhere in the US). It offers multi-country escorted tours from 2 weeks to 52 days. *Contiki Holidays* (1432 E. Katella Ave., Anaheim, CA 92805; phone: 714-937-0611) specializes in vacations for 18- to 35-year-olds; accommodations are in "Contiki Villages" with cabins or tents, and "Contiki Clubs," and itineraries include special stopovers and tours of Great Britain."

Youth fares on transatlantic flights are currently offered by most of the scheduled airlines flying to Europe. Although the situation may change in the future, at press time, the youth fare was almost the same as the standard APEX fare, and there are substantial drawbacks: a 14-day minimum stay, no stopovers, notification of availability and payment in full 24 hours before the flight, and the return can only be left open if this is arranged before the trip, and is again subject to 24-hour notice of availability. This space available restriction means that if you really must be home by a certain date, you are better off opting for a different type of ticket. Discount fares vary from carrier to carrier. To find out about current discounts, contact the individual airlines. Also see *Traveling by Plane,* in this section, for more information on economical flight alternatives.

Students and singles should also keep in mind that youth hostels are plentiful throughout England, Scotland, and Wales. They are generally clean, well situated, always inexpensive, and a sure place to meet other people traveling alone. Hostels are run by the hosteling associations of some 60-plus countries that make up the *International Youth Hostel Federation* (*IYHF*); membership in one of the national associations affords access to the hostels of the rest. To join the American affiliate, *American Youth Hostels* (*AYH*), write to the national office at PO Box 37613, Washington, DC 20013-7613 (phone: 202-783-6161), or contact the *AYH* council nearest you. Membership costs $20 for people between ages 18 and 54, $10 for others. (If joining by mail, add $1 for postage.) The *AYH Handbook,* which lists hostels in the US, comes with the *AYH* card; the *International Handbook,* listing hostels worldwide (volume 1 covers Europe and the Mediterranean), may be purchased for $8.95 (plus $2 postage) each. Those who go abroad without an *AYH* card can get an *IYHF* guest card (for the equivalent of about $18) by contacting one of the national British youth hostel associations in Great Britain. These associations also publish handbooks to hostels in their areas. In addition, the tourist boards of both countries publish information sheets on hostels and on hosteling package holidays. For hostels in England and Wales, contact the *Youth Hostel Association* at Trevelyan House, 8 St. Stephen's Hill, St. Albans, Hertfordshire AL1 2DY, or at 14 Southampton St., London WC2E 7HY; in Scotland, the *Scottish Youth Hostels Association,* 7 Glebe Crescent, Stirling FK8 2JA. These associations also publish handbooks listing hostels in their areas. The British Tourist Authority publishes *Britain: Youth Accommodation,* listing hostels and other budget accommodations including university facilities (where stays of 1 or 2 weeks are permitted). For more information, contact either the British Tourist Authority or the *British Universities Accommodation Consortium* (PO Box U32, University Park, Nottingham, Nottinghamshire NG7 2RD, England).

The *YMCA* and the *YWCA* also run economical accommodations and have separate offices to contact for information. You can get a list of *Y*s in Great Britain by writing to *YMCA/YWCA Accommodations, National Council of YMCAs,* 640 Forest Rd., Walthamstow, London E17 3DZ, or the *Young Women's Christian Association of Great Britain,* 52 Cornmarket St., Oxford OX1 3EJ. These agencies will not make bookings for travelers, however; reservations must be made directly with the specific *Y* of choice.

Many private houses and farms throughout the countryside make a pleasant home base and offer a chance to meet local people. The United States Servas Committee, a non-profit organization designed to promote world peace, keeps a worldwide list of hosts willing to take visitors into their homes as guests for a 2-night stay (see "Home Stays," *Accommodation and Reservations*). The British Tourist Authority (see *Tourist Information Offices*) publishes a booklet, *Britain: Stay on a Farm,* which lists working farms in Great Britain. On many farms, travelers will get a room and a hearty breakfast for as little as $10 a day.

And there's always camping. Virtually any area of the countryside in Britain has a place to pitch a tent and enjoy the scenery. There are numerous national parks, and, with permission, it's possible to camp on private acres of farmland. Many of the campsites have showers, laundry rooms, public phones, eating facilities, and shops. The British tourist boards have booklets listing sites and their facilities, as well as places to rent camping equipment. (For more information, see *Camping and Caravanning, Hiking and Biking.*)

STUDYING ABROAD: Opportunities for study in Britain range from summer or academic-year courses designed specially for foreigners (including those whose school days are well behind them) to long-term university attendance by those intending to take a degree.

Summer study programs are popular and courses are diverse; there are many more than those listed here. For more information on specific courses, colleges, their costs, and requirements, request the booklets *Young Travellers to Britain* from the British Tourist Authority and *Study in Britain* from British Information Services (845 Third Ave., New York, NY 10022; phone: 212-752-5747 in New York City; 800-223-5339 elsewhere in the US).

Special transportation discounts are available to students and youths in Britain. *British Rail* offers the *BritRail* Youth Pass for anyone age 16 through 25. The Youth Pass permits unlimited train travel in economy class throughout England, Scotland, and Wales for periods of 8, 15, or 22 days or 1 month. To buy a pass, contact your travel agent or *BritRail Travel International* offices in North America (see addresses and phone numbers in *Touring by Train*) at least 21 days before departure. Because the passes must be purchased before you leave the US, you will need to have some certainties in your itinerary in order to choose the most economical version.

The British Tourist Authority has a brochure called *Young Britain: A Young Traveller's Guide to Britain,* which includes details on travel, accommodations, temporary work, and more. Other sources of information that may be of help are the following:

American Institute for Foreign Study (*AIFS*), another organization specializing in travel as an educational experience. Students can enroll for the full academic year or for any number of semesters. *AIFS* caters primarily to bona fide high school or college students, but non-credit international learning and continuing education programs are open to independent travelers of all ages. (Approximately 30% of *AIFS* students are over 25.) 102 Greenwich Ave., Greenwich, CT 06830 (phone: 203-863-6087 or 203-869-9090).

Elderhostel is a network of schools, colleges, and universities that sponsors week-long study programs for people over 60 years of age on campuses throughout the US and Europe. Some of its programs are offered in cooperation with the *Experiment in International Living* and involve home stays. Contact Elderhostel, 80 Boylston St., Suite 400, Boston, MA 02116 (phone: 617-426-7788). The University of New Hampshire, the original sponsor of *Elderhostel,* has its own program for travelers over 50; contact *Interhostel,* University of New Hampshire, Division of Continuing Education, 6 Garrison Ave., Durham, NH 03824 (phone: 603-862-1147 weekdays, 1:30-4 PM Eastern Standard Time). For more details about both programs, see *Hints for Older Travelers.*

Experiment in International Living, which sponsors home-stay educational travel. The organization aims its programs at high school and college students, but it can also arrange home stays of 1 to 4 weeks for adults in more than 40 countries. Kipling Rd., Box E-10, Brattleboro, VT 05301-0676 (phone: 802-257-7751 or 800-345-2929).

Institute of International Education (*IIE*), an information resource center that annually publishes several reference books on study abroad, including *Academic Year Abroad* ($19.95), *Vacation Study Abroad* ($19.95), and *Study in the United Kingdom and Ireland* ($14.95). Prices include book-rate postage; first class postage is $4 extra. All volumes are available from IIE headquarters, 809 UN Plaza, New York, NY 10017 (phone: 212-883-8200).

National Association of Secondary School Principals (*NASSP*), an association of administrators, teachers, and state education officials. It sponsors *School Partnership International,* a program in which secondary schools in the US are linked with partner schools abroad for an annual short-term exchange of students and faculty. 1904 Association Dr., Reston, VA 22091 (phone: 703-860-0200).

WORKING ABROAD: Jobs for foreigners in Britain are not easy to come by and in general do not pay well enough to cover all the expenses of a trip. They do provide an invaluable learning experience, however, while helping to make a trip more affordable. Work permits can be obtained through the *Council on International Educational Exchange* (address above) only by students over 18 who are working toward a degree and who are enrolled in a US college or university. The permit allows them to work for 3 months at any time of year, but students must find their own jobs.

Hints for Older Travelers

Special package deals and more free time are just two factors that have given Americans over age 65 a chance to see the world at affordable prices. Senior citizens make up an ever-growing segment of the travel population, and the trend among them is to travel more frequently and for longer periods of time. No longer limited by 3-week vacations or the business week, older travelers can take advantage of off-season, off-peak travel, which is both less expensive and more pleasant than traveling at prime time in high season. In addition, overseas, as in the US, discounts are frequently available.

PLANNING: When planning a vacation, prepare your itinerary with one eye on your own physical condition and the other on a topographical map. Keep in mind variations in climate, terrain, and altitudes, which may pose some danger for anyone with heart or breathing problems.

An excellent book to read before embarking on any trip, domestic or foreign, is Rosalind Massow's *Travel Easy: The Practical Guide for People Over 50,* available for $8.95 (plus $1.75 postage and handling per order, not per book, from AARP Books, c/o Scott, Foresman, 1865 Miner St., Des Plaines, IL 60016; phone: 800-238-2300). It discusses a host of travel subjects, from choosing a destination to getting set for departure, with chapters on transportation options, tours, cruises, avoiding health problems, and handling dental emergencies en route. Another book, *The International Health Guide for Senior Citizens,* covers such topics as trip preparations, food and water precautions, adjusting to weather and climate conditions, finding a doctor, motion sickness, and jet lag. The book also discusses specific health and travel problems, and includes a list of resource organizations that can provide medical assistance for travelers; it is available for $4.95 postpaid from Pilot Books (103 Cooper St., Babylon, NY 11702; phone: 516-422-2225). A third book on health for older travelers, Rosalind Massow's excellent *Now It's Your Turn to Travel* (Collier Books), has a chapter on medical problems; it is now out of print but may be available in libraries. Also, see *Medical and Legal Aid,* in this section. Other excellent books for budget-conscious older travelers are *The Discount Guide for Travelers Over 55* by Caroline and Walter Weintz (Dutton; $7.95) and *The Senior Citizen's Guide to Budget Travel in Europe* ($3.95 plus $1 for postage and handling from Pilot Books, address above).

Travel Tips for Senior Citizens (State Department publication 8970), a booklet with general advice, is available for $1 from the Superintendent of Documents, US Government Printing Office, Washington, DC 20402 (phone: 202-783-3238). The booklet *101 Tips for the Mature Traveler* is available free from *Grand Circle Travel* (347 Congress St., Suite 3A, Boston, MA 02210; phone: 617-350-7500 or 800-221-2610).

If you are traveling in the fall, winter, or spring, bear in mind that you will not always find central heating in public places in Britain and that even if your hotel has it, it may not warm your room up to the temperatures you're accustomed to at home. Bear in mind also that even in summer you will need something warm for the evening in many areas of the country, and rainwear year-round is a good idea, too. However, remember that one secret to happy traveling is to *pack lightly.* (For further hints on what to bring, see *How to Pack,* in this section.)

HEALTH: Health facilities in Great Britain are generally excellent, and a number of organizations exist to help travelers avoid or deal with a medical emergency overseas. For further information on these services, see *Medical and Legal Aid and Consular Services.*

Older travelers should know that Medicare does not make payments outside the US, and — contrary to lingering popular belief — Britain's National Health Service does not provide free medical care to visitors, except in a few instances. If your medical policy does not protect you while you're traveling, there are comprehensive combination policies specifically designed to fill the gap. For a discussion of travel insurance and a list of companies offering attractive combination plans, see *Insurance.*

A pre-trip medical and dental checkup are strongly recommended, particularly for older travelers. In addition, be sure to take along any prescription medication you need, enough to last *without a new prescription* for the duration of your trip; pack all medications with a note from your doctor for the benefit of airport authorities. It is also wise to bring a few common non-prescription over-the-counter medications with you: Aspirin and something for stomach upset may come in handy. If you have specific medical problems, bring prescriptions and a "medical file" composed of the following:

1. A summary of your medical history and current diagnosis.
2. A list of drugs to which you are allergic.
3. Your most recent electrocardiogram, if you have heart problems.
4. Your doctor's name, address, and telephone number.

■ **A word of caution:** Don't overdo it. Allow time for some relaxing each day to refresh yourself for the next scheduled sightseeing event. Traveling across time zones can be exhausting, and adjusting to major climatic changes can make you feel dizzy and drained. Plan on spending at least one full day resting before you start touring. If you're part of a group tour, be sure to check the planned itinerary thoroughly. Some package deals sound wonderful because they include all the places you've ever dreamed of visiting. In fact, they can become so hectic and tiring that you'll be reaching for a pillow instead of a camera.

DISCOUNTS AND PACKAGES: Since guidelines change from place to place, it is a good idea to inquire in advance about discounts for transportation, hotels, concerts, movies, museums, and other activities. The various tourist boards in Great Britain can give the most up-to-date information about discounts and programs for older travelers (see *Tourist Information Offices*).

British Rail offers a Senior Citizen Pass for those 60 and older. It permits unlimited first class train travel through England, Scotland, and Wales at less than the cost of a regular first class *BritRail* pass. Both are available for 8, 15, or 22 days or 1 month and must be purchased before entering Great Britain. (For more information on transportation discounts, see *Traveling by Plane* and *Touring by Bus.*) British Airways offers a 30% discount for senior citizens 60 and older off economy fares. It also offers a Privilege Traveler Card. You must apply and pay a $12 handling fee. It gives the owner 10% off all fares and waives all the penalties. Seniors are also given 10% off *Cunard* cruise line and the *Orient Express.* This card also covers a companion, who must be 50 or older. For information, call 800-AIRWAYS.

Many US hotel and motel chains, airlines, car rental companies, bus lines, and other travel suppliers offer discounts to older travelers. Some of these discounts, however, are extended only to bona fide members of certain senior citizens organizations. Because the same organizations frequently offer package tours to both domestic and international destinations, the benefits of membership are twofold: Those who join can take advantage of discounts as individual travelers and also reap the savings that group travel affords. In addition, because the age requirements for some of these organizations are quite low (or nonexistent), the benefits can begin to accrue early. Among the organizations dedicated to helping you see the world are the following:

American Association of Retired Persons (*AARP*): The largest and best-known of these organizations. Membership is open to anyone 50 or over, whether retired or not. *AARP* offers travel programs, designed exclusively for senior citizens, that cover the globe and include a broad range of escorted tours, hosted tours, and cruises, including regional tours of rural areas of Europe, extended vacations in European cities, and resorts with accommodations in apartments. Dues are $5 a year, or $12.50 for 3 years, and include spouse. For membership information, contact AARP at 1909 K St. NW, Washington, DC 20049 (phone: 202-347-8800); for travel information and reservations, contact AARP Travel Service, PO Box 29233, Los Angeles, CA 90009 (phone: 213-322-7323 or 800-227-7737).

Mature Outlook: This organization has replaced the *National Association of Mature People.* Through its *Travel Alert,* last-minute tours, cruises, and other vacation packages are available to members at special savings. Hotel and car rental discounts and travel accident insurance are also available. Membership is open to anyone 50 years of age or older, costs $9.95 a year, and includes its bimonthly newsletter and magazine as well as information on package tours. Contact the Customer Service Center, 60001 N. Clark St., Chicago, IL 60660 (phone: 800-336-6330).

National Council of Senior Citizens: Here, too, the emphasis is always on keeping costs low. The roster of tours offered by this organization is different each year, and its travel service will also book individual tours for members. Although most members are over 50, membership is open to anyone, regardless of age, for an annual fee of $12 per person or $16 per couple. Lifetime membership costs $150. For information, contact the National Council of Senior Citizens, 925 15th St. NW, Washington, DC 20005 (phone: 202-347-8800).

Certain travel agencies and tour operators specialize in group travel for older travelers, among them the following:

Gadabout Tours: This agency offers escorted tours to many North American destinations but also has tours to Europe, including Britain. See a travel agent or contact Gadabout Tours, 700 E. Tahquitz, Palm Springs, CA 92262 (phone: 619-325-5556 or 800-521-7309 in California; 800-952-5068 elsewhere in the US).

Grand Circle Travel: Caters exclusively to the over-50 traveler, packages a large variety of escorted tours, cruises, and extended vacations. *Grand Circle* also publishes a quarterly magazine (with a column for the single traveler) and a helpful free booklet, *101 Tips for the Mature Traveler Abroad.* Contact Grand Circle Travel, 347 Congress St., Suite 3A, Boston, MA 02210 (phone: 617-350-7500 or 800-221-2610).

Grandtravel: An agency that specializes in trips for older people and their grandchildren (aunts and uncles are welcome, too), bringing the generations together through travel. Ten itineraries (one to England) that coincide with school vacations emphasize historic and natural sites. Transportation, accommodations, and activities are thoughtfully arranged to meet the needs of the young and the young-at-heart. Contact Grandtravel, 6900 Wisconsin Ave., Suite 706, Chevy Chase, MD 20815 (phone: 301-986-0790 in Maryland; 800-247-7551 elsewhere in the US).

Insight International Tours: Packages tours for the mature traveler that emphasize heritage. One of several to Great Britain is called 'Stately Homes, Castles, and Gardens.' Bookings must be made through a travel agent. For details, contact Insight International Tours, 17310 Redhill Ave., Suite 330, Irvine, CA 92714 (phone: 714-261-5373 or 800-792-7209 in California; 800-582-8380 elsewhere in the US).

Saga International Holidays: A subsidiary of a British company specializing in the older traveler, *Saga* offers a broad selection of escorted coach tours, cruises, apartment-stay holidays, and combinations thereof, for people age 60 and over or those 50 to 59 traveling with someone 60 or older. Members of the Saga Holiday Club receive the club magazine, which also contains a column aimed at helping lone travelers find suitable traveling companions (see *Hints for Single Travelers*). A 3-year membership in the club costs $5. Contact Saga International Holidays, 120 Boylston St., Boston MA 02116 (phone: 617-451-6808 or one of the following nationwide toll-free numbers: for reservations, 800-343-0273; for customer service, 800-441-6662; for brochure requests, 800-248-2234).

Many travel agencies, particularly the larger ones, are delighted to make presentations to help a group select destinations. A local chamber of commerce should be able to provide the names of such agencies. Once a time and place are determined, an organization member or travel agent can obtain group quotations for transportation, accommodations, meal plans, and sightseeing. Groups of 40 or more usually get the best breaks.

Another choice open to older travelers is a trip that includes an educational element. *Interhostel,* a program sponsored by the Division of Continuing Education of the University of New Hampshire, sends travelers back to school at cooperating institutions in 33 countries on 4 continents, including — usually — Great Britain. Participants attend lectures on the history, economy, politics, and cultural life of the country they are visiting, go on field trips to pertinent points of interest, and take part in activities meant to introduce them to their foreign contemporaries. Trips are for 2 weeks; accommodations are on campus in university residence halls or off campus in modest hotels (double occupancy). Groups are limited to 35 to 40 participants who are at least 50 years old (or at least 40 if a participating spouse is at least 50), physically active, and not in need of special diets. For further information or to receive the three free seasonal catalogues, contact Interhostel, UNH Division of Continuing Education, 6 Garrison Ave., Durham, NH 03824 (phone: 603-862-1147 weekdays, 1:30 to 4 PM Eastern Standard Time).

Similar to *Interhostel* is *Elderhostel,* a non-profit organization offering educational programs at a huge number of schools in the US and Canada as well as at cooperating institutions overseas, a great many of which are in Great Britain. Most international programs run for 3 weeks and feature a special topic each week at a different location. Accommodations are in residence halls, and meals are taken in student cafeterias. Travel to the overseas programs is by designated scheduled flights, and you can arrange to remain abroad at the end of the program. Age and health qualifications for participation are similar to those for Interhostelers — Elderhostelers must be at least 60 years old (younger if a spouse or companion qualifies), in good health, and not in need of special diets. For information, write to Elderhostel, 80 Boylston St., Suite 400, Boston, MA 02116 (phone: 617-426-7788).

Hints for Traveling with Children

What better way to be receptive to the experiences you will encounter than to take along the young, wide-eyed members of your family. Their company does not have to be a burden or their presence an excessive expense. The current generation of discounts for children and family package deals can make a trip together quite reasonable.

A family trip will be an investment in your children's future, making geography and history come alive to them and leaving a sure memory that will be among the fondest you will share with them someday. Their insights will be refreshing to you; their impulses may take you to unexpected places with unexpected dividends. The experience will be invaluable to them at any age.

The current discount airfares make flights to Great Britain a good deal less expensive than a decent summer camp. In fact, why not send the children to a summer camp for a few days in the British countryside? Riding holidays and pony trekking, as well as traditional camps, are popular, too. Those who would prefer to keep the family together can rent a cottage or visit a family farm in the countryside. The British Tourist Authority has information on how to arrange any of these vacations.

PLANNING: It is necessary to take some extra time beforehand to prepare children for travel. Here are several hints for making a trip with children easy and fun.

1. Children, like everyone else, will derive more pleasure from a trip if they know something about the country before they arrive. Begin their education about a month before you leave. Using maps, travel magazines, and travel books, give children a clear idea of where you are going and how far away it is. Part of the excitement of the journey will be associating the tiny dots on the map with the very real places they will visit a few weeks later. You can show them pictures of streets and scenes in which they will stand within a month. Don't shirk history lessons, but don't burden them with dates. Make history light, anecdotal, pertinent, but most of all, fun. It is not a good idea to overdo the educational approach. If you simply make materials available and keep Britain and your travel plans a topic of everyday conversation, your children will absorb more than you realize.
2. Children should help to plan the itinerary, and where you go and what you do should reflect some of their ideas. If they know something about the sites they'll visit beforehand, they will have the excitement of recognition when they arrive and the illumination of seeing how something is or is not the way they expected it to be.
3. Familiarize the children with pounds and pence (see *Credit and Currency*). Give them an allowance for the trip and be sure they understand just how far it will or won't go.

4. Give children specific responsibilities: The job of carrying their own flight bags and looking after their personal things, along with some other light travel chores, will give them a stake in the journey. Tell them how they can be helpful when you are checking in or out of hotels.
5. Give each child a travel diary or scrapbook to take along. Filling these with impressions, observations, and mementos will pass the time on trains and planes and help to assimilate their experiences.

   There are many books on Great Britain especially for children. The *British Travel Bookshop* (40 W. 57th St., New York, NY 10019) has a *Discovering* series, and some of the titles will especially appeal to children — *Discovering Kings and Queens, Discovering Ghosts,* and *Discovering Preserved Railways* ($4.95 each, plus $2 handling per order). It also offers the nicely illustrated *Stonehenge and Avebury* ($4.35), a history book for children 11 and older, and the new *Children's Guide to London* ($9.95), designed for family trips and featuring information on everything from the Tower of London to the city's unique *Museum of Childhood.* David Macaulay's *Castle* (Houghton Mifflin; $14.95 hardcover, $6.95 paperback), which uses text and drawings to show how castles were built in Wales in the 13th century, is particularly suited to helping children more fully appreciate the many castles they may see in Britain; *Cathedral: The Story of Its Construction* (for children up to grade 5; $14.95 hardcover, $6.95 paperback), by the same author, is also appropriate. Piero Ventura's beautifully illustrated *Great Painters* (Putnam) is an excellent introduction to Italian, Flemish, English, and French painting for older children (ages 12 and up). James Giblin's *Walls: Defenses Throughout History* (Little, Brown) discusses Hadrian's Wall in England and the great defensive walls of World Wars I and II, among others, and will appeal to teenage readers. Many of these books are informative for adults as well.

   And, for parents, *Travel with Your Children* publishes a newsletter, *Family Travel Times,* that focuses on the young traveler and offers helpful hints. Membership is $35 a year. For a sample copy of the newsletter, send $1 to Travel with Your Children, 80 Eighth Ave., New York, NY 10011 (phone: 212-206-0688).

PACKING: Choose your children's clothes much as you would your own. Select a basic color (perhaps different for each child) and coordinate everything with it. Plan their wardrobes with layering in mind — shirts and sweaters that can be taken off and put back on as the temperature varies. Take only drip-dry, wrinkle-resistant items that they can manage themselves and comfortable shoes — sneakers and sandals. Younger children will need more changes, but keep it to a minimum. No one likes to carry added luggage. (Remember that *you* will have to manage most of it!)

Take as many handy snacks as you can squeeze into the corners of your suitcases — things like dried fruit and nut mixes, hard candies, peanut butter, and crackers — and moist towelettes for cleaning. Don't worry if your supply of nibbles is quickly depleted. Airports and train and bus stations are well stocked with such items.

Pack a special medical kit including children's aspirin or acetaminophen, an antihistamine or decongestant, Dramamine, and diarrhea medication. Do not feel you must pack a vacation's worth of Pampers. Disposable diapers (called "nappies") are available in chemist's (drugstores) and supermarkets. A selection of baby foods is also available in most supermarkets, but in the event that you may not be able to find the instant formula to which your child is accustomed, bring along a supply in the 8-ounce "ready-to-feed" cans. Disposable nursers are expensive but handy. If you breast-feed your baby, there is no reason you can't enjoy your trip; just be sure you get enough rest and liquids.

Good toys to take for infants are the same sorts of things they like at home — well-made, bright huggables and chewables; for small children, a favorite doll or stuffed animal for comfort, spelling and counting games, and tying, braiding, and lacing activities; for older children, playing cards, travel board games with magnetic pieces, and hand-held electronic games. Softcover books and art materials (crayons, markers, paper, scissors, glue sticks, and stickers) ward off boredom for children of most ages, as do radio-cassette players with headphones. Take along a variety of musical and storytelling cassettes, extra batteries, and maybe even an extra set of headphones so two children can listen. *Advice:* Avoid toys that are noisy, breakable, or spillable, those that require a large play area, and those that have lots of little pieces that can be scattered and lost. When traveling, coordinate activities with attention spans; dole out playthings one at a time so that you don't run out of diversions before you get where you're going. Children become restless during long waiting periods, and a game plus a small snack — such as a box of raisins or crackers — will help keep them quiet. It is also a good idea to carry tissues, Band-Aids, a pocket medicine kit (described above), and moistened washclothes.

GETTING THERE AND GETTING AROUND: Begin early to investigate all available discount and charter flights, as well as any package deals and special rates offered by the major airlines. Booking is sometimes required up to 2 months in advance. You may well find that charter plans offer no reductions for children, or not enough to offset the risk of last-minute delays or other inconveniences to which charters are subject. The major scheduled airlines, on the other hand, almost invariably provide hefty discounts for children (for specific information on fares and in-flight accommodations for children, also see *Traveling by Plane*).

PLANE: When you make your reservations, let the airlines know that you are traveling with a child. As a general rule, a child under 2 years of age flies to Europe at 10% of the fare paid by the accompanying adult as long as the child is kept on the adult's lap; however, particularly on longer flights, this may not be comfortable. (Don't despair, though. If there are empty seats around you, no one will object to your putting your child down. Armrests on airplanes are generally removable.) A second child under 2 without a second accompanying adult flies to Europe at the same fare applicable to children from 2 through 11, which is usually half an adult economy fare and two-thirds an adult APEX fare.

If traveling with an infant, request a bulkhead seat, and ask for a bassinet. Request seats on the aisle if you have a toddler or if you think you will need to use the bathroom frequently. (Try to discourage children from being in the aisle when meals are served.) Carry onto the plane all you will need to care for and occupy your children during the flight — diapers, formula, "lovies," books, sweaters, and so on. (Never check as baggage any item essential to a child's well-being, such as prescription medicine.) Dress your baby simply, with a minimum of buttons and snaps, because the only place you may have to change a diaper is at your seat. The flight attendant can warm a bottle for you.

Just as you would request a vegetarian or kosher meal, you are entitled to ask for a hot dog or hamburger in lieu of the airline's regular dinner if you give at least 24 hours' notice. Some, but not all, airlines have baby food aboard. While you should bring along toys from home, you can also ask about children's diversions. Some carriers, such as Pan American and British Airways, have terrific free packages of games, coloring books, and puzzles.

When the plane takes off and lands, make sure your baby is nursing or has a bottle, pacifier, or thumb in its mouth. This sucking will make the child swallow and help to clear stopped ears. A piece of hard candy will do the same thing for an older child.

Avoid night flights. Since you probably won't sleep nearly as well as your kids, you risk an impossible first day at your destination, groggily taking care of your rested, energetic children. Nap time is, however, a good time to travel, especially for babies, and try to travel during off-hours, when there are apt to be extra seats. If you do have to take a long night flight, keep in mind that when you disembark, you will probably be tired and not really ready for sightseeing. The best thing to do is to head for your hotel, shower, have a snack, and take a nap. If your children are too excited to sleep, give them some toys to play with while you rest.

■ **Note:** Newborn babies, whose lungs may not be able to adjust to the altitude, should not be taken aboard an airplane. And some airlines may refuse to allow a pregnant woman in her 8th or 9th month aboard, for fear that something could go wrong with an in-flight birth. Check with the airline ahead of time and carry a letter from your doctor stating that you are fit to travel and indicating the estimated date of birth.

SHIP, TRAIN, AND BUS: By ship, children under 12 usually travel at a considerably reduced fare. On British trains and buses, children under 3 years of age travel free and those from age 3 through 15 travel at half fare. For further information, see *Traveling by Plane, Touring by Train,* and *Touring by Bus,* in this section.

ACCOMMODATIONS AND MEALS: Often a cot will be placed in a hotel room at little or no extra charge. If you wish to sleep in separate rooms, special rates are sometimes available for families in adjoining rooms; some places do not charge for children under a certain age. In many of the larger chain hotels, the staffs are more used to noisy or slightly misbehaving children. These hotels are also likely to have swimming pools or gamerooms — both popular with most young travelers. Write the hotel in advance to discuss how old your children are, how long you plan to stay, and to ask for suggestions on sleeping arrangements.

You might want to look into accommodations along the way that will add to the color of your trip. For instance, the many country inns, farmhouses, and cottages in the British countryside prove a delightful experience for the whole family and provide a view of British life different from that gained from staying in a conventional hotel. And don't forget castles, many of which double as hotels. Children will love them. Camping facilities are often in beautiful, out-of-the-way spots and are generally good, well equipped, and less expensive than any hotel you will come across. (See *Accommodations* and *Camping and Caravanning, Hiking and Biking.*)

For the times you will want to be without the children — for an evening's entertainment or a particularly rigorous stint of sightseeing — it is possible to arrange for a baby sitter at the hotel desk. Many British communities have sitter services; check local listings. Whether the sitter is hired directly or through an agency, ask for and check references.

As far as food goes, don't deny yourself or your children the delights of a new cuisine. Encourage them to try new things and don't forget about picnics. There's nothing lovelier than stopping in your tracks at a beautiful view and eating lunch as you muse on the surroundings.

THINGS TO REMEMBER: If you are spending your vacation traveling, rather than visiting one spot or engaging in one activity, pace the days with children in mind; break the trip into half-day segments, with running around or "doing" time built in; keep travel time on the road to a maximum of 4 or 5 hours a day. First and foremost, don't forget that a child's attention span is far shorter than an adult's. Children don't have to see every museum or all of any museum to learn something from their trip; watching, playing with, and talking to other children can be equally enlightening experiences. Also, remember the places that children the world over love to visit: zoos, country fairs and small amusement parks, beaches and nature trails. Let your children lead the way sometimes — their perspective is different from yours, and they may lead you to things you would never have noticed on your own.

Staying Healthy

The surest way to return home in good health is to be prepared for any medical problems that might occur on vacation. Below, we've outlined some things you need to think about before you go.

Obviously, your state of health is crucial to the success of a vacation. There's nothing like an injury or illness, whether serious or relatively minor, to dampen or destroy a holiday. And health problems always seem more debilitating when you are away. However, most problems can be prevented or greatly alleviated with intelligent foresight and attention to precautionary details.

Older travelers or anyone suffering from a chronic medical condition, such as diabetes, high blood pressure, cardiopulmonary disease, asthma, or ear, eye, or sinus trouble should consult a physician before leaving home. A checkup is advisable. A pre-trip dental checkup is not a bad idea, either.

People with conditions requiring special consideration when traveling should consider seeing, in addition to their regular physician, a specialist in travel medicine. For a referral in a particular community, contact the nearest medical school or ask a local doctor to recommend such a specialist. The *American Society of Tropical Medicine and Hygiene* publishes a directory of more than 70 travel doctors across the country. Send a 9-by-12-inch self-addressed, stamped envelope ($1.05 postage) to Dr. Leonard Marcus, Tufts University, 200 W. Boro Rd., North Grafton, MA 01536.

FIRST AID: Put together a compact, personal medical kit including Band-Aids, first-aid cream, antiseptic, nose drops, insect repellent, aspirin, an extra pair of prescription glasses, sunglasses, or contact lenses (and a copy of your prescription for glasses or lenses), over-the-counter remedies for diarrhea, indigestion, and motion sickness, a thermometer, and a supply of those prescription medicines you take regularly. In a corner of your kit, keep a list of all the drugs you have brought and their purpose as well as duplicate copies of your doctor's prescriptions (or a note from your doctor). These copies could come in handy if you are ever questioned by police or airport authorities about any drugs you are carrying and also are necessary to refill any prescriptions in the event of loss. It is also a good idea to ask your doctor to prepare a medical identification card that includes such information as your blood type, your social security number, any allergies or chronic health problems you have, and your medical insurance information. Considering the essential contents of this kit, keep it with you rather than in your luggage.

SUNBURN: Depending on when and where you're vacationing, the burning power of the sun can be phenomenal and can quickly cause severe sunburn or sunstroke. To protect yourself against these ills, wear sunglasses, take along a broad-brimmed hat and cover-up, and use a sunscreen lotion. When choosing a sunscreen, look for one that has a PABA (the para-amino-benzoic acid) base. PABA blocks out most of the harmful ultraviolet rays of the sun.

Some tips on tanning:

1. Allow only 20 minutes or so the first day; increase your exposure gradually.
2. You are most likely to get a painful burn when the sun is the strongest, between 10 AM and 2 PM.
3. When judging if you've had enough sun, remember that time in the water (in terms of exposure to ultraviolet rays) is the same as time lying on the beach.

4. A beach umbrella or other cover doesn't keep all the rays of the sun from reaching you. If you are sensitive to light, be especially careful.
5. As many ultraviolet rays reach you on cloudy days as on sunny days. Even if you don't feel hot, you are still exposed to rays.

If, despite these precautions, you find yourself with a painful sunburn, take a cooling bath, apply a first-aid spray or the liquid of an aloe plant, and stay out of the sun. If you develop a more serious burn and experience chills, fever, nausea, headaches, or dizziness, consult a doctor at once.

WATER SAFETY: Britain is famous for its rocky beaches. It's important to remember that the sea, especially the wild Atlantic or the North Sea, can also be treacherous. A few precautions are necessary. Beware of the undertow, that current of water running back down the beach after a wave has washed ashore; it can knock you off your feet and into the surf. Even more dangerous is the riptide, a strong current of water running against the tide, which can pull you out toward sea. If this happens, don't panic or try to fight the current, because it will only exhaust you; instead, ride it out while waiting for it to subside, which usually happens not too far from shore, or try swimming away parallel to the beach.

INSECTS AND OTHER PESTS: Mosquitoes, horseflies, and other biting insects can be troublesome, so as we have said, be sure to pack a repellent. Insects such as water bugs thrive in warm, damp weather, but pose no serious health threat.

FOOD AND WATER: Water is clean and potable throughout Britain. Ask if water is meant for drinking, but if you're at all unsure, bottled water is readily available in stores. Remember, there may be nothing wrong with the water as far as the residents are concerned, but new microbes in the digestive tract to which the traveler has not become accustomed may cause mild stomach or intestinal upsets. Particularly in rural areas, the water supply may not be thoroughly purified and residents either have developed immunities to the natural bacteria or boil it for drinking. You should also avoid drinking water from streams or freshwater pools. In campgrounds, water is usually indicated as drinkable or for washing only — again, if you're not sure, ask.

Milk is pasteurized throughout Britain, and milk products (cheese, yogurt, ice cream, and so on) are safe to eat, as are fresh produce, meat, poultry, and fish.

Following all these precautions will not guarantee an illness-free trip, but it should minimize the risk. As a final hedge against economic if not physical problems, make sure your health insurance will cover all eventualities while you are away. If not, there are policies designed specifically for travel. Many are worth investigating. As with all insurance, they seem like a waste of money until you need them. For further information, also see *Insurance* and *Medical and Legal Aid and Consular Services,* in this section.

HELPFUL PUBLICATIONS: Practically every phase of health care — before, during, and after a trip — is covered in *The New Traveler's Health Guide* by Drs. Patrick J. Doyle and James E. Banta. It is available for $4.95, plus $2 postage and handling, from Acropolis Books Ltd., 2400 17th St. NW, Washington, DC 20009-9964 (phone: 800-451-7771).

For more information regarding preventive health care for travelers, contact *International Association for Medical Assistance to Travelers* (*IAMAT*), 417 Center St., Lewiston, NY 14092 (phone: 716-754-4883), or write to the US Government Printing Office, Washington, DC 20402, for the US Public Health Service's booklet *Health Information for International Travel* (HEW Publication CDC-86-8280; enclose check or money order for $4.75 payable to Superintendent of Documents).

On the Road

Credit and Currency

It may seem hard to believe, but one of the greatest (and least understood) costs of travel is money itself. If that sounds simplistic, consider that you can lose as much as 30% of your travel dollars' value simply by changing money at the wrong place or in the wrong form. So the one single objective in relation to the care and retention of travel funds is to make them stretch as far as possible. When you do spend money, it should be on things that expand and enhance your travel experience, so that no buying power is lost due to carelessness or lack of knowledge. This requires more than merely ferreting out the best airfare or the most charming budget hotel. It means being canny about the management of money itself. Herewith, a primer on making money go as far as possible overseas.

CURRENCY: The basic currency unit in Great Britain is the pound sterling, which is divided into 100 units called *pence.* These are distributed in a £1 coin as well as 50p, 20p, 10p, 5p, 2p, and 1p coin denominations; the halfpenny ceased to be legal tender at the end of 1984. Paper money is issued in £50, £20, £10, and £5 notes. The Bank of England stopped printing £1 notes on December 31, 1984, and those remaining in circulation ceased to be legal tender in 1985. However, banks in Scotland print a version of the £1 note, and these are likely to continue circulating. Be aware that you may still find shillings, equal to 5p, in circulation, leftovers of the pre-decimal currency system. Note also that the Channel Islands and the Isle of Man have some different coins and notes from the mainland, though the monetary system is the same.

FOREIGN EXCHANGE: Rule number one is as simple as it is inflexible: Exchange your money only at banks, where dollars always buy the greatest amount of foreign currency. Unless someone holds a gun to your head, never (repeat: *never*) exchange dollars for foreign currency at hotels, restaurants, or retail shops, where you are sure to lose a significant amount of your dollars' buying power.

Rule number two: Estimate your needs carefully; if you overbuy you lose twice — buying and selling back. Every time you exchange money, someone is making a profit, and rest assured it isn't you. Although you are allowed to leave Great Britain with as much as you want, anything over $10,000 must be declared. Use up foreign notes before leaving, saving just enough for last-minute incidentals and tips.

Rule number three: Don't buy money on the black market. The exchange rate may be better, but it is a common practice to pass off counterfeit bills to unsuspecting foreigners who aren't familiar with the local currency. It's usually a sucker's game, and you are almost always the sucker; it also can land you in jail.

Rule number four: Learn the currency quickly and keep aware of daily fluctuations in the exchange rate. These are listed in the English-language *International Herald Tribune* daily for the preceding day, as well as in every major newspaper in Europe. Banks post their daily exchange rates, which might vary by a few cents from a neighboring bank's posted rate. Rates change to some degree every day. For rough calculations, it is quick and safe to use round figures, but for purchases and actual currency exchanges, carry a small pocket calculator that helps you compute the exact rate. Inexpensive calculators specifically designed to quickly convert currency amounts for travelers are widely available.

TIP PACKS: It's not a bad idea to buy a *small* amount of British coins and banknotes before your departure. But note the emphasis on the word "small," because exchange rates for these "tip packs" are uniformly terrible. Still, their advantages are threefold: You become familiar with the currency (really the only way to guard against being cheated during your first few hours in a new country); you are guaranteed some money should you arrive when a bank or exchange counter isn't open or available; and you don't have to depend on hotel desks, porters, or taxi drivers to change your money. A "tip pack" is the only British currency you should buy before you leave.

TRAVELER'S CHECKS: It's wise to carry traveler's checks on the road instead of (or in addition to) cash, since it's possible to replace traveler's checks if they are stolen or lost; travelers can usually receive partial or full replacement funds the same day if they have their purchase receipt and proper identification. Issued in various denominations and available in both US dollars and pounds sterling with adequate proof of identification (credit cards, driver's license, passport), traveler's checks are as good as cash in most hotels, restaurants, stores, and banks. However, don't assume that restaurants, smaller shops, or other establishments in small towns are going to be able to change checks of large denominations. Worldwide, more and more establishments are beginning to restrict the amount of traveler's checks they will accept or cash, so it is wise to purchase at least some of your checks in small denominations — say, $20 or the current equivalent in pounds. Also, don't expect to change them into US currency except at banks and international airports.

Every type of traveler's check is legal tender in banks around the world, and each company guarantees full replacement if checks are lost or stolen. After that the similarity ends. Some charge a fee for purchase, others are free; you can buy traveler's checks at almost any bank, and some are available by mail. Most important, each traveler's check issuer differs slightly in its refund policy — the amount refunded immediately, the accessibility of refund locations, and the availability of a 24-hour refund service.

We cannot overemphasize the importance of knowing how to replace lost or stolen checks. All of the traveler's check companies have agents around the world, both in their own name and at associated agencies (usually, but not necessarily, banks), where refunds can be obtained during business hours. Most of them also have 24-hour toll-free telephone lines, and some will even provide emergency funds to tide you over on a Sunday.

Be sure to make a photocopy of the refund instructions that will be given to you by the issuing institution at the time of purchase. To avoid complications should you need to redeem lost checks, keep the purchase receipt and an accurate list, by serial number, of the checks that have been spent or cashed. You may want to incorporate this information in an "emergency packet," also including your passport number and date of issue, the numbers of the credit cards you are carrying, and any other bits of information you can't bear to be without. Always keep these records separate from the checks and original records themselves (you may want to give them to a traveling companion to hold).

Although most people understand the necessity of carrying travel funds in the form of traveler's checks as protection against loss or theft, an equally good reason is that traveler's checks invariably get a better rate of exchange than cash does — usually by at least 1%. The reasons for this are technical, but it is a fact of travel life that should not be ignored.

That 1% won't do you much good, however, if you have already spent it buying your traveler's checks. Several of the major traveler's check companies charge 1% for the privilege of using their checks; others don't — but the issuing institution (i.e., the particular bank at which you purchase them) may itself charge a fee. Thomas Cook checks issued in US currency are free if you make your travel arrangements through its travel agency, for example; and if you purchase traveler's checks at a bank in which you or your company maintain significant accounts (especially commercial accounts of some size), you might also find that the bank will absorb the 1% fee as a courtesy. American Express traveler's checks are available without charge to members of the *Automobile Association of America* (*AAA*) if obtained at an *AAA* office.

American Express, Citicorp, Thomas Cook, MasterCard, and Visa all offer traveler's checks, but not at all locations. Call the service numbers listed below to find a participating branch near you. Note, however, that the exchange rates are usually far less favorable than those available from banks abroad, so it is generally better to carry the bulk of your travel funds overseas in US dollar traveler's checks.

Here is a list of the major traveler's check companies whose checks are accepted in Great Britain and the numbers to call in the event that loss or theft makes replacement necessary:

American Express: To report lost or stolen checks in the US, call 800-221-7282. From Great Britain, American Express advises travelers to call 44-273571-600 in Brighton, England; another (slower) option is to call 801-968-8300, collect; or contact the nearest American Express office. (As we went to press, American Express had just announced a 3-hour replacement of lost or stolen traveler's checks.)

Bank of America: To report lost or stolen checks in the US, call 800-227-3460; elsewhere worldwide, 415-624-5400 or 415-622-3800, collect.

Citicorp: To report lost or stolen checks in the US, call 800-645-6556; from Great Britain and elsewhere worldwide, call 813-623-1709, collect.

MasterCard: To report lost or stolen checks in the US, call 800-223-9920. In Great Britain call the New York office, 212-974-5696, collect, and it will direct you to the nearest branch of MasterCard or Wagons Lits, its European agent.

Thomas Cook MasterCard: To report lost or stolen checks in the US, call 800-223-9920. In Great Britain call the New York office, 212-974-5696, collect, and it will direct you to the nearest branch of Thomas Cook or Wagons-Lits, its European agent.

Visa: To report lost or stolen checks in the continental US, call 800-227-6811; 415-574-7111 collect, worldwide. From Great Britain and elsewhere in Europe, you can also call this London number collect: 01-937-8091.

CREDIT CARDS: There are two different kinds of credit cards available to consumers in the US, and travelers must decide which kind best serves their interests — although they often elect to carry both types. "Convenience" or "travel and entertainment" cards — American Express, Diners Club, and Carte Blanche — are widely accepted. They cost the cardholder a basic annual membership fee ($35 to $50 is typical for these three), but put no strict limit on the amount that may be charged on the card in any month. However, the entire amount charged must be paid in full at the end of each billing period (usually a month), so the cardholder is not actually extended any long-term credit.

"Bank cards" are also rarely issued free these days (with the exception of Sears's Discover Card), and certain services they provide (check cashing, for example) can carry an extra cost. But this category comprises *real* credit cards, in the sense that the cardholder has the privilege of paying a small amount (1/36 is typical) of the total outstanding balance in each billing period. For this privilege, the cardholder is charged a high annual interest rate (currently three to four times the going bank passbook savings rate) on the balance owed. Many banks now charge interest from the purchase date, not from the first billing date (as they used to do); consider this when you are calculating the actual cost of a purchase. In addition, a maximum is set on the total amount the cardholder can charge, which represents the limit of credit the card company is willing to extend. The major bank cards are Visa and MasterCard, with Discover growing rapidly.

Getting any credit card will involve a fairly extensive credit check; to pass, you will need a job (at which you have worked for at least a year), a minimum salary, and a good credit rating.

Note that some establishments you may encounter during the course of your travels may not honor any credit cards and some may not honor all cards, so there is a practical reason to carry more than one when you travel. Also keep in mind that some major US credit cards may be issued under a different name in Europe. For example, in Europe, MasterCard may go under the name Access or Eurocard and Visa is sometimes called Carte Bleue — wherever the equivalents are accepted, MasterCard and Visa may be used. The following is a list of credit cards that enjoy wide domestic and international acceptance:

American Express: Emergency personal check cashing at American Express or representatives' offices (up to $200 cash in local currency, $800 in traveler's checks); emergency personal check cashing for guests at participating hotels (up to $250), and, for holders of airline tickets, at participating airlines in the US (up to $250). Extended payment plan for cruises, tours, and railway and airline tickets, as well as other prepaid travel arrangements. $100,000 free travel accident insurance on plane, train, bus, and ship if ticket was charged to card; up to $1 million additional low-cost flight insurance available. Contact American Express Card, PO Box 39, Church St. Station, New York, NY 10008 (phone: 212-477-5700 in New York; 800-528-4800 elsewhere in the US).

Carte Blanche: Extended payment plan for air travel (up to $2,000). $150,000 free travel accident insurance on plane, train, and ship if ticket was charged to card, plus $1,250 checked or carry-on baggage insurance and $25,000 rental car insurance. Contact Carte Blanche, PO Box 17326, Denver, CO 80217 (phone: 800-525-9135 in the US; 303-790-2433 abroad, cardholders may call collect).

Diners Club: Emergency personal check cashing at participating Citibank branches and other designated banks worldwide (up to $1,000 in a 14-day period); emergency personal check cashing for guests at participating hotels (up to $250 per stay). Qualified card members are eligible for extended payment plan. $350,000 free travel accident insurance on plane, train, and ship if ticket was charged to your card, plus $1,250 checked and carry-on baggage insurance and $25,000 rental car insurance. Medical, legal, and travel assistance available worldwide (phone: 800-356-3448 in the US, or collect from outside the US, 214-680-6480). Contact Diners Club, PO Box 17326, Denver, CO 80217 (phone: 800-525-9135 in the US; 303-790-2433, collect, for customer service; 303-790-8632, collect 24 hours, for lost or stolen cards).

Discover Card: Created by Sears, Roebuck and Co., it provides the holder with cash advance at more than 500 locations in the US and offers a revolving credit line for purchases at a wide range of service establishments. Other deposit, lending, and investment services are also available. For information, call 800-858-5588 in the US (if you can't reach this number by dialing directly, dial for an operator who will be able to place the call).

MasterCard: Cash advance at participating banks worldwide, and a revolving credit line for purchases at a wide range of service establishments. Interest charge on unpaid balance and other details are set by issuing bank. Check with your bank for information. MasterCard also offers a 24-hour emergency lost card service; in the US call 800-336-8472; outside the US, 415-574-7700, collect.

Visa: Cash advance at participating banks worldwide, and a revolving credit line for purchases at a wide range of service establishments provided by issuer. Interest charge on unpaid balance and other details are set by issuing bank. Check with your bank for information. Visa also offers a 24-hour emergency lost card service; in the US call 800-336-8472; outside the US, 415-574-7700, collect.

One of the thorniest problems relating to the use of credit cards abroad concerns the rate of exchange at which a purchase is charged. Be aware that the exchange rate in effect on the date that you make a foreign purchase or pay for a foreign service has nothing at all to do with the rate of exchange at which your purchase is billed to you when you get the invoice months later in the US. The amount American Express (and other convenience cards) charges is ultimately a function of the exchange rate in effect on the day your charge is received at an American Express service center, and there is a 1-year limit on the time a shop or hotel can take to forward its charge slips. The rate at which Visa and other bank cards process an item is a function of the rate at which the hotel's or shop's bank processed it.

The principle at work in this credit card–exchange rate roulette is simple but very hard to predict. You make a purchase at a particular dollar versus local currency exchange rate. If the dollar gets stronger in the time between purchase and billing, your purchase actually costs you less than you anticipated. If the dollar drops in value during the interim, you pay more than you thought you would. There isn't much you can do about these vagaries except to follow one very broad, very clumsy rule of thumb: If the dollar is doing well at the time of purchase, its value increasing against the local currency, use your credit card on the assumption it will still be doing well when billing takes place. If the dollar is doing badly, assume it will continue to do badly and pay with traveler's checks. If you get too badly stuck, the best recourse is to complain, loudly. Be aware, too, that most credit card companies charge an unannounced, unitemized 1% fee for converting foreign currency charges to US dollars.

No matter what you are using — traveler's checks, credit cards, or cash — plan ahead. Also, carry your travel funds carefully. You might consider carrying your money (cash and traveler's checks) in more than one place. Never put money in a back pocket or an open purse. Money should be kept in a buttoned front pocket, in a money purse pinned inside your shirt or blouse, or in one of the convenient money belts or leg pouches sold by many travel shops. It may be quaint and old-fashioned, but it's safe.

SENDING MONEY ABROAD: If you have used up your traveler's checks, cashed as many emergency personal checks as your credit card allows, drawn on your cash advance line to the fullest extent, and still need money, have it sent abroad via the *Western Union Telegraph Company.* A friend or relative can go, cash in hand, to any of *Western Union*'s 9,000 offices in the US, where, for a *minimum* charge of $11 (it rises with the amount of the transaction) plus a $22 international bank fee, the funds will be transferred via a correspondent bank to the main post office branch in a major British city. When the money arrives, you will not be notified; you must go to the post office and ask for a registered letter. The funds will be turned over to you in local currency based on the rate of exchange in effect on the day of receipt. For a higher fee, the US party to this transaction may use his or her MasterCard or Visa card to send up to $2,000 by phone by dialing *Western Union*'s toll-free number (800-325-4176) anywhere in the US. Allow 2 to 5 business days for delivery (faster than any other form of international bank transfer, a method usually so cumbersome and time-consuming that it is of little use to the average traveler).

If you are literally down to your last few pence, the nearest US consulate (see *Medical and Legal Aid and Consular Services*) will let you call home collect to set these matters in motion.

Accommodations

From elegant, centuries-old castle resorts to modest and inexpensive guesthouses, it's easy to be comfortable and well cared for on almost any budget in Great Britain. Admittedly, there are a number of deluxe establishments providing expensive services to people with money to burn, but fortunately, affordable alternatives have always been available, particularly in the countryside.

On the whole, deluxe and first class accommodations in Great Britain, especially in the large metropolitan centers (London and Edinburgh, for instance), are just as expensive as the same types of accommodations in the US (see *Calculating Costs,* in this section). When the dollar is strong, such top-of-the-line establishments are within the range of a great number of travelers who previously would not have been able to afford them. But lately, the rate of exchange has rendered princely accommodations very pricey. Once upon a time, such things as the superiority of New World plumbing made many of the numerous less expensive alternatives unacceptable for North Americans. Today, the gap has closed considerably, and the majority of hostelries catering to the tourist trade are likely to be at least adequate in their basic facilities. When shopping around, also keep in mind that although for all accommodations in Great Britain, the price quoted must include the minimum 15% Value Added Tax (VAT), an additional service charge, usually of 10%, 12½%, or 15%, is often added to hotel and guesthouse bills.

Our accommodations choices are included in the *Best in Town* sections of THE CITIES and in the *Checking In* sections of each tour route in DIRECTIONS. They have been selected for a variety of traveling budgets, but the lists are not comprehensive; with some diligent searching, before you leave and en route, you can turn up an equal number of "special places" that are uniquely yours.

Also consult the brochures and booklets cited in the descriptions below, most of which are available free from the US offices of the British Tourist Authority (see *Tourist Information Offices* for addresses). Other publications can be purchased from the *British Travel Bookshop* (40 W. 57th St., New York, NY 10019; phone: 212-765-0898), which can send you a list of all books in stock and an order form for their purchase by mail through *GHS Inc.* (Box 1224, Clifton, NJ 07012); postage and handling charges vary from $2 to $7.50 according to the size of the order.

RESERVATIONS: To the extent that you are able to settle on a precise itinerary beforehand, it is best to make advance reservations for accommodations in any major British city or resort area, even if you are traveling during the off-season — to be sure of finding space in the hotel of your choice, several months before arrival is not to soon to make the booking. Hotel rooms in other cities should also be reserved in advance year-round. Because many of them are also important convention centers, even off-season travelers may find hotel space scarce and Full signs all over town if a large convention is being held. Also keep in mind that larger hotels are the ones most frequently booked as 2- and 3-day stopover centers for thousands of tour groups.

During the peak travel season — May to October, approximately — and during the Christmas and New Year's holidays, visitors should expect to pay a premium for traveling in Europe. However, not even a willingness to pay for top accommodations will guarantee a room if you don't have reservations. This can also be the case in smaller cities, villages, and throughout the countryside (especially in areas near major summer destinations), where the number of rooms and limited facilities, not the price, is likely to be the qualifying factor. It is wise to make reservations as far in advance as possible for popular tourist areas throughout Great Britain, and this advice becomes particularly compelling during July and August, when the British themselves take to the road, packing vacation spots and coastal resorts.

All the hotel entries in the *Best in Town* sections of THE CITIES chapters include phone numbers for reservations; however, the simplest approach may be to leave it all to a travel agent, who will provide this service at no charge if the hotel or guesthouse in question pays commissions. The accommodations guides published by the British Tourist Authority use a symbol to show which of the establishments listed pay such a commission. If the one selected doesn't, the travel agent may charge a fee to cover costs, or you may have to make the reservation yourself.

Reserving a room yourself is not difficult if you intend to stay mainly in hotels that are members of chains or associations, whether British ones with US representatives or American ones with hotels overseas. Most international hotel chains list their toll-free (800) reservation numbers in the white pages of the telephone directory, and any hotel within a chain can assure reservations for you at sister facilities. Naturally, the more links in the chain, the more likely that an entire stay can be booked with a minimum number of letters or phone calls to one central reservations system. If booking with primarily British establishments, either a travel agent or the British Tourist Authority offices will be able to tell you who in the US represents the chain or a particular hotel.

Hotels that are not represented in the US will have to be contacted directly. If you choose to write rather than telephone, it's a good idea to enclose at least two International Reply Coupons to facilitate a response and to leave plenty of time for the answer. Give full details of your requirements and several alternate dates, if possible. You will probably be asked to send a deposit for 1 night's lodging, payable by foreign draft; in return, be sure to get written confirmation of the reservation. (International Reply Coupons and foreign drafts are available at post offices and banks — check with your branches.)

If the hotel you want has no rooms available on your chosen dates, take heart. The advice to make reservations early is always woven into every travel article; making a *late* reservation may be almost as good advice. It's not at all unusual for hotel rooms, totally unavailable as far as 6 months ahead, to suddenly become available 6 days — or even 6 hours — before your arrival. Cancellations tend to occur closer to rather than farther from a designated date, and somewhat flexible travelers recognize that there will almost always be some cancellation on the day they plan to arrive.

Though not all travelers would face the prospect of arriving in a strange city without a reservation with equal sangfroid, there are services that help book empty rooms for those who risk it. Tourist Information Centres (TICs) at most British ports of entry (seaports, airports, railroad terminals) will reserve a room in the locality for a small fee — usually no more than 80p (about $1.20), except in London — or a refundable deposit or both. The London Tourist Board and Convention Bureau's Tourist Information Centres in the Heathrow Airport underground station, Victoria Railway Station, *Harrods* and *Selfridges* department stores, and the Tower of London will book hotels and budget accommodations such as guesthouses (but not hostels) within a 20-mile radius of central London. The desks of numerous hotel booking agencies, charging similar fees or deposits, are also found in rail stations and airports. These can make same-day or advance reservations for London or other parts of Britain, as can the central reservations offices of the various hotel chains and groups.

The same offices can also be used by those who prefer to give full rein to their wanderlust unhampered by hotel reservations made too far in advance. In Great Britain, any TIC displaying a Tourist Accommodation Service sign (a bed appears on it) can supply information and book a room in its locality once you've arrived. Some provide a further Book-a-Bed-Ahead (BABA) service. Go early in the day before starting out for your destination and, for a fee — usually about £1.85 (around $2.75) or a refundable deposit or both — a staff member will phone ahead to make a reservation — provided you're going to an area that also has a BABA service. You must claim your room relatively early: Bookings are provisional and are usually released at 6 PM each evening. Book-a-Bed-Ahead can also handle bed-and-breakfast accommodations, though these can be found almost as easily by just keeping an eye out for the signs on windows and gateposts or, in small villages, by asking any policeman or shopkeeper who in the area rents rooms.

OVERBOOKING: The worldwide travel boom has brought with it some abuses that are pretty much standard operating procedure in any industry facing a demand that frequently outstrips the supply. Anticipating a certain percentage of no-shows, hotels routinely overbook rooms. When cancellations don't occur and everybody with a reservation arrives as promised, it's not impossible to find yourself with a valid reservation for which no room exists.

There's no sure way to avoid all the pitfalls of overbooking, but you can minimize the risks. Always carry evidence of your confirmed reservation. This should be a direct communication from the hotel — to you or your travel agent — and should specify the exact dates and duration of your accommodations and the price. The weakest form of confirmation is the voucher slip a travel agent routinely issues, since it carries no official indication that the hotel itself has verified your reservation.

Even better is the increasing opportunity to guarantee hotel reservations by giving the hotel (or its reservation system) your credit card number and agreeing that the hotel is authorized to charge you for that room no matter what. It's still possible to cancel if you do so before 6 PM of the day of your reservations (before 4 PM in some areas), but when you do cancel under this arrangement, make sure you get a cancellation number to protect you from being billed erroneously.

If all these precautions fail and you are left standing at the reservation desk with a reservation the hotel clerk won't honor, you have a last resort: Complain as long and as loud as necessary to get satisfaction! The person who makes the most noise usually gets the last room in the house. It might as well be you.

What if you can't get reservations in the first place? This is a problem that often confronts businesspeople who can't plan months ahead. The word from savvy travelers is that a bit of currency (perhaps attached discreetly to a business card) often increases your chances with recalcitrant desk clerks. There are less venal ways of improving your odds, however. If you are traveling on business, ask an associate at your destination to make reservations for you.

There is a good reason to do this above and beyond the very real point that a resident has the broadest knowledge of local hotels. Often a hotel will appear sold out on its computer when in fact a few rooms are available. The proliferation of computerized reservations has made it unwise for a hotel to indicate that it suddenly has five rooms available (from cancellations) when there might be 30 or 40 travel agents lined up in the computer waiting for them. That small a number of vacancies is much more likely to be held by the hotel for its own sale, so a local associate is an invaluable conduit to these otherwise inaccessible rooms.

Hotels, Guesthouses, and Inns – Hotels may be large or small, part of a chain or independent, new and of the "international standard" type or well established and traditional. There are built-for-the-purposes premises and converted stately homes, resort hotels offering plenty of opportunities for recreation, motels offering virtually none. One way to help you select the type of hotel that fits your finances and personal needs is to become familiar with the official hotel grading system recently introduced in Great Britain, which enables prospective guests to sort them all out and determine what might lie behind the doors of any given hostelry. The system consists of six classifications, from five crowns (the highest rating) through four, three, and two crowns to one crown and, simply, "listed" (the lowest rating). The number of crowns rates the *range* of facilities and services offered by an establishment: For instance, in a five-crown hotel, all bedrooms must have private bathrooms (with tub and shower), whereas in a four-crown hotel, only 75% of the bedrooms must have private bathrooms (tub *or* shower). In a one-crown establishment, a guest can expect a washbasin with hot and cold running water in any bedroom without a private bathroom, whereas in an establishment that is merely listed, no private washbasin or bathroom need be provided (the number of public bathrooms depends on the number of bedrooms).

This classification scheme, run by the tourist boards of England, Scotland, and Wales, applies to all types of accommodations, from luxury hotels to humble bed-and-breakfast establishments (see below). The crown rating is posted outside the premises, but before relying on it entirely in choosing a bed for the night, it is important to note two characteristics of the scheme. For one thing, it is voluntary: An establishment requests (and pays for) inspection and rating by the pertinent tourist board, and not all hotels in Britain have yet done so or even intend to do so. For another, the crowns merely guarantee the existence of the facilities and services rated, they do not assess the quality. Thus, a five-crown hotel could be a clean, comfortable, but characterless place to sleep, while a listed accommodation might be simple yet above average in charm, run with attention to detail and a high degree of hospitality. Recognizing this deficiency, the Scottish Tourist Board has added estimates of quality to the basic crown scheme, rating Scottish hotels as "approved," "commended," and "highly commended," and the English and Welsh tourist boards may eventually follow suit.

No matter what their crown rating, all participating establishments are required to supply adequate heating according to the season and to serve breakfast. In any British hotel, whether participating or not, breakfast is apt to be included in the quoted price of the room, and it is usually a full one of juice, coffee or tea, rolls, cereal, eggs, and bacon or sausage, although there is a growing tendency in the larger urban hotels to substitute a continental breakfast (coffee and rolls) or to charge separately for the full one. A service charge of 10% to 15% may be added to bills at some properties in addition to a compulsory 15% Value Added Tax (VAT). Hotels, motels, guesthouses, and inns with four rooms or more are required to display minimum and maximum room prices in a manner that clearly shows what is included. If it is not clear, be sure to ask in advance what the final tab will be, since the extras can add considerably to the bill. (To reduce it, consider traveling off-season, and investigate the hotel "mini-breaks" offered by many British chains. These packages allow a discount for stays of 2 nights or more, usually weekends, and can be in effect at any time of the year.)

At present, the most comprehensive guide to British hotels available to the general public is *Hotels and Restaurants in Britain* ($19.95), published by Britain's *Automobile Association* (*AA*). It lists room prices inclusive of extras and rates hotels according to the *AA*'s own long-established star system. Other books to consult are *Scotland: Hotels and Guesthouses, Wales: Hotels and Guesthouses,* and the British Tourist Authority's *England: Where to Stay/Hotels, Motels, Guesthouses, and Universities in England,* available for $8.95, $6.45, and $11.95 respectively. Listings in all three of these reflect the new crown ratings. A good book for those interested in information on London alone is the London Visitor and Convention Bureau's *Where to Stay in London* ($4.95), which also uses the crown ratings. All the publications mentioned here are available from the *British Travel Bookshop* (address above).

A word about guesthouses: These are to Britain what pensions are to the Continent. They are found everywhere and especially at seaside resorts, where the vacationing British keep them heavily booked all summer long. Also called private hotels or board residences, they are generally small, family-run, and in the budget category. Unlike hotels, guesthouses do not provide meals for non-guests, and unlike inns, they usually are not licensed to serve alcohol. The standard practice is to include breakfast in the room price; some offer an evening meal if desired. Prices are typically from $15 to $30 per person double occupancy, and for this, there is usually no private bath, nor is there always running water in the bedroom. A special group of guesthouses provide outstanding amenities and service and cost more; see *Commended Country Hotels, Guest Houses, and Restaurants,* a free British Tourist Authority publication listing establishments that have won favor in a BTA-operated commendation scheme (which predates the crown scheme and provides one level of award only). Guesthouses are also to be found in the national tourist board and other accommodations guides mentioned above.

Inns are of particular interest to travelers attracted by the prospect of sampling the lodgings of another age. There are inns dating to medieval times and many more not quite so old that have nevertheless been in business for centuries. An inn was, first of all, a wayside watering place for travelers passing on foot, horseback, or by coach, but laws requiring the innkeeper to provide food for the drinkers and accommodations for the diners turned innkeepers into hoteliers. The focal point of an inn is still its public bar; the number of rooms is therefore usually limited, and some in city centers do not provide accommodations at all. What remains of bygone days is the charm of thatched roofs, timbered façades, cobblestone courtyards, beamed ceilings, and the occasional four-poster bed. Heating and hot and cold water in the rooms have been added, though private bathrooms are usually lacking. Inns are found in any price range, from $15 per person double and up. The British Tourist Authority's free *Stay at an Inn* lists a selection of inns found in historic towns all over Britain.

Castles and Country Homes – Found throughout the British Isles, these inns specialize in the traditional atmosphere, service, and hospitality typical of a great country estate. Many were once country homes, ancestral manor houses, or castles, and a number are noteworthy for architectural features, surrounding gardens or parklands, river- or lakeside settings, or locations in dell, dale, and mountain. The real attraction, however, is the history associated with so many of them and their antique decor. Most have modern amenities (television sets, private baths) along with traditional features such as fireplaces and sitting rooms. They are much sought out by the British themselves as weekend retreats. Weekend reservations are a must; midweek reservations are strongly recommended during high season and around the holidays. Prices are not economy class — from $35 up per person double, including breakfast.

Some of these properties are members of the prestigious French hotel association *Relais & Châteaux* (catalogue available for $5 including postage and handling from travel bookshops or from *David B. Mitchell & Company* (200 Madison Ave., New York, NY 10016; phone: 212-696-1323 or 800-696-1323). Others are listed in the British Tourist Authority's free publication *Commended Country Hotels, Guest Houses, and Restaurants.*

Bed-and-breakfast – Bed-and-breakfast establishments (commonly known as B&Bs) provide exactly what the name implies. Though any hotel or guesthouse does the same, it is unusual for a bed-and-breakfast establishment to offer the extra services found in the other establishments, and consequently the bed-and-breakfast route is often the least expensive way to go.

Beyond these two fundamentals, nothing else is predictable about going the bed-and-breakfast route. The bed may be in an extra room in a family home, in an apartment with a separate entrance, or in a free-standing cottage elsewhere on the host's property. You may have a patio, garden, or pool at your door, or only the bare necessities. Accommodations range from private homes and lovely mansions to small inns and guesthouses. Private baths are rare; in recompense, the breakfasts are hearty, home-cooked, and, as often as not, served along with some helpful tips on what to see and do and a bit of family history to add to the local lore.

Bed-and-breakfast houses are a staple of the low-cost lodging scene in Great Britain wherever there is an extra room to rent in a private house and a landlady or landlord willing to attend to the details of this homespun form of hospitality. Prices average from $12 to $20 per person per night, breakfast included, and despite their name, some B&Bs offer an evening meal as well — by prior arrangement and at extra cost, naturally.

The best rule of thumb is to find out as much as you can before you book to avoid disappointment. The British Tourist Authority publishes a leaflet explaining the bed-and-breakfast idea, and the national tourist boards and other organizations publish annual B&B guides. See *Scotland: Bed-and-breakfast* ($6.45), *Wales: Bed-and-breakfast* ($5.25), *Where to Stay: Farmhouses, Bed-and-Breakfast, Inns, and Hostels in England* ($9.75), and the *AA Bed-and-Breakfast in Britain* ($12.95), all available through the *British Travel Bookshop* (address above). If you wish to travel unencumbered, however, the tourist information center in any British town will have a list of bed-and-breakfast establishments nearby.

Farmhouses – In the country, city people rediscover the sounds of songbirds and the smell of grass. Suburbanites get the chance to poke around an area where the nearest neighbor lives miles away. Parents can say to their children, "No, milk does not start out in a carton," and prove it. Youngsters can see people who live differently, think differently, and have different values. But even if there were no lessons to be learned, a stay at a farm would be a decidedly pleasant way to pass a couple of weeks, so it's no wonder that throughout Great Britain there are hundreds of farms welcoming guests.

Farm families often put up guests on a bed-and-breakfast basis — for a night or two or by the week, with weekly half-board plans available. Many of the listings in the British Tourist Authority's free *Stay on a Farm* booklet carry a brief description of the farm, allowing travelers to pick a traditional or a modern farm, a dairy farm over a sheep farm, one with ponies to ride or one near a river for fishing. If the peace and quiet and the coziness of the welcome are appealing, a farmhouse can be an ideal base from which to explore a region by car or by foot and an especially good idea for those traveling with children.

Another useful source of information on bed-and-breakfast establishments overseas is the annual brochure published by the *Bed & Breakfast Reservations Services Worldwide* (a trade association), which provides a list of its members. It costs $3; to order the most recent edition write to Bed & Breakfast Reservations Services Worldwide, PO Box 14797, Dept. 174, Baton Rouge, LA 70898, or call 504-346-1928 or 800-842-1486.

Apartments, Homes, and Cottages – Another alternative to hotels for the visitor content to stay in one spot for a week or more is to rent a house or an apartment (usually called a "flat" overseas). Known to Europeans as a "holiday let" or a "self-catering holiday," a vacation in a furnished rental has both the advantages and disadvantages of living "at home" abroad. It is certainly less expensive than staying in a first class hotel for the same period of time (though luxury rentals are available, too); it has the comforts of home, including a kitchen, which means saving on food; and it gives a sense of the country that a large hotel often cannot. On the other hand, a certain amount of housework is involved because if you don't eat out, you have to cook, and though some holiday lets come with a cleaning person, most don't.

The British Tourist Authority publishes *Holiday Homes* and *Apartments in London,* two free booklets that give information on rental agencies and individual properties in Great Britain. Further guides to self-catering accommodations are published by the British *Automobile Association* (*AA*) and by the English and Scottish Tourist Boards; the Wales Tourist Board includes self-catering accommodations in its *Where to Stay in Wales* guide.

In addition, companies in the US arrange rentals throughout Great Britain. They handle bookings and confirmation paperwork, generally for a fee included in the rental price. Among such agencies are the following:

At Home Abroad: British cottages and country houses, primarily in Sussex and the Cotswolds. Photographs of properties can be requested by mail for a $50 registration fee. 405 E. 56th St., Apt. 6H, New York, NY 10022 (phone: 212-421-9165).

Campus Holidays USA: Home stay accommodations in England, Scotland, and Ireland for those interested in experiencing the British way of life. It includes single, twin, and even triple rooms for friends or family traveling together in typical British family homes. 242 Bellevue Ave., Upper Montclair, NJ 07043 (phone: 201-744-8724 in New Jersey; 800-526-2915 elsewhere in the US).

Castles, Cottages and Flats of Ireland and UK, Ltd.: The specialty is cottages in England's heartland, but also featured are properties elsewhere in England, Wales, and Scotland as well as London flats. Small charge ($3.50) for receipt of main catalogue, refundable upon booking. Box 261, Westwood, MA 02090 (phone: 617-329-4680).

Country Homes and Castles: The specialty is large properties — castles, manor houses, stately homes — throughout Great Britain. 4092 N. Ivy Rd., Atlanta, GA 30342 (phone: 404-231-5837), and 900 Wilshire Blvd., Suite 830, Los Angeles, CA 90017 (phone: 213-629-4861).

Eastone Overseas Accommodations: A huge selection of houses and cottages in England and Scotland and a few in Wales; flats in London and other major towns. 198 Southampton Dr., Jupiter, FL 33458 (phone: 407-575-6991/2).

Livingstone Holidays: Cottages in the Cotswolds, Norfolk, Devon, Cornwall, and other areas of England, as well as London flats. Small charge ($2) for larger brochures. 1720 E. Garry, Suite 204, Santa Anna, CA 92705 (phone: 714-476-2823).

Rent a Vacation Everywhere (*RAVE*): Mostly flats in London, plus houses and cottages in the Cotswolds and elsewhere. 328 Main St. E., Suite 526, Rochester, NY 14604 (phone: 716-454-6440).

Villas International Ltd. (formerly *Interchange*): Specializes in London flats, also has country houses, from cottages to castles, throughout Great Britain. 71 W. 23rd St., New York, NY 10010 (phone: 212-929-7585 in New York State; 800-221-2260 elsewhere in the US).

Home Exchanges – Another alternative for families who are content to stay in one place during their vacation is a home exchange: The Smith family from Chicago moves into the home of the Hansen family in Bristol, while the Hansens enjoy a stay in the Smiths' home. The home exchange is an exceptionally inexpensive way to ensure comfortable, reasonable living quarters with amenities that no hotel could possibly offer; often the trade includes a car. Moreover, it allows you to live in a new community in a way that few tourists ever do: For a little while, at least, you will become a resident.

Several companies publish directories of individuals and families willing to trade homes with others for a specific period of time. In some cases, you must be willing to list your own home in the directory; in others, you can subscribe without appearing in it. Most listings are for straight exchanges only, but each of the directories also has a number of listings placed by people interested in either exchanging or renting (for instance, if they own a second home). Other types of arrangements include exchanges of hospitality while owners are in residence or youth exchanges, where your teenager is put up as a guest in return for your putting up their teenager at a later date. A few house-sitting opportunities are also available. In most cases, arrangements for the actual exchange take place directly between you and the foreign host. There is no guarantee that you will find a listing in the area in which you are interested, but each of the organizations given below includes British homes among its hundreds or even thousands of foreign listings.

International Home Exchange Service/Intervac US: The $35 fee includes copies of the three directories published yearly and a listing in one of them. (Directories are available without a listing for $45.) A 20% discount is given to travelers over 65. PO Box 3975, San Francisco, CA 94119 (phone: 415-435-3497).

InterService Home Exchange: An affiliate of *Intervac International,* this service publishes three directories annually that include more than 6,000 exchanges in over 300 countries worldwide. For $35, interested home-swappers are listed in and receive a copy of the February, March, and May directories; a black and white photo of your home may be included with the listing for an additional $10. Box 387, Glen Echo, MD 20812 (phone: 301-229-7567).

Loan-A-Home: Specializes in long-term (4 months or more — excluding July and August) housing arrangements worldwide for students and professors, business-people, and retirees, although its two annual directories (with supplements) carry a small listing of short-term rentals and/or exchanges. $30 for a copy of one directory and one supplement; $40 for a copy of two directories and two supplements. 2 Park La., 6E, Mt. Vernon, NY 10552 (phone: 914-664-7640).

Vacation Exchange Club: Some 6,000 listings, about half of which are foreign. For $24.70, subscribers receive two directories, one in late winter, one in the spring, and are listed in one. For $16, they receive both directories but no listing. 12006 111th Ave., Suite 12, Youngtown, AZ 85363 (phone: 602-972-2186).

World Wide Exchange: The $45 annual membership fee includes one listing (for house, yacht, or motorhome) and three guides. 1344 Pacific Ave., Suite 103, Santa Cruz, CA 95060 (phone: 408-425-0531).

Home Exchange International (*HEI*), with offices in New York, Los Angeles, London, Paris, and Milan, functions differently in that it publishes no directory and shepherds the exchange process most of the way. Interested parties supply *HEI* with photographs of themselves and their homes, information on the type of home they want and where, and a registration fee of $40. The company then works with its other offices to propose a few possibilities, and only when a match is made do the parties exchange names, addresses, and phone numbers. For this service, *HEI* charges a closing fee, which ranges from $150 to $450 for domestic or international switches from 2 weeks to 3 months and from $275 to $525 for switches longer than 3 months. Contact Home Exchange International, 185 Park Row, PO Box 878, New York, NY 10038-0272 (phone: 212-349-5340), or 22458 Ventura Blvd., Woodland Hills, CA 91364 (phone: 818-992-8990).

HOME STAYS: If the idea of actually staying in a private home as the guest of a foreign family appeals to you, check with the United States Servas Committee, which maintains a list of hosts throughout the world willing to open their doors to foreigners entirely free of charge. The aim of this non-profit cultural program is to promote international understanding and peace, and every effort is made to discourage freeloaders. Servas will send you an application form and the name of the nearest of some 200 interviewers around the US for you to contact. After the interview, if you're approved, you'll receive documentation certifying you as a Servas traveler. There is a membership fee of $45 for an individual, as well as a deposit of $15 to receive the host list, refunded on its return. The list gives the name, address, age, occupation, and other particulars of the hosts, including languages spoken. From then on, it is up to you to write to them directly, and Servas makes no guarantee that you will be accommodated. If you are, you'll normally stay 2 nights.

Servas stresses that you should choose only people you really want to meet and that for this brief period you should be interested mainly in your hosts, not in sightseeing. It also suggests that one way to show your appreciation once you've returned home is to become a host yourself. The minimum age of a Servas traveler is 18 (however, children under 18 may accompany their parents), and though quite a few are young people who've just finished college, there are travelers (and hosts) in all age ranges and occupations. Contact Servas at 11 John St., Room 706, New York, NY 10038 (phone: 212-267-0252).

Another organization arranging home stays is *In the English Manner,* which specializes in home stays with British families, who open their homes to guests. Prospective hosts have been visited by the company to assure that only those genuinely interested in meeting foreigners and making their stay a memorable experience participate. Hosts, in fact, are probably better screened than guests, who need merely supply the company with family members' names and ages, occupations, special interests, and other pertinent data, such as allergies. The company then selects a few possible hosts and lets the client make the final decision. There is a minimum stay of 3 nights, which can be divided among three different families if desired, but no maximum stay except what is mutually agreeable to both hosts and guests. The entire cost of the stay is paid in advance. Meals that guests decide upon in advance are also prepaid; meals and other extras decided upon during the stay are paid in cash on departure (to avoid embarrassment, the company advises clients beforehand what the hosts charge). The program is not for budget travelers, since the cost ranges from small houses at $120 for two up to castle accommodations at $200 per night per couple, with an average of $160 to $170 per night. But the homes in Great Britain — about 80 of them — are not ordinary; they include several country houses, some larger stately homes, and a castle. Single rates are available, and there are reductions for children. Contact In the English Manner, PO Box 936, Alamo, CA 95407 (phone: 415-935-7065 in California; 800-422-0799 elsewhere in the US). For other organizations and services offering home exchanges, contact the local tourist authority.

Time Zones and Business Hours

TIME ZONES: The countries of Europe fall into three time zones. Greenwich Mean Time — measured from Greenwich, England, at longitude 0°0′ — is the base from which all other time zones are measured. Areas in zones west of Greenwich have earlier times and are called Greenwich Minus; those to the east have later times and are called Greenwich Plus. For example, New York City is 5 zones west, or 5 hours earlier, than Greenwich (so it is Greenwich Minus 5); when it is noon in Greenwich, it is 7 AM in New York.

Because the British move their clocks an hour ahead in the spring and an hour back in the fall, corresponding to daylight saving time in the US, the same differential between time zones is maintained nearly all year.

British timetables use a 24-hour clock to denote arrival and departure times, which means that hours are expressed sequentially from 1 AM. For example, the departure of a train at 6 AM will be announced as "0600;" one leaving at 6 PM will be noted as "1800." A noon departure would be "1200," and midnight, "2400."

PUBLIC HOLIDAYS: In England and Wales, the public holidays are *New Year's Day* (January 1), *Good Friday, Easter Monday, May Day* (first Monday in May), *Spring Bank Holiday* (last Monday in May), *Summer Bank Holiday* (last Monday in August), *Christmas Day* (December 25), and *Boxing Day* (December 26).

In Scotland, they are *New Year's Day* (January 1), *Bank Holiday* (January 3), *Good Friday, Bank Holiday* (late May), *Summer Bank Holiday* (early August); *Christmas Day* (December 25), and *Boxing Day* (December 26).

BUSINESS HOURS: Most businesses in Great Britain are open weekdays from 9 AM to 5 or 5:30 PM. Shops follow roughly the same schedule, staying open until 5:30

or 6 PM, and are also open on Saturdays. In small towns and villages, shops may close for an hour at lunchtime, and on at least one weekday they close at 1 PM. Some stores may skip the early closing and simply not open on Mondays; others may close completely or early on Saturdays. Larger stores in shopping centers stay open till 8 or 9 PM at least 1 day a week (Thursdays in most cases, but sometimes Wednesdays). For information on pub hours, see *Drinking and Drug Laws.*

Banks are open from 9:30 AM to 3:30 PM, weekdays. In Scotland, there is a break for lunch (12:30 to 1:30 PM). Most banks are closed on weekends and public holidays, although major airport banks are open 7 days a week and *some* bank branches may open Saturday mornings.

Mail, Telephone, and Electricity

MAIL: The equivalent of US general delivery is called general post office or *Poste Restante* in Great Britain and is probably the best way for travelers to have mail sent if they do not have a definite address. As there are often several post offices in major cities, it is important that the address and/or specific name of the office be indicated (not just the name of the city), and travelers should be sure to call at the correct office when inquiring after mail. Post offices are open weekdays from 9 AM to 5:30 PM and on Saturdays from 9 AM until 12:30 or 1 PM. Main post offices in London keep longer hours and are open on Sundays as well.

If you are an American Express customer (a cardholder, a carrier of American Express traveler's checks, or traveling on an *American Express Travel Service* tour) you can have mail sent to its offices in cities on your route; letters are held free of charge — registered mail and packages are not accepted. You must be able to show an American Express card, traveler's checks, or a voucher proving you are on one of the company's tours to avoid paying for mail privileges. Those who aren't clients must pay a nominal charge each time they ask if they have received mail, whether they actually have a letter or not. There is also a forwarding fee, for clients and non-clients alike. Mail should be addressed to you, care of American Express, and should be marked "Client Mail Service." Additional information on its mail service and addresses of American Express offices in Great Britain are listed in the pamphlet *Services and Offices,* available from the nearest US branch of American Express.

US embassies and consulates abroad do not accept mail for tourists. They will, however, help out in emergencies, if you need to receive important business documents or personal papers, for example. It is best to inform them either by separate letter or cable, or by phone if you are in the country already, that you will be using their address for this purpose.

TELEPHONE: Direct dialing within the country, between nations, and overseas is possible in England, Scotland, and Wales. There are a lot of digits involved once you start dialing outside the national borders, but avoiding operator-assisted calls can cut costs considerably and bring rates into a reasonable range — except for calls made through hotel switchboards. One of the most unpleasant surprises travelers encounter is the amount they find tacked on to their hotel bill for telephone calls, because foreign hotels routinely add surcharges that can be the equivalent of a daily room rate. It's not at all uncommon to find 300% or 400% added on for telephone charges.

Until recently, the only recourse against this unconscionable overcharging was to call collect from abroad or to use a telephone credit card (available through a simple procedure from any local US phone company). Now, *American Telephone and Telegraph* (*AT&T*) offers USA Direct, a service that connects users, via a toll-free number, with an *AT&T* operator in the US, who will then put a call through at the standard international rate. For a brochure and wallet card listing toll-free numbers by country, contact International Information Service, AT&T Communications (635 Grant St., Pittsburgh, PA 15219; phone: 800-874-4000). *International Telecharge* (108 S. Akard, Dallas, TX 75252; phone: 800-234-4840) offers a similar service, Diplomat (formerly, Quick Call USA).

AT&T has also put together Teleplan, an agreement among certain hoteliers that sets a limit on surcharges for calls made by guests from their rooms. Teleplan is currently in effect in selected hotels in Great Britain. Teleplan agreements stipulate a flat amount for credit card or collect calls (currently between $1 and $10), and a flat percentage (between 20% and 100%) on calls paid for at the hotel. For further information, contact *AT&T*'s International Information Service (address above).

Until Teleplan becomes universal, it's wise to ask the surcharge rate *before* calling from a hotel. If the rate is high, it's best to use a telephone credit card or one of the direct-dial services listed above, place the call collect, or place the call and ask the party to call right back. If none of these choices is possible, make international calls from the local post office or special telephone center to avoid surcharges.

Making connections in Europe can sometimes be hit or miss — all exchanges are not always in operation on the same day. If the number dialed does not go through, try later or the next day. So be warned: Those who have to make an important call — to make a hotel reservation in another city, for instance — should do so a few days ahead.

ELECTRICITY: The US runs on 110-volt, 60-cycle alternating current; Great Britain uses 220- or 240-volt, 50-cycle alternating current. The large difference between US and European voltage means that, without a converter, the motor of a US appliance used overseas would run at twice the speed at which it's meant to operate and would quickly burn out. Travelers can solve the problem by buying a lightweight converter to transform foreign voltage into the domestic kind (there are two types of converters, depending on the wattage of the appliance) or by buying dual-voltage appliances that convert from one to the other at the flick of a switch (hair dryers of this sort are common). The difference between the 50-cycle and 60-cycle currents will cause no problem — the appliance will simply run more slowly — but it will still be necessary to deal with differing socket configurations before plugging in.

Sets of plugs for use worldwide can be bought at hardware stores or from the *Franzus Company* (53 W. 23rd St., New York, NY 10010; phone: 212-463-9593). *Franzus* also publishes a useful brochure, *Foreign Electricity Is No Deep Dark Secret,* which provides information about converters and adapter plugs for electric appliances to be used abroad but manufactured for use in the US.To obtain a free copy, send a stamped, self-addressed envelope to *Franzus* at the above address; a catalogue of other travel accessories is available on request.

Medical and Legal Aid and Consular Services

MEDICAL AID ABROAD: You will discover, in the event of an emergency, that most tourist facilities — transportation companies, hotels, and resorts — are equipped to handle the situation quickly and efficiently. Most towns and cities of any size have a public hospital and even the tiniest hamlet has a medical clinic or private physician nearby. The level of medical care available in Great Britain is generally excellent, providing the same basic specialties and services that are available in the US. All hospitals are prepared for emergency cases, and many hospitals also have walk-in clinics to serve people who do not really need emergency service, but who have no place to go for immediate medical attention.

Before you go, be sure to check with your insurance company about the applicability of your policy while you're abroad; many policies do not apply, and others are not accepted in Europe. Older travelers should know that Medicare does not make payments outside the US, and — contrary to lingering popular belief — Britain's National Health Service (NHS) provides free medical aid to tourists *only* for treatment in hospital accident and emergency wards and for the diagnosis and treatment of certain communicable diseases. Most visitors (except citizens of Common Market countries or of those with which Great Britain has reciprocal agreements) are liable for all other medical charges, including hospitalization resulting from an accident or emergency. If your medical policy does not protect you while you're traveling, there are comprehensive combination policies specifically designed to fill the gap. For a discussion of medical insurance and a list of inclusive combination policies, see *Insurance,* in this section.

If a bona fide emergency occurs, the fastest way to receive attention may be to take a taxi to the emergency room (or "casualty department") of the nearest hospital. An alternative is to dial 999, the free nationwide emergency number used to summon the police, fire trucks, and ambulances. Since ambulance dispatchers are accustomed to taking calls from doctors only, state immediately that you are a foreign tourist and then the nature of your problem and your location. Keep in mind that a taxi may be a faster way to reach help at night, however, when emergency service rotates among hospitals; first call 999 to find out which one in a given area is on duty.

If a doctor is needed for something less than an emergency, there are several ways to find one. Ask at the hotel or check at the post office, where neighborhood NHS physicians are supposed to be listed (though they often aren't). Dialing 999 will also be of help. Callers will often be given the name of a general practitioner, since private doctors, usually specialists, may see patients upon referral only. For the seriously ill or injured traveler, however, it is best to see a private doctor. Although it goes beyond the bounds of the NHS system to do so, it's usually possible to find a private doctor without referral from a general practitioner through the US Consulate (see address and phone number below) or directly through a hospital, especially if you are in an emergency situation. If you are already at the hospital, you may see the specialist there, or you may make an appointment to be seen at his or her office (or "surgery").

In addition, though general practitioners deliver primary care, there is no violation of protocol in approaching a specialist directly. Call the appropriate department of a teaching hospital or the US Embassy (address and phone number below), which also maintains a list of doctors. Remember that if you are hospitalized you will have to pay, even in an emergency.

If you are staying in a hotel or motel, ask for help in reaching a doctor or other emergency services, or for the house physician, who may visit you in your room or ask you to visit an office. (This service is apt to be expensive, especially if the doctor makes a "house" call to your room.)

Emergency dental care is also available throughout Great Britain (again, see the front page of the local telephone directory), although travelers are strongly advised to have a dental checkup some weeks before the trip to allow time for any necessary work to be done.

There should be no problem finding a 24-hour drugstore ("chemist") in any major British city — for one thing, chemists who close are required to give the addresses of the nearest all-night drugstores in the window. In the case of minor complaints, British pharmacists may do some prescribing, and some are not averse to filling a foreign prescription; however, do not count on this — you may have to have a local doctor rewrite the prescription. Nevertheless, to make most effective use of the drugstore, it's a good idea to ask your doctor for the generic names of any drugs you use so that you can ask for their equivalents should you need a refill. Americans will also notice that some drugs sold only by prescription in the US are sold over the counter in Great Britain. Though this can be very handy, be aware that common cold medicines and aspirin that contain codeine or other controlled substances will not be allowed back into the US.

Emergency assistance is also available from the various medical programs designed for travelers who have chronic ailments or whose illness requires them to return home. The *Medic Alert Foundation* sells identification emblems that specify that the wearer has a health condition that may not be readily apparent to a casual observer. A heart condition, diabetes, epilepsy, and severe allergy are the sorts of things that these emblems were developed to communicate, conditions that can result in tragic errors if not recognized when emergency treatment is necessary and when you may be unable to speak for yourself. In addition to the identification emblems, the foundation maintains a computerized central file from which your complete medical history is available 24 hours a day by telephone (the phone number is clearly inscribed on the ID badge). The one-time membership ranges from $25 to $45, is tax deductible, and is based on the type of metal from which the emblem is made — the choices ranging from stainless steel to 10K gold-filled. For information, contact the Medic Alert Foundation, Turlock, CA 95381-1009 (phone: 209-668-3333 or 800-ID-ALERT).

International SOS Assistance also offers a program to cover medical emergencies while traveling. Members are provided with telephone access — 24 hours a day, 365 days a year — to a worldwide, monitored, multilingual network of medical centers. A phone call brings assistance ranging from a telephone consultation to transportation home by ambulance or aircraft, and in some cases transportation of a family member to wherever you are hospitalized. The service can be purchased for a week ($15), a week plus additional days ($15, plus $2 for each additional day), a month ($45), or a year ($195). For information, contact International SOS Assistance, PO Box 11568, Philadelphia, PA 19116 (phone: 215-244-1500 or 800-523-8930).

The *International Association for Medical Assistance to Travellers* (*IAMAT*) provides its members with a directory of affiliated medical centers in over 140 countries (500 cities, including London and Edinburgh) to call for a list of participating doctors. A non-profit organization, *IAMAT* appreciates donations; for $25, a set of worldwide climate charts detailing weather and sanitary conditions will be included. To join, write well before your trip (processing takes about 3 weeks) to IAMAT, 417 Center St., Lewiston, NY 14092 (phone: 716-754-4883).

The *International Health Care Service* provides information about health conditions in various countries, advice on immunizations recommended, and treatment if necessary. A pre-travel counseling and immunization package costs $175; a post-travel screening, $75 plus lab work. Appointments are necessary. The service also publishes *The International Health Care Travelers Guide,* available for $4.50 with a self-addressed envelope. Contact the International Health Care Service, New York Hospital–Cornell Medical Center, 440 E. 69th St., New York, NY 10021 (phone: 212-472-4284).

Those who return home ill with a condition they suspect is travel related and beyond the experience of their regular physician should consider seeing a specialist in travel medicine. For information on finding such a specialist in your area, see *Staying Healthy,* in this section.

For a thorough description of the medical services in Great Britain's larger cities, see *Traveling Healthy,* by Sheilah M. Hillman and Robert S. Hillman, M.D. Unfortunately out of print, it may be found in the library.

Practically every phase of health care — before, during, and after a trip — is covered in *The New Traveler's Health Guide* by Drs. Patrick J. Doyle and James E. Banta. It is available for $4.95, plus $2 postage and handling, from Acropolis Books Ltd., 2400 17th St. NW, Washington, DC 20009-9964 (phone: 800-451-7771).

LEGAL AID ABROAD: It is often far more alarming to be arrested abroad than at home for an infringement of the law. Not only are you alone among strangers, but the punishment can be worse. Granted, the US consulate can advise you of your rights and provide a list of lawyers (called "solicitors"), but it cannot interfere with local due process. The best advice is to be honest and law-abiding. If you get a traffic ticket, pay it. If you are approached by drug hawkers, ignore them. The penalties for possession of hashish, marijuana, cocaine, and other narcotics are generally more severe than in the US.

CONSULAR SERVICES: There is one crucial place to keep in mind when outside the US, namely, the American Services section of the US Consulate. If you are injured or become seriously ill, the consulate will direct you to medical assistance and notify your relatives. If, while abroad, you become involved in a dispute that could lead to legal action, the consulate, once again, is the place to turn. And in case of natural disasters or civil unrest, consulates around the world handle the evacuation of US citizens if it is necessary. Keep in mind, though, that nowhere does the consulate act as an arbitrator or ombudsman on an American citizen's behalf. The consul has no power, authorized or otherwise, to subvert, alter, or contravene the legal processes, however unfair, of the country in which he or she serves. Nor can a consul oil the machinery of a foreign bureaucracy or provide legal advice. The consul's responsibilities do include providing a list of lawyers and information on local sources of legal aid, informing relatives in the US, and organizing and administrating any defense monies sent from home. If a case is tried unfairly or the punishment seems unusually severe, the consul can make a formal complaint to the authorities. In a case of what is called "legitimate and proven poverty" — of an American stranded abroad without funds — the consul will contact sources of money, such as family or friends in the US, and, as a last resort, arrange for repatriation at government expense, although this is a loan, which must be repaid.

Do not expect the consulate to help you with trivial difficulties such as canceled reservations or lost baggage. The consulate is primarily concerned with the day-to-day administration of services such as issuing passports and visas; providing notarial services; the distribution of VA, social security, and civil service benefits to resident Americans; depositions; extradition cases; and reports to Washington of births and deaths of US citizens.

The US Embassies in Great Britain are at the following addresses: 24/31 Grosvenor Sq. W., London W1A 1AE (phone: 01-499-9000), and 3 Regent Terr., Edinburgh EH7 5BW (phone: 031-556-8315).

The US State Department operates a Citizens Emergency Center, which offers a number of services to American travelers abroad and their families at home. In addition to giving callers up-to-date information on trouble spots, the center will contact authorities abroad in an attempt to locate a traveler or deliver an urgent message. In case of death, illness, arrest, destitution, or repatriation of an American citizen on foreign soil, it will relay information to relatives here if the consulate is unable to do so. Travel advisory information is available 24 hours a day to people with Touch-Tone phones by calling 202-647-5225. Callers with rotary phones can get travel advisory information at this number from 8:15 AM to 10 PM on weekdays; 9 AM to 3 PM Saturdays. For emergency calls, from 8:15 AM to 10 PM weekdays, and 9 AM to 3 PM Saturdays, call 202-647-5225. For emergency calls only, at all other times, call 202-634-3600 and ask for the Duty Officer.

Drinking and Drug Laws

DRINKING: It is more than likely that some of the warmest memories of a trip to Great Britain will be moments of conviviality shared over a drink in a neighborhood pub. As in the US, national taxes on alchohol affect the prices of liquor in Great Britain. Prices for mixed drinks are somewhat more expensive than at home, although local brews are reasonably priced, so take this opportunity to savor them at the source.

Visitors will find that liquor, wine, and brandies are distilled to the same proof and often are the same labels as those found at home. However, British beers and ales tend to be about 5% higher in alcohol content and have quite a different flavor from those brewed in the US. You'll want to try the specialties: English ale and Scotch whisky (Gaelic for "water of life." Note also the spelling: the Scottish don't like to be called "Scotch" — it's a drink, not a nationality) are the favorites in British pubs. Whisky may be tempered with a little water or ice, and ale comes at room temperature, except when it is called lager, which is usually chilled. (For a more thorough discussion of British beverages, see *Food and Drink,* PERSPECTIVES, and *Pub Crawling,* DIVERSIONS.)

Pub hours in Britain vary slightly and confuse everyone. To make matters even worse, the regulations relating to "opening hours" have recently been changed. In England — and not in any other country in Great Britain — the old regulations allowed a pub to open at 11 AM, serve drinks until 3 PM, then close until 5:30 PM and remain open until 11 PM. A recent amendment eliminated the 3-5:30 PM closing, but *only* for those establishments in which a "real" meal is available and on the table with your beer mug during that period. It's too early to appraise how the broad range of pub owners will adopt this change, since the meal specified under the new rules must be one that is eaten with a knife and fork. Normal "pub grub" munchies — sandwiches, or finger foods such as Scotch eggs, for example — don't qualify. Sunday hours are shorter: noon to 3 PM and 7 to 10 PM. And to confuse you completely, opening and closing hours in Scotland and Wales are entirely different. In addition, there are local quirks to deal with, such as places in Scotland that stay open all afternoon and those in parts of Scotland and Wales that close all day Sunday.

- **Two warnings:** The legal age for drinking is 18. Those under 18 are allowed into pubs but cannot be served alcoholic beverages. When setting off to do some serious pub crawling, visitors should leave their cars behind and make alternate plans for transportation back to the hotel. Britain has strict laws against drunk driving, and they are zealously enforced.

DRUGS: Illegal narcotics are not as prevalent in Great Britain as in the US, and the moderate legal and social acceptance that marijuana has won in the US has no counterpart in Great Britain.

The best advice we can offer is: Don't carry, use, buy, or sell illegal drugs. The dangers are clear enough when indulging in your own home; if you take drugs while traveling, you may endanger not only your own life but also put your fellow travelers in jeopardy. And if you get caught, you may end up spending your hard-earned vacation funds on bail and attorney's fees — and wind up in jail.

Those who carry medicines that contain a controlled drug should be sure to have a current doctor's prescription with them. There isn't much that the American consulate can do for drug offenders beyond providing a list of lawyers. Having broken a local law, an offender puts his or her fate in the hands of the local authorities.

Ironically, travelers can get into almost as much trouble coming through US customs with over-the-counter drugs picked up abroad that contain substances that are controlled in the US. Cold medicines, pain relievers, and the like often have codeine or codeine derivatives that are illegal except by prescription in the US. Throw them out before leaving for home.

Tipping

Throughout Europe, you will find the custom of including some kind of service charge as part of a meal more common than in North America. Restaurant menus usually state whether a service charge is added to the bill automatically (in some cases, it is already calculated in the menu prices). Unfortunately, not every restaurant notes that the charge is added, but you should feel no embarrassment about asking a waiter when the bill is presented. This service charge generally ranges from 15% to 20%. If it isn't added, a 15% tip — just as in the US — is usually a safe figure, although one should never hesitate to penalize poor service or reward excellent and efficient attention by leaving less or more. If the tip has been added, no further gratuity is expected — though it's a common practice in Great Britain for diners to leave a few extra pence on the table. The emphasis is on *few,* and 75p (roughly $1) is usually quite adequate.

Although it's not necessary to tip the maître d' of most restaurants — unless he has been especially helpful in providing a table or arranging a special party — when tipping is appropriate, the lowest amount should be £3 (about $5). In the finest restaurants, where a multiplicity of servers are present, plan to tip 5% to the captain in addition to the standard 15% for the waiter. The sommelier (wine waiter) is entitled to a gratuity of approximately £1 (about $1.50) per bottle of wine.

In allocating gratuities at a restaurant, pay particular attention to what has become the standard credit card charge form, which now includes separate places for indicating gratuities for waiters and/or captains. If these separate boxes do not appear on the charge slip presented, simply ask the waiter or captain how these separate tips should be indicated. Be aware, too, of the increasingly common, devious practice of placing the amount of an entire restaurant bill (in which service has already been included) in the top box of a charge slip, leaving the "tip" and "total" boxes ominously empty. Don't be intimidated: Leave the "tip" box blank and just repeat the total amount next to "total" before signing.

There is virtually no tipping in pubs — unless you become something of a regular and care to offer the barman an occasional drink. It is not uncommon, however, to leave a few pence for a barmaid; and for those served at a table in a bar or cocktail lounge, a small gratuity — 75p (about $1) — is usual for the server.

As in restaurants, visitors will normally find a service charge of 10% to 15% included in their final bill at most British hotels. No additional gratuities are required — or expected — beyond this billed service charge. It is unlikely, however, that a service charge will be added to bills in small guesthouses or modest bed-and-breakfast establishments. In these cases, guests should let their instincts be their guide; no tipping is expected by members of the family who own the house, but it is a nice gesture to leave something for others — such as a dining room waiter or a maid — who may have been helpful. A gratuity of 75p to £1 (around $1) per night is adequate in these cases.

If a hotel does not automatically add a service charge, it is perfectly proper for guests to ask to have an extra 10% to 15% added to their bill, to be distributed among those who served them. This may be an especially convenient solution in a large hotel, where it's difficult to determine just who out of a horde of attendants actually performed particular services. For those who prefer to distribute tips themselves, a chambermaid is generally tipped at the rate of 75p (about $1) per day, or £3 to £4 (about $5 to $6) per week. Tip the concierge or hall porter for specific services only, with the amount of such gratuities dependent on the level of service provided. Doormen and/or porters are generally tipped at the rate of 75p (about $1) per bag for carrying luggage, along with a small additional amount if a doorman helps with a cab or car. Other miscellaneous tips to hotel staff depend entirely on the service rendered.

Once upon a time, taxi drivers in Great Britain would give one a rather odd look if presented with a tip for a fare, but times have changed, and 10% to 15% of the amount on the meter is now a standard gratuity. Porters in airports expect to be compensated at the rate of about 75p (about $1) per bag, as do porters who carry bags in railway or bus stations.

Theater ushers are not tipped, though it is common practice to purchase a program from the person who shows you to your seat. Sightseeing tour guides are usually tipped; members of a group may discuss a total amount among themselves and contribute equally to the gratuity.

Shopping

Browsing through the department stores, street markets, small shops, and craft centers of Great Britain will undoubtedly be one of the highlights of a trip. Visitors from the US may not be quite as enthusiastic about prices as they might have been a few years ago, but there is still plenty of value left for the money and enough quality and craftsmanship to make many an item irresistible. To help steer visitors toward the best, several sections of this book are devoted to shopping. In THE CITIES, individual reports include a list of specific stores, boutiques, and markets, as well as descriptions of special shopping streets where they exist. And sections in DIVERSIONS describe not only where to find antiques and other collectibles, but also — for those who have yet to experience this stimulating form of acquisition — how to buy them at auctions.

WHAT TO BUY: In Great Britain, crafts are thriving. Products in traditional and modern styles and combinations of the two are found in craft centers, workshops, and stores throughout the country. Cashmere sweaters and Shetland wool knits are enduring British classics, as are Harris tweeds, ancestral tartans, and cotton and silk *Liberty* prints, whether sold by the yard or made up into fashionable clothes. *Burberrys* and *Jaeger* are good labels, and there are lower-priced sports clothes at *Marks & Spencer* stores around the country. *Harrods* in London is Europe's largest department store, and it should be on your sightseeing list even if it's not on your shopping list. Its motto, *Omnia, Omnibus, Ubique* (Everyone, Everything, Everywhere), gives a pretty good idea of the range of its activities. Shopping can also be mixed with sightseeing in the famous food department at *Fortnum and Mason,* purveyor of groceries to the royal family — which may explain the formality of swallowtail coats on its salesclerks (pronounced "clarks"). There are still some antiques left in Britain, in spite of the shiploads consigned to US dealers. In London, try the Bermondsey–New Caledonia Market — a dealers' market — very early Friday mornings for a chance at what might turn up in an expensive shop later in the day, unless you spot it first. The showrooms of *Sotheby's* and *Christie's,* probably the most famous art and antique auctioneers in the world, are open for viewing. If you attend the daily sales, however, don't move a muscle or blink an eye unless you've brought money — lots of it. New and used books can be found in any number of shops on London's Charing Cross Road, including one (*Foyles*) with a stock of over 4 million volumes.

HOW TO SHOP ABROAD: The goods are enticing, but even so, top-quality goods are not necessarily less expensive in a fashionable boutique in the capital city of the country from which they came than they are in an equally fashionable US store. To be sure, visitors should do some homework before going and should arrive with a list of the goods they want — as specific as possible, with brands or labels — and the cost of each in the US. In some cases, visitors will find it less expensive to buy abroad, but frequently they will find it is not, and knowing the difference is crucial to a successful shopping trip. On arrival, it is still necessary to comparison shop as much as time permits, bearing in mind that articles can be less costly the closer the buyer gets to the point of manufacture, and least expensive of all in the factory that makes the item — if it sells to the public. You'll get a better price on Scottish woolens and knitwear at mill outlets in Scotland than in the Edinburgh and London shops. On the other hand, although the *Royal Doulton, Spode, Minton,* and *Wedgwood* ceramics and china factories at Stoke-on-Trent have retail shops on the premises, they do not sell at discounted prices, in order not to undercut their own retailers. (Two of them — *Wedgwood* and *Spode* — have "seconds" shops, where china with slight imperfections sells for as little as half the ordinary retail price.)

If your itinerary won't allow combing the countryside in search of sources, and if you can time your visit accordingly, perhaps the best bargains in almost anything British may be had at sale time: 2 weeks in January and 1 week in July, when the majority of London's department stores and specialty shops offer their wares at substantial reductions. Londoners wait for the sales, not to mention the rest of the British and hordes of shoppers from the Continent, so expect some of the usual local reserve to disappear as all engage in a frantic fight for some of the world's most coveted merchandise.

DUTY-FREE SHOPS: If common sense says that it is always less expensive to buy goods in an airport duty-free shop than to buy them at home or in the streets of a foreign city, travelers should best be aware of some basic facts. Duty-free, first of all, does not mean that the goods will be free of duty when the travelers return to the US. Rather, it means that the shop has paid no import tax acquiring goods of foreign make because the goods are not to be used in the country, which is why duty-free goods are available only in the restricted, passengers-only area of international airports or are delivered to departing passengers on the plane. In a duty-free store, travelers save money only on goods of foreign make because they are the only items on which import tax would be charged in any other store. There is usually no saving on locally made items, although in countries that impose VAT taxes (see below) that are refundable to foreigners, the prices in airport duty-free shops are also minus this tax, sparing travelers the often cumbersome procedures they otherwise have to follow to obtain a VAT refund. Beyond this, there is little reason to delay buying local souvenirs until reaching the airport. In fact, because airport duty-free shops usually pay high rents, the locally made goods sold in them may well be more expensive than they would be in a downtown store. The real bargains are foreign goods, but — let the buyer beware — not all foreign goods are automatically less expensive in an airport duty-free shop. Spirits, smoking materials, and perfumes are fairly standard bargains, but when buying cameras, watches, clothing, chocolates and other foods, and luxury items, be sure to know what they cost elsewhere. Terrific savings do exist (they are the reason for such shops, after all), but so do overpriced items that an unwary shopper might find equally tempting. Among the airports with duty-free shops in Great Britain are Heathrow, Gatwick, Manchester International, and Scotland's Prestwick.

VALUE ADDED TAX: Commonly abbreviated as VAT, this is a tax levied by various European countries and added to the purchase price of most merchandise. The standard VAT rate in Great Britain is 15% (children's clothes, books, food, and transportation are exempt). The tax is intended for residents (and is already included in the price tag), but visitors are required to pay it, too, unless they have purchases shipped directly to an address abroad by the store. If visitors pay the tax and take purchases with them, however, they are entitled to a refund under retail export schemes that have been in operation throughout Great Britain for several years. In the past, returning travelers have complained of delays in receiving the refunds and of difficulties in converting checks written in foreign currency into dollars, but a new service (called Tourist Tax Free Shopping — TTFS), has recently been introduced and greatly streamlines the refund procedure.

To obtain a refund through the new service, visitors must shop only in participating stores — there are some 12,000 of them nationwide, distinguished by the red, white, and blue TTFS symbol. Show the salesperson your passport and ask for a tax-free shopping voucher, which the shopkeeper will fill out with details of the purchase and the amount of VAT refund due (a small administration charge will be deducted). It's then up to you to fill out the back of the voucher with your name and address and instructions concerning how the payment is to be made — by check in dollars or pounds sterling or to a credit card account. At departure time, all of your vouchers must be presented with the merchandise (so don't pack it in the bottom of your suitcase) to the customs desk that's usually next to passport control. The customs official will stamp the vouchers, after which you mail them to Tourist Tax Free Shopping headquarters, using the already addressed (and postpaid if mailed in Britain) envelope supplied by the store (you can mail all the vouchers in one envelope). Refunds are processed within 5 working days of receipt of the vouchers. Note that if you have too little time at the airport to take care of customs formalities, it is possible to have a notary public certify the vouchers after your return home. For further information, or to trace a delayed refund, write to Tourist Tax Free Shopping, Europa House, 266 Upper Richmond Rd., London SW15 6TQ.

Should you happen to shop in a store that is not part of the TTFS system, don't despair. Visitors are still entitled to a VAT refund under the old retail export scheme, although they may have difficulty collecting it unless the store is willing to do the paperwork. Again, show the salesperson your passport and ask for a retail export form (also known as a VAT relief form), which will be filled out on the premises. At departure, have the form validated at the customs desk and mail it back to the *store* (which will have supplied a stamped, self-addressed envelope for this purpose). Note that stores are under no obligation to perform this service, and those that do may require a minimum purchase below which they refuse to process the form. They will also most likely deduct a small charge from your refund for doing so. The refund comes as a check, usually in British currency (although some shops offer dollar checks, often for an extra fee), mailed to your home address or, if the purchase was made by credit card, as a credit to your account.

A VAT refund by dollar check or credited to a credit card account is relatively hassle-free, but should you receive a check in pounds sterling, you'll probably find that your US bank will assess a fee, as much as $15 or more, for converting it into US dollars. Far less costly is sending the foreign currency check (after endorsing it) to *Ruesch International* (1140 19th St. NW, Suite 320, Washington, DC 20036; phone: 202-887-0990 or 800-424-2923), which will convert it to a dollar check for a $2 fee (deducted from the dollar check). *Ruesch* also has offices at 1925 Century Park E., Suite 1925, Los Angeles, CA 90067 (phone: 213-277-7800), and 450 Park Ave., Suite 2301, New York, NY 10022 (phone: 212-421-7100).

Customs and Returning to the US

The duty-fee allowance for US citizens returning from abroad is $400, provided your purchases accompany you and are for personal use. A flat 10% duty based on the "fair retail value in country of acquisition" is assessed on the next $1,000 worth of merchandise brought in for personal use or gifts. Amounts over $1,400 are dutiable at a variety of rates. The average rate for typical tourist purchases is about 12%, but you can find out rates on specific items by consulting *Tariff Schedules of the United States* in a library or any US Customs Service office.

Families traveling together may make a joint declaration to customs, which permits one member to exceed his or her duty-free exemption to the extent that another falls short. Families may also pool purchases dutiable under the flat rate. A family of three, for example, would be eligible for up to a total of $3,000 at the 10% flat duty rate (after each member had used up his or her $400 duty-free exemption) rather than three separate $1,000 allowances. This grouping of purchases is extremely useful when considering the duty on a high-tariff item, such as jewelry or a fur coat. Individuals are allowed 1 carton of cigarettes (200) and 1 liter of alcohol if over 21. Alcohol above this allowance is liable for both duty and an Internal Revenue tax. Antiques, if they are 100 or more years old and you have proof from the seller of that fact, are duty free, as are paintings and drawings if done entirely by hand.

Personal exemptions can be used once every 30 days; in order to be eligible, an individual must have been out of the country for more than 48 hours. If any portion of the exemption has been used once within any 30-day period or if your trip is less than 48 hours long, the duty-free allowance is cut to $25. The allotment for individual "unsolicited" gifts mailed from abroad (no more than one per day per recipient) has been raised to $50 retail value per gift. These gifts do not have to be declared and are not included in your duty-free exemption.

Tourists have long been forbidden to bring into the US foreign-made US trade-marked articles purchased abroad (if the trademark is recorded with customs) without written permission. It's now possible to enter with one such item in your possession as long as it's for personal use.

Clearing customs is a simple procedure. Forms are distributed by airline or ship personnel before arrival. If your purchases total no more than the duty-free $400 limit, you need only fill out the identification part of the form and make an oral declaration to the customs inspector. If entering with more than $400 worth of goods, you must submit a written declaration. It is illegal not to declare dutiable items; not to do so, in fact, constitutes smuggling, and the penalty can be anything from stiff fines and seizure of the goods to prison sentences. It simply isn't worth doing. Nor should you go along with the suggestions of foreign merchants who offer to help you secure a bargain by deceiving customs officials in any way. Such transactions are frequently a setup, using the foreign merchant as an agent of US customs. Another agent of US customs is TECS, the Treasury Enforcement Communications System, a computer that stores all kinds of pertinent information on returning citizens. There is a basic rule to buying goods abroad, and it should never be broken. If you can't afford the duty on something, don't buy it. Your list or verbal declaration should include all items purchased abroad as well as gifts received abroad, purchases made at the behest of others, the value of repairs, and anything brought in for resale in the US.

Do not include in the list items that do not accompany you, i.e., purchases that you have mailed or had shipped home. These are dutiable in any case, even if for your own use and even if the items that accompany your return from the same trip do not exhaust your $400 duty-free exemption. In fact, it is a good idea, if you have accumulated too much while abroad, to mail home any personal effects (made and bought in the US) that you no longer need rather than your foreign purchases. These personal effects pass through customs as "American goods returned" and are not subject to duty. If you cannot avoid shipping home your foreign purchases, however, the US Customs Service suggests that the package be clearly marked "Not for Sale" and that a copy of the bill of sale be included. The customs examiner will usually accept this as indicative of the article's fair retail value, but if he or she believes it to be falsified or feels the goods have been seriously undervalued, a higher retail value may be assigned. Remember, the examiner is empowered to impose a duty based on his or her assessment of the value of the goods. The duty owed is collected by the US Postal Service when the package is delivered. More information on mailing packages home from abroad is contained in the US Customs Service pamphlet *International Mail Imports* (see below for where to write for this and other useful brochures).

Gold, gold medals, bullion, and up to $10,000 in currency or negotiable instruments may be brought into the US without being declared. Sums over $10,000 must be declared in writing. Drugs are totally illegal with the exception of medication prescribed by a physician. It's a good idea to travel with no more than you actually need of any medication and to have the prescription on hand in case any question arises either abroad or when reentering the US.

Customs implements the rigorous Department of Agriculture regulations concerning the importation of vegetable matter, seeds, bulbs, and the like. Living vegetable matter may not be imported without a permit, and everything must be inspected, permit or not. Processed foods and baked goods are usually okay. Regulations on meat products generally depend on the country of origin and manner of processing. As a rule, commercially canned meat, hermetically sealed and cooked in the can so that it can be stored without refrigeration, is permitted, but not all canned meat fulfills this requirement. Be careful in buying pâté, for instance. Goose liver pâté in itself is acceptable, but the pork fat that is often part of it, either as an ingredient or a rind, is not. Even canned pâtés may not be admitted for this reason. (The imported ones you see in US stores have been prepared and packaged according to US regulations.)

Customs also enforces federal laws that prohibit the entry of articles made from the furs or hides of animals on the endangered species list. Beware of shoes, bags, and belts made of crocodile and certain kinds of lizard, and if you're shopping for big-ticket items, beware of fur coats made from the spotted cats. All can be found in Europe, but they will be confiscated upon your return, and there will be no refund. For information about animals on the endangered species list, contact the Department of the Interior, US Fish and Wildlife Service, Office of Management Authority, PO Box 27329, Washington, DC 20038-7329 (phone: 202-343-5634), and ask for the free publication *Facts About Federal Wildlife Laws.*

Customs agents are businesslike, efficient, and not unkind. During the peak season, clearance can take time, but this is generally because of the strain imposed by a number of jumbo jets disgorging their passengers at the same time, not because of unwarranted zealousness on the part of the customs people. Efforts to streamline procedures include the Citizens' Bypass Program, which allows Americans whose purchases are under $400 to go to the "green line," where they simply show their passports to the customs inspector. This, in effect, completely eliminates the old obligatory inspection, although inspectors still retain the right to search any luggage they choose, so don't do anything foolish and illegal.

The US Customs Service publishes a series of free pamphlets with customs information. It includes *Know Before You Go,* a basic discussion of customs requirements pertaining to all travelers; *International Mail Imports; Travelers' Tips on Bringing Food, Plant, and Animal Products into the United States; Importing a Car; GSP and the Traveler; Pocket Hints; Currency Reporting; Pets, Wildlife, US Customs; Customs Hints for Visitors* (*Nonresidents*); and *Trademark Information for Travelers.* For the entire series or individual pamphlets, write to the US Customs Service, PO Box 7407, Washington, DC 20044, or contact any of the seven regional offices, in Boston, Chicago, Houston, Los Angeles, Miami, New Orleans, and New York. The Customs Service has a recorded message whereby callers using Touch-Tone phones can get more information on various topics; the number is 202-566-8195. These pamphlets provide great briefing material, but if you still have questions after you're in Great Britain, you can contact the US Customs representative at the US Embassy in London, 24 Grosvenor Sq., London W1A 1AE (phone: 493-4599).

Sources and Resources

Tourist Information Offices

Tourist authorities in Great Britain are generally the best sources of travel and entry information, and the literature offered is usually free. When requesting brochures and maps, state the areas you plan to visit and your interests regarding hotels, restaurants, special events, tourist attractions, guided tours, and sports facilities. The British Tourist Authority in North America is best equipped to handle written or telephone inquiries from potential visitors. (Also note that the British Tourist Authority previously handled tourism for Northern Ireland, and although this is no longer the case, earlier publications may focus on both countries.)

There are numerous regional tourism organizations as well as more than 600 tourist information centers in towns throughout England, Scotland, and Wales. These furnish information and handle inquiries by mail and, where numbers are listed, also by telephone. Offices are generally open on weekdays. Some are open in summer only and others year-round. For a complete list of all local information centers, seasonal and otherwise, contact the British Tourist Authority. Below is a list of national tourist offices in the US and in Great Britain.

IN THE US

British Tourist Authority, 40 W. 57th St., New York, NY 10019 (phone: 212-581-4700); World Trade Center, 350 S. Figueroa St., Suite 450, Los Angeles, CA 90071 (phone: 213-628-3525); John Hancock Center, Suite 3320, 875 N. Michigan Ave., Chicago, IL 60611 (phone: 312-787-0490); Cedar Maple Plaza, Suite 210, 2305 Cedar Springs, Dallas, TX 75201-1814 (phone: 214-720-4040).

ENGLAND

London Tourist Information Centre, Victoria Railway Station Forecourt, London SW1 (phone: 01-730-3488).

English Tourist Board, Thames Tower, Black's Rd., Hammersmith, London W6 9EL (phone: 01-730-3400).

Cumbria Tourist Board, Ashleigh, Holly Rd., Windermere, Cumbria LA23 2AS (phone: 09662-4444).

East Anglia Tourist Board (includes Cambridgeshire, Essex, Norfolk, and Suffolk), Toppesfield Hall, Hadleigh, Suffolk 1P7 7DN (phone: 0473-822922).

East Midlands Tourist Board (includes Derbyshire, Leicestershire, Lincolnshire, Northamptonshire, and Nottinghamshire), Exchequergate, Lincoln LN2 1PS (phone: 0522-531521).

Heart of England Tourist Board (includes Gloucester, Hereford and Worcester, Shropshire, Staffordshire, Warwickshire, and West Midlands), 2-4 Trinity St., Worcester, WR1 2PW (phone: 0905-613132).

Northumbria Tourist Board (includes Cleveland, Durham, Northumberland, and Tyne and Wear), Aykley Heads, Durham DH1 5UX (phone: 091-3846905).

North West Tourist Board (includes Cheshire, High Peak District of Derbyshire,

Greater Manchester, Lancashire, and Merseyside), The Last Drop Village, Bromley Cross, Bolton, Lancashire BL7 9PZ (phone: 0204-591511).

South East England Tourist Board (includes East Sussex, Kent, Surrey, and West Sussex), 1 Warwick Park, Tunbridge Wells, Kent TN2 5TA (phone: 0892-40766).

Southern Tourist Board (includes Eastern and Northern Dorset, Hampshire, and the Isle of Wight), Town Hall Centre, Leigh Rd., Eastleigh, Hampshire SO5 4DE (phone: 0703-616027).

Thames and Chilterns Tourist Board (includes Bedfordshire, Berkshire, Buckinghamshire, Hertfordshire, and Oxfordshire), 8 Market Pl., Abingdon, Oxfordshire OX14 3HG (phone: 02352-2711).

West Country Tourist Board (includes Avon, Cornwall, Devon, West Dorset, Somerset, and Wiltshire, and the Isles of Scilly), Trinity Ct., 37 Southernhay E., Exeter, Devonshire EX1 1QS (phone: 0392-6351).

Yorkshire and Humberside Tourist Board (includes Humberside and North, South, and West Yorkshire), 312 Tadcaster Rd., York YO2 2HF (phone: 0904-707961).

SCOTLAND

Scottish Tourist Board, 23 Ravelston Terr., Edinburgh EH4 3EU (phone: 031-332-2433).

Aviemore and Spey Valley Tourist Organisation, Main Rd., Aviemore, Inverness PH22 1PT (phone: 0479-810363).

City of Edinburgh District Council, Waverley Market, Princes St., Edinburgh EH2 2QP (phone: 031-557-1700).

Dumfries Tourist Board, Whitesands, Dumfries-shire DG1 2SB (phone: 0387-53862).

Fort William and Lochaber Tourist Board, Travel Centre, Fort William, Inverness-shire PH33 6AJ (phone: 0397-3781).

Greater Glasgow Tourist Board, 35-39 St. Vincent Pl., Glasgow G2 1ES (phone: 041-227-4880).

Inverness, Loch Ness and Nairn Tourist Board, 23 Church St., Inverness IV1 1EZ (phone: 0463-234353).

Isle of Skye and South West Ross Tourist Board, Tourist Information Centre, Portree, Isle of Skye IV51 5VZ (phone: 0478-2137).

Loch Lomond, Stirling and Trossachs Tourist Board, Dumbarton Rd., Stirlingshire FK8 2LQ (phone: 0786-75019).

Oban, Mull and District Tourist Board, Boswell House, Argyll Sq., Oban, Argyll PA34 4AN (phone: 0631-63122).

Orkney Tourist Board, Information Centre, Broad St., Kirkwall, Orkney KW15 1NX (phone: 0856-2856).

Outer Hebrides Tourist Board, 4 S. Beach St., Stornoway, Isle of Lewis PA87 2XY (phone: 0851-3088).

Perth Tourist Board, The Round House, Marshall Pl., Perth PH2 8NU (phone: 0738-38353).

St. Andrews and North East Fife Tourist Board, 2 Queens Gardens, St. Andrews, Fife KY16 9TE (phone: 0334-72021).

Scottish Borders Tourist Board, Municipal Buildings, High St., Selkirkshire TD7 4JX (phone: 0750-200555).

Shetland Tourist Office, Information Centre, Market Cross, Lerwick, Shetland ZE1 0LU (phone: 0595-3434).

Note: Scotland has more than 30 regional tourism bodies. Those listed above handle areas most frequently of interest to visitors.

WALES

Mid Wales Tourism Council (includes parts of Dyfed, Gwynedd, and Powys), Canolfan Owain Glyndwr, Machynlleth, Powys SY20 8EE (phone: 0654-2401).

Wales Tourist Board, Brunel House, 2 Fitzalan, Cardiff CF2 1UY (phone: 0222-499909).

Wales Tourist Board, North Wales Regional Office (includes Clwyd and most of Gwynedd), 77 Conway Rd., Colwyn Bay, Clwyd LL29 7LN (phone: 0492-531731).

Wales Tourist Board, South Wales Regional Office (includes parts of Dyfed and Powys, Gwent, Mid, South, and West Glamorgan), Ty Croeso, 6 Gloucester Pl., Swansea SA1 1TY (phone: 0792-465204).

CHANNEL ISLANDS

Alderney Recreation and Tourism Committee, States Office, St. Anne's, Alderney, Channel Islands (phone: 0481-822994).

Herm Island Administrative Office, Herm Island, Via Guernsey, Channel Islands (phone: Herm 4 or 0481-22377).

Sark Tourist Information Officer, Sark, Channel Islands (phone: 0481-83-2262).

States of Guernsey Tourist Board, PO Box 23, White Rock, Guernsey, Channel Islands (phone: 0481-26611).

States of Jersey Tourist Committee, Weighbridge, St. Helier, Jersey, Channel Islands (phone: 0534-78000).

ISLE OF MAN

Isle of Man Tourist Board, 13 Victoria St., Douglas, Isle of Man (phone: 0624-74323).

ISLE OF WIGHT

Isle of Wight Tourist Office, Quay Store, Town Quay, Newport, Isle of Wight PO30 2EF (phone: 0983-524343).

Sports

Grand castles, stately homes, ruined monasteries, and ancient tombs convey a sense of the British past. But for showing off the present — the British at their most energetic, most passionate best — there's nothing like one of the nation's sporting events. The British, perhaps more than any other nation, still cherish the concept of amateur sports as "honest endeavor." National sports include games that are hardly known in the US as well as games that are the ancestors of our own national pastimes.

RUGBY FOOTBALL: The irony of rugby football is best expressed in an old saying that holds, "Rugby is a game for ruffians played by gentlemen, while soccer is a game for gentlemen played by ruffians." A schoolboy at the great English public school of Rugby invented something new in 1823 by picking up a soccer ball and running forward with it, contrary to the rules. Soccer was basically a kicking game, but carrying the ball and tackling became part of the new sport, formalized in 1871, when the Rugby Football Union came into being. Exported to the US, rugby developed into American football, which it resembles — somewhat. In Britain, rugby is played from September to April on Saturday afternoons by school and university teams, county teams, hospital teams, and by anyone else who can bring together the requisite 15 players per side. Once you've seen the game played, you will remember the "set scrum," one means by which play begins, when forwards of opposing teams, like two compact and only apparently disorderly phalanxes, push and shove against each other for possession of the ball. The Welsh are justly proud of their amateur Rugby Union national team, which they regard as the best in the world — with some justification, given their record over the years of winning the Triple Crown (a hotly contested designation awarded to the winner of the European rugby league championships).

The rugby season begins slowly in early autumn, picks up momentum after Christmas (when tryouts for places on the English, Welsh, and Scottish teams are held), and climaxes in February with the Internationals, which draws huge crowds. These competitions — the Triple Crown — take place, on a home and away basis, among Scotland, Ireland, England, Wales, and France. There are also occasional visits from teams from New Zealand (the *Allblacks*) and Australia (the *Wallabies*), who play the British team (made up of players from the national teams within Great Britain) called the *British Lions.* The most important matches are played in southwest London at *Twickenham,* headquarters of Rugby Union's controlling body (Whitton Rd., Twickenham; phone: 01-892-8161 for information, 01-571-6880 for tickets). In Wales, the place to see a match is *Cardiff Arms Park;* in Edinburgh, go to the *Murrayfield* rugby ground.

Rugby League — a semi-professional version — is played largely for and in the working class areas of Northern England using a smaller number of players on a team (13 men). The League stronghold is in Lancashire and Yorkshire, principally, but the Rugby League Challenge Cup Final takes place at London's *Wembley Stadium* in May.

SOCCER: Soccer, in recent years, has become a sport many prefer to watch on TV from the comfort of their armchairs, for fear of trouble at the grounds. This reputation, however, comes mainly from the supporters of a few inner-city teams. If attendance records are a guide, this is the most popular sport in Great Britain, where it was called football long before Americans began to play anything remotely resembling it. After rugby came on the scene, the London Football Association was formed (in 1863) to protect the purity of the original football, which then became known as "association football" and eventually as "soccer," through constant repetition of the abbreviation for the word "association."

Competitions in Britain and on the Continent are exciting, particularly when the European Cup and World Cup tournaments are in progress or the English First Division Cup Final takes place. The tough competition of the English First Division in particular shows what an entertaining, skillful sport soccer can be at its best.

Almost every medium-size town has a local soccer team of either professional or amateur standing. For instance, stouthearted visitors to London determined to see what it's all about can follow the crowds to the grounds of some of the most popular professional clubs: *Arsenal, Highbury Stadium* (Avenell Rd., N5; phone: 01-226-0304); *Chelsea, Stamford Bridge* grounds (Fulham Rd., SW6; phone: 385-5545); *Tottenham Hotspur* (748 High Rd., N17; phone: 01-801-3411); *West Ham United, Boleyn Park* (Green St., E13; phone: 01-472-0704).

The Football Association Cup Final, the equivalent of the World Series, takes place at *Wembley Stadium,* London (phone: 01-902-1234), before a crowd of 100,000 in May. Tickets are usually bought at the stadium about an hour before the match, but for the Cup Final they're usually sold out in advance to club members. Rest assured it will be on the telly. The season runs from August to May, with games played on Saturday afternoons. For a schedule, contact the Football Association Ltd., 16 Lancaster Gate, London W2 3LW (phone: 01-262-4542), or any British Tourist Authority office in the US.

CRICKET: For many visitors, cricket is idiosyncratically English — and far too slow to bother with. The game dates to the 12th or 13th century, and rules existed by 1744. Yet baseball fans will discover that while outwardly the two games appear different, there are many parallels, especially now that 1-day matches are played, usually on Sundays. There was a time when a Test Match — an international competition held at home and away between Britain and teams from its former colonies, such as Australia, India, Pakistan, New Zealand, or the West Indies — could last a week and end in a draw. With this in mind, several years ago the Marylebone Cricket Club (MCC) — the body controlling cricket — changed the rules to speed up the game.

If you want to understand the English character — its emphasis on understatement, good sportsmanship, team spirit, skill, courage, and endurance — there is nothing quite so traditionally *English* as spending an afternoon sipping beer in the shade with friends on a warm summer day listening to the *thwack* of leather on willow. Whether it's a local cricket match on the village green, a county match, or the country's best players matching wits and stamina with teams from abroad at *Lord's Cricket Ground* in London, ideally, watch the game with someone who can explain it. Cricket is slow enough that there is plenty of time to learn what is happening without missing any of the action — and if you're lucky, the action can be explosive and spectacular.

The season runs from mid-April to early September, and matches are played by university teams and professional county teams. International, or Test, matches take place annually. Perhaps the most famous was the game at the *Oval* won by Australia against Britain in 1882; the morning after, London's shocked *Sporting Times* ran an obituary for British cricket, announcing that its remains would be cremated. Since then, any England-Australia Test Match is played for the "Ashes," which repose in an urn that never leaves the Cricket Memorial Gallery at *Lord's Cricket Ground* — not even if Australia wins. *Lord's Cricket Ground,* home of the MCC, is *the* place to see a game (St. John's Wood Rd., London NW8; phone: 01-289-1611). The next best place is the *Oval* (Kennington, London SE11; phone: 01-582-6660), home of the Surrey County Cricket Club and site of the 1882 humiliation.

POLO: No one is sure where it came from — somewhere in central Asia probably — but it got to Britain via India, where enthusiastic British army officers discovered it. The first match seems to have been played on the outskirts of London in 1871. From the beginning it has been a rich man's sport, since it takes a lot of money to maintain a string of polo ponies — and a string of them is necessary: The game is a fast and punishing one for the horses, and the player will change mounts more than once during a game. There are some 500 players in Britain, and the fact that Prince Charles is among them helps to keep the game very much alive. The Hurlingham Polo Association (Ambersham Farm, Ambersham, Midhurst, West Sussex GU29 0BX; phone: 07985-277) is polo's governing body. To see a match, go to *Smith's Lawn,* Windsor Great Park, Windsor, or to *Cowdray Park,* Midhurst, West Sussex, on summer weekends.

CURLING: Scotland participates in the football and Rugby Union frenzy, but it has its own pastimes, too. Besides golf, which began here, there is curling, a major winter sport that probably began here, and if not, at least developed here. Curling is somewhat related to shuffleboard and has been almost as successful an export as golf. There are now many more curlers in Canada than in Scotland, but the Scots have been curling since the 16th century; the Royal Caledonian Curling Club, founded in 1838, is the governing body of the sport. The game is played on a 46-yard-long ice rink with 40-pound stones (also known as "granites"). Two players or "curlers" slide eight stones toward a circular target, while assistants vigorously brush the ice with brooms along the path of the stone in an attempt to place a stone nearest the center.

HIGHLAND GAMES: You'll see plenty of kilts and plenty of sheer brute strength at these traditional annual athletic meets. The history of the games goes back as far as the 11th century. They take place along with clan gatherings and bagpipe and dance competitions all over the Scottish Highlands during the summer; the calendar is especially busy in August and early September. Even the queen attends the Braemar Royal Highland Gathering, the best known of the Highland games, held not far from Balmoral Castle on the first Saturday in September. Most of the games are running and throwing events and they're usually entered by professionals. The main event at many a gathering is a sport called "tossing the caber," actually a tree trunk of considerable weight that must be "tossed" from a vertical position — if the athlete can manage it. The caber at the Braemar games, all 19 feet and 120 pounds of it, has been tossed, but rarely. The rules of the Scottish Games Association require that the caber start out bigger and heavier than any of the athletes can handle, but that it can be cut down if it can't be tossed. Once someone has been successful, however, the caber stays as it is. Besides those at Braemar, other important games are the Portree Highland Games on the Isle of Skye, the Cowal Highland Gathering at Dunoon, and the Aboyne Highland Games.

Theater and Special Event Tickets

The British Tourist Authority can supply information on the many special events and festivals that take place in Britain, though they cannot in all cases provide the actual program or detailed information on ticket prices. In more than one section of this book you will read about events that spark your interest — everything from music festivals and special theater seasons to sporting championships — along with addresses to write to for descriptive brochures, reservations, or tickets. Since many of these occasions are sometimes booked well in advance, if there is something you do not want to miss, you should think about having your booking in hand before you go. If you do write, remember that any request from the US should be accompanied by an International Reply Coupon to ensure a response (send two of them for an airmail response). Actual tickets can usually be paid for by an international money order or by foreign draft. These international coupons, money orders, and drafts are available at US post offices and banks.

Tickets for shows, sports events, and opera, ballet, and concert performances that are part of the regular cultural seasons in London and elsewhere can be bought before you go from the following agencies. (They may also be able to supply tickets to some of the more popular special events.) Also note that British Airways passengers can reserve theater and special event tickets through the British Airways Box Office Service (phone: 800-AIRWAYS).

Edwards & Edwards, 1 Times Sq. Plaza, New York, NY 10036 (phone: 212-944-0290 in New York State; 800-223-6108 elsewhere in the US). Provides tickets for Edinburgh's *International Festival* and the Stratford-upon-Avon Shakespeare season as well as theater and cultural events in London. Books best available seats, generally in the orchestra.

Keith Prowse & Co., 234 W. 44th St., New York, NY 10036 (phone: 212-398-1430 in New York State; 800-669-7469 elsewhere in the US). Theater, concerts, and sporting events, including the *Edinburgh Military Tattoo* and performances at Stratford-upon-Avon. Booking fee of $15 per ticket.

London Showline, 130 Skyline Dr., Suite 103, Ringwood, NJ 07456 (phone: 201-962-9246 in New Jersey; 800-962-9246 elsewhere in the US). Theater, opera, and performing arts tickets, including the West End theaters and Shakespeare season at Stratford-upon-Avon; also sightseeing tours and the *Edinburgh Military Tattoo.* Service charge of $18 per ticket.

London Stages, 18455 Burbank Blvd., Suite 5-N, Tarzana, CA 91356 (phone: 818-881-8433 or 800-729-0029). Handles events in London and Stratford-upon-Avon; also stagecraft, theater courses and study groups in London. Service charge of about $5 per ticket.

Books and Magazines

Throughout GETTING READY TO GO, numerous books and brochures have been recommended as good sources of further information on a variety of topics. In many cases, these are publications of the British Tourist Authority and are available free through British Tourist Authority offices both here and abroad. Others may be found in the travel section of any good general bookstore. If you still can't find something, the following bookstores and mail order houses specializing in books on travel are a further resource.

British Gifts, PO Box 26558, Los Angeles, CA 90026 (phone: 213-666-7778). Mail order only. Stocks a large selection of maps and books on Britain, including *Automobile Association of Great Britain* (*AA*) and British Tourist Authority publications.

British Market, 2366 Rice Blvd., Houston, TX 77005 (phone: 713-529-9889). Stocks maps and British Tourist Authority literature as well as a wide range of guidebooks published in both Britain and the US. Selected price lists are available. Open 9 AM to 6 PM, Mondays through Saturdays, 12AM to 5PM on Sundays.

British Travel Bookshop, 40 W. 57th St., 3rd Floor, New York, NY 10019 (phone: 212-765-0898). Carries a complete line of books and maps on all areas of Britain, especially the *AA* and British Tourist Authority material as well as other books by little-known publishers. Book list available. Open 9:30AM to 5 PM weekdays.

The following stores and/or mail order houses also specialize in travel, but not in travel to any particular country or continent. They offer books on Great Britain along with guides to the rest of the world, and in some cases, even an old Baedeker guidebook or two.

Book Passage, 51 Tamal Vista, Corte Madera, CA 94925 (phone: 415-927-0960 in California; 800-321-9785 elsewhere in the US). Travel guides and maps to all areas of the world. A free catalogue is available.

The Complete Traveller, 199 Madison Ave., New York, NY 10016 (phone: 212-685-9007). Travel guides and maps. A catalogue is available for $2.

Forsyth Travel Library, PO Box 2975, 9154 W. 57th St., Shawnee Mission, KS 66201-1375 (phone: 913-384-0496 or 800-367-7984). Travel guides and maps, old and new, to all parts of the world. Ask for the Europe-only catalogue or the more extensive, worldwide catalogue.

Gourmet Guides, 2801 Leavenworth St., San Francisco, CA 94133 (phone: 415-771-3671). Travel guides and maps, along with cookbooks. Mail order lists available on request, including one about Great Britain.

Phileas Fogg's Books and Maps, Stanford Shopping Center, Palo Alto, CA 94304 (phone: 415-327-1754). Travel guides, maps, and language aids.

Thomas Brothers Maps & Travel Books, 603 W. Seventh St., Los Angeles, CA 90017 (phone: 213-627-4018). Maps (including road atlases, street guides, and wall maps), guidebooks, and travel accessories. Catalogue available.

Traveller's Bookstore, 22 W. 52nd St. (lobby), New York, NY 10019 (phone: 212-664-0995). Comprehensive collection of travel guides and maps. A catalogue is available for $2.

The Travel Suppliers, 727 N. Placentia Ave., Fullerton, CA 92631 (phone: 714-

528-2502). Books and maps, plus travel paraphernalia from money belts and pouches to voltage and currency converters. Catalogue available.

Before or after your trip you may want to subscribe to a publication that specializes in information about Britain. *In Britain,* a monthly magazine published by the British Tourist Authority, spotlights the smaller cities and towns and various parts of the countryside and contains sketches about contemporary and historical personalities. To subscribe, write to *In Britain,* PO Box 1238, Allwood, Clifton, NJ 07012 ($32.95 for 1 year). Single copies cost $3.50 at the *British Travel Bookshop* (address above). Concerned with London almost exclusively is *Letter from London,* an 8-page newsletter published independently roughly once a month by Mary Anne Evans, a native Londoner, who reports on a wide variety of topics — hotels and restaurants, shopping, current and upcoming gallery exhibitions and theater productions, and the like. Each issue also contains a "Country Letter," featuring an event or place out of town. For a sample issue or a subscription ($5 for a sample issue; $69 for 10 yearly issues), write: *Letter from London,* 63 E. 79th St., Apt. 4A, New York, NY 10021. (Note, there is no telephone number to call.)

Genealogy Hunts

For those interested in their British heritage, it's possible to trace British ancestors by mail or to hire a professional genealogist. Stateside, researchers can go to the Church of Latter-day Saints' genealogical library in Salt Lake City, where thousands of reels of microfilmed records are filed. But nothing is quite as satisfying as going to the British Isles, flipping through the records, and actually visiting the area where your ancestor lived. Thanks to an abundance of records kept throughout the ages in Britain, the descendants of yeoman and middle class families can trace their heritage back to the 1400s; but even if your pedigree is not quite so grandiose, there's a good chance that you'll be able to worship in a church where some great-great-great-great-grandfather was married, walk up to the house where his children were born, read a will written in his own hand, or photograph his moss-covered gravestone in some peaceful country churchyard. Doing the research in person, on the spot, rather than by mail, is more efficient, since clues can be followed up immediately.

It goes without saying, however, that it isn't possible to even begin to search in Great Britain until the groundwork has been laid at home. It is necessary to know not only the name of the emigrant ancestor, but also the dates of his or her birth and emigration. It is also important to have a general idea of where he or she came from. The names of your ancestors' relatives can also be useful. From there, it will be possible to consult parish registers and the archives of various public record offices and genealogical libraries. *Note:* Don't forget about the realignment of British counties that took place in 1974; many records were relocated at that time.

Birth certificates give the date and place where the event occurred; the child's forenames; the father's name and occupation; the mother's name and maiden surname; her usual residence if the birth took place elsewhere; and the name and address of the person providing the information.

Marriage certificates give the names of the contracting parties; their ages (most of the time, that is — remember that some people stretched the truth a bit); their fathers' names and occupations; the date and place of the marriage; and the names of the witnesses.

A death certificate records the date, place, and cause of death, plus the deceased's name, age, occupation, and usual residence (if different from the place of death), and the name and address of the person furnishing the data.

The details on a birth certificate usually tell you enough so that you can look for the parents' marriage certificate, and the marriage certificate will usually give you the information you need to find the records of the births of the two parties.

ENGLAND AND WALES

In the 13th century, England united with Wales, so although the Welsh have their own language, the two countries' records are essentially one and the same.

The search is easiest if your ancestor emigrated after 1837, when civil registration of births, marriages, and deaths was introduced in both countries. The General Register Office (St. Catherine's House, 10 Kingsway, London WC2B 6JP) houses the records. Like most in Britain, they're indexed, but to get particulars you have to request a certificate, the preparation of which takes a day or two. A certficate costs £10 (about $15) if applied for by mail, £5 (about $7.50) if in person.

Once you know the addresses, you may get further information from returns of the censuses taken decennially from 1841 and now housed at the Census Room of the Public Record Office (Land Registry Bldg., Portugal St., London WC2) as far as the year 1881. Later returns are held by the General Register Office (address above). Complete data from later returns become available only after a century has passed from the census date, but partial information from the 1891 and 1901 censuses is available in some circumstances.

These and other British records should lead you, if your American research did not already, to the period before 1837. In this era, it's the registers of the 14,000 parish churches in England and Wales that are your most valuable source. Gaps in their listings of baptisms, marriages, and burials do exist, but some volumes date from as early as 1538, when the law requiring the clergy to keep such records went into effect. Copies of many of them are at the *Society of Genealogists,* a private genealogical library open to the public for a fee at 14 Charterhouse Buildings, Goswell Rd., London EC1M 7BA (phone: 01-251-8799); it has catalogues of the copies that can be found here and elsewhere. Where no copies exist, you can find out the originals' whereabouts from the appropriate County Record Office. (A list of County Record Offices' addresses has been published by Her Majesty's Stationery Office, London.) When you do locate the parish, use *Crockford's Clerical Directory* to find the name and address of the clergyman who currently has custody of the records. Make an appointment as far in advance as possible to be sure that the clergyman will have time to show you his records.

The County Record Offices provide other valuable information. Many well-to-do folk were married by license in the good old days, and records of the proceedings can often be found in the County Record Offices. Others are housed in the Lambeth Palace Library (London SE1 7JU; phone: 01-928-6222) and the Guildhall Library (Aldermanbury, London EC2P 2EJ; phone: 01-606-3030), which has an extensive collection of the material on London.

Various central indexes of vital records, available in genealogical libraries, can also be useful. *Boyd's Marriage Index,* which covers the period from 1538 to 1837, is only one.

Among the genealogist's best tools are wills, especially in Wales, where, until the mid-19th century, surnames changed with each generation, as in Scandinavian countries. The information in a will can often clarify relationships of people whose names you've found mentioned elsewhere, and the particulars are almost always reliable.

Sometimes you can make up charts for several generations of a family from just one will. If the document (or a copy) was proved since 1858, you'll find it at the Principal Probate Registry (Somerset House, The Strand, London WC2; phone: 01-936-6000). Before 1858, wills were proved in a variety of courts, depending on the deceased's holdings. If these were varied and widespread and the deceased lived in the southern half of England, the will was generally proved in the Prerogative Court of Canterbury (PCC); if he lived in the north, in the Prerogative Court of York. The PCC records, which begin in 1383 and are indexed, are at the Public Record Office (Chancery La., London WC2A 1LR; phone: 01-876-3444). The York probate records, which date from 1389, are at the Borthwick Institute (St. Anthony's Hall, Peasholme Green, York YO1 2PW; phone: 9046-42315), and are indexed to 1858. (By appointment only, so write well before your visit.)

When, sooner or later, you hit a snag in your research, you can get help at the *Society of Genealogists.* In addition to the parish register transcripts, it houses a vast general index of names, a 7-million-entry marriage index, and a collection of documents relating to some 13,000 families, plus material for Scottish and Welsh families and for English families abroad. When you need professional help, consult the College of Arms (Queen Victoria St., London EC4V 4BT; phone: 01-248-2762). The *British Travel Bookshop* carries *Discovering Your Family Tree* ($5.95) and *Discovering Surnames* ($4.95 each); postage depends on the amount ordered; call 212-765-0898 or write 40 W. 57th St., New York, NY 10019, and ask for its book list.

SCOTLAND

Many Scots, including boatloads of prisoners boarded against their will, crossed the Atlantic in the 17th and 18th centuries during the political turmoil that followed the deposition of the Catholic King James II and the struggle of his grandson Charles Edward Stuart — "Bonnie Prince Charlie" (1720–88) — to regain the throne. Flora Macdonald, who helped this romantic fellow escape after his defeat in 1746 at Culloden Moor, was just one of the Scottish immigrants of this period.

Tracing these families, and others, can be relatively simple here, for in addition to the fact that the records are remarkably thorough to begin with, they're all centrally located. The General Register Office for Scotland (New Register House, Edinburgh EH1 3YT) contains not only the records of births, marriages, and deaths since the beginning of compulsory registration in 1855, but also information from about 4,000 old parish registers dealing with Scotland's 900 parishes before compulsory registration. The earliest of these dates to 1553, although more commonly they begin in the 17th or 18th century. The fact that married women are also often listed under their maiden names makes the task just that much easier. Better yet, New Register House is also the repository for the returns of the decennial census, from 1841 onward, and those up to and including that of 1891 may be consulted.

Wills, justiciary records, deeds, services of heirs, and other legal documents are also in Edinburgh, at the Scottish Record Office in H. M. Register House, Princes St., Edinburgh EH1 3YY. Registers of sasines, a Scottish document dealing with the descent of land, are also available here.

Although these records may be all you need, there are also many books, articles, and unpublished materials that may help you work out any knotty problems you encounter. The *Scots Ancestry Research Society* (3 Albany St., Edinburgh EH1 3PY) and the *Scottish Genealogogist Society* (write to the Honorary Secretary, 21 Howard Pl., Edinburgh EH3 5JY) can help you directly or provide the names of professional searchers. Margaret Stuart's *Scottish Family History: A Guide to Works of Reference on the History and Genealogy of Scottish Families* (1930), Joan Ferguson's *Scottish Family Histories*

Held in Scottish Libraries (1960), and G. F. Black's *Surnames of Scotland* (1962) may also prove helpful. You may also be interested in contacting the *Museum of Scottish Tartans* (Davidson House, Drummond St., Comrie, Perthshire PH6 2DW; phone: 0764-70779), a non-profit cultural organization that maintains an enormous fund of information about tartans.

SPECIAL PROBLEMS

If your ancestor did not belong to the established church of the land, you may have difficulties at first, but there are special genealogical societies and/or guides for just about any sect you can name. The records of the Society of Friends, for instance, are a dream — superbly indexed and organized. Information about the Huguenots, the French Protestants who came in great waves from the late 16th century and especially around 1685, following the revocation of the Edict of Nantes, can be pursued by writing to the *Huguenot Society of London* (c/o University College, Gower St., London WC1 E6BT; phone: 01-387-7050). Research into Jewish ancestry can be slow going because of frequent name changes. The *Jewish Historical Society of England* (33 Seymour Pl., London W1H 5AP; phone: 01-723-4404) is a great resource. For help in finding societies concerned with other groups, contact the big genealogical libraries in the country of your ancestors' origin.

Weights and Measures

When you are traveling in the Great Britain, you'll find that just about every quantity, whether it is length, weight, or capacity, may be in an unfamiliar figure. In fact, this is true for travel almost everywhere in the world, since the US is one of the last countries to make its way to the metric system. It may happen soon in the US, and your trip to Great Britain may serve to familiarize you with what will one day be the weights and measures at your grocery store.

There are some specific things to keep in mind during your trip. The British still use the pre–Common Market system, which is more familiar to US travelers, though they are adapting to European standards because of a uniformity of measurement needed by 1992. Fruits and vegetables at a market are recorded in pounds and ounces, but your luggage at the airport and your body weight may well be in kilos (kilograms). (This latter is particularly pleasing to people of large build, who instead of weighing 220 pounds hit the scales at a mere 100 kilos.) A kilo is 2.2 pounds and 1 pound is .45 kilos. Body temperature is measured in degrees Centigrade or Celsius as well as on the more familiar Fahrenheit scale, so that a normal body temperature may be expressed as either 37C or 98.6F, and freezing is either 0 degrees C or 32F. Highway signs are written in several styles: in black and white for miles; in green and white for kilometers; or in miles and kilometers (1 mile equals 1.6 kilometers; 1 kilometer equals .62 mile). Where speed limits are in kilometers per hour, think twice before hitting the gas when you see a speed limit of 100 (which means 62 mph). Gasoline is sold either by the liter (approximately 4 to a gallon) or by the gallon; and remember that a British or "imperial" gallon is 20% larger than an American gallon. Weights are given not only in pounds but also stones; one stone equals 14 pounds.

The tables and conversion factors listed below should give you all the information you need to understand any transaction, road sign, or map you encounter on your travels.

CONVERSION TABLES
METRIC TO US MEASUREMENTS

Multiply:	by:	to convert to:
LENGTH		
millimeters	.04	inches
meters	3.3	feet
meters	1.1	yards
kilometers	.6	miles
CAPACITY		
liters	2.11	pints (liquid)
liters	1.06	quarts (liquid)
liters	.26	gallons (liquid)
WEIGHT		
grams	.04	ounces (avoir.)
kilograms	2.2	pounds (avoir.)

US TO METRIC MEASUREMENTS

LENGTH		
inches	25.	millimeters
feet	.3	meters
yards	.9	meters
miles	1.6	kilometers
CAPACITY		
pints	.47	liters
quarts	.95	liters
gallons	3.8	liters
WEIGHT		
ounces	28.	grams
pounds	.45	kilograms

TEMPERATURE

$°F = (°C \times 9/5) + 32$ $°C = (°F - 32) \times 5/9$

APPROXIMATE EQUIVALENTS		
Metric Unit	**Abbreviation**	**US Equivalent**
LENGTH		
meter	m	39.37 inches
kilometer	km	.62 mile
millimeter	mm	.04 inch
CAPACITY		
liter	l	1.057 quarts
WEIGHT		
gram	g	.035 ounce
kilogram	kg	2.2 pounds
metric ton	MT	1.1 ton
ENERGY		
kilowatt	kw	1.34 horsepower

Camera and Equipment

Vacations are everybody's favorite time for taking pictures. After all, most of us want to remember the places we visit — and show them off to others — through spectacular photographs. Here are a few suggestions to help you get the best results from your picture-taking.

BEFORE THE TRIP: If you're taking out your camera after a long period in mothballs or have just bought a new one, check it thoroughly before you leave to prevent unexpected breakdowns and disappointing pictures.

1. Shoot at least one test roll, using the kind of film you plan to take along with you. Use all the shutter speeds and f-stops on your camera, and vary the focus to make sure everything is in order. Do this well before you leave so that there will be time to have the film developed and to make repairs if necessary. If you're in a rush, most large cities have custom labs that can process film in as little as an hour. Repairs, unfortunately, take longer.
2. Clean the camera thoroughly, inside and out. Dust and dirt can jam mechanisms, scratch film, and mar photographs. Remove surface dust from the lenses and camera body with a soft camel's-hair brush. Next, use at least two layers of crumpled lens tissue and your breath to clean lenses and filters. Don't rub hard and don't use water, saliva, or compressed air on lenses or filters because they are easily damaged. Persistent stains can be removed by using a Q-tip moistened with liquid lens cleaner. Anything that doesn't come off easily needs professional attention. Once your lenses are clean, protect them from dirt and damage with inexpensive skylight or ultraviolet filters.
3. Check the batteries for the light meter, and take along extras just in case they wear out during the trip.

EQUIPMENT TO TAKE ALONG: Keep your gear light and compact. Items that are too heavy or bulky to be carried comfortably on a full-day excursion will likely stay in your hotel room.

1. Most single lens reflex (SLR) cameras come with a 50mm, or "normal," lens, a general purpose lens that frames subjects within an approximately average angle of view. This is good for street scenes taken at a distance of 25 feet or more and for full-length portraits shot at 8 to 12 feet. You can expand your photographic options with a wide-angle lens, such as a 35mm, 28mm, or 24mm. These give a broader than normal angle of view and greater than normal "depth of field," that is, sharp focus from foreground to background. They are especially handy for panoramas, cityscapes, and for large buildings or statuary from which you can't step back. For extreme closeups, a macro lens is best, but a screw-on magnifying lens is an inexpensive alternative. Telephoto lenses, 65mm to 1000mm, are good for shooting details from a distance (as in animal photography), but since they tend to be heavy and bulky, unless you anticipate a frequent need for them, omit them from vacation photography equipment. A zoom, which is a big lens but relatively light, has a variable angle of view so it gives a range of options. Try a 35mm to 80mm; beware of inexpensive models that give poor quality photographs. Protect all lenses with skylight or ultraviolet filters, which should be removed for cleaning only. A polarizing filter helps to eliminate glare and reflection and to achieve fully saturated colors in very bright sunlight. Take along a couple of extra lens caps (they're the first things to get lost) or buy an inexpensive lens cap "leash."
2. Travel photographs work best in color. Good slide films are Kodachrome 64 and Fujichrome 50, both moderate- to slow-speed films that provide saturated colors and work well in most outdoor lighting situations. For very bright conditions, try slower film like Kodachrome 25. If the weather is cloudy or you're indoors with only natural light, use a faster film, such as Kodachrome or Ektachrome 200 or 400. These can be "pushed" to higher speeds. There are even faster films on the market for low-light situations. The result may be pictures with whiter, colder tones and a grainier image, but high-speed films open up picture possibilities that slower films cannot.

   Films tend to render color in slightly different ways. Kodachrome brings out reds and oranges. Fujichrome is noted for its yellows, greens, and whites. Agfachrome mutes bright tones, producing fine browns, yellows, and whites. Anticipate what you are likely to see, and take along whichever types of film will enhance your results. You might test films as you test your camera (see above).

   If you prefer film that develops into prints rather than slides, try Kodacolor 100 or 400 for most lighting situations. Vericolor is a professional film that gives excellent results, especially in skin tones, but it suffers shifts in color when subjected to temperature extremes; take it along for photographing people *if* you're sure you can protect it from heat and cold. All lens and filter information applies equally to print and slide films.

   How much film should you take? If you are serious about your photography, pack one roll of film (36 exposures) for each day of your trip. Film is especially expensive abroad, and any leftovers can be bartered away or brought home and safely stored in your refrigerator. Processing is also generally more expensive away from home — and not always as good. If you are concerned about airport security X-rays damaging your undeveloped film (X-rays do not affect processed film), store it in lead-lined bags sold in camera shops. This possibility is not as much of a threat as it used to be, however. In the US, incidents of X-ray damage to unprocessed film (exposed or unexposed) are minimal because low-dosage X-ray equipment is used virtually everywhere. As a rule of thumb, photo industry sources say that film with speeds up to ASA 400 can go through security machinery in the US five times without any noticeable effect. Overseas, the situation varies from country to country, but at least in Western Europe the trend is also toward equipment that delivers less and less radiation. While it is doubtful that one exposure would ruin your pictures, if you're traveling without a protective bag you may want to ask to have your photo equipment inspected by hand, especially on a prolonged trip with repeated security checks. (Naturally, this is possible only if you're carrying your film and camera on board with you; it's a good idea anyway, because it helps to preclude loss or theft or the possibility at some airports that checked baggage will be X-rayed more heavily than hand baggage.) In the US, Federal Aviation Administration regulations require that if you request a hand inspection, you get it, but overseas the response may depend on the humor of the inspector. One type of film that should never be subjected to X-rays, even in the US, is the new, very high speed film with an ASA rating of 1000. If you are taking some of this overseas, note that there are lead-lined bags made especially for it. Finally, the walk-through metal detector devices at airports do not affect film, though the film cartridges will set them off.

3. A small battery-powered electronic flash unit, or "strobe," is handy for very dim light or at night, but only if the subject is at a distance of 15 feet or less. Flash units cannot illuminate an entire scene, and many museums do not permit flash photography, so take such a unit only if you know you will need it. If your camera does not have a hot-shoe, you will need a PC cord to synchronize the flash with your shutter. Be sure to take along extra batteries.
4. Invest in a broad camera strap if you now have a thin one. It will make carrying the camera much more comfortable. For safety and ease of use, keep the camera strapped around your neck (not on your shoulder) whenever it is out of its bag.
5. A sturdy canvas or leather camera bag, preferably with padded pockets — not an airline bag — will keep equipment clean, organized, and easy to find.
6. For cleaning, bring along a camel's-hair brush that retracts into a rubber squeeze bulb. Also, take plenty of lens tissue and plastic bags to protect equipment from dust.

SOME TIPS: For better pictures, remember the following pointers:

1. *Get close.* Move in to get your subject to fill the frame.
2. *Vary your angle.* Shoot from above or below — look for unusual perspectives.
3. *Pay attention to backgrounds.* Keep it simple or blur it out.
4. *Look for details.* Not just a whole building, but a decorative element; not just an entire street scene, but a single remarkable face.
5. *Don't be lazy.* Always carry your camera gear with you, loaded and ready for those unexpected memorable moments.

Words to the Wise

"Two people divided by the same language" is how Oscar Wilde described the transatlantic relationship between Britain and the US. He had a point. Below are some common British terms followed by their standard American translations. For definitions of terms that do not necessarily have American equivalents — such as "bubble and squeak" (a dish of leftover cabbage and potatoes) and "royal duke" (a duke who, as a member of the royal family, is also a prince) — consult the *Dictionary of Britain: An A to Z of the British Way of Life,* by Adrian Room (Oxford University Press; $24.95; $8.95 paperback). It can also take the mystery out of the local newspapers by supplying the meanings of all sorts of British acronyms, from CAMRA (Campaign for Real Ale) to USDAW (Union of Shop, Distributive, and Allied Workers).

The following words and phrases should help you:

aubergine: eggplant
bespoke: custom-made
biscuit: cookie or cracker
bonnet (car): hood
boot (car): trunk
candy floss: cotton candy
car park: parking lot
chemist's shop: drugstore
chips: French fries
coach: long-distance bus
cotton: thread
cotton wool: absorbent cotton
crisps: potato chips
cul-de-sac: dead end
dual carriageway: divided highway
dynamo (car): generator
face flannel: washcloth
flat: apartment
flyover: overpass
fortnight: 2 weeks
gear lever: gearshift
hire purchase: installment plan
joint (meat): roast
jumper (or jersey): sweater
left luggage office: baggage room
lemonade: general term for soda
lemon Squash: what Americans call lemonade
lift: elevator
loch: lake
loo, lavatory, WC: bathroom
lorry: truck
mackintosh, mac: raincoat
nappy: diaper
off licence/wine merchant: liquor store
overtake: pass
petrol: gasoline
pram: baby carriage
public school: private school
queue: stand in line
quid: pound
rasher: slice of bacon
reception: front desk
return ticket: round-trip ticket
roundabout: traffic circle
rubber: eraser
silencer (car): muffler
single ticket: one-way ticket
stalls (theater): orchestra seats

stone: measure of weight equal to 14 pounds
surgery: doctor's or dentist's office
trainers: sneakers
trunk call: long-distance call
underground, tube: subway
wally: a fool
wellingtons or wellies (sometimes called galoshes): rubber boots

PERSPECTIVES

History

Who built Stonehenge? Alas, we don't really know. Britain is an island and its earliest history is a succession of invasions and immigrations. In one of these waves the original inhabitants of Britain disappeared, leaving behind great stone circles like those at Stonehenge and Avebury, built about 2000 BC, and primitive flint tools, but no trace of their language or heritage.

The Bronze Age reached Britain sometime after 1600 BC, brought by a race of people known as the "Beaker Folk," identified by their tools fashioned from Cornish tin and Irish copper, and pottery of a distinctively idiosyncratic shape.

THE CELTS

In the 7th century BC there arrived on the island the first tribes for whom there is a definite historical record. These were the Celts, a race of warriors, artists, and bards who decorated their shields with intricate abstract designs and forged their weapons from iron. They brought with them a priestly caste called the Druids, who led them in worshiping a pantheon of nature spirits in groves of trees and administered the tribes' systems of law and education. Remains of an Iron Age village can be seen at Maiden Castle in Dorset.

About 75 BC the Belgae (present day Belgium is named for them) settled in England. A chief of the Belgae, Cymbeline (ca. AD 5–40), who gave his name and very little else to a play by Shakespeare, is the first identifiable figure in British history. He minted coins that bore his own image and established a tribal capital at Colchester. Cymbeline died just before the second Roman invasion in AD 43.

THE ROMANS

Julius Caesar landed in Britain at Dover with an expeditionary force in 55 BC primarily to cut off communication between tribal chiefs on the island and those in Gaul. But it was not until Claudius's personal expedition nearly a century later that a permanent garrison was established and that conquest began in earnest.

At first the Celtic tribes resisted the Romans fiercely, chiefly under Caractus, son of Cymbeline, who was captured and taken to Rome, and Boadicea, the first of a series of remarkable women in British history, who was the chief of a Norfolk tribe, the Iceni. It was only after Boadicea's defeat and suicide by poison in AD 61 that the Pax Romana finally prevailed in the southern part of England.

In the north, skirmishes continued for decades, prompting Emperor Hadrian, who had visited Britain in 121, to build (ca. 122–127) the 73½-mile-long wall that stretches from the Tyne River in northeast England to Solway Firth in southwest Scotland and is named for him.

Until 450, Britain south of the wall was the Roman province of Britannia, a source for the empire's Cornish tin, grain, and slaves.

The impact of Roman civilization was indelible, not least in the establishment of a capital where the Thames River becomes narrow enough to ford. They named it Londinium — London. Other towns flourished too, among them Eboracum (York), Lindum (Lincoln), Devana Castrum (Chester), and Aquae Sulis (Bath), where sections of the ancient baths can still be seen. In addition, the conquerors built for military purposes the famous Roman Roads, among them the Fosseway, part of which is today a quiet country road in southern Warwickshire.

The street plans of many English towns betray Roman origins, although the schools where Greek and Roman law were taught and the villas with their remarkably sophisticated central heating systems lie buried beneath rubble and grass.

ANGLES, SAXONS, AND JUTES

In the middle of the 4th century, piratic raids of the province of Britannia by the Scoti, an Irish race, and the Picts, inhabitants of present-day Scotland, increased, while a series of Saxon tribes of the Teutonic race penetrated the southeast of the country. Cut off from supply routes by the Teutonic conquest of Gaul and faced with the disintegration of the empire in Rome, the Roman legions withdrew from Britain. Lacking a trained army of their own, the native Celts fled to the western fringes of their land, where their descendants flourish today. The territory they left was occupied not only by the Saxons, but also by their kinfolk from northern Germany, the Jutes, and by the tribe that gave its name to the southern half of Britain, the Angles. These loosely knit tribes gradually coalesced into what became known as the Heptarchy — the seven kingdoms of Wessex (the West Country), Essex (southeastern England north of London), Sussex, Kent, East Anglia, Mercia (the midlands) and Northumbria (northern England). Occasionally one king among the seven would achieve primacy, and it was during the supremacy of Ethelbert of Kent that Augustine the Monk (St. Augustine of Canterbury) arrived in southeast England in 597.

CHRISTIANITY

There had been Roman Christians in the service of the Empire, among them the father of Patrick, the Apostle of Ireland, and Irish missionaries had established isolated Christian settlements on the Celtic fringe in the northwest of England and the west of Scotland. But the descendants of the Teutonic invaders in most parts of England had not been converted.

Much of English history can be told in a series of anecdotes and the first is probably that concerning the conversion of England. The story goes that Pope Gregory I (St. Gregory the Great) was walking in Rome one day when he spotted some handsome flaxen-haired youths in chains.

"Who are they?" he asked.

"Angles," he was told, "pagans."

"Not Angles," the pope replied, "angels!" And he decided that their country belonged to Christ.

Thus, Augustine the Benedictine, charged with the task, presented himself to King Ethelbert, who gave the monk and his companions some land at Canterbury, and founded the see that is still first in authority in England.

Contact with the Celtic church led to conflict. The customs of the Roman monks were less austere than those of the Irish and they calculated the date of Easter by different means. When they met at the Synod of Whitby in 664 the differences were settled and the Celtic church submitted to Rome, which was to dominate England spiritually for the next 870 years.

There followed a golden age of monastic learning and religious art, especially manuscript illumination. Missionaries from the British church were known all over Europe. Theodore of Tarsus, Archbishop of Canterbury from 690 to 699, introduced the Roman system of bishoprics and parishes and initiated national synods that brought the rival kingdoms together for the first time. How well he succeeded is proven by the title of St. Bede's Ecclesiastical History of the English People, published ca. 731, which suggests that by this date the inhabitants of the country were accustomed to thinking of "England" as a unit.

Certainly the Mercian King Offa (reigned 757–796) thought so. He was the first king to sign himself on charters as Rex Anglorum (King of the English), the existence of other kings notwithstanding. Offa is perhaps best remembered for Offa's Dyke, the entrenchment he built as a barrier against the Welsh on the border of England and Wales. Parts of the dyke are well preserved. Offa's burial place, Offchurch in Warwickshire, is an exquisite village not far from Stratford-upon-Avon.

It was in Offa's reign that the first of the Danish raids on the English coast took place. These were followed by a series of Viking onslaughts, until only the kingdom of Wessex, under the first English national hero, Alfred the Great (849–899), was offering resistance. Alfred is remembered in legend by all English schoolchildren. The story goes that after an especially unsuccessful skirmish with the Danes, he was forced to flee to the Somerset fens, where he took refuge with an old peasant woman who did not recognize him. The woman gave him shelter and food and asked him to watch some oaten cakes that she had placed on the fire. Alfred began to think of his next campaign and the cakes started to burn. When the old woman returned, she scolded the shabby king roundly. Whether or not the story is true, it is certain that his mind was frequently occupied with defeating — or compromising with — the Danish invaders. At the Peace of Wedmore in 878, defeat and compromise came hand in hand. Having temporarily bested the Danes, Alfred extracted a promise from their chief, Guthrun, that he would become a Christian and leave England in peace, and they divided the country between them. The line of demarcation ran roughly from southeast to northwest, with Alfred taking the southern part, including London. The northern part was ceded to Danish immigrants and became known thereafter as the Danelaw, the territory where the rules and customs of Denmark flourished.

Alfred was not only a warrior, he was also a scholar; as the first translator from Latin to English of St. Bede's History, he is acknowledged to be one of the fathers of English literature. He invited European scholars to his court, instituted schools, and directed the foundation of the Anglo-Saxon Chronicle, ca. 891, the sole source of much of our knowledge of early Christian England.

Alfred's son, Edward (reigned 899–924), began the reconquest of the Danelaw, which was completed under Edward's son, Athelstan (reigned 924–939). The Vikings were christianized and absorbed into Anglo-Saxon society. One Dane, Oda, became Archbishop of Canterbury in 924.

In 991 the Viking raids began again, led by Sven Forkbeard, King of Denmark. By 1013 Sven was acknowledged ruler of England and Ethelred the Unready, the English king, fled to Normandy. Sven's son Canute (reigned 1017–35), although the son of a conqueror, was revered by subsequent generations of Englishmen, largely because of his treatment of some sycophantic courtiers. Legend has it that among Canute's entourage were some who considered him to be — or said that they considered him to be — semi-divine. They claimed that if he wished, he could turn back the tide. When the rumor came to Canute's ears, he took his court to the shore, where he sat in his throne commanding the tide to recede. When it didn't, he reminded the offenders of the difference between the honor that belonged to God and that which belonged to the king.

Canute, through his sons, also ruled Norway and Denmark. When he died, ruling such a large northern empire proved too difficult for his heirs. In 1042 Danish rule ended in England and Ethelred's son, Edward (reigned 1042–66), came from Normandy to claim his crown.

The saintly Edward, known as the Confessor, had little taste or flair for kingship. His main preoccupation was with religion (in 1065 he founded the Church of St. Peter, which later became famous as Westminster Abbey), and he was politically and physically dominated by the powerful Earl Godwin of Wessex, whose son Harold succeeded the childless Edward to the throne in 1066.

THE NORMAN CONQUEST

When Harold Godwinsson (1022?–66) arrived at Hastings to meet the Norman invaders, he was already the triumphant victor over his brother Tostig and Harold III of Norway in a decisive battle at Stamford Bridge on September 25, 1066. He was killed at the Battle of Hastings on October 14, by a Norman arrow that penetrated one of his eyes. A 230-foot-long embroidery attributed to William the Conqueror's wife, Matilda, illustrates the incident. Called the Bayeux Tapestry, it is housed in the Bayeux Museum in Normandy.

By Christmas Day, the Conqueror, William I (1027?–87), the illegitimate son of Robert I of Normandy and a tanner's daughter, had been crowned King of England. There were to be other invasions of England, but this was the last to succeed. It is from this point on that England stops being constantly on the defensive, and becomes a country determined to expand. The culmination of this desire was reached in the vast empire ruled from London in the reign of Victoria.

Resistance to William was never very effective. The Saxon rebels, ill-equipped and generally disorganized, were no match for the Norman cavalry clad in chain mail and garrisoned in fortified keeps. The most famous outlaw was Hereward the Wake, a Saxon chieftain from Lincolnshire, who made one valiant last stand in the fens of the Isle of Ely. Hereward's exploits made him a folk hero. He is known as the Last of the English.

Perhaps the greatest legacy William left was the Domesday (or Doomsday) Book, a record of a survey made in 1085–86 of every parcel of land in England, who owned it, and who had owned it.

William was succeeded in England by his son, William II (reigned 1087–1100), called William Rufus because of his ruddy complexion. William II made enemies of the church by the sale of church lands, and of the people by ruthless taxation. He was killed while hunting in the New Forest by what history has politely termed a stray arrow, and was followed by his brother, Henry I (reigned 1100–1135), known as Henry Beauclerk (the fine clerk) for his ability to read and write. During Henry's reign an accounting system for administering the income and expenditure of the realm was introduced. This system was the nucleus of the modern exchequer. Henry also appointed justices to travel into the provinces to see that the laws of the realm were administered fairly, causing him to be known as the Lion of Justice. Henry's only son, William, died in 1120 in what has become known as the Wreck of the White Ship in the English Channel. Legend has it that after the death of his heir, the king was never again known to smile. His only remaining child was a daughter, Matilda (1102–67), who at the age of 23 became the widowed empress of Germany and at 26 the Countess of Anjou. In 1126, 1131, and again in 1133, Henry had required a group of powerful English barons — and, most notably, his nephew Stephen of Blois (1097–1154) — to acknowledge Matilda as Henry's successor to the throne. On Henry's death in 1135, Stephen repudiated his oath and had himself declared king. The result was an era of civil war and anarchy during which, men said, "the heavens slept." Following the death of Stephen's son, Eustace (1153), Matilda's son Henry was accepted as heir apparent.

Henry II (1135–89), by his marriage to the remarkable Eleanor of Aquitaine and through his succession to possessions in Normandy and Anjou, was the lord of a large part of France, a fact that was to dominate English history for nearly 250 years. Henry is best remembered for his quarrel with Thomas à Becket, his former crony, which brought to a head the conflict between church and state.

THE CHURCH IN THE MIDDLE AGES

The church in Henry's time was an almost autonomous organization existing side by side with the secular authority represented by the king. The right to invest archbishops and bishops with symbols of their office had been won for the church by Thomas's predecessor, St. Anselm, in 1107, making the pope, and not the king, supreme authority in ecclesiastical matters. The visible power of the church in Henry II's day was everywhere. Many of the cathedrals that are one of England's glories today were in their infancy in Henry's reign: Durham Cathedral, the most perfect example of Norman architecture in Britain, was consecrated in 1093, Ely in 1083, Winchester in 1093, and Norwich in 1096. In addition the great Cistercian abbeys of Rievaulx, Jervaulx, and Fountains, and the Benedictine houses at Selby and Whitby and other places, served to remind the king of the power of the church. The crisis with Becket reached its climax over who should prosecute those men in Holy Orders who had broken the law — "criminous clerks," as they were called. The crown and its justices, said Henry. The church, said Thomas. It was more than a matter of church and state, however. Thomas à Becket had been Henry's closest friend and as chancellor of England had lived as a sybarite. On his appointment to the Archbishopric of Canterbury, his personal habits had become austere and the authority he acknowledged was not Henry's but that of the church. Henry, so the story goes, was heard to mutter, "Will no one rid me of this troublesome priest?" and shortly afterward Thomas was murdered by four knights of Henry's entourage. The murder shocked the whole Christian world. Within 3 years Thomas had been canonized and Henry was forced to do penance at his shrine. Canterbury became a place of pilgrimage surpassed in Europe only by Santiago de Compostela in Spain. Its importance was immortalized in Chaucer's *Canterbury Tales,* while the crisis between the two former friends has inspired numerous biographies and dramas, the most famous of which are Anouilh's Becket and T. S. Eliot's *Murder in the Cathedral.*

Henry's son Richard I, called Richard the Lion-Hearted (1157–99), has appealed to movie-makers rather than dramatists — especially as the king who reigned during the exploits of the legendary Robin Hood. Although he was king for 10 years, Richard spent only two of them in England. In the popular imagination Richard is a benign and just monarch, the very antithesis of his sinister brother, John Lackland. The truth about Richard is more complicated. He was chivalrous, brave, war loving, and homosexual. His devotion to the Third Crusade seems to have arisen from a taste for military combat as much as a desire to bear witness to the glory of God. The most romantic story concerning Richard tells of his release from captivity in Germany. On his way home from the Crusade in 1190, he was taken prisoner by Leopold II, Margrave of Austria. Richard's favorite troubador, Blondel de Nesle, wandered through Europe singing a song known only to the two of them. As he sang outside Dürstein Castle, Blondel heard a voice responding to his song and was able to tell Richard's friends where he was incarcerated.

There are no romantic stories about King John (1166–1216). He is best known as the king who was forced to accept the Magna Carta by his barons at Runnymede in June 1215. The charter set forth the principle that the king was not absolute and that he was required to observe the rights of subjects and communities. There is no written constitution in Britain and to this day the Magna Carta is one of the most important documents in British constitutional history.

John's son, Henry III (1207–72), succeeded to the throne as a 9-year-old boy. The quarrels with powerful barons that had marred his father's reign were even more serious during that of Henry. In 1258, a group of noblemen under the leadership of Henry's brother-in-law, Simon de Montfort, forced

Henry to acknowledge the Provisions of Oxford, which effectively handed over power to a council of 15 members. Henry repudiated the provisions in 1261 and thereby started a 6-year struggle with his barons, during which de Montfort was killed at the battle of Evesham in 1265.

In spite of the constant atmosphere of crisis between the king and the barons, cultural life in England flourished during Henry's reign. Three great colleges of Oxford University were founded during this period: University College (1249); Balliol (1263); and Merton (1264). At the same time the Franciscan philosopher and scientist Roger Bacon (ca. 1214–94) made Oxford the greatest center of learning in Europe.

Henry's son, Edward I (1239–1307), found himself more often in conflict with his Welsh and Scottish neighbors than with his barons. He completed the conquest of Wales in 1282, and in 1301 had his son (later Edward II, 1284–1327), who had conveniently been born in the castle at Carnarvon in North Wales, declared prince of that country. The title Prince of Wales has usually been given to the eldest son of the sovereign ever since. Edward's struggle to become overlord of Scotland was ultimately less successful, although history remembers him as the Hammer of the Scots and he removed the ancient coronation stone of the Scottish kings from Scone, the Scottish royal seat. It now sits under St. Edward's chair in Westminster when the sovereign is crowned.

Edward II is best remembered from the play by Elizabethan dramatist Christopher Marlowe that depicts the monarch's infatuation with his favorite, Piers Gaveston, Earl of Cornwall, and his murder in particularly brutal circumstances at Berkeley Castle in Gloucestershire. His son, Edward III (1312–77), came to the throne in 1327 when he was 15 years old, though he was effectively controlled by his mother, Isabella, and her lover, Roger de Mortimer, Earl of March, until the latter's execution in 1333.

THE HUNDRED YEARS WAR

Much of Edward's reign was focused on the series of wars that became known as the Hundred Years War, caused by disputes over English holdings in France; trouble between the great weaving cities of Flanders, which were allies of the English, and their French overlords; and French aid to the Scots. To exacerbate matters, Edward assumed the title of King of France, claiming that the Salic law, which debars succession to or through females, applied in France. (It did, and even if it didn't, there were at least five senior claimants.) The title of King of France remained incorporated in the English crown until the reign of George III in the 19th century. The two most famous battles of the Hundred Years War — Crécy in 1346 and Poitiers in 1356 — did much to establish the reputation of the king's heir, Edward, the Black Prince, as a legendary figure of heroism and chivalry in English history.

The other single dominating feature of Edward III's reign was the Black Death, the epidemic disease that according to some estimates reduced the population of England by one-half. The resulting labor shortage accelerated the change from a society of laborers bound to a single master to one where freelance services could be offered, and the country never again returned to the system of servile tenure. When during the reign of the Black Prince's son, Richard II (1377–99), landlords tried to resurrect that system, they were repulsed by the Peasants' Revolt of 1381. (It was led by two men of Kent, Wat Tyler and Jack Straw; a pub called Jack Straw's Castle now stands on the high point of Hampstead Heath, London, where he is said to have assembled his followers.)

Richard's reign ended in abdication; he was replaced by his first cousin, Henry Bolingbroke (IV), son of John of Gaunt (who was the Duke of Lancaster and fourth son of Edward III). Taking advantage of Richard's unpopularity, Henry had himself "elected" king by Parliament, thereby bringing the house of Lancaster to the throne.

Between 1400 and 1406 Henry had to contend with four rebellions against his authority. His son Henry V (1387–1422) — Shakespeare's Prince Hal — avoided such occurrences by concentrating his subjects' minds once again on the long-drawn-out struggle with France. Following his victory over vastly superior French forces at Agincourt on October 25, 1415, Henry was assured of the support of his countrymen for the house of Lancaster. He had himself declared Regent of France and heir to Charles VI, whose daughter, Isabella, he married.

The son they produced, the ill-fated Henry VI (1421–71), succeeded his father in 1472 when he was barely 9 months old. "Henry VI, in infant bonds crowned king/Of whose state so many had the managing/That they lost France and made his England bleed," wrote Shakespeare accurately in his epilogue to Henry V.

Henry VI's appetite for war was minimal. He was more concerned with religion and literature, and in spite of the virtually endless turmoil of his reign, managed to found Eton College near Windsor in 1440 and King's College at Cambridge in 1441. The military successes of his father in France were gradually whittled away as France rallied under Joan of Arc (burned 1429) and other leaders. By the end of the Hundred Years War in 1453, Gascony, Maine, Normandy, Bordeaux, and Bayonne were controlled by the French, leaving Calais as the only English possession in France.

In England, the great nobles made rich by the wars and by the recently introduced raising of sheep kept increasingly large retinues that amounted to small private armies. These semi-independent chieftains, uncontrolled by the king or the council that ruled in his name, fought with one another and terrorized their neighbors. In 1450, tired of the virtual anarchy around them, about 30,000 men from Kent and Sussex marched on London under one Jack Cade and demanded that Henry's kinsman and heir, Richard, Duke of York, be admitted to the ruling council. During two brief periods in which Henry was judged insane, Richard acted as Lord Protector of the realm. In 1454 when the king recovered, Richard was unwilling to yield his power and there followed what is probably the most famous family feud in history, the Wars of the Roses (1455–85).

THE WARS OF THE ROSES

To understand the rationale behind this struggle, it is necessary to resort to some genealogy. Both Henry VI and Richard were descended in the direct male line from Edward III, Henry via Edward's fourth son, John of Gaunt (Duke of Lancaster), Richard from the fifth son, Edmund (Duke of York). In addition, however, Richard was descended through his mother from Edward's third son, Lionel, Duke of Clarence, giving him the superior claim according to the English laws of succession. The white rose on the crest of the house of York and the red rose adopted as the badge of the house of Lancaster gave this dreary 30-year quarrel its name.

Henry's antipathy to war notwithstanding, his wife, Margaret of Anjou, was determined to secure the inheritance for their son, Edward, born in 1453, even after Henry was taken prisoner following the battle of Northampton in 1460 and had acknowledged Richard as his heir. A year later Richard was dead and his son was proclaimed king as Edward IV (lived 1442–83), and the kings of the house of Lancaster were declared by Parliament to have been usurpers. Except for a brief period in 1470–71 when Henry was restored, Edward managed to hold on to his throne for 20 years, although until Henry's death (probably by murder) in the Tower of London in 1471, the picture was one of battles, victories, reversals, and more victories.

A dozen years later in 1483, another king of the Yorkist dynasty, Edward V, who had succeeded his father when he was 12 years old, was to die in the tower. Whether he and his younger brother (known to history as the "little princes in the tower") were murdered by command of their uncle, Richard III (1452–85), has never been satisfactorily established. We do know that Richard was prepared to go to the extraordinary lengths of marrying his niece, Elizabeth of York, Edward V's sister, to secure his position. (He was refused.) Although Richard's dealings with his people were remarkable for his sense of justice and his accessibility (Shakespeare's monster is largely a brilliant invention), the old dynastic rivalry ruined him. In 1485, at Bosworth Field in Leicestershire, he was killed in battle by the forces of Henry Tudor, Earl of Richmond, the surviving heir to the claims of the house of Lancaster. The crown of England was found in a bush, and the Wars of the Roses ended.

THE TUDORS

Henry Tudor (1452–1509) was crowned Henry VII and married Elizabeth of York, thus uniting the two houses. His reign was remarkable for an expansion in learning and knowledge of the outside world. William Caxton's printing press had been established at Westminster in 1477 and Thomas Malory's *Le Morte d'Arthur* was published in 1485. Under a patent from Henry VII dated March 15, 1496, John Cabot sailed from the West Country port of Bristol and reached North America in the vicinity of Cape Breton in Canada. English claims on the American continent were later based on this discovery.

Henry Tudor's son Henry VIII (1491–1547) is probably the best-known king in English history, not least for his six wives. Henry's struggle with the papacy over his divorce from Catherine of Aragon and his marriage to Anne Boleyn has tended to obscure his early religious fervor. In 1521 he wrote the *Assertion of the Seven Sacraments,* a rebuttal of Martin Luther. For his pains he received the title Defender of the Faith from Pope Leo XI, a title that the English sovereign bears to this day.

Thirteen years later in 1534, the Defender of the Faith became the founder of the Church of England when Henry caused the Act of Supremacy to be passed. The act declared that the king and his successors were the supreme head of the church and clergy in England. Among those executed for refusal to take the oath confirming the act were the bishop of Rochester, John Fisher, and Henry's erstwhile friend and chancellor St. Thomas More. Religious orders were dissolved and many great abbeys and monasteries sold to the highest bidder. The hauntingly beautiful ruins of Fountains Abbey in Yorkshire and Tintern Abbey in Wales date from this period. Henry's marital exertions notwithstanding, all his descendants were dead by the end of 1603.

In the meantime there were three more Tudor monarchs. The first was Edward VI (1537–53), Henry's sickly son by Jane Seymour, who gave his name to the King Edward VI Grammar Schools, i.e., free college preparatory schools around England, the most famous of which is the school that William Shakespeare attended in Stratford. Edward was succeeded by Henry's daughter by Catherine of Aragon, Mary I, whose attempt to restore Catholicism and consequent decimation of the Protestant bishops caused her to be known as Bloody Mary. And finally there was Elizabeth I, the Virgin Queen (1533–1603). During Elizabeth's reign the European Renaissance came into full bloom in England, most notably in the person of William Shakespeare (1564–1616). The school where he learned his little Latin and less Greek still stands in Stratford and is one of the most perfect spots in the country for soaking up the atmosphere of Elizabethan England.

This period also saw the ascendancy of England's sea power as demonstrated by Sir Francis Drake, who became the first Englishman to circumnavigate the globe (1577–80), and Sir Walter Raleigh, who in 1596 sailed 300 miles up the Orinoco River in Central America. The English superiority at sea culminated in the defeat in 1588 of the Great Armada from Spain — a fleet of 362 ships and 3,165 cannon — which had been sent to conquer England in the name of Catholicism.

Both Elizabeth and her people were victims of inflation. An influx of precious metals from the New World and the expansion of the wool trade had brought enormous changes to the economic structure of England. The value of the revenues that by tradition and hereditary right accrued to the Crown dwindled. To save money Elizabeth was frequently obliged to take to the road, traveling with her court from great house to great house to be entertained at the cost of the leading noblemen of England. One such "progress," or journey, to Lord Leicester's at Kenilworth Castle, has been immortalized in the novel *Kenilworth* by Sir Walter Scott.

The poor took to the road, too, in Elizabeth's reign, though in rather less luxury than the queen. Land that had traditionally been put under the plough was enclosed for sheep pasturage, which required a smaller labor force. The displaced laborers — "sturdy beggars," as they were known — wandered from place to place seeking employment and, quite incidentally, inspired the children's nursery rhyme "Hark, hark, the dogs do bark, the beggars are coming to town. . . ."

In 1601 Parliament passed the Poor Law charging individual parishes with the welfare of the needy.

Elizabeth's reign was marred only by the execution of her cousin, Mary,

Queen of Scots (1542–87), at Fotheringhay Castle in Northamptonshire. Mary had been a rallying point for Catholics after Elizabeth was declared a bastard by Pope Paul IV. Mary's apparent implication in a plot to assassinate Elizabeth forced the Tudor Queen to sign her death warrant, a decision that biographers tell us was to haunt her for the rest of her life.

It was to James VI of Scotland, who as Mary's son was the real heir in any case, Elizabeth left the throne in her will, and he hurried to London to be also crowned King James I of England in 1603. His accession united the two kingdoms in his person, though they were to have separate parliaments for another 104 years.

THE STUARTS

There had been a Stuart on the throne of Scotland ever since Robert II succeeded in 1371. Robert was the grandson through his mother of the famous Robert the Bruce who, according to legend, regained hope and courage after defeat in battle by observing the patience with which a spider wove its web. He was the descendant also of King Duncan, who had been slain in 1040 by Macbeth, who in turn was the descendant of the ancient Irish High Kings. For several hundred years the single outstanding feature of Scottish history was one of wars with England, often in alliance with France. Mary, Queen of Scots, was herself half French, had spent her childhood in France, and was the widow of a French king before marrying James VI's father. In Scotland to this day there are French words in use — gigot for a leg of lamb comes to mind — that are not heard in England outside French restaurants.

James I was pedantic — the Wisest Fool in Christendom, men called him — superstitious, and susceptible to the flattery of many male favorites. The warm reception the English initially offered him cooled when it became clear that he did not understand the English parliamentary system or the religious changes taking place. He managed to offend both Puritans and Catholics by his intransigence, and the latter prepared to assassinate him when he opened Parliament on November 5, 1605. The gunpowder to be used in the plot was discovered in the cellars of the Houses of Parliament and one of the conspirators, Guy Fawkes, was arrested. On every November 5, Guy Fawkes Day, visitors can see bonfires dotting the countryside and effigies of Fawkes being burned.

James authorized the publication of the Bible that bears his name and is one of the masterpieces of written English.

Charles I (1600–1649), who succeeded James in 1623, had even less success in dealing with Parliament than his father. In 1628 it adopted the Petition of Right, a statement of civil liberties that prohibited the billeting of soldiers with civilians; arrest on unspecified charges; martial law in peacetime; and all forms of taxation not approved by Parliament itself. Charles assented to the petition in return for financial subsidies for which he was desperate, then promptly violated it by exacting by force the ancient taxes known as "tonnage and poundage."

From 1629 to 1640 he ruled without Parliament; in 1641 Parliament in turn issued the Grand Remonstrance, which set out in full its grievances against the king. On January 3, 1642, Charles went to the House of Commons in an attempt to arrest five of its members. He failed, and the Commons withdrew to the Guildhall (in the heart of the city of London), where they were protected by citizens of the metropolis. Charles made his way to York, where he was joined by 65 members of the Commons and 32 peers. When he raised the standard at Nottingham in August 1642, the Civil War had begun.

THE CIVIL WAR, 1642–46

English schoolboys used to reenact the Civil War between the Cavaliers (the Royalists) and the Roundheads (Puritan Parliamentarians under Oliver Cromwell) the way American schoolboys play cowboys and Indians. The romantic hero in this otherwise bleak period was Prince Rupert of the Rhine, Charles's nephew, who distinguished himself first of all at the bloody Battle of Edgehill in northern Oxfordshire. Charles's strength was further diminished by defeats at Marston Moor in 1644 and Naseby in 1645. In 1647 he fell into the hands of parliamentary forces and was tried and convicted of treason "for laying war against Parliament." On January 30, 1649, he was beheaded in Whitehall, London, an act regarded by Royalists then and now as regicide.

THE COMMONWEALTH, 1649–60

The Commonwealth was dominated from the start by Oliver Cromwell, who in 1653 assumed the title of Lord Protector. The title and office of king, as well as the House of Lords, were abolished. Parliament met regularly but acted merely as the instrument for Cromwell, who was virtually a dictator, rigidly enforcing the puritanical laws that had been enacted and using the army to collect taxes. When he died in 1659 his son, Richard, became Protector. Richard managed to hold the office for only a few months, since he was unable to control the army. He became known to history as Tumbledown Dick.

THE RESTORATION

Puritan supremacy and military control engendered a strong reaction and by the spring of 1660 public opinion was clearly in favor of inviting Charles II to return to England from the Continent, to which he had fled. His resumption of the crown, however, was subject to certain conditions; these were accepted by Charles in the Declaration of Breda (April 14, 1660), in which he proclaimed among other things an amnesty to all not especially excluded by Parliament. When Charles entered London on May 29, 1660, there were several days of rejoicing. His reign is remembered in the popular imagination as a kind of English bacchanalia. Public dancing was permitted once more and the theaters were reopened.

The licentious mood of the times was superbly chronicled by Samuel Pepys (1633–1703), the Prince of Gossips, in his diaries.

The era was not entirely frivolous, however. In 1662 the Royal Society, generally agreed to be the world's most celebrated organization for stimulating scientific research, was founded. In 1665–66, Sir Isaac Newton formulated the theory of gravity, thus changing our understanding of physical laws.

More somber was the Great Plague of April 1665 and the Great Fire of London, which burned 450 acres of the city between September 2 and 9, 1666. It is because so many structures were destroyed by the fire that there exist today the present St. Paul's Cathedral as well as 40 or so other beautiful churches designed by the brilliant architect Sir Christopher Wren in an effort to rebuild London.

Charles left no legitimate heirs, although by one of his many mistresses he is an ancestor of the current Princess of Wales, the former Lady Diana Spencer.

Charles's brother, James II (1633–1701), assumed the throne in 1685. He was a convert to the Roman Catholic faith in a country where Parliament had passed in 1673 the Test Act, which excluded from public office all those who refused, among other things, to take communion according to the rite of the Church of England. He was moreover formed in the same autocratic Stuart mold as his father and grandfather. By his first wife, he fathered two daughters, both brought up as Protestants. A subsequent marriage (after his conversion) to a devout Catholic, and the birth of his son, James (known in history as the Old Pretender), on June 10, 1688, proved intolerable to both the Tory and Whig parties in England. On June 29 seven Whig and Tory leaders invited William of Orange (who was James's son-in-law and also his nephew) to come to London and take the throne. He arrived there on December 19, and on December 22 James fled to France.

William and his wife, Mary, were crowned in February 1689 and reigned jointly until Mary's death in 1694, after which William reigned alone until 1702. In 1701, when it seemed clear that both William and his successor, Princess Anne (James II's younger daughter, later Queen Anne; reigned 1702–14), would die childless, Parliament passed the Act of Settlement declaring that the sovereigns of Great Britain were to be Protestant. The crown was settled on Sophia of Hanover, a granddaughter of James I, and her Protestant heirs.

Some Scottish Jacobites — supporters of the house of Stuart; Jacobus is Latin for James — objected to the act and planned to offer the Scottish throne to James Stuart, the Old Pretender. To avoid this, in Queen Anne's reign an Act of Union was passed (1707), establishing one parliament for the United Kingdom and adopting one flag, the crosses of St. George and St. Andrew, known as the Union Jack.

THE HANOVERIANS

In spite of the union, Jacobite risings were launched in 1715 just a few months after the son of Sophia of Hanover came to the throne as George I (reigned 1714–27) and again in 1719. Both failed miserably and Jacobite aspirations lay dormant until 1745 when the Young Pretender, James's son, Charles, popularly called Bonnie Prince Charlie (1720–88), landed in Scotland and penetrated as far south as Derby in England before he and his army were dispersed.

Neither George I nor his son George II (reigned 1727–60) cared much for living in Britain, and public affairs fell increasingly into the hands of ministers. Chief among these was Sir Robert Walpole (1676–1745), First Lord of the Treasury to George I and George II, and generally recognized as the first British "Prime Minister and First Lord of the Treasury." Since Walpole's day the British cabinet has usually been drawn from the party forming the majority in the House of Commons.

Ministers controlled not only affairs in the United Kingdom but an increasingly vast overseas empire based largely on the European demand for sugar and tobacco, and on the slave trade. By the Treaty of Paris (1763), which ended the Seven Years War between Britain and France, the United Kingdom gained Canada and all the French territories east of the Mississippi, Grenada in the West Indies, Florida, Senegal, and confirmation of her possessions in India.

Twenty years later, by another Treaty of Paris (September 23, 1783), Britain was forced to acknowledge the independence of the United States. This act represented the final repudiation of the North American policy of George III (1738–1820). Throughout the struggle with the colonists, the king had displayed a stubbornness and shortsightedness that were not always characteristic of the way he tried to rule at home. By 1782, however, much of the popularity he had once enjoyed in England had waned. His acquiescent minister, Lord North, who had mismanaged the war with the colonies, resigned, and in 1783 George, whose mental instability was becoming more obvious, was forced to accept the younger William Pitt (1759–1806) as prime minister. Pitt's rise to power marked the end of any significant influence that the British sovereign could exercise over Parliament.

The loss of the United States was assuaged by the addition to the colonial map of Australia and New Zealand, discovered by Captain James Cook in 1771, and by the territories won as a result of the Napoleonic Wars, 1803–15. These wars had added two names to the long litany of English heroes: Lord Nelson, victor of the sea battle of Trafalgar on October 21, 1805; and the Duke of Wellington, who defeated Napoleon at Waterloo on June 18, 1815. The territories awarded to Britain in the subsequent carve-up of the world included Ceylon, Trinidad, Tobago, Malta, Mauritius, and the Cape Colony of South Africa.

THE INDUSTRIAL REVOLUTION

The final defeat of Napoleon naturally inspired a period of national rejoicing. It also added 400,000 men to the ranks of the unemployed — and the dissatisfied.

Since George III's accession in 1760, England had changed radically. Technology based on the use of wood for fuel and the use of wind and water for power had given way to one in which power was based on steam, particularly for raising coal from mines. The appearance of James Watt's steam engine in 1769 marked the summit of this development.

The all-important cotton textile industry was revolutionized by a series of inventions that resulted in a tremendous increase in output. The landscape in the mining areas of the North and the midlands changed completely. The midland coal fields became known as the Black Country.

In Lancashire large cotton mills sprang up across the county. Birmingham, equidistant from England's main ports, became a large manufacturing center.

People poured from the countryside to find jobs in the new urban industrial areas. Legislation controlling conditions of employment was nonexistent. Women and children, as well as men, could be required to work for as long as they were able to stand up. With a pool of cheap female and child labor available, male breadwinners and their families often starved. By 1843, during Queen Victoria's reign (1837–1901), there were 200,000 inmates in workhouses.

The sort of life led by the poor in the early 19th century has been brilliantly described in the novels of Charles Dickens (1812–70).

REFORM

The population shifts caused by the Industrial Revolution had done nothing to change the way that Britain was represented geographically in Parliament. "Rotten boroughs" — districts where the population had declined considerably — still returned two members, whereas big industrial cities such as Birmingham elected none.

Ninety-nine percent of the 400,000 soldiers demobilized in 1815 had no vote. They were, moreover, to suffer like their fellow countrymen from two pieces of legislation designed to favor the rich, especially landowners. One was the 1815 Corn Law, which virtually excluded all foreign corn from Britain, thereby raising the price of bread. The other was the abolition in 1816 of the 10% income tax. The popular agitation, food riots, and calls for reform that followed culminated in the Peterloo Massacre of 1819, when armed horsemen cut down listeners at a large open-air parliamentary reform meeting at Manchester.

The reign of George IV (1820–30) saw two pieces of legislation that signaled that Parliament and the small segment of the population it represented (about 420,000 out of 23 million people) were resigned to change. One was a more favorable Corn Law (1828) permitting grain to be imported at any time and fixing the duties so that prices remained reasonably low. The other was the Catholic Emancipation Act (1829), which restored to Catholics many of the privileges that had been removed by the Test Act, including the right to sit in Parliament.

It was the Great Reform Bill of 1832 in the reign of William IV (1830–37) that marked the beginning of democracy in Britain. Although it added only 800,000 people to the rolls, it redistributed 143 seats. Among the large cities finally enfranchised were Manchester and Birmingham.

Parliament's social conscience prevailed. The following year, in 1833, slavery was abolished in the colonies and a Factory Act was passed forbidding the employment of children under 9 and regulating work hours.

Under two of Queen Victoria's prime ministers, Benjamin Disraeli (1804–81), a Conservative, and William Gladstone (1809–98), a Liberal, reform bills in 1867 and 1884 added close to 3 million male voters to the electoral rolls, most of them from the working classes.

Women over 30 were given the vote in 1918, but it was not until 1928 that they shared the franchise equally with men and were permitted to vote at 21.

The Victorian era produced a number of remarkable men and women besides those responsible for electoral reform, among them Florence Nightingale (1820–1910), the founder of modern nursing; the poet Lord Tennyson (1809–1902), who is buried in Westminster Abbey; and the social reformer Lord Shaftesbury (1801–85). It was also the era when Karl Marx (1818–83) sat for years in the Reading Room of the *British Museum* writing *Das Kapital* while the peaceful revolution he declared impossible got under way all around him.

The enfranchisement of urban workers under Disraeli and Gladstone resulted in the formation of the Labour Party in 1900, which has always tended to prefer a mild, pragmatic form of socialism to the more revolutionary kind proposed by Marx. Since 1924 the Labour and Conservative parties have alternated in office with almost predictable regularity except for periods of National Government — government with ministers drawn from all major parties — during times of national emergency. The last of these was from 1940 to 1945, during World War II, under the leadership of Winston Churchill (1874–1965), whose panache as a wartime leader made him a hero along the lines of Nelson and Wellington.

The House of Lords — the upper house of Parliament — lost the last vestiges of its power in 1911 during the administration of Prime Minister David Lloyd George (1863–1942). In that year the Parliament Act was passed denying the lords any power over a bill involving finance and circumscribing the delay they could exercise over other legislation.

The creation of hereditary peers (lords who can pass on to their heirs their titles and the privileges of sitting in the House of Lords) was discontinued during the 1960s when a system of life peerages was introduced to provide the chamber with able men and women who could contribute to national debates. The House still provides the government with senior ministers, however. Lord Carrington, foreign secretary (appointed 1979) in the administration of Margaret Thatcher, Britain's first woman prime minister, is a hereditary peer who sits in the House of Lords.

The other hereditary institution, the Crown, appears likely to flourish. Victoria's heirs — Edward VII (1901–10), George V (1910–36), Edward VIII (1936; abdicated and became the Duke of Windsor), George VI (1936–52), and Elizabeth II (1952–present) — have all succeeded to the throne quite smoothly. Even the sting of the abdication crisis was quickly overwhelmed by the impending threat of World War II.

The monarchy today has little more than the power "to be consulted, to encourage, and to warn," as political theorist Walter Bagehot wrote in 1867. But although the monarch no longer has the right to dissolve Parliament, she has the right to refuse to dissolve it. That is, if a prime minister should resign because of lack of support in the House of Commons, the monarch has the right to ask someone else to form a government if she believes that person can command a majority in the House.

Perhaps the most useful function of the monarchy in the 20th century is its role as the head of the Commonwealth, that loosely knit group of countries that were formerly a part of the British Empire.

As the ranking member of the Commonwealth and a comparatively recent member of the European Economic Community (the Common Market), Britain forms a political bridge between its former possessions and Western Europe. In addition, it still frequently serves as arbiter and mediator in disputes among and between its former possessions. British influence, though clearly diminished, remains a substantive force in world affairs.

Literature

Until the late 18th century, it was fashionable for cultivated British travelers to be appalled by much of the local scenery. They dismissed mountain landscapes as "horrid" — a word that, to Latin scholars of the day, meant "uncouth" or "shaggy." They preferred to pull down the carriage blinds, or better still, to remain in London.

Then along came Wordsworth and Scott. William Wordsworth (1770–1850) set forth the Lake District as nourishment for the eye, and found in mountaintops an inspiration for the spirit. Meanwhile, Walter Scott (1771–1832) quite consciously turned the Scottish Highlands and borders to literary ends in his novels and poems. Thus, in the 19th century, cliffs suddenly became glamorous, mountains fashionable, and ravines a romantic enthusiasm. Nineteenth-century excursionists filled the Scottish Trossachs, armed with Scott's popular narrative poem *The Lady of the Lake.*

Even today, our perceptions of British landscapes are shaped by the experience of literature. What would the world think of the Lake District if Wordsworth, Coleridge, and Southey had not lived and worked there? Similarly, the novels of Thomas Hardy (1840–1928) have bestowed a cosmic significance on the heaths and tumuli of Dorset: "To persons standing alone on a hill during a clear midnight such as this, the roll of the world eastward is almost a palpable movement" (*Far from the Madding Crowd*).

Authors such as Hardy impose an image of their own creation on a countryside. Readers traveling through the region cannot escape it. Are they seeing Dorset or are they experiencing Hardy's Wessex? A more fantasy-minded tourist might even pursue the haunts of the fictional characters. For example, Dorchester, where Hardy was educated and where he lived for the first 40 years of his life, is the Casterbridge of his novels; Woolbridge Manor, near Wool, has been identified as the Wellbridge Manor of *Tess of the D'Urbervilles*; and in Bindon Abbey you can see the empty stone coffin in which Angel Clare laid Tess.

The traveler in a more cheerful mood might follow Mr. Pickwick and the Pickwick Club on their Dickensian travels. Eatanswill, of the Eatanswill Election, where Mrs. Leo Hunter gave her fancy-dress breakfast, is actually Sudbury, in Essex. And so on . . .

A BRIEF CHRONOLOGY: MEDIEVAL TIMES

"Anon." was the first English author, and among the first literary figures were monastic chroniclers who — working chiefly at Canterbury, Peterborough, and Winchester — laboriously compiled *The Anglo Saxon Chronicle,* that mixture of history, rumor, and poetry drawn from earliest times to the 12th century. England then was a country of marsh and forest.

Chaucer (ca. 1345–1400), the author of *The Canterbury Tàles,* is the first great name among English poets. He is known to have gone to France with Edward III's army, to have served in the medieval equivalent of the diplomatic service, and to have been appointed, in 1374, controller of customs in the City of London. There he lived above Aldgate, one of the eastern gateways to that then walled city. Aldgate is now just another commercial street, and the closest one can come to Chaucer is a plaque on an undistinguished building in Whitechapel that marks his former residence.

During the 15th century, in Westminster, William Caxton set up his famous printing press, the first in England. English literature in the vernacular was given a tremendous boost, and the reading public greatly increased. *The Canterbury Tales* was one of the works that were set on Caxton's press. Another was Sir Thomas Malory's *Le Morte d'Arthur*, a prose translation of a French story that has permeated English literature. The legend of King Arthur is memorably retold in Tennyson's *Idylls of the King and in Camelot,* the modern musical version. Sir Thomas wrote his Arthurian work in Newgate Prison, where the wayward knight was jailed for a variety of crimes that included assault, extortion, jail breaking, poaching, a cattle raid, armed robbery, and attempted murder. Newgate Prison is no more; the Old Bailey, London's Central Criminal Court, now stands in its place.

SHAKESPEARE AND STRATFORD-UPON-AVON

In the 16th century, during the reign of Queen Elizabeth, Shakespeare burst upon the stage, and the English language reeled. There are those who would argue that Shakespeare, an actor with no education beyond that provided by Stratford's grammar school, could not have written Shakespeare's plays. They must be the works of Francis Bacon — too well born to admit their authorship. Or else they must be the works of Christopher Marlowe. But let us accept, along with the vast majority, that the Shakespeare who wrote the plays, and who seems to have coined half the English language, was that same young man who came to London from Warwickshire in the 1580s and found employment as an actor.

The Elizabethan age already was one of popular enthusiasm for the theater — an English enthusiasm that has continued to the present day. But the theaters were regarded with suspicion by city government, and so they were built in what were then the rural suburbs of London. The first, *The Theatre,* was erected in 1577 at Shoreditch, to the east of the city. *The Globe* was in Southwark, on the far bank of the Thames. Just north of the City — for 16-century London has now become merely the banking quarter of a much greater whole — a blue plaque is set into a blank wall in an undistinguished street. It reads: GOOD MASTER EDWARD ALLEYN'S FORTUNE THEATRE STOOD ON A SITE NEAR HERE IN 1600.

The stage was then patronized by men of culture and by the populace, the "groundlings" — by the circle and the pit. Thus the Shakespearean plays alternated elevated themes with scenes of low comedy. With a flourish of trumpets, the captains and the kings depart, stage left; enter stage right the drunken porters, the punning clowns.

Although his theatrical career was centered in or near London, Shakespeare has put Stratford-upon-Avon on the map. If Shakespeare had not been born there, Stratford would be no more than a Warwickshire market town, much like a hundred other small English towns.

In 1769 the actor David Garrick — mindful, no doubt, of how much his own career owed to parts like Richard III — superintended the first annual celebration of Shakespeare's birthday. Stupendous rainfalls dimmed the event slightly; several persons were drowned and several events had to be abandoned. Nevertheless, the town caught on as a focus of literary pilgrimage. No building associated with Shakespeare is not a museum. The site of his own demolished house has become a memorial garden, and even Anne Hathaway's cottage has been visited by millions paying tribute to literature.

April 23, the feast day of England's patron saint, George, is also celebrated, by happy chance, as the birthday of its patron poet. On the nearest Saturday to that date, the whole town still turns to ceremony: The diplomatic corps journeys up from London; flags of all the nations are flown; processions are formed; and wreaths are laid. Even before Garrick, Stratford was becoming a place of literary enthusiasm. A subsequent owner of New Place — an imposing residence in the center of Stratford that Shakespeare bought in 1597, retired to in 1610, and died in in 1616 — was much harassed by curious tourists. Strangers would knock at his door and want to see the mulberry tree under which the great man wrote. So, in 1756, the new owner cut the mulberry tree down. (A local opportunist bought the timber and turned it into souvenirs, for which there was already a demand.) In 1759, mainly to spite his fellow townsmen, he demolished the house itself. Its site is now a garden, stocked with the trees, herbs, and flowers mentioned in the plays.

Meanwhile, the curious — having paid their orthodox respects at the tomb in Stratford Church — were already visiting Shakespeare's birthplace in Henley Street. There were no birth certificates in those days; but Stratford must be reckoned Shakespeare's birthplace, since his parents, John and Mary Shakespeare, are known to have been living there in 1564. The house was passed from his granddaughter (and last direct descendant) to his great-nephew's family, to whom it belonged until 1806. In the late 18th and early 19th centuries, the tenants of the house were not above exhibiting spurious relics, and at least one made a good income from favoring visitors with fragments cut from "Shakespeare's very own chair."

On Thursday, September 16, 1847, the house was put up for auction as "the truly heart-stirring relic of a most glorious period, and of England's immortal bard." The sale was not unforeseen. Committees had been set up, and theatrical benefits and charity concerts had been held to raise money. The house was bought for £3,000.

It was a solid 16th-century house, half-timbered and mullioned, built of local materials. A surprising amount of the original fabric remains: The flagstones knew Shakespeare's feet; the timbers were familiar to his hand.

The original intention was to entrust the house to the government. Instead, the committees found themselves perpetuated as the Shakespeare Birthplace Committee (recognized by Act of Parliament in 1891 as the Shakespeare

Birthplace Trust). Between 1857 and 1864 much was done to restore the house to its original condition. An 18th-century brick facing on part of the building was removed. Dormer windows were restored in accord with the evidence of the earliest engraving (published in 1769). When Shakespeare was born, the house was part of a row, but now thc adjoining properties were removed to reduce the risk of fire.

In the ensuing years the same Trust acquired the home of Shakespeare's wife, Anne Hathaway; Hall's Croft, a medieval house in which the poet's daughter Susanna lived after her marriage; and Mary Arden's house, birthplace of the poet's mother at Wilmcote, a few miles northwest of the town. The trust has also established the Shakespeare Centre and a reference collection.

In 1879 the *Shakespeare Memorial Theatre* was built beside the river. Burned down in 1926 (the surviving library wing is a monument to the florid architectural piety of the 19th century), it was replaced by the present theater in 1932. This is the home of the *Royal Shakespeare Company,* which presents the plays of Shakespeare and others in both London and Stratford.

In the villages that surround Stratford, idyllic cottages are inhabited by nationally known actors and actresses. With Shakespeare himself as the principal local industry, the town has an abundance of hotels, many with Shakespearean names, and a superabundance of gift shops and craft centers.

THE SEVENTEENTH CENTURY

Meanwhile, a whole school of metaphysical poetry was flourishing — with religious subject matter; neatly turned verse; and sharp, direct, and often elaborate metaphor. John Donne (1573–1631) was the central figure among these poets. In youth he was a dissolute man about town; in age, a saintly city preacher and Dean of St. Paul's Cathedral. You will find his effigy in St. Paul's — it is one of the few monuments to have survived the 1666 Fire of London. Characteristically, he sat for it in life, wearing his shroud.

Donne was the first chaplain of Lincoln's Inn, one of the Inns of Court to which English barristers belong. Each of the Inns of Court has many literary associations, for many English authors have studied law. An appetite for the picturesque will take the visitor to London to Lincoln's Inn. There, when a senior member dies, it is the custom for the chapel bell to be tolled, and the visitor might call to mind Donne's most celebrated lines: "Never send to know for whom the bell tolls; it tolls for thee."

The 17th century was also the time of John Milton (1608–74), a giant in English literature, a university man (Christ's College, Cambridge), and a poet in Latin and Hebrew as well as English. Born in London, Milton lived there when he wrote *Paradise Lost* and its sequel, *Paradise Regained.* He was buried in St. Giles, Cripplegate, a medieval church that survives in the middle of the extravagantly modern architecture of London's Barbican. He was a first-rate scholar, and one of the last men ever to master just about all that was known. (Today, of course, that would be impossible.) When he was a very young man, he decided to become the greatest English poet of all time — and he did.

THE EIGHTEENTH CENTURY

A dominant figure of the second half of the 18th century was Dr. Samuel Johnson (a doctor of laws) — essay writer, pamphleteer, novelist, and author of the very influential *Dictionary of the English Language* (1755). Dr. Johnson is, perhaps, most renowned as one of the greatest conversationalists who ever lived. Fortunately, much of his talk was faithfully recorded for us by his biographer, James Boswell. To cite just one example, Dr. Johnson once declared, with typical authority, "When a man is tired of London, he is tired of life, for there is in London all that life can afford."

This man, who rejoiced so vigorously in the sociability of literary London, lived for a time (1749–59) in a house in Gough Square, an alley to the north of Fleet Street. That house still stands and here the visitor may intrude into the past, for it is open to the public. The house contains not only a collection of portraits and letters but also something much less tangible, the flavor of the man's life.

THE NINETEENTH CENTURY

The last century was a time of many literary greats — so many, that we cannot even attempt to mention all of them. They ranged from the Romantic poets — Wordsworth, Coleridge, Byron, Shelley, and Keats — to such novelists as Charles Dickens, the Brontë sisters, and Jane Austen. It can hardly have occurred to Jane Austen that Chawton Cottage, where she lived from 1809 to 1817, would become a place of public show, for her work was secret and her novels were published anonymously. Jane Austen died in obscurity in 1817, at the age of 42.

The cottage still stands in the Hampshire village of Chawton, where Austen lived with her widowed mother and her sister Cassandra. Today it is owned by the Jane Austen Trust. While living there she revised *Sense and Sensibility* and *Pride and Prejudice* and wrote *Emma and Persuasion.* She worked in the common sitting room, where she was always ready to slip her paper under a blotter when she heard that famous creak of the door. (The door is there; the creak has gone.) This sitting room, though a small and unassuming room in a small and seemly house, has seen the creation of those perfect portraits of provincial life and universal character.

Long before the Austens moved in and fitted it up, Chawton Cottage may have been a posting inn; the road that idles past was then the main road to Winchester. It is known that the house declined into laborers' dwellings before it was restored by the Trust. Today, however, it is as nearly as possible the house that Jane Austen knew. Some of the original furniture has found its way back. On the table stands part of a dinner service whose purchase is recorded in a surviving letter. Her bedroom upstairs still overlooks the yard, the bakehouse/laundry, and the outhouse containing her mother's donkey cart.

There may be souvenirs on sale in the parlor, letters in frames on the walls, yet one feels that at any moment Jane Austen may return from walking up to the big house. No matter that the village pond opposite has long been filled in. No matter that the motorway whines past a few hundred yards away.

A scant mile from Chawton is the town of Alton, with its main street bedizened with shopfronts. Here it is still possible to imagine the younger Miss Bennets (*Pride and Prejudice*) walking in search of officers, to imagine good Miss Bates (*Emma*) about her marketing.

Finally, there is Bath — the place where nearly all her marvelous characters "take the waters." Before she moved to Chawton and after her father retired from his rectorship, Jane Austen's family actually lived in Bath. One of their homes, 4 Sydney Place, is marked with a plaque. The beauty of Bath today is that so little has changed. Fashionable society abandoned Bath in about 1840 and began to take other waters abroad. So where the honeyed stone terraces of the 18th century end, the suburbs of the 1920s begin. Apart from a vast new hotel in the center of town, few thought it worthwhile to tear down, redevelop, or embellish 19th-century Bath.

If Jane Austen were to do anything so uncharacteristic as to haunt a place, her sprightly specter in sprigged muslin would find everything in Bath just as she remembered it. And one could do worse than follow her as one's guide — to walk, "with great elasticity," down Milsom Street with Catherine Morland, to wait opposite Union Passage for John Thorpe to pull up in his gig, to loiter outside the Pump Room until Isabella and Catherine appear in hotly indifferent pursuit of young men (all from *Northanger Abbey*) . . . or to enter the Assembly Rooms and see exactly where Anne Elliot encountered Captain Wentworth (*Persuasion*).

Bath remains to this day a trim, precise city, peopled by characters, whether fictional or historic, who lived at precise addresses. Dickens's Mr. Pickwick and his party settled in lodgings in the Royal Crescent; Mr. Pickwick, like Isabella and Catherine, frequented the Pump Room. It was out of a house in Royal Crescent that his friend Mr. Winkle was locked while only half awake and half dressed. It was from No. 11 Royal Crescent that the playwright Sheridan went off with the singer Elizabeth Linley. Does it matter which is fiction and which is fact?

Fiction has inspired many a reader to dream about the Yorkshire moors. The most renowned of these dreamers, the 19th-century American poet Emily Dickinson, wrote "I never saw a moor/I never saw the sea" — and indeed, she never did. Airplane and railroad, however, have brought many a 20th-century visitor to the heather-studded moors.

And with good reason. Even if the domineering Reverend Patrick Brontë had never been incumbent of the Yorkshire village of Haworth in the 1840s, the moors around it would now be accounted scenic. But the Reverend Mr. Brontë had three daughters (not to mention a dissolute son who was Emily's model for the fictional Heathcliff). By writing *Wuthering Heights, Jane Eyre,* and *The Tenant of Wildfell Hall,* Emily, Charlotte, and Ann Brontë imbued mere topography with literary associations and implications; and the Brontë Society, restoring the parsonage and opening it to the public, has turned a minor entry in the gazetteer into an international shrine.

You can draw your own map of 19th-century literary Britain — almost infinitely. For example, Salisbury in Wiltshire is a much visited town. It has a cathedral; it has history; it has Stonehenge nearby. But as good a reason as any for visiting Salisbury is the small fact that "wandering one midsummer evening round the purlieus of Salisbury Cathedral," Anthony Trollope (1815–82) "conceived the story of *The Warden*." And from *The Warden* grew all of Trollope's *Barchester* novels.

Thomas Hardy's birthplace is a small thatched cottage on the outskirts of Dorchester. It is approached by a 10-minute walk through woods; the interior is open by appointment only, and then only the parlor.

No doubt the greatest English novelist of all, however, was Charles Dickens, whose work greatly influenced a legion of writers — including one as remote from him in time and place as Dostoyevsky. Dickens began life as a journalist and wrote his novels at a hectic rate in weekly parts. Like Shakespeare, Dickens was enormously popular. Many thousands of readers on both sides of the Atlantic eagerly awaited those weekly installments.

Dickens (1812–70) lived much of his life in London. The tourist who goes down to the Thames at Blackfriars where the cars now speed along the riverbank, cannot be sure whether he is seeking out the young David Copperfield, sent to wash and label bottles at Murdstone and Grinby's warehouse, or the young Charles Dickens, miserably employed in a blacking factory a little farther upstream. But success came to the young Dickens, and he established his reputation — with the completion of *The Pickwick Papers* and the writing of *Oliver Twist* and *Nicholas Nickleby* — at about the time he, his wife, and his young son came to live at No. 48 Doughty Street, near the Gray's Inn Road (1837). The house, now owned by the Dickens Fellowship, is open to the public.

Walter Scott (1771–1832), as any traveler in Scotland discovers, made much of this country in his own image, or at least in the image of ancient romance, which he marshaled in his novels. His novels take the characters of history — some of it quite recent in his day — and turn them into a more compelling reality. It would be difficult for many people to say whether the character of, for example, Jeannie Deans, heroine of *The Heart of Midlothian,* was an invention or not. For it is a novel, like so many of Scott's, full of real events (in this case Edinburgh's Porteous Riots of 1736) and historical characters, among them Queen Caroline.

One finds the same imprecision about location. In *The Bride of Lammermoor* the castle, Wolf's Crag, is taken by many to be Fast Castle on the east coast. The author himself wrote evasively that the position of Fast Castle "seems certainly to resemble that of Wolf 's Crag as much as any other, while its vicinity to the mountain ridge of Lammermoor renders the assimilation a probable one." (Mountain ridge is a bit steep for the Lammermuir Hills, but that is the effect that Scott has on scenery.) Certainly Ellen's Isle in Loch Katrine owes much of its fame to its part in *The Lady of the Lake.*

There is no imprecision about Scott's own residences. For most of his active life he lived in Edinburgh, at 39 Castle Street, a house identified by a small statuette above the door. Otherwise, it is inaccessible, for it is now a legal office. From there, having made a fortune and lost it, he finally retired to the baronial pile he had designed at Abbotsford, near Galashiels. This is now a monument to Scott the novelist and antiquarian, opened to the public by his descendants.

Relics of Scott, Robert Louis Stevenson, and Robert Burns are in Edinburgh in a museum called *Lady Stair's House*, romantically situated in an alley off the High Street. Much of Burns's literary output was produced in Edinburgh, although Ayrshire, from whence he came, and to which he returned, is scattered with memorials to him, and places associated with him.

Robert Louis Stevenson (1850–94) was perhaps the writer who described the city of Edinburgh with the greatest sympathy. He was born at 8 Howard Place, then on the northern fringes of the town, but grew up at 17 Heriot Row, just across Queen Street Gardens from 39 Castle Street. From the Heriot Row windows he looked down on Leerie the lamplighter (*A Child's Garden of Verses*). In consumptive adulthood he lived in Bournemouth (*Hardy's Sandbourne*), in America, and in Samoa. But he always looked back to Edinburgh.

Even *Treasure Island* is said to have its Edinburgh associations: The map of the island, it is claimed, was based on an island in a small ornamental pond in Queen Street Gardens. *Kidnapped,* that most Scottish of books, follows the Lowlander David Balfour in his flight with Alan Breck, during the aftermath of the Jacobite uprising of 1745. *Kidnapped* is an exhilarating adventure yarn, but its account of the journey from the western coast of Mull, through Appin, over Rannoch Moor and down through Balquhidder to Stirling also constitutes an excellent guidebook for any visitor to the Highlands.

THE TWENTIETH CENTURY

The London of today has grown into an amorphous region. But even its remotest suburb has some literary interest, some chance association with authorship. Among its greatest literary interpreters have been Charles Dickens and Virginia Woolf. The novels of Dickens were written at a journalistic gallop; Virginia Woolf composed hers with agonizing care. Her novels are often accounted "difficult," but in them, and in her shorter writings, she creates a scene, composed of random moments in time, which lives more strongly than the actual streets she is describing. One cannot board a No. 11 bus down the Strand without remembering Elizabeth Dalloway's taking an impetuous, allusive omnibus ride from Westminster to Chancery Lane (*Mrs. Dalloway*).

Virginia Woolf was a Londoner. She was born, in 1882, at 22 Hyde Park Gate, a tall confident house that still overlooks the south side of the park. After her father's death she moved to Bloomsbury, living first with her brother and sister, later with her husband, Leonard Woolf, in a number of houses: 46 Gordon Square, 29 Fitzroy Square, 52 Tavistock Square (Dickens, too, had once lived in this square; both their houses have been demolished), and finally in Mecklenburgh Square.

Her eye was acute, and her imagination imposed its own enhancing order on the streets and squares of the London of 60 years ago. In *Mrs. Dalloway* she has pinned down Mayfair — every brick, every leaf — on an early summer morning. In *Night and Day* and *Jacob's Room* she has done the same for the Strand, Bloomsbury, and Holborn.

There may be little of the picturesque in the town of Eastwood and the Nottinghamshire coalfields, but D. H. Lawrence was not only born there but set many of his novels in the area and peopled the novels with characters drawn from life. You can walk the streets of Eastwood and pass from *The White Peacock* to *Women in Love* to *Sons and Lovers.* Here, in Devonshire Drive, is the very house in which the Brangwen sisters lived. Here at Gresley, just a few hundred yards off the M1 motorway, is the church where they came to watch the wedding (*Women in Love*) . . .

The 19th century was the great age of English theater. Ornate palaces were built in every suburb and provincial town and theatrical companies toured the country by way of the recently developed railways. However, the 19th century produced no great playwrights until the last couple of decades, when Oscar Wilde and George Bernard Shaw began to write for the stage.

Yet Shaw, who lived until 1950, rightly belongs to the 20th century. And it was Shaw himself, with that unflappable sense of his own importance, who left his house at Ayot St. Lawrence, just north of London, to the National Trust. This was his home from 1906 until 1950, and it came to the Trust exactly as he had lived in it, with his books, his papers, and his furniture.

Harold Nicolson's *Diaries and Letters* records the rather macabre story of how he, as Chairman of the Trust, went down to inspect Shaw's bequest in 1950. There he found "all his hats, and coats and nailbrushes etc." and, on the garden paths, spread a few days before, the ashes of Shaw himself, "like the stuff put down for slugs."

BLUE PLAQUES AND THE NATIONAL TRUST

Unleashed on his or her literary trail, a visitor to London will find a number of buildings marked with blue commemorative plaques. Some, on modern structures, merely hint that someone — Coleridge or Dryden — "lived in a house on this site." Others designate a surviving house: These very steps up to this very door represented security to some great writer; this doorknob was familiar to his or her hand; these, perhaps, were the very panes of glass through which he or she viewed the passing world. A few literary figures are remembered by more than a plaque affixed to a wall. The National Trust is the custodian of many a literary shrine; it preserves and opens to the public such important homes as No. 24 Cheyne Row, London, where Thomas Carlyle lived from 1834 until his death in 1881; Wordsworth's birthplace in Cockermouth, Cumbria; and Lamb's House, Rye, East Sussex, where Henry James spent the summers from 1898 until his death in 1916, and where he wrote *The Ambassadors* and *The Golden Bowl.*

Architecture

Britain has castles and cathedrals that can hold their own with those of Europe, but its domestic architecture — stately homes, farms, cottages, and parish churches — best expresses the character of the people and the progress of British life through the ages. Many stately homes are open to the public and can be visited and viewed in detail. Take a half-day's trip out of London — no matter the direction — and you can enjoy the rich heritage of old homes and cottages that everywhere remain part of Britain's daily life. Many a village pub — where you can stop for a beer, lunch at the bar, or partake of a more formal dining room repast — will date from Elizabethan times or earlier. (Some say the Old Chesil Rectory pub at Winchester is the oldest in the country.)

Many of these indigenous buildings have grown or have been altered over the years, so that their style is not pure, nor their history unalloyed. Tales of their derivation may be as varied as the people you talk to about them — but their authenticity and their central role in the life of their localities are beyond dispute.

Walk through the village streets, go into the pubs, spend some moments in the parish churches, and you will begin to experience the flavor of English life, as articulated in its buildings. Get off the main road, take almost any byroad in Kent, Surrey, or Sussex, and you will be surprised at the number of old village centers that survive on the very fringes of the major metropolitan areas in this very crowded land.

Remains of Roman villas can be seen here and there in England; a particularly fine one is found at Bignor in Sussex.

In addition, quite a number of Saxon churches or parts of churches survive in England, predating the Norman Conquest of 1066. The earliest Saxon churches were built of timber with neither aisles nor towers. Later versions, such as Bradford on Avon in Wiltshire or Earl's Barton in Northamptonshire, have blunt, crudely decorated towers and reproduce in stone the earlier types of wooden ornamentation. An interesting part-Saxon church, in the attractive sailing village of Bosham on Chichester Harbour, Sussex, is said to commemorate the spot where the Saxon King Canute "told the sea to go back." And many churches in East Anglia have the round towers that hark back to Saxon times.

Brought in by William the Conqueror in 1066, Norman architecture is equivalent to the style known on the Continent as Romanesque. In Britain, the Norman period extended from the Conquest to the latter part of the 12th century, when the Gothic style was born. Norman abbey churches and cathedrals are numerous in England, for the period of the conquest was a period of building and rebuilding.

Romanesque structures of this period are typically heavy and solid, with round arches. Architectural historian Nikolaus Pevsner described their Englishness as "an articulation . . . that conveys to us at once a feeling of certainty and stability . . . There is no wavering here — as there was none in the ruthless policy of William the Conquerer in subduing and normalizing England. Blunt, massive, and overwhelmingly strong are the individual forms which architects used in these early buildings, sacred as well as secular."

Winchester Cathedral (1080–90) is an example of early Norman architecture; Durham Cathedral (1093–1130) is High Romanesque. The latter anticipates the Gothic style in its vaulting over the choir. This is probably the earliest example of rib vaulting in Europe. Pevsner cites the White Tower at the Tower of London and the keep of Colchester Castle in Essex as examples of the massive, almost brutal English secular architecture of the Norman period.

During the latter part of the 12th century, Gothic architecture flowered in England as it did in Europe. With its pointed arches, flying buttresses, fully developed rib vaulting, and its elaborate stained glass windows, this style introduced a new concept of religious space. The Gothic combined structural clarity with a coherent expression of interior space and an honest use of materials. So much engineering skill was martialed in its soaring surge toward heaven, that even today "Gothic" and "cathedral" are almost synonymous in most people's minds.

The earliest English example of developed Gothic is the east end of Canterbury Cathedral, which was started by William Sens in 1175. Lincoln (begun 1192) and Salisbury (about 1220) are fine, mature examples of the early English Gothic period. Wells (dedicated in 1239), with its carved west front, was one of the few to escape the ravages of Oliver Cromwell. In the 14th century its famous inverted arches were added to support the tower, which was then in danger of collapse.

Wells marks the transition to the decorated style of the middle Gothic period. This was the period when the famous octagon at Ely Cathedral was built to replace an earlier tower that had collapsed into the church. (Some of the most dramatic feats of ecclesiastical architecture were corrections of earlier structural deficiencies!) Many of the boldest and most celebrated castles in Wales were also erected at the end of the 13th century, among them Harlech, Conway, and Caernarvon.

The Gothic period went out with the perpendicular style, which was almost the antithesis of its immediate predecessor. Here the emphasis was on strong, simple vertical and horizontal elements, large windows with fine, repetitive tracery, and fan vaulting. St. George's Chapel, Windsor (1474), and King's College Chapel, Cambridge (1446–1515), are supreme examples of this architectural period. Do not miss King's College Chapel. The whole of Cambridge, easily accessible by train from London, is well worth a visit — but King's College Chapel, with its powerfully simple exterior and delicately ornate interior, speaks directly to the heart. If you get there in the afternoon, try to catch evensong at about 3 or 3:30, sung in candlelight by one of the finest men-and-boy's choirs in the world.

The return to classical (especially Italian) principles and influences, known as the Renaissance, swept Europe in the 15th century, began to appear in

England during the reign of Henry VII, and took hold in the reign of Henry VIII.

Throughout the Tudor and Jacobean periods, several influences combined to shape English architecture: the devotion to large, mullioned windows, typical of the perpendicular Gothic style; the French and Italian Renaissance preoccupation with symmetry; and decorative motifs — especially an ornamentation known as strap-work, that originated in the Netherlands. Longleat House in Wiltshire (1568), Hardwick Hall in Derbyshire (1591–97), Hatfield House in Hertfordshire (1608–12), and Audley End in Essex (1603) each in its own way demonstrates a balance between these architectural forces.

Inigo Jones (1573–1652) — painter, stage designer, and architect — introduced the purity of Palladian forms to English architecture, marking this important transition with his Queen's House, Greenwich (1616). But it was Sir Christopher Wren (1632–1723), England's most renowned architect, who created England's own unique expression of classical and baroque architecture. Wren's masterpieces are fortunately very much in evidence today, notably St. Paul's Cathedral and numerous fine city churches. Many of Wren's structures suffered severe damage in the blitz of World War II, and have since been faithfully restored and rebuilt.

The classical purity of Palladianism reappeared in Bath, with John Wood the Elder's (1704–54) planning of Queen Square and with his son John Wood the Younger's (1728–81) design of the Royal Crescent. Also in the classical tradition was John Nash (1752–1835), whose Regent Street and Regent's Park frontages in London are world famous. There are Georgian or Regency squares in many cities, but perhaps the most beautiful are in Dublin. These too are designed in the spirit of classical symmetry.

Architecturally, the late 18th century and most of the 19th century must be characterized as a period of historical revival and a looking back to the past for inspiration. At first, neoclassicism appeared with a return to "first principles," meaning the nobility and simplicity of Greek art. As the 19th century advanced, neoclassicism was abandoned in favor of the revival of specific — and sometimes superficially applied — styles of the past.

Pattern books were produced to enable architects to provide their patrons with buildings designed in the style of their choice, whether this was Gothic, Norman Provincial, Greek Revival, or French Renaissance. Among the 18th and 19th-century stylistic revivals, however, there were vigorous and original architects and approaches to architecture that, to some extent, anticipated the future. Robert Adam (1728–92), generally considered a master of the purest neoclassical expression, in fact interpreted Greek and Roman themes in a highly personal way. His Syon House, Middlesex, is an example of the delicacy of his detail and the transparent quality of his space. Sir John Soane (1753–1837), who clothed his buildings in overtly neoclassical forms, could not quite conceal his romantic and picturesque leanings. His No. 13 Lincoln's Inn Fields, London (now the *Sir John Soane Museum*), is not to be missed.

At the same time, in the mid-19th century, another influence was sweeping away much of the fabric of the past. Industrialization brought new construction techniques, using iron and glass with apparently limitless possibilities, and causing as much anxiety as optimism. Joseph Paxton exploited this technology in his daring design of the famed and ill-fated Crystal Palace (1851). Structural tours de force were also displayed in a number of new iron bridges.

Initially, these developments caused architects to retreat in fear into increasingly effete imitations of the past, leaving the real breakthroughs in design to the engineers. But ultimately, modern architecture was born in response to both the perils and the challenges of the machine.

At first this response took the form of an attempt to master or to arrest the power of the machine by a deliberate return to hand craftsmanship in every aspect of life. Author, art critic, and social reformer John Ruskin thought that handicrafts would reawaken the medieval pride in collective work and ameliorate the impersonal effects of industrialization. And in 1861, British designer, socialist, and poet William Morris formed the Arts and Crafts Movement, which aimed to bring the beauty of individual craftsmanship into every home in the land. Morris's home, The Red House at Bexley Heath in Kent, was designed by Philip Webb in 1859, and set a standard for the picturesque style of residential architecture that was to follow.

Richard Norman Shaw (1831–1912) and Charles Annesley Voysey (1857–1941) were the chief exponents of the picturesque architectural style. Sometimes, a certain austerity appeared in their work that can be regarded as foreshadowing the modern movement in England. In Glasgow, Charles Rennie Mackintosh (1868–1928) was also influenced by Morris, and created his own highly original, historically premodern designs. His most notable works include the tea shops he did for Miss Cranston and the now-famous Glasgow School of Art (1897–99).

Two parallel developments, the work of the Chicago School in America, and that of the Bauhaus in Germany, finally brought modern architecture to the attention of the whole world. In Chicago in the 1880s and 1890s, the skyscraper evolved — a tall building with steel skeletons that removed any load-bearing function from the walls. A parallel development was the elevator. These two inventions changed the face of corporate architecture.

At about the same time, at the Bauhaus in Germany, architect Walter Gropius (1883–1969) was introducing a new architectural aesthetic based on industrial technology and modern materials. He preached the doctrine that a building's form must be lean and clean, derived from and expressive of its essential function.

Britain was comparatively slow to embrace the international style of the modern movement. However, in the 1950s, such men as Sir Leslie Martin, Eric Lyons, and Lord Llewelyn-Davies were pioneers in prefabricated schools and housing. The postwar housing at Roehampton has achieved world renown. Britain has also been in the vanguard of modern town planning, taking a leadership role in the evolution of the concept of the garden city or the new town. These self-contained communities do not depend, as the typical suburbs do, on London or on other metropolitan centers. Sir Ebenezer Howard (1850–1928) was the father of this movement, and Letchworth, started in 1903, was the earliest garden city and is worth a visit. Welwyn Garden City, Hampstead Garden Suburb, and, more recently,

Cumbernauld New Town in Scotland, are interesting examples of the evolution of the idea of the new town.

The bombing of London, especially in the area around St. Paul's, created opportunities for postwar urban development. A number of high-rise towers have been built, against the strenuous opposition of those who viewed them as destructive to London's lovely skyline, and to the scale and environmental quality of the city. The towers have gone up, nonetheless, though few have any architectural distinction. The Barbican development, the new Stock Exchange, and Chartered Accountants Hall are some of the most interesting high-rises in the City of London area. New Zealand House, the Docklands development, Lloyd's Bank, Thamesmead, Brunswick Center, The Economist Building, and the Institutes of Education and Law are also new London buildings worth a second look.

Having attempted in a few short pages to trace the history and development of English architecture — with its chief exponents and some pivotal buildings of each period — we must return to the starting point — to England's domestic architecture. The grand and not-so-grand country houses, the town squares, the villages, country towns, inns, and farmhouses — these are the soul of English architecture. One sees them wherever one travels. Many grand and more modest houses are open to the public. Although there are a number of books about them, the best source of basic information is the British National Trust, which owns and operates so many.

As you travel through England, you will be struck by regional differences in building styles and materials. If you study some of these buildings, you will learn something about their local character and about the periods of their origin. Especially striking are the black-and-white timbered houses of Cheshire and Shropshire. Gawsworth Hall near Macclesfield, Little Moreton Hall near Congleton, and the Feathers Inn, Ludlow, are three of the finest. In Kent, the oasthouses for drying the hops to make beer are indigenous architectural forms worth a detour to see.

The Cotswolds (chiefly Gloucestershire) are noted for the yellowish-gray stone used on almost all buildings, old and new. Some Cotswold villages, such as Bibury, Broadway, Castle Combe, and Stow-on-the-Wold represent English vernacular architecture at its most enchanting. Here brick, flint, tile, slate, timber, and thatch make their appearance throughout the country. Their color palettes and patterns weave themselves into their background with an environmental integrity that we strive for in modern forms and materials and cannot find.

Traditional Music and Dance

There's more to dance in Britain than Scotland's Highland Fling: England and Wales both have traditions of their own which mirror distinctive cultures. It all adds up to a rich inheritance — surprising, perhaps, in so small an island.

The origins of British ceremonial dance are said to lie in pagan and primitive rituals — in magic and myths, in seasonal celebrations, and in fertility and luck-bringing rites. Historians argue about dates and derivations, but certainly some of the oldest surviving ceremonial dances are rooted in the Stone, Neolithic, and Iron ages. Later the dances were variously influenced by the invading Celts, Jutes, Angles, Saxons, and Scandinavians.

Probably the earliest music for dance was provided by the chanting of the dancers, and rhythmic sounds produced on any domestic or hunting implements at hand. Primitive instruments included drums, bagpipes, other pipes such as flute and recorder, and reed instruments.

In pagan times ritual dancing was essential to existence, and later both ritual and social folk dances were enjoyed as a form of merrymaking and as a relief from the daily battle for survival. The early Christian church abhorred pagan revelry, as did the Puritans in later times, but neither group succeeded in putting an end to dancing. It was the Industrial Revolution in the 19th century that did the most damage, shifting communities toward a more impersonal lifestyle. All was not lost, however.

Imagine a tranquil village amidst England's verdant Oxfordshire countryside on a warm spring day, the village green lined with spectators intently watching six dancing men who are dressed in white trousers and shirts, with bells tied below their knees, wearing black bowler hats decorated with flowers and ribbons, and carrying white handkerchiefs. In this scene you have one of the most famous of all surviving English ritual ceremonial dances, the Cotswold morris.

The costume described is the one worn by the Bampton morris dancers, who perform annually in Bampton each *Spring Bank Holiday Monday.* The dancers are accompanied by a single musician, playing either a fiddle or a melodeon (a Viennese accordion), and by two "characters," one of whom bears a cake impaled on a sword and the other, a Fool, who carries a pig's bladder and teases people. The whole performance is wrapped in an atmosphere of jollity, with everyone reacting good-humoredly to the Fool's mocking taunts and acting as if they believe that tasting the cake will bring good luck.

There are other traditional Cotswold morris teams near Bampton, which also perform locally in spring and summer, in Abingdon, Chipping Camden, and Headington. The dancers usually wear white costumes, black shoes, and bells; they carry either handkerchiefs or, for use in rhythmic "combat," wooden sticks — but there are many differences in the colorful accessories peculiar to the individual teams. There are variations too in each team's dances, and although the steps themselves are simple, the skill lies in coping with the changing rhythms and patterns; any irregular ringing of the bells soon draws attention to the offender. Though the dancers are amateurs they take enormous pride in their performances.

No one is certain whence came the word *morris.* There was a widely held belief that it derived from the dark-skinned Moors of Spain, and though this is now dismissed, it did seem to make sense in connection with another tradition, the *Processional Morris of the Britannia Coconut Dancers,* for which the dancers blacken their faces.

The Britannia Coconut Dancers or, as they are often called, the *Britannia Nutters*, perform throughout the Saturday before Easter in the Lancashire town of Bacup. The eight men of the team carry mill bobbins and garlands of colorful rags. They dress in a ritual disguise of white hats, red and white decorated shirts, black breeches, long white socks, and clogs, and dance through the streets to the accompaniment of a brass band.

Since the 16th century traditional instruments that accompanied morris dancing have been the pipe and tabor (a small drum), which are played simultaneously by a single musician; but fiddles, melodeons, and concertinas are also popular nowadays.

Sword dances are a tradition of the northeast, having developed in all probability from the weapon dances of the ancient Romans, which in turn were once part of a pagan rite possibly even older than the forerunners of the morris dance. Sword dances used to be associated with sword plays, and though the plays as such have now disappeared the dances still contain an element of drama that is exemplified by the retention of characters such as Tommy (a king) and Betsy (a half-man, half-woman creature).

There are two distinct types of sword dance, the long sword (stiff), which is danced in Flamborough (Humberside), Grenoside and Handsworth (South Yorkshire), and Loftus, Skelton, and Guisborough (Cleveland); and the short or rapper sword (flexible), which is the specialty of the *Royal Earsdon Sword Dancers* at Earsdon near Newcastle-on-Tyne.

The steps consist of complex mixtures of walks, runs, and (in the rapper) fast "jigging with shuffles." Swords are linked to symbolize the unbroken ring of life, and periodically they are plaited together into a many-sided lock, which is then held up by the captain of the team for the approval of the crowd. The rapper sword dance has no counterpart elsewhere. It is a more athletic dance than the long sword dance, which might be said to resemble the style of "soldiers at the double."

Sword dances are performed between *Boxing Day* (the first day after Christmas) and *Plough Monday* (the first or second Monday in January), to the accompaniment of a single musician with pipe, accordion, or fiddle, by teams of five to eight men. Dancers wear either military-type uniforms or white shirts and stylish versions of miners' "long shorts" with colorful sashes and rosettes for decoration.

The *'Obby 'Oss Procession* may be seen in two towns in the West Country: Padstow (Cornwall) and Minehead (Somerset). Both ceremonies are held in early May and involve men dressed as horses parading through the town with their attendants. Of the two, the Padstow 'Obby 'Oss ceremony on May 1 is the more celebrated. It starts at midnight the night before when selected "mayers" go round the town singing, and then early next morning they decorate the streets with festive greenery. The 'Oss emerges midmorning and dances through the streets for the rest of the day accompanied by the mayers, a teaser, and a memorable *May Day* tune, played on melodeons, accordions, and drums. Superstition plays an integral part in these dances, and the locals enter into the ceremonies with enthusiasm, convinced that the 'osses are lucky.

Each year, on the first Monday after the first Sunday after September 4, you can see the ancient Abbots Bromley (Staffordshire) horn dance. It is believed to have originally been a fertility ritual, but this is played down nowadays — the villagers prefer to associate it more with the traditions of the deer hunt. Six male dancers, dressed in Tudor costume, carry reindeer horns, and since three are clothed in white and three in black it is supposed that they symbolize good and evil. Four characters escort the dancers, the Fool, the Hobby Horse, the Maid Marian (a man-woman figure), and Robin Hood with his bow and arrow, and they all parade through the village streets entertaining the crowds with plenty of dancing and tomfoolery. The Horse ensures that the two musicians with melodeon and triangle are kept up to snuff by persistently and rhythmically clacking his jaws!

There is another form of dance tradition in England quite separate from these ritual ceremonial dances, the social or country dances. These are done purely for enjoyment, by men and women together, and even by children. They developed in the rural communities and, quite separately, in the ballrooms and drawing rooms of the aristocracy.

Among the most popular country dances were those which celebrated *May Day.* To this day people still enjoy the traditions that have developed from the old customs, such as dancing round the Maypole and choosing the May Queen. Oldest of all the surviving dances is the world-famous Helston furry dance, which is performed each year on or about May 8 in Helston (Cornwall) to celebrate the passing from darkness (winter) into light (spring). The dance, which is accompanied by the *Helston Town Band,* is processional and during the day there are three separate processions: for children, for formally dressed adults, and for anyone in the mood to make merry.

In the 16th century court dances were formal and dignified, but during the reign of Elizabeth I the courtiers were introduced to rustic dances, first as entertainment and then for participation; and almost inevitably the traditions began to mingle and lived on under the collective title of country dances.

These dances enjoyed their greatest popularity in the 18th century, after which they gradually went out of favor. In the early 20th century they were revived by Cecil Sharp. With tireless enthusiasm he collected and chronicled hundreds of dances, tunes, and songs. He founded the English Folk Dance Society, which later became the English Folk Dance and Song Society and which rekindled interest everywhere. From this countless affiliated clubs have sprung, and nowadays you may be sure that every night somewhere in town or country there are informal dances or ceilidhs (evenings of traditional music, song, and dance).

If you come to England looking for folk dance and music, you would do well to begin your search at Cecil Sharp House, home of the English Folk Dance and Song Society (2 Regents Park Rd., London NW1 7AY, phone: 485-2206). They welcome visitors and will let you browse in the library among the specialized books (predominantly British and American). There are also magazines, photographs, tapes, pamphlets advertising events and festivals, and a bookshop — and if you peep into the main hall you may even see some dancing! Overseas members currently pay an annual subscription of about $8.95.

In Scotland there are no longer either ritual ceremonial dances or dance-dramas: The only traditional dances that survive come from the Highlands and undoubtedly most famous of all is the Highland fling.

The name comes from the flinging action made by the working foot as it moves sharply inward to the lower calf of the supporting leg. Though its origins probably lie in battle traditions, it is an elegant dance. But there must be a "fire in the feet," and the dancer, his weight balanced on his toes, must make intricate cutting, beating, kicking, and flinging movements with enough verve and agility to astonish his audience.

Seann triubhs ("shabby trousers") is another favorite Highland dance. It is said that during the '45 Rebellion (the Jacobite uprising of 1745) men had to wear tartan trews (trousers) instead of kilts, and this dance is symbolic of that period and the attempts that were made to "shake off" the trousers. However much truth there is in that story, seann triubhs is an extremely graceful traveling dance that mixes cutting, beating, and kicking movements with pirouettes, balances, and attractive circlings of the arms.

There is only one hilt-and-point sword dance in Scotland that resembles the English tradition: the Papa Stour sword dance, still performed in the Shetland Island of Papa Stour. The Highland sword dance is performed between the angles made by two swords placed on the ground in the form of a cross, and though the dancer must show plenty of vigor he also has to be extremely delicate so as to avoid touching the swords with his feet as they beat, step, and jump.

Elaborate costumes are worn for these dances, consisting of kilt, velvet jacket (or shirt and tie), plaids (lengths of tartan placed over the shoulders), a sporran (animal-skin pouch) attached to a chain round the waist, and ghillies (soft flat black shoes). Women wear similar costumes, but without the sporran. Traditionally the most popular accompanying instrument is the bagpipe, though jew's-harp, fiddle, and melodeon are also common. The best place to see Highland dancing is at one of the many Highland Games that take place between mid-July and mid-September. The Games of Braemar and Dunoon are especially popular for dancing.

Just when country dances began to go out of vogue in England in the early

19th century they became immensely popular in Scotland, and have remained so to this day, although had it not been for the formation in 1923 of the Scottish Country Dance Society, less authenticity might have prevailed.

These dances are vivacious or graceful, and in the main they fall into three groups: strathspeys, reels, and jigs, with hundreds of variations of each. The men wear kilts and the women white dresses and tartan sashes. Originally the bagpipe was the most popular accompanying instrument, but it has now been superseded by the fiddle.

Scottish country dancing has a worldwide following these days, and many foreign visitors join the (now) Royal Scottish Country Dance Society's annual summer school at St. Andrews. There are performances and casual gatherings all over Scotland throughout the year as well as competitions, festivals, and displays at Highland Games. During the summer months, there is even dancing in the streets of Edinburgh. For more information contact Miss M. Gibson, the Royal Scottish Country Dance Society, 12 Coates Crescent, Edinburgh EH3 7AF (phone: 225-3854), and the Scottish Tourist Board, 23 Ravelston Terr., Edinburgh EH4 3EU (phone: 332-2433).

Surprisingly, since the Welsh are renowned for their musical traditions, there is less apparent love of dance, and little is known about the early folk dances. In the Middle Ages there were many popular dances including chains, rounds, reels, and morris dances, but with the establishment of the Chapel in Wales in the late 18th century these merrymakings were forced to a halt. The people were obliged to concentrate on religion, and consequently their musical talents became vested in their great choral tradition.

The instrument that dominates is the harp. Wales boasts the triple harp which, with its three rows of strings, is considered by some to be the finest harp in existence. Undoubtedly it lends itself to dancing, though the fiddle and flute are also popular. The only dance that has survived in an unbroken tradition is the clog and broom dance. It is vigorous, and quite tricky to perform: The dancer makes fast tapping steps around the broom as it lies on the ground, or he may pick it up and jump over it. Nowadays some of the best dancers delight in introducing inventive tricks into it.

It was not until 1949, with the formation of the Welsh Folk Dance Society, that attempts were made to salvage what was left of the dances. It also has made great efforts to ensure that authentic costumes survive, and these are usually quaint and charming: breeches, waistcoats, and shirts for men; and pretty blouses, long skirts with lace aprons, and caps, or the well-known, tall, flat-topped black hats for women.

You'll find plenty of dance displays at the *International Musical Eisteddfod* in July at Llangollen or the *Royal National Eisteddfod of Wales* (which alternates each August between North and South Wales), and the many smaller ones which crop up all over Wales during the summer. Information can be obtained from Mrs. Jean Huw Jones, Dolawenydd, Betws, Ammanford, Dyfed SA18 2HE (phone: 2837), and the Wales Tourist Board, 3 Castle St., Cardiff CF1 2RE (phone: 27281).

Food and Drink

The image most Americans have of British food is that of a massive roast beef, surrounded by plainly cooked vegetables, mashed potatoes, and a little gravy. No elaborate sauces or violent flavors. Unfortunately, cost has driven the roast beef of old England into decline, but you can still sample its splendor in "carvery" rooms in major London hotels, where huge joints of beef, pork, and lamb are featured. Many "medieval banquet" restaurants also serve meals styled to resemble feasts of the past — from the 16th century to Victorian times. These, however, aim more for drama than for authenticity, and the visitor must go elsewhere for genuine "Old English" dishes. In an effort to promote traditional foods and recipes, the British Tourist Board created the "Taste of England, Scotland, and Wales" distinction. You'll see this noted on many menus, and tourist board booklets list the establishments that serve traditional fare.

BREAKFAST: A SUBSTANTIAL MEAL

"Breakfast first, business later," declared British writer William Makepeace Thackeray. Standard breakfast fare includes grapefruit or juice, eggs and bacon, with tomatoes, mushrooms, or sausages, followed by toast, marmalade, and tea or coffee. But some country house hotels have preserved the Edwardian tradition of serving kidneys and kedgeree. (The latter, a fish and rice mixture flavored with curry, is particularly good for soaking up and salving any excesses of the night before.) A mixed grill of lamb chops, sausages, liver, kidney, mushrooms, and tomatoes also may be served as a late breakfast dish, and potted and cold meats, brawn (a cold, pressed pig meat), and finnan haddock are also popular.

Regional sausages, such as Cumberland ring sausages, can still be found. And in Lancashire and Scotland, Suffolk, or black, pudding is famous. It's made with pig's blood and served sliced with grilled bacon and eggs. Potato cakes, crisply fried, are served in some places, and in Wales and north Cornwall, a seaweed called "laverbread" is fried with the bacon. Kipper, a bony smoked fish that's quite salty, is another breakfast staple.

Is it any wonder that novelist Somerset Maugham once commented that to eat well in Britain, one should eat breakfast three times a day?

TEA: A BRITISH TRADITION

"Everything stops for tea" is an English saying, and rare is the worker who can get through his day without tea breaks. The afternoon tea meal was started in about 1780 by the Duchess of Bedford as a gossipy way of filling in the time between early lunch and late dinner. A whole industry of teacups, special china, cake stands, embroidered cloths, linen, and tea forks for the cakes grew up, and a precise ritual soon evolved around a silver teapot and sugar bowl with little tongs.

This graciousness has disappeared in today's hurried times. Visitors, however, can still test out Rupert Brooke's lines "Stands the church clock at ten to three?/And is there honey still for tea?" Honey or country preserves, particularly strawberry jam, go with scones, which are rather like an American biscuit. Other cakes include Victoria sponge rock and fairy (iced) cakes, Battenburg, and Madeira. In Scotland, teas are substantial, and they include fruitcakes like Dundee and tea breads, which are halfway between cakes and breads in consistency. In Wales, bacon, fish, pancakes, and *bara brith* ("speckled bread") are eaten.

In Devon and Cornwall, tea is served with thick, clotted cream, and regional cakes follow sandwiches and scones. "Tea" also refers to the early evening meal in the north, and in country districts (especially in Shropshire) one may still find signs for "farm teas." These are often quite substantial — including salads, ham, or fish. The "strawberry tea" is a happy summer event during the Wimbledon tennis fortnight and the Henley regatta: A bowl of fresh strawberries and cream is served with tea.

In the smaller villages and towns, there used to be many shops where local ladies served tea and homemade cakes; this was considered a respectable occupation for "spinsters" ever since a Miss Cranston set up the country's first tea room in Glasgow's Sauchiehall Street in 1904. These days, tea shops come and go, and some consider tea to be an endangered meal.

Nevertheless, the afternoon tea ritual is still maintained in all its glory by such hotels as the *Lygon Arms* in Broadway in the Cotswolds, which serves crumpets and tea cakes in winter. And teas at the *Ritz,* or *Brown's* hotels in London are tops: At any one of these hostelries, monogrammed Irish linen covers the high little round tables (the stiffly corseted Edwardian ladies sat higher than today's women) and thin cucumber, cress, cheese, tomato, egg, or smoked salmon sandwiches are followed by scones, clotted cream, and strawberry jam. Finally, delicate petit fours and pastries are served. A choice of Indian and China teas is traditional. (For a more extensive selection of tea shops and tea gardens see DIVERSIONS.)

THE MAIN COURSE

As we have said, Britain is famous for its good roast meats, such as chicken, turkey, and duckling, as well as game in season — pheasant, grouse, quail, partridge, venison, and hare. Welsh lamb deserves special mention, as does English mutton. However, there are many outstanding meat dishes besides the traditional roast, including meat pies, puddings, and stews.

In the little Cotswold village of Broadway, the butcher shop called *Collins* still practices the old art of making raised pies. Typically, the pies have carefully molded, high sides and are filled with game from local shoots. So special are *Collins*'s pies that *Harrods* and *Fortnum and Mason* keep specially monogrammed pie molds there.

Perhaps more familiar to most Americans is the steak and kidney pie, which when served in London sometimes also contains mushrooms or oysters. More economical recipes use less expensive cuts of meat. For example, Lancashire hot pot utilizes the neck end of lamb, and tripe and onions is a northern favorite. On the banks of the Mersey River the word *scouse* may be heard more than seen on a menu. It is a diminutive for *lobscouse,* a lamb, beef, and vegetable stew and is such a favorite with Liverpudlians that they are nicknamed Scouses. And Robert Burns called the Scottish favorite, haggis, the "chieftain o' the puddin race." It is a dish made of the innards of a sheep, minced with suet and oatmeal, and it's traditionally served with "tatties and neeps," or potatoes and turnips. Haggis is now often offered on hotel menus as an appetizer.

In the midlands, where ham and bacon are especially loved, little pieces of bacon turn up in boiled, hot, gray peas. Pork crackling is rendered down to make "scratchings" and is often sold in pubs in packets and eaten like potato chips. The great hams of the country are in York, where they are cured by dry salting. York hams are said to have derived their original flavor from smoking in the oak sawdust of timbers used in the building of York's cathedral. Bradenham ham, made since 1781, is dry-cured, pickled in molasses for a month, and matured for 3 months thereafter. Suffolk Seager ham is rounded with a dark brown finish. It is cured in brine, black treacle, and molasses and then it is smoked.

The Dunmow flitch is a side of bacon traditionally presented every 3 years to the most harmoniously married couple in this Essex town. You may also come across the bacon "clanger," a pastry roll of bacon, onion, and herbs that originated in Oxfordshire. Sometimes it has a sweet filling at one end and is savory at the other, so that a worker in the fields could take his whole meal in one neat pack.

Practicality mixed with poverty was the origin of the Cornish pasty that was made for the tin miner (many of whom immigrated to Colorado, where pasties are still served at the miners' festival). Triangular in shape, so it can slip into a pocket, the pasty contained potato, vegetables, and whatever scraps of meat were available. It was said that the pasty was hard enough to withstand a fall down the mine shaft.

And now a word about the trimmings: *Tracklement* is the lovely old English word for a condiment to go with meat. Cumberland sauce with ham or pâté is one old delight; red currant jelly goes with lamb, and there are many chutneys. Mustard is the major meat accompaniment, declared by George I to be his favorite. *Colman's* mustard ship in Bridewell Lane, Norwich, is a replica of a 19th-century grocer's shop and sells many blends. Other English mustards include Taylors, English vineyard mustards, and whole grain mustards by Crabtree and Evelyn. Horseradish cream — they say the best horseradish root comes from country graveyards — is a pungent root that is grated, mixed with cream, and served with roast beef.

Because it's an island, Britain has a plentiful supply of fish and seafood. Cod is king and it is usually served up as the ubiquitous fish fingers. Turbot is served with hollandaise sauce, and Dover sole and mackerel are traditionally served with gooseberry sauce. Herrings, pilchards (which are popular tinned in oil for teas), bloaters from Yarmouth, and sprats are traditional fish.

Salmon is the luxury fish, caught in Scotland and Wales and in bigger English rivers like the Wye. In summer it is served poached hot with hollandaise sauce or cold with mayonnaise and cucumber. Smoked salmon is a glory that is principally found in Scotland, and smoked mackerel and trout are served as appetizers with horseradish sauce.

Oysters from East Anglia and Cornwall, shrimp from Lancashire's Morecambe Bay, lobsters, mussels, and Dublin Bay prawns are all popular, if expensive. Londoners like small shellfish such as whelks or cockles; these are skewered on a pin and sold from stalls in the East End. They also enjoy eels, jellied or made into pies with a green parsley sauce. Whitebait may open a meal, and on the Severn River in spring, elvers (baby eels) are eaten in competitions to see who can consume the most.

Fish and chips, the age-old British favorite, can be enjoyed in impressive, chandelier-hung surroundings at *Harry Ramsden's* in Guisley, Yorkshire. Other recommended places for a fish-and-chip pilgrimage are the *Gainsboro* at Hull, *Bryan's* fish restaurant at Headingly, and *Mother Hubbard's* at Girlington near Bradford.

Eleanor Roosevelt once remarked, "The English have ten green vegetables and eight of them are brussels sprouts." Although vegetables are often a weak spot on the British menu, there are some exceptions. Spring is heralded by the arrival of little new potatoes cooked with a sprig of mint and served with melted butter. Cold mashed potatoes and leftover cabbage are often mixed together and fried for breakfast or for light family meals. In England this is known as "bubble and squeak" and in Scotland as "rumbledethumps" — because of the elbow grease that goes into beating it. And "pan haggerty" — thinly sliced potatoes, onions, and grated cheese — is pan fried in Northumbria. Early in the summer there is samphire, a marsh plant that is eaten like asparagus in East Anglia. Asparagus itself is ready in June and is expensive, but like strawberries and salmon, it's a sign of the British summer.

DESSERTS

A "good pud" is seen as a threat to most dieters, but traditional puddings live on in Britain, aided by memories of the nostalgic treats of childhood. Before North Sea oil and central heating, Britons kept warm with a whole repertoire of suet puddings: Kentwell pudding, in which a lemon and butter and sugar were encased in suet pastry; spotted dicks, suet with dried fruit; or castle, treacle, mattress, and cabinet puddings. Bread and butter pudding cooked with dried fruit and milk was another favorite, and Christmas pudding served after the turkey is probably the richest of all: It's dark with fruit and alcohol and it is served with custard, rum, or brandy butters.

Not all puddings are heavy. Syllabub was made originally by pouring fresh cow's milk from a height onto lemon and wine mixtures. Junkets are a light, creamy affair made in the West Country: Indeed, visits to the dairy to eat this became so popular that the word *junket* is now synonymous with a party outing. Another confection was a puree of rhubarb and gooseberries mixed with thick cream. And trifle is a year-round favorite — it's sponge cake, soaked in sherry, layered with raspberry jam or fruit, and topped with custard and cream.

A most famous pudding — which can also be eaten cold with jam for dessert — is the Yorkshire pudding usually served with roast beef. Yorkshire women claim only they can make it properly, though a local competition to find the champion pudding maker was won lately by a Chinese chef.

But puddings are by no means the only dessert specialties to be found in Britain. Many baked products can be sampled and bought from the weekly Women's Institute markets (a list is available from the National Federation of Women's Institutes, 39 Eccleston St., London SW1W 9NT). These small, friendly regional markets are a good way to meet local people.

Gingerbread, a specialty of the Lake District, is made daily in *Sarah Nelson's* shop in Grasmere. In this area, gingerbread alphabets were once used to teach children to read. Shortbread is Scotland's favorite, while in Richmond, Surrey, "maids of honour tarts," named for Anne Boleyn's ladies, are still sold. The *Old Bakewell Pudding* shop in Bakewell, Derbyshire, sells tarts with almonds and raspberry jam. Yorkshire's parkin, based on oatmeal, treacle, and ginger, is made traditionally on November 5, Bonfire Night. Also in Yorkshire, apple pie is a favorite dish customarily eaten with a slice of cheese. The locals are fond of the rhyme: "Apple pie without a slice of cheese is like a kiss without a squeeze."

As for fruit, Scottish raspberries from Speyside are excellent in flavor. Outstanding among the late summer fruits in Britain are apples, pears, and plums, particularly damsons and greengages. Britons often mix soft fruits with black and red currants to make a "summer pudding;" the fruit is puréed and put in a crust made of dried bread.

BREADS AND CHEESES

Among British breads are bloomers, baps (soft Scottish breakfast rolls), coburgs, cobs, pistols (round-shaped loaves), and cottage loaves (two rounds on top of each other). Biscuits (cookies and crackers) include Dorset knobs — dried, rusklike tidbits that go with cheese — and Bath Olivers — thin water biscuits invented in the 18th century for dieters by Dr. Oliver, Bath's first spa physician.

England has nine national cheeses, of which Stilton is king. A veined blue cheese from Leicestershire, it is traditionally served with port. Cheshire cheese, which comes in patriotic red, white, and blue versions, was much loved by Samuel Johnson; his favorite Fleet Street pub in London is named *The Cheshire.* Lancashire cheese spreads and toasts well. Derby is the rarest, and sage Derby, veined with the herb, was originally made for Christmas. Caerphilly was once made in Wales, and now it's made in Somerset. Easily digestible, Caerphilly was the chosen snack of coal miners cramped at the pit face. Cheddar from the Mendip Hills goes well in a fruit pie pastry.

"New" cheeses are brought out regularly. These include red Windsor, veined with red wine; Cotswolds, a double Gloucester with onions and chives; Walton, a blend of Cheddar and Stilton; Ilchester, a cheddar mixed with beer, spices, and chives; and Labra, the first ewe's milk cheese to be made since the Middle Ages.

In certain areas, you can visit farms to see cheeses being made. In Scotland many national cheeses are made in Orkney, including Dunlop, Caboc (rolled in oats), and Castle Stuart blue cheeses.

A NOTE ON BEVERAGES

The pub or "local" is a Briton's home away from home; it's an informal place to talk and drink. Most British beer is warm and heavy, so often the lagers served chilled are more to the visitors' taste. Local breweries persist and such brews as Adnams of Southwold with their Fishermen's ale, Doddington, Theakstons, Ruddles, Toby Cobbold of Ipswich, and Greene King of Bury St. Edmunds are served mainly in their own regions. "Real ale" bars are springing up around the country these days — even at some railway stations. A few unusual pub drinks are black beer from Leeds, which is made from malt and cane sugar mixed with rum, whisky, or lemonade; shrub, which was used as a West Country mix to sweeten sea-tainted rum in the old smuggling days; and lovage, an herbal pick-me-up that is also from the West Country.

Cider is a traditional drink from the West Country and Hereford. It's based on fermented apples and is sold fresh. (The sweetness varies.) Some leading cider producers own pubs that specialize in cider. In the West Country, some pubs sell "scrumpy," the raw farm-brewed cider that has a deceptive ox-felling power; so much so, that the police are not eager that it be sold to tourists. Mead is a honeysweet drink dating from before Christian times. It is still made in Cornwall and on the island of Lindisfarne, where the factory is open to the public.

Although Britain has always been thought of as a beer-drinking country, wine is rapidly becoming popular as well. Today you can find wine lists that offer selections from California to Australia, and from Chile to Charente. In addition, Britain is reviving its native vineyards, which declined during the Middle Ages, when most of France — and French wine — was under the control of the English crown. The English Vineyards Association numbers over 400 growers, who produce 180,000 bottles per year. Among the best-known names are Hambledon and Pilton Manor in Somerset, both of which have days when they are open for visitors. Adgestone from the Isle of Wight is one of the most prized wines, and Beaulieu comes from Lord Montagu's estate in Hampshire. Merrydown in Sussex also produces English country wines made from elderberries, red currants, and apples, as well as a rich, sweet mead.

And though pubs advertise Harvey Wallbangers and other cocktails, the more conservative Briton will have a sherry before a formal meal and a glass of port (known as the "Englishman's drink") afterward. On hot summer days, many find a gin and tonic cooling, and a whisky and soda is good any time. But even though gin, vodka, and other spirits are made in Britain, Scotch is the most popular — more than 200 brands are produced and consumed. So much Scotch is sold that they say the duty on its sale pays for the nation's defense budget! (For a more complete discussion of beers, ales, and liquors, as well as the selection of the best watering holes in Britain, see *Pub Crawling,* DIVERSIONS.)

THE CITIES

ABERDEEN

With a population approaching a quarter of a million, Aberdeen is Scotland's third largest city and is among the most distinctive in Britain. Well known among the British for its striking granite architecture, bracing clean air, and 15th-century university (not to mention, more recently, its soccer team), this North Sea port unexpectedly became familiar to a far wider audience as the oil capital of Europe during the 1970s. Aberdeen's good fortune in becoming the major service and supply base for the oil-drilling industry in the North Sea made it Scotland's most prosperous city in the short space of a decade and allowed it — until the decline of world oil prices — to ride out Britain's economic recession more successfully than most other cities.

Still, Aberdeen is no Houston or Dallas, since the oil boom in Great Britain is only skin deep. Beneath this new outer layer are more traditional commercial mainstays: a fishing industry important enough to make the city the third largest fishing port of the United Kingdom, and a small but thriving shipbuilding industry that had its greatest days in the mid-19th century. Even longer established are textiles and papermaking, and last, but not least, is Aberdeen's enduring role as market town for the agricultural products raised in the surrounding countryside of northeastern Scotland.

Also worthy of note is the granite industry. Aberdeen stands on and is built of granite. Until seen first-hand, few travelers realize what that means: Its streets look and are clean; its magnificent granite buildings perennially present the finish of fresh renovation. The effect is chilling or cheerful, depending on the weather, but always spectacular. Britain's late poet laureate, Sir John Betjeman, spoke of the city as "a strange textured place . . . so remote, so windswept and of such a solid, grey strangeness." Others have compared it to Leningrad — hardly an unreasonable comparison, considering that, at a distance of 540 miles from London, Aberdeen lies at the same latitude as that most beautiful of Russian cities, and its Georgian and Victorian neo-Gothic architecture has something of the same stateliness.

Granite and gray are not all that predominate, however. Beauty of a more natural variety is rife. As the city's tourist authorities proudly boast, Aberdeen's numerous splendid parks and gardens — with their abundant floral displays, magnificent roses, and heaths and heather — are nine-time winners of the prestigious Britain in Bloom competition. Between them, almost every conceivable kind of plant life is represented, from the exotic tropical and desert plants found in the Winter Gardens to the alpine flora of the Johnston Gardens.

Another feature adding to Aberdeen's special appeal is its unique location astride not one, but two rivers, neatly named Dee and Don. The Dee is the more famous because of its association with Balmoral, the Scottish holiday retreat of British kings and queens, 50 miles away. What's more, it is the Dee that holds the harbor and docks of Aberdeen in its mouth. Yet both rivers have contributed substantially to the fortunes of the city, and in the words of the old rhyme, "Ae mile o'Don's worth twa o'Dee except for salmon, stane and tree." Had Aberdeen been built closer to the sea, much of its charm would be wanting. As it is, a spacious esplanade stretches for two miles from Don to Dee, with the golden sandy beach on one side and a stretch of golf courses on the other.

Aberdeen's promotional slogan "City for Lovers" has an up-to-date ring, but its official motto is "Bon Accord," which dates from the night in 1308 when Aberdonians attacked the English garrison in the castle (no longer extant) and razed the fortifications, using the French phrase as a password. The origins of the city can't be traced back much earlier than this event — only to the 12th century — yet by the end of the 13th century, a succession of charters had created and reaffirmed all the trappings of a medieval royal burgh. The 14th century was turbulent — the English, expelled in 1308, returned in 1336 and devastated the town, causing such great damage that widespread reconstruction was required — and the distinction between "Old" and "New" Aberdeen may well have been born then.

That the unruly times continued into the 15th century can be seen in buildings such as St. Machar's Cathedral, a church resolutely constructed for defense. Still, it was precisely in the late 15th century, in "Old" Aberdeen — then known as the Kirktoun of Seaton, the ecclesiastical community by the Don — that the most important single event in Aberdeen's development took place. In 1494, Bishop Elphinstone obtained a papal bull allowing the establishment of a university, the third in Scotland after St. Andrews (1411) and Glasgow (1450). Within a century, in 1593, George Keith, the Earl Marischal of Scotland, set up a rival, Protestant university on the site of a Greyfriars monastery in "New" Aberdeen. The two institutions, King's College and Marischal College, finally merged into the University of Aberdeen in 1860.

During the Reformation of the 16th century, St. Machar's and other churches fell into decay; the cathedral was again damaged in the 17th century, during Oliver Cromwell's Commonwealth, when stones from its buttresses were used to fortify the city. The Jacobite risings of the first half of the 18th century — when, after the Act of Union of 1707 had made England and Scotland one kingdom, followers of James Stuart, the Old Pretender, sought to restore him to the throne — also touched Aberdeen. In 1716, defeated Jacobite army chiefs gathered here after the Battle of Sheriffmuir to learn that their "king" had slipped out of the country. In 1745, the drunken followers of the Young Pretender, James's son, Bonnie Prince Charlie, proclaimed the Old Pretender at the Mercat Cross and rudely poured wine down the shirt front of Aberdeen's provost, who, loyal to George II, had refused to drink. The next year, the Duke of Cumberland stayed in Aberdeen with his army en route to defeat Bonnie Prince Charlie's Highland army at Culloden Moor.

The Act of Union meant the end of Scottish independence, but it did open up the English market to Scotland and gave a great boost to Aberdeen's docks. This, along with the onset of the Industrial Revolution, enabled local industries to develop. Woolen mills were established first; the manufacture of linen, cotton, and paper followed in the late 18th century. Granite quarrying came to the fore in 1741, with the opening of the Rubislaw quarry, which would supply most of the material used to build the city's elegant and austere granite houses.

The city's first shipyard was built in 1753, but it wasn't until the next century, when several notable ship designers were at the drawing boards, that the shipbuilding industry reached its zenith. William and James Hall can be credited with launching the world's first clipper schooner, the *Scottish Maid,* in 1839. This milestone ushered in Aberdeen's clipper era, a period when beautiful, fast, Aberdeen-built sailing ships, including the tea clippers that kept American ships from monopolizing the China tea trade, won the city an international reputation. When, in 1872, the *Thermopylae* proved to be the fastest sailing ship in the world (in a race against the famous Glasgow-built *Cutty Sark*), the end of the era was already at hand, but it had established a shipbuilding tradition that has lasted to the present day.

At about the same time, from the mid-18th century to the mid-19th century, Aberdeen was also Scotland's leading whaling port. Overfishing destroyed whaling, but the city quickly recouped with its herring fleets. By 1900, the introduction of steam trawling made Aberdeen a boom town — and Scotland's leading fishing port — with whitefish rather than herring the prime catch. The city retains this premier status despite a decline in the fishing industry since the 1920s. Even postwar modernization of the fleet was not enough to offset the loss of fishing grounds, thus the city had cause to be grateful that the local oil boom ensured its continued prosperity.

Aberdeen is hardly the first place that travelers to Scotland consider visiting, but it shouldn't be given short shrift. Not only is it an attractive city, rich in historical and natural interest, it is also (especially since the oil boom) a cosmopolitan city, possessed of ample restaurants, hotels, shops, sports facilities, pubs, entertainment, and cultural events. Furthermore, its location offers the best of several worlds: Aberdeen has the convenience of a modern city with its own many tourist attractions, the holiday atmosphere of a seaside resort (yes, there is plenty of sunshine, but be prepared for icy water and, in general, stimulating summer weather — freshness rather than great heat), and, finally, proximity to the magnificent scenery of the Highlands and "Castle Country." (In Royal Deeside and the Cairngorms alone there are some 60 castles.)

ABERDEEN AT-A-GLANCE

SEEING THE CITY: Though it is no longer possible to climb the university's Mitchell Tower or the tower of Aberdeen Town House for a truly panoramic view, the approach to Aberdeen by the main road from the south (A92) is dramatic compensation. According to Cuthbert Graham in his book Portrait of Aberdeen and Deeside, the city "signals its approach by the appearance, poking up over the brow of a ridge, of a spikey corona of skyscrapers." As the highway descends to the 16th-century Bridge of Dee, "a wide spreading silver-veined city arising from a river's brim" appears. To the left, fertile fields, wooded slopes, and ever higher hills stretch almost to the Cairngorms.

SPECIAL PLACES: A good many of the city's sights are to be found in two fairly compact areas. Aberdeen's most famous thoroughfare, Union Street, runs about a mile east and west across the city center, with Telford Bridge (or Union Bridge) midway in its course and the fine prospect of Union Terrace Gardens just above. At the eastern end of the street is an open space known variously as the Castlegate or Castle Street, the city's historic marketplace since the 12th century and still the heart of town. Another essential area for any visitor is Old Aberdeen, or Aulton, as it was once known locally, about 1½ miles north of the city center. Despite the modern architecture that surrounds it, Old Aberdeen dates from the Middle Ages and contains a mixture of buildings from the 16th century on. It is made up of what is, in effect, almost a single line of streets, beginning with College Bounds, which runs into High Street, then Don Street, and, finally, Chanonry.

CITY CENTER

The Old Tolbooth and Aberdeen Town House – The oldest building still extant on the Castlegate is the Old Tolbooth, which dates from 1627, although earlier versions of it go back to the reign of Robert III (1390 –1406), when the monarch gave permission for the erection of a tolbooth, or burgh jail. The Old Tolbooth, in turn, its tower and steeple rising to a height of 120 feet, is incorporated into a newer building, the handsome Aberdeen Town House. Completed in 1874, this ornate edifice, in Flemish-Medieval style, has been the home of the Aberdeen City Council for over a century and has a massive tower that is more than 200 feet tall. A free tour of the combined structures can be arranged by telephoning the town sergeant between 9 AM and 5 PM weekdays. Corner of Broad and Castle Sts. (phone: 642121).

Mercat Cross – What is considered the finest old burgh cross surviving in Scotland was designed and built by John Montgomery in 1686. The focal point of the city, it stands on a hexagonal platform in the center of the Castlegate and is topped by a unicorn. Its charm and interest derive from both the detail of its decoration — the medallions adorning it contain portraits of the Stuart kings — and the rich pageant of history associated with the site. Castle St.

Marischal College – Part of the University of Aberdeen since 1860, it was founded in the late 16th century as a Protestant rival to the earlier King's College. It was built on the site of a Greyfriars monastery, only one gable of which remains (incorporated into the Greyfriars Church, completed in 1903, which forms part of the college's south front). The college itself is a quadrangle, and the buildings on the inner courtyard were mostly completed by 1844, but the primarily granite façade that opens onto Broad Street was completed in 1906. This great Broad Street frontage, designed in Perpendicular Gothic by A. Marshall Mackenzie, has been called "a tour de force of the granite carver's art," a remarkable work of architecture that is a must for any visitor to Aberdeen. Broad St.

Provost Skene's House – This townhouse, built in the mid-16th century, was extensively altered during the 17th century, when it was the residence of Sir George Skene, Provost of Aberdeen, from whom it takes its name. In the 18th century, the Duke of Cumberland, known as Butcher for his ruthless treatment of his enemies, stayed here for 6 weeks on his way to defeat the army of Bonnie Prince Charlie at Culloden. Now restored and functioning as a museum, the house contains furnished period rooms, displays highlighting local history, and a beautiful painted ceiling dating from 1630. Another definite must-see, it also has a kitchen that is open for tea, coffee, and light meals. Closed Sundays. Guestrow, off Broad St. (phone: 641086).

Provost Ross's House (Aberdeen Maritime Museum) – One of the oldest buildings in Aberdeen, Provost Ross's House was built in 1593. As the home of the *Aberdeen Maritime Museum,* it contains a splendid variety of exhibits that provide the visitor with an excellent survey of Aberdeen's maritime past. Models of famous ships associated with Aberdeen port, including the lovely sailing ships of the clipper era, are a major feature. Closed Sundays. Shiprow, off Castle St. (phone: 585788).

St. Andrew's Episcopal Cathedral – Although built in 1816–17, the interior covers several periods. The cathedral is of special interest to Americans because it contains the Seabury memorial, a gift of the American Episcopal Bishops in commemoration of Samuel Seabury of Connecticut, who was consecrated the first bishop of America in Aberdeen in 1784. Open for church services, and Mondays through Saturdays from 10 AM to 4 PM from mid-May through September. 28 King St.

Aberdeen Art Gallery – The permanent collection contains paintings by Scottish artists from the 16th century to the present, a series of 18th- and 19th-century British portraits, 20th-century British works, and some French Impressionist paintings. Contemporary foreign and British sculpture is also well represented, plus decorative arts, including an interesting collection of silver and glassware from northeastern Scotland. Open Mondays through Saturdays from 10 AM to 5 PM, Thursdays to 8 PM, and Sundays from 2 to 5 PM. Schoolhill (phone: 646333).

Union Terrace Gardens – This delightful sunken Victorian garden runs along Union Terrace. Slap bang in the city center, there is no more convenient or picturesque place to relax after a hard day of sightseeing or shopping.

OLD ABERDEEN

King's College – This complex of buildings, the older part of the University of Aberdeen, was founded by Bishop Elphinstone in 1495, a year after he received the foundation bull from Pope Alexander VI of the notorious Borgia family. Various additions have brought it up to the second half of the 19th century, but for the visitor, the most memorable part is the delightful chapel begun in 1501, when the founder was still alive to further the work. The chapel has a tower and spire topped by a detailed replica of a king's crown. Open for services during university terms and Mondays through Fridays from 8 AM to 5 PM. High St.

Cruickshank Botanic Gardens – Next to the Chanonry in Old Aberdeen are the University of Aberdeen's botanic gardens, begun in the late 19th century. A splendid collection of exotic plants, shrubs, and trees, a rockery, a water garden, and a heather garden make this a spot for a delightful walk. Open Mondays through Fridays from 9 AM to 4:30 PM year-round; also open Saturday and Sunday afternoons (2 to 5 PM) from May through September. Off the Chanonry (phone: 272704).

St. Machar's Cathedral – Described as one of the finest examples of a fortified church in Western Europe, it dates from the 14th, 15th, and early 16th centuries. According to legend, the site was consecrated in the 6th century by Machar, a missionary from Iona, instructed by St. Columba to go north through the land of the Picts until he came to a place where a river made a curve similar to that of a bishop's crozier, which is precisely what the Don does here (as can be seen by looking from St. Machar's northeast side). The cathedral was founded in the 12th century, but work on the present building began in 1357 and was finally completed about 1520, when Bishop Dunbar installed the magnificent heraldic ceiling, the most striking feature of the interior (bring binoculars). Outside, it is the West Front, with its two great western towers, that is a particularly impressive sight. Open daily from 9 AM to 5 PM. Chanonry, off St. Machar Dr.

Seaton Park – North of St. Machar's Cathedral and adjacent to Don Street, it has several attractions, including the Wallace Tower, or Benholme's Lodging, a worthy example of a 16th-century Scottish tower-castle (172 such towers still exist in Scotland — this one's name comes from Sir William Wallace, a famous 13th-century liberator of Scotland, although no specific connection made between the two is known), and the Chapter House, built between 1653 and 1655 by George Cruickshank of Berriehill. The park itself is well worth a stroll. It contains woodland, gardens, an adventure playground, and a picnic area, and the grass-covered knoll at the Motte of Tillydrone affords an especially fine view of the river Don. Open year-round.

Brig o' Balgownie (Old Bridge of Don) – Across Seaton Park and reached via Don Street, the Old Bridge of Don is one of Aberdeen's most famous relics of the Middle Ages. The brainchild of two early provosts of the city, Richard the Mason and Malcolm de Balgownie, it was begun in 1286 and completed in 1329. The bridge is 72 feet wide and 60 feet tall at the top of its Gothic arch, and it is still in use today — a tribute to medieval workmanship.

ELSEWHERE

Beach Esplanade – With its 2 miles of sandy beach between the estuaries of the Don and the Dee, the Beach Esplanade has all the facilities expected of a typical British seaside resort. These include a children's "fishing village" and adventure playground, along with the £6-million Beach Ballroom complex. Opened during the spring of 1989, the complex contains two swimming pools, a flume, sauna, multi-purpose gym, and a lounge bar, all in a tropical setting; as we went to press, an ice skating rink was under construction. The beach Esplanade also has an amusement park with a funfair and video and slot machines (open daily from 2 PM in June, July, and August and on weekends in May and September; phone: 595910); and the *Holiday Inn Amusement Centre* (open daily from 11 AM year-round; phone: 581909), with more video and slot machines (which no self-respecting British holiday resort is ever without!), bingo, and a snack bar. This is a place to bring kids, but be sure to have plenty of change for the videos and slots. Still in the works is the Oil Experience Centre, which will have drills, rigs, and other oil equipment for visitors to operate; it's slated to open in 1992.

Footdee Village – Known locally as Fittie, this model village was built in 1808–1809 to house fishermen and their families. Designed by John Smith, city architect of Aberdeen, Footdee consists of two squares of single-story cottages, simple but robustly constructed examples of Georgian architecture that have survived to the present day. Over the past half century, the village has become a popular spot with summer visitors, particularly city dwellers attracted by the secluded atmosphere of this traditional Scottish fishing village, just a short bus ride away from the center. Off the southern end of the Beach Esplanade.

Walker Park and Girdleness Lighthouse – On the opposite side of the Dee from the village of Footdee is the grassy headland of cliffs and coves called Walker Park. Among its attractions are the Balnagask Golf Course and the Torry fort, a military battery of 60 guns built in 1860, which now serves as a pleasant vantage point. Girdleness Lighthouse, designed by Robert Stevenson (the grandfather of Robert Louis Stevenson), was built in 1832–33.

Loirston Country Park – Near the coast, on the same grassy headland as Walker Park, this is the place to take children who like animals, because Doonie's Farm, where they can see and handle pets and domesticated farm animals (open daily from daylight to dusk), is contained within the park boundaries. There is also a convenient picnic area. Follow Greyhope Rd. south of Walker Park.

Duthie Park and Winter Gardens – Overlooking the river Dee, this place makes for a splendid family outing and is Scotland's most visited attraction. Duthie Park is a large grassy area containing playgrounds, trampolines, flower gardens, exotic plants and birds, an aquarium, a boating pond, and a self-service restaurant (all open from July through September), as well as the Winter Gardens — lush, tropical gardens inside heated glasshouses, which have just undergone a major extension from ¾ acre to 1¼ acres (open year-round from 10 AM to dusk). The cactus house, which boasts among other attractions a talking cactus, has won three awards. Duthie Park is also the site of the annual *Santa Lucia Festival of Light,* held throughout December, which includes a spectacular laser show. Access from Polmuir Rd. or Riverside Dr.

Bridge of Dee – Built between 1520 and 1527 by the enterprising Bishop Dunbar, this formidable piece of 16th-century engineering has seven semicircular arches of identical size. The bridge is famous as the site of the 1639 battle between the Covenanters under the Earl Marischal and the Earl of Montrose (one of Scotland's most heroic and romantic historical figures) on one side and the Royal army under the Earl of Aboyne on the other. The outcome was a Royalist defeat, leaving Aberdeen open to the Covenanters. On the Dee at the southern tip of Holburn St. and Riverside Dr.

Ruthrieston Pack Horse Bridge – A short walk north along Riverside Drive from the Bridge of Dee is the picturesque Ruthrieston pack horse bridge. Built by the Aberdeen Town Council in 1693–94, it's made up of three arches and squat buttresses and was used to carry the old South Road northward into the city center.

Old Deeside Line Walkway – This is a nature walk along the Dee that was formed by lifting the track from a disused railway line. It begins at Duthie Park and ends about 4 miles away outside the village of Cults, to the west of Aberdeen. For those who are in the city for any length of time, especially during the spring and summer, the walk is a must. A book describing it and its wildlife is available from the City of Aberdeen Information Centre.

Victoria Park and Westburn Park – Yet further evidence of Aberdeen's wide open spaces are these two adjoining parks just north of the central area. Features include flowerbeds, a paddling pool, a picnic area, a playground for disabled children (play leaders organize games during the summer), and a restaurant. Westburn Rd.

Hazlehead Park – About 2½ miles west of the center, the city's largest park offers rose and heather gardens, exotic trees and shrubs, extensive woodlands, nature walks (booklets are available from the City of Aberdeen Information Centre), and an unusual collection of rare birds and animals. Other assets include a maze, electric cars, putting green, trampolines (open May through September), and a restaurant. In addition to the putting green, the Hazlehead Park Golf Courses are here — two 18-hole courses and a 9-hole course. Access at the corner of Hazlehead Ave. and Groats Rd.

Johnston Gardens – Another fine example of Aberdeen's numerous parks and gardens is this sweet little green space, known for its alpine plants, with a rustic bridge crossing a stream. Viewfield Rd.

■ **EXTRA SPECIAL:** For a look at a little Aberdonian local color, get up at 4 AM any weekday and hasten down to the Aberdeen Fish Market, between the railway station and the harbor. Hundreds of tons of fish will be landed by a platoon of trawlers to the accompaniment of the shouts of sailors and the barks of the auctioneers who sell off the catch. Aberdeen fishwives (who run fish stalls and everyone else within earshot of their tongues) are so famous for their bumptious personalities that writers of Scottish skits and pantomimes practically pour them into their scripts. It's not unusual to meet a few ersatz examples in *His Majesty's Theatre* at night, having met the real thing in the morning. Off Market St.

SOURCES AND RESOURCES

TOURIST INFORMATION: The friendly, helpful staff of the City of Aberdeen Information Centre, St. Nicholas House, Broad St. (phone: 632727), offers information, guidebooks, maps, leaflets, and assistance with accommodations. Some helpful and relatively inexpensive publications are *Aberdeen: Historical Walkabout* by Cuthbert Graham, available at the information center, and *A Visitors' Guide to Aberdeen* by R. E. H. Mellor and J. S. Smith, available in local bookshops. A good detailed map of Aberdeen is published by Geographia and is also available in bookshops.

Local Coverage – *The Aberdeen Press and Journal* is the morning daily. For a rundown on local events, call the "Aberdeen What's On Line" (phone: 636363).

Telephone – The area code for Aberdeen is 0224.

GETTING AROUND: Quite a few of Aberdeen's attractions are well away from the city center, so visitors will do a great deal of walking unless they use mechanical modes of transportation.

Airport – Aberdeen Airport, approximately 6 miles northwest of the city center at Dyce, is served by flights from London and other British and northern European cities. There is a cabstand and regular bus service to the Guild Street Bus Station.

Bus – *Grampian Transport,* headquartered on King St. (phone: 637047), serves most local routes. *Northern Scottish,* the other major company, operates mainly longer-distance coaches from the Guild Street Bus Station (phone: 591381), next to the train station.

Car Rental – All the major firms are represented. See the yellow pages for details.

Taxi – There is a cabstand at the train station. Otherwise, call City Taxis (phone: 494949), TODA Taxis (phone: 633535), or Mair's Taxis (phone: 724040).

Train – The mainline station with connections to London, Glasgow, Edinburgh, and most other British cities is on Guild Street, a 5-minute walk from Union Street. The phone number for general information is 594222; for sleeper and Motorail inquiries, call 582005.

SPECIAL EVENTS: In keeping with its horticultural tradition, the *Aberdeen Spring Flower Show* is held every March. The major annual happening is the *Aberdeen Festival,* also called the *Bon Accord Festival,* which lasts for a week in mid-June. The Aberdeen Highland Games, in Hazlehead Park, are the highlight of the festival, but the blowout also involves a parade of floats down Union Street, pipe bands at the St. Nicholas Shopping Centre off Union Street, more music, dancing, and shows, plus the *Riding of the Marches,* a 500-year-old ceremony in which horses pull coaches around the boundaries of the city, the whole thing led by a lone piper. Other events include the youth *Football Festival* in July and the *Aberdeen International Youth Festival* in early August. The latter, 10 days long, draws young performers from many countries and ends with a fireworks display in Hazlehead Park. Two 1-day events in August are the *Fish Festival,* with displays on ways to cook and serve fish, and the *Clydesdale Horse Show,* which has pony rides for kids and demonstrations by blacksmiths, in addition to the fine horses. In December, the *Christmas Festival* sets the mood for the season with carolers, bands, chestnut stalls, and a carnival.

MUSEUMS: In addition to those mentioned in *Special Places,* Aberdeen has a number of other museums of interest.

Aberdeen Arts Centre Gallery – Two galleries concentrating on the works of local artists and craftsmen. Open daily. King St. (phone: 635208).

Anthropological Museum – Exhibits of local archaeology and antiquities from Egypt, Europe, Asia, Africa, and America. Closed Saturdays. Marischal College, Broad St. (phone: 273131).

Artspace Galleries – Contemporary Scottish art housed in an early-18th-century building. Closed Sundays. 21 Castle St. (phone: 639539).

Blairs College Museum – Portraits of the legendary Mary, Queen of Scots, and other 16th-century memorabilia. Four miles from the city center. Open the last Saturday of the month, other times by appointment. Blairs College, S. Deeside Rd. (phone: 867626).

James Dun's House – An 18th-century townhouse that has been renovated and decorated to reflect its period, with permanent displays and special exhibitions. Closed Sundays. 61 Schoolhill (phone: 646333).

Natural History Museum – A broad collection of invertebrates and vertebrates, housed in a modern gallery. Closed weekends. University of Aberdeen, Tillydrone Ave. (phone: 272850).

Peacock Printmakers – Major printing processes since the invention of the printing press in the 15th century are on permanent display. Closed Sundays. 21 Castle St. (phone: 639539).

SHOPPING: Union Street and its connecting streets comprise the main shopping area, with a broad spectrum of stores represented, including most of the major department stores. There are also small specialty shops, such as antiques dealers and traditional Scottish shops selling woolens and tartans, plus maritime shops on Trinity Quay and Regent Quay. Aberdeen also offers two recently opened shopping malls: St. Nicolas Centre, off St. Nicolas Street, and the Bon Accord Shopping Centre, off St. George St., which opened in the fall of 1989. Both centers house major department stores. To boost business throughout Aberdeen, shopkeepers have introduced some imaginative promotional events, such as the *Rose Festival* in August, when 250,000 roses are handed out free, and the *Scottish Connection,* an Easter-time festival celebrating all things Scottish in shops, restaurants, and events throughout the city.

J. W. Baker Ltd. – Northeastern Scotland's specialist in china, crystal, and pottery, with export and postal facilities. 136 Union St. (phone: 640648).

Burberrys – Top-of-the-line men's and women's clothing, including the famous raincoats. 454–456 Union St. (phone: 646034).

Debenham's – A large department store with a wide selection of better-quality goods and a restaurant. Trinity Centre, 155 Union St. (phone: 573111).

Hebridean Workshop – This suburban shop is stocked with products of the traditional crofting communities of the islands — handmade jerseys, tweeds, handspun wools, all from the wool of Hebridean sheep. 74–76 High St., Banchory (phone: 0942-4795).

Marks & Spencer – Good quality and value for the money are offered at this branch of the well-known chain. 2 St. Nicholas St. (phone: 644281).

Pitlochry Knitwear – An excellent selection of Scottish clothing, tartans, foods, and souvenirs. 187 Union St. (phone: 575380).

Rosslyn Sports – Everything for the sportsperson. 419 Union St. (phone: 593574).

SPORTS: For full details on the wide range of local sports facilities, especially for outdoor sports, consult the free guide offered at the City of Aberdeen Information Centre.

Golf – The most prestigious of the several courses in and around Aberdeen is the *Royal Aberdeen Golf Course* at Balgownie (phone: 702571), which is of championship standard. Others are the *Links Golf Course,* along the Esplanade; the *Balnagask Golf Course,* south of the Dee; and the *Hazlehead Park Golf Courses.* Full details on these courses are available at the information center.

Skiing – A sport rapidly increasing in popularity. Artificial skiing — on a slope carpeted with a slippery, manmade white material — is available Saturday afternoons at Garthdee Rd. (phone: 318707).

Soccer – *The Aberdeen Football Club,* nicknamed the Dons and based at Pittodrie Stadium (phone: 632328), has dominated Scottish soccer for the past decade, achieving its most important success when it triumphed at the 1982 European Cup Winners Cup Final. The season runs from September to May.

Swimming – There is an indoor swimming pool (and a sauna) at *Bon Accord Baths,* Justice Mill La. (phone: 587920 or 575676). The recently opened Beach Ballroom Leisure complex has 2 pools (see Special Places).

THEATER: The splendid *His Majesty's Theatre,* Rosemount Viaduct (box office phone: 637788), opened in 1906 and was recently refurbished. It hosts prestigious performances by visitors, such as the *National Theatre of London,* the *Scottish Ballet,* and the *Scottish Opera.* Tragedies, farces, plus a variety of other familiar and contemporary productions share the stage at the Capitol Theatre, 431 Union St. (phone: 583141).

MUSIC: Besides *His Majesty's Theatre* (see above), where the visiting *Scottish Opera* and *Scottish Ballet* perform, there is the *Music Hall,* Union St. (box office phone: 641122), where the fare runs the gamut from performances by the *Scottish National Orchestra* for classical devotees to major rock and pop concerts for fans of contemporary music.

NIGHTCLUBS AND NIGHTLIFE: The oil boom has livened up Aberdeen's nightlife considerably. However, note that, as elsewhere in Britain, nightclub owners tend to spend vast sums of money on sophisticated lighting and sound effects, and then let them deteriorate rapidly. Furthermore, the music selection is usually banal, admission prices are expensive, and so are drinks (beer drinkers will find a much better pint in any pub). Try *Mr. G's,* 70–78 Chapel St. (phone: 642112), and Ritzy's, Bridge Pl. (phone: 581135).

BEST IN TOWN

CHECKING IN: The City of Aberdeen Information Centre has a booking service to help anyone arriving in town without a reservation. Expect to pay $105 and up nightly for a double room with breakfast in a hotel listed below as expensive, from $80 to $105 in a hotel listed as moderate, and from $55 to $80 in one listed as inexpensive. All hotels accept major credit cards. All telephone numbers are in the 0224 area code unless otherwise indicated.

Caledonian Thistle – One of the city's premier hotels, this elegantly furnished and centrally located establishment of many years' standing has 80 rooms, now with every convenience — TV sets, video movies, coffee- and tea-making facilities. Also within the hotel are a new conference suite, sauna, and a "Taste of Scotland" restaurant. Union Terrace (phone: 640233). Expensive.

Copthorne – Very modern and centrally located hotel, it has recently undergone major refurbishment. Occupying a converted warehouse, it has 89 rooms and provides such facilities as a swimming pool, solarium, and a fitness room. 122 Huntly St. (phone: 630404). Expensive.

Holiday Inn Aberdeen Airport – A large (154 rooms), modern hotel, which offers the facilities expected in a first class establishment, including a fitness room and an indoor swimming pool. For those keen on bodybuilding, this is the place. Riverview Dr., Dyce (phone: 770011). Expensive.

Stakis Tree Tops – West of the city center, this is a modern hotel that has recently been renovated and enlarged. Among the facilities is a fully equipped leisure center. There are 114 rooms and a "Taste of Scotland" restaurant. 161 Springfield Rd. (phone: 313377). Expensive.

Altens Skean Dhu – Aberdeen's largest hotel (220 rooms) was built in the early 1880s and is 3 miles south of the city (via A956). It's generously appointed, with all the modern conveniences and facilities that would be expected in an upper-bracket hotel, including a heated outdoor pool. Souter Head Rd., Altens (phone: 877000). Expensive to moderate.

Bucksburn Moat House – This converted mill, 4 miles northwest of town (near the airport), makes an interesting and pleasant stay for the visitor. It has all the modern facilities, including an indoor swimming pool; 99 rooms. Old Meldrum Rd., Bucksburn (phone: 713911). Expensive to moderate.

Station – Every major railway station has a station hotel, and Aberdeen is no exception. This one, built in traditional granite style, has 59 bedrooms. Guild St. (phone: 587214). Expensive to moderate.

Craighaar – Convenienty situated just a mile from the airport, this modern hotel has 41 rooms and a full range of basic facilities, including phones, private bath, hair dryers, and trouser presses. It also has a reputation among locals for good, fresh food. Waterton Rd., Bucksburn, Aberdeen (phone: 712275). Moderate.

Douglas – This 87-room hotel has been completely refurbished. It includes 2 suites for meetings and social functions. Market St. (phone: 582255). Moderate.

New Marcliffe – An old, recently renovated Aberdeen house, west of the city center, with 28 rooms and a restaurant that has earned the "Taste of Scotland" seal of approval. The building is constructed of granite and is designed in traditional style. Through the hotel, guests can enjoy temporary membership in the *Royal Aberdeen Golf Club,* salmon fishing on the Dee, and a private box at the *Aberdeen Football* (soccer) *Club.* 53 Queens Rd. (phone: 321371). Moderate.

Swallow Imperial – With 108 rooms, it offers all the modern fittings and facilities of a large city-center hotel. Stirling St., near the station (phone: 589101). Moderate.

Norwood Hall – This one-time mansion, built in 1881, is popular with visitors who like to wine and dine in surroundings recalling the romantic past. The hotel stands on 15 picturesque acres in a southwestern suburb of Aberdeen, yet it's only 5 minutes' drive from the city center. There are 46 rooms; parking is no problem. Garthdee Rd., Cults (phone: 868951). Inexpensive.

EATING OUT: Whether the choice be Italian, French, Indian, Chinese, Turkish, or even Scottish cuisine, it's possible to find both excellent food and friendly service in Aberdeen's wide range of restaurants, pubs, cafés, and wine bars. To guarantee quality, however, a safe bet is to stick to hotel restaurants — or look for the "Taste of Scotland" sign, awarded to and displayed only in hotels and restaurants where the very best Scottish dishes are served. Expect to pay over $55 for a meal for two with wine in restaurants listed below as expensive, from $30 to $55 in a restaurant listed as moderate, and under $30 in a restaurant listed as inexpensive. All telephone numbers are in the 0224 area code unless otherwise indicated.

Gerard's – A first class French restaurant with an excellent reputation. Closed Sundays. 50 Chapel St. (phone: 639500). Expensive to moderate.

Silver Darling Fish Restaurant – Recently opened, it's already acquired a fine reputation for French food. As the name suggests, it specializes in fish, which is delivered fresh each morning. The chef also prepares delicious barbecued foods. Reservations necessary. Pocra Quay (near the lighthouse), Footdee (phone: 576229). Expensive to moderate.

Atholl – For a fine selection of traditional Scottish food made from local produce that has earned the approval of the "Taste of Scotland." Open for lunch and dinner daily. Atholl Hotel, 54 Kings Gate (phone: 323505). Moderate.

Light of Bengal – An Indian restaurant serving imaginative, aromatic Indian cuisine, catering to the upper end of the market. Open for lunch and dinner daily. 13 Rose St. (phone: 644963). Moderate.

Shishmahal Tandoori – Exotic tandoori (clay oven) dishes contribute to the excellent reputation of this Indian restaurant. Open for lunch and dinner daily. 468 Union St. (phone: 643339). Moderate.

Turkish Nargile – Take-out kebab houses have grown popular in Aberdeen in recent years, but this is a more exclusive restaurant presenting Turkish delights in a much more varied light. Open for dinner daily. 77–79 Skene St. (phone: 636093). Moderate.

Yangste River – This topnotch establishment serves Cantonese, Peking, and Szechwan cuisine as well as dim sum. Open for lunch and dinner daily. 8 Bridge St. (phone: 583377). Moderate.

Jaws Café – For vegetarians and health-conscious visitors. Tasty snacks, meals, and home baking are provided at reasonable prices. Open from noon to 3 PM on Mondays, Tuesdays, Wednesdays, and Saturdays, and from noon to 9 PM on Thursdays and Fridays; closed Sundays. St. Katherine's Centre, 5 W. North St. (phone: 645676). Inexpensive.

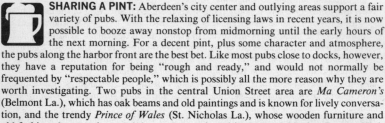

SHARING A PINT: Aberdeen's city center and outlying areas support a fair variety of pubs. With the relaxing of licensing laws in recent years, it is now possible to booze away nonstop from midmorning until the early hours of the next morning. For a decent pint, plus some character and atmosphere, the pubs along the harbor front are the best bet. Like most pubs close to docks, however, they have a reputation for being "rough and ready," and would not normally be frequented by "respectable people," which is possibly all the more reason why they are worth investigating. Two pubs in the central Union Street area are *Ma Cameron's* (Belmont La.), which has oak beams and old paintings and is known for lively conversation, and the trendy *Prince of Wales* (St. Nicholas La.), whose wooden furniture and old-fashioned atmosphere and decor are popular with students. *Machar Bar,* on High St., in Old Aberdeen — more or less opposite King's College — once had sawdust on the floor and was for men only. Now it has been modernized and pleasantly decorated, making it a cozy nook patronized by liberal arts academics.

BATH

Bath was meant to be a beautiful city, and it is. Anchored in the valley of the river Avon and reverberating up seven surrounding hills in the southwest corner of the Cotswolds, its location alone would have been promising. But for more than 1,600 years, the ancient city — known as Aquae Sulis to its Roman founders — remained undistinguished except as the site of Britain's only hot springs, a place to come and "take the waters." It was a remarkable 18th-century urban planning effort that made Bath the splendid Georgian city that it is today. Then the haphazard parts, including the striking abbey, were unified along classical lines in tier upon tier of crescents, terraces, and squares climbing from the banks of the river. As a result, Bath still calls itself the first planned city in England, and visitors who see its warm, honey-colored stones set against the rich green of lawn, tree, and wooded hillside will probably agree.

The city's past emerges from legend with the Romans who, in approximately AD 54, established an elaborate system of baths here, along with a temple to Sulis Minerva, a combination of the Celtic deity Sul and the Roman goddess of wisdom, Minerva. The town grew to become a famous health resort and remained one until the Romans left Britain in the early 5th century. After that, Aquae Sulis declined rapidly, and the Roman baths sank back into the warm mud.

The Saxons built an abbey in 781, such a fine one that it was chosen as the site of the coronation in 973 of King Edgar as the first King of England, in a ceremony that has remained a model for the coronation of all subsequent English kings and queens. The city's fame was short-lived, however, though the sick continued to be drawn to medieval baths raised over the salubrious mineral springs by builders unaware of the ancient prototypes buried underground. As the visitors soaked in the Cross Bath (dating from the 7th century), the King's Bath (built smack on top of the Romans' reservoir in the 12th century), and others, Bathonians made a better living in the wool trade — Chaucer's Wife of Bath was one of the successful makers of cloth.

With the patronage of royalty in the late 17th century, Bath began to regain its reputation as a first class spa. The wife of King James II, Mary of Modena, bore a healthy son after a stop at the Cross Bath. His daughter, Queen Anne, later made several trips. Once kings and queens and their entourages, members of court, country gentry, and notables from all walks of life began to take the cure or just luxuriate, Bath was suddenly fashionable among both the healthy and the sick.

Today's city of elegant squares and crescent streets is the labor of love of three 18th-century gentlemen. Richard "Beau" Nash arrived in 1705. He was an honest gambler from Wales, a social catalyst who found his calling when he took on the job of master of ceremonies, in charge of public entertainments. Nash was the equivalent of a modern fund-raiser and public relations person for Bath. He found the money to pave roads, light streets, and endow the Royal Mineral Water Hospital, which survives as the Royal National Hospital for Rheumatic Diseases. He became an arbiter of taste and comportment, laying down rules of etiquette that were not to be broken. Duels were suppressed, smoking in public prohibited, improper dress ridiculed, corruption in the sedan chair business wiped out. Within a generation, the sheer force of his personality had made Bath the second capital of English society.

A Cornish postal clerk named Ralph Allen arrived next. He eventually became postmaster, made a fortune from the mail business, and bought the limestone quarries on the southern hill of the city, Combe Down. Bath's pale stone was as yet untested for building purposes, so Allen engaged a Yorkshire architect, John Wood, as technical adviser. It was a master stroke. Thus supplied with financial backing and building material, the talented Yorkshireman proceeded to impose architectural order on the gay whirl of the city, designing not simply single buildings but entire rows, crescents, and squares in accordance with the neoclassical principles of the Palladian style. Queen's Square, North and South Parade, and the Circus are all his.

Wood's grand conceptions were not realized in full, not even by his son, another John Wood, who carried on the father's work and added his own to the Bath landscape. The younger Wood's Assembly Rooms enclosed the Georgians' amusements and dalliance in aesthetically suitable wrappings. While the frivolity endured, they were the essence of Bath. But his ultimate expression was the Royal Crescent, a beautiful scimitar of a street whose grandeur seems almost out of keeping with a city this size, one that was never in itself of great consequence in the affairs of state, though almost anyone of consequence — in government, the arts, or society — spent time here.

Visitors to Bath today see much of it as the Georgians left it, despite bombing damage during World War II, population growth (now at 85,000), and the development of light industry. Bathonians have a history of carefully safeguarding their heritage and preserving their architecture, even to the point where residents whose tree-lined gardens are visible to tourists receive a maintenance grant from the city's "tree fund." Blending the past with the present to create a congenial whole is one of the marvels of Bath. It still provides the feeling of a city truly built in a gentler age, a time immortalized in the novels of Jane Austen and Tobias Smollett. It's a pervasive feeling that's hard to shake in Bath — as if one would want to. Instead, reinforce it by walking up to the Royal Crescent at dusk. As the honey-colored stones darken to gray, the lights of the city twinkle across the dark shadows of Royal Victoria Park as softly as gas lamps. It's easy to imagine you're in an England of another time.

BATH AT-A-GLANCE

SEEING THE CITY: The up-and-down setting of this city on seven hills provides more than one spot for an overall view. If you have a car, drive north up Lansdown Road and see Bath unfold beneath you or, even better, go to the opposite side of town: From Widcombe Hill or North Road you face directly onto Bath Abbey, the Royal Crescent, and the Pump Room.

SPECIAL PLACES: Bath's tourism "musts" are conveniently situated right in the heart of town. The hot baths of Aquae Sulis may have given the city its start in the 1st century, but the most commanding building is undoubtedly the later abbey, a massive square-towered edifice that dwarfs its surroundings from almost every angle. Still later came the Assembly Rooms, the Pump Room, and glorious streets, squares, and crescents that have helped to make Bath the architectural gem that it is.

Roman Baths – The baths are Britain's most complete Roman remains, fed by the country's only hot water springs. The establishment, with its magnificent Great Bath measuring 83 feet by 40 feet, flourished between the 1st and 5th centuries AD as one of the most famous health resorts of the Roman Empire, then fell into ruin. The springs themselves — gushing to the surface at a temperature of 110F and a rate of more than 300,000 gallons a day — remained in use for various later baths, however, including the King's Bath, built by 12th-century Normans over the Roman reservoir and spring, next to the by-then-buried Roman baths. Rediscovery of the latter began in the 18th century, and they are still being excavated today. The treasures preserved in the accompanying museum include coins, gemstones, pewter tableware, mosaics, and a gilt-bronze head of the goddess Sulis Minerva, to whom a temple on the site was dedicated. Many of the objects were found in excavations beneath the floor of the King's Bath, where the ancients had thrown them as offerings to the sacred spring. (Among the more unusual finds are the curses inscribed on lead, invoking the aid of the goddess in bringing grief to an enemy.) Excavations in the area of the original temple precinct, underneath the Pump Room, are now complete. Open daily except Christmas Day and Boxing Day. Admission charge includes entrance to the Roman Baths and the Pump Room. Abbey Church Yard (phone: 461111).

Pump Room – Upstairs from the baths, this grand hall was built at the end of the 18th century. It was one of the town's social centers and continues as a meeting place for both natives and tourists. The mineral water pumped to the fountain in the bay window is the same therapeutic drink that Sam Weller of *Pickwick Papers* thought tasted like "warm flat-irons." Glasses of the tepid, cloudy water are available for sampling in the Pump Room for about 40¢. Or enjoy some Bath buns and coffee and listen to the *Pump Room Trio* play its daily morning concert on the platform under the balcony, a tradition dating to the days of Beau Nash. There's a grand piano recital and tea every afternoon. Open daily. The admission charge to the Roman Baths includes the Pump Room; a combined ticket covers admission to the Assembly Rooms and the *Museum of Costume* on Bennett St. as well. Abbey Church Yard (phone: 461111).

Sally Lunn's House – When you've partaken of Bath buns in the Pump Room, indulge further with a Sally Lunn (a pastry not quite as sweet as a Bath bun, eaten toasted with butter or clotted cream). Sally's house is supposed to be the oldest in Bath (built in 1482, and recent excavations of the basement have unearthed kitchenware dating back to Roman times). The buns have been served here since she, a pastry cook herself, first dreamed them up in the 17th century. On North Parade Passage (phone: 461634).

Bath Abbey – A Saxon abbey and a Norman cathedral occupied this site before the present church was begun in 1499. The cathedral had fallen into ruin when Oliver King, Bishop of Bath and Wells, was inspired by a dream to rebuild the church; the dream is represented by the angels ascending ladders into heaven, carved on the west front. Though its predecessor was much larger, Bath Abbey is no disappointment. Inside, daylight pours through sparkling panes of glass in the tall clerestory windows (the abbey is sometimes called the Lantern of the West for this reason), illuminating the famous fan vaulting, a pale and delicate example of English Perpendicular architecture. The 19th-century east window over the altar, unusual for its square top, was damaged in World War II and restored by the great-grandson of its original designer. Note also the medieval carving of the Prior Birde Chantry next to the sanctuary and, at the northeast corner of the church, the modern Edgar Window, showing the coronation in 973 of the man thought to have been the first king of all England. (Visitors cannot wander around during services.) Abbey Church Yard.

Assembly Rooms – Designed by John Wood the Younger, these opened in 1771 as a fashionable gathering place where concerts, dancing, card games, and light refreshments could be enjoyed in surroundings of appropriate elegance. Such light-mindedness was scorned in the Victorian age, and from the mid-19th century on the Bath Assembly Rooms fell into disrepair, then were restored to their former splendor in 1938 only to be gutted, except for the shell, by a World War II bombing raid. The Assembly Rooms have been closed for ceiling restoration, but are scheduled to reopen this year, when visitors will see a faithful reconstruction of the rooms carried out with the aid of detailed 18th-century engravings. The ballroom, lit by five crystal chandeliers that were safely packed away at the outbreak of the war, looks like a giant blue and white Wedgwood confection, and the tearoom is no less delectable a creation in a pinkish tone. Downstairs is the *Museum of Costume,* with an array of 18th-century finery along with exhibitions dating from 1560 to the present, making up one of the largest costume collections in the world. The museum is expected to reopen this year. Admission charge for museum only. Bennett St. (phone: 461111).

Royal Crescent – The sheer stateliness of Bath's showpiece of residential architecture rarely fails to impress. The Royal Crescent is the supreme achievement of John Wood the Younger and is considered to be the finest crescent in Europe. Begun in 1767, it consists of 30 pale amber Georgian stone houses whose 114 Ionic columns support a continuous cornice the length of the curving whole. Ironwork fences, the sidewalk, and the cobblestone street repeat the curve, wrapping it around a sweeping segment of Royal Victoria Park. The Bath Preservation Trust has restored No. 1 Royal Crescent as a Georgian residence and museum of 18th-century cooking. Open daily except Mondays, March through October. Admission charge. At the end of Brock St. (phone: 28126).

Circus – Another example of Georgian town planning, this is possibly the greatest achievement of John Wood the Elder, who began it in 1754. It is a stately ring of regally proportioned and identically faced stone townhouses surrounding a circular green of lawn and huge spreading plane trees. Each of its three sections is composed of 11 houses fronted by columns in Doric, Ionic, and Corinthian tiers. Wood designed one of the houses — No. 7 — for William Pitt, MP for Bath and later Prime Minister of England, and many other celebrities have lived here over the years, including the painter Thomas Gainsborough (No. 17) and the explorer David Livingstone (No. 13). At the north end of Gay St.

Pulteney Bridge – Bath's version, on a smaller scale, of the Ponte Vecchio in Florence. Built in 1770 by Robert Adam, this shop-lined structure on three arches connects Grand Parade and Bridge Street to Argyle Street, and even if you don't window-shop, you'll be across it before you know it. Below the bridge is the boomerang-shaped Pulteney Weir, recently redesigned for the purposes of flood control.

Holburne of Menstrie Museum – The former *Sydney* hotel (built in 1796–97) houses a superb collection of silver, glass, porcelain, bronzes, furniture, and paintings by such English masters as Sir Joshua Reynolds and Thomas Gainsborough. A wide range of 20th-century craftwork, including textiles, pottery, furniture, and calligraphy, is on display in a crafts study center. Open 11 AM to 5 PM Mondays through Saturdays and 2:30 to 6 PM on Sundays; closed mid-December through mid-February and Mondays November to Easter; afternoon teas are served in the garden in summer. Admission charge. Great Pulteney St. (phone: 66669).

Prior Park – A handsome Georgian mansion overlooking the city, Prior Park was designed for Ralph Allen by John Wood the Elder. Allen had bought the local Combe

Down stone quarries, and Wood was a proponent of the Palladian style in architecture. When stone and style came together in early buildings such as Prior Park, begun in 1735, it was a forecast of things to come for Bath. Alexander Pope and Henry Fielding visited here (Allen is Squire Allworthy in Fielding's *Tom Jones*), but today Prior Park is a boys' school. The grounds and chapel are open daily. Admission charge to the grounds. About 1 mile southeast of Bath (phone: Combe Down 832752).

American Museum in Britain – Its 18 period rooms range from a 17th-century New England saltbox to a mid-19th-century New Orleans mansion, plus such other curiosities as a Colonial Massachusetts tavern, a replica of George Washington's garden at Mount Vernon, the captain's cabin of a Yankee whaling boat, and an old-fashioned country store. The museum is in Claverton Manor, a neoclassical home of 1820. Open afternoons April through October, daily except Mondays; otherwise by appointment. Admission charge. 2½ miles east of town (phone: 460503).

Huntingdon Heritage Centre – Exhibitions of Bath's city model, as well as its architectural heritage. Open Tuesdays through Fridays. Admission charge. The Vineyards, at the top end of town on Paragon St. (phone: 333895).

Sheldon Manor – A few miles east of Bath on A4, this medieval manor house was a cozy family home for 700 years. Now the house plus its terraced gardens shaded by ancient yew trees and old-fashioned roses, its 13th-century porch, and its 15th-century chapel are open to the public. Homemade buffet lunches and afternoon tea are served in the barn. Open Sundays, Thursdays, and bank holidays from 12:30 to 6 PM, April through early October. 1½ miles west of Chippenham (phone: 0249-653120).

■ **EXTRA SPECIAL:** Just outside Bath, the Kennet and Avon Canal winds lazily along leafy banks. Opened in 1810, the long-neglected canal has now been re-dredged and brought back to life for pleasure craft. On Saturday and Sunday afternoons in spring and summer, a waterbus plies between Bath and Folly Swing Bridge, the prettiest section of the canal. In the spring passengers stand an excellent chance of passing broods of newborn ducklings and cygnets splashing about under their mothers' watchful gaze. You can also enjoy a cruise on the river Avon aboard the *Scenic I,* which runs daily on the hour from 11 AM to 7 PM, upstream from Pulteney Weir opposite the Parade Gardens. For details on other boat trips, check with the tourist information center. It's also lovely to walk alongside the canal on the old towpath where horses drew barges long ago.

SOURCES AND RESOURCES

TOURIST INFORMATION: On-the-spot details about Bath can be obtained from the tourist information center (phone: 462831) opposite the Roman Baths and Pump Room in the Abbey Church Yard. An excellent *Bath Official Guide Book* is available from the information center and most bookstores. Christopher Ansley's *New Bath Guide,* a satirical look at 18th-century Bath society, was an immediate hit when it was first published in 1766, and it is still carried in some local bookstores.

City of Bath honorary guides — known as the mayor's guides — will take you on a free, approximately 2-hour walking tour; they're carefully trained, unpaid volunteers, and they frown on tips. Tours leave the Abbey Churchyard (outside the Pump Room); for exact times, consult the notice board outside the Pump Room entrance or ask at the information center.

Marion Carter provides a private guide service using qualified, registered professional guides for walks in Bath and car tours in the surrounding area (phone: 312901).

Local Coverage – The daily (except Sundays) *Bath & West Evening Chronicle* has details of events taking place in the city. The tourist information center also publishes the monthly *What's On.*

Telephone – The area code for Bath is 0225.

GETTING AROUND: Airport – London's Heathrow and Gatwick airports have a direct rail link with Bath via Reading. Bristol Airport, at Lulsgate, 15 miles west of Bath, is the airport nearest to Bath (phone: 027587-4441). Other local airports are at Cardiff, Plymouth, Exeter, and Southampton.

Bus – *Badgerline* and *National Express* operate the city buses and long-distance coaches, which leave from the bus station on Manvers St. Open-top bus tours are offered in warm weather. For tour and bus information, call the station (phone: 464446).

Car: Among Bath's most reputable car rental dealers is *Avis* (phone: 446680).

Train – High-speed trains destined for London's Paddington Station and other major cities leave regularly from Bath Spa Station on Dorchester St. at Manvers St. Traveling at 125 mph, the trains make the trip to London in 70 minutes. For information, call British Rail (phone: 463075).

SPECIAL EVENTS: The highlight of the year is the *Bath International Festival of Music,* 2 weeks of musical events of exceptional quality in late May and early June, rounded out by various non-musical doings, such as the *Bath Contemporary Art Fair.* For concerts and operas, the festival uses the town's handsome old halls, including the Assembly Rooms, the Guildhall Banqueting Room, and the *Theatre Royal,* while choral and organ performances take place in Bath Abbey or in nearby Wells Cathedral. Reservations are required, and bookings can be made by mail from the first week in April. For details, write to the Bath Festival Office, Linley House, 1 Pierrepont Pl., Bath BA1 1JY. The schedule of the *Bath Georgian Festival Society,* which holds concerts throughout the year, is available in the *Pump Room. The Royal Bath and West Show,* the biggest agricultural show in the West Country, is held each year at the end of May at Shepton Mallet, 20 miles south of the city. Several antiques fairs are also held in Bath each year.

MUSEUMS: In addition to those mentioned in *Special Places,* others include the following:

Artsite Gallery – Reopened in 1985 after extensive refurbishment, it features a number of exhibitions accompanied by recorded interviews with the artists. Closed Mondays. No admission charge. Linley House, 1 Pierrepont Pl. (phone: 460394).

Beaux Arts Gallery – Works by contemporary artists and ceramicists. Closed Sundays. 13 York St. (phone: 464850).

Burrows Toy Museum – Children's games, dolls, and other toys of the last 2 centuries. Open daily. York St. (phone: 461819).

Bath Industrial Heritage Centre – The 190-million-year history of Bath Stone, the preserved contents of a Victorian brass foundry, an aerated mineral water factory, and engineering works. Open daily from 2 to 5 PM February through November, weekends only December and January. Admission charge. Julian Rd. (phone: 318348).

Geology Museum – Fossils from the rocks of North Somerset. Closed Sundays. 18 Queen Sq. (phone: 28144).

Herschel House and Museum – Former home of Sir William Herschel, the astronomer who discovered the planet Uranus. Astronomical and musical exhibits. Open daily. 19 New King St. (phone: 336228).

Museum of English Naive Art – The first museum of English folk painting by traveling artists of the 18th and 19th centuries, situated in a 19th-century schoolhouse. Open April through October; Mondays through Saturdays, 11 AM to 6 PM; Sundays, 2 to 6 PM. Admission charge. Countess of Huntingdon Chapel (phone: 446020).

Museum of Bookbinding – A reconstruction of a 19th-century bindery. Open Mondays through Fridays. Manvers St. (phone: 466000).

National Centre of Photography – The Royal Photographic Society's display of original Victorian photographs, early cameras, and changing contemporary exhibitions. Open daily. Milsom St. (phone: 462841).

Victoria Art Gallery – Paintings, etchings, prints, porcelain, and Bohemian glass. Closed Sundays. Bridge St. (phone: 461111 or 465024).

SHOPPING: Bath, quite justifiably, claims to be one of Britain's premier shopping centers, and the window displays alone make a day of leisurely browsing nearly as much fun as a buying binge. Antiques shops are numerous, and there are also markets where the private shopper may spot something exquisite before the dealer from London or overseas does. The *Great Western Antique Centre,* Bartlett St., is one of these; closed Sundays. Its many stalls sell everything from Victrolas and antique tiled stoves to old buttons still on the card. The *Bartlett Street Antique Market,* just across the street, is another, full of stalls doing business also daily except Sundays. *The Bath Antique Market,* Guinea La., occurs only on Wednesdays, as does the nearby *Paragon Antiques Market,* both of which attract dealers from all over the west of England.

A taste of old Bath can be found at the *Bath Market,* in the Guildhall on Bridge St. Butchers, fishmongers, secondhand books, and fruit-and-vegetable stalls spill over one another in an atmosphere that reeks of tradition and is authentic right down to the sawdust scrunching beneath your feet. A cheery, bustling place, especially on dark winter evenings, it's open daily, except Sundays, from 9 AM.

A short selection of Bath's many fine shops follows. Milsom Street is the main shopping artery. A new mall on Bath St., the *Colonnades,* has 35 shops and a restaurant. Another complex, the elegant, new *Shire Yard,* is far more in keeping with the town's Georgian style in the 1740s; the shops here are elegant and expensive. The majority of the city's stores stay open 6 days a week, closing on Sundays, but a few also close on Mondays.

Bath Stamp & Coin Shop – For collectors or beginners. 12–13 Pulteney Bridge (phone: 463073).

Catherine – Quite simply the best place for delicious Belgian Leonidas chocolates — so precious that they are sold by the gram. 18 Northumberland Pl. (no phone).

Chapter and Verse Bookshop – The proprietors claim to be able to procure any book from any place faster than anyone else, but with more than 25,000 titles in stock, there can't be many left. The shop has a huge section devoted to Bath and local history. 9–10 High St. (phone: 464654).

Corridor Stamp Shop – Similar to the *Bath Stamp and Coin Shop,* but stamps only. Look for it, if only to make sure you pass through the narrow, glass-covered arcade where it is located. 7a The Corridor (phone: 463368).

Jim Garrahy's Fudge Kitchen – It's difficult to wait until you're back out on the street before sampling the results of this shop's 1830s recipes for chocolate, mint, walnut, and other mouth-watering fudge flavors. Union Passage (phone: 462277).

General Trading Company – A twin of the Sloane Street shop in London, famous for all kinds of gifts, from traditional to modern to Oriental, it devotes a large portion of space to antiques, kitchenware, and stationery. 10 Argyle St.

Global Village – Bright handicrafts, kitchenware, folk art, and costumes from near and far. 4–5 Green St. (phone: 464017).

Highland Clothing Co. – The place for cashmere, lambswool, Braemar knitwear, and tartans. Rooftop restaurant. 2a Bath St. (phone: 466144).

Jolly's – A department store with everything from fashion to food. Milsom St. (phone: 466201).

Liberty – A branch of the famous fabric store with an unusual line of ready-to-sew garments; sew up one seam and the skirt is ready! 12 New Bond St. (phone: 462224).

E. P. Mallory & Son – Two shops. Old jewelry and silver at 5 Old Bond St. (phone: 465443); modern jewelry, silver, and china at 1–4 Bridge St. (phone: 465885).

Mementos of Bath – Souvenirs of the Roman Baths and the rest of Bath — even a record of the *Pump Room Trio.* Roman Baths (phone: 461111).

National Trust Shop – Linens, preserves, toiletries, crafts, and hand-knit woolens, many produced exclusively for the National Trust. 14 Abbey Church Yard (phone: 460249).

Nectar – Artistically presented baskets of goodies and shelves of bottles — containing body lotions, scents, perfumes, bath oils — surrounded by a fiery red decor. Shire Yard (phone: 447401).

Papyrus Fine Paper – For stationery, scrolls, handmade books and albums, pens, and inks. 25 Broad St. (phone: 463418).

Poppy at the Glove Shop – One of the few specialty glove shops in England, the shop also stocks leather handbags, scarves, belts, and costume jewelry. Northgate St. (phone: 465320).

Rossiter's – A row of several shops that sell lovely housewares and decorative items for the home — kitchenware, china tea services, chintz fabrics, and more. 40 Broad St. (phone: 460170).

Secret Garden – Dedicated to aromatherapy and herbal skin care, guests can create their own personalized skin creams. 17 New Bond St. (phone: 465514).

Stamps – A new shop, featuring ultramodern kitchenware. 26 Milsom St. (phone: 466066).

Silver Gift Shop – Interesting silver gifts and jewelry, curiously displayed against a background of furry toys. Union Passage (phone: 466093).

Timothy Solloway – Fine linens, British and imported, for kitchen, bed, and bath. 3 Church St. (phone: 466463).

Tumi – The first floor houses a changing exhibition of Latin American crafts and artifacts, including wall hangings, tapestries, pottery, and jewelry. New Bond Street Place (phone: 462367).

SPORTS: The *Sports and Leisure Centre* on the Recreation Ground has some indoor sports and swimming as well as a sauna, a solarium, and an electric golf trainer. Across the river via North Parade Bridge (phone: 462563).

Boating – *Bath Boating Company,* Forester Rd. (phone: 66407), has skiffs and punts for hire. Information about boat trips on the Avon as well as on the Kennet and Avon Canal is available at the tourist information center (phone: 462831).

Cricket – The *Bath Cricket Club* (phone: 25935) plays at the North Parade Cricket Ground across the river and just to the south of the *Sports and Leisure Centre.* The *County Cricket Festival* is held in June, when you'll see some even better teams compete on the Recreation Ground. Consult the newspaper or the monthly events list put out by the information center.

Fishing – For a license to fish in the river Avon and the Kennet and Avon Canal, apply at the Wessex Water Authority, Broad Quay (phone: 313500), or at a local fishing tackle dealer.

Golf – *Entry Hill,* just a mile from downtown, is Bath's newest golf club. The 9-hole course is open daily and membership is not necessary (phone: 834248). Bath's other leading golf clubs are on the outskirts of town. The *Lansdown Golf Club,* an 18-hole course about 2 miles north of town on Lansdown Hill, accepts visitors (phone: 22138); the *Kingsdown* course (18 holes) is a century old and overlooks Box Valley (phone: 742530); another 18-holer, the *Bath Golf Club* is the oldest of them all, next door to Sham Castle (phone: 463834).

Horse Racing – The *Bath Races* take place a few times each month from April through September at the racecourse on Lansdown Hill, 2 miles north of town (phone: 466375).

Rugby – The *Bath Rugby Football Club* (phone: 25192) plays its home games on the Recreation Ground. The monthly events list keeps track of the dates and times.

Soccer – Twerton Park, about a mile west of Bath via the Lower Bristol Rd., is the scene of the *Bath City Football Club* games (phone: 23087). Consult the events list.

Swimming – The pool at the *Sports and Leisure Centre* on the Recreation Ground (North Parade Rd.; phone: 462563) is open year-round.

THEATER: Bath's *Theatre Royal,* in The Sawclose at the end of Barton St. (phone: 465065), dates from 1805 and has reopened after major renovations. Once again it provides an intimate setting for comedy, drama, musicals, opera, ballet, concerts, and a traditional Christmas pantomime. The theater also stages pre-London openings and is a regional base for the *National Theatre.* The *Bath Puppet Theatre* (phone: 312173) overlooks the picturesque Pulteney Weir (beside the famous bridge), and performs on weekends and school holidays.

MUSIC: Concerts of classical music presented in unusual surroundings by leading artists are part of the 2-week *Bath International Festival of Music* beginning in late May (see *Special Events*). The rest of the year, music by local and visiting groups can be heard at the *Theatre Royal* and elsewhere. The *Pump Room Trio* holds forth with concerts of light orchestral music in the Pump Room mornings throughout the year and on summer afternoons, piano recitals take place every afternoon, and during the summer there are band concerts in the Parade Gardens on Sunday afternoons. Pubs with live jazz nightly or several nights weekly include *The Entertainer, North Parade,* next door to the *Fernley* hotel (phone: 461603), and *The Bell,* 103 Walcot St. (phone: 25998).

NIGHTCLUBS AND NIGHTLIFE: The quiet dignity of the place means that Bath is unlikely to win an award as Britain's most swinging city. What happens, happens in the pubs, and in nightspots such as *Rumours,* opposite the *Theatre Royal* (phone: 463993), and *Moles,* 14 George St. (phone: 333423), which features a live band.

BEST IN TOWN

CHECKING IN: Bath has a number of memorable hotels and a few truly outstanding ones. Summer visitors, particularly in July or August, must book well in advance. The tourist information center, Abbey Church Yard (phone: 460521), can help make arrangements. Expect to pay $110 or more for a double room with breakfast at hotels listed in the expensive category; between $70 and $105 at those listed as moderate; and under $70 at any listed as inexpensive. All telephone numbers are in the 0225 area code unless otherwise indicated.

Fountain House – This former Georgian mansion dating from 1735 became Bath's first all-suite hotel. Set in the city's center, it has 14 one- and two-bedroom apartments with spacious kitchens, marble bathrooms with brass fixtures, and living rooms with fireplaces; some even have washing machines. Come morning, there's a basket with a pint of milk, a loaf of Hovis bread, and the newspaper on every apartment's doorstep. 9–11 Fountain Bldgs., Lansdown Rd. (phone: 338622). Expensive.

Priory – Without a doubt, one of Britain's best country hotels. A Gothic house built in 1835, its 21 rooms — most of them suites — are furnished with antiques. In the quiet gardens is a heated swimming pool in use from spring through fall. The restaurant is divided in two: *Brown Dining Room* and the *Terrace* (see *Eating Out*). It's about a mile from the center of Bath. Closed the first 2 weeks in January. Weston Rd. (phone: 331922). Expensive.

Queensbury – In the city center, this elegant 26-room hotel is comprised of three Georgian-period houses, replete with 18th-century stucco ceilings and cornices, iron railings, and colorful window boxes. Russel St. (phone: 447928). Expensive.

Royal Crescent – The centerpiece of the Royal Crescent, this elegant and historic Georgian hostelry is part of Bath's architectural heritage. There are 36 super-deluxe rooms, but to really splurge, spend a night in one of the extra-special apartments. The Sir Percy Blakeney Suite, for example, has a 17th-century canopied bed, pale blue sofas, an Oriental carpet, and a white and gold ceiling of intricate gesso swirls. On summer days, cocktails and tea are served in the garden. 15–16 Royal Crescent (phone: 319090). Expensive.

Ston Easton Park – Peter and Christine Smedley's Palladian country manor, 12 miles outside of Bath, won the Egon Ronay Hotel of the Year award within months of opening in 1982. A grandfather clock ticks in the library, a log fire crackles throughout the winter, and the 20 guestrooms (several with four-poster beds) overlook 300 acres of landscaped parkland. Ston Easton (phone: 076121-631). Expensive.

Fernley – This 18th-century building opposite the Parade Gardens is just a 2-minute walk to the Pump Room, Roman Baths, and Bath Abbey. Just over half the 47 rooms have private baths. There's also a salad bar, a French brasserie called *Magnums,* and *No. 3 North Parade,* an adjoining restaurant with a tearoom. 1 North Parade (phone: 461603). Expensive to moderate.

Francis – In an entirely different spirit, this 94-room property forms the southern side of Queen Square, built by John Wood the Elder between 1729 and 1736. Damaged by World War II, the hotel has been rebuilt in its original style, and furnishings reflect the period. Queen Sq. (phone: 24257). Expensive to moderate.

Hilton International – Bath's most modern hotel has 184 rooms and is built over a municipal parking lot on the banks of the Avon overlooking the river and Pulteney Bridge. There is no period charm here; its main lure is efficiency, convenience, and comfort. Walcot St. (phone: 463411). Expensive to moderate.

Number Nine – Tucked away on one of Bath's most charming, secluded walkways in the heart of the city, this building is a bona fide historical property with scores of antiques to prove it. The 8 rooms are individually decorated, one with a four-poster bed; another has a Jacuzzi. Miles Bldgs. (phone: 25462). Expensive to moderate.

Bath – Only minutes from the city center, Bath's newest hotel has 96 luxurious rooms and is superbly sited alongside Widcombe Basin and the river. Widcombe Basin (phone: 338855). Moderate.

Gainsborough – A mile from the center, here is a small country house providing bed and breakfast set in an acre of garden. All 16 rooms have private baths and two have four-poster beds. Weston La. (phone: 311380). Moderate.

Lansdown Grove – A modernized Georgian mansion, this is on Lansdown hill, facing south over the city. The 46 rooms are pleasantly decorated; all have private baths, and some have balconies with lovely views. Lansdown Rd. (phone: 315891). Moderate.

Pratt's – As historic as any hotel in Bath, it is in South Parade, and is a John Wood design of the 1740s. There are 47 modern, comfortable rooms, all with private baths. Saturday night dinner dances are held during the winter months. South Parade (phone: 460441). Moderate.

Redcar – Not far from the center of town, near Henrietta Park, the hotel is part of a mellowed stone Georgian terrace and has 31 well-equipped rooms. 27 Henrietta St. (phone: 469151). Moderate.

Royal York – Queen Victoria slept here in 1830, when she was still a princess and the hotel was still an old coaching inn. More than half of the 52 large rooms have private baths. George St. (phone: 461541). Moderate.

County – Friendly and unpretentious, this 25-room hotel has a restaurant, grill room, and 3 bars. Only half the rooms have private baths. 18–19 Pulteney Rd. (phone: 466493). Inexpensive.

Parkside Guest House – Nicely placed on the fringe of Royal Victoria Park, close to the Royal Crescent and the Botanical Gardens, this pleasant bed-and-breakfast offers vegetarian meals on request. 11 Marlborough La. (phone: 29444). Inexpensive.

Somerset House – This small Georgian house with a no-smoking policy has just 1 single and 8 double rooms, which accounts for the personal service of owners Jean and Malcolm Seymour and the very good home-cooked meals (ingredients come from their garden). 35 Bathwick Hill (phone: 466451). Inexpensive.

EATING OUT: The range of restaurants in Bath is broad: English, French, Italian, Greek, Indian, Chinese, and many more. Expect to pay $105 and up for a meal for two with wine at restaurants listed below as expensive; from $70 to $100 at the moderate ones; and less than $60 at the inexpensive ones. At the numerous wine bars and fast-food establishments, two people can eat simply for less than $25. All telephone numbers are in the 0225 area code unless otherwise indicated.

Hole in the Wall – It doesn't sound like much, but this beamed restaurant with flagstones in the basement of a Georgian building has been one of Bath's most prestigious eating spots for a number of years. The cuisine is mostly French and usually superb, and there is great variety. Reservations are advised, especially for Saturday nights. (There are also 8 rooms available.) Closed for lunch on Sundays and 3 weeks over the Christmas holidays. 16 George St. (phone: 25242). Expensive.

Old Mill – This is a hotel-restaurant on the river Avon about 2½ miles from town. Good English cooking is the specialty; traditional Sunday lunches are served, too. Open daily. Tollbridge Rd., Batheaston (phone: 858476). Expensive.

Priory – Dinner is a grand occasion here, and you can choose to have it either in the Georgian *Brown Dining Room* with period furniture and paintings or in the *Terrace* overlooking the courtyard. The cuisine is primarily French, and there is an extensive wine list. Open daily. Priory Hotel, Weston Rd. (phone: 331922). Expensive.

Flowers – On the ground floor of three beautifully converted 18th-century courtesans' houses, this restaurant is brightly decorated in pastel colors, and its walls are crammed with artwork. Traditional English food is the specialty. Closed Sundays and Mondays, a week at Easter, 2 weeks at Christmas, and most of August. 27 Monmouth St. (phone: 313774). Expensive to moderate.

Clos du Roy – French food, neither classic nor nouvelle, but imaginative creations by owners Philippe and Emma Roy. Open Tuesdays through Saturdays; closed during the last week in January and the first week in February. 7 Edgar Buildings, George St. (phone: 464356). Moderate.

Circus Restaurant – An upscale café that serves morning coffee, lunch, and dinner and features some interesting items like mussel pâté. Closed Sundays. 33 Brock St. (phone: 330208). Moderate.

Ménage à Deux – This lively, plant-filled restaurant prepares both English and French dishes. The poultry and fish specialties are among the best choices, particularly the turbot in Cornish crab sauce. Closed Sundays and for lunch on Mondays. 2 George St. (phone: 63341). Moderate.

La Pentola – Down the stairs at the river end of North Parade, the stone-vaulted room that is the restaurant's dining area was once a cellar for the patrician home above. The fare is strictly Italian and rated among the town's better values. Closed Sundays and Mondays. 14 North Parade (phone: 24649). Moderate.

Popjoy's – Beau Nash lived with his mistress Juliana Popjoy in this Georgian house, which is now one of the best restaurants in Bath. High-quality English dishes are made from seasonal produce (the menu changes every 2 months). Closed Mondays in winter. Sawclose (phone: 460494). Moderate.

Il Romano – One of Bath's few upmarket Italian restaurants, this is a friendly, efficient establishment where plates are piled high with steak, fish, and pasta. Closed Sundays and Mondays. 1 Barton St. (phone: 26572). Moderate.

Theatre Vaults – This restaurant, in the vaults of the restored *Theatre Royal,* has quickly gained a good reputation for reasonably priced and tasty lunches and suppers. Open daily except Sundays. Barton St. (phone: 65074). Moderate.

Woods – The two dining rooms, basically Georgian including the fireplaces, have been attractively updated with modern cane seating and finished in tones of beige, burnt orange, and dark red. English and French cooking are featured; it's advisable to book. Closed Sundays and Mondays. 9–13 Alfred St. (phone: 314812). Moderate.

KT's – Places like this are now a familiar High Street sight, featuring a light and airy decor combined with such hearty, healthy fare as hamburgers, stuffed potatoes, lentil lasagna, and vegetarian moussaka. Open for lunch and dinner daily. 4–5 Grand Parade (phone: 461946). Moderate to inexpensive.

Pasta Galore – This eatery serves pasta in all shapes and forms. Open lunch and evenings daily except Sundays. 31 Barton St. (phone: 63861). Moderate to inexpensive.

Sweeney Todd's – A friendly, boisterous restaurant on Bath's main shopping street, it serves good pizza and hamburgers. Open daily. 15 Milsom St. (phone: 62368). Moderate to inexpensive.

Bink's – Although it calls itself a coffee shop, this place serves remarkably good hot and cold meals in a pleasant atmosphere. Afternoon tea is served here in true English style — including scones, jam, and clotted cream. Lunches to go are also available. Open daily. Abbey Church Yard (phone: 66563). Inexpensive.

Canary – Peer through the multipaned windows facing the narrow street to see a profusion of small tables set in a bower of flowery wallpaper. This busy, licensed tea shop serves one-dish meals such as quiche, omelettes, and salads as well as a wonderfully confusing selection of cakes for tea. Closed Sundays and evenings. 3 Queen St. (phone: 24846). Inexpensive.

Clarets – A downstairs wine cellar and restaurant with contemporary styling and a youngish, sophisticated clientele. In summer, tables are set up outside. 7 Kingsmead Sq. (phone: 66688). Open daily except Sundays for drinks, meals, or snacks. Inexpensive.

David's Coffee Shop – A handkerchief-size café serving homemade continental cakes and pastries and delicious sandwiches. Open daily except Sundays. 17 Pulteney Bridge (phone: 64636). Inexpensive.

Francis – Even if you're not staying here, stop by for the weekday buffet lunch in the elegant surroundings of the *Roman Bar.* Pile your plate with cold cuts and salad, add a pint of ale, and consume it smugly — it's not at all a bad deal. Open daily. Queen Sq. (phone: 24257). Inexpensive.

Monk's Coffee House – Strategically set opposite the Pump Room and Roman Baths, a good place for light meals, coffee, and snacks. Closed evenings. 7 Abbey Church Yard (phone: 60759). Inexpensive.

Moon and Sixpence – This is an attractive wine bar–restaurant in a restored courtyard (self-service during the day; waiters in the evenings) serving enticing fish, meat, and salads. During the summer, outdoor tables surround a lovely fountain. Open daily. 6A Broad St. (phone: 60962). Inexpensive.

Rajpoot Tandoori – A quiet, elegant restaurant featuring Raj curries and tandoori barbecues. 4 Argyle St. (phone: 66833). Open daily. Inexpensive.

Walrus and Carpenter – Beefburgers, chili con carne, and steaks are the choices in this attractive restaurant on a corner near the *Theatre Royal.* Open evenings only; closed Sundays. 28 Barton St. (phone: 314864). Inexpensive.

SHARING A PINT: At first glance, the *Saracen's Head,* 42 Broad St., looks like an ersatz antique. In fact, it is said to be the oldest pub in town. The building was completed in its present form in 1713, and Charles Dickens stayed here in 1835 while it was still an inn. (The display case in the wall has a few items from his time.) While bending your elbow, be sure to appreciate the original plasterwork in the beamed ceiling. Around the corner on Green St., there's the *Old Green Tree,* and if business is brisk, you'll have to squeeze in. Its tiny bar, smoking lounge, and snug are paneled in dark wood, and all is very friendly, intimate, and cozy. The *Rummer,* in a renovated Regency building on Newmarket Row along Grand Parade opposite the Pulteney Weir, looks like a restaurant in someone's living room. Actually, it, too, is a pub, and although bar snacks are served all day, you can sit graciously at those tables with just a drink. The *Grapes,* Westgate St., occupies a lovely old building — white walls, dark beams, etched glass in the doorway — and the mood is lively. The *Huntsman,* North Parade, manages to be almost all things to all people. The main lounge bar of this establishment is filled at lunch with office workers and with tourists who come for the great variety of fast, honest food. Downstairs, the noisy *Cellar Bar* is frequented by students and other youth. Upstairs, there's a quiet restaurant. The *Huntsman* is sprawling and comfortable, and the entrance toward the river is claimed to be the oldest shopfront in Bath.

BIRMINGHAM

According to the *Domesday Book,* the historic census of England ordered by William the Conquerer, Birmingham was one of the poorest manors in England in 1085–86. It had a mere ten inhabitants and was valued at only 20 shillings — just £1! By the 16th century, the town's population was still not especially impressive (probably about 1,500), although it already included a fair number of blacksmiths, who made the air ring with their diligence. Then, 200 years ago, the onset of the Industrial Revolution brought boom times. Perfectly situated at the very center of England, with abundant quantities of coal, iron, and wood nearby, a knack for manufacturing, and energetic inhabitants, Birmingham quickly established itself as "the city of 1,001 trades," described by de Tocqueville in the early 19th century as "an immense workshop, a huge forge." Today its population numbers over a million, making this manufacturing metropolis the second largest city in Britain.

Although Birmingham makes an excellent geographic base for travelers, with attractive countryside all around, it is not an obvious place for visitors to put on their itinerary. It has neither a picturesque setting nor famous ancient buildings. Instead, its attraction is simply that of a bustling industrial city getting on with the serious business of making a living. As visitors rub shoulders with Brummies (as citizens are known) in the streets or shops, they hear the famous local accent and get a firsthand glimpse of the down-to-earth flavor of real British working people. Indeed, should they get into conversation, they are sure to find themselves again and again being addressed as "mate" or "luv."

Large areas of the city center, built during Victorian times, were destroyed by Hitler's World War II bombs. Now, surrounded by a high-speed ring road, the center is a mixture of styles, and the few old ornate red brick buildings that remain look rather forlorn amid the tall modern blocks and multistory car parks. The site known as the Bull Ring, Birmingham's original marketplace (still serving the same purpose after 8 centuries), was extensively developed in the early 1960s, becoming the first symbol of the city's post-war modernization, and is now undergoing further dramatic redevelopment. Similarly, the style of broad Corporation Street, the pride of the Victorian city, has been radically changed by the arrival of modern shops and traffic-free areas. Gone, too, are most of the narrow back streets, having been replaced by wider, straighter ones. Yet while some Brummies regret the enormous changes, there is no denying that a great deal has changed for the better and that there is now plenty for visitors to see and do.

Scores of familiar British business names have their roots in "Brum" — from Cadbury chocolates, HP sauce, and Typhoo tea to Austin Rover and Wolseley cars and Dunlop tires. Indeed, a quarter of Britain's exports originate here, although many of the city's 5,000 factories and workshops were badly hit by the national recession in the early 1980s. The National Exhibition Centre, opened on the eastern edge of town near the airport in 1976, has taken up some of the slack: With typical Brummie entrepreneurial vigor, the City Council invested millions of pounds to build it, and now 80 percent of the UK's major exhibitions are held here, bringing crowds of visitors and spawning new hotels, restaurants, and conference centers. A major new International Convention Center is due to open in 1991 close to the city center; it will include 11 halls, a spectacular mall, and a 2,200-seat concert hall. The Brummies are very proud of all their new facilities, so it was disappointing when the city failed to be chosen as the site for the 1992 Summer Olympic Games, particularly as the preparations would have been a welcome economic boost in the face of some industrial decline. Nevertheless, just being the British nominee has encouraged the city to advertise itself widely, with a subsequent boost for tourism.

Birmingham's fortunes have always centered on crafts and trade. In 1166, Henry II granted Peter de Bermingham a charter to hold a regular market in the Bull Ring. (Today its outdoor stalls, together with the large covered shopping mall, are still among Birmingham's busiest.) During the 16th century, the town was notable for the number of blacksmiths counted among its residents, and during the next century, the English Civil War enhanced the city's reputation as a manufacturing center. Birmingham supplied swords, pikes, and armor to the Parliamentary forces — enough of them, unfortunately, to anger King Charles and prompt Royalist soldiers to burn down and loot the city. Afterwards, gunmaking was established as an important trade, and by 1754 one factory alone was exporting 600 firearms a week.

Toward the end of the 18th century, such pioneering scientists as Joseph Priestley, who discovered oxygen, William Murdock, who invented gas lighting, and James Watt, who developed the double-action steam engine, made Birmingham their home, giving the Industrial Revolution and Birmingham's part in it no small boost. Watt's work was financed by the Birmingham industrialist Matthew Boulton, who, in 1762, had set up his Soho Manufactury to make buttons, buckles, and other small metal items. Boulton's interest in a new power source for his factory led him to buy a share in Watt's patent, and from 1775 to 1800 the two were partners in the manufacture of steam engines. Eventually the Soho works grew to be the engineering showplace of Europe, partly because (thanks to Murdock) it was the first factory in the world to be lit by gas, an advancement that allowed production to continue after dark.

During the late 18th and early 19th centuries, the city became the center of the canal system that revolutionized the transport of heavy goods in England. Even today, Birmingham has more miles of canals than Venice, although they are rather less scenic, hidden away behind old wharves and warehouses. When railways superseded the canals, the city became the natural hub of England's rail network, too. Commercial enterprises multiplied; industrial wealth grew; and in the prosperous times of the late 19th century, most of the city's municipal buildings took shape. Joseph Chamberlain, lord mayor from 1873 to 1876 (and father of Neville, also lord mayor and, later, Prime Minister of Britain), was a central figure in pushing through ambitious plans for the Council House developments at Victoria Square as well as in founding Birmingham University in the leafy suburbs at Edgbaston. An imposing memorial fountain with a white marble spire in Chamberlain Square commemorates his achievements — and the university's clock tower is also affectionately called Joe.

The small tea and coffee shop on Bull Street, where the Cadbury family started their business in 1824, had disappeared long before the redevelopment of the 1960s, when landmarks such as the British Telecom went up. However, the unique "garden factory" George Cadbury opened to manufacture chocolate at Bournville in 1879 still thrives today. Its setting, less than 5 miles from the city center, remains almost unchanged, surrounded by neatly kept grounds and the small houses he built as a social duty for his workers. So, too, the car factory that Herbert Austin built at Longbridge in 1906 — one of the world's first mass-production car factories and the one that made Birmingham the center of Britain's automobile industry — is still in operation today. Just beyond it are the woods and moors of the Lickey Hills, providing a lovely breath of countryside.

In fact, the city is well endowed with parks and open spaces, boasting 6,000 acres of parkland and 6 million trees, which provide a much-needed contrast to the industrial areas and drab inner city. Cannon Hill Park, Edgbaston, ablaze with daffodils and tulips in spring, is the largest, while pretty Queens Park, Harborne, has a fragrant garden for the blind. The woodland trails and lakeside pathways of Sutton Park, constituting 2,400 acres on the northeastern edge of the city, also seem far removed from both the noise and smell of heavy industry and the roar of traffic.

Like the canals and railways before them, Britain's main motorways now converge on Birmingham, providing local links right into the center. Appropriately for the home of the nation's automobile manufacturing industry, the most famous road junction in the country is the interweaving mass of motorway overpasses and concrete pillars at Gravelly Hill, nicknamed Spaghetti Junction. Appropriately, too, the best view of it is from a traditional narrowboat chugging along the canal directly underneath. Cut there 200 years earlier, the canal provides a vivid reminder of Birmingham's much slower, more peaceful era.

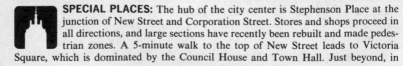

BIRMINGHAM AT-A-GLANCE

SEEING THE CITY: The city center has no towers to climb to gain a vantage point for an all-encompassing view, but since the center itself is built on high ground, watch out for views over the industrial suburbs from the top floors of shops and car parks.

SPECIAL PLACES: The hub of the city center is Stephenson Place at the junction of New Street and Corporation Street. Stores and shops proceed in all directions, and large sections have recently been rebuilt and made pedestrian zones. A 5-minute walk to the top of New Street leads to Victoria Square, which is dominated by the Council House and Town Hall. Just beyond, in

Chamberlain Square, are the *Birmingham Museum and Art Gallery* and the remarkable Central Library. A short stroll away on Broad Street are the other main civic buildings: the white Anglesey marble Hall of Memory, a war memorial to local soldiers who fell during World War I, and Baskerville House, a 20th-century neo-Georgian building housing city offices. A ring road encircles the whole of the central area, making the drive from one side to the other very easy, though parking is very restricted. The road has also transformed parts of Birmingham into a confusing concrete jungle that many older Brummies complain has made the Victorian city they knew almost unrecognizable.

CITY CENTER

Town Hall – The city's main concert hall, styled on the model of the Temple of Castor and Pollux in Rome, has neoclassical columns and arches on all four sides and is faced with Anglesey marble. Opened in 1834, it was designed by Joseph Hansom, more famous as the inventor of the Hansom cab. Inside, the white and gold baroque decorations provide a superb setting for the *City of Birmingham Symphony Orchestra,* whose home this is until the concert hall in the new International Convention Center opens in 1991. Mendelssohn conducted the first performance of his *Elijah* here in 1847. Paradise St. (phone: 236-3889).

Council House – This is the most impressive public building in town, naturally enough, since it's the headquarters of Birmingham's city government. Built in 1879 in an Italian Renaissance style, it has an elaborate portico, Corinthian columns, and a large dome, all reflecting the industrial prosperity of the last century. Inside are elaborately decorated banquet rooms, as well as the Council Chamber. The building is open to the public one weekend in September only, when the civic plate — official silverware and other regalia — is on display. Victoria Sq., Colmore Row (phone: 235-2040).

Birmingham Museum and Art Gallery – Around the corner from the Council House (but connected to it), this is immediately recognizable by the "Big Brum" clock tower on top. The art collection, which includes paintings and drawings from the 14th to the 20th century, is ranked among the most important in Britain outside London, and the fine collection of works by the pre-Raphaelites is especially notable. Natural history, archaeology, and local history exhibits are also on display, along with costumes, textiles, and ceramics. Open Mondays through Saturdays from 9:30 AM to 5 PM, and Sundays from 2 PM. Tours of the clock tower are conducted on the same September weekend when the Council House is open to the public. Chamberlain Sq. (phone: 235-2834).

Central Library – This imposing, modern white stone building is the largest library complex in Europe. Built in 1974, it has 34 miles of bookshelves and 1½ million books. Specialist sections include a large Shakespeare collection, the Samuel Johnson collection, and music and local studies collections. Open Mondays through Fridays from 9 AM to 8 PM and Saturdays from 9 AM to 5 PM. Chamberlain Sq. (phone: 235-4227).

Museum of Science and Industry – Features an impressive collection of scientific and industrial items reflecting the city's achievements since the Industrial Revolution. Exhibits range from steam engines (including the oldest working one in the world, a 1779 Watt beam), machine tools, old cars, motorcycles, and bicycles, to firearms and mechanical musical instruments. Many are still in working order and can be operated by visitors. Steam engines are run on the first and third Wednesdays of each month, and special steam engine events take place regularly. Open Mondays through Saturdays from 9:30 AM to 5 PM and Sundays from 2 PM. Newhall St. (phone: 236-1022).

St. Philip's Cathedral – The city's Anglican cathedral, built in 1715, is a fine example of the Palladian style. It has four magnificent 19th-century stained glass windows by Sir Edward Burne-Jones. Colmore Row (phone: 236-4333).

St. Chad's Cathedral – The first Roman Catholic cathedral to be built in England after the Reformation, this was begun in 1839 and dedicated in 1841. It is the work of Augustus Pugin, who pioneered the Victorian-Gothic style and also designed the Houses of Parliament in London. St. Chad's Queensway (phone: 236-5535).

St. Martin's-in-the-Bull-Ring – Birmingham's parish church stands on the edge of the city's centuries-old market area, so shoppers bustle past it all day long. A church has been here for 900 years, though the present one, in Gothic style, dates from only 1873. It has a Burne-Jones stained glass window and the ancient tombs of the de Bermingham family. Bull Ring (phone: 643-5428).

Gas Street Basin – The 260 miles of the narrow Birmingham Canal Navigation network, which threads its way through the city, are the heart of an English waterways system that reaches as far as the Mersey, the Humber, the Severn, and the Thames. Built from the mid-18th to the mid-19th century to serve and expand the Industrial Revolution, most are still in good repair, with recently restored towpaths alongside for walking. A particularly interesting stretch through the center of the city is that from Gas Street Basin (Gas St., off Broad St.) to the newly restored Cambrian Wharf, which leads to the Farmer's Bridge flight of 13 locks (off Newhall St.). The canal guide (*Brum Trail 7*) sold by the Birmingham Convention and Visitor Bureau (about $1.50) is a handy reference. Narrowboats for holidays afloat can be hired by the week (or for shorter periods during the off-season) from *Brummagem Boats,* Sherbourne St. Wharf (phone: 455-6163). In summer, short excursions from Gas Street Basin are run by *Brummagem Boats* and *Second City Canal Cruises* (phone: 643-4384).

SUBURBS

Aston Hall – This fine 17th-century Jacobean mansion is in Aston Park, about 2½ miles north of the city center. Built by a wealthy squire, Sir Thomas Holte, it was attacked by Parliamentarians during the English Civil War, and the marks of their cannon shot can still be seen. The grand balustraded staircase, long gallery, and period furniture are notable — as is the resident ghost, presumably that of one of the squire's daughters, who refused to marry the man chosen for her and was locked in a tiny room in the attic, where she went mad and died. Open daily from 2 to 5 PM; closed November through March. Trinity Rd., Aston (phone: 327-0062).

Birmingham University – In the pleasant residential suburb of Edgbaston, about 3 miles southwest of the center, this institution dates from the turn of the century, though the campus was greatly enlarged during the 1960s. The Byzantine-style buildings in characteristic red brick are the oldest. The clock tower, nicknamed Joe after Joseph Chamberlain, the lord mayor responsible for founding the university, is one of the city's most famous landmarks. It also includes the *Barber Institute,* a notable collection of art. (The city has another university at Aston; only 20 years old, it specializes in technology.) Bristol Rd., Edgbaston.

Botanical Gardens – These contain beautifully landscaped ornamental gardens and glasshouses with tropical plants, as well as aviaries with exotic birds. Open daily from 9 AM to 8 PM or dusk, Sundays from 10 AM. Admission charge. Westbourne Rd., Edgbaston (phone: 454-1860).

Cannon Hill Park – The largest park proper in Birmingham, it has 80 acres with lovely floral displays, a boating lake, and a nature center where trees and plants are accompanied by explanatory notes. The various theaters of the *Midlands Arts Centre* (see *Theater*) are also here. Pershore and Edgbaston rds., Edgbaston.

Bournville Village – George Cadbury built his famous chocolate factory 4½ miles south of the city center in 1879. It was a pioneering project, since he also built houses there for his workers, surrounding everything with gardens. The sample-laden factory visits, for which it used to be well known, are no longer offered. Bournville.

Blakesley Hall – This typically Elizabethan timber-framed house was built by a rich yeoman farmer during the latter part of the 16th century. Period rooms and items of local historic interest are on display inside, while the area around the house, only 4 miles east of the city center, retains its old-time village atmosphere, with quaint farmhouses and cottages clustered around a 15th-century spired church. Open Mondays through Saturdays from 9:30 AM to 5 PM, Sundays from 2 PM. Blakesley Hall Rd., Yardley (phone: 783-2193).

National Exhibition Centre – Built on a 400-acre site on the outskirts of the city about 8 miles southeast of the center, the NEC opened in 1976. Now 80% of Britain's major exhibitions are held here, attracting over 3 million visitors a year from all over the world. With nine exhibit halls and several more planned, the NEC also stages conferences and large-scale entertainments such as pop music concerts, ice shows, and horse shows. Other facilities include a manmade lake, two hotels, and an adjacent railroad station. Bickenhill (phone: 780-4141).

Black Country Museum – New and still growing, this museum is located roughly 10 miles west of central Birmingham, in the heart of the Black Country, an ironworking area so covered with the black smoke of its industries during the 18th and 19th centuries that the name has stuck, even though the grime has long since lifted. To illustrate the hard life of those times, old buildings and industrial objects from throughout the Black Country are now being salvaged and reconstructed at this open-air site, and the result is an entire Black Country village, 19th-century vintage. It contains houses, shops, a chapel, a pub, an old tram and canal boats to ride, and a fairground. Regular demonstrations of chainmaking, glass cutting, and baking complete the picture. Open daily except Christmas from 10 AM to 5 PM (hours shorter in winter). Admission charge. Tipton Rd., Dudley (phone: 557-9643).

■ **EXTRA SPECIAL:** To sample the flavor of one of the city's oldest industries, walk 15 minutes down Newhall Street from Colmore Row to Birmingham's famous jewelry quarter. The area, centered around Frederick and Albion streets, is a warren of converted houses and small workshops, some of them in modern factory blocks but many dating from Victorian times. Priceless gold and silver items as well as less expensive costume jewelry are manufactured here, even though the majority of the businesses employ fewer than ten people. For security reasons, factory visits are possible only at *Barker Ellis,* 44 Harford St. (for an appointment, phone: 523-4211), who make and engrave silver items and also have a retail shop. A few other shops in the area offer jewelry bargains. Further information is available from the British Jewelers Association, 27 Frederick St. (phone: 236-2657), or from the jewelry quarter guide (*Brum Trail 6*) sold by the Birmingham Convention and Visitor Bureau (about $1.50).

SOURCES AND RESOURCES

TOURIST INFORMATION: The Birmingham Convention and Visitor Bureau (BCVB) has two information offices. One, the ticket shop and tourist information center (phone: 643-2514), is in the city center at 2 City Arcade, off Corporation St., and is open Mondays through Saturdays from 9:30 AM to 5:30 PM. It not only dispenses tourist information and helps with travel arrangements such as car rental and restaurant reservations but also provides a booking service for theaters, concerts, and sports events. The other office (phone: 780-4321) is at the Piazza entrance to the National Exhibition Centre, adjoining Birmingham International Station, and is open Mondays through Fridays from 9:30 AM to 5:30 PM, with more extensive hours during exhibitions. It provides similar services and can make accommodations reservations.

The *Birmingham Souvenir Guide,* a 36-page illustrated guide to the main places of interest, is available from the BCVB for about $1; *Brum Trail* booklets, describing walking tours of specific areas such as the city center, the canals, and the jewelry quarter, cost about $1.50 each. *What's On,* a free entertainment guide published every 2 weeks, is available from BCVB offices as well as from hotels, theaters, and libraries. You can also call *What's On* (phone: 643-8921) for up-to-date information. The free *International Visitor Magazine* is another useful publication distributed at BCVB offices, hotels, and other outlets. It contains articles on tourist attractions in the city, along with comprehensive listings of restaurants, nightclubs, and sports and leisure facilities. The free *Birmingham Visitors' Guide* lists hotels, restaurants, and other services.

Local Coverage – The *Birmingham Post,* the *Evening Mail* (both published every weekday), and the *Sunday Mercury* are the local newspapers.

Telephone – The area code for Birmingham is 021.

GETTING AROUND: Because traffic can be heavy, the best way to explore the city center is on foot. The *Centrebus* service (Route 101), which connects the main car parks with the center, leaves every few minutes; fixed fare is about 25¢. Transportation options for sights that are farther afield are listed below.

Airport – Birmingham International Airport (phone: 767-5511), 9 miles southeast of the city center along Coventry Road, serves both domestic and international flights. Departing every 2 minutes, a free MAGLEV train (the world's first magnetic suspension rapid transport system) links the airport building to the adjacent National Exhibition Centre and Birmingham International Station.

Bus – Local service throughout the city and surrounding area is provided by *West Midlands Travel* and other operators. For information on schedules and fares, phone 236-8313 between 7 AM and 10 PM. Exact change is required; fares vary depending on the distance traveled, and discounts go into effect from 9:30 AM to 3:30 PM and from 6PM to 11:30 PM. Longer-distance buses around the area are operated by *Midland Red Bus and Coach Services* (phone: 643-0088), with departures from the Bull Ring. *National Express,* a national network of long-distance coaches, runs from the *Digbeth Coach Station* (phone: 622-4373). *Flightlink* airport coaches make numerous trips daily to Heathrow, Gatwick, Luton, and Manchester airports from various pickup points (phone: 554-5232). There are also *London Liner* buses from Colmore Row to London (phone: 236-2707).

Car Rental – The major companies have offices in the city center and at the airport. Arrangements can also be made through the Birmingham Convention and Visitor Bureau or by using the free phone at Birmingham International Station.

Taxi – There are several taxi ranks in the city center as well as at the airport, the National Exhibition Centre, and railway stations. Any hotel or restaurant can also call a cab for you, or phone 427-8888.

Train – The main railway station is New Street Station, in the city center. Birmingham International Station serves the National Exhibition Centre. Trains between Birmingham and London (service is every half hour) stop at both. For exact times of trains to London, call 643-4466; for information on trains to other cities, call 643-2711.

SPECIAL EVENTS: The *Birmingham Super Prix,* when Formula 3000 cars tear along a 2½-mile circuit through the city center, is the city's newest annual event. (It took an act of Parliament in 1985 to allow the city streets to be used for racing.) Held on the August bank holiday, it already attracts leading drivers from all over the world. The *Birmingham Jazz Festival* is another big draw: It takes place in May and/or June and features a week or more of concerts in pubs, nightclubs, hotels, and in the open air. There's also the *Film and TV Festival* in October and a *Readers and Writers Festival* in November. Exhibitions and trade fairs are year-round events at the National Exhibition Centre — most are geared to a specific audience, but some, including the *British International Antiques Fair* (April), the *Royal International Horse Show* (June), and the *International Motor Show* (every other year in October) appeal to and are open to the general public.

MUSEUMS: In addition to those mentioned in *Special Places,* there are several others of interest in Birmingham and vicinity.

Birmingham Railway Museum – A working museum featuring 11 steam locomotives, historic carriages, and workshops where visitors can watch restoration work in progress. Open daily; engines are steamed up the first Sunday of each month and bank holidays. Warwick Rd., Tyseley (phone: 707-4696).

National Motorcycle Museum – A unique collection illustrating the development of British motorcycles from 1901, including racing models. Open daily. Bickenhill, adjoining the National Exhibition Centre (phone: 704-2784).

Patrick Collection – Classic vintage cars displayed in appropriate settings, and a section devoted to modern racing cars. Open April through October; closed Tuesdays. Lifford Lane, Kings Norton (phone: 459-9111).

Sarehole Mill – An 18th-century water-powered corn mill restored to working order. Open daily Easter through November. Cole Bank Rd., Hall Green (phone: 777-6612).

Weoley Castle – Excavations of the ruins of a 13th-century fortified manor house, with a small museum of finds. Open Easter through October, Tuesday through Friday afternoons. Alwold Rd., Northfields (phone: 422-4270).

SHOPPING: Shoppers from all over the Midlands crowd into Birmingham's city center, attracted by its markets, department stores, excellent clothing and shoe shops, and branches of leading chain stores, such as *British Home Stores, Boots, C & A, Littlewoods, W. H. Smith's,* and *Marks and Spencer.* New Street, Corporation Street, and High Street are the main shopping areas, with several traffic-free market squares leading off them, such as *Corporation Market,* with stalls selling inexpensive clothes and household goods. There are also malls of better quality specialty shops, such as the ornate *Great Western Arcade,* which is patrolled by a beadle in Victorian dress, the modern *Pavilions,* High St., which has four floors of stores and a good selection of restaurants serving snacks, and *City Plaza* in Needless Alley, close to St. Philip's Cathedral. The *Pallasades* is a large, partially carpeted mall over New Street Station, reached from either the station or New Street. It has a wide selection of individual shops selling clothing in particular, and it leads directly into the Bull Ring market complex, a pedestrians-only zone also approached by underground walkways from New Street and Smallbrook Ringway. Open Mondays through Saturdays, it includes the *Bull Ring Open Market* — 160-odd outdoor stalls selling fruits and vegetables, plants, fabrics, and china — and the *Bull Ring Centre Market Hall,* whose 190 indoor stalls house the best inland fish market in the United Kingdom, together with a wide variety of meat and other foods, garden accessories, crockery, jewelry, and clothing. The *Rag Market,* on Edgbaston Street opposite the Bull Ring, is the largest covered market in the UK. Open on Tuesdays, Fridays, and Saturdays, its 550 stalls offer everything from sheepskin coats to curtains. On Monday mornings it becomes the site of an antiques market, the largest in the UK, attracting buyers from all over Europe, and every 2 months (Wednesdays from 2:30 to 8 PM), an antiques fair offers a significant selection of antique clothes, lace, pottery, and furniture. Next to the *Rag*

Market are the *Row Market,* selling clothing and accessories for teenagers, and the *Flea Market,* the place for secondhand goods and bric-a-brac. Both are in action Tuesdays, Fridays, and Saturdays.

Below are some individual stores of note. In general, shopping hours in Birmingham are from 9 AM to 6 PM and until 8 PM on Thursdays.

Beatties – Hobbies and models, especially trains and aircraft. The Pallasades (phone: 643-8604).

Halcyon Gallery – Original paintings and fine art prints. The Pallasades (phone: 643-4474).

High and Mighty – Clothes for tall and large men. Smallbrook Queensway (phone: 643-1940).

Hudsons – One of Britain's leading bookshops, particularly good for paperbacks and academic and local books. New St. (phone: 643-8311).

Lewis's – A department store, not as luxurious as *Rackhams* (see below) next door, but very popular among Brummies in the market for household items of every sort. Bull St. (phone: 236-8251).

Nathan – Famed for over 100 years as "the jewelers under the clock," it's the best in town for top quality watches, clocks, and gems as well as fine antiques and silver. 31 Corporation St. (phone: 643-5225).

West End Stamp Company – A haven for stamp collectors, specializing in British Commonwealth, European, and American stamps. Cigarette cards and old postcards are also sold. 23 Needless Alley, off New St. (phone: 643-1364).

William Powell – Hand-crafted guns, rifles, and fishing tackle, since 1802. Also sells the accessories and clothes required for shooting, including traditional tweed jackets, woolens, and leather. 35 Carrs La., off High St. (phone: 643-0689).

Rackhams – The city's leading department store, the largest outside London, is part of the *Harrods* group and is famed for its superb window displays. Excellent for clothing, perfumery, and fine foods. Corporation St. (phone: 236-3333).

Sweet Indulgence – Handmade chocolates and traditional candies. Great Western Arcade (phone: 236-4274).

Things Australian – High-quality goods, including bushmen's jackets, made down under. Fletchers Walk (phone: 236-4468).

SPORTS: Leisure centers throughout the suburbs are equipped with gyms, swimming pools, squash and badminton courts, and facilities for other pursuits. In the city center, private health clubs offering aerobics, weight training, and power workouts include the *Albany Hotel Club,* Smallbrook Queensway (phone: 643-8171); *Corinthians,* Smallbrook Queensway (phone: 643-8712); and *Pat Roach,* Piccadilly Arcade (phone: 643-8888).

Cricket – The *Warwickshire County Cricket Club* (phone: 440-4292) plays at the County Ground, Edgbaston Rd., from April through early September. Test matches and 1-day internationals also take place at the County Ground.

Golf – Visitors can play for a small charge at the city's eight municipal courses. Call the Birmingham Convention and Visitor Bureau for phone numbers. There are also more than 40 private courses in the area, including the two championship courses at the *Belfry* hotel complex near Sutton Coldfield, headquarters of the Professional Golfers' Association (phone: 0675-70333) and host of the Ryder Cup, for the second time, in 1989.

Greyhound Racing – Call *Hall Green Stadium,* York Rd. (phone: 777-8439), for the latest schedules.

Ice Skating – Three public sessions are held most days at the centrally located *Silver Blades Ice Rink,* Pershore St. (phone: 622-4325), and the *Solihull Ice Rink,* Hobbs Moat Rd., which is 10 miles south of the city center (phone: 742-4315).

Rugby – Saturday matches take place during winter at *The Reddings,* Moseley (phone: 449-0048).

Soccer – The *Birmingham City Football Club* plays at St. Andrews, Bordesely Green (phone: 772-0101); the *Aston Villa Football Club* at Villa Park, Aston (phone: 327-6604); and the *West Bromwich Albion Football Club* at The Hawthorns, Birmingham Rd., West Bromwich (phone: 525-8888).

Squash – All the leisure centers have courts, but most have to be booked in advance. Private clubs include the *Metropole Hotel Squash Club* at the National Exhibition Centre (phone: 780-4242) and the *North Birmingham Center,* Chester Rd., Sutton Coldfield (phone: 373-7185).

Swimming – In addition to pools at the leisure centers, there are 19 municipal baths open Mondays through Fridays from 9 AM to 9 PM, Saturdays until 5 PM, and Sundays from 8 AM to 12:30 PM. For details, call the Recreation Community Services Department (phone: 235-3022).

Tennis – Most parks have public courts that can be booked inexpensively by the hour. Private clubs include the *Edgbaston Priory Club,* where international tournaments are held (phone: 440-2492).

THEATER: The *Birmingham Hippodrome,* Hurst St. (phone: 622-7486), presents large-scale musicals, variety shows, and opera; it is the new home of the *Sadlers Wells Royal Ballet,* Britain's national ballet company; in addition, there is usually a traditional pantomime from Christmas through February. Built as a music hall in 1899, it was recently refurbished, and its seating capacity was expanded to 1,950. The *Alexandra Theatre,* Suffolk St. (phone: 643-1231), hosts national touring companies and London West End productions, with a different program scheduled each week (except from Christmas through February, when a pantomime runs). Most productions are plays, although it boasts that it presents everything from Shakespeare to nude shows. (Backstage tours are free.) The *Birmingham Repertory Theatre,* Broad St. (phone: 236-4455), however, is *the* place for drama, either classical or contemporary — it has an international reputation. Performances take place in the *Main House;* experimental productions are staged in the small *Studio Theatre.* The *Midlands Arts Centre,* Cannon Hill Park, Edgbaston (phone: 440-3838), is the home of the famous *Cannon Hill Puppet Theatre,* which stages productions for children every morning and afternoon; it has three theaters, one open air. The *Crescent Theatre,* Cumberland St. (phone: 643-5858), is the city's leading amateur theater, while the *Triangle Media and Arts Centre* at Aston University, Gosta Green (phone: 359-3979), has its own *Youth Theatre* and stages "fringe" productions by touring companies. Tickets for all theaters are available from the BCVB Ticket Shop, 2 City Arcade (phone: 643-2514).

MUSIC: The *City of Birmingham Symphony Orchestra,* Britain's first municipal orchestra, came into being in 1920 and now enjoys international renown. Under the baton of Simon Rattle (who became principal conductor in 1980, at the age of 25), it performs regularly in *Town Hall,* Paradise St., from September through May; during June and July, informal Promenade Concerts, including programs by visiting orchestras, take place every evening. Concert tickets are available from the box office (phone: 236-1555) or the BCVB. Visiting opera and ballet companies (from the *Welsh National Opera* to the *Bolshoi*) show up at the *Birmingham Hippodrome* (address and phone number above). The *Midland Youth Jazz Orchestra* and the *Maestros Steel Band* perform at the *Midlands Arts Centre* (address and phone number above). Live pop concerts and other star attractions generally take place at the *Birmingham International Arena,* National Exhibition Centre (phone: 780-4133).

NIGHTCLUBS AND NIGHTLIFE: Birmingham has more than two dozen nightclubs, most of them in the city center or the nearby suburb of Edgbaston. In town, *Bobby Brown's at the Lock,* Gas St. (phone: 643-0691), is an imaginatively converted warehouse overlooking the canal, with various small bars, a discotheque, a bistro-style restaurant (free buffet on Wednesdays), and an intimate, friendly atmosphere. Open from 9 PM to 2 AM. *Liberty's,* Hagley Rd. (phone: 454-4444), is a large stylish club with the *Piano Bar* restaurant for dinner (French menu), cocktail bar, champagne bar, several other bars, and a disco. Open Mondays through Saturdays from 9 PM to 2 AM. *The Dome,* Horsefair (phone: 622-2233), features a geodesic dome above the dance floor and has three restaurants (French, Italian, and traditional) and two lounges. Disco on Mondays and Thursdays through Saturdays from 9 PM to 2 AM . For a night out of town, the *Bel-Air* nightclub at the *Belfry* hotel (phone: 0675-70301) is well worth the 9-mile journey to Wishaw.

Birmingham has four casinos, two in the city center — *Cromwells* (part of the *Grand* hotel, Colmore Row; phone: 236-7951) and *Stakis* (Hill St.; phone: 632-5465) — and two in Edgbaston. They're open every evening until the early hours and are busiest during the week, when businessmen are in town.

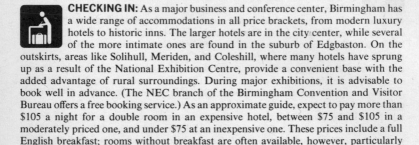

BEST IN TOWN

CHECKING IN: As a major business and conference center, Birmingham has a wide range of accommodations in all price brackets, from modern luxury hotels to historic inns. The larger hotels are in the city center, while several of the more intimate ones are found in the suburb of Edgbaston. On the outskirts, areas like Solihull, Meriden, and Coleshill, where many hotels have sprung up as a result of the National Exhibition Centre, provide a convenient base with the added advantage of rural surroundings. During major exhibitions, it is advisable to book well in advance. (The NEC branch of the Birmingham Convention and Visitor Bureau offers a free booking service.) As an approximate guide, expect to pay more than $105 a night for a double room in an expensive hotel, between $75 and $105 in a moderately priced one, and under $75 at an inexpensive one. These prices include a full English breakfast; rooms without breakfast are often available, however, particularly in the larger hotels, as are rooms with continental breakfast. All telephone numbers are in the 021 area code unless otherwise indicated.

Albany – Built in the 1960s with the businessman in mind, this 13-story establishment has a convenient New Street Station location and a high percentage of single rooms (178 out of a total 254), plus 3 luxury suites. All rooms are elegantly furnished, with private bath, color TV sets, coffee- and tea-making facilities, and air conditioning. There are two restaurants — the *Carvery,* where diners carve their own main course and select appetizers from a buffet, and an à la carte English restaurant — plus a leisure club with swimming pool, gym, and squash courts. Smallbrook, Queensway (phone: 643-8171). Expensive.

Belfry – Visitors have only to venture 9 miles northeast of the city center to find a country-manor-house atmosphere, complete with lovely gardens, a championship golf course, and a leisure club with a pool and squash courts. Some of the 168 bedrooms even sport four-poster beds. Its French restaurant has a very good reputation, and there is also a piano bar, appealing to an older crowd. Lichfield Rd., Wishaw, near Sutton Coldfield (phone: 0675-70301). Expensive.

Birmingham Metropole – On the grounds of the NEC, this modern hotel complex caters primarily to business travelers. With 692 rooms and 12 suites, this is the city's largest hotel. (It's also Britain's largest conference hotel, with a capacity for

1,800 delegates.) The bedrooms are comfortably appointed, with private bath, color TV sets, and coffee- and tea-making equipment, but the general atmosphere is impersonal. There are 2 restaurants, squash courts, a sauna, and a cinema. National Exhibition Centre (phone: 780-4242). Expensive.

Holiday Inn – A member of the worldwide chain, with 290 rooms (including 64 reserved for non-smokers), 5 suites, a restaurant, 2 bars, and atmosphere and facilities similar to those of its fellows. On the west side of the city center, a 5-minute walk from the shops on New Street. Holliday St. (phone: 631-2000). Expensive.

New Hall – Set in its own 26-acre park, this hotel is the oldest inhabited house with a moat in England. Built during the 13th century, it has sandstone battlements and a drawbridge and, fortunately, has lost none of its character in the transformation to a hotel. There are 12 luxurious suites in the oldest part of the house, and most have a view of the moat; a new wing with 50 rooms has been built around an attractive courtyard on the site of the old kitchen garden. There is a restaurant (see *Eating Out*), croquet lawn, and putting green; riding and clay pigeon shooting can also be arranged. Despite the rural surroundings, it is only 7 miles northeast of the city center, and the M6 and M42 motorways are only a few minutes' drive away. Walmley Rd., Sutton Coldfield (phone: 378-2442). Expensive.

Strathallan – Modern high-rise hotel in a striking polygonal shape at busy Five Ways, Edgbaston, a mile west of the city center (buses pass regularly). The majority of its 166 rooms are singles, and all have bathrooms. There is an American-style bar, and the French restaurant, *Le Mange Tout,* features live entertainment on Saturday evenings. 225 Hagley Rd., Edgbaston (phone: 455-9777). Expensive.

Cobden – Like its sister hotel, the *Norfolk,* this was until recently a temperance hotel, but it now has a license to serve alcoholic beverages. Originally a Victorian house with a large garden, it has been expanded to accommodate 241 rooms, half of them singles with bath, and a fitness club. It offers a convenient location on the main road west from the city center. 166 Hagley Rd., Edgbaston (phone: 454-6621). Moderate.

George – Once an old coaching inn but now one of several small hotels on the outskirts, convenient to the National Exhibition Centre. It's in the center of Solihull, a smart, middle-class borough 8 miles south of the city center with good shopping and within a few minutes' drive of pretty countryside. Although a wing of new rooms has been added (there are 74 in all, most with baths), the inn's traditional character still prevails in the main dining and lounge areas. Some rooms have four-poster beds, and the hotel has its own bowling green. High St., Solihull (phone: 711-2121). Moderate.

Grand – A traditional city center hotel in a splendid Victorian building, this was recently refurbished in the appropriate style. The genteel atmosphere is enhanced by long corridors, and each of the 167 bedrooms has a private bath, color TV set, and coffee- and tea-making facilities. The hotel has 2 restaurants and 3 bars; the ornate Grosvenor suite, which has hosted such statesmen as Lloyd George, Joseph and Neville Chamberlain, and Winston Churchill, has banquet facilities. Colmore Row (phone: 236-7951). Moderate.

Marston Farm – Only 7 miles from town, this place is surrounded by quiet farmland, yet is still within easy reach by car of the National Exhibition Centre and motorways. Attractively converted, it has a modern bedroom wing (all 19 rooms have baths), an outdoor swimming pool, and a barbecue restaurant in summer. Bodymoor Heath, Sutton Coldfield (phone: 0827-872133). Moderate.

Midland – A city center, privately owned hotel, long established and recently refurbished, it caters primarily to businesspeople with 112 rooms (including a few new small suites) with private baths. Several lively bars include one serving real ale, which is well patronized by Brummies. New St. (phone: 643-2601). Moderate.

Asquith House – A snug hostelry typical of a number of small, owner-run establishments in the Edgbaston area, 2 miles from the city center. With only 10 rooms, most with baths, the atmosphere is homey, and since it's off the main Hagley Road, it is also quiet. 19 Portland Rd., Edgbaston (phone: 454-5282). Inexpensive.

Campanile – Built with the business traveler in mind, this modern, 51-room hotel offers no frills but good value. Centrally located near New Street Station. Irving St. (phone: 622-4925). Inexpensive.

Saracens Head – A small, comfortable inn-style hotel, 6 miles south of the city center. All 34 rooms have private baths. Stratford Rd., Shirley (phone: 744-1016). Inexpensive.

EATING OUT: The city has come a long way since the 1960s, when the only places to eat out were hotel dining rooms and a few Chinese restaurants. Now its restaurants reflect its status as an international business center and offer many cuisines — particularly European, Indian, and Chinese. Many are comparatively new, however, so the city has yet to establish a reputation for good eating. A meal for two without wine will cost more than $60 in a restaurant listed as expensive, between $30 and $60 in a moderate one, and under $30 in an inexpensive one. All telephone numbers are in the 021 area code unless otherwise indicated.

Jonathans' – The area's most unusual restaurant serves traditional English dishes in a setting that's a deliberate re-creation of the genteel world of the 1880s. Victorian decor, furniture, and objets d'art prevail in several dining rooms, including the secret "Boardroom," hidden behind a book-lined wall, and smaller rooms for private meals. The two owners are both called Jonathan; one does the cooking, the other looks after the guests. Open for lunch (except Saturdays) and dinner daily. Reservations advised. 16 Wolverhampton Rd., Oldbury (phone: 429-3757). Expensive.

Lombard Room – Housed in the *Patrick Collection* automobile museum, there is an airy conservatory area for pre-dinner drinks and an elegant dining room in a converted Victorian hall. The imaginative menu specializes in nouvelle cuisine, and guests can choose from over 200 excellent wines. Open Tuesdays through Sundays, except lunch on Saturdays and dinner on Sundays. The Patrick Collection, 180 Lifford Lane, Kings Norton (phone: 459-9111). Expensive.

New Hall – Dining in this hotel's 400-year-old oak-paneled restaurant surrounded by a 13th-century moat is a special experience. The food, prepared by chef Allan Garth, is delicious; fish and game are the specialties, cooked with fresh, home-grown herbs and watercress taken from the moat. Open daily. Walmley Rd., Sutton Coldfield (phone: 378-2442). Expensive.

Penns Hall – About 6 miles from the city center, in a large country-house hotel surrounded by lakeland, this sophisticated dining room offers English and international fare. Open for lunch (except Saturdays) and dinner daily. Reservations advised. Penns Hall Hotel, Penns La., Walmley, Sutton Coldfield (phone: 351-3111). Expensive.

Plough and Harrow – Part of an elegant old inn that dates from 1704 and is one of Birmingham's oldest, this award-winning restaurant features classic French cuisine. The food and service are both excellent and the decor is dramatic, with views over a large garden. Open for lunch (except Sundays) and dinner daily. Reservations necessary. Plough and Harrow Hotel, Hagley Rd., Edgbaston (phone: 454-4111). Expensive.

Sloans – In the modern Chad Square shopping center, this is the place for intimate, sophisticated dining amid attractive decor. It specializes in interesting fish dishes.

Open for lunch and dinner Mondays through Fridays, dinner on Saturdays, and lunch on Sundays. Reservations necessary. Hawthorne Rd., Edgbaston (phone: 455-6697). Expensive.

Bobby Brown's in Town – In a large vaulted cellar with inglenook fireplaces and a minstrel gallery, the city center's most interesting restaurant attracts a cosmopolitan clientele who feast on beefsteak and Guinness pie — a house specialty — as well as steaks, creamy sweets, and alcoholic coffees. Open daily for lunch and dinner until 11 PM. Reservations advised. Burlington Passage, New St. (phone: 643-4464). Moderate.

Bull's Head – In an old, timbered coaching inn, 11 miles from the city center at Meriden (the center of England), this is one of the highly successful low-priced steak bars of the Berni Inn chain, offering grills and a selection of salads to which diners help themselves. The setting is delightfully rural and an easy drive from the NEC. Open daily for lunch and dinner. Meriden (phone: 0676-22541). Moderate.

Le Provençal – Owned and run by René Ernst, a young Swiss chef who named it after the famous hotel where he trained at Juan-les-Pins, in the south of France. The French and Swiss "bourgeois" cuisines that are his forte are definitely not for calorie counters. Very popular with local businessmen. Open daily, except Sundays, for lunch and dinner (last orders 10 PM). Reservations advised. Albany Rd., Harborne (phone: 426-2444). Moderate.

Rustie's – A colorful place where Caribbean food gets star billing on a menu that includes such dishes as Devil Creek (very hot spicy lamb curry) and Jamaica-style cod sautéed with ackee, a tropical pod, as well as "Aphrodisiac" cocktails. When she is not performing elsewhere, comedienne Rustie Lee livens up the atmosphere even more with songs and jokes. Open daily for lunch, Caribbean afternoon tea, and until after the theaters close (last orders, 11:30 PM). 69–71 Hurst St. (phone: 622-4137). Moderate.

The Square – Many of the regular customers of this wine bar and restaurant liken its vibrant decor and informal but smart atmosphere to that found on an ocean liner. Installed in an attractive Georgian building in the Victorian jewelry quarter, it is becoming distinctly trendy. The wine bar serves simple snacks at lunchtime; the restaurant, with bistro-style menus, is open for lunch and dinner Mondays through Fridays and for dinner on Saturdays (last orders, 10 PM). St. Paul's Sq. (phone: 236-3717). Moderate.

Arthurs Bar – An old brick warehouse bordering the canal has been cleverly converted and dressed up in stunning black and white decor. Long and narrow, it has a marble floor in a bold check and an intricate wrought-iron balustrade along a balcony with white Italian tables and chairs overlooking the water. The menu features bistro food, including salads and gooey "afters." Open daily for lunch and dinner. Gas St. (phone: 643-5567). Inexpensive.

Branegans – Racks of barbecued ribs and steaks are the specialties of this new American-style restaurant and bar whose emphasis is on good value and efficient service. Decor is strikingly neo-Victorian. 192 Broad St. (phone: 643-5100). Inexpensive.

Chung Ying Garden – Considered one of the best Chinese restaurants in Britain, it's decorated in exotic Oriental tea room decor, and the menu offers 350 dishes, including dim sum; the special rice and barbecued duck are outstanding. 17 Thorp St. (phone: 666-6622). Inexpensive.

Days of the Raj – Northern Indian cuisine, including a huge buffet at lunchtime. The furnishings are of delicate bamboo. Open daily for dinner and Mondays through Fridays for lunch. Dale End (phone: 236-0445). Inexpensive.

Salamis – Genuine Greek food, including excellent kebabs and other specialties. The atmosphere is always jolly, thanks to live bouzouki and guitar music, and the owner, known to everyone as Harry, is happiest when he has everyone up on the tables dancing. Open Mondays through Saturdays from 6:30 PM to 1 AM. Broad St. (phone: 643-2997). Inexpensive.

■ **Note:** There is no better place to sample the traditional British take-out meal than *Bedders Fish and Chips,* Coventry Rd., Small Heath (phone: 772-1532). Expect to "queue," since it's patronized by Brummies from all over the city. The fish is delivered fresh, direct from coastal fishing ports, but no longer does it come wrapped in newspaper, as in days gone by. Open for lunch daily, except Sundays, from 11:30 AM to 2 PM and from 4 to 7:30 PM on Fridays. Inexpensive.

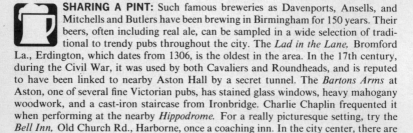

SHARING A PINT: Such famous breweries as Davenports, Ansells, and Mitchells and Butlers have been brewing in Birmingham for 150 years. Their beers, often including real ale, can be sampled in a wide selection of traditional to trendy pubs throughout the city. The *Lad in the Lane,* Bromford La., Erdington, which dates from 1306, is the oldest in the area. In the 17th century, during the Civil War, it was used by both Cavaliers and Roundheads, and is reputed to have been linked to nearby Aston Hall by a secret tunnel. The *Bartons Arms* at Aston, one of several fine Victorian pubs, has stained glass windows, heavy mahogany woodwork, and a cast-iron staircase from Ironbridge. Charlie Chaplin frequented it when performing at the nearby *Hippodrome.* For a really picturesque setting, try the *Bell Inn,* Old Church Rd., Harborne, once a coaching inn. In the city center, there are several new pubs overlooking the canal, among them the *James Brindley* on Bridge St. and the *Longboat* at the Cambrian Wharf junction.

BOURNEMOUTH

By English standards, Bournemouth is an infant of a city, not much more than a hundred years old. Yet for all its youth, until recently Bournemouth had a reputation for Victorian primness. Unlike Brighton, its good-time sister just down the coast, it became associated with a picture-postcard stereotype of a bluff Colonel Blimp (retired) taking the air in a Bath chair on the promenade, his heavily bandaged, gouty foot protruding stiffly in front of him.

It's still possible to encounter such people here, refugees from the pages of the Jeeves books of P. G. Wodehouse, their voices like "good sound port made audible," but the only Bath chair likely to be seen is in the museum. Bournemouth has been at some pains to rid itself, once and for all, of the Colonel, and to a great extent, it has succeeded. It is now something of a pacesetter among English seaside resorts, making its way toward the 21st century. A genuinely year-round town, it has few monuments of historic interest, but it has a wider range of hotels and restaurants than any English place outside London and ample conference and leisure facilities both indoors and out.

And it still has the mild, yet bracing, climate that made it a resort in the first place — the sort of fresh air that a certain Dr. Granville recommended in the mid-19th century to those "in delicate health." It still has the beach, too — 7 miles of golden sand that perfectly fulfilled the Victorian concept of the seaside. The sand was (and is) excellent for molding into castles and moats or sand pies. And the gentle slope of the shore permitted the easy use of the bathing machines by which the ladies of the time preserved their modesty when entering the sea for a dip.

Little wonder that a contemporary writer called Bournemouth "this most decorous and dull of watering places." Dances and concerts were positively discouraged, although Punch and Judy shows were allowed on the beach. The future King Edward VII, then Prince of Wales, brought a discreet breath of scandal to the town when he built a house for his mistress, the actress Lillie Langtry, among the mansions with their armies of live-in servants on the pine-clad heights of East Cliff. She was known as the Jersey Lily because of her flawless white skin and her birth on the largest of the Channel Islands. Whenever the prince could slip away from London, he came down to Bournemouth to the house on Derby Road that is now known as the *Langtry Manor* hotel.

Bournemouth then was a parvenu. Until the early 19th century, this stretch of heathland and pinewoods beyond the sands was virtually uninhabited, the haunt of smugglers and cutthroats who dodged riding officers and revenue cutters and landed contraband tea, brandy, and tobacco in the steep tree-lined "chines," or valleys, along the coast. The local gentry — squires, clerics, doctors, and town clerks — were not averse to bribery in the form of a keg or two, since in this way they avoided paying duty.

At the same time, when the threat of invasion by Napoleon was at its height, one Captain Lewis Tregonwell was dispatched with a troop of Dorset yeomanry to patrol the coast between Christchurch and Poole. Captain Tregonwell was destined to become the founder of Bournemouth when, in 1810, he bought 8 acres of land to build the mansion that is today the central part of the *Royal Exeter* hotel. The town grew into a residential resort as wealthy Victorians, encouraged by Dr. Granville's advice, built their villas around this foundation.

It was not until the railway station opened in 1870, however, that Bournemouth became a full-fledged seaside resort. Then speculators came in and found the tops of the hundred-foot-high cliffs, split by those wooded chines, the perfect place to build hotels. In 1876, the first *Winter Gardens,* a concert hall in imitation of the Crystal Palace in London, was built, and 4 years later the building of the present Bournemouth Pier attracted more entertainments to the seafront. In the second half of the 19th century Bournemouth's population grew from a few hundred to 59,000. Today it is in excess of 150,000.

Over the years, Bournemouth has been associated with more than a few notable people. Robert Louis Stevenson lived here for a few years during the 1880s — on what is now R.L. Stevenson Avenue — and wrote *Kidnapped* and *The Strange Case of Dr. Jekyll and Mr. Hyde* while in residence. The heart of the poet Percy Bysshe Shelley was buried here. Disraeli stayed at the *Royal Bath* hotel for the sake of his health, while his archrival, Gladstone, made his last communion at St. Peter's Church. Winston Churchill nearly killed himself in a boyhood prank in Alum Chine. John Galsworthy sang in a choir at St. Swithun's and attended a local preparatory school before going to Harrow. Francis Kilvert wrote of Bournemouth in his celebrated *Diary 1870–79.*

In his novel *Tess of the D'Urbervilles,* Thomas Hardy immortalized the place as "Sandbourne" and wrote of its eastern and western stations, its gaslit piers, promenades, and covered gardens. It was, he said, "a glittering novelty." Thus Bournemouth's reputation spread far and wide, helped by the promotion of the railway companies, as were its sister resorts. Unlike them, however, it did not attract the hoi polloi, and it shunned "What the Butler Saw" machines and cotton candy. Instead, it developed an awe-inspiring gentility that survived through the Jazz Age.

During World War II, the old *Winter Gardens* was occupied by the Royal Air Force as Bournemouth, along with the rest of the south coast, became the front line of Britain's defenses. When peace returned, the large gaps blown out of Bournemouth and Boscombe piers when invasion seemed likely in 1940 were filled in, and both structures were restored to their Victorian splendor.

Modern Bournemouth has expanded east and west to reach the older towns of Christchurch and Poole, but its heart is still the green valley of the Bourne stream (which flows into the sea here, hence the name Bournemouth), landscaped to form the Upper and Lower Bourne Gardens. To the east and west of Bournemouth Pier, the cliffs are lined with the grand hotels built by the Victorians and Edwardians. Many of the chines that interrupt the cliffs can be negotiated by winding paths and steps descending through pine-scented glades and subtropical vegetation to the undercliff drives and promenades, traffic-free in summer, giving access to beaches that are safe from both off-shore winds and fumes of the automobile.

Festivals and entertainment featuring top show business names are part of the Bournemouth calendar. The town center and the suburbs of Westbourne and Boscombe have Victorian shopping arcades festooned with flowers in hanging baskets, tubs, and troughs, and in the Bohemian quarter of Pokesdown, antiques and curio shops abound. At night, the clubs and casinos open their doors and keep them open into the wee hours. Bournemouth has done an admirable job keeping up with the competition from other resorts, and maintaining its popularity.

The resort has its own airport at Hurn, operating regular services to France and the Channel Islands, so it attracts hordes of continental visitors, many of whom attend the numerous English-language schools that flourish here. Indeed, the whole town has a continental air about it. A stroll down the main street, beneath the pine trees, heading toward the bandstand and the brightly striped deck chairs, makes it easy to imagine what it feels like to be in the south of France. Bournemouth has come a long way from its origins in early Victorian times, when, as the *Hampshire Advertiser* phrased it, "the magic hand of enterprise converted the silent and unfrequented vale into the gay resort of fashion and the favoured retreat of the invalid."

BOURNEMOUTH AT-A-GLANCE

SEEING THE CITY: The best view is from the heights of either the West Cliff or the East Cliff, from which the 7-mile sweep of sands fringing Poole Bay can be seen to full advantage. To the west the view extends to Sandbanks, a spit of land at the entrance to Poole Harbour, with the limestone hills of the Isle of Purbeck, an island in name only, beyond. To the east, down the shore to Hengistbury Head, the green hills of the Isle of Wight, beyond Christchurch Bay, can be seen on a clear day. Beneath the vantage point on the cliffs, footpaths zigzag down through the trees to the promenade below.

SPECIAL PLACES: Bournemouth is a garden city: There are 2,000 acres of them within the city limits, and they are at the heart of it. If it is a good morning, take a seat among the pines in the Lower Gardens and listen to the birds or to the military band tuning up for the first of the daily concerts at the bandstand, or browse among the portraits and landscapes by local artists on show in Pine Walk. On the far side of the square, the azaleas, magnolias, and rhododendrons follow the Bourne through the Central Gardens into the willow-shaded Upper Gardens to Coy Pond. The best way to take in the sights is from the breezy, open-top deck of one of the yellow buses that ply the coast regularly, or head off on foot. Organized walks leave from the tourist information center on Westover Road.

CENTRAL BOURNEMOUTH

The Pier – No English seaside resort is complete without one, and Bournemouth's is as fine as any to be found. The original iron structure, which was mentioned by Thomas Hardy in *Tess of the D'Urbervilles* and which replaced previous wooden piers serving pleasure steamers, is still part of the framework. It has a theater, a restaurant, and bars, as well as all kinds of fun and amusements for children. To the left and right of Bournemouth Pier is sandy beach lapped by warmish waters. This is a "Eurobeach," meaning that it meets the standards laid down by the European Economic Community for avoiding pollution. To keep the beaches even cleaner, dog-free zones between Fisherman's Walk and Durley Chine have been introduced from May through September, and motor traffic is banned from the undercliff drives and promenades during the summer school holidays and peak season. Lifeguards patrol between Alum Chine and Bournemouth Pier on summer weekends, and there is no shortage of deck-chair attendants. There are also freshwater showers, a seafront pizzeria, and a *patisserie,* with baking done on the premises.

The Pavilion – It took 53 years of argument before this building became brick and mortar. Eventually opened by the Duke of Gloucester in 1929, it has been the pride of Bournemouth ever since, its terraces looking out over the Lower Gardens. It has a theater seating 1,600, a large ballroom also used for banquets, and restaurants and bars. Westover Rd.

The Winter Gardens – The Victorian "Crystal Palace" on this site was dismantled in 1935 and replaced by a municipal indoor bowling green, at that time a considerable novelty and the first of its kind in Great Britain. After World War II, during which it was commandeered by the Royal Air Force, it was restored to its original use as a concert hall, seating 1,800. The quality of the acoustics turned out, more or less by chance, to be excellent, and it became the home of the *Bournemouth Symphony Orchestra.* Exeter Rd.

Bournemouth International Centre – Rivaling Brighton's conference and exhibition complex, this is Bournemouth's most emphatic statement that it is looking to the future. Apart from major conferences, the BIC stages topnotch entertainments in its two auditoriums, Windsor Hall and Tregonwell Hall, the latter named after the city's founding father. It also contains a gymnasium, solarium, and sauna, and a lagoon-style indoor swimming pool that simulates the waves breaking on the beach outside. West Cliff (phone: 22122).

Russell-Cotes Art Gallery and Museum – Occupying a Victorian Gothic monstrosity on a cliff top, formerly the home of the mayor Sir Merton and Lady Russell-Cotes, this museum specializes in Victoriana, including the last remaining example of the invalid carriage known as the Bath chair, the symbol of Bournemouth's origins. It also has a collection of Japanese art as well as burial urns from Bronze Age barrows unearthed in the locality. The Henry Irving theatrical collection is a reminder that the great actor-manager was a close friend of the Russell-Coteses and often stayed at this house. Outside is a remarkable geological terrace made up of rocks, stones, and ores spanning 2,600 million years. Closed Sundays. Admission charge. East Cliff (phone: 21009).

St. Peter's Church – This Victorian building with a tower and a spire, the parish church of Bournemouth, was completed in 1879, in the same decade as the town's first railway station. It contains a beautiful chapel and stained glass window (commemorating the Reverend John Keble of the Tractarian movement at Oxford, who was a daily communicant here during the last months of his life). In the churchyard is the Shelley Tomb, where the heart of the poet Percy Bysshe Shelley is said to be interred together with his wife, Mary, who wrote *Frankenstein,* and his son, Sir Percy Shelley, who lived at Boscombe Manor. Shelley senior drowned in Italy in 1822 and was cremated, his ashes buried in Rome — his heart was snatched from the fire by his companion, Edward John Trelawney. Hinton Rd.

St. Stephen's Church – With its ornate screens and reredos, this church is acknowledged to be Bournemouth's most beautiful building. Although begun in 1881, it was not completed until 1908, and the spire that was to have soared above the tower was never built. St. Stephen's Rd.

ENVIRONS

Southbourne – Three miles east of Bournemouth, this quiet seaside suburb has a good, sandy beach; a shell house plastered with shells, mosaics, and tiles; and bowling greens fringed with pines, including a clifftop crown (top-quality) green. Its large Victorian villas are now mostly hotels and guesthouses, but the river Stour still flows sweetly beneath the weeping willows in Tuckton Tea Gardens, where small boats can be hired.

Hengistbury Head – East of Southbourne, on the 2-mile crooked finger of low hills, mud flats, and beaches that form the southern side of Christchurch Harbour, this was one of England's busiest ports during the Iron Age. The Noddy Train, a mock locomotive hauling rubber-tired carriages, transports visitors from Southbourne to this archaeological, wildlife, and leisure area.

St. Andrew's Church – Built on the site of a Saxon mission, the parish church at Kinson, a suburb on the northern outskirts of town, is the oldest in Bournemouth. The 12th-century tower still bears the marks of ropes used to hoist contraband into hiding inside, and in the churchyard lies Robert Trotman, barbarously "Murdered on the Shore near Poole 2nd March 1765." A verse on the headstone proclaims his innocence with regard to tea smuggling. Wimborne Rd., Kinson.

Compton Acres – These beautiful gardens overlooking Poole Harbour are 3 miles west of the city center. There are seven individual gardens landscaped in different styles, including Japanese, Italian, and Roman, a rock and water garden, and a subtropical woodland glen. Open daily from April through October. Admission charge. Canford Cliffs (phone: 708036).

Poole – Suburban development has virtually merged this ancient seaport with its younger neighbor, Bournemouth, but it jealously retains its antiquities in the old town. Once a principal port for trade with Newfoundland and the rest of the New World, the old town and harbor are now a conservation area embracing the Georgian Custom House and Guildhall, warehouses, and harbor offices. There are three museums to be seen: the *Guildhall Museum,* Market St., tracing the development of the town; *Scaplen's Court Museum,* High St., showing everyday life in Poole across the centuries; and the *Maritime Museum,* Paradise St., housing exhibits of the town's colorful seafaring history in 15th-century cellars (all open daily year-round, except certain holidays; admission charge). In addition, there is an aquarium with sharks, piranhas, and crocodiles, as well as a zoo. Poole Pottery, on the quay, offers guided tours of its crafts center.

Poole Harbour – An enormous natural anchorage, as much as 100 miles around, crammed with thousands of yachts and small boats so that in summer it is difficult to move on the water. The entrance is guarded by a spit of land called Sandbanks, whose beaches, stretching toward Branksome Dene Chine and back to Bournemouth, are some of the best on the south coast. Within the harbor is Brownsea Island, 500 acres of heath and woodland owned and protected by the National Trust. In 1907, Lord Baden Powell held a summer camp for boys on the island, and so began the Boy Scouts. It is still a nature lovers' delight, open from Easter through September and reached by ferry from Sandbanks or Poole Quay.

■ **EXTRA SPECIAL:** Bournemouth's candle illuminations are unique. Four times a year (on four separate nights in July, August, and September), children flock to the Lower Gardens to light candles — there are 21,000 of them in multicolored honeypot jars hung on large wooden frames, some as tall as 23 feet. Each candle contributes its part to a picture within the frame, which might be a flower, a ship, or a flag, or even a kangaroo, elephant, or maple leaf, since, in keeping with Bournemouth's Victorian origins, a portion of the display usually represents countries that once were part of the Empire. The custom is believed to have begun during a visit of Princess Eugenie of Austria in 1896, when the gardens were lit with "fairy lights," which were expanded into pictures for the Diamond Jubilee of Queen Victoria a year later. On a midsummer night, the overall effect is enchanting.

SOURCES AND RESOURCES

TOURIST INFORMATION: Bournemouth's main tourist information center, in the middle of town on Westover Rd. (phone: 291715), is open year-round from 9:30 AM to 5:30 PM Mondays through Saturdays (to 7 PM from June through August), Sundays from 10 AM to 3 PM. The office provides full details of tours and excursions, transport, shows and special events, as well as free maps and guides, while its Accommodation Desk supplies up-to-the-minute information and can make provisional bookings. The *What to Do Handbook* ($1.25/80p including postage), published annually in March, is also available here.

Local Coverage – The *Bournemouth Evening Echo* goes on sale in the early afternoon.

Telephone – The area code for Bournemouth is 0202.

GETTING AROUND: The best way to negotiate downtown Bournemouth is on foot, with the bus used for longer stretches. Besides the numerous footpaths leading down the chines to the seafront, there are also cliff lifts for the weary.

Bus – Yellow buses fan out at frequent intervals from the square, which is actually a *roundabout,* where seven roads converge into the valley at the heart of the town. A "Day Tripper" ticket, allowing a whole day's unlimited travel, can be bought for about $3 from the driver (weekly tickets are available, too). *Centeride* is a yellow minibus service that operates between the shopping centers and car parks. In summer only, open-top yellow buses provide a coastal service between Sandbanks and Christchurch or Hengistbury Head, affording marvelous views of the English Channel en route. Bus information offices (phone: 27272) are on Avenue Rd. and at the Pier Terminal on Exeter Rd. in Bournemouth and at Havilland Rd. W, Boscombe.

Car Rental – All the major companies have branches in Bournemouth.

Paddlesteamer – In September, the *Waverley,* a restored Scottish craft, operates pleasure cruises from the pier (phone: 041-221-8152).

Taxi – Metered cabs ply from ranks on the square and on Westover Road.

Train – Bournemouth's train station is Central Station (phone: 292474) on Holdenhurst Rd. The trip from London's Waterloo Station, via express services, can take as little as 96 minutes. Every Saturday from May through September, the *Bournemouth Belle,* which first ran in 1931, makes the nostalgic journey from Waterloo, using carriages from the *Venice–Simplon Orient Express.*

SPECIAL EVENTS: The ever-changing calendar of festivals and theme weeks encompasses everything from nostalgic indulgence to flower arranging, dancing girls, and marching bands. There is a leaflet giving dates and details from the tourist information center. The *Regatta and Carnival,* held the first week in August, marks the high point of Bournemouth's summer season with fireworks, flying displays by the RAF "Red Arrows," the election of Miss Bournemouth, and one of the four occurrences of the candle illuminations (see *Extra Special*).

MUSEUMS: Considering that it is a relatively modern city, Bournemouth is well endowed with museums, including two mobile museums in converted yellow buses. In addition to those mentioned in *Special Places,* the following may be of interest:

Big Four Railway Museum – Over 1,000 railway relics, including nameplates. Closed Sundays. Dalkeith Steps, off Old Christchurch Rd. (phone: 22278).

Shelley Museum – Said to be the only museum in the world devoted to Percy Bysshe Shelley, it consists of books, furniture, paintings, and personal effects brought from his Italian villa (Casa Magni) and installed in his son's former home. Open Mondays through Saturdays from June through September; Thursdays, Fridays, and Saturdays the rest of the year. Shelley Park, Beechwood Ave., Boscombe (phone: 303571).

Transport Museum – A collection of vintage Bournemouth tramcars, trolley buses (1933–69), and buses covering a century of public transport. Open on Wednesdays during high season only (and only to guided parties). Mallard Rd., off Castle La. (phone: 21009).

SHOPPING: Bournemouth prides itself on its range of shopping opportunities. Indeed, surveys by tourism authorities show that as many people come here for the stores and shops as for the seaside attractions, given the choice and the quality available. The main shopping area, with all the major chain stores as well as a local, family-run department store, is gathered around the square in the city center. Better ladies' boutiques are dotted among the household names (*Marks & Spencer, C & A,* and an upgraded *British Home Stores*), and there is a new, ultra-smart complex known as the *Quadrant* specializing in housewares. The ornate Victorian arcades in the center and also at Boscombe and Westbourne are another feature of Bournemouth shopping. Antiques, curios, and Victoriana should be sought either at Boscombe, a 5-minute drive from the city center, or in the Bohemian quarter of Pokesdown, where there are such items as Oriental lacquerwork, Art Deco teapots, stuffed bears, and decorated headboards to bargain over. It could be an indication of the romantic nature of the resort that there seems to be a jewelry shop around every corner. Many shops are open until 9 PM on Thursdays in high season.

Absolute Chic – A boutique that lives up to its name for those who are looking for women's clothing in the upper price range. 14 Post Office Rd. (phone: 298077).

Antique Centre – Some 20 stalls under one roof in the Pokesdown area on the outskirts of town. Look for the collectible Clarice Cliff pottery, hand-painted in the 1930s. 837–839 Old Christchurch Rd. (phone: 421052).

Beales – An independent department store owned and run by the same family since 1881. It's up-to-the-minute, whether the object of desire be an Aquascutum raincoat or a pair of Kurt Geiger shoes. Old Christchurch Rd. (phone: 22022).

Boscombe Militaria – One of the numerous antiques and curio shops in Boscombe, specializing in items handed down by members of the armed forces. 86 Palmerston Rd. (phone: 304250).

Charlotte – A boutique in the 19th-century arcade at Westbourne, but one in which to expect late 20th-century prices on women's clothing, such as skirts at $150 plus, for instance. 118 Poole Rd. (phone: 766555).

Purbeck Pottery – Here's a good place to buy locally produced wares. Poole Quay, Poole (phone: 760867).

SPORTS: Angling, athletics, boating, bowls, cricket, croquet, cycling, football, golf (serious and not so serious), hockey, horseback riding, sailing, shooting, skating (ice and roller), squash, swimming, rugby, running, tennis, table tennis, and windsurfing — all these and more can be done in Bournemouth. The town also hosts a number of national and international sports challenges, among them powerboating and windsurfing (World Fun Board Championships), bowls, tennis, squash, and badminton. The Parks and Recreation Department, Town Hall (phone: 22066), can supply full details.

Bowling – The tenpin variety, not the kind played on outdoor greens, is available at *Wessex Bowl,* Poole Rd., Branksome (phone: 765489).

Cricket – The *Hampshire County Cricket Ground,* where home matches are played throughout the summer, is in Dean Park.

Fishing – Daily or weekly permits are available for coarse fishing on the river Stour. The pier is a good place to fish for bass, cod, conger, flatfish, garfish, mackerel, mullet, and whiting. Boats can be hired for offshore fishing, too (phone: 708068). No permit is required for sea angling.

Football and Soccer – American football, a relative newcomer, is now played regularly at *Kings Park,* where the Bournemouth Bobcats turn out with their cheerleaders. The English variety (soccer) has a ground at *Dean Court.*

Golf – Bournemouth has two championship courses. The *Meyrick Park Golf Club* (phone: 20871), whose fine course in open parkland welcomes visitors. The municipal *Queens Park Golf Club* (phone: 36198) has 18 holes (par 72) open to everyone and is also easily accessible by bus.

Ice Skating – There is an all-year rink on Westover Rd. (phone: 22611).

Sailing – Canoes, small sailing boats, sailboards, and wetsuits can be rented at *Salterns Marina* in Poole Harbour (phone: 700503). The *Royal Motor Yacht Club* (phone: 707227) offers temporary membership to visitors introduced by members.

Swimming – After exhausting the beaches and the many hotel pools, try jumping the waves in the Leisure Pool at the Bournemouth International Centre (phone: 22122).

Tennis – The pride of at least a dozen tennis courts is the new *Bournemouth Tennis Centre,* Central Gardens, where professional coaching is available. It is heavily booked in summer (phone: 298318). *West Hants Lawn Tennis Club,* Rosslyn Rd. (phone: 519455), has indoor courts and accepts temporary members.

THEATER: At the *Pavilion* and *Pier* theaters and at the Bournemouth International Centre, the names of television and stage stars are up in lights (phone for all three: 297297).

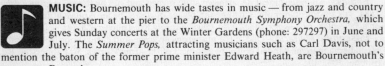

MUSIC: Bournemouth has wide tastes in music — from jazz and country and western at the pier to the *Bournemouth Symphony Orchestra,* which gives Sunday concerts at the Winter Gardens (phone: 297297) in June and July. The *Summer Pops,* attracting musicians such as Carl Davis, not to mention the baton of the former prime minister Edward Heath, are Bournemouth's answer to Boston's.

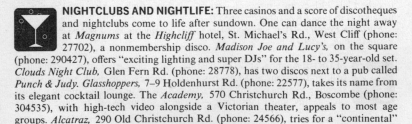

NIGHTCLUBS AND NIGHTLIFE: Three casinos and a score of discotheques and nightclubs come to life after sundown. One can dance the night away at *Magnums* at the *Highcliff* hotel, St. Michael's Rd., West Cliff (phone: 27702), a nonmembership disco. *Madison Joe and Lucy's,* on the square (phone: 290427), offers "exciting lighting and super DJs" for the 18- to 35-year-old set. *Clouds Night Club,* Glen Fern Rd. (phone: 28778), has two discos next to a pub called *Punch & Judy. Glasshoppers,* 7–9 Holdenhurst Rd. (phone: 22577), takes its name from its elegant cocktail lounge. The *Academy,* 570 Christchurch Rd., Boscombe (phone: 304535), with high-tech video alongside a Victorian theater, appeals to most age groups. *Alcatraz,* 290 Old Christchurch Rd. (phone: 24566), tries for a "continental"

atmosphere. *Zig-Zags,* Fir Vale Rd. (phone: 28954), is a members-only club that insists on smart dress. The *Bournemouth Casino* (phone: 25052) is attached to, but separate from, the *Royal Bath* hotel (entrance on Russell-Cotes Rd.). The *Curzon Sporting Club Casino,* 9 Yelverton Rd. (phone: 293188), is well appointed and has its own restaurant. Another casino operates at the *Victory Sporting Club,* Terrace Rd. (phone: 26065). Note that many Bournemouth clubs are for members only — for temporary membership, 48 hours' notice is usually required.

BEST IN TOWN

CHECKING IN: Bournemouth has more hotels than anywhere else in Britain, outside London. Expect to pay around $80 and up for a double room in those places listed as expensive; from $50 to $80 in moderate; and under $50 in inexpensive. Self-catering apartments range from $50 to $500 per week, depending on size, location, and season. Those who arrive in town without a reservation can contact the Accommodation Desk at the tourist information center on Westover Rd. for assistance. All telephone numbers are in the 0202 area code unless otherwise indicated.

Dormy – North of Bournemouth and close to the scenic New Forest area, but within easy reach of town, this establishment is more like a holiday village than a hotel, with some of its 134 rooms in bungalows on the grounds. It offers squash and tennis courts, swimming pool and solarium, and reduced greens fees for guests at the adjacent golf club. Amenities also include a restaurant and an assortment of bars. New Rd., Ferndown (phone: 872121). Expensive.

Marsham Court – In a quiet spot overlooking the bay, only minutes from the city center. All 80 rooms have either bath or shower and color TV set, and there is a heated outdoor pool. Mini-putting, snooker, weekly barbecues, dances, and video shows are among the activities. Free nanny service. Russell-Cotes Rd., East Cliff (phone: 22111). Expensive.

Norfolk Royale – The city's newest hotel, it's conveniently located near shopping, the convention center, and the beach. Of its 95 rooms, all with private bath, 15% are for non-smokers, and 8 are reserved for women guests only. There are 2 restaurants, an indoor swimming pool, steam room, sauna, and Jacuzzi. Richmond Hill (phone: 21521; in the US, 1-800-228-5151). Expensive.

Royal Bath – In 1912, Bournemouth's oldest hotel was awarded five stars by the Automobile Association, and it has maintained that high ranking ever since. Disraeli stayed here for 3 months in 1874 and reported to Queen Victoria that his health had greatly improved. Oscar Wilde and H.G. Wells were also guests here. Its top-of-the-line amenities include 133 rooms with bath, 2 restaurants, 3 bars, games rooms, a heated swimming pool, sauna and gymnasium, nanny service, and splendid sea views from the garden. Bath Rd. (phone: 25555). Expensive.

Langtry Manor – The house that the future King Edward VII built for his mistress, Lillie Langtry, is now a hotel whose accommodations include Lillie's suite, with a lace-flounced four-poster bed and corner bath, and Edward's suite, with vaulted ceiling and Jacobean four-poster. The Edwardian atmosphere extends to the dining room, where the menu and wine list are of high quality and where regular six-course Edwardian dinner parties are offered, Edwardian dress optional. In all, there are 17 rooms with bath. 26 Derby Rd., East Cliff (phone: 23887). Expensive to moderate.

Cliff End – Modern wings have been added to this 19th-century villa, which has direct access to the beach through pine-filled gardens with nary a road to cross.

All 40 rooms have private baths and color TV sets. Restaurant; babysitting service. Manor Rd., East Cliff (phone: 309711). Moderate.

Cumberland – With its tiers of white balconies, its sunblinds, and the Union Jack flying, here is a reincarnation of thirties' chic. The lounges overlook the bay, and there is a 60-foot swimming pool, plus a children's pool. All 103 bedrooms have bathrooms. Restaurant. E Overcliffe Dr. (phone: 290722). Moderate.

Harbour Heights – This balconied Deco hotel has 49 rooms (nearly all with bath) and is but a stroll from some of the best beaches in England. The restaurant features an evening carvery at which non-residents are also welcome. 73 Haven Rd., Sandbanks, Poole (phone: 707272). Expensive.

New Ambassador – A Jewish family-run hotel with 112 rooms, all with bath. The dining room serves kosher food and wines only, and there is a synagogue on the premises. East Cliff (phone: 25453). Moderate.

Chinehead – Close to pine-scented walks where gray squirrels play and within walking distance of the sea and shops, this hotel has just 27 rooms, most of them with baths. There is a bar for residents and a TV lounge. 31 Alumhurst Rd. (phone: 752777). Inexpensive.

Durley Grange – A trim, modern building with a dormered red roof, this family-managed hotel attracts numbers of bowls players and golfers. Traditional English breakfasts and four-course dinners can be included. 6 Durley Rd., West Cliff (phone: 24473). Inexpensive.

Montague – Barbara and Geoff Ramsden, the proprietors, live on the premises, which are within easy walking distance of the city center and the beaches. A half-acre garden and a well-kept swimming pool (heated from May to October) are at guests' disposal. Varied choice of menus. Durley Rd. S (phone: 21074). Inexpensive.

Studland Dene – For those who want to be very near a sandy beach, this old-fashioned family hotel stands on a gentle slope just 150 yards from one. The dining room and terraces overlook the sea and Alum Chine. Dogs are welcome by arrangement. Alum Chine, West Cliff (phone: 765445). Inexpensive.

EATING OUT: Bournemouth is a cosmopolitan city with restaurants to appeal to every palate — French, Italian, Greek, and, yes, American, plus more than a whiff of real Indian curry to complement the traditional fish and chips wrapped in paper and seasoned with salt and vinegar. A meal for two, not including wine and service, will cost $50 and up in a restaurant listed as expensive, from $25 to $50 in a restaurant listed as moderate, and $20 or less in an inexpensive place (which includes fast-food spots and take-outs, where it is possible to eat for $5 to $10 a head). Many of the hotels open their restaurants to non-residents. All telephone numbers are in the 0202 area code unless otherwise indicated.

Sophisticats – Although rather small and about 3 miles from the city center, this is one of the most stylish of Bournemouth's many ambitious restaurants. Menu choices range from fish in delicate sauces to veal Normandy style and Javanese steaks marinated in soy sauce and wine. Closed Sundays, Mondays, the last week in June, the month of October, and 2 weeks in January. 43 Charminster Rd. (phone: 291019). Expensive.

Crust – Set in a split-level building furnished with cane furniture and ferns, this is the place for shellfish from local boats; the chef cooks lobster, scallops, mussels, crab, and fresh vegetables to order. Service is sometimes leisurely, but there is a good choice of reasonably priced wines, including some from Australia. Open daily for lunch and dinner. Bourne Ave., on the square (phone: 21430). Moderate.

Fishnets – Scandinavian smorgasbord in a picturesque old mill: One fixed price covers the whole evening. Closed Sundays and Mondays. The Quay, Poole (phone: 670066). Moderate.

Solent – The restaurant at the Bournemouth International Centre allows diners to watch the waves in Poole Bay, as well as the artificial waves in the center's own pool, while tucking into meat and two vegetables. Closed Sunday evenings. Exeter Rd. (phone: 22122). Moderate.

Zorbas – Highly recommended for its varied Greek menu and Aegean ambience, this restaurant is open for dinner daily, except Mondays. 218 Old Christchurch Rd. (phone: 28125). Moderate.

Poets Corner – For those who like music and dancing while they dine, this hotel restaurant lays it on every night except Sunday. The food is plain English. County Hotel, Westover Rd. (phone: 22385). Moderate to inexpensive.

Fatty Arbuckle's – "Giant" portions are available here to satisfy the appetites expected of American diners. Open daily for lunch and dinner. 146 Old Christchurch Rd. (phone: 293355). Inexpensive.

Flossies & Bossies – An unusual combination of a vegetarian restaurant, offering good fresh food and take-out, with a French-style bistro. Closed Sundays. 73 Seamoor Rd., Westbourne (phone: 764459). Inexpensive.

Henry's – Its health food, vegetarian, and strict vegan menus cater to those on special diets. Closed Sundays and for dinner on Mondays. 6 Lansdowne Rd. (phone: 297887). Inexpensive.

Salad Centre – All home cooking, concentrating on vegetarian and health food recipes. Open for lunch and dinner in the summer; lunch and snacks in the winter. Closed Sundays. Post Office Rd. (phone: 21720). Inexpensive.

Seashells – A good bistro for devotees of fresh seafood. Closed Mondays. 34 Panorama Rd., Sandbanks (phone: 700610). Inexpensive.

SHARING A PINT: Bournemouth is not really a "pubby" place, since wine bars such as *Alcatraz* (Post Office Rd.), *Cruisers* (on the triangle), and a trio on Old Christchurch Road seem to have taken over. For picture-postcard inns with Old World character, it is necessary to drive out into the Dorset countryside or head for the nearby New Forest. The *Old Barn Farm Inn,* Three Legged Cross, Wimborne, 12 miles away, has a skittle alley. The *Old Beams* (Salisbury Rd., Ibsley), serves country beers, and the *Royal Oak* (North Gorley, near Fordingbridge), overlooks a duck pond. Another *Royal Oak,* this one at Okeford Fitzpaine, Blandford, 24 miles from Bournemouth through delightful country, serves magnificent pub grub with its ales. *Scott Arms,* on a hilltop at Kingston on the Isle of Purbeck, looks out over Poole Harbour and the ruin of Corfe Castle. Back in Bournemouth, the *Inn in the Park,* Pinewood Rd., near Branksome Dene Chine, is a family-owned house serving real ale. For a family outing, take A35 out of Bournemouth for Hinton St. Michael and the *Oak,* which serves not only pints of real ale but afternoon teas as well, and has a model railway and a children's room.

BRIGHTON

Brighton straddles 7 miles of breezy English Channel coast, and although it is England's oldest and most famous seaside resort, it is also a colorful cosmopolitan town in its own right, with great character, style, and vitality. No winter ghost town this; it bustles all year-round.

Brighton has never been prim. In less permissive days, when an illicit weekend was still naughty, Brighton was the place for it. Only an hour's train journey from London left the maximum time available for a romantic interlude in one of the numerous private and discreet (though distinctly unromantic) hotels. Famous men kept their mistresses here in elegant bay-fronted houses bordering quiet seaview squares. The city people brought their manners, fashions, and entertainments with them and nicknamed their coastal capital London-on-Sea. This liberal attitude lingers. Brighton has more than its fair share of amusements, hotels, restaurants, theaters, pubs, shops, and sports facilities.

None of this happened by chance, for Brighton was established by one of the greatest eccentrics of all time — the Prince Regent who eventually became King George IV of England. This spoiled, wayward, and extravagant libertine first visited Brighton in 1783, lured by the new fashion for sea bathing hailed as a cure-all by another eccentric, Dr. Richard Russell of nearby Lewes. The prince loved the place and promptly set about building the most exotic palace in Europe, just across the fields from the narrow, cobbled streets that once made up the original medieval fishing town of Brighthelmstone.

Famous worldwide for its bizarre beauty, the Royal Pavilion he conjured up sits like a creamy Oriental fantasy in the middle of a formal English garden. Outside, it resembles a Mogul palace bedecked with minarets, onion domes, terraces, and trellises; inside, the decor carries a fancy for lavish chinoiserie to the limit. It became the hub of the Prince Regent's glittering and cultured social circle, but not everyone thought it beautiful. Wags at the time not only commented on its onion domes but also referred to turnips and a "considerable number of bulbs of the crown-imperial, the narcissus, the hyacinth, the tulip, the crocus, and others." To one critic it seemed the dome of St. Paul's had gone to Brighton and pupped. When the Prince Regent became king in 1820, he lost interest in the completed palace, but his successor, King William IV, enjoyed summers here; Queen Victoria stayed here, too, though reportedly was not amused.

The Royal Pavilion set the tone for the future: Regency Brighton was extravagant and gay. The narrow streets of the fishing village became the home of hostelries, restaurants, and boutiques. Theaters, music halls, parks, and gardens sprouted around the Pavilion, and Brighton became the country's most fashionable resort, graced by a splendid pier at each end of the seafront.

Its popularity has continued from those Regency days. Although most of its 3 million yearly visitors now come only for the day or weekend instead of the traditional fortnight, a new university and arts college, an impressive new yachting marina, and a growing convention trade have all combined to add another dimension to the town, making it far more vital and cultured than most resorts. Brighton also has a distinct cosmopolitan flavor, thanks to its proximity to the Continent. French, German, Italian, Spanish, and Scandinavian students were quick to take advantage of Brighton, using it as a first base for their English-language schooling.

Most visitors still head directly for the beaches, but these are for the hardy rather than the knowledgeable sun worshiper. The shorefront consists of shingle stones rather than soft sand, and the tides can be strong, fueled by bracing breezes. To the west the beaches are cleaner, quieter, and fringed by the lawns of Brighton's stately and (dare one say it) staid neighbor, Hove.

The central beaches are boisterous, friendly, and the first to become crowded with families. Here are the amusement arcades, bumper cars, fish and chip cafés, cockles and whelks stalls, paddling pools, putting greens . . . in short, all the slightly sleazy glories of the traditional English seaside resort that are not to be missed. The crowning glory of this candy-floss (cotton candy) mile is the Palace Pier, complete with café, fishing platforms, and boat rides as well as endless slot machines and fun fair thrills. Sadly, the West Pier — far prettier but less well placed for attracting day-trippers — has been closed for some time, although plans to restore it are under way.

To the east, past the center of town, England's famous white cliffs begin their gradual climb toward Dover. The beaches become rockier and narrower and virtually disappear at high tide. But at low tide they are a delight for shrimp catchers and seapool ponderers. The quaint and largely unspoiled village of Rottingdean, 4 miles east of the center of Brighton in the gentle, rolling hills of the Sussex Downs, is the perfect focal point for these uncommercialized, untamed beaches that still belong to the true sea lover.

Lining Brighton's main seafront and stretching into spacious garden squares behind it are hundreds of hotels and guesthouses, large and small, good and bad. Most are in Regency style with bay fronts, balconies, and wrought-iron trimmings, but there are some good modern hotels as well, a result of the thriving conference trade. Beyond the seafront, the heart of the town lies focused on the narrow streets of the original village and the shopping streets that grew up around it and the Royal Pavilion. Cosmopolitan Brighton lives in these "Lanes," with art shops, bookstores, boutiques, antiques stalls, and the best restaurants, cafés, pubs, and wine bars. There's something for every taste and pocketbook here, and the whole area of the Lanes is perfect for people-watching or browsing. Residents use this part of town as much as visitors, even in high summer, and if prices are a little inflated, perhaps the atmosphere is worth it!

Real local color is still farther afield, however, and is very easy to miss. It centers on Gloucester Road and Kensington Gardens, in the area between Brighton's railway station and the Dome. This whole section was once nearly a slum until a timely preservation order made it trendy again. Now the little flat-fronted laborers' houses are snapped up by aspiring executives who commute to London. It is also the main student quarter and the starting point for many of the newest fashions, and it is certainly the best place for spotting the real eccentrics or one of the many famous actors who live or retire here. It is still possible to find bargains in the junk shops, and the local pubs and cafés may be scruffy, but they're full of interesting people.

Between this highly metropolitan scene and the seaside razzmatazz, Brighton offers a full range of entertainments, holiday sports, and sights. Few visitors have sufficient time to see it all, let alone the beautiful surrounding Sussex countryside. But the beauty of this lovely, liberal place is that you can spend as little as a day or as much as a year here and still come away satisfied.

BRIGHTON AT-A-GLANCE

SEEING THE CITY: The best view is from the end of the Palace Pier, which is at the junction of Marine Parade and the Old Steine. On the clearest days you can see the whole sweep of the coast from Worthing to Beachy Head. To the west, the Peace Statue marks the boundary of Brighton and the start of Hove Lawns. To the east is the impressive seawall of the Marina with the white cliffs above. In between is the entire Brighton seafront. Don't neglect the pier itself, a splendid Victorian structure of iron and steel, wood and glass, lined with amusement halls, slot machines, sun decks, fishing platforms, and endless candy-floss (cotton candy) and hot doughnut stalls. The Palace Pier is open every day of the year, though hours depend on the season.

For a spectacular, if expensive, night view, hotels such as the *Metropole* or the *Norfolk,* both on King's Road, have rooftop rooms for dinner and dancing. After attending a concert at the *Brighton Centre,* stop in at its less expensive *Skyline* restaurant, which also has a very good view.

SPECIAL PLACES: You'll be doing a lot of walking — browsing through the old quarter, ambling along the seafront promenade, visiting the dazzling Brighton Pavilion — within a fairly centralized area of an otherwise sprawling town. For the sights outside the center, take the bus, unless something more characteristic, such as the electric railway or the open-top excursion buses mentioned below, is indicated.

CENTRAL BRIGHTON

Royal Pavilion – The creation of Brighton's prime mover and shaker, the prince regent who became King George IV of England. It was begun modestly in 1786 and was rebuilt in its present extravagant form by the English architect John Nash (who also laid out Regent's Park and Regent Street in London and redesigned Buckingham Palace) from 1815 to 1822. The state and private apartments are arranged with superb Regency and Chinese furniture and works of art, including many original pieces on loan from Queen Elizabeth II.

The showpiece of the Regency Exhibition, now at the Pavilion year-round, is the spectacular Banqueting Room, set with silver, porcelain, and glass from the period and containing what is probably the best collection of gold plate in all of England. Other marvelous rooms include the Saloon, the North and South Drawing Rooms, the King's Apartments, and the Great Kitchen, which has the original mechanical spits, over 500 pieces of copperware, and tables showing the preparation of a banquet. The magnificent Music Room, tragically destroyed by fire in 1975, has been restored. The Royal Pavilion Lawns have deck chairs and regular summer performances by the *Pavilion Trio* band. The Royal Pavilion is also the scene of some of the musical events of the *Brighton Festival,* held in May. Admission charge. As we went to press, the Royal Pavilion was undergoing extensive restoration, and some rooms may be temporarily closed in 1990. Open daily from 10 AM to 5 PM (6 PM in summer).Town center, above the Old Steine (phone: 603005).

The Lanes – The roughly square mile of narrow, paved alleys that made up the original village can be visited only on foot. This area is Brighton's Old Town, and it's full of atmosphere and character, with countless shops for buying or browsing, including particularly good ones for books or antiques. Shop around to find the best price, however, especially if you're looking at antique jewelry. Entrances to the Lanes are all clearly marked, and the easiest to spot are on East Street, North Street, Ship Street, and Middle Street. Look for Duke's Lane, just off Ship Street, cunningly created out of backyards and filled with boutiques. Brighton Square, another of the more modern additions, is the center of the Lanes, with benches and a café-bar ideal for watching the world go by, continental style. Guided walking tours, which last about 1 hour, are available throughout the year. They depart from the Tourist Information Centre (phone: 23755).

King's Road – This is the main seafront road. Steps and slopes descend from it to the central beaches and the lower promenade with cafés, amusement halls, and all the traditional seaside entertainment. Fish and chips wrapped in newspaper, jellied eels, peanuts, ice cream, cotton candy, and Brighton rock candy are the things to eat, washed down with a pot of tea that will be served on a tin tray for transporting to the beach. It's inexpensive and very cheerful, but rent a deck chair because there are bits of tar on the pebbles. The Palace Pier end of the King's Road is most rowdy. Opposite the beach at East Street, the Old Fish Market is used for mending nets, and fishermen sell their wares from the beach, about 100 yards away. The Beach Deck near the *Grand* hotel is another entertainment area with outdoor concerts and games for children. Toward Hove, the scene becomes more sedate, with singsong pubs replaced by boating ponds and putting greens. For grass instead of stony beaches, try the Lawns at Hove.

Volk's Railway and Peter Pan's Playground – Britain's first public electric railway opened in 1883 and still runs along the edge of Brighton's easterly beaches. The track starts 200 yards east of Palace Pier and extends 1½ miles to the western perimeter of the Marina. The ride is inexpensive, and passengers travel in little wooden carriages with open sides and yellow roofs. Take it out to the Marina, then stroll back at sea level along Madeira Drive, passing *Peter Pan's Playground and Fun Fair.* The alternative is to return via the high-level Marine Parade with its ornate Victorian ironwork — the walk is quieter and gives better views. There is a temperamental lift opposite *Peter Pan's*; don't rely on it to work. *Volk's Railway* runs from late March to late September and during the Christmas period; Peter Pan's Playground is open from Easter through October.

Brighton Art Gallery and Museum – Close to the gardens of the Royal Pavilion and housed in buildings originally intended as stables for the palace, the gallery contains Brighton's fine collection of Old Masters and English watercolors and a good collection of pottery and porcelain. It also has the most important collection of 20th-century continental and English decorative art in the country. Worth seeing as well — the history of Brighton's seaside and the inspired *Costume Museum.* Closed Mondays. Church St. (phone: 603005).

Brighton Centre – One of Europe's largest conference and exhibition complexes, the Centre also hosts major concerts and entertainment. There's the *Skyline* restaurant, a cocktail bar that overlooks the English Channel, and facilities for banquets and dances. King's Rd. (phone: 203131; box office: 202881).

Brighton Marina Village – This ambitious construction, the largest yachting marina in Europe, was built against the odds of gale force winds and tumultuous seas and was opened in May 1979, by the queen. Immense breakwaters protect the inner harbor and have an enviable record for fishing catches. The marina has berths for nearly 2,000 yachts, as well as a Marina Village development with restaurants, bars, and bistros surrounding a pleasant piazza where visitors can sip drinks and watch the world go by. Open daily from 9 AM until dusk. Reach it by *Volk's Railway,* any of the city's open-top buses, or by car — there is good parking. Admission charge. Marine Dr., Black Rock, 1½ miles east of the Palace Pier (phone: 693636).

St. Nicholas's Churchyard – Brighton is full of quiet green corners tucked away out of sight of the main roads and easy to miss. St. Nicholas's Churchyard is one of the prettiest and is perfectly placed for a rest after shopping in nearby Western Road. It's a short walk up the steep hill of Dyke Road (which starts just above the Clock Tower) to the shallow brick steps that lead into the peaceful grounds surrounded by the gray flint walls characteristic of the area. The church itself is not always open but has a 12th-century Norman font and some excellent stained glass windows. The top end of the churchyard leads into a small park.

ENVIRONS

Preston Manor – Two miles out from the Old Steine along the main London Road is this charming 18th-century country house set in beautiful parkland. It has original furnishings of the 18th to 20th centuries, including some fine silver and paintings, all arranged as they would have been during the life of the family that owned it. Open Tuesdays through Sundays from 10 AM to 5 PM; closed Mondays, except bank holidays. Admission charge. Buses No. 5a or No. 5b from the Old Steine take about 10 minutes (phone: 552101).

Booth Museum of Natural History – Not too far from Preston Manor, this is an entirely different kind of museum. It houses a large collection of British birds, stuffed and displayed in their natural habitats, an exhibit of both British and exotic butterflies, an exhibit of skeletons illustrating evolution, and a Geology of Sussex gallery. Open weekdays except Thursdays from 10 AM to 5 PM, Sundays from 2 PM to 5 PM. Admission charge. 194 Dyke Rd., close to the Seven Dials (phone: 552586).

British Engineerium – Various Victorian steam engines — and the impressive Easton and Anderson steam engine of 1876 — puff efficiently away every Sunday in the engine houses of this museum. A huge number of Victorian mechanical inventions and other engineering exhibits are displayed in the restored 19th-century water pumping station. Open daily except Christmas from 10 AM to 5 PM. Admission charge. Nevill Rd., Hove, 3 miles from Brighton center (phone: 559583).

Stanmer Park – A natural park in the downland of Sussex is the setting for a village preserved as it was at the turn of the century. There are farmyards, a duck pond, a woodland park, and a rural museum that's open Sundays and Thursdays in summer; most other parts are open daily. Lewes Rd., 4 miles northeast of Brighton center, just before the University of Sussexcampus.

Devil's Dyke – This famous beauty spot is 700 feet above sea level. The devil is supposed to have dug a chalk pit here to let in the sea and drown the pious folk of Sussex. The attempt failed, but the view is spectacular. Near Poynings, 8 miles from Brighton center.

Charleston Farmhouse – This 18th-century building was the favorite country retreat of the Bloomsbury group of artists, writers, and intellectuals during the 1920s and 1930s. Regular visitors to the house in its heyday included Virginia Woolf, economist John Maynard Keynes, Benjamin Britten, T. S. Eliot, and Bertrand Russell. The house was fully restored by Vanessa Bell (Virginia Woolf's sister) and Duncan Grant. Open Wednesdays, Thursdays, Saturdays, and Sundays from April through October. Admission charge. Firle, 6 miles east of Lewes (phone: 0321-83265).

■ **EXTRA SPECIAL:** When the weather allows, open-top excursion buses run along the seafront to Rottingdean, a picturesque Sussex village set on the cliff tops in downland countryside. Steps and slopes lead to the undercliff walk edging narrow rocky beaches and to the open-air saltwater swimming pool — a sun trap that catches reflections off the white cliffs above it. A very pretty High Street has some good pubs and curio shops as well as the general stores typical of a small village. The *Plough Inn* is on the village green. Rudyard Kipling lived in Rottingdean, and adjoining his house on the green is the *Grange,* a small art gallery and museum that has displays of his letters and books as well as frequent temporary exhibitions. *The Grange* is open Mondays, Tuesdays, Thursdays, and Saturdays from 10 AM to 5 PM, Sundays from 2 PM to 5 PM (phone: 31004). Rottingdean village is 5 miles east of Brighton, easily reached by several buses, including the open-top ones.

SOURCES AND RESOURCES

TOURIST INFORMATION: The main tourist information center is at Marlborough House, 54 Old Steine, Room 19, near North St. (phone: 23755). There is an information kiosk open in the summer only on King's Rd. opposite West St. Hove's tourist information centers are at the Town Hall, Norton Rd. (phone: 775400) and at *King Alfred Leisure Center,* Kingsway (phone: 720371). All three carry books, maps, guides, and leaflets. The British Tourist Authority's *Guide to Brighton* (about 30¢) gives a brief outline of attractions and lists accommodations. It has an adequate map, but a better one will cost about 85¢, or there are various street-by-street guides for about $1.50, all available at bookstores and newsstands. *In and Around Sussex* (75¢) is good for attractions up to 30 miles from Brighton. There is also a guide for disabled visitors. The information center distributes all of these.

Local Coverage – The *Brighton Evening Argus* is on sale everywhere from noon on, usually with a good entertainment section.

Telephone – The area code for Brighton is 0273.

GETTING AROUND: Central Brighton is ideal for walking — the best parts are all fairly close together. Outside the main center, the town gets hilly.

Airport – Gatwick Airport is 24 miles north of Brighton, and trains operate between the two (about a 40-minute journey). There are also buses and express coaches. For information, call 0293-28822.

Bus – The best way to get around both the town and the county. Three private companies (*Brighton and Hove Buses, Southdown Services,* and *Brighton and Hove Bus and Coach Company*) operate from either the Pool Valley bus station (schedules and ticket offices are here) or the Old Steine. Some buses require the exact fare, so take loose change with you or buy a Travelcard for unlimited weekly travel in the Brighton area ($12 from any post office or at the bus station). A MasterRider card allows unlimited travel on all buses within a 35-mile radius of the city (about $25 per week). Regular local fares start at 40¢/25p. For information on local, regional, and long-distance services, call the Travel Enquiry Service at 206666.

Car Rental – All main firms are represented, but traffic is congested, and car parking is scarce and by meter in the center. Unless you're planning an excursion, you're better off without a car.

Sightseeing Tours – Brighton offers a taxi guide service with drivers who take parties of 4 in each car for tours of the town and surrounding countryside. For details, phone Jim Fleet at 304321.

Taxi – There are reliable taxi ranks at the railroad station and at the intersection of East and North streets. You may be able to hail a cab in the street, and they are good at responding to telephone calls. To order one, phone *Streamline Cars* at 27282.

Tourbus – From mid-June to mid-September, guided tours aboard double-decker buses provide a good introduction to the city. Tickets and timetables are available at the tourist information center.

SPECIAL EVENTS: The *Brighton Festival* in May provides a full program of music, theater, dance, and other entertainment, all detailed in the festival program available from February on. For information, write to the Brighton Festival Office, Marlborough House, 54 Old Steine, Brighton, East Sussex BN1 1EQ, England.

The *London to Brighton Veteran Car Run* takes place the first Sunday in November. Antique cars — the "Old Crocks" — make their annual pilgrimage from Hyde Park Corner in London to Madeira Drive in Brighton in celebration of the day in 1896 when a law requiring all motor cars to be preceded by a man waving a red flag was finally dropped. A *Historic Commercial Vehicle Rally,* every year in May, is a runner-up to the Old Crocks. Trucks, fire engines, ambulances, and the like take part.

MUSEUMS: In addition to those mentioned in *Special Places,* there are several other museums of interest.

Aquarium and Dolphinarium – Performing dolphins in the 1,000-seat dolphinarium and a varied display of freshwater, marine, and tropical fish, sea lions, and turtles in the mock Gothic underground galleries of Britain's largest aquarium. Other attractions include a flight simulator and an indoor children's adventure playground. Marine Parade (phone: 604233).

Hove Museum of Art – Coins, medals, watches, dolls, miniatures, plus a good modern exhibition. 19 New Church Rd., Hove (phone: 779410).

Pastimes – A collection of seaside postcards featuring the work of Mabel Lucy Atwell, the queen of Seaside Postcards, and of Donald McGill, the undisputed king are here. Located in the center of town in one of its oldest houses. Tours on Friday, Saturday, Sunday, and Monday afternoons from 2 to 5 PM April through October; Sunday afternoons November through March. 22 Charles St. (phone: 687183).

SHOPPING: Churchill Square is Brighton's pride — a new, modern precinct with all the major chain stores including *Habitat* (called *Conran's* in the states), the furniture and housewares store. It's next to the original shopping street off Western Road, near its eastern end. In the vicinity of Churchill Square, Western Road runs into North Street, giving almost 2 miles of prime shopping; the inexpensive and cheerful shops and stalls of Gardner Street, Bond Street, and the Lanes lead off North Street. Best buys are antiques, bric-a-brac, secondhand books, and local paintings and crafts, plus traditional English glass, china, and woolens. Most shops stay open until 8 PM on Thursdays.

Avison's Belgian Chocolates – Morello cherries, hazelnut pralines, and specialty chocolates tempt the eye and the mouth in an enticing window display. 19 Preston St. (phone: 28015).

Friends – A fascinating leather shop, either for buying things ready-made or the materials to make them yourself. The store also does first class repairs on all leather goods. 29 Bond St. (phone: 27607).

Graffiti – An assortment of brightly colored novelty gifts — including cards, bags, notepaper, and balloons. 17 Cranbourne St. (phone: 27777).

Hanningtons – The smartest store in town, selling furniture, china, and glass as well as men's and women's clothing. North St. (phone: 29877).

Colin Page Books – A rare antiquarian bookshop with some precious volumes. 36 Duke St. (phone: 25954).

Lawleys – Good for china and glass. 25 North St. (phone: 26068).

Pecksniff's Bespoke Perfumery – Bath salts, perfumes, soaps, skin care products, and a wide range of self-serve potpourri. 45–46 Meeting House La. (phone: 28904).

Jo Webb – An unusual collection of old and new music boxes in every shape and size. Prince Albert St. (no phone).

SPORTS: You can wear yourself out at the *King Alfred Leisure Centre* playing badminton or table tennis, bowling, swimming in the palm-fringed pool, scooting down the waterslides called flumes, or taking a sauna, then finishing off in the café or bar. Open all year. Kingsway, Hove (phone: 734422).

Cricket – For a modest entry fee you can watch a match — called a fixture — at the *Sussex County Cricket Ground,* Eaton Rd., Hove. The local tourist office has a calendar of fixtures.

Fishing – Good catches are sea whiting, mackerel, occasionally plaice, and very occasionally cod. The best place to fish is at the free *Brighton Marina* (phone: 693636). During the summer, only angling club members can fish from the Palace Pier: Try your luck at the groynes (breakwaters) instead. Those toward Hove, where there are fewer boats and swimmers, are preferable. No charges or permits for this.

Golf – The *East Brighton Golf Club,* Roedean Rd., has one of the best courses in the area, with magnificent views over sea, downs, and Marina. Visitors are welcome. Several buses from the Old Steine pass it (phone: 603989). The municipal *Hollingbury Park Golf Club,* Ditchling Rd., has 18 reasonable holes open to all. The No. 26 bus from the Old Steine takes you right there (phone: 552010). For a more casual game, try the two pitch-and-putt courses on either side of the Roedean school on the way to Rottingdean. You can rent clubs, balls, and tees, and hit away happily without embarrassment.

Greyhound Racing – *Coral Stadium,* Nevill Rd., Hove, has races three times a week from 7:45 PM. Telephone 204601 or 204605 for a table in the excellent restaurant that overlooks the course.

Horse Racing – The *Brighton Races* meet frequently between April and October at the *Brighton Racecourse,* Race Hill (phone: 0444-441111). Admission charge.

Soccer – There's good support for the *Brighton and Hove Albion* — known locally as the *Seagulls.* Games are played from late August to mid-April at the *Brighton and Hove Albion Ground* on Goldstone Rd., Hove (phone: 739535).

Tennis – Twelve parks have public courts. The main ones are in *Preston Park,* ten hard courts in all, easily seen from the London Road. Another ten courts are on the other (west) side of the road, away from the main park in a section called the Rockery. There's no racquet rental, nor can you book any of the public courts. Just take a chance and turn up, but be prepared to wait during July and August.

THEATER: The *Theatre Royal,* New Rd. (phone: 27480), has pre-London runs and variety, with weekly changes in the program. Other productions are at the *Gardner Centre Theatre,* a modern theater-in-the-round at the University of Sussex, Falmer (phone: 685447).

MUSIC: You can hear all kinds. Big pop and rock concerts are at the 5,000-seat *Brighton Centre,* Russell Rd. (phone: 202881). The *Dome,* 29 New Rd., slightly smaller with 2,000 seats, stages classical, pop, rock, and variety events, including some with international celebrities (phone:

674357). Both have an Entertainments Line, which provides details of forthcoming performances (phone: 0898-800-6666). St. Peter's Church, London Rd., has occasional organ concerts, and several pubs have folk, jazz, and rock groups and informal sing-songs.

NIGHTCLUBS AND NIGHTLIFE: This tends to be bright, breezy, and informal, with the emphasis on the young and noisy. Apart from the pubs, which are crowded in summer, activity centers on *Kingswest,* an entertainment complex on King's Road close to the West Street intersection. It contains a restaurant complex and two night spots. *Busbys* (phone: 25899) is for the smartly dressed (no jeans) over-21 crowd. The music is live, usually pop and rock. The *Top Rank Suite* (phone: 732627) varies from night to night, sometimes live music, sometimes disco. Farther along the King's Road, the *Metropole* hotel's lively club, the *Metro,* is open until 2 AM (phone: 775432). The *Pink Coconut* (phone: 21628) on West Street is the South Coast's most exotic discotheque for the over-20's crowd. Check the *Argus* for details. There are four casinos: one in the *Metropole* hotel (phone: 775432), *Sergeant York's,* 88 Queen's Rd., near the station (phone: 26514), the *International Casino Club,* 6 Preston St. (phone: 725101), and *Hove Sporting Club,* 28 Fourth Ave., Hove (phone: 72026). Several hotels and restaurants have dinner dances or cabarets.

BEST IN TOWN

CHECKING IN: The best hotels are those with a sea view, and even inexpensive ones can be found overlooking the eastern or western ends of the beaches. At an expensive hotel a double room with private bathroom and TV set will cost about $180 and up for two, including breakfast, tax, and service. A moderate hotel will cost $90 to $120, and the simplest private hotel (guesthouse) will run from $40 to $60, but this may not include a private bathroom. The better hotels offer reduced weekly rates in late June, July, and early August, when there is no convention business in town, and many also offer year-round holiday (including weekend) bargains. (The *Brighton for All Seasons and All Reasons* brochure, available at the tourist information center, lists them all.) Do not turn up without a reservation from late August through early June, which is traditionally the prime convention season. There are also holiday flat-lets available with prices from $120 to $400 per flat per week, depending on the size. All telephone numbers are in the 0273 area code unless otherwise indicated.

Bedford – Tall, modern, spacious, comfortable, and a little impersonal, but one of the best in town, with 125 rooms. King's Rd. (phone: 29744). Expensive.

Grand – Right in the center of the seafront, this is the old and very attractive queen of Brighton hotels. Its Victorian architecture is at its best in the lobby and on the landings. Reopened in the fall of 1986, the hotel has undergone extensive restoration since the IRA bombing of 1984 and now features an indoor pool, sauna/solarium, fitness center, and nightclub. King's Rd. (phone: 21188). Expensive.

Granville – Several of the 25 rooms contain Jacuzzis, Greek baths, and four-poster beds. A solarium is also on the premises. *Trog's* restaurant, a separate entity below the hotel, serves imaginative French food and fine wines. 123–125 King's Rd. (phone: 26302). Expensive.

Metropole – A large, modernized period hotel, it has good facilities, including its own health club and casino, plus a garage. White columns and murals surround a beautiful indoor swimming pool. With an attached exhibition hall, and since it's the main conference hotel in Brighton, it's one of the first to fill up. King's Rd. (phone: 775432). Expensive.

Norfolk – Toward the Hove end of the seafront and recently reconstructed, it still sports its attractive and bright Regency exterior. An expansion has increased the room total to 117, and facilities now include a swimming pool, health club, and American-style cocktail bar, plus a rooftop nightclub and restaurant. King's Rd. (phone: 738201). Expensive.

Old Ship – On the seafront close to the Lanes, much of its original style and charm is intact, especially in the 200-year-old banquet room once used by the Prince Regent. The 155 rooms vary from simple singles to lavish delights with antique four-poster beds. King's Rd. (phone: 29001). Expensive.

Queens – Now under new ownership, this luxury hotel has 78 rooms, 12 suites, and a seaview restaurant. Extensive leisure facilities include a health club and a nightclub. 1–5 King's Rd. (phone: 21222). Expensive.

Ramada Renaissance – An exciting, modern structure on the seafront, with an airy, plant-filled atrium lounge. Its Leisure Club features a swimming pool and 2 restaurants — the *Promenade,* for hot buffet lunches, and the more formal *La Noblesse*). The hotel's *Le Pavillon* restaurant, located in the adjacent Bartholomew Square, serves savory pancakes and ice cream. King's Rd. (phone: 206700). Expensive.

Royal Crescent – One mile from the center, this 52-room hotel has a strong Regency flavor, a friendly atmosphere, and excellent views. It's close to the Kemptown area, with some interesting little shops nearby. 100 Marine Parade (phone: 606311). Expensive.

Wheeler's Sheridan – This is a landmark of red Edwardian brick at a noisy corner of the seafront, but its location is outweighed by its plushness — velvet, brass, and crystal — and atmosphere. Its 60 rooms are very popular with regular customers, so book ahead. 64 King's Rd. (phone: 23221). Expensive.

Royal Albion – Built in 1826, this hotel became one of the town's most fashionable properties during the 1920s. All 121 rooms overlook either the sea or Steine Gardens. Old Steine (phone: 29202). Expensive to moderate.

Lanes – This hotel has 42 rooms, all with bath; most have an excellent sea view. 71 Marine Parade (phone: 674231). Moderate.

Olde Place – If you can't stay here or prefer to be in the center of town, this traditional oak-beamed village inn (21 rooms) is still worth a visit for a meal. High St., Rottingdean (phone: 31051). Moderate.

Prince Regent – There are many small hotels in the elegant, airy square facing the West Pier. This one with 18 rooms was recently restored in full Regency style, and the accent is on friendly service. 29 Regency Sq. (phone: 29962). Moderate.

Le Flemings – Small (11 rooms) but enterprising, with a bar, comfortable furnishings, and a pretty courtyard. 12A Regency Sq. (phone: 27539). Inexpensive.

Marina House – Just a few yards from the seafront, this nicely furnished little hotel is run by a cheery husband and wife team. 8 Charlotte St. (phone: 605349). Inexpensive.

Preston Resort – Two miles from the town center, close to Preston Manor and Park, this is a good stop for the motorist. It's a modern, attractive 24-room hotel with parking, and it's close to the main London–Brighton Road. 216 Preston Rd. (phone: 507853). Inexpensive.

Twenty One – A tiny (7-room) Victorian house with a terrace, it has built a solid reputation as a fine hotel in a style reminiscent of a sophisticated private house. Lots of stairs, so don't arrive with heavy suitcases. Closed December to mid-January. 21 Charlotte St. (phone: 686450). Inexpensive.

EATING OUT: Brighton is fortunate to have a greater variety of restaurants than most cities its size. Just about every style of cooking is available, including the usual range of Indian, Chinese, and Italian, and better than average Greek. Local fish is delicious. There are some good spots with inexpensive fast food, and there's a healthy sprinkling of better restaurants with excellent and imaginative fare. At the less expensive restaurants you can still get a simple English three-course set meal for under $40 for two, excluding wine. In the moderate ones, a meal for two with a fair amount of skill in its preparation and presentation will cost up to $90, including house wine. The most expensive meals in town cost about $100 to $140, including wine, with service added. All telephone numbers are in the 0273 area code unless otherwise indicated.

English's Oyster Bar – If you can treat yourself well only once, do it here. The restaurant is 150 years old, converted from 400-year-old fishermen's cottages in the Lanes. Reservations necessary. Closed Sundays. 29–31 East St. (phone: 27980). Expensive.

French Connection – Once a Georgian fisherman's cottage, this is now an intimate and romantic restaurant known for its unusual French, English, and fish dishes. Service is especially friendly. Closed Sundays. 11 Little East St. (phone: 24454). Expensive.

Wheeler's Oyster Rooms – The seafood is unsurpassed, and it's served in Edwardian elegance. Reservations are necessary, since this is one of the oldest (1856) and best-known restaurants in the region. Open daily. 17 Market St. (phone: 25135). Expensive. The management here also runs *Wheeler's Sheridan Tavern,* a hotel restaurant serving similar fare. Open daily. 64 King's Rd. (phone: 28372). Expensive.

Fudges – On the seafront, in the basement of a grand Victorian building that was rescued from dereliction in 1984, and hugely popular for its good, traditional English fare, including salads, grills, and fish. Open daily for lunch and dinner. 127 King's Rd. (phone: 205852). Expensive to moderate.

Langan's Bistro – An offshoot of London's internationally famous celebrity eatery, it serves haute dishes at not-so-haute prices. 1 Paston Place (phone: 606933). Expensive to moderate.

Al Forno – Owned by two brothers (who also run *Al Duomo,* at 7 Pavilion Building; phone: 26741), this simple and crowded Italian place is great for pizza and pasta. Outdoor dining in summer. 36 East St. (phone: 24905). Moderate to inexpensive.

Le Grandgousier – This is tiny, too, and informal. Everyone shares one huge table and tucks into the simply cooked food. The choice is limited, but it's great fun and good value. Open daily, except Sunday lunch. 15 Western St. (phone: 772005). Moderate to inexpensive.

Lum Thai – The room is full of Thai ornaments that perfectly complement the food, which includes maize, chicken wings, and bamboo shoots; the chef was trained in Thailand and all the waiting staff are Thai. Special set menus at lunchtime. Open daily. 196 Church Rd., Hove (phone: 772072). Moderate to inexpensive.

Browns – The atmosphere is light, bright, and busy, with sanded floors, white walls, and palms. This is the best of the hamburger-spaghetti palaces, open every day with continuous service. 3–4 Duke St.(phone: 23501). Inexpensive.

Crusts – The kind of bistro now familiar on the British restaurant scene — decorated with plants, elegant coatstands, and bentwood chairs — serving hot, substantial, value-for-your-money food: burgers, baked potatoes, and salads. Bring your own wine (corkage charge) or visit *Crusts Wine Bar,* opposite. Open daily. 24 Market St. (phone: 26813). Inexpensive.

Food for Friends – Tulips on the tables, still lifes on the walls, plants hanging from the ceiling, classical music on the turntable, and delicious casseroles and wholesome salads served by a young, cheerful staff to a fast-moving (but never-ending) queue of students and Brightonites. Open daily. 17A–18 Prince Albert St. (phone: 736236). Inexpensive.

Themes – Owners Jon and Anne offer delicious English roast dishes as well as seafood (including smoked Scotch salmon) and a range of specials. The restaurant is tucked away in the heart of the Lanes. Closed Sunday evenings and Mondays for lunch. Reservations advised. Boyces St. (phone: 25195). Inexpensive.

SHARING A PINT: It's difficult to choose from the wide selection of pubs in Brighton. The *Belvedere,* 159 King's Rd. Arches, close to the Palace Pier, is a boisterous, beachside bar — don't dress up. The *Colonnade Long Bar,* New Rd., is next to the *Theatre Royal* and is used during intermissions; it has Victorian decor and a good selection of playbills. Don't miss *Cricketers* on Black Lion St., the town's oldest pub. The original parts, dating from 1549, include the stables and coachyard, and there are old mirrors and marble and brass tables. The *Bedford Tavern,* 30 Western St., is simple and unassuming; if you're passing by, pop in to see its collection of heraldry. *Dr. Brighton's,* on King's Rd. by Market St., is a traditional-looking pub with good, hot food. The *Druid's Head,* Market Pl., The Lanes, is an Old World pub with beams and decorative horse brasses. Once a smugglers' haunt, it now belongs to the fashionable young set. The *King and Queen,* Marlborough Pl., an amusing imitation of a Tudor beer garden, overlooks the Victoria Gardens. It's good for families — there's an aviary for diversion. The *Royal Pavilion Tavern,* Castle Sq., is a popular central pub with old oak panels and beams and extensive hot and cold snacks. In Rottingdean, the *Black Horse,* High St., is a genuine village pub, with a comfortable and friendly large bar and the original snug — the tiny bar for women.

BRISTOL

As described in the pages of Robert Louis Stevenson's *Treasure Island,* a wide-eyed visitor of a century or so ago could wander the docks of Bristol, sniffing in the smell of tar in the salt air, marveling at the figureheads of ships that had been far over the world and the "many old sailors, with rings in their ears, and whiskers curled in ringlets, and tarry pigtails, and their swaggering, clumsy sea-walk . . ." It was a scene that any movie mogul would have been proud to conjure up on a Hollywood back lot.

Naturally, Bristol looks like that no more. Now it's a large, modern, lively city with isolated patches of medieval antiquity reaching through the centuries. Walk along the quayside of the harbor today and see characteristic warehouses, old, deserted, and decaying until recently, now restored as museums and arts and exhibition centers. The once-busy freight yards and great cranes are now idle — poignant reminders of Bristol's former prowess as a great trading port — but these, too, are being restored to preserve an important part of the city's railway and dockside heritage. Pleasure craft, visiting naval warships, and even a few restored traditional sailing boats now grace the harbor, creating a striking scene that is further enhanced by the backdrop of Bristol's city center, dominated by the towers of the cathedral and, behind them, the university buildings.

Bristol had been an important port since the 11th century. During the Middle Ages, its merchants and seafarers traded in wine, stacking the wharves and cellars with Bordeaux from France, sherry from Spain, and port from Portugal. By the 15th century it was known for an enterprising maritime boldness that attracted sailors from Europe bent on discovery. John Cabot came from Italy, found backing by a local merchant, and set sail in 1497 to become the first explorer to reach the American mainland. The customs officer who awarded Cabot a pension was Richard Ameryck, and to this day some Bristolians believe that it was he, and not Amerigo Vespucci, who gave his name to the New World.

Cabot was followed by other explorers, then by thousands of early American settlers who stepped off European soil here and sailed to a new life. Having played a part in the discovery of America, Bristol did its share in developing it, financing colonization efforts, trading in Virginia tobacco and West Indian sugar. A less glorious chapter was getting involved in the black slave trade; the Bristol merchants grew fat on the proceeds from it, while the Quakers and John Wesley and his Methodists, who were all influential in the colonies, railed against it.

"All shipshape and Bristol fashion" is an English phrase meaning everything methodical and orderly, recalling the days when this West of England city was dominated by the masts of tall ships from all corners of the world.

In Bristol, unlike most other seafaring cities, the docks are in the heart of the town rather than at its edge. That the ships are no longer there is the result of an error of judgment on the part of the earliest Bristolians. The city grew at the confluence of the Avon and Frome rivers, 7 miles inland from where the Avon — which rises and falls with close to the highest tide in the world — flows out into the Severn estuary. Fear of piracy caused the medieval inhabitants to plant themselves far upstream, a less than ideal location that made docking a tricky business of picking the right moment to set out upriver or risk getting stuck in the mud at low tide. Even berthed ships were in danger of breaking up in the tidal sweep.

To remedy this, the city channeled the Avon into a new cut in the early 18th century, creating a "floating harbor" with a constant level of water for ships to tie up in. But by then, much transatlantic trade had already been lost to Liverpool. Ironically, the situation was not helped by the presence of Isambard Kingdom Brunel, the pioneering British engineer who built the largest vessels of his day, thereby inspiring even larger ones that couldn't make it up the Avon to Bristol. By the end of the 19th century, new docks had been built downstream at Avonmouth and Portishead, but, alas, they came too late to prevent the decline in Bristol's maritime fortunes.

The cityscape underwent further change as a result of World War II. The blitz of 1940–41 damaged some 9,000 buildings, including the medieval core. (The original castle that used the Avon and the Frome as its moat had been razed centuries before on the orders of Cromwell.) Throughout history the tallest structures in Bristol had been the spires and towers of churches, but with postwar reconstruction came the first tall office blocks. Now it is necessary to walk between walls of concrete and glass for a glimpse of the churches, as fine as those in any medieval city, and the other reminders of Bristol's heritage — remains of early monasteries and Georgian squares and terraces — that survive.

For many devotees, Bristol's most charming part is suburban Clifton, perched on the Clifton and Durdham Downs above the city and the Avon Gorge. Begun as a dormitory in the healthful high air for visitors to the Hot Well spa at the foot of the gorge, Clifton then became a fashionable place to live. The spa had only a brief moment of glory in the early 18th century (Bath was more popular), but Clifton was left with Georgian crescents to compete with those of Bath, and large, graceful Victorian villas. When the wealthy moved out early in this century, Clifton lost its cachet, but many of its houses have since been restored, and it is now a quiet residential quarter with shops and bistros and a villagelike atmosphere appealing to young sophisticates.

Still, Clifton is far from the reality of a commercial, manufacturing city of nearly half a million people. The more distant suburb of Filton, one of the largest aerospace capitals in the world and the hub of Bristol's aircraft industry (the supersonic *Concorde* came off the production line here), is closer to the old spirit of adventure, perhaps, but the heart of the city is really in the waterways, its most characteristic visual feature. Although life in the harbor is only the ghost of what it once was, the docks remain a museum of Britain's mercantile past.

BRISTOL AT-A-GLANCE

SEEING THE CITY: From the top of the Cabot Tower on Brandon Hill there is a spectacular bird's-eye view of the center of Bristol and much of the surrounding area. It's quite a climb, however, and the view is almost as good from the base of the tower. The panorama is dominated by church spires, venerable stone buildings, and waterways, and it provides a surprise. Bristol has a generous amount of open space for a city whose past has been linked so strongly with commercial and maritime matters, and you'll see a lot of greenery among the old buildings and new office blocks.

SPECIAL PLACES: The best starting point for exploring Bristol is the vast junction known to residents as the Centre. If it's not marked as such on your map, look for its boundaries: St. Augustine's Parade and Broad Quay to the west and east, Colston Avenue to the north, and the Bridgehead (or Quay Head) to the south, at the tip of St. Augustine's Reach. In recent years the Centre has been taken over by cars, but if you can bear the exhaust fumes and the incessant roar of traffic, you are well placed here to reach the older sections of town, the waterfront, the dignified buildings of College Green, and the shops of Park Street and Queens Road. Most buses to other parts of the city also stop here, and there are plenty of waiting taxis. A plaque on the Bridgehead commemorates the spot from where John Cabot set out on his historic voyage of discovery to the New World, and the park benches around the statue of Neptune provide a welcome chance for modern-day explorers to sit down while deciding in which direction to explore.

CENTRAL BRISTOL

Bristol Cathedral – The Cathedral Church of the Holy and Undivided Trinity was founded in the 12th century as an Augustinian monastery. The Norman chapter house, which dates from this earliest period, should not be missed. Other older parts are the 13th-century Elder Lady chapel and the 14th-century choir and Eastern Lady chapel (with the Jesse window), while the nave is the work of a Victorian architect faithful to the original style. Particularly interesting, if you have the time to study them, are the 16th-century misericords in the choir on which monks — who were not allowed to sit during services — leaned. They're beautifully carved and all different, some with serious and some with humorous scenes. Open daily from 8 AM to 6PM. College Green (phone: 264879).

Council House – This graceful, curved, 20th-century red brick building across the street from the cathedral is the headquarters of Bristol's municipal administration. The golden unicorns on either end of the roof are symbolic of the city; they are also found on its coat of arms. Since this is a working building, tours of the interior are by special arrangement and for groups only. College Green (phone: 266081).

Georgian House – Once the home of a merchant wealthy from West Indian trade, this is now a museum maintained as though the merchant and his family still lived in it. It was built in 1790, and the furnishings, all of local manufacture, are Georgian in period. Open daily except Sundays from 10 AM to 1 PM and 2 PM to 5 PM. 7 Great George St. (phone: 299771, ext. 237).

City Museum and Art Gallery – The major museum in the area, it has extensive collections in the fine and applied arts, archaeology and history, geology and natural history, but visitors pressed for time will find exhibits of Bristol blue — and green, amethyst, and white — glass not too far beyond the lobby. The building next door to the museum, looking much older than it is, is the 20th-century neo-Gothic Wills Memorial Building of the University of Bristol. It houses the 10-ton Great George bell, which sounds hourly in E flat. Open daily except Sundays from 10 AM to 5 PM. Queens Rd. (phone: 222000).

King Street – This cobbled street was laid out in the 1660s and remains one of the most picturesque in Bristol. The pink buildings at its western end are the Merchant Venturers' Almshouses, built in the 17th century for retired seamen. Next is the 18th-century Old Library, now a restaurant. Farther along, the Palladian Coopers' Hall, a guildhall built in 1743, has become the entrance to the *Theatre Royal,* since 1766 one of the leading stages in the country and the present home of the *Bristol Old Vic Company.* Several other 17th-century edifices line the street, which ends with a group of buildings as appealingly half-timbered and gabled as you'll see anywhere. Built in 1664, these houses eventually became *Ye Llandoger Trow,* an inn where Daniel Defoe is supposed to have met the man he transformed into Robinson Crusoe, and which still operates as a pub and restaurant. King Street stops at an original stretch of Bristol quayside known as the Welsh Back.

Corn Street – The four bronze "nails," or trading tables, on which 16th- and 17th-century merchants counted out their money ("paid on the nail") characterize this section of Bristol. The heart of the medieval city was at the crossing of Corn, Broad, High, and Wine Streets; the area later became Bristol's center of banking and commerce. Corn Street, especially, is an amalgam of worthy and workaday 18th- and 19th-century buildings. Two to compare are the Exchange (1743), behind the nails, designed by John Wood the Elder as a market and meeting place for merchants, and the ornately carved palazzo (1854) across from it, now Lloyd's Bank. Behind the Exchange is the St. Nicholas Market, a warren of stalls covered over in the 18th century and still going strong daily except Sunday. Several interesting churches include All Saints (Corn St.), with Norman foundations; *St. Nicholas's* (St. Nicholas St.), dating from the 1760s and now a museum; and Christ Church (Broad St.), an 18th-century replacement of an earlier church. (The mechanical men who strike the quarter hours on its clock were on the older building, too.) Walk to the end of Broad Street and you'll come to St. John's Gate, the only survivor of Bristol's nine medieval gateways.

John Wesley's New Room – In contrast to the other, imposing churches to be visited in Bristol, the world's first Methodist chapel is a spare and simple house of worship. John Wesley built it in 1739, and he and his brother preached here for 40 years. Their living quarters are upstairs. Open daily except Wednesdays and Sundays from 10 AM to 1 PM and 2 PM to 4 PM. 36 The Horsefair.

THE HARBOR

Bristol Maritime Heritage Centre – This striking, modern building was opened in 1985 and houses artifacts and displays that tell the city's maritime history and the SS *Great Britain*'s story. Open daily from 10 AM to 6 PM. Great Western Dock, Gas Ferry Rd., off Cumberland Rd. (phone: 260680).

SS *Great Britain* – Following the SS *Great Western,* the SS *Great Britain* was the second nautical accomplishment of Isambard Kingdom Brunel. When it floated out from Bristol in 1843, not only was it the first iron-hulled screw steamship in the world, it was also the largest liner on the seas. The *Great Western,* which had been the first transatlantic steam vessel, is no more; the *Great Britain,* fortunately, is. It was shipwrecked and abandoned in the Falkland Islands in 1886, and its return to the city in 1970 was a nostalgic and emotional occasion. It is now being restored at the British Maritime Heritage Centre dock, where it was built. Open daily from 10 AM to 6 PM in summer and to 5 PM in winter. Admission charge. Great Western Dock, Gas Ferry Rd., off Cumberland Rd. (phone: 20680).

St. Mary Redcliffe – The church Queen Elizabeth I described as "the fairest, goodliest, and most famous parish church in England" was built mostly in the 14th and 15th centuries near enough to the city docks to be a merchant seaman's last and first call at the beginning and end of a voyage. It is an outstanding example of Perpendicular architecture, and it positively presides over what has since become a rather dull stretch of the Bristol cityscape. Inside, the nave and choir soar to a ceiling ornamented with more than 1,200 carved and gilded bosses. As you enter, note the unusual hexagonal shape and the very pretty stained glass windows of the outer north porch, which dates from 1290, and the black marble pillars of the late-12th-century inner north porch, the oldest part of the church. Open 8 AM to 8 PM (6 PM in winter). Redcliffe Way.

CLIFTON

Clifton Suspension Bridge – Bristol's most famous landmark is another of Isambard Kingdom Brunel's achievements. The bridge has a 702-foot span, 245 feet above the high-water level of the limestone Avon Gorge, which is famous for rare trees and plants; although it adds an attractive focal point to the Clifton scene, it is entirely functional. Before it opened in 1864, people crossed the river in a basket on a cable. Since then, pilots have flown underneath it and suicides have been attempted (some successfully) from it. The city's favorite story is that of the young woman who jumped after a lover's quarrel in 1885 — she parachuted gently in her petticoats to a soft landing in the mud and lived to a ripe old age.

Clifton Cathedral – The Cathedral Church of Saints Peter and Paul is the headquarters of the Roman Catholic diocese of Clifton. Completed in 1973, it is considered an important work of contemporary church architecture, designed to reflect the most recent changes in the form of liturgical worship. Visitors are welcome inside to see its modern works of art. Open 7:30 AM to 10 PM. Visit the Tourism Information Center for details. Clifton Park (phone: 738411).

Clifton and Durdham Downs – Bristol's largest and most popular open space covers more than 400 acres on the north side of the city. Bristolians play football on the Downs in winter, cricket in summer, and walk on the green expanse year-round.

Zoological Gardens – The Bristol zoo is one of the best in Britain. It has more than 1,000 animals, birds, reptiles, and fish, but it is most famous for its white tigers. There are also extensive gardens. Open daily 9 AM (10 AM on Sundays) to 6 PM (5 PM in winter); closed Christmas Day. Admission charge. Clifton Down (phone: 738951).

ENVIRONS

Blaise Castle House Museum – Blaise Castle itself is nothing but a Gothic folly, a sham structure built in 1766 to decorate the grounds of this estate. *Blaise Castle House Museum,* set up in the estate's real 18th-century mansion, is a folk museum of costumes, toys, crafts, and other reminders of West Country life in days gone by. The landscaped grounds contain woodlands, walkways, the remains of an Iron Age hill fort, and a number of attractions for children. Open Wednesdays to Saturdays from 10 AM to 1 PM and 2 to 5 PM. Henbury, 4 miles northwest of Bristol (phone: 506789).

■ **EXTRA SPECIAL:** You can sample dockside Bristol easily enough on foot by walking from the Bridgehead along Narrow Quay, over the Prince Street Bridge and onto Prince's Wharf, beyond which is Wapping Wharf with the SS *Great Britain* at its far end. (A helpful *Maritime Walks* guidebook is available at the tourist information center.) Another choice is the ferrybus. During the season it plies the Floating Harbour from Narrow Quay, making various stops, including one at the *Great Britain.* A tour of the dockside pubs also operates during the summer.

SOURCES AND RESOURCES

TOURIST INFORMATION: The tourist information center at 14 Narrow Quay (phone: 260767) can supply brochures, maps, and general information. It's open weekdays from 9 AM to 5 PM and on Saturdays from 9 AM to 12:30 PM. For about 75¢, you can pick up the *Bristol Official Visitors Guide,* which is a comprehensive introduction to all aspects of the city and includes several walking tours to cover its sights. Other walking tour guides are available, including a "Walkabout" series on individual routes. *The Bristol Heritage Walk* brochure (about $1.50) describes a route that is marked on the streets it follows. From late April through September, try one of the regular walking tours led by Bristol's Corps of Guides. Visit the tourist information center for details. All walks cost about $1 and last approximately 1½ hours. The exact time of departure is posted outside the information center, at the Exchange, or near Neptune's statue at the Bridgehead.

Local Coverage – The morning *Western Daily Press* and the *Bristol Evening Post* are the two dailies, while the fortnightly *Venue* magazine covers what's on and where to go in and around the city.

Telephone – The area code for Bristol is 0272.

GETTING AROUND: You may want to take a bus or taxi to Clifton, but the rest of Bristol is walkable, with one word of warning. Traffic speeds around and out from the Centre in all directions, and little provision seems to have been made for pedestrians to interrupt it. There are a few traffic lights (all pedestrian operated) and a few striped zebra crossings (where the pedestrian has the right of way once he or she steps from the curb), but you'll see many a Bristolian paused on the verge of a dash at the sight of any break in the two-way onslaught.

Airport – Bristol's Lulsgate Airport, about 6 miles southwest of the city on A38 (phone: 027587-4441), has flights to Dublin, Cork, Belfast, Channel Islands, Glasgow, Cardiff, Isle of Man, and other domestic destinations. In summer, 40 or more flights per week depart Lulsgate for the Continent.

Bus – The *Bristol City Line* operates bus services within the city and throughout the surrounding area, including the inexpensive and friendly yellow minibuses that run approximately every 10 minutes, and also conducts sightseeing tours during the summer months. Most city bus routes include a stop in the Centre; long-distance coaches operate out of the bus station on Marlborough Street, north of the Broadmead shopping center. (For schedule information, phone: 553231 from 8 AM to 9 PM, or 558211 for tour details.)

Car Rental – The major national and international companies are represented, including *Avis* (phone: 292123), *Budget* (phone: 277614), and *Hertz* (phone: 294044).

Taxi – You'll have no trouble getting a taxi in the Centre for the trip out, but for the return, you'll probably have to call one. Numerous cab companies are listed in the local yellow pages.

Train – Temple Meads Railway Station is at Temple Gate in the city center. (Visitors may want to visit the display on the history of Bristol here). Frequent trains connect it with London's Paddington Station, South Wales, and Britain's major cities. The trains from London Paddington are among the fastest and most efficient in the country (journey time: 90 minutes). Several services also stop at Parkway Station, on Bristol's northern outskirts; travel time is about 10 minutes shorter. For information, call Temple Meads Railway Station, Temple Gate (phone: 294255), from 8 AM to 10 PM.

SPECIAL EVENTS: The water and wine that played such a part in Bristol's past come together fittingly 1 week in July in the *World Wine Fair and Festival,* the city's biggest annual event. Exhibitors from all over the world come to the Bristol Exhibition Complex, two refurbished warehouses on the Floating Harbour just below the Bridgehead; stands are set up for visitors to sample wines not usually available for general consumption, and fireworks displays light up the city docks. The docks are also the focus of other events, including the *Bristol Boat Show* in April or May, the *Bristol Grand Prix* powerboat race in June, and the *Bristol Harbour Regatta and Rally of Boats* in July. In August, the sky over Ashton Court Estate, 825 acres of park on the other side of the Clifton Suspension Bridge, is full of multicolored hot-air balloons taking part in the *Bristol International Balloon Fiesta.*

MUSEUMS: In addition to those discussed in *Special Places,* Bristol has a number of other interesting museums.

Bristol Industrial Museum – Machinery, especially that connected with transport — including horse-drawn carriages and a model of the Concorde cockpit — in a transit shed in the city docks. The Bristol Harbour Railway links the museum to the Maritime Heritage Center. Other steam engines and rolling stock are on display outside the museum. Open Saturdays through Wednesdays from 10 AM to 5 PM, but closed from 1 to 2 PM. Prince's Wharf (phone: 299771, ext. 290).

Exploratory – Recently moved to its new home in Brunel's magnificent engine sheds at Temple Meads, the best thing about this science museum is its series of "hands-on" experiments. Open Wednesdays through Saturdays, 10 AM to 5 PM. Admission charge. Temple Meads.

Harvey Wine Museum – An illustration of how wine is made, plus collections of old wine bottles, glasses, decanters, and silver decanter labels. The well-known wine company has set up the museum, which can be visited by appointment, Mondays through Fridays. 12 Denmark St. (phone: 277661).

National Lifeboat Museum – Britain's only museum dedicated to housing and restoring rescue vessels. On the quayside of the historic harbor, next to the Industrial Museum (phone: 213-389).

St. Nicholas Church Museum – A church converted to an ecclesiastical museum of silver, vestments, and church art, including an altarpiece by William Hogarth. Open daily except Sundays from 10 AM to 5 PM. Admission is free, but there is a charge to do a rubbing in the Brass Rubbing Centre downstairs. 20St. Nicholas St. (phone: 299771, ext. 243).

Red Lodge – A 16th-century house preserved with its 18th-century alterations and furnishings of both periods, including superb, carved paneling and stone fireplaces. Open daily, except Sundays, from 10 AM to 1 PM and 2 to 5 PM. Park Row (phone: 299771, ext. 236).

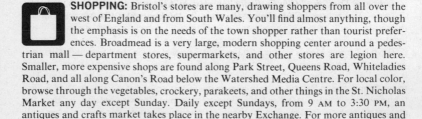

SHOPPING: Bristol's stores are many, drawing shoppers from all over the west of England and from South Wales. You'll find almost anything, though the emphasis is on the needs of the town shopper rather than tourist preferences. Broadmead is a very large, modern shopping center around a pedestrian mall — department stores, supermarkets, and other stores are legion here. Smaller, more expensive shops are found along Park Street, Queens Road, Whiteladies Road, and all along Canon's Road below the Watershed Media Centre. For local color, browse through the vegetables, crockery, parakeets, and other things in the St. Nicholas Market any day except Sunday. Daily except Sundays, from 9 AM to 3:30 PM, an antiques and crafts market takes place in the nearby Exchange. For more antiques and small boutiques, visit the Mall and its environs in Clifton. The Clifton Antiques Market, 26–28 the Mall, is open Tuesdays through Saturdays from 10 AM to 6 PM.

Alexander Gallery – Fine arts dealers and publishers. 122 Whiteladies Rd. (phone: 739582).

Banks of Bristol – Antiques reproduction specialists selling chairs, tables, and household goods. 71 Park St. (phone: 28306).

Barometer Shop – Specialists in barometers of all shapes and sizes, they also sell kits for making your own. Park Row (no phone).

Boules – One of several trendy clothes stores along Queens Rd. (phone: 264085).

Bristol Craft Centre – Jewelers, potters, weavers, leatherworkers, an embroiderer, and others market what they make on the same premises at 6 Leonard La., an exceedingly narrow passage from Corn to Small St., entered from the opening beside 31 Corn St. (phone: 23182).

Bristol Guild – All manner of arts and crafts shops sell their wares here, from kitchenware and decorative furnishings to basketware and pottery. The traditional (but hard to find) Bristol chocolates called Guilberts can also be purchased here. 66–70 Park St. (phone: 25548).

Les Chatteries – Health food galore as well as nuts, coffee, preserves, mustards, handmade chocolates, and their own brand of multiflavored ice cream. Canon's Rd. (phone: 20969).

City Museum and Art Gallery Shop – Handmade reproductions of Bristol blue glass are on sale here, as well as posters, prints, and other souvenirs. Queens Rd. (phone: 222000).

Debenham's – An excellent department store with goods from furs to furnishings. The Horsefair (phone: 291021).

Dingles – Also a department store, more exclusive than *Debenham's,* and with a noteworthy food hall. Queens Rd. (phone: 215301).

George's – Three very good bookshops, all on Park Street: No. 89 for general books, No. 81 for academic books, and No. 52 for fine arts books (phone: 276602).

Global Village – Unusual pottery, crafts, and wickerwork. Park St. (phone: 290963).

SPORTS: Five sports centers provide facilities for squash, badminton, bowls, and various team games. The largest of these is the *Whitchurch Sports Centre,* Bamfield, Whitchurch (phone: 833911), south of the city. Whitchurch is open daily and has four squash courts, an indoor bowling green, a fitness room, a sauna, and a bar. It is also the scene of spectator events such as basketball and hockey games and karate matches.

Cricket – The *Gloucestershire County Cricket Club* (phone: 46743) plays at the *County Ground,* Nevil Rd., from the end of April through early September.

Greyhound Racing – Call the *Bristol Stadium,* Stapleton Rd. (phone: 511919), for the latest racing schedule.

Rugby – The *Bristol Rugby Club* (phone: 514448) is based at the *Memorial Ground,* Filton Ave.; the *Clifton Rugby Club* (phone: 500445), at Cribb's Causeway.

Soccer – The *Bristol City Football Club* plays at Ashton Gate (phone: 632812); the *Bristol Rovers Football Club* plays at Twerton Park (phone: 511050). Most games are on Saturdays at 3 PM.

Swimming – Bristol has 10 indoor pools open daily (closing at noon on Sundays). The outdoor *Clifton Pool* at Oakfield Place, Clifton (phone: 737538), is open daily from July to early September.

THEATER: Bristol has made a name for itself in British theatrical history. The famous *Theatre Royal,* King St. (phone: 250250), opened in 1766, is the oldest continuously active theater in Britain. Since World War II it has been the home of the *Bristol Old Vic Company,* one of the most respected repertory groups in the land. The *Bristol Old Vic* does both classic and new plays, but if you have a choice, see a Shakespearean or other old comedy, because they're especially suited to the splendor of the Georgian setting. The company also plays at the *New Vic,* a second, modern auditorium next door (but sharing entrance and box office with the *Theatre Royal*). While almost as large, the *New Vic* is meant for informal and experimental theater and can be used for theater-in-the-round. Finally, you'll see smaller productions at the *Little Theatre* (phone: 291182), inside *Colston Hall* on Colston St., where the *Little Theatre Company* presents its productions as well. The Bristol Old Vic Theatre School (phone: 733535) gives several performances yearly at all the aforementioned theaters or at the *Vandyck Theatre* on Park Row, home of the University of Bristol Drama Department. As the first such department in a British university, this is another part of Bristol's theatrical tradition. The *Bristol Hippodrome,* St. Augustine's Parade (phone: 299444), seats 2,000 and hosts touring companies such as the *Royal Shakespeare Company* and the *National Theatre Company.* It is also the stage for visiting opera and ballet. The *Watershed,* Britain's first media and communications center, at 1 Cannon's Rd. (phone: 276444), and the *Arnolfini Arts Centre,* 16 Narrow Quay (phone: 299191), are dockside warehouses that have been converted to contemporary arts centers, with cinemas, galleries, and stage facilities, restaurants, and bars.

MUSIC: *Colston Hall,* Colston St. (phone: 262957), is Bristol's main venue for all types of musical performances, from classical to pop. The *Bournemouth Symphony Orchestra* and the *Bournemouth Sinfonia* play a regular season of concerts — the Harveys Bristol Series — from October to April. *St. George's,* a refurbished neoclassical church on Brandon Hill (phone: 230359) serves as an important classical music site with a full program of lunchtime concerts. Touring opera and ballet companies stage their productions at the *Bristol Hippodrome* (address above), and concerts of 20th-century music are the specialty of the *Arnolfini Arts Centre* (address above), which showcases the contemporary in all the arts. Recitals are held in many of Bristol's churches, including Bristol Cathedral, Clifton Cathedral, St. Mary Redcliffe, the Lord Mayor's Chapel on College Green, and St. George's Church on Charlotte Street. University of Bristol students put on concerts, often at lunchtime, in the Wills Memorial Building, Queens Rd.

NIGHTCLUBS AND NIGHTLIFE: Bristol's nightlife compares well with that of any city outside London. There are more than 20 nightclubs, including *Yesterdays,* 15 King St. (phone: 297670), which has five bars, two discotheques, a restaurant, and a fast-food counter; the *Reeves Club and Cabaret Room* at *Arno's Court* hotel, 470 Bath Rd. (phone: 711461); *Misty's* at 48 Park St. (phone: 24422); *Platform One,* Clifton Down Station (phone: 739171); and *Chasers,* 63–65 Regent St., Kingswood (phone: 608191), where you can usually catch a live band in the evening.

BEST IN TOWN

CHECKING IN: Bristol is not the prime tourist destination that prestigious Bath is, but as an important commercial center and the object of many an expense-account traveler, it's no less expensive than its neighbor. A wide range of accommodations is available, however, and if you book in advance, you should be able to find a room at the right price almost any time of the year. Look in Clifton for the broadest choice of reasonably priced small hotels and guesthouses. Few of Bristol's hotels are right in the center of town, and those that are tend to be in the expensive category. As a rough guide, expect to pay more than $110 a night for a double room at an expensive hotel, between $80 and $110 at a moderate one, and $50 to $80 at an inexpensive one. A hearty English breakfast should be included in the rate, but a growing number of the top hotels now offer room only. All telephone numbers are in the 0272 area code unless otherwise indicated.

Grand – This large, lovely Victorian has had a facelift and now sports a scrubbed stone exterior above the row of brown-and-gold striped awnings that line the street. Gracious and extensively modernized inside, with 179 rooms; right in the historic center. Broad St. (phone: 291645). Expensive.

Holiday Inn – Just like every other member of the chain. This modern, multi-story hotel has 284 rooms, a sauna, indoor swimming pool, gym, restaurants, and bars. It's convenient to the Broadmead shopping center, with a courtesy car operating to and from the railroad station on weekdays. 2 Lower Castle St. (phone: 294281). Expensive.

Bristol Hilton – Elegant and modern, with almost 200 luxurious rooms — all of them suites — it's close to the city center and convenient to the railroad station. Traffic races by out front and the setting is unglamorous, but the beautiful church of St. Mary Redcliffe does dress up the neighborhood. Redcliffe Way (phone: 260041). Expensive.

Thornbury Castle – A 16th-century country house 12 miles out of town, it once played host to King Henry VIII and Anne Boleyn. Originally it was known as a restaurant that served bacon from its own pig farm and wine from its own vineyard. While the pigs have gone, the highly regarded wine remains, and the castle now offers 12 cozy rooms above the restaurant. Castle St., Thornbury (phone: 0454-418511). Expensive.

Avon Gorge – This solid-white block of Victoriana perches on the edge of Clifton, overlooking the Avon Gorge and the Clifton Suspension Bridge. A recent expansion has brought the total number of rooms to 83, all with private bath. If you don't get one gorge-side, enjoy the view at tea on the terrace. Sion Hill, Clifton (phone: 738955). Moderate.

Hawthorns – In Clifton, only about half a mile from the Park Street shops. It has 160 rooms (100 with bath) and a wide range of entertainment. Woodland Rd., Clifton (phone: 731260). Moderate.

St. Vincent Rocks – This Regency hotel is a smaller (46 rooms, all with private bath) alternative to the *Avon Gorge* down the road. It, too, overlooks the river's chasm and has an enviable view of the Clifton Suspension Bridge. Sion Hill, Clifton (phone: 738544). Moderate.

Unicorn – It's smarter than its unappealingly modern front on Prince Street would lead you to believe. Go around back and you're right among the cobblestones, chains, and bollards of Narrow Quay and the harbor. Contemporary styling inside (194 rooms) and a popular waterfront bar. Prince St. (phone: 230333). Moderate.

Glenroy – Comfortable and small, and part of one of Clifton's attractive 19th-century squares. Fifty-four rooms, 45 with private bath. 30 Victoria Sq., Clifton (phone: 739058). Inexpensive.

Seeley's – A serviceable place, this, too, is in Clifton, not far from the Park Street shops. About half of the 65 rooms have private baths (some have Jacuzzis) and all have TV sets, radios, and tea-making facilities. Finishing touches include a sauna, solarium, and invigorating spa baths. 17–27 St. Paul's Rd., Clifton (phone: 738544). Inexpensive.

EATING OUT: As one of the largest cities outside London, you'd expect Bristol to be well endowed with good restaurants, and it is. There are some excellent eating places in the hotels and some equally good ones outside, in central Bristol and Clifton, offering traditional English, Chinese, French,

Indian, and Italian cuisines, among others. In addition, the city has two floating pub-restaurants. To sample local fare, try Severn salmon, Cheddar-cooked ham, jugged hare, and pigeon pie. A meal for two with wine will cost more than $70 at a restaurant listed as expensive, $55 to $70 at one listed as moderate, and less than $50 at one listed as inexpensive. A number of Bristol's restaurants close on bank holidays, as do many eating places throughout Britain. All telephone numbers are in the 0272 area code unless otherwise indicated.

Gornys – Friendly service and imaginatively cooked food are what draw people to this Swiss-French restaurant that is run by a German. Open for dinner only; closed Sundays, Mondays, the month of August, and 2 weeks at Christmas. Reservations necessary. 13 Cotham Rd. (phone: 426444). Expensive.

Harveys – The wine cellar of the famous firm of wine merchants is no ordinary place: frogs' legs among the appetizers, specialties such as beef Wellington or venison cutlets with juniper berries and gin, and four sauces for the duck. The bill of French and English fare is bountiful and the wine list will never cramp your style. Closed Saturday lunch, Sundays, and public holidays. 12 Denmark St. (phone: 277665). Expensive.

Kiln – Part of the *Ladbroke Dragonara* hotel, this unusual round restaurant with a fixed-price carvery as well as an à la carte menu, is actually a 200-year-old kiln for the making of Bristol glassware. Dancing on Saturdays. Redcliffe Way (phone: 260041). Expensive.

Restaurant du Gourmet – Three floors of a terraced house make up this French restaurant. The atmosphere is intimate but the menu is extensive. Closed Sundays and Mondays; dinner only on Saturdays, when you should be sure to reserve a table. 43 Whiteladies Rd. (phone: 736230). Expensive.

The Bridge – In the *St. Vincent Rocks* hotel, this restaurant has a wall of windows from which to admire the Clifton Suspension Bridge. English and French dishes are featured and roast meats are served from a carving trolley. Closed for lunch on Saturdays. Sion Hill, Clifton (phone: 739251). Moderate.

Colley's Supper Rooms – Arrive punctually at 7:45 PM for a wonderful six-course supper. There is no menu in the conventional sense, but plenty of variety. Judging by the fact that the place is often booked solid weeks ahead, people are happy with the arrangement. Closed Sundays for lunch and all day Mondays. 153 Whiteladies Rd. (phone: 730646). Moderate.

51 Park Street – Owner Bruce Isaacs is a firm believer in the motto "Come in and eat as much or as little as you like, when you like." His young staff rush between the potted plants, elegant chairs, tables, and coatstands to serve continental breakfast and brunches (including eggs Benedict) to a never-ending stream of students, Bristolians, and tourists. The paddle fans and soft music add to the atmosphere. Open daily from 11 AM to 11PM. 51 Park St. (phone: 268016). Moderate.

Michael's – Here you can feast on such delicacies as cream of Stilton soup, fresh salmon trout in a mushroom sauce, and passion fruit sorbet. The ornate Victorian dining room, converted from an old garage, is filled with flowers, curios, and tables of assorted shapes and sizes; the bar with chaise longues, stuffed birds, and a fireplace. Open for dinner daily except Sundays and for lunch on Sundays from mid-September until Easter. Reservations advised. 129 Hotwell Rd. (phone: 276190). Moderate.

Papa Lou's – The emphasis here is on roominess and relaxation. Guests can enjoy a full meal, a snack, or simply a glass of wine. Park Street Ave. (phone: 272876). Moderate.

Rajdoot – Authentic Punjabi cuisine — including the charcoal, clay oven barbecues of tandoori cooking — is served in an elegant setting. Test your palate on a quail or lobster curry. Open for lunch and dinner daily, though not for Sunday lunch.

Reservations necessary for the evening meal. 83 Park St. (phone: 268033). Moderate.

Vintners – Despite the rather cavernous atmosphere, good wines and delicious hot food are served here. Open for breakfast, with live music at lunchtime and seating in the back garden during summer. Open daily. St. Stephen's St. (phone: 291222). Moderate.

Bloomers – The 18th-century Old Library premises are now fresh and folksy inside, with lights hanging low over antique pine tables, chairs copied from those in an old farmhouse kitchen, and lots of potted plants. Stick to the fish and meat pies or have one of the more imaginative entrées, such as pan-fried veal coated in Stilton and bread crumbs. Three-course special meals are served for the customer in a hurry. Open daily. Old Library, King St. (phone: 291111). Inexpensive.

McCreadies Whole Food – It's small and friendly, with some interesting alternatives to the staple health food menu. Open 8:30 AM to 5 PM. Broad St. (phone: 265580). Inexpensive.

Trattoria da Renato – Actors and actresses from the *Old Vic* across the street congregate here. The walls are covered with their photos and the tables are attractively covered with pink napery topped by white lace. Food is Italian. Closed Sundays and for lunch on Saturdays. 19 King St. (phone: 298291). Inexpensive.

Woodes – A bustling coffee shop with a style all its own, it has two big wooden staircases, unique old furniture, and a slightly Bohemian atmosphere. Park St. (phone: 264041). Inexpensive.

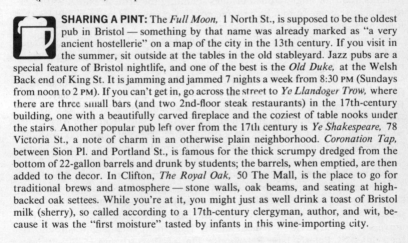

SHARING A PINT: The *Full Moon,* 1 North St., is supposed to be the oldest pub in Bristol — something by that name was already marked as "a very ancient hostellerie" on a map of the city in the 13th century. If you visit in the summer, sit outside at the tables in the old stableyard. Jazz pubs are a special feature of Bristol nightlife, and one of the best is the *Old Duke,* at the Welsh Back end of King St. It is jamming and jammed 7 nights a week from 8:30 PM (Sundays from noon to 2 PM). If you can't get in, go across the street to *Ye Llandoger Trow,* where there are three small bars (and two 2nd-floor steak restaurants) in the 17th-century building, one with a beautifully carved fireplace and the coziest of table nooks under the stairs. Another popular pub left over from the 17th century is *Ye Shakespeare,* 78 Victoria St., a note of charm in an otherwise plain neighborhood. *Coronation Tap,* between Sion Pl. and Portland St., is famous for the thick scrumpy dredged from the bottom of 22-gallon barrels and drunk by students; the barrels, when emptied, are then added to the decor. In Clifton, *The Royal Oak,* 50 The Mall, is the place to go for traditional brews and atmosphere — stone walls, oak beams, and seating at high-backed oak settees. While you're at it, you might just as well drink a toast of Bristol milk (sherry), so called according to a 17th-century clergyman, author, and wit, because it was the "first moisture" tasted by infants in this wine-importing city.

CAMBRIDGE

Cambridge's bold claim to being the most beautiful city in Britain is based on the majestic architecture of its several colleges. The distinction is not often disputed (except by its rival, Oxford, the country's other bastion of knowledge and medieval design). Each year, millions of visitors flock to this small city to marvel at its masterpieces of cut stone, stained glass, and carved wood, and to breathe its rarefied and scholarly atmosphere. They also come to Cambridge for an experience Oxford cannot match: a quiet punt ride up the "Backs" on the river Cam, which slides lazily past the colleges' back lawns (hence the name), and is edged by lush green banks and drooping willows. One 19th-century tourist, Henry James, described the Backs as "the loveliest confusion of gothic windows and ancient trees, of grassy banks and mossy balustrades, of sun-checquered avenues and groves, of lawns and gardens and terraces, [and] of single arched bridges spanning the little stream . . ." Lesser tourists have come to much the same conclusion on postcards written to the folks back home.

This city of great tranquillity and beauty has deep historical roots. Cambridge was established in AD 43 as a Roman camp on a hill overlooking a natural ford in the river Cam at its upper navigable limit. The camp blossomed into a trading town, as the Romans built roads connecting Colchester, the garrison town to the southeast, with Lincoln, a settlement in the north. In the 5th century, the area was overrun and conquered by the Saxons. St. Bene't's (a contraction for St. Benedict's) Church dates from this period; its Saxon tower stands today. In the 11th century, the Normans, too, invaded Cambridge, and under instructions from William the Conqueror built a castle to defend the town against rebels led by Hereward the Wake.

Details about early scholarly stirrings in Cambridge are vague. There was a monastery in the nearby town of Ely, and in 1209, when students retreating from a hostile townsfolk streamed here from Oxford, these monks may have set up a center of learning. Whatever the case, by the mid-13th century the university was firmly established, and by 1284 the first college was founded, then called St. Peter's, later Peterhouse. During the 14th and 15th centuries, 11 more colleges were founded and several hostels were built to house the students.

Today, education is Cambridge's main industry (there are 35 colleges and about 12,000 students), but the university, like Oxford, retains its original medieval organization. Each of the colleges is a self-governing entity within a decentralized university system. Each drafts its own rules and holds title to its own property. While the university provides lectures, conducts examinations, and awards degrees, the individual colleges control admissions and determine the subjects an undergraduate should "read."

Strictly speaking, the term "university" refers not to its imposing granite structures but rather to the community of people involved — the chancellor, masters, and fellows and scholars, to be exact. The chancellor governs the university as a whole, aided by the vice chancellor, who supervises the administrative personnel and is chairman of the principal university bodies. Each college is presided over by a master, who heads a staff of fellows (commonly referred to as "dons"). The dons conduct weekly tutorials (discussions of an assignment with a student), give lectures, and do their own research. The position of don is as much an identity as a job; one tried to explain the mystique in this way: "Being a don at Cambridge is more than a job. It is a way of life. If he will never be rich, he is at least his own master . . . He lives in surroundings compared to which any other city whose university tempts him to move appears so often shabby and ugly. That is why so few move."

Many scholars feel the same attachment to Cambridge — with good reason. Ever since the Middle Ages the colleges have traditionally provided for their members' every need. Each self-sufficient enclave includes a dining room, with an imposing high table where the master and fellows dine apart from (and a bit above) the undergraduates; a chapel; a library; and common rooms as well as private rooms where students live. More important, many colleges have remained unchanged over the centuries. Cambridge has spawned some of the most influential figures in politics, the arts, and science — people like Cromwell, Pepys, Newton, Darwin, Wordsworth, and Byron. What undergraduate would not delight in writing at Samuel Pepys's desk or wielding the same silverware as Oliver Cromwell?

Cambridge, like any institution that reaches so far into the past, is plagued as well as enriched by traditions out of step with the modern world. Perhaps because of its monastic beginnings, the university has always disciplined students rather rigorously. For example, until fairly recently, the college gates were locked at 11 PM. As each college is surrounded in a rather prisonlike way by high walls often crowned with a row of spikes, there was no easy way to get in if you tarried too long. This hardly deterred spirited carousers, however, and the famous night climbs of Cambridge have spawned many a British mountaineer.

As a result of this and other episodes, the emphasis at Cambridge upon dignity and discipline has become somewhat legendary. Consider the oft-told tale of the student who tried to turn the ancient rules to his own advantage. In studying the university statutes he discovered that he had the right, while sitting for an examination, to demand a tankard of ale from the proctor. His request was grudgingly granted and the ale brought in . . . but not without a price. For it seems that the statute, set down in the 14th century, also made it compulsory to wear a sword after dark. The next evening the student was found and fittingly — if somewhat uncomfortably — attired.

CAMBRIDGE AT-A-GLANCE

SEEING THE CITY: Head straight for Great St. Mary's, the University Church in King's Parade, and climb to the top for a fine view of the city. For an alternative perspective stroll up Castle Mound, once the site of Cambridge's castle, whose stonework was gradually removed over the years and used in the construction of the colleges.

SPECIAL PLACES: Every tour of Cambridge should begin at its heart — the colleges, all of which are open in part to the public. A word of warning, however: The colleges are not museums but private places where people live and work, and Cambridge's 3 million yearly visitors create an enormous problem, especially in spring and summer when students are preparing for exams. To some extent, the situation would be like finding your own backyard on the itinerary of every tour of England. What's more, the colleges receive no income from tourists, so visiting their courts (the counterparts of Oxford's quads) should be considered a great privilege and quiet behavior only common courtesy.

In general, visitors are allowed to walk around the courts (but not on the grass, which remains the privilege of fellows only); visit the chapels and some gardens; and occasionally go into other designated areas, such as libraries or dining halls. Members of the college live off a "staircase," as the names at the bottom will indicate, but unless you are visiting a friend or relative in residence, you won't be allowed to wander into these private quarters. The colleges are also sometimes closed to visitors — for example, from about mid-May to mid-June, when examinations are being taken. Notices to this effect are posted at the gate; if in doubt, check with the porter in the college lodge.

The selection of colleges below, arranged in walking tour order, is by no means exhaustive, but it does include those most interesting architecturally and most centrally located. If you have time to visit only a few of them, King's and Trinity should be at the top of the list. Nearby Queens' and St. John's (and perhaps the entire area between them) would be both worthwhile and easy to reach, and you'd still have time to explore the Backs. Some of the colleges not mentioned below are Peterhouse (founded in 1284); Gonville and Caius, pronounced *kees* (1348); St. Catherine's (1473); Sidney Sussex (1596); and Downing (1800). Then there are the three colleges founded for women, namely, Girton (1869; out of town and far removed from the lusty male population); Newnham (1871; novelist Margaret Drabble studied here); and New Hall (1954; at the time it was probably Cambridge's most controversial building — judge for yourself). Last, the three newest colleges are Churchill (1960; way out of town, inspired by Sir Winston's wish to encourage scientific and technological studies); Fitzwilliam (1966; affectionately called Fitzbilly); and Robinson, opened by the Queen in 1981.

THE COLLEGES

Corpus Christi College (1352) – Because the Old Court has changed little since it was built in the 14th century, it provides a glimpse at medieval college organization. Then four students shared a room but each had his own study cubicle — hence the difference in the size of the windows. In the 16th century, one of the cubicles would have been used by the great English dramatist Christopher Marlowe when he was a student here. The library, containing a priceless collection of Anglo-Saxon manuscripts (nearly 40 of them, saved from the libraries of monasteries dissolved by Henry VIII and including an important copy of the *Anglo-Saxon Chronicle*), is open Tuesdays and Thursdays during the term. The chapel is open daily. Be warned: The college is said to have a resident ghost. Trumpington St.

Pembroke College (1347) – The college was founded by Marie de Valence, Countess of Pembroke, and some of the buildings of her time survive. The chapel (built in 1663–66) was Sir Christopher Wren's first building, designed while he was a professor at Oxford. Wren's uncle, who had been imprisoned in the Tower of London and intended the chapel as thanksgiving for his release, told his nephew that since he was a mathematician, he ought to be capable of building a chapel. Wren was and did, in a classical style new to Cambridge. The college is also known for its gardens. Trumpington St.

Queens' College (1448) – Founded by Margaret of Anjou and Elizabeth Woodville, the respective Queens of Henry VI and Edward IV, Queens' has a lovely red brick

First Court built in the 15th century and decorated with a sundial in the 17th century. But its pièce de résistance is the New Court. The cloister around it, also 15th century, supports a wonderful example of 16th-century domestic architecture called the President's Lodge (Queens' does not have a master), an evocative building of timber and plaster that is put to good use in *May Week* as a backdrop for the college's productions of Shakespeare. Also of interest is the Mathematical Bridge, a copy of an original (1749) that was held together on geometrical principles without nails, nuts, or bolts but that, once taken apart by some curious Victorians, couldn't be put back together without the fastenings. Sir Basil Spence's Erasmus Building (1959) was one of the first modern contributions to college architecture. (Erasmus, the Renaissance theologian, lived at Queens' in 1511–14.) Queens' La.

King's College (1441) – Of the grand design that Henry VI had for the college he founded, only the chapel was ever realized. It was not until 1724, when the Fellows' Building was added, that an actual court began to take shape where Henry intended one; until then, students lived in an older court that is no longer part of the college. But the magnificent Gothic chapel, begun in 1446 and completed 90 years later, largely as the founder planned it, is not only Cambridge's best-known building, it is also often acclaimed the finest building in England — and all this majesty had been meant initially for the private worship of only 70 scholars. The initial stage of construction ended in 1461 when Henry was deposed. (The level that had been reached at that point is visible in a change in color of the stone.) Edward IV and Richard III financed further work, but it was Henry VII who began the final stage and left money for its completion, which explains the rose of his Tudor father and the portcullis of his Beaufort mother, symbols carved everywhere as decoration. The chapel has the largest fan-vaulted ceiling in existence; original 16th-century stained glass, the gift of Henry VIII, in all but one (and part of another) of its windows; and an intricately carved wood organ screen bearing the initials of Henry VIII and Anne Boleyn, another gift. Behind the altar is Rubens's *Adoration of the Magi,* donated in the 1960s after having set a (then) record for the highest price ever brought by a painting at auction. The chapel is open daily, but be prepared for unpredictable closings because of choir practice or recording sessions. The King's College Chapel choir is very well known, so if you get a chance, go and listen. Notices of concerts are usually posted on the doorway. Evensong is held at 5:30 PM on weekdays (excluding Mondays) and at 3:30 PM on Sundays during university terms only. King's Parade.

Clare College (1338) – Though one of the oldest colleges, its original buildings were destroyed by fire, and the present ones date only from the 17th century. They rank among the university's most handsome, however, and Clare's bridge is the oldest (1640) and one of the prettiest on the Cam. The college is also known for the elegance of its 18th-century wrought-iron gates and for the delightful Fellows' Garden on the other side of the river. The garden is normally open on weekdays from 2:45 to 4:30 PM. Trinity La.

Trinity Hall (1350) – Originally all the colleges were called halls, and the people who lived in them were the college. Gradually the latter word became more inclusive in meaning, and by the 19th century, most of the halls had changed their names. Because a Trinity College already existed, Trinity Hall, traditionally the college for lawyers, is the only Cambridge college known by its old name. Its Front Court dates from the 14th century but was refaced in the 18th century. You'll get a better idea of Trinity's early days by seeing the 16th-century Tudor brick library, especially pretty in summer when the flowers bordering it are in bloom. Trinity La.

Trinity College (1546) – Founded by Henry VIII, Trinity is the largest college in Cambridge and home to more than 800 students. The school has a distinguished roster of alumni: Francis Bacon, John Dryden, Isaac Newton, Thomas Macaulay, Alfred Lord Tennyson, Bertrand Russell, six British prime ministers, over 20 Nobel Prize winners, and Prince Charles, not to mention Lord Byron, who was eventually "sent down," expelled, for rooming with a pet bear and bathing naked in the fountain at the center of the Great Court, the source of the college's water supply. The Great Court, the largest court or quad in either Cambridge or Oxford, is the creation of Thomas Nevile, master of the college in the late 16th and early 17th centuries. He also began Nevile's Court; the long cloister on the north side is where Newton worked out his theory of sound (stand at its west end and stamp your foot to hear the echo he timed to measure the speed of sound). Nevile's Court became complete only at the end of the 17th century with the addition of Christopher Wren's library — and the sight of the sun resplendent on the glass of the Wren Library's many windows is still one of the most memorable in Cambridge. The library is open to the public on weekdays from noon to 2 PM and on Saturdays during term from 10:30 AM to 12:30 PM. (It's lavish with carved wood inside, and some of its treasured manuscripts are usually on display.) Nevile's dining hall (again, Cambridge's largest) is between the two courts and is normally open from 2 to 3 PM during the summer vacation, except on Sundays. Trinity St.

St. John's College (1511) – An enormous, rather austere place, this is the second largest of the Cambridge colleges, with buildings spanning the centuries. The beautiful gatehouse, ornate with the arms of the founder, Lady Margaret Beaufort (mother of Henry VII), is in its original state, the Second and Third courts date from the late 16th and early 17th centuries respectively, but across the river Cam are the 19th-century neo-Gothic New Court and the ultramodern Cripps Building. The two parts of the college are connected by the covered Bridge of Sighs (1831), picturesque despite the bars on the windows to keep undergraduates inside. William Wordsworth was a St. John's student; he later wrote of its "three gloomy courts," in the first of which (much altered since the founding) he had an "obscure nook." St. John's St.

Magdalene College (1542) – Built in the 15th century to house Benedictine monks studying at Cambridge, Magdalene (pronounced *mawd*-len) was founded as an actual college in the 16th century, and its First Court has buildings of both centuries. It is a favorite of the British aristocracy, but its most famous student was Samuel Pepys, who left his library to his old school, including the manuscript of his famous diary. The library — arranged in presses Pepys provided — is open daily except Sundays from 11:30 AM to 12:30 PM and from 2:30 to 3:30 PM. Across the street from the college are old buildings that Pepys himself would have seen. Magdalene St.

Jesus College (1496) – This is another college with a religious background. Founded on the site of a convent that dated from the 12th century, Jesus, too, has parts that are older than it is, including the chapel — though the pre-Raphaelite stained glass (by Edward Burne-Jones and Ford Madox Brown) and ceilings (by William Morris) came about during a 19th-century restoration. The college is approached via a long brick-walled avenue known as the "chimney," but once past the 15th-century gate tower, the grounds are spacious, with gardens and a delightful Tudor Cloister Court. Alistair Cooke, a journalist and commentator on the American scene, was a Jesus undergraduate, as was Samuel Taylor Coleridge. Jesus La.

Christ's College (1505) – The first of the two colleges Lady Margaret Beaufort founded at Cambridge, and as at St. John's, her coat of arms above the gate makes a highly ornamental entranceway. John Milton was a student at Christ's (he wrote many of his early poems here; a later one, *Lycidas,* was written in memory of a college fellow), as was Charles Darwin. The beautiful Fellows' Garden (open weekdays from 10:30 AM to noon and from 2 to 4 PM) contains a mulberry tree, traditionally associated with Milton. St. Andrew's St.

Emmanuel College (1584) – Sir Walter Mildmay, Queen Elizabeth I's chancellor of the exchequer, founded this college on the site of a 13th-century Dominican friary that had been dissolved by Henry VIII. The monastic buildings were converted to college use (the friary church became the dining hall), then other buildings followed, including the chapel and its colonnade (1668–73), designed by Sir Christopher Wren. Emmanuel was meant to educate clergymen and it became a center of Protestant theology, but because of their Puritan sympathies, many of its graduates went to America in the early 17th century. Among them was John Harvard, who died at the age of 31, leaving $1,600 and 320 books for the foundation of Harvard University. St. Andrew's St.

OTHER CAMBRIDGE SIGHTS

Fitzwilliam Museum – The private treasure trove that Viscount Fitzwilliam donated to the university, along with the funds for a building to house it, is one of the oldest public museums in the country. Founded in 1812, it contains Middle Eastern, Egyptian, Greek, and Roman antiquities and European ceramics, manuscripts, paintings, drawings, and miniatures of all periods. The paintings and drawings — from Flemish and Italian Old Masters through French Impressionism to modern English art — are in the gallery upstairs, open daily from 2 to 5 PM. The rest is in the downstairs gallery, open from 10 AM to 5 PM. Both galleries are open Sundays from 2:15 to 5 PM, and closed Mondays. The museum also sponsors temporary exhibitions. Trumpington St. (phone: 332900).

Senate House – This classical Georgian building of the 1720s was designed by the English architect James Gibbs (who also designed the Fellows' Building next to the King's College Chapel), and it, too, belongs to the university. When illuminated at night, its Corinthian details make it look almost like an edible confection, and each June it becomes the suitably stylish setting for the ceremony of General Admission to Degrees — graduation, that is. King's Parade.

Round Church – Built in the same distinctive shape as the Holy Sepulcher Church in Jerusalem, the Norman Round Church dates from about 1130. It is one of only five Round Churches still surviving in England. Bridge St.

Folk Museum – Crafts, tools, kitchen and farm equipment, toys, and furniture are among the many objects on display in a series of rooms meant to illustrate life in Cambridge and the surrounding countryside in the last few hundred years. The building itself was formerly a pub (*The White Horse Inn*) and in the courtyard is an 18th-century shopfront, one of several large relics salvaged from Cambridge's past. Open Mondays through Saturdays and Sunday afternoons. Admission charge. Corner of Castle and Northampton sts. (phone: 355159).

Brass Rubbing Centre – Don't let the thought of working in a cold, damp, and dimly lit church put you off the idea of brass rubbing; in Cambridge, there's a cozy do-it-yourself workshop with 70 brasses to choose from. The brasses are replicas of monuments to real people (mostly minor gentry — the very wealthy invested in more elaborate stoneworks) dating from the time of the Crusaders. The price for making your own rubbing ranges from about $3 to $9, depending on the size of the brass you choose, and includes the use of all materials plus basic instruction for novices. If you can't summon the necessary effort — and brass rubbing is hard work — the Center also sells finished rubbings. Open 12 to 5 PM, Mondays through Saturdays. Groups can visit anytime by special request. St. Giles Church, Castle St. (phone: 835055).

Scott Polar Research Institute – The small museum here is dedicated to the famous explorer and to polar exploration. Letters, diaries, and photographs of Robert Falcon Scott's expedition to the South Pole are on display along with souvenirs of other expeditions and displays describing the geography and geology of the Antarctic and current polar research. Open daily except Sundays from 2:30 to 4 PM. Lensfield Rd. (phone: 337733).

Botanic Gardens – These are the university's research gardens, open to the public Mondays through Saturdays from 8 AM to dusk (6:30 PM in summer) and summer

Sundays from 2:30 to 6:30 PM. You'll find the hothouses very inviting on cold days (in winter, the Cambridge east winds seem to blow uninterrupted all the way from Siberia). Entrances on Bateman St., Trumpington Rd., Brooklands Ave., and Hills Rd. (phone: 337733).

American Military Cemetery – More than 3,800 American servicemen who fought in World War II from British bases are buried in these beautifully landscaped grounds. The names of another 5,125 who lie in unknown graves are inscribed on the Memorial Wall. On the Madingley Rd., 4 miles outside the city (phone: 0954-210350).

■ **EXTRA SPECIAL:** One of the most stylish ways to enjoy Cambridge is to hire a punt — a long, flat-bottomed, square-nosed boat that is both steered and propelled by means of a long pole that you push into the mud of the river bottom. It sounds difficult, looks easy, and, in practice, is somewhere between the two. Be prepared for ridicule from the onlookers along the grassy banks, especially if you go around in circles or, heaven help you, get the pole stuck in the mud and forget to let go. Either explore the Backs, a beautiful stretch of river behind the college and past splendid lawns, gardens, and drooping willows, or go on a lengthier excursion up the river to Grantchester for tea. The two routes are separated by a weir. *Scudamore's Boatyards,* a famous Cambridge name in punting since 1910, offers punts for self-drive hire at two locations, one at Quayside, off Bridge Street, and another at Mill Lane, near Silver Street (but go to the latter if you're aiming for Grantchester). The cost is about $5.50 an hour, plus a $45 deposit. Punts are available from Easter through early October. Don't forget to stand at the back of the boat, especially if you have recently been to Oxford, where they stand at the front. The deposit is deductible *if* you return. There is also a 40-minute guided tour through the Backs and a chauffeured punt service with champagne, strawberries, and cream.

SOURCES AND RESOURCES

TOURIST INFORMATION: The tourist information center, on Wheeler St. (phone: 322640), is open weekdays from 9 AM to 6 PM (9 AM to 5:30 PM November through February) and on Saturdays from 9 AM to 5 PM. From Easter through September, it is also open on Sundays (10:30 AM to 3:30 PM). The center offers guided walking tours to the major colleges and through the intricate maze of small streets and alleyways around them. The tours last approximately 2 hours, cost about $3.50, and depart several times a day, Mondays through Saturdays, April through December, and Sundays April through September. You can check the schedule by calling the number above. It's wise to make reservations at least a half hour in advance. Evening walking tours of historic Cambridge are conducted daily during July and August; tours leave from the center at 6:30 PM and also cost about $3.50. For information on all university departments, including museums, use the general university phone number: 337733.

The center sells a comprehensive selection of guides to Cambridge. These include the *Cambridge Official Guide, A Brief Guide to Cambridge,* and *Where to Eat In and Around Cambridge.* Available free are a city map and pamphlets on the area's events, accommodations, campsites, bike rentals, car rentals, bookshops, and antiques shops.

Most of Cambridge's bookstores (see *Shopping*) carry a broad range of guidebooks including many "picturebooks" filled with lush photographs. Try to find *Look at Cambridge* and *Historic Cambridge* by John Brooks, *Cambridge* by Kenneth Holmes, and *Royal Cambridge* by Marion Colthorpe, which describes the many royal visits to the city since Queen Elizabeth I.

Local Coverage – The *Cambridge Evening News* is the city's daily paper.

Telephone – The area code for Cambridge is 0223.

GETTING AROUND:

Bicycle – Most students and some academics travel around by bike. You can rent one from *University Cycles,* 9 Victoria Ave. (phone: 355517); *Geoff's Bike Hire,* 65 Devonshire Rd. (phone: 65629); or *Ben Hayward and Son,* Laundress La. (phone: 352294). A day's hire will run about $4, and a week's $7.50, with a deposit of around $30.

Boat – A sightseeing alternative for enjoying Cambridge and the surrounding countryside is a 3-day or a 1-week cruise aboard the *Westover Boat Company*'s converted narrowboats. Summer only (phone: 0860-516343).

Bus – For inexpensive links to other towns in East Anglia and London, try the bus; the station is on Drummer St. (phone: 423554). The information office is open Mondays through Saturdays from 8:15 AM to 5:30 PM.

Car Rental – Try *Godfrey Davis* at 315 Mill Rd. (phone: 248198) or *Marshall's Car Hire,* Jesus La. (phone: 62211).

Taxi – Two of the biggest taxi companies are *Camtax,* 26 Victoria Rd. (phone: 313131), and *United,* 123a Hills Rd. (phone: 352222). Apart from the trip into town from the station or visits to places outside the city, such as the American Military Cemetery, you're unlikely to need a cab, since most of the places of interest in town are within walking distance of each other.

Train – Cambridge and London are linked by frequent trains from Liverpool Street Station, travel time about 1½ hours. The Cambridge railway station is at the far end of Station Rd., a long walk from the center of town, so take the bus that waits in the front of the station or a taxi (which will cost roughly $4). For information, phone 311999; for a recorded announcement of the London rail timetable, call 359602.

SPECIAL EVENTS: Most university events take place during the university terms — there are three a year — and more toward the end of the term than the beginning. The most celebrated is *May Week,* which actually takes place in June and is closer to a fortnight than a week. It is the busiest time on the social calendar, enhanced by a general feeling of relief at the end of the working year, particularly in the wake of final examinations. Many college and university societies put on displays of their activities, the most delightful of which are the plays and concerts held on the college lawns (which the public may attend). Each year several colleges hold elaborate balls — the *May Balls* — at which members and their guests (though outsiders can sometimes buy tickets — ask at the porters' lodge) dance from dusk till dawn, enjoy champagne buffets, and, if still going strong, punt up to Grantchester for breakfast.

Late in June, the *Midsummer Fair* takes place on Midsummer Common — as it has since the Middle Ages. Also in June are the students' boat races (the Bumps) and the *Footlights Revue,* a series of comedy dramas at the *Arts Theatre,* most famous as the one-time launching pad for John Cleese and the Monty Python gang. On June 30 and July 1 graduates congregate at the Senate House for their ceremonial awards. During the last 2 weeks in July, the city sponsors the *Cambridge Festival,* the most important part of which is a series of concerts and recitals in such historic settings as the King's College and St. John's College chapels and the Senate House. There are also art exhibitions, dramatic presentations, a fireworks display, and an Elizabethan feast. The weekend *Folk Festival* at Cherry Hinton Hall closes the month. The most important winter event is the King's College *Festival of Nine Lessons and Carols* on Christmas Eve, which is broadcast live worldwide. Festival details and tickets are available from the Festival Box Office, the Corn Exchange, Wheeler St. (phone: 358977).

MUSEUMS: In addition to those described in *Special Places,* Cambridge has a number of other interesting museums. The best of these are the following:

Gallery on the Cam – Local artists' paintings, prints, batiks, and ceramics are displayed aboard a converted barge. Open Tuesdays through Saturdays from 10 AM to 5 PM, Sundays from noon to 5 PM. Near Jesus Lock, Chesterton Rd.

Kettles Yard Art Gallery – Permanent collection of modern art including works by Henri Gaudier-Brzeska, Ben Nicolson, and Christopher Wood, and changing exhibits of contemporary art and crafts. Permanent collection open daily from 2 to 4 PM; exhibition gallery open daily except Sundays from 12:30 to 5:30 PM, Sundays from 2 to 5:30 PM. Northampton St. (phone: 352124).

Museum of Classical Archaeology – Casts of Greek and Roman sculpture. Open weekdays from 9 AM to 1 PM and from 2:15 to 5 PM, and Saturdays from 10 AM to 1 PM, when the university is in session. Sidgwick Ave. (phone: 62253).

National Horseracing Museum – Five galleries house a collection of art, trophies, and horsy objects, many of which have been owned by famous riders. The galleries, the Jockey Club rooms, the stud, and the training yard are featured in morning tours of and all-day visits to the museum. Open daily except Mondays April through early December. Admission charge. 99 High St., Newmarket, 10 miles NE of Cambridge (phone: 0638-667333).

Sedgwick Museum of Geology – Geological specimens by the hundreds. Open weekdays from 9 AM to 1 PM and from 2 to 5 PM, Saturdays during the university's full term from 9 AM to 1 PM. Downing St. (phone: 333456).

University Museum of Zoology – Displays on marine life, birds, insects, and mammals, as well as fossil specimens. Open weekdays from 2:15 to 4:45 PM. Downing St. (phone: 336600).

Whipple Science Museum – Early microscopes, telescopes, astronomical and navigational equipment, surveying instruments, slide rules, and electrical apparatus. Open weekdays from 2 to 4 PM, during university term only, as well as the first Sunday in every month. Free School La. (phone: 334500).

SHOPPING: The marketplace in Market Square, on ever-so-flat Market Hill, has been a shopping area since medieval times. The stalls, sheltered by brightly colored canopies, are open for business year-round daily except Sundays. Most sell fruits and vegetables, inexpensive clothing, and plants, but some sell items of interest to visitors, including gifts, records, and secondhand books.

Bookstores abound in Cambridge, stocking much more than just academic tomes. *Heffers of Cambridge,* an establishment with many branches, has its main bookstore at 20 Trinity St. (phone: 358351); other branches include a children's bookshop at 30 Trinity St. (phone: 356200) and paperback shops at 13 Trinity St. (phone: 61815) and 31 St. Andrew's St. (phone: 354778). *Sherratt & Hughes* (formerly *Bowes & Bowes*), the oldest bookshop in England, has presided over its corner location on Trinity and Market streets for the last 400 years (phone: 311243); *Deighton, Bell & Co.* at 13 Trinity St. (phone: 353939) offers rare and fine books; *Quinto* specializes in old leatherbound books and ancient prints at 34 Trinity St. (phone: 358279); and *G. David,* a Cambridge institution for secondhand books, has shops at 3 and 16 St. Edward's Passage (phone: 354619).

The city has five main shopping areas. The first starts at St. John's Street and continues down Trinity Street, along King's Parade (with colleges on one side and old shop buildings, some dating from the 16th century, on the other), and into Trumpington Street. A second begins at Magdalene Bridge and runs down Bridge Street, Sidney Street, St. Andrew's Street, and Regent Street. Chic, expensive shops line the newly renovated Rose Crescent, a wide alleyway leading from Market Square to Trinity Street. The Lion Yard pedestrian precinct, between Market Square and St. Andrew's Street, is served by its own multilevel parking lot. The fifth shopping area is the recently developed Grafton Centre, 10 minutes from downtown, with department stores, small, exclusive boutiques, and a handful of cafés and restaurants.

Antiques Etcetera – A magpie's nest of Victoriana, including watches and clocks, silver, and jewelry. 18 King St. (phone: 62825).

Cellini – One of England's leading pearl specialists and jewelry designers. The workshop is next door, so the finishing touches to a design can be tailored to suit the customer. 4 Rose Crescent (phone: 350600).

Choice – Every inch of space is taken up with titanium jewelry, Liberty print goods, Chelsea and Moorcroft potteries, local artists' paintings, and a commendable range of Cambridge souvenirs. 18 Rose Crescent (phone: 315214).

Culpeper the Herbalists – A large store of the Cambridge-based chain famous for its herbal cosmetics, soaps, teas, honeys, and fresh herb jellies. Gift wrapping is free. 25 Lion Yard (phone: 67370).

Fitzbillies – Selling cakes, pastries, homemade bread, handmade chocolates, mouth-watering fudge, and souvenirs — T-shirts, sweatshirts, aprons, and tea towels. Many shoppers purchase the leftover bread and feed it to the ducks in Mill Pond across the road. There's been a *Fitzbillies* in Cambridge since 1924; this one's at 52 Trumpington St. (phone: 352500), and there's a younger branch at 50 Regent St. (phone: 64451).

The Friar's House – Crammed with fine crystal and porcelain and the best selection of collector's paperweights in East Anglia. Open daily. Bene't St., behind King's Parade (phone: 60275).

Marr's – For all things chic and leather, from handbags, wallets, and hip flasks to voluminous jackets. 16 Rose Crescent (phone: 355499).

Primavera – A contemporary gallery, stocking pottery, glass, cards, ceramics, tiles, clothes, toys, corn dollies, clay Suffolk cottages, and other folk art. There are exhibitions in the basement. 10 King's Parade (phone: 357708).

Ryder and Amies – Caters to the university's demand for badges, plaques, cufflinks, crested ties, and college rugby shirts (various colors); also carries Shetland tweed ties and tartan berets. 22 King's Parade (phone: 350371).

Scots Corner – Shelves and tables piled high with kilts, tartans, tweeds, and fine Scottish knitwear. 11 Bridge St. (phone: 61534).

W & G Taylor – Tweeds and tartan items as well as a range of deerstalker hats and 6-foot-long striped scarves (available in different colors, depending upon college allegiance). It also has the largest selection of hats in Cambridge. 5 Trinity St. (phone: 350510).

Textile Studio – An exclusive collection of stunning ball gowns and wedding dresses (all designed to order) in addition to an assortment of textiles, knitwear, and other gift items. 3 Free School La. (phone: 313583).

SPORTS: Both the university and town hold regular sporting events throughout the year. During the winter months, soccer and rugby are the most popular, and in the summer, cricket. The college playing fields are dotted around the town; you'll find many of these indicated on the tourist office map. Schedules of events are posted on the notice boards in the porters' lodges of the individual colleges.

Fishing – In the Cam, naturally. A rod license can be obtained for about $6 wherever you rent tackle.

Golf – There are public courses at Gog Magog, Babraham Rd., Bar Hill, and Girton.

Riding – Several stables operate in the area, including *Miss E. Pickard's School* at New Farm Stables, Bourn (phone: 934501), 8 miles west of Cambridge. The charge is around $12 per hour.

Rowing – A major university sport. Competition reaches a crescendo in March when eights from Oxford and Cambridge clash on the Thames in London. The rest of the year, college boat clubs as well as local school and town clubs row downriver from Midsummer Common. You'll often see eights, fours, pairs, and single sculls practicing on the river, but watch out for the almost equally frequent coach bicycling along the towpath. With one hand gripping the handlebars and the other clutching a megaphone, he won't be looking where he's going, so be sure to keep out of his way. Traditional racing can't be done on the Cam because it isn't wide enough for two boats to row side by side. Instead they race in a line. Sometimes as many as 15 boats participate in a single competition, each starting off at 1½-length intervals behind the other. The object is to catch up with the one in front and overlap the stern — hence the name of the race, "Bumps." University Bumps take place in February and during *May Week* (in June), city Bumps in July, on a course between Baitsbite Lock and Stourbridge Common. The best place to watch is from the towpath at Fen Ditton.

Tennis – Outdoor grass and hard courts are available for public use at Jesus Green; hard courts are available at Lammas Land, off Fen Causeway.

Walking – Choose from among the area's several enjoyable walking trails — along the Cam towpaths; across the meadows to Grantchester, so beloved by the poet Rupert Brooke; down the Coe Fen Nature Trail, which starts at the bridge near the rough car park off Barton Road. Other trails are recommended in the tourist information center's booklet *More Country Walks Around Cambridge.*

THEATER: The *Arts Theatre* at Peas Hill (phone: 352000) puts on modern and classic plays, ballet, opera, light opera, and other musical productions by local and touring companies. It also stages the annual *Footlights Review* in June, a satirical presentation that gave birth to such eminent wits as David Frost, Dudley Moore, Jonathan Miller, and John Cleese. The university's *Amateur Dramatic Club* (*ADC*) *Theatre* on Park St. (phone: 359547) has an excellent reputation and puts on a broad selection of plays during the university term.

MUSIC: There are many concerts and recitals in Cambridge throughout the year, including large choral works by the Cambridge University Music Society and the King's College Chapel choir, organ recitals in Great St. Mary's and the King's College Chapel, and many other solo appearances. Details and times are posted on notice boards in the college porters' lodges as well as in several restaurants, cafés, bookstores, and the various faculty buildings.

NIGHTCLUBS AND NIGHTLIFE: Despite the city's youthful population, there isn't much taking place in the small hours, mainly because the undergraduates have to be back in their dorms then. The few discos in town include *Ronelles* in Heidelberg Gardens, Lion Yard (Thursday night is for the "oldies" — those over 25; Wednesdays are free for women); and *Route 66* on Wheeler St. (opposite the tourist information center). Both places serve reasonably priced meals and cocktails. Note that no jeans, T-shirts, or sneakers are allowed, and men must wear jackets and ties.

BEST IN TOWN

CHECKING IN: Cambridge offers few moderate or expensive hotels but numerous inexpensive bed-and-breakfast establishments. During the summer and particularly toward the close of the school year (about mid-May to mid-June), when the influx of tourists is further bolstered by parents and other relatives visiting students, it is difficult to get a room. Reserve at least 2 months in advance for *May Week.* Although the tourist office provides a booking service for visitors who arrive without a room reservation, don't expect it to perform miracles on short notice. In Cambridge and environs you'll pay $100 and up for a double room at an expensive hotel; between $70 and $100 at a moderate one; under $60 at an inexpensive one. All telephone numbers are in the 0223 area code unless otherwise indicated.

Cambridgeshire Moat House – It more than compensates for its out-of-town location with a plethora of sports facilities — an 18-hole championship golf course, tennis courts, squash courts, a sauna, and a large, heated, indoor swimming pool. All 100 rooms have private bath and shower. Bar Hill, 7 miles northwest of Cambridge on A604 (phone: 0954-80555). Expensive.

Garden House – The town's most luxurious hotel, it's close to the city center yet set amid 3 acres of gardens that reach down to the river, where punting and fishing are possible. At dusk, sip cocktails on the lawn before tackling the extensive restaurant menu which includes typical English dishes. All the 117 bedrooms (there are 10 suites, each named after a Cambridge college) have private bath and shower, and most have small balconies overlooking the gardens and river. Granta Pl. and Mill La. (phone: 63421). Expensive.

Post House – Overlooking a lake, just 1½ miles from the center of town, this relatively new establishment has an appealing countrified atmosphere, 120 rooms, a restaurant, and a heated indoor pool. Lake View, Bridge Rd., Impington (phone: 0223-7000). Expensive.

Royal Cambridge – Spanning several Regency houses, this completely modernized hotel is on the main London–Cambridge road (A10), close to the city center. 74 rooms, most with private baths. Trumpington St. (phone: 351631). Expensive.

Gonville – Next to the green called Parker's Piece, this modern, 60-room hotel is lacking in atmosphere but has a good restaurant. Light refreshments are served on the sheltered patio during summer. Gonville Pl. (phone: 66611). Expensive to moderate.

University Arms – An imposing structure on the edge of Parker's Piece, the *Arms* has belonged to the same family since 1891. The oak-paneled dining room, which overlooks the park and has a grand fireplace, also boasts an impressive wine list that includes several house wines bottled by the proprietor. There are 3 bars, one with 100 different types of whiskey. 116 rooms, all with bath. Regent St. (phone: 351241). Expensive to moderate.

Arundel House – This converted Victorian terrace building overlooks the river and Jesus Green and offers a cozy atmosphere, friendly service, all modern conveniences, and 70-plus rooms. 53 Chesterton Rd. (phone: 67701). Moderate.

The Coach House – Catherine Child converted a coach house into an intimate, 4-room bed-and-breakfast establishment, beautifully set on 2 acres of lawns in a charming village 6 miles northwest of Cambridge on A604. No smoking or children are permitted. Closed January and February. Scotland Rd., Dry Drayton (phone: 0954-82439). Moderate.

Helen – There is a charming Italian-style garden in front of this 25-room hotel, a mile from town and a 10-minute walk from the railway station. 167–69 Hills Rd. (phone: 246465). Moderate.

Rosswill Guest House – Guests receive a warm, friendly welcome from Bill and Muriel Halliday in their comfortable townhouse overlooking the river Cam and Jesus Green. With 13 spacious rooms and ample parking, it's a 10-minute walk from the city center. 17–19 Chesterton Rd. (phone: 67871). Moderate.

Five Gables Farm – This Tudor farmhouse has oak beams, working fireplaces, and a relaxing rural setting. Open May through September only. Buck's La., Little Eversden, about 7 miles southwest of Cambridge (phone: 022026-2236). Inexpensive.

May View Guest House – One of the city's best bargains, a few minutes from the center, overlooking Jesus Green, this is a quiet, comfortable, Victorian house with attention to detail, including antiques — one of which is a four-poster bed. During the summer guests can sip drinks in an attractive Italianate garden. 12 Park Parade (phone: 66018). Inexpensive.

EATING OUT: Although Cambridge is generally rated poorly as an eating town, it is well served by eating houses in the inexpensive (less than $35 for dinner for two without wine) and moderate (between $35 and $70) categories. Most of these places offer extremely good value and large helpings — the latter is an especially important consideration in a town where most of the potential customers are students. Two people can expect to pay over $70 for dinner at a restaurant listed here in the expensive category, some of the best of which are in the more expensive hotels. All telephone numbers are in the 0223 area code unless otherwise indicated.

Midsummer House – Cambridge's newest, smartest eatery is owned by TV celebrity Chris Kelly, a host on the weekly "Food and Drink" program. The restaurant has an enviable location tucked into a corner of Midsummer Common on the riverside. Dress smart to eat upstairs or relax among the leaves in the downstairs conservatory. Food is imaginative, with plenty of fresh vegetables and several fixed-price menus. Closed Mondays, Saturdays for lunch, and Sunday evenings. Midsummer Common (phone: 69299). Expensive.

Don Pasquale – One of the city's top restaurants, with a somewhat Italian menu. The pheasant roasted with capers, onions, parsley, and white wine sauce is especially recommended. Closed Sundays. 12 Market Hill (phone: 67063). Expensive to moderate.

Jean Louis – This classic French restaurant has lots of eye appeal since it's housed in one of Cambridge's cottages at the foot of Castle Hill. The menu has delicious meat and fish dishes. 15 Magdalene St. (phone: 315232). Expensive to moderate.

Brown's – Sunk behind the colonnaded façade of the city's old hospital, this is Cambridge's version of the Oxford *Brown's.* Inside it's bright and airy, with ceiling fans, masses of plants, and a cocktail bar. The cuisine is eclectic, and the portions gargantuan. Open daily. 23 Trumpington St. (phone: 461655). Moderate.

Fagin's – A French restaurant with a river view and an interior richly decorated with retired cinema seats and marble-topped tables. Open daily. 33 Bridge St. (phone: 62054). Moderate.

Michel's Brasserie – One of the few harbingers of nouvelle cuisine in Cambridge, serving such treats as *anticanabale* (pancake filled with zucchini, peppers, and eggplant) and poached filet of lemon sole in cream sauce with grapes. Great people-watching from the first floor. Open daily. 25–26 Bridge St. (phone: 64961). Moderate.

Taj Mahal – The best of Cambridge's dozen-plus Indian restaurants. Try the spicy Lamb Pasanda. 37 Regent St. (phone: 353835). Moderate.

Twenty-Two – In what looks like an ordinary house, a smart, intimate eatery favored by locals celebrating special occasions. The 3-course menu (fixed price about $25) features fresh meat, fish, and game. Closed Sundays and Mondays. 22 Chesterton Rd. (phone: 351880). Moderate.

Eraina – A cosmopolitan taverna with a menu composed of multiple choices, including Italian, French, and Greek dishes as well as charcoal-broiled steaks, roasts, and a selection of 21 omelettes. A favorite among office workers. Open daily. 2 Free School La. (phone: 68786). Moderate to inexpensive.

Old Orleans – Get your tortilla chips and Dixie desserts at this new Southern-style barbecue smokehouse, serving everything from seafood gumbo soup to char-grilled barbecue ribs and a wide selection of cocktails. Open daily from 11 AM to midnight. Miller's Yard, 10–11 Mill La. (phone: 322777). Moderate to inexpensive.

Varsity – Another Greco-Cambridge restaurant, with Franco-Anglo influences, and chips served more or less with everything. The clientele is and has been for generations composed mainly of students enjoying a break from college dinners. There are three dining rooms; the main floor is the best for people-watching. A charming, faded atmosphere, just the right side of seedy, pervades. 35 St. Andrew's St. (phone: 356060). Moderate to inexpensive.

Belinda's Coffee/Wine Bar and Beer Cellar – This self-service restaurant is actually a renovated underground maze of spacious passages. Selections are from a freshly prepared hot and cold buffet, and seating is at counters and tables. Good wine list. Open daily. 14 Trinity St. (phone: 354213). Inexpensive.

Carrington's Coffee House – A popular lunchtime café that serves far more than coffee: hot soups, quiches, meat dishes, cakes, and crêpes. It's in the basement of *Carrington's China Shop,* so mind your elbows on the way down. Closed Sundays. 23 Market St. (phone: 62106). Inexpensive.

Crusts – One of the 18th-century cottagelike buildings that line Northampton Street. Open fires are lighted in winter; outdoor dining is the norm in summer. Filling but uneventful fare: grills, pies, and salads. Open daily. 21–24 Northampton St. (phone: 353110). Inexpensive.

Fitzwilliam Museum Coffee Room – Pâté with tasty breads, homemade quiche, cheesecake, French pastries, and good coffee are among the fare. Closed Sundays and Mondays; otherwise open from 10:30 AM to 4 PM. Trumpington St. (phone: 321443). Inexpensive.

Footlights – A restaurant–bar that claims to serve "the only real Mexican and Texan food in Cambridge." Shoppers' lunch, business lunch, and afternoon tea are featured; 25 different cocktails are mixed at the bar. Wednesday through Saturday evenings showcases live entertainment: jazz, blues, piano music, and Mexican "fiesta." Open daily. Grafton Centre, Fitzroy St. (phone: 323434). Inexpensive.

Hobb's Pavilion – A converted cricket pavilion named after famous cricketer Jack Hobbs, overlooking Parker's Piece, is now *the* Cambridge crêperie. Crêpes come sweet and savory — even filled with Mars bars and cream. Many vegetarian dishes available. Closed Sundays and Mondays. Parker's Piece (phone: 67480). Inexpensive.

Martin's Coffee House – Its rock cakes and homemade doughnuts are in constant demand; hot meals and thick sandwiches are also available. The place is filled with students during the school term but looks a little empty and sad at other times. Closed evenings. 4 Trumpington St. (phone: 61757). Inexpensive.

Nettles – A minuscule vegetarian–health food café with a delicious range of foods, including nut loaf and *muesli* with fruit, and a busy carry-out service. Open from

9 AM to 8 PM; closed Sundays. 6 St. Edward's Passage (phone: 350983). Inexpensive.

Pentagon – An impressive array of hot and cold dishes is displayed. Halfway up the stairs to the *Arts Theatre,* it features photos of actors past and present. Further up, the *Roof Garden* serves coffees and light lunches on a flower-decked terrace. Both closed Sundays. 6 St. Edward's Passage (phone: 359302). Inexpensive.

Sweeney Todd's – A pizza and hamburger joint in an old water mill — you can watch the water gushing over the wheel as you eat. Open daily. Newnham Rd. (phone: 67507). Inexpensive.

For cream teas, try *Auntie's Tea Shop* in St. Mary's Passage (open daily); *The Orchard* at Grantchester (open summers only; closed Wednesdays); and *The Barn* at Fen Ditton (open summers only; closed Mondays and Fridays). An even creamier affair can be enjoyed at the *Copper Kettle,* 4 King's Parade (open daily), where the treats include American-style cheesecake and baba au rhum with pineapple and fresh cream.

SHARING A PINT: Cambridge has many more pubs than colleges, and most of them serve real ale. On Bene't St. is the *Bath,* with traditional bitter and draught cider as well as mature cheeses and hearty breads. The *Baron of Beef* on Bridge St. is a woody, beamy, Old World student haunt. Tucked away at the end of Thompsons La., the *Spade and Beckett* has a peaceful garden looking onto the river. The *Fort St. George in England,* Midsummer Common, is a gathering spot for rowing enthusiasts; you can sip ale and watch the boats at the same time. The *Free Press,* Prospect Row, is a cozy little pub with excellent, inexpensive food, and the *Ancient Druids* in Grafton Centre brews its own beer on the premises. Five miles northwest of the city in the village of Madingley, the pub *Three Horseshoes* has a reputation for good food. During the summer cold drinks are served outside on the lawn.

CANTERBURY

Despite the vast damage inflicted by World War II bombing raids (and subsequent rebuilding and development), there remains enough sheer history in Canterbury to give the impression of time's having stopped somewhere along the line and only recently started again to admit the automobile, electricity, and indoor plumbing. The cathedral, begun in the 11th century and finally completed in the 16th, towers moodily over the pubs and shops crouching nearby; half-timbered, whitewashed little houses line the narrow streets; and the river Stour, long ago plied by seagoing ships, now drifts slowly past brilliant flowerbeds and under arching stone bridges. Countless ghosts walk the passageways unseen, and after dark you can almost hear the chanting of monks on their journey from cloister to dining hall.

But Canterbury's history stretches a good deal farther back than the Middle Ages. The first settlement of any size known to have flourished in the area dates from about 300 BC. In about 75 BC, these poorly organized natives were conquered by the Belgae, a tribe from across the Channel; still later, in 54 BC, Roman troops led by Julius Caesar stormed and took one of the Belgic fortified camps. A full-scale invasion was launched by Emperor Claudius during the next century, and it was after this victory that the Romans settled in permanently. They called the place Durovernum Cantiacorum and built roads connecting the city with other settlements to the north and south. Traces of the Roman period can still be seen around Canterbury. For example, the medieval city walls were built upon the original Roman foundations, and an intricately tiled Roman pavement is found in Butchery Lane.

During the 5th century Britain was invaded and conquered by the Saxons; by 560 the city had forsaken its Roman identity to become Canterbury (actually Cantwarabyrig), the capital of the Saxon kingdom of Kent, ruled by Ethelbert. It was with the arrival in 597 of St. Augustine — sent by the pope to convert Ethelbert and his subjects to Christianity — that Canterbury assumed its new and final role of cathedral city. For in the years that followed, Augustine became archbishop (and primate of all England), founded the Abbey of Sts. Peter and Paul (now called St. Augustine's Abbey), and established the first cathedral.

The city was racked by several invasions during the ensuing years — the Vikings, Danes, and Normans all destroyed much that they found and built anew (including the cathedral). The incident that really put the city on the map, however, was the murder of Thomas à Becket in 1170.

Becket, for years a trusted adviser to King Henry II, was named Archbishop of Canterbury in 1162. Thus began a long power struggle between the two over who was the final authority on church matters. Regarded by some as a traitor, Becket was slain in his own cathedral by four of the king's knights. He was soon canonized and the place where he fell declared a shrine.

(The shrine was destroyed in 1538, and now only a plaque marks the spot.) People from all over the world began to flock to the shrine by the thousands to honor the martyr. So popular was the pilgrimage to Canterbury that Geoffrey Chaucer chose it as the narrative vehicle for his bawdy classic, *Canterbury Tales,* in which each pilgrim tells his story as the group journeys together to the shrine.

Canterbury can claim many literary connections in addition to this most famous one to Chaucer: The dramatist Christopher Marlowe was born here in 1564 and educated at the King's School; you may be able to catch a performance of one of his plays at the new *Marlowe Theatre* in The Friars. Some 3 centuries later, the playwright and novelist W. Somerset Maugham, also a King's alumnus, sent the protagonist in *Of Human Bondage* to school here. R. H. Barham, the 19th-century humorist, was born in St. George's Parish and set parts of his series *The Ingoldsby Legends* in Canterbury. Joseph Conrad, although born in Poland, became one of England's great adventure writers and is buried near Westgate. St. Dunstan's is the setting for several episodes of Charles Dickens's novel *David Copperfield;* in fact, the hotel called the *House of Agnes* on St. Dunstan's Street is supposedly the building Dickens had in mind when he described the home of Agnes Wickfield.

A day's stroll will take you past most of these landmarks, retracing the real or fictitious footsteps of the city's illustrious native sons. If you just let your imagination run a bit as you wander through Canterbury's prim gates and gardens, you'll soon begin to sense its less decorous past — when the pious thronged the city's crowded streets, the taverns roared a welcome, and the scaffold threatened the woebegone wrongdoer.

CANTERBURY AT-A-GLANCE

SEEING THE CITY: As you approach Canterbury — by car on A2 from London, from Dover in the southeast, or from Whitstable a few miles to the north — you are immediately aware of the towering hulk of the cathedral, floodlit by night and somberly gray in the daytime, and no less impressive than it was at the true dawn of England's history. Three viewpoints should not be missed. The first, for a panorama, is the high plateau called Eliot Causeway on the campus of the University of Kent-at-Canterbury, about 2 miles along the road to Whitstable. Admission is free, but visitors are not particularly encouraged. The second is the summit of the Westgate Towers, a massive piece of fortification abutting the City Wall. Admission charge. The third is the roof of the multistory parking lot on Gravel Walk. From here the town's remaining ancient buildings (most were wiped out by wartime bombing) can be seen. Admission by courtesy of the management.

SPECIAL PLACES: Although you've seen the splendor of the cathedral from a distance, you haven't experienced the vastness of its frontage. Walk along the busy shop-lined stretch of Mercery Lane, leading from the middle of High Street, and into the broad patio called Buttermarket. Immediately opposite is the Christ Church Gate; through here you enter another world. From west to east ranges the South West Tower, built in 1460, and behind it the North West Tower of 1840. Then comes the Nave, dating from 1400, and east of that the noble Bell Harry

Tower, raised in 1500. Next are the South East Transept, originating in 1126, and the Choir, put up during the restoration of 1184. The dates given relate only to the superstructure; the main work was started more than 400 years earlier. It is here, in the open, away from the clamor of traffic and trade, that you first experience the sensation of stepping into medieval history.

CANTERBURY CATHEDRAL

The traceable story goes back to the time of Ethelbert, King of Kent, who in 597 granted the site now occupied by the cathedral to St. Augustine, the Christian missionary from Rome. Building began in 602. Little is known of subsequent events until the disastrous fire of 1067, the year following the conquest, after which the cathedral was completely rebuilt from its foundations. The history of the present fabric therefore starts with the work of reconstruction carried out by the first Norman archbishop, Lanfranc, in 1070. A hundred years later the infamous murder of Archbishop Thomas à Becket led to continuing pilgrimages and the common acceptance of Canterbury Cathedral as the "Mother Church of the realm." The cathedral is open Mondays through Saturdays 9 AM to 5 PM (6:30 PM in summer), Sundays 12:30 to 2:30 PM and 4:30 to 5:30 PM. Contact Cathedral House (phone: 762862) for further information.

The Nave – Take a good look at this cavernous, majestic, peaceful enclosure. Designed in about 1400 by Henry Yevele, the architect of Westminster Hall and the nave of Westminster Abbey, it is an example of Perpendicular Gothic and has long been regarded as one of the greatest architectural masterpieces in the world. An interesting and unexplained oddity is that if you stand near the center, at the western end, and view the whole length of the building through the choir screen, the presbytery, and Trinity Chapel, you will notice that the cathedral is not set in a straight line. The eastern part inclines toward the south, or, from your point of view, the right. Exactly behind you is the West Window, with its figure of Adam in the act of digging (removed for restoration but due to be returned). Dating from 1178, it is probably the earliest action picture in existence, for until then, all church windows showed only nonsequential, immobile and flat outlines. Similar illustrated windows appear in all parts of the vast church, forming a rich gallery of medieval artwork. The brilliant jewel-tone windows high in the clerestory look merely decorative from floor level, but with good binoculars you can see more detail, and the fascinating and often lighthearted tales unfold like a newspaper cartoon. The so-called Poor Man's Bible illustrates scenes from the Old and New Testaments for the illiterate populace, miracles supposedly performed at Becket's shrine, and homely little accounts of 13th-century life.

The Tomb of the Black Prince – Edward of Woodstock, son of King Edward III, became Prince of Wales, but was survived by his father and never succeeded to the throne. He is remembered as a hero of the battles of Crécy and Poitiers and a tireless patron of the cathedral. It was under his sponsorship that Henry Yevele was able to carry out major rebuilding in the crypt and also design the Westgate and a considerable portion of the city walls. In 1363 the Black Prince married Joan, the Fair Maid of Kent; this match and the subsequent marriage of their daughters to almost all claimants to the throne resulted in the start of the York and Tudor dynasties. His shrine and tomb, with a replica of all the royal knightly regalia displayed nearby, may be seen in the south aisle of Trinity Chapel. It is considered among the most splendid memorials in England.

The Crypt – This is the oldest part of the cathedral, with a low roof and rounded arches in pure Norman style, its rather frightening severity relieved by grotesque and deliberately humorous carvings on the capitals (top part) of the pillars. Also on view is the original regalia of the Black Prince.

The Martyrdom – The site where Thomas à Becket was slain by four French knights — Fitzurse, de Moreville, de Tracy, and le Breton — on December 29, 1170, is in the northwest transept at the western end of the crypt. The four, with their retainers, were sent on this evil mission because Archbishop Becket refused to place the demands of his king, Henry II, above those of the church. A shrine venerating the saint was erected after his death, although only the original steps remain, worn down by countless thousands of feet over the centuries.

The Canterbury Pilgrims Way – Spend an hour reliving the Thomas à Becket pilgrimage of Chaucerian England in a medieval church 3 minutes from the cathedral. With the help of audio-visual extracts from *The Canterbury Tales,* this permanent exhibition accurately describes a most extraordinary journey. Open daily from 9 AM to 7 PM April through October, to 5:30 PM in winter. Admission charge. St. Margaret's St. (phone: 454888).

The Choir (or Quire) – This might be called the jewel of the cathedral, because of the sparkling beauty of its glasswork, the oldest examples of which are the Twelve Miracle Windows.

The Cloisters, the Chapter House, the Green Court, the King's School – To see the cathedral's entire interior takes the better part of a day, but be sure to make time for the peripheral buildings that date from when the whole was a Benedictine monastery. The Cloisters, leading from the Chapter House, are virtually "corridors in the vale of time." If as you stroll through the passageway called the Dark Entry you encounter the ghost of a certain Nell Cook, don't be alarmed — you're not the first. The story of her origin is obscure, and her occasional appearances are rarely sinister. The Chapter House was the place where Prime Minister Margaret Thatcher and France's President François Mitterand met to sign the treaty that set in motion the Channel Tunnel. Beyond the Green Court, and traditionally associated with the cathedral itself, is the King's School, the oldest public school in the land. (The term "public" is really a misnomer for "private"; this is a very expensive and exclusive private boys' school.) The King's School is notable architecturally for its handsome staircase and stages its own *King's Week Arts Festival* yearly in mid-July.

WITHIN THE OLD CITY WALLS

About half of the initial wall structure still stands; the walkway atop it makes a fascinating hike in good weather.

The Westgate – The next most imposing of Canterbury's historic buildings is at the extreme end of St. Peter's Street, as it joins St. Dunstan's Street, following on from High Street, 5 minutes' walk in a westerly direction from the cathedral. As a relic and the last of the city's fortified gatehouses, it is magnificent, but it has a grisly history: Construction of the Westgate Towers was started at the order of Simon of Sudbury in 1380, during the reign of Richard II. In the following year, it became the city gaol (jail), which it remained until 1829. Today it is a museum exhibiting a collection of arms and armor, shackles, manacles, fetters, and instruments of torture; and the old prison cells still retain their original doors and fittings. Even the timbers of the dreaded gallows are here, a macabre reminder that prisoners were hanged for sometimes quite trivial offenses. Open daily except Sundays from 10 AM to 1 PM and from 2 to 5 PM April to September, from 2 to 4 PM October to March. Admission charge. St. Peter's St. (phone: 452747).

Dane John Mound – Nothing to do with Danes, but a prominent feature of central Canterbury, the top of the prehistoric rise giving fine views of the red tile Tudor houses in the neighborhood. The name comes from the Norman-French word *donjon,* meaning a castle or keep, or — more chillingly — a dungeon. Dane John Mound lies southwest of the cathedral on Pin Hill, about 5 minutes' walk from Christ Church Gate.

The Norman Castle – A vast ruin now, but it still possesses one of the largest Norman keeps in the country. It was built between 1070 and 1094 and has been several times surrounded and captured and was once the royal prison for the County of Kent. Like the Westgate, it has a grim history of cruelty and mayhem. When the fanatical

Mary I was on the throne, many Protestants were imprisoned here before being burned at the stake for their religious opinions. The Norman Castle is at the junction of Castle St. and Rheims Way.

OUTSIDE THE PERIMETER

St. Dunstan's – The section of Old Canterbury beyond the Westgate and leading toward the railway crossing on Whitstable Road. A good place of call is the *House of Agnes,* now a hotel on St. Dunstan's Street (see *Eating Out*), reputedly the one Dickens had in mind as the house of Agnes Wickfield in *David Copperfield.* The interesting old *Falstaff Inn* is nearly opposite, and a door or so away is a small, cozy pub called the *Bishop's Finger.* (The name refers to the ring worn by medieval bishops.)

St. Augustine's Abbey – Founded by St. Augustine, with the support of King Ethelbert, in AD 602. Though largely a ruin, it is an important and still beautiful relic of Canterbury's past, particularly the finely restored Fyndon Gate. Reached from the Quenin Gate of the cathedral.

ENVIRONS

Chilham Castle Keep – A 10-mile drive southwest of Canterbury is Chilham Castle, the home of Viscount Massereene and Ferrard and one of the finest houses in Kent. Neither the Jacobean house nor the adjacent splendidly preserved Norman keep is open to the public, but the surrounding gardens remain an attraction for visitors. Open daily from 11 AM to 5 PM April to mid-October, with jousting displays on Sundays. Admission charge. Chilham (phone: 730319).

Howletts and Port Lympne Zoo Parks – The largest breeding colony of gorillas outside the US is contained within these two zoo parks, run by John Aspinall and his family. Also here are a fine collection of other rare, endangered species, including great cats and free-roaming herds of deer and antelope. Open daily except Christmas Day from 10 AM to 5 PM or dusk. Admission charge. Howletts is at Bekesbourne, 3 miles south of Canterbury (phone: 721286); Port Lympne is off A20 between Ashford and Folkestone (phone: 64646).

Fordwich – Drive to Sturry, 4 miles north of Canterbury on Rte A28. Turn right at the signpost. The tiny former Cinque Port on the river Stour is less than a minute away. It is an exquisite little town of some 300 inhabitants and is remarkable for having the smallest town hall in England, delightful to look at and scarcely bigger than a farmworker's cottage. Nobody knows how old the structure is, but the records show that extensive repairs were carried out as recently as 1474. Here again, you'll see instruments of torture. The stocks are outside in the courtyard, their oaken clamps worn slim from centuries of use; the small prison is in one corner; and overlooking the river stands the crane that once lowered condemned miscreants into the water for drowning. Beside it is the ducking chair for the correction of shrewish wives, and in the town hall itself you can inspect the room set aside for drying them off. An excellent place for lunch is the *George and Dragon,* round the corner from the town hall (see *Best in Town*).

Badges Hill Fruit Farm – While exploring the orchard country around Canterbury, call in at this farm where they make pippin cider. There are local crafts and farm produce for sale, and you can join the English in one of their favorite summer hobbies — picking fruit. Chilham, 6 miles from Canterbury (phone: 730573).

■ **EXTRA SPECIAL:** During the third week of July, a series of choir and orchestra concerts are given at the King's School and in the environs of the cathedral. The musical performances are very well done and performed in glorious surroundings, but wear something warm — it can get very chilly in the evenings. Buy tickets at Forwood Bookings, 37 Palace St. (phone: 55600).

SOURCES AND RESOURCES

TOURIST INFORMATION: The tourist information center is at 34 St. Margaret's St. (phone: 766567), close to the cathedral. It stocks the usual helpful guidebooks, brochures, and maps; has a 24-hour computerized information service; and is open daily from 10 AM to 5 PM year-round, except on Sundays September through April. Guided tours of the city, including cathedral precincts, leave St. Margaret's Street daily at 2:15 PM from May until September; there is a fee. Guided tours of the cathedral only are conducted several times daily, except Sundays, and Easter through October. To arrange additional or out-of-season tours, consult the Guild of Guides, Arnett House, Hawks La. (phone: 459779). The city's Leisureline Information Service can be reached at 767744.

Local Coverage – The weekly *Kentish Gazette* includes a useful *Town Crier* supplement, which lists all local events. Available at *Kent County Newspapers Ltd.,* 9 St. George's Pl. (phone: 768181).

Telephone – The area code for Canterbury is 0227.

GETTING AROUND: As Canterbury is very small, walking is the best form of transportation. To visit some of the outlying areas, you'll need to know about alternate modes of conveyance, discussed below.

Bus – From the bus station on St. George's Lane (near *Riceman's* department store), you can catch National Express coaches to London's Victoria Station (about 2 hours) and buses to Dover, Folkestone, Deal, and Margate (all about an hour's ride). For information, call 766151.

Car Rental – There are many car rental firms in Canterbury: among them *U-Drive Rentals* (phone: 463700), *Canterbury Motor Co. Ltd.* (phone: 451791, ext. 51); *Hertz* (phone: 765654), *Invicta* (phone: 762780), *Dane Valley* (phone: 710590). There is adequate, low-cost parking in the city.

Taxi – Quick and courteous cab service is available at all times. Try *Austen's Taxis* (phone: 454105); *Bishop's Taxis* (phone: 65566); *Canterbury Radio Taxis* (phone: 760333), or *Taylor's Taxis* (phone: 456363).

Train – *Britrail's* InterÇity 125 trains run frequently from London's Victoria Station to Canterbury East Station (Station Rd.), continuing on to Dover. London–Canterbury travel time is 1 hour and 20 minutes. Regular service between London's Charing Cross Station and Canterbury West Station (Station Rd. W) takes about 2 hours. For information, phone: 454441.

SPECIAL EVENTS: In mid-July the *King's Week Arts Festival* is held at the King's School. In late September or early October the annual *Canterbury Festival* takes place, with a costumed procession through the streets, followed by events such as plays and concerts. For details, write to Canterbury Festival, 59 Ivy Lane (452853). At Easter and during the summer the *Chaucer Festival* is celebrated with various medieval events; contact the tourist information center for more details (phone: 766567).

MUSEUMS AND GALLERIES: Religious articles are displayed in Canterbury's churches and cathedral. Besides the Westgate and the Canterbury Cathedral mentioned in *Special Places,* other interesting museums include the following:

Royal Museum and Art Gallery(the Beaney Institute) – Incorporates *Buff's*

Regimental Museum and chronicles the area's history and archaeology. Closed Sundays. 18 High St. (phone: 452747).

Roman Pavement – Shelters the remains of a Roman mosaic floor and other artifacts. Closed Sundays. Butchery La. (phone: 452747).

Heritage Museum – Housed in the 13th-century Poor Priests' Hospital on Stour St., it offers a walk through the city's history: The museum contains the 150-year-old *Invicta,* a steam-powered locomotive designed by George Stephenson, and a working remnant of one of the earliest passenger railways in the world. Open Mondays through Saturdays and Sunday afternoons during summer (phone: 452747).

Drew Gallery – Holds exhibitions of contemporary paintings, sculpture, prints, and ceramics by local, national, and international artists. Closed Thursdays and Sundays. 16 Best La. (phone: 458759)

A medieval church provides the setting for guided tours recreating the Thomas Becket pilgrimage from London to Canterbury Cathedral at the Pilgrims Ways Center on St. Margaret's Street. A reduced-price, combined ticket is available for entry to *Canterbury Heritage, The Royal Museum and Art Gallery,* and *Roman Pavement.* Contact the museum secretary (phone: 452747).

SHOPPING: Wednesday is market day, although Canterbury's compact size makes any day here a shopper's dream. Thursday is late-shopping night; the stores are open until 8 PM. For a wide selection of the basic necessities, try *Riceman's* department store, opposite the bus station; *Debenham's,* on Guildhall St.; or *Marks & Spencer,* 4 St. George's St. If your hobby is antiques, spend a morning in Palace St. — turn right out of Christ Church Gate of the cathedral and then right again. There are many old buildings here now housing antiques such as *Parker-Williams Antiques,* No. 22. Other specialty shops we recommend include the following:

Ardennes – For authentic French bread, baked fresh daily. 16 Burgate.

Canterbury Pottery – Pottery collectors should be sure to stop in at this shop whose wares are handmade on the premises. On the far side of Buttermarket, just before Mercery La.

Chaucer Bookshop – The place to pick up your copy of *Canterbury Tales* as well as out-of-print, antiquarian, and general secondhand tomes. 6 Beercart La.

Culpepper – A a branch of the well-known herbal specialists shops. 11 Marlowe Arcade.

Fudge Kitchen – At Jim Garrahy's shop visitors can see fudge being made and try a free sample. On Burgate.

Indoor Market – Usually a collector's and bargain hunter's paradise.St. Peter's St.

Kynttila – Stocks a wide selection of interesting candles and candlesticks. 30 Palace St.

Liberty – A branch of the the famous London store specializing in quality fabrics and clothes is in a fine old building; upstairs visitors can enjoy refreshments among the rafters and beams in the tea room. Corner of Burgate and Butchery Lane.

Next – One of Britain's most popular designer fashion chains. On St. Margaret's St.

Tube – For the trendiest clothes. Marlowe Arcade.

Villa Toscana – Stocks china vases, jardinières, stoneware, terra cotta, reproductions of antique furniture, and a huge range of classic Italian leather handbags. 1 Roper Rd.

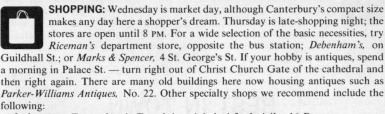

SPORTS: Cricket – Canterbury is cricket territory; to watch this very British game at its best, go to the *Kent Country Cricket Club* at St. Lawrence Ground, off Old Dover Rd. (phone: 63421). Tickets are available at the gate.

Golf – The well-kept 18-hole *Canterbury Golf Club,* Littlebourne Rd.

(phone: 63586), is open to the public. Players with established handicaps are preferred, but novices are not discouraged. Clubs may be rented.

Horseback Riding – Horses can be hired at two stables about 5 miles due north of Canterbury: *High Rews Equestrian Centre,* Canterbury Rd., Herne Common (phone: 02273-62678), and *Homecroft Riding Stables,* Canterbury Rd., Herne Common (phone: 02273-2065).

Swimming – The Kingsmead indoor swimming pool on Kingsmead is open to the public. Admission charge (phone: 69817).

THEATER: Canterbury has only one commercial playhouse, the *Marlowe,* at The Friars, which opened in the spring of 1984 (phone: 767246). The *Gulbenkian Theatre* of the University of Kent on St. Giles La. (phone: 69075) is generally open to the public during the university terms only; its offerings include plays, recitals, concerts, and lectures. Check the newspapers for schedules.

NIGHTCLUBS AND NIGHTLIFE: There's not much after-dark entertainment in Canterbury. However, one possibility is *Alberry's Wine and Food Bar,* 38A St. Margaret St. (phone: 452378), for an enjoyable evening of eating and drinking and, on Monday, Tuesday, and Thursday nights, listening to live music downstairs in its Roman cellar. *Crotchets Wine Bar,* 59 Northgate (phone: 458857), has more than 60 wines on its list, a garden, and, most nights, live jazz. *Studio Three Nightclub and Midnight Bar,* in the Invicta Radio Building (15 Station Rd. E.; phone: 462520), is the town's classiest music venue. Over 21 only.

BEST IN TOWN

CHECKING IN: Book well in advance, because the city welcomes about 2 million visitors during the summer. Most of the hotels listed below are smallish but make up for this shortcoming with their cheerful and attentive service. None, however, is in the true luxury class, except for nearby *Eastwell Manor,* in Ashford. For a double room in the hotels we list below, expect to pay $80 to $150 per night in those noted as expensive; $45 to $80, moderate; and $30 to $45, inexpensive. All telephone numbers are in the 0227 area code unless otherwise indicated.

County – First licensed in 1629, it is considered the best in Canterbury and is richly decorated and furnished in antiques. The hotel's restaurant specializes in continental cuisine. 74 rooms; parking available. High St. (phone: 66266). Expensive.

Eastwell Manor – This turreted, rambling country-house hotel offers 24 luxurious, spacious rooms furnished with antiques, and an accomplished kitchen, all set amid extensive gardens. It's about 10 miles southwest of Canterbury and a first class choice for visitors who long to experience life in an elegant rural setting. Eastwell Park, Boughton Aloph, near Ashford (phone: 0233-35751). Expensive.

Slatters – Part Tudor, part Queen Anne, part Roman, but mostly modern, this 32-room hotel is just 200 yards from the cathedral and continuously busy. Parking is available. St. Margaret's St. (phone: 463271). Expensive.

Abbots Barton – At this large country house surrounded by its own 2 acres of attractive grounds, guests will find log fires and a quiet, old-fashioned ambience, good food, and solid, comfortable furniture. In short, it's the perfect home base for families. Facilities include 50 modern rooms (all with private bath) and parking. 37 New Dover Rd. (phone: 760341). Moderate.

George and Dragon – This charming 16th-century inn near the river Stour has 13 rooms. Its restaurant, which serves steak dinners, also offers a very fine hot and cold buffet lunch and is open daily. Fordwich, near Sturry (phone: 710661). Moderate.

Ann's Guest House – A family-run, Victorian house featuring four-poster beds in most of its 19 rooms and good parking facilities. 63 London Rd. (phone: 68767). Inexpensive.

Georgian Guest House – If you're a little eccentric, you'll find yourself one of the family at this 15th-century antiques-filled bed-and-breakfast establishment. 69 Castle St. (phone: 461111). Inexpensive.

EATING OUT: Although it's a country town, Canterbury boasts a few very fine restaurants that serve expertly prepared meals for reasonable prices. There are also some cozy little eateries in the surrounding area, which you may decide to include on a day tour out of town. In general, a meal for two, excluding wine, tips, and drinks, will run about $60 to $80 in a place listed as expensive, $35 to $60 in a moderate one, and under $35 in an inexpensive one. All telephone numbers are in the 0227 area code unless otherwise indicated.

Beehive – During the Middle Ages, this was a pub conveniently located across the way from the cattle market; during the 18th century, it was a smugglers' lair. Today it's one of Canterbury's best restaurants — a small and intimate place specializing in continental food. Closed Saturdays for lunch and Sundays. Reservations necessary. 52 Dover St. (phone: 61126). Expensive.

Duck Inn – This snug little restaurant, set in a 16th-century cottage in the midst of a farm field, is warmed by a roaring fire and is noted for its very good French cooking. It's about 5 miles outside Canterbury, near the village of Bridge on the road to Dover. The best way to reach it is by taxi. Closed Mondays and Tuesdays. Reservations necessary. Pett Bottom (phone: 830354). Expensive.

Ristorante Tuo e Mio – Just the place for a rich, satisfying Italian lunch or dinner with plenty of fresh produce and pasta. Top it off with a sinful *zubaglione.* Parking is not too good, so walk instead. Closed Mondays for lunch and from late August to early September. Reservations necessary. 16 The Borough (phone: 61471). Expensive.

House of Agnes – Referred to in Dickens's *David Copperfield,* it's now a hotel as well as a restaurant. The kitchen prepares good hearty English home cooking. Reservations necessary. 71 St. Dunstan's St. (phone: 65077). Moderate.

Marlowe's – A friendly eatery that features health food, a salad bar, and a cocktail bar. Open daily. St. Peter's St. (phone: 464569). Moderate.

Pranzo e Cana – This Italian restaurant is a newcomer to the scene. Expect the usual, but very tasty, pasta and sauces. Closed Mondays. 41 Broad St. (phone: 459174). Moderate.

Queen Elizabeth – In an authentic Tudor building, once the cathedral's guesthouse where Elizabeth I reputedly stayed, there is now a pleasant restaurant known for its good lunches and teas. Closed Sundays. High St. (phone: 464080). Moderate to inexpensive.

Caesars – A student haunt, with huge hamburgers and generous portions of ribs and other transatlantic dishes. Open daily. 46 St. Peter's St. (phone: 456833). Inexpensive.

Teapot – It's well worth taking a walk up to the end of St. Peter's Street to find this charming tea room and restaurant. In a cottage-like interior with lacey tablecloths and old wooden chairs 170 different teas are sold as well as cream teas and vegetarian meals. Open daily, 10 AM to about 9 PM. 34 St. Peter's St (phone: 463175). Inexpensive.

SHARING A PINT: For a special experience, stop by the *Millers Arms,* Mill La. (phone: 452675); it's an authentic oak-beamed, flagstone-floored pub that even has its own minuscule brewery. Possibly the friendliest and most atmospheric pub, which also serves tea and coffee all day, is the *Olive Branch,* 39 Burgate (phone: 462170), opposite the cathedral gates. The *City Arms,* Butchery La. (phone: 457900), has very good bar lunches, real ale, and live music on Wednesday evenings.

CARDIFF

"A proper fine Towne" was how the 17th-century cartographer Christopher Saxton described Cardiff. And today it's a proper fine city: handsome, spacious, and genial, with a definite sense of its own importance. It is, after all, the capital city of the principality of Wales. And it has a capital feel about it. You sense right away that it is at the center of things. It is a busy headquarters for commerce, industry, government, the arts, and communications. And it has perhaps the most attractive city center in all of Britain — the Welsh Washington, as it's called.

From London, Cardiff is 2½ hours away on the M4 (Swansea) motorway, or less than 2 hours by the 125-mph super-train, nicknamed the *Welsh Bullet.* And the Central Station sign says *Caerdydd/*Cardiff in salute to the two languages of Wales, hinting at the history, pride, and fascination of this singular land. Welsh, spoken by one-fifth of the principality's 2.8 million people, is Wales's distinction among nations; and its story is a central part of the history of the Welsh people.

In Cardiff you'll see the language (it's older than English, dating from the 6th century) written on all manner of signs. You're sure to see the word *Croeso* — "welcome" — and the Welsh mean it. And you'll hear the language spoken in the streets and shops and on radio and television.

But you won't hear it a lot. For one thing, Cardiff is in southeast Wales, and the strongly Welsh-speaking areas are in the north and west. Cardiffians, however, have their own distinctive twang, one of the many strands from which the city's character is woven. It is a multilayered and cosmopolitan place (twinned with Nantes in France, Stuttgart in Germany, and Xiamen in China), an outward-looking, modern European city of warm people, as well as a storehouse of the history of a fascinating area — three of the thirteen Welsh signatories of the Declaration of Independence were sons of Cardiff, and Dr. Richard Price, who wrote pamphlets supporting the colonists' cause, came from nearby Bridgend.

Cardiff is Europe's youngest capital city, awarded the status by Queen Elizabeth in 1956, at a time when nationalist feeling in Wales was demanding some recognition of the principality's special identity within the United Kingdom. Other towns applied for the honor, but Cardiff was the home of the Welsh Office, headquarters of all Welsh administration, and the Temple of Peace, which administers all liaison between Wales and the United Nations. With such administrative prowess and a population of 277,000, the city had the scale, background, and facilities to make it a realistic contender.

Diligent Romans built a no-nonsense little Cardiff beside the river Taff as part of their network of conquest. The thick-walled stone fortress they constructed around AD 76 served as a defense and trading post. The Roman stones, still visible around the first 2 feet of the castle walls, were already old when the Normans arrived in the 11th century and established their own stronghold on the site of the old Roman fort.

On a mound they raised a keep, a noble medieval fist, and it remains intact: one of the finest examples of its kind in Britain. Castle, moat, and green are right in the city center, and Cardiffians like to saunter or doze on the green on summer days.

King Edward I of England conquered stubborn Wales in the 13th century. But a hundred years or so later, in 1404, the Welsh political comet Owain Glyndwr fanned the embers of resistance, started a war of independence, and sacked Cardiff. Eventually he lost his struggle, but 5 centuries later Cardiff was generous enough to erect a marble statue of the hero in its opulent city hall.

Roundheads took the town from Royalists in Britain's 17th-century civil war. But for nearly 200 years after that, life was peaceful enough. Cardiff bloomed quietly, a market town, seaport, and occasional bolt-hole for pirates prowling the Bristol Channel.

Then the Industrial Revolution came. Up in the winding green valleys, spoking from Cardiff's hub, men tore out coal to fuel factories, furnaces, mills, ships. The coal was sent to Cardiff, first by mule, then barge, then rail, for shipment to British cities and the world.

The new Cardiff soared on the dizzy spiral of the great coal rush, the central event in post-1800 Welsh history. The riches of the valleys poured in. The river Taff ran black. Tycoons multiplied. With Welsh coal at the heart of British economic expansion, Cardiff became the world's greatest coal port. The Cardiff Coal Exchange is still there in dockland, monument to an age, a stately Victorian edifice in Coalowner Gothic. Look at it, and in your mind's eye you can see the frock-coated financiers making their fortunes.

In its heyday, Cardiff's dockland was called Tiger Bay. It was a teeming, noisy, rumbustious Dodge City of pubs, little houses, and bordellos. Today old Tiger Bay has gone, for it was a time as well as a place. The slums have been cleared and the area is often cited as an example of an integrated multiracial community of long standing. And its people prefer you to use its proper name: Butetown.

During Cardiff's Victorian and Edwardian expansion, its top citizens consolidated its position as chief city of Wales. Among lawns, shrubs, and boulevards they built their halls of government and culture: city hall, county hall, museum, law courts, university, and others, all laid out in a grand, magisterial sweep. Meanwhile, the burgeoning middle classes built lovely villas in places like Cathedral Road.

One of the most pleasant things about Cardiff is that its heart remains village-size. And the castle, the business center, shops, restaurants, pubs, hotels, station, rugby stadium, museum, theaters, galleries, and parks can all be reached comfortably on foot.

You can traverse the city by way of parks, greens, and footpaths; and the stroll across Llandaff Fields to Llandaff, the secluded village within the city, with its cathedral, pubs, and cottages, is a great favorite (see *Special Places*).

One of the famous parks, though, is not a park at all: Cardiff Arms Park is a temple of rugby football, a game to which Welshmen devote blood, sweat, and tears. On big-match Saturdays the city seems to vibrate with emotion, song, and excitement. The Red Dragon flag of Wales is hoisted aloft and almost everyone seems to have a leek or a daffodil, the national emblems, pinned to hat or coat. To be in Cardiff on one of these days is to experience a certain kind of Welshness, humorous and exuberant, in the raw.

CARDIFF AT-A-GLANCE

SEEING THE CITY: Right in the middle of town is the best place to get a feel for Cardiff: the exhilarating castle. It is open almost every day of the year. Cross the moat bridge, go through the gate house, turn left, and make for the clock tower. From here you get a sentry's-eye view of the castle itself, the river Taff, the Arms Park, *Sophia Gardens Cricket Ground,* and busy shopping streets. You can also see the famous "animal wall" — a row of sculptures of beasts and birds perched on battlements. You can see Bute Park, stretching off in the direction of Llandaff cathedral; and the pristine towers, domes, and greenery of Cathays Park (pronounced "*catt*-hays"). Much the same view can be had from a slightly different vantage point, the roof garden of the castle. This is a piece of delicious Victorian extravagance, with its delightful shrubs, murals, mosaics, and fountains. On the northwest edge of Cardiff is The Wenallt, an area of rolling woodland that offers a superb view of Cardiff, laid out on its coastal plain, and of the Bristol Channel.

SPECIAL PLACES: Although Cardiff owes much of its importance and growth to coal, there has been over the years a conscious effort to keep its center free of grime. The city fathers of the last century dreamt they dwelt in marble halls — and set about making that dream come true. As a result, Cardiff is, at its center, a place of gracefulness, greenery, and wide avenues. Its compactness means that, for the most part, you can park the car and walk to the principal sights and that you are never far from a little restaurant, a jolly pub, or a stretch of grass where you might do as the locals do and chat, read, gaze, or snooze.

CITY CENTER

In 1898, the city fathers bought 60 acres from the Marquess of Bute — Cathays Park, in fact — and planned what is today's Civic Centre. A short walk from the main shopping area and just northeast of the castle, it includes all of Cardiff's most impressive public buildings: City Hall, the *National Museum,* and the Welsh Office, plus the University College and the Institute of Science and Technology. Built with white Portland stone, these are all grouped around a war memorial on the fringe of Bute Park.

Cardiff Castle – Nineteen hundred years of history are stored here. The Roman walls are 10 feet thick, and the Norman stone keep on its *motte,* or mound, was built to last when it was erected in the 11th century to show the locals who was boss. In the 19th century, the third Marquess of Bute, one of Wales's great coal moguls, ordered the renovations and extensions of the castle that give the place its unique appearance. He commissioned the architect William Burges to design a nobleman's indulgence. The result is the baroque and charming place of today, full of color, exquisite murals, carvings, and painted ceilings and windows. There is a table with a hole in it, through which a vine emerged, enabling the marquess and guests to pluck fresh grapes. Part of the castle is now used for civic receptions and banquets. (Medieval banquets are held every evening except Sundays year-round; phone 372737 for booking and information.) Other rooms and towers house the *Museum of the Welch Regiment.* A visit to the castle includes an excellent conducted tour, although you can wander on your own among the peacocks, if you prefer. Open daily; admission charge. Castle St. (phone: 822083).

National Museum of Wales – A short walk from the castle is one of Britain's finest museums. Huge and airy, it offers a broad-ranging and detailed introduction to Wales in all aspects. It has a remarkable collection of carved Celtic standing stones and crosses; a host of national treasures; and a gallery housing, among much else, the work of artists like Augustus John and his sister Gwen and an outstanding collection of Impressionist paintings, the centerpiece being Renoir's *La Parisienne.* Apart from its large permanent collection, the *National* hosts touring art exhibitions. Open daily except Mondays from 10 AM to 5 PM, Sundays from 2:30 to 5 PM. Museum Ave., Cathays Park (phone: 397951).

City Hall – Next to the museum and the first building to go up in Cathays Park (1905), it is distinguished by its clock tower and ornate stonework. Inside is the Marble Hall with its statues of the great men of Welsh history. Closed weekends. City Hall Rd., Cathays Park.

Welsh Industrial and Maritime Museum – Four acres of Pier Head in Cardiff's dockland are devoted to the museum, which tells the story of Welsh industrial progress. The exhibits range from coal mines, iron and steel works, and tinplate mills, plus several outdoor displays. Open daily except Mondays from 10 AM to 5 PM. Bute St. (phone: 481919).

Cathays Park – Pink-surfaced avenues, blossoms, shrubs, walks, statuary, and buildings of an almost Athenian aspect. The Welsh are rightly proud of it.

St. John's Church – A landmark in Cardiff since the 15th century, with its tall pinnacled tower in the Perpendicular style. It is the heart of the city's commercial and shopping district and is a 2-minute walk from the castle.

ENVIRONS

Llandaff Fields – On these tree-lined meadows in summer, boys are playing baseball (surprisingly popular in these parts) or cricket, maybe dreaming of playing first class cricket one day at *Sophia Gardens,* the handsome ground in the city center. This is a lovely setting for the game that is a British passion and a mystery to foreigners. Why not go for a few hours and enjoy trying to understand the ritual? In winter the boys will be playing rugby and dreaming of playing in the red shirt for Wales at Cardiff Arms Park.

Llandaff – Two miles from the city center. You can reach it by bus or by walking across Llandaff Fields. Llandaff is a charming enclave: Somehow it has retained a sleepy village air with its neat and solid Victorian houses, inns, whitewashed deanery, and a village green from which a path leads to the cathedral, beautiful and discreet in its hollow. St. Teilo founded a settlement here in the 6th century, which is how Llandaff got its name: *llan* (church) and *taff,* from the river Taff. The cathedral dates from the 12th century. It fell into disrepair and was at one time a beer house and cattle shelter. It was restored in the 19th century, wrecked in an air raid in 1941, and restored once more. One of its most striking features, and still controversial, is Epstein's aluminum figure of Christ, which dominates the nave.

Old Bishops Palace – In keeping with the rest of Llandaff: peaceful gardens among ancient walls, a place for reflection.

Butetown – Cardiff's famous and notorious Tiger Bay of days gone by. Time was when seafaring men from many parts of the world settled in this dockland area and created a vibrant, tough, and often seamy and squalid community. Things have changed a lot, and though Butetown is still a lively, mixed community, it prides itself on its respectability. The coal trade isn't what it was, but the docks are still very important. And it's interesting to see the imposing shipping and banking offices and the Coal Exchange, built in the great days of the coal rush. Butetown is also home to the *Welsh Industrial and Maritime Museum,* which displays the machinery that powered early industrial growth and other pioneering equipment (see "City Center"). From High Street in the city center, you can get a bus to the museum, in the heart of Butetown.

Castell Coch – With its turreted, fairy-tale towers, the Red Castle dominates the northern pass into Cardiff from the South Wales valleys. Built by William Burges, who was also partially responsible for Cardiff Castle, it was designed as a hunting lodge for the third Marquess of Bute (1846–1900), the romantic model for Disraeli's novel *Lothair* (1820). Its remarkable, fantastic (in the literal sense of the word) interior includes a carved wooden ceiling as well as wooden parrots along the gallery. Open daily from 9:30 AM to 6:30 PM mid-March to mid-October; off-season hours are from 9:30 AM to 4 PM, except Sundays from 2 to 4 PM. Admission charge. Taffs Well (phone: 810101).

Roath Park – Some 100 acres, with an attractive lake. You can rent a rowboat very cheaply (just keep away from the serious young lads fishing from the banks). Admire the geese camped on the island and pause at the miniature lighthouse, a memorial to the Antarctic hero Captain Robert Falcon Scott (1868–1912), who sailed from Cardiff to make his ill-fated expedition to the South Pole.

Dyffryn Gardens – These are a few miles west of the city center, on Rte. A48 at St. Nicholas. On the way down the winding country road (where you can get a good feel for the lovely Vale of Glamorgan), stop at the Tinkinswood long barrow, one of the finest examples of a neolithic burial chamber to be found in Wales: It has a 40-ton capstone. Dyffryn House (phone: 593328) is a spacious mansion with 70 acres of spacious grounds to match. It has masses of flowers, shrubs, and trees — and a teahouse, which makes it a perfect place to wind down and draw breath. Open from April through September, and weekends in October; admission charge. You can reach Dyffryn by bus from the station, No. X1 or No. 231.

■ **EXTRA SPECIAL:** Out on the edge of the Vale of Glamorgan, 4½ miles from the city center, at St. Fagan's, is one of Cardiff's most pleasant treats, the *Welsh Folk Museum* (phone: 569441). Among the buildings in the 100-acre estate around the newly renovated Tudor mansion are an original cottage, farmhouses, barns, a smithy, tollhouse, chapel, tannery, cockpit, and a woolen factory. Each one once stood in some part of rural Wales, was carefully taken apart, its stones and slates and beams numbered, then reconstructed in the sheep-grazed meadows of St. Fagan's. The furnishings and equipment are authentic, too, and you can wander through the houses, upstairs and downstairs, to see how Welsh people lived through the centuries. Note the cozy fireside beds and the lovespoons that young men carved for their sweethearts: the more intricate the carving, the deeper the passion! St. Fagan's tells the story of the people of Wales. The attendants are jolly and helpful, and all speak Welsh. In addition to the authentic buildings, St. Fagan's has a large museum, a buttery, and a restaurant. Open daily from 10 AM to 5 PM, Sundays from 2:30 PM; admission charge. Take the No. 32 bus, which leaves from the station every hour on the hour.

SOURCES AND RESOURCES

TOURIST INFORMATION: In the Welsh language the name of the Wales Tourist Board is *Bwrdd Croeso Cymru* — literally translated as Wales Welcome Board. It indicates how the Welsh feel about showing visitors their land. The board's office in Cardiff is in the center, at 8–14 Bridge Street, near the new *Holiday Inn* (phone: 227281). Here visitors can get maps, guidebooks, leaflets, advice, and directions (open Mondays through Saturdays from 9:30 AM to 6 PM). The printed material is first rate, and the advice is bright and friendly. A 24-hour computerized "Infopoint" information display is in the window. Visitors can also get information about Cardiff from the Public Relations Officer, City Hall (phone: 822000).

The Wales Tourist Board publishes an excellent, clear, and colorful map of Wales as well as *The Cardiff Guide* booklet (about $.75), and good inexpensive maps and guides to Cardiff are available from newsagents and bookshops like *W. H. Smith* and *Menzies. Lears,* in the Royal Arcade and *Oriel,* on Charles St., carry a wide selection of books about Wales.

Local Coverage – The city's public relations office publishes brochures, books, and a useful monthly guide called *Events in Cardiff.* Information about restaurants and entertainments is available from the Wales Tourist Board. Daily movie, theater, and concert listings are in the *Western Mail,* published every morning except Sunday, *Wales on Sunday,* and the *South Wales Echo,* Cardiff's afternoon paper.

Telephone – The area code for Cardiff is 0222.

GETTING AROUND: Air – Cardiff–Wales Airport is accessible via Amsterdam's Schiphol Airport from any major world destination. There are also domestic flights to Belfast, Bristol, Guernsey, and Jersey. The airport is 10 miles west of the city center on A4226 (phone: 0446-711211).

Bus – At its heart Cardiff is a walker's city. But there's a bus network that operates until late at night. *Cardiff Buses* (phone: 396521) runs a good variety of tours in summer months using open-top double-decker buses, starting from Greyfriars Road. An information kiosk is in the bus station.

Car Rental – Most major national and international firms have offices in Cardiff: *Hertz* (phone: 24548), *Avis* (phone: 42111), and *Godfrey Davis* (phone: 498978, 497110).

Taxi – Cabs (*thacsis*) don't cruise as a rule. The Wales Tourist Board has a good taxi list, and there are plenty of firms in the yellow pages. *Castle Cabs* (phone: 394929), *City Centre Cars* (phone: 488888), *Amber Cars* (phone: 378111, 378378), and *Metro Cabs* (phone: 464646) are among those offering 24-hour service. There are cab ranks at Central Station and the Friary in the city center.

Train – Good rail services to the suburbs, outlying towns, valleys, and villages and fast intercity services. London is 1 hour and 45 minutes away. *Valley Line* local trains run from both Central and Queen Street stations. A direct line now links Cardiff to Bangor in north Wales, which allows speedy access to Snowdonia. Information from *British Rail,* Central Station, Penarth Rd. (phone: 28000).

SPECIAL EVENTS: The *Llandaff Festival of Music* is growing in stature and is held every June. A big rugby match is always a special event: You're unlikely to get tickets for an international competition, but less important matches are just as passionate and exciting. The *Cardiff Spectacular* will be held for the first time in 1990 and should include military pageantry. As we went to press it was slated to take place in August (phone: 0222-751235; ask for Andrew Kerr). The *Cardiff Festival of Music* (classical) convenes for 3 weeks in late November and December. Under men like the 10th-century King Hywel Dda (Hywel the Good), culture flourished and the *eisteddfod* (pronounced eye-steth-vod), a competitive festival of poetry and song, became part of the Welsh tradition. There are numerous *eisteddfodau* in Wales today, the biggest being the *National Eisteddfod,* which attracts huge crowds. This festival is traditionally a nomadic one, held alternately in north and south Wales. In 1990 it is scheduled to take place in the town of Cwmrumney from August 4 through 11 (phone: 0222-398399). The bardic ceremonies, held on Tuesdays and

Thursdays, were invented in the last century to provide pageantry (but no one takes them *too* seriously), and the winning poets are treated like pop stars, feted by crowds, blinking in the TV lights. The other eisteddfod worth a mention is the *International Eisteddfod,* held every July in a huge field on the boundaries of Llangollen in Clywd, North Wales. Created originally to promote harmony between nations, it now attracts some 30 competing musical teams from all corners of the globe. The *Hay-on-Wye Festival* (about 10 days beginning at the end of May) had its first highly successful runs in 1988. It features international writers, local poets, exhibitions, major theatrical events, and the annual Raymond Williams lecture honoring the great border novelist and critic.

MUSEUMS: In addition to those described in *Special Places,* the following museums are of interest:

Chapter Centre for the Arts – One of the largest in Europe, with cinemas, theater, workshops, and touring exhibitions of contemporary works. Open daily. Market Rd. (phone: 396061).

Fotogallery – Wales' leading photography gallery changes exhibits monthly. Open daily. 31 Charles St. (phone: 41667).

Oriel Art Gallery – Exhibitions change about every 3 weeks. Closed Sundays. 53 Charles St. (phone: 395548).

St. David's Hall – Take the escalators up to all six floors for the free exhibitions of modern art, mostly by local artists. Closed Sundays. Working St. (phone: 42611).

Turner House Art Gallery – A branch of the *National Museum of Wales,* with changing exhibitions. Closed Mondays. Plymouth Rd., Penarth (phone: Penarth 708870).

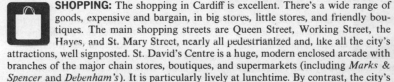

SHOPPING: The shopping in Cardiff is excellent. There's a wide range of goods, expensive and bargain, in big stores, little stores, and friendly boutiques. The main shopping streets are Queen Street, Working Street, the Hayes, and St. Mary Street, nearly all pedestrianized and, like all the city's attractions, well signposted. St. David's Centre is a huge, modern enclosed arcade with branches of the major chain stores, boutiques, and supermarkets (including *Marks & Spencer* and *Debenham's*). It is particularly lively at lunchtime. By contrast, the city's famous shopping arcades (Dominion, Queen Street, Castle, Morgan, Royal, and Oxford) contain smaller specialty shops, many selling Welsh craftwork — woolen products, beautiful bedspreads, flannel, pottery, and woodwork. There's a smaller, fast-developing shopping area out near Roath, on Wellfield Road, with a number of specialty shops and health food restaurants.

Cardiff Indoor Market – All the bustle, noise, and color of Wales, with a wide range of goods and accents. Welsh lamb is a specialty in the butchers' stalls; *bara brith,* a kind of fruit bread, is offered at the bakers' stalls. And try some *laverbread,* a Welsh delicacy. It's a thick black seaweed, something of an acquired taste, delicious with ham or bacon. Cockles, another Welsh favorite, are available here. Closed Wednesdays and Sundays. Enter from St. Mary St. or the Hayes.

Castle Welsh Crafts and Woollens – Designer fashions, plus traditional quality woolens. 1 Castle St. (phone: 43038).

Charisma Chocolates – Thayer's real dairy ice cream is for sale here, as well as icy cold liters of champagne sorbet. 47–48 Royal Arcade (phone: 371081).

Howells of Cardiff – One of the major department stores, with almost everything, including a good range of glassware, china, and gifts. Also a savvy delicatessen and restaurant. St. Mary St. (phone: 31055).

Jacob's Warehouse – A crafts and antiques market. Open Thursdays and Saturdays. W. Canal Wharf.

H. J. Lear Ltd. – The largest bookshop in Cardiff, with two floors of paperbacks and hardcovers, including maps and guidebooks of the area. 13 Royal Arcade (phone: 395036).

David Morgan – Another big department store in the city center. The Hayes (phone: 21011).

Jan Stedman – A modern, friendly shop selling trendy women's lingerie, swimwear, and trinkets. 24 Morgan Arcade (phone: 372537).

Things Welsh – Pottery, crafts, woolens, metalwork, all of good quality. Duke St. Arcade (phone: 33445).

TSP Inter – They will design and print "I'm not a tourist" or any other motif on your baseball cap, T-shirt, or jeans. 14–16 Morgan Arcade (phone: 387013).

Wally's Delicatessen – A well-stocked deli counter at the back (Belgian pâté is a specialty), plus shelves loaded with Oriental delicacies, herbs, whole grains, and wines. 46 Royal Arcade (phone: 29265).

SPORTS: Visitors are welcome to use the wide range of sporting facilities at the *Western Leisure Centre* (phone: 593592) and the *Heath Sports Centre* (phone: 755607).

Ice Skating – Available at *Cardiff Ice Rink,* Hayes Bridge Rd. (phone: 383451).

Riding – Rent horses at *Cardiff City Riding School,* Pontcanna Fields, a few miles west of Cardiff (phone: 383908).

Rugby – This is a national passion, and the immensely popular *Cardiff Rugby Club* plays at the *Cardiff Arms Park National Rugby Stadium.*

Sailing – There's boat rental and anchorage at Penarth, 5 miles south of Cardiff.

Swimming – Go to the *Wales Empire Pool* on Wood St. (phone: 382296), where you can also have a Turkish bath and sauna.

THEATER: The *New,* in Park Pl. (phone: 394844), stages productions by the internationally renowned *Welsh National Opera,* ballet, pre-London plays, and pantomime in the winter. The *Sherman,* in Senghennydd Rd. (phone: 30451), is a modern theater that puts on plays by major professional groups and sometimes by local amateur groups. The small "workshop" theater is known for its fringe productions. The *Chapter Arts Centre,* on Market Rd. (phone: 396061), features regular theater productions and daily movies. There's also a small restaurant on the premises that is well patronized by students. *Moving Being,* Wales's leading experimental theater group, appears regularly at *St. Stephen's Theatre Space,* W. Bute St. (phone: 498885). Show schedules can be found in the local papers. The Welsh College of Music and Drama presents some impressive amateur productions to *Edinburgh Festival* fringe audiences. Visitors fortunate enough to catch a production at the College are often happily surprised by the quality and imagination of the performance.

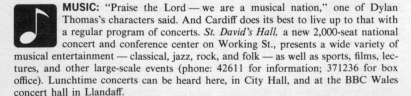

MUSIC: "Praise the Lord — we are a musical nation," one of Dylan Thomas's characters said. And Cardiff does its best to live up to that with a regular program of concerts. *St. David's Hall,* a new 2,000-seat national concert and conference center on Working St., presents a wide variety of musical entertainment — classical, jazz, rock, and folk — as well as sports, films, lectures, and other large-scale events (phone: 42611 for information; 371236 for box office). Lunchtime concerts can be heard here, in City Hall, and at the BBC Wales concert hall in Llandaff.

NIGHTCLUBS AND NIGHTLIFE: Cardiffians take their evening pleasure with some enthusiasm. They like to go out to dinner and take quite a long time over the meal: They're not fast-food folk. And they like propping up a bar, talking, and listening to music. You'll find it easy to join them in any of these activities. Cardiff also has a number of nightclubs; these include *Mont Merence,* 45 Charles St. (phone: 29142), and *Bumpers,* Castle Arcade (phone: 32654). For the wheelers and dealers, there's gambling at *Les Croupiers,* 32 St. Mary St. (phone: 382810), and at *Sloane's,* Westgate St. (phone: 43899).

BEST IN TOWN

CHECKING IN: Wales has always been popular with travelers, and some of its hotels are justly famous. Moreover, standards have improved considerably during the past few years. If you want the tops in comfort and class in Cardiff you'll have to pay top dollar, but in the more modest places you will find considerable comfort, excellent home-cooked food, a warm welcome, and a bill that doesn't make you pale. Consult the tourist board, which has lists of recommended and inspected hotels. A double with breakfast in a hotel in the expensive category will cost about $90 and up; in the moderate, $60 to $90; and in the inexpensive, as low as $60. All telephone numbers are in the 0222 area code unless otherwise indicated.

Celtic Manor – Althoough this 19th-century manor house, comprised of 17 rooms and a 58-room annex, has a commercial atmosphere, special features include large bedrooms, views over Chepstow, flower-filled wooded gardens, and a paneled restaurant. Facilities also include a sauna, gymnasium, and solarium. 12 miles outside Cardiff, off the M4. Coldra Woods, Newport (phone: 0633-413000). Expensive.

Crest – This hotel has 159 smart, modern, and comfortable rooms with all the facilities. Bilingual signs and notices are a pleasant nod of respect to the old language. Castle St. (phone: 388681). Expensive.

Holiday Inn – Cardiff's newest hotel boasts 182 rooms and all the modern conveniences, including a pool, gym, sauna, spa bath, and piano bar. Mill La. (phone: 399944). Expensive.

Inn on the Avenue – Just off the M4, this first class hotel has 144 rooms, all with private bath. Restaurant, pool, gym, beauty salon, and helipad; parking available. Circle Way E., Llanedeyrn (phone: 732520). Expensive.

Park – In the center of town, this hotel is considered the best, with a gracious, spacious air and an attentive staff. There are 108 large rooms with private bath and two very good restaurants — the *Caernarfon Room* and the *Theatre Garden.* Parking. Park Pl. (phone: 383471). Expensive.

Post House – Up-to-date and very comfortable, it's a bit out of town at Pentwyn (4 miles off M4, Junction 29), so you really need a car. Good eating and plenty of sports facilities to work it off. 150 rooms. Pentwyn Rd., Pentwyn (phone: 731212). Expensive.

Stakis Inn on the Avenue – Recently refurbished, this modern, 144-room hotel is off the A48 a few miles east of Cardiff. Facilities include a swimming pool, sauna, solarium, and fax machine. Free morning paper provided. Circle Way East, Llanedeyrn (phone: 0222-732520). Expensive.

Beverley – Comfortable and friendly with a good restaurant. 18 rooms. 75 Cathedral Rd. (phone: 43443). Moderate.

Lincoln – Welshman Keith Baines spent 24 years in the US before returning with his American wife to combine two large Victorian houses into one comfortable 18-room hotel. Guests craving an "authentic" American breakfast will be happy to find that the menu includes such items as honest-to-goodness pancakes with maple syrup and eggs Benedict. 118 Cathedral Rd. (phone: 395558). Moderate.

Royal – One of Cardiff's long-established and most dependable hotels, with 67 rooms; 47 of them have private bath. In the center of town on St. Mary St. (phone: 383321). Moderate.

Cedars – In a pleasant and quiet suburb, this is a comfortable place with a restaurant. 25 rooms. Fidlas Rd., Llanishen (phone: 752163). Inexpensive.

Hayes Court – This is representative of a number of good, clean, comfortable, and rather homey hotels, not far from the city center. It has a restaurant and a liquor license; there's also a sauna. 160 Cathedral Rd. (phone: 30420). Inexpensive.

EATING OUT: Cardiff is a cosmopolitan city, and this is reflected in its restaurants, tastes, and menus. While you're here, though, be sure to try the local specialties, such as Welsh lamb. Also, don't miss fresh Welsh salmon or *sewin,* a kind of trout. Pluck up courage at breakfast and taste *laverbread* — remember, it's not bread but seaweed. For starters, you'll find *cawl* (a thick vegetable, leek, and lamb soup) in its various forms delicious. And to round off a meal, homemade pies and fruit tarts are usually good. Some restaurants — mostly the less expensive ones — serve food throughout the day and evening. Others stick to the usual lunch and dinner hours, and these places accept major credit cards. Eating out in Cardiff is less expensive than in London. Expect to pay $75 and up for dinner for two, including wine and tips, in places listed as expensive; $45 to $75 in a moderate restaurant; and under $45 in an inexpensive one. All telephone numbers are in the 0222 area code unless otherwise indicated.

Spanghero's – Named after a rugby hero, this establishment is known for its accomplished French nouvelle cuisine carefully prepared and beautifully presented by celebrated chef David Evans. For those who need to watch their budgets rather than their waistlines, there are less expensive meals in the informal wine bar. Closed Sundays. Westgate House, Westgate St. (phone: 382423). Expensive.

Gibson's – One of the capital's most enjoyable restaurants, at which the proprietress almost always scores a bull's eye with her French cooking. There's a good atmosphere, a friendly staff, and wines to match. Reservations necessary. Closed Sundays. A little off the beaten track at 8 Romilly Crescent (phone: 341264). Expensive to moderate.

Harvester – Be sure to bring a robust appetite — the food here is British with a Welsh flavor, that is, hearty but rather plain. Try the homemade soup and the delicious game casserole. Open daily except Sundays for dinner; closed for 3 weeks in August. Reservations advised. 5 Pontcanna St. (phone: 232616). Expensive to moderate.

Savastano's – The reason Jimmy Savastano's place is usually busy, and the customers keep on coming back, is because it provides a happy, delicious, and informal eating experience. Italian specialties; veal dishes are especially good. Open daily. Reservations advised. 302 North Rd., Gabalfa (phone: 621018). Expensive to moderate.

Armless Dragon – A bright, cheery place with a number of surprising specialties, including shark curry, Welsh laverbread balls, wild rabbit, and rack of Welsh lamb. Closed Saturday lunch and Sundays. 99 Wyverne Rd. (phone: 382357). Moderate.

Blas ar Gymru – This cozy eatery, whose name means "taste of Wales," serves up generous helpings of good, wholesome, traditional Welsh dishes like cawl (a thick vegetable, leek, and lamb soup) and gower cockle and bacon pie, all washed down with local wine or mead. Open Mondays through Fridays for lunch, Mondays through Saturdays for dinner. 48 Crwys Rd. (phone: 382132). Moderate.

Landaf Celebrity – There are two entrances to this dignified but friendly establishment: one in St. David's Hall and the other on Working Street. The wholesome, if unimaginative, dishes include traditional Welsh roast, shoulder of Welsh lamb with mint, and farmhouse chicken with bacon roll. Closed Sundays. The Hayes (phone: 227211). Moderate.

Riverside – A successful Cantonese restaurant, this place is a cut above average and offers a great variety of dishes, all cooked by talented hands. It also serves an interesting Chinese beer. Open daily from noon to midnight. Reservations advised. 44 Tudor St., Riverside (phone: 372163). Moderate.

Truffles – Has a conservative menu of steaks, fish, and the like, with a tea room downstairs. Closed Sundays. 3 Church St. (phone: 344958). Moderate.

Yr Ystafell Gymraeg – The name means "the Welsh Room," and not surprisingly, the restaurant is furnished with Welsh antiques. You'll find many enjoyable native dishes here: Choose from cockles, laverbread, and lamb. The steak and kidney pie is lovely, and so is the cawl. Closed Saturday lunch and Sundays. Reservations advised. 74 Whitchurch Rd., Gabalfa (phone: 342317). Moderate.

Arnolds – Americans say that this hamburger joint is as good as the best back home. Bright and breezy atmosphere, with All-American desserts like apple pie, colossal ice cream dishes, and cheesecake, too. Open evenings. 167 Albany Rd. (phone: 499893). Inexpensive.

Crumb's Salad – As the name suggests, the house specialty here is salad — of many varieties — including vegetable, rice, and fruit. Open daily except Sundays for lunch only. 33 Morgan Arcade (phone: 395007). Inexpensive.

The Louis – Just the place for a Welsh afternoon tea, with friendly waitresses and plenty of room. It's open all day every day and serves traditional meals from a large menu. 32 St. Mary St. (phone: 225722). Inexpensive.

Peppermint Lounge – Where you go when you have the munchies, it features homemade burgers and a full range of cocktails. Open daily. 34 Woodville Rd. (phone: 374403). Inexpensive.

Tandoori Mahal – Typical of the many Indian restaurants in Cardiff, this restaurant offers authentic tandoori (clay oven) cooking served by a friendly staff. Open daily. 98 Albany Rd., Roath Park (phone: 491500). Inexpensive.

Zio Pin – Three lively Italian restaurants serving pizza, homemade pasta, and calzone. Closed Sundays. 74 Albany Rd. (phone: 485673); 1260 Cowbridge (phone: 220269); 9 Park La. (phone: 340397). Inexpensive.

SHARING A PINT: Cardiff has pubs for all tastes — quiet, noisy, intimate, brash. And it has its own beer, made at Brain's brewery (that's the malty smell in the air on St. Mary Street!). The club-like back bar in the *Park* hotel is busy at lunchtimes and early evenings. The *Old Arcade,* on Church St., (phone: 31740), is a typical large, friendly, Cardiff pub, as is the *Butcher's Arms,* on High St., Llandaff (phone: 561898). The *Conway,* on Conway Rd. (phone: 32797), is a favorite, lively haunt of young Welsh-speaking people. Out at *St. Fagan's* is the elegant *Plymouth Arms* (phone: 569130), where you can eat well, too.

CHESTER

The red sandstone walls surrounding the old city of Chester are the only city walls in Britain to have come down to the 20th century very nearly intact. For the last 3 centuries they have been a pleasant place to walk to get a better view of one of the most medieval-looking of British cities. Before that, however, these walls did their share of preserving it. Though it's now been more than 300 years since Chester's streets have seen any fighting, the walls are a reminder that it has been a military city for all its 19 centuries of existence.

The original town — called Deva or Castra Legionis, fortress of the legions — was laid out by the battle-tested veterans of the Roman Twentieth Legion (conquerors of the Celtic warrior-queen Boadicea) when Britain became the newest province of the Empire only decades after the Crucifixion. Centuries after the Romans had abandoned Britain, Hugh Lupus suppressed the local tribes, thus gaining the Earldom of Chester (a title held ever since by the monarch's eldest son). He built the castle at Chester from which Edward I set out to crush the rebellious Welsh, binding them into submission in the 13th century with a chain of coastal fortresses from Flint to Caernarvon. Later still, Chester's position astride the route to Ireland was of strategic importance to Charles I, who expected reinforcements from his armies there, during the mid-17th-century Civil War between the king and his Parliament. Charles watched the defeat of his army at the battle of Rowton Moor (1645) and fled the city, only to be executed later.

Since Roman times, there have always been soldiers in Chester. Even now it is the home of an active unit, the First Battalion, the King's Regiment, and the permanent depot of its own county regiment, the Cheshire Regiment, formed three centuries ago. This military presence has stamped itself firmly on the city. The four main streets follow the line of the main roadways laid out inside the Roman fort almost 2,000 years ago, and where they meet at Chester Cross, the Church of St. Peter is built on the foundations of the Roman headquarters building and the residence of the military commander. The lines of many of the smaller back streets echo the layout of the Roman barracks, granaries, and storehouses.

Even the Rows, Chester's aboveground network of shopping walkways, may owe their origins to the city's distant past as a military fortress. According to one of the more convincing theories (no one really *knows* why they were built), the ruins of the buildings left by the Romans were so massive that their Saxon successors preferred to build on top of them and in front of them rather than labor to remove the weighty stonework. The surviving rows follow the four main streets — Bridge Street, Watergate Street, Northgate Street, and Eastgate Street — that existed within the Roman fortress, and even the one exception, a now-vanished set of rows down Lower Bridge Street, lies along the Roman road from the fort to the Dee crossing — a road that would also have been lined with Roman buildings. (Complaints that shops in the rows were dark — Daniel Defoe was among the complainers — led to a theory that they were deliberately built to keep the wares of Chester's merchants from scrutiny in broad daylight, but this theory is not taken seriously.)

Chester's military history has left a practical legacy. Before mechanization, armies marched — whatever Napoleon might have said — on their own two feet, and this is a city designed as much for today's pedestrian, shopper, or tourist as it was for yesterday's infantryman. The almost-complete circuit of the city walls, built on the north and east over the original Roman ramparts but extended to the south and west probably by Saxon engineers to take the city's defenses closer to the river, links with the Rows to form a network of walkways completely free from the traffic below. In addition, the four main city streets are now being turned into a pedestrian area, and though it will be some years before cars are finally banished, traffic levels within the walls are already low enough to give a feeling of the city before the coming of the automobile.

One reason Chester still possesses so many links with the past is that it has been in decline, in a sense, ever since the Middle Ages. Originally a major port, the silting-up of the Dee eventually killed the seaborne trade with Ireland and America. Remedies were tried, but in the end, shipping moved to Liverpool (at the time an obscure fishing village) on the nearby river Mersey, and with it went the industrialization and urbanization that would have obliterated the old Chester forever.

Instead, the city found a new role as a prosperous market town, a trading center between northwest England and North Wales, and a destination for 1½ million tourists a year who are treated to the sight of as picturesque a town as any in old England. Boswell told Johnson it pleased his fancy more than any town he ever saw, and Nathaniel Hawthorne wrote of its "houses of very aged aspect, with steep, peaked gables."

Yet in spite of the abundance of black and white half-timbering, Chester's buildings are today largely the work of Victorian restorers and rebuilders. Fortunately, they were enthralled by the traditional Cheshire "magpie" decoration, and their revival designs give the city a unity of style that bridges the centuries. Among the Georgian brick and Victorian plaster are genuine ancient houses such as the Leche House and Bishop Lloyd's House, dating from the 16th and early 17th centuries. Near them is God's Providence House — so called because its inhabitants survived the plague in centuries gone by — built in the same era but rebuilt, more richly decorated, 200 years later. It's entirely typical of Chester that the real and the reproduction are so intermingled and, sometimes, virtually indistinguishable.

CHESTER AT-A-GLANCE

SEEING THE CITY: In a city as tightly packed as Chester, there's no single spot for a panoramic vista. The Grosvenor Bridge across the Dee, the longest single masonry arch in the world when it was completed in 1832, gives a good view down onto the racecourse and the river and across to the city skyline behind the western ramparts of the city walls. But for a closer view of the city's bustle, pick a spot on the Rows overlooking Chester Cross, where you can lean on the old balustrades and watch the world go by. From April through September, at noon and 3 PM, the town crier Michael Chittenden stands by the cross in the 19th-century uniform of the city bellman to bring the citizens up to date on the day's events. Another means of seeing the city is aboard a horse-drawn narrowboat that plies a section of the Shropshire Union Canal. Boats are docked at the Tower Wharf on Whipcord La. (phone: 390059) and run from Easter to September.

SPECIAL PLACES: Chester's compact layout, not to mention its tougher-than-average parking problems, make it an ideal city to explore on foot. Pubs, restaurants, museums, and shops are all within a few minutes' walk of one another. For the more energetic, the 2-mile circuit of the city walls (see *Extra Special*) is a useful connecting link to the cathedral and the river, where tree-lined walks and rows of benches make an ideal spot to end a walking tour.

Rows – Chester's above-pavement-level pedestrian shopping "streets" or galleries were built in the Middle Ages over the main roads of the original Roman fortress. Bridge Street and Eastgate Street Rows have the most cosmopolitan shops; Northgate Street Row has survived, with gaps and changes of level; but Watergate Street Row has the strongest flavor of the past, with its antiques and curio shops and magnificent old houses such as the Leche House. It was built in the mid-16th century as the town residence of the Leche family, so called because they were originally Leeches, or surgeons, to King Edward III in the 1300s. Another magnificent house is Bishop Lloyd's House, built in the early 17th century for Dr. George Lloyd, who was Bishop of Sodor and Man from 1600 to 1604 and Bishop of Chester from 1604 to 1615. The house, reconstructed in the 19th century, contains elaborate carvings (including the three-legged crest of the Isle of Man) and broad windows on the front, which were a local fashion and which turn up again in the *Falcon Inn* and the *Bear and Billet Inn* on Lower Bridge Street, where the original Rows have all but vanished. Leche House is now an antiques shop; visits to Bishop Lloyd's House must be arranged in advance by contacting the Publicity Department, Town Hall (phone: 313126).

Cathedral – Not originally a cathedral at all, this was founded in 1093 by Hugh Lupus, the Norman Earl of Chester and alleged nephew of William the Conquerer, as the Benedictine Abbey of St. Werburgh. The abbey was broken up in 1540 when Henry VIII dissolved England's monasteries, and the following year the church became the cathedral of the new diocese of Chester. You can still see the monks' dining room, the choir stalls, the cloisters where they studied, and part of the shrine to St. Werburgh (an Anglo-Saxon abbess who died ca. AD 700), which attracted pilgrims from all over the north of England during the Middle Ages. There is an audiovisual show for visitors, which provides a 12-minute introduction to the cathedral, plus a bookshop and a refectory offering tea, coffee, and light refreshments in a lovely 13th-century setting. Outside, the new bell tower (1975) is the first separate one to be added to an English cathedral in 500 years. St. Werburgh St.

Castle – At the city end of the Grosvenor Bridge, these colonnaded buildings don't look much like a castle today. The original Norman fortress on its superb defensive position overlooking the river and the Old Dee Bridge was completely transformed between 1788 and 1822 to house the Assize Courts. Behind the Georgian court building (now housing Chester's Crown Courts), the 750-year-old Agricola Tower is the only part of the medieval castle that survives. It can be viewed on request — ask at the *Cheshire Military Museum* — and the court buildings can be seen from the Public Gallery when the courts are in session. Castle St.

Abbey Square – The low arch of the 14th-century Abbey Gateway, where the Chester Miracle Plays were performed in the Middle Ages, is on the eastern side of Town Hall Square. Through the gateway is Abbey Square, a peaceful oasis of cobblestones and Georgian houses, scarcely changed in 200 years. From the opposite corner of the square, Abbey Street leads to the Kaleyard Gateway, a gap in the city walls that once gave access to the abbot's private garden.

Old Dee Bridge – Until the opening of the Grosvenor Bridge 150 years ago, all traffic across the river had to use this narrow medieval bridge, built on the site of the Roman crossing more than seven centuries ago. It leads from the city to the old suburb of Handbridge, called Treboeth or "Burned Town" by the Welsh, who burned it more than once during cross-border raids before they were subdued in the 13th century.

River Dee and the Groves – The name comes from that given by the Romans to both town and river — Deva. Below the city walls is the Groves, Chester's tree-lined riverside promenade, with seats used by fishermen, by audiences for the Sunday brass band concerts (May through September), and by picnickers watching the boats. (Unfortunately, the charm of this beautiful spot is hardly improved by the recent addition of an amusement/games arcade which is, quite frankly, an eyesore.) Motorboats and rowing skiffs can be rented here (but watch out for the weir just above the Old Dee Bridge), or you can leave the navigation to others and book a trip on one of the sightseeing cruises going upriver to Heronbridge and the tranquil charm of Eccleston village. Evening musical cruises, discos, jazz, and parties are available. Cruises depart from the Boating Station, Souters Lane, the Groves. The cruises are operated by *Bithell's Boats* (phone: 25394 or 316388). Return by boat, by city bus from Eccleston, or by foot along the riverbank path through the Meadows on the Handbridge side.

Chester Zoo – On the outskirts of Chester is one of Britain's largest and most comprehensively stocked zoos, also offering guided tours, restaurants, and a shop. A farm area is available to children for petting animals. Off A41 (phone: 380280).

Amphitheatre – On Vicars Lane, opposite Chester Visitors Centre, stands the northern half of the *Roman Amphitheatre,* the largest yet uncovered in Britain. The oval arena measures approximately 64 by 54 yards and once held about 7,000 people. Today it is remarkably well preserved. Open March 15 through October 15; weekdays, 9:30 AM to 6:30 PM; Sundays, 2 to 6:30 PM; from October 16 through March 14, open on weekdays, 9:30 AM to 4 PM and Sundays, 2 to 4 PM.

■ **EXTRA SPECIAL:** Chester's walls are nearly complete, which makes them unique in Britain, and a first class way to explore the city. Start by climbing to the top of the Eastgate arch, crowned by the much-photographed clock commemorating Queen Victoria's Diamond Jubilee in 1897 and symbolizing Chester to exiles all over the world. Follow the wall southward, and near the modern Newgate arch you'll see the foundations of one of the corner towers of the original Roman fort. Across Vicar's Lane is the excavated half of the amphitheater the Romans used for gladiatorial contests as well as for drills and weapons training, while next to the Newgate, the old Wolfe or Wolfeld Gate gives an idea of just how narrow the Roman and medieval city gates must have been. Beyond the Newgate arch you come eventually to six short flights of steps — the Wishing Steps. According to tradition, if you make a wish, run from the bottom to the top, then down and back again without drawing breath, and your wish will come true!

As the walls swing west, there's a good view of the river and the old bridge. After crossing the Bridgegate arch, rebuilt and widened like the other city gates in the 18th century, you come to the only gap in the walls, beside County Hall. Look for the signposts on the other side of the hall and rejoin the ramparts as they turn north beside the Castle. You pass the racecourse on the Roodee — a recreation area first used for racing in 1540, making Chester Races the oldest in the country — and the Watergate arch before reaching the old Bonewaldesthorne's Tower in the northwestern corner of the defenses and the Water Tower at the end of a spur wall. When the Water Tower was built in the 14th century, the river was so close it flowed through the archway.

The northern face of the walls is the most impressive of all, since the original ditch that ran full circuit was widened and deepened here in the 18th century as part of Chester's canal. You'll pass the Goblin Tower, nicknamed Pemberton's Parlour after a rope maker who sat in comfort to watch his workers toiling below, then, close to the Northgate, a bastion called Morgan's Mount, after the commander of a royalist battery placed here in the Civil War siege of 1645. If you look out over the parapet, you'll see the precarious Bridge of Sighs spanning the giddy drop to the canal. It was used to take prisoners from the notorious Northgate Jail across to the Chapel of St. John for a last service before their execution.

Finally, the northeastern corner of the walls is crowned by King Charles's Tower, built on the site of the original Roman tower. Here Charles I is supposed to have stood while his army was crushed on the field of Rowton Moor in September 1645. He fled afterward, begging the city to hold out for 10 more days. When Chester finally surrendered to Parliament 5 months later, its citizens were starving and weak from disease, but its walls still held the enemy at bay. The building now contains displays concerning the English Civil War and the siege of Chester. Open from April through October; weekdays, 1 to 5 PM; Saturdays, 10 AM to 5 PM; Sundays, 2 to 5:30 PM; November through March open Saturdays, 1 to 4:30 PM; Sundays, 2 to 4:30 PM. Admission charge (phone: 21616).

St. John's Church and Ruins – To the east of the *Amphitheatre* is the parish church of St. John the Baptist. From 1075 to 1102 it was Chester's cathedral, and in 1975 celebrated its 900th anniversary. The ruins of the 12th-century choir are among the finest examples of Norman architecture in Europe.

SOURCES AND RESOURCES

TOURIST INFORMATION: Guides, handouts, lists of events, maps, and a monthly *What's On* bulletin are available at the tourist information center at the Town Hall, Northgate St. (open 9 AM to 7:30 PM, May through September; 9 AM to 5:30 PM, October through April; 10 AM to 4 PM on Sundays, May through October; phone: 313126 or 318356). The Tourist Information Centre also provides an accommodations bureau, Bureau de change, and booking service. The latter two services are also available at the Chester Visitors Centre, Vicars Ln. (phone: 351609). If you want to spend an evening in an English home, it can be arranged by calling Mr. and Mrs. Richardson (phone: 678868), Mr. and Mrs. Brockley (phone: 380749), or Mr. and Mrs. Read (phone: 051-3396615), who organize this free friendly service, any day from 5:30 to 7 PM.

Local Coverage – Five newspapers report on town events: the *Chester Chronicle,* whose files include issues that give day-to-day coverage of the American Revolution, appears Fridays; the *Chester Observer* on Wednesdays; the *Chester Express* and the *Chester Mail* on Tuesdays; and the *Evening Leader* on weekdays. There is also some coverage in the *Liverpool Daily Post* (mornings) and the *Liverpool Echo* (evenings).

Food – For advice on where to eat, the publication *Eating Out in the Chester Area,* available at the Tourist Information Centre, is an invaluable source of advice and information.

Telephone – The area code for Chester is 0244.

GETTING AROUND: Bus – The Chester Corporation operates services inside the city area (phone: 474521). Contact one of the city's information centers for details. *Crosville Motor Services,* with an inquiry office (phone: 381515) at the Delamere Street bus station, operates services outside the city.

Airport – The nearest airports are Manchester International Airport (phone: 061-489-3000) and Liverpool (phone: 051-486-8877).

Car Rental – For travel outside the city, it makes sense to rent a car. There are offices of *Avis,* 128 Brook St. (phone: 311463); *Budget,* Lower Bridge St. (phone: 313431); *Hertz,* Sealand Rd. (phone: 374705); *Hawarden Motor Co. Ltd.* (phone: 532452); and *Crane Bank Garage* (phone: 45595).

Sightseeing Tours – There are a wide variety of coach excursions that offer sightseeing tours as far as North Wales and throughout the Northwest of England. The largest operator is *Lofty's Tours Ltd.* (phone: 051-355-2519). Excursions can be booked at the Tourist Information Centre and at Chester Visitors Centre, Vicars Lane. A Pastfinder tour allows visitors to discover where the 20th Roman Legion (which defeated Queen Boadicea) built their fortress and where Hugh the Wolf, the bloodthirsty nephew of William the Conquerer, built a stronghold; a Ghosthunter Trail and an Ale Trail can also be explored. Full details on all three tours are available from the Tourist Information Centre.

Taxi – Chester's complex parking arrangements make cabs a good idea in the city area. Cab ranks are in front of the Town Hall and outside the railway station on City Road. You can flag down the licensed black taxicabs anywhere you see them, or you can book cabs in advance from *Chester Radio Taxis* (phone: 372372 or 325646) or *Kingcab* (phone: 43119).

Train – Chester's station is on the north side of the city on Station Rd. (phone: 40170). Fast InterCity 125 trains connect Chester to London's Euston Station (travel time about 2½ hours).

SPECIAL EVENTS: At the end of April a reenactment of the *Siege of Chester* (1644–46), which took place during the English Civil War, is staged. Attractions include a 1½-hour battle between Parliamentarians and Royalists, a reconstruction of a 17th-century village, and a demonstration of archery and cavalry drills (phone: 336170). For boating enthusiasts, the the *Chester Races* are held in May, June, July, and September. Staged on the Roodee, once the site of a massive Roman Harbour, they're the oldest races in the country. For more information contact the manager, *Chester Race Co. Ltd.* (phone: 323170). In late May, *Beating Retreat,* a military ceremony with a display of massed bands takes place on the castle grounds; check with the Tourist Information Centre for details. The *Chester Summer Music Festival* in mid-July features a week of orchestral concerts, recitals, and choral works. The *Chester Sports and Leisure Festival,* with concerts, theater, dance, displays, and river and canal trips, takes place in Grosvenor Park in late June to early July. The *Film Festival,* featuring new and old movies, is usually held during the last week of August. The nearby village of Kelsall hosts a folk festival in late May.

MUSEUMS: Chester has several museums devoted to preserving and presenting its long history. Among them are the following:

Boat Museum – Several miles north of Chester at the junction of the Shropshire Union and Manchester Ship canals is Britain's largest canal museum, featuring a collection of traditional canal narrowboats and demonstrations of 19th-century living and working conditions on the canals. Open daily 10 AM to 5 PM, April through October; closed Fridays November through March and open 11 AM to 4 PM. Dockyard Rd., Ellesmere Port (phone: 051-355-5017).

Cheshire Military Museum – Three centuries of the Cheshire Regiment, including service in America and India, and the campaign under General Sir Charles James Napier, who annexed the Indian province of Sind for the British in 1843 and announced his success with the terse Latin *Peccavi,* meaning "I have sinned." Chester Castle (phone: 347203 or 327617).

Chester Heritage Centre – A slide show on the history of Chester, before and after photographs of the restoration of its buildings, and a changing exhibition on the city's heritage. It is also the starting point for a series of self-guided heritage walks around Chester. St. Michael's Church, Bridge St. Row (phone: 317948).

Chester Visitor Centre – Video presentations of the city's 2,000-year history and a life-size reconstruction of an 1850s street scene, replete with sounds and smells, old shop and pub fronts transported from the Rows, a brass rubbing center, and a coffee and lunch bar in an old oak-beamed school. Vicars La. (phone: 313126).

Grosvenor Museum – The main museum is named after Hugh Lupus Grosvenor, first Duke of Westminster, who donated part of the site on which the museum was built in the 1880s. It contains many relics of Chester's Roman past, natural history exhibits, paintings, and silver. Open Mondays through Saturdays, 10:30 AM to 5 PM and Sundays, 2 to 5 PM. Grosvenor St. (phone: 321616).

Toy Museum – A fascinating collection featuring 5,000 exhibits, including cars, airplanes, boats, games, dolls, and teddy bears. The toys date as far back as 1830. There is also a Toy Shop and a Dolls Hospital which restores teddy bears and dolls "to full health." Bridge St. Row (phone: 316251).

St. Mary's Centre – Formerly the Parish Church of St. Mary's on the Hill, this 15th-century building is now the home of an exhibition and educational center. It hosts concerts, seminars, and educational videos. Attractions include a 15th-century chapel and painting and a beautifully restored oak-paneled roof. Open Mondays through Fridays, 2 to 4:30 PM or by appointment. St. Mary's Hill (phone: 603320/1).

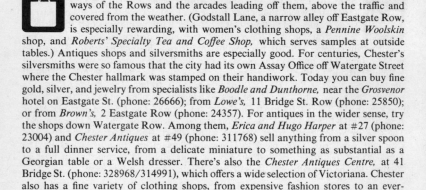

SHOPPING: Most of the best shops are along the elevated, two-tiered walkways of the Rows and the arcades leading off them, above the traffic and covered from the weather. (Godstall Lane, a narrow alley off Eastgate Row, is especially rewarding, with women's clothing shops, a *Pennine Woolskin* shop, and *Roberts' Specialty Tea and Coffee Shop,* which serves samples at outside tables.) Antiques shops and silversmiths are especially good. For centuries, Chester's silversmiths were so famous that the city had its own Assay Office off Watergate Street where the Chester hallmark was stamped on their handiwork. Today you can buy fine gold, silver, and jewelry from specialists like *Boodle and Dunthorne,* near the *Grosvenor* hotel on Eastgate St. (phone: 26666); from *Lowe's,* 11 Bridge St. Row (phone: 25850); or from *Brown's,* 2 Eastgate Row (phone: 24357). For antiques in the wider sense, try the shops down Watergate Row. Among them, *Erica and Hugo Harper* at #27 (phone: 23004) and *Chester Antiques* at #49 (phone: 311768) sell anything from a silver spoon to a full dinner service, from a delicate miniature to something as substantial as a Georgian table or a Welsh dresser. There's also the *Chester Antiques Centre,* at 41 Bridge St. (phone: 328968/314991), which offers a wide selection of Victoriana. Chester also has a fine variety of clothing shops, from expensive fashion stores to an ever-changing but constantly replaced selection of inexpensive boutiques. Below are some of our top choices for a variety of stores.

Adams Antiques – Unusual cabinets, chandeliers, and board games for discerning collectors. 65 Watergate Row (phone: 319421).

Laura Ashley – Victorian-style dresses, children's clothes, wallpaper, and fabrics. Watergate Row (phone: 316403).

Blakes – Old family bakehouse, virtually unchanged since Victorian days. Shop early in the day, as the delicious homemade bread and misshapen but tasty cakes and pies tend to sell out by midafternoon. Watergate St. Row (phone: 325933).

Brown's of Chester – The city's premier department store, founded in the reign of the same George III who presided over the loss of the American colonies. It's now owned by *Debenham's* store chain, but much of the old ambience survives. Particularly good for women's clothes and perfumes. Eastgate St. (phone: 350001).

Chester Candle Shop – The showrooms contain a huge selection of candle ware and gifts. Guests can see carved candles in the making, and children can make candles under supervision. 75 Bridge Street Row (phone: 46011).

Duttons – A fine health food shop. Godstall La., off Eastgate St. opposite *Brown's* (phone: 316255).

Golfers World – Equipment and British woolens for golfers. 15 Watergate Row (phone: 318497).

Indesign – Designers of rustic, knobby wooden chairs and chests that look as though they're still growing. Some textiles and ceramics, too. 38 Watergate St. (phone: 329459).

William Jones – Specialty foods — coffee, Chinese and Indian teas, chocolates, sausages and pies, cheeses, bacon. In Owen Owen's Bridge St. store (phone: 321555).

Liberty's – The exclusive London-based department store specializing in fabrics and giftware has recently opened a branch in Chester. Expensive but well worth a visit. Bridge St. (phone: 350456).

Penhaligon's – A branch of the well-known, exclusive perfumer based in London. Eastgate St. (phone: 320275).

Three Kings Studios – Pottery plus other work from more than 70 local artists and craftsmen. Lower Bridge St. (phone: 317717).

Tudor Antiques – A tiny shop packed with dollhouses, dolls, their clothes, and (increasingly hard to find) teddy bears. Lower Bridge St. (no phone).

SPORTS: Chester's multisport leisure center, *Northgate Arena* has squash courts, badminton courts, and a swimming pool with palm trees, rocks, children's paddling area, and training pool. Corner of Victoria Rd. and St. Oswalds Way (phone: 380444).

Cricket – For those who want to experience the mysteries of the British national game for themselves, *Chester Boughton Hall Cricket Club* has home matches every Saturday afternoon and some Sundays from May to late September at the Filkins Lane ground.

Golf – There are clubs for hire at the 9-hole municipal golf course at Westminster Park (phone: 673071). Visitors with a temporary membership also have access to the 18-hole courses at the *Chester Golf Club,* Curzon Park (phone: 677760); the suburban *Upton-by-Chester Golf Club* (phone: 381183) and *Vicars Cross Golf Club* (phone: 35174); and the *Eaton Golf Club* at Eccleston (phone: 680474).

Horseback Riding – Both experienced riders and novices can try *Waverton Riding and Livery Centre* (phone: 335202).

Soccer – From August through May the *Chester Football Club* plays on most Saturday afternoons. The team is currently in the English League, division 3. *The Stadium,* Sealand Rd. (phone: 371376).

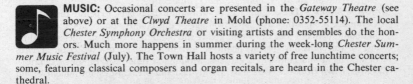

THEATER: Local repertory productions and some touring productions take place in the *Gateway Theatre,* Hamilton Pl. (phone: 40393), and in the *Clwyd Theatre* at Mold, 12 miles away (phone: 0352-55114). Liverpool's wider choice of theaters is only 45 minutes away by car.

MUSIC: Occasional concerts are presented in the *Gateway Theatre* (see above) or at the *Clwyd Theatre* in Mold (phone: 0352-55114). The local *Chester Symphony Orchestra* or visiting artists and ensembles do the honors. Much more happens in summer during the week-long *Chester Summer Music Festival* (July). The Town Hall hosts a variety of free lunchtime concerts; some, featuring classical composers and organ recitals, are heard in the Chester cathedral.

NIGHTCLUBS AND NIGHTLIFE: *High Society,* Love St. (phone: 43448), is predominantly a disco with occasional live music, as are *Caverns,* 39–41 Watergate St. (phone: 20619); *Blimpers,* City Rd. (phone: 314794); *Rendezvous,* Northgate St. (phone: 27141); and *Cinderella Rockerfella,* 144 Foregate St. (phone: 314981). For a more refined atmosphere, the *Plantation Inn* hotel, Liverpool Rd. (phone: 374100), has dinner and dancing 6 nights a week from 7:30 PM, and the *Rowton Hall* hotel, Whitchurch Rd. (phone: 335262), has a dinner dance every Saturday from 8 PM. In the city, there are dinner dances on Saturday nights at the *Chester Grosvenor* hotel, Eastgate St. (phone: 324024). For folk music buffs, there's a folk evening every Monday at 8:30 PM in the *Bear and Billet,* Lower Bridge St. (phone: 21272) and at 8 PM every Friday in the *Bull and Stirrup,* Upper Northgate St. (phone: 371167). There is live cabaret at the *Merseyview Country Club* (phone: 0928-33108).

BEST IN TOWN

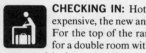

CHECKING IN: Hotels in Chester fall into three categories: the old and expensive, the new and moderately expensive, and the small and inexpensive. For the top of the range hotels in the city center, expect to pay up to $245 for a double room with bath (expensive). This includes breakfast, which rates as a meal in its own right. Out-of-town hotels and motels charge about $130 for a double, but with breakfast extra (moderate). Best values are found at the smaller hotels, which charge about $80 to $130 per night for a double (inexpensive). All telephone numbers are in the 0244 area code unless otherwise indicated.

Chester Grosvenor – Built between 1863 and 1866, this has a reputation as the city's best hotel, an old and luxurious establishment with superb service and an excellent restaurant. Sadly, the traditional pianist and tea lounge have been lost to a £12-million face-lift, which included the renovation of the ground floor *La Brasserie* restaurant (see *Eating Out*) and its à la carte counterpart, *Arkle.* All 87 bedrooms and suites have private baths. Access to nearby health club. Eastgate St. (phone: 324024). Expensive.

Soughton Hall – What used to be a stately home is now a 12-room hotel, complete with luxurious fixtures and fittings, antique furniture, and aristocratic gardens. At night the front windows glow from the warm light of chandeliers. Northop, 10 miles from Chester (phone: 0352-86207). Expensive.

Blossoms – Built in the 16th century, with later facelifting outside, modernized inside, this remains a hotel in the traditional manner — sweeping staircases, thick carpeting, and 69 comfortable rooms, all with private baths. St. John St. (phone: 323186). Expensive to moderate.

Queen – Originally built to serve the adjacent railway station, this is a classic Victorian hotel, though it has been brought well into the 20th century. All its 90 rooms have private baths. City Rd. (phone: 328341). Expensive to moderate.

Abbots Well – This converted country house is an elegant hotel-motel on the southern edge of the city. It has a good restaurant and 128 rooms, all with private bath. Whitchurch Rd. (phone: 332121). Moderate.

Crabwall Manor – The original hall or farmhouse dates back to before the Norman Conquest, though the castellated frontage of this country-house hotel was added in about 1600 and looks modern, giving the building a strangely ageless quality. All 32 bedrooms have private facilities. Two miles outside of Chester on 11 acres of woodland and landscaped gardens. Mollington (phone: 851666). Moderate.

Chester Town House – A friendly, trendy bed-and-breakfast establishment within the city walls in a conservation area of cobbled lamplit streets and alleyways. All rooms have private baths. 23 King St. (phone: 350021). Moderate to inexpensive.

City Walls and Cromwell Court – An elegant Georgian house next to the walls on the western side of the city. In addition to 17 rooms (all with bath), 10 apartments have been added next door, along with a restaurant, sauna, and gym. City Walls Rd. (phone: 313416). Moderate to inexpensive.

Ye Olde King's Head – One of the city's oldest inns (it dates from the 16th century), with a lovely timbered dining room. There are only 10 rooms, none with private bath. 48 Lower Bridge St. (phone: 324855). Moderate to inexpensive.

Cavendish – This is actually a beautifully restored and elegantly furnished Edwardian house with 20 rooms, set in its own landscaped gardens on the edge of town. There is tennis, croquet, boating, fishing, and golf nearby. 42 44 Hough Green (phone: 675100). Inexpensive.

Pied Bull – Passengers used to board the stage for London at this old coaching inn. It's a cheerful pub with 8 rooms. Northgate St. (phone: 325829). Inexpensive.

EATING OUT: Chester's choice of restaurants is surprisingly good. You could eat in a different place every night for a month and still not cover the whole list. Generally prices are lower than in larger British cities: $90 for two, including wine, is the absolute top (expensive). Most restaurants will set you back less than $70 (moderate), and by choosing carefully you can get away with a meal for two for $50 or less (inexpensive). Some of the foreign restaurants — Swiss, French, Italian, Greek, Mexican — offer a lot for the money, and the best value of all must be the hot and substantial Indian curries and the more exotic Chinese specialties. All telephone numbers are in the 0244 area code unless otherwise indicated.

Craxton Wood – A delicious meal in the French restaurant of this country house hotel might consist of *bûchette de saumon, truite en papillote,* fresh vegetables, and a Black Forest tart. (There are also 14 guestrooms and a suite with lots of antique furnishings.) Closed Sundays, bank holidays, the last 2 weeks in August, and 1 week at Christmas. Puddington, 5 miles north of the city on the main Parkgate Rd. (A540) (phone: 051-339-4717). Expensive.

Chester Grosvenor – The main hotel dining room serves classic French cooking (trout, veal, lamb) and does it impeccably. Closed December 24–26. Down in *La Brasserie,* there is lighter fare, such as fillet of salmon with sorrel and scallop stew. Open daily. Eastgate St. (phone: 324024). Main restaurant: expensive; *La Brasserie:* moderate.

Rossett Hall – This is a luxury restaurant in a Georgian country house, with first class cooking and top-quality local cheeses. Follow the A483 road south 5 miles to the village of Rossett, then look for *Rossett Hall* behind the long wall on the right-hand side, in the center of the village. Open 7 nights a week. Wrexham Rd., Rossett (phone: 570867). Expensive.

Boat Inn – Every inch of the 15-mile drive to this country pub and restaurant is worth it. The setting above the beautiful upstream reaches of the Dee is incomparable. Pheasant and fresh Dee salmon are on the menu in season, along with vintage clarets and Burgundies. Follow A483 to Wrexham (12 miles south), then take A539 and look for the sign for Erbistock. Erbistock, Clwyd (phone: 0978-780143). Expensive to moderate.

Pippa's – The menu is French bistro, the setting stylish, and the resident jazz pianist provides excellent entertainment. Closed Sundays. 58 Watergate St. (phone: 313721). Expensive to moderate.

Blue Bell – In the city's oldest medieval inn, this restaurant offers a traditional menu of English fare, such as halibut with grapes or orange and lemon pork, with not a chip to be seen. Afternoon tea available. Closed Sundays. 65 Northgate St. (phone: 317758). Moderate.

Abbey Green – Set in a Victorian house, organically grown vegetables and quiches made with the eggs of free-range chickens are on the inventive vegetarian menu at this eatery, which won the National Vegetarian Restaurant of the Year Award in 1988. Apéritifs and coffee are served in the "withdrawing" room. Closed Sundays and Monday evenings. 2 Abbey Green, Northgate St. (phone: 313251). Moderate to inexpensive.

Jade Cantonese – The only restaurant in Chester to offer a full Cantonese menu. Behind its rather garish façade are delicious, subtle flavors, crisp vegetables, and a genuine mixture of Chinese diners among the clientele. Closed Sundays. 43 Watergate St. Row (phone: 321455). Moderate to inexpensive.

Paris Brioche – A French patisserie serving delicious breakfasts only. Or take out their delicious cakes, sandwiches, or French filled rolls. Closed Sundays. 39 Bridge St. Row (phone: 48708). Moderate to inexpensive.

Watergate Wine Bar – Below street level in an oak-filled, 12th-century crypt, this eatery is popular for its atmosphere and its extraordinary menu, featuring curried parsnip soup, pears with Stilton mousse and tarragon, and pheasant with wine and grapes. The wine bar is open evenings, but food is served only at lunchtime. Closed Sundays. Watergate St. (phone: 320515). Moderate to inexpensive.

Aphrodite's – Here you can dine in the same room as Charles I, though not from the same menu. This Greek restaurant is in the restored Gamul House, which was the home of Sir Francis Gamul, mayor of Chester and host to the king during the mid-17th-century Civil War siege. Greek specialties such as dolmades and moussaka and Greek and Cypriot wines are served in the main restaurant. Lower prices prevail in the street-level *taverna.* Closed Sundays. Gamul House, Lower Bridge St. (phone: 319811). Inexpensive.

Great American Disaster – As close as you're likely to get to a genuine hamburger and definitely the only place in Chester for anything approaching American cooking. Other specialties are steaks and chicken, French fries (chips), baked potatoes, salads, apple pie, American beer, and coffee. Open daily. 14 Lower Bridge St. (phone: 318973). Inexpensive.

Sidoli's – Spread over two floors, this restaurant serves homemade pasta and other Italian dishes, including pizza. The ice cream is also homemade. Closed Sundays. 25 Northgate St. (phone 44068). Inexpensive.

60's – Southern-style chicken and Mexican burritos are served in a dark, cocktail-bar ambience. Open daily. Music Hall Passage (phone: 318515). Inexpensive.

SHARING A PINT: Pubs are the center of Chester life. In the old days they were simply places to drink and chat, but now most of them serve food, too, and the best of them give even good restaurants a run for their money. The *Boat House,* at the upstream end of the Groves next to the school and club boathouses, used to be a real rowing man's pub, with faded photographs of long-gone oarsmen and autographed oars on the wall. The noisy, cheerful, busy river bars — serving an excellent selection of American food — have been added, full of young people and music, and an unmatchable view of the Dee. The *Bear and Billet* on Lower Bridge St. is a beautiful 17th-century half-timbered house turned into a popular and friendly pub offering food as well as drinks. It once belonged to the Earls of Shrewsbury who enjoyed the profits from the tolls of the adjacent Bridgegate. (Before going in, look up: Payment was often in kind, hence the doors high in the gable where a hoist was used to lift goods to and from the roof.) *Duke's,* set in modern surroundings in Mercia Sq., is one of the new generation of wine bars. It serves wine by the glass, draught and bottled beers, plus a hot dish of the day. The *Albion Inn,* close to the walls on Park

St., is just the opposite; a real, old-fashioned, cozy, back-street Chester pub with draught beer from the wood and the traditional steak and kidney pie, black pudding and mushy peas, bread and cheese, and treacle tart. The *Town Crier,* opposite the railway station on City Rd., is a newly renovated establishment that serves traditional ales as well as meals. The *Falcon,* set in a 17th-century timber-framed building, also serves excellent beer. Other drinking haunts favored by locals include the *Pied Bull* on Northgate St., *Custom House Inn* on Watergate St., and *Boot Inn* on Eastgate St.

EDINBURGH

Other beautiful and famous urban centers such as Rome or San Francisco may share the distinction of being built on hills, but Edinburgh, a stark and in some ways still medieval city whose streets have often flowed with blood, alone can claim to be built on extinct volcanoes.

Astride one of these, high above the houses where Edinburgh's 440,000 inhabitants dwell, looms Edinburgh Castle, a portentous fairy tale structure that often makes visitors gasp the first time they see it. It seems almost supernatural, with ancient stonemasonry rising out of volcanic rock as if there were no dividing line between the two.

From the 7th century on, there was a fortress where Edinburgh Castle now stands, and as life in the Middle Ages became more civilized, life within the fortress spilled onto the long sloping ridge — carved by glaciers ages after the volcanic era — that runs down from Edinburgh Castle to the foot of Arthur's Seat, another extinct volcano, crowning Edinburgh's central park. The ridge, with its clusters of high stone and wood tenements, its one thin, snakelike public street, its cathedral, and its tollbooth, was (and still is) the securing knot at the center of Scotland's legal, commercial, and artistic fiber.

Walking around central Edinburgh today is sheer joy. There's very little need for a map; it's hard to get lost. Every time you reach a hilltop, there's a glorious vista of the sweeping fusion of earth, sky, and sea, and every glance up an alley reveals fantastic steeples, jagged, smoking, chimney-potted skylines, or beauteous rotund domes. The city lights its most imposing public buildings at night, and they are legion, spread out over a series of precipices and valleys. Nature provides incredible sunsets, the product of Scotland's unique slowly fading evening light (the "gloaming") and rapid change in the evening temperature. Legend and romance are at every hand. Somebody famous lived in almost every residence.

At the head of the legend and romance brigade are the arch Presbyterian John Knox and Mary, Queen of Scots, who together dominated life in the Edinburgh of the late 16th century. (Not that they dominated it together. When Mary arrived in Edinburgh in the autumn of 1561 as Scotland's very young and very Catholic new queen, Knox described the event in his diary as God having fouled the air with black fog and seeping rain.) The political and religious strife attendant upon Mary's reign is notorious, as are her two marriages and the three deaths associated with them, the last of these her own (she was beheaded by her cousin Queen Elizabeth I of England, to whom she had fled for asylum). Mary lived in Holyrood Palace, by the abbey at the base of Arthur's Seat. John Knox lived up the ridge from her near St. Giles's Cathedral, within the city gates. Both residences still stand, and are open to the public today.

Their Edinburgh reached its full flower around the end of the 17th century, when the tenements along the ridge had grown 15 (or more) tottering stories high and housed uncounted numbers of people, all of whom threw their garbage into the central street, warning those below with nothing more than the terse cry *"Gardez-loo!"* Buildings frequently collapsed. Water could be had only from one of the city's six wells, called *pennywells* (their sites are still marked today), and inhabitants would line up with buckets from 3 AM on to be sure of some water.

These cramped and malodorous conditions, plus a plethora of alehouses and a police force made up of decrepit Highlanders back from European wars, no doubt had something to do with the locals' favorite sport, rioting on fete days, parade days, and the king's birthday. Riots occasioned by more serious events were frequent also and occurred regularly in every age up to the Victorian and even beyond. Famous instances are the assassination of a wealthy councillor, John MacMorran, by dissatisfied youths at the Royal High School (16th century); "Cleanse the Causeway," a battle in the streets between two noble families, the Douglases and Hamiltons (17th century); the Jenny Geddes affair, in which a Presbyterian fishwife caused pandemonium by throwing a stool at a dean who was reading the new Episcopal service book in St. Giles's Cathedral — the first event in the British Civil War (17th century); the Porteous Riots, immortalized by Sir Walter Scott in *The Heart of Midlothian* (18th century); and the trial of William Burke, whose sale of his victims' corpses to the University of Edinburgh's medical luminaries did so much to further the international reputation of that great institution (19th century). Religious riots have scarred the city's history repeatedly, although the last one was in the 1930s.

Obviously this wizened medieval town had to spread out somehow, and luckily, in the second half of the 18th century, its by now thoroughly Protestant God sent it an increase in trade and prosperity. City fathers erected a wealth of new buildings on another ridge to the north — known as the New Town, connected to the Old Town by bridges. The classically proportioned beauty of New Town buildings, many of which were designed by the world-renowned British architect Robert Adam, is a testament to what is generally regarded as Edinburgh's golden age, part of the so-called Scottish Enlightenment. It was a great age not only for architects but for writers, publishers, philosophers, and politicians. Throughout the city, taverns became the sites of ongoing seminars. Among many other well-known people of the time, David Hume, Adam Smith, and James Boswell were Edinburgh men.

Today's Edinburgh has lost some of its traditional vibrancy and color, though it is certainly safer and cleaner. The near stranglehold the Presbyterian Church of Scotland attained on the social institutions during Queen Victoria's reign meant that industriousness, temperance, and respectability — all the middle class virtues — took supreme command of the city. About 60% of the present inhabitants are white-collar workers, an unusually high proportion, which helps keep the local flavor staid.

Nonetheless, signs are that things are livening up. Since 1979, an avalanche of flashy pubs, nightspots, and restaurants has shattered the city's sober air. Edinburgh has always been favored by geography, situated as it is on the Firth of Forth, an inlet in the North Sea, and surrounded by woods, rolling hills, and lochs (lakes). It is not only a national capital but a port whose chief exports include whisky, coal, and machinery; a large brewing center; and a center for nuclear and electronics research.

And though the idea of a Scottish Assembly at Edinburgh — favored by a majority of Scottish voters — was set aside on a technicality a few years ago, a groundswell of agitation for Scotland's greater control of its own affairs remains. Who can say whether Edinburgh's second golden age is at hand? Perhaps not all its volcanoes are extinct.

Certainly the smell of sulfur has been ominously in the air, as the ancient capital has been made a battleground for the local repercussions of Thatcherism's bitter conflicts. Increased government pressure on the BBC has resulted in the shelving of plans for a National Broadcasting Centre for Scotland, and the transfer of news and current affairs to Glasgow. Labour party victories in local government elections have been offset by government privatization of Edinburgh city transport, which has led to at least temporary transport chaos, if not actual Streetcar Wars. The *Edinburgh Festival* (see *Extra Special*) has been caught in the crossfire, weakened by government slashing of arts budgets and local Labour Council charges of elitism. In fact, the *Festival* has continued to maintain high standards and has reached out to embrace populism, increased internationalism, and the avant-garde. It would seem that, despite continuing pressure, the theater pageant is reviving, rejuvenated.

If anything, occasional disasters heighten the innumerable triumphs of what is undoubtedly the world's greatest arts festival. The low-budget *Film Festival* can't be Cannes, but its stature increases steadily. Unfortunately, mismanagement, anti-apartheid boycotts, and underfunding made the Commonwealth Games of 1986 a financial disaster, and Edinburgh's complacency has been additionally jolted by a growing preference for Glasgow as the site of future sporting events. The old Glasgow taunt that Edinburgh is "fur coat and nae knickers" has all too much relevance in a cold financial climate. The capital has had to look to its laurels, which means, among other things, that tourists are currently taken far less for granted.

EDINBURGH AT-A-GLANCE

SEEING THE CITY: Edinburgh has many wonderful views; on a clear day, there are striking panoramas from the top of any of its extinct volcanoes. To the north lies the sparkling Firth of Forth and, beyond it, the ancient kingdom of Fife. To the south are the lovely Pentland Hills and surrounding plowed farmlands. Look eastward, where the giant Bass Rock, off the coast of Berwickshire, meets your eye. Look westward to see across the whole nation to Ben Lomond, nearly on the west coast of Scotland! If you have a car, drive up Arthur's Seat (the road begins just by Holyrood Palace), park at Dunsapie Loch, and walk to the uppermost height (a steep and furzy climb — wear flat shoes and watch out for falling sheep). If you have no car, see the city from Edinburgh Castle.

SPECIAL PLACES: The "Royal Mile" is the name given to the oldest part of the city, the road that runs downhill from Edinburgh Castle to Holyrood Palace. It comprises four contiguous streets: Castle Hill, the Lawnmarket, High Street, and the Canongate. Since the entire citizenry of Edinburgh lived and worked for centuries either on or just off these four streets, the Royal Mile is practically groaning with objects and sites of historic fascination: 16th- and 17th-century houses, well preserved, with their adjacent courtyards and closes; residences of famous writers and distinguished thinkers; St. Giles's Cathedral, the High Kirk of Edinburgh, with its 17th-century spire in the shape of the Scottish crown; excellent museums; the classical City Chambers; and the building where Scotland's Parliament met from 1639 until union with England's in 1707.

THE ROYAL MILE

Edinburgh Castle – The oldest building in Edinburgh is part of the castle structure, a tiny ethereal chapel built by Queen Margaret, the wife of the Malcolm who features in *Macbeth.* King James VI of Scotland (later James I of England) was born here. The Scottish Regalia, including Sceptre and Crown, are on display. These disappeared after the union of Scotland with England and were found, over 100 years later, by Sir Walter Scott (who was leading a government commission appointed to look for them) in an old locked box. Emotion ran so high that his daughter, who was present on the occasion, fainted when he lifted the lid. Also in the castle is the Scottish National War Memorial, honoring Scots who died in the two world wars (phone: 225-9846).

Outlook Tower Visitor Centre – A short distance east of the castle, climb up 98 steps, walk outside, and find yourself face to face with church spires. The camera obscura, actually a periscope, throws a revolving image of nearby streets and buildings onto a circular table, while one of the tower's denizens gives an excellent historical talk. Downstairs is a very good book shop carrying everything from Lady Antonia Fraser's best-selling biography of Mary, Queen of Scots, to gleaming coffee table volumes about one of the national obsessions, Scotch whisky. Open daily on weekdays from 10 AM to 5 PM and on weekends to 4 PM. Admission charge. Castle Hill (phone: 226-3709).

Parliament House – Built from 1632 to 1640, after Charles I suggested that it replace the Collegiate buildings of St. Giles's Cathedral, this historic sanctum once housed Scotland's Parliament and is today the country's supreme court. Until 1982, tourists could enter only by written request. Its showpiece is the Great Hall, with a fine hammer-beam roof and walls laden with portraits by Raeburn and other famous Scottish artists. Also of interest is the Signet Library, a splendid example of interior decoration, with an exquisite ceiling. Written permission of the librarian is required to visit, however. Closed Saturdays through Mondays. Admission charge for library. Upper High St. (phone: 225-2595).

St. Giles's Cathedral – A church of some sort has stood here for over 1,000 years. The medieval building here was named for the Athenian saint Egidius (Giles). St. Giles's has often been showered by flying religious fur, especially at the time of the Reformation. In 1559–60 soldiers were put on guard at the church and many of its treasures hidden in private Catholic homes; Protestant nobles nonetheless ravaged the altars. Later, English troops came to their aid and stripped St. Giles's from top to bottom. It was at this stage that John Knox, a prime mover in this sequence of events, was made minister of St. Giles's. His unmarked grave is believed to be under Parliament Square, just outside St. Giles's. Open Mondays through Saturdays, 9 AM to 5 PM, (7 PM in summer); Sundays, open afternoons only. Upper High St. (phone: 225-4363).

Mercat Cross, or Market Cross – Near the east door of St. Giles's stands a monument restored in 1885 by W. E. Gladstone, prime minister of Britain off and on from 1868 to 1894. Here was the crossroads at which proclamations were read out and public hangings took place, until well into the 19th century. It was also the commercial focal point of old Edinburgh, the place being so thick with butchers, bakers, merchants, burgesses, lawyers, tinkers, tailors, farmers, drovers, and fishmongers that the town council issued ordinances requiring each trade to occupy its own separate neighboring street or close (hence the names you see on the entrances to the closes as you go down the Royal Mile: Fleshmarket Close, Advocates' Close, and so on). City tradesmen never obeyed these ordinances, however, and the Mercat Cross remained as colorful as ever until the city began to spread out in the second half of the 18th century. High St., by St. Giles's.

Advocates' Close and Anchor Close – These are typical of the many narrow alleys that gave access to the inns and taverns that were so much a part of Edinburgh's 18th-century cultural life. Doors to these places (taverns no longer) were topped by stone architraves dating from the 16th century and bearing inscriptions like "Blissit Be God of Al His Gifts" or "Spes Altera Vitae" (these two examples are still in Advocates' Close today). In Anchor Close was Douglas's, where the poet Robert Burns habitually drank. Entrances of both closes are from High St.

John Knox's House – Legend says that Scotland's fieriest preacher of all time lived here, but historians say no. However, legend has won, and this attractive 15th-century dwelling was preserved when most of its neighbors were razed during the widening of High Street in 1849. Open October through March, 10 AM to 4 PM; 10 AM to 5 PM the rest of the year. Closed Sundays. Admission charge. 45 High St. (phone: 556-6961).

Acheson House – When King Charles I was crowned at Edinburgh in 1633, Sir Archibald Acheson, baronet, was his secretary of state. Acheson built this house, a small courtyard mansion, the only one of its kind in Edinburgh, in the same year. It was the height of elegance in its day, yet 100 years later it had become a popular brothel and 200 years after that was inhabited by 14 families, though it had been built to house one. It was bought and restored by the Marquess of Bute in 1935, whereupon, despite its history, it was leased to the Canongate Kirk for a manse! Today it houses the *Scottish Craft Centre,* where you can buy all sorts of attractive, handmade items. Closed Sundays. No admission charge. 140 the Canongate (phone: 556-8136).

Canongate Kirkyard – Opposite Acheson House. Pause long enough to read the long list — mounted on a plaque — of notables buried there. The Canongate.

Brass Rubbing Centre – Visitors may rub any of the brasses or stones on show. Materials are provided for a fee that probably won't come to over about $8. The brass commemorating Robert Bruce, King of Scotland from 1306 to 1329, is very impressive. In addition to being nice souvenirs, your own finished products make beautiful gifts. Closed Sundays, except from 2 to 5 PM during the *Edinburgh Festival.* In Trinity Apse, Chalmers Close, off High St. (phone: 556-4364).

Holyrood Palace – A royal retreat since the beginning of the 16th century, the palace is where Queen Elizabeth II stays when she is in residence in Edinburgh. It is made of stone, a huge, imposing round-towered edifice befitting kings and queens. Most of what you see of it now was built by Charles II from 1671, but it is chiefly associated with Mary, Queen of Scots, who lived in it well before that for 6 contentious, sensational years. The old part, still extant, contains her bedroom and the supper room in which David Riccio, her secretary, was brutally murdered before her very eyes by a gang of armed men that included her jealous husband, her cousin Lord Darnley. By the side of the palace, within its spacious grounds, are the picturesque ruins of Holyrood Abbey and the lodge known as Queen Mary's Bath House, where she reputedly bathed in red wine. A guide will take you through it all, sparing no gory details. Closed Sundays from November through March and when the Queen is in town. Admission charge. At the bottom of the Canongate (phone: 556-7371).

Scotch Whiskey Heritage Centre – Just next door to the entrance to the Edinburgh Castle, this new tourist attraction features an hour-long tour, in an electric barrel-car, that shows the role of whiskey in Scotland's turbulent past. The sounds and even the smells of the distilling industry are tantalizingly reproduced. You will emerge knowing exactly how to make whiskey. 358 Castlehill (phone: 220-0441).

Scottish Poetry Library – For anyone who visits Britain to explore America's literary ancestry, an hour or two browsing here should bring rich pleasure. An extensive collection of books, magazines, and tapes with Scottish works in English, Scots, and Gaelic is housed in this 18th-century building in a courtyard off the Royal Mile. The building was formerly owned by Edinburgh's most famous burglar, Deacon William

Brodie, a respectable town councillor by day and a criminal by night, who was hanged in 1788. No admission charge. 14 High St. (phone: 557-2876).

BEYOND THE ROYAL MILE

Princes Street Gardens – Princes Street is modern Edinburgh's Main Street, its Broadway, and its Fifth Avenue. The gardens stretch nearly the street's whole length on the south side, where the old Nor' Loch, which was used in medieval times as the castle moat, once stood. The city spends thousands of pounds every year to keep the gardens opulent with flowers. In summer months (June–September) there are concerts, children's shows, variety acts, and do-it-yourself Scottish country dancing (to professional bands) here. Gates close at dusk. Princes St.

National Gallery of Scotland – Smack in the middle of Princes Street Gardens, on a manmade embankment called the Mound, is this exquisite museum, opened in 1859. It contains paintings by British and European masters from the 14th century to Cézanne. Open daily, except Sunday mornings. The Mound (phone: 556-8921).

Scott Monument – Sir Walter Scott is certainly one of Edinburgh's favorite sons — his face even decorates all Bank of Scotland notes, even though he was the most famous bankrupt in Scottish history. The elaborate 200-foot Gothic monument on the east end of Princes Street Gardens helps make Edinburgh's skyline the ornamental marvel it is. Its 287 steps take you to the summit. (Don't attempt it if you suffer vertigo.) Closed Sundays. Admission charge. Princes St. (phone: 225-2424, ext. 6596).

New Town – To the north of Princes Street lies the largest neoclassical townscape in Europe, built between the 1760s and 1830s. Assiduous conservation means that little has changed externally in these streets, squares, and crescents. Three of the more interesting ones are Charlotte Square (designed by Robert Adam), Moray Place, and Ann Street. The New Town Conservation Centre, 13A Dundas St. (phone: 557-5222), conducts personalized tours Mondays through Fridays; call in advance to arrange a time. The Centre also offers exibitions, a reference library, and various publications.

Georgian House – On the most gracious square in the elegant New Town, the National Trust for Scotland has furnished a house in period style and opened it to the public. The kitchen is a wonderland of utilitarian objects that would have belonged to a typical high class late-18th-century ménage. Fascinating audio-visual sessions on the history and topography of the New Town come with the admission price. Open daily April through October; weekends only in November; closed December through March. 7 Charlotte Sq. (phone: 225-2160).

Edinburgh Zoo – Opposite the Pentland Hills, away from the city center, en route to the western suburb of Corstorphine, is a zoo with a view and the world's most famous penguins, the largest colony in captivity. Every afternoon at 2:30, from April through September, they perform their delightful Penguin Parade through the park grounds. Open daily. Admission charge. Corstorphine Rd., Murrayfield (phone: 334-9171).

Grassmarket – This ancient street is flanked by many cozy eateries, elegant shops, and seedy-looking flophouses. The West Bow, off the street's east end, has some intriguing boutiques. Leading from the Grassmarket is Cowgate, with the 16th-century Magdalen Chapel (phone the Scottish Reformation Society to see it: 220-1450).

Dean Village – This 800-year-old grain milling town on the Water of Leith is over 100 feet below the level of much of the rest of the city and a good place to soak up local color. In summer the woodland walk along the river is popping with bohemians who live in the next village, Stockbridge. End of Bell's Brae (turn left off Queensferry St. onto Bell's Brae as you approach Dean Bridge from the west end of Princes St.).

Water of Leith Walkway – The Walkway extends from the outlying Edinburgh district of Colinton, on the southwest side of the city, near the Water of Leith's source, to the mouth of the Water of Leith at Edinburgh's chief seaport, a distance of over 10 miles. The Stockbridge section of the Walkway, including the woodland path from Dean Village, features St. Bernard's Well, so named to honor 12th-century St. Bernard of Clairvaux, said to have restored himself to health with the Well's healing waters after a frosty reception by the Scottish court, which followed his attempt to raise a Scottish army for the Second Crusade. The Well is encased in an impressive Doric rotunda featuring a marble statue of Hygeia, Goddess of Health.

Greyfriars Kirk – This historic Presbyterian church, dedicated on Christmas day in 1620, was the site of a pre-Reformation Franciscan friary. It is also where Presbyterians declared their opposition to the prescribed Episcopalianism of Charles I by signing the National Covenant in blood in 1638. Open March through September. George IV Bridge (phone: 225-8839).

Edinburgh Crystal Visitors Centre – Cut-glass items sell like hotcakes in the Edinburgh shops, and here's a chance to see how the objects are made. Operating in a town about 12 miles (19 km) south of Edinburgh, the *Centre* offers guided tours on weekdays; guests can see the glass blown, sheared, and cut. There is also a factory shop and a restaurant. Children under 10 are not allowed. At Eastfield near Penicuik; take Straiton Rd. south from town (phone: 0968-75128).

■ **EXTRA SPECIAL:** The *Edinburgh International Festival* is held every year during the last 3 weeks of August. It features the best-known, most highly regarded performers in opera, music, theater, and dance. Each year brings different orchestras, soloists, theater and opera companies — all are usually top-notch.

Accompanying the festival proper is the phenomenal *Edinburgh Festival Fringe,* an orgy of over 900 productions by amateur and lesser-known professional companies from Europe, Great Britain, and the US who come to Edinburgh at their own expense to strike a blow for art and for themselves. The *Edinburgh Military Tattoo,* a spectacular concert in full Highland dress by the massed pipe bands of Her Majesty's Scottish regiments, blasts forth most nights during the festival on the Castle Esplanade.

Coinciding with the first 2 weeks of the *International Festival* is the *Edinburgh International Film Festival.* Entries are screened at 88 Lothian Road, where the rest of the year *Filmhouse* (phone: 228-2688) offers a varied diet of classics and art movies in bijou surroundings with outstanding restaurant and bar facilities. The *Edinburgh International Jazz Festival* convenes during the second week of the festival. Pick up the succession of lively concerts at the Edinburgh Festival Club, in the Edinburgh University Staff Club, 9/15 Chambers St. (phone: 226-5639).

Those interested are advised to reserve tickets — and hotel space — as far in advance as possible, especially for the most popular attractions such as the *Tattoo.* A detailed *Festival* brochure is available at the British Tourist Authority in the US (see *Sources and Resources*) by May or June. Book reservations through a travel agent or write directly to the individual events. For the International Festival, it's the Festival Box Office, 21 Market St., Edinburgh EH1 1BW (phone: 226-4001); for the Tattoo, the Ticket Centre, 31-33 Waverly Bridge, Edinburgh EH1 1QB (phone: 225-3732); and the Edinburgh Festival Fringe Society, 180 High St. (phone: 226-5257 or 226-5259; reservations, 226-5138). The Film and Jazz festivals are more informal and easier to get tickets for once you're in Edinburgh.

SOURCES AND RESOURCES

TOURIST INFORMATION: The City of Edinburgh Tourist Centre, Waverley Market, 3 Princes St., Edinburgh EH2 2QP (phone: 557-1700), offers information, maps, and leaflets, and stocks all City of Edinburgh publications. On sale there is the *Edinburgh Official Guide,* updated annually. In it is a reasonable working map of downtown areas, with places of interest marked. A good, more detailed map is the Edinburgh number of the *Geographia Street Atlas and Index* series, on sale at most local bookshops. The pamphlets on Edinburgh history and legend at the *Camera Obscura* bookshop (see *Special Places*) will add greatly to your appreciation of what you see of the city. Each costs about $3. For a selection of other publications of local interest, also check the Ticket Centre, Waverley Bridge (phone: 225-1188), open weekdays 10 AM to 4:30 PM; Saturdays, 10 AM to 12:30 PM; during high summer, open later and on the weekends.

The US Consulate is at 3 Regent Ter. (phone: 556-8315).

The Tourist Centre also has leaflets on guided walking tours available in Edinburgh, including tours of the Royal Mile, the New Town, Leith, and a Robert Louis Stevenson trail. Among the offerings is a small foray into the dark side of Edinburgh's history entitled *Ghosts, Ghouls, Gallows.*

For information concerning travel in other parts of Scotland, drop by the new Scottish Travel Centre in St. Andrews Square (phone: 557-5522).

Local Coverage – The *Scotsman,* morning daily; the *Edinburgh Evening News,* evening daily; *What's On,* published monthly by the city, listing forthcoming happenings; another *What's On,* a free, privately owned monthly, available in most hotel lobbies; and *The List,* a comprehensive Glasgow and Edinburgh events guide (phone: 558-1191). Also see the *Festival Times* during the *Edinburgh Festival.*

Food – See *Restaurants in Edinburgh,* sold by the Tourist Board.

Telephone – The area code for Edinburgh is 031.

CLIMATE AND CLOTHES: A day with no rain is a rarity, even in summer. When the wind blows, put millstones in your shoes. Mists are not unknown either. Temperatures usually don't go below freezing in winter or over 70F (21C) in summer. A raincoat with a zip-in wool lining that fits over all the clothes you own is part of a recommended survival kit.

GETTING AROUND: Airport – Edinburgh Airport is about a half-hour from the center of town; the average taxi fare is $11. An "Airlink" bus, #100, travels from the airport to Waverley Bridge, making stops en route at the *Caledonian* hotel and at Haymarket and Murrayfield (phone: 226-5087). The tourist desk at Edinburgh Airport (phone: 333-2167) will provide information.

Bus – *Lothian Region Transport* headquarters is at 14 Queen St. (phone: 554-4494), parallel to Princes St., 2 blocks away. Route maps are no longer available, because routes are subject to change every 3 months. The Ticket Centre at Waverley Bridge also houses a City Transport Information Bureau, where details on each current bus route (except for St. Andrew Square Bus Station) can be obtained (phone: 226-5087). Passengers can reach most places from Princes St.; exact fare required. The Tourist Board office can provide information on bus tours of the city and countryside. Longer-distance buses go from St. Andrew Square Bus Station, St. Andrew Sq. (phone: 556-8464).

Car Rental – All major national firms are represented at the airport and in town.

Taxi – There are cabstands at St. Andrew Square Bus Station and in Waverley Station, off Princes St. To call a cab, phone *City Cabs* (phone: 228-1211), *Central Radio Taxis* (phone: 229-2468), or *Radiocabs* (phone: 225-6736 or 225-9000).

Train – The main railway station is Waverley Station at Princes St. and Waverley Bridge (phone: 556-2451). All trains *not* bound for London also stop at Haymarket Station, about 3 blocks west of Princes St. To catch a train here, add about four minutes to departure time from Waverley Station.

SPECIAL EVENTS: The *Edinburgh International Festival* and the concurrent *Edinburgh Festival Fringe,* the *Edinburgh Military Tattoo,* the *Edinburgh International Film Festival,* and the *Edinburgh International Jazz Festival* are held every year during the last 3 weeks in August. (For details, see *Extra Special.*) The *Edinburgh Folk Festival* occurs in early spring. For details, contact the Folk Festival office, 16A Fleshmarket Close (phone: 220-0464).

MUSEUMS: The city runs two museums of local history: *Huntly House,* the Canongate (phone: 225-2424, ext. 6689) and the *Lady Stair's House* (a Burns, Scott, and Stevenson museum), Lawnmarket (phone: 225-2424, ext. 6593). The *National Gallery of Scotland,* one of the three Scottish national galleries, is described in *Special Places.* Other museums include the following:

Central Library – An outstanding collection of maps, prints, photographs, books, and newspapers. The Reference, Scotland, and Edinburgh rooms are invaluable. George IV Bridge (phone: 225-5584).

City Art Centre – A particular pride and joy of the City of Edinburgh, this beautifully converted former fruit warehouse now houses Scottish paintings and sculpture, temporary exhibitions of fine arts, and a popular café. Opposite the *Fruitmarket Gallery* at 2–4 Market St. (phone: 225-2424, ext. 6650).

DeMarco Gallery – Headquarters for avant-garde art. 17–21 Blackfriars St. (phone: 557-0707).

Edinburgh Wax Museum – With every notorious Scot from Macbeth to Billy Connolly, and a particularly effective gruesome Chamber of Horrors that makes Mme. Tussaud's look like a high school prom. Admission charge. 142 High St. (phone: 226-4445).

Fruitmarket Gallery – A venue near the railway station with a changing program of avant-garde exhibitions from various countries. 29 Market St. (phone: 225-2383).

Holography Gallery – This exhibition above the *Wax Museum*'s knickknack shop has the finest range of holography in north Britain. 140 High St. (phone: 220-1566).

Lauriston Castle – A fine 16th-century tower enlarged to become a historic home; good art and furniture collections. Open Saturdays and Sundays only, 2 to 4 PM; visits with guided tours only. Admission charge. Off Cramond Rd. S. (phone: 336-2060 or 225-2424, ext. 6689).

National Library of Scotland – Exhibits on Scotland's literati through the ages. Temporary admission to the reading room may be obtained by serious inquirers. George IV Bridge (phone: 226-4531).

Museum of Childhood – Antique toys, games, dolls, and costumes, all beautifully explained and arranged. 38 High St. (phone: 225-2424, ext. 6646).

National Library of Scotland – Exhibits on Scotland's literati through the ages. George IV Bridge (phone: 226-4531).

The People's Story – Tells the story of the working class of Edinburgh through the centuries, including sections on the development of trade unions, health, welfare, and leisure. At the Canongate Tollbooth, 163 Canongate (phone: 225-2424, ext. 6679).

Royal Scottish Museum – A museum of natural history, science, and technology, great for kids. Chambers St. (phone: 225-7534).

Russell Collection of Harpischords and Clavichords – A feast for those who appreciate early keyboard music. Housed in *Saint Cecilia's Hall,* a restored 18th-century concert hall, the collection is owned by Edinburgh University. A faculty member leads tours of the collection at 2 PM on Wednesdays and Saturdays, and at 10:30 AM daily except Sundays during the *Edinburgh Festival.* Admission charge. Corner of Cowgate and Niddry Sts. (phone: 667-1011, ext. 4577).

Scottish National Gallery of Modern Art – Matisse to Picasso. Belford Rd. (phone: 556-8921).

Scottish National Portrait Gallery – Features paintings of Mary, Queen of Scots, Robert Burns, Sir Walter Scott, and more. 1 Queen St. (phone: 556-8921).

SHOPPING: Princes Street is Edinburgh's main shopping street, chock-a-block with a variety of stores. In addition, at the east end of Princes Street is Waverley Market, a large, modern shopping mall with Waverley Station at its base and the Tourist Office on the roof. Open daily until 6 PM, except Thursdays until 7 PM. The best buy is in Scottish tartans and woolens. Also worth a look are antiques — particularly Victoriana — in the area around St. Stephen's Street in Stockbridge. Bone china and Scottish crystal are attractive, and don't miss the shortbread, which is on sale everywhere. We especially recommend the following shops:

Debenham's – A branch of the London firm, with clothes, accessories, cosmetics, and more. 109-112 Princes St. (phone: 225-1320).

Edinburgh Woollen Mill – A good, inexpensive alternative to the *Scotch House,* with three locations, 62 Princes St. (phone: 225-4966); 453 Lawnmarket (phone: 225-1525); and 139 Princes St. (phone: 226-3840).

James Pringle's Woolen Mill – If it's made of wool, it's probably sold here! Offering low prices for top quality goods is the policy of this factory outlet, which also provides free taxi service from your hotel to their door. 70–74 Bangor Rd. (phone: 553-5161).

Jenner's Department Store – Sells everything, especially bone china and Scottish crystal. A particularly good selection of fine food items, ideal for packing fancy picnics. Princes and St. David's Sts. (phone: 225-2442).

Pitlochry Knitwear – Bargains in Scottish products, especially sweaters, kilts, and ladies' suits. 28 North Bridge (phone: 225-3893).

Scotch House – Classy, expensive woolens such as kilts, sweaters, tweeds, scarves, shawls, and mohairs. 60 Princes St. (phone: 556-1252).

Whiskey Shop – This connoisseurs' paradise claims to have the largest selection of whiskies anywhere in the world. In Waverly Market (phone: 558-1588).

Also worth visiting is St. Mary's Street. Leading off the Royal Mile, it's rapidly becoming famous for shops selling secondhand clothes, jewelry, and objets d'art.

SPORTS AND FITNESS: Fitness Center – *Meadowbank Sports Centre,* 139 London Rd. (phone: 661-5351), has a large gym with weights and exercise equipment, a 400-meter track, and classes in archery, boxing, fencing, and judo.

Golf – Scotland's national mania. A letter from your home club president or pro should get you into any of the city's 22 courses (you'll usually need it only for the posh, private ones like *Royal Burgess, Bruntsfield,* both in suburban Barnton, and *Muirfield* — home of the world's oldest group of players, the *Honourable Company of Edinburgh Golfers* — in nearby Gullane). Clubs can be rented. Full details on public courses are listed in the *Edinburgh Official Guide,* in the map *Golf Courses of Scotland,* and in the free leaflet *Golf Courses in Scotland,* all available at the tourist office.

Jogging – A good bet is *Holyrood Park,* near the huge stone palace at the foot of Canongate. An especially popular run is around Arthur's Seat, an extinct volcano in the center of the park.

Skiing – *Hillend Ski Center* on the Pentland Hills is the largest artificial slope in Great Britain. Equipment for hire. Open daily, 9:30 AM to 9 PM, weekends May through August, 9:30 AM to 5 PM (phone: 445-4433).

Swimming – Have a dip in the luxurious *Royal Commonwealth Pool,* built for the 1970 Commonwealth Games. Open weekdays, 9 AM to 9 PM, weekends, 10 AM to 4 PM. Dalkeith Rd. (phone: 667-7211). For other sports, consult the *Edinburgh Official Guide* and the Edinburgh Tourist Centre's *What's On.*

THEATER: The *King's,* 2 Leven St. (phone: 229-1201), and the *Royal Lyceum,* Grindlay St. (phone: 229-9697), are Edinburgh's two main venues. The *King's* presents everything from occasional touring productions of the finest of London's *National Theatre* to unfunny, patronizing junk. On the other hand, the *Royal Lyceum* has been gaining an increasingly high reputation for presenting interesting productions, primarily of established plays. The *Playhouse,* 20 Greenside Pl. (phone: 557-2590), is a converted cinema where musical productions are staged. The *Traverse,* 112 West Bow (phone: 226-2633), is a small theater which has become internationally known for its productions of avant-garde theater pieces and for presenting the work of new playwrights from all over the world. The *Netherbow,* 43 High St. (phone: 556-9579), and *Theatre Workshop,* 34 Hamilton Pl. (phone: 225-7942), mount small-scale, artistic productions. Schedules are in the dailies and in *The List.*

MUSIC: Classical music is the city's overriding passion. Highbrow musical events are held at *Usher Hall,* Lothian Rd. (phone: 228-1155), where the *Scottish National Orchestra* holds performances on Friday nights at 7:30. The *Scottish Opera Company,* which has excellent standards, has seasons at the *King's,* and also at the *Playhouse* (see *Theater* for addresses), where other famous names in both classical and nonclassical music give concerts. For chamber music and occasional jazz, try *Queen's Hall,* Clerk St. (phone: 668-3456). At *St. Mary's Cathedral,* Palmerston Pl. (phone: 225-6293), evensong is sung on weekday afternoons at 5:15 by a trained choir with boy sopranos. Also, countless amateur groups swell the city's halls and churches. Details are available in the dailies and in *The List.*

NIGHTCLUBS AND NIGHTLIFE: Edinburgh isn't exactly Las Vegas; it isn't even Philadelphia. Discos here are usually filled with a very young crowd, but you could risk the following if you're under thirty: *Zenatec,* 56 Fountainbridge (phone: 229-7733); *Cinderellas Rockerfellas,* 99 St. Stephen St. (phone: 556-0266); and *Outer Limits* (teenagers leave at 11 PM so others can roll up to an after-hours bar), W. Tollcross (phone: 228-3252). *Amphitheatre,* in a deconsecrated movie theater, is officially a nightclub and, as we go to press, *the* place to go; it's on the Lothian Rd. between *Usher Hall* and Princes St. (phone: 229-7670). Jazz and folk music can be heard at bars and hotels around the city; check the *Evening News'* Nightlife page or *What's On* magazine.

BEST IN TOWN

CHECKING IN: In Scotland, it is practically impossible to get a room without an accompanying kippers-to-nuts Big Scottish Breakfast (you pay for it whether you eat it or not). Expect to shell out $155 and up for a double with breakfast in the hotels listed below as expensive; $90 to $155 for those in the moderate category; between $55 and $90 for the cheapies-but-goodies in the inexpensive range. Unless otherwise noted, hotels accept all major credit cards. Should you find it impossible to get into any of our selected hotels, the City of Edinburgh District Council at the airport and in town at the Tourist Centre, Waverley Market, 3 Princes St. (phone: 557-1700), has an accommodations service covering all of Edinburgh and the surrounding district. All telephone numbers are in the 031 area code unless otherwise indicated.

Caledonian – A large Edwardian former railroad hotel with 254 rooms, 2 dining rooms, and 3 bars. Recently completely refurbished, it boasts great views of

Edinburgh Castle. The new decor is very engaging, and the rooms have been made infinitely more appealing. Celebrities love it. Phones in rooms. West end of Princes St. (phone: 225-2433). Expensive.

Carlton Highland – This building has been remarkably transformed from an old department store into a grand and sophisticated Victorian hotel. Recently opened with 207 rooms, 2 dining rooms, and a bar. North Bridge, off Princes St. (phone: 556-7277). Expensive.

Dalhousie Castle – Originally built during the 12th century and enlarged ever since (Queen Victoria once stayed here). Now it's a luxury country house hotel with 24 rooms. About 8 miles (13 km) south of Edinburgh (phone: 087-520153). Expensive.

Edinburgh Sheraton – This honey-colored hotel, just off Princes Street, seems architecturally incongruous in the neighborhood, but it can't be beat for its range of modern amenities: 263 very well equipped rooms, a health club and gym, sauna and whirlpool bath, swimming pool, parking, bar, and restaurant. 1 Festival Sq. (phone: 229-9131). Expensive.

George – In the New Town, between Charlotte and St. Andrew Squares, it's known for its gracious comfort. It has 195 bedrooms, 2 dining rooms, and a long bar. Phones in rooms. 19–21 George St. (phone: 225-1251). Expensive.

Hilton National – A flashy, contemporary property away from the center of things but with a beautiful view of the Water of Leith and close to Dean Village and the *Museum of Modern Art.* There are 146 rooms and 2 restaurants. 69 Belford Rd. (phone: 332-2545). Expensive.

King James Thistle – An oasis of charm and friendliness in St. James Centre (otherwise known as Edinburgh's leading eyesore). Guests are treated graciously by the staff of this 147-room hotel; the *St. Jacques* restaurant offers Scots food prepared *à la France.* Top of Leith Walk at Princes St. (phone: 556-0111). Expensive.

Ladbroke Dragonara – A flashy, contemporary property away from the center of things but with a beautiful view of the Water of Leith and close to Dean Village and the *Museum of Modern Art.* There are 146 rooms (with phones) and 2 restaurants. 69 Belford Rd. (phone: 332-2545). Expensive.

Post House – An ultramodern, all-conveniences affair, this is a good place to be if you have a car (it's beside the zoo, outside the city center). Its low-priced coffeehouse is less stuffily British than almost anywhere else. Breakfast optional. All 208 rooms have phones. Corstorphine Rd. (phone: 334-0390). Expensive.

Royal Scot – This 252-room modern structure is the epitome of the faultless airport hotel. Direct access to M8 for Glasgow. 111 Glasgow Rd. (phone: 334-9191). Expensive.

Howard – Its flower-filled window boxes are the last word in winsomeness. It has 25 rooms, with phones (and, surprisingly for a hotel this size, private baths). 32–36 Great King St. (phone: 557-3500). Expensive to moderate.

Braid Hills – Muriel Spark fans will remember that this is where Miss Jean Brodie, by then past her prime, took tea. An old, established, family-run 68-room hotel in the southern suburbs toward the Pentland Hills. 134 Braid Rd. (phone: 447-8888). Moderate.

Donmaree – This sweet little family hotel, in a respectable suburb, has 17 rooms. 21 Mayfield Gardens (phone: 667-3641). Moderate to inexpensive.

Galloway Guest House – Not as well equipped as the *Donmaree* (none of the 10 rooms has a phone), but more centrally located, just off the panoramic Dean Bridge, and the room rate includes breakfast. Dinner served off-season only, but guests have limited access to the kitchen. No credit cards accepted. 22 Dean Park Crescent (phone: 332-3672). Inexpensive.

EATING OUT: Reports on Scottish food vary from calling it a joke to claiming it is at least superior to English cooking. Still, visitors might want to try some of the following specialties: cock-a-leekie soup (chicken and leek), salmon, haddock, trout, and Aberdeen Angus beef. Skip any offering of haggis (spicy intestines), except on a purely experimental basis. Scones originated in Scotland, and shortbread shouldn't be missed. Restaurants usually keep the city's formal hours (lunch until 2:30, dinner anywhere from 6 on). Expect to pay $45 and up for dinner for two, excluding wine and tips, in establishments listed as very expensive; $30 to $45 for expensive; $30 to $50 in moderate establishments; and under $30 in inexpensive places. All telephone numbers are in the 031 area code unless otherwise indicated.

L'Auberge – A discreet, indeed positively diplomatic, restaurant that serves French fare, most notably fish and game. Open daily. 56 St. Mary's St. between Cowgate and Canongate (phone: 556-5888). Expensive.

Pompadour – The fascinating lunch menu here is a steadily unfurling history of Scots cooking, while dinners feature French cuisine. In the *Caledonian* hotel, Princes St. (phone: 225-2433). Very expensive.

Beehive Inn – Among the fittings in this Old Town restaurant is a cell door from the very old town jail. Steaks and fish are served from an open charcoal grill and are followed by luscious desserts. Closed Sundays. Major credit cards accepted. 18 Grassmarket (phone: 225-7171). Expensive.

Cosmo's – Edinburgh's link to Rome. Everybody who works here is fiercely Italian, as is the menu, with fabulous seafood and veal. The cocktail bar is made of imported Italian marble. Closed Sundays and Mondays. Reservations necessary. Major credit cards accepted. 58A Castle St. (phone: 226-6743). Expensive.

Howtowdie – White tablecloths and glass cases full of taxidermists' birds set the tone at this Highland-style establishment long famed for its ritzy image and traditional Scottish cooking. Closed Sundays, October to April. Reservations necessary. 27A Stafford St. (phone: 225-6291). Expensive.

Merchant's – A trendy French restaurant with white tablecloths, silver, crystal, and waitresses wearing trousers; there's also a green parrot that sleeps at lunchtime and can be pacified at dinner with a monkey-nut. Closed Sundays. 17 Merchant St. (phone: 225-4009). Expensive.

Prestonfield House – A 300-year-old country estate within its own peacock-laden park grounds. Candlelit dinners in rooms with tapestries, paintings, and blazing open fires. French cooking. Reservations necessary. Major credit cards accepted. Off Priestfield Rd. (phone: 667-8000). Expensive.

Arches – The dining room adjoining this bustling university-area bar has very good lunches and elegant dinners. Open daily. 66–67 South Bridge (phone: 556-0200). Moderate.

Blake's – An upmarket establishment (formerly *Nimmo's*) serving à la carte seafood, steaks, and rack of lamb. There's also a charming wine bar. Closed Saturdays for lunch. Reservations advised. 101 Shandwick Pl. (phone: 229-6119). Moderate.

Shamiana – Tandoori (Indian) food at its finest. Everything is cooked from scratch with delicate spices. Pale pink tablecloths, bone china, waitresses in saris, give the place a rarefied air. Open daily from 6 to 11:30 PM and on weekdays from 12 to 2 PM. Reservations necessary. Major credit cards accepted. 14A Brougham St. (phone: 228-2265). Moderate.

Skipper's Bistro – A jolly waterfront seafood restaurant in Leith, justly famous for its imaginative preparations and the freshness of its ingredients. Reservations necessary. Closed Sundays. 1A Dock Pl., Leith (phone: 554-1018). Moderate.

Stockbridge Steak House – Offering steaks but also stressing other examples of Scottish and Irish cuisine. 42 St. Stephen St. (phone: 226-5877). Moderate.

Helios Fountain – Among other specialties featured at this trendy café are a selection of vegetarian pies and goulashes invented each morning by the hip proprietors; the dishes are ready in time for lunchtime guests. It's a great spot for eavesdropping on intellectual conversations or for watching people browse over the books and jewelry-making materials also sold here. Open daily 10 AM to 6 PM; closed Sundays. 7 Grassmarket (phone: 229-7884). Inexpensive.

Henderson's Salad Table – This cafeteria-style vegetarian's heaven-on-earth may keep diners standing in line for as long as 15 minutes, but it's worth it. Piles of salads, hot pots, opulent desserts available continuously day and evening. Closed Sundays. 94 Hanover St. (phone: 225-2131). Inexpensive.

SHARING A PINT: Until recently, boozing was restricted to puritanical hours. But now it's possible to imbibe from 11 AM to 11 PM, and a few places have opened up where the taps keep flowing until the wee hours. Among the best pubs: the *Abbotsford,* 3 Rose St. (phone: 225-5276), is a haunt of Scotland's "Makars" (playwrights and poets) and journalists; *Bennet's,* Leven St. (phone: 229-5143), is a noisy but atmospheric theater-district pub with a Victorian hangover; the *Beau Brummel,* 99 Hanover St. (phone: 225-4680), is a neo-Regency plush artifact in mid-city; and the *Tilted Wig,* 1-2-3 Cumberland St. (phone: 556-1824), facetiously known as the Wilted Twig, is notable for its uncompromising trendiness and has a clientele of bar-hogging English smoothies, whom you can scatter at a stroke by standing in the doorway shouting, "Nigel, your MG's on fire!" And for enjoyable courtyard drinking facilities, join the crowd of university students at the *Pear Tree,* 36 W. Nicolson St., off Buccleuch St. (phone: 667-7796). If you enjoy folk music, try the *Fiddler's Arms,* 9–11 Grassmarket (phone: 229-2665).

Rutherford's, Drummond St., off South Bridge opposite Old College, was much frequented by Robert Louis Stevenson and Arthur Conan Doyle when they were Edinburgh University students in the 1870s, although while within its portals they never knowingly met. *Stewart's,* across the road, is a fine working-class pub, and if the private back room is free, you and your friends can occupy it for an old-fashioned disputatious Scottish enquiry into philosophy — see Scott's *Guy Mannering. Preservation Hall,* 9 Victoria St. (phone: 226-3816), opposite the *Bookfare* bookshop, is large, commodious, ornamented with fine epigraphs against drink, and offers rock and jazz music evenings. *Mather's,* 25 Broughton St. (phone: 556-6754), is the ecumenical watering hole for left-wing labour, nationalist, and sexual politicos. Opulent barges sometimes carry licenses in tourist season on the Leith waterfront. Find out at the *Waterfront Wine Bar,* 1C Dock Pl., Leith (phone: 554-7427). Also try *The Malt Shovel,* 57 Shore, Leith (phone: 554-8784). Both offer bar lunches.

GLASGOW

"The Second City of the Empire" — this grand sobriquet belonged to Glasgow through the long and glorious reign of Queen Victoria, when only London surpassed the famous northern megalopolis in size, wealth, and might. From a tiny 7th-century cathedral town on a tributary of the river Clyde, Glasgow grew to be an international industrial capital, the world's foremost shipbuilding center, and a pioneer in mining, railroading, canal cutting, ironworking, steam engineering, and scientific invention and development. From the time of James Watt (1736–1819), who was a Glaswegian, the city never looked back.

Today Glasgow is Britain's third most visited city (after London and Edinburgh), renowned for its magnificent and extensive Victorian architecture. Greek, Gothic, Venetian, Beaux-Arts, Renaissance, Art Nouveau — you name it, Glasgow's effervescent coterie of 19th-century architects copied it and went it one better. All over central Glasgow, public buildings the size of a chain of Alps capture the pomp and circumstance of the Victorian age, while in the west end, private residences from the same period show an unrivaled variety and graceful delicacy of line. Unbelievably, many of the elaborate string-corniced wonders in the city center were built as warehouses!

Although Scottish nationalists today bitterly lament the union of the English and Scottish parliaments in 1707, it was in fact this move that put Glasgow on the capitalist map. Freed at last from stringent laws prohibiting Scottish trade with the American colonies, city merchants now exploited Glasgow's relative proximity to the open sea. While cargoes from London were attacked by pirates in the English Channel, and London's ships waited days for each other to load so they could sail in fleets for protection, Clyde clippers zoomed, carefree, to Virginia. In exchange for Scottish muslins and linens, Glasgow merchants acquired tobacco, and acquired it much faster than their English competitors, whom they undersold. Soon Glaswegian tobacco merchants were supplying half of Europe. They became known as tobacco lords, married into each others' families, and produced dynasties that endured to corner many a new kind of market when the American Revolution severely curtailed tobacco profits.

As the Industrial Revolution gathered momentum, pressure to increase the efficiency of the Clyde, which was too shallow to allow heavy ships to service Glasgow's ports, became fierce. Parliament approved a plan to strip away miles of adjacent factories and build in their stead high quaysides acting as dikes. Steam dredgers and the development of underwater blasting did the rest. By 1886, 58 million cubic yards of waste and sludge had been dispatched, and the whole riverbed had been lowered by about 29 feet. No mere "muddling through" was good enough for Glasgow in those iron-willed days; when

Man fought Nature, Nature lost. As Glaswegians put it, "The Clyde Made Glasgow and Glasgow Made the Clyde."

Daniel Defoe glowingly described Glasgow's spacious streets and beautifully proportioned houses (a striking contrast to the Edinburgh of the same period), and visiting writers in later generations noted how eager the natives were to point these out. Signs of civic pride, past and present, are everywhere. Glaswegians have long had a penchant for showing off; witness, since Victorian times, the large number of official and unofficial parades, elaborate world's fair–type exhibitions, and crowded sailings down the Clyde in open boats. The city crest, bearing symbols associated with Glasgow's founder and patron saint, St. Mungo, appears on everything, even the sides of city buses. Museums are municipal, free, and very special, especially the *Museum of Transport* (see *Special Places*), where you can sense how wheels have become an absolute cult for Glaswegians in the climate of nostalgia and waning power that is the aftermath of their enormous share of the Industrial Revolution.

Perhaps logically, perhaps paradoxically, the gargantuan civic pride of Glaswegians is nowhere more evident than within the city's widely famous slum subculture, associated primarily with a southside district called the Gorbals. Its raw, swaggering, laugh-loving idiom is epitomized today in the art of comedian Billy Connolly. The virile mix of football, folklore, hard drink, and Red politics was fanned and molded in the 19th century by whole new populations that poured into the Clyde Valley from Catholic Ireland and the Scottish Highlands. The small, staid old Presbyterian Glasgow of tobacco lord days, in which stick-brandishing officials known as bum baillies beat the bottoms off offenders caught strolling in the streets during church, hardly knew how to absorb the shock. This was the origin of much of Glasgow's present orange-green antipathy, exemplified by the rivalry between the *Rangers* and *Celtic* soccer teams.

Glasgow's slums have been of momentous importance to British political history. In 1922, Glasgow constituencies elected ten Socialist MPs, all local orators who had become noted for their high-minded, left-wing ideals. They and their followers were known as the Red Clydesiders. Two years later, Ramsay MacDonald, a native Scot, became Britain's first Labour prime minister. Today the Labour party, often eclipsed in England in parliamentary elections, would sink without Glasgow's support.

But the road to political significance was a hard one for Glasgow. During World War I the city was *urbs non grata* at Westminster because of strikes in its ship and munitions yards. Public rallies, furthermore, exhorted Glaswegians to enlist for no form of combat short of a full-scale workers' revolution. With years of exploitation behind them, Glasgow's slum dwellers were on a galloping high. Housewives organized a rent strike by shouting propaganda from the tops of middens (shacks containing communal garbage) in tenement backcourts. By Bloody Friday, January 31, 1919, strikes of all kinds were widespread in Glasgow, and multitudes gathered in George Square to hear Prime Minister Lloyd George, up from London for the purpose, speak from the steps of the City Chambers. Rioting ensued, 50 people were injured, two important Red Clydesiders went to jail, and the next day armed troops and tanks blazed into the city. Yet somehow this token taste of blood had cleared the air, and within a few days most strikers returned to work and the tanks disappeared.

Glasgow today is a mass of contradictions. It has a greater variety of high-quality cultural events than Edinburgh (except during the *Edinburgh Festival*), yet it also has one of the highest crime rates in Europe. Right in its middle, near its most elegant buildings, are streets in a state of shameful dereliction. The Gorbals and other tenement areas have been bulldozed and refitted with faceless skyscraper apartments, yet the rambunctiousness and camaraderie of the days when 30 people shared one toilet, and every drink was a half of whisky knocked back with a pint of beer to chase it, linger on.

The Second City, however, is gone. Elevated motorways on concrete slabs thread their way over parts of Glasgow's once-majestic urban scene, and the Clyde, which sent the ringing din of riveting from its busy docks all over the city, is still. Population has declined from over a million to around 750,000, and Birmingham has outstripped Glasgow as London's runner-up in size. Yet at least half of all Scots still live within 20 miles of Glasgow, and engineering and printing, to say nothing of textile, food, drink, tobacco, and chemical industries, soldier on, despite rising unemployment. Whither now? The key to Glasgow's future seems to lie in tourism. With the international fame of the *Burrell Collection* (see *Museums*) and the European Parliament's selection of Glasgow as the European City of Culture for 1990 (see *Special Events),* there is talk all over Britain of a Glasgow renaissance.

GLASGOW AT-A-GLANCE

SEEING THE CITY: Getting an overhead gander at Glasgow is almost like finding the Holy Grail. The city is devoid of rooftop restaurants and publicly accessible steeples. Make your way to Glasgow University (buses No. 44 and No. 59 leave frequently from the city center for University Avenue), and storm the Gothic vaults of the main university building, architect Sir George Gilbert Scott's elephantine monstrosity built on Gilmorehill in 1870. Ask for the lodge of the "Bedellus," who with his magic key will unlock a door that leads up 252 steps to the top of Glasgow University Tower. If you can stand the climb, the reward is spectacular: Just below you is lovely Kelvingrove Park, with the river Kelvin winding through. Across the river is *Kelvingrove Art Gallery,* on a hill above a wooded glade. South of you is the river Clyde, and southeast is downtown Glasgow. Be sure to phone the Bedellus to make arrangements beforehand, otherwise you'll be in for a long wait. The best time to visit is Fridays at 2 PM. University of Glasgow (phone: 339-8855, ext. 452).

SPECIAL PLACES: One way to see Glasgow is to take it period by period. But start in the middle of things, with Victorian Glasgow, because it is this era that is the essence of the city. Except for the *Museum of Transport,* the surviving Victoriana listed below is quite conveniently placed. The rest of the sights — Medieval Glasgow, the Old Merchants' City, Modern Glasgow, and Clydeside attractions — are not far afield either, but don't expect to cover everything the same day. If you visit from April through October, hop aboard *Discovering Glasgow,* the zany 2-hour, 14-mile bus tour of the city that costs about $6 for adults and departs at 10 AM Mondays, Tuesdays, Thursdays, and Fridays from the Glasgow tourist information office at 35 St. Vincent Pl. (phone: 227-4880).

VICTORIAN GLASGOW

George Square – Also called Glasgow's Valhalla, this intriguing mix of equal parts statues, flower plots, picnickers, and pigeons was originally laid out in 1781 and named after King George III. It came into its own in Victorian times, when most of the grandiose buildings now surrounding it were constructed. Since Bloody Friday it has been the undisputed central focal point of the city.

City Chambers – William Young, a local boy who made good in London, designed Glasgow's Italian Renaissance city hall, and Queen Victoria officially opened it in 1888 to the roars of 600,000 spectators. Inside, the loggia, staircases, and grand banqueting hall, with their sumptuous interplay of granite, mosaics, marble, and stone, make a millionaire's mansion look like a log cabin. Guided tours begin at 10:30 AM and 2:30 PM weekdays (except when a banquet is in progress). George Sq. (phone: 221-9600).

Merchants' House – Opposite George Square's west side is the Glasgow Chamber of Commerce building, built in 1877 by native architect John Burnet. (The ungainly upper three stories spoiling the effect of the domed turret were added later.) Glasgow invented chambers of commerce in 1659 when its Merchant Guild erected a house, unique at that time, from which to minister to the widowed and orphaned of the collective merchant poor. That building — and that institution — was this one's ancestor. (Glasgow's Trades Guild, not to be outdone by its archrival, followed suit with a similar institution and eventually built the elegant Trades House of 1794, designed by the renowned Scottish architect Robert Adam. This is on nearby Glassford St. and is well worth a look.) Trades House is open 10 AM to 5 PM, Mondays through Fridays (phone: 552-2418); Merchant's House is open Mondays through Fridays from 10 AM to 4 PM May through September, unless a special meeting is taking place. 7 W. George St. (phone: 221-6779).

Buchanan Street, Gordon Street – For row after nonstop row of massive, public architectural Victoriana, nowhere in the world beats this!

Tenement House – Recently opened by the National Trust for Scotland, this is an example of a Scottish middle class turn-of-the-century household and provides an interesting look at life in Victorian Britain. Open daily from 2 to 5 PM, April through October. Admission charge. 145 Buccleuch St. (phone: 333-0183).

Museum of Transport – In 1962, a huge turnout of Glaswegians wept openly as they watched a parade of trams from all eras make a farewell memorial run through the streets. The trams were then lovingly roundhoused and became the nucleus of this museum. Also present are vintage cars, trains, and fire engines of Scottish design, plus a bevy of brightly painted Victorian items: traction engines, craftsmen's carts, carriages, even a one-horse open sleigh. The oldest bicycle in the world is here, looking like a couple of mill wheels. There's also a reproduction of a 1938 Glasgow street and an extensive nautical exhibition — pictures and models only — at which you can brush up your Clydeside history. Open Mondays through Saturdays from 10 AM to 5 PM, Sundays from 2 to 5 PM. Kelvin Hall, Bunhouse Rd. (phone: 357-3929).

Necropolis – Every tombstone is a virtual Parthenon in this graveyard of Glasgow's wealthy Victorian industrialists. Save a few gasps for the pièce de résistance, the huge, round, double-decked Menteith Mausoleum (date: 1842; recipe: gingerbread) on the east side beside a bird's-eye view of a brewery. The towering statue of John Knox was erected in 1833 (before the brewery). Keep clear of the place after 4:30 PM, when it fills up with imbibers, petty thieves, and (possibly) resurrectionists. Open all day. Across the Bridge of Sighs off Cathedral Sq.

MEDIEVAL GLASGOW

Glasgow Cathedral – A perfect specimen of pre-Reformation Gothic architecture, this was the only church on the Scottish mainland to have its inner structure spared during pillaging by 16th-century Protestant zealots bent on destroying "monuments of idolatry." Its 15th-century carved stone choir screen, separating the aristocracy at the front of the building from the plebeians at the back, was saved through petitioning by Glaswegian stonemasons: Such was the prestige of the Glasgow trade guilds. Have a look also at the remarkable fan vaulting in the crypt over the tomb of Glasgow's patron saint, St. Mungo, and at the chair Oliver Cromwell sat in when he visited Glasgow in 1650. (Glasgow was lucky because at most places he visited he was too busy burning and wrecking to sit down.) The chairs Queen Elizabeth and Prince Philip sit in when they worship in Glasgow Cathedral can be seen. (The Queen turns Presbyterian automatically when she hits the Scottish border.) Open Mondays through Saturdays from 9:30 AM to 7 PM and Sundays from 2 to 5 PM April through September; to 4 PM daily October through March. Cathedral Sq. (phone: 552-0220).

Provand's Lordship – Just opposite the cathedral is the oldest house in Glasgow, built about 1471. It was the townhouse of the prebend, or provand, of a nearby country see. Imagine a colony of such buildings extending up and down the adjacent streets and you will have an idea of Glasgow at the time of Mary, Queen of Scots. The house is now a period museum with displays of Scottish furniture. Open Mondays through Saturdays from 10 AM to 5 PM, Sundays from 2 to 5 PM. 3 Castle St. (phone: 552-8819).

THE OLD MERCHANTS' CITY

Glasgow Cross – This was the heart of the city in the 18th century, before George Square took over. The large reproduction of an etching that hangs on a wall of Merchants' House shows what it used to be like looking west down the Trongate. Today the Tolbooth steeple (1626) and the Tron Church steeple (1636) are all that's left from earlier times. The Edinburgh stagecoach stopped in Glasgow Cross, carrying newspapers from the capital, and Glasgow's merchants conducted their morning business and sipped their "meridians," or noonday rums, in the *Tontine* hotel, opposite the Tron Church. If you see the "scaffies," or city street sweepers, leaning on their brooms chatting garrulously together at 4:30 each afternoon, eating ice cream bought from a van beside the Tolbooth steeple, they are perhaps acting under the influence of a folk memory two centuries old. You can't see anything better than this for local color! Intersection of Gallowgate, Trongate, Saltmarket, and High St.

Stirling's Library – The main part of this structure, now a library, was the mansion of William Cunningham, the most famous tobacco lord of all. Ask at the front desk for the historical pamphlet. Closed Wednesdays and Sundays. Royal Exchange Sq., off Queen St. (phone: 221-1876).

MODERN GLASGOW

Glasgow School of Art – This is the most famous building in Glasgow and one of the most famous buildings of its period in the world — Charles Rennie Mackintosh's finest example of the style poet laureate Sir John Betjeman called "Beardsley-esque baronial." Its east wing was completed in 1899, the rest, with additions to the east wing, in 1909. Ironically, Mackintosh, an architect, interior designer, and artist of the avant-avant-garde, won the competition for the design of the school because his plan was the cheapest to build! Today, few dispute his unqualified genius. Although the public is not currently admitted inside, there are plans to open the doors in the future. Phone the porter for details. 167 Renfrew St. (phone: 332-9797, ext. 214).

John Logie Baird Plaque – You'll find it by the door of the room where Baird invented television (if he invented it — he is said to have been anticipated by an obscure Irish curate), in the main hall of the University of Strathclyde. The Scottish inventor demonstrated a true television system in 1926. The University is open to the public

Mondays through Fridays from 9 AM to noon and from 2 to 4 PM. George St., just east of George Sq. (phone: 552-4400).

BY CLYDESIDE

Custom House Quay – The Glasgow Corporation has fitted out its disused docksides with flower-decked walkways. Bands play here in summer and discos blare at night, while the anchored *Carrick* casts a silent eye upon all. The *Carrick,* a contemporary of the famous clipper *Cutty Sark,* holds the world sailing ship record of 65 days from Australia to London. Custom House Quay adjoins Clyde St.

Clyde Street – Continuing east, you'll see on your left the 17th-century Dutch tower of Glasgow's *original* Merchants' House, preserved for its magnificence when the house itself was razed. At No. 64 to No. 76, the world's most pretentious fish market, dated 1873, is dripping with sculpted rosettes and topped with winged horses. The building, once derelict, has been transformed into a classy new market, similar to London's Covent Garden, called Briggait (phone: 552-3970). At the end of Clyde Street, around the corner to the left along the Saltmarket, are the Justiciary Courthouses, with Doric porches, where the last public hanging in Glasgow, that of the dashingly notorious conman and poisoner Dr. Edward William Pritchard, occurred in 1865.

Glasgow Green – This is the oldest public park in Europe, and it has certainly seen a lot of action! The heart-rending statue at the west entrance was erected in 1881 by temperance reformers, after which massive turnouts of public temperance pledgers were a common sight on the green for decades. During World War I, you couldn't see the grass for the sea of tweed caps at Red Clydesiders' rallies. The green was also for centuries the site of Glasgow's chief washhouse and bleaching lawn: Foreign visitors commented on the brazenness of the local washerwomen, who lifted their skirts about their thighs to dance barefoot on the dirty clothes stewing in their tubs. It was on Glasgow Green one fine Sunday afternoon in 1765 that James Watt, playing hookey from church, had a vision of the steam condenser that changed the history of the world. Open all day. The west entrance is opposite the Justiciary Courthouses in the Saltmarket.

People's Palace – You never know what you'll find at this museum of local history, since the city owns more objects than it can possibly display at once and keeps changing the show. The place is impressionistic and fun, with everything from theatrical bills and political pamphlets to elaborate wrought-iron streetlights and fountains and the ridiculous pouting stone faces that once adorned the façade of the *Tontine* hotel. There are exhibits from every century. Open Mondays through Saturdays from 10 AM to 5 PM, Sundays from 2 to 5 PM. East side of Glasgow Green (phone: 554-0223).

Scottish Exhibition and Conference Centre – The Queen opened this structure in 1985 as a site for major auto and trade shows as well as top-name entertainment. Five interlinked halls are grouped around a glass-covered concourse housing restaurants, cafeterias, and gift shops. Off Finnieston St. at the site of the old *Queen's Dock,* on the banks of the river Clyde (phone: 248-3000 or 204-2161 for recorded up-to-the-minute information on the Centre's exhibits).

■ **EXTRA SPECIAL:** How about a trip on the last seagoing paddle steamer in the world, the *Waverley?* From spring until early fall, the Paddle Steamer Preservation Society operates this charming craft on 1-day round trips from Anderston Quay, Glasgow, to scenic spots beyond the Firth of Clyde. As you cruise the Clyde you'll see the cranes and derricks in the dockyards that once supplied over half the world's tonnage of oceangoing ships. Have lunch in the restaurant (with bar) on board, or bring sandwiches. For full details, contact *Waverley Excursions Ltd.,* Waverley Terminal, Anderston Quay (phone: 221-8152).

SOURCES AND RESOURCES

TOURIST INFORMATION: The Greater Glasgow Tourist Board office, 35 St. Vincent Pl. (phone: 227-4880), has stacks of free leaflets recommending things to see and do not only in Glasgow but throughout Scotland. Open from 9 AM to 9 PM Mondays through Saturdays and from 10 AM to 6 PM Sundays in summer; from 9 AM to 6 PM Mondays through Saturdays in winter. Ask at the desk for the official city guidebook, *Greater Glasgow,* and for *What's On,* a bimonthly booklet with a comprehensive diary of local entertainment (no charge for these items). Bartholomew publishes a complete map of Glasgow, available at the tourist board office for the reduced price of about $2.30 (higher in bookshops). John Smith and Son, booksellers, 57–61 St. Vincent St. (phone: 221-7472), carries *Glasgow at a Glance* (about $7.50). This is your bible, chronologically wrapping up every important building in town with an erudite blurb and a stunning picture, so don't leave it behind in the hotel. Short historical paperbacks about Glasgow are on sale, too, plus a selection of touring and restaurant guides and maps.

Local Coverage – The *Glasgow Herald* is the one respectable morning daily; the evening daily is the *Evening Times.* A valuable fortnightly guide to Glasgow and Edinburgh events is *The List,* available at newsstands for about 90¢. It also contains excellent features and reviews.

Telephone – The area code for Glasgow is 041.

GETTING AROUND: Rule number one is to use your feet in the George Square district — you can't view Victorian architecture properly unless you wallow in it. Buchanan, Gordon, and Sauchiehall streets are pedestrian zones. For information (including timetables) about available public transport (bus, rail, and subway) within the Strathclyde region, contact the Transclyde Travel Center, St. Enoch Sq. (phone: 226-4826).

Airport – Prestwick Airport (phone: 0292-79822) serves transatlantic flights, and Abbotsinch Airport, also called Glasgow Airport (phone: 887-1111), serves European and domestic flights. Buses shuttle passengers between the airports and Buchanan Bus Station. Service to Prestwick train station operates every hour (the 30-mile trip takes 40 minutes) with a transfer there to another bus to the airport, and service to Abbotsinch operates twice an hour (the 9-mile trip takes about 20 minutes).

Bus – Glasgow's bus system was once a model of urban transport, but since deregulation in October 1986, it leaves something to be desired. Schedules change every 3 months, and some routes have too many buses, causing traffic congestion, while other areas are left without adequate service. For information, phone 332-7133 or 226-4826.

Buses for destinations outside the Strathclyde region depart from the Anderson Bus Station on Argyle St. (phone: 248-7432) and the Buchanan Bus Station on N. Hanover St. (phone: 332-9191).

Car Rental – Renting a car is recommended because there is plenty to lure you out of downtown Glasgow. All the major firms are listed in the local yellow pages.

Subway – Subway trains run every 5 minutes Mondays through Saturdays until 10:30 PM; check at the tourist office for Sunday times. The system's stops are listed in *Greater Glasgow* or on a city center map. Hillhead Station is a good alighting point for west-end shops and restaurants.

Taxi – Taxis are still reasonably priced at about $1.35 for the first mile and about 30¢ for each additional 1/6-mile. There is increasing demand for taxis following the chaos caused by deregulation of the buses, and at night they are harder to find than ever. To visit places such as the *Burrell Collection,* phone for a taxi in advance: *Croft Radio Cars* (phone: 331-2769), *Radio Cars* (phone: 881-6666), or *Radio Cars Glasgow* (phone: 649-3333).

Train – Central Station on Gordon St. (phone: 204-2844) and Queen Street Station (phone: 204-2844) are the city's major British Rail terminals. Both stations provide regular service, and a bus connects the two.

SPECIAL EVENTS: Parades, band concerts, sports competitions, beauty contests, and disco dancing are what goes on in summertime at community festivals, and every Glasgow district has one, usually in late May or June. Get the complete list from the Greater Glasgow Tourist Board office. Every May there is the *Mayfest,* a major international arts festival that may soon be on a par with the *Edinburgh Festival* (46 Royal Exchange Sq.; phone: 221-4911). The *Scottish National Orchestra (SNO) Proms* have nothing to do with dancing. These 14 concerts with famous guest soloists and conductors alternate among Edinburgh, Glasgow, Aberdeen, and Dundee in summer. Contact the SNO, 3 La Belle Pl., Glasgow G3 7LH (phone: 332-7244). The *Glasgow International Folk Festival* takes place in early July; for details, contact the Arts Centre, 12 Washington St. (phone: 221-4526). In addition, a wide variety of events will be held throughout the year to celebrate Glasgow's naming as the European City of Culture for 1990. Some of these events include special performances by the *Scottish Opera,* the *Scottish Ballet,* and the *Scottish National Orchestra,* along with various theatrical shows celebrating Glasgow's past, a major exhibition at Central Station, and a program of sporting events, including the European Indoor Athletic Championship. For details write to PO Box 88, Glasgow, Scotland.

MUSEUMS: The *Museum of Transport* and the *People's Palace,* described in *Special Places,* are high on the list of things to see. But the most important of Glasgow's museums is the fabulous *Burrell Collection,* listed below with others worth a visit. Admission is free; opening hours, unless otherwise stated, are Mondays through Saturdays from 10 AM to 5 PM, Sundays from 2 to 5 PM.

Glasgow Museums & Art Gallery – British and European paintings, including Rembrandt's *Man in Armor* and Dali's *Christ of St. John of the Cross,* in addition to natural history, ethnography, and the decorative arts. Kelvingrove Park (opposite Kelvin Hall) on Dumbarton Rd. (phone: 357-3929).

Burrell Collection – Bequeathed to Glasgow by Sir William Burrell, a millionaire ship owner (and opened to the public in 1983), this dazzling 8,000-piece collection contains Cézannes, Rembrandts, Ming vases, Halses, sculptures, and tapestries. The building that houses the collection is itself a work of art. A shuttle bus takes visitors to the Collection every 20 minutes from Pollokshaws Rd. On the Pollok House grounds, 2060 Pollokshaws Park (phone: 649-7151).

Haggs Castle – An ornate castelated late-16th-century structure containing the original kitchen with cauldrons, spits, and barrels, and a Victorian nursery. A children's activity workshop — butter making, spinning, weaving, and more — takes place on Saturday afternoons (reservations necessary on local holidays) in a nearby cottage, and the landscape includes a knot garden. 100 St. Andrews Dr. (phone: 427-2725).

Hunterian Museum – Geological, anthropological, and historical collections, and Roman relics. Open Mondays through Fridays from 9:30 AM to 5 PM, Saturdays from 9:30 AM to 1 PM. In the main building of Glasgow University, Gilmorehill, off University Ave. (phone: 330-4221).

Hunterian Art Gallery – Paintings, drawings, prints, and furniture by (among others) Whistler and Charles Rennie Mackintosh. Open Mondays through Fridays from 9:30 AM to 5 PM, Saturdays from 9:30 AM to 1 PM. The gallery's Mackintosh

House is closed Mondays through Saturdays from 12:30 to 1:30 PM and charges admission afternoons and Saturday mornings. Hillhead St. (phone: 330-5431).

Pollok House – Works by El Greco, Goya, Murillo, and William Blake, plus antique furniture, silver, porcelain, and glass, all displayed in a house designed by William Adam, the father of the famous family of Scottish architects, and completed in 1752 (later additions by Sir Rowand Anderson were begun in 1890). It is surrounded by extensive park grounds. 2060 Pollokshaws Rd. (phone: 632-0274).

Royal Highland Fusiliers Museum – Three centuries of the Glasgow and Ayrshire Regiment: uniforms, weapons, medals, and pictures. Open Mondays through Fridays, 9 AM to 4 PM. 518 Sauchiehall St. (phone: 332-0961).

SHOPPING: Tuesday or Saturday is early closing day (1 PM) for some shops, though most city-center establishments remain open daily, often including Sundays. Local wares include woolens, pottery, crystal, Victorian bric-a-brac, jewelry, shortbread, and whisky. The *Argyle Arcade,* the L-shaped passage between Argyle and Buchanon Streets, is home to Glasgow's famous diamond and jewelry center, but it also has clothing and gift shops. The arcade itself is something to see: built in 1828 by John Reid, it has a magnificent mosaic roof best viewed from the Buchanon Street entrance. Also of interest is the historic *Sloan's Arcade Café. Savoy Centre,* a new self-contained shopping complex off Sauchiehall Street, is clean and well maintained, with 160 shops selling almost anything. *Candleriggs Market,* at 71–73 Albion St., is a good place to hobnob with residents and inspect local wares. It was recently converted from an old fruit market and is open Fridays, Saturdays, and Sundays only. *Paddy's Market,* operating daily by the railway arches in Shipbank Lane, is, however, the place for an authentic taste of old-fashioned Glasgow street-vending. So, too, is the *Barras* ("barrows"), a weekend flea market east of Glasgow Cross where they sell everything from "wee fleas" to white elephants.

Fraser's – This four-tiered, balconied, Victorian-vintage department store with central court, glass-paneled ceiling, and a couple of hundred feet of suspended chandelier offers English bone china, clothes, linens, Edinburgh crystal, food delicacies, or just a beautiful breath of rarified air. 21 Buchanan St. (phone: 221-3880).

Lawrie's – The sort of place where the landowning milord buys his deerstalking "breeks" (breeches). Kilts, skirts, jackets, pure wool plaids, tweeds, mohairs, accessories, and souvenirs. Highland dress made to order and clan tartans traced for visitors unsure of their Scottish connections. 110 Buchanan St. (phone: 221-0217).

Saltoun Pottery – Hand-thrown mugs and jugs designed by talented Glaswegian Nancy Smillie and a fine array of ceramics and glass. 24 Ruthven St. (phone: 334-4240) and Princes Sq. (phone: 248-3874).

Catherine Shaw – Specialists in Celtic jewelry, including hand-crafted pieces of silver and polished Scottish stone. In the Argyle Arcade (phone: 221-9038).

Upstairs Downstairs – Eastern objects and imported Indian clothes for women, in joyous native designs. 625 Great Western Rd. (phone: 334-9623). Visit also *Eurasia Crafts,* 528 Great Western Rd. (phone: 339-3933).

Victorian Village – Antiques, roomfuls of ornaments and old lace. Beethoven's *Pastoral* wafts through the adjoining corridors while you browse or dawdle in the charming tearoom. 53–57 W. Regent St. (phone: 332-0808).

SPORTS: Boating – Try Hogganfield Park and Queen's Park.

Fishing – The Firth of Clyde, the ocean, and the upland waterways near Glasgow are all popular. The Greater Glasgow Tourist Board office has details.

Golf – Get *Golf in Scotland,* a free leaflet, from the Greater Glasgow Tourist Board office. It supplies details of the championship courses along the Ayrshire coast as well as the Glasgow courses. Rent equipment from a pro shop and have ready an introductory letter from your home club secretary.

Hiking – Glasgow has 7,000 acres of municipal green space, much of it woodland, in over 70 parks. *Greater Glasgow* describes attractions in the larger parks.

Horseback Riding – The *Kilmardinny Farm and Riding Establishment Ltd.*, Milngavie Rd., Bearsden (phone: 942-4404), is the best bet.

Soccer – It's called football here, and in Glasgow football is just about synonymous with the two home teams, the *Celtic* and *Rangers.* Kickoff is 7:30 PM on Wednesdays and 3 PM on Saturdays from August through May. Celtic Park, at 95 Kerrydale St., is the *Celtic* home stadium, and Ibrox Park, on Edmiston Dr., is the home of the *Rangers.* Get tickets from the turnstiles prior to the games and take no intoxicating beverages; police may search you. League playoffs and cup finals are at Hampden Park on Somerville Dr. It's fair to say that football violence is now much less evident in Scotland than in England, but *Rangers* crowds still make anti-Catholic noises.

THEATER: Since 1942, the *Glasgow Citizens Theatre,* in deepest Gorbals on Gorbals St. (phone: 429-5561), has been famous throughout Scotland for its vigorous experimentalism, high standard of performance, and lusty approach to what are usually considered highbrow classics. The *Pavilion,* Renfield St. (phone: 332-1846), is the inheritor of the rich "Scotch comic" music hall tradition — typified by the late Harry Lauder — that Glasgow has given the world. Pre-London runs and large amateur (dramatic society) productions are at the *King's,* Bath St. (phone: 248-5153, stage door; or 227-5511 for ticket information). *The Mitchell Theatre,* Granville St. (phone: 227-5511), has variety acts and light musicals. There is also a handful of locales where the flower of upcoming young artistic Glasgow unfolds its petals: the *Glasgow Print Studio and Drama Centre,* 22–25 King St. (phone: 552-0704); the *Royal Scottish Academy of Music and Drama,* 100 Renfrew St. (phone: 332-4101); and the amazing *Third Eye Centre,* 350 Sauchiehall St. (phone: 332-7521), which publishes its own glossy monthly brochure describing events on its premises including plays, mime, dance, cabaret acts, jazz, films, talks, poetry readings, appearances by folk and rock groups, and workshops in dramatic arts for all ages. Open Tuesdays through Saturdays from 10 AM to 5:30 PM, Sundays from 2 to 5:30 PM, and evenings when events are scheduled; while you're there, stop in at the bar, café, or bookshop. The *Glasgow Film Theatre* (for art films) is at 12 Rose St. (phone: 332-6535). The *Tron Theatre Club,* 38 Parnie St. (phone: 552-4267), stages trendy new productions by small professional companies.

MUSIC: The restored *Theatre Royal* on Hope St. (phone: 331-1234), originally built in 1882, is the elegant headquarters of the prestigious *Scottish Opera Company.* Other national opera companies perform there, too (as do professional theater groups). City Hall, Candleriggs (phone: 227-5511), and *Henry Wood Hall,* Claremont St. (phone: 221-4952), are the places for important orchestral and classical concerts, supplemented by Glasgow Cathedral, which often hosts choral and sacred works. Also on Candleriggs is the ticket center (phone: 227-5511 or, for credit card bookings, 227-5015), where theatergoers can reserve tickets for the *King's* and *Mitchell* theaters and City Hall. Rock rolls in the Scottish Exhibition and Conference Centre. Bagpiping and Highland and Scottish country dancing must be traced to city parks and to small parish halls — have a look at a copy of *What's On.* Several locally popular jazz bands play the pub and restaurant circuit. Check the dailies for where. The City of Glasgow *Municipal Club* runs a *Grand Ole Opry* house on Friday, Saturday, and Sunday nights at Paisley Road Toll (phone: 429-5396).

NIGHTCLUBS AND NIGHTLIFE: The safest course is to chart a theater evening with a restaurant meal afterward. This will steer you clear of the restless natives whose idea of a Big Night Out is a long crawl from one mobbed, fuming pub to another, the progression marked by rantings, singing, and battles of wit. Gambling halls and dance hangouts can have an unadorned and, to a tourist, tawdry air. Oasis in the wilderness: *Charlie Parker's,* 21 Royal Exchange Sq. (phone: 248-3040), specializes in drinks and dinner; upstairs is the *Pzazz* disco (phone: 221-5323); open Friday and Saturday nights until 3:30 AM.

Scotland's Secretary of State has asked city councils to avoid granting late-hour operating licenses to pubs. Consult a copy of *Restaurants in Glasgow,* available at the Greater Glasgow Tourist Board office, for restaurants that have extended-hours licenses to serve drinks with food after the pubs close. You can drink until 2 AM in the overnight-guests-only bar of your hotel without having to eat.

BEST IN TOWN

CHECKING IN: A well-known Scottish television executive recently defined a typical Glasgow hotel as a "reasonable, functional, bathroom's-got-a-bath, bedroom's-got-a-bed kind of place." Comfort you'll certainly get, but don't expect to be overwhelmed by the picturesque. The price of a room includes breakfast, whether you eat it or not, and top class establishments will want you to show your mettle by consuming prunes, porridge, herrings, eggs, bacon, sausages, tomatoes, coffee, and toast, all in one sitting. Hotels in the expensive range charge anywhere from $135 and more a night per double; moderate hotels charge $90 to $135; and inexpensive hotels, $60 to $90. Guesthouses and bed-and-breakfast inns are a lot less expensive. Lists of these for Glasgow, Renfrew, Strathkelvin, and Monklands are available in *Greater Glasgow.* All telephone numbers are in the 041 area code unless otherwise indicated.

Albany – Where the visiting pop stars stay — this is a slick 248-room flat-topped box with a big-city image. Inside, it's soft lights, carpets, and chrome. One of the two dining rooms is a popular carvery serving Scottish fare. Bothwell St. (phone: 248-2656). Expensive.

Copthorne – New owners have restored this former railway hotel, which until recently was called the *North British,* to its original grandeur. After a few nights of sheer elegance here, you'll pretend you own half of Glasgow. Perpendicular to the City Chambers, it has 140 rooms, a restaurant, and a café. On George Sq., adjacent to Queen St. Station (phone: 332-6711). Expensive.

Holiday Inn – Yes, it's one of *those* and has everything from individual mini-bars in the 296 rooms to a heated indoor Jacuzzi. Argyle St. (phone: 226-5577). Expensive.

One Devonshire Gardens – A stately, distinguished townhouse where guests can feel like 19th-century aristocrats. It has 8 unusually designed rooms and an excellent restaurant. 1 Devonshire Gardens, W. Glasgow (phone: 339-2001). Expensive.

Stakis Grosvenor – This pure white 93-room Victorian showpiece in the west end, opposite the Botanic Gardens, is elegance incarnate. Grosvenor Terr. (phone: 339-8811). Expensive.

Beacon's – Consider it a bit of historic Glasgow in the form of a charming Victorian terraced house with 36 rooms and period decor. Edward VII once stayed here. The view across Kelvingrove Park to the town of Paisley and the hills beyond is glorious. 7 Park Terr. (phone: 332-9438). Moderate.

Central – An architecturally distinguished railway hotel of the 1880s, next to Central Station, it's spacious and gracious in the Victorian mode, but it was built right over a streetful of slum houses, so it may be haunted by the home-loving ghosts of the dispossessed. Sumptuous bedrooms (219). Gordon St. (phone: 221-9680). Moderate.

Hospitality Inn – Glasgow's largest hotel has 316 rooms that contain all the ultra-modern conveniences. It also has 2 restaurants, *Prince of Wales,* which serves French food, and *Garden Café,* which has an American-style menu of steaks, burgers, chili, and fried chicken. 36 Cambridge St. (phone: 332-3311). Moderate.

Stakis Pond – There are 134 rooms in this somewhat lethargic modern hotel in the west end. The name comes from the usable boating pond, which it overlooks, and it's a good place for kids. Great Western Rd. (phone: 334-8161). Moderate.

Marie Stuart – Bill Tennent, a local television personality, runs this grand old house with 8 rooms well south of the Clyde. Glaswegians like it for wakes and weddings. 46–48 Queen Mary Ave. (phone: 424-3939). Inexpensive.

Sherbrooke Castle – The bar here is the neighborhood pub, ideal for helping you forget you're a tourist. This 25-room Scottish baronial mansion-house is on a knolltop on the city's south side. 11 Sherbrooke Ave. (phone: 427-4227). Inexpensive.

EATING OUT: Native food, dismissed with a laugh by the ignorant because of the names of some of its dishes ("haggis," "powsowdie," "cullen skink"), can actually be delicious. Top of the Scottish gastronomic pops are Aberdeen Angus steak, lamb with rowanberry jelly, venison, moor grouse, salmon, and trout. For a meal for two expect to pay over $50 at restaurants listed as expensive; $30 to $50 at restaurants listed as moderate; and under $30 at restaurants listed as inexpensive. This selection does not include any of Glasgow's numerous pubs with catering facilities, fish and chips shops, and plastic-age fried chicken or burger joints. Time your hunger pangs carefully. Most restaurants are open for lunch from noon until 2:30 PM and for dinner from 5 PM or 7 PM until 11 PM or so. Few are open continuously throughout the day, and few are open on Sundays. All telephone numbers are in the 041 area code unless otherwise indicated.

Colonial – This establishment, which prides itself on being Glasgow's top restaurant, serves modern Scottish food. Eat here and you'll see the unseen face of business Glasgow. Closed Sundays. 25 High St. (phone: 552-1923). Expensive.

Rogano – Seafoods are a specialty, and there's an oyster bar in this pub-restaurant, which media people and talkative about-towners have claimed as their own. Its antique fixtures include mirrors and glass paneling adorned with sea themes. Closed Sundays. 11 Exchange Pl. (phone: 248-4055). Expensive.

Ubiquitous Chip – No, this is not a fish and french fries outlet. The menu caters to the discriminating palate, featuring local delicacies when they are in season. And the glassed-in courtyard with a fountain and an Art Deco water lily mural pleases the eye, too. Closed Sundays. 12 Ashton La. (phone: 334-5007). Expensive.

L'Ariosto – High-backed pine chairs, tiled floor, dim lighting, soft music, and lots of lovers' nooks make this romantically Italian. The bill of fare doesn't stop at spaghetti. Dancing Tuesday through Saturday nights. Closed Sundays. 92–94 Mitchell St. (phone: 221-8543 and 221-0971). Expensive to moderate.

Fountain – Small and unpretentious, this restaurant is in the London image, known for its expense-account lunches. Menu is international, with emphasis on French cuisine. Closed Saturday lunch and Sundays. 2 Woodside Crescent, Charing Cross (phone: 332-6396). Expensive to moderate.

La Parmigiana – Italian cuisine served here, by jolly Italian waiters. Striped awning outside, bijou-type intimacy within. Dining is accompanied on Fridays and Saturdays by the strains of "O Sole Mio" and other gems sung to the strings of a small guitar. Closed Sundays. 447 Great Western Rd. (phone: 334-0686). Moderate.

L'Arena di Verona – Food is Italian plus basic British. Across the street from the *Theatre Royal,* this is popular with actors and theatergoers. An extension to the dining area is a chic pizza parlor. Closed Sundays. 311–313 Hope St. (phone: 332-7728). Moderate to inexpensive.

Ad Lib Mid Atlantic – Steaks and real beef hamburgers, piped disco music, and posters of glamorous American celebrities are all part of the effort to make Yankees feel at home and Glaswegians feel they're not. Cocktails are a specialty. Open Mondays through Saturdays from noon to the "wee" hours; closed Sundays. 111 Hope St. (phone: 248-7102). Inexpensive.

Café Gandolfi – Genuine 1930s bits and pieces (like the overhead propeller fan), a larger-than-life delicatessen, comestibles, taped 1930s jazz, and animated intellectual chat. Closed Sundays. 64 Albion St. (phone: 552-6813). Inexpensive.

Cul de Sac – A little, university-area coffeehouse, bar, and *crêperie* with a mellow social ambience and occasional live accordion music. Open Mondays through Thursdays and Sundays from noon to 11:30 PM, Fridays from noon to midnight, and Saturdays from noon to 1 AM. 44–46 Ashton La. (phone: 334-4749). Inexpensive.

Willow Tea Room – Another great hideaway to recuperate in during a hectic day, it serves light meals and beverages. Particularly noteworthy, it was designed by Charles Rennie Mackintosh, the noted Art Nouveau architect from Glasgow. Open Mondays through Saturdays from 9:30 AM to 5 PM. 217 Sauchiehall St. (phone: 332-0521). Inexpensive.

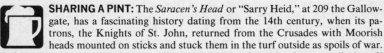

SHARING A PINT: The *Saracen's Head* or "Sarry Heid," at 209 the Gallowgate, has a fascinating history dating from the 14th century, when its patrons, the Knights of St. John, returned from the Crusades with Moorish heads mounted on sticks and stuck them in the turf outside as spoils of war. *Babbity Bowster* hotel, a traditional inn at 16–18 Blackfriars St., features a lively café bar (without the usual din-creating machinery) with live music, mainly traditional and classical, in an 18th-century building. For a touch of the Franco-Scottish "auld alliance," try *Fouquet's Wine Bar and Brasserie,* 7 Renfield St. *Scotch Corner,* Bath and Buchanan sts., offers local color, including "live weekend entertainment," somewhat obviously with the tourist in mind. Intellectuals make themselves at home in the bar at the *Tron Theatre Club* (closed Mondays), 63 Trongate. The *Waterloo Bar,* 308 Argyle St., recently refurbished, has a live DJ Thursdays and Sundays and is open to midnight except Sundays. *Bon Accord* (North St.) is known for its wide range of traditional beers. Glasgow is crawling with pubs, and if you stay any length of time, you will soon find your own favorites.

INVERNESS

Despite the flatness of its center and the "plain Jane" look of its streets (a visual adjustment for the traveler, after the scenic grandeurs experienced en route), Inverness is still an exhilarating place to visit and explore. It is northern Scotland's commercial and administrative center, the "Capital of the Highlands," where kilt often passes bowler hat in the square beside the Town House in the course of the ritual biddings of good day. The river Ness courses through the city's center beside high-spired "kirks," and the sun, which never quite goes down in midsummer, bathes its shining water in an exquisite golden half-light.

No newcomer, Inverness dates from at least the 4th century BC, when the entire Highland region was ruled from here by Pictish kings. St. Columba of Iona was en route to Inverness to convert King Brudei to Christianity in AD 565 when his boat supposedly was nearly capsized by the Loch Ness monster. According to legend, he firmly rebuked the animal, and it bashfully resubmerged — or so reported St. Adamnan, Abbot of Iona, writing a century later. During the 12th century, Inverness became a royal burgh under the patronage of King David I, son of King Malcolm III (Macbeth's successor) and the Normanized English St. Margaret. This ascendancy of the Norman–Scot influence over Gaelic tradition, represented in part by Macbeth (or "Maelbeatha," in his national tongue), caused trouble for centuries. All too often the peaceful patterns of Invernessian trading, fishing, and farming were disrupted by yet another highland chieftain or Norman–Scot adventurer sacking the town, hoping to annex it to his neighboring fief. The king's keeper of law and order at Inverness, the "Justiciar of the North," lived at Inverness Castle, which it was his duty to defend. But quite often these justiciars were more loyal to local forces than to the crown. One, a follower of the fourth Earl of Huntly, was put to death by Mary, Queen of Scots, in 1562 when he closed his portals against her.

During more recent times, while the North Sea oil boom of the 1960s and early 1970s was thriving, Inverness was again "sacked" by government officials, who, in the interest of short-term profit, razed massive portions of the old town to make way for the construction of low-cost concrete office blocks. Luckily, a concentration of Victorian buildings still survives in the area around Station Square.

Again, in 1966, city fathers suffered a lapse of foresight and old-fashioned ideals when they squandered the opportunity to have a new Scottish university built here; the proposed institution was eventually built in Stirling instead. Not surprisingly, as the dominance of oil has waned during the last decade, so has the orgy of expedience and greed, and the old churchgoing respectability of Inverness — and the reserved but trusting neighborliness of its historic families — quietly have regained control. (A stranger, by Inverness standards, is anyone whose family has resided here for less than a century.)

It has always been the churches — not the king's justiciars, the merchants, the bankers, or the lawyers — that have knitted the Invernessian social fabric. During the 13th century, the town was dominated by the Dominican Black Friars, who held extensive properties and, at the request of King Alexander III, sent ambassadors to Norway. Although they fell afoul of the Abbot of Abroath in the late 14th century (when their church buildings were pillaged by the abbot's men), the Black Friars continued to dominate Inverness until the Reformation, when they finally were forced to surrender their holdings to the burgh council. Rubble from the priory was later used by Cromwell's men to build a citadel on Shore Street (see *Special Places*).

The final smack in the face to the Black Friars' sacred precinct came as late as 1977, when a hideous concrete footbridge between two unaesthetic government buildings was constructed right over it. Meanwhile, 20 Protestant churches now polka-dot Inverness, including Baptist, Christian Brethren, Presbyterian, Free Presbyterian, Methodist, Episcopalian, and Salvation Army. Their bookshops are everywhere; it is impossible to walk through the streets without seeing lintels painted "Church of Scotland Bookshop," "Scripture Union Bookshop," "Christian Literature Crusade," and so on. Roman Catholicism still does maintain a tenuous foothold in Inverness, however, with two churches that bring the town's full complement of places of worship to 22.

It is questionable whether the wild blood of the highlanders, who lent so much turbulence to the history of Inverness, has truly been quelled in modern times. Scottish newspapers still occasionally carry stories of murders and other unthinkable crimes in out-of-the-way farmhouses in remote districts north of Inverness. (These cases are then tried in Inverness and the criminals imprisoned here.) But on the whole, it is the wild blood of *tourists* with which Invernessians currently contend: The permanent population of 40,000 swells like a party balloon to 100,000 in summer, as tourists pack local hotels. However, the good townsfolk show no eagerness to construct a string of casinos and other concessions to tourism on the shores of Loch Ness. They have gone so far as to open some new shops, many small, personalized tour agencies, two Loch Ness cruise companies, and some firms that rent boats, bicycles, and ponies. Otherwise, Invernessians go about their business without taking much notice of tourists. They continue to leave the vestibules of their residences invitingly open, making visitors feel a million miles from the strict security and suspicions of more cosmopolitan communities.

INVERNESS AT-A-GLANCE

SEEING THE CITY: Nature has provided no fewer than three completely different views of the city. A favorite is 220-foot-high Tomnahurich Cemetery, off Glenurquhart Rd. (A82), where cypress and yew trees sigh melodiously, and fairies reportedly cavort at night upon the old mud tracks that may one day soon be paved. (As the number of car owners in the area grows, locals have been protesting to the district council that the funeral corteges of the bereaved are having to "squelch their way" to the graves.) Also impressive is Craig Phadrig, to the west of town, which has a steep forest-trail climb to an ancient vitrified fort, double-walled, from about 350 BC. Or be lazy: Just nip up Castle Hill, a few hundred yards from the High St., for a bird's-eye view of those two sentinels on opposite banks of the fast-flowing Ness, St. Andrew's Cathedral and Ness Bank Church. Across Moray Firth, behind them in the distance, is the towering form of Ben Wyvis.

SPECIAL PLACES: Most visitors find they can wrap up sightseeing in Inverness in half a day and still be wanting more. So in addition to attractions in the town itself, we have selected some special places within 15 miles of town.

IN THE CITY

Town Centre – On the High St., a block from the river, is an area that has been the town center since medieval times. It consists of a cluster of three interesting structures — the townhouse, steeple, and destiny stone. The small but ornately Gothic townhouse of 1882 contains an interesting array of former coats-of-arms of the burgh of Inverness and other heraldic paraphernalia, as well as paintings, portraits, and busts of former dignitaries. The council chamber within contains a document with the signatures of members of David Lloyd George's cabinet (including Winston Churchill's). Lloyd George interrupted a highland holiday in September 1921 to convene his cabinet here during a knotty skirmish (by post) with Eámon de Valera (whom he refused to recognize as "President of the Irish Republic"). Opposite, the town steeple of 1791 has a 150-foot spire of particularly arresting Georgian elegance; on the site of the old tollbooth, it was originally built as a jail. The locals call the belfry chimes the *skellats* ("tin-pans"). Next to the townhouse is the *Clach-na-Cuddain* ("Stone of the Tubs"). In olden times the women of the town stopped to gossip here on their way home with tubs of water from nearby wells; hence the plebeian name for what has historically been the town talisman, bringing good luck. It is thought to have been brought here from a prehistoric stone circle. The old mercat (market) cross, restored in 1900, stands atop.

Church Street – Beginning at its junction with High St., walk north along Church St. to Abertarff House, Bow Court, Dunbar's Hospital, the parish church, the old Gaelic church, and the Dominican friary graveyard. Restoration work in this area has recently turned the tide of legalized vandalism that has wiped out so much of the old town.

Abertarff House: A whitewashed 16th-century building with the characteristic corkscrew stairwell of fashionable residences of the time. Today it is the highland headquarters of the National Trust for Scotland. Open Mondays through Fridays, 9 AM to 4:30 PM (phone: 232034).

Bow Court: Dating from 1722, it is now a complex of shops and apartments. Its former Trades Hall wing is on land owned by the Inverness "Six Crafts" (hammermen, wrights, shoemakers, tailors, skinners, and weavers).

Dunbar's Hospital: A particularly fine 17th-century grammar school and weighhouse, with a hostel above for bedesmen (beggars), who were cared for by the parish church. The ornamentation on the façade is composed of mythical beasts peering out of fleurs-de-lys and thistles.

Parish Church of Old High Church: An 18th-century edifice, built onto a medieval tower with a 17th-century balustraded spire. Its graveyard is interesting, too, with mausoleums of some of the hoariest Invernessian clans. A good view of the parish church can be had from the nearby footbridge across the river Ness.

Old Gaelic Church: As close to the parish church as a hatpin to a hat, this house of worship was built in 1649 for speakers of Gaelic. It now has a free, or sabbatarian, congregation.

Black Friars Priory: Nothing is left of the splendors of this 13th-century structure — that rich Dominican house with exclusive fishing rights on the adjacent stretch of Ness — except a 13-foot sandstone pillar. To get there, turn left at the end of Church St. for Friars St. Built into the south wall of the graveyard is an effigy of an armored knight, the tombstone of Alexander Stewart, bastard son of the Wolf of Badenoch (see *Northeast Scottish Highlands,* DIRECTIONS), who was sheriff of Inverness and Justice of the North during the 15th century.

Castle Hill – Inverness Castle, a lovely pink chess piece dominating the town, was built during the 19th century on the site of David I's medieval castle, blasted by Jacobites in 1745. Today it is the Inverness Sheriff Court. In summer, people picnic on its grassy lawns, not in the least intimidated by its violent history or the proximity of Her Majesty's prison. Only in Inverness could a cluster of sleepy Victorian townhouses rub sides with a slammer. It's fun to walk through the area, glorying in the architecture. Try Old Edinburgh Rd., Mitchell St., and Gordon Terr.

Shore Street – This is the road along the part of the river called the "Cherry," a corruption of *curach,* the Gaelic word for boat. The quay here has been in use since the 16th century and once harbored myriad small craft. Jutting up among today's depots, factories, and warehouses is Oliver Cromwell's Tower, on Cromwell Rd., a continuation of Shore St. Thirty feet high, it was the crowning glory of the famous Puritan's "Pentagon," a five-sided fort blown up during the Restoration.

Ness Islands – A place for sunlit serenity and dalliance among daffodils, these islets in the middle of the river have views of small waterfalls from various footpaths. Bridges to the islands are from the Island Bank and Bught rds.

James Pringle Woolen Mill – *James Pringle Ltd.* continues to produce topnotch woolen goods here at its picturesque 200-year-old factory on the Ness. They offer tours of the mills and then turn visitors loose among a trove of purchasable cashmeres, lambswools, and Shetlands. There is also a cafeteria. Open daily during tourist season. On B862, Dores Rd. (phone: 223311).

Kiltmaker – Another purveyor of fine Scottish wools, this establishment has crystal, china, lace, pendants, pottery, and perfumes from highland flowers. Its pièce de résistance, a scientific Loch Ness monster video show incorporating official archive footage, is offered free. 4–9 Huntly St. (phone: 222781).

EAST OF THE CITY

Culloden Battlefield and Visitor Centre – This historic site of the last pitched battle fought in Britain, with its clan graves, Well of the Dead, Memorial Cairn, and *Old Leanach Farmhouse* (a small war museum), lies 5 miles outside town. A day of infamy that will live in Scots' memories forever, April 16, 1746, saw a ragged band of supporters of "Bonnie Prince Charlie" (heir to the Royal Scots House of Stuart, the "Young Pretender" to the British throne) butchered while Prince Charlie himself, a desperate fugitive, barely managed to return to the European mainland via Skye, at one point disguised as a maidservant. The full, harrowing story is told at the visitor center by a multimedia show produced by the National Trust for Scotland. Battlefield open year-round; museum and visitor center open Easter through mid-October. Admission charge to the visitors center and museum. On B9006 (phone: 790607).

Clava Cairns – This impressive group of Bronze Age standing stones and burial chambers is found near Culloden, off B9006, 6½ miles from Inverness.

Culloden Pottery – On varying days of each week, the colony of stone- and earthenware potters near Culloden, in the Old Smiddy at Gollanfield, provides visitors with a chance to throw pots, too, then fire and glaze their products to be taken home. They also do commissioned works. It's all informal and fun. Gift shop and buffet lunchroom attached. Open daily except 3 weeks at Christmas. On A96 (for more information about days, hours, and instruction phone 62340).

Fort George – Erected after the Battle of Culloden in order to enforce proscriptions against highlanders, this remarkable 12-acre garrison, designed by the famous architect Robert Adam (whose creations are found as far away as Charleston, South Carolina), is polygon-shaped and cost (in its own day) the whopping sum of £160,000. It sits on the Moray coast with a fine view out to sea and contains a regimental museum of the Queen's Own Highlanders. Visitors can sally around the tops of the defenses. Open daily year-round. Admission charge. On B9039; turn off A96 at Gollanfield (phone: 0667-62777).

Cawdor Castle – The location where Shakespeare believed that Macbeth stabbed King Duncan (although, if true, Lady Macbeth must have made the fastest house move — or "flit," as it is called here — in British drama, since she had barely received the news of Macbeth's being made Thane of Cawdor before being discovered at home in their castle). In any case, if this is the spot that Shakespeare meant, Duncan spoke truly on his last evening: "This castle hath a pleasant seat." It's the castle with everything: a drawbridge, a tower built around a tree, a freshwater well inside the house, gardens, nature trails, a pitch-and-putt golf course, a picnic area, snack bar, licensed restaurant, and gift shop. It's been the seat of Thanes of Cawdor for 600 years (which rules out a home for the real Macbeths, but could certainly make it a castle described to Shakespeare). Open daily May through September. Admission charge. 13 miles from Inverness on B9090 (phone: 06677-615).

Castle Stuart – Opened to the public for the first time in 1989, this is the ancestral home of the Earls of Moray, who were relatives of the Scottish Stuart kings. It houses some magnificent oil paintings of Bonnie Prince Charlie. Open daily May through September. On B9039, about 7 miles from Inverness (phone: 0463-790745).

SOUTH OF THE CITY

Tomatin Distillery – Stop at Tomatin, by the river Findhorn, for a demonstration of the process through which *Uisge Beatha,* "The Water of Life," comes into existence. Tours of the *Tomatin Distillery,* including a wee sample dram and bottles at factory prices, are given weekdays several times a day, Easter through September. On the old A9 (phone ahead: 08082-234).

Tomatin Smiddy – Also at Tomatin is a traditional blacksmith's shop, used today to produce items commissioned by architects as features of buildings. Visitors can view decorative ironwork made by proprietor Mike Crummy. Open daily. On the old A9, down from the distillery (phone: 08082-261).

Knocknagael Boar Stone – Though partly weathered away, this 7-foot survivor of the Pictish civilization that was dominant in Inverness around AD 300 is exhilarating to see *in situ,* rather than in a museum. On B861, 2 miles from Inverness.

Urquhart Castle – Nobody comes to Inverness without also coming here. Right on Loch Ness, by the village of Drumnadrochit, this is the point from which "Nessie," the Loch Ness monster, has most often been glimpsed. Take binoculars to the top of the castle shell. (One of the largest edifices in Scotland from the 13th century onward, the castle was blown up by Williamite forces in 1692.) Waters on this stretch of Loch Ness are deeper than the North Sea and perfect for prehistoric inhabitants. But hunts by midget submarine, radar, tungsten TV lamp, strobe light, time-lapse camera, and Spectra Polaroid systems have as yet proven nothing. Open daily year-round, except Sunday mornings. Admission charge. On A82, 15 miles from Inverness.

Loch Ness Monster Exhibition – Lack of proof has not deterred the Inverness Department of Recreation and Tourism from extensively presenting the case for Nessie's existence, even to constructing a fake stuffed plesiosaurus and anchoring her in a Drumnadrochit lily pond. The official exhibition can be found among a welter of shops, eateries, hotel facilities, sideshow exhibitions on other topics, and gimmicky invitations such as the one from Photo Kilt ("Have your picture taken wearing full highland dress"). Open daily. Admission charge. On A82, 15 miles from Inverness (phone: 04562-573).

WEST OF THE CITY

Monaick Castle Winery – Within this attractive, historic country seat of the Clan Fraser of Lovat, an entrepreneurial descendant, Philippa Fraser, runs a unique and growing business. Combining research and development techniques with folk recipes handed down through many generations, she now bottles silver birch, elder flower, and rowanberry wines. Ms. Fraser also makes traditional mead, from honey, that for centuries was mixed with whisky and drunk in these parts for weeks after weddings, giving rise to the term "honeymoon." Visitors are invited to tour, taste, and buy, from 10 AM to 5 PM daily except Sundays. Off an approach road to A862, near Kirkhill (phone: 83283).

Highland Aromatics – Wines in an old castle, soaps in an old church . . . the attractively packaged toiletries for sale here at the former Drumchardine Village Kirk are handmade, scented with flowers of hill and glen. Visitors can watch the production weekdays. On A862, near Kirkhill (phone: 83625).

Beauly Priory – The impressive ruins of a Valliscaulian Priory of 1230 dominate Beauly village, to which the local lairds, the Norman-aristocrat Fraser barons Lovat, gave its French name (from *Beaulieu,* "lovely place," here pronounced *bew*-lee). Notice especially the arcaded windows. Closed Sunday mornings and in winter. Admission charge. On A862, 13 miles from Inverness.

NORTH OF THE CITY

For sights north and northwest of Inverness, see *Northwest Scottish Highlands,* DIRECTIONS.

SOURCES AND RESOURCES

TOURIST INFORMATION: Practically a museum, with expensively prepared murals depicting local history, the Inverness, Loch Ness, and Nairn Tourist Board is at 23 Church St. (phone: 234353). There are books and maps for sale and an endless selection of free leaflets. Additional publications are available at *Melven's Book Shop* on Union St. (phone: 233500). The tourist board is open daily May through October, Mondays through Saturday noons in April and March, and weekdays only November through February.

Local Coverage – Newspapers hereabouts may strike some people as quaint. There are: the *Inverness Courier* (Tuesdays and Fridays, with birth announcements, weddings, obituaries, and offers of free turnips to pensioners published on the front page); the *Nairnshire Telegraph* (Tuesdays); the *Highland News* (Thursdays); and the *People Journal* (Thursdays). The tourist board distributes weekly comprehensive events guidesheets in summer. Tune in to Moray Firth Radio daily in summer at 9 AM for tourist information broadcasts.

Telephone – The area code for Inverness and environs is 0463.

GETTING AROUND: Walking is best for most areas of town, although occasionally there is excess traffic on some streets.

Airport – Inverness Airport — serving the Western Isles, Aberdeen, Glasgow, Manchester, London, Jersey, Orkney, and Shetland — is at Dalcross, 6 miles northeast on A96, or Inverness-to-Nairn road (phone: 232471). Contact the airline companies directly for flight arrivals and departures. A bus from Inverness meets most flights.

Bicycle – Rent from *Academy Motor Co. Ltd.,* 122 Academy St. (phone: 225800), or *Ness Motors,* King St. (phone: 222848).

Bus – The bus station is at Farraline Park, off Academy St. (phone: 233371). *Highland Scottish Omnibuses* conduct afternoon tours to Strathpeffer, Aviemore, or the Black Isle, and short tours around Inverness. Local buses depart from here as well. Timetables are available at the station.

Car Rental – Over a dozen companies rent cars in Inverness, including *Hertz* and *Swan National.* Lists of these, plus lists of firms with private chauffeurs, are available from the tourist board.

Sightseeing Tours – The *Loch Ness Monster Tour* leaves from the Inverness railway station parking lot and boards a cruiser at the *New Clansman* hotel marina for a 3½-hour trip down the Loch to Urquhart Castle and the Loch Ness Monster Exhibition at Drumnadrochit. Tours leave daily at 10:30 AM and 2:30 PM. The cost is about $10.50 (phone: 233999).

Taxi – The largest telephone taxi firm is *Rank Radio Taxis,* 111 Academy St. (phone: 220222, 239777, or 230331). Many small taxi firms conduct personalized tours on request at prices that are negotiable.

Train – British Rail and the Highland Line (which offers scenic tours) operate from Station Sq. (phone: 238924).

SPECIAL EVENTS: The *Inverness Folk Festival* is held sometime between the third week in March and mid-April at various venues (details available from the tourist board). The *Police Gala Day* and *Highland Tug of War Championships* are at Police Headquarters on Old Perth Rd. in mid-June. *Beauly Gala Week* takes place in Beauly during the last week of July. The *Inverness Tattoo* (massed pipers) in Northern Meeting Park and the annual *Highland Antiques Fair* at a hotel in Inverness (details available from the tourist board) are in early August. Bught Park is the scene of the *Highland Shinty Cup Final* (shinty is a ruthlessly macho, Celtic type of hockey) in early summer, the *Inverness Highland Games* in mid-July, and the *Northern Meeting* solo piping competition (also see *Music* below) in late August or early September.

MUSEUMS: Besides those mentioned in *Special Places,* Inverness has one other museum of interest:

Inverness Museum and Gallery – Exhibits depict the history of the highlands and feature works by modern artists, including sculpture and paintings. There are many interesting views of old Inverness. Visiting exhibitions, lecture series, coffee shop. Open Mondays through Saturdays from 9 AM to 5 PM. Castle Wynd (phone: 237114).

SHOPPING: In addition to those establishments mentioned in *Special Places,* there are many other good stores in Inverness. The best buys are crafts, tweeds, tartans and woolens, antiques, and sporting goods. Wednesday is the early closing day; Tuesday is Market Day.

Barney's – Open till 10 PM for whiskies, chocolates, cigarettes, magazines, provisions. Castle St. (phone: 232249).

Campbell and Company – Exclusive designs in tweeds and knitwear; "bespoke tailors" (goods custom-made). Worth traveling to Beauly. Early closing Thursday. Highland Tweed House, Beauly (phone: 782239).

Duncan Chisholm & Sons Ltd. – Highland dress, kilts, capes, jackets, Norwegian sweaters, accessories, and gifts. 47–51 Castle St. (phone: 234599).

Eastgate Shopping Centre – New and beloved by the locals, with branches of large British chains like *Marks & Spencer.* On display is an elaborate, oversize animated nursery clock featuring rolling cut-out waves, a tinkling rhyme, Noah's Ark, and a deckswab monkey that ascends a mast and chimes a bell on the hour. 11 Eastgate (phone: 226457).

Edinburgh Woollen Mill – Branches throughout Scotland; low prices on a wide range of pure woolens. 28–30 High St. (phone: 237545).

Jack Hesling Highland Antiques – Dealers throughout the highlands lodge stock here, including paintings, silver, out-of-print and antiquarian books, prints, and maps. 15 Tomnahurich St. (phone: 231316).

Highland Heirlooms – Attractive kitsch from local Victorian attics. Castle St. (phone: 224467).

Inter Sport – Bright, trendy sports clothes, including shorts, tracksuits, and swimsuits, as well as a rainbow selection of sneakers. Inglis St. (phone: 239427).

Island Woollens – Individual designs in sweaters and other knitted goods; small and select. Church St. (phone: 230659).

Clive Rowland Mountain Sports – Heavy-duty sports and camping equipment; waterproof jackets, boots, tents, rucksacks; books, guides, maps, and information. 9–11 Bridge St. (phone: 238746).

Shetland Originals – Sweater specialists, with hand-knits in Fair Isle, Aran, Icelandic, and mohair yarns. Bridge St. (phone: 234660).

Spean Bridge Mill Shop – All-purpose variety of skirts, jackets, sweaters, accessories. Bridge St. (phone: 236517).

SPORTS: Canoeing – Hire from *Inverness Watersports Centre,* Coulmore Bay, North Kessock, on the south shore of the Black Isle, across the Beauly Firth from Inverness. Take A9 north across the Kessock Bridge (phone: 046 373-313).

Cruising – Two pleasure-cruising companies offer tours of Loch Ness: *Jacobite Cruises Ltd.,* Tomnahurich Bridge, Glenurquhart Rd. (phone: 241730); and the British Waterways Board's *Scot II Cruises,* Caledonian Canal, Clacknaharry, on the north shore of Inverness (phone: 233140). Or pilot it yourself: 2- to 8-berth cabin cruisers are available March through October from *Caley Cruisers,* Canal Rd. (phone: 236328); yachts are available from *Highland Holiday Boats,* Dochgarroch pier, at the southern tip of the Caledonian Canal, south of Inverness on A82 (phone: 046386-265).

Field Trips – Daily and weekly expeditions are conducted by trained naturalists to the great outdoors of surrounding districts to view highland wildlife. April through October. Contact Caledonian Wildlife, 30 Culduthel Rd. (phone: 233130).

Fishing – There is excellent salmon and trout fishing in the area. The *Inverness Angling Club* leases a stretch of the river Ness; permits for the river are sold at tackle shops and at the tourist board. Permits for Loch Ness fishing are available from *Glenmoriston Estate Office,* in the village of Glenmoriston, on A82 south of Inverness (phone: 0320-51202). River Beauly permits are available from the *Lovat Estate Office,* Beauly (phone: 782205). A wide selection of tackle is available from *Graham's,* 71 Castle St. (phone: 233178); closed Wednesday afternoons. For a free leaflet listing local fishing possibilities, contact the tourist board.

Flying – Lessons for flying are given at the *Highland Aero Club,* Dalcross Airport (phone: 0667-62230). Open daily year-round. No previous experience needed.

Go-Karting – Vehicular fun for families is to be had at *Bught Park Go-Kart Track.* Go-karts, bounce-abouts, four-wheel fun cycles (phone: 223960).

Golf – *Inverness Golf Club* maintains an 18-hole championship course off Culcabock Rd., on the east side of town (phone: 233422). *Torvean Golf Course,* another 18-hole course, is off Glenalbyn Rd., on the west side of town (phone: 239882 or 231989 for the pro shop).

Pony Trekking – Pony rides are available at *Highland Riding Centre,* Mondays through Saturdays. Borlum Farm, Drumnadrochit (phone: 04562-220).

Shooting and Deerstalking – Details, equipment, and shooting permits are available from *Graham's,* 71 Castle St. (phone: 233178). Closed Wednesday afternoons.

Skating – *Inverness Ice Centre* offers ice skating in winter and roller skating in spring, weekends only September through June. Bught Park (phone: 235711).

Swimming – The *Inverness Swimming Pool* is a 25-meter pool, with adjacent kids' pool, sunbeds, gyms, saunas, Jacuzzis, and a cafeteria. By the river Ness at Glebe St. (phone: 233799).

Tennis and Squash – *Inverness Lawn Tennis and Squash Club,* Bishops Rd. (phone: 230751), maintains 3 tennis courts (all hard) and 4 squash courts; open daily (even on Sundays, a minor miracle in this sabbatarian community). Also try the 10 (hard) municipal tennis courts in Bellfield Park, off Island Bank Rd. (no phone).

Track – Work out at the new All-Weather Athletics Park, Queen's Park, off Bught Dr. (no phone).

Water Sports – The *Loch Insh Watersports Centre* has rental equipment available for canoeing, windsurfing, water skiing, and dinghys from May through September. There is an eatery on the premises. At Kincraig, about 30 miles south of Inverness on the A9 (phone: 05404-272).

THEATER: Inverness playgoers are dependent on its one impressive venue, the *Eden Court Theatre,* a graystone-and-glass creation incorporating a medieval bishop's palace on the river Ness. In winter the productions are usually excellent, as many touring companies play here, but in summer all is suddenly tartanized for the tourists. There are lightning conversions of space in galleries, foyers, and even the restaurant for film shows, discos, cabarets, art exhibitions, and sales of local craftsmen's work. Bishops Rd. (phone for box office: 221718; phone for restaurant and administration: 239841).

MUSIC: The *Folk Club* meets in the *Beaufort* hotel, 11 Culduthel Rd. (phone: 222897), on Sundays at 8:30 PM. The *Inverness Country and Western Club* meets at *Inverness Ice Centre* at Bught Park on Tuesdays at 8:30 PM. The *Inverness Jazz Platform* hosts concerts at various locations throughout the year; watch the papers or contact Jim Love, the secretary (phone: 238113). When in town, opera and rock are anchored to *Eden Court Theatre.* Mid-May through mid-September, a lone piper struts his stuff on Castle Hill Mondays through Saturdays at 7PM. But the pride and joy of Inverness's music scene is the September *Northern Meeting* solo piping competition (see *Special Events*); here the high art of the ancient classical *pibroch* ("pee-brock," or bagpipe) players, who composed their own works, is performed by their descendants — not only Scottish, but American, Canadian, and New Zealandian.

NIGHTCLUBS AND NIGHTLIFE: Nightlife in Inverness is characterized by plenty of hootch and "Hoots, Mon!" Many hotels put on cabarets, also called "Scots Nights," which feature Scottish country dancing, traditional music, and stand-up Scots comics. The most famous of these is the *Cummings* hotel's *Scottish Showtime* (Church St.; phone: 232531). The tourist board has details of the town's frequent dances and discos. In summer, Northern Meeting Park, on Ardross St., is the site of an outdoor "Scots Night" Tuesdays, Wednesdays, and Thursdays at 8 PM.

BEST IN TOWN

CHECKING IN: Not long ago, the typical Inverness hotel was a former private house with a bar that had all its seats set up around a piano. Expect to pay over $205 for a room for two with breakfast in those places listed as very expensive, $115 to $125 in expensive, $75 to $115 in moderate, and under $75 in inexpensive. All telephone numbers are in the 0463 area code unless otherwise indicated.

Culloden House – Residents feel like kings in the spacious, light rooms of this beautiful 18th-century palace, complete with ornate plasterwork and priceless antique furniture. There are 20 bedchambers, extensive park grounds, and a sauna. On Culloden Moor (phone: 790461). Very expensive.

Caledonian – This popular modern riverfront all-rounder has a bouncy local clientele, convivial staff, 120 rooms, cabarets, and dancing. Church St. (phone: 235181). Expensive.

Craigmonie – Adjacent to *Inverness Golf Course,* this delightful family-owned turn-of-the-century townhouse has 30 bedrooms, a patio with wrought-iron garden furniture shaded by dainty umbrellas, a leisure complex, and a setting on tree-lined grounds. Annfield Rd. (phone: 231649). Expensive.

Kingsmills – Only a 10-minute drive from downtown is this striking 200-year-old time capsule, whose main entrance is in an architraved turret. It has 70 rooms (some in recently built extensions), private squash courts, and 4 acres of gardens. Culcabock Rd. (phone: 237166). Expensive.

Station – The comfortably plush Victorian grandeur of this centrally located 66-room relic has been heightened by the recent refurbishment of its public rooms. The restaurant has excellent "Taste of Scotland" fare. Academy St. (phone: 231926). Expensive.

Loch Ness Lodge – Near Urquhart Castle, this 54-room hotel is the Drumnadrochit version of the *Cummings* (see entry below), with "Taste of Scotland" cuisine, mini-cruises on Loch Ness, and elaborate frothy Scots *ceilidhs* (folk music evenings). Open April through October. On A82, Drumnadrochit (phone: 04562-342). Moderate.

Polmaily House – An Edwardian country house on its own grounds, with 9 rooms and delicious traditional fare. Open April to October. Glen Urquhart (phone: 04562-343). Moderate.

Beaufort – Half of Inverness is laid out below this 31-room hilltop mansion in a first class residential area. Private showers and color television sets. Enormous steaks are the chef's specialty. 11 Culduthel Rd. (phone: 222897). Inexpensive.

Cummings – The complete ordinariness of this 34-room rectangle somehow manages to be endearing. Nightly Scottish cabarets here, April through September, have been wowing audiences for years. Church St. (phone: 232531). Inexpensive.

Drumnadrochit – With an imposing view overlooking Drumnadrochit village, this 20-room hotel offers comfort, reasonable prices, and a restaurant. Off A82 (phone: 04562-218). Inexpensive.

Firs Guest House – This delicious Italian-influenced piece of Victorian architecture right on the river looks like a movie set, inside and out. What is lost in amenities is gained in atmosphere! It has 6 bedrooms. Dores Rd. (phone: 225197). Inexpensive.

Redcliffe – A friendly family-run establishment, with 6 bedrooms and big, bright windows, it has a bar that is "home" to many Castle Hill inhabitants. Its location affords a lovely, elevated view of the river, despite its proximity to the town center. 1 Gordon Terr. (phone: 232767). Inexpensive.

EATING OUT: A meal for two with wine will run over $45 in an expensive restaurant, $30 to $45 in a moderate establishment, and up to $30 in an inexpensive one. All telephone numbers are in the 0463 area code unless otherwise indicated.

***Dunain Park* –** Guests of this family-owned country house are treated to sumptuous breakfasts, snack lunches in the garden, teas with homemade jams, and outstanding, imaginatively prepared dinners. Non-residents with the necessary reservations may partake of the latter; those who are willing to risk gout in this oasis with its hint of sniffy respectability, may spend the week in one of its 6 rooms. Open year-round. On A82, 2½ miles south of Inverness (phone: 230512). Expensive.

***Dickens* –** The decor in this fashionable mid-city restaurant — a classic medley of browns and whites — is glossily smart. Its Chinese proprietors are equally adroit at Chinese and European cooking, including vegetarian. 77–79 Church St. (phone: 224450). Expensive to moderate.

***Brookes Wine Bar* –** Recently selected by a popular consumer magazine as "Scottish Wine Bar of the Year." Just by the castle, it has an open-plan feel to it, with customers encouraged to drop into the kitchen to chat with the cooks. The wine list is longer than a litany, the food — including watercress mousse and beetroot soup — elegantly delicate. There are no-smoking areas, and patrons can put their feet up and read a newspaper or the *Bible,* both of which are supplied by the management. Closed Sundays in winter. 75 Castle St. (phone: 225662). Dinner: moderate; lunch: inexpensive.

***Whinpark* –** This outwardly unassuming-looking eatery, in a once routine Victorian abode, calls itself a "restaurant with rooms." The food is a voyage of discovery, including traditional steaks, venison, and salmon, and also creative nouvelle cuisine. 17 Ardross St. (phone: 232549). Moderate to inexpensive.

SHARING A PINT: The *Criterion* (16 Church St.) is an intact survival from Victorian times, spangled everywhere with decorative stained glass. On a corner of Academy St. is the *Moray,* cozy and old-fashioned, a busy lunchtime hub of Invernessian pub grubbers.

LIVERPOOL

Anyone even remotely within range of the sounds of the 1960s knows that Liverpool is synonymous with the *Beatles.* The "Fab Four" — John, Paul, George, and Ringo — turned a provincial city, struggling with the decline of its maritime commerce, into a place at the forefront of a decade. "The Pool" was on the map again, and no Liverpudlians, no matter how strong their accent, ever had to explain where in the world they came from.

Prior to the arrival of the *Beatles,* Liverpool had not enjoyed a similar level of international renown since the century between 1830 to 1930, when its pre-eminence was intimately tied to the growth of the New World. Then the great port city on the river Mersey, from which ships reach the Atlantic by way of the Irish Sea, was the principal European embarkation point for emigrants to the United States, Canada, and Australia, and it forged more links with America than any other city in Britain. More than 9 million emigrants passed through Liverpool's docks during this period, driven by poverty, hunger, unemployment, religious persecution, or just plain ambition to find a more comfortable life, a more democratic government, or a new beginning across the water.

The tiny chapel where Richard Mather, a 17th-century Puritan minister and one of the earliest emigrants to New England, preached is still much as it was over 350 years ago, when he sailed across the Atlantic in the wake of the *Mayflower.* His son, Increase, became Rector of Harvard; his grandson, Cotton, became President of Yale and a key figure in the Salem Witch Trials. Lowly born Robert Morris, another Liverpool emigrant, was the financial genius behind the American Revolution and a signer of the Declaration of Independence.

All, however, were not so fortunate. Many would-be emigrants failed to reach their "Promised Land," either because they ran out of money or because they found work and decided to stay in Liverpool or the Northwest of England. Thus, the names of many of the shops and businesses in contemporary Liverpool can be traced to Irish, German, Lithuanian, Polish, and Russian founders who had not planned to settle here, and the city still has Norwegian and Swedish churches whose congregations come from all over the area.

The last view of England for some of those who did leave was Liverpool's "Big Three," a trio of famous buildings grouped around Pier Head: the green-domed Port of Liverpool Building, the Cunard Building, and the Royal Liver Building, the last topped by the mythical Liver Birds that have become the symbol of the city. These three landmarks, dating from the early 20th century, when Liverpool had reached the height of its mercantile might, are still the dominant features of the waterfront and are still best seen from the water. Most people see them now from one of the ferries crossing the river to Birkenhead.

From its humble beginnings as a tiny fishing village on a muddy tidal creek (the pool from which it takes its name), Liverpool has always had its fortunes closely linked to the river that wends its way south of the city. King John, who granted the village a charter in the early 13th century, used it as a jumping-off place for Ireland. Growth was slow for several centuries, but once trade began with the Americas in the late 17th century, Liverpool was on its way to becoming the second most important city in the British Empire. The first dock opened in 1715, and a string of them followed, trading mainly with the American colonies and the West Indies in sugar, spices, and tobacco, as well as supplying plantations there with slaves from Africa. The slave traffic became illegal in the early 19th century, but immigration to the New World and the dawn of transatlantic steamship traffic filled the gap. Eventually Liverpool's docks stretched for 7 unbroken miles.

Although changing world economics and the arrival of the jumbo jet put an end to almost all transatlantic passenger service — *Cunard* suspended service from Liverpool to New York in 1966, and the last transatlantic liner left for Canada in 1967 — Liverpool is still one of Britain's principal commercial ports. Nowadays, rather than human cargo, the ships are full of everything from antiques to engineering products, Wedgwood pottery to Jaguars, much of it still America bound. Most of the port business has shifted to those docks nearest the mouth of the river, however. The old floating landing stage in the heart of the city has been cut back and plays host only to Mersey ferry boats. City developers, meanwhile, have been quick to seize the opportunity to develop the original, superfluous dockside buildings for new uses, making the Albert Dock area a "second city centre," offering shops, restaurants, museums, boat trips, and other waterside activities.

In addition to the docks, several city streets have managed to retain their distinctive characters. Among the magnificent Victorian buildings on William Brown Street, built in true classical style, are the *Liverpool Museum,* the Central Library, the *Walker Art Gallery,* and the old County Sessions House, which now contains the *Museum of Labour History.* Rodney Street, named after Admiral Rodney, the British naval hero, is Georgian. (The birthplace of William Gladstone, four times British prime minister, is at No. 62 Rodney Street.) Nelson Street and Great George Square form the center of Liverpool's Chinatown, the oldest such enclave in Europe.

It is only recently that outsiders, English as well as foreign, have begun to discover Liverpool. Britain's first *International Garden Festival,* held here in 1984, was a giant step on the road to a future in tourism — it attracted 3 million visitors. Probably some who came thinking only of the city's industrial outskirts and lingering slums (gradually being razed) were surprised to find that Liverpool can be an attractive place. True, the marks of a harsh downturn in its economic fortunes over the last decade will take years to fade, but the city's maritime legacy is intact, and redevelopment of the dockland area is just one of the facelifts that are adding a new dimension. Already a highly individualistic city, known for its quick wit and dry sense of humor (many famous British comedians have hailed from hereabouts) and its distinctive nasal "Scouse" accent, Liverpool now has shops to match any thriving High Street, trendy wine bars humming alongside well-preserved Victorian and Edwardian pubs, and playwrights, artists, and musicians plugging their vibrant hometown.

LIVERPOOL AT-A-GLANCE

SEEING THE CITY: There is a spectacular bird's-eye view of the city, the river, and the docks from the top of the Anglican Cathedral tower. For an all-encompassing view of Britain's equivalent of the Manhattan waterfront, look back from one of the Mersey Ferries that depart every 20 minutes from Pier Head. They cross the river to either Wallasey or Birkenhead, on the Wirral Peninsula. The trip takes 8 minutes each way, which is why so many visitors go just for the ride.

SPECIAL PLACES: The historic waterfront, with its trio of signature buildings and the reclaimed Albert Dock, is a suitable place to begin any tour. Then head inland to the city center, most of whose sights, including the city's two cathedrals, are reachable on foot. The Festival Gardens are a bit farther afield. The Wirral Peninsula, where the port of Birkenhead and the residential district of Wallasey are located, is across the river Mersey. The 100-square-mile peninsula separates Liverpool from the Chesire Plain and comprises acres of open countryside, country parks, towns, villages, seaside resorts, and wide, sandy beaches that attract holidaymakers from all over the North West of England and Wales. Besides Mersey Ferries, two road tunnels and one railway line connect Liverpool to the Wirral.

CITY CENTER

Royal Liver Building – Liverpool's most photographed building is easily recognized by its two towers, each with one of the legendary Liver Birds poised for flight on top. Built in 1908, it was among the world's first multistory concrete buildings, and those who believe Big Ben is Britain's biggest clock soon discover that they are mistaken. It's occasionally possible to climb up behind the two clock faces on either of the towers for an excellent view of the waterfront, but check with the tourist information center for details on opening times. Otherwise, since the building houses working offices, only the lobby is accessible. The ground floor has undergone a $3,600,000 refurbishment, and now includes a café and gift shop. Pier Head.

Cunard Building – This magnificent structure, the middle of the three waterfront landmarks, dates from 1915. It was built by Nova Scotia–born Samuel Cunard, who came to Liverpool in 1840 to start the first transatlantic liner service, carrying passengers and mail between Liverpool, Halifax, and Boston on his famous ship, *Britannia.* The coats of arms of Britain's allies during World War I are carved between the windows on the top floor. (The United States is absent, since work was completed before the US entered the war.) The massive eagles and the company's shield were carved out of a chunk of stone weighing 43 tons. Since the demise of all *Cunard's* trade in the city, the building now serves as a regular office block. Pier Head.

Port of Liverpool Building – The blueprint was a serious but ultimately unsuccessful contender in the design competition for Liverpool's Anglican Cathedral, so don't be surprised by the ecclesiastical elements of its architecture, including the green copper dome. Built at the turn of the century and now the central office for all port administration, it's worth a visit just for its impressive marble interior and its window emblems depicting all the Commonwealth countries. Pier Head.

Albert Dock Village – The city's showplace attraction on the waterfront, this was the first of Liverpool's old docks to be reclaimed from decay. Albert Dock originally opened in 1845 and closed during the early 1970s. It's now a tall ships center, providing a berth for several square-rigged vessels. The *Maria Asumpta,* the oldest wooden square-rigged vessel in the world, is docked here and is open to the public for an admission charge. The magnificent Victorian warehouses are undergoing restoration and constitute the largest group of "Grade 1 Listed" buildings in the country. Only a short walk from the city's main shopping streets, the area that was once the heart of "sailortown" and was also frequented by slave traders, privateers, and the feared Press Gangs (who "persuaded" unwilling men to join the navy), has become a focal point of the city's leisure activities, boasting wine bars, restaurants, small specialty shops, museums, and exhibition areas. One of the warehouses serves as an extension of London's *Tate Gallery,* a brand-new permanent home for some of the gallery's contemporary painting and sculpture collections and a major venue in the north for touring exhibits of modern art (open 11 AM to 7 PM, Tuesdays through Sundays; phone: 709-3223). Another houses the *Merseyside Maritime Museum* (see below). The transformed Albert Dock is fairly new on the Liverpool scene; it opened in 1984 in time for the Cutty Sark Tall Ships Race, which returns to the city in 1992 (also the 500th anniversary of Columbus's first voyage), by which time even more extensive restoration of the docks complex will be complete. A major advantage of the Albert Dock scheme is the huge, free car-parking facility adjacent to it, making Liverpool one of the easiest cities in Britain in which to find a parking place. Open daily from 10 AM to 8 PM; some restaurants are open in the evening. Albert Dock (phone: 709-9199).

Merseyside Maritime Museum – The star of the Albert Dock redevelopment is housed in a warehouse but spills over much of the quayside. Follow the quayside trail through the surrounding maritime park, which now looks much as it did when sailing ships loaded and unloaded here; see the museum's growing collection of ships and boats rescued from the breaker's yard because of their one time connection with the port (several are now open to the public); and visit the restored Piermaster's House and other dockside buildings for demonstrations of coopering and boatbuilding as it used to be done. Inside, displays include the original builder's model of the *Titanic* and a nameplate from one of her lifeboats, preserved in a glass case in the main hall, and the "Emigrants to a New World" exhibition downstairs. The latter includes a reconstructed dockland street peopled with actors as the sorts of hawkers and porters that the emigrants would have encountered, a section of a packet ship providing a glimpse of their traveling conditions, and an Emigration Bureau to give American visitors advice on how to trace their ancestors. The museum is open daily from 10:30 AM to 5:30 PM (last ticket sold at 4:30 PM). Admission charge. Albert Dock (phone: 709-1551).

Liverpool Town Hall – A palatial Georgian building, topped by a golden dome and a statue of Minerva, it is possibly Liverpool's finest building and the second oldest in the city center (dating from 1754). It was the unlikely setting for the last act of the American Civil War — the surrender of the British-built Confederate raider *Shenandoah* to the Mayor of Liverpool. As a working building, it is open to the public only 2 weeks in August, but it's impressive enough outside. Water St.

Bluecoat Chambers – The oldest building in the city center, dating from 1717, is a beautiful specimen of Queen Anne style. Built as a school for poor children by Bryan Blundell, a tobacco merchant, privateer, slave trader, and sea captain in the American trade, it's now an arts center with a permanent exhibition of ceramics, jewelry, and textiles by British craftsmen; a concert hall, coffee shop, and a bistro. A pamphlet entitled "The Bluecoat — Today and Yesterday," gives an excellent history of this building. It is open daily from 10:30 AM to 5:30 PM. School La. (phone: 709-5297).

St. George's Hall – This giant Greco-Roman building of the mid 19th century (the first building visible upon exiting the railway station) reflects Liverpool's former prosperity and civic pride. It has the proportions of a mausoleum; it once housed the law courts, but it now stands empty, awaiting a new use. Lime St.

Walker Art Gallery – The best of its kind outside London and ranked among the top in the world. It contains a notable collection of European art dating from the 14th century to the present day and is particularly rich in Flemish and Italian works, as well as those by progressive 19th-century British artists such as Millais, Leighton, and Sickert. Open Mondays through Saturdays from 10 AM to 5 PM, Sundays from 2 to 5 PM. William Brown St. (phone: 207-0011).

Anglican Cathedral – There are two modern cathedrals in Liverpool (hence the popular local folk song lyric, "If you want a cathedral, we've got one to spare"), but this one, also known as Liverpool Cathedral, looks far too Gothic for its youth. The reason is that although its foundation stone was laid in 1904, the church was not completed until 1978. Designed by Sir Giles Gilbert Scott and built of locally quarried pink sandstone, the structure is massive: It is the largest church in Britain and nearly the largest in Europe — only St. Peter's in Rome and the cathedrals of Milan and Seville exceed it — and it contains the largest church organ and the highest and heaviest peal of bells to be found anywhere. There is a guided tour up the 331-foot tower, which provides spectacular views; admission charge. Homemade snacks are served in the refectory, with all profits going to the church. Open daily from 9 AM to 6 PM; the refectory is open Mondays through Saturdays from 10 AM to 4:30 PM and Sundays from noon to 5 PM. St. James' Mount (phone: 709-6271).

Metropolitan Cathedral of Christ the King – The Roman Catholic cathedral is a more strikingly modern building than its Anglican counterpart. Designed by Frederick Gibberd and completed in 1967 (having taken only 4½ years to build), it is a circular structure towering up to a spiked crown of brilliant stained glass by John Piper. At night, when illuminated from within, the glass glows magically, adding to the building's space-age appearance. It's a rare example of fine modern architecture, but it didn't stop the locals from nicknaming it "Paddy's Wigwam." What is seen today is the third attempt at building a Roman Catholic cathedral in Liverpool, and it rests on the foundations of a 1930s' design still visible in the crypt. The cathedral is open daily from 8 AM to 6 PM (5 PM in winter); the bookshop is open daily from 10 AM to 5 PM; the tea room is open Sundays through Fridays from 10 AM to 5 PM and Saturdays from 10 AM to 3 PM. Mount Pleasant (phone: 709-9222).

Liverpool University – Opposite the Metropolitan Cathedral and founded over a century ago, this institution is home to some 6,000 students. It is Britain's original "red brick" university (see Alfred Waterhouse's red brick and terra cotta Victoria Building, built in 1890), after which all other provincial universities came to be referred to colloquially as red brick universities (and Waterhouse himself came to be nicknamed, unfairly, Slaughterhouse Waterhouse). The *University of Liverpool Art Gallery,* Abercromby Sq., features changing displays from the university's own collections. Open Mondays, Tuesdays, and Thursdays from noon to 2 PM and Wednesdays and Fridays from noon to 4 PM. The university is located in and around Brownlow Hill (phone: 794-2000, ext. 2324).

ELSEWHERE

Knowlsley Safari Park – A large and impressive wildlife park, with a selection of all the animals one would expect to see on the prairie or in the jungle, including lions, tigers, zebras, rhinos, African elephants, and monkeys. Facilities include a pets' corner, amuseument park, café, and souvenir shop. Open daily from 10 AM to 4 PM, March 1 through October 31. Prescot, Merseyside (phone: 430-9009).

Festival Park – The park created for Britain's first *International Garden Festival* in

1984 is now open to the public from May through September. A few miles south of the city center, it contains 75 landscaped, fountain-filled acres permanently divided into gardens, including the Japanese Garden with its fragile pagoda-style house; an exhibition hall for horticultural shows; a waterfront esplanade; and a model of the *Beatles'* own *Yellow Submarine* for children to play on. Open from 10 AM to dusk. Admission charge. Riverside Dr. (phone: 709-3631).

Speke Hall – This pretty black-and-white timbered manor house, owned by the National Trust, is near the airport, about 8 miles southeast of the city. Begun in 1490 and finished largely in the 16th century, it looks much as it did when the Norris family occupied it in Elizabethan times, except that it was formerly surrounded by a moat. Notable features include the rich patterning of the timberwork and such interior details as the plaster ceiling of the Great Parlour. Also of interest are the 17th-century furnishings, with which later owners, the Watt family, wealthy West Indian merchants, nostalgically furnished the house in the 19th century. Open Tuesdays through Sundays from 1 to 5:30 PM, March 25 to November 5; November 11 through December 17, open Saturdays and Sundays only, 1 to 5 PM. Admission charge. The Walk, Speke (phone: 427-7231).

Seaforth Nature Reserve – On the edge of Liverpool's dockland and within sight of the city center is this fine nature reserve that is a mecca for bird watchers. It attracts a wide variety of plants, birds, and animals, including the Little Gulls for which it is famous. Two hides are located on the banks of the reserve's two large pools. Open from 9 AM to 5 PM during winter and 8 AM to 6 PM during summer (phone: 920-3769).

Croxteth Hall and Country Park – Just 5 miles from the city center, this 500-acre country park is well worth a day's visit. The hall, with its fine 18th- and 19th-century architecture, is the ancestral home of the Earls of Sefton. Other attractions include the Home Farm, with its huge collection of farm animals, the walled garden, and the parkland with a miniature railway picnic area and footpaths. Special events are held throughout the year; ask for a free brochure. Open from 11 AM to 5 PM, April through September. Off Muirhead Ave. E. (phone: 228-5311).

THE WIRRAL

Port Sunlight Village – This planned village was built during the 19th century by William Lever, first Lord Leverhulme and founder of Lever Brothers, to house his employees when he moved the small family soap business from Warrington to larger premises on the marshy Wirral Peninsula. After strolling through the streets of the benevolent industrialist's vision of a Utopian town, stop at the Port Sunlight Heritage Centre to see a fascinating record of the creation and life of the community. Open Mondays through Fridays from noon to 4 PM and weekends from 2 to 4 PM from Good Friday through October (phone: 644-6466). Admission charge. The famous *Olde Bridge Inn,* the village pub, serves coffee and lunches (and alcohol — Lever's religious beliefs originally condemned its consumption). Port Sunlight Village can be reached by taking the ferry to Birkenhead and then the 41, C1, C3, or C4 bus from Hamilton Square. Bebington.

Lady Lever Art Gallery – Built by Lord Leverhulme in memory of his wife, this gallery contains their magnificent private collection of 18th- and 19th-century paintings by British artists — Reynolds, Gainsborough, Turner, Constable, the pre-Raphaelites — and other works of art, including a superb collection of Wedgwood china and English furniture. Open Mondays through Saturdays from 10 AM to 5 PM and Sundays from 2 to 5 PM. Admission by voluntary donation. Port Sunlight Village (phone: 645-3623).

Willamson Art Gallery – Fine collections of 18th- and 19th-century British watercolors, ceramics, glass, furniture, and pottery are contained in this excellent museum. There are also displays of local and maritime history. Open Mondays through Saturdays from 10 AM to 5 PM; Sundays from 2 to 5 PM. Slatey Rd., Birkenhead (phone: 652-4177).

Boat Museum – Winner of the Council of Europe's "Museum of Europe" award in 1984, this splendid museum houses the world's largest collection of traditional canal boats. Open daily from 10 AM to 5 PM during the summer; from 11 AM to 4 PM during the winter (closed Fridays). Admission charge. Dockyard Rd., Ellesmere Port (phone: 355-5017).

Ness Gardens – Owned by Liverpool University, these 60-acre gardens afford charming views over the Dee Estuary and house the most comprehensive collection of plants in northwest England. Attractions include a visitors center, café, lecture theater, and gift shop. Open daily from 9 AM to sunset. Admission charge. Near Neston, South Wirral (phone: 336-2136).

Wirral Country Park – Tracing the old West-Kirby-to-Houton railway line, this 12-mile linear country park is a fine place to relax, fish, walk, ride horses, and picnic. There are excellent views across the Dee Estuary. Facilities include a visitors center, café, and parking lot. The visitors center is open daily from 10:30 AM to 3:30 PM, November through March; until 5 PM in April, May, September, and October; and until 8 PM June through August (phone: 648-4371).

■ **EXTRA SPECIAL:** Although the old *Cavern Club* — where the *Beatles* played 292 times — has been torn down, Mathew Street is still something of a Liverpudlian tribute to the city's world-famous offspring. In the place of the old club, there is now a new shopping development, Cavern Walks, whose tiny atrium contains a statue of all four *Beatles* by John Doubleday and a pub fittingly called *Abbey Road.* (A new version of the *Cavern Club* is down below — see *Nightclubs and Nightlife.*) Also on Mathew Street are the *John Lennon Memorial Club* (a cellar bar full of mementos that's actually a membership organization, although visitors can drop by and sign in) and the *Beatles Shop* (see *Shopping*). Beatles City, which formerly took visitors on a journey through the *Beatles* era, from their earliest days to world acclaim, is no more. However, as we went to press, the rights to the name "Beatles City" had been purchased and plans were underway to make it into a traveling exhibition, opening in London at a future date. There also has been talk of a brand new *Beatles* exhibition/museum opening on the Albert Dock, though at press time construction of the exhibit hadn't begun.

A cadre of BeatleGuides — local fans with exhaustive knowledge of all places of interest to visiting fans — lead guided *Beatles* tours by minibus every afternoon throughout the year (they can also be booked for private tours). The itinerary includes Sefton Park, Penny Lane, Strawberry Field (now a children's home), the *Beatles*' houses, and the *Blue Angels* pub, where they played their first professional audition. The tour lasts approximately 2 hours and departs at 2:30 PM. Inquire at the tourist information center at 29 Lime St.

SOURCES AND RESOURCES

TOURIST INFORMATION: The main offices of the Liverpool Tourist Information Centre, 29 Lime St. (phone: 709-3631), are open Mondays through Saturdays from 9 AM to 5:30 PM, Sundays from 10 AM to 5 PM. A smaller branch in the Atlantic Pavilion at Albert Dock (phone: 708-8854) is open daily from 10:30 AM to 5:30 PM. Both locations dispense general information, run an accommodations booking service, and sell show and concert tickets, as well as *Beatles* souvenirs. If you want to chat with a local about what to do and where, ask the tourist information center for details of a free service called "Friends of Merseyside" (phone: 336-6699). Qualified Mersey Guides and BeatleGuides for coach, minibus, car, or walking tours can also be arranged here, though tours actually depart only from the Lime Street location. The free monthly magazine *What's on Merseyside,* which has listings of what's on and where, is available from the tourist offices, and a number of guidebooks to the city are on sale, including *The American Connection,* by Ron Jones, which tells the story of Liverpool's links with America from Christopher Columbus to the Beatles (about $4.50). There is a series of books called the *Liverpool Dossier* that gives an excellent description of local history, legends, and characters (about $3). A useful source for information on the arts is *Arts Round Merseyside* (phone: 709-1534).

Local Coverage – *The Liverpool Echo* is the daily evening newspaper.

Telephone – The area code for Liverpool is 051.

GETTING AROUND: Those who plan to be in Liverpool for a few days can purchase weekly tickets for bus, rail, and ferry travel from the Merseytravel shops in Williamson Square and Pier Head (phone: 236-7676). Besides the ferry and the train (see below), two road tunnels — the Queensway Tunnel to Birkenhead (at just over 2 miles, it was the longest in the world until the Japanese exceeded it a few years ago) and the Kingsway Tunnel to Wallasey — connect Liverpool to the Wirral Peninsula (50p toll each way).

Airport – Liverpool Airport (phone: 486-8877), 6 miles southeast of the center, serves both international and domestic flights, with daily departures to London, the Isle of Man, Belfast, Dublin, and, in summer only, Jersey.

Bus – The Merseytravel office (phone: 236-7676) in Williamson Square has information on all local buses, which run frequently and are inexpensive. Most pass through Roe Street, the best place to hop aboard. A city center/Albert Dock bus link No. 22, taking in the Albert Dock and Lime Street stations on a circular route, runs every 15 minutes daily, from 10 AM to 8 PM. Long-distance buses use Northwestern Station, Skelhorne St. (phone: 709-6481).

Car Rental – Most major companies are represented, including *Avis,* 113 Mulberry St. (phone: 709-4737) and at Liverpool Airport (phone: 427-4142); *Budget,* 39 Leece St. (phone: 709-3103); and *Hertz,* Mount Pleasant Car Park, 8 Brownlow Hill (phone: 709-3337) and at the airport (phone: 427-5131). Consult the yellow pages for full details.

Ferry and Boat – The *Isle of Man Steam Packet Company* operates ferries to Douglas, the island's capital, with return crossings twice weekly (Tuesdays and Saturdays) from Pier Head, mid-May through mid-September. For details, contact the tourist information center or the Isle of Man Steam Packet Company, PO Box 5, Imperial Bldg., Douglas, Isle of Man (phone: 0624-23344). *Mersey Ferries* offers services to Birkenhead and Wallasey from Pier Head, with departures every 20 minutes. Between May and September, weather permitting, the company also operates daily 2-hour afternoon cruises aboard the *Royal Iris.* Information is available from Mersey Ferries, Victoria Pl., Seacombe, Wallasey (phone: 630-1030) or from the *Merseytravel* office in Williamson Square (phone: 236-7676). A water taxi connects various points on the Albert Dock.

Sightseeing Tours – A 1-hour city sightseeing coach tour departs daily at 1 PM from the tourist information center. 29 Lime St. (phone: 709-3631).

Taxi – There are several firms, including *Davy Liver* (phone: 709-4646), *Huyton Radio Cars* (phone: 480-8888), *City Kabs* (phone: 263-8282), and *ABC Taxis* (phone: 480-4800). Centrally located cabstands can be found outside Lime Street Station and the *Britannia Adelphi* hotel, or call 733-3393.

Train and Subway – Most mainline trains come into Lime Street Station (phone: 709-9696), which connects with a modest subway system stopping at Moorfields,

Central, and James Street underground stations. There are frequent rail links from Liverpool to London (2½ hours), the Wirral (including Birkenhead), Chester, North Wales, Manchester, and most major cities. Pick up trains for Birkenhead at Lime Street, Moorfields, Central, or James Street stations.

SPECIAL EVENTS: The *Grand National Steeplechase,* Britain's (and the world's) most important jumping race, takes place in late March or early April at Aintree, only 6 miles away; it's one of the world's major sporting events, so book seats well in advance. (For information, write to the Aintree Racecourse Company Ltd., Aintree, Liverpool, England L95AS.) Liverpool itself has a parade of horses through the town center early in May. The 3-week-long *Mersey River Festival* in June is the highlight of the year for the nonhorsey crowd: Its activities include a regatta, an international powerboat race, air displays, and fireworks, all focusing on the river and dockland area. The annual *Mersey Beatle Convention,* approximately 4 days in August, gives Beatlemaniacs a chance to indulge themselves in singing, dancing, filmgoing, souvenir hunting, and reminiscing. For details on this and other *Beatles* weekends, contact Cavern City Tours Ltd., 4th Floor, 31 Mathew St., Liverpool L2 BRE, England (phone: 236-9091). For bargain hunting and local color, including street entertainers, visit the flea market and craft fair that takes place every Sunday at Stanley Dock (phone: 207-1711).

MUSEUMS: Liverpool's rich cultural heritage is displayed in numerous museums and galleries, many of which are underrated and underpatronized. Visitors could easily spend hours in any one of Liverpool's museums and still not cover it adequately — they are that good. In addition to those mentioned in *Special Places,* other museums of note include the following:

Large Object Collection – A rocket satellite launcher, a 2-ton telescope, a tunnel cleaning machine, and other heavyweights from the *Liverpool Museum* collection. Open April 2 through October 31 from 10 AM to 5 PM. Princes Dock (phone: 207-0001).

Liverpool Museum – One of Britain's finest, with diverse collections which include antiquities, archives, botany, decorative arts, geology, zoology, physical sciences, social, and industrial history, and a transport gallery. The transport gallery houses the museum's most celebrated item — the 150-year-old steam engine, *The Lion.* Built in 1838 for the Liverpool and Manchester Railway Co., it is the oldest working steam engine in the world. (Visitors wishing to see the engine actually steam must arrange this in advance.) The aquarium, vivarium, and planetarium appeal particularly to younger visitors. Closed Sunday mornings. William Brown St. (phone: 207-0001).

Museum of Labour History – Exhibits illustrating the life of ordinary working people in Merseyside over the last 150 years and their struggle to win legal and political rights. Closed Sunday mornings. Former County Sessions House, William Brown St. (phone: 207-0001).

Open Eye Gallery – A continually changing program of work by local and international photographers. Whitechapel (phone: 709-9460).

Sudley Art Gallery – A 19th-century merchant's house with a collection of 18th- and 19th-century paintings by such artists as Gainsborough, Turner, and Reynolds. Closed Sunday mornings. Mossley Hill Rd. (phone: 207-0001).

SHOPPING: Pedestrians-only Church Street, Lord Street, Whitechapel, and Paradise Street are Liverpool's main shopping arteries. Most of the nationwide chain and department stores can be found here, including *Marks & Spencer, C & A, W. H. Smith's, Habitat, Mothercare,* and *British Home Stores.* Liverpool's own *George Henry Lee* is in the vicinity, on Basnett Street. There are more shops on Elliot Street and Parker Street, as well as in the massive St. John's shopping center, which also has a bustling fruit, vegetable, fish, and meat market; it has recently undergone major refurbishment and now includes a large "food court." The modern and luxuriously appointed Cavern Walks complex, on Mathew Street, features small specialty stores. Albert Dock Village, worth a separate shopping expedition, contains dozens of specialty shops that make it a haven for the selective shopper. For a change from the ordinary souvenir shops it is a must. A very important development was the opening (in 1988) of the Clayton Square Shopping Centre in the city center off Church Street. Elegantly laid out, it attracts big names such as *Principles Ltd, Boots, Next Jewellery,* and *Laura Ashley,* and designer boutiques such as *Oasis, Dash,* and *Knickerbox.* It will eventually house 50 shops.

Albert Dock Souvenir Shop – Recently opened, this gift shop offers a variety of gifts and ornaments related to nautical activity and Albert Dock. The Colonnades, Albert Dock (no phone).

Beatles Shop – Posters, photos, sheet music, records, T-shirts, scarves, blow-up models, and other Beatlemania memorabilia, sold to the tunes of a working jukebox devoted exclusively to the lads. Mathew St. (phone: 236-8066).

Boodle and Dunthorne – An old clock above the doorway, marked 1798, distinguishes this old-fashioned jeweler. Boodle House, Lord St. (phone: 227-2525).

Cigarette Card Company – A fascinating shop carrying a huge collection of full cigarette card sets dating back to their heyday in the 1920s and '30s. The card collections cover topics as diverse as transportation, sports, and celebrities to wild animals. Individual cards are also available. Atlantic Pavilion, Albert Dock (phone: 709-3929).

Frank Green's – Paintings, prints, and cards — the Liverpudlian artist's impressions of the city's changing scene since the early 1960s. Edward Pavilion, Albert Dock (phone: 709-3330).

Glass Corner – Upscale and expensive, this retailer offers beautifully crafted designer glass ornaments and giftware. Anchor Courtyard, Albert Dock (phone: 709-6900).

Hologram Experience – An exhibition and gift shop with a vast array of holograms. The Colonnades, Albert Dock (phone: 708-5561).

Kabuki – Japanese products, including teapots, sake sets, kimonos, fans, delicate lampshades, and books. Upstairs is a small tea room where authentic tea ceremonies are performed (by reservation). Cavern Walks (phone: 236-0226).

Milan Leather – A comprehensive selection of leatherware. Very upscale. Edward Pavilion, Albert Dock (phone: 708-7154).

Quiggins – Under one roof are several stalls selling antiques, collectibles, and jewelry. 75 Renshaw St. (phone: 708-6934).

W. Richards – An old-fashioned hunting, shooting, and fishing emporium, in business since the 18th century. It's one of the places British yuppies buy their Barbours — dark green, oiled, waterproof, expensive coats designed for country walking. India Buildings, 2 Brunswick St. (phone: 236-2925).

David M. Robinson – One of the city's most exclusive diamond and gold jewelers. 24 Church Alley (phone: 708-9725) and 24 North John St. (phone: 236-2720).

Rushworth's Music House – Records, instruments, and sheet music sprawled over four floors. Whitechapel (phone: 709-9071).

J. Sewill – Nautical instruments, such as telescopes and barometers, as well as carriage clocks and other items for the landlubber. 36 Exchange St. E. (phone: 227-1376).

Sweet Talk – Candies (treacle taffy, clotted cream caramels, etc.) sold by weight. Britannia Pavilion, Albert Dock (no phone).

Truffles – A bewildering range of jams, honeys, coffees, teas, and chocolates are sold here and in a sister shop, the *Quartermaster's Store,* opposite the atrium. Cavern Walks, Mathew St. (phone: 236-5668).

Youngs – Established in 1849, this bookshop is the best place in town to find maps of the surrounding area. 15 N. John St. (phone: 236-2048).

SPORTS: Besides the possibilities listed below, the *Oval Sports Centre,* Old Chester Rd., Bebington, Wirral (phone: 645-0551), has a full range of facilities, from a swimming pool to a dry ski slope. For the Liverpool sports information line, phone: 724-2371.

Boating and Sailing – The *Liverpool Watersports Centre* at Salthouse Dock (phone: 708-9322), next to Albert Dock, offers sailing, sailboarding, and canoeing. A narrowboat, *Caterpillar,* can be hired from the center. There are also boats for hire at the *Crosby Sailing Club,* Cambridge Rd. (phone: 928-7150), 6 miles north of the city.

Golf – At least 35 golf courses dot the map of Liverpool's environs. The *Liverpool Municipal Golf Course,* Moor La., Kirkby (phone: 546-5435), has 18 holes and is open daily. Most private clubs admit visitors, including the *Royal Liverpool Golf Club,* Meols Dr., Hoylake (phone: 632-3101), one of Britain's top courses and a frequent venue for the British Open championship. Another world-famous course, the *Royal Birkdale Golf Club* (phone: 0704-67920), is among the six courses at Southport, along the coast about 20 miles north of town. There's a ladies' course within a gentlemen's course among the sand dunes at Formby (phone: 07048-73493), between Liverpool and Southport.

Rugby – Fans can watch one of the country's top professional Rugby League clubs at St. Helens, 20 miles east of Liverpool, and there are Rugby Union clubs at Waterloo, Birkenhead Park, New Brighton, and Liverpool.

Soccer – The two famous home teams are the *Liverpool Football Club* (nicknamed the "Reds," after their red shirts) and the *Everton Football Club* (the *Toffees* or *Blues*). On most Saturdays during the season, one or the other team is playing a home game, either at Anfield (phone: 263-2361) or at Goodison Park (phone: 521-2020). Details of Soccer Weekends, which include a match, a visit to the club's trophy room, and a guided coach tour of Liverpool, are available from the tourist information center, or phone the reservations hotline, open daily from 10 AM to 6 PM (phone: 708-7086).

Tennis – The Wirral International Tennis Tournament, which has attracted such pros as John McEnroe, Kevin Curran, and Ken Flach, is now an annual event that takes place in June, 1 week before Wimbledon. Ashton Park, West Kirby (phone: 647-2366, Wirral Sports Information).

Walking – The Wirral Peninsula has superb coast walks, including the Wirral Way, 12 miles down the west coast.

THEATER: Many of the country's top playwrights and actors began their careers here, and the city's largest theater, the *Liverpool Empire,* Lime St. (phone: 709-1555), regularly premiers shows that end up hits in London's West End. It also attracts such major touring companies as the *Scottish Opera and Ballet* and the *Welsh National Opera,* plus musicals and pop concerts. As Britain's oldest surviving repertory theater, the *Liverpool Playhouse,* Williamson Sq. (phone: 709-8363), is the place to see the classics and contemporary plays, while the *Everyman Theatre,* Hope St. (phone: 709-0338), stages more avant-garde productions.

MUSIC: Ask any schoolboy in Liverpool what he wants to be when he grows up, and he'll reply, "a musician." The city that gave rise to the *Beatles* and the Mersey Sound still has a flourishing live music scene, with the *Royal Court Theatre,* Roe St. (phone: 709-4321), the biggest rock venue. Other musical groups, from pop to opera, book into the *Liverpool Empire,* Lime St. (phone: 709-1555). The *Royal Liverpool Philharmonic Orchestra* plays in *Philharmonic Hall,* Hope St. (phone: 709-3789), and performs smaller concerts at the *Bluecoat Concert Hall,* Bluecoat Chambers, School La. (phone: 709-5297). There's usually live folk and jazz at one of the pubs and clubs, and in summer there are string ensembles that play regularly in Cavern Walks and outdoor bands that perform around the Albert Dock.

NIGHTCLUBS AND NIGHTLIFE: Liverpool offers a rich variety of nighttime entertainment ranging from discos and live acts to cabarets and casinos There are dozens of venues in Liverpool city center. Check *What's On Merseyside* and at the tourist information center. Sadly, the original *Cavern Club* was torn down in order to build a rail tunnel underneath it, but there's plenty of activity in the wee hours in the new *Cavern Club* (Cavern Walks, Mathew St.; phone: 236-1964), on the same site, which features live music most nights (and is also open for lunch). Other discos include *Snobs* (phone: 709-9172) and *Tuxedo Junction* (phone: 709-9526), both on Parr Street, and *Saturdays,* at the *Britannia Adelphi* hotel.

BEST IN TOWN

CHECKING IN: There are plenty of smart hotels in Liverpool and plenty of empty rooms, particularly on weekends. Expect to pay $115 and up for a double room with bath in hotels listed as expensive, $75 to $105 for those classed as moderate, and under $75 for those listed as inexpensive. A full English breakfast is usually included in the room price. All telephone numbers are in the 051 area code unless otherwise indicated.

Atlantic Tower Thistle – Locals consider it the best in town. Modern, distinctively shaped like the bow of a ship, and not long ago refurbished, it has 226 newly refurbished rooms (several with magnificent views of the river and all with private baths), an elegantly styled marble foyer, 2 restaurants, and the *Tradewinds Bar* with a nautical theme. Dinner dancing every Saturday evening. 30 Chapel St. (phone: 227-4444). Expensive.

Britannia Adelphi – Built in 1914, during the Edwardian heyday of transatlantic passenger traffic, this 344-room hotel reflects the style of that era: The marble foyer with mirrored ceiling is huge, and there is a magnificent lounge, complete with chandeliers and parlor palms, where there's no chance of hearing a conversation at the other end of the room. Ranelagh Pl. (phone: 709-7200). Expensive.

Liverpool Moat House – A former *Holiday Inn* now owned by the British Queens Moat House chain, only a short walk from Albert Dock. The style falls short of elegant, but it's warm, comfortable, and modern, right down to the piped music in the elevator. In addition to 258 rooms, there's a sauna, solarium, and an indoor swimming pool. Paradise St. (phone: 709-0181). Expensive.

Trials – Based in an imposing Victorian building that once served as a bank, this has 20 luxuriously appointed rooms with all the expected modern conveniences. 56 Castle St. (phone: 227-1021). Expensive.

Cherry Tree – Located 5 miles east of the city center, this 50-room hotel has recently undergone a complete refurbishment. The building is set in expansive gardens, and each room has a private bath. East Lancashire Rd., Knowlsley Prescot (phone: 546-7531). Expensive to moderate.

Crest – Like its fellows up and down the country, what it lacks in distinctive character it makes up for in practical facilities. There are 160 bedrooms, 15 of which are dubbed "Lady Crest" rooms, equipped with hair dryers, skirt presses, and so on. Lord Nelson St. (phone: 709-7050). Expensive to moderate.

Aachen – Tucked into a row of townhouses, this small establishment (17 rooms, 9 with private bath) is popular with visiting Americans. 89–91 Mount Pleasant (phone: 709-3477). Moderate.

Feathers – A friendly place with 160 bedrooms (57 with private bath) and 2 restaurants. The proprietors also own the *Bradford* and *Alicia* hotels. 119–125 Mount Pleasant (phone: 709-9655). Moderate.

Leasowe Castle – On the Wirral peninsula near Wallasey, just a short drive off the M53 motorway and within easy reach of the city center via the Mersey tunnel, this excellent hotel is situated in a 400-year-old castle offering much old charm and character along with modern comfort. All basic facilities are included in the 40 rooms. A fine restaurant and the newly opened *Castle Bar* offering a variety of bar lunches are also on the premises. Leasowe, Moreton, Merseyside (phone: 606-9191). Moderate.

St. George's – This Trusthouse Forte property stands at the top of a flight of steps in St. John's shopping center. It has 155 modern rooms, a large *Carvery* restaurant, and a reliable baby-sitting service. St. John's Precinct, Lime St. (phone: 709-7090). Moderate.

Shaftesbury – Those who have seen the film *Letter to Brezhnev* may recognize one of the hotel's 67 bedrooms. The hotel's restaurant is known for its flambé dishes ignited at your table. Mount Pleasant (phone: 709-4421). Moderate.

Solna – Overlooking Liverpool's largest natural park, this Victorian house offers peace and quiet a couple of miles away from the bustle of the city center. Of the 36 rooms, 24 have private bath. Ullet Rd., Sefton Park (phone: 733-1943). Moderate to inexpensive.

Antrim – Family-run, homey, and friendly, with 20 rooms. 73 Mount Pleasant (phone: 709-9212). Inexpensive.

University – Single bed-and-breakfast rooms and fully-equipped self-catering apartments are available from 1 night to 3 months at the university's Hall of Residence, July through September. University of Liverpool, PO Box 147 (phone: 794-3201/2 or 794-6440/1). Inexpensive.

EATING OUT: The restaurant that used to revolve at the top of Liverpool's skyscraping ventilation tower is now closed, but its demise hardly bankrupted the city of good eating places. Rumor has it that some 140 nationalities live in the 1 square mile of the Toxteth Quarter alone, spawning the city's wealth of ethnic restaurants. There is a wide choice of Chinese restaurants, particularly in Chinatown, at the top of Bold Street (where there is no dearth of Chinese-owned fish and chip shops). More traditional English restaurants are everywhere, and even the city's hotel restaurants are slowly attracting locals. And don't be surprised to find "scouse" on a menu; it is the traditional dish of stewed lamb, beef, and vegetables that earned Liverpudlians their famous nickname. A meal for two with wine will cost more than $75 at a restaurant listed as expensive, $50 to $65 at one listed as moderate, and less than $50 at an inexpensive one. All telephone numbers are in the 051 area code unless otherwise indicated.

Del Secolo – The most ambitious of a trio of family-run restaurants, but whereas the other two more moderate eateries (see *Villa Italia* and *Casa Italia* below) serve Italian food, the menu here offers a massive selection of international dishes. Closed Saturday evenings and Sundays. 36–40 Stanley St. (phone: 236-4004). Expensive.

Wharf – Ideal for a special occasion, this superbly decorated French restaurant serves a wide variety of seafood and meat dishes. It has become one of the best in town. Britannia Pavilion, Albert Dock (phone: 708-6841). Expensive to moderate.

L'Alouette – An imaginatively decorative bistro, it serves a wide selection of French cuisine. Reservations necessary well in advance on weekends. Closed Mondays. 2 Park La. (phone: 727-2142). Moderate.

Armadillo – In a converted warehouse, it has a self-service, student-like atmosphere by day, but in the evening it becomes a bustling grown-up restaurant. Imaginative vegetarian dishes include a vegetable and cheese pie and pease pudding served with cream, dry vermouth, and a julienne of vegetables. Good value. Closed Sundays and Monday evenings. 20–22 Mathew St. (phone: 236-4123). Moderate.

Far East – A good part of the city's large Chinese population flock here for dim sum at Sunday lunchtime — a reliable recommendation for visitors. It's above the Chinese supermarket in Chinatown, so diners can check out what they'll be eating on their way in. Open daily. 27–35 Berry St. (phone: 709-3141). Moderate.

Lau's – The best Chinese restaurant in town is *not* in Chinatown but in a large, detached house opposite Sefton Park. Family-run (Mr. Yuk Shan Lau can often be seen making noodles), it specializes in Peking cuisine — the basic banquet menu will defeat even the healthiest of appetites. Closed Sundays. Rankin Hall, 44 Ullet Rd. (phone: 733-3096). Moderate.

L'Oriel – Housed in the distinctive Oriel Chambers Building, an office block, but the first in the country to be constructed with "picture" windows. The basic menu is French. Closed Sundays. Oriel Chambers, Water St. (phone: 236-5025). Moderate.

Villa Italia – The basic Italian menu features pasta dishes and charcoal grilled meats served at small marble-topped tables set on sewing machine stands. Closed Sundays. 9–13 Temple Ct. (phone: 227-5774). Moderate.

Churchill's – In the basement of a modern office block, it's hardly distinctive architecturally, but the kitchen produces good English cooking. Closed Saturdays for lunch and Sundays. Churchill House, Tithebarn St. (phone: 227-3877). Moderate to inexpensive.

Jenny's Seafood – A modest basement entrance belies the excellent reputation here. Among the best preparers of fish in town, it's housed in an old building where lines for ships used to be stretched; hence the address. Closed Saturdays for lunch, Sundays, and Mondays for dinner. Old Ropery, Fenwick St. (phone: 236-0332). Moderate to inexpensive.

Mandarin – An extensive range of mainly Cantonese dishes is served in attractive surroundings. Open daily. 40 Victoria St. (phone: 236-8899). Moderate to inexpensive.

Qué Pasa – Wooden floors, bare brick walls, and the occasional sombrero and other evocative decoration distinguish this small, attractive Mexican restaurant. Open daily. 94–96 Lark La. (phone: 727-0006). Moderate to inexpensive.

Casa Italia – Essentially a pizzeria, serving 19 different combinations of pizza, plus homemade ice cream. Closed Sundays. 36 – 40 Stanley St. (phone: 236-4004). Inexpensive.

Everyman Bistro – An excellent value for the money, this self-serve bistro offers a wide variety of freshly produced meat and vegetarian produce. Hope St. (phone: 708-9545). Inexpensive.

La Grande Bouffe – A basement bistro that livens up most nights to the rhythms of a good jazz pianist, although there's a hideaway Impressionist Room for those seeking a quieter, more intimate evening. The menu includes daily vegetarian specials. Closed Sundays and Monday evenings. 48A Castle St. (phone: 236-3375). Inexpensive.

Ye Olde Patisserie – Not really as ancient as its name implies. The fare consists of cakes, coffee, and tea. A convenient retreat after exertions on the main shopping streets. Closed Sundays. 27 Tarleton St. (phone: 708-5416). Inexpensive.

SHARING A PINT: Interesting old pubs in which to imbibe include sailortown haunts such as the 18th-century *Pig and Whistle* (Covent Garden), which served ale to thousands of emigrants on their way to the New World (see the "Emigrants Supplied" sign inside). Similar flavor can be found at *The Eagle* (Paradise St.) and *The Baltic Fleet* (Wapping). *Rigby's,* on Dale St., is old, although not as old as might be expected, given the 1726 emblazoned across the top of the building. Nautical in theme, the pub even owned a bill of sale belonging to Nelson (it was later stolen). A nautical theme continues at *Ye Hole in Ye Wall* on Hackins Way; it's one of Liverpool's oldest sailortown pubs, and at least one sailor has been killed in a gang fight. *The Vines* (Lime St.) is a beautiful Edwardian pub that still sports wooden fixtures made by carpenters who worked on the great ocean liners at the turn of the century, while the *Philharmonic* (Hope St.) is particularly ornate and known for its gents' marble lavatories (ladies are allowed to inspect when unoccupied). Other pubs in this style include the *Beaconsfield* (Victoria St.) with its tastefully appointed interior, the *Libson* (Victoria St.) which is fitted with ornate brass and woodwork and is renowned for its spectacular ceiling, and the *Central* (Ranelagh St.), a carefully preserved Victorian pub with sumptuous decorations. *Penny Lane* is a wine bar serving food at 116 Penny La. Just off Hope St., on Rice St., is the tiny *Ye Cracke,* at one time frequented by the *Beatles.* Also formerly patronized by the *Beatles* is the *Grapes* (Matthew St.). Even Chinatown has its pubs — try *The Nook,* on Nelson St. A place that has become a Liverpool institution with its bizarre mixture of poets, punks, trendy models, and yuppies is the famous *Kirklands Café Bar* (Hardman St.). The building used to be a bakery that supplied, among others, Queen Victoria. Now it offers good food and entertainment.

LONDON

British author and journalist V. S. Pritchett noted that the essence of London was contained in the very sound of its name: Lon-don, a weighty word, solid, monumental, dignified, even ponderous. London is a shapeless city without a center; it sprawls anarchically over 620 square miles and brims over with a variety of neighborhoods and people. One of its sharpest observers, Daniel Defoe, portrayed London in the 18th century much as it could be described today: "It is . . . stretched out in buildings, straggling, confused . . . out of all shape, uncompact and unequal; neither long nor broad, round or square."

London can best be understood not as one city but as a conglomeration of villages that were incorporated whole, one by one, as the monster expanded — Chelsea, Battersea, Paddington, and Hampstead are just a few. Fortunately, all of its important parks and squares have remained inviolate, but not without a struggle, for London's merchant class — its backbone and its pride — often resisted and defeated town planners, ever since Parliament turned down Sir Christopher Wren's splendid plan to rebuild after the fire of 1666. It was royalty and aristocracy that created and preserved the parks — St. James's Park, Hyde Park, Kensington Gardens, Regent's Park, and Kew Gardens were all royal parks — and their enthusiasm became contagious. The passionate regard of Londoners for their green spots has been one of the city's saving graces as it grew so helplessly and recklessly, more in the spirit of commerce than of urban planning.

Today's London — though marred by soulless high-rise intruders of glass and concrete — boasts more greenery than any metropolis could reasonably hope to retain in these philistine times. Aside from its many garden squares and the meticulously tended plots of so many Londoners' homes, the city is punctuated by a series of large parks and commons; besides those already mentioned, there are Wimbledon Common, Richmond Deer Park, Primrose Hill, Hampstead Heath — the list goes on and on. And to make even more certain that citification does not intrude too far into London life, a green belt, almost 100 square miles of forest and grassland, virtually encircles the city and, to the chagrin and impatience of developers, is meticulously preserved by law.

London's other natural resource, the River Thames, has not been so fortunate. As any glance at a map will show, London follows the serpentine meanderings of the Thames, England's principal river. Nearly everything of interest in London is on or near the Thames, for London is London because it is a natural port. The river has always been London's mainstay, for centuries its only east-west road, and it has justifiably been said that "every drop of the Thames is liquid history." At the site of the Naval College in Greenwich, for example, there once stood a royal palace where Henry VIII and

Elizabeth I were born, and where tournaments, pageants, and banquets were held.

A great river port and a city of gardens, London is also a city of stately squares and monuments, of royalty with its pomp and ceremony, a cosmopolitan city of the first rank. Until World War II, it was the capital of the mammoth and far-flung British Empire upon which, it was said, the sun never set. For many centuries, a powerful Britannia ruled a considerable section of the globe — the largest since Roman times — and the English language spread from the inconsiderable British Isles to become the dominant language all over the world, from North America to India.

If the British Empire has contracted drastically, it has done so gracefully, among memories of its greatest days. And if once-subject peoples hated their oppressor, they still love London, and many have chosen to live there. London is still the center of the Commonwealth of independent nations that were once British colonies, and its cosmopolitan atmosphere owes a great deal to the ubiquity of former colonials. Their presence is felt in the substantial Indian-Pakistani community in the Southall district of West London; in the strong Caribbean flavor in Brixton; in Chinatown in and around Gerrard Street — a hop, skip, and a jump from Piccadilly Circus; in the Cypriot groceries and bakeries of Camden Town; and in the majestic mosque on the fringe of Regent's Park.

A tantalizing diversity of accents flavors the English language here — accents from Australia and Barbados, Bangladesh and Nigeria, Canada and Malaysia, Kenya and South Africa, Sri Lanka and Ireland, Hong Kong and the US. And then the various inflections of Britain itself are also to be heard in the streets of London — the lilt and rasp of cockney, Oxford, Somerset, Yorkshire, the Scottish Highlands, and the Welsh mining towns.

London's somewhat onomatopoeic name derives from the Celtic term *Llyn-din,* meaning "river place," but little is known of London before it was renamed *Londinium* by the Romans in AD 43. The rather fantastical 12th-century historian Geoffrey of Monmouth may have originated the myth widespread in Shakespeare's day — that London was founded by Brute, a direct descendant of Aeneas in 1108 BC, who named it Troynovant, New Troy, or Trenovant. Even in medieval times, London had grandiose notions of its own importance — a prideful self-image that has been amply justified by history. Nevertheless, yet another chunk of Roman London has recently been uncovered by archaeologists from the *British Museum.* While excavating the foundation of the 15th-century Guildhall chapel, they found Roman works more than 1 meter wide that have been identified as Roman London's missing amphitheater. The site should be open to visitors early this year (phone: 660-3699).

The city was sufficiently prominent for the Norman invader William the Conqueror to make it his capital in 1066. During the Middle Ages, the expansion of trade, population growth, and the energetic activities of its guilds of merchants and craftsmen promoted London's prosperity. Indisputably, London's golden age was the English Renaissance, the 16th century, the time of Queen Elizabeth I, Shakespeare, and Drake's defeat of the Spanish Armada. Most of the Tudor buildings of London were wiped out in the great fire of 1666. Christopher Wren, the architect of genius, undertook to rebuild many buildings and churches, the most outstanding of which is St. Paul's Cathedral. The 18th century, a highly sophisticated age, saw the building of noble homes and stately squares, many of them part of a grand expansion program developed by the prince regent's principal architect, John Nash. One of the best examples of his work is the terrace of largely crown-owned Regency houses surrounding Regent's Park. In the early 19th century, interest continued in homes and squares; and only in the Victorian age, the height of the Empire, were public buildings like the Houses of Parliament redesigned, this time in grand and fanciful neo-Gothic style.

London has seen whole catalogues of heroes and villains, crises and conflagrations, come and go, sometimes swallowed whole in the passage of time, sometimes leaving relics. Still on elegant display is stately Hampton Court Palace, the most magnificent of England's palaces, where Henry VIII lived now and again with five of his six wives. There is a spot downtown — in front of the Banqueting House on Whitehall — where another king, Charles I, was beheaded by his subjects, who were calmly committing dreaded regicide 150 years before the presumably more emotional and explosive French across the English Channel even contemplated such a gesture.

London has lived through the unbounded permissiveness of the flamboyantly royal Restoration period (1660-85), when even King Charles II frequented brothels and didn't care who knew it, and it has survived the stern moral puritanism of the Victorian era, when it was downright rude to refer to the *breast* of chicken or a piano *leg.* And most recently, London stood up with exemplary courage under the devastating effects of the Nazi bombings, which destroyed a great many buildings and killed thousands of people.

Many of our images of London, taken from old movies, actually mirror its realities: Big Ben rises above the Houses of Parliament, somberly striking the hour; ramrod-straight scarlet-uniformed soldiers half hide their faces in towering black bearskin hats; waiters at the Bank of England still sport the kinds of top hats and tailcoats their predecessors wore for a century; lawyers in court still don wigs and black robes. A few images, however, are outdated: The bowler hat has been slipping steadily out of fashion for years, and rigidly enforced environmental regulations have made London's once-famous pea soup fog a thing of the past.

London's nearly infinite variety of urban moods includes the sturdy edifices lining Whitehall, center of the British government, with Trafalgar Square at its head and Parliament at its foot; the elegant shopping areas of Knightsbridge, Bond Street, Kensington, and the Burlington Arcade; suburban chic in Barnes and Blackheath; handsome squares in Bloomsbury; melancholy mystery in Victoria and Waterloo train stations with their spy-movie atmosphere; the vitality of East End street markets; and the riparian tranquillity of Thames-side towpaths in Putney and along Hammersmith Mall.

The British have a talent that amounts to a genius for government — for democracy and political tolerance — a talent that has been developing ever since the Magna Carta was signed in 1215 and one that makes London's ambience easy and relaxed for individualists of all sorts. It is no wonder that the eccentric and inveterate Londoner of the city's 18th-century heyday, Dr.

Samuel Johnson, once declared, "When a man is tired of London, he is tired of life, for there is in London all that life can afford."

Johnson's opinion, though somewhat overblown, was essentially shared by one of several modern American writers who chose to live in London. Disillusioned with New York, Boston, and Paris, Henry James decided in favor of London in 1881. Somehow he concluded that London was a place eminently suited to human life: "It is not a pleasant place; it is not agreeable, or cheerful, or easy, or exempt from reproach. It is only magnificent. You can draw up a tremendous list of reasons why it should be unsupportable. The fogs, the smoke, the dirt, the darkness, the wet, the distances, the ugliness, the brutal size of the place, the horrible numerosity of society . . . but . . . London is on the whole the most possible form of life."

LONDON AT-A-GLANCE

SEEING THE CITY: London has, for the most part, resisted the temptation to build high. Aside from a handful of modest gestures toward skyscraping, there aren't many towering structures to obscure panoramic overviews of the city from its higher vantage points, which include:

London Hilton International – There were discreet noises of disapproval from Buckingham Palace when it was realized that the view from the roof bar of the *Hilton* included not only the palace grounds but, with high-powered binoculars, the inside of some of the royal chambers as well. In fact, the view over Mayfair, Hyde Park, and Westminster is breathtaking. Park La. (phone: 493-8000).

Westminster Cathedral – Not to be confused with Westminster Abbey. The top of the bell tower of London's Roman Catholic cathedral looks down on a broad expanse of the inner city. An elevator takes visitors up for a token charge (from April to September only). Off Victoria St. near the station, at Ashley Pl., SW1.

Hampstead Heath – Climb to the top of Parliament Hill, on the southern rim of this "wilderness" in north London. On a clear day, the view south from the Heath makes the city look like a vast village.

South Bank Arts Center – On the south bank of Waterloo Bridge is the bunkerlike complex of cultural buildings, including the Royal Festival Hall, the *National Theatre,* the *National Film Theatre,* the *Hayward Gallery,* and other cultural attractions. For a view of London, look across the Thames — upriver to the Houses of Parliament, downriver to St. Paul's Cathedral.

Tower Bridge Walkway – The upper part of one of London's famous landmarks is open to visitors. In addition to the viewing gallery, there is an exhibition on the history of London's bridges and a museum that includes the bridge's Victorian steam pumping engines. Open November through March, 10 AM to 4:45 PM; April through October, 10 AM to 6:30 PM. Admission charge. Tower Hill Underground Station.

St. Paul's Cathedral – The reward for climbing the 600 steps into the dome of this cathedral — the largest in the world after St. Peter's in Rome — is a panoramic view of London.

Docklands – The development of this area is so extensive that it even includes its own railroad; new apartment, commercial, and office buildings stretch seemingly without end. As we went to press, the landscape still contained a forest of construction cranes, but even now it's a wonderful place to explore. The *Docklands Light Railway,* a high-tech, overhead train, runs from Tower Hill to Greenwich, speeding over the fast-developing and fascinating terrain. If food shopping is on your agenda, visiting the

Docklands will put to rest forever the image of British homemakers buying the family's food in tiny neighborhood greengrocers and small butcher shops. There's a market here called the *Super Store,* a British interpretation of a California supermarket, and the *Billingsgate Market,* originally on Lower Thames St., has moved here. It's the place where some of London's premier chefs pick out their produce and fresh fish early in the morning, and it's the best place to pick up a side of smoked Scottish salmon to cart home.

SPECIAL PLACES/ATTRACTIONS: Surveying London from the steps of St. Paul's Cathedral at the turn of the 19th century, a visiting Prussian general commented to his English host: "What a place to plunder!" Even those who are less rapacious will appreciate the extraordinary wealth of sights London displays for visitors to inspect. Though some are dispersed in various corners of this vast city, most are clustered reasonably close together in or near the inner districts of Westminster, the City, and Kensington. Twenty Photospot locations — places to stand to get the best photographs of famous sights — have been indicated throughout Westminster with blue and white signs fixed to lampposts.

WESTMINSTER

Changing of the Guard – An American who lived in London once said, "There's just no better way to convince yourself that you're in London!" This famous ceremony takes place daily from April to mid-August (alternate days in winter) promptly at 11:30 AM in the Buckingham Palace forecourt, at 11:15 AM at St. James's Palace, and at 11:30 AM at the Tower of London. (In very wet weather, it may be canceled.)

Horse Guards – If you haven't had enough, you can see a new guard of 12 members of the Household Cavalry troop in with trumpet and standard, daily at 11 AM, 10 on Sundays, on the west side of Whitehall. Incidentally, they come from stables not far from Hyde Park and make a daily parade along the south roadway of Hyde Park, past Buckingham Palace, and then on to Trafalgar Square to turn into Whitehall. Their progress is as much fun to watch as the actual ceremony.

Buckingham Palace – The royal standard flies from the roof when the monarch is in residence at her London home. Although George III bought the palace in 1762, sovereigns officially still live in St. James's Palace around the corner in Pall Mall, and Buckingham Palace did not become the actual principal regal dwelling until 1837, when Queen Victoria moved in. The palace, unfortunately, is open only to invited guests (the *Queen's Gallery* and Royal Mews are open to the public; see below). The queen's summer garden parties are held on the palace lawns. The interior contains magnificently decorated apartments, a superb picture gallery, and a throne room (66 feet long), where foreign ambassadors are received and knights are knighted. The palace grounds contain the largest private garden in London (40 acres). And the gate that originally was built for the entrance, too narrow for the coaches of George IV, now marks the Hyde Park end of Oxford Street and is known as Marble Arch. Buckingham Palace Rd.

State Visits – If you aren't going to be in London for the queen's official birthday in June, you might want to see her greet a foreign dignitary in full regalia. This happens quite frequently and is announced in the royal calendar in *The Times.* The queen meets her guest at Victoria Station, and they ride to Buckingham Palace in a procession of horse-drawn coaches, followed by the colorful Horse Guards. Meanwhile, at Hyde Park Corner, the cannoneers on horseback perform elaborate maneuvers before their salute thunders through the whole city.

Queen's Gallery – Treasures from the royal art collection are on display in this room of the palace only. Exhibitions change about once a year. Open Tuesdays through Saturdays from 10:30 AM to 5 PM, Sundays from 2 to 5 PM. Admission charge. Buckingham Palace Rd., SW1.

Royal Academy – Housed in a building that resembles a cross between a mausoleum, a railroad station, and a funeral parlor are the works of *the* established, leading fashionable painters of the past. It's also the place where some of the major exhibitions to visit London are mounted. Admission charge. Burlington House, Piccadilly, W1 (phone: 439-7438).

Royal Mews – The mews is a palace alley where the magnificent bridal coach, other state coaches, and the horses that draw them are stabled. The public is admitted on Wednesdays and Thursdays from 2 to 4 PM. Admission charge. Buckingham Palace Rd. SW1.

St. James's Park – Parks are everywhere in London and Londoners love them. This is one of the nicest, where at lunch hour on a sunny day you can see the impeccably dressed London businessmen lounging on the grass, their shoes and shirts off. With its sizable lake (designed by John Nash) inhabited by pelicans and other wild fowl, St. James's was originally a royal deer park, drained under Henry VIII in 1532 and laid out as a pleasure ground for Charles II.

The Mall – The wide avenue parallel to Pall Mall and lined with lime trees and Regency buildings leads from Trafalgar Square to Buckingham Palace. This is the principal ceremonial route used by Queen Elizabeth and her escort of Household Cavalry for the State Opening of Parliament (October/November) and the *Trooping the Colour* (see *Special Events*). It is closed to traffic on Sunday afternoons.

Trafalgar Square – One of London's most heavily trafficked squares is built around the towering Nelson's Column — a 145-foot monument that honors Lord Nelson, victor at the naval Battle of Trafalgar in 1805. At the base of the monument are four huge bronze lions and two fountains. Flanked by handsome buildings, including the *National Gallery* and the 18th-century church of St. Martin in the Fields, the square is a favorite gathering place for political demonstrations, tourists, and pigeons.

Piccadilly Circus – Downtown London finds its center here in the heart of the theater district and on the edge of Soho. This is the London equivalent of Times Square — lots of it is just as tacky — and at the center of the busy "circus," or traffic circle, is the restored statue of Eros (moved about 40 feet from its original perch), which actually was designed in 1893 as *The Angel of Christian Charity,* a memorial to the charitable Earl of Shaftesbury — the archer and his bow were meant as a pun on his name. The Trocadero, a recently converted 3-story shopping and entertainment complex featuring the *International Village Restaurant,* has lent Piccadilly a new level of bustle. Popular exhibitions include the *Guinness World Records* display and the London Experience, for a look at the city's history. Separate admission charges.

National Gallery – One of the world's great art museums, this is an inexhaustible feast for art lovers. In the vast collection on display are works by such masters as Uccello, da Vinci, Titian, Rembrandt, Rubens, Cranach, Gainsborough, El Greco, Renoir, Cézanne, and Van Gogh. Open daily, 10 AM to 6 PM; Sundays, 2 to 6 PM. Trafalgar Sq., WC2 (phone: 839-3321).

National Portrait Gallery – Right behind the *National Gallery* sits this delightful museum. Nearly every English celebrity from the last 500 years is pictured here, with the earliest personalities at the top and the 20th-century notables at the bottom. Open daily, Mondays through Fridays, 10 AM to 5 PM; Saturdays, 10 AM to 6 PM; Sundays, 2 to 6 PM. 2 St. Martin's Pl., WC2 (phone: 930-1552).

Whitehall – A broad boulevard stretching from Trafalgar Square to Parliament Square, lined most of the way by government ministries and such historic buildings as the Banqueting House (completed in 1622, with a ceiling painted by Rubens) and the Horse Guards (whose central archway is ceremonially guarded by mounted troopers).

Detective novel fans may be interested to know that from 1890 to 1967 Scotland Yard occupied the Norman Shaw Building at the Trafalgar end of Whitehall; it now houses offices for members of Parliament. The Yard has moved to Victoria Street near St. James's Park.

Downing Street – Off Whitehall, a street of small, unpretentious Georgian houses includes the official residences of the most important figures in the British government, the Prime Minister at #10 and the Chancellor of the Exchequer (Britain's secretary of the treasury) at #11.

Cabinet War Rooms – Constructed to resemble its wartime appearance, this underground complex of 20 rooms was Winston Churchill's auxiliary command post during World War II, which he used most often during the German Luftwaffe's blitz on London. Of special note are the map room, with maps pinpointing the positions of Allied and German troops in the final stages of the war, and the cabinet room, where the prime minister met with his staff. Open daily. Admission charge. Beneath the government building on Great George St., SW1 (phone: 930-6961).

Westminster Abbey – It's easy to get lost among the endlessly fascinating tombs and plaques and not even notice the Abbey's splendid architecture, so do look at the structure itself and don't miss the cloisters, which display its Gothic design to advantage. Note also the fine Tudor chapel of Henry VII, with its tall windows and lovely fan-tracery vaulting, and the 13th-century chapel of St. Edward the Confessor, containing England's Coronation Chair and Scotland's ancient coronation Stone of Scone.

Ever since William the Conqueror was crowned here in 1066, the Abbey has been the traditional place where English monarchs are crowned, married, and buried. You don't have to be an Anglophile to be moved by the numerous tombs and memorials with their fascinating inscriptions — here are honored (not necessarily buried) kings and queens, soldiers, statesmen, and many other prominent English men and women. Poets' Corner, in the south transept, contains the tombs of Chaucer, Ben Jonson, Tennyson, Browning, and many others — plus memorials to nearly every English poet of note and to some Americans, such as Longfellow and T. S. Eliot.

The Abbey is itself a lesson in English history. A church has stood on this site since at least AD 170; in the 8th century, it was a Benedictine monastery. The current early–English Gothic edifice, begun in the 13th century, took almost 300 years to build.

Guided tours are offered six times a day, except Sundays. Admission charge to the royal chapels and Poet's Corner. Broad Sanctuary SW1 between Victoria and Millbank (phone: 222-5152).

Houses of Parliament – The imposing neo-Gothic, mid-19th-century buildings of the Palace of Westminster, as it is sometimes called, look especially splendid from the opposite side of the river. There are separate chambers for the House of Commons and the House of Lords, and visitors are admitted to the Strangers' Galleries of both houses by lining up at St. Stephen's Entrance, opposite Westminster Abbey. Big Ben, the world-famous 13½-ton bell in the clock tower of the palace, which is illuminated when Parliament is in session, still strikes the hours. The buildings themselves are closed to the public, although Westminster Hall, with its magnificent hammer-beam roof, can be seen by special arrangement with a member of Parliment. The gold and scarlet House of Lords is also well-worth seeing. St. Margaret St., SW1 (phone: 219-3000).

Tate Gallery – London's fine art museum includes an impressive collection of British paintings from the 16th century to the dawn of the 20th century, as well as modern British and international art. Best of all are masterpieces by Turner, Constable, Hogarth, and Blake. The Turner collection is housed exclusively in the ultra-modern Clore Gallery extension. Millbank, SW1 (phone: 821-1313).

Soho – This area of London is full of character; lively, bustling, and noisy by day; indiscreetly enticing by night. Its name comes from the ancient hunting cry used centuries ago when the area was parkland. The hunting, in a way, still goes on, particularly by undercover detectives. Soho lacks the sophistication and glamour of its counterparts in Europe, but it's not all sleazy either. The striptease clubs vie for customers with the numerous restaurants serving moderately priced food (mostly Italian and Chinese). Soho offers a diversity of entertainments: Shaftesbury Avenue is lined with theaters and movie houses. Gerrard Street abounds with Chinese restaurants, and it is the place to go for Chinese New Year celebrations. London's liveliest fruit and vegetable market is on Berwick Street (if you shop here, never touch the produce, as the vendors will get furious). Frith Street is a favorite Italian haunt, the best place for a foaming cappuccino and a view of Italian TV at the *Bar Italia.* Old Compton Street has several good delicatessens, perfect places to buy a picnic lunch to take to Soho Square.

Covent Garden – Tucked away behind The Strand, Covent Garden was the site of London's main fruit, vegetable, and flower market for over 300 years. The area was immortalized in Shaw's *Pygmalion* and the musical *My Fair Lady* by the scene in which young Eliza Doolittle sells flowers to the ladies and gents emerging from the *Royal Opera House.* The *Opera House* is still there, but the market moved south of the river in 1974 and the Garden has since undergone extensive redevelopment. The central market building has been converted into London's first permanent late-night shopping center with emphasis on all-British goods. In the former flower market is the *London Transport Museum,* whose exhibits include a replica of the first horse-drawn bus and a steam locomotive built in 1866. Boutiques selling quality clothes for men and women are springing up all over, along with discos, wine bars, and brasserie-style restaurants. On weekends the whole area is packed with young people. One nice touch: Just to remind everyone of the Old Covent Garden, there are about 40 of the original wrought-iron trading stands from which the home-produced wares of English craftsmen and women are sold.

Bloomsbury – Well-designed squares — Bloomsbury Square, Bedford Square, Russell Square, and others — surrounded by pretty, terraced houses form this aristocratic district. Within its confines are the *British Museum* and the Centre of the University of London. The Bloomsbury group of writers and artists included Virginia Woolf, her husband Leonard Woolf, her sister Vanessa Bell and her husband Clive Bell, Lytton Strachey, E. M. Forster, Roger Fry, and John Maynard Keynes. Living nearby and peripheral to this central group were D. H. Lawrence, Bertrand Russell, and others. Unfortunately, none of the original buildings in Bloomsbury Square have survived, but the garden is still there, and nearby Bedford Square remains complete. Virginia Woolf lived at 46 Gordon Square before her marriage.

British Museum – One of the world's largest museums offers a dazzling array of permanent exhibitions — including the legendary Elgin Marbles (from the Parthenon) and the Rosetta Stone. In 1985 seven new sculpture galleries were opened, exhibiting some 1,500 Greek and Roman treasures. This magnificent collection includes two of the seven wonders of the ancient world: the Mausoleum of Halicarnassus and the Temple of Artemis at Ephesus. There is an equally impressive parade of temporary displays. The Egyptian and Mesopotamian galleries are especially stunning. The manuscript room of the British Library, within the museum, displays the original Magna Carta, together with the signatures of a great many famous authors — Shakespeare, Dickens, Austen, and Joyce among them — and numerous original manuscripts, including *Alice in Wonderland.* The British Library has an enormous collection, since every book published in Britain must be sent there. If you wish to use the library, consult a copy of the library's catalogue, stocked by major world libraries. Send in your requests with call numbers; many books often take 2 days to arrive from storage or other branches. The library also has a remarkable, gigantic Reading Room where so many of the world's great books — Marx's *Das Kapital,* for example — were written (access is limited; you must call or write to the museum's British Library Reference

Division for permission). Open Mondays through Saturdays, 10 AM to 5 PM; Sundays, 2:30 to 6 PM. Great Russell St. WC1 (phone: museum, 636-1555; library, 636-1544).

Oxford, Regent, Bond, and Kensington High Streets – London's main shopping streets include large department and specialty stores (*Selfridges, Debenhams, John Lewis, Liberty, D. H. Evans*), chain stores offering good value in clothes (*Marks & Spencer, C & A, British Home Stores, Littlewoods*), and scores of popular clothing chains (*The Gap, Laura Ashley, Benetton, Principles*).

Burlington Arcade – A charming covered shopping promenade dating from the Regency period (early 19th century), the arcade contains elegant, expensive shops selling cashmere sweaters (we recently saw some here that were 10-ply!), antique jewelry, and other expensive items. One entrance is on Piccadilly (the street, not the circus), the other near Old Bond St., W1.

Hyde Park – London's most famous patch of greenery (361 acres) is particularly well known for its Speakers' Corner at Marble Arch, where crowds gather each Sunday afternoon to hear impromptu diatribes and debates. Among the park's other attractions are sculptures by Henry Moore; an extensive bridle path; a cycle path; the Serpentine lake, where boats for rowing and sailing can be rented and where there's swimming in the summer; a bird sanctuary; and vast expanses of lawn.

Madame Tussaud's – The popularity of this wax museum (recently voted Britain's favorite indoor attraction) is undiminished by the persistent criticism that its effigies are a little bland, and visitors are quite likely to find themselves innocently addressing a waxwork attendant — or murderer. Madame moved to London from Paris in 1802, when she was 74, crossing the Channel with her waxwork effigies of heads that had rolled during the French Revolution. The current museum includes many modern and historical personalities and the gory Chamber of Horrors, with its murderers and hangmen. Open daily 10 AM to 5:30 PM; in July and August, 10 AM to 6 PM. Admission charge. Marylebone Rd., NW1 (phone: 935-6861).

London Planetarium – During 30-minute shows, visitors travel through space and time under a huge starlit dome. Interesting commentary accompanies the display. Guests can save money by purchasing a combination ticket to the planetarium and *Madame Tussaud's* — both at the same address, Marylebone Rd., NW1. There is also a Laserium show at 6 PM. Closed Mondays (phone: 486-1121).

THE CITY

The difference between London and the City of London can be confusing to a visitor. They are, in fact, two distinctly different entities, one within the other. The City of London, usually called only the City, covers the original Roman London. It is now the "square mile" financial and commercial center of the great metropolis. With a Lord Mayor (who only serves in a ceremonial capacity), a police force, and rapidly growing new developments, it is the core of Greater London. The governing council, the London Residuary Body, administers 32 boroughs including the City.

St. Paul's Cathedral – The cathedral church of the London Anglican diocese stands atop Ludgate Hill and is the largest church in London. This Renaissance masterpiece by Sir Christopher Wren took 35 years to build (1675-1710). Its domed exterior is majestic and its sparse decorations are gold and mosaic. The interior contains particularly splendid choir stalls, screens, and, inside the spectacular dome, the "whispering gallery," with its strange acoustics. Nelson and Wellington are buried below the main floor, and there is a fine statue of John Donne, metaphysical poet and dean of St. Paul's from 1621 to 1631 — he stands looking quite alive on an urn in an up-ended coffin which, typically, he bought during his lifetime and kept in his house. Wren himself was buried here in 1723, with his epitaph inscribed beneath the dome in Latin: "If you seek his monument, look around you."

A gorgeous monument it remains; though damaged by bombs during World War II, it became a rallying point for the flagging spirits of wartime Londoners. More recently, St. Paul's raised British spirits as the site for the wedding of Prince Charles and Lady Diana Spencer in July 1981. The Golden Gallery at the top of the dome, 542 steps from the ground, offers an excellent view of the city. St. Paul's Churchyard, EC4.

Old Bailey – This is the colloquial name for London's Central Criminal Court, on the site of the notorious Newgate Prison. Visitors are admitted to the court, on a space-available basis, to audit the proceedings and to see lawyers and judges clad in wigs and robes. Old Bailey, EC4 (phone: 248-3277).

Museum of London – Exhibits and displays depict London history from the Roman occupation to modern times. The museum is in the Barbican area and was opened in 1976. It includes Roman remains, Anglo-Saxon artifacts, Renaissance musical instruments, a cell from old Newgate prison, Victorian shops and offices, audiovisual recreation of the 1666 Great Fire, and the Lord Mayor's Golden Stage Coach. Closed Mondays. Open Tuesdays through Saturdays, 10 AM to 6 PM; Sundays, 2 to 6 PM. 150 London Wall, EC2 (phone: 600-3699).

Barbican Centre for Arts and Conferences – Served by underground stations Barbican, St. Paul's, and Moorgate, the Barbican, which opened in 1982, includes 6,000 apartments, the Guildhall School of Music and Drama, and the restored St. Giles' Church (built in 1390). The *Barbican* also features the 2026-seat *Barbican Hall* doubling as conference venue (with simultaneous translation system), and *Concert Hall* (*London Symphony Orchestra*); the 1166-seat *Barbican Theatre* (the *Royal Shakespeare Company*'s London performance venue); a 200-seat studio theatre; sculpture courtyard; art exhibition galleries; seminar rooms; three cinemas; two exhibition halls; a municipal lending library; restaurants and bars. Silk St. EC2 (phone: for guided tours and general information, 638-4141; recorded information, 628-2295; credit card bookings, 638-8891 or 628-8795; *Royal Shakespeare Company* performances, 628-3351.

Bank of England – Banker to the British government, holder of the country's gold reserves in its vaults, controller of Britain's banking and monetary affairs, "the Old Lady of Threadneedle Street" is the most famous bank in the world. Bathed in tradition as well as the mechanics of modern high finance, its porters and messengers wear traditional livery. Visits by appointment only. Threadneedle St., EC2 (phone: 601-4444).

Mansion House – The official residence of the Lord Mayor of London, containing his private apartments, built in the 18th century in Renaissance style. Permission to view the house may be obtained by writing, well in advance of your visit, to the Public Relations Office, City of London, Guildhall, London EC2P 2EJ. Mansion House St., EC4 (phone: 626-2500).

Lloyd's – A new, strikingly dramatic, futuristic building now houses the world's most important seller of international maritime and high-risk insurance. The exhibition and gallery overlooking the trading floor is open to visitors (advance booking required for groups) on weekdays from 10 AM to 4 PM. Corner of Lime and Leadenhall Sts., EC3 N7 DQ (phone: 623-7100, ext 3733).

Stock Exchange – The second largest exchange in the world can be seen from the viewing gallery on weekdays from 9:45 AM to 3:15 PM. Old Broad St., EC2 (phone: 588-2355).

The Monument – A fluted Doric column, topped by a flaming urn, was designed by Sir Christopher Wren to commemorate the Great Fire of London (1666) and stands 202 feet tall. (It was allegedly 202 feet from the bakery on Pudding Lane where the fire began.) The view from the top is partially obstructed by new buildings. Closed Sundays in winter. Admission charge. Monument St., EC3 (phone: 626-2717).

Tower of London – Originally conceived as a fortress to keep "fierce" Londoners at bay and to guard the river approaches, it has served as a palace, a prison, a mint, and an observatory as well. Today the main points of interest are the Crown Jewels; the White Tower (the oldest building), with its exhibition of ancient arms, armor, and torture implements; St. John's Chapel, the oldest church in London; the Bloody Tower, where the two little princes disappeared in 1483 and Sir Walter Raleigh languished from 1603 to 1616; an exhibit of old military weapons; Tower Green, where two of Henry VIII's queens — and many others — were beheaded; and Traitors' Gate, through which boats bearing prisoners entered the castle. The yeoman warders ("Beefeaters") still wear historic uniforms. They also give excellent recitals of that segment of English history that was played out within the tower walls. You can see the wonderful Ceremony of the Keys here every night at 9:30 PM; reserve tickets several months ahead. Closed Sundays in winter. Admission charge. Send a stamped, self-addressed envelope to: Resident Governor Constable's Office, HM Tower of London, EC3N 4AB (phone: 709-0765).

Fleet Street – Most native and foreign newspapers and press associations once had offices here — in the center of London's active newspaper world — and some still do, despite the growing exodus to more technologically advanced plants elsewhere. The street also boasts two 17th-century pubs, the *Cock Tavern* (#22) and the *Cheshire Cheese* (just off Fleet St. at 5 Little Essex St.) where Dr. Samuel Johnson held court for the literary giants of his day.

Johnson's House – In nearby Gough Square is the house where Johnson wrote his famous *Dictionary;* the house is now a museum of Johnsoniana. Admission charge. 17 Gough Sq., EC4 (phone: 353-3745).

Inns of Court – Quaint and quiet precincts house the ancient buildings, grounds, and gardens that mark the traditional center of Britain's legal profession. Only the four Inns of Court — Gray's, Lincoln's, and the Inner and Middle Temple — have the right to call would-be barristers to the bar to practice law. Especially charming is the still-Dickensian Lincoln's Inn, where young Dickens worked as an office boy. In its great hall the writer later set his fictional case of Jarndyce v. Jarndyce in *Bleak House.* John Donne once preached in the Lincoln's Inn chapel, designed by Inigo Jones. Both hall and chapel can be seen on weekdays if you apply at the Gatehouse in Chancery Lane WC2 (phone: 405-1393). Also lovely are the gardens of Lincoln's Inn Fields, laid out in 1618 by Inigo Jones. The neo-Gothic Royal Courts of Justice in the Strand, better known as the Law Courts, are home to the High Court and the Court of Appeal of England and Wales, which pass judgment on Britain's most important civil cases. The courts, unlike the Old Bailey, are closed to the public, but the vaulted, cathedral-like great hall is open to all.

OTHER LONDON ATTRACTIONS

Regent's Park – The sprawling 472 acres just north of the city center has beautiful gardens, vast lawns, a pond with paddleboats, and one of the finest zoos in the world. Crescents of elegant terraced homes border the park. Admission charge.

Camden Passage – This quaint pedestrian alleyway lined with antiques and specialty shops has an open-air market — pushcarts selling curios and antiques — on Tuesdays, Wednesday mornings, and Saturdays. Just off Upper St. in Islington, north of the city, N1.

Hampstead Heath – The North London bucolic paradise of wild heathland, meadows, and wooded dells is the highest point in London. Kenwood House, an 17th-century estate on the heath, is home to the Iveagh Bequest, a collection of art (Gainsborough, Rembrandt, Turner, and others; see "Museums" in *For the Mind,* DIVERSIONS) assembled by the first Earl of Iveagh. Lakeside concerts, both classical and jazz, are held on the grounds in summer (for details, call 734-1877).

Kew Gardens – Here are the Royal Botanic Gardens, with tens of thousands of trees and other plants (though the freak hurricane of October 1987 severely damaged hundreds of prize specimens and several sections of the gardens are still closed to the public). The gardens' primary purpose is to serve the science of botany by researching, cultivating, experimenting, and identifying plants. There are shaded walks, floral displays, and magnificent Victorian glass greenhouses — especially the Temperate House, with some 3,000 different plants, including a 60-foot Chilean wine palm. Open daily. Admission charge.

Portobello Road – This area is famous for its antiques shops, junk shops, and outdoor pushcarts; it is one of the largest street markets in the world. The pushcarts are out only on Fridays and Saturdays, which are the best and most crowded days for the market. Less well known is Bermondsey Market, Long Lane at Tower Bridge Rd. SE1, on Fridays from 7 AM on; this is where the antiques on Portobello Road or Camden Passage were probably purchased.

Victoria and Albert Museum – Born of the 1851 Exhibition, the museum contains a vast collection of fine and applied arts (probably the largest collection of the latter in the world) — an amalgam of the great, the odd, and the ugly. Especially delightful are the English period rooms. There are superb collections of paintings, prints, ceramics, metalwork, costumes, and armor in the museum, which also contains English miniatures and famous Raphael cartoons. The museum's new Henry Cole Wing (named after its founder) houses a broad selection of changing exhibitions as well as an interesting permanent display of printmaking techniques. Jazz concerts and fashion shows are held in the Italianate Pirelli Garden at the heart of the museum. Closed Fridays. Entry donation suggested. Cromwell Rd., SW7 (phone: 938-8500 or 938-8441 for recorded information).

Greenwich – This Thames-side borough is traditionally associated with British seapower, especially when Britain "ruled the waves"; it includes such notable sights as the *National Maritime Museum* on Romney Rd. (phone: 858-4422), containing superb exhibits on Britain's illustrious nautical past (see "Museums" in *For the Mind,* DIVERSIONS); the Old Royal Observatory, with astronomical instruments; *Cutty Sark,* a superbly preserved 19th-century clipper ship that's open to visitors; Royal Naval College, with beautiful painted hall and chapel; and Greenwich Park, 200 acres of greenery sloping down toward the river.

Richmond Park – The largest urban park in Britain is one of the few with herds of deer roaming free. (Hunting them is illegal, though this was once a royal hunting preserve established by Charles I.) It also has large oaks and rhododendron gardens. From nearby Richmond Hill there is a magnificent view of the Thames Valley.

Manor Houses – Six beautifully maintained historic homes are in Greater London. Notable for their architecture, antiques, grounds, and, in the case of Kenwood, an 18th-century art collection, these homes are all accessible by bus and subway: Kenwood House (Hampstead tube stop; open daily), Ham House (Richmond tube stop; closed Mondays; admission charge), Chiswick (Turnham Green or Chiswick Park tube stop; open daily; admission charge), Syon House (Gunnersbury tube stop; open daily; admission charge). Osterley Park House (Osterley tube stop; closed Mondays; admission charge), and Apsley House, home of the Duke of Wellington (149 Piccadilly; open Tuesdays through Sundays from 11 AM to 5 PM; admission charge).

Hampton Court Palace – On the Thames, this sumptuous palace and gardens are in London's southwest corner. Begun by Cardinal Wolsey in 1514, the palace was appropriated by Henry VIII and was a royal residence for 2 centuries. Its attractions include a picture gallery, tapestries, state apartments, Tudor kitchens, the original tennis court, a moat, a great vine (2 centuries old), gardens, and a maze. You can get there by bus, by train, or, best of all, in summer by boat from Westminster Pier. Open daily. Admission charge. East Molesex, Surrey (phone: 977-8441).

Freud Museum – This house was the North London home of the seminal psychiatrist after he left Vienna in 1938. His antiquities collection, library, desk, and famous couch are all on display. Open Wednesdays through Sundays, 12 to 5 PM. 20 Maresfield Gardens, NW3 (phone: 435-2002).

Highgate Cemetery – The awe-inspiring grave of Karl Marx in the new cemetery (open until 3:45 PM in winter, dusk in summer) attracts countless visitors, who can then stroll past the overgrown gravestones and catacombs of the not-so-famous in the old cemetery across the road (open until 3 PM in winter, dusk in summer). Entrance to the latter is by guided tour only (hourly). No admission charge. Highgate Hill, NW3.

Thames Flood Barrier – A massive and intriguing defense structure across the river at Woolwich Reach near Greenwich. Boats regularly leave Barrier Gardens Pier (or the riverside promenade nearby) for visits up close. Visitors are not allowed on the barrier itself, but audiovisual displays at the Visitor Centre, on the river's south bank just downstream, explain its background and illustrate the risk to London of exceptionally high tides. Open weekdays from 10 AM to 5 PM, weekends to 5:30 PM. Admission charge. Accessible from London by road, by river (from Westminster Pier to Barrier Gardens Pier), and by rail (to Charlton Station). 1 Unity Way, Woolwich (phone: 854-1373). While on the south bank, make a day of it with lunch at *Tides,* near the flood-defense system.

■ **EXTRA SPECIAL:** Windsor Castle is the largest inhabited castle in the world. It is the queen's official residence and was built by William the Conquerer in 1066 after his victory at the Battle of Hastings. Among the royal sovereigns buried here are Queen Victoria and her consort, Albert. Windsor looks like a fairy tale castle in a child's picture book: The huge Norman edifice looms majestically above the town; visitors feel awed and enchanted as they climb up the curving cobblestone street from the train station, past pubs and shops, toward Henry VIII's Gateway. The castle precincts are open daily, and there's a regular changing of the guard. The State Apartments, which can be toured when they're not in use, are splendidly decorated with paintings, tapestries, furniture, and rugs. There is also an exhibition of drawings by Leonardo da Vinci, Michelangelo, and Raphael, and a room displaying Queen Mary's dollhouse. Separate admission charges. For information, call 075-386-8286.

The castle is bordered by 4,800 acres of parkland on one side and the town on the other. While the town still has a certain charm, heavy tourism is beginning to have a deleterious effect. Across the river is Eton — considered by some to be the more attractive town — which is famous as home to the exclusive boys' school founded by Henry IV in 1440.

The train from Paddington stops right in the center of Windsor (travel time is 39 minutes), or there's a Green Line coach from Victoria (1½ hours).

Don't miss taking one of the many boat trips along the Thames to places like Marlow, Cookham, or Henley (where the first rowing regatta in the world was held in 1839). The Royal Windsor Safari Park is also southwest of London. Once a royal hunting ground, it's now a drive-through zoo, whose residents include baboons, camels, rhinos, cheetahs, and Bengal tigers. Be forewarned: In summer the park is very popular and traffic is bumper-to-bumper. An alternative would be to take the safari bus. Open daily. Admission charge.

For a spectacular side trip out of London, there is nothing quite like Oxford and Stratford-on-Avon, Shakespeare's birthplace — both of which can be seen in a 1-day organized bus tour. Otherwise you can choose one; the regular bus from Victoria Coach Station to Stratford (90 mi/144 km) travels via Oxford (65 mi/105 km), so you can catch a glimpse of the ancient colleges if you try hard.

Shakespeare's birthplace is still an Elizabethan town, and even if there's no time to see a play at the *Shakespeare Memorial Theatre,* the Tudor houses, with their overhung gables and traditional straw roofs, are a very pleasant sight. The poet's birthplace is a must, as is the grave at charming Holy Trinity Church. The Great Garden of New Place, said to contain every flower that Shakespeare mentioned in his plays, and Anne Hathaway's Cottage are both enjoyable.

Oxford is England's oldest university town; its fine Gothic buildings have cloistered many famous Englishmen. Most of the great colleges are on High Street (the High) or Broad Street (the Broad). See Queen's College, Christ Church, Trinity College, the Bodleian Library, and the marvelous *Ashmolean Museum of Art;* be sure to look in a bookstore too — and *Blackwell's* on Broad Street is one of the finest in the world. Students usually guide the university tours.

Another highly recommended day trip, less ambitious than Stratford and Oxford, is Cambridge, only 1 hour and 20 minutes from London by train. Cambridge is even more delightful than Oxford because the town takes full advantage of the River Cam. So don't fail to walk along "the Backs" — the back lawns of several colleges, leading down to the river; or better yet, rent a canoe or a punt, a flat-bottomed boat that is propelled by a long pole. (It's easier than it sounds.) The town has two parallel main streets that change their names every 2 blocks; one is a shopping street and the other is lined with colleges. Don't miss *Heffer's* on Trinity Street; it's the biggest branch of the best bookstore in Cambridge. Stroll through the famous colleges — King's, Trinity, Queens, Jesus, Magdalene, and Clare. King's College Chapel is a 15th-century Gothic structure that is a real beauty. Also see at least one garden and one dining hall.

The last of the notable attractions in the area, 5 miles (8 km) to the southwest of London, are the Savill and Valley gardens — 35 acres of flowering shrubs, rare flowers, and woodland. Open daily. Admission charge.

SOURCES AND RESOURCES

TOURIST INFORMATION: In the US, contact the British Tourist Authority, 40 W. 57th St., New York, NY 10019 (phone: 212-581-4700). The London Visitor and Convention Bureau is the best source of information for attractions and events once you get to London. Its Tourist Information Centre on the forecourt of Victoria British Rail Station is open Mondays through Saturdays, 9 AM to 7 PM; Sundays, 9 AM to 5 PM. Many leaflets and brochures on the city's landmarks and events are available; staff people are also on hand to answer questions on what to do, how, and when. Other branches are at the tube station at Heathrow Airport Terminals 1, 2, and 3, *Harrods* and *Selfridges* stores, and the Tower of London (Easter to October only). A Telephone Information Service is offered daily except Sundays, 9 AM to 6 PM (phone: 730-3488).

The British Travel Centre books travel tickets, reserves accommodations and theater tickets, and sells guidebooks. It offers a free information service, including an information hotline covering the whole of Britain. Open 9 AM to 6:30 PM, daily except Sundays. 4 Lower Regent St. (phone: 730-3400).

Among the most comprehensive and useful guidebooks to London are the *Blue Guide to London* (Benn); *London Round the Clock* (CPC Guidebooks); and *Londonwalks* (Holt, Rinehart & Winston). *Naked London* (Queen Anne Press) lists the city's more unusual, less visited sights for dedicated sleuths. The annual *Good Food Guide* ($16.95) and *Egon Ronay's* hotel and restaurant guide ($19.95) are available in most bookstores (prices slightly lower in Great Britain). For detailed information on 200 London museums, including maps, consult the *London Museums and Collections Guide* (CPC Guidebooks; $12). The *Shell Guide to the History of London* (Michael Joseph) bristles with exciting, accurate details on the city. *London: Louise Nicholson's Definitive Guide*

(Bodley Head) comes surprisingly close to the claims of the title. Susie Elms's *The London Theatre Scene* (Frank Cook) gives fair coverage of an essential aspect of the city.

London A-Z and *Nicholson's Street Finder,* inexpensive pocket-size books of street maps (available in bookstores and from most "newsagents"), are very useful for finding London addresses. Also helpful are maps of the subway system and bus routes and the *London Regional Transport Visitors Guide* — all available free from the London Transport information centers at several stations, including Victoria, Piccadilly, Charing Cross, Oxford Circus, and Heathrow Central, and at the ticket booths of many other stations (phone: 222-1234 for information).

The US Embassy is at 24–31 Grosvenor Sq. W. (phone: 499-9000).

Local Coverage – Of London's several newspapers, the *Times,* the *Sunday Times,* the *Observer* (Sundays only), the *Guardian,* the *Independent,* and the *Daily Telegraph* are the most useful for visitors. Also helpful are the weekly magazines *City Limits, Time Out,* and *New Statesman.* The *Evening Standard* is the paper most read by Londoners. For business news, read the *Financial Times* and the *Economist.*

Telephone – The area code for London is 01.

CLIMATE AND CLOTHES: Conventional wisdom has it that Britain doesn't have climate — it only has weather. The weather in London is often unreliable and unpredictable, with beautiful sun-drenched mornings regularly turning into dreary afternoons — and vice versa. The televised weather reports aren't much help — with their lugubrious references to possible "sunny intervals." Still, legends about incessant rain in London are exaggerated (though having a raincoat or umbrella is advisable). In fact, London has less rain than Rome, which is known as a sunny city. It's just that the rain is spread out over more days. The British capital is very much a city of the temperate zone. With occasional exceptions, summers tend to be moderately warm, with few days having temperatures above 75F (24C), and winters moderately cold, with few days dropping below 30F (–1C). Spring and autumn tend to be most comfortable, with little more than a sweater or light overcoat required (and a raincoat ready for contingencies). In this age of informality, no place still requires formal evening dress, though nightclubs and a few haute cuisine restaurants may insist that men wear jackets and ties and women be appropriately attired.

GETTING AROUND: Airports – London's two main airports are Heathrow, which opened its $20 million Terminal 4 in April 1986, and Gatwick, both of which handle international and domestic traffic. Heathrow is 15 miles and about 50 minutes from downtown; a taxi into town will cost about $30 to $40 unless you share: Two passengers to the West Central district, for example, pay about $15; three pay $12 each; four $11 each; and five (the maximum) $10 each. (When sharing, the cab meter is turned off and passengers agree beforehand on the order of destinations. There's a shared-cab rank at Terminal 1, and they're also available at London's 200 taxi stands.) The trip downtown can easily be made on the London underground (subway) from two stations at Heathrow: One serves terminals 1, 2, and 3; the other serves Terminal 4. Piccadilly Line trains leave every 4 to 10 minutes and operate between 5 AM (6:45 on Sundays) and 11:30 PM; the trip takes about 45 minutes. Stops are convenient to most of London's main hotel areas, and the line feeds into the rest of the London underground network. Airbus A1 and scheduled bus #767 run between Heathrow and Victoria (one of the city's main and most central railway stations); airbus A2 goes from the airport to Paddington (another major rail station); and airbus A3 connects with a third mainline station, Euston.

Gatwick Airport is 29 miles and 40 minutes from downtown; a taxi into the city will cost about $45. Gatwick is not connected to the underground system, but it does have its own rail station, with express trains leaving for Victoria Station every 15 minutes from 6 AM to 10 PM during the day and hourly through the rest of the night. The journey takes about 30 minutes and is by far the best transportation alternative between airport and town. Green Line bus 777 travels between Gatwick Airport and Victoria Station (phone: 668-7261 for information) and costs about $5.50 for the 70-minute trip. If you prefer the royal treatment, phone *Friends in London;* they'll meet you at the airport in a Rolls-Royce, whisk you to your hotel with champagne to sip on the way, and spend up to an hour answering questions about London. The service costs about $120 to $182, depending on the airport. Phone 240-9670; in the US, contact Wilson and Lake Tours International, 1 Appian Way, Suite 704-8, South San Francisco, CA 94080 (phone: 415-589-0352).

Boat – The *Riverbus,* a high-speed riverboat service run by the *Thames Line,* links east London to west, between Greenland Pier and Chelsea Harbour. It runs at approximately 15-minute intervals, weekdays from 7 AM to 10 PM, weekends from 10 AM to 6 PM, calling at 8 piers (phone: 941-6513).

For a leisurely view of London from the Thames, tour boats leave roughly every half hour from Westminster Pier at the foot of Westminster Bridge and from Charing Cross Pier on Victoria Embankment; they sail (summers only) upriver to Kew or downriver to the Tower of London, Greenwich, and the massive Thames flood barrier. An inclusive ticket covering a round-trip boat ride from central London to Greenwich and entry to the *National Maritime Museum,* the Old Royal Observatory, and the *Cutty Sark* clipper is available for about $10 from the British Travel Centre, the Victoria Tourist Information Centre, and at Charing Cross, Westminster, and Tower piers. A journey along Regent's Canal through north London is offered (summers only) by *Jason's Trip,* opposite 60 Blomfield Rd., Little Venice W9 (phone: 286-3428). For further information about these and other boat trips, contact the London Visitor and Convention Bureau's River Boat Information Service (phone: 730-4812).

Bus and Underground – The London public transport system gets sluggish now and then but is normally reasonably efficient. Its subway, called the underground or tube, and its bus lines cover the city pretty well, though buses suffer from traffic congestion, and the underground is notoriously thin south of the Thames. The tops of London's famous red double-decker buses do, however, offer some delightful views of the city and its people. The underground is easy to understand and to use, with clear directions and poster maps in all stations. Pick up free bus and underground maps from tourist offices or underground ticket booths. The fares on both trains and buses are set according to length of the journey. On most buses, conductors take payment after you tell them where you're going; some require that you pay as you enter. Underground tickets are bought on entering a station. Retain your ticket; you'll have to surrender it when you get off (or have to pay again), and bus inspectors make spot checks to see that no one's stealing a free ride. There are also Red Arrow express buses, which link all the mainline British Rail stations, but you'll have to check stops before you get on. With just a few exceptions, public transport comes to a halt around midnight; it varies according to underground line and bus route. If you're going to be traveling late, check available facilities. For 24-hour travel information, phone 222-1234.

A London Transport Visitor Travelcard can be purchased in the US from travel agents and *BritRail Travel International* offices in New York, Dallas, and Los Angeles, or in London from London Regional Transport travel information centers. The card provides unlimited travel on virtually all of London's bus and underground networks and costs about $4 for 1 day (available only in London), $12 for 3 days, $16 for 4 days, and $26 for 7 days. If purchased in the US, a book of discount vouchers for many of the city's sights is included; for purchase in London, a passport-size photo must be provided.

The underground links Heathrow, London's main airport, with central London. The Piccadilly Line zips from Piccadilly Circus to the airport in about 40 minutes. (The underground does not connect with Gatwick Airport but there are trains to Victoria Station every 15 minutes from 6 AM to 10 PM during the day and hourly through the rest of the night. The ride takes about 30 minutes.) Buses also link Heathrow with the city. For bus and underground information, call 222-1234.

One of the least expensive and most comprehensive ways to tour the city is to take *London Transport's* 2-hour unconducted bus tour, which leaves every hour from four sites: Marble Arch, Piccadilly Circus, Baker Street tube station, and Victoria Station (phone: 222-1234). Other guided bus tours are offered by *American Express* (phone: 930-4411), *Frames* (phone: 837-6311), *Harrods* (phone: 581-3603), and *Thomas Cook* (phone: 499-4000).

From June through October, a Tourist Trail ticket serves the three daily coach routes from London to Edinburgh (via Oxford, Stratford, Chester, and Windemere), London to Edinburgh (via Cambridge, Lincoln, York, and Durham), and London to York (via Stratford and Lincoln). The ticket allows unlimited travel on the luxury coaches for 15 days and costs $115, with a discount for holders of Britexpress coach passes. Tickets are available at Victoria Coach Station (phone: 730-0202).

Car Rental – Several agencies, including *Hertz,* at 35 Edgware Rd. W2 (phone: 402-4242), and *Avis,* 35 Headford Pl. SW1 (phone: 245-9862), are represented in London. *Swan National,* 305 Chiswick High Rd. W4 (phone: 995-4665), and *Thrifty,* 67 Brent St. NW4 (phone: 202-0093), are less expensive, or try *Guy Salmon Car Rentals,* 7-23 Bryanston St., Marble Arch (phone: 408-1255), or *Godfrey Davis,* Davis House, Wilton Rd. SW1 (phone: 834-8484). In addition, *Budget Rent-A-Car* has four reservation desks at Heathrow Airport terminals (phone: 759-2216 or 759-0069). And for riding in style, call *Avis Luxury Car Services* (phone: 235-3235) for chauffeur-driven Rolls-Royces and Daimlers.

Helicopter Flights – See London from the air. Sightseeing tours are available for about $230 (plus VAT) per hour. The standard flight includes an aerial tour of the major London sites; special views available on request. Make a reservation with *Cabair Air Taxis Ltd.,* Elstree Aerodrome, Borehamwood, Hertfordshire, WD6 (phone: 953-4411).

Taxi – Those fine old London cabs are gradually being supplemented with more "practical" models. It is one of life's great tragedies. Although dashboard computers in cabs are becoming increasingly more common, too, London cabbies seem generally pleased with the new system; the computers allow communication between driver and dispatcher so that the cab's home office knows who's empty and who's closest to a prospective fare. Riders will be happy to know that the computer also allows drivers to check on possible traffic problems and to obtain basic route instructions. Whether you end up in a computerized or "regular" cab, taxi fares in London are increasingly expensive (though you don't mind the price so much if you're riding in the big, old comfortable vehicles), and a 15% tip is customary. Tell a London cabbie where you're going *before* entering the cab. When it rains or late at night, an empty cab (identifiable by the glow of the roof light) is often very difficult to find, so it is wise to carry the telephone number of one or more of the cab companies that respond to calls by phone. There are also many "minicab" companies that do not respond when hailed on the street, nor do they use meters. They operate on a fixed fare basis between their home base and your destination, and you have to call their central office to book one. Hotel porters or reception desks usually can make arrangements to have such a car pick you up at a specified time and place. Be aware that taxi rates are higher after 8 PM (and sometimes even higher after midnight) and on weekends and holidays.

Several firms and taxi drivers offer guided tours of London; details are available at information centers. You can arrange for the personal services of a member of London's Guild of Guides by phoning the London Visitor and Convention Bureau's Guide Dept. (phone: 730-3450).

Train – London has 11 principal train stations, each the starting point for trains to a particular region, with occasional overlapping of routes. The ones you are most likely to encounter include King's Cross (phone: 278-2477), the departure point for Northeast England and eastern Scotland, including Edinburgh; St. Pancras (phone: 387-8537), for trains going north as far as Sheffield; Euston (phone: 387-7070), serving the Midlands, North Wales, including Holyhead and ferries for Dun Laoghaire, Ireland, Northwest England, and western Scotland, including Glasgow; Paddington (phone: 262-6767), for the West Country and South Wales, including Fishguard and ferries to Rosslare, Ireland; Victoria (phone: 928-5100), for Gatwick Airport and, along with Charing Cross Station (phone: 928-5100), for departures to Southeast England; and Liverpool St. Station (phone: 283-7171), for departures to East Anglia and to Harwich for ferries to the Continent and Scandinavia. All of these stations are connected via London's underground.

BritRail's Travelpak transportation program is intended for travelers who wish to venture out of London. It includes round-trip journeys from Gatwick or Heathrow airports to central London; the London Explorer; and a 4-day *BritRail* pass for unlimited train travel within Britain. Maps and timetables are also included. *BritRail* Travelpaks must be obtained before leaving the US from any North American *BritRail* office. Write *BritRail*, 630 Third Ave., New York, NY 10017 (phone: 212-599-5400).

Walking Tours – A trained guide can show you Shakespeare's London or that of Dickens or Jack the Ripper — many different themes are offered. These reasonably priced tours last up to 2 hours, generally in the afternoon or evening. *City Walks* offers a Sherlock Holmes Trail of Mystery and Whodunit Tour departing from the Baker St. underground station, Baker St. exit, on Tuesdays and Saturdays at 10:30 AM (phone: 937-4281). *Citisights* (phone: 739-2372) start from the *Museum of London,* London Wall. *Streets of London* (phone: 882-3414) start from various underground stations. *Londoner Pub Walks* (phone: 883-2656) start from Temple underground station (Dist. and Circle) on Fridays at 7:30 PM. *London Walks* (phone: 882-2763) provides tours leaving from a variety of points.

SPECIAL EVENTS: Dates vary marginally from year to year and should be checked — together with details — with the London Visitor and Convention Bureau. In late March/early April, the Oxford and Cambridge rowing "eights" race through the waters from Putney to Mortlake, an important competition for the two universities, whose respective teams practice for months beforehand. The world-famous *Chelsea Flower Show* takes place in late May. In early June you can enjoy the annual *Trooping the Colour,* England's most elaborate display of pageantry — a Horse Guards' parade, with military music and much pomp and circumstance — all in celebration of the Queen's official birthday. You can see some of the parade without a ticket, but for the ceremony you must book before March 1 by writing to the Brigade Major, Headquarters, Household Division, Horseguards, Whitehall SW1 (do not send money). The 2-week long *Greenwich Festival,* also held in June, includes mime and dance performances, poetry readings, a wide variety of music, and children's events. (For more details see "The Best Festivals" in *For the Mind,* DIVERSIONS.) Late June heralds the *Wimbledon Lawn Tennis Championship* — the world's most prestigious — complete with a member of the royal family presenting the prizes. The *City of London Festival* is held for 2½ weeks in July within the old city's square mile. It features choirs, orchestras, chamber groups, and leading soloists of international repute, along with a popular jazz program, dance, street theater, and a wide range of exhibitions. The *Henley Royal Regatta,* in early July (at Henley-on-Thames, a 1-hour train ride from London), is an international rowing competition and one of the big social events of the year. Watch from the towpath (free) or from within the Regatta enclosure (about $3 to $5). The *Royal Tournament,* a military pageant, takes place at Earl's Court for 3 weeks in July. The *Early Music Centre Festival* — featuring orchestral, chamber, and choral music — is usually held at the end of September through early October. October or November is the time for the *State Opening of Parliament; Guy Fawkes Day* is on November 5, when fireworks and bonfires mark the anniversary of the plot to blow up both houses of Parliament and King James I in 1605; and on the second Saturday in November, an inaugural procession for the new lord mayor, who rides in a golden carriage, followed by floats and bands. On the first Sunday in November, the *London-To-Brighton Veteran Car Run* features shiny antique autos undertaking the 50-mile drive.

MUSEUMS: Many of London's museums and galleries have no admission charge; others charge $1.50 to $3. A number of the museums are described in *Special Places.* Others of note include:

Bethnal Green Musem of Childhood – Impressive collection of more than 4,000 toys, including dolls and dollhouses, games, and puppets. Cambridge Heath Rd., E2 (phone: 980-3204).

Courtauld Institute Galleries – A remarkable collection of French Impressionist and post-Impressionist paintings. Somerset House, the Strand (phone: 580-1015).

Design Museum – The best examples of everyday items of today's consumer society are on display at this new museum in The Docklands. Tea kettles, tables and chairs, cars and bikes are all part of the permanent exhibit. Closed Mondays. Butler's Wharf, SE1 (phone: 403-6933).

Dickens's House – Manuscripts of early works, first editions, and personal memorabilia. 48 Doughty St., WC1 (phone: 405-2127).

Dulwich College Picture Gallery – Works by European masters in one of England's most beautiful art galleries. The college itself boasts such famous alumni as P.G. Wodehouse and Raymond Chandler. College Rd., SE21 (phone: 693-5254).

Institute of Contemporary Arts – Exhibitions of up-to-date British art, film, theater, manifesto. Closed Mondays. Nash House, Duke of York Steps. The Mall, SW1 (phone: 930-3647).

Jewish Museum – Art and antiques illustrating Jewish history. Woburn House, Upper Woburn Pl., WC1 (phone: 388-4525).

London Toy and Model Museum – This charming Victorian building houses a fine collection of model trains and mechanical toys. October House, 23 Craven Hill, W2 (phone: 262-7905).

Museum of Mankind – Ethnographic exhibitions. 6 Burlington Gardens, W1 (phone: 323-8043).

Musical Museum – One of Europe's most comprehensive collections of pianos and mechanical musical instruments, all in good working condition. 368 High St., Brentford, Middlesex (phone: 560-8108).

Natural History Museum – Exhibits of native wildlife, plants, fossils, and minerals. Cromwell Rd., SW7 (phone: 589-6323).

Sir John Soane's Museum – Its collection includes Hogarth's series *The Rake's Progress.* 13 Lincoln's Inn Fields, WC2 (phone: 405-2107).

Science Museum – The development of science and industry, including an "Exploration of Space" exhibit. Exhibition Rd., SW7 (phone: 589-3456).

Space Adventure – Aims to offer all the sights, sounds, and sensations of space travel. What is claimed to be Europe's — perhaps even the world's — largest flight simulator re-creates the movements of space travel, complemented by audiovisual effects. Step inside and experience countdown, launch, G-forces, interplanetary travel, reentry, and landing. Open daily. 92-94 Tooley Street (phone: 378-1405).

Theatre Museum – Britain's newest collection of theatrical material has been given its own home. Everything from circus to pop, grand opera to mime, straight theater to Punch and Judy and pantomime is here, as well as an excellent informal café/ restaurant on the main floor. 1E Tavistock St., WC2 (phone: 836-7891).

Wallace Collection – Sir Richard Wallace's fine collection of European paintings, sculpture, and armor. Hertford House, Manchester Sq., W1 (phone: 935-0687).

Whitechapel Art Gallery – An East End haven for modern art, including works by Moore, Hepworth, and Hockney. Includes exhibitions of contemporary British artists, along with third world and ethnic minority artists. 80 Whitechapel High St., E7 (phone: 377-0107).

SHOPPING: Stores are generally open from 9 AM to 5:30 or 6 PM, daily except Sundays, but the shops in the West End stay open until about 7:30 PM on Thursdays, and Covent Garden stays open until 7 PM Mondays through Saturdays. Although London is traditionally one of the most expensive cities in the world, savvy shoppers can still find good buys. The current lure, however, is more for fine British workmanship and style than very low prices.

The favorite items on any shopping list in London are cashmere and Shetland knitwear; fabric (tweeds, blends, men's suitings); riding gear; custom-made men's suits, shirts, shoes, and hats; shotguns; china and crystal; umbrellas; antiques; sporting goods; English food specialties (jams and marmalade, various blended teas, Stilton cheese, shortbread, and others). Books published by British houses, once a fine buy, are now far higher in price, and you probably will do better to buy the US editions. For secondhand books, though, London still hides treasures. The Charing Cross Road is a good place to start, and even pricey establishments may have basements with long out-of-print paperbacks in good condition, along with unfashionable Victoriana at very inexpensive prices. See Sheppard's *Directory of Second-Hand and Antiquarian Bookshops of the British Isles* for tips. But as all bargain hunters know, there is no substitute for your own voyages of discovery.

Devoted bargain hunters recognize that the best time to buy British is during the semiannual sales that usually occur from *Boxing Day* (December 26) through the early part of the New Year and again in early July. The Christmas/New Year's sales offer by far the best bargains in the city, and the crowds can be the equal of the low prices. Many stores remain open on *New Year's Day* to accommodate the bargain hunters, and the best-publicized single sale is that held by *Harrods* for 3 weeks beginning the first Friday in January. That opening day is an event in itself.

Be sure to take your passport when you shop, and always inquire about the VAT refund application forms when you make a purchase of over $25. The VAT (Value Added Tax) is a 15% surcharge payable at the sales counter, but foreign customers usually will be reimbursed for it at home. For purchases at any of the 10,000 shops displaying the London Tax Free Shopping logo, retailers issue vouchers that will be stamped by Customs when you leave the country and then posted to LTFS (21–24 Cockspur St., SW1); a refund is issued in local currency in as few as 4 days.

Though scattered about the city, the most appealing shops tend to center in the West End area, particularly along Bond, Oxford, South Molton, Regent, and Jermyn streets and Piccadilly. Other good areas are Kings Road, Kensington High Street, and Kensington Church Street, along with Knightsbridge and Covent Garden.

This is a city of markets; we have already described Portobello Road and Camden Passage in *Special Places.* Also worthy of note is Camden Lock Market (Camden High St. NW1) on Saturdays and Sundays for far-out clothes, leather items, antiques, and trinkets. The restored Jubilee Market on the south side of Covent Garden piazza is one of the largest indoor markets in the country. It features antiques and a flea market on Mondays; housewares, clothing, and jewelry Tuesdays through Fridays; and crafts on weekends. Or get up early on a Sunday morning and head for the East End to sample a typically English transport café ("caff") breakfast at *Fred's* (40 Aberfeldy St., E1) before tackling the very famous Petticoat Lane for food, inexpensive clothes, crockery, and even the proverbial kitchen sink.

The following stores are only a sampling of London's treasure houses.

Anderson and Sheppard – Reputable "made-to-measure" tailor for men's clothes. 30 Savile Row, W1.

Antiquarius – A good place for antiques. 135–141 King's Rd., SW3.

Aquascutum – Famous for raincoats and jackets for men and women. 100 Regent St., W1.

Laura Ashley – A relatively inexpensive women's boutique specializing in romantic styled skirts, dresses, and blouses. 183 Sloane St. SW1; plus other branches on Hampstead High St., Oxford St., 47–49 Brompton Rd., and Fulham Rd.

Asprey & Company – Fine jewelry, silver, and luggage. 165–169 New Bond St., W1.

Bates – A gentlemen's hatter, and our favorite. Check out the eight-part caps. 21A Jermyn St., SW1.

W. Bill Ltd. – Shetland sweaters, knit ties, argyle socks, club mufflers, gloves. 28 Old Bond St., W1.

Body Shop – More than 150 different beauty products (perfumes, soaps, hair and skin care products — famous for not having been tested on animals), from the worldwide chain that started in Brighton. 32 Great Marlborough St., W1.

Browns – Beautiful but expensive women's clothes, at 23–27 S. Molton St., W1; and a cosmetics branch on Hampstead High St., NW3.

Burberrys – Superb but expensive men's and women's raincoats and traditional clothes, and home of the now nearly ubiquitous plaid that began life as a raincoat lining. 18 Haymarket, SW1.

Church & Co. – Superior men's shoes. 58–59 Burlington Arcade, W1.

Conran's – Terence Conran has transformed the beautiful Michelin Building into a larger, more exclusive and expensive version of his well-known *Habitat* stores. However, the export of larger furniture and furnishings is probably better arranged through a New York branch. 77 Fulham Rd., SW3.

Jasper Conran – Top British designer clothes from Terence Conran's son. 37 Beauchamp Pl., SW3.

Crocodile – Chic and expensive women's clothes. 57 Beauchamp Pl., SW3.

Justin De Blank – Excellent specialty foods, especially cheese and take-out dishes. 42 Elizabeth St., SW1.

Dillon's – A good bookstore, London's most scholastic, partly owned by London University. 1 Malet St., WC1.

Emmanuel – Creative designers of Princess Diana's wedding dress and other clothing for members of the aristocracy. 10 Beauchamp Pl., SW3.

Feathers – French and Italian designer clothing for women. 40 Hans Crescent, SWI.

Fortnum and Mason – Boasts designer originals (usually of the rather dowdy variety), an appealing soda fountain-cum-restaurant, and one of the most elegant grocery departments in the world (where the staff wears striped morning trousers and swallow-tail coats). 181 Piccadilly, W1.

Foyle's – London's largest bookstore. 119 Charing Cross Rd., WC2.

Thomas Goode and Company – London's best china and glass shop first opened in 1827. Even if you don't plan to buy anything, you may want to look at their beautiful 1876 showroom. 19 S. Audley St., W1.

Grays Market – The hundreds of stalls here and at the annex down the street sell everything from antique playing cards to 16th-century furniture. 1-7 Davies Mews, W1 and 58 Davies St., W1.

Gucci – Outposts of the famous Italian fashion, leathergoods, and shoe manufacturer are found on Old Bond St., W1 and at 200 Sloan St., SW1.

Habitat – Up-to-the-minute designs with realistic prices for furniture and household goods. 156 Tottenham Court Rd., W1 and 206 King's Rd., SW3.

Halcyon Days – The best place to find authentic Battersea boxes — both antique and brand-new. 14 Brook St., W1.

Hamley's – The largest toy shop in the world. 200 Regent St., W1.

Harrods – The ultimate department store, although it does tend to be quite expensive. It has everything, even a mortuary and a bank, and what it doesn't stock it will get for you. The "food halls" particularly fascinate visitors, and traditional British merchandise is available in abundance. For those interested in trendy styles, it has the Way In boutique. Its annual January sale is legendary. Or splurge on a $320 tour of London in the store's vintage Rolls-Royce, the "Flying Lady." 87-135 Brompton Rd., Knightsbridge, SW1.

Douglas Hayward – A reputable made-to-order tailor. 95 Mount St., W1.

Heal's – Furniture and fabrics in the best modern designs. (It also has a popular lunch-meeting restaurant.) 196 Tottenham Court Rd., W1.

Jaeger – Tailored (and expensive) men's and women's clothes. 204 Regent St., W1.

Herbert Johnson – Men's hats. 13 Old Burlington St., W1.

Peter Jones – Another good, well-stocked department store, offering moderately priced, tasteful goods. Sloane Sq., SW1.

John Keil – Lovely, expensive antiques. 25 Mount St., W1.

Kent & Curwen – The place to buy authentic cricket caps, Henley club ties, and all sorts of similarly preppy raiment. 39 St. James's St., SW1 and 6 Royal Arcade, W1.

Kilkenny – All things Irish, including Paul Costelloe linen shirts and tweeds, hand knits, rugs, pottery, and Waterford crystal. 150 New Bond St., W1.

John Lewis – Another good department store, "never knowingly undersold" and particularly noted for its fabrics and household goods. 278 Oxford St., W1.

Liberty – Famous for print fabrics. Scarves and ties a specialty. 210 Regent St., W1.

Lillywhites – The whole gamut of sporting goods. Piccadilly Circus, SW1.

John Lobb – World-famous for made-to-order shoes that will last 10 years or more, with proper care. 9 St. James's St., SW1.

James Lock and Company – The royal hatters. They fitted a crown for the queen's coronation, and they'll happily fit you for your first bowler. 6 St. James's St., SW1.

Lord's – Tops in ties. 66–70 Burlington Arcade, W1.

Marks & Spencer – Locally nicknamed "Marks & Sparks," this chain specializes in clothes for the whole family, made to high standards and sold at very reasonable prices. Its linens and sweaters (especially cashmere and Shetland) are among the best buys in Britain. 458 Oxford St., W1 (and many other branches).

Moss Bros. – Men's formal attire (including dress tartans) and high-quality riding clothes for sale and hire. Bedford St., WC2.

Harvey Nichols – Lady Di's favorite luxury department store, specializing in women's haute couture. Knightsbridge, SW1.

Partridge Ltd. – Fine (but expensive) antiques. 144 New Bond St., W1.

Paul Smith – Britain's number one men's designer has two adjacent shops in Covent Garden. 43–44 Floral St., WC2.

James Purdey and Sons – The place to go for custom-made shotguns and other shooting gear. 57 S. Audley St., W1.

Reject China Shop – Good buys in slightly (invisible) irregular, name-brand china. Glassware, crystal, and flatware, too. For a fee, the shop will ship your purchases back home. 33–35 Beauchamp Pl., SW3 or 134 Regent St., W1.

Peter Robinson Top Shop – Young, trendy, moderately priced women's clothing. 216 Oxford St., W1.

Scotch House – Famous for Scottish cashmeres, sweaters, tartans — a wide selection of well-known labels. 2 Brompton Rd., SW1 and many branches.

Selfridges – This famous department store offers somewhat less variety than *Harrods,* but it has just about everything too — only a little less expensive. The extensive china and crystal department carries most patterns available. Oxford St., W1.

David Shilling – His one-off (a tad eccentric) hat creations always create a stir at Ascot. 44 Chiltern St., W1.

Shirin – The best designer cashmeres in town. 51 Beauchamp Pl., SW3.

Simpson's – Standard garments for men and women. 203 Eagle Pl., W1.

James Smith and Sons – The oldest umbrella shop in Europe. 53 New Oxford St., WC1.

Smythson of Bond Street – The world's best place to buy diaries, note pads, and calendars, many in Florentine marbled paper; also exotic ledgers in which to record odd data. 54 New Bond St., W1.

Sotheby Parke Bernet – The world's oldest art auctioneer, interesting to look at even if you don't plan to buy. They auction books, porcelain, furniture, jewelry, and works of art; at times, even such odd items as vintage cars and wines. Viewing hours are between 9:30 AM and 4:30 PM on weekdays, at Bloomfield Pl., W1 (phone: 493-8080).

Henry Sotheran Ltd. – Now incorporates *Cavendish Rare Books.* The large stock includes books on voyages and travel, Weinrab architectural books, finely bound literature, early English and continental titles. 2 Sackville St., W1.

Swaine, Adeney, Brigg, and Sons – Riding gear and their famous pure silk umbrellas. 185 Piccadilly, W1.

Turnbull and Asser – Men's shirts made to order. 71–72 Jermyn St., SW1.

Twinings – Tea — and nothing but — in bags, balls, and bulk. 216 Strand.

Waterstone's – Look for the maroon canopy of this huge chain of bookstores, whose instant success is due mainly to enterprising, well-informed staff and late, late hours (it's open till midnight in Edinburgh, for example). There are many branches, including ones on Hampstead High St., Old Brompton Rd., Charing Cross Rd., and High St., Kensington.

Wedgwood – Porcelain. 266 and 270 Regent St., W1.

Westaway and Westaway – Cashmere and Shetland wool kilts, sweaters, scarves, and blankets. 65 Great Russell St., WC1 and 29 Bloomsbury, WC1.

SPORTS AND FITNESS: Soccer (called football hereabouts) and cricket are the most popular spectator pastimes, but London offers a wide variety of other sports.

Cricket – The season runs from mid-April to early September. The best places to watch it are at *Lord's Cricket Ground,* St. John's Wood Rd. NW8 (phone: 289-1615), and *The Oval,* Kennington, SE11 (phone: 582-6660).

Fishing – Several public ponds right in London are accessible to the angler. A permit is required from Royal Parks Department, the Storeyard, Hyde Park, W2 (phone: 262-5484). The department can also provide information on where to fish.

Fitness Centers – *David Morgan Health Club,* 3 Hanover Sq. W1 (phone: 639-3353); *Pineapple Dance Studios,* 7 Langley St., WC2 (phone: 836-4004) and several other locations around town.

Golf – Aside from private clubs, for which membership is required, there are several municipal courses, some of which rent clubs. Try *Pickett's Lock Center,* Pickett's Lock La. N9 (phone: 803-3611), *Addington Court,* Featherbed La., Addington, Croydon (phone: 657-0281), and *Beckenham Place Park,* Beckenham, Kent (phone: 650-2292).

Wentworth, Virginia Water, Surrey (phone: Wentworth 2201), and *Sunningdale,* Ridgemount Rd., Sunningdale, Berkshire (phone: Ascot 21681), are the best courses within driving distance of London, and a letter from your home club pro or president (plus a polite phone call) may gain access to their courses.

Greyhound Racing – *Empire Stadium,* Empire Way, Wembley (phone: 902-1234), and others. There are evening races, so check the afternoon newspapers for details.

Horse Racing – Nine major racecourses are within easy reach of London, including *Epsom,* where the Derby (pronounced Darby) is run, and *Ascot,* where the Royal Ascot takes place — both in June. The flat racing season is from March to November; steeplechasing, August to June. Call the *Jockey Club,* 42 Portman Sq., W1 (phone: 486-4921) for information.

Horseback Riding – Try *Bathurst Riding Stables,* 63 Bathurst Mews, W2 (phone: 723-2813) and *Ross Nye's Riding Establishment,* 8 Bathurst Mews, W2 (phone: 262-3791).

Ice Skating – There is the *Queen's Ice Skating Club,* 17 Queensway, W2 (phone: 229-0172) and *Silver Blades Ice Rink,* 386 Streatham High Rd., SW16 (phone: 769-7861). Skates are for rent at both rinks.

Jogging – Most pleasant for running are Hyde Park, bordered by Kensington Rd., Park La., and Bayswater Rd.; Hampstead Heath, North London; and Regent's Park, bordered by Prince Albert Rd., Albany St., Marylebone Rd., and Park Rd.

Rugby – An autumn-through-spring spectacle at *Rugby Football Ground,* Whitton Rd., Twickenham (phone: 892-8161).

Soccer – *The* big sport in Britain. The local football season is autumn to spring and the most popular clubs are *Arsenal,* Highbury Stadium, Avenell Rd., N5 (phone: 359-0131); *Chelsea,* Stamford Bridge, Fulham Rd., SW6 (phone: 381-0111); *West Ham United,* Boleyn Ground, Green St., E13 (phone: 470-1325). As a spectator, be careful at games. Violence and overcrowding has been a major problem in recent years.

Swimming – Several excellent indoor public pools include: *Swiss Cottage Center,* Adelaide Rd., NW3 (phone: 586-5989); *Putney Swimming Baths,* 376 Upper Richmond Rd., SW15 (phone: 789-1124); and *The Oasis,* 167 High Holborn,, WC1 (phone: 836-9555). There is outdoor swimming in the Hyde Park Serpentine, and Hampstead Heath, in the summer.

Tennis – Aside from private clubs, more than 50 London public parks have tennis courts available to all. Get information from the London Visitor and Convention Bureau (phone: 730-3488).

THEATER: London remains the theater capital of the world, with about 50 theaters regularly putting on plays in and around its West End theater district and a vigorous collection of "fringe" theaters in various parts of town. Best known, and most accomplished, are the two main repertory theater companies — the *National Theatre Company* at the *National Theatre,* South Bank, SE1 (phone: 928-2252) and the *Royal Shakespeare Company* (*RSC*) at the Barbican Centre, The Barbican, EC2 (phone: 638-8891); from time to time both present dazzling versions of classics and new plays, although they sometimes trade on their reputations — the *National* mistaking dreariness for realism, and the *RSC,* staidness for reliability. (For reliable critical reviews, consult the *Observer*'s Michael Ratcliffe and the *Guardian*'s Michael Billington.) Shakespearean plays are also performed in summer at the open-air theater in Regents Park, NW1 (phone: 935-5756).

In the West End, presentations include both first class and second-rate drama and comedy, a fair sprinkling of farce (for which the British have a particular fondness), and the best of imports from the American stage. Visitors from the US often find attending theater in London easier — and somewhat less expensive — than it is at home. Except for the small handful of runaway box office successes, tickets are usually available for all performances. In most cases, you can reserve by telephone, but tickets must be picked up well before curtain time. *The West End Theatre Society* operates a half-price ticket kiosk in Leicester Square. It posts a list of shows for which remaining seats may be purchased at half-price on the day of the performance. Ticket agencies that offer tickets to all shows, charging a small commission, include *Keith Prowse & Co.* (phone: 437-8976), *Dial-A-Ticket* (phone: 930-8331/2), and *Ace Tickets* (phone: 223-8173).

The quality of London's fringe theater varies from accomplished and imaginative to amateurish. Theaters in pubs are at the *King's Head* in Islington, 115 Upper St., N1 (phone: 226-1916), and at the *Bush,* in the *Bush* hotel, Shepherd's Bush Green (phone: 743-3388). The *Riverside Studios* in Hammersmith, Crisp Rd., W6 (phone: 748-3354), the *Tricycle Theatre* at 269 Kilburn High Rd., NW6 (phone: 328-8626), and the *New End Theatre* in Hampstead, 27 New End, NW3 (phone: 435-6054), have established reputations for the excellence of their productions, which often move on to the West End and sometimes even directly to Broadway. Also keep an eye on the *Donmar Warehouse* for major transfers from the *Edinburgh Festival Fringe* (features an enormous collection of amateur films) or for exciting avant-garde companies such as *Cheek by Jowl;* at 41 Earlham St., Covent Garden (phone: 836-3028). Lunchtime fringe theater presentations offer an alternative to sightseeing on rainy days.

A visit to *St. Martin's* is now tantamount to seeing a major London landmark, as it houses the late Agatha Christie's *The Mousetrap;* transferred from the *Ambassador* next door, there's a fresh cast each year, and it's been running since 1952 — the longest run ever in nightly theater. The play is an exciting, tantalizing, and mildly frightening mystery-thriller. If you tell whodunit, you are ruined socially. West St., Cambridge Circus, WC2 (phone: 836-1443).

Check *Time Out* or *City Limits* for comprehensive lists, plot summaries, and theater phone numbers. Daily papers list West End performances.

Show tours to London are very popular in season; see your travel agent for package deals. If you want to reserve specific tickets before you arrive in London, there are agencies in the US that keep a listing of what's on in London. For a service charge of about $5 per ticket, they will sell you the best seats only. Contact *Edwards & Edwards,* One Times Square Plaza, New York, NY 10036 (phone: 212-944-0290 or 800-223-6108) or *Keith Prowse & Co.,* 234 W. 44th St., New York, NY 10036 (phone: 212-398-1430 or 800-223-4446).

Note: For more London theatre listings see "The Performing Arts" in *For the Mind,* DIVERSIONS.

CINEMA: London may not be the equal of Paris as a movie metropolis, but many say it's stronger when it comes to very good, little-known films, often from the US or Commonwealth countries. British film is startling in both similarities and contrasts to that of the US. In Great Britain, Chaplin, Hitchcock, and Laughton are regarded as English. The *British Film Institute* (21 Stephen St., Soho; phone: 255-1444) has an incomparable British and international film library, administers the National Film Archive, contains first class documentation and filmographic material, and publishes the monthly *Film Bulletin* and the quarterly *Sight and Sound,* as well as running the *London Film Festival* (November), which takes place in the *National Film Theatre* (*NFT*) on the South Bank near Waterloo Station and Bridge (phone: 928-3232). Membership is required at the *NFT* (about 65¢ a day or $15.70 for a year), but it's well worth it for its two cinemas; wide variety of old and new British, US, and international movies; good film bookshop; and eating facilities. The success of the *NFT*'s *London Film Festival* in past years testifies to the high caliber of London's critics, who include the *Evening Standard*'s Alexander Walker, the *Guard-*

ian's Derek Malcolm, the *Financial Times*'s Nigel Andrews, and, above all, the *Observe*r's Philip French; the *Film Festival* appoints one of them as its *supremo* of the year.

As with the theater, there are big divisions between West End and fringe (or independent) cinema. The West End strives for probable box-office smash hits, so watch out for long lines at Friday openings, and head for early showings, some of which begin not long after noon. Monday admission prices are less expensive. For sheer luxury, the *Curzon Mayfair* on Mayfair's Curzon St. in the West End is unbeatable for both low budget and commercial films (phone: 499-3737). The most exciting film fare usually is found in independents, and sometimes you must travel to remote parts of London to see outstanding work in an almost empty cinema. If independent films interest you, check what's showing in places like *Everyman* at Hampstead (phone: 435-1525); the *Museum of London* at London Wall near Barbican (phone: 600-3699); the luxurious, comfortable *Barbican Cinema* (phone: 638-8891); *Screen* on Baker St. (phone: 935-2772); *Screen on the Green* at Islington (phone: 226-3520); and *Screen on the Hill* at Hampstead (phone: 435-3366). All feature late-night showings and children's screenings on Saturdays (as do the *Barbican and NFT*). In some cases you may have to pay moderate club fees. Most British cinemas now ban smoking in the auditorium. Telephone the theaters for show times.

Alongside the *National Film Theatre* is the new *Museum of the Moving Image* that, among other sites, shows fine movies sidestepped by big distributors. The museum has over 50 exhibits and over 1,000 clips from various old and recent films and TV shows. There's also a good bit of movie memorabilia, including Charlie Chaplin's hat and cane. Open Tuesdays through Saturdays, 10 AM to 8 PM; Sundays, 10 AM to 6 PM; closed Mondays. Admission charge (phone: 928-3535).

MUSIC: Few cities offer a greater variety of musical performances — both classical music and the many varieties of popular music. For classical music, the focus of attention is the *South Banks Arts Center* with its three concert halls — *Royal Festival Hall, Queen Elizabeth Hall,* and the *Purcell Room* — (phone: 928-3191 for all three); the *Barbican Hall,* home of the *London Symphony Orchestra* (phone: 628-8795); and the *Royal Albert Hall,* Kensington Gore, SW7 (phone: 589-8212). The latter is the home of the *Henry Wood Promenade Concerts,* or more simply, the *Proms,* an 8-week series of orchestral concerts that has been a popular feature of the London summer scene (July to September) for decades. Tickets are inexpensive, because the Proms came into being to give students and other people who are not affluent an opportunity to dress up and be part of a grand musical event. The performances are tops (some broadcast live by the BBC), and the SRO audience is large and enthusiastic. *Wigmore Hall,* Wigmore St., W1 (phone: 935-2141), is best known for recitals of chamber music and performances by some of the world's most accomplished instrumental and vocal soloists. Concerts are also often held in the dignified, splendid setting of St. John's Church, Smith Sq., SW1 (phone: 222-1061). The *London Symphony Orchestra* performs at *Barbican Hall,* The Barbican, EC2. During the summer outdoor concerts are given at Kenwood, Crystal Palace, and Holland Park, and bands play in many of London's parks.

Operas at *Covent Garden Royal Opera House,* Floral St., WC2 (phone: 240-1066), are internationally famous. The *English National Opera Company* offers its performances at the *London Coliseum,* St. Martin's La., WC2 (phone: 836-3161). The best of London's ballet performances are presented at *Covent Garden,* the *Coliseum,* and at *Sadler's Wells,* Roseberry Ave., EC1 (phone: 837-1672), as well as at *The Place,* 17 Duke Rd., WC1 (phone: 387-0161), home of the *London Contemporary Dance Theatre* and the *London School of Contemporary Dance.* Details about concert, recital, opera, and ballet performances are listed in the arts sections of the Sunday newspapers.

Although superstar musicians and vocalists usually appear in the city's larger halls, good live popular music can be heard in London's music pubs. Among the best of them are the *Dublin Castle,* 94 Parkway, NW1 (phone: 485-1773); *King's Head,* 4 Fulham High St., SW6 (phone: 736-1413); *Kensington,* 54 Russell Gardens, Holland Rd., W14 (phone: 603-3245); and *Hope and Anchor,* 207 Upper St., N1 (phone: 359-4510).

NIGHTCLUBS AND NIGHTLIFE: It used to be that they virtually rolled up the sidewalks in London at 11 PM. Now there's a very lively and often wild nightlife, including nightclubs, jazz clubs, historical feast entertainments, and gambling casinos. Some wind up around midnight; most go on until well into the early morning hours. In Covent Garden and still-trendy-after-all-these-years Chelsea, particularly along King's and Fulham roads, are fashionable pubs, wine bars, and restaurants. Two nightclubs with floor shows are the *London Room,* Drury La., WC2 (phone: 831-8863) and *Omar Khayyam,* 177 Regent St., W1 (phone: 734-7675). There is dancing at both. There's a show but no dancing at *Madisons,* Camden Lock, Chalk Farm Rd., NW1 (phone: 485-6044). The best jazz clubs are *Ronnie Scott's,* 47 Frith St., W1 (phone: 439-0747), and *The 100 Club,* 100 Oxford St., W1 (phone: 636-0933). For jazz and a slice, try *Pizza Express,* 10 Dean St., W1 (phone: 437-9595), with live music nightly except Mondays. *Dingwalls,* Camden Lock, Chalk Farm Rd., NW1 (phone: 267-4967) and the *Town and Country Club,* 9 Highgate Rd., NW5 (phone: 267-3334), have a continually changing program of much-acclaimed performers of rock music.

For a special treat, London offers the *medieval banquet,* complete with traditional meals served by costumed waiters and waitresses. Menus resemble those of traditional Elizabethan feasts, and there is period music, horseplay, occasional mock sword fights, Shakespearean playlets, and other light entertainment. Try *Tudor Rooms,* 17 Swallow St., W1 (phone: 240-3978); *Beefeater,* St. Katherine Dock, E1 (phone: 408-1001); and *Shakespeare's Tavern,* Blackfriars La., EC4 (phone: 408-1001).

The disco scene is a rapidly changing one, and many places — such as expensive and exclusive *Annabel's,* 44 Berkeley Sq., W1 (phone: 629-3558) — are open only to members. Clubs of the moment include: the *Hippodrome,* Charing Cross Rd., WC2 (phone: 437-4311); *Stringfellows,* 16–19 Upper St. Martin's La., WC2 (phone: 240-5534); *Legend's,* 29 Old Burlington St., W1 (phone: 437-9933); *Crazy Larry's,* Lots Rd., SW10 (phone: 352-3518); *Xenon,* 196 Piccadilly, W1 (phone: 734-9344); *Tramp,* 40 Jermyn St., SW1 (phone: 734-0565), where the chic social set meets to disco (members only); and *Limelight,* at 136 Shaftesbury Ave., W1 (phone: 434-0572). A smart addition to the West London night scene is the *Broadway Boulevard* club in Ealing, particularly convenient for guests at the Heathrow hotels (phone: 840-0616).

Female impersonators regularly perform at the *Union Tavern,* 146 Camberwell New Rd., SE5 (phone: 735-3605); *Jongleurs Cabaret Club* at the *Coronet,* Lavender Gardens, SW11 (phone: 585-0955); and *Black Cap,* 171 Camden High St., NW1 (phone: 485-1742). Phone for details.

BEST IN TOWN

CHECKING IN: Visitors arriving in London between early spring and mid-autumn without hotel reservations are in for an unpleasant adventure. For many years now, there has been a glaring shortage of hotel rooms in the British capital during the prime tourist season, which each year seems to begin earlier and end later. (For a small fee, the Tourist Information Centre at Victoria Station Forecourt, or at the underground station in Heathrow, will try to help you locate a room.) This fact, plus years of general inflation and the difficulty of finding suitable hotel staff are largely responsible for often excessive hotel charges, generally out of keeping with other costs in Britain. As a rule, expensive hotels do not include any meals in their prices; moderate and inexpensive hotels generally include continental breakfasts. Prices — with bath, English breakfast, VAT, and a 10% service charge sometimes included — are $130 to $250 and up for a double room in an expensive hotel; $85 to $120 in moderate; and $60 to $80, inexpensive. All telephone numbers are in the 01 area code unless otherwise indicated.

As an alternative to conventional hotel accommodations, it's easy to stay in one of 500 private homes and apartments through a program called "Your Home in London." These vary from a single in a bed-and-breakfast establishment for $30 a night to a 2-bedroom apartment in central London for $140 a night. For information, in the US phone 301-269-6232. If you are particularly interested in service flats (apartments with close-to-traditional hotel services — mostly daily maid service), contact *Eastone Overseas Accommodations,* 6682 141st Lane N., Palm Beach Gardens, FL 33418 (phone: 407-575-6991) or *Hometours International,* 1170 Broadway, New York, NY 10001 (phone: 212-689-0851 or 800-367-4668). Service flats range from the very elegant to the very modest at a bed-and-breakfast establishment.

Blakes – A row of Victorian townhouses has been transformed into this 55-room refurbished hotel, where many employees wear warrior-like uniforms. There's black antique furniture on the lower level, while the upper floors are decorated in pale gray and pastels. The bathrooms are made of marble, and there are black and red silk sheets in many rooms. Facilities include a first rate restaurant, a glass-enclosed courtyard, FAX machine, laundry service, and 24-hour room service. 33 Roland Gardens, SW7 (phone: 370-6701). Expensive.

Basil Street – A relic with a reputation for graceful, old-fashioned service and beautiful antique furnishings to match. It draws a faithful international clientele who, if they can reserve one of its 94 rooms, prefer staying here to patronizing any of the modern, impersonal, newer hotels. It has a women's health club and sits just down the street from *Harrods.* 8 Basil St., SW3 (phone: 581-3311). Expensive.

Beaufort – A tranquil and very elegant hotel comprised of two Victorian houses in Beaufort Gardens, the heart of fashionable Knightsbridge. It offers 28 comfortable and attractively decorated rooms, each with a plenitude of facilities: stereo/cassette player; TV set; direct-dial phone; hair dryer; magazines and books; a decanter of brandy; and even a teddy bear for the youngsters. Breakfast is brought on a tray each morning. Convenient to restaurants and shops (*Harrods* is just around the corner). 33 Beaufort Gardens, SW3 1PP (phone: 584-5252). Expensive.

Berkeley – Remarkably understated, this 150-room hotel manages to preserve its impeccably high standards while keeping a low profile. Soft-spoken service complements the tastefully lavish, traditional English decor. There are also a health club and a new gymnasium. Wilton Pl., SW1 (phone: 235-6000). Expensive.

Britannia – Mahogany furniture, velvet armchairs, rooms painted in colors you might choose at home — all very tasteful and solid, despite the anonymity of the spacious foyer with the pretentious chandeliers. This is where the American Embassy — also on the square — often puts up visiting middle-ranking State Department officials. Now part of the Inter-Continental chain. Grosvenor Sq., W1 (phone: 629-9400). Expensive.

Brown's – As English as you can get, retaining pleasing, quaint, Victorian charm, and not at all marred by heavy, sturdy furniture or the somewhat hushed atmosphere. Strong on service. If it's an English tea you're after, this is the place (tie and jacket required). Dover St., W1 (phone: 493-6020). Expensive.

Cadogan Thistle – Very comfortable, older, 69-room place, redolent of Edwardian England. Oscar Wilde was arrested here, and Lillie Langtry, who was having an affair with the Prince of Wales (later Edward VII), lived next door. The furniture and decor are original, but modern conveniences are offered as well. 75 Sloane St., SW1 (phone: 235-7141). Expensive.

Capital – Only a stone's throw from *Harrods,* this 45-room hotel has recently been beautifully refurbished. All rooms have air conditioning, color TV sets, radios, and elegantly appointed bathrooms. There is an intimate lounge, a lively bar, and an excellent French restaurant (see *Eating Out*). 22 Basil St., Knightsbridge, SW3 (phone: 589-5171). Expensive.

Cavendish – Famous as the *Bentinck,* the hotel run by Louisa Trotter (in real life, Rosa Lewis) in the TV series "The Duchess of Duke Street," this modern replacement offers one of the most attractive locations in central London, near Piccadilly. Its 253 rooms are comfortable, though hardly elegant. Jermyn St., SW1 (phone: 930-2111). Expensive.

Chesterfield – In the heart of Mayfair and near Hyde Park, this small, recently rebuilt Georgian mansion has a certain exclusive elegance. Its 113 bedrooms are thoroughly modernized and well equipped. Amenities include a restaurant, a wood-paneled library, and a small bar that opens onto a flower-filled patio. 35 Charles St., W1 (phone: 491-2622). Expensive.

Churchill – Inside, a turn-of-the-century mood is reflected in the discreet decor. This is a well-run, efficient place, with a pleasant restaurant and a snack room that serves the best bacon and eggs in London. Very popular with Americans. Portman Sq., W1 (phone: 486-5800). Expensive.

Claridges – This plush 209-room outpost for visiting royalty, heads of state, and other distinguished and/or affluent foreigners is an Art Deco treasure. The line of chauffered limousines outside the main entrance sometimes makes traffic seem impenetrable. Wrought-iron balconies and a sweeping foyer staircase help provide a stately setting for one of London's most elegant hostelries. Liveried footmen serve afternoon tea. Brook St., W1 (phone: 629-8860). Expensive.

Connaught – A touch too sober for high livers; a trifle too formal for the rough-and-ready crowd. But there aren't many hotels left in the world that can rival it for welcome, elegance, and comfort — particularly in its luxurious suites. Unfortunately, though, the restaurant's food is losing its once high reputation. Carlos Pl., W1 (phone: 491-0688). Expensive.

Dorchester – Closed while undergoing an ambitious £70-million renovation, this Mayfair classic is scheduled to reopen by spring of 1990 — more luxurious than ever. Park La., W1 (phone: 629-8888). Expensive.

Dorset Square – Set in a lovely garden (formerly Thomas Lord's cricket grounds) in the heart of London, this Georgian country house is one of the city's most elegant and charming hotels. Guests can choose from the 37 rooms in the main hotel or truly treat themselves by staying in one of the suites across from the hotel. The suites include sitting and drawing rooms and are elegantly furnished with marble bathrooms, working fireplaces, and antiques. The Royal Suite features a grand piano. 39–40 Dorset Sq., NW1 6QN (phone: 723-7874). Expensive.

Draycott – The 26 rooms here are each distinctively decorated. While there's no restaurant, there is a breakfast room and 24-hour room service. Staying here is like living in a fashionable London townhouse. 24–26 Cadogan Gardens, SW3 (phone: 730-6466). Expensive.

Drury Lane Moat House – Near the theater district and fashionable Covent Garden, this 153-room hotel is ultra-modern with a cool, sophisticated decor. There's an elegant bar, and lunch is served on the terrace. 10 Drury La., High Holborn, WC2 (phone: 836-6666). Expensive.

Dukes – Despite its modest size (only 39 rooms and 18 suites), this is an establishment where nobility and prestige shine through. The exterior has an exquisite Edwardian façade, there's a peaceful flower-filled courtyard, and some suites are named for former dukes. A virtual total reconstruction has produced accommodations of great taste and warmth, and the snug location, down a quiet cul-de-sac, does its best to seem authentically British. Piccadilly, Buckingham Palace, Trafalgar Square, Hyde Park Corner, and the shops of Bond Street and the Burlington Arcade are all within walking distance. 35 St. James's Pl., SW1A (phone: 491-4840 or 800-223-5581). Expensive.

Fenja – In this new first class Victorian townhouse, each of the 14 bedrooms is named for a writer or artist with associations in the locality (Jane Austen, Hilaire Belloc, Henry James, John Singer Sargent). There are private bath/showers with luxury fittings, erystal decanters filled with liquor, and terrycloth bathrobes. Rooms service is also available 24 hours a day. 69 Cadogan Gardens, SW3 (phone: 589-7333). Expensive.

Forty-Seven Park Street – One of our most cherished secrets, these "service flats" are a favorite of folks who are staying for more than a few days; the accommodations are small apartments perfect for extended visits. Breakfast alone is worth crossing the Atlantic, since "room service" here is provided by the elegant *Le Gavroche* restaurant, which flourishes downstairs. Owned by the Roux Brothers, who also own the restaurant (and the *Wayside Inn* out in Bray), the furnishings are luxurious in the best English taste. The location, roughly between Hyde Park and Grosvenor Square, is also ideal. 47 Park St., W1Y (phone: 491-7282). Expensive.

Gatwick Hilton International – Part of the airport's expansion program, this 552-room hotel provides much-needed accommodations for the ever-increasing number of visitors using the Gatwick gateway. Connected to the terminal by an enclosed walkway; facilities include many services for business travelers: bars, health club, 24-hour room service, and more. Gatwick Airport (phone: 0293-518080). Expensive.

Grosvenor House – This 472-room grande dame facing Hyde Park has a health club, a swimming pool, some interesting shops, the much-lauded *Pavilion* restaurant, the *Park Lounge,* which serves traditional afternoon teas, and the exclusive *Crown Club* on the top floor for members only — usually businesspeople who require special services — with rooms, suites, a lounge, and complimentary extras. Park La., W1 (phone: 499-6363). Expensive.

Halcyon – A $15-million restoration brought back to glamour the two Belle Epoque mansions that are the foundations of this property. Some of the guestrooms feature four-poster beds and Jacuzzis, plus all modern conveniences. Its *Kingfisher* restaurant is among London's best. 81 Holland Park, W11 (phone: 727-7288). Expensive.

Hilton International Kensington – A bit out of the way, this modern hotel offers a great deal of comfort at prices below those of most Hiltons. Services include a restaurant, piano lounge, a Japanese restaurant, and a lavish brunch on Sundays. Rooms are well designed and well maintained. 179–199 Holland Park Ave. (phone: 603-3355). Expensive..

Hyde Park – The only hotel set in Hyde Park, this establishment — formerly apartments in Victorian times — played host to Rudolph Valentino in the 1920s and George VI and Queen Elizabeth in 1948. Today it continues to offer some of the finest accommodations in London. The spacious bedrooms are furnished with lovely antique furniture, modern bathrooms, and mini-bars. Some rooms also have spectacular views of the park. Marble stairs, chandeliers, and beautiful plants are all part of the hotel's elegant decor. Visit the *Park Room* overlooking Hyde Park for delicious meals, including breakfast and afternoon tea. There is also a grill room, drawing room, and business lounge, which provides international communication services. 66 Knightsbridge, SW1 Y7LA (phone: 235-2000). Expensive.

Inn on the Park – Don't be deceived by the modern exterior; everything is traditional (and wonderful) within. A fine example of the superb service routinely offered by members of the Four Seasons chain, the rooms are comfortable, tastefully furnished, and spacious. The breakfast buffet is delightful; the restaurant is first rate. Hamilton Pl., Piccadilly, W1 (phone: 499-0888). Expensive.

Inter-Continental – Smack-dab in the middle of the West End, right on Hyde Park Corner, with windows overlooking the route of the Royal Horse Guards as they go cantering off for the Changing of the Guard each morning. Its 490 well-proportioned rooms are equipped with refrigerated bars. Modern and comfortable, particularly the Art Deco *Le Soufflé* restaurant, but the location is the chief lure. 1 Hamilton Pl., Hyde Park Corner, W1 (phone: 409-3131). Expensive.

London Hilton International – Well situated off Hyde Park Corner, near shopping and theater, this contemporary high-rise offers comfortable accommodations (445 rooms) and spectacular views of the park and the city. Special attention to excecutives includes a multilingual switchboard, secretarial staff, office equipment, and private dining rooms. There's every conceivable service, plus 3 restaurants — the *Roof,* with a view; the *Polynesian;* and the new *British Harvest,* serving organically grown traditional British produce; plus a disco, and a snack bar. 22 Park La., W1 (phone: 493-8000). Expensive.

London Marriott – Close to the American Embassy and West End shopping, Marriott's recent refurbishment has transformed this modern hotel. It's bright and busy, and it has everything — lounge, bar, two restaurants, shops, 227 very comfortable rooms, and good service. Grosvenor Sq., W1 (phone: 493-1232). Expensive.

Londonderry – This deluxe hotel overlooks Hyde Park; it recently reopened after an extensive tasteful refurbishment. Its 3 penthouse suites and 150 rooms feature a French Mediterranean decor, a theme echoed in both the *Isle de France* restaurant and adjoining bar. Park La., W1 (phone: 493-7292). Expensive.

Mayfair Holiday Inn – Renovation hasn't damaged the hotel's all-pervading Regency style, unusual for this chain. Sitting in London's highly prestigious property belt, it has 192 rooms, the à la carte *Berkeley* restaurant, and an evening pianist in the *Dauphin* cocktail bar. 3 Berkeley St., W1 (phone: 493-8282). Expensive.

Le Meridien – Formerly the *New Piccadilly,* located between the Royal Academy and Piccadilly Circus, this hotel recently underwent a £16-million refurbishment, though the rooms remain mostly modest in size and rather dark. A lofty, Edwardian marble entrance hall leads to the 284 rooms and 24 suites. The *Terrace* restaurant, on the second floor, seats 140 under a glass roof, and the space beneath the hotel has been transformed into the biggest health club in Europe. There is also a less formal restaurant, a bar, and a cocktail lounge. Piccadilly, W1 (phone: 734-8000). Expensive.

Montcalm – A smaller, elegant hotel that has a lovely façade, a warm-toned and understated interior, and top-notch service. Its 114 rooms have all the usual comforts, and many of its 6 suites are especially luxurious. There's a bar, and in *Les Célébrités* restaurant, chef Gary Houiellbecq brings to bear all the skills he employed at the acclaimed *Compleat Angler* in Marlow. Great Cumberland Pl., W1 (phone: 402-4288). Expensive.

Mountbatten – The life and times of Earl Mountbatten of Burma is the theme throughout this refurbished, wonderfully eccentric hotel's public rooms, all with exhibitions of various mementos from India. All 127 rooms feature Italian marble bathrooms, satellite color TV and in-house movies, while 7 suites have whirlpool baths. Monmouth St., Covent Garden, WC2 (phone: 836-4300). Expensive.

Park Lane – If you don't mind the noise of the city streets, the site of this hotel, in the heart of the West End, is appealing. Some of the 324 rooms have views of Green Park across the street. Piccadilly, W1 (phone: 499-6321). Expensive.

Ritz – The fellow who was heard to mutter snootily "Nobody stays at the *Ritz* anymore" was off-base, especially since the recent renovation restored much of the old luster and certainly got the "bugs" out. With 130 rooms, it now ranks among London's finest stopping places, and it's hard to find another hotel in London with more elegant surroundings. Tea is a particularly pleasant experience; the dining room is equally splendid, with its elegant interior columns, opulent ceiling frescoes, and the view of Green Park. There was a time when the quality of the cuisine wasn't quite equal to the decor, but that has largely changed. Piccadilly, W1 (phone: 493-8181). Expensive.

Royal Court – Clean, comfortable, and recently refurbished, the hotel has a courteous, helpful staff, at the head of London's fashionable Chelsea shopping and residential district and within quick, easy reach of the rest of the action in town. Sloane Sq., SW1 (phone: 730-9191). Expensive.

Royal Horseguards Thistle – This 262-room hotel overlooks the Thames with views of the South Bank. Recently modernized, it is a good base for those interested in the changing of the Buckingham Palace guard, Westminster Abbey, and the Houses of Parliament. Riverside rooms have balconies and there's a pleasant terrace. 2 Whitehall Ct., SW1 (phone: 839-3400). Expensive.

Savoy – A favorite of film and theater performers, some of whom check in for months. Still one of London's top addresses, it's a 200-room hotel with armies of chambermaids and porters to keep things running, and the reputation of its famous *Savoy Grill* has been restored through a beautiful resuscitation of the decor and a revitalization of the kitchen. The Thames Suites are the most beautiful accommodations in the entire city. The Strand, WC2 (phone: 836-4343). Expensive.

Selfridges – Just behind the department store of the same name, modern in both furnishings and tone, with a refreshing, unaffected courtesy. Convenient for shopping. Orchard St., W1 (phone: 408-2080). Expensive.

St. James's Club – For about $480 ($320 per year thereafter) and an introduction by a member, you can join this exclusive residential club in the heart of London (though you don't need to bother for your first stay). Guests have full use of club suites. Some of the best food in the city is served in the downstairs dining room. 7 Park Pl., SW1 (phone: 629-7688). Expensive.

Stafford – In a surprisingly quiet side street close to the city center, this is where many American television and newspaper organizations often lodge visiting correspondents to give them efficient, friendly, British small-hotel management at its best. Owned by Cunard, which has refurbished the 62 rooms in smashing style. 16 St. James's Pl., SW1 (phone: 493-0111). Expensive.

White House – A very big hotel, converted from apartments, in a quiet spot near Regents Park. Modernized and efficiently run, its facilities include a coffee shop and wine bar. Albany St., NW1 (phone: 387-1200). Expensive.

White's – What used to be three 19th-century merchant bankers' private homes have been transformed into one of London's most charming small hotels. It has personality that the larger ones lack — a cobbled forecourt, a glass-and-iron-covered entryway, even a wood-paneled writing room where tea is served in the afternoon. Choose a room at the front, overlooking Hyde Park, and take breakfast on the balcony. Lancaster Gate, W2 (phone: 262-2711). Expensive.

Abbey Court – In the Notting Hill Gate area near Portobello Market, this elegant hotel has 24 bedrooms of various sizes, all with private bath, TV sets, hair dryers, and trouser presses. The flowers on display in the common areas are especially lovely. Breakfast is served in the room, and 24-hour room service is also available. No restaurant. 20 Pembridge Gardens, W2 (phone: 221-7518). Expensive to moderate.

Alexander – This South Kensington hotel in an agreeable off-Brompton retreat — a peaceful place to escape from the world — was recently tastefully refurbished. Its elegant yet unpretentious decor includes fine fabrics, tiled bathrooms for each of the 40 bedrooms, and somc four poster beds In-house movies are offered, along with 24-hour room service and a garden for fine weather. 9 Sumner Place, SW7 (phone: 581-1591). Expensive to moderate.

Number Sixteen – Housed in four adjoining townhouses, this is a delightfully comfortable hotel with an accent on personal service. The 32 rooms feature fresh flowers and full bath/showers. Continental breakfast is served in all rooms, some of which have terraces leading to the conservatory and garden. There is a small bar. No children under 12 are permitted to stay in the hotel. 16 Sumner Place, SW7 (phone: 589-5232). Expensive to moderate.

Durrants – This elegant Regency-style hotel has a splendid location behind the Wallace Collection and is only a few minutes' walk from the shopping on Oxford Street. It has been family-run for over 50 years and all 95 rooms have retained their character while being kept comfortably up to date. George St., W1 (phone: 935-8131). Moderate.

Ebury Court – A small hotel with smallish but cozy rooms and an intimate atmosphere (the owners dine with guests in the restaurant). Its faithful clientele testifies to its comfort, suitability, and "country house in London" touches. Hard to beat — all things considered — in a town where hotel prices tend to be unreasonable. Fewer than half of the 39 rooms have a bath or shower. 26 Ebury St., SW1 (phone: 730-8147). Moderate.

Embassy House – Over a million dollars has just been spent on renovating this Edwardian building on a wide tree-lined street in Kensington. It is very near the *Albert Hall* and all the main museums and an easy walk from *Harrods* and Hyde Park. There are 68 rooms, and although the decor is modern, there are elaborate high ceilings and elegant staircases. There's also a restaurant and bar. 31 Queens Gate, SW7 (phone: 584-7222). Moderate.

Harewood – This small, modern hotel is well maintained by a pleasant and efficient staff. Some of its 93 rooms have private terraces. Restaurant and wine bar. Harewood Row, NW1 (phone: 262-2707). Moderate.

Pastoria – In the very center of the West End, near all theaters, this pleasant, comfortable little hotel has 52 rooms, most with baths and TV sets; it has a bar and a restaurant. St. Martin's St., WC2 (phone: 930-8641). Moderate.

Ramada Inn – Completely refurbished, redecorated, and generally upgraded, all 510 rooms have private bath and in-house movies. There's also a comfortable Victorian pub. Lillie Rd., SW6 (phone: 385-1255). Moderate.

Wilbraham – A charming, authentic, 52-room bed-and-breakfast establishment, just around the corner from *Harrods* and Sloane Square. 1 Wilbraham Place, SW3 (phone: 730-8296). Moderate.

Claverley – Named the "Best Bed and Breakfast Hotel" in 1987 by the British Tourist Authority, this establishment, in the middle of London, has 36 rooms, 30 of which have private baths; some rooms have four-poster beds. All bedrooms have floral decor, and each has a heated towel rack in the bathroom. In the reading room guests are invited to help themselves to newspapers, coffee, tea, and cookies. A fine British breakfast is served in the morning. 13 Beaufort Gardens, SW3 (phone: 589-8541). Moderate to inexpensive.

Blanford – This pleasant bread-and-breakfast establishment has 33 rooms, decorated in pastel greens and pinks, each with a color TV set and direct dial telephone. A British-style breakfast is served in the morning, and complimentary newspapers are available. 80 Chiltern St, W1M 1PS (phone: 486-3103). Inexpensive.

Delmere – Nearly 200 years old, this lovely hotel was designed by architect Samuel Pepys Cockerell, the student of Benjamin H. Latrobe, who designed the south wing of the Capitol building in Washington, DC. The hotel has 40 rooms equipped with private showers or baths, hair dryers, and the makings for tea and coffee. There is also a bar and a restaurant, *Le Sous Sol,* where food is grilled on stones — hot slabs of Matterhorn rock. The staff, mostly from Holland, is very friendly. Paddington station, where trains depart to Bath and South Wales, is a mere 5-minute walk away. 130 Sussex Gardens, Hyde Park, W2 1UB (phone: 706-3344). Inexpensive.

Diplomat – Small, with no restaurant and only 24 rooms — all with baths — it is nonetheless comfortable, friendly, and affordable. In Belgravia at 2 Chesham St., SW1 (phone: 235-1544). Inexpensive.

Hotel la Place – A fine bed-and-breakfast establishment with 24 rooms, including private baths, TV sets, and king-size or two double beds; some rooms also have mini-bars. British breakfast is served in the morning. 17 Nottingham Place, W1M 3FB (phone: 486-2323). Inexpensive.

Hotel 167 – Redecorated in 1987-88, this bed-and-breakfast establishment is housed in a brick Victorian building and has been lovingly and uniquely furnished with both modern and antique pieces, along with a color scheme of soft grays and creams. Double rooms include private bath, and singles have baths opposite the rooms. The hotel is conveniently located near good shopping on Fulham Road, the *Victoria and Albert Museum,* and the Gloucester Road underground station. 167 Old Brompton Rd., SW5 OAN (phone: 373-0672). Inexpensive.

Observatory House – This bed-and-breakfast establishment was once owned by Count Dangerville of France, and many members of royalty have slept here since then, including the exiled King of Yugoslavia. In 1988 the hotel was renovated in Victorian decor, and all 27 rooms have private showers, color TV sets, telephones, trouser presses, and tea and coffee supplies. Some rooms are for nonsmokers only. 37 Hornton St., Kensington, W8 7NR (phone: 937-1577). Inexpensive.

Winchester – Near Victoria Station, this bed-and-breakfast establishment is in an old townhouse with a Victorian-style façade; the interior was completely refurbished with, among other facilities, modern bathrooms and new furniture. The 18 bedrooms include showers, color TV sets, and radios. Guests are treated to an English breakfast in the morning. 17 Belgrave Rd., Victoria, SW1 (phone: 878-2972). Inexpensive.

YMCA – This relatively new "Y" could be the best and most comfortable low-cost hotel in the middle of London. The 168 adequate, tidy rooms, are complemented by a series of facilities not often found in hotels — including squash courts, a gym, billiard room, swimming pool, and sauna. Close to the *British Museum* and Oxford Street shopping district. Men and women of all ages are welcome, and triple rooms are available. 112 Great Russell St., WC1 (phone: 636-8616). Inexpensive.

EATING OUT: Few London restaurants were ever known for the excellence of their cuisine — and some visitors of times past might call that a charitable understatement. But there's been a notable transformation in recent years. While restaurants offering really good English cooking — and not simply "chips with everything" — are still not easy to find (some are listed below), there has been a veritable explosion of good foreign restaurants in town (some of which are also noted below).

A meal for two will cost about $150 at a restaurant listed as very expensive; $100, expensive; $50 to $75 is moderate; and $30 and under inexpensive. Prices do not include drinks, wine, or tips. Most London restaurants have developed the continental habit of automatically adding a service charge to the bill, so make certain you're not tipping twice. Reservations are necessary in all restaurants below. All telephone numbers are in the 01 area code unless otherwise indicated.

Le Gavroche – Probably the best French restaurant in London and, according to *Guide Michelin,* one of the best in the entire country, with three stars to its credit (only one other establishment in Britain has received such a high rating). The food is classic French; many of the dishes by those chefs extraordinaires, the Roux brothers, qualify as genuine masterpieces. Reserve well in advance. Closed weekends. 43 Upper Brook St., W1 (phone: 408-0881). Very expensive.

L'Arlequin – A tiny establishment that offers unusual and innovative Gallic cooking by proprietor Christian Delteil, who reputedly makes the best sorbets in London. Closed weekends. 123 Queenstown Rd., SW8 (phone: 622-0555). Expensive.

Bibendum – Located on the second floor of the former Michelin building, renovated by Sir Terence Conran of the *Habitat* chain of stores. Chef Simon Hopkinson's good taste ranges beyond the classic French dishes. Michelin House, 81 Fulham Rd., SW3 (phone: 581-5817). Expensive.

Le Bistroquet – A chic, French-ish brasserie. Ceiling fans rotate and spiky-haired waiters and waitresses whiz between tables as fish dishes cooked in parchment are cut open, filling the air with the scent of capers and fresh fennel. Open daily. 273–275 Camden High St., NW1 (phone: 485-9607). Expensive.

Capital Hotel Restaurant – The elegant, comfortable, small dining room in this hotel near *Harrods* offers well-chosen, admirably prepared French dishes. Some discriminating Londoners consider it the best place to eat in town. Shuns the aren't-you-lucky-to-get-a-table attitude flaunted by some other better London restaurants. 22–24 Basil St., SW3 (phone: 589-5171). Expensive.

Cavaliers' – Sue and David Cavaliers' restaurant, south of the river in upwardly mobile Battersea, serves French fare prepared by an accomplished British chef. Closed Sundays and Mondays. 129 Queenstown Rd., SW8 (phone: 720-6960). Expensive.

Connaught – Very dignified and very proper, this restaurant, with one Michelin star, has a fine reputation for both its cuisine and elegant service. Frankly, these guys carry stuffy to sometimes excessive lengths, but it's hard not to appreciate the masterful culinary performance. The setting — lots of rich paneling and crystal chandeliers — matches the distinction of the menu. Closed weekends. At the *Connaught* hotel, Carlos Pl., W1 (phone: 499-7070). Expensive.

Gay Hussar – Among the best Hungarian restaurants this side of Budapest, its substantial menu offers a varied selection: chicken ragout soup, goulash, roast pork, and lots more. The food here is extremely filling as well as delicious. Informal atmosphere, with a regular clientele drawn from London's newspaper and publishing world. Closed Sundays. Make reservations early. 2 Greek St., W1 (phone: 437-0973). Expensive.

Guinea Grill – This unimposing restaurant substitutes displays of its fresh food — steaks, chops, fresh vegetables — for a menu. It's as good as it looks, cooked with care. A name change was contemplated at press time. Closed Sundays. 26 Bruton Pl., W1 (phone: 629-5613). Expensive.

Hilaire – Once serving only superb French food, this spot now also offers impressive English dishes, imaginatively prepared and charmingly served. Closed Saturdays for lunch and Sundays. 68 Old Brompton Rd. (phone: 584-8993). Expensive.

Leith's – A fine continental restaurant in an out-of-the-way Victorian building northwest of Kensington Gardens, this spot serves very good entrées, hors d'oeuvres, and desserts as part of a fine *prix fixe* dinner. An excellent vegetarian menu is also available, and its wine selection is very good. Open daily for dinner. 92 Kensington Park Rd., W11 (phone: 229-4481). Expensive.

Lichfield's – Fish and game are the chef's specialties here: Try galantine of quail, for example, set on a bed of apples and bathed in Calvados sauce. As an alternative to the train, take a boat to Richmond from Westminster Pier, lunch at *Lichfield's,* and walk it off on Richmond Green. Open Tuesdays, Fridays, and Sundays for lunch; Tuesdays through Saturdays for dinner. 13 Lichfield Terrace, Sheen Rd., Richmond (phone: 940-5236). Expensive.

Poons – This Cantonese restaurant has built a reputation for good, authentic cooking and specializes in top-quality fish dishes and wind-dried food. You can even watch the chefs at work through a glass partition. Closed Sundays. 41 King St., WC2 (phone: 240-1743) and 4 Leicester St., WC2 (phone: 437-1528). Expensive.

Rue St. Jacques – Lavishly decorated with huge gold-framed mirrors. The food here is marked by rich cream sauces. A delicous vegetarian main course is also available. Pricey, but well worth it. The formality stretches to jacket-and-tie requirement and a doorman who provides parking service. Closed Saturdays for lunch and Sundays for dinner. 5 Charlotte St., W1 (phone: 637-0222). Expensive.

Savoy Grill – Renowned as a celebrity-watching ground, but actually inhabited mostly by a male, business clientele. Although the menu features some classic French dishes, the English grills and roasts are its specialty. The lovely, newly restored decor resembles a luxurious ship's dining room (first class, natch) of 50 years ago. Perfect for after theater. Closed Sundays. At the *Savoy* hotel, The Strand, WC2 (phone: 836-4343). Expensive.

Tante Claire – Run by chef Pierre Koffman and his wife, Annie, this newly expanded establishment has been awarded two Michelin stars as well as many other honors. While fish dishes are the chef's specialty, everything — especially the duck, calves liver, and *Pied de Cochon farci aux Morilles* (pig's foot stuffed with foie gras and mushrooms) — is excellent. The *prix fixe* lunch is a remarkably good value at around $20. Closed weekends. 68 Royal Hospital Rd., SW3 (phone: 352-6045). Expensive.

Wilton's – Good food, skillfully prepared, elegantly served in a plush, rather formal Victorian setting. Game, fish, oxtail, steak and kidney pie — what the best of English cooking can be all about. Closed Sundays and 3 weeks in July/August. 55 Jermyn St., SW1 (phone: 629-9955). Expensive.

Langan's Brasserie – Still trendy after all these years, and still a popular haunt for celebrities. Ask for a downstairs table and take your time studying the lengthy menu. Reservations necessary. 1 Stratton St., W1 (phone: 491-8822)). Expensive to moderate. *Langan's Bistro* serves slightly simpler and less expensive dishes prepared in the same style. Both closed Sundays and Saturdays for lunch. 26 Devonshire St., W1 (phone: 935-4531). Moderate.

Bloom's – A large restaurant specializing in Jewish food, *Bloom's* has a bright and bustling atmosphere, a bit like the dining room of a large hotel, with waiters who almost — but not quite — throw the food at you. The popular take-out counter serves up the best hot salt beef (like corned beef) sandwiches in town. House wine is Israeli. Closed Friday evenings and Saturdays. 130 Golders Green Rd., NW11 (phone: 455-1338) and 90 Whitechapel High St., E1 (phone: 247-6001). Moderate.

Bombay Brasserie – At lunchtime there is an Indian buffet; at dinner, classic cooking from the Bombay region. Parsi dishes, rarely found outside of India itself, are also included. And the setting is lovely, with lots of banana plants, wicker chairs, and ceiling fans. Popular with both the American and British show-biz colonies. Open daily. Courtfield Close, Courtfield Rd., SW7 (phone: 370-4040). Moderate.

Camden Brasserie – The daily specials are posted on a board outside this restaurant, located in an increasingly fashionable part of town. Among the selections are meat and fish grilled over an open fire. 216 Camden High St., NW1 (phone: 482-2114). Moderate.

Chuen Cheng Ku – At this huge restaurant in the heart of Chinatown, the overwhelming majority of the clientele is Chinese. The specialty here is dim sum, served every day until 6 PM. Also try the pork with chili and salt, duck webs, steamed lobster with ginger, and shark fin soup. 17 Wardour St., W1 (phone: 734-3281). Moderate.

Hungry Horse – This is the place to discover what a properly made English meat pie and Yorkshire pudding should taste like, as well as other English goodies. Don't be put off by having to pass under an archway and climb down a flight of stairs to get there — if anything, the inside looks a touch too tidy. Closed Sundays for dinner. 196 Fulham Rd., SW10 (phone: 352-7757). Moderate.

123 – One block away from the Japanese Embassy, this is where the staff eats, a sure sign of quality. But be warned that there are two menus, one in English, the other in Japanese, and they are vastly different. The latter offers a far more extensive array of sashimi. Ask the waiter to translate. Closed weekends. 27 Davies St., W1 (phone: 409-0750). Moderate.

Porters – A very English eatery in Covent Garden, famous for its home-cooked pies — steak, mushroom, and vegetable are a specialty. The kitchen, bar, and basement are even more spacious since the restaurant was completely redecorated. Open daily. 17 Henrietta St., WC2 (phone: 836-6466). Moderate.

Le Routier – The English equivalent of a truck stop, with an interesting location overlooking the craft workshops and canal at Camden Lock. Inside you'll find a brasserie atmosphere, with specialties of the day chalked up on a blackboard. Very popular for lunch on weekends. Open daily. Commercial Pl., Chalk Farm Rd., NW1 (phone: 485-0360). Another branch, closed weekends, is at Foley St., W1 (phone: 631-3962). Moderate.

La Ruelle – Just off Kensington High Street, this small French restaurant recently introduced an imaginative selection of vegetarian dishes to its classic menu. Closed weekends. 14 Wright's La., W8 (phone: 937-8525). Moderate.

Shezan – A quiet, brick and tile restaurant just below street level that prepares some very fine Pakistani food. Specialties include marinated-in-yogurt *murg tikka Lahori* (chicken cooked in *tandoori,* or clay ovens) and *kabab kabli* (minced spiced beef). An enthusiastic staff will explain the intricacies of tandoori cooking, help with your order, and lavish excellent service upon you. Closed Sundays. 16 Cheval Pl., SW7 (phone: 589-7918). Moderate.

Sweetings – A special London experience, this traditional fish restaurant is one of the great lunchtime attractions in London's financial district. You may have to sit at a counter with your lobster, brill, or haddock — but it will be fresh and perfectly prepared. Weekday lunchtime only; no reservations, so expect a wait. 39 Queen Victoria St., EC4 (phone: 248-3062). Moderate.

Tate Gallery Restaurant – Who would expect one of London's better restaurants to be in a fine art museum? But there it is — a genuine culinary outpost (leaning toward French cuisine) with a very good wine list. Not just another meal between the masterpieces. Lunch only. Closed Sundays. Tate Gallery. Millbank, SW1 (phone: 834-6754). Moderate.

La Trattoria dei Pescatori – A busy atmosphere pervades this restaurant, whose decor includes a boat, terra cotta tiles, copper pans, and chunky ceiling beams. The menu is enormous, with trout, halibut, salmon, shrimp, turbot, and lobster appearing in several guises. A typical specialty is *misto dei crostacei alla crema* — Mediterranean prawns, scallops, shrimp, and mussels sautéed with onions and herbs, simmered in fish stock and Asti, with a touch of cream. Closed Sundays. 57 Charlotte St., W1 (phone: 580-3289). Moderate.

Treasure of China – In a landmark Georgian building, this restaurant is a leader in original Peking and Szechwan cuisine. Owners Tony Low and Roger Norman offer a selective daily menu as well as superb banquets celebrating Chinese festivals. Open daily. 10 Nelson Rd., SE10 (phone: 858-9884). Moderate.

Tuttons – One of the few restaurants in London that serves food all day, it's a very popular and lively brasserie in a former Covent Garden warehouse and a handy snack spot for theatergoers. Open from 10 AM to 11:30 PM Sundays through Thursdays; 10 AM to midnight Fridays and Saturdays. 11 Russell St., WC2 (phone: 836-1167). Moderate.

Wheeler's – One of the chain of London seafood restaurants with the same name, this is the original and the best of the lot. It's an old-fashioned, narrow establishment, on three floors, which specializes in the many ways of preparing Dover sole, most of them delicious. The oyster bar on the ground floor is our favorite perch. Closed Sundays. Duke of York St. at Apple Tree Yard (phone: 930-2460). Moderate.

Chiang Mai – Thai restaurants are a rarity in London. This one is easy to spot since it's the only eatery in Soho (and probably the whole of Britain) with a carved wooden elephant poised on the sidewalk. The menu offers such dishes as coconut chicken and galanga soup. Those unfamiliar with Thai cooking should inquire about the spiciness of individual dishes before ordering. Closed Sundays. 48 Frith St., W1 (phone: 437-7444). Moderate to inexpensive.

HQ – An unusual (for London) Créole-style menu is the main attraction at this new restaurant/wine bar in trendy Camden Lock. Its location above the art and craft shops affords guests good views of the canal and weekend street performers. Open daily. Commercial Pl. (phone: 485-6044). Moderate to inexpensive.

Kettner's – As you check your coat, you have to make your choice — a bottle of champagne at the bar (25 labels in stock), a humble but tasty salad in the brasserie-style café, or a pizza in the beautifully furnished dining room reminiscent of an Edwardian hotel. Open daily. 29 Romilly St., Soho, W1 (phone: 437-6437).

Khyber – A wide selection of Indian Punjabi specialties as well as tasty vegetarian dishes are served here. Try the *pannir,* mild cheese cooked with peas, meat, and spices, and the *aloa gobi,* a cauliflower dish. Open daily. 56 Westbourne Grove, W2 (phone: 727-4385). Moderate to inexpensive.

Last Days of the Raj – This popular restaurant on the eastern fringe of Covent Garden serves dishes from India's Punjabi region. Punjabi cuisine is rather mild, and one of its specialties is meat prepared *tandoori* style — marinated in yogurt and spices, then baked in a special tray oven. Some kind of tandoori cooking is usually on the menu in addition to other specials, which change every few months. The exotic mango-based cocktails are powerful, and the service is extremely friendly. Be sure to dine at the Drury Lane *Raj,* as other restaurants are now trading on the original restaurant's good name. Closed Sundays. 22 Drury La., WC2 (phone: 836-1628). Moderate to inexpensive.

Smolensky's Balloon – This American-owned cocktail bar/restaurant with a 1930s piano-bar atmosphere is guaranteed to make you feel homesick. Steaks and fries figure largely on the menu, offset by some interesting vegetarian dishes. Open daily, noon to 11:45 PM, Sundays noon to 10:30 PM. 1 Dover St., W1 (phone: 491-1199). Moderate to inexpensive.

Bangkok – Known for its *saté* — small tender slices of beef marinated in a curry and soy sauce and served with a palate-destroying hot peanut sauce. From your butcher block table you can watch your meal being prepared by chefs in the windowed kitchen. Closed Sundays. 9 Bute St., SW7 (phone: 584-8529). Inexpensive.

Café Maxim's – In the same building as *Maxim's de Paris,* it aims to combine the atmosphere of a brasserie with the already familiar *Maxim's* style. Live jazz in the evenings. Closed Saturdays at lunch and Sundays. Clareville House, Panton St., SW1 (phone: 839-4809). Inexpensive.

Calabash – West African cuisine gives this restaurant a unique position on London's restaurant map, especially since it's in the bubbling Covent Garden district. The service is accommodating and helpful and the food is both good and different. Closed Sundays. Downstairs at London's Africa Centre, 38 King St., WC2 (phone: 836-1976). Inexpensive.

La Capannina – Homemade pasta is offered by this unpretentious, friendly Italian restaurant, typical of those that flourish in Soho. Closed Saturdays for lunch and Sundays. 24 Romilly St., W1 (phone: 437-2473). Inexpensive.

Chicago Pizza Pie Factory – A little while ago, an American advertising executive turned his back on the ad world to bring London deep-dish pizza Windy City style, along with Budweiser beer and chocolate cheesecake. Londoners beat a path to his door and haven't yet stopped clamoring to get in. Open daily. 17 Hanover Sq., W1 (phone: 629-2669). Inexpensive.

Cosmoba – A small and friendly family-run Italian restaurant that is basic in every respect — except for its food. Tucked down a tiny alleyway and always packed with regulars. Closed Sundays. 9 Cosmo Pl., WC1 (phone: 837-0904). Inexpensive.

Cranks – There are four branches of this self-service vegetarian restaurant. All are popular and serve good homemade desserts as well as salads, quiches, and other hot food. Drop in for coffee or afternoon tea. Closed Sundays. 8 Marshall St., W1 (phone: 437-9431), open for dinner Mondays through Saturdays; 11 The Market, Covent Garden, WC1 (phone: 379-6508), open daily; Tottenham St., W1 (phone: 631-3912), closed Sundays; and Unit 11, Adelaide St., WC2 (phone: 631-3192), closed Sundays. Inexpensive.

Dumpling Inn – This Peking-style restaurant serves excellent Oriental dumplings, and most of the other dishes are equally good. Try the fried seaweed; it's got lots of vitamins and tastes terrific. The service, though efficient, is a little brisk. Open daily. 15A Gerrard St., W1 (phone: 437-2567). Inexpensive.

Geales' – This place serves up truly English — and fresh — fish and chips in a setting that looks like a 1930s tearoom. Go early, because *Geales'* is no secret. Closed Sundays and the last 3 weeks in August. 2 Farmer St., W8 (phone: 727-7969). Inexpensive.

Hard Rock Café – This is the original. An American-style eating emporium with a loud jukebox and good burgers. It's always crowded, and the lines stretch well out into the street. As much a T-shirt vendor (at the shop around the corner) these days as a restaurant. Open daily. 150 Old Park La., W1 (phone: 629-0382). Inexpensive.

Kalamaras Taverna – A small friendly eatery with authentic Greek food prepared under the watchful eye of the Greek owner. The menu here is more varied than that in most of the other Greek/Cypriot restaurants in London. Bouzouki music is sometimes played in the evenings. Closed Sundays. 66–76 Inverness Mews, W2, off Queensway (phone: 727-5082 or 727-9122). Inexpensive.

My Old Dutch – This authentic Dutch pancake house serves endless varieties of sweet and savory pancakes on genuine blue Delft plates. Loud music. Open daily. 132 High Holborn, WC1 (phone: 242-5200). Inexpensive.

Oodles – A "country food" restaurant with branches on four of London's busiest streets. Wholesome quiches, spicy curries, and unusual salads are served under ceilings hung with (fake) country flowers and branches. Closed Sundays. 42 New Oxford St. WC1 (phone: 580-9521); 31 Cathedral Pl. EC1 (phone: 248-2550); 113 High Holborn WC1 (phone: 405-3838); and 128 Edgeware Rd., W2 (phone: 723-7548). Inexpensive.

Standard – Possibly the best Indian restaurant value in London, so it tends to get crowded quickly. There are no reservations, so dine early to beat the rush. Open daily. 23 Westbourne Grove, W2 (phone: 727-4818). Inexpensive.

Widow Applebaum – Not an authentic New York Jewish delicatessen, but this place serves pretty good herring, cold cuts, chopped liver, potato salad, dill pickles, and apple pie. Closed Sundays. 46 S Molton St., W1 (phone: 629-4649). Inexpensive.

SHARING A PINT: There are several thousand pubs in London, the vast majority of which are owned by the six big brewers. Most of these pubs have two bars: the "public," which is for the working man who wants to get on with the business of drinking, and the "saloon" or "lounge," which makes an attempt at providing comfort and may serve good food and wine as well as beer. Liquor at the latter may cost more. Among the means by which pubs are appraised is the brand and variety of draft brews that spew forth from its taps. The extraordinary variety can easily perplex the uninitiated. There's ale: bitter, mild, stout; and lager, whose varying tastes provide a perfect excuse to linger longer in pubs you find particuarly convivial. Eating in a crowded pub is not always easy because the limited number of tables are barely large enough to hold all the empty beer glasses, let alone food. Pub food is hearty but not especially imaginative: a ploughman's lunch, which is a hunk of bread and cheese plus pickle; cottage pie, which is ground meat with mashed potato on top baked in the oven; sausages; and sandwiches. The number (and quality) of pubs serving more upscale food is increasing, since British law has recently expanded opening hours for pubs offering food; the law used to require pubs to close for several hours during late afternoon to early evening, whereas now most open at 10:30 or 11 AM and remain open all day.

Here are the names of pubs where we like to raise a pint or two: *Dirty Dick's,* 202 Bishopsgate, EC2, is offbeat but popular, with fake bats and spiders hanging from the ceilings, sawdust on the floor, and good bar snacks; and *Sherlock Holmes,* 10 Northumberland St., WC2 (phone: 930-2644) is the pub that Holmes's creator, Arthur Conan Doyle, used to frequent when it was still the *Northumberland Arms,* and which he mentioned in *Hound of the Baskervilles;* a glass-enclosed replica of Holmes's Baker Street study is there, along with Holmes memorabilia. *The Audley,* 41 Mount St., W1, is our favorite luncheon stop in the high-rent district, with fine sandwiches and salad plates in an atypically hygienic environment. Other fine spots include *The Antelope,* 22 Eaton Terrace, SW1, where the Bellamys (or even Hudson, their butler) might have sipped a lager on the way home to nearby 165 Eaton Place; *The Grenadier,* 18 Wilton Row, SW1, perhaps the poshest pub site in town, just off Belgravia Square; *Admiral Codrington,* 17 Mossop St., SW3, is large and Victorian, with brass beer pumps, engraved mirrors, and good food; *Dickens Inn* by the Tower, St. Katherine's Way, E1, is a converted warehouse overlooking a colorful yacht marina and serving shellfish snacks; *George Inn,* 77 Borough High St., SE1, dates from 1676 and retains the original gallery for viewing Shakespearean plays in the summer; *The Flask,* 77 Highgate West Hill, N6, serves drinks at three paneled bars and on its outside patio; *The Lamb,* 94 Lambs Conduit St., WC1, is also paneled and hung with photos of past music hall performers; *Museum Tavern,* 49 Great Russell St., WC1, is across the road from the *British Museum* and decorated with hanging flower baskets; *Princess Louise,* 208 High Holborn, WC1, has live music, cabaret, and a wine bar upstairs with good food; *Bull and Bush,* North End Way, NW3, owes its fame to the Edwardian music-hall song "Down at the Old Bull and Bush." Former customers include Thomas Gainsborough and Charles Dickens. It has an outdoor bar and barbecue for balmy summer evenings. *Prospect of Whitby,* 57 Wapping Wall, E1, the oldest riverside pub in London, was once the haunt of thieves and smugglers (now it draws jazz lovers); *Ye Olde Cheshire Cheese,* 5 Little Essex St., EC4 (just off Fleet St.), is a 17th-century pub with paneled walls and sawdust floors popular with the Fleet Street set.

WINE BARS: An innovation on the London scene, they serve wine by the glass or bottle, accompanied by such light fare as quiche and salad, and occasionally full meals. Prices tend to be lower in wine bars than in restaurants, and tables can often be reserved in advance. Here's a selection of the finest: *Boos,* 1 Glentworth St., NW1, combines rustic decor with simple homemade food; *Cork and Bottle,* 44–46 Cranbourn St., WC2, is patronized by the London wine trade and has a classical guitarist providing background music; *Draycott's,* 114 Draycott Ave., SW3, has tables grouped outside on the pavement and is frequented by the smart London set; *Ebury Wine Bar,* 139 Ebury St., SW1, in the heart of Belgravia, serves good food (try the English pudding) and offers live music nightly; *Le Bistroquet,* 273–275 Camden High St., NW1, is one of London's trendiest spots, popular with the city's yuppies; *Shampers,* 4 Kingly St., W1, is near the famous *Liberty* department store and sometimes has a classical guitarist in the evenings; *Bar des Amis,* 11–14 Hanover Pl., WC2, is a crowded watering hole in fashionable Covent Garden; *Crawford's,* 10–11 Crawford St., W1, is a lively basement bar serving full cold buffet lunches and suppers; *Penny's Place,* 6 King St., WC2, can be too crowded for comfort, but always has good wines, food, and music; *Julie's,* 137 Portland Rd., W11, has become a landmark for aging flower children of the '60s; *El Vino,* 47 Fleet St., EC4, is *the* haunt for journalists, and is most famous for refusing to serve women at the bar.

NORWICH

Drive for miles across the empty, pan-flat landscapes of Norfolk, the ever so English county that forms the great eastern belly of Britain, and eventually you arrive at Norwich, a city that seems to exist without any obvious reason. No community within a 40-mile radius of the city's commanding cathedral spire comes close to challenging Norwich's scale, and apart from its perch atop one of the few modest hills in East Anglia — which may once have offered some strategic military advantage in pre-missile days — the reason for Norwich's very existence is hard to understand.

From its hazy origins as Northwick ("wick" is the old English word for a small settlement), this "Fine City" — as the boundary road signs proclaim — grew to rival York as the second largest city in England, after London. Settled by Saxons and sacked by Danes, Norwich (pronounced *nahr*-ich) began to build up some civic momentum in the 11th century. Its position on the river Wensum, which flows to the sea some 20 miles away, was a vital link to the rest of the world. So when William the Conqueror sailed from Normandy in 1066, first landing on the country's southern shores, Norwich was already a busy town, importing timber, stone, steel, wine, and cloth from the far corners of Europe and exporting the products of the rich, thickly populated agricultural hinterland of Norfolk. The Normans threw up the castle in the center of town and then set about building a monastery and church. French stone from Caen, William's hometown, was shipped across the Channel and up the river to construct the church — the magnificent cathedral that now stands just off a street called Tombland, the original Saxon marketplace.

During the 13th century, Norwich surpassed York as a commercial center, although it rapidly lost its place after the Black Death of the 14th century decimated the population. It was not until the wool trade flourished on the surrounding lands during the 15th and 16th centuries, and Norwich became the industry's chief point of export, that the city recuperated and expanded again. Half-timbered inns, ancient squares, countless churches built by wealthy merchants, and street names like Charing (Shearing) Cross recall these prosperous times when Norwich grew rich on thickly coated sheep.

When the rest of the country prospered during the Industrial Revolution, however, Norwich's fortunes ebbed. Unable to compete with the booming industries in the Midlands and the far north, where higher wages and standards of living lured most of its skilled craftsmen, the city diversified — into brewing (the huge Norwich Brewery still stands on King Street), mustard (the *Colman's Mustard Shop and Museum* tells the whole story), banking, insurance, and confectionery. Today there's even a small Turkish Delight factory run by two Turks called, appropriately enough, the Sultans.

Despite these industrial inroads, a distinctly medieval air still clings to

Norwich, which has more Grade One Listed buildings than any other comparable city in the country, save historic York. Its heart is a labyrinth of ancient alleys, among which narrow, cobbled Elm Hill is the most picturesque. Lined with unspoiled buildings housing interesting shops, the whole area seems to be from another era. There are still four thatched buildings within the city center, and clustered around Upper St. Giles Street is a "village" within the city, its winding lanes lined with antiquarian bookshops, craft shops, tiny candlelit restaurants, and pretty, half-timbered houses. Portions of the old city wall are glimpsed at the ends of alleyways, the largest portion running down to the river between Bracondale and King Street. Even the city's street system, which also dates from the Middle Ages, is finding it hard to support modern rush-hour traffic.

But the most ubiquitous examples of medieval life in Norwich are the churches its merchants built to show off the wealth they had accumulated in textile trading. Five hundred years ago, there were more churches here than in any other European city, at least one for every Sunday of the year. Today, even in the wake of Henry VIII's Reformation (when numerous ecclesiastical buildings in England were demolished), there are still around 30, although several are no longer places of worship: The St. Simon and St. Jude Church, for example, is now a Boy Scout headquarters; All Saint's on Westlegate is a coffee bar and all-purpose community center; St. Michael-at-Plea is used for exhibitions; and St. Peter the Hungate is part museum of church arts and part brass-rubbing center. One church now serves as a health club, another a club for martial arts, and several more stand empty.

Medieval buildings and glorious churches are the prime reason for visiting Norwich, but they are by no means the city's only asset. The hub of the city is the Market Place, a sea of striped awnings lined on one side by the 14th-century Guildhall (now home of the tourist information center), on another by the rather harsh lines of the modern City Hall, and on a third by the colossal proportions of St. Peter Mancroft, considered one of the finest churches in the country. The market held here is the largest daily (except Sundays) open-air market in the country, though it may not be as interesting to visitors as the weekly cattle market held on the Ipswich Road every Saturday morning. This harks back to the city's historic agrarian roots — and it's still a far cry from being just a show for the tourists. In fact, greenhorns aren't likely to understand a word that's said — so don't raise your arm at the wrong moment or nod hello to the auctioneer unless leaving Norwich with a four-legged memento is on your agenda.

NORWICH AT-A-GLANCE

SEEING THE CITY: To do the job properly, the tip of the tower of the neo-Gothic Roman Catholic St. John's Cathedral on Earlham Road, on the western edge of the center, is technically the highest point in the city, but those with less energy may drive (or walk) up to Mousehold Heath, just to the northeast of town. The Heath, which first rose to fame as the site of Ketts Rebellion, a 1549 uprising of 20,000 angry peasants that disrupted Norwich and unnerved the monarchy, is to Norwich what Hampstead Heath is to Londoners — there are still local inhabitants who have yet to explore all the leafy dells, undulating hills, and coppices of this huge expanse of common. From St. James Hill it is possible to see all the old buildings clustered around the cathedral and to put Norwich into proper perspective.

SPECIAL PLACES: The cathedral and its close, the castle, and the market square are the three major focal points of central Norwich, an area defined by the river Wensum and the line of the old city walls.

CITY CENTER

Norwich Cathedral – This beautiful church was begun in 1096 by Herbert de Losinga, first Bishop of Norwich. According to the old chronicles, the bishop founded the church and the monastery attached to it in atonement for an act of simony — he had bought his bishopric. Unfortunately, Losinga, whose tomb can be seen before the high altar, did not live to see more than the first three bays of the nave, which was finished by his successor during the first half of the 12th century. Measuring only 250 feet long and 95 feet high, it is not the longest nor the loftiest nave in England, but in this instance grandeur has nothing to do with statistics. The huge square pillars, the great semi-circular arches, and the splendid proportions of the triple arcade of white stone are a superb example of the talent of Norman builders. Because the early cathedral was repeatedly damaged by fire and storm — traces of ancient flames can be seen in the pinkish tinge of some of the stonework — the vaulted stone roof, a replacement for a burnt wooden one, dates from the 15th century. The carvings of Old and New Testament scenes on the roof bosses are notable; unfortunately, they can be seen only with binoculars. The bosses of the adjoining cloisters, the only 2-story monastic cloister (built from the late 13th to the early 15th century) in England, are equally remarkable and much more accessible to the naked eye. Exit the south door to Life's Green to best appreciate the cathedral's 315-foot stone spire (the second tallest in the country, topped only by that of Salisbury Cathedral). The 15th-century builders who erected it (the original wooden spire had blown down in a hurricane) pulled off a daring architectural feat, since the 120-foot Norman tower on which it rests was never intended to support such a soaring structure. The cathedral is open daily from 7:30 AM to 6 PM and until 7 PM during the summer. The Visitors Centre sells refreshments and houses an exhibition on the cathedral. Open Mondays through Saturdays, 10:30 AM to 4:30 PM.

Two medieval gateways, the Erpingham, with its much eroded statue of Sir Thomas Erpingham (he fought at the Battle of Agincourt), and the Ethelbert, lead off Tombland to the Cathedral Close, the "home farm" of the former monastery. Filled with Georgian houses, creeper-covered cottages, and converted stable blocks that lead down to the river, this is a world removed from busy crowds, shops, and traffic. The deanery was once the prior's house, but old-fashioned brass plaques now advertise the offices of solicitors. The other old houses on the north side of the Lower Close stand on the site of the monks' granary. Also inside the close are a statue of Nelson, who was once a pupil at the nearby school, and the grave of Dame Edith Cavell, a nurse shot in Belgium in 1915 for helping British prisoners escape from the Germans.

Norwich Castle and Castle Museum – Another focal point of the city stands 500 yards or so from the cathedral on top of manmade Castle Mound, which is particularly beautiful when covered in daffodils in spring. A wooden castle was probably built here by Ralph de Guader, the only Anglo-Saxon traitor at the Battle of Hastings, but the great square stone keep seen today, albeit much restored, dates from the time of Henry I (1120–30). From the 12th through the 19th centuries, part of the castle was used as the official county jail, and since 1894 it has been used as a museum, housing natural history and archaeology exhibits, as well as some of the finest art collections outside

London. Of particular interest are the two *Colman Galleries,* which display works by painters of the Norwich school, a 19th-century movement whose major exponents were John Crome and John Sell Cotman. Open Mondays through Saturdays from 10 AM to 5 PM, Sundays from 2 to 5 PM. Admission charge. Castle Meadow (phone: 611277).

St. Peter Mancroft – Often mistaken for the cathedral, this church, built between 1430 and 1455, is the largest and grandest in the city. The massive tower, dramatically floodlit at night, houses the famous set of 12 bells that rang the first true "peal" of 5,040 changes in 1715. Inside, look up to the fine hammerbeam roof, with its angels, fan vaulting, and stone corbels, and then look east, to the flowing medieval glass in the great window above the altar. The 15th-century font has a massive wooden canopy topped by a Victorian dome. Market Place (phone: 610443).

St. Peter Hungate Church Museum – This tiny former church houses a museum of ecclesiastical art, but its beautiful and unusual roof, the Norfolk tiles on the floor, and the Norwich-made 15th- and 16th-century glass in the windows also make it an exhibit in itself. The objects on display include a collection of rare medieval items, manuscripts, an early Anglican communion plate, Russian icons, and musical instruments. There's also a brass-rubbing center. Open Mondays through Saturdays from 10 AM to 5 PM. Princes St. (phone: 667231).

St. Andrew's and Blackfriars – These two civic halls began as the nave and the chancel of a huge 15th-century Dominican church. The most complete friary complex in the country, they survived Henry VIII's Dissolution of the Monasteries because they were given to the city and adapted for municipal purposes. Now they're used for concerts, exhibitions, craft fairs, and an antiques market every Wednesday. St. Andrew's St. (phone: 57348).

Bridewell Museum – Before it was finally turned into a museum, this 14th-century merchant's house had quite a checkered history. In the 16th century, it served as a "bridewell" (a prison for tramps and beggars), as evidenced by the initials and dates its inmates scratched in the walls of the courtyard, and, later, as a factory. Now its galleries feature exhibits on Norwich's textile, shoe, food, drink, and other industries over the past 200 years. Special displays include a steam fire engine and a Victorian bar. Open Mondays through Saturdays from 10 AM to 5 PM. Admission charge. Bridewell Alley (phone: 667228).

Strangers' Hall – Another old merchant's house turned museum, this one dedicated to urban English domestic life. The mansion's stone-vaulted undercroft dates from about 1320, but constant enlargement by wealthy owners in later centuries left it a complex, rambling structure in which there are numerous period rooms, from Tudor to Victorian, open for inspection. Two cellars house permanent exhibitions of inn and tradesmens' signs as well as a motley collection of old vehicles. Protestant Flemish weavers, fleeing religious persecution and taking refuge here during the reign of Queen Elizabeth I, may have been the "Strangers" who gave the house its name. Open Mondays through Saturdays from 10 AM to 5 PM. Admission charge. Charing Cross (phone: 611277).

American (USAAF) Memorial Library – Commemorates the more than 6,000 Americans of the 8th United States Army Air Force who were killed during World War II flying from East Anglian bases. Included is a collection of mostly American-published books donated in their memory. Open Mondays through Fridays from 10 AM to 5 PM, Saturdays from 9 AM. Norwich Library, Bethel St. (phone: 611277).

Assembly House – An 18th-century Georgian building with a fountain playing in the elegant courtyard, this was at one time a meeting place for fashionable society, but it also saw duty as a dancing academy and a school. It is now possible to take tea in the restored ballroom, whose elegance makes it an experience no visitor should miss. There is also a small art gallery, a music room in which concerts are held, and an adjacent cinema. Theatre St. (phone: 626402).

ENVIRONS

Sainsbury Centre for Visual Arts – A radical and exciting building, designed by Norman Foster, that houses the collection of ethnographic and modern art donated to the University of East Anglia by Sir Robert and Lady Sainsbury, founders of Britain's principal supermarket chain. About 2 miles west of the town, the building, financed by the Sainsburys' son, has been compared to the Beaubourg in Paris — and acclaimed or derided with the same passionate adjectives. In addition to the Sainsbury collection (from African and Eskimo art to Picasso and Henry Moore), the exhibits include the university's collection of 20th-century art and Art Nouveau. Buses run every half hour to the university campus from the railway station on Thorpe Road. Open Tuesdays through Sundays from noon to 5 PM. Admission charge. University of East Anglia (phone: 0603-56060).

■ **EXTRA SPECIAL:** The Wensum meanders through Norwich before joining the river Yare, a few miles away, for its final journey to the sea at the popular holiday resort of Great Yarmouth. Although the river played an important role in the city's trade until the coming of the railway in the late 18th century, it now entertains far more pleasure craft than cargo vessels. The Riverside Walk follows the Wensum from Carrow Bridge, in the southeast section of Norwich, through the historic heart of town to Hellesdon, 5 miles upstream (there are directional signs in a number of places). *Southern River Steamers* (phone: 501220) runs 1- to 3-hour riverbus cruises from Easter to September. Boats leave either from the end of the quay at the back of Roaches Court, off Elm Hill, or from outside Thorpe Station.

SOURCES AND RESOURCES

TOURIST INFORMATION: Norwich's tourist information center (in the Guildhall, Gaol Hill, opposite the market; phone: 666071) can supply brochures, maps, and general information, as well as help with rooms through its accommodations booking service. From June to September, the center is open Mondays through Saturdays from 9:30 AM to 6 PM and Sundays from 9:30 AM to 1 PM; off season, it's open Mondays through Fridays to 5:30 PM, Saturdays to 1 PM. The *Norwich Official Guide* (about $2.30), a comprehensive introduction to all aspects of the city, and the free *What's On in Norwich,* produced by the tourist office every month, are both available here. The tourist information center also supplies brochures on walking trails with themes (about 30¢ to 50¢), which include the *Knobs and Knockers Trail* (a look at the homes of famous people), the *Macabre Trail* (a search for the ghosts that are part of the city's history), and the *Norwich Silver Trail* (a tour of the most beautiful of the city's treasures). Full details of the most important churches are in the *Old Churches of Norwich* brochure. There's also a useful leaflet describing how best to see the city after dusk — Norwich has won many international awards for its nighttime floodlighting of key attractions.

Local Coverage – The morning *Eastern Daily Press* and the *Eastern Evening News* are the two daily papers. The *Norwich Mercury* is published once a week.

Telephone – The area code for Norwich is 0603.

GETTING AROUND: It takes only 15 minutes to walk across Norwich, but a bus or taxi may be necessary to visit points farther afield.

Airport – Although London's Heathrow is only a 2½-hour drive away, Norwich Airport, Fifers La. (phone: 411923), 4 miles north of the center via

Cromer Road, has become an important international hub, with frequent flights to Amsterdam and several other European cities, as well as connections with the rest of the world.

Bus – The local bus company, *Eastern Counties,* operates four City Line minibus services in addition to its other routes (among which numbers 26 and 27 are especially useful, since they run from the center of town to the university campus). Long distance (and local) buses use the bus station on Surrey St. (phone: 620491), but for information on either, phone or visit the Bus Users Information Centre at All Saint's Centre, Westlegate (phone: 613613), open Mondays through Saturdays from 10 AM to 4 PM.

Car Rental – All the usual car hire firms are represented, including *Avis,* Terminal Building, Norwich Airport, Holt Rd. (phone: 416719); *Budget Rent-A-Car,* Clarence Garage, Thorpe Rd. (phone: 66986); *Kenning,* 106–110 Prince of Wales Rd. (phone: 628271); and *Willhire,* Station Garage, Thorpe Rd. (phone: 660587).

Taxi – There are taxi ranks on Guildhall Hill as well as outside the train station, and there are plenty of taxi firms, including *Beeline* (phone: 623333), *Bell* (phone: 622677), *Bestway* (phone: 620260), and *Courtesy* (phone: 620666).

Train – Prince of Wales Rd. links the city center with Norwich Station (phone: 620255), across the river at the corner of Riverside and Thorpe Rd. There are hourly trains to London (a 2-hour journey on the new electrified line), to the coast, and to Peterborough, where connections to several other major destinations in Britain can be made.

SPECIAL EVENTS: The calendar includes a *Mammoth Fete* in May, a *Raft Race* in June, and a *Horse Show* and the *Lord Mayor's Procession* in July. Giant games of chess and draughts — the pieces are as big as young children — go on every day throughout the summer in Chapelfields Gardens, the city's central public gardens.

MUSEUMS: In addition to those discussed in *Special Places,* Norwich has two other interesting museums:

Mustard Shop Museum – Exhibits illustrating the history of Colman's Mustard, begun over 150 years ago, with *Colman's Mustard Shop* on the same premises. Mustard tastings can be arranged. Closed Thursdays and Sundays. 3 Bridewell Alley (phone: 627889).

Royal Norfolk Regiment Museum – Weapons and regimental memorabilia, in a former military hospital on Mousehold Heath. Open Mondays through Fridays. Brittania Barracks, Britannia Rd. (phone: 628455).

SHOPPING: Since it is the largest urban center for miles around, Norwich draws shoppers from all over the surrounding county. The core of the city is the open-air market on the Market Place, a sea of 200 brightly striped canopies (known locally as "tilts") concealing stalls that sell everything from fresh fruit and vegetables to flowers, fresh fish, clothing, books, and basketware. It convenes every day except Sunday. The big chain stores — including *Boots, Marks & Spencer,* and *British Home Stores* — are a few minutes' walk away, augmented by five department stores — *Jarrolds, Bonds, Debenham's, Littlewoods,* and *Garlands.* London Street, the first street in Britain to be closed to traffic and given over to pedestrians alone, is lined with jewelers and boutiques such as *Laura Ashley* and *Habitat,* whereas the old shops on Elm Hill, Swan Lane, and Bridewell Alley are well stocked with local arts and crafts, jewelry, and souvenir bottles of old Norfolk Punch — a concoction prepared using natural underground waters and dozens of herbs. The most attractive thoroughfare of all is the Royal Arcade, a covered walkway designed in beautiful Art Nouveau style right down to the lettering on the individual shops and elegant hanging lamps.

The *Shopping in Norwich* leaflet produced by the tourist information center lists the city's most interesting shops and includes a map. Some shops in Norwich close on Thursdays.

Body Shop – Shampoos, rubs, herbs, perfumes, and bath foams. Davy Pl. (phone: 617991).

Brambles – Plenty of gift items, several with amusing themes, plus cards, posters, and a basement café. 16–22 Exchange St. (phone: 624350).

Clan – Fair Isle knitwear and cashmere, skirts, suits, and tartan kilts (the real thing). All imported from Scotland, despite Norwich's own wool trading history! 7 Westlegate (phone: 620332).

Colman's Mustard Shop – Gift items and 13 different types of mustard are sold in an attractive interior that incorporates a mustard museum. Closed Thursdays. 3 Bridewell Alley (phone: 627889).

Contact Gallery – Small, modern, and cheerful, it features only local artists. 56 St. Benedict St.

Charles Cubitt – Antiques, coins, glass and china trinkets on the ground floor; fine and rare books on art, natural history, and old Norfolk upstairs. 10 All Saint's Green (phone: 622569).

Elm Hill Stamps and Coins – Its wares date back as far as Roman times. Sells old postcards, too. Elm Hill (phone: 627413).

Camilla Hepper – Herbal cosmetics specialist for delicate skin. Dove St. (phone: 627688)

Hovells – A wealth of traditional wicker baskets, hampers, and dried flowers, as well as the pine and cane furniture found across the street in *Skippers* restaurant. Bedford St. (phone: 626676).

T. M. Lincoln – An old-fashioned pharmacist specializing in homeopathic and herbal preparations. 76 Upper St. Giles St. (phone: 620612).

Little Shop – A.J. Podolski, the jeweler and silversmith, sells and repairs interesting old baubles. Tucked away on St. Andrew's Hill, off Bedford St. (phone: 622853).

Movie Shop – It describes itself as "an antiquarian and nostalgic center." Lots of kitsch, as well as genuine antiques and film books and annuals. 11 St. Gregory's Alley (phone: 615239).

National Trust – Wildlife calendars, nature diaries, woolens, and soaps. Information on local National Trust properties is available. Dove St. (phone: 610206).

Thorntons – Derbyshire chocolates, gift boxes or full-blown slabs of toffee, and other things for the sweet tooth. 1 Orford Pl. (phone: 612576).

James and Ann Tillett – A reputable stock of pewter, solid antique silver, jewelry, glass decanters, and tiny enamel pieces, just opposite the cathedral. Tombland House, Tombland (phone: 624914).

Waterstone's – Norwich's newest bookstore, housed in an ornate building (look up before entering), with several shelves devoted to travel. 30 London St. (phone: 632462).

SPORTS: Norwich has several parks with facilities for outdoor sports. Eaton Park, for example, offers tennis, bowls, football, hockey, and cricket. Three leisure centers — the *Duke Street Leisure Centre* (phone: 623469), the *Crome Leisure Centre* on Telegraph La. E. (phone: 36697), and the *Norman Leisure Centre* on Bignold Rd. (phone: 401840) — offer saunas, spa baths, solariums, gyms, and squash courts.

Cricket – The Norfolk County Cricket team plays at *Lakenham Cricket Ground,* Hall Rd., from May through the summer.

Golf – The *Royal Norwich Golf Club,* Drayton Rd. (phone: 649928), the *Eaton Golf Club,* Newmarket Rd. (phone: 651686), and the *Costessey Park Golf Club,* West End, Old Costessey (phone: 746333), all allow visitors to play, but the abilities of transient players may be "tested" by the resident professional.

Rugby – The Norwich Rugby Club meets September through May at *Beeston Hyrne,* North Walsham Rd. (phone: 646259).

Soccer – The local "Canaries" play at the *Carrow Road Stadium* (phone: 612131) from August through May.

Swimming – The *Norwich City Baths,* St. Augustines, (phone: 620164), also has 2 squash courts and a sauna. Open 7 days a week.

Tennis and Squash – The *Norfolk Tennis and Squash Centre,* Lime Tree Rd. (phone: 653532), offers both. For squash only, try *Hunters Squash Club,* Edward St. (phone: 613185), *Norman Recreation Centre,* Bignold Rd. (phone: 640810), or the *Norwich City Baths* (see above).

THEATER: Norwich's *Theatre Royal,* Theatre St. (phone: 628205), is one of the most successful provincial groups in the country, with many of its plays and other productions going on to become major hits in London's West End. Everything from circus to vaudeville to opera and ballet, with some of the world's leading companies and artists performing, also takes place at this theater, built in 1935 on the site of the 18th-century original. The *Norwich Players,* an amateur company, produce about ten shows a year at the *Maddermarket Theatre,* St. John's Alley (phone: 620917). The *Da Silva Puppet Company* performs at the *Norwich Puppet Theatre,* housed in a former church on St. James, Whitefriars (phone: 629921), while the *Sewell Barn Theatre,* named for local author Anna Sewell (who wrote *Black Beauty*), is, as the rest of its name suggests, a converted barn seating around 100 people on Constitution Hill (phone: 411721). The *Sewell Barn Theatre Company* is also the main group performing in summer at Norwich's fifth theater, the open-air *Whiffler,* in the Castle Gardens (phone: 622233).

MUSIC: The superb acoustics of Norwich Cathedral make it the perfect place for choral concerts and organ recitals; the huge medieval St. Andrew's and Blackfriars halls on Elm Hill are venues for choral, symphony, band, and pop concerts; other performances are held in the *Music Room* of the Assembly House on Theatre Street. The University of East Anglia is the most popular place for pop concerts and bands playing the university circuit. A series of brass band concerts takes place in Norwich's parks most Sunday afternoons during the summer.

NIGHTCLUBS AND NIGHTLIFE: Norwich's most popular discotheque, the neon-lit *Ritzy and Central Park* (phone: 621541), in a handsome, white-washed, gabled building on Tombland, is open 7 nights a week. Other discos are *Hy's,* also on Tombland (phone: 621155); *Pennies,* Edward St. (phone: 612909); and *Santanas,* Magdalen St. (phone: 617890). Nightclubs include *Le Valbon,* Magdalen St. (phone: 630760); *Moulin Rouge,* St. Stephen's Rd. (phone: 628708); and *Springfields,* Oak St. (phone: 660220).

BEST IN TOWN

CHECKING IN: Norwich is not Britain's most popular tourist destination, but it does have a handful of top hotels catering to a regular business clientele. It also has several comfortable smaller hotels that may not offer as many "mod cons" but possess a whole lot more character. Earlham Road, leading west out of the center, is lined with guesthouses and bed-and-breakfast establishments. As a rough guide, expect to pay more than $100 a night for a double room at an expensive hotel, between $70 and $100 at a moderate one, and $35 to $60 at an inexpensive one. A full English breakfast should be included in the rate, but a growing number of the top hotels now charge separately for this repast. All telephone numbers are in the 0603 area code unless otherwise indicated.

Arlington – A superb Georgian building with 41 rooms, sitting pretty in a quiet countryside setting only a 10-minute walk from the town center. Two French restaurants on the premises mean that guests don't even have to venture out in the evening. Newmarket Rd. (phone: 617841). Expensive.

Maids Head – Opposite the cathedral, it claims to be the oldest continuously inhabited inn in England, with its roots going back 7 centuries. Some of the 80 bedrooms have original oak beams, but most are modern. The *Minstrel Gallery* restaurant serves a traditional Sunday lunch, and a courtyard bar, converted from the original coach "garage," is popular with locals. Tombland (phone: 628821). Expensive.

Nelson – A modern hotel within convenient suitcase-lugging distance of the railway station (across a bridge over the river). From the lounge and many of the 122 bedrooms, patrons can watch the boats floating downriver. The new Executive Rooms come with a fridge well-stocked with milk, Perrier, and OJ. Prince of Wales Rd. (phone: 628612). Expensive.

Norwich – Thoroughly modern and primarily a businessman's retreat, it's on the ring road around Norwich, about 3 miles northwest of the city center. Thanks to an energetic manager and a very friendly staff, however, it's far from anonymous. The 102 bedrooms are well equipped, from cable TV to trouser presses, and the *Rouen* restaurant competes with Norwich's best. 121 Boundary Rd. (phone: 410431). Expensive.

Post House – It offers excellent service, 116 warm, comfortable rooms, all with private facilities, and every modern convenience, plus a health and fitness club with a sauna and swimming pool — all about 2 miles south of the center. Ipswich Rd. (phone: 56431). Expensive.

Sprowston Hall – There has been a manor house on this site — about 3 miles northeast of the center — since 1559, although most of the present building is 19th century. Walk through 8 acres of lawns to reach the 18-hole golf course next door. The 41 newly decorated bedrooms ooze character from every timber beam and sloping ceiling. Wroxham Rd. (phone: 410871). Expensive.

Castle – In the town center, with plenty of parking, easy access to shops, and a promising restaurant. Note that less than half the 78 rooms have private baths. Castle Meadow (phone: 611511). Moderate.

Cumberland – A friendly, family-run, whitewashed hotel with 26 bedrooms, 10 of which boast private bathroom facilities. It's particularly attractive in summer, when guests can dine in the glass-paneled verandah dining room. 212–214 Thorpe Rd. (phone: 34550). Moderate.

Beeches – Mr. and Mrs. Cunby's stolid, gray hotel is a homey-looking building on busy Earlham Road. Yet inside the traffic seems miles away, and people who stay here have a privileged view over Norwich's "secret garden," a Victorian plantation carefully restored to its original state but rarely open to public view. 6 Earlham Rd. (phone: 621167). Inexpensive.

Crofters – A welcoming, self-service cold buffet is laid out in the kitchen every evening for late arrivals who haven't the energy to go out to a restaurant. With 15 rooms, on private grounds next to St. John's Cathedral. 2 Earlham Rd. (phone: 613287). Inexpensive.

Fuchsias Guest House – John and Jenny Davies bring boundless energy to bear in the running of this friendly Victorian guesthouse, a modest affair with 6 rooms. Facilities are far superior to the prices, and they'll prepare a delicious evening meal if requested. 139 Earlham Rd. (phone: 651410). Inexpensive.

EATING OUT: By no stretch of the imagination can Norwich be considered a gastronomic center, and although there's plenty of interesting produce to be found in the surrounding countryside, the city's restaurants rarely manage to use it to best advantage. Look, if possible, for menus featuring samphire, a salt-marsh plant harvested on the nearby coast and, served with butter or vinegar, better known as the poor man's asparagus. Look, also, for crabs from Cromer, cockles and mussels from Moreston, Great Yarmouth herring, Lowestoft kippers, Stiffkey (pronounced *stoo*-kee) Blues or oysters, Norfolk dumplings served sweet or savory, and wild duck and geese from the fens. Don't forget to accompany everything with a generous dollop of mustard — they say Mr. Colman made his fortune from the mustard that people *left* on their plates. A meal for two with wine will cost more than $60 at a restaurant listed as expensive, $45 to $60 at one listed as moderate, and less than $40 at an inexpensive one. All telephone numbers are in the 0603 area code unless otherwise indicated.

Marco's – One of Norwich's smartest restaurants. Proprietor/chef Marco Vessalio makes superb zabaglione to follow other Italian specialties. Closed Sundays. 17 Pottergate (phone: 621044). Expensive.

Green's Seafood – One of the best of a poor bunch of "top" restaurants, it has a menu devoted to fish, with the exception of one vegetarian dish, one chicken dish, and two steak dishes. Closed Sundays. 82 Upper St. Giles St. (phone: 623733). Expensive to moderate.

Old Princes Inn – Despite its name, this is a restaurant, not a pub or hotel, and — hurray, hurray — it does serve such traditional English dishes as Norfolk duckling and Dover sole in, what's more, a crypt of 12th-century origins done up in Tudoresque decor. Closed Sundays. 20 Princes St. (phone: 621043). Moderate.

Pacifico's Mexican Restaurant and Cocktail Bar – On the busy but attractive section of Tombland near the cathedral, this 2-room eating place specializes in Mexican cocktails. Tombland (no phone). Moderate.

Savoy – A Greek restaurant, with some Malaysian specialties to add extra spice to the selections. The choice of hors d'oeuvres is huge, and there are lots of fish dishes. Live music in the downstairs *Cella Taverna* where there is sometimes a special "Greek Night" with cabaret and bouzouki music. Closed Sundays. 50 Prince of Wales Rd. (phone: 620732). Moderate.

Skippers Wine Centre – The à la carte restaurant and wine bar are part of a trio that also includes a coffee shop, the lifelong ambition of wine connoisseur Bernard Skipper. His wine list is endorsed by four prizes for "Wine List of the Year." Dianne Skipper prepares the food, served daily from breakfast on. Closed Sundays. 18 Bedford St. (phone: 622836). Moderate.

Boswell's – This old creeper-covered pub next door to the cathedral is almost a Norwich institution. Keeping pace with changing times, its carvery serves well-presented hot and cold meats and salads, while the desserts are served at a DIY (Do It Yourself) sweet bar. Open daily. Tombland (phone: 626099). Moderate to inexpensive.

Eat Naturally – "Open from coffee time till bedtime," this eatery serves imaginative variations on the vegetarian and health food theme. Closed Sundays. 11 Wensum St. (phone: 660838). Moderate to inexpensive.

Morello's – The stall partitions in this ex-stable still stand, the hay racks now display dried flowers, and the walls are hung with brasses and tack. Two menus are short but sweet, one devoted to vegetarian dishes, the other to pasta, Burmese spiced rice, and chili con carne, all described with flowery adjectives. Closed Sundays. 3 Orford Yard, off Red Lion St. (phone: 616106). Moderate to inexpensive.

Oscar's – An All-American restaurant, as if it were not obvious from the Stars and Stripes draped across the ceiling, the wooden Statue of Liberty model in the window, and the Bogart and Bacall wall posters. Plus the hash browns, burgers, steaks, and dips to whet the appetite. Open daily from 11 AM to 11 PM (midnight on Saturdays). Upper Goat La. (phone: 620829). Moderate to inexpensive.

Siam Bangkok – Dine beneath a ceiling of painted paper parasols in this small Thai restaurant. Hot and sour soups, perfumed rice, and the dubious-sounding *cow pat bohw* appear on the menu. Closed Sundays. 8 Orford Hill (phone: 617056 or 617073). Moderate to inexpensive.

Swelter's – In a basement down a pretty Georgian alley, this former newspaper press room has been converted into an attractive wine bar serving salads and snacks at lunchtime (weekdays) and light meals in the evening (Wednesdays through Saturdays). It's the proud possessor of Norfolk's only "Cruvinet," a device to keep the contents of open wine bottles from oxidizing. Woburn Ct., 8 Guildhall Hill (phone: 612874). Moderate to inexpensive.

Assembly House – Take tea — or a hot or cold lunch — in the ballroom of this Norwich landmark, a meeting place for fashionable society during the 18th century. Closed after 7:30 PM and Sundays. Theatre St. (phone: 626402). Inexpensive.

Briton's Arms – Morning snacks, light lunches, and tea in the classic English manner are served around a real fire in winter in this 15th-century cottage. Closed evenings and Sundays. Elm Hill (phone: 623367). Inexpensive.

Crypt Coffee Bar – The old crypt walls meet a modern glass roof laced with red framing, the whole creating an attractive, if rather bizarre, setting for hot lunches, snacks, cakes, and coffee, served until about 5 PM. On Saturdays, there's often a crafts fair going on in the same building. Closed Sundays. St. Andrew's Hall, Elm Hill (phone: 628477). Inexpensive.

Gedge – The full name is *Gedge of Elm Hill,* where it sits perched on the corner at the top. The smell of coffee and home-baked cakes, scones, pastries, and rolls wafts outside the door, a hint of things to come. Tables are available outside. Closed after 5 PM and Sundays. 2 Elm Hill (phone: 624847). Inexpensive.

Lloyd's – Convenient for lunch as you shop along the street, it serves seasonal and regional dishes. There's a minimum charge at lunchtime. London St. (624978). Inexpensive.

Piglet's Pasta Bar – Serves, guess what, in all shapes and sizes, which, for the uninitiated, are displayed in their raw state in the window. Open daily. 21 Tombland (phone: 621822). Inexpensive.

Pink Rose – The place for simple dishes such as quiche, in surroundings that suggest a tearoom. Closed Sundays and Mondays. 68 St. Benedict St. (phone: 615581). Inexpensive.

SHARING A PINT: In 1892, the local Temperance Society listed more than 800 pubs in the city. Today there are a "mere" 200 within the city walls. Many have several centuries of history, and some have resident ghosts as part of their pedigree. The *Adam and Eve* (17 Bishopsgate) is the oldest pub in Norwich, dating from 1249, when it was used as a brewhouse for builders working on the cathedral. Cozy low beams and bare-tiled floors are reminiscent of its "spit and sawdust" wherryman days. The *Bell,* Timberhill, one of the city's most famous, is the place where the notorious "Hell-Fire Club" met in the 18th century to plot against the Methodists. The *Coach and Horses* (Bethel St.) is an old coaching inn whose exterior walls still carry the medieval parish boundary marks and whose interior woodwork dates from 1400, while the *Lamb Inn,* another old coaching inn down a passageway (Orford Place), was the scene of the infamous murder of one of its landlords in 1787. The yuppie crowd frequents the brightly decorated *Drummonds* (Queen St.), which is open for breakfast as well as lunch, tea, and supper. *Micawbers Tavern* has a cozy old dark wooden interior but remains more offbeat, situated at the quiet end of Pottergate on the corner of Cow Hill. Chris Gudgin's *Walnut Tree Shades* cocktail bar, Old Post Office Ct. (phone: 620166), serves sangria, daiquiris, Mocktails, Harvey Wallbangers, Street Machines, or, for the really daring, 2-pint "party pitchers" — "one of these, and you're anybody's" says the menu.

OXFORD

For 600 years, England had only two universities, and though more than 40 institutions of higher learning have opened their doors since the early 19th century, the two venerable ancients are still so embedded in the British psyche that they are often called by one name, Oxbridge, put asunder only by scholars debating questions of academic supremacy or by tourists comparing their visible merits. Although neither argument is likely to come to a conclusion soon, the casual visitor will notice a difference between Oxford and Cambridge. Whereas Cambridge, often described as a "city within a university," has the atmosphere of a small country town, Oxford is larger and bustling, not quite a metropolis, but transformed by a 20th-century auto industry on its outskirts into a "university within a city."

Fortunately, Oxford University, though only part of present-day Oxford, remains its historic core, one of the great living architectural treasures of the world, where examples of every building style from the 11th century on are preserved in less than 1 square mile. Oxford is Britain's oldest university, but age coupled with academe has not produced a dark, dreary collection of moss-covered monoliths. A much-quoted line by the 19th-century poet Matthew Arnold — "That sweet city with her dreaming spires" — aptly describes the university's towers, domes, and constant repetition of pinnacles when seen from afar or above. Close up, as the visitor stands before a single façade of ribbed golden stone, limpid panes of glass, or alternating panels of the two, any sense of the laborious process of study fades, and Oxford becomes the idea of learning incarnate, all light, clarity, and brilliance, even in the most inclement weather.

No one knows why scholars began to gather here. The city was probably in existence on the banks of the river Thames (called, in Oxford, the Isis) and its tributary, the Cherwell, long before the first reference to it appeared in the *Anglo-Saxon Chronicle* in 912. In 1121, the Priory of St. Frideswide was founded, and it was possibly the presence of scholarly monks that drew English students to Oxford after a quarrel between Henry II and the French resulted in the closing of the Sorbonne to Englishmen in 1167. The university then developed quickly. By 1300, the first colleges had been established (University, Balliol, and Merton), and there were 1,500 students on hand.

Relations between town and gown were immediately antagonistic. Early students lived in lodging houses at the mercy of price-gouging townspeople; townspeople saw their city taken over by a young and boisterous occupying army. An outbreak of hostilities in 1209 caused some students to flee and set up a university at Cambridge. Even greater trouble in 1355, on *St. Scholastica's Day,* resulted in the deaths of 62 students and in the rest being driven from town. That the dispute was eventually resolved in favor of the university was a measure of its royal protection (because scholars became the basis of a king's loyal civil service, the gown-crown connection was strong). Thereafter, on every *St. Scholastica's Day* from 1357 to 1825, city dignitaries performed the humiliating penance of placing 62 pennies on the altar of the university church of St. Mary the Virgin, and for nearly 500 years the university virtually ruled Oxford.

Rivalry between town and gown is now light-hearted, but the structure of the university has scarcely changed since the Middle Ages. By 1400, every student was required to be listed on the roll (matricula) of a master (or teacher — later to be called a don, from the Latin *dominus* for "master") responsible for him, and all were required to live in colleges or halls rather than in scattered lodging houses. The proliferating colleges became self-contained communities — behind the gates of each were living quarters, chapel, library, kitchen, dining hall, and even a brewery. This collegiate system in its modern guise continues to baffle visitors. Many an undergraduate popping out of Worcester or Wadham has been accosted by lost tourists looking for Oxford College, unaware that Oxford's colleges are part of Oxford University. Young men and women (the first of five women's colleges opened in 1878, and most of the colleges are now open to both sexes) seeking admission to the university have to be accepted, usually after an examination, by individual colleges, and live in them or in lodgings approved by them. But the university arranges academic curricula, administers financial aid from the government, and awards degrees.

This medieval organization also accounts for the type of sightseeing experience to be had in Oxford. More than 600 buildings in the city are considered to be of outstanding architectural merit, and most belong to the university. Your time in Oxford will be spent wandering through gateways into "quadrangles," or courtyards (the students live up numbered staircases around the quads), discovering gardens, cloisters, and chapels, visiting the occasional open library or hall, following a passageway through still another arch and into one more quadrangle, often a spacious green lawn coaxed to perfection by centuries of loving care and hardly any pounding of feet — the sign will say who's allowed to walk on the grass, and it's usually dons, sometimes postgraduates, occasionally undergraduates, never visitors.

Much of Oxford's history is brought to life by the anecdotes of local guides well versed in the city's folklore: How Dr. Johnson, a poor student at Pembroke College, was ashamed to walk into nearby Christ Church — always a grand college — because of his run-down shoes, yet threw away a pair of new ones left at his door by a rich scholar. Or how (the story everyone tells) one would-be undergraduate, up for an interview, was greeted superciliously by a don who turned from the awed youth, opened a copy of *The Times,* and said, "Right, impress me" — at which the boy took out a box of matches, set fire to the paper, and won a scholarship.

Oxford is primarily its students, and they do occasionally use humor to relieve the weight of tradition that is everywhere. At times, even on their backs. If exams are under way, visitors will see them going around in *subfusc* — dark suits or skirts with short black gowns on top, the age-old traditional dress for formal occasions. Some of the weightier traditions, in fact, seem actually born of silliness: "The Mallard Song," sometimes sung by the fellows of All Souls, celebrates a duck that flew out of a drain when the college was built. The Boar's Head Ceremony, held at Queen's College at Christmas, honors a legendary scholar who saved himself from a wild boar's attack by stuffing a Greek book down the animal's throat.

None of this, however, changes the fact that Oxford's stock-in-trade is the pursuit of knowledge, and visitors tiptoeing around quadrangles are constantly reminded of this by the firm signs asking them to be quiet. Such a polite command is not hard to obey, especially if it's all the better to hear the choristers of Christ Church singing in the cathedral. But even without the background sound, the sight of the sun glinting off the exalted architectural complex of Radcliffe Square, or of the progression of college façades on High Street coalescing to a magnificent skyline, is an inspiration.

OXFORD AT-A-GLANCE

SEEING THE CITY: An initial bird's-eye view of Oxford is absolutely essential, since it gives a clear idea of the layout of the colleges. Four of the best vantage points for such a perspective are the gallery near the top of the spire of St. Mary's Church, on High Street — colloquially known as The High — the cupola at the top of Christopher Wren's *Sheldonian Theatre* on Broad Street, Carfax Tower in the very center of town (closed in winter), and the tower of St. Michael's at the North Gate. From St. Mary's you see much of High Street, with its gentle curve that is fancifully said to reflect most people's natural stroll: All Souls College; University College; and the Radcliffe "Camera," or Library. From the Sheldonian you look onto Broad Street (better known as The Broad); across to Balliol and Trinity colleges; closer by, down at Exeter College, the Bodleian Library, and the Clarendon Building — once the home of the university printers, later to become the Oxford University Press. The view from South Park (east of Magdalen Bridge) of the "dreaming spires" set amid the trees is lauded in many a guidebook. For another traditional view of Oxford's spires, find the slightly unkempt piece of common land called Port Meadow, between the river Thames and the railway line. Or, closer and more congenial, though slightly less panoramic, Christ Church Meadow, near the southernmost point of the city, to the east of St. Aldate's.

SPECIAL PLACES: Ask any but the most disenchanted Oxford graduate about special places and he or she will answer "my college." Virtually all 35 of them are worth a visit, but happily the most impressive are the most central. Not one is too distant from Carfax (from the French *quatre voies,* "four ways," or from the Latin *quadrifurcus,* "four-forked" — where the four main streets of Oxford met in Saxon times and still do) to be visited on foot. Most offer a glimpse of inner sanctums: quadrangles, chapels, and dining halls hung with portraits of distinguished former students and benefactors. Opening times vary.

For an overview of the entire university over the past 8 centuries, the "Oxford Story" describes important events and personalities involved with Oxford. Life-size tableaux with dramatic sound and lighting effects are accompanied by commentary by Sir Alec Guinness, which visitors listen to on headphones. Everything is included from Archbishop Cranmer being burned at the stake to the development of penicillin and a modern undergraduate wondering which clubs and societies to join. The entire presentation is given in one location. There's an excellent gift shop. Open daily. Admission charge. 6 Broad St. (phone: 790055).

THE HEART OF OXFORD

Magdalen College – Magdalen (pronounced *mawd*-lin) Tower, guarding the eastern end of High Street, was called by King James I, "the most absolute building in Oxford." An anthem is sung from the top of the tower at 6 AM every *May Day* morning. The college was established in 1458 by William of Waynflete, a bishop of Winchester, who was one of the first college founders to emphasize the importance of a chapel. There is a famous deer park, where the animals are fairly tame. Across High Street from Magdalen, also on the banks of the river Cherwell, is the Botanic Garden, the oldest in Britain, laid out in 1621 with approximately £5,000 given by Henry Danvers, Earl of Danby, primarily for the study of medicinal herbs. Open daily from 2 to 6:15 PM. High St.

All Souls College – Founded 21 years before Magdalen by Henry Chichele, Archbishop of Canterbury, All Souls does not have undergraduates, only 60 fellows engaged in research and teaching. Because of its great academic distinction, it has been called "the most exclusive club in Britain." (A member of the college once remarked that he never needed an encyclopedia; if he wanted to know anything he just had to ask a colleague.) Behind All Souls' small 15th-century front quadrangle is the 18th-century great quadrangle, with twin towers and the magnificent Codrington Library whose central adornment is a sundial made by Christopher Wren. Open daily from 2 to 5 PM. High St.

University College – Across High Street from All Souls, "Univ," as it is known, has the oldest building foundation in Oxford (1249). It used to be believed that it was founded by Alfred the Great, though the most telling comment on that occurred when one don — on being asked to a formal dinner to celebrate the millennium of Alfred's "foundation" — declined to come and sent two burned cakes instead. There's also a memorial to the poet Shelley (although he was expelled from the college). Open from 10 AM to 6 PM summer; from 10 AM to 5 PM winter. High St.

Church of St. Mary the Virgin – St. Mary's 14th-century spire is one of the dominant features of the Oxford skyline (climb to the tower at the top for a magnificent panorama of the city), and the church is a fine example of Perpendicular Gothic. Alongside the church, and sharing the same entrance, stands the old Congregation House, built during the 1320s. The university's first building, it housed the original library. High St.

Radcliffe Camera – This building commemorates Oxford's most generous 18th-century benefactor, Dr. John Radcliffe. It's such a distinctive building that when seen from miles away under the right conditions and from the right viewpoint, it compares as a landmark with Cambridge's King's College Chapel. Designed by James Gibbs — influenced by plans for a projected mausoleum for Charles I at Windsor — and completed in 1749, it was originally called the Radcliffe Library and is now a reading room for the Bodleian, the university library. Radcliffe Sq., behind St. Mary's.

Bodleian Library – Ball games are not allowed on the grass between the Radcliffe Camera and the Bodleian Library, and strollers are discouraged, because the earth here is only a thin crust: Below it are massive stores of books and underground railways that bring books, on request by readers, from their shelves. The creation of the Bodleian Library was the outstanding achievement of 17th-century Oxford. It was founded by Thomas Bodley, born in 1545 and a fellow of Merton at 19, and opened in 1602, using an older library (Duke Humfrey's Library, built over the 15th-century Divinity School) as a core. It is one of the greatest libraries in the world and has the right, like the *British Museum Library* and the Cambridge University Library, to a copy of every book published in the country. Only readers may enter the library, although conducted tours can be arranged. For details, contact the City of Oxford Information Centre, St. Aldate's opposite the Town Hall (phone: 726871). Across the road from the *Sheldonian*

Theatre is an extension to the Bodleian, the New Bodleian, built in all its ugliness in the late 1930s. Radcliffe Sq.

Sheldonian Theatre – The degree-giving ceremony is held in the *Sheldonian,* which was designed by Christopher Wren in 1669, then professor of astronomy at the university. Based on a classical amphitheater, it is enhanced by its own courtyard, entered from Broad Street, which it shares with the Clarendon Building. Its interior, also used for concerts, is magnificent, among the most attractive of its features being a famous ceiling by Robert Streeter, "sergeant-painter" to King Charles II. You can climb a wide wooden stairway to the cupola for a partial view of central Oxford's spires and gargoyles. Open Mondays through Saturdays from 10 AM to 4:45 PM (to 3:45 PM November through February). Broad St.

New College – Its full name is St. Mary College of Winchester in Oxenford, but when it was completed in 1386, the full effect was so stunning that the college, founded by William of Wykeham, Bishop of Winchester, has always been known as New College. The front quadrangle is the original one (the first quadrangle built as such in Oxford, following the example of Merton's Mob Quad, which became a quad bit by bit), though the top story on three of its sides was added in the late 17th century. The other side is formed by the chapel, which should be seen inside, too, for various treasures including the bishop's crosier. New College's garden quad, also added in the late 17th century, incorporates a stretch of 13th- and 14th-century city wall. Open daily from 2 to 5 PM (termtime), and 11 AM to 5 PM (vacation). New College La.

Balliol College – Apart from All Souls, which does not admit undergraduates, Balliol is academically the most impressive college in the university, with a long list of distinguished graduates, particularly in the field of politics (Lord Curzon, Harold Macmillan, Edward Heath). The college originated in 1255 when the Bishop of Durham levied a fine upon John de Balliol, a powerful landowner. He was to pay a sum of money for several years toward the support of poor Oxford scholars. After his death in 1269, his wife continued the project. Balliol, founded in approximately 1263, was actually a living quarters, not a college as we know it today. Outside Balliol, in the middle of Broad Street, a cross on the ground marks the spot where three Protestant martyrs, Thomas Cranmer, Nicholas Ridley, and Hugh Latimer, were burned at the stake during the reign of Mary Tudor in 1555. Open daily from 10 AM to 6 PM. Broad St.

Exeter College – In the Fellow's Garden of Exeter is one of Oxford's most famous trees, a horse chestnut that reaches over the boundary wall toward Brasenose. It is said that when the branches of the tree *touch* Brasenose, Exeter will beat Brasenose on the river. The tradition is scoffed at, but Brasenose undergraduates are known to clip the branches just in case. The college is associated with the rise of the pre-Raphaelite movement: William Morris and Burne-Jones were fellow students and later close friends. There is a William Morris tapestry in the chapel. Open from 2 to 5 PM (termtime), and from 10 AM to 5 PM (vacation). Broad St. at Turl St.

Christ Church – Lesson one: If you don't want to be taken for a complete country bumpkin, never say "Christ Church College," but simply "Christ Church." Lesson two (very subtle, this one): Contrary to usage at the other colleges, fellows, or dons, here are known as "students," but undergraduates never are. Christ Church was founded on the site of the Priory of St. Frideswide by Cardinal Wolsey in 1525, was refounded by Henry VIII in 1532 and 1546, and includes among its august alumni such names as Sir Philip Sidney, Richard Hakluyt, John Locke, John Wesley, John Ruskin, Lewis Carroll, and W. H. Auden. Its exquisitely vaulted chapel is also Oxford's cathedral, one of the smallest cathedrals in England, while its 16th-century Great Quadrangle (or Tom Quad) is Oxford's largest. Great Tom, the imperious bell in Tom Tower, hangs right above the main Christ Church entrance and resounds 101 times at 9:05 each night, the original curfew time for the 101 undergraduates it summoned by its first peal. See, also, the paneled and gilded medieval dining hall and the 18th-century Palladian Peckwater

Quad, behind Tom Quad. Open weekdays from 9:30 AM to 4:30 PM, Saturdays to 12:30 PM. St. Aldate's.

Merton College – University College was founded in 1249, Balliol in 1263, but if it's a question of official papers, then Merton (founded in 1246, with final statutes dated 1274) can claim to be the oldest college in Oxford. It has, at any rate, Oxford's oldest quadrangle, Mob Quad (begun 1304), whose south and west sides are formed by a curious medieval library — no lending library, some of the books are still chained to desks as they were for the early scholars. Merton also has Oxford's first collegiate chapel, containing original 13th-century stained glass. Intimate, quiet, and less neatly laid out than the other colleges, Merton's buildings only gradually assumed the familiar quadrangle form, but once this pattern was copied by New College, it was the model for all the colleges that followed. Open weekdays from 2 to 5 PM, weekends from 10 AM to 5 PM (to 4 PM in winter). Merton St.

St. Edmund Hall – A few yards off High Street, this college has what may be the prettiest quadrangle in the university. Though quite small, it has a well, a sundial, window boxes, flowers, and wisteria climbing the walls. The college's architecture ranges from the 16th to the 20th centuries. An archway leads to the former church of St. Peter's in the east, a beautiful building which is now the college's library. Open daily. A short tunnel leads into it from Queens Lane.

Ashmolean Museum of Art and Archaeology – This collection of paintings, sculpture, musical instruments, artifacts of the Stone and Bronze Ages, and other objets d'art originally belonged to John Tradescant (d. 1638), then his son, who in turn left it to Elias Ashmole, also a collector. Among the treasures are Michelangelo and Raphael drawings, the Pomfret and Arundel marbles, Oliver Cromwell's death mask, and Guy Fawkes's lantern. Perhaps the most famous item in the whole museum is the exquisite Alfred Jewel, found in a field in 1693 and marked with an old English inscription "Alfred Had Me Made." The Ashmolean's wealth of rarities and curiosities outgrew its original building in the 19th century and moved to these premises. Closed Mondays. Beaumont St. (phone: 278000).

The *Ashmolean*'s former quarters, next to the *Sheldonian Theatre* on Broad Street, now house the *Museum of the History of Science* (phone: 277280). Open Mondays through Fridays, 10:30 AM to 1 PM and 2:30 PM to 4 PM.

OFFBEAT OXFORD

Covered Market – Built in 1774, this is a busy and charming if down-to-earth street market recently relinked (after 250 years) to the Cornmarket shopping street by a pedestrian route through the Golden Cross courtyard. In its maze of tiny lanes crammed with tiny shops, the aroma of just-ground coffee and fresh fish mingles with that of ripe cheese and bloodstained sawdust from the butcher's shops and that of a game dealer's shop half-buried in fur and feathers. Wander among the banks of fresh fruit and vegetables, salami, mussels, carp, and silver sprats. After a colorful morning's stroll, drop by at the rough-and-ready but popular *George's Cafe,* 77 The Market (phone: 249527). Downstairs is a basic coffee and tea shop selling pies, sandwiches, and cakes, while the upstairs caters to a health-conscious clientele with salads and home-made soups. Both claim a cult following among undergraduates. The tables may be covered in crumbs, the service offhand, the floor unswept, the other customers morose or argumentative, but the place has style.

Blackwells Bookshop – One of the world's biggest bookshops, virtually an Aladdin's cave filled with books, *Blackwells* is where tourists buying paperback guides to the city rub shoulders with fellows of All Souls collecting esoteric tomes ordered on their behalf, and undergraduates dutifully gathering up texts recommended by their tutors. 52 Broad St., opposite the *Sheldonian Theatre;* other branches are 27 Broad St. (for art and posters) and 88 Holywell St. (for music).

■ **EXTRA SPECIAL:** Early summer sees Oxford at its best and brightest, and although most undergraduates have exams on their minds, that does not seem to obtrude — perhaps it even helps. Oxford has all kinds of activities and fetes during this season; check the *What's On* brochures as well as the college notice boards. There are open-air plays in college gardens; "commem" balls — grand, all-night, black-tie affairs to which you may have trouble obtaining tickets, especially for the more popular ones; picnics and madrigals on the river; garden parties; church festivals, and much more. Tickets are available from *Tickets in Oxford* (see *Sources and Resources,* below). (*A word of caution:* Because hotel rooms are at a premium at this time, be prepared to accept hotel accommodations some distance from the city center or even in the surrounding countryside. Woodstock, Abingdon, Witney, and Weston-on-the-Green, for example, have good hotels.)

SOURCES AND RESOURCES

TOURIST INFORMATION: The City of Oxford Information Centre, St. Aldate's (opposite the Town Hall, about 100 yards from Carfax; phone: 726871), is excellent, and the staff is very helpful. It's open Mondays through Saturdays (and Sundays in summer), 9 AM to 5:30 PM, and stocks a massive amount of tourist literature, guides, maps, and *What's On* brochures; there is also a 24-hour informational video screen. Very informative 2-hour guided walking tours, including the popular "American Roots in Oxford" tour, depart from here daily. The cost is approximately $4. *Tickets in Oxford* (phone: 727855) is also based here, with tickets for plays and concerts in town as well as in London and Stratford-upon-Avon. The inexpensive *Oxford Guide* and the *Oxford Vade Mecum,* on sale in most bookstores, are both useful and detailed. Both the information center and Thames and Chilterns Tourist Board, the Mount House, Church Green, Witney, Oxfordshire 0X8 6DZ (phone: 0443-778800) have essential background information on the surrounding area.

Local Coverage – The *Oxford Mail* (whose editor, incidentally, is traditionally allowed to dine in All Souls when the mood takes him) is the evening newspaper. Also available are the magazine *What's On* and the free leaflet *This Month in Oxford. Daily Information,* a city-published sheet, is available for reference from the information center.

Telephone – The area code for Oxford is 0865.

GETTING AROUND: Except for the trip from the train station, for which you will need a taxi or a bus to Carfax, in the city's historic core, and unless you choose a hotel out of the center, you will not need transport. Everyone goes on foot or by bicycle. In fact, 2-hour guided walking tours of the city are popular and a good means of orientation. They are available in the morning and afternoon; the information center has details.

Bus – The new, air conditioned *CityLink 190* and Oxford Tube nonstop coaches run every 20 minutes from Oxford's Gloucester Green to London's Victoria Station (phone: 248190). The *X70* bus runs several times daily to both London's Heathrow and Gatwick airports (phone: 722270). The *South Midlands Bus Company,* which provides very good service linking the city center with its outskirts, is at 395 Cowley Rd. (phone: 711312). For information, contact the Travel Shop, 5 Gloucester St. (phone: 772250).

Car Rental – You can rent a car from *Europcar,* Seacourt Tower, Botley Rd. (phone: 246373); *Hertz,* Woodstock Roundabout (phone: 510933); *Kenning,* Oxford TraveLodge on Woodstock Rd. (phone: 511232); *Motorlux, Ltd.,* 265 Iffley Rd. (phone:

240101); or *Swan National,* St. Clement's Garage, Dawson St. (phone: 240471). Others are listed at the information center and in the yellow pages. Parking in Oxford is difficult to find, but day-trippers can take advantage of the "Park and Ride" scheme. Leave your car free of charge in the parking lots clearly marked as you enter Oxford, then take the blue and white buses that run frequently (weekdays from 7:30 AM to 6:30 PM, Saturdays from 8:30 AM to 6:30 PM) to the city center.

Taxi – Unfortunately, cabs in Oxford are expensive compared with most other cities. There are cab ranks in several locations around the city; one convenient spot is the taxi rank near the *Randolph* hotel. To order by phone, call *Radio Taxis* (phone: 249743) or *ABC Taxis* (phone: 770077).

Train – London's Paddington Station is a quick, 1-hour ride from Oxford by train. For frequent trips, discount Saver Return tickets, available at Paddington Station, are valid for 1 month for travel any time after 9:30 AM. The Oxford railway station is west of the city center just off Park End St. (phone: 722333).

SPECIAL EVENTS: Late May sees one of the biggest events of the Oxford calendar — *Eights Week,* when crews from the colleges compete over 4 days for the coveted title of Head of the River. The annual *May Day Morning* is celebrated on May 1, with traditional morris dancing and madrigal singing beginning at 6 AM. *Encaenia* takes place in the *Sheldonian Theatre,* most spectacularly at the end of the summer term, when honorary degrees are awarded to distinguished men and women. In late August the *Oxford Regatta* monopolizes the river Thames. Each September, the *St. Giles' Fair* is held in St. Giles', between the *Randolph* hotel and the point at which the Woodstock and the Banbury roads fork off to the north. Traffic has to be diverted to accommodate this centuries-old fun fair.

MUSEUMS: In addition to those mentioned in *Special Places,* other museums of note are the following:

Bate Collection of Historical Instuments – A comprehensive collection of woodwind, brass, and percussion instruments. Open Mondays through Fridays from 2 to 5 PM. Faculty of Music, Floyds Row (phone: 276139).

Christ Church Picture Gallery – Old masters, glassware, antiques. Open daily. Admission charge. In Canterbury Quad, Christ Church (phone: 276172).

Museum of Modern Art – Gallery, cinema, and a bookshop. Closed Mondays. 30 Pembroke St. (phone: 722733).

Museum of Oxford – The history of the city from Norman times by means of photographs and models. Closed Sundays and Mondays. St. Aldate's (phone: 815559).

Pitt Rivers Museum – General Pitt-Rivers' renowned 19th-century collection, including ethnological and archaeological items, musical instruments, and weapons. Open Mondays through Saturdays, 1 to 4:30 PM. Parks Rd. (phone: 270927).

Rotunda Museum of Antique Dolls' Houses – A private collection featuring more than 40 historic dollhouses, complete with period furniture and "inhabitants." Open Sundays, summer only. Admission charge. Grove House, Iffley Turn (phone: 777935).

University Museum – Mainly natural history, in what was once Oxford's most architecturally controversial building. Open Mondays through Saturdays, 12 to 5 PM. Parks Rd. (phone: 272950).

SHOPPING: Just off Cornmarket, the 12th-century courtyard of the old *Golden Cross Inn* was converted into a precinct of specialty shops in 1987; particularly notable are the *Oxford Collection,* which sells quality souvenirs, and *Neal's Yard Wholefood Warehouse.* Inspired by the droves of academe, you will probably want to buy books and possibly paintings or prints, too. Besides *Blackwells,* there are several other bookstores on Broad Street, including the *Dillons* and the well-stocked *Paperback Shop,* and the city's largest secondhand bookstore, *Robin Waterfield's,* is at 36 Park End St. Along High Street, you'll find many antiques and picture shops; the *Oxford Gallery* sells as well as exhibits paintings (mostly contemporary). Also on High Street are *Reginald Davis* (No. 34), for silver and jewelry; *P. Audley-Miller* (No. 46), for antiques; *Magna Gallery* (No. 41), for old maps and prints; *Shepherd and Woodward* (Nos. 109–114), for Oxford University paraphernalia (sweat shirts, scarves, ties, etc.); and *Frank Cooper Shop and Museum* (No. 84), an Oxford institution and makers of a delicious marmalade since 1874. Just off High Street, Turl Street (No. 6) has *Ducker & Son,* with top-quality shoes for men. Little Clarendon Street, just north of the Ashmolean, has a couple of good crafts shops — *Tumi* (No. 1–2), which carries Latin American items, and *Oriental Crafts* (No. 21). Here you'll also find the well-known *Laura Ashley* (No. 26), along with *Sylvester* (No. 23), with a huge selection of interesting housewares, and the *Malvern Cheese Shop* (No. 32). For a picnic lunch visit the cheese shop, then pick up some other interesting comestibles at the *Covered Market* off High St., or the Wednesday morning open market off St. George St. (near the bus station). A jug of wine to accompany that picnic can be found at *Oddbins,* 108 High St. Both the *Westgate Shopping Centre* and the new *Clarendon Centre* contain several well-known chain stores. One of the coziest places to rest weary shopping legs is *Rosie Lee,* 51 High Street, where an afternoon tea of toasted teacakes and Earl Grey or *Rosie Lee*'s own blend of tea is served, as well as snacks, from 10 AM to 6:30 PM.

SPORTS: Biking – Bicycles can be rented from *Bee Line Bikes,* 33 Cowley Rd. (phone: 246615); *Denton's,* 294 Banbury Rd. (phone: 53859); *Penny Farthing,* 5 George St. (phone: 249368); *Reg Taylor,* 285 Iffley Rd. (phone: 247040); or *Broadrib,* 6 Lincoln House, Market St. (phone: 242624). (Though biking around Oxford may seem romantic, it isn't very safe, so unless you're confident on two wheels, skip it.)

Boating – The sport most popularly associated with Oxford is rowing, especially in view of the Boat Race held every year against Cambridge. At Oxford, the river Thames is too narrow to accommodate teams racing side by side, so the colleges have devised "Bumps," a series of rows in which 13 crews start together, one behind the other, and each tries to catch up and "bump" the one in front. But the best way for visitors to get properly acquainted with the river is to hire a punt (a flat-bottomed boat propelled and steered by a pole) at *Cherwell Boathouse,* Bardwell Rd. (phone: 515978), *C. Howard & Son,* Madgalen Bridge (phone: 61586), or *Hubbocks,* Folly Bridge (phone: 244235). Although unlikely, it is possible to fall into the river, and only competent swimmers are advised to venture out. Motorboats can also be rented for longer excursions from *Medley Boat Station,* Port Meadow (phone: 511660), or *Salters,* Folly Bridge (phone: 243421).

Golf – The *Southfield Golf Club* on Hilltop Rd., Headington (phone: 242158), welcomes visitors who are members of other golf clubs, weekdays only.

Ice Skating – The *Oxford Ice Rink* hires out skates. Oxpens Rd. (phone: 248076).

Swimming – Take a dip at the *Ferry Pool* (indoor and outdoor) near Ferry Centre, Summertown (phone: 510330). *Ferry Pool* also has squash courts, and rents racquets. *Temple Cowley Pool,* Cowley Rd. (phone: 716667), has the only ozone-sterilized pool in the area, as well as a sauna/solarium and fitness rooms.

THEATER: The *Apollo* on George St. plays host to drama, opera, ballet, and popular music shows (phone: 244544), while the *Pegasus Theatre* on Iffley Rd. (phone: 722851) presents "fringe" productions. Univeristy drama groups also stage plays regularly in various colleges. Check the *Daily Information* sheet at the Information Center, the *Oxford Mail,* or *What's On.*

MUSIC: Virtually all the colleges have a chapel of considerable architectural interest, and many of these showcase classical concerts and recitals. The best Oxford music is church music, however, and visitors are welcome at services in the three college chapels that have choir schools — Christ Church, Magdalen College, and New College. Several colleges are used for orchestral and choral concerts as are the *Sheldonian Theatre,* the *Town Hall,* and the *Holywell Music Rooms,* said to be the oldest of their kind in Europe. *Music at Oxford* (phone: 864056) has a regular program of chamber concerts, and the *City of Oxford Orchestra* also performs regularly. For more details, consult the *Daily Information* sheet or *Tickets in Oxford* at the information center.

NIGHTCLUBS AND NIGHTLIFE: During the university term Oxford is a young city, so there's a lot going on. Both *Boodles,* 34–35 Westgate (phone: 245136), which is fairly dressy, and *Bogarts,* the Plain (phone: 241047), are open Thursdays through Saturdays from 9 PM to 2 AM. *Cape of Good Hope,* the Plain, features disco groups. Non-members of clubs should try to arrive before 10:30 PM.

BEST IN TOWN

CHECKING IN: Perhaps it is because members of the university (which includes anyone who has graduated from it) can always get a room in their old college, or perhaps it is because during the vacation there are so many university landladies whose merits are passed by word of mouth — whatever the reason, Oxford is short of top-grade hotels, especially in the city center, and for the few that do exist, it's usually necessary to make reservations well ahead. You need never go without a bed, however; if you are having trouble, consult the information center in St. Aldate's (phone: 726871). Expect to pay $120 and up for a double room in a hotel listed as expensive; $70 to $120 at a moderate one; and under $70 in an inexpensive establishment. All telephone numbers are in the 0865 area code unless otherwise indicated.

Le Manoir aux Quat' Saisons – At the top of the country house hotel league, this dining-and-lodging establishment, 12 miles from Oxford, boasts a two-Michelin-stars restaurant. The 10 luxurious guestrooms feature half-testered beds and views overlooking nearly 30 acres of meadows and gardens. It is possible for two people to spend as much as $500 a night half board, but this discourages few, as booking months in advance is a necessity. Church Rd., Great Milton (phone: 0844-278881). Very expensive.

Ladbroke Linton Lodge – A short bus or taxi ride from the city center, this modernized Edwardian townhouse has 70 bedrooms, including some "Gold Star" luxury rooms; an oak-paneled dining room with a traditional English menu; and pleasant, peaceful gardens. 13 Linton Rd. (phone: 53461). Expensive.

Oxford Moat House – This modern hotel plays host to many conventions. For the casual tourist, however, it also offers 155 sleek rooms, a health club, and a convenient bistro-bar. This is a good starting point for a Cotswolds journey, as it is outside Oxford on A40 Wolvercote Roundabout (phone: 59933). Expensive.

Randolph – The best in town, this is a Victorian Gothic monument with an efficient staff and a very good location, directly opposite the *Ashmolean Museum.* Richly and elegantly furnished throughout, its 109 rooms are spacious and come with television sets and phones; other facilities include two luxury suites and the lofty *Spires* restaurant, which serves both à la carte and fixed-price dinners, a coffee shop for quick meals, a bar, and a lounge in which cream teas are served every afternoon. Beaumont St. (phone: 247481). Expensive.

Eastgate – Not quite as luxurious as some, but newly refurbished, with an excellent location near Magdalen and Queens colleges. Although the 35 rooms here are smallish, the staff is friendly. The High, entrance on Merton St. (phone: 248244). Expensive to moderate.

Cotswold Lodge – On the main road to Banbury, about a half-mile north of the city center, is this comfortable, privately-owned hotel. All 55 rooms have private bath; a modern wing is behind the original Victorian building. 66A Banbury Rd. (phone: 512121). Moderate.

Cumnor – In a hilltop-village setting on the edge of Oxford, this 6-room hotel has very comfortable surroundings and serves good, fresh food in its dining room. Off A420 Swindon Rd. at 76 Abingdon Rd., Cumnor (phone: 862216). Moderate.

TraveLodge – It's one of those standardized, no-frills motels that offers efficient service, 24-hour snack service, outdoor pool, and a 24-hour gas station. 3 miles north of Oxford center at Peartree Roundabout (phone: 54301). Moderate.

Westwood Country – Although its grounds are filled with all kinds of wildlife, like badgers and deer, this is still a peaceful 26-bedroom place just a few minutes from the city center. Four of the rooms have four-poster beds, and you can tone up in the multi-gym and wallow in a whirlpool bath before dinner. Price includes entry to the Cotswold Wildlife Park. Hinksey Hill Top (phone: 735408). Moderate.

The Lawns – The very name evokes the peaceful surroundings of Derek and Audrey Cotmore's little bed-and-breakfast establishment right on the city's doorstep. Guests are free to lounge in the garden and use the outdoor swimming pool. Breakfasts are filling and delicious, and a nearby pub offers hearty evening meals for those who want a night off the town. 12 Manor Rd., South Hinksey (phone: 739980). Inexpensive.

Old Parsonage – A kind of gem situated at the point where the main Banbury Road quiets down, this small, creeper-covered, former 13th-century hospital has 34 rooms, a simple decor, and tranquil atmosphere. Oscar Wilde was a frequent patron. 1–3 Banbury Rd. (phone: 54843). Inexpensive.

EATING OUT: Oxford offers more in the way of restaurants than it does hotels. If you cannot secure an invitation to dine at High Table with a don in one of the colleges (gastronomically it may not be tops, but for atmosphere it's unbeatable), you can still eat very well indeed. This is, after all, a very sophisticated community, and fine food is much appreciated. On the other hand, it's also a youthful community and has lots of hamburger joints and pizza parlors. Expect to pay $60 and up for dinner for two, excluding wine and tips, in establishments listed as expensive; $30 to $60 in moderate establishments; and under $30 in inexpensive places. All telephone numbers are in the 0865 area code unless otherwise indicated.

Le Manoir aux Quat' Saisons – In 1984, Oxford's best restaurant moved 12 miles away to Great Milton, into a beautiful 14th-century manor house hotel of the same name. Its two-star Michelin menu is among the best in Britain, featuring skillfully prepared haute cuisine and game in season, and there's an extensive wine list. Reservations necessary. Closed Mondays, Tuesdays for lunch, and December 24 through January 20. Church Rd., Great Milton (phone: 08446-8881). Very expensive.

Elizabeth – This chic little restaurant has a good location opposite Christ Church and is housed in one of Oxford's finest late-15th-century buildings. The sophisticated menu features French cooking; house specialties include trout stuffed with seafood, mousse, *suprême de volaille au vin blanc,* and *caneton aux abricots.* Open daily except Mondays, Christmas, and bank holidays. Reservations necessary. 84 St. Aldate's (phone: 242230). Expensive.

La Sorbonne – Occupying the second floor of a beautifully preserved half-timbered 17th-century house with overhanging eaves, this place offers classic French fare in a friendly, informal atmosphere. The wine list, as well as the service, is very good. Its Casse-Croute Room is somewhat less expensive than the main restaurant but also serves excellent French cuisine. Closed for 10 days at Christmas. Reservations necessary. 130A High St. (phone: 241320 or 242883). Expensive.

Blue Coyote – The new American owner has brought a flavor of California to the decor and the food. Indian artifacts adorn sunny orange walls, and the menu features everything from blue corn pancakes and clam chowder to Maryland crab cakes and pecan pie. Open daily. 36 St. Clements St. (phone: 241431). Moderate.

Cherwell Boathouse – Perched on the Cherwell, a tributary of the Thames, this restaurant is in a refurbished boathouse that rents punts and a gondola; they put out eight rooftop tables for summer dining. Two imaginative and set menus of three courses are offered daily — a recent example included hot vichyssoise, West Indian deep-dish meat pie, and Caribbean apple and grape dessert. Open daily for dinner except Sundays; also lunchtime buffets. Reservations necessary. Bardwell Rd. off Banbury Rd. (phone: 52746). Moderate.

Michel's Brasserie – Tucked away from the hustle and bustle, this eatery serves good French fare at reasonable prices. Open daily. 10 Little Clarendon St. (phone: 52142). Moderate.

Saraceno – Handily located (but easily overlooked) near the *Apollo Theatre,* this modern, white-walled French/Italian restaurant is popular with theatergoers, who pause here for a taste of the warm Mediterranean — be it scampi, scaloppine, zabaglione, or anything else on the extensive menu. Closed Sundays. In the basement under the *Jaeger's* boutique at 15 Magdalen St. (phone: 249171). Moderate.

Le Bistro du Marche – An informal place that serves delicious, reasonably priced French regional cuisine. Open daily. Market Avenue One, 9A High St. (phone: 723342) Moderate to inexpensive.

Brown's – This sprawling row house restaurant decorated with lots of mirrors and hanging plants is a popular place for students to entertain their parents. It's always crowded, so be prepared to wait in line and share tables. The entrées are wholesome and filling — spaghetti, steak and mushroom pie, hot sandwiches — and the desserts are homemade. String quartets accompany meals in the afternoons, and there's usually live jazz late at night. Open daily. No reservations. 5–9 Woodstock Rd. (phone: 511995). Moderate to inexpensive.

Crypt – One of a new breed of wine bars in town, this is in the cellars of the Oxford Union Society. It has imaginative Anglo-French dishes such as the Mungo Bagger, steak wrapped around prawns, and scampi in white wine and Madeira. The wine list has 45 choices. Closed Sundays. Frewin Passage (phone: 251000). Moderate to inexpensive.

Maxwell's – This faintly Art Deco, American-style diner is the place to go when you suffer a Big Mac attack. The menu features rib steaks, skewered lamb, burgers, milkshakes, and banana splits. Open daily. 35A Queen St. (phone: 242192). Moderate to inexpensive.

Brewery and Bakehouse – There is a strong emphasis on food in this pub, which brews its own beer and sells its own freshly baked bread and pizza. Live jazz is featured on Thursday nights and Sunday lunchtimes. Open daily. 14 Gloucester St. (phone: 727265). Inexpensive.

Fasta Pasta – This tiny Italian restaurant and shop perfectly captures the spirit of the old country. There's fettuccine and other fresh pasta, olive oil, wine, and salami to take away; or enjoy a plate of fresh pasta accompanied by a giant-size cappuccino. Open daily for lunch and dinner. 3 Little Clarendon St. (phone: 57349). Inexpensive.

Go Dutch – The pancakes served here are a meal in themselves — 12 inches in diameter and thick with a variety of fillings. Owner Rowena Greenwood recommends the bacon-and-apple. It looks rather like Grandma's dining room, with heavy gate-leg furniture and plant-filled windows. Open weekdays from 6 to 11 PM, weekends from noon. No reservations on weekdays. 18 Park End St., opposite the train station (phone: 240686). Inexpensive.

Head of the River – The ground floor of this converted wharf house beside Fully Bridge is a pub, the second a bistro/cocktail bar, and the top a 40-seat restaurant overlooking the river. The whole is linked by a spiral staircase and decorated with Laura Ashley–style furnishings and an abundance of dried flower arrangements. St. Aldate's (phone: 721600). Inexpensive.

Heroes Sandwich Bar – Good sandwiches on whole wheat, rye, or pita are available here, as are interesting soups, milk drinks, and fruit juices. Closed Sundays. 8 Ship St. (phone: 723459). Inexpensive.

Munchy Munchy – Spicy Malaysian dishes that change every day and a good selection of fish and fresh vegetables are served in this unpretentious eatery. The surroundings and very reasonable prices are reminiscent of food centers in the owners' home city of Singapore. Closed Sundays and Mondays. 6 Park End St. (phone: 245710). Inexpensive.

Nosebag – Oak-beamed ceilings, handmade pottery, and classical music make this eatery a pleasant respite in a busy sightseeing day. The soups, salads, and daily hot and cold specials are all very reasonably priced. Lunch draws a big crowd. Open daily until 5:30 PM. 6–8 St. Michael's St. (phone: 721033). Inexpensive.

Pastificio – This bright, modern restaurant serves great fresh pasta. Special lunch menus (such as minestrone, garlic bread, and spaghetti) are a real bargain, and a Pasta Pronto menu offers dishes ready in 4 to 5 minutes for people in a hurry. Open daily. 14–16 George St. (phone: 791032). Inexpensive.

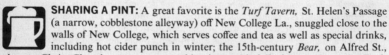

SHARING A PINT: A great favorite is the *Turf Tavern,* St. Helen's Passage (a narrow, cobblestone alleyway) off New College La., snuggled close to the walls of New College, which serves coffee and tea as well as special drinks, including hot cider punch in winter; the 15th-century *Bear,* on Alfred St., close to Christ Church, was once a coaching inn and is full of atmosphere; the *Eagle and Child,* St. Giles, was frequented by literary lights such as J. R. R. Tolkien; the *White Horse,* in Broad St. next door to Blackwells, is handy and historic, despite the addition of electronic games; and the *King's Arms,* on the corner of Holywell St. and Parks Rd., close to Wadham, is a convenient spot for a little nip.

PERTH

The world knows Edinburgh, Glasgow, and Aberdeen; Perth needs a little finding. To be in Perth means to be both physically and spiritually *inside* Scotland. Stationed at the head of the river Tay estuary, in the east central part of the country, the city calls itself the Heart of Scotland, a distinction with coordinates in time as well as space. Perth is indeed rich in historical associations, if not in actual remnants, and geographically speaking, it is one of several gateways to the Highlands. Many travelers stumble upon it for the latter reason only, but those who prolong the encounter find that Perth has its own special charm. In many ways, it is something of a magic town.

Perth is set in what is perhaps the oldest inhabited part of Scotland. The discovery here of a dugout canoe dating from 8,000 years ago suggests that, even for Stone Age hunting and fishing people, the river Tay made this a traveler's natural point of entry. Walk out into the dawn of Perth today and it's possible to sense the security of a residential, confident, and comfortable city, while still seeing in the river the same purity and bewitchment that must have dazzled the eyes of those ancient folk.

Seven main roads converge on Perth, which afforded anyone going north or south the first opportunity to bridge the Tay. The great Roman general Julius Agricola came here in AD 80 and established at Inchtuthill (just up the river) the biggest legionary fort north of York. And well he might. The Picts, a Celtic tribe of obscure origin (descendants of Iron Age invaders) who inhabited central and northern Scotland, had been driven from here by the Romans but were biding their time and would return. The name of the town itself marks their frontier dispute: Possibly it comes from Agricola's fort, "Bertha," or possibly it is some mutation of a word in the fragmentary and largely lost Pictish language.

Christian missionaries came, as did traders and invaders, and the Tay's dawn-red color soon ran blood red. Scone Palace (pronounced *skoon*), 2 miles north of the city, is associated with King Kenneth MacAlpin (usually rendered "MacAlpine"), the great 9th-century ruler of the Scots (descendants of Irish settlers in western Scotland), who was prodded by the necessity of defense against the invading Vikings to impose his rule also on the Picts, thus establishing a united Pict-Scot kingdom, the traditional nucleus of the kingdom of Scotland. Scone became the seat of government and the coronation place of Scottish kings from Kenneth I himself to Charles II in 1651, even though the Stone of Destiny, the Stone of Scone on which the coronations actually took place, was stolen by Edward I of England in 1296 and made the Coronation Chair in Westminster Abbey. Officially, the stone is still in Westminster Abbey, but it is a sardonic Scottish legend that it is not the *real* stone, for when some Scots stole the original in 1951, it is said that they returned a substitute.

As a key to the Highlands even in the Middle Ages, Perth was a walled town with a castle that overawed it until Old Perth was swept away by storm and flood in 1209. King William the Lion (1165–1214) then extended the town to the west in a "new burgh." War, trade, and remarkable religious devotion — medieval records often refer to Perth as St. John's Toun — characterized the period. Edward I, in his campaign to make the English king also the ruler of Scotland (which included carrying off the Stone of Scone), fortified the town in 1298. And it was, in fact, the capture of Perth from the English in 1313 — in pursuit of which the Scottish king, Robert the Bruce, after a feigned retreat, plunged up to his neck in the moat's icy waters and set his scaling ladder against the ramparts — that completed the reconquest of Scotland, clinched the following year with the defeat of Edward II at Bannockburn. The next English king, Edward III, ousted Bruce's son, David II, and from 1333 to 1339 Perth was the English headquarters. But it was soon retaken and its walls cast down after the surrounding country had been so badly devastated as to cause starvation and inspire cannibalism.

Perth then became the scene of clan warfare, when, in 1396, 30 men each from the Chattan and Kay clans gathered on the North Inch and fought to the death of almost every last man. The thousands of spectators included King Robert III and his queen, who watched from Blackfriars Monastery nearby, and the bloody combat was later described in Sir Walter Scott's novel *The Fair Maid of Perth,* the heroine of which is supposed to have lived in a house in the North Port that now serves as a crafts center. The same monastery was the scene of the murder of Robert's son, James I (1406–37), whose attempts to impose order over warring clans and militant nobles led to his being hacked to pieces by some of the latter in a sewer under the monastery, where he had taken refuge. The padlocks had been treacherously removed, and a brave lady, Catherine Douglas, used her arm to bar the gates, breaking it in the vain effort to stop the King's pursuers.

Blackfriars, a Dominican friary founded by Alexander II in 1231, was one of Perth's many royal foundations for the clergy: James himself had founded a Charterhouse near the railway station, the present site of the King James VI Hospital. There were also monasteries of the Greyfriars and the Whitefriars. No stone of the medieval friaries survived the 16th century, however, because it was in Perth that John Knox preached some of his most incendiary Reformation sermons, rousing the mob to a frenzy of destruction that leveled them all.

On the westerly outskirts of Perth is Huntingtower Castle, formerly known as Ruthven Castle, where the Raid of Ruthven took place. A band of conspirators led by Lord Ruthven, first Earl of Gowrie, invited the 16-year-old James VI (later James I of England) here in 1582, "kidnapped" him, and held him prisoner in the castle for several months. For this, the earl was beheaded a few years later, and James took further revenge in 1600 at Gowrie House (no longer extant) in Perth, when another attempt to kidnap him, this time by the sons of the first earl, ended in the death of the two brothers at the hands of James's attendants. Full particulars of the episode, which went down in history as the Gowrie Conspiracy, remain a mystery, but it did result in the proscription of the very name Ruthven, hence the castle's name change.

Through all these vicissitudes of history, Perth retained its strong commercial character and is today known for its insurance, textile, and dyeing industries, as well as for its cattle markets and world-famous whisky. During the early 19th century, Arthur Bell turned a small family whisky business into a great export concern; another family distilling business was begun at the same time by John Dewar. The story is told that Bell and Dewar were once on their way to a church meeting and decided to stop for a dram beforehand. Bell asked Dewar what he would have, to be told: "A Bell's. It would not do to go into the meeting smelling of whisky." According to members of the Bell family, it was Bell who made the remark, just after he ordered a Dewar's.

PERTH AT-A-GLANCE

SEEING THE CITY: To experience the magic of Perth, climb to the top of 729-foot Kinnoull Hill, east of the river, a very simple feat. Take the easy side (unless you are a geologist or a botanist, in which case you will have fun on the precipitous side). There is a tower on the edge of the precipice, placed there by the ninth Earl of Kinnoull, who had been impressed by the castles on the Rhine, though he thought the river inferior to his own Tay. He also put a stone table on the top of the hill and dined there frequently because of his love of the view. The hill now belongs to the city, which, for spectators standing by the table, lies directly below, with the Grampians to the right, the fields and woods to the left, and the river in front. Lord Kinnoull seems to have been quite right.

SPECIAL PLACES: Perth is small enough to be seen on foot. The city lies on the west bank of the river Tay, with two large green spaces — North Inch and South Inch — to the north and south of it. Between these two parks is something of a grid. Tay Street runs along the river, beginning in the south as Shore Road and eventually passing Queen's Bridge (which connects with the Dundee Road, A85, across the river) and then Perth Bridge (cross it to get to Kinnoull Hill). High Street runs westward off Tay Street midway between the two bridges. South Street runs westward from Queen's Bridge, becoming County Place, then York Place, and then turning south for the Glasgow Road (A9). The city's tourist information center is at Marshall Place, which runs westward from Tay Street along the top of the South Inch, becoming King's Place and ending at the railroad station.

CITY CENTER

St. John's Kirk – Perth's oldest building, and one of it's few surviving medieval structures, St. John's Kirk was founded in 1126 and largely rebuilt during the 15th century. It suffered badly from a wave of destruction of religious property after John Knox, the great Protestant orator, denounced church idolatry here in 1559 and virtually launched the Reformation from its pulpit. The Royalist general (and poet) James Graham, Marquis of Montrose, used it as a camp in 1645, and during the 1650s the Cromwellians made it into a courthouse. It was put to use as an Episcopalian church for the Young Pretender, Prince Charles Edward, or Bonnie Prince Charlie, in 1745 (although he was then a Roman Catholic). Again in use for the Church of Scotland, the church was a triumph of restoration in the 1920s, and the present queen (who, by law, becomes Presbyterian when in Scotland) took part in a *Thanksgiving* service here for her Silver Jubilee in 1977. Open 10 AM to 12 PM and 2 to 4 PM, Mondays through Saturdays. Enter by the west door. St. John's Pl., off High St.

Salutation Hotel – Built in 1699 and still in full commercial use as a hotel, it became famous as the headquarters of Bonnie Prince Charlie during the Jacobite rising of 1745. 34 South St.

Watergate – The Vikings left their imprint on Perth in the name of this street (*gate* means "street"), which lies between High Street and South Street and offers fragments from the medieval town. Look at the wall in Fountain Close, off the east end of South Street, where there is a map of the old narrow passages or "vennels," the most interesting of which is Oliphant's Vennel. Then, for a change of pace, cross High Street to George Street, which contains some interesting early Victorian work.

Fair Maid's House – This fine stone house near the North Inch dates from the Middle Ages. In its early life, it was the guild hall of the glovers, but ever since Sir Walter Scott depicted it as the home of a 14th-century glover's daughter, the heroine of his novel *The Fair Maid of Perth,* it has been known by Scott's appellation rather than the historical one. Inside are a street-level crafts shop, where the works of local craftsmen are exhibited and sold, and an upstairs art gallery, with changing exhibitions of paintings by Scottish artists. Open Mondays through Saturdays, 10 AM to 5 PM. North Port, off Charlotte St. (phone: 25976).

Old Academy – The impressive façade is all that remains of the Old Perth Academy, built in 1807; the rest of the rebuilt structure currently consists of expensive apartments. A one-time rector (headmaster) of the famous school, the physicist Adam Anderson, designed Perth's first piped-water system, brought to completion in 1832, and was also responsible for the introduction of the city's gas lighting system. The academy building is on Rose Terrace, overlooking the North Inch, and both the street and its environs contain some fine 18th-century houses, including one (10 Rose Terr.) in which John Ruskin, the great essayist and critic of art and architecture, spent part of his youth. Atholl Street and Barossa Place, at either end of Rose Terrace, also have architectural charms worth investigating. Rose Terr., west of North Inch.

Balhousie Castle – A 15th-century castle, restored during the 17th century, is the home of the *Black Watch Regimental Museum,* whose collection commemorates many formidable engagements in British imperial and military history over the last 2½ centuries. Colorful uniforms are on display, as well as some interesting silver. Open Mondays through Fridays from 10 AM to 4:30 PM and Sundays from 2 PM to 4:30 PM Easter through September; Mondays through Fridays from 10 AM to 3 PM October to Easter. Hay St. (phone: 21281, ext. 30).

St. Ninian's Episcopal Cathedral – The first cathedral built in Scotland since the Reformation (it was begun in 1849) contains some truly fine stained glass. North Methven St.

King James VI Hospital – The site of the old Carthusian monastery (Charterhouse), founded by James I during the 15th century and destroyed in 1559, is now occupied by a hospital originally endowed by James VI in the 16th century, although the present structure is from the mid-18th century, with a cupola added in 1764. The building was for a time broken up into flats but has been restored and is well worth a look. Hospital St., off County Pl.

Greyfriars' Cemetery – Behind the tourist information center, this interesting old burial ground occupies the site of another vanished religious house, this time that of the Franciscans, endowed by Sir Laurence Oliphant, first Baron Oliphant, who was Sheriff of Perthshire in 1470. The tourist information center itself occupies the Round House, the old city waterworks, another of Adam Anderson's achievements. Canal St.

ENVIRONS

Fairways Heavy Horse Centre – This delightful little activity center features rides in wagons pulled by Clydesdale horses, video shows, a display of horse-drawn implements, and the opportunity to see newborn foals and to watch a blacksmith at work.

Open daily from 10 AM to 5 PM April through September. Admission charge. Walnut Grove, 2 miles east of Perth on A85 (phone: 25931).

Scone Palace – The ancient historic site of Scone, the traditional coronation place of Scottish kings, has been at the center of Scottish history since Pictish times, although what is seen here today is Scone Palace, a castellated mansion built largely during the first decade of the 19th century. The palace is the last of several structures that occupied this spot, beginning with a 12th-century Bishop's Palace and adjoining abbey that were destroyed in 1559 — along with the rest of Perth's religious foundations. The Earls of Gowrie, subsequent owners of the property, built a new palace here in the 16th century but were forced to forfeit it after the Gowrie Conspiracy (see Huntingtower Castle, below), when James VI gave the estate to the Murray family, later Earls of Mansfield and the present owners.

The palace interior is famous for its rare porcelain, needlework, furniture, clocks, ivories, and the Vernis Martin collection of 18th-century French papier mâché objets d'art. Outside, magnificent daffodils, rhododendrons, bluebells, roses, and rare trees share 100 acres of grounds with Highland cattle, ornamental fowl, veteran agricultural machinery, a picnic park, and an adventure playground. Of particular interest is Moot Hill, opposite the palace, where the Stone of Destiny was kept and where a replica now stands. The chapel beside the imitation stone, built in the 19th century as the Murray family chapel, incorporates a 17th-century aisle of the old parish church of Scone village, which was re-sited — yes, the *village* was re-sited — when the present palace was built. Also on the grounds is the Old Gateway, part of the original Bishop's Palace; the ancient Graveyard, where Robert II (who reigned from 1371 to 1390), first of the Stuart line of Scottish Kings, is buried; and the Pinetum, a grove with 130-year old conifers and the original Douglas fir, grown from seeds sent home by botanist David Douglas, who was born on the estate and worked on it as a young gardener. Gift shops and a coffee shop complete the enclave. Open Mondays through Saturdays from 9:30 AM to 5 PM and Sundays from 1:30 PM to 5:30 PM Good Friday until the second Monday in October, with extended hours on Sundays during July and August, 10 AM to 5:30 PM; off-season and evening tours by arrangement. Admission charge. Two miles northeast of Perth by A93 (phone: 0738-52300).

Huntingtower Castle – Known until 1600 as Ruthven Castle, this is a splendid 15th- and 16th-century building consisting of two towers joined by a later structure, with a painted ceiling that dates from 1540 among its notable features. The castle was the site, in 1582, of the Raid of Ruthven, a conspiracy led by its owner, Lord Ruthven, first Earl of Gowrie, who lured the young James VI (later James I of England) here and held him prisoner, later paying with his head for his act of treason. An attempt by the sons of the earl to kidnap James again in 1600 — the Gowrie Conspiracy — ended in their death and the end of the Ruthven name. An even earlier occupant of the castle was Patrick Ruthven, third Baron Ruthven, Provost of Perth from 1553 to 1566. He played a major part in bringing the Reformation to Scotland, assisted in the capture of Perth from the French in opposition to the Regency of Queen Mary's mother, and rose from his deathbed to take part in the murder of Mary's favorite, Riccio, in 1566. Open Mondays through Saturdays from 9:30 AM to 7 PM (to 4 PM October through March), Sundays from 2 to 7 PM (to 4 PM October through March). Admission charge. Three miles northwest of Perth by A9 and A85 (phone: 27231).

Elcho Castle – Wrought-iron window grills characterize this well-preserved, 16th-century stately home on the south bank of the Tay. Elcho Castle was the ancestral seat of the Earls of Wemyss, a family whose members took up very different political positions over the generations (and included one earl, a Jacobite agent and follower of Bonnie Prince Charlie in the rising of 1745, who afterward produced memoirs that caused considerable controversy because of their forthrightness and critical character). Open April through September, Mondays through Saturdays, 9:30 AM to 7 PM, and

Sundays, 2 to 7 PM; October through March, Mondays through Saturdays, 9:30 AM to 4 PM, and Sundays, 2 to 4 PM. Admission charge. 4½ miles southeast of Perth.

Pitheavlis Castle – The family seat of the Oliphants, endowed with crow-stepped gables and a small turret, is a fine example of what passed for grandeur in a late 16th-century townhouse. It's not open to visitors, but those interested can walk west out of the center of town, beyond the railroad station, and admire it. Needless Rd.

Branklyn Garden – Within walking distance of the city, southward on the Dundee Road (A85), this small, beautiful garden houses over 3,000 species of rare shrubs and plants. Open daily from March through October, 9:30 AM to sunset. Admission charge (no phone).

Bells Cherrybank Gardens – Trees, heather, shrubs, and an aviary are set on 18 acres of ground. There are also decorative sculptures, pools, a waterfall, and a children's play area. On the A9, about 3 miles south of the city. Open Tuesdays, Thursdays, Saturdays, and Sundays, 11 AM to 5:30 PM, from mid-April through September.

■ **EXTRA SPECIAL:** Non-teetotalers can take in one of the free tours, including free samples, offered by Dewar's blending plant. The 1½-hour tours depart at 10:15 AM and 2:15 PM Mondays, Tuesdays, and Wednesdays; at 10:15 AM and 2 PM Thursdays; and at 10:15 AM on Fridays. Call ahead. (Bell's has only an office in Perth.) On the Perth outskirts at Iveralmond (phone: 21231).

SOURCES AND RESOURCES

TOURIST INFORMATION: Perth's tourist information center, Marshall Pl. (phone: 38353), is in the Round House, a converted waterworks from the 19th century. From April through June and September through October, the office is open Mondays through Saturdays, 9 AM to 6 PM; Sundays, 12 to 6 PM. In July and August, it's open from 9 AM to 8 PM daily. From November through March, open Mondays through Fridays, 9 AM to 6 PM; closed weekends. Besides a slide program that describes the attractions of Perth and surrounding Perthshire places of interest, the office operates a full accommodations booking service. The indispensable annual *Perth Guide* is available here, too.

Local Coverge – The Perth *Evening Telegraph* is the daily newspaper. The *Dundee Courier* is the local morning daily and is idiosyncratic enough to be entertaining. The *Perthshire Advertiser* comes out on Tuesdays and Fridays.

Telephone – The area code for Perth is 0738.

GETTING AROUND: The city itself is easy to see on foot, but wheels are necessary for points in the environs. Note that Wednesday is early closing day and that on market days, Mondays and Fridays, moving around may be less easy — but more entertaining.

Bus – For information on local bus service, including service to much of the rural area around Perth, contact *Strathtay Scottish Omnibuses Ltd.* at the bus station, Leonard St. (phone: 26848). The station, from which longer-distance buses to Edinburgh, Glasgow, Inverness, and other cities also depart, is north of King's Place, the westward continuation of Marshall Place.

Car Rental – *SMT*, Dunkeld Rd. (phone: 26241), can arrange both car and van hire.

Taxi – Cab ranks are located on Mill Street, in the center of Perth. To call by phone, try *A & B Taxis* (phone: 34567), *Ace Taxi* (phone: 33033), or *Perth Radio Taxis* (phone: 28171).

Train – Direct trains to Aberdeen, Inverness, Glasgow, Edinburgh, and Dundee (and through Dundee to the Inter City 125 network) leave from the railroad station at the far end of King's Place (phone: 37117 for information; 37228 for reservations).

SPECIAL EVENTS: The *Perth Festival of the Arts,* held during the last half of May, includes drama, music, and visual arts at sites all over the city. The *Perth Agricultural Show* is held on a Friday and Saturday at the end of July at Lesser South Inch. The *Perth Highland Games,* held in early August, also take place at Lesser South Inch. Check with the tourist information center for exact dates.

MUSEUMS: Besides those mentioned in *Special Places,* Perth offers these two:

Perth Museum and Art Gallery – Local archaeological discoveries, relics of the glovers guild, and a well-regarded Perthshire natural history section. Open Mondays through Saturdays, 10 AM to 5 PM (closed 1 to 2 PM for lunch); closed Sundays. 78 George St. (phone: 32488).

Sandeman Library – Repository of the local archives and venue for occasional exhibitions. Closed Saturday afternoons and Sundays. Kinnoull St. (phone: 23329).

SHOPPING: Wednesday is the early closing day, but most shops are open 6 days a week during the summer. Sundays are more traditionally observed, Sunday mornings especially. Leave major shopping for the big cities and coastal towns; local tourist items are the main interest here. There is St. John's Centre, however, which houses 42 shops, mostly branches of chain stores. It has a historical mural on the wall inside and a clock that chimes as two figures emerge and dance to celebrate the hour.

Caithness Glass – The factory produces glassware and paperweights, and the factory shop offers splendid bargains. In addition, it is possible to watch glassmaking (Mondays through Fridays) and view the *Paperweight Collectors Gallery.* Open Mondays through Saturdays from 9 AM to 5 PM and Sundays from 1 AM to 5 PM (from 11 AM July and August). Two miles northwest of Perth (off A9) at Inveralmond (phone: 37373).

County Classics – A rich selection of Scottish knitwear and men's and women's tweeds. The accent is on what the "county," that is, the aristocratic and landed gentry, wears, but with warmth and durability in mind. 8 South St. (phone: 25290).

Hogg's Fife Footwear – Necessities for the conquest of Kinnoull Hill and the streets of Perth, again with the accent on comfort and durability. 32 High St. (phone: 25045).

House of Gowrie – Offers an enticing selection of fine cigars, tobacco, snuff, clay and wooden pipes, and other related paraphernalia. 90 South St. (phone: 26919).

McArthurs – An interesting, if somewhat conservative, selection of woolen goods. 32 St. John St. (phone: 28802).

W. and M. Patterson "Foot Comfort" Shop – Near to and similar to *Hogg's.* 39 High St. (phone: 27414).

SPORTS: Facilities for many activities, from archery, badminton, basketball, and gymnastics to table tennis and volleyball, are at *Bell's Sports Centre,* Hay St., North Inch (phone: 22301), which offers a full program of events. If your sport is not on the list, check anyway, because new athletic diversions are continually being introduced.

Bowls – There are public greens for lawn bowling at North Inch, South Inch, Darnhall, Scone Recreation Park, and Moncreiffe, all with bowls for hire. *Perth Ice Rink,* Dunkeld Rd. (phone: 24188), has a full-size indoor green.

Curling – The ancient Scottish game, in which players twirl polished granite stones over the ice, is popular and worth discovering, also at *Perth Ice Rink,* Dunkeld Rd. (phone: 24188).

Fishing – The Tay is well known as a superb angling site, so only 20 daily permits are issued at one time. Apply well in advance, especially from August through October, at the Leisure and Recreation Office, open weekdays from 8:45 AM to 12:45 PM and from 1:45 to 4:30 PM. The tourist information center issues holiday fishing permits. Fishing is also extensive on the Tay's tributary rivers, the Earn and the Almond, and at lochs, rivers, and even Highland streams nearby. (See the tourist information center for details.) There is fly-fishing for trout in well-stocked ponds at the *Sandyknowes Fishery,* Bridge of Earn (phone: 813033), where there are also nearby picnic areas, and at the *Crook of Devon Fish Farm and Restaurant,* near Kinross (phone: 05774-297), and the *Drummond Fish Farm,* Comrie (phone: 0764-70500).

Golf – The famous links at St. Andrews, Carnoustie, Gleneagles, Rosemount, and Blairgowrie are nearby, and Perth itself is home to good 18-hole courses. The public course at North Inch may be the granddaddy of all, because the game has been played there since the 16th century; its martyrs including a Mr. Robertson, who had to sit at the seat of repentance in 1604 for "playing at the gowf on the Sabbath on the North Inch at the time of preaching afternoon." Private clubs encourage visitors. The *King James VI Golf Club* (phone: 25170) is on Moncrieffe Island in mid-Tay; *Craigie Hill Golf Club* (phone: 22644 or 24377), Cherrybank, involves higher ground with hilly undulations; and there's also the *Murrayshall Golf Club* (phone: 52784) at Scone.

Horse Racing – The most northerly horse racing in Britain takes place at the *Perth Hunt Racecourse* at Scone Palace (phone: 51597) on certain dates from April through September. Ask at the tourist information center.

Ice Skating – Visit the *Perth Ice Rink* on Dunkeld Rd. (phone: 24188).

Water Skiing – For a small fee, visitors are welcome at the *Perth Water Ski Club,* Shore Rd. (phone: 30598), a family and recreational club with powerboat facilities.

THEATER: The *Perth Theatre,* High St. (phone: 21031), many of whose performers and directors have gone on to considerable success in Glasgow, Edinburgh, and London, has a reputation for work that's enjoyable, if not too harrowing or intellectually demanding. Expect to see an Agatha Christie thriller more often than an avant-garde experimental play. The theater is comfortable, with good restaurant facilities.

MUSIC AND NIGHTLIFE: Nightclubs here can be booked and patronized only by large local parties. However, traditional Scots Gaelic folk music events — *ceilidhs* (pronounced *kay*-leez) — take place in some of the hotels. They can be pretty upbeat, featuring singers, dancers, pipe bands, and do-it-yourself Highland flings. Check the Perth *Evening Telegraph* for details. The Perth tourist board also organizes participatory Scottish country dancing weekly, from May through August; check with the tourist office for details.

BEST IN TOWN

CHECKING IN: Perth is not a jet-set kind of place and doesn't try to be. The accent here is on comfort and common sense rather than luxury, even though Scotland's poshest hotel, *Gleneagles,* is in the vicinity. Hotels listed below in the expensive category start at $150 and can run as high as $300 for a double room, but most are at the less expensive end. A double room in a hotel categorized as moderate is from $100 to $120; and one in the inexpensive range, from

$50 to $100. Guesthouses and bed-and-breakfast establishments are good and less expensive still. The annual *Perth Guide* has an excellent accommodations register listing maximum charges. All telephone numbers are in the 0738 area code unless otherwise indicated.

Gleneagles – This truly palatial resort, Scotland's most luxurious hotel, is about 15 miles southwest of Perth and may not be ideal as a base for exploring the city. Nevertheless, those who wish to experience the best, imagine themselves the aristocratic masters of all they survey, and perhaps get in some golf on the 4 world-renowned courses (about to be reduced to 3 by the new Jack Nicklaus track that will combine the Prince's and Glendevon layouts), may wish to make the sacrifice. Although there are 241 rooms, no one feels crowded or neglected; space and service are lavish. And the 800-acre grounds hold facilities for enough other activities besides golf to keep anyone from getting bored. Try not to forget about Perth. Auchterarder (phone: 0764-62231). Very expensive.

Murrayshall – This completely refurbished, baronial country-house hotel is making the faithful standbys among the Perth hostelries look frantically to their laurels. Presiding over 300 acres of magnificent parkland, it offers amenities that include an 18-hole golf course, tennis courts, nature walks, croquet lawn, local fishing rights, and a restaurant serving Tay salmon and vegetables from the estate's walled garden. There are 20 bedrooms. At Scone, just north of Perth (phone: 51171). Expensive.

Royal George – Queen Victoria stayed here and was impressed enough to allow the establishment to add "Royal" to its name. The most expensive hotel in town, it has a central location, a magnificent view of the Tay, and pleasant cuisine (see *Eating Out*), while the 43 bedrooms all have TV sets, telephones, and tea- and coffee-making facilities. Tay St. (phone: 24455). Expensive.

Huntingtower – About 3 miles west of town off A85, this half-timbered country house is smallish but restful. There are 24 rooms, as well as a good restaurant that specializes in Scottish cooking. Crieff Rd., Almondbank (phone: 073883-771). Moderate.

Isle of Skye – Overlooking the river Tay, just across Queen's Bridge, this recently renovated hotel has 55 bedrooms, all with private baths or showers, and a restaurant. 18 Dundee Rd. (phone: 24471). Moderate.

Lovat – This 35-room hotel enjoys an excellent reputation, and while it stresses conferences, weddings, dinner dances, and its restaurant, it's also a good place for a family retreat. On a busy entrance road to Perth, it's a 20-minute walk from the town center. Guests may avail themselves of the facilities of the Leisure Club at *Queen's* hotel, which shares the same management. Glasgow Rd. (phone: 36555). Moderate.

Queen's – Near the railway station and less secluded than the *Lovat.* There are 60 bedrooms, each with tea and coffee-making facilities, TV set, hair dryer, and trouser press. Other amenities include a Leisure Club with a swimming pool, spa bath, steam bath, sauna, solarium, and gymnasium. Leonard St. (phone: 25471). Moderate.

Salutation – Bonnie Prince Charlie stayed here back in the 18th century, but they have since upped the number of bedrooms to 65 and have installed such things as TV sets, radios, telephones, and tea makers as well as private baths. Restaurant. 34 South St. (phone: 30066). Moderate.

Beechgrove Guest House – In addition to a peaceful, attractive setting, this 6-bedroom former manse is a "listed building," which is equivalent to "landmark status" in the US. Dundee Rd. (phone: 36147). Inexpensive.

Sunbank House – Bounded by rolling green lawns above the river Tay, this charming early Victorian family house in gleaming white stone offers 6 bedrooms, all with sumptuous views. Friendly resident proprietors. 50 Dundee Rd. (phone: 24882). Inexpensive.

EATING OUT: Although Perth thinks of itself as a city, it can be absolutely rural when it comes to food: The Tay salmon may have been caught that morning, the bread baked last night, the bacon cured locally (and recently). Game is particularly reliable, since restaurant and hotel folk have generations of wisdom on which to draw in selecting venison, grouse, pheasant, and partridge. Consequently, meals in Perth can be excellent as well as fresh and nutritious. As in other Scottish cities, look for the "Taste of Scotland" sign as a further guarantee of quality. At the restaurants listed below, expect to pay $70 and up for a meal for two with wine in an establishment tending toward the expensive end, and from $50 to $70 in a moderate one. All telephone numbers are in the 0738 area code unless otherwise indicated.

Coach House – Behind the old-fashioned stone façade are the additional charms of "Taste of Scotland" cuisine and something of the gentility of former days. At once popular and understaffed, the restaurant serves good food that is worth the slight sacrifice in efficiency. Closed Sundays, Mondays, and the first 2 weeks in January, plus 2 weeks in July. 8 North Port (phone: 27950). Expensive.

Italian Corner – A favorite of Perth residents, this jolly restaurant, run by Italian-speaking Italians, offers a fine array of pizza and pasta. Open for lunch Fridays and Saturdays and for dinner daily, except Mondays. Canal St. (phone: 29645). Moderate.

Littlejohn's – A popular eatery purveying American dishes to Perth locals. Closed Sundays at lunch; reservations necessary. South Methven St. (phone: 39888). Moderate.

Royal George – Magnificent views of natural and artificial waterscape, agreeable (but anonymous) surroundings captivatingly laid out, and fine "Taste of Scotland" food to recommend it. Open daily for lunch and dinner. Royal George Hotel, Tay St. (phone: 24455). Moderate.

SHARING A PINT: *The Granary* (Canal Crescent) is in an interesting old building whose historic granary features have been retained. It has a small restaurant, too. The pub in the *City Mills* hotel (West Mill St.) also sports architectural features denoting its working origin: Look through the glass panels in the floor to see the old mill wheel. *Lovat's* (Glasgow Rd.) has a jukebox and a pool table.

STRATFORD-UPON-AVON

Even without William Shakespeare's pervasive presence, Stratford-upon-Avon would be a very pleasant stopping point on a tour through the Warwickshire heart of England. It is a charming town, set congenially in the midst of peaceful green countryside on a bend of the gentle river Avon. It is filled with the elegance of lovely, early-16th-century half-timbered buildings. In its picture prettiness, swans glide by the spire of its riverside parish church, and trees, flowers, and gardens further soften its aspect. It is small enough to be seen in a day's stroll but large enough to have all the attributes of a busy market town — which it is and has been since receiving its first royal market charter in 1196, fully 368 years before William Shakespeare's birth ensured its enduring fame.

Stratford was first a Celtic settlement, then a small Roman town, its name — a mixture of the old Welsh for river and the Roman for street — meaning "the place where the street (or *straet*) fords the river (*afon*)." In the 13th century, the Guild of the Holy Cross, an Augustinian religious fraternity, was formed, and it fostered the development of industries and crafts. It also maintained the grammar school and had almshouses and its own chapel, all of which were built by citizens of the town and are still among Stratford's most interesting buildings today.

The town has always been fortunate in the generosity of its citizens. John de Stratford, an archbishop of Canterbury in the 14th century, is thought to have rebuilt Holy Trinity Church and to have established a college of priests to serve it. Later on, Hugh Clopton, who was to become Lord Mayor of London at the end of the 15th century, built the nave and tower of the Guild Chapel and the splendid 14-arch Clopton Bridge, which still takes the heavy traffic of the 20th century into and out of town. More recent benefactors have been Charles Edward Flower, whose patronage made the first *Shakespeare Memorial Theatre* a reality in 1879, and his grandson Sir Archibald Flower, who was the major contributor to the present theater, opened in 1932.

Stratford's most illustrious citizen was undoubtedly William Shakespeare, son of John Shakespeare — "Gulielmus filius Johannes Shakespere," as the parish register puts it. Though he has been dead for more than 3½ centuries, his attraction is as strong as when he was a famous writer of plays in Elizabethan and Jacobean London. England's, and probably the world's, greatest playwright dominates the life of Stratford-upon-Avon: His houses and his children's houses are visited by hundreds of thousands of people every year; the big theater on the river, one of the world's most famous, bears his name and its actors perform his works; hotels and restaurants are named after him;

and shopkeepers live on the proceeds from the sale of books, prints, portrait busts, trinkets, and souvenirs with a Shakespearean theme. The Shakespeare Connection is a lucrative one, and it is to the credit of Stratford's residents that they have not allowed it to overwhelm and cheapen their delightful town.

The Shakespeare Connection in a nutshell? Well, he was born here, on or about April 23, 1564, and he died here on April 23, 1616. In between, he grew up, went to school, moved to London to seek his fortune, and came back wealthy enough at 33 to buy a large house, New Place, in 1597, to which he retired in 1610, and where he died of a fever caused, it is said, by too strenuous an evening of eating, drinking, and being merry.

Shakespeare's father was a glovemaker, and his mother, Mary Arden, came from a respectable family of small landowners at Wilmcote, 3 miles from Stratford. The family house, from which John Shakespeare conducted his business, was on Henley Street, slightly to the north of the center of the busy little town. Young William went to school at the King Edward VI Grammar School on Church Street, and in 1582 married Anne Hathaway, a yeoman farmer's daughter 8 years older than himself. They had three children, Susanna and the twins, Judith and Hamnet (the latter died at age 11 in 1596). Then came the years of fame and glory in London, followed by a short period of happy retirement tending his garden in Stratford.

After his death, the town's interest in its brilliant native son subsided somewhat, though there was always a steady trickle of people to see his house and his garden with its famous mulberry tree. The turning point in the town's long-range fortunes came with David Garrick's *Shakespeare Jubilee* in 1769. The event could be called the original *Shakespeare Festival,* and it grew out of Stratford's plans to decorate its rebuilt town hall.

Garrick was then England's foremost Shakespearean actor and as such was offered the honorary "Freedom" of the borough if he would provide a portrait or bust of Shakespeare to be hung in the town hall along with a portrait of himself. To no one's surprise, he accepted this opportunity to appear before an admiring posterity and organized his great jubilee — 3 days of celebration that, though marred by torrential rain, helped secure the future of Stratford as a great tourist attraction. The two portraits that were the occasion for the jubilee were both destroyed by fire in 1946, but a bust of Shakespeare that Garrick presented to Stratford can still be seen in the town hall.

The Shakespeare revival in Stratford grew apace during the 19th century, helped by interest from abroad and especially from the US. The first *Shakespeare Memorial Theatre* opened in 1879 to the sneers of the London theater establishment, but it was not long before they had to swallow their pride and take a serious interest in the little provincial theater, especially once the prominent producer Frank Benson began putting on the Bard's works here in 1886. His company remained for 30 years and established a performing tradition that became influential throughout the theater world.

Today Stratford-upon-Avon may be devoted to Shakespeare, but it has not been swamped by his cult. Its other side, its ancient existence as a very lively market town continues unabated and almost undisturbed. Once a week, as has happened for centuries, Cotswold farmers bring their produce to market and shoppers come in from the surrounding villages. Branches of many of the large chain stores and a shopping mall blend with the Shakespearean sites, hotels, and restaurants. It's a comfortable mix of commerce and culture, of modern and medieval, that allows life to go on for its inhabitants while preserving for visitors the feel of countless generations that have gone before, and for the pilgrims who seek it, a shrine.

STRATFORD AT-A-GLANCE

SEEING THE CITY: The towers of Holy Trinity Church and the Guild Chapel are not open to visitors and there are no tall modern buildings from which to get a bird's-eye view of the town, but the layout of the center of Stratford is simple. Most visitors start their tour at Shakespeare's Birthplace on Henley Street, which runs diagonally down to intersect Wood Street/Bridge Street, one of the four main thoroughfares that cut east-west across Stratford. The other three are Ely Street/Sheep Street, Scholars Lane/Chapel Lane, and Chestnut Walk/Old Town. Running north to south starting at the river are Waterside/Southern Lane, High Street/Chapel Street, and Rother Street/Windsor Street/Shakespeare Street.

SPECIAL PLACES: The Shakespeare Birthplace Trust is the official body that, on behalf of the nation, owns the five most important buildings connected with William Shakespeare. These are the Birthplace itself, New Place (with Nash's House), Hall's Croft, Anne Hathaway's Cottage, and Mary Arden's House. The Shakespeare Centre, the Trust's headquarters on Henley St., is also an academic center, opened in 1964, for anyone wishing to study its splendid collection of books and documents relating to Shakespeare, including translations of his plays in 67 languages. There is usually an exhibition in the front hall, where the engraved glass panels by John Hutton (depicting characters from the plays) are well worth a look. The Shakespeare Centre is open daily except Sundays; admission is free to the library and records office, but there is a charge for the exhibitions. There is an individual admission charge for each of the Birthplace Trust buildings, but it's possible to lower the cost by buying an inclusive ticket for entrance to all five. The phone number for the Shakespeare Centre and all Trust buildings is 204016.

Most of Stratford's special places, including the ones without Shakespearean connections, are in the center of town within easy walking distance of each other. In the course of a day's stroll, you can see everything listed here (with the exception of Anne Hathaway's Cottage and Mary Arden's House), as well as experience the everyday workings of a typical English market town. Alternatively, you can take the *Guide Friday* "open-top" Double-Decker Bus Tour (see *Sources and Resources*), which runs every 30 minutes and links all the Shakespeare properties, including Mary Arden's House and Anne Hathaway's Cottage.

THE SHAKESPEARE BIRTHPLACE TRUST

Shakespeare's Birthplace – The spiritual center of Stratford-upon-Avon lies in this modest, half-timbered and gabled Tudor building where William Shakespeare was born on or about April 23, 1564. The house, visited by more than half a million people of all nationalities every year, is beautifully maintained and furnished with objects typical of Shakespeare's period. The bedroom in which the Bard is assumed to have been born is upstairs, its window scratched with the signatures of famous people who have visited it, including those of Sir Walter Scott, Alfred, Lord Tennyson, and the actress Ellen Terry. The Birthplace also houses a museum of relics and records of

Shakespeare's day and a fine library as well as an exhibit of period costumes used in Shakespearean plays produced by BBC television. Don't miss the well-kept garden behind the house; in it grow many of the flowers, herbs, and plants Shakespeare knew. Open daily. Admission charge. Henley St. (phone: 204016).

New Place – Shakespeare's house stood on this site. The building passed out of the family's hands in 1670, and its last owner, constantly irritated by the numbers of admirers wanting to see it, demolished it in 1759. All that can be seen today are part of the foundations and the once-extensive gardens. There is a replica of an Elizabethan knot garden — an elaborately laid-out formal garden typical of those times — and the Great Garden, which contains topiary work and a mulberry tree said to have been grown from a cutting from Shakespeare's original tree. The young mulberry in the center of the lawn was planted by Dame Peggy Ashcroft to mark the 200th anniversary of David Garrick's jubilee. Nash's House, adjoining the gardens, was once owned by Thomas Nash, husband of Shakespeare's granddaughter Elizabeth Hall, and is furnished with items of their period. It also houses *New Place Museum,* devoted mainly to local archaeological material. Open daily April through October. Admission charge. Chapel St. (phone: 292325).

Hall's Croft – A short walk from New Place to Old Town, a quietly elegant residential street, brings you to Hall's Croft. Shakespeare's elder daughter, Susanna, and her physician husband, Dr. John Hall, lived in this lovely house with its gabled front and overhanging upper floor from 1607 to 1616. Inside, it is the beautifully furnished house of a well-to-do Jacobean family, immaculately kept, with brass and copper glowing and flowers in the living rooms. Don't miss the bedroom with its four-poster, and Dr. Hall's dispensary, stocked with pottery jars of herbs and potions, mortars and pestles, and surgical instruments. A large walled garden behind the house, again immaculate, provides an oasis of sweet-scented calm. Open daily, April through October. Admission charge. Old Town (phone: 292107).

Anne Hathaway's Cottage – So many hundreds of drawings, prints, engravings, and plaques portray this pretty, thatched house, that it is something of a surprise to come across the building itself on the outskirts of Stratford. It's about a 1-mile walk from town (take the footpath from Evesham Pl.), but it can also be reached by bus from Bridge Street, or even by bicycle. The trip is worth it, because Anne's cottage retains a charming English country air, with roses, jasmine, and other scented flowers in the garden, and Tudor furnishings in the house. Open daily. Admission charge. Shottery village (phone: 292100).

Mary Arden's House – Shakespeare's mother lived in this lovely gabled farmhouse in Wilmcote village before her marriage. The house is set in a garden, and the barns in back house a museum devoted to rural life and farming. About 3 miles from Stratford, Wilmcote can be reached by road, train, or even by boat along the canal. Open daily April through October. Admission charge. Wilmcote village (phone: 293455).

OTHER STRATFORD ATTRACTIONS

Drinking Fountain and Clock – The ornate fountain and clock in the center of the Market Place was the gift of George W. Childs, a Philadelphian who presented it to the town in Queen Victoria's jubilee year of 1887. It was unveiled by the famous actor Henry Irving.

Holy Trinity Church – On the bank of the river Avon, this stately parish church dates from the 13th century. Shakespeare was baptized and buried here, and photocopies of the church register entries of both events are on display. On the north wall of the chancel is a bust of the poet carved by his contemporary Gerard Jannsen, a memorial erected by the Shakespeare family in 1623. Shakespeare's grave is below the bust, flanked by those of his wife and other members of his family. Open daily. Admission charge to the chancel. Old Town.

Gower Memorial – An imaginative statue of William Shakespeare crowns this impressive memorial, which its creator, Lord Ronald Sutherland Gower, labored over for 12 years. Unveiled in 1888, it stands with its back to the *Royal Shakespeare Theatre* in Bancroft Gardens near Clopton Bridge. The four life-size bronzes at its base are of Hamlet, Lady Macbeth, Falstaff, and Prince Hal.

King Edward VI Grammar School – This half-timbered building on Church Street can trace its origins back to the 13th century, and it was here that Shakespeare learned his Latin and Greek. Since it is still a school, it can be visited by special arrangement only, but don't walk by without pausing for a glimpse through the gateway or without noticing the ancient almshouses that border it (phone: 293351).

Guild Chapel – The beautiful gray stone tower of the Guild Chapel is one of the finest landmarks in Stratford. It rises above the austerely elegant chapel, which was rebuilt by Hugh Clopton about 1496, on the site of a building dating from the mid-13th century. Today it is used by the grammar school, which holds a daily service there during the school term. Paintings that once covered the walls have mostly disappeared, except for one, *The Day of Judgment,* over the chancel arch. The chapel adjoins the grammar school and almshouses on Church St. and is open daily.

Harvard House – The Stars and Stripes flying from a flagpole above the front door indicates the special importance of this old half-timbered building, dating from 1596. It was the home of a wealthy Stratford alderman, Thomas Rogers, whose daughter Katherine was the mother of John Harvard, the first benefactor of the university. The house now belongs to Harvard and is furnished in the style of the Elizabethan period. Open irregular hours; phone for details. Admission charge. High St. (phone: 204026).

Motor Museum – Nothing to do with Shakespeare at all, but it's worth a visit. The museum's specialty is cars from a bygone golden age, the 1920s. There are about 30 cars, and bicycles and motor bicycles as well. Gift and bookshop on site, plus a picnic garden. Open daily. Admission charge. 1 Shakespeare St. (phone: 69413).

Shrieve's House – Halfway down Sheep Street, stop for a moment outside this imposing late-16th-century private house with its great studded door and gateway. Shakespeare undoubtedly knew the owners of this Stratford townhouse and may well have attended the wedding feast of their daughter here in 1613.

Stratford Brass Rubbing Centre – Here is an opportunity to make your own souvenir of Stratford. The center has exact replicas of a large number of brasses, many from the Stratford area, and supplies paper and wax as part of the charge for doing a rubbing. Open daily April through October and weekends only in March. Royal Shakespeare Theatre Summer House, Avonbank Gardens (phone: 297671).

Stratford Butterfly Farm and Jungle Safari – This specially created jungle has nearly 1,000 free flying butterflies, birds, and insects, including the world's largest species of spider, the Therathosa Leblondi (goliath bird eater). Open daily. Admission charge. Tramway Walk (phone: 299288).

Teddy Bear Museum – A new collection of hundreds of antique, modern, and famous bears from around the world. Admission charge. 19 Greenhill St. (phone: 293160).

Warwick Castle – Situated 8 miles outside of Stratford (take the open-top bus from Stratford Wood St.), this is one of England's most visited stately homes. It houses a superb art collection of old masters. The grounds boast a re-created Victorian rose garden with more than 700 rose trees of at least 70 varieties. Saturday afternoons Easter through August, *Morris Dancers* perform on the castle grounds. Open daily; rose garden closed November through February. Admission charge. Warwick (phone: 0926-495421).

■ **EXTRA SPECIAL:** A visit to the *Royal Shakespeare Theatre* at its imposing riverside location is a major event for theater and Shakespeare lovers from all over the world. You can be sure that the production you'll see will have been thought out in meticulous, often controversial, detail and will be excitingly staged and beautifully acted by the *Royal Shakespeare Company.* The season, during which several Shakespeare plays are presented, generally runs from the end of March to January. Tickets should be bought as far in advance as possible from the box office, through *Guide Friday Ltd.* (see *Sources and Resources*), or through a ticket agency. Tickets go on sale in early March, though it is often possible to buy them at the last minute. The theater holds back a few medium-price tickets (maximum two per person) and some standing-room tickets for sale on the day of performance. Bona fide students (with identification to prove it) may chance upon an unsold ticket immediately before the performance. The theater has 2 restaurants and a shop selling a good range of books and other items about the theater in general and *Royal Shakespeare Company* productions in particular. The attached *Theatre Picture Gallery and Museum* has interesting paintings, portraits, and relics of famous theater personalities. Backstage tours are also available daily except Sundays. The Royal Shakespeare Theatre, Stratford-upon-Avon, Warwickshire CV37 6BB (phone: 295623 for booking and for telephone credit card purchases; 69191 for 24-hour information on seat availability).

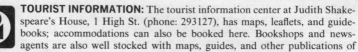

SOURCES AND RESOURCES

TOURIST INFORMATION: The tourist information center at Judith Shakespeare's House, 1 High St. (phone: 293127), has maps, leaflets, and guidebooks; accommodations can also be booked here. Bookshops and newsagents are also well stocked with maps, guides, and other publications of interest to the visitor. The Stratford-upon-Avon Tourist (Telephone) Service (phone: 67522) gives prerecorded information such as opening times, telephone numbers, and other details of places of interest in and around the town. *Guide Friday Ltd.* (Civic Hall, Market Place, 14 Rother St.; phone: 294466) runs tours via open-air, double-decker buses to the Shakespeare sites outside town. Buses depart during the summer every 15 minutes. Tours to Warwick Castle, the town of Warwick, and Charlecote Park leave every hour. Tours of the surrounding countryside, including the Cotswolds and Blenheim Palace, are also available. Most departures are from the company office, but car tours with a personal driver/guide can be arranged. *Guide Friday Ltd.* also operates walking tours and has a tourism center at 14 Rother St. that provides visitors with town maps and area brochures.

Local Coverage – The *Stratford-upon-Avon Herald* is helpful, as is the free weekly publication called *Why?* available at most hotels.

Food – A leaflet published by the tourist board, *Food and Drink in the Heart of England,* tells where you can pick your own fruit and sample cider, wine, and cheese in the Stratford area, and provides some recipes for meals prepared in local restaurants.

Telephone – The area code for Stratford is 0789.

GETTING AROUND: The best way to see central Stratford-upon-Avon is on foot. Most of its important streets are laid out in a simple grid pattern, so it's not easy to get lost. In the town center, street numbers often ascend on one side and descend on the other, rather than one side being even-numbered and the other odd.

Bicycle – Stratford and its surrounding countryside are ideally suited to exploration by bike. *Clarkes,* Bancrofts Esso Station, Guild St. (phone: 205057), rents bicycles. Along with renting bikes, *Pashley's,* Henley St. (phone: 297044), also provides guides and suggests routes.

Boat – Short trips for an hour or so or a holiday lasting several weeks are possible on the Avon and the historic early-19th-century Stratford Canal. Rowing boats, punts (propelled by poles), and canoes can be rented at *Bancroft Cruises,* 25 Meer St. (phone: 292459), *Rose's Boathouse,* Swan's West La. (phone: 67073) and *Stratford Marina Ltd.,* Clopton Bridge (phone: 69669). One-hour and half-hour cruises are also available through these companies.

Bus – *Midland Red (South) Ltd.,* Warwick Rd. (phone: 204181), serves Stratford and the surrounding villages. The bus departure point is on Bridge St. near Clopton Bridge. *National Express Coaches* (phone: 021-622 4373) operates daily service from Midland Red's Garage to London's Victoria Station.

Car Rental – Two local firms are *Arden Motors,* Arden St. (phone: 67446), and *Suparent Ltd,* Western Rd. (phone: 414447). *Guide Friday Ltd.,* Civic Hall, Market Place, 14 Rother St. (phone: 294466), will arrange rentals through the major national and international companies.

Taxi – Taxis are relatively expensive and can't be flagged down on the street. Go to the cab rank at the intersection of Rother and Wood sts. (the Market Place) or at Bridgefoot by the *Pen and Parchment* pub. Phone *Guide Friday Ltd.* at 294466 or 69999. Your hotel can also get you a taxi.

Train – Fast InterCity 125 trains run from London's Euston station to Coventry and connect with an express motorcoach to Stratford. Called the *Shakespeare Connection,* the service is coordinated to suit theatergoers. It runs four times a day and twice on Sundays (about $23 one-way, $26 round trip). For details, phone 294466. Slower trains run from Stratford station on Station Rd. to London's Paddington Station (phone: 204444).

SPECIAL EVENTS: Every spring, usually on the Saturday nearest April 23, Stratford and the world unite to honor Shakespeare. A procession that includes ambassadors from many countries walks from his Birthplace to Holy Trinity Church to lay floral tributes on his grave. Flags of the nations are unfurled in the center of town, and there is a special performance at the *Royal Shakespeare Theatre.* The Boat Club holds its Regatta in June (heralded by a popular raft race), and the *Stratford Festival* of music, plays, and poetry readings takes place during the last 2 weeks in July (for details contact the festival office at Civic Hall, Market Place, 14 Rother St.; phone: 67969). In October (usually on the 12th) there's the *Mop Fair,* when stalls, sideshows, and amusements take over the town center.

SHOPPING: Look for high-quality handicrafts — including pottery, stained glass, and carved woods — as well as English sheepskins, leather clothing, and china. Sheep Street has several elegant antiques shops, and the Antique Centre arcade off Ely St. has nearly 50 dealers' booths.

Avon Wools – Hand-knitted sweaters and quality wools. 31 Henley St. (phone: 204428).

Peter Dingley – Good-quality British-made crafts, including pottery and carved wood. 8 Chapel St. (phone: 205001).

Edinburgh Woollen Mill – A wide range of Scottish woolens and tweeds, usually at very reasonable prices. 31 Bridge St. (phone: 205949).

Lamberts of Stratford – Comprehensive selection of English chinas and crystal. 1 Henley St. (phone: 293174).

Minories – It's a group of crafts shops off Meer Street; be sure to stop in at *Pretty Presies,* which specializes in English lace, dolls, and dried flowers; also visit *Camilla Hepper* for herbal cosmetics.

Sentre Arts – Another shop where everything is handmade. The stained glass is unusual and attractive. Centre Craft Yard, off Henley St. (phone: 68731).

Shakespeare Centre Bookshop – Specializes in Shakespearean books and other publications and sells gifts and souvenirs. Henley St. (phone: 204016).

Sheepskin Shop – Leather jackets, coats, sweaters, children's toys, and other items. 33 Sheep St. (phone: 293828).

Spinning Wheel – Woolen cloaks, scarves, and ties, handwoven on the premises. 10 Chapel St. (phone: 293375).

Sweet Indulgences – A tempting array of sugar delights. Meer St. (phone: 204407).

Teahouse – Vast choice of teas and coffees; also teapots and mugs. Red Lion Shopping Court, off Sheep St. (phone: 414038).

Tappit Hen – Broad range of English pewter. 57 Henley St. (phone: 69933).

Thornton's – Famous for its handmade chocolates and toffee. 15 Bridge St. (phone: 295251).

Tradition of Wales – Welsh pottery, carvings, and woolen goods. 22 Henley St. (phone: 68758).

Robert Vaughan – Antiquarian bookshop specializing in the theater and English literature, including first editions. 20 Chapel St. (phone: 205312).

SPORTS: Stratford has facilities for many kinds of sports; ask at the information center for a complete list.

Cricket – Matches take place at the *Stratford Cricket Club* on Swan's Nest La. (phone: 29768).

Fishing – Go to 37 Greenhill St. for daily and season fishing tickets, the necessary fishery board license, too.

Golf – Visitors pay greens fees to play on the 18-hole courses at the *Stratford-upon-Avon Golf Club,* Tiddington Rd. (phone: 205749), and the *Welcombe* hotel, Warwick Rd. (phone: 295252).

Horse Racing – Races are held about once a month at the *Stratford Race Course.* Luddington Rd. (phone: 67949).

Swimming – The district council's Leisure Center at Bridgefoot has 2 pools as well as squash courts, a sauna, and a solarium, and is open daily. Admission charge (phone: 67751).

Tennis – Stratford's Leisure Center has lighted tennis courts, along with squash courts, a gym, and swimming pool. Admission charge. At Bridgefoot (phone: 67751).

THEATER: At the *Royal Shakespeare Theatre,* along the river, the *Royal Shakespeare Company*'s main season starts in late March (phone: 295623). The new *Swan Theatre,* built within the shell of the old *Memorial Theatre* at the back of the *Royal Shakespeare Theatre,* features the works of Shakespeare's contemporaries, and the season lasts from April through January.

MUSIC: Stratford's tradition is drama rather than music, but the town plays host to orchestras, bands, and soloists throughout the year. In July, in conjunction with the *Stratford Festival,* the *Royal Shakespeare Theatre* presents occasional concerts.

NIGHTCLUBS AND NIGHTLIFE: Evenings are fairly quiet in Stratford; pubs close at 11 PM. The *Toll House* restaurant, Alcester Rd. (phone: 297812), has a disco on weekends that's popular with young people and stays open until the early hours. *Debut,* 21 Sheep St. (phone: 293546), is a Greek restaurant featuring a trio and belly dancer on Saturday nights. Along with Chinese food, *As You Like It,* 4–5 Henley St. (phone: 293022), has a large bar and dancing nightly.

BEST IN TOWN

CHECKING IN: For visitors who intend to stay in a modest bed-and-breakfast establishment, there is no need to make reservations in advance; many of these worthy British establishments line the main roads leading into town. Those who want a good hotel, however, should book ahead, especially at the height of the season, June to September. The tourist information center, 1 High St. (phone: 293127), supplies copies of the official *Accommodation Register* and can help you find somewhere to stay. For a small fee, *Guide Friday Ltd.,* Civic Hall, Market Place, 14 Rother St. (phone: 294466), will also help you book a room.

A bed-and-breakfast establishment offers a comfortable room (some with private bath) and a good breakfast for about $45 for two per night. For the same accommodations in an inexpensive hotel, you will pay about $55. Moderately priced hotels — most have private bathrooms in every room and all have hot and cold water — run about $60 to $95 for two per night. And expect to pay $95 and up in the large, expensive hotels. The smaller bed-and-breakfast establishments usually don't accept credit cards. All telephone numbers are in the 0789 area code unless otherwise indicated.

Alveston Manor – Reputedly the setting for the first production of *A Midsummer Night's Dream,* this modernized Elizabethan manor with oak paneling and leaded windows is set on spacious grounds across the Avon from the theater and the center of town. There are 108 rooms, all with private bath, and a 9-hole putting course. Clopton Bridge (phone: 204581). Expensive.

Ettington Park – This newly converted Victorian Gothic building (listed in the *Domesday Book*) is considered *the* place to stay in the Stratford vicinity; it retains many features reminiscent of 18th- and 19th-century gracious living. The 49 luxurious rooms and suites overlook the 40-acre Ettington Estate. Fresh herbs and salads from the garden are served at the imposing restaurant, and leisure activities include riding, fishing, tennis, and swimming in the indoor pool. Alderminster, 5 miles from Stratford (phone: 0789-740740). Expensive.

Moat House International – Behind the somewhat pedestrian façade lie all the comforts and services expected of a major hotel chain. Color TV sets, individual climate control, and a mini-bar are in all 250 rooms; guests are permitted free use of an adjacent leisure center. It's a short walk to the *Royal Shakespeare Theatre.* Bridgefoot (phone: 414411). Expensive.

Shakespeare – A Stratford landmark, this gabled, timber-fronted 16th-century building is the place to stay if you want a taste of Elizabethan England. David Garrick stayed here in 1769, and since then most of its rooms have been named after Shakespeare's plays: You could find yourself sleeping in the *Midsummer Night's Dream* room and eating in the *David Garrick* restaurant. The 70-room hotel has been carefully modernized so that the authentic atmosphere endures. Chapel St. (phone: 294771). Expensive.

Welcombe – This elegant 81-room hotel set in extensive parkland on the outskirts of Stratford was once a private mansion and retains the atmosphere of an English country house. The menu in its paneled restaurant is classic French. The park has room for an 18-hole golf course plus a heli-pad with connections to nearby Birmingham airport, and also offers coarse fishing and croquet; the hotel's garage has car-servicing facilities and gas. Warwick Rd., 1¼ miles from town center (phone: 295252). Expensive.

White Swan – One of the oldest inns in town, it dates from the 15th century — beautifully evident from its medieval, gabled façade to the sturdy wood beams within. All 42 rooms have private bath, and two have large four-posters. Rother St. (phone: 297022). Expensive to moderate.

Falcon – One of those stunning, half-timbered buildings that make Stratford so picturesque, the 73-room hotel overlooks the gardens of New Place, Shakespeare's house. Inside, it is less elegant than the *Shakespeare* hotel, and all but 20 of the rooms are in the modern extension. Nevertheless, it has a charm of its own. Chapel St. (phone: 205777). Moderate.

Haytor – A smallish, family-run hotel with a quiet, friendly atmosphere and lovely private gardens; 18 rooms, almost all with bath. On the edge of town, a 10-minute walk from the center. 20 Avenue Rd. (phone: 297799). Moderate.

Sequoia House – Situated across the river, opposite the *Royal Shakespeare Theatre,* this 21-room Victorian hotel is only a 5-minute stroll along the old tramway path from the town center. 51–53 Shipston Rd. (phone: 68852). Moderate.

Stratford House – Once a private Georgian home, this charming 10-room hotel has been recently modernized in delightful style, including the incorporation of the *Shepherd's Garden* restaurant. Sheep St. (phone: 68288). Moderate.

Grosvenor House – On the main Warwick Road, yet close to the center of town, it's actually several large houses imaginatively linked into one big, comfortable hotel. Included — besides 57 rooms — are a sauna, fitness center, spa baths, a beauty salon, a restaurant, and parking. 12 Warwick Rd. (phone: 69213). Moderate to inexpensive.

Coach House – On a main road out of town, this rambling, 22-room hotel on several floors, has a pleasant dining room and a friendly atmosphere. 17 Warwick Rd. (phone: 299468). Inexpensive.

Glenavon Private – Just up the road from Holy Trinity Church and Hall's Croft, this is a congenial 15-room family-style hotel in a quiet part of town. 6 Chestnut Walk (phone: 292588). Inexpensive.

Hardwick House – A cozy, family-run Victorian house (12 rooms) in a quiet area, only a few minutes' walk from the town center and Shakespearean attractions. 1 Avenue Rd. (phone: 204307). Inexpensive.

Payton – Another well-maintained little hotel with a homelike atmosphere, it, too, is in a quiet part of town, though only a short walk from the back gate of Shakespeare's Birthplace. 6 John St. (phone: 66442). Inexpensive.

Salamander – Overlooking a small park about 10 minutes from the center of town, this 7-room Victorian guesthouse is pleasant and well run. 40 Grove Rd. (phone: 205728). Inexpensive.

EATING OUT: With the help of a range of fast-food and snack restaurants, Stratford manages to feed its hundreds of thousands of visitors pretty well. Those arriving just for the day find that the coffee houses and tearooms are generally good, and many of them stay open long enough to provide an evening meal. Pizza, hamburgers, and the glass-of-wine-with-food places have all found their way into town, and the sausage-egg-and-chip cafés offer good value for the money. At midday, there is the ploughman's lunch (bread, cheese, and pickle) to be sampled with a pint of beer in one of Stratford's typical pubs, many of which also offer an array of hot and cold food at the bar.

Those staying overnight can expect the full British breakfast — fruit juice, cereal, sausage, bacon and eggs, toast, and tea or coffee — in the morning, though a lighter continental breakfast — usually fruit juice, croissants or toast, and coffee — is also available. Evening meals range from a standard "meat and three vegetables" to international cuisine. Prices for a three-course meal for two, without drinks will cost over $60 in the expensive category, $30 to $60 in the moderate category, and under $30 in the inexpensive category. All telephone numbers are in the 0789 area code unless otherwise indicated.

Da Giovanni – A discreetly curtained front and restrained gold lettering hide a plush restaurant very much in the Italian grand manner, complete with leather sofas and chairs, flocked wallpaper, and bronze statues. Delicious Italian cooking. Closed Sundays. 8 Ely St. (phone: 297999). Expensive.

Moat House International – The hotel's *Warwick Grill* was conceived on a luxury scale and has an impressive central buffet. Check the menu for re-creations of authentic Elizabethan dishes. Open daily. Bridgefoot (phone: 67511). Expensive.

Marlowe's – Approached down a narrow alley off the High Street, Marlowe's is in a house that dates from Shakespeare's time. Once an inn, it's now a restaurant with a distinguished air, where oak paneling and wood fires in winter add to the atmosphere. The food is standard international cuisine, the wine list is good, and at its bar, the *Loose Box Tavern,* a meal can be had for about $12. Open daily. 18 High St. (phone: 204999). Expensive to moderate.

Arden – The restaurant here draws theatergoers (the *Royal Shakespeare* is just across the road), and both restaurant and bar are good places to spot celebrities. The food is simple, based on the best available fresh ingredients. Open daily. 44 Waterside (phone: 294949). Moderate.

Bobby Browns – Snack lunches, cream teas, and à la carte dinners, are served in this versatile eatery housed in a 16th-century building with beamed ceilings and mullioned windows. Soups, cakes, and puddings are creatively prepared. 12 Sheep St. (phone: 292554). Moderate.

The Opposition – A bistro-style restaurant that has won a following for its imaginative and regularly changing menu. Closed Sundays and Mondays for lunch. 13 Sheep St. (phone: 69980). Moderate.

Sorrento – Set in a beautiful, historic building, this Italian restaurant offers classical fare in an intimate atmosphere. Closed Sundays. 13–14 Meer St. (phone: 69304). Moderate.

Welcombe – Just outside of town, this hotel's restaurant is famous for its Saturday and Sunday afternoon cream teas, replete with hot scones, pancakes, and other goodies. Warwick Rd. (phone: 295252). Moderate.

Box Tree and River Terrace – Both are in the *Royal Shakespeare Theatre* building and are open to non-playgoers — if you can't get tickets, at least you can say you've been there. The *Box Tree* is open for lunch on matinee days and Sundays, and every evening before and after performances except Sundays; the *River Terrace,* on the ground floor with a view of the river, is open from midmorning for snacks and light meals. Waterside (phone: 293226). Moderate to inexpensive.

Horseshoe Buttery – A favorite of locals — the best recommendation it could garner — the fare is good old-fashioned English, like steak and kidney pie, chops, and grills, all presented in a Tudoresque setting of wooden beams and brocaded furniture. Two bed-and-breakfast rooms available. 33–34 Greenhill St. (phone: 292246). Moderate to inexpensive.

Boat House – Set above *Rose's Boathouse,* this attractive wine bar and restaurant offers a limited menu of entrées and salads and has splendid views of the river and theater gardens. Open daily; the bar stays open late. Swan's Nest La., Bridgefoot (phone: 297733). Inexpensive.

Casa Bonita – Partly a shop that sells an interesting variety of gifts, this is also a small café serving tasty sandwiches and other light snacks. In summer months there's outdoor dining on the patio. Open Mondays through Saturdays; closed evenings. 59–60 Henley St. (phone: 205880). Inexpensive.

Centre Coffee House – A spotless coffee shop where the salads are fresh and the pâté homemade. Opposite Shakespeare's Birthplace. Open daily (except Mondays in winter). Henley St. (phone: 297490). Inexpensive.

Cobweb – Above a cake and confectionary shop, in a building so old that both the floors and the beamed ceilings have distinct slopes, this charming restaurant offers omelettes, grills, and salads as well as a typically English afternoon tea. Closed Sundays. 12 Sheep St. (phone: 292554). Inexpensive.

Hills – Emulating a mini-theater, the tables are arranged in a pit and a balcony, and since it is open very late, this restaurant is popular with a post-theater crowd. The imaginative menu is prepared with all fresh produce. Closed Sundays. 3 Greenhill St. (phone: 293563). Inexpensive.

Mistress Quickly – At this coffeehouse specializing in tasty salads, simple hot dishes, and cream teas guests choose from a large buffet-style display and then order from waitresses. Open daily. 59–60 Henley St. (phone: 295261). Inexpensive.

Old Tudor House – Your basic English sausage, eggs, and chips with everything, but nicely prepared and presented. A good family place — they will even provide a highchair for the baby. Open daily. High and Ely Sts. (phone: 297140). Inexpensive.

Richoux – Waitresses dressed in Victorian pinafores serve a good selection of salads and sandwiches at this pretty new coffeehouse. Open daily. Red Lion Shopping Court, off Bridge St. (phone: 415377). Inexpensive.

Vintner Wine Bar – A bistro with beamed ceilings, it serves snacks and informal meals; hot dishes include homemade soups and French-style vegetables. Open daily. 5 Sheep St. (phone: 297259). Inexpensive.

SHARING A PINT: Among Stratford's array of pubs, two are particularly worth raising an elbow in. The *Garrick Inn,* next to Harvard House on High St., dates back to late Elizabethan times, but its ambience is delightfully Dickensian, with several small bars (phone: 292186). The *Black Swan* (commonly known as the *Dirty Duck)* is Stratford's theatrical pub, where actors and actresses come for their post-show pints and the atmosphere can become charged with the euphoria engendered by a good performance. Waterside (phone: 297312). *The Windmill,* on Church St., is one of Stratford's oldest pubs and serves good food and real ale. For something trendy, try the *Slug and Lettuce* (also a bistro), 38 Guild St. (phone: 299700).

YORK

"The history of York," according to King George VI, "is the history of England." In 1971, York celebrated its 1,900th birthday, and each successive epoch of the country's past is still legible in its ruin sites, buildings, and monuments. The Middle Ages are especially well represented, and for many visitors, it is this aspect of York that is the most interesting. Within the 3 miles of ancient defensive wall is perhaps the best-preserved medieval city in Great Britain, containing its largest medieval church, York Minster, and its best-preserved medieval street. The quirky, timbered, slightly akimbo buildings in the Shambles — once the butchers' quarters — may look like a stage set, but they are as authentic as the day they were built.

In AD 71, the Romans chose the meeting point of the rivers Ouse and Foss as the site of Eboracum, at first a temporary camp, then a permanent fort. From that it grew to become a major Roman city that Emperor Hadrian (of Hadrian's Wall fame) used as a home base and where Constantine the Great was proclaimed Emperor. It flourished as a trade center at the hub of a network of roads and as a port for seagoing ships that navigated the 50-mile stretch up the river Ouse. The most inspiring physical legacy of those times is the surviving Multangular Tower in the museum gardens (though its upper stonework is "merely" medieval).

The Romans left to defend their own country in the early part of the 5th century, and little is known of the next slice of history until the Saxons gained control of the city in the 7th century. They built a wooden church, the first York Minster, predecessor of the present building. The conquering Danes, arriving in the 9th century, further developed the city as an important port, called it Jorvik, and gave the name *gate,* Norse for "street," to several of its thoroughfares. Some of Jorvik's original Viking buildings have been excavated recently, superbly preserved in the peaty earth. The Normans' 11th-century presence is recorded in today's landscape as two humps of earth on which William the Conqueror raised two wooden castles. One hump remains as Baile Hill; the other supports Clifford's Tower, a later structure in stone.

It was in the 13th century, however, that the city began to assume its familiar shape. Though it had earlier been surrounded by an earth mound and a wooden stockade, these were now replaced by the actual limestone walls, together with the four principal gateways (called bars, just to confuse matters): Monk Bar, Micklegate Bar, Walmgate Bar, and Bootham Bar. Within the boundaries, several churches, friaries, nunneries, and an abbey established York as a cradle of European Christianity and as the country's second city. The minster, growing grander and grander over the 250 years of its construction, was finally completed in 1472, and has been York's crowning glory ever since.

Medieval city planners developed their roads along the main Roman streets. Stonegate was, for example, the Via Praetoria; Petergate, the Via Principalis; and Micklegate, meaning the Great Street, was the main route from London where the only bridge over the Ouse stood. The medievals then built connecting alleyways and the characteristic timber-framed buildings that overhang them, each story projecting farther than the one below. The Shambles is one such street, now restored not as a lifeless museum piece but as a busy commercial artery.

During the 15th century the Dukes of York were deeply indentified with the city and its shire in their own minds, those of their enemies, and the people of Yorkshire. During the mid-15th century, the House of York and the House of Lancaster struggled for the throne of England. Richard, the then Duke of York, led the opposition to Lancaster's King Henry VI, and thus began the extended historic scrap over the royal succession — known as the Wars of the Roses (the house of Lancaster's emblem was a red rose, and the house of York, white). Since those battles, the dukedom of York has been awarded to the second son of the royal family; Queen Elizabeth conferred the title on Prince Andrew the day he married Sarah Ferguson.

The prosperity of medieval York stemmed from its thriving wool trade. With the slow decline of this industry, and in the wake of Henry VIII's purge against the power of the church, the city was doomed for some time to play only a minor role in English history until it became a fashionable social center in 18th-century Georgian Britain. The racecourse, Assembly Rooms, and many splendid townhouses belonging to large, landowning families were part of this scene. The aristocracy, and those who could, chose to live in York rather than other more grimy and industrialized cities perched on the rich coal seams and deposits found almost everywhere in Yorkshire except York itself.

Because it was widely favored by wealthy northerners as a refuge from the grime of early industrialization, York remained relatively factory-free, with candy works a notable exception. It did, however, spawn George Hudson, a railway inventor and entrepreneur who was largely responsible for making the city a keystone in Britain's expanding railway network. Today a plaque commemorating his life and work can be seen outside the *Railway King* hotel on George Hudson Street. (The house of Joseph Hansom, inventor of the first horse-drawn cab, is in Micklegate.)

To absorb York's antiquated atmosphere, simply wander around, particularly in the labyrinth of streets and alleyways in the shadow of the minster. Stroll along the gates — the activities that once took place in them are evident in their names: Colliergate was the street of the charcoal dealers, Spurriergate belonged to the spurmakers, and Stonegate was the route used to carry building materials to the minster. Whip-ma-whop-ma-gate is the longest name for the shortest street, one named after a whipping post where criminals were punished.

Everywhere are curiosities of the past. In Deangate, for example, there is a working gas lamp in front of the minster's south door. At Nos. 5 and 7 Petergate, and at several other points in town, you can see the original firemark signs put there in Georgian days, when each insurance company had its own fire engine, which would only go to the rescue of its own blazing customers. Above all, be sure to allow your ears to work, as well as your eyes, as you roam this unique city; the Yorkshire accent is as much a part of the local atmosphere as the historic buildings.

York does have its shabbier, modern appendages (and some less shabby, including a modern university), but it has managed more successfully than most cities to conserve its age-old character. Whether it can continue to resist pressures to keep up-to-date by widening streets and building taller buildings remains to be seen. In the meantime, it is not unusual for over 2 million visitors a year to step into York's time capsule to enjoy its ancient airs and graces. You will not be alone in admiring this most historic of cities.

YORK AT-A-GLANCE

SEEING THE CITY: For those who need an aerial perspective before tackling some of York's inner alleyways, the city walls offer a 2½-mile-long vantage point. The route along the crest of the barricades dates from the 1200s and is still the traditional promenade for both natives and visitors. The path — 3 feet wide and often without handrails, so be careful — can be reached from the bars, or gateways, where the walls join the major roads (Bootham, Monk, Walmgate, Fishergate, Victoria, and Micklegate bars). The stretch between Bootham Bar and Monk Bar is particularly attractive and affords a good view of the spires and buttresses of York Minster. The walk, which is delightful in springtime when clouds of daffodils hug the grassy banks, is open daily from dawn till dusk.

SPECIAL PLACES: Nearly everything you'll want to see in York is in the medieval heart of the city. The only exception is the *National Railway Museum* on the west side of the Ouse near the railway station, which is just outside the old city walls.

York Minster – York without the minster's imposing skyline presence would be like Paris denied its Eiffel Tower. This grandiose church — the Cathedral of St. Peter — is the largest medieval cathedral in northern Europe. It was built over a period of 250 years, from 1220 to 1472, but even before that, there was a church on the spot, several in fact: The first was a wooden one built in the 7th century (the word *minster* is Anglo-Saxon for a mission from which the surrounding country was evangelized). York Minster contains the finest collection of medieval stained glass in England. Of the 130 windows (most were removed at the outbreak of World War II and painstakingly put back together again), the 13th-century Five Sisters Window of delicate grisaille glass is the most famous, although the West Window, with its heart-shaped tracery, is perhaps the most beautiful. The Rose Window, commemorating the 15th-century War of the Roses, was badly damaged in the 1984 fire that swept through York Minster. However, an exhibition of its upcoming restoration is on display. Among the minster's other proud features are the late-15th-century choir screen with its sculpted Kings of England, and the undercroft. The church was in danger of collapsing until desperately needed renovations were begun in 1967. During the course of the repairs, the foundations of an early Norman cathedral were revealed, and it was discovered that the medieval church had been raised right above the city's Roman headquarters. There is now an *Undercroft Museum,* where visitors can see the massive 20th-century concrete underpinnings as well as an exhibit on the history of the minster and its site. York Minster is open daily from 7 AM to dusk, though sightseeing is restricted during services. It costs nothing to wander around the minster itself, but there is an admission charge for the *Undercroft Museum* and Chapter House (the neighboring 13th-century meeting place of the dean and chapter), which contains a small collection of medieval stone carvings; open Mondays through Saturdays from 10 AM to dusk, Sundays to 1 PM.

Treasurer's House – The official residence of the treasurer of the minster (until the post was abolished in 1547) is behind the minster on the site of a Roman building. Though it dates from the 13th century, most of what exists today is from the 17th century. The last owner, Frank Green, renovated the building and gave it to the National Trust in 1930. Visitors can walk through about 20 rooms furnished with period pieces and take in a lively exhibition showing some of the personalities associated with the house. Open daily from April through October. Admission charge. On some summer evenings (contact the tourist information center for details) you can enjoy coffee by candlelight in the main hall and music in the drawing room. Minster Yard (phone: 624247).

St. William's College – One of York's many picturesque half-timbered structures, this was built in 1453 to lodge the minster's chantry priests and has been restored as a meeting place for church convocations. Its Tudor quadrangle is a particularly remarkable feature. Those interested in becoming more directly involved in the city's history, and possibly returning home with a 14th-century archbishop in tow, will find a wide selection of replicas in the *York Brass Rubbing Centre* here (phone: 645137), a few taken from original brasses found in local churches. Materials and advice, from $1.50. Open daily from 10 AM to 5 PM and Sundays, 9:30 AM to 5 PM, when not being used for meetings. College St. (phone: 624426).

Holy Trinity Church – Completed before 1500, this picturesque church on a picturesque street contains a split-level pulpit and 18th-century wooden box pews, each with its own door enabling it to be occupied by a single family. Goodramgate.

Shambles – Mentioned in the *Domesday Book,* this narrow cobblestone alleyway is one of the best-preserved medieval streets in Britain, if not in Europe. Originally it was a street of butcher shops, known as "fleshammels," but it is now lined with antiques, crafts, and gift shops (some still have the sloping wooden shelves in front that were used to display meat). People living in the upper stories of these typically medieval overhanging buildings can shake hands with their neighbors across the road if they lean out the windows far enough. The Shambles leads from King's Square (at the foot of Petergate) to The Pavement.

Jorvik Viking Centre – Small electric cars transport visitors underground to Jorvik — an old Viking city that's been uncovered by archaeologists. A bustling market, a busy wharf, houses with smoking chimneys, as well as reconstructions of the original excavation are on display; so are scores of objects — tools, kitchenware, shoes, and fragments of clothing — that have lain untouched since the Vikings lived here 1,000 years ago. Open daily from 9 AM. Admission charge. Coppergate (phone: 643211).

Fairfax House – An 18th-century townhouse displaying the famous Terry collection of Georgian-era furniture and clocks, entitled "Life in Georgian York." Now owned by the York Civic Trust, the house was used as a movie house and dance hall from 1920 to the mid-1960s. Open daily, except Fridays; closed January and February. Castlegate (phone: 655543).

The York Story – York from pre-Roman times to the present day is the subject of exhibits in the city's Heritage Center, housed in the former St. Mary's Church. Lots of lavishly constructed models, a slide show, and audio presentations are included in the center, which was designed as York's contribution to the European Architectural Heritage Year in 1975. See this before you explore the real thing. Open daily. Admission charge. Castlegate (phone: 628632). Joint tickets for the York Story and the *Castle Museum* (see below) are available from the latter. Castlegate (phone: 653611).

Clifford's Tower – A confusing history is attached to this remnant of York Castle. William the Conqueror erected a wooden fortress on a manmade earth mound here in 1068. In 1190, a rioting anti-Jewish mob burned it down, killing 150 of the Jews of York who had taken refuge inside. The existing quatrefoil stone tower, actually the medieval keep of the castle, was built in the 13th century, gutted by fire in the 17th century, and later restored and named after a Roger de Clifford, who had been executed here in 1596. In the 19th century, the tower was used as a prison. Open daily. Admission charge. Tower St. (phone: 646940).

Castle Museum – The private collection of everyday "bygones" accumulated by a country doctor from Pickering, 25 miles northeast of York, and donated to the city in 1925, forms the basis of this museum which has become one of the most important folk museums in the country. Stars of the show are the reconstructed streets: a Victorian cobbled one complete with Hansom cab (the original taxi, whose inventor, Joseph Hansom, lived in York), candlemaker's, blacksmith's, and other shop fronts, and an Edwardian street with gaslighted pub. Among the other, diverse displays are a Victorian parlor, a Georgian dining room, snuffboxes, policemen's truncheons, old musical instruments, vintage candy bars that include sugar pigs and spice mice, firearms, and unintelligible tape recordings of the local Yorkshire dialect. All this is housed in a former 18th-century prison for women, with various craftsmen's workshops set up in the converted cells — except for one that remains untouched. In it Dick Turpin, the notorious highwayman who, legend has it, rode Black Bess and terrorized travelers in the early stagecoaches, was imprisoned before being executed in 1740. Open daily from 9:30 AM, Sundays from 10 AM. Entry for the last tour, April through October, is 5:30 PM; November through March, 4 PM.. Admission charge. Tower St. (phone: 653611).

Merchant Adventurers' Hall – The wealthiest and most powerful of the city's trade guilds built this excellent example of a medieval guildhall in the 14th and 15th centuries. It has lovely timberwork inside and out. Open Mondays through Saturdays year-round and Sundays from March 21 to November 6; closed December 21 to January 4. Fossgate (phone: 654818).

Assembly Rooms – Built in the 1730s, this was once the most fashionable social center in the north of England. It was *the* place to go in Georgian times to play cards and dice, drink tea, or attend a grand ball. Today dances are still held here, though exhibitions and conferences are more usual. The design of the building is Italian Palladian, and the colonnaded Egyptian Hall is its chief interior feature. Open weekdays only, except when functions are taking place. Blake St. (phone: 613161).

Yorkshire Museum and Botanical Gardens – The museum contains exhibits that date back 160 million years, but apart from the geological items, it is probably best known for its collection of archaeological remains, particularly finds from Roman York. The Roman Life galleries, opened in 1985, display relics — including a Roman kitchen, mosaics, and priceless gold and silver jewelry — from one of Britain's most fascinating periods. In the 10-acre botanical gardens, in which the museum stands, are the ruins of St. Mary's Abbey (founded ca. 1080), once the most important Benedictine monastery in the north of England. (It was suppressed by Henry VIII's Dissolution of the Monasteries and thereafter lost many of its stones to local building projects.) The Multangular Tower and a section of the city walls, their lower portions Roman, are also in the gardens. Open daily, except Sunday mornings. Admission charge for the museum. Museum St. (phone: 629745).

City Art Gallery – The collection includes minor old masters dating from the 14th century, but works of 19th- and 20th-century European painters tend to be the specialty. The building itself is Victorian. Open daily. Admission charge. Exhibition Sq. (phone: 623839).

National Railway Museum – One of the few national museums outside London, it is packed with reminders of the days of steam and appropriately housed in the old depot where the locomotives went for maintenance and repairs. The most famous items are the *Pacific Mallard* locomotive, which still holds the world's steam speed record at 126 mph, and Queen Victoria's luxuriously appointed *Pullman* carriage. Many of the locomotives and carriages on display stand on two giant turntables in the 2-acre Great Hall, and lots of other aspects of railway history are covered by the exhibits in the museum galleries. There is a shop and an upstairs restaurant overlooking the main London–Edinburgh line. Open Mondays through Saturdays from 10 AM to 6 PM, Sundays from 11 AM. Leeman Rd. (phone: 621261).

■ **EXTRA SPECIAL:** The oldest inhabitants of York are its ghosts — the city is widely reckoned to be the most haunted in Europe. Monks, black cats, a duke, a 13th-century mayoress, the headless Earl of Northumberland, and marching Roman soldiers have all been seen by upstanding and sober members of the community. Several buildings are steeped in ghostly tales. The modern *Theatre Royal,* for example, stands on the ruins of St. Leonard's Hospital whose medieval crypt is now a theater club room inhabited by the Grey Lady, the ghost of a young nun said to have been buried alive in the walls for having an affair with a monk. You can see for yourself: Jayne and Trevor Rooney's 2-hour walking tour, led by an expert guide, leaves daily from outside the *Anglers Arms,* Goodramgate, at 8 PM, March through October, in search of "haunted and historic York." The tour costs about $3, and reservations are not required (phone: 426767). There are also more general guided walking tours and bus tours of the area, even 15-minute clip-clops around the town on a horse-drawn carriage, with en route commentary by the driver. They leave from opposite the front of the minster and cost approximately $1.50 (phone: 769490). Yorktour, 12A Coney St. (phone: 641737), offers a variety of tours — open-top bus tours, walking tours, double-decker boat tours.

SOURCES AND RESOURCES

TOURIST INFORMATION: The tourist information center in the De Grey Rooms, Exhibition Sq. (phone: 621756), has lots of free or nominally priced pamphlets on the city and the surrounding area, including the *Official York Guide* (about $2.30). A free 2-hour walking tour, led by members of the Association of Voluntary Guides, leaves here two or three times a day from Easter through October. The tourist information center is open in June through September from 9 AM to 8 PM, Mondays through Saturdays; in October through May from 9 AM to 5 PM, Mondays through Saturdays; year-round from 2 to 5 PM on Sundays. Except for Venice and Florence, York has probably been the subject of more books and guides than any other single non-capital city in Europe. A broad selection is for sale at the *York Minster Bookshop* and at the bookstore in the *Castle Museum.* Among the shorter booklets worth reading are *The City of York and the Minster,* by A. L. Laishley; *Georgian Houses in York,* by the York Georgian Society; *Roman York from AD 71,* by the Yorkshire Architectural and York Archaeological societies; and *York Mystery Plays,* by Eileen White. The two historical works called simply *York* — one by George Benson, the other by Angela Fiddes — are meatier tomes.

Local Coverage – The *Yorkshire Evening Press* is the city's daily newspaper, on sale at various newsstands and from street-corner venders (whose cry doesn't sound anything like "*Yorkshire Evening Press*").

Telephone – The area code for York is 0904.

GETTING AROUND: York is to be explored on foot, especially since parking is virtually impossible on the street and most of the major car parks are outside the walls, away from where you really want to be. Because it is a compact city, with all places of interest within strolling distance, you won't be logging mammoth mileages.

Bicycle – Not at all an unusual mode of transportation in York. Rent one from *Cycle Scene,* 2 Ratcliffe St., Burton Stone La. (phone: 653286), or the *York Cycleworks,* 14–16 Lawrence St. (phone: 626664).

Boat – Several companies operate river tours. From mid-March through September, *Hills Boatyard,* Lendal Bridge (phone: 623752), has hour-long, 6-mile cruises on double-decker boats up the Ouse to Bishopthorpe Palace, the 13th-century home of the archbishop of York, and back. Times of the sailings are posted on the notice board by the boatyard gates. *White Rose Line* (Foss Basin, St. George's Field; phone: 628324) arranges riverboat jazz cruises, supper cruises, and floodlit evening cruises from King's Staith. For those who prefer to be on their own, *York Marine Services* in Bishopthorpe rents self-drive motorboats and rowboats by the hour, day, or week (phone: 704442).

Bus – The railway station is really the hub of the bus network. The *West Yorkshire Bus Company* sells a 2-day tourist ticket allowing unlimited travel on any of its city bus routes for about $4.50. Buy it from the driver on the city tour bus, from the company's head office on Rougier St. (phone: 624161), or from the tourist information bureau in the British Rail station, where you can also pick up information on the company's city center coach tours, which depart daily from outside the *Royal York* hotel (about $2.70), and their morning "Super City" tours, which combine a walking tour with travel by bus (open-top double-decker on fine days) and riverboat (about $5.50).

Car Rental – A car isn't necessary to see the city, but they are available if you plan an excursion into the countryside. Major firms represented include *Godfrey Davis,* Station Garage, Leeman Rd. (phone: 620394); *Avis,* at the railway station (phone: 610460); *Tern Car Rentals,* Clarence St. (phone: 611767); and *Kenning,* Micklegate Bar (phone: 659328).

Taxi – Centrally located cab ranks are at St. Sampson's Sq. (phone: 622333), by the *ABC* cinema on Piccadilly (phone: 654579), by the *Odeon* cinema on Blossom St., next to the *Windmill* hotel on Queen St., at the railway station, and at Bootham Bar.

Train – It takes only 2 hours to travel from London's King Cross Station to the York terminus, which is west of the city on Station Rd. (phone: 642155).

SPECIAL EVENTS: During the last week in January and the first 3 weeks of February join the locals in the growingly popular *Jorvik Viking Festival,* which features an ancient ritual boat-burning on the Ouse and many community events, including parades and pageants. The *York Races,* run a few days each month from May through October (the most important race, the *Ebor Handicap,* takes place in August), are usually the biggest events on the calendar. They are regularly upstaged, however, by the *York Cycle of Mystery Plays,* a reenactment that traditionally takes place every 4th year in tandem with the *York Festival* (see below). The 48 plays — first performed in the mid-14th century and repeated for about 200 years thereafter — tell the story of man from the Creation to the Last Judgment. Originally presented by the medieval guilds, each of which chose a Biblical story to illustrate, the revived plays are still performed by local citizens, 200 of them, along with a handful of professional actors. Most of the plays are set dramatically against the ruins of St. Mary's Abbey, but some are presented on authentically built wagons drawn around the city as in medieval times. The performances go on for 3 weeks and coincide with the *York Festival* of symphony, chamber, opera, and choral music, dance, art exhibits, and other entertainment. The next festival will take place in 1992. For details, contact the York Festival Office, 1 Newgate, Off Kings Square, York Y01 2lA (phone: 610266).

MUSEUMS: In addition to the museums described in *Special Places,* you may want to visit *Impressions.* When it opened in 1972, it was the first photographic gallery outside London, and there still aren't many others. Apart from its changing exhibitions, there are cards, prints, and specialist books on sale. Open Tuesdays through Saturdays, plus Mondays in August and December. 17 Colliergate (phone: 654724). There's also the York Dungeon, a spine-chilling, permanent historical exhibition of "blood, death, and torture." Open daily from 10 AM to 6 PM. Admission charge. 12 Clifford St. (phone: 632599).

SHOPPING: York's Newgate marketplace has been the focal point of all trading activities since medieval times. The setting is beautiful and the variety of wares is bound to interest browsers of all dispositions. Among the stalls you'll find antiques, clothing, bric-a-brac, and homemade Yorkshire foods as well as fish, fowl, and vegetables. The market is in full swing every day except Sunday. More conventional shop premises range from Georgian frontages in the city's older thoroughfares to modern shopping center facilities. The Coppergate pedestrian mall around St. Mary's Square contains shops, restaurants, branches of most chain stores, and exclusive jewelers, as well as the Jorvik Viking Centre. Early closing day in York is Wednesday, although many of the larger stores now stay open 6 days a week.

Antiques shops abound. Most carry a wide selection of pieces and periods, though they may be known for a specialty. Among them are *Greenwoods* in Stonegate (jewelry), *York House* in Petergate (furniture and paintings), *Trinity* in Goodramgate (dolls), *Morrison* in The Mount (furniture), *Donald Butler* in Goodramgate (fine china), and several others. There are lots of antiquarian bookshops, too, including *Spelman's* in Micklegate, *O'Flynn* in Bridge St., and *MacDowell and Stern* in Grapelane.

Laura Ashley – A branch of one of Britain's most popular stores for women's ready-to-wear. Davygate (phone: 627707).

Cox – Sheepskin: Slippers, gloves, rugs, coats, hats, footmuffs, and powder puffs are among its variations on a theme. 19 The Shambles (phone: 624449).

Deco – Original pottery, jewelry, glass, and various decorative household items from the 1920s and 1930s. 39 Stonegate (phone: 631960).

Ralph Ellerker's – Famous since 1796, then as a saddler and harnessmaker, now as a store for the modern equestrian who rides for pleasure. Apart from its ancient beams and rich leathery fragrance, you'll also discover ropes and canvasses, a macrame or yachting enthusiast's dream. Lots of regular gift ideas, too. The Shambles (phone: 654417).

Liberty – The famous London store now has a branch in York, with printed fabrics and a variety of gifts. 15 Davygate (phone: 633093).

Little Gallery – "All gifts shipped to all countries" is the motto of this well-stocked souvenir emporium where solid English pewter, historical dolls, bone china, glass, copper, and brass are offered. 71–73 Low Petergate (phone: 623150).

Mulberry Hall – One of the finest medieval buildings in York (it was a private house from the 15th to the 18th century, when it became a shop), it is now one of England's most respected porcelain dealers. Twelve elaborate showrooms sprawl over three floors. 17 Stonegate (phone: 620736).

Preston's of Bolton – Established in 1869, this shop now calls itself "The Diamond Centre of the North," selling a wide range of watches and jewelry. Coppergate (phone: 634315).

Alan Stuttle Gallery **–** Original oils, watercolors, and limited edition and other prints, including many of York. 42 Stonegate (phone: 624907).

Wooden Horse **–** An interesting collection of diverse ethnic items ranging from African tribal rugs to Nepalese clothing, Chinese kites, and Mexican silver. 9 Goodramgate (phone: 626012).

SPORTS: Cricket – To see a first class match, go to Leeds, 25 miles away. Yorkshiremen have always been fanatical cricketers, and the *Yorkshire County Cricket Club* is based at the *Headingley Cricket Ground,* St. Michael's La., Leeds (phone: 0532-52865). When Yorkshire meets Lancashire, it's the Wars of the Roses all over again — check local papers for the date of the annual "battle."

Fishing – Licenses to fish the river Ouse and others can be bought at *Hookes,* 28–30 Coppergate (phone: 655073), *G. E. Hill,* 40 Clarence St. (phone: 624561), or *Bulmers* at Monk's Bar (phone: 654070).

Golf – There are more than 60 courses within an hour's drive of York, but four within easy reach of the city center are the *Fulford Golf Club,* Heslington La. (phone: 413579), the *Heworth Golf Club,* Muncastergate, Malton Rd. (phone: 422389), the *Railway Institute,* Pike Hills, Tadcaster Rd. (708756), and the *York Golf Club,* 6 miles out of town at Strensall (phone: 490304). All allow temporary visitor membership, but phone ahead. There is also a driving range at Wiggington Rd.; open daily from 10:30 AM (phone: 659421).

Horse Racing – The *York Racecourse* is the most important racetrack in northern England. Entrance to the grounds costs about $1.50, but if you don't want to take advantage of the facilities inside, you can watch from the common land around the track, even stroll almost to the winning post, without payment. The races begin in May and reoccur for a few days each month through October. Peak of the season is the running of the Ebor Handicap in August. On the Knavesmire, 1 mile south of the city (phone: 620911).

Swimming – The *Barbican Pools* are the city's most modern, with three separate pools. Open daily. Admission charge. Paragon St. (phone: 630266).

Tennis – Courts are available at Rowntree Park, Hull Rd. Park, Glen Gardens, Scarcroft Rd., and at the university. Book at the courts.

THEATER: The *Theatre Royal,* St. Leonard's Pl., was built in 1740 and became one of the country's leading theaters in Georgian times. Rebuilt by the Victorians, it is still York's main theater, offering a range of dramatic performances by both local groups and leading actors and actresses. The box office is open Mondays through Saturdays (phone: 623568), and most performances begin at 7:30 PM or 8 PM. The *Arts Centre,* housed in a converted medieval church in Micklegate, has much more varied entertainments — films, exhibitions, music, and other events — in addition to plays (phone: 623568).

MUSIC: With the exception of the University of York Music Department, which gives twice-weekly concerts during term time in *Lyons Concert Hall,* York is generally a poor city for all kinds of music. A few pubs and restaurants have live folk or jazz performances and there are several discos, but lovers of classical music will be extremely fortunate if they hear any during their stay. The *Theatre Royal* and the *Arts Centre* are the most likely settings for musical events and the tourist information center will know of any others. Also consult the free monthly publication, *Your K Music,* available from various outlets, including the tourist information center.

NIGHTCLUBS AND NIGHTLIFE: York is not a night town. If you crave action in the wee hours, your best bet is to drive to Leeds, which thrives on things happening when most of its respectable citizens are tucked into their beds. However, York does have a few discos worth visiting. Most require jackets and ties; some allow informal attire other than jeans. Entrance charges vary according to the DJ and night of the week, but generally they are inexpensive and membership, if necessary, is nominal for the transient visitor. *Roxy Nightclub,* 25 Bootham Rd. (phone: 627319), offers dinner and dancing in a Georgian house Mondays through Saturdays from 10 PM. *Ziggy's,* 55 Micklegate (phone: 620674), has two bars and a disco; open Mondays through Saturdays from 10 PM to 2 AM. *Winning Post* hotel (Bishopthorpe Rd.; phone: 625228), has entertainment every night from Wednesdays through Sundays, including live bands most Friday and Saturday nights.

BEST IN TOWN

CHECKING IN: August is a hopeless time to visit York if you want to stay in the city center. Not only is it the peak time for tourists, but their numbers are swelled by racegoers, here for the most important meeting on the calendar. Rather than try to squeeze into too few city beds, car drivers are advised to travel out and find smaller hotels in the Vale of York, the flat band of land to the north of the city, or even to go to Harrogate, a half-hour ride to the west, where there's bound to be a room, even at the height of the summer. The tourist information center can give on-the-spot advice about room availability and operates a booking service for a fee, for those who apply in person. A double room with breakfast costs $110 and up at hotels listed as expensive; from $80 to $100 at moderate ones; and less than $75 at inexpensive ones. All telephone numbers are in the 0904 area code unless otherwise indicated.

Crest – A four-star haven of luxury in the city center that caters to business travelers. It features 136 superbly furnished bedrooms. 1 Tower St. (phone: 648111). Expensive.

Judges Lodging – The stone head above the doorway represents Aesculapius, the Greek god of healing, because the building was once the town residence of a well-known physician. Later it was the residence of the Assize Court judges, hence the name. Built about 1710 in Georgian style and appointed with period furnishings and antiques, it has 13 lavishly decorated rooms, including 6 with four-poster beds. Cuisine is French and the wines are personally imported by the proprietor, who is also French. 9 Lendal (phone: 638733). Expensive.

Post House – Large, modern, and built close to the ground, this is about 1½ miles south of the center of town. Part of it faces the racecourse; the restaurant and other public rooms are arranged around a cedar of Lebanon tree planted in the garden of the manor house that used to occupy the site. There are 147 rooms. Tadcaster Rd. (phone: 707921). Expensive.

Royal York – The place to go to experience Victorian charm at its most overwhelming. This magnificent 126-room railway hotel has been in operation just over 100 years, and although necessary steps toward modernization have been taken, the traditional air remains, especially at teatime in the high-ceilinged lounge. There is a fitness room and a putting green in the formal gardens. Naturally, it's convenient to the station. Station Rd. (phone: 653681). Expensive.

Viking – Large (187 rooms), centrally located (on the river Ouse), and with excellent service, this hotel is an expanse of Scandinavian modernity right down to the sauna and whirlpool bath. The restaurant specializes in local dishes, including apple pie and Wensleydale cheese, which you can consume with some Theakston's Old Peculier ale and round off with a taste of Brontë liqueur. North St. (phone: 659822). Expensive.

Abbey Park – A 5-minute wander away from the city center, this 84-room hotel is a vintage Georgian brick building with updated bedrooms. The restaurant serves typical Yorkshire fare, including Yorkshire pudding and syllabub. The Mount (phone: 658301). Expensive to moderate.

Whitwell Hall Country House – This magnificent Tudor-Gothic–style hotel is set amidst 18 acres of wooded garden. There's a log fire burning in the grand entrance hall, game in season, fresh garden herbs and salads, a heated indoor swimming pool, and a sauna. Pre-dinner drinks are served in the Orangery near the pool. Whitwell-on-the-Hill (phone: 065381-551). Expensive to moderate.

Abbots Mews – Located in a quiet cul-de-sac a few minutes' walk from the city center, this hotel occupies a Victorian coachman's cottage and the adjoining stable block. 6 Marygate La., Bootham (phone: 634866). Moderate.

Chase – The building is 19th century with later additions, and it overlooks the Knavesmire racecourse. This is a pleasant, traditional sort of hostelry, about 1½ miles from the center. All 80 rooms have private tubs or showers. Tadcaster Rd. (phone: 707171). Moderate.

Hill – This Georgian establishment is family run, and since it has only 10 rooms (2 with four-poster beds), staying here is like staying in a private home — with private bath or shower, use of a delightful garden, and traditional cuisine. About 2 miles from the city center. 60 York Rd., Acomb (phone: 790777). Moderate.

Hudson – A large 4-story Victorian building just a few minutes' walk from the city center. Most of the 28 rooms have TV sets and private tub or shower. Typical English fare is served in the downstairs restaurant amid Victorian-era kitchen decor. 60 Bootham (phone: 621267). Moderate.

Coach House – The 17th-century origins of this guesthouse are still much in evidence, with oak-beamed ceilings throughout. It's located in the same, traffic-free cul-de-sac as the *Abbots Mews* hotel. There are 13 rooms, 10 with private bath or shower. 20–22 Marygate, Bootham (phone: 652780). Moderate to inexpensive.

Ashcroft – The 2½-acre setting with a view of the river Ouse compensates for this lovely Victorian hotel's distance from the city center (1 mile). All 15 rooms have private baths or showers. 294 Bishopthorpe Rd. (phone: 659286). Inexpensive.

Jorvik – Small and modest — most of the 18 rooms have private bath. The hotel faces the Abbey Gate and the 11th-century St. Olave's Church. 52 Marygate, Bootham (phone: 653511). Inexpensive.

Youth – Catering to the budget traveler, this unassuming place offers meals, bike rentals, and dormitory–style rooms at prices of $7 and up per night (bed only). 11–13 Bishopshill Senior (phone: 630613). There is also an international hostel at 13 Bootham (phone: 622874). Very inexpensive.

EATING OUT: Yorkshire's reputation for mountainous portions of everything is as apparent in its major city as anywhere else in the county, although the more cosmopolitan restaurants are less likely to plump you out of all proportion than those that pride themselves on real Yorkshire kitchens. The most renowned local specialty is Yorkshire pudding. Despite it's name, it isn't a dessert but a traditional accompaniment to roast beef served at Sunday lunch. The secret of a successful "pud" lies in its lightness, and everyone seems to have his or her own secret recipe to achieve the same end. (To make yours, whisk one egg, add a little milk, and gradually work in 3 ounces of flour, beating well. Add the rest of a half-pint of milk, leave it for an hour, then heat up some beef drippings in a baking tin. When very hot, pour in batter and cook in a hot oven — around 425 degrees — until the pudding rises and turns crispy brown at the edges). And if you thought there was nothing as American as apple pie, be advised that — topped with a slice of Wensleydale cheese — it is just as much of an institution here as it is back home. Parkin (an oatmeal, molasses, and ginger-rich cake) is another Yorkshire institution, traditionally made for *Guy Fawkes Day* (see *Sharing a Pint*). Expect to pay $65 to $85 for a full meal for two, including wine, in a restaurant listed below as expensive, $35 to $55 in those listed as moderate, and less than $30 at those listed as inexpensive. In addition to its restaurants, several of York's pubs serve good quality bar snacks at lunchtime. All telephone numbers are in the 0904 area code unless otherwise indicated.

19 Grape Lane – Despite it's name, this is a French restaurant with a small, discriminating menu that includes bouillabaisse and Normandy pheasant. 19 Grape La. (phone: 636366). Expensive.

Bess's – "Bess's Impresses" is its motto, and it does, with views over York Minster and beautiful large gardens not least among its attractions. Sandwiches are the specialty. Open daily. At the *Royal York* hotel, Station Rd. (phone: 653681). Expensive to moderate.

Tanglewood Inn – "A haven for the hungry," located 5 miles from York on the Malton Road. The menu — served by a small, friendly staff — includes tanglewood pie (an original steak and kidney pie, cooked in Guinness stout), salads, and light lunches. Open daily. Malton Rd. (phone: 86318). Expensive to moderate.

Betty's Tea Room – There's nothing better than to come in from York's chilling winter air and wallow in the coziness of toasted, home-baked tea cakes and crumpets puddled in butter, Yorkshire parkin, Brontë-rich fruitcakes, and *Betty's* famous rarebit, made from farmhouse Cheddar and Yorkshire ale, grilled on toast, and all according to a secret recipe. Open for main meals, too, either in the licensed restaurant or the cafeteria. Closed from 5:30 PM and Sundays. St. Helen's Sq. (phone: 659142). Moderate.

Plunkets – With some very tasty food, this place has a friendly ambience, good music in the background, lots of plants, and excellent hamburgers. 9 High Petergate (phone: 637722). Moderate.

Aquarium – *The* place for all dishes fishy. 25 Tanner Row, Rougier St. (phone: 645839). Inexpensive.

Cross Keys – One of the city's few authentically Edwardian pubs, this one has some of the best authentic homemade Yorkshire cooking in town, including shepherd's pies (ground beef crowned by mashed potato and lightly grilled). Goodramgate (phone: 659408). Inexpensive.

Danish Kitchen – Fittingly adjacent to the Jorvik Viking Centre, this is the place for Danish-style open sandwiches as well as cakes and pastries. High Ousegate (phone: 637752). Inexpensive.

Grunts' – A taste of Chicago pizza in York. 12 Clifford St. (phone: 648144). Inexpensive.

King's Manor – The historic Tudor setting of the York University refectory is open to the public for lunch Mondays through Fridays from noon to 2 PM. Both salads and hot meals are available. Exhibition Sq. (phone: 430000). Inexpensive.

Medio's Pizzeria – Enormous pizzas, baked in a brick oven, complete with pasta choices and a few other temptations besides. The atmosphere is lively. Open for lunch and dinner daily. 115 Micklegate (phone: 34765). Inexpensive.

St. William's – Once a medieval house for chantry priests, the surroundings are monastic with a hint of luxury. A very popular luncheon spot for salads, quiche, teatime tea, and cakes. Stop in after visiting the nearby minster or when you tire of brass rubbing. Enjoy a glass of elderberry wine at one of the festive tables outside, during the summer. Open daily, daytime only. 3 College St. (phone: 34830). Inexpensive.

SHARING A PINT: York has an embarrassment of riches when it comes to pubs. There are some 150 all told, quite a few of them crammed with character and characters. The drink is beer, especially beer from the local breweries and especially the famous Theakston's Old Peculier. Pubs are usually open from 11 AM to 3 PM and 5 to 11:30 PM; Sundays, 2 to 4 PM and 7 to 10:30 PM. *Ye Old Starre Inn,* easily located at 40 Stonegate by the gallows right across the road, is York's oldest alehouse. Its name was first recorded in 1644, and it has been a popular lodging house both for actors from the *Theatre Royal* and for church dignitaries visiting the minster. Today's interior is Victorian. The *Bay Horse* pub, 55 Blossom St., where you can try the locally brewed John Smith beer, and the *Bootham Tavern,* Bootham, are other places to imbibe in a Victorian setting. The *King's Arms,* on King's Staith, is still sometimes flooded in winter with waters from the adjacent embankment — a board records the various flood levels. At the *Roman Bath,* St. Sampson's Sq., customers can view genuine Roman steam baths, or rather their 2,000-year-old remains. General Wolfe, who lost his life winning Québec for the British, spent part of his youth in the *Black Swan Inn,* his mother's home in Peasholme Green. It was built as a merchant's house in the 16th century, and a room upstairs was used for illegal cockfighting. *Young's* hotel, 25 High Petergate, is reputedly on the site of the birthplace of Guy Fawkes, the man who tried (unsuccessfully) to blow up the British Parliament in 1605, bequeathing to children all over England an annual (November 5) excuse to burn him in effigy to the accompaniment of firecrackers.

DIVERSIONS

For the Body

Great Golf

True golf devotees contend that many of the finest — and most traditional — golf courses in the world are found in Britain. This is hardly surprising since the sandy land along its coasts was the terrain that spawned the game. It's hard to believe that less than a century ago golf was virtually unknown anywhere outside Scotland, though the Scots proved great apostles, spreading the word from Perth (where the first recognizable 6-hole course is thought to have been constructed on the city's North Inch), St. Andrews, Prestwick, and Dornoch.

These are the icons of a game that has gripped the attention of an entire planet. And even now, the courses found in Scotland and England provide a very different sense of the game than can be acquired anywhere else on earth. Nature was the architect of these courses. As a writer remarked in *The World Atlas of Golf,* "To this day nobody knows who laid [the courses] out . . . there were no fairways, no tees, and no greens, simply agreed starting and finishing points. The game had reached St. Andrews, Carnoustie, Leith, Dornoch, Montrose, North Berwick, and Musselburgh by the beginning of the 16th century. Golf thus became established on linksland . . . St. Andrews became — and still is — one long fairway, with nine holes out to a distant point, and nine holes back . . . designs incorporated stone walls, blind shots, hedges, irregularly shaped mounds and greens in geometric shapes."

But it's more than history that lures generations of modern golfers to the game's breeding grounds. The intensity of the challenge remains as vital as ever, and the chance to pit one's own skill against the achievements of golf's greatest historic figures is nearly irresistible. Not to play these courses at least once in a lifetime is not to know the real horizons of the game.

ALDEBURGH, Aldeburgh, Suffolk, England: Now 1½ miles inland, this immensely popular course, laid out by persons unknown, was undoubtedly once a part of the shore, and for nearly a century the name Aldeburgh has been synonymous with the classic sandy links — sea turf covered by the first markers of heathland, clumps of trees, and bright gorse. The first of *Aldeburgh*'s short holes features a kidney-shaped green set right behind a great sleepered bunker that extends to the right. The flag can be set at the back of the green close to still more bunkers. And while the fourth's 140-yard length may not intimidate, finding the green certainly will. Details: The Aldeburgh Golf Course, Aldeburgh, Suffolk IP15 5PE, England (phone: 0728-452890).

GANTON GOLF CLUB, Ganton, North Yorkshire, England: The east coast of England is not well known for its golfing venues, but this Yorkshire course is one of Britain's finest inland layouts. The holes are positioned on open heathland. The prime hazards here are bunkers and gorse, especially those placed alongside and amid fairway landing areas. Straight hitting is a must. Perhaps the greatest lure is the variety of challenge that requires accurate play and consummate concentration. Details: Ganton Golf Club, Ganton, North Yorkshire YO12 4PA, England (phone: 0944-70329).

ROYAL LIVERPOOL, Hoylake, Merseyside, England: This was the site of the first British amateur championship — which has been held here on 15 occasions since — and the first international golf competition (played between England and Scotland in 1902). In 1921, "Hoylake," as it's generally called, played host to the first international match between Great Britain and the US, which was dubbed the Walker Cup the following year. The club has hosted 10 British Open championships and is considered by many to be one of the best tests of golf in Britain. Not for the faint of heart. Details: Royal Liverpool Golf Club, Meols Dr., Hoylake, Merseyside L47 4AL, England (phone: 051-632-3101).

HUNSTANTON GOLF COURSE, Hunstanton, Norfolk, England: The town of Hunstanton has two distinctions: First, it is the only east coast resort that faces west (because it is on the cusp of Norfolk as it dips into the Wash). Second, it is home to *Hunstanton Golf Course.* Shaped by George Fernie in 1891 along the shore north of town, this layout is sure to challenge with its formidable set of bunkers. Details: Hunstanton Golf Course, Hunstanton, Norfolk PE36 6JQ, England (phone: 04853-2811).

ROYAL LYTHAM & ST. ANNES GOLF CLUB, Lytham St. Annes, Lancashire, England: Possessed of little visual splendor and set in an essentially urban setting, this course remains one of the most difficult of all the tracks in Britain and has maintained a special place on the British Open championship rota. Don't be deceived by the apparent tranquillity; the course is a test of golf that's among the finest in Britain, and nerve and subtlety are both required. For male guests, a special package including accommodations, golf, breakfast, dinner, and VAT is available; book early. Details: Royal Lytham & St. Annes Golf Club, Links Gate, Lytham St. Annes, Lancashire FY8 3LQ, England (phone: 0253-724206).

ROYAL ST. GEORGE'S GOLF CLUB, Sandwich, Kent, England: This corner of Kent is rich in history, and no course has a more constant involvement with the evolution of English championship golf. Often called "Sandwich," it was the site of the first official Walker Cup matches ever held in England. It was also the scene of the first ever American victory in the British Amateur championship and in the British Open (by Walter Hagen). It was here that Henry Cotton ended American postwar domination of the Open by winning the first of his three titles. And it was here in 1949 that the Open saw the memorable tie between Henry Bradshaw and the South African Bobby Locke (who won the 36-hole playoff). This is a place where golf history buffs will want to make their mark. Those interested in completing a tour of Kent's triumvirate of Open championship courses (or those who cannot be accommodated at the *Royal St. George*'s) should try their skills at two other fine layouts nestling cheek by jowl with it on the county's eastern shore, the *Royal Cinque Ports* and the beautiful *Prince's.* Details: Royal St. George's Golf Club, Sandwich, Kent CT13 9PB, England (phone: 0304-613090); Royal Cinque Ports Golf Club, Golf Rd., Deal, Kent CT14 6RF, England (phone: 0304-374007); and Prince's Golf Club, Sandwich Bay, Sandwich, Kent CT13 9QB, England (phone: 0304-611118).

SUNNINGDALE, Sunningdale, Berkshire, England: While the Old Course is considered the championship layout here, the New is probably the more challenging of the two. When you play them, you will discover that the decision on difficulty is an arbitrary one at best. Fairways and greens are meticulously maintained, and this is perhaps the finest single brace of courses in England. Private but approachable. Details: Sunningdale Golf Club, Ridgemount Rd., Sunningdale, Berkshire SL5 9RR, England (phone: 0990-21681).

WENTWORTH, Virginia Water, Surrey, England: Generally considered the prettier of the layouts here, the East Course can do wonders for a shaky backswing. But it's the West Course, with its relatively narrow tree-lined fairways, that is sometimes not so affectionately called the "Burma Road." For a high-handicap player, the West is not unlike putting an innocent's head into the mouth of an unfriendly lion, and especially from the back tees, the cry of "You can't get there from here!" is continually heard. (A third course will be ready for play in 1990.) The World Match Play Championship has been held here every year since 1964. Again, it's a private club; access is available to traveling players on weekdays with prior notice — upon presentation of your own club membership card and, if possible, a letter from your club president. With its dozen tennis courts, swimming pool, and equally well-maintained 9-hole, par-30 course, the *Wentworth Golf Club* is probably the nearest thing to an American country club in the south of England. Details: Wentworth Club, Virginia Water, Surrey GU25 4LS, England (phone: 0990-42201).

FULFORD, York, North Yorkshire, England: For an inland course in a county with more than its share of ups and downs, Fulford is remarkably flat. Many of the fine copper beech and oak trees that dominate it define the shape of the visitor's shot both from the tee and to the green; the good driver is always rewarded. There are two distinctly different sets of holes, one starting from the first to the sixth on the way out, the other from the twelfth homeward to finishing green near the clubhouse. Details: Fulford Golf Club, Heslington La., York, North Yorkshire YO1 5DY, England (phone: 0904-413579).

ROYAL BIRKDALE GOLF CLUB, Southport, Merseyside, England: This Lancashire coast setting in a stunning expanse of dunes is one of the most popular and demanding championship courses in the country, and it recently received top honors in England in a survey conducted by Golf World. It has hosted many international competitions, as many as any other course in Britain, since the end of World War II. The final 6 holes cover almost 2½ miles, and it takes supreme accuracy, rather than raw power, to avoid the fairway bunkers. Formby and Hillside, two other notable layouts, are a mere 5 miles away. Details: Royal Birkdale Golf Club, Waterloo Rd., Southport, Merseyside PR8 2LX, England (phone: Southport 0704-67920).

GLENEAGLES, Auchterarder, Perthshire, Scotland: Few hotels in the world can match *Gleneagles'* range of facilities. There are four 18-hole golf courses, a driving range, and a 9-hole pitch and putt course. The Queen's Course was restored in 1983 to James Braid's original design, the King's Course is an absolute joy to play (in 1987 it became home to the Bell's Scottish Open tournament), and all the *Gleneagles* links are also consistently in the best condition of any Scottish course. But the extraordinary hotel here would itself be reason enough to visit. Details: Gleneagles Hotel Golf Course, Auchterarder, Perthshire PH3 1NF, Scotland (phone: 0764-62231).

CARNOUSTIE, Carnoustie, Tayside, Scotland: Just 5 miles from St. Andrews as the crow flies (or 25 miles by road) is this site of half a dozen British Open tournaments. If the Championship Course (the best of the trio of tracks here) is the least impressive of the championship Scottish courses at first glance, its true value is easily appreciated in a single round. It encompasses the very essence of what's best about playing golf in Scotland, and the back nine in particular — with the famous fourteenth hole, called "Spectacles" because of two yawning twin bunkers in mid-fairway — as well as the three back-breaking finishing holes leave memories (not necessarily pleasant) that do not soon fade. Details: Carnoustie Golf Links, Links Parade, Carnoustie, Tayside DD7 7JE, Scotland (phone: for reservations, 0241-53789).

ROYAL DORNOCH, Dornoch, Highland Region, Scotland: No course in the world offers more wild beauty than this northernmost of the globe's great golf layouts. The course sweeps in a great curve along the shores of the Dornoch Firth, a site of splendid isolation that seldom fails to inspire a feeling of singular elation; many players echo the sentiments of Tom Watson, who remarked that the three rounds he played during one 24-hour visit were more fun than any other golfing experience of his life. Details: Royal Dornoch Golf Club, Dornoch, Sutherland IV25 3LW, Scotland (phone: 0862-810219).

THE HONOURABLE COMPANY OF EDINBURGH GOLFERS, Gullane, East Lothian, Scotland: The single best course in Scotland, this is home to the golf club with the longest continuous history in the world, one that has grown in status with each decade since its formal beginnings in 1744. Tucked along the south shore of the Firth of Forth, the course — most commonly called "Muirfield" — is totally challenging as well as beautifully simple. (For an idea of just how challenging it can be, know that the Committee recently imposed a maximum handicap of 18 for men and 24 for women because so many visitors, "unable to cope with the difficulty of the championship course," took 4½ hours or even longer to get around it.) Note that access is granted to non-members only by advance arrangement, and then only on Tuesdays, Thursdays, and Friday mornings. Still, getting to play at this wonderful place is considerably less problematic than it once was; when writing, include alternate playing dates. Details: The Honourable Company of Edinburgh Golfers, Muirfield, Gullane, East Lothian EH31 2EG, Scotland (phone: 0620-842123).

PRESTWICK, Prestwick, Strathclyde, Scotland: This famed course was the site of the first 12 British Open championships, and another dozen in subsequent (but not consecutive) years up until 1925. It has been taken off the Open rota because of its limited facilities for handling crowds, but it is still worth playing for its historic associations and for its challenges — long carries, deep bunkers, tough weather, rolling sand dunes, and the insidious Pow Burn, and the wind, which prevails from the direction of the Ailsa Craig in the southwest. However, on the admittedly rare occasions when the wind comes out of the east, you may need earplugs to drown out the din from neighboring Prestwick Airport, which can be seen across the railway line bordering the first hole. There are no ladies' tees, but women are welcome in the Cardinal Room for light refreshments. Bookings must be made well in advance. Details: Prestwick Golf Club, 2 Links Rd., Prestwick, Strathclyde KA9 1QG, Scotland (phone: 0292-77404).

THE OLD COURSE, St. Andrews, Fife, Scotland: Dating at least from the 15th but more likely from the late 14th century, this is the sport's greatest magnet, drawing all of the world's golfers, and its aura is only slightly diminished by the bathers and strollers who frequently cross the first and eighteenth fairways of *The Old Course* — it's the shortest route to the beach. Once on the course, golfers soon become aware of its extreme difficulty and subtle layout, which was fashioned by nature, with the help of the sheep and rabbits who created bunker locations when burrowing underground to escape the offshore winds that blow year-round. There are four other courses on the same site — the Balgove, Eden, Jubilee, and New (which was *opened* in 1894) — but it's the Old (the site of no less than two dozen British Opens, and now the permanent home of the Dunhill Nations Cup tournament held each October) that any dedicated golfer must play. Make plans carefully to be here on the right day (the Old Course is closed Sundays), and confirm tee-off times well in advance — a year in advance is not too early. Details: Links Management Committee, Golf Pl., St. Andrews, Fife KY16 9JA, Scotland (phone: 0334-75757).

ROYAL TROON, Troon, Ayrshire, Scotland: Laid out along the beach, with the outgoing nine heading virtually straight down the strand and the closing nine paralleling it only a few yards inland, the only distraction — aside from the view of the Firth of Clyde, the Isle of Arran, and the flaming sunsets — is the course's location directly below the flight path into Prestwick Airport. So it sometimes seems as though players are about to be sucked up into the jet wash. Another classic Open layout, it is one of the few important private clubs in Scotland open to visitors (in limited numbers). Playing privileges are offered Mondays through Thursdays only to members of clubs in the US who can produce a letter of introduction and a respectable certificate of handicap, and only upon advance arrangement, which is essential. The day-ticket greens fee also covers a round of play on the Portland, which some have pronounced even tougher than the Old Course. No women are permitted. Plan to book well in advance. Details: Royal Troon Golf Club, Craigend Rd., Troon, Ayrshire KA10 6EP, Scotland (phone: 0292-311555).

TURNBERRY HOTEL GOLF COURSE, Turnberry, Strathclyde, Scotland: The two courses here, the Ailsa and the Arran, are quite close in quality, but it's the Ailsa on which the British Open was played in 1977 and 1986. The wind blows in from the sea, and it sometimes takes an act of courage just to stand up on the craggy tees and hit out into the teeth of what occasionally seems like a major gale. The beautiful *Turnberry* hotel — built at the turn of the century in the Edwardian style and now completely refurbished — provides some respite from the elements. It has recently been sold to a Japanese investment group. But the golfing challenge is the real lure. Details: Turnberry Hotel Golf Courses, Ayrshire, Scotland KA26 9LT, Scotland (phone: 0655-31000).

ROYAL PORTHCAWL, Porthcawl, Mid Glamorgan, Wales: Not a links course in the strictest sense, though there are occasional sandhills. The main hazards, however, are gorse, hummocks, heather, and deep bunkers. The good news is that the lay of the land permits players to look across Bristol Channel to the long, dark line of the Somerset coast — and see the sea from any tee or green. Founded in 1891, the course combines links and heathland play, and there's a particularly high premium on a golfer's ability to place shots accurately against often furious natural elements. Just trying to find the fairway here can be a humbling experience. Details: Royal Porthcawl Golf Club, Rest Bay, Porthcawl, Mid Glamorgan CF36 3UW, Wales (phone: 0656-712251).

ST. PIERRE GOLF AND COUNTRY CLUB, Chepstow, Gwent, Wales: Two fine 18-hole courses here. The beautiful, old parkland course is laid out within the tree-studded bounds of an old deer preserve, with an 11-acre lake. Its quality is such that major events have been attracted to it from its birth; it has been the venue for the Dunlop Masters Tournament, the Curtis Cup, the Silk Cup Masters, and the Epson Grand Prix of Europe. The opening holes are played between daunting ranks of chestnuts, which seem to move, according to many visitors, specifically to block their shots. The New course is on a pleasant meadowland with a meandering stream, which comes into play on most of the holes and provides a good challenge. The club is on the A48, the main Chepstow-to-Newport road. Details: St. Pierre Hotel Golf and Country Club, St. Pierre Park, Chepstow, Gwent NP6 6YA, Wales (phone: 0291-625261).

Tennis

Britain practically closes down in late June and early July, the fortnight of the All England Lawn Tennis Championships at Wimbledon.. Ticket scalpers do a brisk trade outside the gate (and even advertise in the personal columns of the newspapers), and those who aren't lucky enough to secure tickets stay home and watch the competition on television. (For travelers, the best source of tickets is one of the package programs offered by British ticket broker/tour operator *Keith Prowse & Co.*)

This passion has definitely had its effect on the number of participants in the sport, and the population of courts, players, and clubs has soared in the last few years. Although tennis still has a long way to go before it becomes the national mania in Britain that it is in the US, there are now hundreds of thousands of players, and courts are seldom hard to find. While Britain is not a tennis polestar, buffs should be sure to pack their racquets and tennis whites, since a tennis match is a fine, rapid way to get off the standard tourist circuit and into local life (which, in the case of British tennis clubs, is most often that of the upwardly mobile middle classes). In these circles, playing well is considered important — but playing as if you mean to win at all costs isn't the style. If you pass muster, you may end the match with at least an invitation to tea.

WHERE TO PLAY

Municipal courts abound in Britain; tourist literature can provide their locations in the towns you'll be visiting. In addition, many of the more luxurious hotels have their own courts. The best source of information, including lists of affiliated private tennis clubs where visiting players may be able to get a game, is *Britain's Lawn Tennis Association,* Queens Club, West Kensington, London W14 9EG, England (phone: 01-385-2366).

Those who want to spend more than just a casual hour a day on the courts may want to plan their trip around stops at a handful of resorts, tennis schools, and other spots at which the game is given more than just a passing nod, such as the following:

BEACONSFIELD SCHOOL OF LAWN TENNIS, Beaconsfield, Buckinghamshire, England: Established 25 years ago, this school is open year-round and offers individual and group courses at modest cost. Principal Suzan Livingston, who is also president of the British Women's Tennis Association and women's executive of the European Tennis Association, does not push a single style but works to encourage the skills of each individual player, whether beginner or pro. Lodging is in hotels or with local families; the setting is the rolling, wooded Chiltern Hills, only 30 minutes from Heathrow and 40 minutes by train or car from central London. Details: Beaconsfield School of Lawn Tennis, Beaconsfield, Buckinghamshire HP9 2BY, England (phone: 0494-674744).

EUROPA CLUB AND TENNIS CENTER, Southampton, Hampshire, England: Residential junior and adult courses at every level on eight indoor and seven outdoor courts in the heart of the Hampshire countryside; videotapes record your efforts against ball machines. Full bar and restaurant on the premises. Details: Europa Club and Tennis Center, Frogmore La., Nursling, Southampton SO1 9XS, England (phone: 0703-731713).

FREETIME SUMMER CAMPS, Surrey, England: Tennis camps for boys and girls, ages 4 to 16, in Hampshire and Surrey. Includes full board accommodations and one instructor for 6 children. Details: Freetime Summer Camps, 149–151 Goldsworth Rd., Surrey GU21 1L5, England (phone: 04862-70800).

HOLBROOK HOUSE, Holbrook, Wincanton, Somerset, England: This is your chance to see how it feels to play on grass: This family-run hotel has a good grass court in addition to its all-weather court. Lodgings are in a former country house dating from 1530. No coaching is available. Details: Holbrook House, Holbrook, Wincanton, Somerset BA9 8BS, England (phone: 0963-32377).

INSIDE OUT TENNIS, Hammersmith, London, England: For players at all levels, there are short courses based on the Inner Tennis concept developed in the US, which addresses motivation and outlook as well as physical skills. Course prices, if staying more than one day, include accommodations in a highly rated nearby hotel. Details: Inside Out Tennis, 32 Tabor Rd., Hammersmith, London W6 0BW, England (phone: 01-741-7950).

JONATHAN MARKSON OXFORD TENNIS CAMP, Oxford, England: Resident professionals at Oxford teach students at all levels on hard and grass courts. Instructors also include former Wimbledon players. Jonathan Markson is a former Scottish International who coached both Oxford University's men's and ladies' teams to victory in the 1988 varsity match against Cambridge. Much emphasis is placed on teaching pupils to hit the ball early — the "early ball technique." Camp convenes in July and August, with two special weeks for adults. Accommodations are private rooms in University housing. Details: Jonathan Markson Tennis Camp, Hertford College, Oxford University, Oxford OX1 3BW, England (phone: 01-386-8682).

TENNIS COACHING INTERNATIONAL, Milton Ernest, near Bedford, Bedfordshire, England: This leading tennis school, an hour from London in a pretty village alongside the river Ouse, offers an extensive program of courses at private and municipal clay, asphalt, and grass courts in the area. Instructors are picked for their patience, technical know-how, and teaching abilities. Videotape, ball machines, and backboards are available, and adult and junior L.T.A. Tournament holidays are offered. Accommodations are in an evocative building that dates from 1694, in private apartments or hotels, or with English families. Details: Tennis Coaching International, Thurleigh Rd., Milton Ernest, near Bedford, Bedfordshire MK44 1RF, England (phone: 02302-2914).

WHERE TO WATCH

The big deal is unquestionably the All England Lawn Tennis Championships, which take place from June 25 to July 8 (excluding June 1) in 1990 at the *All England Lawn Tennis and Croquet Club* in Wimbledon. Still a magnet to players who compete for much bigger cash prizes elsewhere, this tourney is an experience even for those who have never held a racquet. Grass courts, strawberry teas, and the legendary Centre Court make for such a spectacle that visitors may find the world class matches that are going on quietly on all the outlying lawns no more than a diversion. Advanced seat tickets for Centre Court and Number One Court are distributed by public ballot. Ticket applications, available from the end of September 1989, can be obtained by sending a self-addressed, stamped envelope to the Club: PO Box 98, Church Rd., Wimbledon SW19 5AE, England. The Club must receive completed forms by midnight, January 31. For the first 9 days of the tournament, some tickets are available on the day of play for Number One Court; for Number Two Court and the remaining outside courts, tickets are always available on the day of play. For more details contact the All England Lawn Tennis and Croquet Club (phone: 01-946-2244); a self-addressed, stamped envelope or international postage coupons should be included with any correspondence.

By far the most certain and efficient means of seeing the match of your choice is to purchase one of the many packages of Britain's *Keith Prowse & Co.,* 200 Galleria Parkway, Suite 720, Atlanta, GA 30339 (phone: 800-669-8687), which offers a wide range of selection for first-week, second-week, and men's and women's finals play. Similar offerings with close-to-the-court grandstand seats are available for the Stella Artois (men's) championships at *Queens Club* and for the Pilkington Glass Cup (women's) at *Eastbourne.*

Horsing Around

Britain is among the world's most horse-mad nations — and has been practically ever since the Romans, and later the Normans, brought horses to Britain many centuries ago. There were races as early as the 12th century at London's Smithfield Market. Period romances speak of races between knights and noblemen. Later, Henry VIII and James I kept stables (the latter's at Newmarket), and from James II on down, English monarchs have been horse fanciers. Elizabeth II, who keeps a stable and rides regularly, can be at her most animated when urging on her horse. Princess Anne, who ranks in the international class in the demanding game of 3-day eventing, competes in shows all over the country with her husband, Captain Mark Phillips, who also conducts equestrian weekends at the *Gleneagles* hotel's new equestrian center, which he helped plan.

For travelers, the ubiquity of the mania for horses means that equestrians will never want for a common ground for conversation in village pubs and that horse-oriented vacations abound.

MEETS, SHOWS, AND RACES

You'll be meeting Britons on their favorite turf when you take in one of the dozen international shows and hundreds of national events held in Britain every year. Britain alone has some 59 racecourses — 17 devoted solely to flat racing (whose season runs from the third week in March to the first week in November), 24 solely to National Hunt racing (or steeplechasing, whose season begins early in August and ends in June), and the rest with facilities for both. Major courses include *Ascot,* near Windsor in Berkshire (see below); *Doncaster's Town Moor* course, in South Yorkshire (the successor to two other courses that flourished in the area as early as 1595), home of the William Hill Futurity, a mile-long contest for 2-year-olds, and of the St. Leger Stakes, a September race for 3-year-old colts and fillies and the last classic of the flat racing season and the third in Britain's Triple Crown; *Epsom,* in Surrey (see below); the lovely *Goodwood,* in Sussex in the Duke of Richmond's Park, especially noted for the 1-mile Sussex Stakes, held in late July; *Newmarket,* the celebrated old course in Cambridgeshire, England's flat-racing headquarters; and *Sandown Park,* founded in 1875, now the home of the Eclipse Stakes, a 1¼-miler run every July since 1886 and named to honor the 18th-century nonpareil from whom all of the world's thoroughbred race horses are said to be descended. (This animal, who prompted his owner's now apocryphal remark "Eclipse first, the rest nowhere," didn't compete until he was 5 years old — but won every race he entered.) The Triple Crown of the British racing season goes to the horse that wins Newmarket's Two Thousand Guineas, the Epsom Derby, and Doncaster's St. Leger. (Newmarket, the center of flat-track racing in England and the focal point of British training, is also the home of the new *National Horseracing Museum,* which tells the story of racing's development in England and shows videos of classic races. There are also a number of stud farms in the area, including the National Stud, open to the public on special days during August. Tattersalls, the celebrated English horse auctioneers founded in London in 1766, conducts a number of sales throughout the year, the most important being the two Yearling Sales held in the fall.)

Tracks are always grass — rather than dirt or a synthetic surface as in many countries — so that meetings last only 4 or 5 days at a stretch (just 3 days in winter) and are spaced far enough apart to give the turf time to recover between meetings; the nationwide schedule is arranged so that there's always something going on in each region of the country. For dates and locations of upcoming weeks' fixtures (as racing events are called here), consult listings in newspapers such as the *Sporting Life* and the *Racing Post.* Following is a list of major events; a season-long fixtures calendar, which includes smaller events such as the Great Yarmouth Races in July, is available from the Racecourse Publicity Association, Winkfield Rd., Ascot, Berkshire SL5 7HX, England (phone: 0990-25912).

GRAND NATIONAL, Aintree, near Liverpool, Merseyside, England: The grueling steeplechase described in Enid Bagnold's *National Velvet* — the most famous race of its kind and the premiere event of the steeplechase season — subjects competitors to 4½ lung-tearing miles over wickedly mischievous fences and ditches and extremely high fences reputed to be bigger than those of any other steeplechase course in the world; it's so tough that only a small percentage of competitors even finish, and only a half-dozen horses have won the competition even twice in more than a century. Fences such as the Chair, grim and formidable, and Becher's Brook, named after the brilliant jockey who fell there during the first Liverpool steeplechase in 1839, make for the sort of race that warms even those who don't know a Totalisator from a tic-tac man. At least, it will help you understand the comment of the *Liverpool Courier:* "All men of ardent feelings love moderate danger for the very excitement it produces and the intrepidity it brings to action." On the night before, be sure to stop in at the cavernous cocktail lounge of the immense, rococo *Adelphi* hotel to see the jockeys who will prove the point on the morrow. The Grand National takes place annually at the end of March or early in April over a Thursday, Friday, and Saturday. (The main event is held on Saturday.) Details: Aintree Racecourse, Aintree, Liverpool, Merseyside L9 5AS, England (phone: 051-523-2600).

ROYAL ASCOT, Ascot, Berkshire, England: The June meeting at this racecourse on the southern edge of Windsor Great Park, 25 miles west of London, has enjoyed royal patronage ever since Queen Anne drove over to watch the first races on the Ascot Common in 1711 — and it is still considered a high point of the London social season. Ascot is where Eliza Doolittle (of George Bernard Shaw's *Pygmalion* and Lerner and Loewe's *My Fair Lady*) first encountered high society; things are as oh-so-social even today. In the Royal Enclosure — the pricey part of the seating area — men wear top hats and morning coats and women, their smartest dresses and hats. Models come here hoping to catch a photographer's eye and launch a career; while other females, including more than one dowager, show up in bonnets that some might call preposterous. The sovereign and members of the royal family drive in state carriages from Windsor Castle on each day of the 4-day meeting. The key race in the meeting is the Ascot Gold Cup — a 2½-mile race that ranks as one of the most important of British flat racing's season. The King George VI and the Queen Elizabeth Stakes, a 1½-miler first run in 1951, takes place each July. Packages that include admission to the Grandstand Enclosure and the Paddock for the Ascot Gold Cup are available from *Keith Prowse & Co.,* 200 Galleria Parkway, Suite 720, Atlanta, GA 30339 (phone: 800-669-8687). Other details: Ascot Racecourse, Ascot, Berkshire SL5 7JN, England (phone: 0990-22211).

BADMINTON HORSE TRIALS, Badminton, Avon, England: Three-day eventing is one of the toughest tests that horse and rider can face; the trials held annually since 1949 at the Duke of Beaufort's lovely green park in Badminton — the small West Country village that has become something of a fox-hunting magnet because the Duke's world-famous pack of foxhounds make their home here — are so important that they're regularly televised, and in prime time no less: Certainly, the trials are the world's longest running and most famous. Competitors come from all over the world, and over 250,000 spectators attend. The first 2 days are devoted to dressage and the fourth to the jumping test, both in the main arena. But the main feature is the speed and endurance test, which takes place on Saturday. The cross-country section takes riders over about 30 terrifying obstacles of every description. They are fixed and can't be knocked down. And though there are always several brand-new fences to test competitors' courage, hardy annuals like the famous Jump into the Lake and the Quarry reappear frequently in different guises — and still manage to send riders' hearts into their throats. While the competitors are risking their necks, spectators can watch on closed-circuit television sets in several marquees or follow the event's progress, fortified by visits to the several large refreshment tents around the course. It's also fun to see the Deer Park, full of red and fallow deer, and to browse through the veritable village of shops and exhibits that go up for the duration in Badminton Park. The competition lasts 4 days and takes place in the first half of May. Ticket application forms are available in early January. Details: Badminton Horse Trials Office, Badminton, Avon GL9 1DF, England (phone: Badminton 045-421272 or -421375).

ROYAL INTERNATIONAL HORSE SHOW, Birmingham, West Midlands, England: Even those who sit in the stands and refer to the dressage display as "those circus horses who dance" — as more than one spectator has been known to do at this immensely popular June annual, over 70 years old and among the most prestigious shows in the international equestrian calendar — find that its magic wins their hearts in a twinkling. Dressage, Arabians, hackney ponies in single harness, pairs of ponies, weight-carrying cobs, heavy horse turnouts, and children's ponies ridden sidesaddle can all be seen, along with lightweight, middleweight, and heavyweight hunters, small and large hacks, ladies' hacks, and costers' turnouts. Jumping competitions keep spectators on the edge of their seats from start to finish: Sometimes the outcome is in doubt right up until the last sleek animal has taken the last fence. The site is Birmingham's National Exhibition Centre. Details: Royal International Horse Show, 35 Belgrave Sq., London SW1 8QB, England (phone: box office and tickets, 021-780-4141; information, 01-235-6431).

THE EVER READY DERBY STAKES, Epsom, Surrey, England: The race after which the Kentucky Derby was named, itself named for one of the men who founded it in 1780, the sporting 12th Earl of Derby, is a carnival as much as a 1½-mile speed trial for 3-year-old colts and fillies. All kinds of people turn up: ancient Gypsy families come to settle debts and arrange marriages; the top-hatted and tail-coated with their Rolls-Royces and picnic hampers; families with children; Cockneys from the East End just out for a good time; fortunetellers; gaudy tipsters predicting the winners; and bookies with bulging Gladstones stuffed with fivers quoting the odds, their helpers peering through binoculars to the other side of the course, where white-gloved tic-tac men are using age-old hand movements to signal how the money is going. The spectacle of this national festivity — the event that Benjamin Disraeli himself called the Blue Riband of the Turf — has hardly changed a bit since the 18th-century English painter George Stubbs memorialized it on canvas. Ever since Sir Charles Bunbury's horse Diomed won the first race in 1780, the Derby Stakes has had a history punctuated with colorful characters, among them the early-19th-century Jem Robinson, who won a thousand pounds on a bet that within a single week, he would win the Oaks and the Derby (the latter for a seventh time), and marry; and Miss Emily Davison, a suffragette who died in 1913 after hurling herself under the hoofs of King George V's Anmer. The meeting usually takes place during the first week in June; the Ever Ready Derby is staged on a Wednesday, and the Gold Seal Oaks — Epsom's other major contest, a 1½-miler for fillies which is named after the Earl of Derby's shooting box — 3 days later. Buy a grandstand ticket if you must, but it's more fun to watch the goings-on from the hill in the middle of the course. *Keith Prowse & Co.,* 200 Galleria Parkway, Suite 720, Atlanta, GA 30339 (phone: 800-669-8687, has packages. Details: United Racecourses, Ltd., Racecourse Paddock, Epsom, Surrey KT18 5NJ, England (phone: 03727-26311).

THE SILK CUT DERBY, Hickstead, West Sussex, England: This August event at the *All England Jumping Course* ranks as the nation's premiere show-jumping event. The fact that only 24 horses have jumped clear rounds on the course since 1961 suggests its difficulty; the Derby Bank, one of several permanent obstacles in the International Arena here, is famous among horse folk. Novice jumping, showing classes, and driving take place in other arenas. The whole production is fast and easily understood. Details: The Secretary, All England Jumping Course, Hickstead, West Sussex RH17 5NU, England (phone: 0273-834315).

BURGHLEY HORSE TRIALS, near Stamford, Lincolnshire, England: The European 3-day championships take place on the grounds of the famous Elizabethan mansion, Burghley House, and attract the top international riders. The cross-country phase includes many new fences, plus old favorites such as Capability's Cutting (named after the celebrated 18th-century landscape architect "Capability Brown" who created the grounds of Burghley Park itself). Details: Burghley Horse Trials, Stamford, Lincolnshire, PE9 2LH, England (phone: 0780-52131; FAX: 0780-52982).

HORSE OF THE YEAR SHOW, Wembley, near London, England: Hunters, hacks, and ponies show up in October for this premier fixture of the British equestrian calendar. The Horse Personalities of the Year awards are always popular, but the whole event presents a wonderful display of horseflesh, an equine extravaganza if ever there was one. Details: Horse of the Year Show, Wembley Arena, Wembley HA9 ODW, England (phone: 01-902-8833, or for tickets, 01-900-1234).

RIDING HOLIDAYS AND PONY TREKKING

The British flock to horse holidays with exactly the same enthusiasm that Americans flock to dude ranches — except that they are more likely to wear jodhpurs than jeans, swing into saddles without horns as well as with, and do their riding at a stable that doesn't always have anything more than a casual arrangement with their lodging place. Top-notch horses, delightful scenery, and the chance to join the natives in one of their favorite pastimes are the main attractions.

When you do begin to look into the possibilities of an equestrian holiday, you may at first find the lingo bewildering. The term *riding holiday,* for instance, refers to not just any vacation spent on horseback, but specifically to one where you'll trot, canter, occasionally even take small jumps, and get basic instruction either by a full-fledged instructor accredited by the British Horse Society (BHSI), a British Horse Society–designated assistant instructor (BHSAI), or, in smaller establishments, horse folk who instruct as a summer job. The organizations that sponsor such activities, called "riding holiday centres," may also arrange for guests to compete in local shows and contests — great fun — where they may find themselves engaging in horse talk with anyone from a local farmer to the squire's lady. Some riding holiday centers — those termed "residential" — have accommodations on the premises; some arrange for lodging in nearby guesthouses, old coaching inns, quaint hotels, or with local families. Rank beginners and advanced equestrians alike can sign up for riding holidays, which are available year-round.

Pony trekking, on the other hand, involves day-long trips on the back of a sturdy native pony or cob (a stocky, short-legged horse) and has participants traveling mainly at a walk — partly because most are inexperienced riders, partly because the riding is across moors, through dense forests, and in steep mountain country mainly in Scotland, the Lake District, the north of England's Dales, and sections of Wales, along narrow trails and roads that don't lend themselves to a faster pace. Absolute novices may be provided with some instruction, but it will ordinarily be at a relatively elementary level. The season generally runs from mid-April until late September or early October. Note that Ponies of Britain, a nonprofit organization that inspects both trekking and riding holiday centers in Britain — an expert on the subjects — suggests that children under 12 will get tired and bored while pony trekking and are generally better off at a riding holiday center that specializes in youngsters. The real joy of pony trekking is the scenery en route, for on horseback, it's possible to cover great sweeps of terrain — forests, fields, and meadows full of ferns or bracken, or spotted here and there with a clump of rosy heather or purplish foxglove and thistle — that may not otherwise be accessible to any but the most intrepid of Wordsworthian walkers. With saddles squeaking, the horses' hooves pounding out a soothing rhythm, the smell of leather and sweat perfuming the sweet clean air, you'll pass through forest dells to wild clear streams with whitewater lacy as a Renaissance lady's collar, struggle up steep rocky hillsides, and then promenade across their flat summits, with the woods-and-farms countryside spread out like a piece of green velvet patchwork.

The following include some of the best of British centers offering riding holidays and pony trekking. There are many others, but not all are as well-run as those listed here. To get other ideas, send a stamped, self-addressed envelope to *Ponies of Britain,* Ascot Racecourse, Ascot, Berkshire SL5 7JN, England (phone: 0990-26925); or send $6 (£4) to the British Horse Society (British Equestrian Centre, Stoneleigh, Kenilworth, Warwickshire CV8 2LR, England; phone: 0203-696697) to get its list of 580 inspected centers.

Flanders Farm Riding Centre, Silver St., Hordle, Lymington, Hampshire SO41 6DF, England (phone: 0590-682207). Adult riding courses with instruction in show jumping and cross-country. Beginners welcome.

Gooseham Barton Stables, Gooseham, Morwenstow, near Bude, Cornwall EX23 9PG, England (phone: 028-883204). Lovely riding through quiet, scenic countryside and forests, with a sandy beach nearby. For experienced riders and unaccompanied children age 12 and older; beginners off-peak season only. One cottage with a kitchen is available. The name derives from one Sir William de Gooseham, who is said to have owned the farmhouse around 1310.

Harrogate Equestrian Centre, Brackenthwaite La., Burn Bridge, Harrogate, North Yorkshire HG3 1PW, England (phone: 0423-871894). Situated in a pretty area, 3 miles from the ancient spa town of Harrogate. Facilities include a large covered school and an outdoor school. All types of instruction available for adults and children, including dressage, show stadium jumping, and cross-country riding over the more than 100 fences on 70 acres of grassland, including an official horse trials course.

Hoofbeats International Inc., 182 Hillside Ave., Englewood, NJ 07631 (phone: 800-526-4789 or 201-568-3471). Former teacher Ellie Phayer leads groups on 1-week to 10-day horseback holidays in England, Scotland, and Wales.

Lea Bailey Riding School, Byeways, Lea Bailey, Ross-on-Wye, Herefordshire HR9 5TY, England (phone: 0989-81360). Riding holidays in the Royal Forest of Dean and lessons in side-saddle, jumping, driving, and stable management.

Lyncombe Lodge, Churchill, Avon BS19 5PG, England (phone: 0934-852335). The place for a farmhouse holiday and long rides away from towns and traffic in the heart of the Mendip Hills, midway between Bath and the sea.

Moat House, Benenden, Kent TN17 4EU, England (phone: 0580-240581), or, in the US, Patricia Grindle, 22 Pleasant St., South Natick, MA 01760 (phone: 617-655-7000). An English riding school in the traditional mold. Princess Anne took riding lessons here while a student at the Benenden School nearby.

North Wheddon Farm, Wheddon Cross, near Minehead, Somerset TA24 7EX, England (phone: 0643-84224). Riding at all paces is provided here on the wild moors of surrounding Exmoor National Park, which has been called "the riding playground of England." Lodging is in a fine, attractive, old Georgian farmhouse.

Pakefield Holiday Centre, London Rd., Kessingland, Lowestoft, Suffolk NR33 7PF, England (phone: 0502-565117). Weeklong holidays (May 30 to July 4 and August 22 to September 12) with 5 days' riding at nearby stables, often on nearby beaches, plus videotapes and discussion groups. For a small extra charge, riders can use the indoor and outdoor rings, which are floodlit.

Porlock Vale Equitation Centre, Porlock, near Minehead, Somerset TA24 8NY, England (phone: 0643-862338). Courses are available in general equitation and dressage, and instruction covers all aspects of equitation, among them sidesaddle, stable management, the training of the young horse, and more. The object is to produce thinking riders who can continue to progress on their own. Facilities include two indoor schools, an outdoor manège, show jumps and jumping grids, permanent cross-country fences, and a lecture room. A location in the delightful country between the northern fringe of Exmoor and the Somerset coast, with paddocks running down to the sea, provides the opportunity to ride over nearly 100 square miles.

Shilstone Rocks Stud, Widecombe-in-the-Moor, Newton Abbot, Devon TQ13 7TF, England (phone: 0364-2281). A riding and trekking center and stud on a Dartmoor farm with a history that goes back to 1244. With its granite tors, deep bogs, and untamed ponies grazing on the open moorland, Dartmoor has a reputation for wicked storms and thick, swirling mists, making it the perfect setting for Sir Arthur Conan Doyle's eerie novel, *The Hound of the Baskervilles.* It's one of Britain's greatest authentic wildernesses, a hill range of remarkable beauty.

Silverdown Riding School, Harwell, Didcot, Oxfordshire OX11 0LU, England (phone: 0235-835377). Riding holidays, with dressage courses and gymkhanas in addition to the more usual instruction.

Triple Bar Riding Centre, Home Farm Cottage, Broadmoor, Abinger Common, Dorking RH5 6JY, England (phone: 0306-730959). Hacking by the hour and day rides over adjacent 6,000 acres of National Trust land. Riding holidays, including accommodations nearby.

Wheal Buller Riding School, Buller Hill, Redruth, Cornwall, TR16 6ST, England (phone: 0209-211852). Offers a 6-night holiday, "Own a pony for a week," that includes room and board. Instruction in jumping, dressage, and cross-country. Also, holidays for adults, hourly hacking lessons, and day rides. Four miles from the beach.

Blair Castle Trekking Centre, Blair Atholl, Pitlochry, Tayside PH18 5SR, Scotland (phone: 079-681263). Experienced guides lead hour-long, half-day, and day-long treks on sure-footed Highland ponies. Instruction is available. Open from April to mid-August.

Bowmont Centre, Belford-on-Bowmont, Yetholm, Kelso, Roxburghshire TD5 8PY, Scotland (phone: 057382-362). Situated in the Cheviot hills of the Scottish borders, the center offers accommodations in an 18th-century farmhouse with log fires on a 1,350-acre sheep farm. There are 2,000 ewes, along with three brood mares and their foals. Guests can walk, fish, or pony trek through the spectacularly scenic hills of the Scottish borders. Children over 12 are particularly welcome.

Highland Riding Centre, Borlum Farm, Drumnadrochit, Highland IV3 6XN, Scotland (phone: 045-62220). In one of the loveliest parts of Scotland, overlooking Loch Ness, this center is especially good for families. There are Shetland ponies for small children and livelier mounts for the experienced. Instruction, which is available indoors as well as out, can be tailored to all levels. Disabled riders are welcome, and ramps and mounting facilities for guests in wheelchairs are available. And when chore time rolls around — grooming the ponies, cleaning tack, mucking out the stalls, helping the blacksmith, herding cows and calves, caring for lambs, searching for eggs, even making hay — guests are welcome to lend a hand. Long established and well run.

Abergwynant Farm Trekking Centre, Penmaenpool, Dolgellau, Gwynedd LL40 1YF, Wales (phone: 0341-422377). Scenic treks over the mountains and foothills of Cader Idris, up valleys, past lakes and derelict gold mines, and through woods and Forestry Commission land overlooking the superb Mawddach Estuary. Over 60 horses and ponies are available at this peaceful farm, which has won awards for its location and facilities. Book well in advance.

Cae Iago Trekking Centre, Farmers, Llanwrda, Dyfed SA19 8LZ, Wales (phone: 055-85303). Excellent trekking through beautiful wild country for all levels of riders, as well as trail rides for the experienced.

Cwmyoy Pony Trekking Centre, Cornmill, Llanthony, Gwent NP7 7NN, Wales (phone: 0873-890565). Pony trekking through the heather-purpled Black Mountains and Brecon Beacons National Park. Near the ancient Llanthony Priory.

Golden Pheasant Riding Centre, Tal y Garth Farm, Glyn Ceiriog, near Llangollen, Clwyd LL20 7AB, Wales (phone: 069172-408). Accommodation is in a comfortable 18th-century stone farmhouse on 65 acres. The center provides instruction in riding as well as stable management. Facilities include an enclosed outdoor manège, a cross-country course, and, for those who want to soothe their overworked muscles, a swimming pool. Children's riding holidays are a specialty.

POST TREKKING

There's nothing quite as delightful as seeing the country from the back of a horse or sure-footed native pony, heading from inn to inn through narrow trails, along abandoned train beds, and down wide sandy beaches — and staying away from the trekking center for up to a week at a time. *Post trekking,* or *trail riding,* as this activity is called, is not widely available, and it is not generally recommended for riders without experience, as it usually involves good horses and a fast enough pace to cover about 25 miles a day. Usually a warm camaraderie develops en route, so that you become one of a cohesive band of pilgrims straight out of *The Canterbury Tales* as you traverse the miles. That's one reason for going. Post trekking is also a practically worry-free holiday: There are guides to keep you going at a reasonable pace, to make sure you don't get lost, and to arrange for your luggage to be transported from one hostelry to the next. And at the end of each day, there's always a hot bath, a rustic feast, a good night's sleep in a clean-sheeted bed, and one of those massive breakfasts (the kind that make you feel as if it's going to take an Act of Parliament to get you into the saddle) before you hit the trail once again. For a booklet containing information about post treks other than the one described below, send $1 (to cover postage) to Ponies (UK), 56 Green End Rd., Sawtry, Huntingdon, Cambridgeshire PE17 5UY, England (phone: 0487-830278).

ROB ROY COUNTRY, Scotland: This is post trekking at its best. After day-trekking in Queen Elizabeth Forest Park at Aberfoyle to check the compatibility of ponies and riders, participants travel through Duke's Pass to Loch Achray in the Trossachs, then by Loch Finglas, through Glen Mann to Balquhidder (where Rob Roy MacGregor is buried), over the Kirkton Pass and the eastern shoulder of Ben More to Killin, the spectacular falls of Dochar, then down through Glenogle to Lochearnhead and Bonnie Strathyre — returning to Aberfoyle via Brig-o'-Turk. The terrain is magnificent throughout, and the views are superb. Accommodations, in comfortable inns and hotels, are provided from Saturday to Saturday, with the post trek running from Sunday to Friday in May, September, and October. Details: Equiventure, Achinrier, Baracaldine, Argyllshire, Scotland (phone: 0631-7232).

CARAVANNING

Meandering along a narrow lane flanked by billowing meadows and fields, in a horse-drawn wagon, with grand vistas stretching off toward a purple-hazed horizon, is one of the most relaxed ways around to spend a week — especially where the roads are small, traffic-free, and punctuated here and there with quaint old pubs, interesting restaurants, and historic sites. Agencies that rent well-equipped caravans, many of them brightly painted in gypsy fashion, make this possible in a number of areas for about $350 a week; the agent can usually direct you along the most scenic routes and overnight spots. A good one to try is *Waveney ValleyHorse Holidays,* Air Station Farm, Pulham St. Mary, near Diss, Norfolk IP21 4QF, England (phone: 0379-741228). *Welsh Covered Wagon Adventure Holidays,* Rhydybont, Talgarth, Powys LDE OEE, Wales (phone: 0874-711346). *Welsh Horsedrawn Holidays,* Greystone, Bell St., Talgarth, Brecon, Powys LD3 OBP, Wales (phone: 0874-711346). For trips in the Brecon Beacons area of Wales.

HUNTING

In Britain, hunting has nothing to do with shooting. Here, shooting involves going after game with firearms. Hunting means riding to hounds, and it is extremely popular, with so many meetings scheduled from November until spring that the ardent follower could hunt every day of the week with a pick of locations.

Quite apart from the quality of the horses, there is stupendous scenery awaiting the visitor, and a rider may be forgiven for taking a tumble if distracted by the view — say, over the rolling farmlands of Leicestershire, England's best hunting country.

The pack of hounds — usually 30 to 40 in number and counted in "couples" — are under the control of the huntsman, who may be the Master or a professional hunt servant. The huntsman is assisted by his "whippers-in" (usually two in number). The mounted spectators, or "followers," are usually led by the Field-Master who's responsible for seeing that the hounds are not ridden over and that the farmers' land, used for the hunt, is not abused. Non-riders often follow the action by bicycle, on foot, or in their cars and stand by for the chance to watch the hounds and the horses passing. From the stirrup cup that almost invariably precedes each meet to the rendezvous afterward in some favored hostelry, the atmosphere is at once efficient, orderly, friendly, and convivial; the participants are judged as much by their sportsmanship as by other qualities such as dress and "turnout" for both the rider and the horse, which should be neat, clean, and "workman-like" at all times.

Some hunts exclude all non-members; others accept only visitors who live locally. However, there are many that admit visiting non-members temporarily upon payment of the "cap" — a day's hunting fee. The hunt secretary can advise on horse hire and correct clothing.

One organization that has information about which hunts welcome guests in various parts of Britain is *Master of Foxhounds Association,* Parsloes Cottage, Bagendon, Cirencester, Gloucestershire GL7 7DU, England (phone: 0285-83470).

Riding to foxhounds is not the only way to follow hunting in England. It is also possible to ride with one of the three packs of staghounds or with one of the 25 packs of harriers. Of the latter, 11 hunt only hares, 9 hunt only foxes, and 5 hunt both. There are also 10 packs of draghounds, which follow an artificial trail. Hunters who do not ride can still participate with one of the 90 packs of beagles, 11 packs of bassets, or 15 packs of minkhounds, all of which are followed only on foot. The season for hare is September to March; for mink, it's summer.

The following associations can provide further details on these forms of hunting:

Association of Masters of Harriers and Beagles, Horn Park, Beaminster, Dorset DT8 38B, England (phone: 0308-862212).

Masters of Basset Hounds Association, Yew Tree Cottage, Haselton, Cheltenham, Gloucestershire GL54 4DX, England (phone: 0451-60500).

Masters of Deerhounds Association, Honeymead, Simonsbath, Minehead, Somerset TA24 7JX, England (phone: 064-383242).

Masters of Minkhounds Association, Selby, High Street, Hemingford Abbots, Huntingdom, Cambridge PE18 9AH, England (phone: 0480-69902).

FOR MORE INFORMATION: To get additional details on these and other forms of field sports, contact the *British Field Sports Society,* 59 Kennington Rd., London SE1 7PZ, England (phone: 01-928-4742).

Wonderful Waterways and Coastal Cruises

Whether you're dangling your hand from a dinghy or slicing through the waves underneath a billowing sail, being on a boat is something special. People wave and sing and talk to each other, the winds whip at your hair, the waves rock you like a baby in a cradle. The pace seems closer to man's own than that of the *Concorde,* slowing you down rather than speeding you up, and when your foot touches shore again, you can't help but feel supremely relaxed.

Britain's varied and often rugged coastline and its complex weather patterns provide a challenge to even the most experienced sailor, while novice crew members find the sport here both invigorating and exciting. Consequently, British vacationers head for the water in droves — and support all manner of boat rental operations, sailing schools, and cruising establishments. Once a sport reserved only for the wealthy, sailing has become so democratized that you no longer have to own your own craft to enjoy the nation's offshore pleasures.

SAILING

Many sailors do sail in the English Channel — and they savor the challenges posed by its changeable winds, fierce tides, heavy shipping traffic, and busy harbors. But Britain offers more forgiving waters that don't, like these, require such stout seagoing yachts and solid sailing experience. There are the sheltered bays along the notched Devon, Essex, and western Scotland coasts; the celebrated Solent, the 3-mile-wide arm of water between the north coast of the Isle of Wight and England's southern shore, south of Southampton, known as the cruising ground of the rich ever since the mid-19th century when Queen Victoria started summering there in a palace-sized "cottage" designed by her husband, Prince Albert; and the coastal waters of East Anglia, where splendid sprit-rigged sailing barges — once used for cargo and now revamped to accommodate passengers — are common sights. (The sailing barge *Victor,* built in 1895, rerigged in 1974, and refurbished every year, departs for cruises from Strood Pier out of the river Medway. Art and birding cruises are other possibilities.

The best sources of suggestions for sailing in any given area are always local yacht clubs and harbormasters. Another is whichever pub is patronized by the local branch of the Royal National Lifeboat Institution's members, who are apt to be experienced watermen whose families have fished in the area for hundreds of years; their advice will come salted with tales of shipwrecks, which can be contemplated over a pint of beer.

SAILBOAT CHARTERS: These are widely available in resort centers of the most popular sailing areas; experienced sailors can charter bareboats for cruises, while novices can hire their craft with a professional crew. Information regarding charters can be obtained from the following:

Summer Isles Charters, Castle Hill Farm, Hickleton, near Doncaster, S Yorkshire DN5 7BG, England (0709-895051). Based in one of the most delightfully remote parts of the country.

Yacht Charter Association, 60 Silverdale, New Milton, Hampshire BH25 7DE, England (phone: 0425-619004). Gives details on member charter operators throughout Britain that offer insured craft that meet Association standards.

Since no registration exists in the United Kingdom, and charter yachts are not required to carry any specific safety equipment — not even a compass — it is highly advisable to charter only from *YCA* members, who achieve such membership by meeting its safety standards.

SAILING SCHOOLS: Week-long sailing courses in dinghies and cruisers, for novices and more advanced sailors alike, are available at reasonable cost at dozens of sailing schools and clubs in Britain. The largest organization setting minimum safety standards and levels of instruction for these is the *Royal Yachting Association,* RYA House, Romsey Rd., Eastleigh Hampshire S05 4YA, England (phone: 0703-629962); upon request, it will send a complete list of recognized schools. Among the noteworthy are the following:

British Performance Sailing, Lymington Marina Unit 3, Bath Rd., Lymington, Hampshire SO41 9YL, England (phone: 0590-79011). Offshore racing and cruising courses at all levels. Recognized by the Royal Yachting Association, whose 1-ton yacht *Griffin* is the school flagship.

Club UK, West Cowes, Isle of Wight PO31 7PQ, England (phone: 0983-294941 or -290154). Formerly the *National Sailing Centre,* and still one of the country's best-known sailing schools, it offers 5-night and weekend programs in dinghy sailing, board sailing, and racing, from March through October. Royal Yachting Association certificates at all levels are awarded upon successful completion of the respective course. Accommodation is in waterside premises that include a bar and marina.

Dolphin Sailing School, The Foreshore, Woodside, Wootton, Isle of Wight PO33 4JR, England (phone: 0983-292580). Dinghy sailing in the scenic Solent for beginners and for more seasoned sailors, with all equipment and training meeting Royal Yachting Association standards. Lodging is in the *Foreshore,* a century-old former boathouse between the woods and the water, with lawns running down to the sea.

Emsworth Sailing School, The Port House, Port Solent, Portsmouth, Hampshire P06 4TH, England (phone: 0705-210510). Weekend to multi-week courses using cruising dinghies or yachts. Accommodation is provided.

Fowey Cruising School, 32 Fore St., Fowey, Cornwall PL23 1AQ, England (phone: 072-683-2129). Courses in theory and practice, approved by the Royal Yachting Association, are taught year-round. Skippered cruises available from April through October; the sailing area includes the coasts of lush South Devon, Cornwall, the Scilly Isles, the Channel Isles, and Brittany. Shore accommodations date back to the 16th century.

Hayling Sailing School and Windsurfing Centre, Northney Marina, Hayling Island, Hampshire PO11 0NH, England (phone: 0705-467334).

Island Cruising Club, 10 Island St., Salcombe, Devon TQ8 8DR, England (phone: 054-884-3481). The club offers cruising, keelboat, dinghy sailing, and windsurfing to individuals, families, and groups. Accommodations are available on the floating ship *Ergemont.* Season runs from March through October.

John Sharp Sailing, Brockles Quay, St. Veep, Lostwithiel, Cornwall PL22 0NT, England (phone: 0208-872470).

Ocean Youth Club, Ltd., The Bus Station, South St., Gosport, Hampshire PO12 1EP, England (phone: 0705-528421/2). Some of Britain's finest sailing in eleven 50- to 76-foot vessels; mainly for young people aged 12 to 24 (though some programs exist for older vacationers). Cruising grounds include the coast of Britain and continental waters.

Jersey Cruising School, PO Box 531, Jersey, Channel Islands, England (phone: 0534-78522). Sail an Anglo-French cruising ground with the third-highest tidal range in the world. Bareboat and skippered charters are also available. A full range of Royal Yachting Association certificates have been awarded here.

Tighnabruaich Sailing School, Tighnabruaich, Argyll, Strathclyde PA21 2BD, Scotland (phone: Tighnabruaich 0700-811396). This large sailing school specializes in dinghy sailing and offers courses for novices and experienced sailors alike, along with programs in windsurfing and coastal cruising. The scenery is nothing short of magnificent.

Plas Menai National Watersports Centre, Caernarfon, Gwynedd LL55 1UE, Wales (phone: 0248-670597). The only year-round, sea-based center in the country, it offers courses at all levels in dinghy sailing, windsurfing, canoeing, cruising, diving, and mountaineering in its facilities. Also featured are adventure activity and sailing camps with 24-hour supervision for 8- to 18-year olds.

Twr Y Felin Outdoor Centre, St. Davids, Pembrokeshire, Dyfed SA62 6QS, Wales (phone: 0437-720391). Open year-round for surfing, windsurfing, and canoeing.

EVENTS: Not only do all the sailing craft look picture postcard perfect against the blue sky and the blue water on a breezy summer's day, but the well-tanned yachting folk striding around in Topsiders, toasting their victories at the local pub, also make for an entertaining spectacle. One of the biggest of the British events is *Cowes Week,* which takes place in the Solent the first week of August. It is sponsored by the Cowes sailing clubs, among them the Royal Yacht Squadron, an organization so exclusive that even royalty has been barred from membership. True, you don't see the 300-foot spectator craft — floating hotels, really — that once appeared at Cowes every year in August, or the grandiose racing yachts that used to accompany them; and gone is the era when you might have seen four bearded gentlemen promenading along the waterfront and later learned that all of them were kings, as in Edwardian days. But the event still brings literally millions of pounds' worth of yachts to the area, along with an equally high sum's worth of somebody's rich uncles. The goings-on are as toney as ever, and the race is remarkably easy to see from shore, especially around the Royal Yacht Squadron's esplanade and Egypt Point, where the racers nearly touch land. The tough Fastnet Race, held every other year, is also important.

CRUISING THE INLAND WATERWAYS

Salt air isn't the only tonic that will enliven a vacation: While thousands of Britons descend on the coast, just as many more head for waters inland to spend their holidays floating down narrow canals or streams, or navigating lakes and broads such as those described below. This extensive system of waterways, some 2,200 miles in England alone, takes in the most wonderful scenery — castles of kings and queens, universities renowned around the globe, exquisite gardens manicured to perfection, nature preserves, and tranquil lakes and fens. While many of the noteworthy streams of other countries carry too much ship traffic to be enjoyable for pleasure boaters, most of Britain's canals are free of commercial craft and ideal for recreation.

There are basically two ways to go — by self-skippered boat or on a fully catered hotel boat cruise. The self-skippered arrangements work like this: You hire a craft, with berths for 2 to 12 — a cabin cruiser or a steel-hulled narrowboat (so-called because they are only about 7-feet wide in order to pass through the locks, which you work yourself, please note). Someone shows you how to operate the craft and tells you whom to call if you need any help. You hire a bicycle for countryside explorations, buy a pile of groceries, some fishing tackle, and a few books, then cast off for a floating holiday that will take you along as many miles of waterways as you choose, at the rate of about 15 to 20 miles per day. There are plenty of places to moor, to walk and bicycle in the countryside, and to buy fresh supplies. If you fear you'll feel as if you're driving at *Indy* after only an hour of Driver's Ed., you can sometimes hire a skipper to do the piloting (a skippered charter). And if you don't feel like cooking, you can stop in restaurants and pubs along the way. Alternatively, you can join a group on one of the many hotel boats that cruise some of the waterways and let the hotel staff provide your meals (still another option — charter the hotel boat yourself). The cruising life is simple, idyllic, and restorative, any way you slice it. And everyone who does it goes home talking about next year. The *British Waterways* (Melbury House, Melbury Ter., London NW1 6JX, England; phone: 01-262-6711) can supply a great deal of general information about the cruising possibilities in Britain as well as maps and charts of the entire system. Bookings for a variety of types of craft on a wide assortment of British waterways can be arranged through the following:

Bargain Boating, Morgantown Travel Service, 127 High St., PO Box 757, Morgantown, WV 26505 (phone: 304-292-8471). Agent for *Blakes Holidays.*

Blakes Holidays, Wroxham, Norwich, Norfolk NR12 8DH, England (phone: 0603-783221).

Blakes Vacations, 4939 Dempster St., Skokie, Illinois 60077 (phone: in Illinois, 312-539-1010; elsewhere, 800-628-8118). Agent for *Blakes Holidays* (see above).

Boat Enquiries Ltd., 43 Botley Rd., Oxford, Oxfordshire OX2 0PT, England (phone: 0865-727288).

Dial Travel, Dial Britain, PO Box 1034, Hunt Valley, MD 21030 (phone: in Maryland, 301-683-4310; elsewhere, 800-424-9822). Agent for *UK Waterway Holidays.*

Hoseasons Holidays Ltd., Sunway House, Oulton Broad, Lowestoft, Suffolk NR32 3LT, England (phone: 0502-500505).

Skipper Travel Services, 210 California Ave., PO Box 60309, Palo Alto, CA 94306 (phone: 415-321-5658). Agent for *Hoseasons Holidays Ltd.* and *UK Waterway Holidays.*

UK Waterway Holidays Ltd., Welton Hythe, Daventry, Northants NN11 5LG, England (phone: 0327-843773). This firm, which is jointly owned by the British Waterways Board and the Association of Pleasure Craft Operators, has a special information service to help make its clients' visits to the UK more enjoyable.

Be sure to review sales material thoroughly to determine what exactly is included: Some firms offer a discount for two consecutive weekly bookings, and some include linen, fuel, car parking, and VAT, for which others may charge, in their rates. Also find out if there is a cancellation penalty.

NORFOLK BROADS, England: Described in a Nature Conservancy Report as "an extensive system of marshland, interconnected waterways and shallow lakes or Broads lying in the valleys of the rivers Bure, Yare, and Waveney and their tributaries," this area — formed as a result of medieval peat digging — was discovered by vacationers at the end of the 19th century, and has been booming as a recreational center ever since. The villages are full of establishments where you can park your car, have a meal and a good night's sleep, and rent or moor a boat. Thousands of British families do just that every summer; along with fishing, boating is the prime recreational activity in the Broads. They are the finest inland sailing waters in Europe, with the exception of Holland, and the rivers and lakes teem with cruisers chugging along at about 5 miles an hour. When dusk falls, boats are tied up in force along the riverbanks, the pubs do a booming business as vacationers come in off the water for a pint and some talk, and the moorings take on an eerie blue glow as those who have stayed aboard switch on their televisions for another sort of evening's relaxation. Certainly, most Broads cruisers don't come here to get away from the crowds but to join them. That fact notwithstanding, the months of April, May, June, September, and October are peaceful throughout the area, and even in season, there are a number of areas in this lacework of dykes and rivers, some 140 miles of navigable waterways in all, where it is possible to get off by yourself for a bit among the reedy swamps, scrubland, and occasional patches of forest. Acle, Potter Heigham, Horning, Stalham, Norwich, and Wroxham are the centers for most commercial facilities. Most boats are floating bungalows, complete with television sets, showers, cooking facilities, and central heating; prices vary according to the time of year and the size of the boat. For more information, contact the two major area liveries, *Blakes Holidays* or *Hoseasons Holidays Ltd.* (addresses above).

ENGLISH RIVERS: Of all the nation's rivers, three warrant special attention because of their navigability and accessibility. The Thames, which stretches across the breadth of the southern part of the country and is navigable for about 125 miles, winds its long way through pastoral green landscapes punctuated by villages so quaint you'll think you've stepped into a photograph from *National Geographic;* there are lovely estates, grand old houses, medieval churches, marvelously well-tended gardens — and even a few gray cities where the roar of traffic may blot out the memory of the birdsongs that accompany you the rest of your trip. As John Burns once commented, "Every drop of the Thames is liquid history." Commercial traffic along most of the Thames's navigable length is light, and the current is almost nonexistent in most seasons. A recorded announcement of Thames River cruises can be heard by calling the River Boat Information Service of the London Tourist Board (phone: 01-730-4812).

Also delightful is the river Avon, between Stratford and Tewkesbury, which meanders through a string of delicious 16th-century villages and towns (including none other than Stratford-upon-Avon, where it's possible to take in performances of the *Royal Shakespeare Company*); the river proper is linked to a system of narrow canals that give the option of making loop cruises. The Severn, England's longest river, travels through towns like Worcester, noted for its splendid cathedral and its porcelain manufactory, and Upton-upon-Severn, a market town full of houses dating to the Georgian era and earlier, as it meanders for 42 navigable miles from Stourport to ancient Gloucester. *UK Waterway Holidays Ltd., Hoseasons Holidays, Blakes Holidays,* and *Boat Enquiries Ltd.* (addresses above) lease craft here. Also consult the Upper Avon Navigation Trust, Avon House, Harvington, Evesham, Worcestershire, England (phone: 0386-870526), regarding the river Avon between Stratford-upon-Avon and Evesham; the Lower Avon Navigation Trust, Ltd., Mill Wharf, Mill La., Wyre Piddle, Pershore, Worcestershire WR10 2JF, England (phone: 0386-552517), for information about the Avon between Evesham and Tewkesbury; and Thames Water, Nugent House, Vastern Rd., Reading, Berkshire RG1 8DB, England (phone: 0734-593777), regarding the Thames above Teddington.

BRITAIN'S CANALS: The Industrial Revolution brought many changes to Britain, not the least of them being the lacing together of the country by literally hundreds of miles of canals — waterways abandoned not long afterward when the railroads began to prove their greater speed. Many of the canals continued to be used for freight, but it has been only recently that they have seen anything approaching the traffic they did at first. Boats that now thread the waters transport holidaymakers, and their primary function is not commerce but leisurely pleasure in the now-pastoral scene along the route. Some cruisers take bikes along on the cabin tops for cycling into villages along the way for a drink in a pub or a foray to the local greengrocer's. Children work the locks by which the craft journey uphill. All along the route are old buildings whose impressive size or construction testify to the canals' former importance. Some have been converted to contemporary uses: The canal-side granary on the Grand Union Canal at Stoke Bruerne in Northamptonshire now houses the *Waterways Museum,* with exhibits relating to the canals' heyday.

The Grand Union Canal, the major transportation artery between London and the Midlands for a century and a half, is the longest canal in England. The main line leaving the Thames at Brentford suffers some urban suffocation but comes into its own about 10 miles out when it starts its long climb through increasingly rich countryside toward a summit in the Chiltern Hills, 55 wide locks up. It continues to the aforementioned Stoke Bruerne, and the Northampton arm joins the river Nene soon after. There are other arms well worth exploring at Aylesbury, Welford, Market Harborough, and Trent Junction; the landscape on the Leicester arm is remarkably beautiful. Also consider the Regent's Canal, which winds past the London Zoo to the Thames.

A good publication to take along on any canal crawl is the British Waterways *Canal Architecture in Britain.* To order a copy, and for more information about planning a cruise, contact the British Waterways ($3.40/£2.20 includes postage), Melbourne House, Melbourne Terrace, London NW1 6JX, England (phone: 01-262-6711); or write to *UK Waterway Holidays* for a copy of their brochure (address above).

CALEDONIAN CANAL, Scotland: This 60-mile-long waterway, one of the grandest in Britain, joins the east and west coasts of Scotland and links Loch Ness, Loch Lochy, and Loch Oich through the heart of the Great Glen, a valley rich in history and wildlife, once occupied by clans like the MacDonalds, the Camerons, and the Stewarts. In the pretty, loch-side communities, villagers sell crafts; restaurants purvey venison, salmon, pheasant, and other local specialties; and the pubs serve single malt whiskies. Will Nessie make an appearance? You may develop your own theory about who she really is. It's a beautiful trip, whether you come for the vivid greens and brilliant yellows of spring, the wildflowers and heather purpling the mountainsides in summer, or the splashes of color in autumn, when you'll appreciate the heating in your boat. The cabin cruisers in which most people make the trip can be hired from *UK Waterway Holidays.*

Gone Fishing

It's not hard to understand the overwhelming popularity of Izaak Walton's sport given just how much water there is in Britain, how pretty most of the angling hot spots are, and how good the fishing is. Though long past is the day that a monster 72-pound, 8-ounce salmon can be caught in the London section of the Thames — as it was in the early part of the 19th century — most of the streams and lakes here are remarkably pollution-free, and conditions in those that used to be like England's Thames are improving. The game fishing — that is, for salmon, sea trout, brown trout, and rainbow trout — is some of the best in the world, and the sea fishing and coarse fishing — for bream, carp, chub, dace, perch, pike, roach, tench, eel, and other species — are excellent.

Each section of Britain offers a different proportion of these three types of angling, and where to go will depend on the objective. In Scotland and Wales, the rivers are thought of entirely as game fishing streams. Scottish rivers are world famous for their salmon (though other game species are taken), particularly because of the consistent excellence of the fisheries; Britain's record salmon, a 64-pounder bagged in 1922, was caught in Scotland's Tay. In Wales, salmon, and to an almost equal extent sea trout (which the Welsh call "sewin"), are the big deal. English streams stand out for the sheer variety of angling offered: Some streams are consecrated primarily to game fishing; some entirely to coarse fishing; and some are mixed fisheries, offering both coarse and game species. There are many reservoirs, and many waters are stocked.

Game fishing is the glamour sport on the local angling scene, and while many vacationers do some coarse fishing or some sea angling as a sidelight to a sightseeing vacation, game fishing is something to plan a trip around. In Britain, that's all the more true because of the existence of many quaint and comfortable old fishing hotels, the perfect answer to one pressing problem encountered by most avid fishermen hankering for an exciting angling vacation — that of the fed-up fishing widow. Attractively situated within a short drive of all the shops, ruins, and cathedrals an inveterate sightseer could desire, the best of these hostelries offer spacious chambers with high ceilings, French doors, balconies entwined with wisteria, or similar features. Cucumber sandwiches and currant scones, fruitcakes and jam tarts, may be standard fare at tea; and at dinner, guests discuss not just the best flies of the day but also where to get the best buy on a pair of sheepskin gloves or a handmade tapestry.

For details about fishing in England, Scotland, and Wales, consult the excellent *Where to Fish* ($23/£14.95 from Thomas Harmsworth Publishing, 13 Nicosia Rd., London SW18, England; phone: 01-874-1357). Published biannually, its 480 pages contain thousands of entries with information supplied by hoteliers, tackle dealers, club secretaries, and other on-the-spot sources. A number of publications covering angling in various regions of England are available, among them *Fishing in the North West* (available for $1.50/£1 from the North West Water Authority, Dawson House, Great Sankey, Warrington, Cheshire WA5 3LW, England; phone: 092-572-4321) and the *Northumbrian Angling Guide* (available free from Northumbrian Water, Northumbria House, Regent Centre, Gosforth, Newcastle-upon-Tyne, Tyne & Wear NE3 3PX, England; phone: 0912-843151).

GAME FISHING

At its best, Britain can provide such good fishing for salmon, trout, and sea trout that it can make anglers sound as if they're telling fish stories when they talk about it back home. However, nearly all game fishing waters in England, Wales, and Scotland are private, with the fishing rights controlled by clubs and associations. Some permit no outsiders at all; some charge a fee high enough to implement the same situation; and some sell day tickets, weekly tickets, or short-term memberships at prices rising — usually with the quality of the fishing — from the nominal to the expensive-but-still-not-exorbitant range. These are generally available in advance through the association's office or on the spot through hotels, pubs, and tackle shops.

In addition to permission, game fishers also usually need, for salmon, sea trout, and brown trout, Water Authority–issued rod licenses, available through fishing hotels, post offices, pubs, and tackle shops. When purchasing a license, be sure to inquire about local rules on season, minimum sizes, permissible bait and tackle, and Sunday fishing.

ENGLAND: Hatchery-raised trout can be found almost everywhere in the country in lakes, reservoirs, and a variety of rivers. Native brown trout proliferate in the famous chalk streams of the southeast, which offers some of the world's best dry-fly trout fishing. Fast, clear-flowing, and highly alkaline, these streams are generally ideal for nurturing big ones that rise freely even when they reach 4 pounds or more.

It's usually necessary to wait a decade to fish more famous rivers like the Itchen and the Test. But *The Orvis Co., Inc.* (The Mill, Nether Wallop, Stockbridge, Hampshire SO20 8ES, England; phone: 0264-781212) offers exceptional, though inevitably expensive, fishing with guides (unusual for trout rivers in England) to an international clientele on private stretches of these two legendary streams, which flow practically in the shadow of Winchester Cathedral, Izaak Walton's burial place. Orvis waters include a short stretch on the celebrated Itchen, which produces extra-wily wild trout, and several on the Test, including one that ranks among the best free-rising stretches in the country, good for large and exceptionally active trophy fish. *Orvis* will also outfit anglers by mail order or from their shops located in Stockbridge, Hampshire and 27 Hackville St. (off Piccadilly) in London's West End. *J. C. Field & Stream* (604 Fulham Rd., London SW6, England; phone: 01-736-0015) also offers guided fishing expeditions on the Test and will outfit anglers from reel to waders. They'll even provide an antique pole for good luck!

Other well-known area streams include the Derwent, an important and especially scenic tributary of the immense Trent; the Dove, where Walton fished, though it's generally not the stream it once was; the Eden, famous for its January-to-May salmon run; the Kennet; the Lune; the Ribble, especially in the middle reaches; and the Wharfe. The Camel and the Fowey are two of Cornwall's important sea trout rivers, and some hotels have good water on the Tamar, among southwest England's most important game fisheries; the Taw, a game river known for a March-to-May spring salmon run, with good sea trout action beginning in July, with some roach and dace downstream; and the Torridge, where the same salmon-in-spring, sea-trout-in-July patterns prevail. In the northeast, the Coquet and the Tweed are the best-known salmon streams.

In general, closed season in England is from October 1 to March 24 for trout and November 1 to January 31 for salmon. However, dates vary from area to area, so it's always a good idea to check with the local region of the National Rivers Authority. The salmon fishing season is closed March 15 through June 15.

Whatever the venue, the first thing to do is get a license, available from local fishing tackle suppliers, or from the appropriate NRA. Then find out who owns the fishing rights to the water and get permission to angle there from whomever owns them, a task that usually involves the purchase of a temporary membership or angling ticket. Regions of the NRA in England and Wales include the following:

Anglican Water — NRA unit — regional headquarters, Aqua House, London Rd, Peterborough PE2 8AG, England (phone: 0733-555667). Covers the counties of Bedfordshire, Cambridgeshire, Essex, Lincolnshire, Norfolk, Northamptonshire, Suffolk, and part of Buckinghamshire and Hertfordshire; and controls the Blackwater, Bure, Cam, Chelmer, Colne, Crouch, Great Ouse, Nene, Stour, Waveney, Welland, Witham, Yare, and tributaries; also Kielder Water, northern Europe's biggest manmade lake.

Northumbrian Water, Northumbria House, Regent Centre, Gosforth, Newcastle-upon-Tyne, Tyne & Wear NE3 3PX, England (phone: 091284-3151). Covers Cleveland, Durham, Northumberland, and part of Cumbria Tyne & Wear and North Yorkshire; and controls the Aln, Byth, Coquet, Tees, Tyne, Wansbeck, Wear, and tributaries.

North West Water, Rivers Division, Dawson House, Great Sankey, Warrington, Cheshire WA5 3LW, England (phone: 092-572-4321). Covers Cheshire, Greater Manchester, Lancashire, Merseyside, and part of Cumbria, Derbyshire, and Staffordshire; and controls the Calder, Derwent, Eden, Esk and Esk (Border), Greta, and Lune, as well as the following lakes: the Bassenthwaite, Brotherswater, Buttermere, Coniston, Crummock Water, Derwentwater, Elterwater, Ennerdale Water, Grasmere, Haweswater, Loweswater, Rydal Water, Thirlmere, and Ullswater.

Severn-Trent Water, Rivers & Regulation Division, Sapphire East, 550 Streetsbrook Rd., Solihull B91 1QT, England (phone: 021-711-2324). Covers Leicestershire, Nottinghamshire, Shropshire, Warwickshire, the West Midlands, and part of Derbyshire, Gloucestershire, Hereford and Worcester, Powys, and Staffordshire; and controls the Warwickshire Avon, Churnet, Dove, Derbyshire Derwent, Dove, Manifold, Soar, Teme, Trent, Vrynwy (excluding Lake Vrynwy and streams running into it), Derbyshire Wye, and their tributaries.

Southern Region — NRA, Guildbourne House, Worthing, West Sussex BN11 1LD, England (phone: 0903-205252). Covers Hampshire, East and West Sussex, and parts of Dorset and Kent; and controls the Adur, Arun, Beaulieu, Cuckmere, Hamble, Itchen, Lymington, Medway, Meon, Ouse, Rother, Stour, and Test.

South West NRA, Manley House, Kestrel Way, Sowton, Exeter, Devon EX2 7LQ, England (phone: 0392-444000). Covers Cornwall, Devon, and parts of Dorset and Somerset; controls the rivers Camel, Dart, Erme, Exe, Fowey, Lyn, Tamar, Taw, Teign, and Torridge.

South West Water, Peninsula House, Rydon La., Exeter, Devon EX2 7HR, England (phone: 0392-219666). Controls reservoir fishing throughout Cornwall and Devon.

Thames Water, Fisheries Manager, National Rivers Authority, Kings Meadow House, Reading, Berkshire RG1 8DQ, England (phone: 0734-593333). Covers Berkshire, Greater London, Hertfordshire, Oxfordshire, Surrey, and parts of Buckinghamshire, Essex, Kent, and Wiltshire; and controls the Cherwell, Colne, Kennett, Lea, Mole, Roding, and Wey.

Wessex Water, Wessex House, Passage St., Bristol, Avon BS2 0JQ, England (phone: 0272-290611). Covers Avon and part of Dorset, Somerset, and Wiltshire; and controls the Bristol and Hampshire Avon, Axe, the Piddle, and the Hampshire Stour.

Yorkshire Water, West Riding House, 67 Albion St., Leeds, West Yorkshire LS1 5AA, England (phone: 0532-448201). Covers North (James Herriott country) West, South Yorkshire and North Humberside; and rivers Swale, Ure, Derwent, Ouse, Nidd Wharfe, Aire, Esk, Calder, Don, Hull. Fishing rod licenses are available from the Fisheries Manager, 21 Park Square South, Leeds LS1 2QG, England (phone: 0532-440191). Humberside, South and West Yorkshire, and part of North Yorkshire; and controls the Aire, Calder, Con, and Yorkshire Ouse.

SCOTLAND: Exclusiveness is the hallmark of the very finest Scottish angling — some streams are so closed that even rich folk and VIPs may find the door barred — but it does not prevail along all of the Tay, the King of Scotland's salmon rivers, or along the entire length of its rivals: the Aberdeenshire Dee, noted by some fly fishermen as Britain's best major salmon stream; the fast-flowing Spey, Scotland's most thrilling fishery; and the prolific Tweed. Also good are the aptly named Awe; the Don, superb for dry-fly trouting; the Northern Esk, which produces abundant numbers of medium-sized salmon; the Findhorn, among the more outstanding of the smaller Scottish salmon streams, with brown trout sport rivaling that of the nearby Spey and good sea trouting in summer; the fairly exclusive, fly-only Helmsdale; the good-quality Naver, especially for salmon and sea trout; and the 30-mile-long Ythan, an excellent sea trout fishery. Many huge freshwater lochs and reservoirs are also rich in trout.

In Scotland, closed season is October 7 through March 14 for trout and late August through February, depending on the area, for salmon. Also, throughout the year, most localities prohibit Sunday fishing. No rod licenses are required for Scottish angling, but to fish for salmon, trout, or sea trout, written permission from the water's owner is necessary.

Local district fishery boards can spell out the rules on seasons and permissible fishing days, and provide information about who owns fishing rights for a given stretch of water. To locate district fishery offices, see a local tackle shop or contact the area tourist board (the address of which can be obtained from the Scottish Tourist Board, 23 Ravelston Terr., Edinburgh EH4 3EU, Scotland; phone: 031-332-2433).

WALES: Here, the Wye is justly famous for salmon, and several hotels have water on the main river and on its tributaries. The Dee, which yields good-sized salmon and smaller browns and sea trout, and the swift Usk, which has an average rod catch per season of some 800 salmon, usually averaging 10 pounds, are Wales's other important salmon rivers. The prolific Towy, and the Dovey and the Conwy, both of which hold numerous records, are the counterparts of the Dee and the Usk for sea trout sport. Offering good opportunities for both sea trout and salmon action are the Clwyd; the Glaslyn, which rises in Snowdon; the Mawddach; the Taf, whose source is on Mynydd Prescelly; and the important Teifi, which claims some of the principality's top trout fly fishing.

On the whole, there are fewer big fish in Welsh reservoirs and lakes than in English and Scottish still waters. Most of the reservoirs and many lakes are in the mountainous districts of Snowdon and the Brecon Beacons, where visitors may well find that fishing is free, the only requirement being the owner's permission to fish.

Welsh Water regulates fishing on Welsh rivers and issues licenses from St. Mellons, Cardiff, Wales (phone: 0874-3181). It controls the Alwen, Alyn, Arrow, Bala Lake, Ceiriog, Ceirw, Clwyd, Conway, Welsh Dee, Dovey, Elwy, Irfon, Ithon, Lliw, Lugg, Neath, Rhymney, Taf, Teifi, Towy, Tryweryn, Twrch, Usk, Wye, and tributaries.

COARSE FISHING

All the fish in freshwater rivers and lakes that are not trout or salmon — bream, carp, chub, dace, perch, pike, roach, rudd, eel, and tench — go by the name of coarse fish, and there are millions of anglers who have made this quarry their specialty, using rods and lines with natural bait such as maggots, worms, or bread. The almost total absence of coarse fish in the streams and still waters of Scotland and Wales is compensated for by their abundance in England, where they often may be fished free of charge, and where the range of possibilities is enormous, particularly in the eastern and central regions: the giant and sluggish Great Ouse, where there is almost every kind of fish (although some stretches boast larger populations of a given species than others), with the town of Huntingdon among the most favored angling centers; the Nene, primarily for bream and roach; the Norfolk Broads and the Broadland rivers, like the Bure, the Waveney, the Yare, and their tributaries (except during the daytime in summer, when boat traffic makes the angling fairly slow), especially for bream and roach; and the Welland, another important coarse fishing stream.

Refer to *Where to Fish* ($23/£14.95 from Thomas Harmsworth Publishing, 13 Nicosia Rd., London SW18, England) for more information.

Fishermen may also take advantage of unused sand and gravel pits, England's foremost fishing grounds. In these still waters, roach and bream, tench, eel, rudd, and some pike are commonly found. Angling is also available in Britain's canals, most of which are controlled by the British Waterways (Principal Fisheries Officer, Willow Grange, Church Rd., Watford, Hertfordshire WD1 3QA, England; phone: 0923-226422). However, canal fishing tends to be more difficult, the fish smaller, and anglers are in competition with pleasure boats.

SEA ANGLING

Among all types of fishing in Britain, sea angling has grown most rapidly in the last few years. That's not surprising: Britain has hundreds of miles of ragged coastline, and anglers reel in an abundance of fish in species that come and go throughout the season, from half-pound flounders and sand dabs to giant mako sharks, 200-pound skate, and 300-pound halibut, plus wrasse, pollack, and mackerel, as well as sea bass, common in southern England and a favorite. No license is necessary, and few advance arrangements are required; tackle can usually be hired; and the chefs in most hotels will cook a guest's prize on request. For trips out over the wrecks and sunken reefs where some of the bigger fish lurk, boats and professional skippers are readily available, and a day out with a group in a boat with a local who knows how to rendezvous with fish can be a most rewarding (and reasonably priced) experience. All that's required is a stomach strong enough to hold up through a day on the short choppy seas.

Shore fishing with a powerful rod and reel for sea bass or cod, also known as beach casting, requires a little more equipment, namely good oilskins, since these delicious creatures favor "storm beaches," and the best fishing is done when there's a strong onshore wind that will drench an angler to the skin with salt spray.

In the majority of coastal fishing hot spots, experienced anglers man Angling Times Report Stations, which dispense valuable advice on local conditions. Many areas also have sea angling festivals; the British Tourist Authority or regional tourist office can provide details.

For more information, consult *Sea Angler* and *Sea Angling Weekly,* available at newsstands. The National Federation of Sea Anglers (14 Bank St., Newton Abbot, Devon, England TQ12 2JW; phone: 0626-331330) organizes over 100 competitions annually, to which visitors are welcome, and will answer questions about them. For Scottish sea fishing information, contact the Scottish Federation of Sea Anglers, Caledonia House, South Gyle, Edinburgh EH1 9DQ, Scotland (phone: 031-317-7192). In Wales contact Welsh Water (phone: 0874-3181).

ENGLAND: In England, the best areas include the Channel ports of Dover and Deal, in Kent; the small resorts of New Haven and Littlehampton, in Sussex; Salcombe, on a many-branched estuary with wooded hills in rolling Devon; Fowey and Looe, among the rocky cliffs of Cornwall; and the mountainous Isle of Man, in the middle of the Irish Sea between England and Ireland. Off the coast of Cornwall alone, there are four species of shark; those interested can arrange to go for them on any number of organized trips.

SCOTLAND: The coarse fishing potential in Scotland is largely unexploited. Shetland and Orkney have Britain's best common skate action, and the Pentland Firth, which separates Orkney and the mainland, produces large halibut. In the southeast, there's plenty of good shore fishing from the rocks and beaches.

WALES: In Wales, the best shore fishing is found west of Cardiff, and the fishing offshore in the south can be superb. In the north and west, boat fishing is quite good.

FISHING SCHOOLS

CHARLES BINGHAM (FISHING), LTD., West Down, Warren's Cross, Tavistock, Devon, England: Mr. Bingham, who has landed more than 200 salmon on the fly and thousands of trout from some of England's most famous rivers, has fished on Dartmoor rivers for more than 40 years. He has written the best-selling books *Salmon and Sea Trout Fishing* and *The Game Fishing Year* (Batsford, 1988 and 1989). The school, which emphasizes fly fishing, teaches beginners the basics, but Charles will also take out experienced anglers. Groups are limited to 3 or 4 people, so each participant gets plenty of personal attention. March to October is the season. Lodging is availble in hotels or farmhouses on Dartmoor. Details: Charles Bingham (Fishing), Ltd., West Down, Warren's Cross, Tavistock, Devon, England (phone: 0822-613899).

ARUNDELL ARMS, Lifton, Devon, England: This traditional West Country hotel pioneered fishing courses many years ago and now offers them for beginning, intermediate, and advanced anglers. Courses are taught by a Cornish champion tournament caster who is reckoned to be one of the best fly-fishing instructors in the country and, as lecturer, *The London Times*'s fishing correspondent Conrad Voss-Bark, who is married to the proprietor (herself a passionate fly fisher and an author of books on the waters of the area). All of the courses, which are run on the inn's extensive river, mix fly-fishing theory with a great deal of on-the-water experience. In addition, there are always two bailiffs on the property to advise visiting fishermen. Weekend fly-tying courses are available in winter. Details: Arundell Arms Hotel, Lifton, Devon PL16 0AA, England (phone: 0566-84666).

GLEN AFFRIC, Cannich, by Beuly, Highland, Scotland: Beginners are welcome at this family-run roadside hotel's summer course, where instruction is given in casting and in trout and salmon fishing. Guests should provide waterproof jackets, hats, Wellingtons, and fishing equipment; the hotel can advise on particulars. The nearest rail and bus stations are 27 miles away at Inverness; transport to the station may be arranged for a small charge. Reserve well in advance. Details: Glen Affric Hotel, Cannich, by Beauly, Highland 1V4 7LW, Scotland (phone: 0456-5214).

OSPREY, Aviemore, Highland, Scotland: Introductory fly-fishing courses, weekend-long crash courses in fly fishing, and salmon fishing courses are available, along with game fishing holiday packages, at this Scottish Highlands fishing school, presided over by one Jim Cornfoot, an amiable Scotsman who has been fishing these waters since he was 10 — nearly 36 years. Participants learn casting, watercraft, fly tying, spinning, knots, entomology, rod, reel, and line construction, how to choose the right tackle and equipment for their needs, how to use a landing net. There's plenty of casting practice, both on the waters adjacent to the school and on the famous river Spey, and there's plenty of time to wash down a dram or two of famous Grouse whisky with a pint of good beer — the favored local method of raising good cheer. Details: Osprey Fishing School, The Fishing Centre at the Aviemore Centre, Aviemore, Highland PH22 1QP, Scotland (phone: 0479-810911 or 0479-810132).

PEEBLES, Peebles, Borders, Scotland: This small county town in the beautiful rolling Borders area is just 25 miles from Edinburgh. A popular center for fishing on the river Tweed, it offers Friday-through-Sunday trout fishing courses presided over by former British Open casting champion Andy Dickison, Tweed Valley born and bred, in April and May. There are also Sunday-to-Sunday salmon week courses in November, when the large salmon, usually weighing in between 10 and 30 pounds, are running. Private instruction in both bait and fly-casting techniques is also available, and Melrose Abbey (for more details, see *Ancient Monuments and Ruins*) and Abbotsford, the former home of novelist Sir Walter Scott, are nearby. Accommodation is at the *Tontine* hotel, a three-star Trusthouse Forte establishment. Details: Peebles Angling School, Craigiedene, 10 Dean Park, Peeblesshire EH45 6DD, Scotland (phone: 0721-20331).

TWEED VALLEY, Walkerburn, Borders, Scotland: Attached to a handsome Edwardian country-house hotel known for its Scottish cuisine, this school offers a syllabus that varies with the season — trouting from April through September and salmon fishing in October and November. Weekend and weeklong casting courses are also available. No experience is necessary, and rods, reels, and lines may be hired; guests will need their own Wellingtons, waders, and waterproof clothing. Rail and bus stations are 32 and 6 miles away, respectively; transport to the center, available at a small charge, can be provided. Book as far ahead as possible. Details: Tweed Valley Hotel (Outdoor Sports Centre), Galashiels Rd., Walkerburn, Borders EH43 6AA, Scotland (phone: 089687-636).

GWYDYR, Betws-y-Coed, Gwynedd, Wales: Anglers interested in perfecting their techniques in salmon, trout, and sea trout fishing can do so here; tuition covers casting, knots, rod and reel care, and night fishing. The hotel has waters along 8 miles of the rivers Conway and Lledr. Details: Gwydyr Hotel, Betws-y-Coed, Gwynedd LL24 0AB, Wales (phone: 069-02-777).

GAME FISHING HOTELS

Anglers can simplify the complicated process of arranging to fish in areas where the angling rights are privately held by basing themselves at a special fishing hotel, which may either control a stretch of a nearby stream or be able to carry out the necessary negotiations with owners of local estates. Most of the following establishments are country house hotels in attractive settings; waters to which they control rights are indicated. Hotels mentioned in areas where fishing is free are conveniently located with respect to the best local waters — and, like the rights-owning establishments, are exceptionally hospitable to anglers: Enthusiasts who want to haul out their tales of that day's triumphs will be sure to find a willing ear.

CAVENDISH, Baslow, Derbyshire, England: The angling available on the rivers Derwent and Wye, by courtesy of the Duke of Devonshire, provides only part of the charm at this establishment, where diners eat off Wedgwood china with Sheffield silver and rest up from a day on the stream in lounges with open fires, oak beams, fresh flowers, and fine views of the adjacent Chatsworth estate. Local fishing celebrity Arnold Mosley is available for coaching by prior arrangement, and guests may borrow fishing tackle if they forget their own. The hotel itself was restored and decorated by the Duchess of Devonshire and has 23 superbly furnished rooms. The setting is Chatsworth, described in *Stately Homes and Great Gardens,* and the magnificent Derbyshire Peak District. Details: Cavendish Hotel, Baslow, Derbyshire DE4 1SP, England (phone: 024688-2311).

TILLMOUTH PARK, Cornhill-on-Tweed, Northumberland, England: This Victorian mansion-turned-inn occupies over 1,000 acres of rolling Northumberland border countryside — and boasts 9 miles of water on the rivers Till and Tweed. Good for salmon, grilse, and sea trout fishing. Spring season lasts from February 1 through mid-May, and following it is the summer season. Details: Tillmouth Park Hotel, Cornhill-on-Tweed, Northumberland TD12 4UU, England (phone: 0890-2255).

IZAAK WALTON, Dovedale, Derbyshire, England: In the heart of the Peak District National Park, this comfortable hotel started its life in the 17th century as a farmhouse. It offers 3 miles on the river Dove. Details: Izaak Walton Hotel, Dovedale, Derbyshire DE6 2AY, England (phone: 0335-29555).

CARNARVON ARMS, Dulverton, Somerset, England: This fine English country sporting hotel, built in 1873 by the fourth Earl of Carnarvon at one of the entrances to the Exmoor National Park, occupies 50 acres along the banks of the river Barle and offers its guests some 7 miles of bank on that stream and along the rivers Exe and Haddeo. In the heart of Negley Farson country, these typical moorland rivers run clear, bright, and shallow between pools. Late May, June, and early July are the best months for wild brownies — small but excellent fighters. In July, August, and September 1988, 156 salmon were taken, with numbers currently increasing, ranging from 5-pound grilse to 8 to 12 pounds. The hotel itself — a warm and friendly family-run establishment for nearly 3 decades — has spacious lounges with open log fires and is furnished with comfortable armchairs and fine antiques. There's also an outdoor swimming pool, hard tennis court, and a handsome full-size billiard table. Details: Carnarvon Arms Hotel, Dulverton, Somerset TA22 9AE, England (phone: 0398-23302).

HACKNESS GRANGE, North Moors National Park, near Scarborough, Yorkshire, England: With 11 miles on the river Derwent in North York Moors National Park, this peaceful hotel occupies a stately limestone residence built in the mid-19th century and more recent additions. Details: Hackness Grange Hotel, Hackness, near Scarborough, Yorkshire YO13 0JW, England (phone: 0723-82345).

HOLNE CHASE, Ashburton, Devon, England: Surrounded by woodlands and by the Dartmoor National Park, this singularly secluded and romantic hotel on an 11th-century hunting estate has about a mile of fishing on the river Dart, whose valley the principal rooms overlook. Sea trout in the 1½- to 4½-pound range as well as salmon weighing from 8 to 15 pounds, have been taken in the last couple of years. The season is April to September, although the hotel is open year-round. Details: Holne Chase, Holne Ashburton, Devon TQ13 7NS, England (phone: 0364-3471).

DEER PARK, Weston Honiton, Devon, England: This family-run country house hotel in a 17th-century hillside Georgian manor stands on 40 acres of Devonshire countryside. Overlooking the valley of the river Otter, it offers 5 miles of private fishing for brown trout; additional fishing includes a 2-acre lake for Rainbow Trout and a mile on the River Coly, where sea trout and salmon can be caught. The hotel can also arrange hunting trips (see *Stalking and Shooting*). Details: Mr. Gilbert Barratt, Deer Park Hotel, Buckerell Village, Honiton, Devon EX14 0PG, England (phone: 0404-41266).

ARUNDELL ARMS, Lifton, Devon, England: Some 20 miles of private salmon, sea trout, and brown trout fishing on the river Tamar and its tributaries, and a 3-acre lake stocked with rainbow and brown trout. Details: Arundell Arms, Lifton, Devon PL16 0AA, England (phone: 0566-84666). See also *Rural Retreats.*

WHITE HART, North Tawton, Devon, England: This tiny inn, located 100 yards from the river Taw, arranges fishing excursions and lessons in angling for trout and salmon. Details: The White Hart Inn, Fore St., North Tawton, Devon EX20 2DT, England (phone: 0837-82473).

LEE PARK LODGE, Romsey, Hampshire, England: In the heart of the late Lord Mountbatten's 6,000-acre Broadlands estate, this sporting lodge is 200 yards away from the river Test and owns the rights on 4 miles of the famous chalk stream. Fishing is on selected beats varying from slow to fast, deep to shallow, wide to narrow. The ghillies who look after guests are expert anglers, knowledgeable in local fishing. The period farmhouse where guests lodge has four double bedrooms and comfortable facilities. Packages that include transport to and from central London and Heathrow Airport are available, as are guided tours to local points of interest for non-fishing partners. Details: Lee Park Lodge, Broadlands, Romsey, Hampshire SO51, England (phone: 0794-517888).

WHITTON FARM HOUSE, Rothbury, Northumberland, England: This charming country hotel, which occupies a converted farm built in 1829, has a mile-long beat on the Coquet and, by special arrangement with the Northumberland Angler's Federation, access to some of the river's lower stretches (described by *Trout and Salmon* magazine as some of the top club-owned waters in Britain). After guests have had their fill of fishing, they can have a drink in the former calf house, eat dinner in the former milking parlor, and then go to bed in a converted stable. There are beamed ceilings, stone walls, and polished pine floors throughout. A stable with 20 horses and ponies for trekking and trail riding is on the premises. Details: Whitton Farm House, Rothbury, Northumberland NE65 7RL, England (phone: 0669-20811).

HALF MOON INN, Sheepwash, Beaworthy, North Devon, England: This quaint, friendly, and comfortable village inn has been owned by the Inniss family for over 30 years. All 14 rooms have private facilities. Nine miles of privately owned salmon and trout fishing on the river Torridge, a small river renowned for its spring run of salmon, its dry-fly fishing in May and June, and its excellent run of sea trout in July and August. Details: Charles Inniss, Half Moon Inn, Sheepwash, Beaworthy, North Devon EX21 5NE, England (phone: 040923-376).

RISING SUN, Umberleigh, Devon, England: The 13th-century *Rising Sun,* a personable cottage-style fishing hotel, has 3½ miles of salmon, sea trout, and brown trout fishing on the river Taw — the first waters above the tides. The salmon action is liveliest from March through May, with the average catch weighing in at 10 to 12 pounds. Large sea trout averaging 4 or 5 pounds run in mid-April; small sea trout of 1½ pounds are running from the third week in June until late September. Grilse run at the end of July and summer salmon in August and September. Details: Rising Sun, Umberleigh, Devon EX37 9DU, England (phone: 0769-60447).

ANGLERS ARMS, Weldon Bridge, Morpeth, Northumberland, England: A mile of fishing for trout and salmon on the river Coquet. The hotel, in an 18th-century building, has 17 recently refurbished rooms, plus a restaurant that serves traditional Northumbrian and English fare. Half of the restaurant occupies a converted Pullman car reminiscent of the Orient Express, and train noises are piped in over the PA system. Four luxurious cottages are also available. Details: Anglers Arms Hotel, Weldon Bridge, Morpeth, Northumberland NE65 8AX, England (phone: 066570-271 and -655).

ALTNAHARRA, Altnaharra, by Lairg, Southerland, Scotland: One of the country's most celebrated angling hotels, this 20-room establishment has been welcoming anglers since 1887 to the tiny hamlet of Altnaharra and the superb private fishing on 4 miles of the rivers Mudale and Mallart. Salmon and brown trout are the quarry here. There are also private beats on several nearby lochs, where there is also sea trout to be taken. Best times are late June through late September for sea trout, late May into September for brown trout, and April through June and September for salmon. Details: Altnaharra Hotel, Altnaharra, by Lairg, Southerland IV27 4UE, Scotland (phone: 0549-81222).

BANCHORY LODGE, Banchory, Grampian, Scotland: At this 24-room country house hotel full of Georgian charm, fishing is on the river Dee, one of the world's most celebrated salmon rivers, and anglers come from the far corners of the earth to experience the salmon season here, from the first of February through the end of September (only fly fishing is permitted after April). The dining room and lounges of the hotel itself are furnished in period style, have open log fireplaces, and overlook the river, as do many of the bedrooms (some of which even have four-poster beds). Details: Banchory Lodge, Banchory, Grampian AB3 3HS, Scotland (phone: 0330-22625).

TULCHAN LODGE, Grantown-on-Spey, Highland, Scotland: Edward VII used to come here to shoot and fish. Recently refurbished, this Scottish country house hotel, overlooking the Spey Valley in the midst of Highland malt whisky distilling country, is as delightful as it was then, with its magnificent paintings, paneled hall and library, and elegant drawing and billiard rooms. There are 11 rooms and 8 miles of private fishing for salmon and sea trout on the river Spey. Fishing seasons run from mid-February through September, with April to August the best for salmon, June and July for sea trout. The hotel opens mid-April. Details: Tulchan Lodge, Grantown-on-Spey, Highland PH26 3PW, Scotland (phone: 08075-200).

EDNAM HOUSE, Kelso, Borders, Scotland: This stately 32-room establishment built in 1761 has a high percentage of repeat business, thanks to the excellent sport in the river Tweed, which flows just outside (so that all the bars and public rooms and half of the guest quarters have river views). Most anglers come for the salmon fishing in spring and fall; however, rights are privately owned and difficult to negotiate. For trout, 8 miles of the Tweed and the Teviot and numerous other small streams in the district are available to hotel guests at a nominal sum; best sport is in May and June. Details: Ednam House Hotel, Kelso, Borders TD5 7HT, Scotland (phone: 0573-24168).

KENMORE, Kenmore, by Aberfeldy, Tayside, Scotland: Handsomely situated in one of Scotland's prettiest villages and surrounded by pristine countryside, this 39-room inn, established in 1572 (Scotland's oldest) on the banks of the river Tay in an area of impressive natural beauty, stands out for more than its setting. It offers 4 miles of private salmon fishing on the river Tay and has rights for salmon and brown and rainbow trout for the entire 16 miles of Loch Tay. Salmon season runs from mid-January through mid-October (and is best from April through June and in September and October); brown trout may be taken from mid-March through mid-October. Those who tire of aquatic pursuits can enjoy the establishment's 18-hole golf course. Details: Kenmore Hotel, The Square, Kenmore, by Aberfeldy, Tayside PH15 2NU, Scotland (phone: 08873-205).

INVERESHIE HOUSE, Kincraig, Kingussie, Highland, Scotland: Occupying a lovely Georgian building at the foot of the Caringorm mountains overlooking Loch

Insh and the river Spey, this establishment offers angling on both bodies of water, as on well as on the Lower Feshie, for salmon, sea trout, brown trout, and Arctic char. Instruction is available. Shooting, deer stalking, and other field sports are available. Details: Invereshie House, Kincraig, Kingussie, Highland PH21 1NA, Scotland (phone: 0540-4332).

CROOK INN, Tweedsmuir, by Biggar, Borders, Scotland: This 16th-century coaching inn, set on 5½ acres of the border hills, was where the Scottish poet Robbie Burns wrote *Willie Wastle.* Now it has 8 rooms and 8 miles of private fishing on the river Tweed for salmon and sea trout, with an additional 30 miles of association and club brown trout waters available. November is the best month for salmon and sea trout; May through July is tops for brown trout. Details: The Crook Inn, Tweedsmuir, by Biggar, Borders ML12 6QN, Scotland (phone: 0899-7272).

TWEED VALLEY, Walkerburn, Borders, Scotland: Traditional Scottish food is one of the major attractions of this former Edwardian country house — along with the area being a significant Atlantic salmon and sea trout fishing center for the past 30 years. Private salmon beats are also available, and guests may purchase permits to fish for brown trout and grayling on more than 30 miles of the river and its tributaries. Best times are from February through May, with peak runs of sea trout and salmon in late September, October, and November. Guides, lessons in both fly and bait casting, and tackle hire are available to guests. Details: Tweed Valley Hotel, Walkerburn, Borders EH43 6AA, Scotland (phone: 089687-636).

GLIFFAES COUNTRY HOUSE, near Crickhowell, Powys, Wales: The river Usk, celebrated for its wild brown trout season, is a prime attraction of this stately, late-19th-century private-home-turned-inn. The average brown trout catch is 10 ounces, but there are three good stretches of salmon water as well, with average annual catches at around 25 to 30 fish. Eight reservoirs stocked by the Welsh Water Authority lie within a 15-mile radius. Details: Gliffaes Country House Hotel, near Crickhowell, Powys NP8 1RH, Wales (phone: 0874-730371).

THE LAKE, Llangammarch Wells, Powys, Wales: Besides 50 acres of sweeping lawns and thick woods, this elegant 19-room country house — including 9 suites — offers a 3-acre trout lake and 5½ miles on the rivers Wye and Irfon, two of the best salmon streams in Wales, with the latter passing through the grounds of the hotel. Salmon fishing comes into its own in the latter part of the season, which runs from late January to late October on both streams. The spring fish are very powerful and can occasionally run over 30 pounds. Trout — mostly wild local fish weighing up to 34 pounds — can also be taken on the Irfon. Those on the smaller Chewfru also provide interesting sport, while the Wye often provides specimens weighing 1 pound and more. The largest salmon ever caught on hotel waters weighed in at a whopping 28 pounds, 8 ounces. Guests won't lack for food or wine here either. The wine list offers 350 varieties, and the kitchen serves homemade chocolates, sausages, and bread. Details: The Lake Hotel, Llangammarch Wells, Powys LD4 4BS, Wales (phone: 0591-2202).

LAKE VYRNWY, via Oswestry, Powys, Wales: It is the fishing on Lake Vyrnwy, which is best in May, that brings some guests to this 30-room establishment, whereas others are drawn by the very fine Bechstein grand piano, the unusual fishing and working holidays, and other special programs such as bird-watching weekends, hot air ballooning, clay pigeon shoots, and the like. The atmosphere is old-fashioned and unpretentious; the view is spectacular. One American visitor implored his hosts, "For heaven's sake, don't modernize the place! It's perfect!" Details: Lake Vyrnwy Hotel, via Oswestry, Shropshire SY10 0LY, Wales (phone: 069173-692).

TYN-Y-CORNEL, Talyllyn Tywyn, Gwynedd, Wales: Angling on Talyllyn Lake is the prime attraction of this lakeside hotel. Owned by the hotel, the lake contains wild brown trout as well as hatchery-bred fish. The hotel is owned by the Welsh Water Authority, and plans for refurbishment, which will retain the character of the hotel, are underway. Parts of the building date back to the 1500s, but the plumbing is strictly 20th century. Details: Tyn-y-Cornel, Talyllyn Tywyn, Gwynedd LL36 9AJ, Wales (phone: 0654-77282).

Freewheeling by Two-Wheeler

The landscapes seen from the roads of Britain unfold with such endless diversity at every bend and turn that traveling through quickly in a car seems a real shame: The villages full of ancient half-timbered houses, the heather-clad plateau country with its deep valleys and minuscule settlements, the rolling hills, the quaint seacoast towns, and the regions of moors and mountains all beg to be explored at bicycle speed, that is, fast enough to cover a fair amount of terrain, but slow enough to stop to inspect a wildflower or admire a view. It's lovely to be able to pull over to the side of the road or to pop into a tea shop with a minimum of fuss or bother. Cycling provides all that. There's something quite special about the rhythm of days on the road: the slow but steady ticking away of the miles, the lure of the unknown just over the next hill, the ready meetings with fellow cyclists on the road or at pubs and hostels, and the special camaraderie that prevails.

The fact that Britain offers not only a great variety of scenery in a relatively compact area, but also an abundance of well-surfaced, little-trafficked secondary roads, as well as many facilities for rental and repair and hundreds of small restaurants and informal hotels that are no less than delighted to welcome bedraggled pedalers, makes the country a well-nigh perfect candidate for cycling vacations — for beginning tourers and experts alike. Even those who are not particularly experienced and postpone their planning until the last minute can still enjoy a two-wheeling vacation here: Just travel light, start out slowly, and don't give up just because of saddle-soreness and tender muscles.

Rentals are widely available outside London, though it may not be possible to hire bikes for children; prices begin at about $7 a day for basic machines in rural towns and move upward when brand-new bikes, locks, lights, panniers, and insurance are supplied and in larger cities, where the broader selections are usually available. In London, *Bike UK* (phone: 01-839-2111) and *Chelsea Cycles* (phone: 01-352-3999) rent bicycles by the day or week. *London Cycling Campaign* (Tress House, 3 Stamford St., London SE1 9NT, England; phone: 01-928-7220) is also a good source.

Since the amount of pleasure at least partially depends on the bike, cyclists may well want to bring their own. Airlines will generally transport bikes as part of passengers' personal baggage, but may insist that the whole machine be crated. At any rate, be sure to check your insurance coverage before leaving home. If you have none, consider joining the *Cyclists' Touring Club* (Cotterell House, 69 Meadrow, Godalming, Surrey GU7 3HS, England; phone: 04868-7217), which has a plan for its members. Cyclists will also need to bring a basic set of tools and spares, including tire pump, puncture repair kit, tire levers, spanners/wrench, spoke key, chain rivet extractor, chain links, inner brake cables, pliers, odd nuts and bolts, brake blocks, oil can, batteries and bulbs, freewheel block remover, rag, extra spokes, inner tubes and outer tires, and a small file for honing spokes. British law requires cycles to have two independent brakes and a red rear light and reflector, as well as a white light in the front for night riding; since riding is on the left here, it's a good idea to fix the front light onto the right-hand side. Not required by law — but certainly eminently practical — are a padlock and chain, though theft is not the problem in rural areas that it is in centers such as Birmingham, Glasgow, Liverpool, Manchester, Sheffield, and, of course, London.

To get out of these cities without battling the traffic is a relatively simple matter, since bikes are allowed to accompany passengers on the train at no extra charge. The procedure is simple: Buy a ticket, take the bike onto the platform, and ask the guard's permission to put it in the luggage van — a request usually refused only when the car is full of other goods. There are a few exceptions, and they change occasionally, so check with *British Rail* for specifics. And always label your bike with your name, address, and the station of origin and destination.

BEST CYCLING AREAS

The touring possibilities are extensive. In England, for instance, any number of "B" and unclassified roads connect nearly every community in the country. In Wales, only the trunk routes in the southeast are too busy for cycling. In Scotland, their counterparts in the south are generally busy. In summer, Scotland's "A" routes in the north can be congested, more because of their narrow and winding nature than because of the quantity of traffic they carry, as can the north and west coast routes and some of the interior highways in Wales. In addition, there are unsurfaced tracks, cattle drovers' routes, bridleways, and woodland paths that lend themselves to two-wheeling (though the going can be a bit rough). Britain has, for instance, hundreds of miles of towing paths along the canals that ribbon the countryside, waterways constructed during the Industrial Revolution and now largely deserted by commercial transport. For information about necessary permits, contact the Information Centre and Canal Shop, British Waterways Board, Melbury House, Melbury Ter., London NW1 6JX (phone: 01-262-6711).

Here are some of the best cycling areas in Britain. Bike rentals, routes, lodgings and camping, and repairs for most of these are covered by the invaluable publications of *Cycling World* magazine ($2.75/£1.80, from Andrew House, 2a Granville Rd., Sidcup, Kent DA14 4BN, England).

LAND'S END TO JOHN O'GROATS, England: The 3-week challenge known as "the End to End" covers approximately 1,000 miles from the southwest to the northeasternmost corners of a country crowded with traffic, towns, estuaries, motorways, and hills. There is no officially designated route, but most cyclists who make this varied trip pedal via Bath, Stratford-upon-Avon, Lincoln, York, Durham, Galashiels, Pitlochry, and Inverness, taking in the Cotswolds, the Yorkshire Moors, the Cheviot Hills, and the Grampian Mountains. Stick to the east side and travel from south to north to take advantage of the prevailing wind. A cyclist can expect to average 50 miles a day at first, more as the journey builds strength.

LONDON, England: Bicycling may not be everyone's idea of the best transportation here, and in fact, it can prove a nightmare to newcomers not forewarned about patterns of flow and congestion. But it's also true that there's no better way of seeing the real London — away from the main thoroughfares used by most buses and taxicabs. Traveling by bike, more than any other mode of transport, will provide a good feel for the way London's "villages" all fit together. The London Cycling Campaign's excellent booklet *On Your Bike* (£2.80, including postage) is full of maps of central London on which are designated streets good for bicycling as well as the official cycle routes through the city. Though aimed at Londoners who use their bikes as transportation, it can be useful to sightseers as well — and serves as an excellent primer on English laws pertaining to cyclists and on cycling safety, maintenance, and repairs. Cycling shops are also listed. In addition, the Campaign publishes a bimonthly newsletter providing up-to-date information on cycling in London as well as a listing of shops where L.C.C. members can get a 10% discount. Fold-out cycling route maps of south, east, and northwest London ($1.50/£1 each) are also available. Details: London Cycling Campaign, Tress House, Stamford St., London SE1, England (phone: 01-928-7220).

EAST ANGLIA, England: The generally low-lying terrain of Suffolk and Norfolk, which, along with parts of neighboring counties, used to be an old Saxon kingdom, seems custom-made for cycling — though there are enough gentle hills to keep the horizons constantly changing. East Anglia is a land of farms, isolated villages full of thatched houses, grand mansions, and inspiring Gothic churches. Where these flatlands slip gently into the sea, there are salt marshes and sand dunes teeming with birds, deserted beaches, and The Broads. Details: East Anglia Tourist Board, Toppesfield Hall, Hadleigh, Suffolk IP7 5DN, England (phone: 0473-822922).

COTSWOLDS AND THE HEART OF ENGLAND: Here is a region that shows a number of faces to the world: There are the chalk hills known as the Chilterns, billowing up out of the valley of the Thames; the jagged blue-hazed Malvern Hills; the Avon valley, with Stratford, the Bard's hometown, and nearby villages full of thatched-roof cottages — not to mention the Cotswolds, where cyclists will roll past dotted pastures and shallow trout streams that look like ribbons of silver when viewed from on high, through placid hamlets (some almost *too* picture-postcard pretty), and alongside occasional fuzzy patches of beech trees that shimmer in the sunshine. Everywhere there is the limestone characteristic of the area — intricately fitted as cottage walls and stone fences, and colored the mellow hues of cream and honey and slate so that the structures seem to grow out of the earth itself. There are ups and downs enough that beginners may find themselves stretched to the limits; intermediate pedalers should find the challenges just about right. Details: Heart of England Tourist Board, PO Box 15, Worcester WR1 2JT, England (phone: 0905-29512), also at 2–4 Trinity St., Worcester WR1 2PW, England (phone: 0905-613132); and the Thames & Chilterns Tourist Board, the Mount House, Church Green, Witney, Oxfordshire 0X8 6DZ (phone: 0993-778800).

NORTH YORK MOORS, England: This roughly oval moorland plateau, barren-looking until the summer blossoming of heather makes it glow purple and blue, is broken up by inviting dales where cozy accommodations can be found. A 553-square-mile national park, bounded on the east by the North Sea, it is generally a country of sheep-dotted, stream-crossed pastures, with fine views in the uplands and tiny villages. National park information centers are at Danby Lodge, not far from Grosmont; in the market town of Pickering, the site of ruined Pickering Castle; and at Sutton Bank, on the western edge of the park, with magnificent views of the Vale of York. The roads between Pickering and Whitby and Whitby and Scarborough can be busy in summer, but most other north–south routes over the moors are quiet enough, and dead-end valley lanes are idyllic. Details: Yorkshire & Humberside Tourist Board, 312 Tadcaster Rd., York, North Yorkshire YO2 2HF, England (phone: 0904-707961).

PEAK DISTRICT, England: The Pennine Hills, England's great backbone, begin in this wild upland practically within shouting distance of the great industrial centers of the Midlands. The more southerly area offers steep-sided valleys; in the north, the characteristic formations are the sharp-edged gritstone cliffs that inspired Daniel Defoe to dub them the nation's Andes. Farther north, the Pennines become wilder, more remote, and harder to cycle. Details: East Midlands Tourist Board, Exchequergate, Lincoln, Lincolnshire LN2 1PZ, England (phone: 0522-531521).

SOUTHEAST, England: Even as close as this area is to London, the countryside is still given over to orchards and hop fields, woods, and farmlands green and fertile enough to warrant the nickname the "Garden of England." Most cycling is on roads and country lanes through the ranges of low chalk hills known as the North and South Downs, which stretch eastward to the high cliffs on the shores of the English Channel and are separated by The Weald — the farm- and village-dotted remains of a once-large regional forest. At practically every turn, the land is fine for beginning cyclists. Much of the area has been designated an "Area of Outstanding Natural Beauty"; Canterbury, Chichester, Guildford, and Rochester Cathedrals, the area associated with the Norman invasion and the Battle of Hastings, and a number of seacoast castles and fortifications are among the points of interest. Details: South East England Tourist Board, 1 Warwick Pk., Tunbridge Wells, Kent TN2 5TA, England (phone: 0892-40766).

LAKE DISTRICT, England: Unquestionably one of England's grandest regions, this mountain mass, its valleys bejeweled with lakes, is a favorite among Britain's national parks — and with reason: The ravines and their sapphire tarns, and the volcanic peaks, stark and jagged, sometimes rising abruptly from just above sea level so that they seem even bigger than they really are, create an effect of striking grandeur. Considering the manmade landscape as well — the velvety pastures laced with lichen-splotched drystone walls, the antique farmhouses, and the lovely villages — it's not hard to see why William Wordsworth, a native son whose various cottages are preserved and open for tours, was so inspired (as were countless other poets and artists down through the years). The hills can be steep — but then, some of those whistle-fast descents from the tops rank among the country's most exhilarating. Despite the area's popularity, there are still plenty of quiet roads. To detour farther from the beaten path, a good bet is the Cumbria Cycle Way, wending along the Smugglers' Coast and through the secluded hamlets of the Eden Valley. There are information offices throughout Cumbria. Details: Cumbria Tourist Board, Ashleigh, Holly Road, Windermere, Cumbria LA23 2AQ, England (phone: 0966-24444).

SOUTHWEST, England: From the cathedral cities and Stonehenge, on the Salisbury Plain, to the New Forest, through the peaceful towns of Dorset (Thomas Hardy's Wessex), and on to the Somerset and Devon uplands — among them Exmoor and Dartmoor — and rugged Cornwall, the southwest of England will challenge even expert cyclists, though less so along the coast than throughout the hilly inland areas. But toward Land's End the scenery rewards cyclists amply for their efforts. The villages are lovely, the vistas unfailingly grand or pastoral, the traditional cream teas scrumptious, and the seacoast wonderfully varied. There are desolate moors, medieval churches, and the prehistoric ruins described in *Ancient Monuments and Ruins.* Details: West Country Tourist Board, Trinity Ct., 37 Southernhay E, Exeter, Devon EX1 1QS, England (phone: 0392-76351).

YORKSHIRE DALES, England: Rivers flowing down from high in the Pennine Hills have cut out a wondrous landscape of steep mountains and deep valleys whose finer points are not well known even in Britain. Like Teesdale, the northernmost of the dales, most boast impressive waterfalls. Swaledale is generally ranked as one of the lovelier dales, but the others have their particular charms as well: Wensleydale, its local cheese; austere, lonely-looking Wharfedale; Nidderdale, with its impressive How Stean gorge; Airedale, with its spectacular Craven Country, Malham Cove's gigantic limestone bluffs, and the heavily visited Gordale Scar gorge; and not too well known Ribblesdale, in the center of the Pennines, where there are abundant potholes and waterfalls — to name only a few. Nearly 700 square miles of this water-carved wonderland have been designated as a national park. Details: Yorkshire & Humberside Tourist Board, 312 Tadcaster Rd., York, North Yorkshire YO2 2HF, England (phone: 0904-707961).

NORTHEAST, England: Apart from a few urban areas near the coast, this is a quiet, sparsely populated region that boasts more ancient remains and medieval castles than any other part of Britain: Hadrian's Wall, Bamburgh Castle, Alnwick Castle, Dunstanbugh Castle, Lindisfarne Priory, Durham Cathedral, the 8th-century churches at Hexham and Jarrow, and Scotland's Melrose, Jedburgh, and Kelso abbeys (described in *Ancient Monuments and Ruins*) are among the notable sites. Roads through the grass-covered Cheviot Hills offer particularly challenging cycling; the rest of the area, mainly given over to forests, farms, and beaches, is more rolling. Details: Northumbria Tourist Board, Aykley Heads, Durham City, Durham DH1 5UX, England (phone: 0913-846905).

WELSH MARCHES, England: In this area between Chepstow, on the Bristol Channel to the south, and Liverpool Bay, just north of Chester, the green and gentle hills of the valley of the meandering Wye and the country north of that offer some pleasant cycling. There's the Forest of Dean, the wild woods between the rivers Severn and Wye; Hay-on-Wye, a town full of second-hand bookshops, including "the world's largest"; the Shropshire Hills; and historical towns like the ancient religious center of Hereford, picturesque Ludlow, and Shrewsbury, full of half-timbered houses. Castles and abbeys are abundant. In few places in England will visitors find so little motor traffic. Details: Heart of England Tourist Board, PO Box 15, Worcester, Hereford & Worcester WR1 2JT, England (phone: 0905-29512); also at 2–4 Trinity St., Worcester WR1 2PW, England (phone: 0905-613132).

HIGHLANDS, Scotland: This region of ridges and glens, many loch-filled, are really restricted to cyclists with plenty of pedal power and a love of wilderness wandering: There are relatively few major roads (though hundreds of miles of narrow lanes), particularly in the west, and those that exist get somewhat more crowded during the summer; outside the main towns, there are few bicycle shops, so it's necessary to carry all spares. The rewards are many, however: the northwest coast, looking much like Norway with its fjords; the vistas of snow-capped peaks; the islands, where it is flatter, less crowded, and even wilder; ancestral castles with long histories of the Scottish clans; and vast blue lakes like Loch Ness, Loch Long, and Loch Lochy — to name only a few. Details and advice: Hi-Line, Bridgend Rd., Dingwall, Ross-shire IV15 9SL, Scotland (phone: 44-349-63434).

NORTH, Wales: Apart from the highway along the north coast, the roads here — as elsewhere in the country — are not at all heavily trafficked as they twist and climb into wild, mysterious mountains that are some of the most beautiful in all of Britain — slate brown and full of foaming rivers, huge smooth lakes, castles, and prehistoric sites. The Isle of Anglesey, across a narrow channel to the north, is more rural than rugged, making for a pleasant contrast. Details: North Wales Regional Office, Wales Tourist Board, Colwyn Bay, 77 Conway Rd., Colwyn Bay, Clwyd LL29 7LN, Wales (phone: 0492-531731 or -534626 for lodging reservations).

MID AND SOUTH WALES: Inland, the terrain is peaceful: Farms are interspersed with patches of woods; rolling hills climb out of pastoral valleys; the neat hamlets scattered here and there are woven together by country lanes and "rough stuff" tracks — unsurfaced but bikeable by the adventurous. But in the south, the countryside is dramatic. There are the mountains of the Brecon Beacons, with their thundering cascades, lakes, forests, moorlands, passes, and deeply incised valleys rich in industrial and cultural heritage; and the Pembrokeshire coast, where mountains plunge to the sea and rocky headlands are interspersed with delightful sandy beaches punctuated by ancient towns such as Cardigan, Pembroke and its castle, St. Davids with its historic cathedral, and delightful Terby. For intermediate cyclists, this is Wales's must — an experience of a lifetime, to boot. Worth a look is the new National Mountain Bike Centre at Llanwrtyd Wells, which stages a number of "fat tyre" competitions in season. Details: Mid Wales Regional Office, Wales Tourist Board, Canolfan Owain Glyndwr, Machynlleth, Powys SY20 8EE, Wales (phone: 0654-2401), and the South Wales Regional Office, Wales Tourist Board, Ty Croeso, Gloucester Pl., Swansea, West Glamorgan SA1 1TY, Wales (phone: 0792-465204).

HOW TO PLAN A TOUR

After choosing a region to explore, it's a fairly easy matter to sketch out an itinerary. For ideas, review local tourist literature and articles about touring in bicycling magazines such as the following:

Cycle Touring, published bimonthly by the Cyclists' Touring Club, Cotterell House, 69 Meadrow, Godalming, Surrey GU7 3HS, England (phone: 0486-87217). \$2.30/£1.50 per copy on newsstands or from the club.

Cycling World, published by Stone Industrial Publications, Ltd., 2a Granville Rd., Sidcup, Kent DA14 4BN, England (phone: 01-302-6150 or 01-302-6069). \$1.80/£1.20 per copy on the newsstands, or \$2.75/£1.80, including postage, from the publisher.

Also consult specialized bikers' books such as the following:

Bike Touring by Raymond Bridge. \$8.95 from Sierra Club, San Francisco.

The Cyclists' Touring Club's Route Guide to Cycling in Britain and Ireland by Christa Gausden and Nicholas Crane lists 365 connecting routes based on minor roads and lanes throughout Britain that are suitable for tours lasting anywhere from a single day to several months. \$12/£7.95 from the Oxford Illustrated Press, Sparkford, Yeovil, Somerset BA22 7JJ, England (phone: 0963-40635).

Cycling World magazine also publishes a *Bed & Breakfast Series* outlining routes and facilities for lodging, camping, and cycle rental (\$3/£2 each).

Weekend Cycling by Christa Gausden. \$10.60/£6.95 from Oxford Illustrated Press.

Once a general itinerary has been sketched, plot out the tour on a large-scale highway map of the country — the sort of map supplied by a national tourist office. Base the daily mileage on the distance usually covered on the road at home, but be sure to allot time for en-route dawdling — chatting with the locals, long stops for admiring the panoramas from a picnic spot, walks through ruined abbeys, and the like.

Then tackle detailed route finding with small-scale topographical maps that will not only display the smallest country lanes, but also indicate the contours of the land and the steepness of the hills throughout the area to be covered. The 1:100,000-scale Leisure Map (\$4/£2.50 from John Bartholomew & Son, 12 Duncan St., Edinburgh EH9 1TA, Scotland; phone: 031-667-9341), key contours to colors and are excellent; they can be ordered directly from the company or from the Cyclists' Touring Club (address above). These can be used in conjunction with lodging guides, such as the BTA publications *Britain: Stay on a Farm; Britain: Stay at an Inn;* and *Cycling;* as well as the CTC's annual handbook for members, which lists not only some 3,000 inexpensive hotels and bed-and-breakfast establishments that extend particularly warm welcomes to cyclists but also bicycle repair shops throughout the country. The CTC Touring Department also provides its members with excellent help in planning trips.

CYCLING HOLIDAYS

Several organizations in Britain offer inclusive packages that include bed and breakfast, bikes, itineraries, and niceties such as repair kits; sometimes luggage is transported to the next night's destination as well. Among them are the following:

Bicycle Beano, 59 Birch Hill Rd., Clehonger, Hereford HR2 9RF, Wales (phone: 0981-251087). Small-group camping and biking tours of mid-Wales and the Welsh Borders. No frills, but rich in spirit.

Bike Events, PO Box 75, Bath, Avon BA1 1BX, England (phone: 0225-310859). The best known recreational cycling organization in the country, this outfit arranges the London-to-Brighton Bike Ride, a 1-day event, which usually is held in mid-June, listed in the *Guinness Book of World Records* as the world's largest of its type (33,906 people participated in 1989). They also organize a variety of adventure rides, including the Great British Bike Ride (Land's End to John O'Groats). Participants receive route maps and full back-up service, and all baggage is transported in a truck.

Cadence Café and Cycle Hire, Worcester Foregate Street Station, Foregate St., Worcester WR1 1DB, England (phone: 0905-613501). Cycling tours from 1-day to full holidays arranged for cyclists at all levels. A full range of equipment is available for hire.

Cyclists' Touring Club, Cotterell House, 69 Meadrow, Godalming, Surrey GU7 3H7, England (phone: 04868-7217). Tours organized by club members.

Cyclorama Holidays, The Grange Hotel, Grange-over-Sands, Cumbria LA11 6EJ, England (phone: 04484-3666). Cycle tours through the Lake District with accommodations in guesthouses and hotels and a sag wagon to transfer gear between overnight stops. A joy for cyclists who want to enjoy superb English countryside, the scenery is wonderfully varied, and there are many places to visit en route. There is a choice of routes with distances to suit individual abilities. Bikes can be supplied, or those who prefer to bring their own can do so. Holidays for cyclists are usually 7 or 8 days long.

East Anglia Cycling Holidays, Ballintuim Post Office, Blairgowrie, Perthshire PH10 7NJ, Scotland (phone: 0250-86201). Run by the same lovely people who run *Scottish Cycling Holidays* (see below), this company provides self-led inclusive tours along the quiet country and coastal byroads of southeast England's East Anglia region — ideal cycling country. Accommodations in pubs, inns, or guesthouses. Cycles and gear can also be supplied.

Pedlars Cycle Tours, c/o Nova Scotia Travel, PO Box 16, Winsford, Cheshire CW7 1AF, England (phone: 0606-592173). Hires tandems and can recommend the best routes around this delightfully green pocket of England. Arranges bikes, itineraries, accommodations, and "collection" for those who break down or lose their way.

Peninsula Bike Tours and Expeditions, Church View Cottage, Church Rd., Bebington, Wirral, Cheshire L63 3DY, England (phone: 051-645-3927). Cycling holidays in Cheshire, North Wales, and Snowdonia.

Scottish Cycling Holidays, Ballintuim Post Office, Blairgowrie, Perthshire PH10 7NJ, Scotland (phone: 025086-201). Inclusive self-led cycling tours throughout Scotland, with multi-speed touring cycles specially geared for the terrain supplied, along with all equipment. Accommodations in a hotel of any standard, guesthouse, or youth hostel, with routes planned accordingly. Cyclists can be picked up at Glasgow or Edinburgh airports.

Youth Hostels Association, Trevelyan House, 8 St. Stephen's Hill, St. Albans, Hertfordshire AL1 2DY, England (phone: 0727-55215). Group trips to favored biking destinations in England and Wales.

Stalking and Shooting

Men have been making sport of their search for game, both large and small, since the time of the pharaohs (who were so enamored of the activity that they looked forward to continuing it in the afterlife) — and the sport's devotees in Britain are no less enthusiastic. In fact, the Glorious Twelfth (of August, of course), which marks the opening of the shooting season for grouse, is something of a national day of festivity in Britain.

But grouse are only one quarry. Also available are species ranging from rabbits and pigeons to wildfowl and pheasants (which were first brought to Britain by the Romans). Scotland and Northern England are known all over the world for their red grouse shooting, and sportsmen from the far corners of the globe come here to participate in shoots at which teams of beaters drive the birds over a line of concealed guns, or to flush them out with the aid of dogs — pointers or setters. (This is known as driven shooting and is distinct from rough shooting, which requires that the huntsman seek out the quarry himself.) Woodcock, some of them resident in Britain and others that overfly the islands during their fall migrations, are another favorite target, challenging because of their predilection for flying erratically between trees. Also sought after are capercaillie, which inhabit pine and fir forests, and fast-flying, unpredictable snipe, which favor marshy areas and are numerous in the boggy country of Wales, Norfolk, and Scotland's Western Isles.

Pheasant shooting is of excellent quality and good value, often with the possibility of guaranteed bags. For a party of six to nine guns, 100- to 250-bird days are typical. These are usually driven out of woodland to the standing guns, and bookings are generally made with a bag expectancy in mind.

Shoreline duck and goose hunting is a chancy affair, and access is fairly unrestricted throughout most of Britain. The principal areas are the Solway Firth in southwest Scotland and The Wash on the east coast of England. However, there are good areas for duck and goose hunting inland, particularly in Scotland for geese. In winter, wildfowlers position themselves by rivers and estuaries to catch the birds at dawn as they fly out to rest and at dusk when they fly inland in search of food.

In Scotland, sportsmen enjoy stalking, the taking of deer with a rifle, as well as shooting. Stalking involves the hunter's creeping up on the animal, taking advantage of all available cover — often over a period of several hours and a distance of several miles — until he is within 120 to 180 yards of it. Though this can be a very expensive proposition, it is one of the most exciting sports that the United Kingdom has to offer, and even though the red deer trophies taken here are not generally as large as those on the Continent, many a sportsman prizes his Scottish trophies far more than larger ones taken more easily. Roebuck and Sika stag trophies are often far superior to continental Europe's because of more selective shooting over the years. The most widely available in Britain, roebuck stalking is also the best value. And the delights afforded by the scenery — everything from flat heather moors to mountainous rocky countryside and wooded farmland — may even outweigh the pleasures of the sport.

For hunting in England, Scotland, and Wales, proper firearms certificates or licenses must be obtained by visitors from overseas; arrangements can be made through reputable agents, such as a holiday tour organizer, with a minimum of a month's notice. Game licenses, available from all main and branch post offices, are also required for most quarry, with the major exceptions of duck, wood pigeon, rabbit, and deer, which are not considered "game."

Shooting and stalking are permitted only during certain seasons, mainly in autumn and winter; dates vary with the quarry. Open season is August 12 to December 10 for grouse, October 1 to February 1 for pheasant, and September 1 to February 1 for partridge (an East Anglian specialty). Deer seasons depend on species and sex. In addition, no shooting of any kind is allowed on Sundays in Scotland, and no shooting of game is permitted on Sundays and on Christmas Day in the rest of Britain.

BOOKING AGENCIES: These organizations can send the particulars describing several estates, including the details of the shooting and fairly complete descriptions of available accommodations. Most shoots are organized for groups of six to eight, and it's common for friends to get together to form a shoot; if a sportsman can't make up a party on his own, the agents can usually fit him into someone else's. (Though, quite naturally, most groups are wary of having an inexperienced sportsman in their midst because of the danger of injury.) The organizers can advise visitors in advance about open seasons and license requirements.

A & C Sporting Services, Burnside Lodge, Port Wenyss, Isle of Islay, Scotland (phone: 0496-86296). U.S. representative: Wild Wing Adventures Ltd., 746 Main St., Monroe, CT 06468 (phone: 203-268-3193).

Macsport Ltd., Macsport House, Ballater Rd., Aboyne, Aberdeenshire AB3 5HT, Scotland (phone: 0339-2896).

Major Neil Ramsay & Co., Tay Terrace, Dunkeld, Perthshire PH8 0AQ, Scotland (phone: 03502-8991).

Peter Readman Sporting Agent, Hirsel Law, Coldstream, Berwickshire TD12 4HX, Scotland (phone: 0890-2139).

Sport in Scotland, Ltd., 22 Market Brae, Inverness, Highland IV2 3AB, Scotland (phone: 0463-222757).

Strutt & Parker Sporting Agency, 13 Hill St., Berkeley Sq., London W1X 8DL, England (phone: 01-629-7282).

Tours and Travel Promotions, 25 Brunstane Dr., Edinburgh EH15 2NF, Scotland (phone: 031-669-5344).

Travel Scotland, 10 Rutland Sq., Edinburgh EH1 2AS, Scotland (phone: 031-229-7366).

HOTELS FOR SHOOTING HOLIDAYS: A number of hotels located in the richest shooting areas can also organize shooting holidays for their guests, among them are the following:

Arundell Arms, Lifton, Devon PL16 0AA, England (phone: 0566-84666). The well-organized program at this sportsman's hotel includes 4-day shoots for driven snipe, as well as driven pheasant shoots, duck flighting, rough and woodcock shooting, and red and roe deer stalking. See also *Rural Retreats.*

Deer Park, West Honiton, Devon EX14 OPG, England (phone: 0404-41266). This Georgian manor, set in 40 acres of Devonshire countryside, can arrange all forms of game shooting, from driven duck to clay shooting. Private fishing is also available (see *Gone Fishing*).

Golden Pheasant, Glynceiriog, near Chirk, Llangollen, Clwyd LL20 7BB, Wales (phone: 069-172-281). Perched in the Berwyn Mountains, one of the finest areas in Wales for shooting high and fast pheasant as well as blackcock, another area specialty. There is also sport for grouse, partridge, and duck from August to November. To arrange for shooting, contact Geoff T. Turner, Aelybryn, Dolywern, near Llangollen, Clwyd LL20 7BB, Wales (phone: 069-172630).

Invereshie House, Kincraig, Kingussie, Highland PH21 1NA, Scotland (phone: 05404-332). Occupying a lovely Georgian building at the foot of the Cairngorm mountains, overlooking Loch Insh and the river Spey, this establishment was built as a shooting lodge in the 1690s, and there is still an abundance of game for shooting and stalking — primarily the magnificent red deer in autumn. (See also *Rural Retreats.*)

Tweed Valley, Walkerburn, Borders EH43 6AA, Scotland (phone: 0896-87636). This former Edwardian country house, with beautiful views of the river Tweed and its valley, can arrange for grouse, pheasant, and mixed shooting as well as for roebuck and Sika deer stalking.

GENERAL INFORMATION: There are a number of sources a sports-minded visitor should contact for more details about shooting-oriented holidays. These include the following:

British Field Sports Society, 59 Kennington Rd., London SE1 7PZ, England (phone: 01-928-4742). A membership organization devoted to hunting, shooting, and fishing, the society can provide lists of shooting agents in the United Kingdom.

Clay Pigeon Shooting Association, 107 Epping New Rd., Buckhurst Hill, Essex IG9 5TQ, England (phone: 01-505-62212). Governs and provides information about the sport in England.

Scottish Clay Pigeon Association, 10 Balgibbon Callander, Perthshire FK17 8EU, Scotland (phone: 0877-31323). Scotland's sister organization to the above.

Scottish Sporting Gazette, 22 Market Brae, Inverness IV2 3AB, Scotland (phone: 0463-222757). A glossy 110-page annual ($10, including airmail) filled with articles on all aspects of Scottish hunting and fishing; advertisements for private hunting estates, country hotels, gunshops, and the like complete the coverage.

Great Walks and Mountain Rambles

Almost any walker will say that it is the footpaths of a country — not its roadways — that show off the landscape to best advantage. Closer to earth than when driving or even biking, those on foot notice details that might not otherwise come to their attention: incredibly tiny wildflowers blossoming cheerfully in a crack between limestone boulders, for instance, or a fox lurking in the shadows of the woods at dawn. There is an enormous range of landscapes, from the sub-Arctic Cairngorms to the tropical gardens at Inverewe, from volcanic forms to dumpling-like Ice Age deposits — and on any given day on the trail, the walker may traverse whole geological epochs.

And the scenery moves by at a relatively slow speed: Hedgerows, fences, and the green velvet pastures can be contemplated at leisure. Churches and barns, old windmills and lichen-crusted stone walls, and farms and villages are seldom far out of sight when treading in the footsteps of Neolithic man or Bronze Age gold traders, traveling along Roman ways, or following tracks first defined by smugglers, cattle drovers, abbots, or coffin carriers, whose ways would often be marked at the tops of passes by the stone piles where they rested their load. Many paths were literally walked into existence by generations of country folk traveling to work, market, church, or the ale house, and in all, over 100,000 miles of public footpaths have been recorded and mapped (a number that swells still further when those in Scotland, where the laws do not require that they be mapped and measured, are considered).

In England and Wales, many footpaths are in the 10 national parks and nearly 40 Areas of Outstanding Natural Beauty (AONB). The national parks, which cover some 5,256 square miles, about 9% of the total acreage of England and Wales, contain some of their most spectacular scenery, a blend of mountain and moor, down and heathland, cliffs and seashore, and all offering plenty of relatively wild mileage for the pedestrian. The land is not owned by the state, as in some countries, but remains in private hands, so that walkers must stick to the public rights-of-way unless a so-called access agreement exists, permitting otherwise (as in over half of Dartmoor and the Lake District, for example). Local planning authorities, responsible for the parks' administration, protect their landscape, clear away eyesores, keep footpaths passable, regulate vehicular traffic, appoint wardens, and alert the public to their recreational potential. AONBs enjoy a looser measure of legal protection. The Countryside Commission, the body responsible for designating these especially scenic areas, has also created several official long-distance trails by negotiating new rights-of-way and linking them to established footpaths. Each of these trails is highlighted by signposts, which announce its beginning and its direction, and by waymarkings, acorn symbols placed at potentially confusing junctures. (The Countryside Commission now advocates a standard system of marking throughout the country, using yellow arrows for footpaths and blue ones for bridleways.)

In Scotland, walkers won't be rambling in national parks as in England, because there are none, despite the fact that the scenery is some of Britain's loveliest and most varied — mountains and moors, lochs, grassy hills, forests and glens, cliffs and sandy beaches, and very few people. The law regarding rights-of-way is complex — and in principle walking just anywhere is not allowed. But in practice, it is possible for walkers to roam more or less freely as long as they respect the obviously off-limits, and keep off the moors during the early August through late October grouse-shooting and deer-stalking season.

The whole experience can be enormously rewarding — even when the weather turns rainy, as it often does at the height of the British summer (which King Charles II once gloomily described as 'three fine days followed by a thunderstorm). But come prepared. Stout walking shoes or boots are essential, as is a good rain parka with leggings. And in addition to the usual walker's gear, a spare sweater is essential, even on a day hike — especially on the British hills, where conditions can turn literally arctic within a matter of hours. Both hiking and backpacking equipment are best bought in the US, where the selection is greater and prices are lower.

WHERE TO WALK

Visitors don't have to dismiss the idea of walking in Britain just because they're not hotshot mountaineers at home. Even novices can share the delights: Just find a hotel in the heart of good walking country, and use it as home base for daily expeditions; at the end of each day, there'll be a hot bath and a hearty meal.

Areas that offer these experiences are delightfully abundant. Among Areas of Outstanding Natural Beauty, a number are really good for walking: the path-crossed, beechwoods-dotted chalk uplands known as the Chilterns, which roll through parts of Bedfordshire, Buckinghamshire, Hertfordshire, and Oxfordshire (for details, contact the Thames & Chilterns Tourist Board, The Mount House, Church Green, Witney, Oxfordshire 0X8 60Z, England; phone: 0993-778800); the 582 square miles of the oh-so-English Cotswolds, full of cozy villages, extending through the counties of Avon, Gloucestershire, Hereford and Worcester, Oxfordshire, and Wiltshire (Heart of England Tourist Board, 2–4 Trinity St., Worcester WR1 2PW, England; phone: 0905-613132); rolling Dorset, with the "far from the madding crowd" scenery of novelist Thomas Hardy and its fine seaside scenery (West Country Tourist Board, Trinity Ct., 37 Southernhay East, Exeter, Devon EX1 1QS, England; phone: 0392-76351); the distinctive Norfolk Coast, a delight to those whose souls resonate to its moody expanses of salt marshes and tidal creeks (East Anglia Tourist Board, Toppesfield Hall, Hadleigh, Suffolk IP7 5DN, England; phone: 0473-822922); the meandering Wye Valley and the Forest of Dean, where there are woodlands and lovely cliffs and gorges along the river to be explored (Heart of England Tourist Board, above). The Wye Valley continues through Wales, the country that is home to the breezy Gower Peninsula, where it's possible to tramp through the coastal dunes and beach country or head inland up into the hills (South Wales Regional Office, Wales Tourist Board, Ty Croeso, 6 Gloucester Pl., Swansea, West Glamorgan SA1 1TY, Wales; phone: 0792-465204).

National parks offer still better experiences — and public transportation is good enough that you don't have to plan all your trips to end back at your starting point.

Despite Britain's dense population, it is remarkably easy to get on a train or bus and, in a few hours, be walking alone through as remote a landscape as can be found almost anywhere — no matter where the starting point. Within a morning's ride of London, for example, there are expanses of land unexploited by agriculture, let alone by industry, which appear just as they would have to Stone Age man. (Don't wait too long to enjoy them. Every year more than 100 square miles of countryside disappear under asphalt or concrete, are inundated by manmade reservoirs, or are spiked by chimneys and telecommunications masts.)

Some of the most interesting of Britain's walking country — at the moment — is described below:

DARTMOOR NATIONAL PARK, Devon, England: The "melancholy moor" of Arthur Conan Doyle's *Hound of the Baskervilles,* a granite upland with bare hills sometimes crowned with weather-wrinkled granite tors, is a beautiful yet mostly savage area, intensely lonely. But there are some 500 miles of foot and bridle paths and 180 square miles of open moorland on which walkers may wander freely. Adventurous perambulators beware: Steer clear of the large chunks in the north that form part of military firing ranges (marked on OS maps); avoid the marshes; and never venture onto the moor without a compass, spare clothing, and emergency rations. Details: Dartmoor National Park, Haytor Rd., Bovey Tracey, Devon TQ13 9JQ, England (phone: 0626-832093).

EXMOOR NATIONAL PARK, Devon and Somerset: Bounded on the north by the sea and a spectacular stretch of the South-West Peninsula Coast Path, the sandstone uplands of Exmoor are less harsh and more varied than Dartmoor: They are covered in grass or heather and bracken; riven by combes, or valleys, dense with scrub oak, birch, ash, elder, holly, and conifers; crisscrossed by lively rivers; patched with farmlands; and scattered with pretty villages. It is a rounded, curvacious world. "The land lies softly," said Lorna Doone. Red deer, a legacy of the days when central Exmoor was a royal hunting forest, can still be seen here, along with herds of wild ponies. Since Exmoor's open moorland is primarily restricted to the west, walkers are more restricted to defined routes than at Dartmoor, but there are still 600 miles of waymarked paths and bridleways from which to choose. Details: Exmoor National Park, Exmoor House, Dulverton, Somerset TA22 9HL, England (phone: 0398-23665).

LAKE DISTRICT NATIONAL PARK, Cumbria, England: This 880-square-mile area, within the county of Cumbria, is the largest of all the national parks. It is also one of the most beautiful, with jewellike lakes and steep mountains rising precipitously from close to sea level so that they seem even higher than they actually are, and dazzling colors, a function of the seasonal changes in vegetation. Poets and writers — among them Coleridge and Ruskin, Hugh Walpole and Beatrix Potter — have been inspired by the landscape for centuries; the area's fame has grown to such proportions that walkers can no longer expect to "wander lonely as a cloud" just everywhere — as did the 19th-century romantic poet William Wordsworth. To experience the real beauties of the Lake District, steer clear of the larger tourist centers such as Ambleside, Keswick, and Windermere; avoid weekends and public holidays; or go just a bit farther afield than everyone else — something that is not too difficult since there are hundreds of miles of footpaths here, ranging from nature trails and level walks along the lakeshore and in the valleys to the strenuous routes that cross the mountains from valley to valley. By tradition, visitors can go almost anywhere on the open highland, and with care, anyone can reach the summits of 3,206-foot Scafell, 3,054-foot Skiddaw, and 3,116-foot Helvellyn — three of the park's more noteworthy peaks. A number of leaflets describing walks from various starting points are available from the park's information office, and guided walks are also available. The best general guidebooks to the area are the *A. A. Ordnance Survey Leisure Guide to the Lake District* ($10.60/£6.95, available from Lake District National Park Visitor Centre, address below) and the *The Lake District National Park* official guide, published by the Countryside Commission (about $9/£13.75, available from the park office); the best footpath guides, which describe the way in delightful illustrated commentary, are in Alfred Wainwright's seven-volume *A Pictorial Guide to the Lakeland Fells* ($9.20/£6 per volume, from Titus Wilson; available through the park office). For general area information, contact the Park Management and Visitors Services National Park Office, Brockhole, Windermere, Cumbria LA23 1LJ, England (phone:

0966-26601); and the Cumbria Tourist Board, Ashleigh, Windermere, Cumbria LA23 2AQ, England (phone: 09662-4444).

NORTH YORK MOORS NATIONAL PARK, North Yorkshire, England: The site of the largest expanse of heather-covered moorland in England and Wales, this 553-square-mile park is a walker's paradise with 1,130 scenic miles of public footpaths. From rolling heather moors, which flower to even higher glory in August, to placid, rich green dales and vale plains full of market towns, villages, neat rows of cottages, and a peppering of distinctive farmhouses looking as solid as fortresses, it offers a naturally beautiful landscape that man's additions have only enhanced. Considering the additional visual rewards offered by the dramatic, cliff-lined coastline that edges the park on the east, it's not hard to understand why, each year, the area attracts some 137,000 visitors on an average summer Sunday. But once on the moors, except at Easter and during the summer, only the occasional sheep staring contentedly through the mists is to be seen. The Cleveland Way, a walk that consists of over 100 miles skirting the coast and the park's inland boundaries on its way around most of the circumference of the park, and the Esk Valley Walk, which follows the river Esk for 30 miles from its source on the high moors to the sea at Whitby, are among the longer footpaths, but there are many others. Details about the park and leaflets describing area long-distance walks are available from the park's Information Service, North York Moors National Park, The Old Vicarage, Bondgate, Helmsley, York YO6 5BP, England (phone: 0439-70657).

NORTHUMBERLAND NATIONAL PARK, Northumberland, England: This long, narrow 398-square-mile region, one of England's least populated, extends southward from the Scottish border, through the lonely sheep-spotted Cheviot Hills and the heather- and bracken-clad Simonside Hills, to Hadrian's Wall — the most spectacular legacy of Britain's 400-year Roman occupation, and one of the world's most important archaeological remains outside Greece and Italy (see *Ancient Ruins and Monuments*). The diversity of landscape results from a lively geological history whose players include the ancient volcano that created the Cheviots, the sea (which subsequently inundated the land), the monumental up-thrusting forces that created the highlands, and the glaciers that carved the terrain into an approximation of its present shape. The Pennine Way, one of the most difficult of England's long-distance footpaths (described below), is among the especially scenic trails in the park. Details: Northumberland National Park Information Service, Eastburn, South Park, Hexham, Northumberland NE46 1BS, England (phone: 0434-605555).

PEAK NATIONAL PARK, Derbyshire, England: An island of rugged countryside standing close to but aloof from the booming metropolises of Manchester, Sheffield, and Derby, the Peak National Park consists of green and grassy limestone uplands, known as the White Peak, and moorlands that form a horseshoe around it, the sharp-edged gritstone Dark Peak. The aggregation offers walking of every grade, from gentle strolls along the river valleys of, say, the Dove and Derwent, through limestone outcrop country, with its caverns and cliffs, to the bracing treks across the moors and wild peat bog of Kinder Scout, Bleaklow, and Black Hill. The Pennine Way begins at Edale, the southern end of the Pennine chain, and works its way up and over the tough plateau. Details: Peak National Park Office, Aldern House, Baslow Rd., Bakewell, Derbyshire DE4 1AE, England (phone: 0629-814321).

BRECON BEACONS NATIONAL PARK, Brecon, Powys, Wales: The national park is centered in southern Powys and extends into the neighboring counties of Dyfed, mid-Glamorgan, and Gwent. These 519 square miles of high hills, crags, and bleak moors in mid-Wales, with the lonely Black Mountain on the west and the flat-topped Black Mountains on the east, embody the sort of imposing area that most people either love or hate. Apart from summits, ridges, and moorland, it encompasses woodlands, farms, lakes, and the valley of the river Usk. Those who like their strolls low and level may enjoy the 30-mile-long Monmouthshire and Brecon Canal towpath. Offa's Dyke Path passes over the Black Mountains. Details: Information Officer, Brecon Beacons National Park, 7 Glamorgan St., Brecon, Powys LD3 7DP, Wales (phone: 0874-4437).

SNOWDONIA NATIONAL PARK, Gwynedd, Wales: Bordered on the west by the beaches and sand dunes of Cardigan Bay, this 838-square-mile expanse of mountains, glacier-scoured passes and valleys, lovely lakes, and white-foaming waterfalls is flecked with hill farms, solid little market towns, and sleepy villages. It is by no means the exclusive territory of climbers — who come here by the score to tackle 3,560-foot Snowdon (the loftiest summit in England and Wales) and the other 14 peaks over 3,000 feet in the challenging Snowdon range. It is also a hiker's paradise, and there are guided walks, nature trails, and scores of footpaths. Details: Snowdonia National Park Information Service, Penrhyndeudraeth, Gwynedd LL48 6LF, Wales (phone: 0766-770274), and, for lodging, the North Wales Tourism Marketing Bureau, 77 Conway Rd., Colwyn Bay, Clwyd LL29 7LN, Wales (phone: 0492-531731), and the Mid Wales Regional Office, Wales Tourist Board, Canolfan Owain Glyndwr, Machynlleth, Powys SY20 8EE, Wales (phone: 0654-2653).

STAR TREKS

If day tripping seems a bit tame, consider a walking tour along one of several long-distance footpaths in England and Wales. Thirteen of them have already been created by the Countryside Commission, and others are being planned. They are created by establishing new rights-of-way to link previously existing trails to form continuous, multi-mile stretches of public footpath, which are then signposted and, at shifts in directions and other potentially confusing points, waymarked with acorn symbols. In addition, there are over 70 other recreational walks devised by local county councils, rambling groups, and even individual enthusiasts eager to share their love of a particular corner of the English landscape, sometimes their own rural backyard. The number of these long-distance delights, both officially and informally arranged, is steadily increasing all the time.

One of the pleasures of traversing these routes is that, while they cover some of the nation's loveliest countryside, they're close enough to civilization that it's possible to stay overnight en route at small hotels, bed-and-breakfast establishments, or huts and mountaineering hostels — or to camp out with tent, sleeping bag, and cookstove. The Ramblers' Association (1–5 Wandworth Rd., Vauxhall, London SW8 2XX, England; phone: 01-582-6878) publishes an annually updated *Ramblers' Yearbook* (available to members, who pay a $15 fee to join), which lists 2,300 bed-and-breakfast houses convenient to long-distance footpaths. Camping is permitted, though it's essential to ask permission of the landowner before pitching a tent for the night, particularly where the surrounding land is cultivated, not only to avoid problems but also to make friends: More than one farmer has been known to show up in the morning bearing a pint of fresh milk for visiting campers to pour over their morning granola. For a free leaflet on long-distance footpaths, *Walking in Britain,* contact the British Tourist Authority or the Countryside Commission (Publications Despatch Department, 19 Albert Rd., Manchester M19 2EQ, England; phone: 061-224-6287). Also contact the Ramblers' Association (address above). A new guidebook series on long-distance routes in both England and Scotland, co-published by the Countryside Commission and Aurum Press, contains detailed maps and local information, available from the Countryside Commission (address above).

A number of walking guides, such as *Remote Walks Around Lakeland, Forty-Four Walks on the Island of Arran,* and *Walks on the Isle of Skye,* are available from the Westmorland Gazette, Attn. Book Publishing Dept., 22 Stricklandgate, Kendal, Cumbria LA9 4NE, England (phone: 0539-20555).

CLEVELAND WAY, from Helmsley to Filey, North Yorkshire, England: This horseshoe-shaped, 100-mile footpath bobs along over moors and down dales, then sweeps along the tops of the cliffs of the county's stunning coastline. The going, while not particularly rough, does demand more than either the North and South Downs trails or the Ridgeway (all described below), and, though rain is not a problem in this relatively dry corner of the nation, occasional chilly spells require warm clothing. For details, consult Ian Sampson's *The Cleveland Way* ($10.60/£6.95 from the Countryside Commission, address above).

COTSWOLD WAY, from Chipping Campden, Gloucestershire, to Bath, Avon, England: The attractions of this route, which runs along the crest of a limestone escarpment — one of those outside the purview of the Countryside Commission — include ever-changing skies, panoramic views out over wooded valleys and lush green fields, and frequent calls at the delightfully mellow yellow villages scattered here and there along the way. The pathway ends at the Roman baths themselves. *The Cotswold Way* by Mark B. Richards describes the route ($2.30/£1.50, or $3.35/£2.25 if ordering by mail from the US, from Thornhill Press, 24 Moorend Rd., Cheltenham, Gloucestershire GL53 0EU, England; phone: 0242-519137).

DALES WAY, from Ilkley, West Yorkshire, to Bowness-on-Windermere, Cumbria, England: Apart from a climb up and over the Pennines' watershed (where only fate determines whether a raindrop finds its way to the North Sea instead of the Irish), this 81-mile-long hike involves low-lying country along the banks of lovely clear rivers. For details, see Colin Speakman's *The Dales Way* ($5.80/£3.80 from Dalesman Publishing, Ltd., Clapham, Lancaster LA2 8EB, England; phone: 046-85225).

HADRIAN'S WALL, near Newcastle-upon-Tyne, Tyne & Wear, England: Constructed by the Emperor Hadrian in AD 122, this ancient Roman barrier against the barbarians survives only in parts: Some are buried by Newcastle, some have been used as a foundation for a military road, and some can be found embedded in the walls of churches and farmhouses in the vicinity. But forts, castles, turrets, signal stations, and other features remain, along with parts of the wall itself, and the Pennine Way actually follows it for 9 of its 73 miles across the neck of England from Wallsend to Bowness, near Carlisle, on the Solway Firth. While there is no continuous right of way along the whole of the wall, enthusiasts of the old can pursue it further on a footpath that runs for 28 miles from Sewingshields Farm, near Hexham, to Wallfoot, near Carlisle; there is a particularly impressive stretch between Chollerford and Gilsand. Accommodations are difficult to find and usually out of the way. Details: Northumberland National Park Information Service, Eastburn, South Park, Hexham, Northumberland NE46 1BS, England (phone: 0434-605555).

LONDON COUNTRYWAY, around London, England: Even the metropolis has its rural back door; this 200-mile circle shows it off. For details, see Keith Chesterton's *The London Countryway* (£5.95, about $9.10, from Constable & Co., 10 Orange St., Leicester Sq., London WC2H 7EG, England; phone: 01-930-0801).

NORTH DOWNS WAY, from Farnham, Surrey, to Dover, Kent, England: This 141-mile-long footpath travels through the rolling Surrey Hills and Kent Downs, along the crest of the North Downs, and across several rivers and highways to its end at Shakespeare Cliff, where the panorama is of the celebrated English Channel. In parts, the footpath follows the medieval Pilgrims' Way. The North Downs Way is similar to its cousin, the South Downs Way (described below), but has more nooks and crannies and fewer grand, obstacle-free stretches in which to develop a steady stride. But the going is relatively easy, as is access to London via train and bus. For details, consult Christopher John Wright's *A Guide to the Pilgrims' Way and the North Downs Way* (£7.95, about $12.80, from Constable, address above).

PENNINE WAY, from Edale, Derbyshire, England, to Kirk Yetholm, Borders, Scotland: The first of the official trails to be designated "expressly for those who seek the call of the hills and the lonely places," this track comprises 270 demanding, often extremely boggy miles, up the backbone of England to a point just north of the Scottish border, traversing the Pennines, the Peak District National Park, and the Cheviots en route. Challenging terrain, however, is not its only attribute; it also offers great diversity, traveling through eerie forests and over high peaks, down old pack horse and shepherds' tracks and old Roman roads, across several rivers, and along well-preserved portions of Hadrian's Wall to a point not far from the impressive fort at Housesteads. Waterfalls and peat bogs, fine views, limestone cliffs, ruined mines, and other landmarks all add still more variety to the pathway. But it's not for everyone: In all, more altitude is gained than climbing Everest, and the weather can be terrible (dangerous, at this latitude, at these altitudes). In addition, although bed-and-breakfast accommodations are plentiful along some of the route, they are scarce enough along other sections to make it essential to plan stops carefully — or to carry camping gear. But for experienced walkers, this famous footpath is a delight. Of the plethora of publications covering the route, one of the best is Tom Stephenson's *The Pennine Way* ($7.50 from Bernan-Unipub, 4611-F Assembly Dr., Lanham, MD 20706; phone: 301-459-7666).

RIDGEWAY, from Overton Hill, near Avebury, Wiltshire, to Ivinghoe Beacon, Buckinghamshire, England: Following the ancient Icknield Way and the Great Ridgeway, first trod by Neolithic man, this 85-mile-long footpath offers an abundance of ancient burial places, religious monuments, Iron Age hill forts, and other evidences of bygone days as it traverses farms, beech woods, and downlands. The section from Overton Hill to Goring has been designated a bridleway, permitting its use by cyclists and horseback riders as well as hikers, but at no point is the going particularly difficult. For details, consult Sean Jennett's *The Ridgeway Path* ($7.50 from Bernan-Unipub, address above).

SOUTH DOWNS WAY, from Eastbourne, Sussex, to Harting, near Petersfield, Hampshire, England: It's true enough that in his *Natural History of Selbourne* Gilbert White referred to the South Downs as "majestic mountains"; and, indeed, when standing on high and looking southward toward the sea or in the opposite direction, across the partly wooded Weald (the remains of an ancient forest), toward the North Downs, most hikers do feel themselves at the top of the world. Nonetheless, the 80-mile route through the range of chalk hills known as the South Downs offers relatively gentle walking. And there's no shortage of places to stay along the way. Most of the South Downs Way is also a bridleway, shared with cyclists and horseback riders — in fact, only the segment across the clifftops of the Seven Sisters near Eastborne is exclusive to walkers. For details, consult Sean Jennett's *South Downs Way* ($7.50 from Bernan-Unipub, address above), or the Society of Sussex Downsmen's *Along the South Downs Way,* which describes the route in both directions and on to Winchester ($3/£2, from Society of Sussex Downsmen, 254 Victoria Dr., Eastbourne, East Sussex BN20 8QT, England; phone: 0323-32227).

SOUTHWEST WAY, from Studland, Dorset, to Minehead, Somerset, England: For lovers of hours spent with the sea as a constant companion, this 567-mile track is not only England's longest long-distance footpath but also its best, and, except for its considerable number of ups and downs, the walking is not difficult. There are four sections: The shortest stretch, at 72 miles, is the Dorset Coast Path. Noted for its special, quiet loveliness, it consists essentially of high cliff walking, nearly always in sight of the sea. The South Devon Coast Path passes largely through the South Devon and East Devon Areas of Outstanding Natural Beauty, which are full of stunning headlands, broad rivers, busy resort towns, quiet bays, and lush greenery. The Cornwall Coast Path leads around Land's End, past spectacular cliffs, lighthouses, stone circles, and more resorts. And the Somerset and North Devon Coast Path, travels through 35 miles of Exmoor National Park, from Minehead into the North Devon Area of Outstanding Natural Beauty as far as Marsland Mouth, bordering Cornwall. The trip is not strenuous, as long as the Woody Bay-to-Coombe Martin leg and the last slog before Marsland Mouth are discounted. On a clear day, the fortunate can catch a glimpse of Wales from Foreland Point and Selworthy Beacon.

Along the length of the path, accommodations and campsites are easy to find. But since this is a resort area, reserve ahead for visits during school holidays.

For more information, consult the Sou'West Way Association's *Complete Guide to the Coastal Path* ($4.50/£2.95 from the Sou'West Way Association, 1 Orchard Dr., Kingskerswell, Newton Abbot, Devon TQ12 5DG, England; phone: 08047-3061), and H. D. Westacott's *South Devon Coast Path,* Edward Pyatt's *Cornwall Coast Path,* and Brian Le Messurier's *South Devon Coast Path* ($7.50 each from Bernan-Unipub, address above).

WOLDS WAY, from Filey, North Yorkshire, to North Ferriby, Humberside, England: This long-distance footpath traverses considerable agricultural land and follows the chalk hills and pretty valleys of the Yorkshire Wolds for 71 miles, from the eastern terminus of the Cleveland Way to the banks of the river Humber to the south. For details, consult David Rubinstein's *The Wolds Way* (£2.80, about $4.30, from Dalesman, address above) or Roger Ratcliffe's *Wolds Way* ($7.50 from Bernan-Unipub, address above).

OFFA'S DYKE PATH, from near Chepstow, Gwent, to Prestatyn, Clwyd, Wales: For 60 of its total 168 miles, this Welsh track follows the distinctive earthwork built in the 8th century by King Offa of Mercia as a frontier between England and Wales. It meanders through the Shropshire Hills and Wye Valley Areas of Outstanding Natural Beauty; climbs up into the imposing Black Mountains; passes through Hay-on-Wye, the town of books (see *Shopping*); and eventually tracks a high ridge through the Clwydian Hills. The walking can be demanding in spots; the terrain is wonderfully varied, taking in everything from wild hills to wooded valleys and peaceful lowlands. For details, consult Christopher John Wright's *A Guide to Offa's Dyke Path* (£7.95, about $12.20, from Constable); Mark Richard's *Through the Welsh Borders Country Following the Offa's Dyke Path* (£4.50, about $7, from Thornhill Press, address above); and the Offa's Dyke Association's *Offa's Dyke Path South* and *Offa's Dyke Path North* (each £6.95, about $11, from the Countryside Commission, address above). For more information on the South Wales region bordered by the path, contact the South Wales Regional Office, Wales Tourist Board, Ty Croeso, 6 Gloucester Pl., Swansea, West Glamorgan SA1 1TY, Wales (phone: 0792-465204).

PEMBROKESHIRE COAST PATH, from St. Dogmaels to Amroth, Dyfed, Wales: Despite the beauty of the wild seascapes of this southwestern part of the country, the area has remained unspoiled by visitors, and often it's possible to walk for many hours along this 180-mile-long footpath without meeting a soul. Not the least of its special offerings, it also provides wonderful scenery: limestone and sandstone cliffs, windswept headlands, jagged inlets and coves, splendid beaches, and blue water (warm in summer, icy the rest of the year). The walking varies from easy to the occasionally strenuous. For details, consult John Barrett's *The Pembrokeshire Coast Path* ($8.95 from Bernan-Unipub, address above), and the National Park (address below) publishes a series of ten Coast Path cards, a mileage chart, and other informational pieces. Also: Pembrokeshire Coast National Park, County Offices, Haverfordwest, Dyfed SA61 1QZ, Wales (phone: 0437-4591).

MAPS AND MORE INFORMATION

When Daniel Boone was once asked whether he had ever been lost, he replied, "Nope, but I was a mite confused once for three days." To avoid that fate, and to help plan a trip, it's essential to have the proper maps and guidebooks.

Some of the most beautiful areas of Britain are covered by 1-inch-to-1-mile Tourist maps and by 1:25,000-scale Outdoor Leisure maps. These are the best choices for those regions for which they exist. Elsewhere, consult the relevant 1:50,000 Ordnance Survey maps. Rights-of-way are indicated by red lines (the dotted lines referring to footpaths, the dashes to bridleways). These symbols and the many others are explained in an elaborate key, a brief study of which will have anyone with even a little aptitude reading these British plans as well as, if not better than, the far less colorful US Geological Survey maps.

In addition, virtually every defined trail in Britain is also covered by one or more step-by-step guidebooks. To find out exactly what's available and what you need, contact the Ramblers' Association (1–5 Wandsworth Rd., London SW8 2XX, England; phone: 01-582-6878) for copies of county Fact Sheets (75p, about $1.20 each, postpaid), which list relevant guidebooks and maps for the main walking areas of the country and include a practical guide to waymarking — an essential for someone who doesn't know the system. Authoritative general books on walking in Britain, such as H. D. Westacott's *The Walker's Handbook* (£2.50, about $3.85, from Penguin), provide information for footpaths, AONBs, and national parks throughout England, Scotland, and Wales.

A good magazine for the hiking enthusiast is *The Great Outdoors,* published monthly by Holmes McDougall, Ltd., Ravenseft House, 302–304 St. Vincent St., Glasgow G2 5NL, Scotland (phone: 03552-42464), which is available by direct subscription and from most major newsstands and outdoor equipment shops. In addition to both informative and descriptive articles on hiking, backpacking, and cycling, each issue includes a useful directory that lists stores specializing in outdoor equipment; reviews of equipment, maps, local guidebooks, and other books; and advertisements for equipment rental agencies and organizations that sponsor walking tours.

As background reading, try to locate a copy of John Hillaby's *A Walk Through Britain* (Houghton Mifflin Co.; currently out of print).

Many useful hiking publications and maps can be bought at *Edward Stanford Ltd.,* 12 Long Acre, London WC2E 9LP, England (phone: 01-836-1321).

GROUP TRIPS

Those who don't want to go it alone — or do all the requisite planning — should contact the following organizations about group treks:

Countrywide Holidays Association, Cromwell Range, Manchester M14 6HU, England (phone: 0612-251000). Founded in 1893, this is Britain's first outdoor and recreational holiday organization, and it owns and operates 14 country houses and coastal hotels in prime walking areas throughout the UK. In addition to long-distance walks, packages include accommodations at one of a number of unusual centers and day trips into the surrounding countryside with an experienced guide.

English Wanderer, Stephen Summers, 13 Wellington Ct., Spencers Wood, Reading, Berkshire RG7 1BN, England (phone: 0734-882515). Guided walking through the hills of England, Scotland, Wales, and Ireland. Walks also available in Herriott, Wordsworth, and Hardy Country. There's also an "In Search of King Arthur" walk. Two- to 14-day trips are offered and accommodations in small country inns and hotels are available.

Footpath Holidays, 4 Holly Walk, Andover, Hampshire SP10 3PJ, England (phone: 0264-52689). Rambles of 5 and 7 nights, approximately 10 miles a day along established footpaths, many in National Parks. Tours are led by experienced guides, and accommodations are available in country hotels.

HF Holidays, Ltd., 142–144 Great North Way, London NW4 1EG, England (phone: 01-203-3381). Choose from an easy, moderate, or strenuous walk, accompanied by a local leader. Accommodations are in 16 beautiful country houses and include evening entertainment. Also available are "Go As You Please" holidays for the independent walker who just wants to use the house(s) as a base.

Lord Winston's Walking Tours, East Wing, The Manor, Moreton Pinkney, Daventry NN11 6SJ, England (phone: 0295-76342). These easy to moderately difficult walks around Land's End, Exmoor, the Lake District, the Cotswolds, and other picturesque destinations are personally guided by the very personable and highly efficient Ken Ward. Accommodations range from simple farmhouses to three-star hotels, and the trek vehicle carries all baggage between overnight stops. For those who prefer to be their own guide, *Lord Winston's* also produces guidebooks to walking in the UK.

Mountain Goat Holidays, Victoria St., Windermere, Cumbria LA23 1AD, England (phone: 09662-5161). Guided rambles through the Lake District, including hotel and guesthouse accommodations. Weekly holidays of both low- and high-level walking are based in Windermere and Keswick.

Ramblers Association Services, Ltd., Box 43, Welwyn Garden City, Hertfordshire AL8 6PQ, England (phone: 0707-331133). Over a hundred guided walking trips in Britain and Europe, ranging from easy to very tough, are offered to small parties of from 8 to 20.

Sussex Seen, 14 Maltravers St., Arundel, West Sussex BN18 9BU, England (phone: 0903-882474). Two- and three-day weekend walking tours in May, June, September, and October. Walkers cover 12 to 14 miles a day, dine on home-cooked food, and overnight in private homes.

The Wayfarers, Braithwaite, Keswick, Cumbria CA12 5TN, England (phone: 0596-82570), and Judy Allpress or Ann Nickerson, 166 Thames St., Newport, RI 02840 (phone: 401-849-5087). Guided walks through Thomas Hardy's Dorset, James Herriot's Yorkshire, Wordsworth's Lake District, the Cotswolds, the border castle country of Wales, the Devon Coast, Dartmoor, Cornwall, and Sir Walter Scott's Borders, with cozy lodging in inns, taverns, hotels, and private homes.

YHA Travel Adventure Holidays, Trevelyan House, 8 St. Stephen's Hill, St. Albans, Hertfordshire AL1 2DY, England (phone: 0727-5521). Watersports, rock climbing, airsports, walking, cycling, riding, golf, and multi-activity holidays throughout Britain, with inexpensive accomodations provided at their 21 adventure centers.

Head for the Hills, Garth, Builth, Powys LD4 4AT, Wales (phone: 05912-388). Celebrated 12-person walks lasting several days are arranged and led by Laurence Golding. Following the ancient and often obscure network of paths and tracks of the more remote parts of the countryside, walkers get a glimpse of history, all the way to the stone age. Areas covered include Dorset, Dartmoor, Exmoor, Cornwall, Avebury, Derbyshire, Shropshire, Yorkshire, and many parts of Wales. Part of the staff travels ahead with luggage to prepare the fully equipped camp and vegetarian food.

For the Mind

Marvelous Museums

It has often been said that when King Charles I died in 1649 and Parliament auctioned off his collection of paintings and other treasures, Britain lost a heritage. But the growth of the great national collections beginning as early as the 17th century with the founding of Oxford's Ashmolean Museum, and the collecting mania of the 18th and 19th centuries — when the rich were really rich and gentlemen made careers of their hobbies, accumulating not only the fine art of Western Europe but also trifles and prizes from the farthest corners of the empire — more than made amends. Today, Britain is home to a staggering agglomeration of artwork from all over the world. And although some of these treasures are privately owned, the majority are on display in the nation's great museums, not to mention the hundreds of country houses whose fine collections are often as stunning as their architecture. (The estimable National Portrait Gallery, for instance, has two collections outside London at Montacute, Somerset, and at Beningbrough, North Yorkshire.) The furnishings in such homes are often in mint condition, and seeing them displayed along with porcelain, silver, and tapestries is indeed a pleasure.

Britain's museums are usually well conceived and designed to provide ideal space and lighting for the works on display. And despite recent cutbacks in government support of the arts, most museums are free (donations are suggested) and open to the public every day except principal holidays. There usually are also special lecture programs designed as much for experts in the fields as for beginners seeking a greater appreciation of what they've seen and admired. Local newspapers and museum calendars are good sources for details.

A museum can be a great deal more pleasurable if a few simple guidelines are kept in mind. Visitors should plan several short visits to a large museum rather than one long one, stay for about an hour, and take in no more than a dozen fine works. There's no fatigue quite like aching, yawny museum fatigue — once described as the dread "museum foot" — and when it has set in, merely sitting for 3 minutes in front of a Rubens won't cure it. Travelers should be well rested when they visit important collections — preferably as soon as the museum opens, before the crowds have arrived. If possible, they should know what they want to see before beginning their rounds, so as not to clutter the experience with too many bleeding saints and blustery seascapes. Most museums publish excellent pamphlets and booklets to steer visitors to the more noted works in their collections. At the very least, visitors will want to stop at the museum shop on their way in, to thumb through the catalogue or look at the postcards to get an idea of what there is to see and where it's to be found.

And everyone should visit an art gallery or an auction house occasionally — just as a reminder that once it was all for sale.

AMERICAN MUSEUM IN BRITAIN, Bath, Avon, England: Oddly enough, this elegant and very English town is home to the country's best collection of things

American — Hopi kachina dolls and Shaker furniture, patchwork quilts and Pueblo pots, and even a teepee and a Conestoga wagon. While British visitors (particularly children) are marveling at these oddities, munching gingerbread baked in a historic oven on the spot, and pondering how their colonies were getting along before the big revolt, Americans admire the quality of the items on display and the thoughtful way the several period rooms are put together. Note that it was at Claverton Manor, the Greek Revival mansion housing these exhibits, that Sir Winston Churchill delivered his first political speech, in 1897. Details: American Museum, Claverton Manor, Bath, Avon BA2 7BD, England (phone: 0225-460503).

MUSEUM OF ENGLISH NAIVE ART, Bath, Avon, England: Those who enjoy the unself-conscious honesty of naive art will be delighted by this collection of innocent images of English life from 1750 to 1900. The paintings, from a boxer caught in a simple, striking pose to charming images of everyday life, are hung in a charming 18th-century schoolhouse adjacent to the Countess of Huntingdon Chapel in the center of Bath. Open April through October. Details: Museum of English Naïve Art, Crane Kalman Collection, the Countess of Huntingdon Chapel, The Vineyard/Paragon, Bath, Avon BA1 5NA, England (phone: 0225-446020).

CECIL HIGGINS ART GALLERY AND MUSEUM, Bedford, Bedfordshire, England: The museum in this fine old Victorian structure, once the home of a local brewer and art lover named Cecil Higgins, spills over into an annex, opened in 1976. Lively and hospitable, it boasts a distinguished collection of English and continental porcelain and glass, and watercolors by Constable, Cotman, Gainsborough, and Turner. Prints by Dürer, Picasso, Rembrandt, the Impressionists, and others are displayed in a succession of changing exhibitions in the new building. The Victorian mansion is set up to show how a family might have kept house about a century ago and has a homey, lived-in look. A fire burns on the hearth, clocks tick throughout, children's toys litter the floor next to a dollhouse, a letter lies half written on the desk, and a white scarf hangs from the hat stand. Upstairs, a newly opened nursery with glowing fire, clothes on the fender, and toys on the floor provides a convincing look at childhood at the turn of the century; a guest bedroom is awry with the recent arrival of a Victorian lady, her baby, and her luggage; and the William Burges room illustrates the eccentricity of the man's work, from its dark-green star-studded ceiling to its rich colors and decoration. Throughout, the captioning helps visitors understand what they are seeing. Details: Cecil Higgins Art Gallery and Museum, Castle Close, Bedford, Bedfordshire MK40 3NY, England (phone: 0234-211222).

BIRMINGHAM MUSEUM AND ART GALLERY, Birmingham, West Midlands, England: Boasting one of the nation's most important art collections outside London, with fine examples from the 17th through 19th centuries, this museum/gallery provides an exceptionally good look at the work of the Pre-Raphaelites, in an assemblage that is likely unequaled anywhere. English watercolorists from the 18th century onward are well represented, and there is a handsomely refurbished gallery dedicated to such applied arts as jewelry, metalwork, stained glass, costume design, and ceramics. The Department of Archaeology and Ethnography presents objects from cultures around the world; the Department of Local History exhibits items from the Birmingham of bygone days; and the Department of Natural History displays a life-size replica of *Tyrannosaurus rex* as well as Britain's finest fossilized triceratops skull. A variety of shops, an Edwardian tearoom, and facilities for the disabled are also available. The associated Museum of Science and Industry on Newhall Street offers old steam engines, aircraft, cars, machine tools, scientific instruments, and the like — a large number of which actually work. These are put into action at the Steam Weekends held in March and October, at the Traction Engine Rally in May, and at the Stationary Engine Rally in September. Details: Birmingham Museums and Art Gallery, Chamberlain Sq., Birmingham, West Midlands B3 3DH, England (phone: 021-235-2834).

ROYAL PAVILION, MUSEUM AND ART GALLERY, Brighton, East Sussex, England: In the former stables and coach houses of the Prince Regent's fantastic "Eastern" palace (now one of the world's great showpieces), the Museum and Art Gallery houses fine collections of Old Masters, watercolors, furniture, musical instruments, costumes, and English pottery and porcelain, as well as archaeological and ethnographic items and displays relating to Brighton history. The collections of applied art from the Art Nouveau and Art Deco periods — in which the museum specializes — and the new Fashion Gallery are particularly interesting. The Hove Amber Cup, found in 1857 in Hove in a Bronze Age barrow carbon-dated to about 1500 BC, is another treasure. The museum's lively exhibition program has presented shows on the Jazz Age, the British in India, the inspiration of Egypt, the Gothic, fairies, and other such subjects. Details: Royal Pavilion, Museum and Art Gallery, Brighton, East Sussex BN1 1UE, England (phone: 0273-603005).

FITZWILLIAM MUSEUM, Cambridge, Cambridgeshire, England: One of the nation's greatest and oldest public museums, the Fitzwilliam was founded in 1816, when Richard, the 7th Viscount Fitzwilliam of Merrion, left his superb collections, his library, and a good endowment to his alma mater, the University of Cambridge. The collections — not to mention the museum's stature — have been growing ever since. Thanks to the innovative spirit of Sir Sydney Cockerell, the museum's fourth director, it is also especially charming and a good deal less chilly and solemn than its peers. Cockerell instituted the policy of enlivening the picture galleries with Oriental rugs, sculpture, period furniture, and even flowers. Visitors can pick up a copy of the museum's brochure guide to lead them through the extensive collections of European applied arts, Islamic and Far Eastern treasures, manuscripts, paintings and drawings, portrait miniatures, prints, European and Oriental fans, and West Asiatic, Egyptian, Greek, and Roman antiquities. Of particular note are the lovely Roman mosaic fountain niche from 1st-century Baiae, the extensively illuminated 13th-century Peterborough Psalter, Frans Hals's *Portrait of a Man,* Delacroix's *Odalisque,* Renoir's *Coup de Vent* and *La Place Clichy,* Stubbs's *Gimcrack,* and masterpieces by the greatest Venetian painters of the 16th century — Palma Vecchio, Titian, Tintoretto, Veronese, and Jacopo Bassano. The music collection, which includes autographed scores of Handel, Bach, Chopin, Britten, and Elgar, is one of Britain's finest, and the collection of works by Blake and the members of his circle is the finest anywhere. Details: Fitzwilliam Museum, Trumpington St., Cambridge, Cambridgeshire CB2 1RB, England (phone: 0223-332900).

MERSEYSIDE MARITIME MUSEUM, Liverpool, Merseyside, England: This cousin to the National Maritime in London's Greenwich emphasizes the history of the nation's merchant marine rather than its Royal Navy, thereby telling the story of the growth of Liverpool, a city founded on the "trade triangle" of cotton, sugar, and slaves that continued to prosper through the 19th century as a stopping point for 9 million emigrants en route between Europe and the New World or Australia. Enter the maritime park, which looks just as it did when sailing ships loaded and unloaded here, and the restored Piermaster's house and other dockside buildings afford an opportunity to see coopering and boat-building as it was done a century ago. "Emigrants to a New World," a permanent exhibition downstairs, includes a reconstructed dockland street peopled with hawkers and porters such as emigrants would have seen; a section of a packet ship showing the traveling conditions of the day; and an Emigration Bureau that advises American visitors on how to trace their ancestry. Outside, in wet and dry dock, is the museum's growing collection of ships and boats rescued from the junkyard, several of which are open to the public. Details: Merseyside Maritime Museum, Albert Dock, Liverpool, Merseyside L3 4AA, England (phone: 051-709-1551).

BRITISH MUSEUM, London, England: Founded in 1753 around the lifetime accumulations of Sir Hans Sloane, a British physician and naturalist, this vast institution is Britain's largest and most celebrated, consecrated to the whole of human history. Trying to cover it all in a single visit is like trying to master nuclear physics while in a barber's chair. The crown jewels of the collection are the renowned Elgin Marbles, massive sculpture and reliefs from the Parthenon that Lord Elgin brought, in the early 19th century, from the Turkish sultan and carted off to safe, civilized England, where they were purchased by the government for £35,000 and presented to the museum. Other treasures on display include the Rosetta Stone, the black basalt tablet that provided the key to Egyptian hieroglyphs; the Royal Gold Cup; the deep blue and white cameo-cut Portland Vase, a great marvel of the glassmaker's art dating from Roman times; gold and silver objects from the Sutton Hoo Burial Ship, found at an East Suffolk archaeological excavation; the Tomb of Mausolus from Halicarnassus, which brought the word "mausoleum" to the English language; the Temple of Diana from Ephesus; and many mummies, among them the one that is widely (and erroneously) believed to have occasioned the legends of the curse of the mummy's tomb. Seven sculpture galleries, opened recently, exhibit some 1,500 Greek and Roman treasures, including two of the seven wonders of the ancient world and represent the bulk of the museum's Greek and Roman collection. Man Before Metals provides an enthralling look at the art and technology of the Stone Age. The departments of Western Asiatic Antiquities and Oriental Antiquities are magnificent. The Magna Carta is on view in the Manuscript Saloon of the British Library (a separate institution since 1973, though still housed in the British Museum), and the King's Library houses a Gutenberg Bible. Depending on what is on display at the time, visitors may see such wonders as the sketchbooks of Dürer or da Vinci, manuscripts of famous composers' famous works and of *Alice in Wonderland,* and the signatures of Shakespeare, Dickens, and Joyce. The British Library Reading Room, where Karl Marx wrote *Das Kapital,* is accessible only to those who come well recommended (preferably by a scholar of some note) and who apply in advance for a ticket, or to those who pay $15.50 and join the National Art Collections Fund, but visitors may view the Reading Room on the hour when it's open. The rest of the museum is also overwhelming; guidebooks to various parts of the collections, for sale in the main lobby, are good investments, as are detailed guides to single aspects of the offerings. Details: British Museum, Great Russell St., London WC18 3DG, England (phone: 01-636-1555; for the library, 01-636-1544).

COURTAULD INSTITUTE GALLERIES, London, England: At first, this institution, established in 1932 to teach art history to University of London students, might not appear to be very special. Yet like a good many museums of its type, this one is approachable and enjoyable in ways that its far larger and more widely known confreres can never be. The setting, replete with Oriental rugs and handsome furnishings, is lovely. The works in the collections are the bequests of industrialist Samuel Courtauld (whose generosity also benefited the Tate Gallery) as well as Lord Lee of Fareham and art critic Roger Fry (who organized London's first post-Impressionist exhibition in 1910). The excellent assemblage of Impressionist and post-Impressionist works includes Manet's *Bar at the Folies-Bergère* and *Le Déjeuner sur l'Herbe;* van Gogh's *Artist with His Ear Cut Off* and *Peach Trees in Blossom;* Cézanne's *Lake of Annecy* and one rendering of the easily recognizable *Card Players;* Tahitian scenes by Gauguin; and wonderful works by Bonnard, Renoir, and Seurat. Recently the Courtauld graciously permitted many works from its Impressionist and post-Impressionist collection to tour in an American exhibition, but these have been returned to their permanent home and are once again on view. In addition, there are early Italian paintings from the Gambier-Parry Bequest and the superb Princes Gate Collection of Flemish and Italian Old Masters. Details: Courtauld Institute Galleries, University of London, Woburn Sq., London WC1H 0AA, England (phone: 01-580-1015). (As we went to press, the Courtauld was slated to reopen by the first of the year at Somerset House, the Strand).

DULWICH PICTURE GALLERY, London, England: Tucked away in Dulwich, a quiet, leafy, almost rural (but easily accessible — 11 minutes by train) suburb of southeast London, this gallery — recently redecorated and rehung in the best Regency manner — boasts a collection of old masters well worthy of a capital city anywhere. The nation's oldest public picture gallery, it contains works bequeathed by the great Shakespearean actor-manager Edward Alleyn, the founder of Dulwich College, plus nearly 400 others from the collection of the French-born art dealer Noël Joseph Desenfans. Many of these had been collected at the behest of Poland's King Stanislas, who abdicated before they could be delivered (or paid for). Among others, there are works by such Dutch painters as Rembrandt, Cuyp, and Hobbema; by 17th- and 18th-century British portraitists such as Gainsborough and Reynolds; by the Flemish painters Rubens and Van Dyck; by the Frenchmen Claude, Poussin, Watteau, and Charles LeBrun; and by Italians such as Raphael, Veronese, Tiepolo, and Canaletto. The austerely neoclassical building that houses the collection was built in 1811 and is often considered to be the masterpiece of its architect, Sir John Soane. Details: Dulwich Picture Gallery, College Rd., London SE21 7AD, England (phone: 01-693-5254).

IVEAGH BEQUEST, London, England: The collection here, assembled by the first Earl of Iveagh, includes works by Cuyp, Gainsborough, Hals, Rembrandt, Reynolds, Romney, Turner, Vermeer, and others. What makes this institution particularly interesting is its setting, a late-17th-century house remodeled beginning in 1764 by the Scottish architect Robert Adam. It's a marvelously stately neoclassical villa that was scheduled for demolition until it was rescued in 1925 by the first earl of Iveagh, who then presented the house and the better part of his own collection to the nation. It has the atmosphere of an 18th-century English country house; and in summer frequently offers chamber recitals, poetry readings, and open-air concerts. Details: The Iveagh Bequest, Kenwood, Hampstead La., London NW3 7JR, England (phone: 01-348-1286).

MUSEUM OF MANKIND, London, England: Only the collections of Berlin's Ethnographic Museum can rival those of *the British Museum,* which are housed in this structure next to the Burlington Arcade in Piccadilly. By far the largest part of its holdings of items relating to African, American, Asian, and Pacific cultures is brought out of the relative limbo of the reserve areas only for special theme exhibitions. However, a selection of the greatest treasures is normally on display, including items such as bronzes from Nigeria, Maori jade ornaments, and a crystal skull probably made by the Aztecs. A new public café opened in the spring of 1989. Details: Museum of Mankind, 6 Burlington Gardens, London W1X 2EX, England (phone: 01-323-8043).

NATIONAL GALLERY, London, England: Among the greatest art museums in the world, the National Gallery was instituted in 1824, when the connoisseur Sir George Beaumont convinced the government to buy the three dozen–plus paintings put up for sale after the death of the wealthy Russian-born merchant-collector John Julius Angerstein — among them Rembrandt's *The Woman Taken in Adultery* and *The Adoration of the Shepherds,* Rubens's *The Rape of the Sabine Women,* and Titian's *Venus and Adonis.* Subsequent gifts and acquisitions have endowed it with a collection that is remarkably balanced and which represents a cross section of the chief schools of Western European art from Giotto to Picasso. Leonardo da Vinci's great cartoon *The Virgin and Child with St. Anne and St. John the Baptist* has a dimly lit room all its own; and here and there masterpieces such as Botticelli's *Venus and Mars,* Holbein's *The Ambassadors,* Breughel's *The Adoration of the Kings,* van Eyck's *Arnolfini Marriage,* and Rubens's *Samson and Delilah* — over 2,000 jewels in all — glow on the walls. As the holdings are highly selective rather than comprehensive, the museum is not huge (though nearly every item it owns is on view at all times). Homan Potterton's *A Guide to the National Gallery* (available at the gallery shop) makes an erudite — and delightful — companion to a visit. Information: National Gallery, Trafalgar Sq., London WC2N 5DN, England (phone: 01-839-3321).

NATIONAL MARITIME MUSEUM, London, England: In a Royal Park by the Thames in Greenwich, and partially in the Queen's House (reopens in spring 1990 after major refurbishment), England's first Palladian building, a beautifully proportioned white structure designed in 1616 by Inigo Jones for James I's consort, Anne of Denmark, this institution tells the story of Britain's long involvement with the sea. There are scores of pictures and silver, porcelain and uniforms, swords and medals, ship models and dioramas. New galleries in the West Wing explore "Discovery and Seapower" and the "Development of the Warship," and the world's largest ship in a bottle is on display in Neptune Hall. There, too, are the steam paddle tug *Reliant,* which rests after a career on the Manchester Ship Canal; the Donola, a 60-foot steam launch; and the smaller *Waterlily.* Next door in the Barge House, Prince Frederick's barge glitters in golden livery. Another must: the uniform that Lord Nelson wore when he was shot at the Battle of Trafalgar in 1805, complete with bullet hole and blood stains. Finally, the Old Royal Observatory — the home of the Greenwich Meridian, which divides the western hemisphere from the eastern — is centered around Sir Christopher Wren's 1675 Flamsteed House andhas exhibits that illustrate the history of nautical astronomy, timekeeping, and Greenwich mean time. The refracting telescope here is the largest in the United Kingdom and is available to visitors. Also in Greenwich, don't miss the *Cutty Sark,* once the fastest clipper in existence; and the *Gipsy Moth* IV, the 53-foot ketch which, in 1966–67, bore Sir Francis Chichester — solo — around the world. Details: National Maritime Museum, Romney Rd., Greenwich, London SE10 9NF, England (phone: 01-858-4422).

NATIONAL PORTRAIT GALLERY, London, England: Established in 1856, this gallery is devoted to the portraits of the most important figures in British arts, letters, history and politics, military life, science, and various other fields. In all, over 9,000 likenesses, arranged chronologically, stare down at visitors from the walls. Elizabeth I is there as a young woman and a dowager, not far from Shakespeare, Mary Queen of Scots, Thomas More, Cardinal Wolsey, Essex, Leicester, and Raleigh. The list of authors portrayed reads like the table of contents in a literature text — Pepys, Milton, Dryden, Pope, Swift, Boswell, Johnson, Tennyson, Dickens, the Brontë sisters, Wilde, Auden, Shaw, and more. Especially since the 1984 opening of a series of galleries devoted to post–World War I portraiture, there's far too much to see in one visit — but it's difficult not to want to give it a try. Special exhibits on historical themes or individual artists are frequently mounted as well. Details: National Portrait Gallery, St. Martin's Pl., London WC2H 0HE, England (phone: 01-930-1552).

QUEEN'S GALLERY, London, England: The British Royal Collection — one of the world's greatest — remained outside the experience of the common man until 1962, when this gallery was created at Buckingham Palace, and even now, only a fraction is on view. But the exhibitions that are mounted here never fail to impress, whether they are devoted to a subject such as royal children, animal paintings, or British soldiers; to single artists — da Vinci or Gainsborough or Canaletto or Holbein, to name a quartet of past shows; or to groups of painters — the Italians or the Dutch, for instance. Exhibitions change about once a year. Details: Queen's Gallery, c/o the Lord Chamberlain's Office, St. James's Palace, London SW1, England (phone: 930-4832, ext. 3351).

SIR JOHN SOANE'S MUSEUM, London, England: On the north side of central London's largest square (a haunt of lawyers since the 16th century), this museum occupies two houses designed by the great architect Sir John Soane (1753–1837) and is a remarkable survival of an early museum. The rooms, ingeniously designed, have curious lighting effects and are packed with objects that were arranged in a very personal manner by Soane himself. The place is full of surprises that the plain and fairly straightforward exterior does not foretell. In the Library, for instance, the spaces behind the flying arches are mirrored, so that a visitor is left with the impression of more space than actually exists. The Monk's Yard, a "Gothick fantasy," is concocted of bits of masonry from the old Palace of Westminster; the Monk's Parlour houses Flemish woodcarvings, casts from medieval sculptures and buildings, and architectural models of some of Soane's own designs; the Sepulchral Chamber contains the alabaster sarcophagus discovered in the tomb of Seti I (d. 1290 BC) by G. B. Belzoni in 1817, purchased by Soane for £2,000 after British Museum authorities decided they could not afford it, having just bought the Elgin Marbles; and the shallow-domed Breakfast Room displays ingenious use of mirrors and indirect lighting. All in all, the place is a hodgepodge — but who ever said a house had to be otherwise? Visitors should not miss Hogarth's famous series *The Rake's Progress,* which recounts the life and hard times of one Tom Rakewell, and his four-part political satire *The Election,* both installed in a small gallery with hinged walls. The Library contains the world's greatest collection of 17th- and 18th-century architectural drawings — works by Sir Christopher Wren, Robert Adam, George Dance, Soane, and many others. There is also a Model Room, open by request, that houses Soane's collection of cork, plaster, and wooden architectural models. (Students wishing to visit the Library, Drawings Collection, and Model Room are advised to make an appointment.) Details: Sir John Soane's Museum, 13 Lincoln's Inn Fields, London WC2A 3BP, England (phone: 01-405-2107).

TATE GALLERY, London, England: Built in 1897 on the site of Millbank Prison, the gift of the sugar broker and art collector Sir Henry Tate, this national collection of British painting and 20th-century painting and sculpture was established less than half a century after the National Gallery, when bequests had swelled the size of the latter's collection to an extent that there was no longer room to house all the paintings — 282 oils and 19,000 watercolors by Turner, among them. Tate bequeathed his own collection plus £80,000 to house it, art dealer Sir Joseph Duveen gave additional funds, and the Gallery was on its way. A major extension was opened in 1979 that increased exhibition space by half. An even newer wing — the magnificent Clore Gallery, designed by James Stirling — houses the Turner Collection. During the summer of 1988, a northern branch of the Tate Gallery opened in Liverpool's Albert Dock. Often overlooked is the fact that the Tate also houses one of the world's best collections of French post-Impressionist works; and the sculpture collection offers excellent examples of the artistry of Rodin, Maillol, Mestrovic, Moore, and Epstein. The British Collection contains the world's most representative collection of works by Blake, as well as works by Hogarth, George Stubbs, John Constable, and the Pre-Raphaelites. The Modern Collection includes works of conceptual, minimal, optical, kinetic, British figurative, pop, and abstract art; it incorporates the most extensive survey of British art of its period in any public collection, including selected examples of very recent art. Rothko, Nevelson, Bacon, Ernst, and Picasso are all represented. Rex Whistler, the noted trompe l'oeil painter, is responsible for the decor of the gallery's excellent restaurant. Details: Tate Gallery, Millbank, London SW1P 4RG, England (phone: 01-821-1313; 01-821-7128 for recorded information).

VICTORIA AND ALBERT MUSEUM, London, England: An offspring of the Great Exhibition of 1851, this museum was originally a repository of the world's finest craftsmanship. The collection, dating from ancient times, was intended to lend inspiration to leatherworkers and ceramicists, furniture makers and woodcarvers, architects and dressmakers, silversmiths and goldsmiths, and other artisans working in the applied arts in the 19th century. Through the original function has not been abandoned even today, the collections are a bit more wide-ranging; they encompass not only textiles and furniture but also watercolors and paintings — among them John Constable's *Salisbury Cathedral from the Bishop's Grounds;* the collections of British art (which include the Constable Collection, presented to the museum by the artist's daughter) stand out for their scope and comprehensiveness. Of particular interest are the Raphael cartoons (designs for tapestries for the Sistine Chapel), the period rooms, Queen Elizabeth I's virginals, the world's first teapot, and the intricately carved, abundantly graffiti'd Great Bed of Ware, which Shakespeare's Sir Toby Belch mentioned in *Twelfth Night* and (measuring about 11 feet square) was purportedly big enough to sleep a dozen couples, half of them at the head, the other half at the foot. Also on exhibit is the Chippendale furniture once owned by David Garrick, pieces by designer William Morris and his followers, Marie-Antoinette's music stand, Russian imperial jewels, patchwork quilts, medieval hangings, and tiles and stained glass. The museum's Henry Cole Wing (named after its founder) houses a broad selection of changing exhibitions, as well as an interesting permanent display of printmaking techniques. There's also a restaurant and super museum shop. Details: Victoria and Albert Museum, Cromwell Rd., London SW7 2RL, England (phone: 01-938-8500 or 01-938-8441 for recorded information).

WALLACE COLLECTION, London, England: The fourth Marquess of Hertford, who died in 1870 after living most of his life in Paris, had one major criterion in collecting: "I only like pleasing paintings," he claimed. But what he called "pleasing" included works of many types — Italian, Dutch, French, Flemish, and Spanish, as well as British — that are now displayed at Hertford House, his former townhouse off Oxford Street, which contains not only the works he amassed, but also the ones he inherited, since the collection was first put together by his great-grandfather in the 18th century and enlarged in the two succeeding generations. The museum's French furniture from the 17th and 18th centuries is very fine, as are the considerable numbers of 18th-century French clocks and the collections of miniatures, gold boxes, and Sèvres porcelain. Painters whose works are represented include Boucher, Canaletto, Fragonard, Gainsborough, Guardi, Hals, Rembrandt, Reynolds, Rubens, Titian, Van Dyck, Velázquez, and Watteau. The famous collection of Oriental and European armor was formed principally by Sir Richard Wallace, the illegitimate son of the fourth Marquess of Hertford. His widow, Lady Wallace, bequeathed the vast collection to the nation in 1897. Details: Wallace Collection, Hertford House, Manchester Sq., London W1M 6BN, England (phone: 01-935-0687).

ASHMOLEAN MUSEUM, Oxford, Oxfordshire, England: Just as Oxford's Bodleian was Britain's first truly public library, the Ashmolean — opened in 1683 — was its first public museum (possibly the first in Europe as well); it celebrated its tercentenary in May 1983. Even today a visitor will find many of the same scenes that Oxford scholars have enjoyed over the years — among them, items from Tradescant's Ark, the "closet of rarities" assembled by John Tradescant the Elder (d. 1638), which forms the nucleus of the collection, as well as odd lots such as Guy Fawkes's lantern, Powhatan's mantle, and the armor-plated hat that belonged to William Bradshaw, president of the court that passed sentence on Charles I. Bronzes (Chinese, Indian, Greek, Roman, Etruscan, Italian Renaissance, later European); ceramics (Chinese, Islamic, Japanese, English, and European); clocks and watches, jewelry, glass, coins and medals, and antiquities (Cretan, Cypriot, Egyptian, Etruscan, Greek, Near Eastern, and Tibetan); paintings (Dutch, English, Flemish, French, Impressionist, Italian, Venetian); other pieces (classical, European, Dark Age, medieval, and Oriental); and weapons are all represented in this *omnium gatherum* of a museum: There's something here for everyone. Details: Ashmolean Museum, Beaumont St., Oxford, Oxfordshire OX1 2PH, England (phone: 0865-278000).

BEAMISH, THE NORTH OF ENGLAND OPEN AIR MUSEUM, Beamish, County Durham, England: The museum, which aims to bring visitors a taste of life in the North of England early in this century, has won the country's British Museum of the Year (1986) and European Museum of the Year (1987) awards. It was founded by enthusiast Frank Atkinson, who collected items and buildings connected with the social, agricultural, and industrial history of the region. The buildings he acquired have been rebuilt on this 200-acre site and furnished as they would have been around the turn of the century. Visitors can take a tram ride to Old Town Street, a working farm, Colliery Village, and the railway station. It's easy to spend a day here, but shorter visits are also possible; routes are marked in the museum guidebook. Details: Beamish, The North of England, Open Air Museum, Beamish, County Durham DH9 0RG, England (phone: 0207-231811).

IRONBRIDGE GORGE MUSEUM, Telford, Shropshire, England: This is not just "another" museum. In 1777–79, when Abraham Darby built England's first iron bridge, from which the town takes its name, he ushered in the great era in industrial architecture that culminated with the construction of Paddington Station and the Crystal Palace in Hyde Park. Today, not only is the bridge itself a tourist attraction, but the whole area — a wooded stretch of the river Severn, all small hills and secret valleys — has been transformed into a beehive of activities reflecting of the days of steam two centuries ago. At Blists Hill, once the site of the most dramatic industrial activity of all, major exhibits focus on relics from the days of coal mines and blast furnaces, and many related artifacts have been brought here and reassembled. Nearby Coalbrookdale, whose foundry produced the components for the famous bridge, was Britain's first coke-smelting center; early castings, cast-iron rails and wheels, and ironmasters' houses and workers' cottages are on display. And at Coalport, site of the china works, visitors can stroll along a bit of disused canal that once linked the factory to the Severn. The workshops that produced the china are open to visitors, and exhibits recount the day-to-day pleasures and tribulations of the local residents who worked here generation after generation. To encourage visits to all the Ironbridge Museum's components, a special Passport to the Gorge ticket allows one visit to each site and is valid indefinitely until all museums have been seen. A good place to start is at Coalbrookdale or the Museum of the River. Details: Ironbridge Gorge Museum, Telford, Shropshire TF8 7AW, England (phone: 0952-453522).

JORVIK VIKING CENTRE, York, North Yorkshire, England: At this second of Britain's two successful "way of life" museums, small electric "time cars" take visitors underground and back a thousand years to see a busy market, houses, and a bustling wharf — all of which have been reconstructed on the excavation site of an old Viking street beneath the modern Coppergate. The reconstructed excavation is also visible from the cars. This amazing and very important find unearthed houses, workshops, kitchenware, tools, fragments of clothing, and other artifacts of daily life in the 9th century, that had been untouched since the Vikings gave the name "gate," Norse for "street," to several of the city's thoroughfares. Sounds and smells are used to evoke an even more authentic atmosphere. Details: Jorvik Viking Centre, Coppergate, York, North Yorkshire YO1 1NT, England (phone: 0904-643211).

NATIONAL GALLERY OF SCOTLAND, Edinburgh, Scotland: One of a trio of National Galleries of Scotland within walking distance of one another, this stands on a manmade embankment known as the Mound at the center of Princes Street Gardens. It has a small but vital collection of European paintings, prints, and drawings that includes works by Verrocchio (*Madonna and Child*), Domenichino (*Adoration of the Shepherds*), Claude (*Landscape with Apollo and the Muses*), Poussin (*Mystic Marriage of St. Catherine*), Gauguin (*Vision of the Sermon*), Andrea del Sarto (*Portrait of Becuccio Bicchieraio*), Velázquez (*Old Woman Cooking Eggs*), Rembrandt (*Woman in Bed*), Vermeer (*Christ in the House of Martha and Mary*), Watteau (*Fêtes Vénitiennes*), Degas (*Diego Martelli*), van Gogh, Renoir, Cézanne, Monet, Goya, Gainsborough, Reynolds, Constable, Millais, and Turner. The collection of works by Scottish artists is particularly good; visitors should not miss Henry Raeburn's *Rev. Robert*

Walker, ice skating through a scene that looks almost luminous. Details: National Gallery of Scotland, The Mound, Edinburgh EH2 2EL, Scotland (phone: 031-556-8921).

SCOTTISH NATIONAL GALLERY OF MODERN ART, Edinburgh, Scotland: Scotland's choice collection of painting, sculpture, and graphic art of the 20th century features works of established masters such as Picasso, Matisse, Ernst, Kirchner, Dix, Moore; major Scottish artists; and the leading figures of the national contemporary scene. Details: Scottish National Gallery of Modern Art, Belford Rd., Edinburgh EH4 3DR, Scotland (phone: 031-556-8921).

SCOTTISH NATIONAL PORTRAIT GALLERY, Edinburgh, Scotland: Portraits — in all mediums — of people who have played a significant role in Scottish history from the 16th century to the present, rendered by the most famous artists of the day, as well as the National Collection of Photography. The gallery shares a splendid neo-Gothic building with the Royal Museum of Scotland (part of the National Museums of Scotland). Details: Scottish National Portrait Gallery, 1 Queen St., Edinburgh EH2 1JD, Scotland (phone: 031-556-8921).

GLASGOW MUSEUMS & ART GALLERY, Glasgow, Scotland: A fine red sandstone building near the banks of the river Kelvin in Kelvingrove Park houses one of Britain's finest civic art collections, graced with a variety of works from many European schools (though the collections of Dutch art of the 17th century, French of the 19th and early 20th centuries, and of Scottish works are particularly strong); Corot, Degas, Monet, Millet, Raeburn, Turner, van Gogh, and Whistler are among those represented. Other works include Rubens's *Nature Adorned by the Graces,* Giorgione's *The Woman Taken in Adultery,* Rembrandt's *A Man in Armour,* and Salvador Dali's *Christ of St. John of the Cross.* The Glasgow Style gallery houses the work of the architect and designer Charles Rennie Mackintosh and his contemporaries. In addition, the building has galleries devoted to natural history (and to British birds and geology in particular), and to Scottish prehistory and history, ethnographical materials from as far away as Africa and Polynesia, decorative arts from Western Europe, and more. The collection of European arms and armor, housed in a striking glass-roofed hall, is especially fine. Details: Glasgow Museums & Art Galleries, Kelvingrove, Glasgow G3 8AG, Scotland (phone: 041-357-3929).

BURRELL COLLECTION, Glasgow, Scotland: Built in 1983 in Pollok Country Park to house the collection given to the city by Sir William and Lady Burrell in 1944, this rich and varied assemblage of art and artifacts reflects the wide-ranging tastes of its collectors. Paintings by Cézanne, Rembrandt, and Hals as well as fine examples of the arts of Egypt, Iraq, Iran, Greece, and Rome highlight the 8,000-piece collection. Pieces of medieval stonework are built into the fabric of the building — the intention of Sir William when he acquired them — and three of the rooms from his home at Hutton Castle, Berwickshire, have been reproduced and are grouped around the courtyard. Details: Glasgow Museums & Art Galleries, Kelvingrove, Glasgow G3 8AG, Scotland (phone: 041-649-7151).

MUSEUM OF TRANSPORT, Glasgow, Scotland: Relocated in Kelvin Hall, the museum contains a fascinating collection of all forms of transportation and related technology. Displays include a simulated Glasgow street of 1938 with period shop fronts and appropriate vehicles on the cobbled roadway; there's also a reconstruction of one of the Glasgow Underground stations. An authentic period motor car showroom has displays of historic automobiles. Superb and varied shop models in the Clyde Room reflect the significance of Glasgow and the river Clyde as one of the world's foremost areas of shipbuilding. Details: Glasgow Museums and Art Galleries, Kelvingrove, Glasgow G3 8AG, Scotland (phone: 041-357-3929).

PEOPLE'S PALACE, Glasgow, Scotland: It features Glasgow history from 1175 to the present in a gallery opened in 1898. The collection covers early Glasgow, the rise of the tobacco trade in the 18th century, and domestic, social, and political life in the 19th and 20th centuries. There's also an important collection of stained glass and a recently commissioned series of paintings on labor history by Ken Curry. Details: Glasgow Museums and Art Galleries, Kelvingrove, Glasgow G3 8AG, Scotland (phone: 041-357-3929).

POLLOK HOUSE, Glasgow, Scotland: Home of the Maxwell family until 1956, this is a neoclassical house built c.1750 with Edwardian additions. On display is the important Stirling Maxwell collection of Spanish and other European paintings, including works by El Greco, Murillo, Goya, Signorelli, and William Blake. Details: Glasgow Museums and Art Galleries, Kelvingrove, Glasgow G3 8AG, Scotland (phone: 041-357-3929).

NATIONAL MUSEUM OF WALES, Cardiff, Wales: One of the largest museums in Britain, this institution, opened to the public in 1927, concentrates on things Welsh — plants and animals, history and prehistory, rocks and minerals, and fine and applied arts. Among archaeological exhibits, the Caergwrle Bowl, noteworthy for its gold embellishments, and the collection of stone monuments and casts from the 5th through the 9th centuries are particularly interesting. A collection of wax models of plants in the botany section ranks among the world's finest, and the displays of the Welsh countryside and the animal kingdom are also musts. The fine-arts galleries include many paintings from the rest of Europe as well — including an impressive collection of Impressionist and post-Impressionist works by Cézanne, Corot, Degas, Monet, Pissarro, and Renoir; Welsh painting is represented by the 18th-century landscape artist Richard Wilson and the 20th-century painters Augustus John, Gwen John, J. D. Innes, Frank Brangwyn, and David Jones. Antiques lovers should be sure to explore the China collection, which contains good examples of Swansea and Nantgarw china and porcelain. Apart from the main building in Cardiff's civic center, the National Museum of Wales comprises nine branches scattered throughout the country, including the Welsh Folk Museum at St. Fagan's and the Welsh Industrial and Maritime Museum in Cardiff's docklands, where the story of the country's industrial progress and the heritage of Wales' rural life over 2 centuries is told in a vast collection of authentically re-created buildings. Details: National Museum of Wales, Cardiff, South Glamorgan CF1 3NP, Wales (phone: 0222-397951).

The Performing Arts

When the summer festival season ends, winter's cultural whirlwind begins. London has lately become something of a dance capital, hosting not just its own progeny — among them the Royal Ballet and the London Festival Ballet — but also visiting companies from home and abroad. *The Royal Opera House,* Covent Garden, ranks among the world's greats. And there's always music in the air, whether it's classical — and played by a symphony orchestra, a chamber group, or a soloist — jazz, or the most traditional folk works. And the theatrical tradition in Britain runs deep and strong. London, for instance, is a hotbed of dramatic affairs, with literally hundreds of offerings in hundreds of playhouses. The dozens of theaters in the West End (London's answer to Broadway) regularly mount ostensibly commercial productions (although many, as a result of British theater's fondness for the experimental, have a long way to go before they make money), and the fare swings wildly: The tiny *Duchess,* for example, for years the host of *Oh! Calcutta,* gave itself over to a glistening *Private Lives* in 1980, and by now may be playing *Hamlet.* The same tradition of eclecticism and experimentation has put the English theater at the forefront of world drama.

With all this going on, deciding on an evening's entertainment (or an afternoon's — or even a morning's, for that matter) can pose some problems. When it comes to theater, one man's meat is another's moan, so before settling on a play, visitors should ask a friend or check newspapers — in London, for instance, the *Observer* or well-regarded tourist magazines such as *What's On and Where to Go* or the BTA's monthly theater guide, the *London Planner.*

But throughout Britain, some theaters reliably turn out productions and concerts that are more interesting or wonderful than others, and some are worth a visit simply because they are particularly beautiful or unusually historic. A few are quite small, so that even the most remote corner (or "gods," as the heights of the balconies are called) affords a fine view of the activities on stage — and the prices are usually relatively low by stateside standards.

We've given a sampling of halls that culture buffs will find worth going out of their way to experience, but there are many other theaters and concert halls in London and the rest of Britain. It's possible to order tickets in advance of arrival in Britain directly through the individual box offices and through *Keith Prowse & Co.,* 234 W. 44th St., New York, NY 10036 (phone: 212-398-1430 or 800-669-7469, except in New York City). This organization, which has been in business for 206 years, is the world's largest entertainment ticket agency and sells some 53,000 tickets a week; its allocations range from a fifth to nearly half of all the seats at London theaters. Tickets to theater and major festival events can also be booked in advance through *Edwards & Edwards,* One Times Square Plaza, New York, NY 10036 (phone: 212-944-0290 or 800-223-6108, except in New York City).

BIRMINGHAM REPERTORY THEATRE, Birmingham, West Midlands, England: A list of the past members of the nation's first repertory company, which makes its home here, reads like a *Who's Who* of British theater. Julie Christie and Albert Finney played here, as did Laurence Olivier, Paul Scofield, Ralph Richardson, and Edith Evans, among others, during the years after Sir Barry Jackson founded the organization in 1913 with his own money "to serve an art instead of making that art serve a commercial purpose." In addition to earning fame for its actors, the Rep also became known for its attention to modern work, particularly plays by George Bernard Shaw, back when Shaw was considered a contemporary; for its successes in London; for Jackson's involvement with the origins of the *Malvern Festival* (described in *The Best Festivals*); and for its modern-dress productions of Shakespeare — all of whose works the company has performed at least once. Set in an attractive, modern home, the Rep's season includes the classics, musicals, and premieres in an 899-seat Main House cunningly designed on a steep tilt so that no one ever sits more than 65 feet from the stage. Assorted new works and innovative restagings of golden oldies are presented in the more flexible 50-by-30 Studio Theatre. At Christmastime, there's always a special show. (*The Wizard of Oz, Treasure Island,* and *Pinocchio* are past successes.) And every year, when the company is not in residence, the Main House hosts a visit by the Rambert Dance Company. Details: Birmingham Repertory Theatre, Broad St., Birmingham, West Midlands B1 2EP, England (phone: 021-236-4455).

THEATRE ROYAL, Bristol, Avon, England: It's Britain's oldest working theater, and since it opened in 1776 many well-known actors have appeared here, ranging from 18th-century greats such as Sarah Siddons (whose ghost is sometimes thought to haunt the building) to present-day stars, including Peter O'Toole, Jeremy Irons, and Jane Lapotaire. The resident company is the respected Bristol Old Vic, which also uses the New Vic Studio on the same site. In addition to contemporary and classic theater productions, the company also hosts art exhibitions, jazz concerts, comedy cabaret, and dance. The theater's Siddons Buttery serves homemade dishes daily from 10 AM, except Sundays. Backstage tours led by expert guides depart at noon on Fridays and Saturdays. Details: Theatre Royal, King St., Bristol, Avon BS1 4ED, England (phone: 0272-250250).

GRAND THEATRE & OPERA HOUSE, Leeds, West Yorkshire, England: This restoration with its elaborately decorated interior is one of the most impressive Victorian theaters in Britain. It is home to Opera North and hosts touring ballet and drama companies when that company is not in residence. Details: The Grand Theatre & Opera House, New Briggate, Leeds, West Yorkshire LS1 6NZ, England (phone: 0532-459351/440971).

BARBICAN CENTRE, London, England: An apparent tribute to modern architecture, this 1982 structure looks like a maze of concrete towers and corridors from the outside. Inside, the lavish decor, the complex design, the exciting potential of the building, and the breadth of artistic activity generated are overwhelming. The Royal Shakespeare Company performs here, as does the London Symphony Orchestra. There are two theaters, cinemas, an art gallery, two shops, a magnificent conservatory of plants, and a concert hall that hosts regular performances of classical music, opera, and more. The Waterside Café, which offers a snack by the fountains in summer, Wine on Six (the Barbican's wine bar), and the more luxurious Cut-Above Carvery all make for a delightful interlude. Details: Barbican Centre, Silk St., London EC2Y 8DS, England (for general information, phone: 01-638-4141; for the box office, phone: 01-628-8795).

LONDON COLISEUM, London, England: There's a sense of occasion surrounding any visit to this floridly Edwardian, 2,358-seat theater, London's largest, at the foot of St. Martin's Lane not far from St. Martin-in-the-Fields and the National Gallery. The interiors are all alabaster and marble, bronze and splendid gleaming mahogany, as posh as those of the ships that once crisscrossed the Atlantic when the theater was first opened. Diaghilev's Ballet Russe performed here, as did Sarah Bernhardt, Mrs. Patrick Campbell, Ellen Terry, and a child star named Noel Coward. The impresario who conceived the place even staged tennis matches and rodeos to keep it filled. Since 1968, the English National Opera Company, which stages classic and contemporary operas in English, has called it home and is in residence from August to June. Details: English National Opera, London Coliseum, St. Martin's La., London WC2N 4ES, England (phone: 01-836-3161 or 01-240-5258).

LYRIC THEATRE HAMMERSMITH, London, England: Though Victorian in style, this theater blends gracefully into its modern shopping center surroundings in Hammersmith's King Street. Classical productions and new plays are presented in the main theater, and the smaller adjacent Studio presents an adventurous program of modern and foreign works. Details: Lyric Theatre Hammersmith, King St., London W6 0QL, England (phone: 01-741-2311).

MERMAID THEATRE, London, England: Founded by actor Bernard Miles in 1951, this theater acquired its present permanent home on the site of an old warehouse on the banks of the Thames 8 years later. It soon gained a reputation for presenting adventurous works and is now completely self-supporting. Details: Mermaid Theatre, Puddledock, Blackfriars, London EC4 V3DB, England (phone: 01-236-5568).

NATIONAL THEATRE, London, England: Anyone who visits this trio of houses in a handsome, large, Thames-side drama complex is sure to have plenty to talk about — even if the fare is not to his taste. That, however, is unlikely, for Albert Finney, John Gielgud, Ian McKellen, Ralph Richardson, Peggy Ashcroft, and Paul Scofield have all appeared here. And plenty of breath-stopping acting takes place, in roles ranging from the soul-stretching to the small, in a selection of plays that embraces the classics; translations of works by European dramatists such as Schnitzler, Horvath, Feydeau, and Brecht; revivals of contemporary plays; new pieces by living playwrights like Pinter, Stoppard, Brenton, Storey, and Bolt; and adaptations of such books as *Lark Rise* and *The World Turned Upside Down.*

The building itself is wonderful, with an interior that feels like a walk-through sculpture, a huge foyer with bars that seems to be London's answer to Paris's sidewalk cafés, and all manner of walks, terraces, and restaurants with fine views of Somerset House and the river curving off toward St. Paul's.

Before performances, ensembles and soloists play for free in the foyers, and it's possible to browse through art exhibitions while listening. There are also almost always so-called platform performances — brief plays, readings, poetry, music, and mime — in all three theaters: the 400-seat Cottesloe, which is otherwise mainly used for works requiring small-scale staging, the 890-seat proscenium-arch Lyttelton, and the 1,160-seat open-stage Olivier. The last two feel almost as intimate as the Cottesloe, thanks to their excellent design. Details: National Theatre, South Bank, London SE1 9PX, England (phone: 01-928-2252).

OLD VIC, London, England: Architects, bombs, and ill-advised alterations had left the Old Vic nothing short of a mishmash when a Canadian named "Honest" Ed Mirvish bought it sight unseen a few years ago and commenced transforming it into one of the most elegant, attractive, and comfortable theaters in central London. The façade was returned to its 1818 incarnation, complete with brick arches, and the interior was restored to a semblance of its 1880s self. Boxes, ceiling, proscenium arch, and tier fronts were elaborately painted in shades of ivory, apricot, coral, pewter, and gold and silver. Velvet house curtains were installed, and the entire auditorium was decked out in wallpaper and carpeting with a period flavor. The house now produces its own subscription season, and, beginning in 1988, Jonathan Miller took over as artistic director, which has ensured interesting — if controversial — theater. The remarkable restoration alone makes a visit worthwhile. Details: The Old Vic, Waterloo Rd., London SE1 8NB, England (phone: 01-928-7616).

OPEN AIR THEATRE (REGENT'S PARK), London, England: It's hard to find a more pleasant way to spend a summer evening in London than to take in a performance of Shakespeare (or a musical) in this lovely amphitheater in the woods near Queen Mary's Rose Garden. Established in 1932, it quickly became an institution among London theatergoers, and actors from Vivien Leigh and Deborah Kerr to Jack Hawkins and Jeremy Irons have played here. Since 1962, the New Shakespeare Company has made its home here and offers three plays, two by Shakespeare, every summer. The new auditorium, which opened in 1975, provides plenty of space for a bar, which serves such fare as Puck's Fizz and mulled wine, barbecue and a cold buffet. Details: Open Air Theatre Regent's Park, London NW1 4NP, England (phone: 01-486-2431).

RIVERSIDE STUDIOS, London, England: This modern arts center alongside the Thames in Hammersmith offers a lively program of drama, music, dance, film, exhibitions, and children's programs in attractive surroundings, which make the Riverside well worth a visit. Details: Riverside Studios, Crisp Rd., London W6 9RL, England (phone: 01-748-3354).

ROYAL ALBERT HALL, London, England: Designed in the classical amphitheater style, and opened by Queen Victoria in 1871 as a memorial to her consort, Prince Albert of Saxe-Coburg, this almost round house is truly splendid and imposing, with a seating capacity for 5,500. The domed building, a quarter of a mile in circumference, has terra cotta moldings imposed on a red brick exterior, an immense Grand Organ, and three tiers of boxes. All kinds of concerts, from a Bach "B Minor Mass" to a spine-tingling, cannon-throttled "1812 Overture," will fill it up. The Henry Wood Promenade Concerts ("The Proms" in local parlance) are particularly special and attract crowds every night from July to September. The Proms programs feature music from all eras. Traditionally, the last night concludes with familiar British music, including Elgar's "Pomp and Circumstance March No. 1." The BBC Symphony Orchestra performs here during most of the season, but every year appearances are made by most of the other major British orchestras, as well as visits by some of the world's most prestigious ensembles, such as the Vienna Philharmonic, the Concertgebouw, the Leipzig Gewandhaus, and the New York Philharmonic. Most concerts at the Hall have remarkably low ticket prices. The Hall has also hosted such popular artists as Frank Sinatra, John Denver, Paul Simon, and Eric Clapton. It's also a venue for championship boxing, tennis tournaments, and grand balls. The Royal Albert Hall Tour allows visitors to savour for themselves the unique ambience and history of this great building; daily guided tours are available from June through mid-September. Details: Royal Albert Hall, Kensington Gore, London SW7 2AP (phone: box office, 01-589-8212; administration/tours, 01-589-3203)

ROYAL COURT THEATRE, London, England: One of the most famous of London's small theaters, this one has made theatrical history more than once — first around 1904, with Harley Granville Barker's stagings of Arthur Pinero farces and George Bernard Shaw plays, and again in the late 1950s, when George Devine's English Stage Company presented John Osborne's *Look Back in Anger.* Even today, the theater is associated with the contemporary and produces the works of new writers such as Caryl Churchill, Edward Bond, and Snoo Wilson. And despite the chronic shortage of money, standards are always high. The Royal Court is a great place for spotting talent, and the audience is lively. *Top Girls* started here before heading for the West End and New York (as did Ron Hutchinson's *Rat in the Skull,* Michael Hastings's *Tom and Viv,* and Wallace Shawn's *Aunt Dan and Lemon*), and the latest *Hamlet* was pronounced revolutionary. Details: The Royal Court, Sloane Sq., London SW1W 8AS, England (phone: 01-730-1745).

ROYAL FESTIVAL HALL, London, England: Opened in 1951, London's premiere concert hall seats an audience of 3,000. It is part of the South Bank Centre, which also includes the nearby National Theatre, the National Film Theatre, Jubilee Gardens, riverside walkways, the Hayward Gallery, and two smaller halls, the 1,065-seat Queen Elizabeth Hall and the 370-seat Purcell Room. In addition to an annual program of 1,200 events that feature most major performers on the international music and lyric arts scenes, there are free foyer exhibitions and lunchtime concerts. Shops and catering facilities are open all day. Details: Royal Festival Hall, South Bank, London SE1 8XX, England (for general information, phone: 01-928-3002; for the box office, phone: 01-928-8800).

ROYAL OPERA HOUSE, COVENT GARDEN, London, England: Worth a look for its grandeur alone, this jewel of a 2,098-seat opera house, the third on the site, is splendidly Victorian, with red plush, shaded lights, scarlet and gold tiers, domed turquoise ceiling, and sweeping horseshoe-shaped balconies. But the play's the thing, and some of the best singers in the world have performed here — among them Dame Nellie Melba, Dame Joan Sutherland, Kirsten Flagstad, and Maria Callas. The tradition of excellence continues unabated, and the hall ranks among the world's half-dozen true greats of its kind. The Royal Opera shares the house with the Royal Ballet, which, under noted choreographers such as Sir Frederick Ashton and Sir Kenneth MacMillan, with dancers like Antoinette Sibley and Dame Margot Fonteyn, Rudolf Nureyev and Anthony Dowell, has become one of the world's most noted companies. Nearby, a silver casket on the south wall of St. Paul's, Covent Garden, contains the ashes of Ellen Terry, the famous actress who died in 1928. Details: The Royal Opera House, Covent Garden, London WC2E 9DD, England (phone: box office, 01-240-1066 or -1911; administration, -1200).

SADLER'S WELLS THEATRE, London, England: Built on the site of two mineral springs discovered in 1683 by Richard Sadler, this member of the trio of the capital's oldest more or less continuously operating halls has seen its jugglers and clowns, ropedancers and performing animals, plays and pantomimes, and even roller-skaters and boxers. The theater once hosted the world premiere of Benjamin Britten's *Peter Grimes* and, in its time, has also been home to the Royal Ballet and the English National Opera. Today, it hosts touring opera and dance companies from all over the world — among them Merce Cunningham, Twyla Tharp, Pilobolus, the Central Ballet of China, and the Sydney Dance Theatre. The London seasons of the country's leading dance companies, including the Rambert Dance Company, the London Contemporary Dance Theatre, the National Youth Music Theater, and the Sadler's Wells Royal Ballet, are also here. Sadler's Wells has recently opened a second auditorium, the Lilian Baylis Theatre, beside the principal building. The new space is small (220 seats) but is fully equipped technically; presentations here are divided between small-scale professional work (music, drama, dance) and community and education projects. The theater's exterior, foyer, and performance areas have all been beautifully redecorated. Details: Sadler's Wells Theatre, Rosebery Ave., London EC1R 4TN, England (phone: 01-278-6563; box office, 01-278-8916).

THEATRE ROYAL (DRURY LANE), London, England: The productions here may not be London's most innovative, but this 2,283-seat theater, with its beautiful symmetrical staircase and domed entranceway, is unarguably one of London's most historic. The fourth playhouse on the site, it was preceded by a theater where Charles II met Nell Gwyn, who once sold oranges at the entrance; another predecessor was designed by Christopher Wren, with John Dryden as chief playwright, and as manager, David Garrick and Richard Sheridan, whose 1777 *School for Scandal* was written upstairs while actors rehearsed completed sections below. The present house, designed by Benjamin Wyatt in 1812, has hosted opera and drama, pantomime and film, and even musicals. Edmund Kean, whom many believe to be the greatest tragedian of all time, played here in 1814, as did Sir Henry Irving, Ellen Terry, Sir John Gielgud, and other famous thespians. The theater has its tradition, the cutting of the so-called Baddeley Cake (named after the actor whose will supplied the funds) in the Grand Saloon after the performance every January 6, and its ghost, a gray-cloaked, high-booted bewigged fellow who haunts the upper circle — in the daytime only, however. For a splurge, theater goers can hire the Royal Box or the Prince of Wales Box, both of which come complete with seating for six and tiny Regency or Adamesque retiring rooms. Tours of the theater can be arranged through its historian, George Hoare. Details: Theatre Royal (Drury Lane), Catherine St., London WC2B 5JF, England (for the box office, phone: 01-836-8108; for tours, phone: 01-836-3352).

THEATRE ROYAL (HAYMARKET), London, England: Architect John Nash, who designed this small, stylish theater, gave it a wonderful Corinthian portico, which looks all the grander when floodlit, as it often is at night. Henry Fielding managed a predecessor on the site around 1737, and the present hall, built in 1821, has been the setting for plays by everyone from Ibsen to Wilde, T. S. Eliot and Tennessee Williams to Noel Coward, J. M. Barrie, and Terence Rattigan; Sir Beerbohm Tree played here in the late 19th century. The hall itself, renovated at the beginning of this century, is all white, rich blue, and gold leaf; there's a wonderfully crafted royal arms above the stage. Details: Theatre Royal (Haymarket), Haymarket, London SW1Y 4HT, England (phone: 01-930-9832).

WIGMORE HALL, London, England: One of Europe's most elegant and intimate concert halls, this fine example of the art nouveau style — full of alabaster, marble, polished mahogany, and brass — was created in 1901 by Carl Bechstein (of piano fame) and is famous for its nearly perfect acoustics. A delightful hall for recitals and chamber music, it has hosted debuts by Elisabeth Schwarzkopf (in 1948) and Daniel Barenboim (in 1958) and recitals by Julian Bream, Peter Pears, Andrés Segovia, and many others. Arthur Rubinstein made his second appearance in England here (in 1912) and also his last public appearance (in 1976). Nowadays, the hall attracts artists such as Olaf Bär, Shura Cherkassy, and the Beaux Arts Trio, and has a regular series of celebrity and early music concerts as well as a very popular series of Sunday Morning Coffee Concerts. Details: Wigmore Hall, 36 Wigmore St., London W1H 9DF, England (phone: 01-935-2141).

YOUNG VIC THEATRE, London, England: This theater, founded more than 15 years ago, is new by London standards, but the spirit of experimentation and the *joie de jouer* that go into the productions are as much a tradition in the British theater as is the Bard himself. David Thacker, the theater's artistic director, is particularly renowned for bringing fresh interpretations and contemporary staging to Shakespeare and modern classics. Among the theater's most recent successes have been Ghosts and A Touch of the Poet with Vanessa Redgrave, Who's Afraid of Virginia Woolf with Billie Whitelaw, and Comedians. The works of William Shakespeare, Henrik Ibsen, Arthur Miller, David Holman, and other modern playwrights are typically presented, along with a comprehensive program of work for younger audiences. It's a lively place and quite different, architecturally, from most theaters. The building includes a café and is easily accessible by public transportation. Details: The Young Vic, 66 The Cut, London SE1 8LZ, England; nearest station: Waterloo (phone: 01-928-6363).

ROYAL EXCHANGE THEATRE, Manchester, England: Housed in a former cotton exchange, the Royal Exchange Theatre Company, whose roots go back to 1959 and a group of actors who had trained at the Old Vic Theatre School, performs Shakespeare, Marlowe, Sheridan, Chekhov, Ibsen, Coward, and a variety of other works old and new, including an occasional world premiere. Several productions, including *The Dresser,* have gone on to London or Broadway, and audiences pack the unusual theater-in-the-round, Europe's largest, to 90% capacity. Concerts of classical and folk music and jazz are also held here, along with a host of other activities. Details: Royal Exchange Theatre, St. Ann's Sq., Manchester M2 7DH, England (phone: 061-833-9333).

THEATRE ROYAL, Newcastle-upon-Tyne, Tyne & Wear, England: Recently refurbished at a cost of £9.6 million, this superbly appointed theater now has extensive conference and catering facilities within the original Victorian building. The theater presents touring performances of drama, ballet, and opera, as well as an annual 5- or 6-week visit by the Royal Shakespeare Company. Details: Theatre Royal, Grey St., Newcastle-upon-Tyne, Tyne & Wear, NE1 6BR England (phone: 091-232-2061).

THEATRE ROYAL, Norwich, Norfolk, England: The atmosphere of the sleek Theatre Royal, a 1970 update of a structure put up in 1935 in the theater and cinema style of the day (the fourth theater on the site), doesn't hold a candle to the grander London halls. Yet, as Europe's most successful provincial theater, it is that remarkable thing, an arts institution that manages to be totally self-supporting. Current management keeps things hopping with a continual and very lively procession of circus, grand opera, ice shows, ballet, pantomime, variety shows, vaudeville, classical music concerts, and programs from the touring companies of the National Theatre Company, Sadler's Wells Royal Ballet, the Glyndebourne Opera, the London Festival Ballet, and foreign dance companies. Charlie Chaplin, as the Lancashire Lad, performed in a previous theater on the site back in 1904, when it was called the Norwich Hippodrome. Open every day except Christmas. Details: Theatre Royal, Theatre St., Norwich, Norfolk NR2 1RL, England (phone: 0603-628205).

ROYAL SHAKESPEARE THEATRE, Stratford-upon-Avon, Warwickshire, England: The senior of the United Kingdom's two national theaters, under the patronage of Her Majesty the Queen, this 1,500-seat hall opened on April 23, 1932, on the Bard's own birthday — appropriately enough, since Shakespeare is the sole fare on these boards throughout the season, from late March through January. The immense Royal Shakespeare Company — the association of actors, directors, and designers who claim the place as one of their principal homes — has numbered almost all the greats of British theater among its members in the course of the past century. The quality of the work is at least professional if not always superb, and often innovative (one season's production of *The Taming of the Shrew* used motorcycles). The Swan Theatre, built within the shell of the old Memorial Theatre, has a horseshoe-shaped auditorium that closely resembles those of 16th-century playhouses, and has been earmarked for performances of Shakespeare and his contemporaries' works, as well as later writers'. And in London, at the Barbican Arts Centre (described above), the RSC performs in the 1,100-seat Barbican Theatre and attached studio space, the 200-seat "Pit"; the almost continuous season includes a mix of Shakespeare (transferred from the previous Stratford season) and new productions of modern and classical works. Details: Royal Shakespeare Theatre, Waterside, Stratford-upon-Avon, Warwickshire CV37 6BB, England (phone: 0789-295623), or the Royal Shakespeare Company, Barbican Theatre, Barbican, London EC2Y 8BQ, England (phone: 01-638-8891).

PALACE THEATRE, Watford, Hertfordshire, England: A restored bit of Edwardiana on the outskirts of London, the Palace offers a fine adventurous program of drama that compares favorably in quality with those in the capital's West End. Details: Palace Theatre, Clarendon Rd., Watford, Hertfordshire WD1 1JZ, England (phone: 0923-225671).

THEATRE ROYAL, York, North Yorkshire, England: The site of this hall, a 20th-century structure, has been occupied by a theater since 1765. Touring companies, Sunday concerts, and an annual Yuletide pantomime flesh out a repertory program of modern and classical drama. Details: Theatre Royal, St. Leonard's Pl., York, North Yorkshire YO1 2HD, England (phone: 0904-623568).

CITIZENS' THEATRE, Glasgow, Scotland: The accolades for this first-rate regional theater just don't stop. The *Times* called it Britain's "most challenging theater," the *Observer* characterized it as "the most unusual and individual theater in the land," the *Daily Mail* noted that it "puts the West End in the shade," and the US's *After Dark* commented on its "outrageously adventurous nature" and its "perverse and avant-garde flair". The century-old playhouse-with-a-past has recently been renovated, and the house is now a stunning example of a traditional proscenium-arch Victorian theater. The company has performed over 140 British and foreign classics since its formation, and has earned a worldwide reputation. Most of the actors have worked with the company for over a decade, and all are paid the same salary. During the summer months, when the company is not in residence, visiting troupes take to the stage. Details: Citizens' Theatre, Gorbals, Glasgow G5 9DS, Scotland (phone: 041-429-5561).

THEATRE ROYAL, Glasgow, Scotland: Those who persist in thinking that Edinburgh is home to everything cultural in Scotland are forgetting that Glasgow is home to the Scottish National Opera, the Scottish National Orchestra, and the Scottish Ballet. The Theatre Royal, Scotland's only opera house, is without question one of the most gorgeous relics of Victorian days in Britain. Now owned by the Scottish National Opera, it has been recently and ingeniously restored so that the most modern theatrical equipment is available but mainly hidden and marvelous plasterwork ornaments the swooping balconies and the domed ceilings — an overwhelming sumptuousness in the scheme of things. Unlike many refurbished opera houses, this one is not done in red and gold but in various shades of cream and brown, highlighted here and there with blue and orange. The Scottish National Opera subscription season runs year-round, and the hall also hosts performances by many other companies including the Scottish Ballet, Sadler's Wells Royal Ballet, the Rambert Dance Company, the English National Ballet, the Dance Theatre of Harlem, the Royal Shakespeare Company, the National Theatre, the Scottish Theatre Company, and others. Details: Theatre Royal, 282 Hope St., Glasgow G2 3QA, Scotland (box office phone: 041-331-1234).

NEW THEATRE, Cardiff, South Glamorgan, Wales: Drama, opera, concerts, and ballet are staged by this large 1,140-seat theater. Major touring companies, including the Royal Shakespeare Company and the National Theatre Company, pay their annual visits, and at Christmas, there is also a family pantomime. Details: New Theatre, Park Pl., Cardiff, South Glamorgan CF1 3LN, Wales (box office phone: 0222-394844).

THE BRITISH FOLK MUSIC SCENE

Folk music is alive and well in England, Scotland, and Wales. There are all manner of outdoor folk music festivals between Easter and September. And every week in the British Isles, singers, guitarists, banjo and mandolin players, and other musicians, as well as aficionados of their music, get together at local pubs to play and sing along at the meetings of the nation's some 1,500 folk clubs. Announcements of the events, which are usually held on weekends, are made via local papers or radio stations, information bureaus, or postings at libraries. The atmosphere is informal, but a strict etiquette prevails: no talking and no service from the bar during songs.

ENGLAND: In addition to folk clubs and festivals, England offers a lively roster of summer folk dance, which derives an additional measure of fascination from its long roots in the past. There are processional dances associated with ancient rituals, such as the famous Furry Dance at Helston in Cornwall on May 8, for instance, which celebrates the passing from the darkness of winter into the light of spring. Morris dancing, the best-known form of English folk dance, probably developed from pagan sacrificial rites. Traditionally, only men take part; they are decked with ribbons and bells and flourish handkerchiefs and garlands as they tread the age-old measures to the accompaniment of custom-honored pipe and tabor (a drum) and the more contemporary fiddles, melodeons, and concertinas. Particularly numerous in the Cotswolds, they also perform in many other parts of England, usually outside public houses. In London, it is a long-standing tradition for Morris dancers to perform outside Westminster Abbey early on Wednesday evenings from May through July.

For a comprehensive list of festival dates and folk clubs, enthusiasts may contact the English Folk Dance and Song Society, Cecil Sharp House, 2 Regents Park Rd., London NW1 7AY, England (phone: 01-485-2206). See also *Traditional Music and Dance,* PERSPECTIVES.

SCOTLAND: Scotland has its own Celtic music tradition featuring pipe, fiddle, clarsach (harp), music, and song. The many festivals, often dedicated to preserving Gaelic language, literature, and culture, frequently include ceilidhs, evenings of traditional music, song, and dance. Performances and casual gatherings that take place all over Scotland throughout the year, as well as competitions, festivals, and Highland Games events, are good places to hear Scottish bagpipes and fiddles.

The Traditional Music and Song Association of Scotland (TMSA) is a group of organizers, tradition bearers, singers, musicians, storytellers, collectors, publishers, and others who are actively concerned with fostering interest in the traditional arts in Scotland. There are branches in Aberdeen, Angus, Perthshire, Fife, Glasgow, and Edinburgh, and festivals are offered in Keith, Newcastleton, Auchtermuchty, and Kirriemuir. Competitions are held at the festivals featuring singing, diddling, and storytelling, such instruments as the fiddle, accordion, tin whistle, mouth organ, Jew's harp, and the art of the ceilidh band. For further details, contact the Traditional Music and Song Association of Scotland, c/o Jane Fraser, National Organizer, St. Katherine's Center, W. North St., Aberdeen AB2 3AT, Scotland (phone: 0224-632978)

The Scottish Folk Directory is also a good resource. It lists folk clubs offering many types of entertainment, from unaccompanied ballads to Cajun music. Also listed is a calendar of festivals, along with artists and what they perform. For details, contact Sheila Douglas, Editor, the Scottish Folk Directory, 12 Mansfield Rd., Scone, Perth, Tayside PH2 6SA, Scotland (phone: 0738-51588). See also Traditional Music and Dance, PERSPECTIVES.

WALES: Wales's folk tradition, distinct from England's, focuses attention on the country's own language. Many nationwide folk festivals and eisteddfodau are held every year, usually in summer. The best-known are the Royal National Eisteddfod, held in North Wales and South Wales in alternate years, and the International Musical Eisteddfod in July at Llangollen. The former offers a particularly good representation of Welsh literature, drama, folk dancing, and music.

For more information on the Welsh folk scene, contact Buddug Lloyd Roberts, Welsh Folk Music Society, Yr Hasan, Cricieth, Gwynedd, or phone Mrs. Jean Huw Jones at 0269-2837.

The Best Festivals

With so much talent in so many fields, it's hardly surprising that Britain is blossoming with festivals. It is surprising, however, that they take place virtually year-round and last anywhere from a day or a week to a month or even a whole summer. Some are devoted to Britain's musical goings-on — jazz, rock, symphonic and chamber music, opera, and the like; others are oddball events that focus on snuff taking or pancake racing; and still others are rooted in centuries-old tradition, with plenty of Morris dancing, craft displays, and brass-band music. The British Tourist Authority publishes *Customs and Pageantry,* which describes a number of these more unusual affairs.

At larger events of all types — in addition to all the listed offerings — visitors will still get, like a plum in a pie, the "fringe." The one at the Edinburgh Festival is world famous (and sometimes more interesting than the main show). Most host towns are often en fête, too, with floral displays everywhere, and there are almost always one or two good restaurants where travelers can socialize over a meal or a drink before and after events. Information about other events may be obtained from the National Trust, the various Garden Schemes, and local tourist boards. Vacationers who get hooked on such activities may want to acquire special publications such as Carol Rabin's *Music Festivals in Europe and Britain* ($8.95 postpaid from the Berkshire Traveler Press, Stockbridge, MA 01262; phone: 413-298-3636).

Even though festivals may be full of "serious events," they are also, in a word, fun — and the opportunity to meet and talk with local people who are delighted to welcome foreign visitors is part of the experience. Therein lies a good deal of the charm and pleasure of a country festival and the memories that go with it. The various tourist boards can provide listings of festivals of all types. Meanwhile, here are some notes on a few of the best.

WORTH A LONG DETOUR

ALDEBURGH FESTIVAL, Aldeburgh, Suffolk, England: Beloved by musicians the world over for its warmth, intimacy, and exceptionally fine acoustics, the remarkable concert hall established by composer Benjamin Britten and tenor Peter Pears is the focal point of this quaint little sea town's annual mid-June festival. A platform for recent developments in British and American music, it also honors the anniversaries of the classical masters. Most of the events take place in the main concert hall, a converted brewery situated 6 miles from Aldeburgh in Snape; nearby churches and stately homes are used for other events. Throughout August each year the British Telecom Maltings Proms are held at Snape featuring a rich variety of artists and programs. The Britten-Pears School for Advanced Musical Studies, also at Snape, is where young artists come to study and participate in festival events. Details: Aldeburgh Foundation, High St., Aldeburgh, Suffolk IP15 5AX, England (phone: 0728-452715).

ARUNDEL FESTIVAL, Arundel, West Sussex, England: Held annually for approximately 2 weeks in August, this festival takes place in a charming South Downs resort dominated by a Norman castle owned by the premier duke of Great Britain. Its panoramic tilting yard is used as an open-air theater for the festival offerings — performances by the New Shakespeare Company and, each year, special emphasis on one other aspect of the arts. There are many other events as well, ranging from concerts of classical music to gymkhanas. Details: Festival Office, The Mary Gate, Arundel, West Sussex BN18 9AT, England (phone: 0903-883690).

BATH INTERNATIONAL FESTIVAL OF MUSIC, Bath, Avon, England: For 2 weeks in late May and early June, this magnificent city, famous for its Roman baths and outstanding Georgian architecture, annually offers a catholic choice of concerts by top musicians of all persuasions, from medieval to jazz; informative tours and lectures in historic buildings, houses, and gardens; performances of opera and dance by leading companies; literary events and lectures; films; many art exhibitions, including Britain's only contemporary art fair; relaxed late-night musical shows; and a candlelight procession through the handsome streets on opening night. What sets this event apart are the concerts' settings. The performances of choral works and the organ recitals are presented in Bath Abbey or Wells Cathedral. There are also concerts and operas in beautiful halls that date from the late 18th or early 19th century — chamber music or dance, for instance, in the city's Theatre Royal, an intimate hall refurbished not long ago to its early-19th-century splendor. During intermissions, visitors promenade through similarly stately, classically proportioned halls, and the route to their hotel leads through streets that seem equally removed from the modern world. Details: Bath Festival Office, Linley House, 1 Pierrepont Pl., Bath, Avon BA1 1JY, England (phone: 0225-462231).

BRIGHTON FESTIVAL, Brighton, East Sussex, England: Brighton, that strange mixture of the beautiful, with its Regency buildings, and the raffishness typical of a popular seaside resort, is always a joy to visit — but never more so than during the 3 weeks in May when the Brighton Festival fills the town with music, both classical and popular, in recitals, chamber and orchestral concerts, and operas, as well as programs of jazz and rock, dance and drama, art exhibitions, and seminars and workshops. There's also a dramatic fireworks display, some sheepdog trials and guided walks, a bric-a-brac market, and open house at local artists' studios. Details: Festival Office, Marlborough House, 54 Old Steine, Brighton, East Sussex BN1 1EQ, England (phone: 0273-26894).

BUXTON FESTIVAL, Buxton, Derbyshire, England: The plays, operas, films, and lectures presented as part of this young and still rapidly developing 3-week midsummer event focus on a figure from the world of literature, such as King Arthur or Shakespeare, highlighting that person's influence on the arts. The attractive Georgian spa town possesses a fine concert hall and an elegant Edwardian opera house. In fact, Buxton's productions of lesser-known operas have put it on the map alongside such events as those in Bayreuth and Glyndebourne. The town nestles amid the rugged hills of central England's Derbyshire Peak District and is easily accessible from Manchester. Details: Festival Office, Hall Bank, Buxton, Derbyshire SK17 6EN, England (phone: 0298-70395).

CHELTENHAM INTERNATIONAL FESTIVAL OF MUSIC, Cheltenham, Gloucestershire, England: This event takes place during 2 weeks in July and presents a wide program of musical offerings, with an emphasis on the contemporary and the British in a continuing classical tradition. The backbone of the festival includes morning chamber concerts in the glorious setting of the historic Pittville Pump Room (the spa waters are still available for tasting), full-scale orchestral concerts in the Town Hall, and opera and dance in the splendidly restored Everyman Theatre. Other events feature mime, film, master classes, composers- and photographers-in-residence, jazz, ethnic music, talks, tours, fringe performances, and more. Details: Town Hall, Cheltenham, Gloucestershire GL50 1QA, England (phone: 0242-521621).

CHELTENHAM FESTIVAL OF LITERATURE, Cheltenham, Gloucestershire, England: For 2 weeks in October some of the world's greatest literary names and curious audiences gather in an enchanting setting to celebrate the written, printed, and spoken word in various venues throughout the region. The breadth of the festival program is an essential part of its wide appeal; it offers conversations, lectures, poetry readings and workshops, theater, children's events, a poetry competition, a bookfair, and exhibitions. Details: Town Hall, Cheltenham, Gloucestershire GL50 1QA, England (phone: 0242-521621).

CHICHESTER FESTIVAL THEATRE, Chichester, West Sussex, England: The repertory of this extremely popular theater festival, which runs from May through September, includes a mixture of the old and the new. The emphasis is on entertaining rather than experimenting, and the most successful plays usually end up in London. During the theater's nearly 30 years of existence, the roster of performers has grown into a veritable *Who's Who* of the English-speaking theater, and the festival has become the most important annual theatrical event outside London, Edinburgh, and Stratford. The theater is attractively modern, hexagonally shaped, and set in a lovely parkland; every seat is a good one. Other pluses: the new alternative productions of the Studio Company, and Chichester itself, a magical place in some of the most enchanting country in Sussex, sophisticated enough that restaurants keep late hours and chefs serve lobster thermidor as well as steak-and-kidney pie. Details: Chichester Festival Theatre, Oaklands Park, Chichester, West Sussex PO19 4AP, England (phone: 0243-781312).

CHICHESTER FESTIVITIES, Chichester, West Sussex, England: In celebration of the founding of Chichester Cathedral, this event, held during the first 2 weeks in July, features artists, musicians, and poets of national and international repute, along with jazz, films, dance, exhibitions, opera, and children's events. Past themes have been "An Anglo French Affair" and "A Touch of Romance." A program for the festivities is published in early April. Details: Chichester Festivities, Canon Gate House, South St., Chichester, West Sussex P019 1PU, England (phone: 0243-785718).

THREE CHOIRS FESTIVAL, Gloucester, Gloucestershire, and Hereford and Worcester, Herefordshire and Worcestershire, England: This August event, which rotates annually among the three cathedral cities, is a tribute to the great English tradition of choral singing and the oldest music festival in Europe. The three cathedral choirs join forces with one another and with world class artists, orchestras, and ensembles from around the world to provide a week of splendid music that ranges from the 16th century to the present. A few works are commissioned especially for the occasion, and there's a varied fringe program. The surrounding countryside — the Cotswolds and the Malvern Hills — is wonderfully scenic and full of beautiful old buildings. Details: Festival Office, Community House, College Green, Gloucester, Gloucestershire GL1 2LX, England (phone: 0452-29819.

GLYNDEBOURNE FESTIVAL OPERA, Glyndebourne, East Sussex, England: Founded in 1934 by John Christie and his wife, the singer Audrey Mildmay, and held on their ancient Sussex country estate some 50 miles south of London, this festival, which now runs from the third week in May to late August, is top drawer musically — with artists from all over the world — and socially as well. The splendid program of opera (six productions each summer) is garnished with a 75-minute supper interval — perfect for a meal in one of the restaurants or for champagne picnics in the gardens and on the velvety English lawns. *BritRail* has service between London's Victoria Station and Lewes. Details: Glyndebourne Festival, Lewes, East Sussex BN8 5UU, England (for information, phone: 0273-812321; for the box office, phone: 0273-541111).

GREENWICH FESTIVAL, London, England: The events of this annual 2-week-long June festival include mime and dance performances; poetry readings; concerts featuring rock, reggae, jazz, classical, and folk music; as well as many children's events. Internationally known artists such as Janet Baker, Claudio Arrau, James Galway, Alfred Brendel, and others perform alongside amateurs and local groups. The Greenwich Festival began as a purely community-oriented affair. Greenwich itself is a historic town on the banks of the Thames, and the magnificence and variety of its concert locations make its festival very special indeed. Details: Greenwich Festival Office, 25 Woolwich New Rd., London SE18 6EU, England (phone: 01-317-8687).

HARROGATE INTERNATIONAL FESTIVAL, Harrogate, North Yorkshire, England: Elegant buildings stand beside modern facilities in this Victorian spa town, whose 2-week festival in July and August embraces all the arts and, from time to time, the sciences as well. The various halls and churches used for the event, among them the 9th-century Ripon Cathedral, host everything from orchestral and chamber music, celebrity recitals, plays, late-night shows, and literary events, to programs for children. A new venture, the Harrogate Spring Music festival in early May, features some of the world's greatest artists performing music in an informal atmosphere. Details: Festival Office, Royal Baths, Harrogate, North Yorkshire HG1 2RR, England (phone: 0423-62303).

CITY OF LONDON FESTIVAL, London, England: London's own festival, held for 2½ weeks in July within the old city's square mile, takes advantage of the area's many fine halls and churches — including the Tower of London, Guildhall, the Barbican Centre, and St. Paul's — for concerts of serious music, featuring choirs, orchestras, chamber groups, and leading soloists of international repute. A popular program of jazz, dance, street theater, poetry, and a wide range of exhibitions runs concurrent with the festival. Details: City of London Festival Box Office, St. Paul's Churchyard, London EC4M 8BU, England (phone: 01-377-0540).

LONDON-TO-BRIGHTON VETERAN CAR RUN, London, England: Until 1896, a British law prohibited the operation of a car unless it was preceded by a man on foot carrying a red flag (so as not to scare horses). Its repeal is the raison d'être for this 50-mile drive full of shiny antique autos, held annually on the first Sunday in November. Details: RAC Motor Sports Association Ltd., Motor Sports House, Riverside Park, Colnbrook, Slough SL3 0HG, England (phone: 0753-681736).

LORD MAYOR'S PROCESSION, London, England: This event, held annually on the second Saturday in November, honors the newly inaugurated lord mayor and the profession that he is leaving for the duration of his term. The lord mayor is transported — in an 18th-century gold State coach drawn by six gray horses — from the Guildhall, to the Royal Court of Justice, where the oath of office is administered. The lord mayor inaugurated in 1989 was the 662nd to hold the position since it was established in 1189. Wonderfully colorful. Details: City of London Public Relations Office, Guildhall, London EC2P 2EJ, England (phone: 01-606-3030).

MALVERN FESTIVAL, Malvern, Worcestershire, England: In 1929, Sir Barry Jackson directed the first Malvern Festival, George Bernard Shaw wrote plays especially for it, and Edward Elgar conducted his own compositions. The festival provides an environment in which new works are presented, new composers heard, and new drama productions introduced. The Fringe is the largest in Britain outside Edinburgh. And Elgar and Shaw still play a part. The picturesque Malvern Hills are within easy reach of the Cotswolds and Wales. Details: Malvern Festival Administrator, Grange Rd., Malvern, Worcestershire WR14 3HB, England (for information, phone: 0684-572725; for the box office, phone: 0684-892277).

KING'S LYNN FESTIVAL, King's Lynn, Norfolk, England: The Queen Mother is the patron of this late-July week of art exhibitions and classical music, both serious and light, plus jazz, puppetry, children's programs, theater, film, talks, and late-night shows — and she usually attends. Street shows and fireworks are part of a fringe that rounds out the program. The site, an ancient market town riddled with quaint streets, curious churches, and historic buildings, is also a delight. Details: King's Lynn Festival, 27 King St., King's Lynn, Norfolk PE30 1HA, England (phone: 0553-773578).

HOBBY HORSE CELEBRATIONS, Padstow, Cornwall, England: Among Europe's oldest festivals, this annual May 1st event brings this sleepy seaport town to life. Caroling and carousing go on all night, but the real highlight is a long parade in which the Hobby Horse — a fabulous creature with a fierce-looking cone-shaped head protruding through a black, sailcloth-covered hoop — acts out a skit in which he dies and is revived over and over, then, at day's end, prances around a Maypole. Details: West Country Tourist Board, Trinity Ct., 37 Southernhay E, Exeter, Devon EX1 1QS, England (phone: 0392-76351).

SALISBURY FESTIVAL, Salisbury, Wiltshire, England: This 2-week-long September event, one of the leading cultural affairs in the South of England, includes lovely concerts by candlelight in the cathedral, operas and plays, a variety of late-evening shows, and assorted outdoor events. There are many points of interest in the region — mysterious, prehistoric Stonehenge and the charming Wilton House among them — and Salisbury itself is a fine ancient town. Details: Salisbury Festival, The King's House, 65 The Close, Salisbury, Wiltshire SP1 2EN, England (phone: 0722-23883).

YORK EARLY MUSIC FESTIVAL, York, North Yorkshire, England: Ancient York is the ideal setting for this annual July event, one of the world's leading festivals devoted to music from medieval to classical. Concert venues are historic — ancient churches in York, the museum gardens, and country houses. Early dance workshops, medieval drama productions, talks, and exhibitions round out the program of concerts. Details: York Early Music Festival, DeGrey House, Exhibition Square, York, North Yorkshire YO1 2EW, England (phone: 0904-658338).

EDINBURGH FESTIVAL, Edinburgh, Scotland: During its 3-week run in late August (August 12 to September 1 in 1990), this grande dame of festivals offers a cornucopia of activities. Most of the city's bigger public buildings, as well as many smaller ones, are taken over for exhibitions, performances, lectures, conferences, master classes, and other cultural affairs of global significance or for nearly 960 more presentations of the Festival Fringe, which the *Guinness Book of World Records* lists as the largest arts festival in the world. The Fringe, nowadays more straightforward than experimental, gives particular encouragement to comics; past performers have included Dudley Moore as well as Michael Palin and Terry Jones, later of the Monty Python team. There, as at the festival proper, patrons can also enjoy music, dance, theater, opera, and the visual arts, as well as many world premieres. The artists are the best in the world, and the audiences are big and international. The colorful Tattoo that takes place at the castle every night is almost as popular as the musical offerings. A book festival, a film festival, and a jazz festival run concurrently. Details: Festival Society, 21 Market St., Edinburgh EH1 1BW, Scotland (phone: 031-226-4001), and the Festival Fringe Society, 180 High St., Edinburgh EH1 1QS, Scotland (phone: 031-226-5257 or 031-226-5259).

FISHGUARD MUSIC FESTIVAL, Fishguard, Dyfed, Wales: The renowned Welsh choral tradition has generated this week-long July annual. The music is mainly classical, but new works are commissioned for performance by visiting musicians from home and abroad; and there's also jazz, poetry, film, and art. The festival often ends with the presentation of a large choral work. Concerts take place in ancient St. David's Cathedral and in Fishguard. The setting for the 1971 filming of Dylan Thomas's *Under Milk Wood* starring Richard Burton, this town on the edge of Pembrokeshire National Park is beautiful — backed by cliffs and partially edged by a shingled beach. Details: Fishguard Music Festival Office, Fishguard, Pembrokeshire, Dyfed SA65 9BJ, Wales (phone: 0348-873612).

INTERNATIONAL MUSICAL EISTEDDFOD, Llangollen, Clwyd, Wales: Music and friendship abound here for a week in July as over 2,000 competitors from 30 countries from Hungary and Bulgaria to Norway, Italy, Japan, the US, and others compete in folk song and dance competitions and choir contests. Evening concerts are given by choirs, dance groups, and renowned singers and instrumentalists. The colors, costumes, and sounds are dazzling, and there's always a special moment — as when an American choir and a Russian chorus got together and sang the Welsh national anthem, in Welsh, or when a group of Zulu dancers swept onstage and interrupted the national anthem to present the festival's music director with their tribe's highest honor. The latest addition to the festival is the Choir of the World competition, in which the title is bestowed on the winning choir. Details: Eisteddfod Office, Llangollen, Clwyd LL20 8NG, Wales (phone: 0978-860236).

IF YOU'RE NEARBY

WINDSOR FESTIVAL, Windsor Castle, Berkshire, England: Concerts, dance programs, readings, lectures, walks, and exhibitions take place in or near Windsor Castle and Eton College and occupy this community every year for 2 weeks in September or October. Details: Dial House, Englefield Green, Surrey TW20 0DU, England (phone: 0784-32618).

BILLINGHAM INTERNATIONAL FOLKLORE FESTIVAL, Billingham, Cleveland, England: This folk festival, whose events take place in four different venues, is unusual because it presents traditional music, song, and dance from many countries in a theatrical setting. Open-air concerts are held daily, and package tours of the area are available. August. Details: Festival Office, Municipal Buildings, Town Centre, Billingham, Cleveland TS23 2LW, England (phone: 0642-558212).

CBSO SUMMER SEASON, Birmingham, West Midlands, England: Each summer, City of Birmingham Symphony Orchestra principal conductor Simon Rattle — one of Britain's most distinguished young conductors — assembles a number of other prominent conductors and soloists for a series of concerts with the orchestra, continuing a tradition inaugurated in 1945. June or July. Details: City of Birmingham Symphony Orchestra, Paradise Pl., Birmingham, West Midlands B3 3RP, England (phone, box office: 021-236-1555).

CAMBRIDGE FESTIVAL OF ARTS, Cambridge, Cambridgeshire, England: A great success since its founding in 1962, the festival is held during the last 2 weeks in July every year. This beautiful and ancient university city plays host to internationally famous jazz and classical musicians, art exhibitions, drama and cabaret, the choirs of King's and St. John's colleges singing in their chapels, activities for children, fairs, fireworks, and more. Details: Cambridge Festival, Mandela House, 4 Regent St., Cambridge CB2 1BY, England (phone: 0223-358977).

CAMBRIDGE FOLK FESTIVAL, Cambridge, Cambridgeshire, England: A well-established festival that does not limit itself to traditional English folk music, it attracts performers from far afield who show off contemporary rock as well as many other musical styles. Held the last weekend in July. Details: Cambridge Folk Festival, Amenities and Recreation Department, Mandela House, Regent St., Cambridge, Cambridgeshire CB2 1BY, England (phone: 0223-358977).

FOLKESTONE INTERNATIONAL FOLKLORE FESTIVAL, Folkestone, Kent, England: For this biennial June event held in odd-numbered years, artists and cultural organizations stage exhibitions, and in one way or another, the whole town gets into the act. The reputation of the musical performances, which take place both indoors and outdoors, is well known throughout Europe. Details: Festival Director, Folkestone International Folklore Festival, Midstreams Green Lane, Hythe, Kent C221 4DY, England (phone: 0303-269119).

TILFORD BACH FESTIVAL, Tilford, Farnham, Surrey, England: Devoted mainly to the music of Bach and organized by the Tilford Bach Society, this village festival has been in existence since 1953. These May concerts are given by the London Handel Orchestra in All Saints' Church, and the intermissions are long enough to allow the audience to stroll over to the local pub for refreshments. Details: Helen Malyron, Festival Secretary, Old Quarry House Seale, Farnham, Surrey GU10 1LD, England (phone: 02518-2167).

ANNUAL BOTTLE KICKING AND HARE PIE SCRAMBLE, Hallaton, Leicestershire, England: When the *Guardian* described this small village's 700-year-old Easter Monday event, the high point on the local calendar, as being "unsurpassed for sheer animal ferocity," it wasn't far from wrong. As the opposing teams from Hallaton and neighboring Medbourne scramble to maneuver two out of three small wooden beer kegs across a goal line, the field is sheer anarchy — a situation that may have something to do with the fact that every now and again each player drops out to have another pint. The event begins with the town rector blessing the Hare Pie at the church gates, then slices are handed out to the villagers. The rest of the pie is carried to Hare Pie Bank, scattered, then comes the scramble. Details: East Midlands Tourist Board, Exchequergate, Lincoln, Lincolnshire LN2 1PZ, England (phone: 0522-531521).

HASLEMERE FESTIVAL, Haslemere, Surrey, England: At this early-music festival held in July, performances follow original manuscripts in the town's Dolmetsch Library and reproduce playing styles of the period in which the various pieces were composed. Arnold Dolmetsch, the library's namesake, founded the event in 1925; Carl Dolmetsch has been festival director for the past 47 years. Details: Festival Secretary, Dolmetsch Foundation, Jesses, Grayswood Rd., Haslemere, Surrey GU27 2BS, England (phone: 0428-2161).

HAXEY HOOD GAME, Haxey, Humberside, England: One of dozens of English festivals rooted in age-old tradition, this one got started some 600 years ago when Lady Mowbray lost her hood to a sudden gust of wind and thanked the 13 men who strove gallantly to rescue it by instituting an annual reenactment of the occasion. Believed by some to have been the origin of rugby, the game is played today — on January 6 — by the descendants of those men and their neighbors. The contest involves a Lord, 13 Boggins, a Fool, a bonfire, a no-holds-barred free-for-all in which writhing and grunting masses of humanity struggle for long hours over a piece of leather stuffed with straw, coins, and other fillings, and equally drawn-out victory celebrations in the local pubs. Details: Tourist Information Centre, Doncaster Central Library, Waterdale, Doncaster, South Yorkshire DN1 3JE, England (phone: 0302-734306).

HENLEY FESTIVAL OF MUSIC AND THE ARTS, Henley-on-Thames, England: This event is timed to follow the Henley Royal Regatta. In fact, it takes place in the Stewards' Enclosure the week immediately after the Regatta in July. Concerts, recitals, and exhibitions make up the fare. Details: Henley Festival of Music and the Arts, 103–109 Wardour St., London W1Z 4HE, England (phone: 01-437-9711).

DANCE UMBRELLA, London, England: A dance treat, this festival has been an important part of the international contemporary dance scene since it was founded in 1978, and it attracts participants from all over the world. During October and November festival events are held in various theaters both in London and around the country. Details: Dance Umbrella, The Riverside Studios, Crisp Rd., Hammersmith, London W6 9RL, England (phone: 01-741-4040).

EARLY MUSIC CENTRE FESTIVAL, London, England: One of Britain's most important early-music events, this festival mixes orchestral, chamber, and choral music — all played on original instruments by professional groups from here and abroad. The concerts are held in a number of important London halls and churches, from the end of September through early October. Details: Festival Secretary, The Early Music Centre, Charles Clore House, 17 Russell Sq., London WC1B 5DR, England (phone: 01-580-8401).

HENRY WOOD PROMENADE CONCERTS, London, England: Better known as "The Proms," it has been so named because this annual festival, since its foundation in 1894, has taken place in an auditorium capable of providing a considerable area of "promenade" or standing places to which the mostly youthful audience is admitted at very reasonable prices. Since 1941, the Proms have been held annually — even throughout WW II — at the Royal Albert Hall in Kensington, a masterpiece of Victorian architecture which accommodates 1,600 people in two promenade areas. The Proms has been promoted by the BBC since 1942, and each night, from mid-July to mid-September, it attracts crowds from all over the world. In addition, several million others listen to live broadcasts of the concerts on the radio and television. The BBC Symphony Orchestra performs most of the concerts — 60 to 70 in all — but every year appearances are made by most of the other major British orchestras, along with prestigious visits by some of the world's most renowned ensembles, such as the Vienna Philharmonic, the Concertgebouw from Amsterdam, the Leipzig Gewandhaus, and the New York Philharmonic. The Proms reflect music from all eras. Traditionally, the last night concludes with familiar British music, including Elgar's "Pomp and Circumstance March No. 1" and the active participation of the audience. Details: Royal Albert Hall, Kensington Gore, London SW7 2AP, England (phone: box office, 01-589-8212; administration, -3203).

LONDON FILM FESTIVAL, London, England: This festival presents the best of British and international movies from the latest international film festivals, with occasional lectures and discussions led by participating film directors after many of the screenings. The National Film Theatre on the South Bank is the principal location, but other London houses are used as well. November. Details: Festival Director, National Film Theatre, South Bank, London SE1 8XT, England (phone: 01-928-3535).

MOULTON VILLAGE FESTIVAL, Moulton, Northamptonshire, England: The traditional May celebrations in this Northamptonshire village have always included the crowning of the May Queen who is pulled around the village in a ceremonial Maycart by all the visiting Morris dancers. In the past few years this small-scale fête has developed into a full-blown event, with folklore such as Morris dancing alongside film, jazz concerts, and art exhibitions. Details: Moulton Village Festival, Rootyhill Cottage, 8 Chater St., Moulton, Northamptonshire NN3 1UD, England (phone: 0604-46818).

PETERBOROUGH DANCE AND MIME SEASON, Peterborough, Cambridgeshire, England: National and international contemporary dance companies converge on this town noted for its large Romanesque cathedral, one of the most distinguished of its kind in Britain. The festival itself, founded in 1982, is a more recent but no less remarkable arrival and has been expanded into two seasons — September to December and January to April. Details: Dance Animateur, Peterborough Arts Council, c/o Peterborough Education Development Centre, Cottesmore Close, Peterborough, Cambridgeshire PE3 6TP, England (phone: 0733-264330).

MINACK THEATRE FESTIVAL, Porthcurno, Cornwall, England: The setting of the open-air Minack Theatre, on the cliffs 3 miles from Land's End, is as provocative as the 16-week season of productions staged by professional and amateur companies. May through September. Details: Minack Theatre, Porthcurno, Penzance, Cornwall TR19 6JU, England (phone: 0736-810471).

SIDMOUTH INTERNATIONAL FOLKLORE FESTIVAL, Sidmouth, Devon, England: The largest folk festival in Britain, this 30-year-old event presents everything from song and dance to crafts, processions, and special children's activities in a selection of venues ranging from pubs to huge open-air theaters. July and August. Details: International Folklore Festival, The Knowle, Sidmouth, Devon EX10 8HL, England (phone: 0395-515134).

STOUR MUSIC, Wye, Kent, England: Founded in 1963, this festival of music, set in the heart of the Garden of England in East Kent, concentrates on music of the Renaissance and baroque periods. Concerts are presented in the 14th-century Pilgrim Church of Broughton Aluph. Late June. Details: Stour Music — Festival of Music in

East Kent, 120 Bridge St., Wye, Ashford, Kent TN25 5EA, England (phone: 0233-812967).

DUMFRIES AND GALLOWAY ARTS FESTIVAL, Dumfries, Scotland: This youthful affair, founded in 1980, offers a program of drama, music, and visual arts in the town's Theatre Royal and in various schools, churches, and halls throughout the region. Late May to early June. Details: Dumfries and Galloway Arts Festival, Gracefield Arts Centre, 28 Edinburgh Rd., Dumfries DG1 1JR, Scotland (phone: 0387-61234, ext. 4447).

EDINBURGH INTERNATIONAL FOLK FESTIVAL, Edinburgh, Scotland: Folk music, dance, drama, a crafts fair, children's events, lectures, courses on traditional instruments, *ceilidhs,* workshops, and an Oral History Conference are the heart of this festival, which takes place over the 10 days that lead up to Easter weekend. The Edinburgh Harp Festival is an integral part of the event, and in 1987 the Festival of European Piping was incorporated as well. Details: Edinburgh International Folk Festival, Shillinghill, Temple, Midlothian EH23 4SH, Scotland (phone: 031-220-0464).

MAYFEST, Glasgow, Scotland: Now the second largest arts festival in Britain, this 3-week event offers popular and classical music, drama, art exhibitions, street theater, cabaret, and community-based events throughout the city. May. Details: Glasgow Mayfest, 46 Royal Exchange Sq., Glasgow G1 3AR, Scotland (phone: 041-221-4911).

PERTH FESTIVAL OF THE ARTS, Perth, Tayside, Scotland: The program of this 2-week festival first held in 1972 includes drama, music, and the visual arts at sites all over the city. Last half of May. Details: Perth Tourist Association, The Round House, Marshall Place, Perthshire PH2 8NU, Scotland (phone: 0738-38353).

PITLOCHRY FESTIVAL, Pitlochry, Tayside, Scotland: Plays in repertory, celebrity concerts, and art exhibitions are presented in Scotland's Theatre in the Hills from May through October. Details: Pitlochry Festival Theatre, Pitlochry, Tayside PH16 5DR, Scotland (phone: 0796-2680).

ORKNEY TRADITIONAL FOLK FESTIVAL, Stromness, Orkney, Scotland: Based on the main island of Orkney, this event attracts both local amateurs and professional musicians from various parts of Britain and has lately spread to other islands. Many competitions and other activities are organized for young performers and children. May. Details: Orkney Traditional Folk Festival, 12 Guardhouse Park, Stromness, Orkney KW16 3DP, Scotland (phone: 0856-850773).

UP-HELLY-AA, Lerwick, Shetland Islands, Scotland: This annual traditional ceremony takes place toward the end of January to celebrate the end of the winter solstice. Dating back to times when the islanders were compelled by their rulers to embrace Christian beliefs but were instead holding on to their pagan Norse ways, this celebration marked the ending of the Christian holy days of Christmas. Each year a Viking galley is built and transported in torchlight procession by up to 900 Shetlanders dressed in Viking or fancy dress costume to the park where the torches are used to set fire to the ship. After the blaze has reached the skies, the "guizers" visit each of several halls open to invited guests, where they perform a sketch inspired by their garb, then dance the night away. Details: Shetland Tourist Organisation, Market Cross, Lerwick, Shetland ZE1 0LU, Scotland (phone: 0595-3434).

FEIS BHARRAIGH, Isle of Barra, Western Isles, Scotland: Devoted to fostering Gaelic language and culture, this event encompasses drama, literature, music, dance, and the visual arts. Traditional instruments like the *clarsach* (harp), bagpipe, tin whistle, and fiddle are featured here, along with Highland and Hebridean dancing. July. Details: Feis Bharraigh, 9 Ardmhor, Northey, Isle of Barra PA80 5YB, Western Isles, Scotland (phone: 08715-237 or 08715-344).

LLANDAFF FESTIVAL, Cardiff, Wales: One of the oldest festivals in Wales, this one offers a series of orchestral and choral music, as well as solo recitals, and attracts orchestras from the rest of Wales and beyond. May to June. Details: Llandaff Festival,

4 Church La., St. Athan, Barry, South Glamorgan CF6 9PL, Wales (phone: 0446-750774).

NORTH WALES MUSIC FESTIVAL, St. Asaph, Clwyd, Wales: New and old music is presented for a week in late September in this quiet town's 6th-century cathedral, the smallest medieval church in England and Wales. Details: North Wales Music Festival, High St., St. Asaph, Clywd LL 17 0RD, Wales (phone: 0745-584508).

ST. DAVID'S CATHEDRAL BACH FESTIVAL, St. David's, Dyfed, Wales: Her Majesty the Queen is the patron of this festival held during the last week in May in Wales's largest cathedral, the shrine of the nation's patron saint, St. David. The building comes as a surprise, because the surrounding area, within the Pembrokeshire Coast National Park, is rural and isolated. But so does its interior, which is far more ornate than the rather plain exterior, and the quality of the music — not only traditional music but also newly commissioned pieces. Details: John Mogford, c/o St. David's Cathedral, St. David's, Haverfordwest, Dyfed SA62, Wales. (phone: 0437-720202

SWANSEA FESTIVAL, Swansea, West Glamorgan, Wales: Wales's most important arts festival is held here annually for 3 weeks in October, in the area where Dylan Thomas grew up and wrote *Under Milk Wood.* It includes ballet, drama, poetry, art, and a week of opera featuring the Welsh National Opera Company. But orchestral music is the main feature. There's always an orchestra from London, another from the Continent, and another from Wales, and past soloists have included Vladimir Ashkenazy and Claudio Abbado. Details: Swansea Festival, The Guildhall, Swansea, West Glamorgan SA1 4PA, Wales (phone: 0792-30130).

FOR MORE INFORMATION

ENGLAND: The following regional arts associations can provide a great deal of additional information about concerts, festivals, and other cultural affairs:

Eastern Arts Association, Cherry Hinton Hall, Cherry Hinton Rd., Cambridge CB1 4DW, England (phone: 0223-215355). Covers Bedfordshire, Cambridgeshire, Essex, Hertfordshire, Norfolk, and Suffolk.

East Midlands Arts Association, Mountfields House, Forest Rd., Loughborough, Leicestershire LE11 3HU, England (phone: 0509-218292). Covers Buckinghamshire, Leicestershire, Northamptonshire, Nottinghamshire, and part of Derbyshire.

Greater London Arts, 9 White Lion St., London N1 9PD, England (phone: 01-837-8808). Covers the London boroughs and the City of London.

Lincolnshire and Humberside Arts, St. Hugh's, Newport, Lincoln, Lincolnshire LN1 3DN, England (phone: 0522-533555). Covers Lincolnshire and Humberside.

Merseyside Arts, Bluecoat Chambers, School La., Liverpool L1 3BX, Merseyside, England (phone: 051-709-0671). Covers the District of West Lancashire, Ellesmere Port, the Halton Districts of Cheshire, and the Metropolitan County of Merseyside.

Northern Arts, 9–10 Osborne Terr., Jesmond, Newcastle-upon-Tyne, Tyne & Wear NE2 1NZ, England (phone: 091-281-6334). Covers Cleveland, Cumbria, Durham, the Metropolitan County of Tyne & Wear, and Northumberland.

North West Arts, 12 Harter St., Manchester M1 6HY, England (phone: 061-228-3062). Covers Greater Manchester, Cheshire, Derbyshire, most of Lancansirek and the High Peak Districk of Derbyshire, and Lancashire.

Southern Arts, 19 Southgate St., Winchester, Hampshire SO23 9DQ, England (phone: 0962-55099). Covers Berkshire, the Districts of Bournemouth, Christchurch, and Poole, Hampshire, Isle of Wight, Oxfordshire, West Sussex, and Wiltshire.

South East Arts, 10 Mount Ephraim, Tunbridge Wells, Kent TN4 8AS, England (phone: 0892-51520). Covers East Sussex, Kent, and Surrey.

South West Arts, Bradninch Pl., Gandy St., Exeter, Devon EX4 3LS, England (phone: 0392-218188). Covers Avon, Cornwall, Devon, Gloucestershire, Somerset, and part of Dorset.

West Midlands Arts, 82 Granville St., Birmingham B12LH, England (phone: 021631-3121). Covers the County of Hereford and Worcester, the Metropolitan County of West Midlands, Shropshire, Staffordshire, and Warwickshire.

Yorkshire Arts Association, Glyde House, Bradford, West Yorkshire BD5 0BQ, England (phone: 0274-723051). Covers North, South, and West Yorkshire.

SCOTLAND: Glasgow has been selected as the 1990 Cultural Capital of Europe, so there will be celebrations and activities in the city throughout the year. Details on this and the wide range of events taking place all over Scotland are available from the Scottish Arts Countil, 12 Manor Place, Edinburgh EH3 7DD, Scotland (phone: 031-226-6051).

WALES: Information on festivals and other arts activities in Wales is available from the following sources:

North Wales Arts Association, 10 Wellfield House, Bangor, Gwynedd LL57 1ER, Wales (phone: 0248-353248). Covers Clwyd, Gwynedd, and Montgomery.

South East Wales Arts Association, Victoria St., Cwmbran, Gwent NP44 3YT, Wales (phone: 06333-75075). Covers Gwent, Mid-Glamorgan, South Glamorgan, and part of Powys.

Welsh Arts Council, 9 Museum Place, Cardiff, South Glamorgan CF1 3NX, Wales (phone: 0222-394711).

West Wales Association for the Arts, Red St., Carmarthen, Dyfed SA31 1QL, Wales (phone: 0267-234248). Covers Dyfed and West Glamorgan.

Antiques and Auctions

Perhaps no nation takes better care of its past than Britain. From the top of the Tower of London to the most remote Scottish crypt, tradition is a cherished possession. So, if you're one of those people who is driven to possess a chunk of history, not simply observe it, and who would rather own a coal scuttle than just ogle the Crown Jewels, grab your checkbook and head for these isles. You'll have the chance to outbid a London dealer at a rural Ayrshire auction, blow dust off a first edition of Dickens at an Aberdeen antiquarian's, and haggle for a special price at the Faversham flea market — if you decide to take *both* the Georgian silver salver *and* the yeoman's crossbow. There's no time like the past — and no time like the present for enjoying it.

Many genuine antiques taken out of the country are subject to duty. Also, an export license may be required; it is available from the Export Licensing Division, Department of Trade and Transport, Kingsgate House, 68–74 Victoria St., London SW1 E6W, England (phone: 01-215-7877).

A REPERTOIRE OF ANTIQUES SOURCES

There are four distinctly different types of dealers in Britain. At the low end of the scale are the flea markets, where true bargains are often available — to those willing to sift through piles of not always interesting miscellanea. Auction houses frequently yield a find, under the right circumstances, to those able to visit the pre-sale exhibition before bidding. Antiques shops offer convenience. A dealer has made the rounds of the markets and has purchased the pick of the auction houses for resale — and a customer pays the price for his time and trouble. Fairs often bring many dealers and many wares together in one place. The quality may be high, with prices to match, but the selection can't be beat. In short, the repertoire of sources for antiques is not so different than that in the US, Canada, and many other countries. What is notable is the selection of these fairs, auction houses, shops, and markets. Below we describe a few of the very best.

SHOPS AND ANTIQUES CENTERS: From Abbotsbury to Zither-on-Thames, there are some 6,000 "olde curiosity shoppes" dappling the landscape of Britain. Whether the quest be for barometers or bond certificates, tools or toy soldiers, enthusiasts will find a shop catering exclusively to their collecting passion. Over the centuries.the antiques trade in Britain has become very sophisticated in many specialties.

Ethical standards are generally high, and usually dealers will spontaneously divulge all the defects of an item a customer is considering buying. A number are members of recognized, reputable national guilds, with clear and rigorous codes in matters of authenticity and quality. But if the caveats aren't offered unsolicited, prospective buyers should be sure to question the dealer about what is original, what has been restored or retouched, and what has simply been replaced. If a purchase involves a significant sum, the buyer should also ask to have the qualifications put in writing.

For advice about purchasing and shipping and customs regulations, and for a list of members, antiques lovers can contact one of the following dealers' associations:

British Antique Dealers' Association, 20 Rutland Gate, London SW7 1BD, England (phone: 01-589-4128). Members of this organization, to which some of the most reputable shops and dealers belong, display a blue and gold plaque engraved with the figure of the Renaissance sculptor and goldsmith Benvenuto Cellini. They also publish a handbook ($20) available from Joyce Golden Associates, 551 5th Ave., New York, NY 10176.

Cotswold Antique Dealers' Association, High St., Blockley, Gloucestershire GL56 9ET, England (phone: 0386-700280).

London and Provincial Antique Dealers' Association, (LAPADA), 535 Kings Road, London SW10 OSZ, England (phone: 01-376-3040). Over 750 members are committed to the strict LAPADA code; look for the chandelier sign.

These organizations can send lists of their members, who adhere to association standards. In addition, a comprehensive list of dealers in Britain is available in the following book — revised annually and for sale at fine bookstores in London:

Guide to the Antique Shops of Britain ($15.25/£9.95), published by the Antique Collectors Club, 5 Church St., Woodbridge, Suffolk IP12 1DS, England (phone: 0394-385501), contains more than 6,000 entries that outline the type of stock, size of showrooms, years in business, hours, and much more.

Miller's Price Guide ($23/£14.95), provides an overview of approximate prices for various items.

Before heading for a small shop in a small town, it's wise for visitors to phone ahead. Most dealers will see prospective buyers by appointment, even outside normal shopping hours.

A recent trend has been the gathering of many small shops into antiques centers — something like tony shopping centers or indoor markets with all the stalls under one roof. These are intriguing places to spend a rainy hour and to get a quick overview of the local market, with no great pressure to buy. There are hundreds of interesting items that rarely make it across the Atlantic.

Bath, Avon, England – There are some 50 antiques shops in this charming spa town, and more than 100 stallholders in the *Great Western Antique Market* (phone: 0225-24243), where dealers purvey everything from antique beds to cameras. It's the largest and most comprehensive antiques center under one roof outside London. Just across the way is the *Bartlett Street Antique Centre.* Bartlett St. (phone: 0225-330267).

Bristol, Avon, England – In this busy city, once a booming port, the 60 dealers at the suburban *Clifton Antiques Market* offer a wide selection at prices that range from the ridiculous to the sublime. 26–28 The Mall, Clifton (phone: 0272-741627).

London, England – There are several antiques centers in London.

Camden Passage Antiques Centre is an 18th-century, traffic-free pedestrian walk that houses 350 dealers. In Islington, north of the city, in Camden Passage, N1. Antiques market days are Wednesdays and Saturdays; book market day is Thursday.

Grays Antique Market, installed in a beautiful terra cotta Victorian structure, houses dozens of stands, and its dealers are more selective than not. There is a fine selection of antique jewelry as well as antiquarian books, maps, prints, arms and armour, lace, scientific instruments, and thimbles. Around the corner, *Grays In The Mews* (1–7 Davies Mews) has Victorian and Edwardian toys, paintings and prints, and Orientalia. 58 Davies St., W1 (phone: 01-629-7034).

Chenil Galleries is increasingly important as a center for art deco and art nouveau objects. But dealers' specialties range from Gothic furniture, tapestries, and textiles, to 18th-century paintings, scientific instruments, and fine porcelain. 181–183 King's Rd., SW3 (phone: 01-352-2123 or 352-2123).

Alfie's Antique Market is housed in what was once a Victorian department store. This warren of 370 stalls, showrooms, and workshops is the biggest covered antiques market in London — and likely the least expensive, since it is where the dealers come to buy. 13–25 Church St., NW8 (phone: 01-723-6066).

Woburn Abbey, Bedfordshire, England – The *Woburn Abbey Antiques Centre* is another good bet. Collectibles are housed in an old stable behind façades that were rescued from demolition, restored, and then re-erected. Items range from furniture to paintings and prints, silver and glassware — most date from before 1870 (phone: 0525-290350).

Brighton, East Sussex, England – In this old fishing town, a famous resort since the days of the Prince Regent, the 22 stalls at the *Brighton Antiques Gallery* sell a wide variety of wares — from Georgian and Victorian silver and jewelry to ceramics, small furniture, antique glass, and other collectors' items. 41 Meeting House La. (phone: 0273-21059).

Edinburgh, Scotland – The Scottish capital bustles with the antiques trade and has its share of shops. The antiques center that stands out is the *Ingliston Market,* on the city's outskirts (Sundays only). Newbridge, Midlothian EH28 8NB (phone: 031-333-3801).

Glasgow, Scotland – At the *Victorian Village,* there are more than two dozen dealers, and roomfuls of antiques, ornaments, and old lace. Beethoven melodies waft through the corridors while visitors browse. Heritage House, 158 Bath St., G2 (phone: 041-332-4033).

FAIRS: There are dozens of fairs in all sizes and qualities. Whether they last 2 days or 10, they attract dealers from all over the region, the country, and Europe. Many dealers make the rounds of these events, beginning in January and continuing throughout the year. The *Antique Dealer and Collectors' Guide* magazine publishes a comprehensive yearly calendar listing antiques fairs throughout the country (01-261-6146).

The most prestigious fairs by far are the *Burlington House Fair,* held in September in odd-numbered years at the Royal Academy in London, and the *Grosvenor House Antiques Fair,* held in June at the Grosvenor House hotel in Park Lane. But there are dozens of others, which include the following:

Bath Guildhall Antiques Fair, Guildhall, High St., Bath, Avon, England. August.

British International Antiques Fair, National Exhibition Centre, Birmingham B40 1NI, England. Late March to mid April.

Buxton Antiques Fair, Pavilion Gardens, Buxton, Derbyshire, England. An old, established antiques fair in the north of England. Early May.

City of London Antiques Fair, Barbican Centre, London EC2, England. Late November.

East Anglia Antiques Fair, Athenaeum, Bury St. Edmonds, Suffolk, England. September.

Edinburgh Annual Antiques Fair, Roxburghe Hotel in Charlotte Sq., Edinburgh, Scotland. Late July.

Kensington Antiques Fair, New Town Hall, Kensington, London W8, England. Early November.

Leicester Antiques Fair, Moat House Hotel, Wigston Rd., Oadby, Leicester, England. February.

Scottish Antiques Fair, Roxburghe Hotel, Charlotte Sq., Edinburgh, Scotland. July.

York Antiques Fair, De Grey Room, Exhibition Sq., York, England. Mid-October.

FLEA MARKETS AND OTHER WEEKLY SPECTACLES: That heady mixture of rubbish and relic known as the flea market is the ultimate paradise for the collector. It offers the chance to find that special, unrecognized rarity, the eye-catching castoff whose true value only a devout aficionado would perceive — say, a yak saddle from the Indian Mutiny, a left-handed pewter monocle, or a chipped 78 rpm recording of Edward VIII's abdication speech. For those who dream of snapping up a precious item before the professionals send it successively to auction, fair, and trendy shop (at prices that spiral ever upward), the weekly markets are a must, especially those that flourish outside London.

The buyer's best allies in this odyssey are bad weather and early arrival. A serious collector should get to the market at dawn and pray for torrential rain, or if the spectacle itself is the main attraction, hope for a sunny morning. Fine days provide such good theater — at such moderate cost — that even the most eager treasure seekers won't be too disappointed at trudging home empty-handed. Though the British have managed to get many of their markets under a roof, thereby sacrificing local color to comforts, the bargains are still there. The curious can try their luck at the following:

Bath, Avon, England – This city is the antiques center of the west of England, and on Wednesdays, over 300 dealers trade in its quartet of markets.

Bartlett Street Antique Centre has 50 dealers that boosts the already estimable number of them at this location. Open Mondays through Saturdays. 7–10 Bartlett St. (phone: 0225-330267 or -66689).

Bath Antique Market is run by the largest group of dealers in the West Country. Its 100 stalls are packed with the rare, the quaint, and the beautiful. Wednesdays. Guinea La., Paragon. (phone: 0225-22510).

Bath Saturday Antiques Market features more than 50 stalls. Saturdays. Walcot St. (phone: 0225-22510).

Paragon Antiques Market also attracts dealers from all over the country every Wednesday. Small, easily carried items are the specialty. 3 Bladud Buildings (phone: 0225-63715).

Birmingham, West Midlands, England – At the *Birmingham Thursday Antique Market,* some 30 dealers sell general antiques, furniture, clocks, and small objects ranging from porcelain to Victoriana. 141 Bromsgrove St. (phone: 021-622-2145).

Brighton, East Sussex, England – The *Old Lanes* offer the widest choice of goods on Saturdays, when the antiques shops concentrated between North Road and Trafalgar Street are augmented by sidewalk stalls.

Dorchester, Dorset, England – The *Dorchester Antique Market* holds forth one Wednesday each month; call ahead for the date. Town Hall, Corn Exchange (phone: 0963-62478).

London, England – Open-air markets flourish all over the city, and for ferreting out curios, they can't be beat.

Bermondsey–New Caledonian Market complex, where several dealers set up every Friday in a good-size open space off Tower Bridge Road at the end of Long Lane and in an erstwhile factory nearby, is known as a dealers' market. Fresh shipments from the country go on sale here first (and, in fact, many of the goods for sale in Portobello Road were purchased here). Arrival after 9 AM means the best will be long gone; regulars try to arrive not much after 5 AM — with flashlights in tow. Tower Bridge Rd., SE1.

Dorchester Antique Market is open once a month on Saturdays in Glastonbury Town Hall (phone: 0963-62478).

Greenwich Antiques Market is a less frenetic place to be on Saturdays (and on Sundays in summer). Greenwich High Rd., SE10.

Jubilee Flea Market at Covent Garden, W2, held on Mondays, is a good bet for small antiques, old jewelry, and crockery. Don't miss the stalls on the south side of the piazza outside the main covered market.

Portobello Road is famous for antiques shops, junk shops, outdoor pushcarts, and legions of antiques lovers from all over the world trying to buy up bits and pieces of England. The activity is astonishing — but eager hunters shouldn't necessarily expect to turn up a treasure at a good price except occasionally in winter, when the weather is so blustery that only the most intrepid antiques hounds venture outside. There are flea markets on Fridays and Saturdays; on Saturdays, there are antiques as well. W11.

Orsett, Essex, England – The *Orsett Antiques Fair* is usually held the second Sunday of each month. Orsett Hall, Prince Charles Ave. (phone: 0702-714649 or 0268-774977).

Edinburgh, Scotland – The major market here is the *Ingliston Market,* which takes place on Sundays on the city's outskirts at Ingliston. This is not a sprawling spread of exquisite antiques; it is a true flea market, with goods ranging from fresh food and clothing to china and toys. The average weekly attendance often tops 25,000. Newbridge, Midlothian EH28 8NB (phone: 031-333-3801).

Glasgow, Scotland – A weekend fixture here since Victorian times, the *Barrows* is one of the most colorful flea markets in Britain, bar none. It takes up a square mile, and it's packed with stalls, up to a thousand of them, almost as colorful as their proprietors. Small wonder that the BBC called it Europe's bargain basement. Saturdays and Sundays. 244 Gallowgate.

Cardiff, Wales – *Jacobs Antique Centre* shelters about 60 dealers and is open on Thursdays and Saturdays. West Canal Wharf (phone: 0222-390939).

AUCTIONS: An auction, as any addict knows, is a mixture of stock market, gambling casino, and living theater. It's the perfect answer to rainy day blues provided newcomers pay attention to these notes:

Don't expect to make a killing. Even Chinese peasant children are hip to the art market today, it seems. But chances of unearthing a real find are better for those who shop at smaller country auctions. Look carefully at mixed lots, and always venture out in inclement weather. Every so often someone picks up a golden goblet for 10p at a Girl Guide (the British version of a Girl Scout) auction and then resells it for £9,000. In any event, there is about a 30% saving on the shop price of a comparable item.

Buy the catalogue before bidding. Catalogues often include a list of estimated prices. Those prices are not a contractual commitment, but they do act as a guide for prospective buyers. An elaborate stylistic code hints at the conviction the house may have about the age and authenticity of an item. The use of capital letters, of artists' full names, and of words like "fine," "rare," and "important" all carry positive connotations. The use of a last name only and of words like "style" and "attributed" should serve as warnings.

Visit the pre-sale exhibition carefully, thoroughly, and even repeatedly. There is the pleasure of browsing in a store without a hovering clerk. Even more important is the prospective buyer's chance to examine the offerings. *Caveat emptor* is the prevailing rule at an auction. Serious buyers should have paintings taken down from the wall and ask to handle objects under lock and key. Those who can't be at the sale can leave a commission bid with the auctioneer or even place a bid by telephone — but if they can't be at the exhibition, they should be wary of buying.

Decide on a top bid before the auction begins, and don't go beyond it. The bidding has its own rhythm and tension. The auctioneer becomes a Pied Piper, with the buyers winking, blinking, and nodding in time to his music. This situation arouses unusual behavior in some people. Suddenly their self-worth is at stake, and they'll bid far beyond what the item is worth — or even what they can afford. A bid may be canceled by promptly calling out "Withdrawn." *Note:* In determining their top price, bidders should remember to add the house commission, which is generally 10%, but can be more, and any value added tax. Fingers rise and hammers fall all over Britain — but the following spots warrant prime attention:

Bath, Avon, England – *Aldridges Auction Galleries* holds sales on Tuesdays, with viewing on Saturday mornings and Mondays until 7 PM. 130–132 Walcot St. (phone: 0225-62830).

Leicester, Leicestershire, England – *Heathcote Ball and Company Castle Auction Rooms* is the prime source of auction action every 6 weeks. A restoration and advisory service is also available. 78 St. Nicholas Circle (phone: 0533-536789).

London, England – London is still the auction capital of the world, and the market price of a work of art or an antique generally refers to the price that other items of its genre have fetched in the London salerooms. Of the auction houses in London, three stand out as the most important.

Christie's was founded in 1766. The fortunes of England's great families can be read in *Christie's* records, and an object's whole lineage can often be traced through its appearances in 2 centuries of *Christie's* sales. No wonder the mother house is something of a national landmark. There are auctions daily, and the exhibition rooms are a constantly changing museum. The clientele includes furred ladies, pin-striped Rembrandt hunters, bespectacled experts from US museums, and ordinary Londoners who do their Christmas shopping here, especially at the South Kensington saleroom, which handles items of recent vintage and some lower value — toys, telescopes, top hats, and the like. Some higher priced sales at *Christie's* in South Kensington include tribal art, Oriental and art deco items, paintings, furniture, and textiles. 8 King St., St. James's, SW1 (phone: 01-839-9060). The South Kensington branch is at 85 Old Brompton Rd., SW7 3LD (phone: 01-581-7611).

Sotheby's is the world's oldest auction house. The little white building in which it is discreetly housed, on the most elegant street in England, is a kind of nerve center of the art world. Its roster of experts in every field rivals the British Museum's. An important sale of Old Masters or Impressionists, with hundreds of thousands of dollars riding on every twitch, beats an evening at the National Theatre, as the chandeliers glitter next to a computer board that translates bids into dollars, yen, marks, lire, and Swiss and French francs as it did November 11, 1987, when Van Gogh's *Irises* sold for $54 million. In its surprisingly large complex of salerooms, auctions of every kind of work of art, including books, manuscripts, coins, medals, and jewelry, take place regularly throughout the year. 34-35 New Bond St., W1 (phone: 01-493-8080).

Phillips is number 3, and it's trying harder and harder. Auctions are held almost daily, and items range from fine works of art to more affordable collectibles. The house also handles a large number of estate sales, held on the owners' premises in fine English country houses. Since they are often sparsely attended by the general public, there's a fair chance of encountering dealer-level prices. The house does a large volume in modestly priced lots, and the staff is extremely helpful to auction novices. Besides the London house (7 Blenheim St., W1; phone: 01-629-6602), there are 20 salerooms throughout the UK. Weekly picture sales are held at Phillips Marylebone Hayes place (Lisbon Grove NW1; phone: 01-723-2647), and collectibles — including toys and dolls — and textiles can be bid on at Phillips West Two, 10 Salem Rd., W2.

Norwich, Norfolk, England – *Aylsham Salerooms* has regular sales of furniture, silver, porcelain and glass, collectibles, and books, and bimonthly sales of paintings, watercolors, and prints. G.A. Key, 8 Market Pl., Aylsham (phone: 0263-733195).

Penzance, Cornwall, England – *W. H. Lane and Son* has about a dozen general sales annually of antiques and objets d'art. In addition, there are a number of special sales devoted to antique books, coins, medals, stamps, and pictures; occasionally there are also treasure trove sales in which pieces of eight and other finds from old wrecks are put on the block. 65 Morrab Rd. (phone: 0736-61447).

Edinburgh, Scotland – *Phillips Scotland* has monthly sales of oil paintings, furniture, Oriental rugs, clocks, bronzes, silver, and other works of art; European ceramics and glass, Orientalia, jewelry, and watercolors are auctioned bimonthly; books, postcards, and maps are offered in eight sales annually, and four annual sales are devoted to dolls, costumes, and textiles. Viewing is usually 2 days prior; on Wednesdays and Thursdays, there's always something to be seen, not least of which is one of the best panoramic views of Edinburgh from the fifth floor. 65 George St. (phone: 031-225-2266).

Glasgow, Scotland – *Christie's Scotland,* Christie's Scottish saleroom, has auctions of jewelry, silver, objets d'art, and furniture, and regular sales of items of special interest — including Scottish silver, collectors' items, and paintings. 164-166 Bath St. (phone: 041-332-8134).

Phillips Scotland holds auctions of furniture, paintings, ceramics, silver, and jewelry every Tuesday; annually they have two special sales of fine jewelry and four of collectors' items. 207 Bath St. (phone: 041-221-8377).

ANTIQUES PEAKS ON THE BRITISH LANDSCAPE

There are a handful of cities and towns in Britain that stand out for their selection of shops, antiques centers, flea markets, and auction houses. These are the places that savvy antiques dealers from the Continent visit when they're on the prowl for newly fashionable 19th-century English furniture and objets d'art — and they are a must on any antiques lover's tour of Britain.

BATH, Avon, England: Bath is the antiques center of the west of England. Its elegant 18th-century squares and crescents are the natural setting for dozens of intriguing antiques shops, and over 300 dealers trade in four antiques markets every Wednesday. Some of the best bets for antiques hunting here include the following:

The Great Western Antique Market adds to any selection. Open 6 days a week, it's a busy bazaar devoted to the old. Bartlett St.

The Guinea Lane Antique Market is a must if you're in town on a Wednesday. Guinea La., Paragon.

Paragon Antiques Market is another fixture of the devoted antiques hunter's Wednesday itinerary. 3 Bladud Buildings, Paragon.

The Bath Saturday Antique Market is also worth a look. Walcot St.

Aldridges Auction Galleries has Tuesday sales, with viewings on Saturday mornings and on Mondays until 7 PM. 130–132 Walcot St. (phone: 0225-62830).

BRISTOL, Avon, England: In addition to dozens of antiques shops, this busy, commercial city has an antiques and crafts market in the Corn Exchange, Corn St. More than 50 stalls there offer a wide selection of glass, china, jewelry, and bric-a-brac. It's open Mondays through Saturdays.

The Clifton Antiques Market in the charming suburb of Clifton is well worth visiting. Open Tuesdays through Saturdays, it is located in a handsome Georgian building near the famous Clifton suspension bridge at 26–28 The Mall (phone: 0272-741627).

The Bristol Antiques and Collectors Fair takes place annually at the Bristol Exhibition Centre on the first day of January. More than 100 dealers exhibit annually. Bristol Exhibition Centre, 2 Canons Rd. (phone: 0272-215206).

CANTERBURY, Kent, England: The compact size of this famous city makes antiques hunting especially pleasant, and the prime destination is Palace Street, not far from the Christ Church Gate of the cathedral, where there are 15 antique shops alone. Good shops on Palace Street include the following:

Five Centuries Antiques, at No. 18.

The Aristocrat, at No. 19. Small and family-run, this shop's specialty is engraved glass and collectors' items (phone: 0227-46435).

Parker-Williams Antiques, at No. 22, sells 17th- to 19th-century English antiques (phone: 0227-68341).

CHESTER, Cheshire, England: The Rows, the centuries-old aboveground network of walkways for which the city is famous, are blessed with some of England's most abundant antiques hunting. Watergate Row, which is the most redolent of the past of all the Rows, offers particularly numerous shops. Good shops along the street include the following:

Erica and Hugo Harper, at No. 27 (phone: 0244-323004). The city's best junk shop, with masses of bric-a-brac, clocks, and furniture in several rooms and prices ranging from the small to the mighty. Mr. Harper can guide you to other shops and answer questions.

Chester Antiques, at No. 49, (phone: 0224-311768). Stocks a large selection of 18th-century grandfather clocks and Victorian clocks as well as Victorian dolls, rosewood furniture, fine English china, barometers, and weapons.

Christopher Pugh, at No. 68 (phone: 0244-314137), is the best dealer in town for 17th- and 18th-century furniture, decorative items, and watercolors.

Goss Street (off Watergate Street) was also the site of the Assay Office, where the city's own hallmark (three wheat sheaves) was stamped on the handiwork of Chester's celebrated silversmiths. Today, fine quality work is available from such specialists as:

Boodle and Dunthorne, next door to the *Grosvenor* hotel, was established in 1798 and is still thriving. Eastgate St. (phone: 0244-326666).

Lowe's, founded 28 years before *Boodle and Dunthorne,* it is the oldest silversmith in Chester and offers the county's largest collection of estate jewelry and silver. 11 Bridge St. Row (phone: 0244-312565).

Brown's, the oldest jeweler in the city, owned by the same family since 1848, focuses on unique items with investment value. 2 Eastgate Row (phone: 0244-324357).

COTSWOLDS, England: The most romantic antiques hunting in Britain is in the Cotswolds, about 100 miles west of London. The area's charming, unspoiled towns, its quaint stone cottages, and its oh-so-English countryside make it very popular with visitors, so bargains are rare. But the antiques shops are so close to one another that visitors can cover quite a few without racking up excessive mileage. An expert shipping service for furniture and other large items is available.

The most important towns for antiquing include Stow-on-the-Wold, a hilltop community whose low houses huddle around a handsome market square (its selection of furniture is so enormous that locals joke that an American who'd just finished a spending spree had labeled his purchases for shipping with "Stow In The Hold"). Nearby Tetbury, home of the Prince and Princess of Wales, has at least a half-dozen good shops. Other good bets are Moreton-in-the-Marsh (particularly High Street); Chipping Norton; Burford (especially on High Street and The Hill); Cirencester, an old market town with a 12th-century church, originally founded by the Romans and second in size to Roman London; and Cheltenham, a genteel spa town with spacious gardens and perfectly preserved Regency buildings.

The Cotswold Antique Dealers' Association members' directory lists information on over 50 reputable dealers and their stock in the Cotswolds. For information, contact CADA, High St., Blockley, near Moreton-in-Marsh, Gloucestershire, GL56 OLL (phone: 0386-700280).

Some well-known dealers in these very special towns and others include:

Peter Stroud Antiques, for 18th- and 19th-century English and French furniture. Station Yard Industrial Estate, Chipping Norton (phone: 0608-41651).

Rankine Taylor Antiques, for 17th-, 18th-, and early 19th-century furniture and objets d'art from France, Italy, and America as well as England, Scotland, and Wales displayed in a series of eclectic room settings that show off the proprietor's eye for the decorative and the unusual. The atmosphere is reminiscent of some 18th-century grande dame's drawing room. A 1961 Silver Cloud II Rolls Royce in racing green, won by the proprietor in a raffle in 1975, is displayed in the backyard. 34 Dollar St., Cirencester GL7 2AN (phone: 0285-652529).

Christopher Clarke Antiques, for furniture, pictures, pottery, and other works of art dating from the 17th to the 19th centuries. The Fosse Way, Stow-on-the-Wold (phone: 0451-30476).

EAST ANGLIA, England: This bulge of coastline to the northeast of London is off the beaten track and little frequented by overseas visitors. Nonetheless, it's rich territory for the antiques collector. The Essex towns of Battlesbridge, Coggeshalle, Colchester, Stansted Mount Fitchett, and Kelvedon (particularly High Street) make for especially happy hunting, as does Cambridge (particularly the Trumpington Street area near Fitzwilliam and Kings Colleges).

In Cambridge, visitors shouldn't miss *Antiques Etcetera,* a magpie's nest of antiques and bric-a-brac from days gone by. 18 King St. (phone: 0223-62825).

The Antiques Centre in Coggeshall has 10 dealers stocking items both large and small, and several others have shops nearby. Open Mondays through Saturdays. The Market Place.

There is also a series of antiques fairs worth attending. Bury St. Edmunds has fairs in March and September as well as one-day events that take place monthly. Cambridge has a major event in July. Ely has a 1-day fair every month. There is also a well-established fair at Snape in July.

Norwich has a weekly market on Wednesdays at St. Andrew's Hall as well as longer events in early January, at Easter, and during July. It also has a sizable antiques center at The Quayside.

LONDON, England: For centuries, London represented a safe haven for things of value. Consequently, it became the unquestioned center of the world's antiques trade. Anything can be bought here, and everything has a market value and instant liquidity.

Best Antiquing Streets – Shops are in greatest supply along Bond Street, Brompton Road, Fulham Road, Jermyn Street, Kensington Church Street, King's Road, and Mount Street.

Antiques Centers – In addition to the enormous variety of flea markets, there are also excellent markets that are open almost any day of the week:

Antiquarius Antique Market. 170 vendors with specialties ranging from theatrical items and delft to faïence and items from the 1950s. 135–141 King's Rd., SW3 (phone: 01-352-8882 or 352-7989).

Bond Street Antique Centre. A source for finely worked antique jewelry, watches, portrait miniatures, silver, porcelain, and other objets d'art. 124 New Bond St., W1 (phone: 01-493-1854).

Chelsea Antique Market. The original indoor antiques market, and still one of the best. 253 King's Rd., SW3.

Gray's Antique Market. Davies Mews and 58 Davies St., W1 (phone: 01-629-7034).

Street Markets – London is unique in its great variety of street markets, and each one has its own flavor and appeal.

Petticoat Lane, London's largest Sunday market, has a special antiques section in Goulston Street. It is known as the New Cutler Street Market and is well known for the sale of scrap gold and silver, as well as coins, stamps, and medals. Open until 2 PM.

Camden Lock, not to be confused with Islington's *Camden Passage* (below), is now the trendiest of the city's markets. Though less important for very old antiques, it is chockablock with items from the thirties and forties, along with masses of second-hand furniture, clothing, and crafts. Saturdays and Sundays, Camden Town, NW4.

The *Jubilee* antiques market, in Covent Garden, W2, has a good selection of small items such as silver and glassware.

Camden Passage in Islington, N1, is not a market for bargains but offers good-quality porcelain, clocks, prints, and silver. Some of the 350 dealers and 150 stalls packed into this mere 200-yard passageway are indoors in *The Georgian Village,* others are in *The Mall.* Wednesdays and Saturdays are the days to browse; there's little to see at other times.

The Bermondsey–New Caledonian Market is open Fridays, and dealing starts briskly at dawn or before. It's a market for the dedicated and the knowledgeable and is frequented primarily by dealers. Flashlights are essential in the wee hours. There is also some activity throughout the week in the area's furniture warehouses. Bermondsey St. at Long Lane, off Tower Bridge Rd., SE1.

Portobello Road often turns up merchandise that you could have had for less at the *Bermondsey–New Caledonian Market* the day before. W11.

Shops – London is not only auction action and wearying market mobs. It is also the cushioning courtesy of some of the world's most distinguished antiques shops. Visitors can browse in their carpeted serenity and examine some of the world's best wares:

Alexander Juran, a continuation of a business started in Prague during the reign of Emperor Franz Josef II. The showrooms are small and shabby, but the textiles, rugs, and carpets on display here can be exceptional. 74 New Bond St., W1 (phone: 01-493-4484).

Antique Porcelain Company Ltd., for 18th-century English and continental porcelain. 149 New Bond St., W1 (phone: 01-629-1254).

Asprey. Much like Tiffany's coveted blue box, a purple box from Asprey means luxury goods. Antiques, china, glass, silver, jewelry, clocks, and leather goods are available here. The company holds three royal warrants. 165 New Bond St., W1 (phone: 01-493-6767).

Grosvenor Prints resembles a great aunt's attic with more than 100,000 prints, on all subjects. The antique print shop also holds four annual exhibitions covering dogs from 1660–1940 (February), portraits (April), mixed subjects (June), and London and topographical views (November). 28–32 Shelton St., Covent Garden, WC2 (phone: 01-836-1979).

London Silver Vaults, for silver. An underground warren of dealers of fine china, objets d'art, and silver (new, old, secondhand), in the strongrooms of the original Chancery Lane Safe Deposit Company, which opened its doors in 1885 and started serving as a secure base for silver vendors during World War II. 53-65 Chancery La., WC2 (phone: 01-242-3844).

Lucy B. Campbell features 17th- to 19th-century decorative prints of birds, animals, plants, and architecture as well as contemporary watercolors. 80 Holland Park Ave., London W11 3RE (phone: 01-727-2205).

Mallett and Son, sells almost all things antiques but specializes in the finest English antique furniture, choosing every item with consummate taste. The shop is a miniature museum displaying wares ranging from the late 17th century to the early 19th. 40 New Bond St., W1 (phone: 01-499-7411). Another shop, selling French and continental furniture and a large, eclectic stock of works of art and decorative items, is at Bourdon House, 2 Davies St., W1 (phone: 01-629-2444).

Milne and Moller deals in British and continental watercolors by 19th- and 20th-century artists. By appointment only and Saturdays. 35 Colville Terrace, London W11 2BU (phone: 01-727-1679).

Partridge, for the absolutely best 18th-century French and English furniture, paintings, and objets d'art. 144–146 New Bond St., W1 (phone: 01-629-0834).

Pickering and Chatto, for antiquarian books in English literature of the 17th and 18th centuries, economics, science, and medicine. 17 Pall Mall, SW1 (phone: 01-930-2515).

S. J. Phillips, for silver, jewelry, and objets d'art from the 16th to the early 19th centuries. 139 New Bond St., W1 (phone: 01-629-6261).

Temple Gallery, for Byzantine, Greek, and early Russian icons. 6 Clarendon Cross, London W11 (phone: 01-727-3809).

Vigo-Sternberg Galleries, for tapestries. 37 S. Audley St., W1 (phone: 01-629-8307).

At Auction – The great auction houses, *Christie's* (8 King St., SW1; phone: 01-839-9060) and *Sotheby's* (34–35 New Bond St., W1; phone: 01-493-8080), are instrumental in setting market prices; they're superb places to develop a feel for the market.

At the Fair – The *Grosvenor House Antiques Fair,* held for 10 days every June at Grosvenor House, Park Lane, London W1, is a sun in the antiques dealer's solar system, where everything from Etruscan heads to Victorian bustles are found, and every piece has been authenticated by independent experts. For more information, contact the British Antiques Dealers' Association, 20 Rutland Gate, Knightsbridge, London SW7 1BD (phone: 01-589-4128).

Burlington House Fair, held in September of odd-numbered years at the Royal Academy of Arts, Piccadilly, London W1, has acquired similar prestige.

OXFORD, Oxfordshire, England: Some of England's happiest antiques hunting is found in this ancient university town along High Street. A number of the shops offer paintings as well as furniture, porcelain, silver, and the like.

YORK, North Yorkshire, England: It's perhaps the best-preserved medieval city in England and the site of the nation's largest medieval church, York Minster. And the curiosities of the past available in York are not restricted to unusual street names like Whip-ma-whop-ma-gate or to the museums. Antiques shops stocking a selection of pieces from all periods are in abundance as well — though the concentration is slowly moving from Goodramgate (and its rising rents) to Micklegate. Among the city's more noteworthy are the following:

MacDowell, for antiquarian books. 56 Micklegate (no phone).

Robert Morrison and Son Antiques, for furniture. Its 18th- and 19th-century rosewood, walnut, mahogany, and oak pieces — together with its case clocks and decorative items — are in immaculate condition, restored as necessary before going on sale. Trentholme House, 131 The Mount (phone: 0904-655394).

O'Flynn, for York's biggest stock of antique maps and prints of York, Britain, and the world. There are also manuscripts dating from the 15th century and a broad selection of antiquarian books. 35 Micklegate (phone: 0904-641404).

Spelman's, for antiquarian books. Fifty thousand volumes occupy the handsome oak breakfront shelving. A coal fire warms visitors in season. 70 Micklegate (phone: 0904-624414).

Trinity, for Victorian memorabilia. Now trading along with nearly three dozen other dealers at the *York Antiques Centre* at 2 Lendal (phone: 0904-641445).

EDINBURGH, Scotland: Stark yet startlingly beautiful, Edinburgh is a seductive site for antiques shopping. Its dour custodian, Edinburgh Castle, sets such a sober tone as it looms over the city that all things light and modern seem trivial, and the mood is just right for buying solid old objects of silver and pewter, dueling pistols, and the like. Edinburgh is also Britain's second city when it comes to the antiquarian book trade.

Best Antiquing Streets – Dundas, Grassmarket, Randolph Place, St. Stephen's, Thistle, and West Bow are full of antiques shops offering everything from furniture and Sheffield plate to Scottish paintings and leatherbound books.

Antiques Centers and Markets – *Ingliston Market,* a Sunday experience. On the city's outskirts at Ingliston.

Shops – There are dozens in the city, but there are a few of particular interest which include the following:

Joseph H. Bonnar, Antique and modern jewelry. 72 Thistle St. (phone: 031-226-2811).

Eric Davidson, period furniture, ceramics, paintings, and clocks. 4 Grassmarket (phone: 031-225-5815).

John R. Martin, an eclectic assortment of wares that has included gold thimbles and a stuffed elephant alongside the more usual breakfronts. Sells largely to the trade. 96 West Bow (phone: 031-226-7190).

The Scottish Gallery, 20th-century Scottish works of art. 94 George St. (phone: 031-225-5955).

At Auction – There are regular sales at several houses:

Lyon and Turnbull is based locally. 51 George St. (phone: 031-225-4627).

Phillips has weekly sales. 65 George St. (phone: 031-225-2266).

At the Fair – The major annual events are held in the *Roxburghe Hotel* in Charlotte Square.

The Edinburgh Annual Antiques Fair. Late July.

The Scottish Antiques Fair. April.

HAY-ON-WYE, Powys, Wales: Visitors to this tiny town in the Wye Valley are always astonished to discover that it is the center of the European antique book trade. Business is concentrated in the lanes of the old town center, and most shops are open on Sundays. It's easy to spend an entire day browsing or even finishing a whole book.

RULES OF THE ROAD FOR AN ODYSSEY OF THE OLD

Buy for sheer pleasure and not for investment. Treasure seekers should forget about the carrot of supposed resale value that dealers habitually dangle in front of amateur clients. If you love an object, you'll never part with it. If you don't love it, let someone else adopt it.

Don't be timid about haggling. That's as true at a Bond Street jeweler's as at the most colorful flea market. It's surprising how much is negotiable — and the higher the price, the farther it has to fall.

Buy the finest affordable example of any item, in as close to mint condition as possible. Chipped or tarnished "bargains" will haunt their buyers later with their shabbiness.

Train your eye in museums. Museums that specialize in items dear to a collector are the best of all, though they may break his or her heart. The coins and medals of the Fitzwilliam in Cambridge or the furniture and clocks of London's Wallace Collection, for instance, all help to set impeccable standards against which to measure purchases. Special tours of Historic Homes of Britain are also offered (described in *Stately Homes and Great Gardens,* DIVERSIONS).

Peruse British art books and periodicals. Among the best are the following:

The Antique Collector, available from National Magazine Company, 72 Broadwick St., London W1V 2BP (phone: 01-439-7144), and on newsstands.

The Antique Dealer and Collector's Guide, available from King's Reach Tower, Stamford St., London SE1 9LS, England (phone: 01-261-6894), and from W. H. Smith and leading newsagents.

The Antiques Trade Gazette, available from 17 Whitcomb St., London WC2H 7PL, England (phone: 01-930-4957). A weekly newspaper listing and reporting on auctions and shows in Britain and on the Continent. Available at the newsstand adjoining *Sotheby's* on Bond St. and at other antiques centers.

Apollo, an international magazine of arts and antiques available on newsstands or from 22 Davies St., London W1Y 1LH, England (phone: 01-629-3061).

The Burlington Magazine, available by subscription, 6 Bloomsbury Sq., London WC1A 2LP, England (phone: 01-430-0481), and at selected newsagents.

Buying Antiques in Britain, published by the London and Provincial Antique Dealers' Association, 525 King's Rd., London SW10 O5Z, England (phone: 01-823-3511). Lists 770 dealers. Free in return for valid antiques business card; subscription is $4.60//3 (surface), $15.30//10 (airmail) purchased by sterling checks only.

The International Herald Tribune art pages, particularly on Saturdays.

Get advice from a specialist when contemplating a major acquisition. The various dealers' guilds can be helpful. Major auction houses like *Sotheby's* and *Christie's* have fleets of resident specialists who can be consulted. So does the British Museum. Those who are interested might enroll in a special instructional program to become experts in their own right. *Christie's Education* (63 Old Brompton Rd., London SW7 3JS; phone: 01-581-3933) is actually two intensive year-long courses on the fine and decorative arts, one covering Greek and Roman antiquity to AD 1450, and the other covering the period from AD 1450 to the present day. Evening courses are also available in specialized subjects, including wine. Sotheby's Educational Studies also offers day-long, weekend, and week-long courses at 30 Oxford St., London W1R 1RE (phone: 01-408-1100) and holds *Works of Art Courses,* which include 3- and 9-month studies on fine and decorative arts and styles in art, and study weeks on topics such as "Collecting on a Limited Budget" and "Contemporary Painting and Sculpture." The British Tourist Authority offers a list of special interest holidays that includes several others.

Ancient Monuments and Ruins

Britain has been inhabited for thousands of years, and scarcely a single one of the population groups who have settled here has disappeared without leaving a trace. The countryside is littered with their remains: stone walls, tombs and burial chambers, barrows and henges, hilltop forts, castles, abbeys, crosses, churches, and towers. Ruined and crumbling, they stand as reminders of a turbulent and fascinating past.

An independent body called the Historic Buildings and Monuments Commission for England (and Scotland), more briefly known as English Heritage, was recently established to record and preserve many of these important sites. Several now ask for admission charges to cover upkeep. The organization's *Guide to English Heritage Properties* can be helpful. It is available for \$3/£1.95 from English Heritage, PO Box 43, Ruislip, Middlesex HA4 0XW, England (phone: 01-845-1200).

AVEBURY STONE CIRCLE, Avebury, Wiltshire, England: Eighteen miles from Stonehenge, the map explodes with prehistory. Not only is the area the site of Silbury Hill (Europe's most massive artificial earth mound), but there is also an abundance of long barrows, standing stones, and stone circles — among them, just off the A4 between Marlborough and Calne, the Avebury stone circle. One of the largest in the world, and certainly the greatest among Britain's some 900 megalithic rings, it encloses approximately 28 acres, at the center of which are traces of two smaller stone circles. The whole is ringed by an earthen bank that stands 20 feet high in spots, and, abutting it, a ditch up to 30 feet deep. About 200,000 tons of earth were moved to create the ditch and bank; some of the heaviest of the 27 stones that remain from the group of 100 that once completed the ring weigh over 40 tons and would have required about 200 people to raise. It has been estimated that if 750 people worked here for 10 hours a day for 2 months of every year (after the harvest was in), the enclosure would have taken about 4 years to complete. And this was during the second millennium BC, a time when the population of the surrounding region, according to some estimates, numbered only about 1,500. Why such a whole society of small farmers was prepared to take time off to create such a place in an age when merely subsisting was a struggle is not known; nor is the nature of the ceremonies that took place there, or the type of beliefs that governed them, or even the ring's exact function, though speculation suggests that it was probably used as a meeting place or a temple, or to fulfill some astronomical function. As is the case with most stone circles, there is no evidence of human sacrifice. Yet Christians who sought to eliminate all records of their pagan past attempted in the 14th century to break up and bury many of the stones (and at least one of them, a man whose trade as a barber was identified by a pair of scissors found alongside him, was crushed to death in the effort, when a pillar toppled over on him). Other early efforts to destroy the great stone circle never entirely succeeded. Though it probably ceased to serve its original purpose in the first millennium BC, the tradition of its importance persisted, and it was still in use as late as the 19th century, when maypoles were erected within the circle and children frolicked there, waiting for the midsummer sun to appear, as their ancestors might possibly have done. The stones here are smaller than those at Stonehenge and natural rather than hewn; Avebury exceeds the more widely known circle, in the words of one 17th-century observer, "as a cathedral doeth a parish church." Today, one of the wide avenues of stones that led to the site is practically obliterated, but much of the one to the south, now West Kennet Avenue, has been restored. Overton Hill, a huge cemetery site once reached along this former processional route, is now accessible via A4 at West Kennet. The barrows can still be seen clearly, and the site of the Sanctuary, a hill-topping Bronze Age religious building of some importance, is now marked with concrete blocks and pillars. For information about the region, contact the West Country Tourist Board, Trinity Ct., 37 Southernhay E., Exeter, Devon EX1 1QS, England (phone: 0392-76351).

ROMAN BATHS, Bath, Avon, England: Britain's most complete Roman remains, unknown until the 18th century, still gush to the surface at 110F at a rate of more than 300,000 gallons a day. Established by Britain's new Roman overlords in AD 54 using waters from the nation's only hot springs, the whole system created Aquae Sulis, which was named to honor the Celtic goddess Sul and was one of the spa centers of the Roman Empire for the next 500 years. When the Romans pulled out of Britain, the baths sank beneath the mud. But the Normans built the King's Bath right over the Roman reservoir and spring, and in medieval times, builders unaware of the ancient prototypes put still other baths over the spring. When it was rediscovered, Jacobean and Georgian visitors put the town, Bath, at the top of their list of fashionable resorts. One million pounds has been spent to improve and upgrade the Roman Baths in an effort to "ease the summer flow." Excavations are still going on, and a nearby museum displays interesting discoveries — coins, gemstones, mosaics, and a gilt-bronze head of Sulis Minerva, whose name was an amalgam of the Celtic deity Sul and the Roman goddess of wisdom, Minerva. Many of these had been thrown as offerings to the sacred spring — some to call down curses upon enemies. Details: Roman Baths, Abbey Church Yard, Bath, Avon, England (phone: 0225-461111).

BATTLE ABBEY, Battle, Hastings, East Sussex, England: Here, 6 miles northwest of the coastal resort of Hastings, between the South Downs and the Channel, William of Normandy launched the last successful invasion of Britain in September 1066 against Harold of Wessex, who had succeeded Edward the Confessor 9 months earlier. Harold, a distant cousin and the son of Edward's advisor, had an equal size army of spear carriers who marched here from the north of England, where they had been defending the country against the onslaughts of yet another claimant to the throne. William, who felt his was the stronger suit, had archers and cavalry, and where his cavalry charges failed against Harold's wall of shields, a rain of Norman arrows succeeded. Harold and his supporters perished, and a new era began for England.

Built by William 4 years after the battle, with its High Altar poised on the spot where Harold was killed, the abbey was colonized by the Benedictine Order until the dissolution of the monasteries; it was then granted to a courtier of Henry VIII, who pulled down the church and remodeled the abbey. The oldest remains are the battlemented Gatehouse, the monks' dormitory with lancet windows, and the Undercroft, with its beautiful English vaults. Surviving parts of the Abbot House are now used as a school, but the grounds are open to the public daily, and the building is open to the public during the school's summer holiday's. Beyond the dormitory to the right, a broad walk looks out over the battlefield and across the valley to the heights of Telham and Senlac (as the invaders called Battle), where the Normans pitched camp the night before the battle. An 8-minute audiovisual presentation on the Battle of Hastings is shown year-round. Details: Battle Abbey, Battle, near Hastings, East Sussex TN33 0AD, England (phone: 04246-3792).

GLASTONBURY ABBEY, Glastonbury, Somerset, England: Romance and tradition cling to this historic site like ivy to the walls of a Harvard dormitory. The site itself was probably sacred in pre-Christian days; later, progressively larger churches were built as the abbey became increasingly wealthier. One of Britain's more irreverent observers once noted that the first son born of a marriage between the Abbot of Glastonbury and the Abbess of Shaftesbury would own more land than the king. Under Dunstan, who introduced the Benedictine rule after he was chosen as abbot in the year 940, the abbey became a center of learning, producing many great ecclesiastics, and for many years, England's premier abbot was Glastonbury's. His greatness endured for centuries afterward, and his importance diminished only with the dissolution of the monasteries in 1539 under Henry VIII, when Thomas Cromwell (later executed at the Tower of London) ordered the elderly abbot Richard Whiting, the 60th abbot of Glastonbury, hanged on the Tor. In the words of the 18th-century writer William Stukely: "For every week a pillar or buttress, a window jamb or an angle of fine hewn stone is sold to the best bidder . . . they were excoriating St. Joseph's Chapel for that purpose, and the squared stones were laid up by lots in the Abbot's Kitchen; the rest goes to paving yards and stalls for cattle, or to the highway." Lead stripped from the roofs was melted down in fires fueled by priceless manuscripts and carved wooden screens that were antique even then.

Legend has elaborately embellished the known history of the millennium before this debacle. One story reports that Christ came here as a child in the company of Joseph of Arimathea, the wealthy trader in whose garden tomb Christ's body was placed when it was taken from the cross. According to another story, Joseph of Arimathea came alone; landing here in the winter, and, wearily, planting his staff into the ground, he saw it sending up leaves and blossoms. It was he who, as legend would have it, brought to England the Holy Grail, which Arthur's knights sought so avidly in later years. Tradition also records that King Arthur was buried at Glastonbury, and it is widely told that toward the end of the 12th century, when Henry II ordered excavations here, monks found a stone inlaid with a leaden cross that had been inscribed according to Gerald the Welshman: "Here lies buried the renowned King Arthur in the isle of Avalon with Guinevere his second wife." There were two skeletons, one of a man of gigantic size, and one of a woman with a bit of golden hair that crumbled at the touch. The bones were reburied at Glastonbury's high altar, but the tomb was broken up at the dissolution, and the bones were dispersed; the leaden cross no longer exists, but a drawing made at the beginning of the 17th century does. As to the veracity of the whole story, no one can say, but Cadbury Castle, believed to be Arthur's Camelot, is not far away, and roads can still be traced between the two sites. As historians keep speculating, the impressively large ruins of the abbey, surrounded by manicured lawns ringed by a stone wall, are open to visitors; they can walk down into an ancient crypt, take in a performance of a play or pageant (in summer), climb the 525-foot Tor for a view out over Wiltshire Downs and the Mendips all the way to Bristol (on a clear day), poke around at the Chalice Well where the Holy Grail is believed to be lost, and see a thorn tree grown from a cutting of the one that sprouted from Joseph of Arimathea's staff. Glastonbury proper is not a very exciting town, filled as it is (like Stratford-upon-Avon and other towns with a past) with souvenir shops, but the Glastonbury Thorn still flowers in midwinter. The abbey now belongs to the Church of England, the Tor to the National Trust. The Abbey Barn, which contains a Rural Life Museum, and the historic *George and Pilgrim's Inn,* which opened in 1475, are nearby. Details: West Country Tourist Board (address above) or the Custodian, The Abbey Gatehouse, Glastonbury, Somerset BA6 9EL, England (phone: 0458-32267).

TOWER OF LONDON, London, England: The Tower — known in some quarters as the world's most famous castle — is actually a complex of buildings. Begun during the days of William the Conquerer and expanded many times over the years, it has figured in British history for a millennium as palace, fortress, treasury, mint, bank, arsenal, munitions factory, garrison, library, museum, observatory, and even zoo. Its most famous function, however, has been that of a prison, and many people came through the so-called Traitor's Gate hoping to be ransomed or pardoned and thereby avoid the fate — endless incarceration or death — of those who had passed that way before them. Many hoped in vain. The stories of the executions, murders, and suicides within these walls are legion. Henry VI, imprisoned during the Wars of the Roses, was stabbed to death during his prayers, allegedly on the order of Richard, Duke of Gloucester, the "usurper of the realm" who became Richard III after the murder of the about-to-be-crowned Edward V and his brother the Duke of York. (The youngsters disappeared from public view in 1483 while lodged in the Tower; the next trace of them was two sets of bones found under a staircase in Charles II's time.) Henry VIII hustled wives, dissidents, and possible claimants to the throne into the Tower, the first step in the journey that usually ended at the executioner's block. Among those who made that journey were Anne Boleyn and Catherine Howard, the monarch's second and fifth wives, who were executed on the Tower Green and buried in the chapel of St. Peter ad Vincula; Sir Thomas More ("the king's good servant but God's first"), who met his end after rejecting his sovereign's claim to the leadership of the English church; and Thomas Cromwell, the not-always-so-jolly king's chief administrator. Later, Lady Jane Grey was beheaded on Tower Green after the Duke of Northumberland, the father of her husband, Lord Guilford Dudley, persuaded her young cousin Edward VI to pass his crown to the 17-year-old Jane rather than to Elizabeth's half-sister Mary, the rightful heir to the throne; she reigned for 9 days, beginning on July 10, 1553, until the English rallied around Mary. In the days of Elizabeth I (who herself had been imprisoned in the Tower on the orders of Mary), the Earl of Essex was executed at the age of 34 after the discovery of a plot to kidnap the aging queen he had courted. James I dispatched Sir Walter Raleigh to the Tower in 1603; Raleigh passed the time writing *A History of the World* until his release in 1616, which was then followed by his death in 1618 when the monarch finally had him beheaded. In modern times, German spies were executed in the courtyards during the two world wars, and in 1941, Rudolf Hess, Hitler's deputy, was imprisoned there for a few days. Today, such colorful episodes of the Tower's history are hard to imagine amid the multitudes of tourists and guides milling about, as they do most of the year. It's most atmospheric when there are few visitors — on a rainy day, for instance, or at night for the Ceremony of the Keys. (Travelers may book ahead by writing to the Resident Governor, Queen's House, HM Tower of London EC3N 4AB, England, and enclosing the appropriate international postage coupons.) Rapiers, clubs, maces and flails, longbows and crossbows, cannon and muskets, shields, daggers, and all manner of other weapons as well as glittering armor, are displayed in the White Tower, the 92-foot-high structure begun by William the Conqueror in 1078 as his palace and fortress and renamed in the mid-13th century when Henry III had the structure whitewashed; the collections are among the finest of their kind in the world. In the Jewel House, a later addition to the complex (closed annually in February), visitors can see the Crown Jewels — the splendid St. Edward's crown worn only during coronations; the Imperial State, which contains over 3,500 precious stones, including four large pearls that probably belonged to Elizabeth I; the ancient Black Prince's Ruby, which Henry V wore at Agincourt; the Stuart Sapphire; and the 317-carat Second Star of Africa, the second-largest of the nine major stones cut from the 3,106-carat Cullinan. The largest Star, a 530-carat, pear-shaped bit of glitter, which is not only the world's biggest cut diamond but also, according to some experts, its most perfect, embellishes the Royal Sceptre, which is also in the Jewel House, along with countless swords, bracelets, ewers, dishes, and other dazzling items. Details: HM Tower of Hill, London EC3 4AB, England (phone: 01-709-0765).

HADRIAN'S WALL, near Newcastle-upon-Tyne, Tyne & Wear, England: Any road west of this Northumberland shipbuilding city leads to the country of Hadrian's Wall, that phenomenal fortification put up by the Romans in the 2nd century AD to mark the northern limit of the Roman Empire and protect the legions from the northern barbarians. A standout even in an empire full of impressive fortifications, whose construction required 16,000 men to quarry and cart to the site over a million cubic yards of stone, it stretched over 70 miles across the neck of England, from what is now Bowness-on-Solway, on Solway Firth in the west, to Wallsend, near the mouth of the river Tyne in the east. It consisted of a broad V-shaped ditch (the vallum) and a stone barrier 15 feet high, up to 9 feet thick (enough to drive a chariot along), and punctuated at third-mile intervals by so many guard towers, massive forts, and "milecastles" that some 5,500 cavalry and over half that many infantry were required to man it. Surprisingly enough, considering the wars and skirmishes that have taken place on and around it in the centuries since the Romans abandoned the country, many of these fortifications are still standing. The ditch is almost entirely intact; the wall itself can be seen from the Military Road, and the remains are particularly extensive in the area between Housesteads and Greenhead (where the wall runs along the border of Northumberland National Park for some 15 miles). There are fine views into the hills, and, at Housesteads, site of the most impressive remains of the 17 forts that once punctuated the wall, there are the remainders of the barracks, the commandant's offices, the granaries, hospital, and a latrine. Similarly well preserved are the remains west of Housesteads at Peel Crag and Walltown Crags. At Vindolanda, near Bardon

Mill, and farther west near Greenhead, two fine museums depict life on Hadrian's Wall during the Roman Army's occupation. Roman artifacts are on display alongside the Roman fort at Corbridge. As an introduction to what visitors will see on the wall itself, the scale models and exhibits at Newcastle University's Museum of Antiquities at Newcastle-upon-Tyne are a must. Details: Northumbria Tourist Board, Aykley Heads, Durham DH1 5UX, England (phone: 091-3846905).

VERULAMIUM, St. Albans, Hertfordshire, England: Built alongside the river Ver to the west of the present St. Albans, the *municipium* of Verulamium was one of the leading cities of Britain during Roman times — its full municipal status confirmed its importance. Britain's first Christian martyr, a pagan Roman soldier named Alban who had given shelter to a Christian and was converted by him, was executed here on a small hill in the year AD 209, 500 paces from Verulamium. A church was built on the site in his honor, and in the 8th century, King Offa II rebuilt this structure to include a special repository for the martyr's bones. Adrian IV, the first English Pope, enthroned in 1155, was the son of a tenant of this abbey, which became a Cathedral in 1877.

While the town of St. Albans grew up around the Abbey and shrine, the original Roman town was left to crumble undisturbed in the fields to the southwest. But though sections of walls, gateways, and part of the basilica, grouped near St. Michael village, remained, they were generally ignored until the 1930s, when archaeologists were able to date them to the 1st through 4th centuries AD. The most impressive of the Verulamium discoveries was the Roman Theatre, the only one now visible in Britain; with a little imagination, the present-day visitor to the ruined walls and now-grassy seating area can envision the spectacle of 1,600 Roman citizens being entertained with cockfights, pantomime, and an occasional classical drama. Beneath a modern building is preserved, in even better condition, a hypocaust — a Roman underground heating system that used channels of hot air beneath a mosaic floor. The on-site Verulamium Museum is a must; the important material it contains can make the Roman city spring vividly to life. Details: Verulamium Museum, St. Michael's, St. Albans, Hertfordshire AL3 4SW, England (phone: 0727-66100/54659/59919, ext. 2419).

CADBURY CASTLE, South Cadbury, Somerset, England: A century ago, when a party of Oxford archaeologists climbed the hill above this village 2 miles from the Wincanton-to-Ilchester A303, an old man met them at its foot and asked tearfully whether they had come to take the old king away. He was referring to Arthur. For this hill fort, one of the many occupied by a farming community since the 8th century BC and stormed by Vespasian, is believed by some to have been Camelot. Fortified for over five centuries, it was defended on the eve of the Roman invasion by four massive earth banks that the Romans partially dismantled before slaughtering the inhabitants and leaving the settlement to lie derelict for the next 200 years. Then, in the late 3rd or early 4th century, activity here — perhaps in the form of pilgrimages — resumed, and, toward the end of the 5th century, the innermost of the four ancient banks was greatly strengthened by the addition of a new rampart held together with timber framing, a new gateway was built, and a small wooden tower was created above it, in building styles that reflected the manners of the Celts and the Romans. When men moved back into the old forts, it was usually to take advantage of the abandoned defenses to provide themselves with an attack-proof homestead. But the prehistoric ramparts here enclose some 18 acres — enough space, suggests archaeologist Leslie Alcock, to have accommodated an army as large as Arthur's. If Arthur was truly the military leader for several small kingdoms, as some historians have surmised, this isolated hill near South Cadbury would have made an ideal base, situated as it was high enough to send signals by lantern to distant Glastonbury, where allies could then, in turn, summon armored horsemen from the hill forts of South Wales. Even the traditions of the Round Table find their corroboration at South Cadbury, with the excavation of a great hall, 63 feet by 34 feet, wooden and thatched. During the digging, fragments of imported pottery and broken wine pitchers were found, and it's easy to imagine these early Britons carousing in the days of darkness brought down around them during these years of warfare. Be forewarned: This is the "site" of the fort, and a good imagination is essential. After the uphill climb, all that is is visible is a grass hill used for the fort. For local tourist information, contact the West Country Tourist Board (37 Southernhay E., Exeter, Devonshire EX1 1QS (phone: 0392-76351).

STONEHENGE, Wiltshire, England: It's hard to appreciate this fantastic monument, not far from magnificently spired, equally celebrated Salisbury Cathedral, surrounded as it is by fences and gates — and all the more so when tour buses are disgorging masses of tourists on day trips from London. Yet the mysterious pull exerted by England's most famous prehistoric monument — two concentric circles of stones, some over 20 feet high, ringed by a ditch 300 feet in diameter — is so strong that it's hard to ignore the myths that explain its origins in terms of Merlin and magic. Certainly the fiction is only a little stranger than the fact — that it was constructed in stages beginning in about 2750 BC, with stones that were rafted and dragged for many long miles (some from as far away as southwestern Wales) and then raised with wooden levers and rollers and ropes made of leather thongs. Its function is similarly unknown; some archaeologists — remarking about the way various stones are aligned with midsummer sunrise and midwinter moonrise — point out that it might possibly have served as a sort of vast open-air observatory. Or perhaps it was used for worship. Until recently, in midsummer, English druids still came here to celebrate their antique rites. Dressed in hooded white robes and carrying mistletoe and holly and banners emblazoned with mystical signs, they sang their hymns and chanted strange runes as they marched in procession among the megaliths, awaiting the coming of dawn. For details about the region, contact the West Country Tourist Board (address above).

GLENELG BROCHS, Glenelg, Highland, Scotland: The palindromic name of this hamlet by the sea ranks with the lovely rocky mountain scenery as one of its more fascinating aspects. Archaeologists and lovers of antiquities, however, are most drawn by the presence of two of the best preserved of Scotland's defensive stone towers known as brochs. Many now are little more than piles of rubble; the ones at Glenelg are not too different than they were when the Picts built them all over the country during the Iron Age, with their 30-foot-high dry stone inner and outer walls, hollow between; their stone lintels; and their center courtyard. Nearby Dun Grugaig, another broch, occupies a lovely site close by a roiling cascade and affords fine views southward toward Ben Sgriol. For local information, contact the Portree Tourist Office, Portree, Isle of Skye IV51 9BZ, Scotland (phone: 0478-2137).

ISLE OF IONA, Inner Hebrides, Strathclyde, Scotland: The whole island, a place of pilgrimage since the Irish missionary St. Columba came here in 563 AD, has become a modern shrine popular with crofters, pilgrims, and tourists under the protectorship of the National Trust. It is still a haven of peace, even an idyll, and an aura of the spiritual hangs over the ruined Benedictine nunnery and the fully restored cathedral, also known as the abbey, now the home of the Iona Community. This resulted in large part from the work of St. Columba, who brought Christianity to this island, and who also made it his headquarters during the 34 years that he traveled throughout Scotland converting the nation to Christianity. It was in testament to the impact of his work in the area that almost every Scottish king through the 11th century, including Duncan (slain by Macbeth) and several Norwegians — some 40 in all — are buried in the abbey graveyard. St. Columba's cell and the slab of stone on which he slept have been excavated; three magnificent Celtic crosses of the hundreds that once bristled in the abbey cemetery remain. And in the almost deserted southern corner of the island, visitors can see the Bay of the Coracle where St. Columba landed, the marble quarry from which the abbey's communion table was cut, and Martyr's Bay, where the island's monks were slaughtered by the Norsemen who periodically raided and ravaged Iona for centuries. A passenger ferry crosses regularly from Fionnphort on the Isle of Mull. Details: Scottish Tourist Board, 23 Ravelston Terr., Edinburgh EH4 3EU, Scotland (phone: 031-332-2433).

MELROSE ABBEY, Melrose, Borders, Scotland: "If thou would see fair Melrose aright/Go visit it by the pale moonlight," wrote Sir Walter Scott in his *Lay of the Last Minstrel* about the ruins here. Among the finest and best-preserved in Scotland, they move present-day visitors just as they did that celebrated 19th-century Scottish poet, who spent the last two decades of his life at nearby Abbotsford in a turreted, baronial sort of manse that is now open to the public for tours. Melrose Abbey, one of four Border abbeys founded for a group of Cistercian monks by David I in 1136 just after the return of Roman Christianity to Scotland, was destroyed during English raids in 1322, restored by Robert Bruce in 1326, battered again in 1385, and ultimately destroyed in invasions in 1543 and 1544 — except for the few sections that stand today in mute testimony to its past beauty. The reddish stonework in parts of the nave is particularly lovely: the large five-light window in the south transept, the elaborately carved foliage embellishing the capitals nearby, the flying buttresses, and the porcine gargoyle playing bagpipes on the roof. According to tradition, the heart of Robert Bruce — which Sir James Douglas was taking to the Holy Land when he was killed — was buried under the east window, and Tom Purdie, the forester for Scott's estate, and Peter Matheson, the writer's coachman, are interred in the abbey cemetery. The choir is believed to be the resting place of Douglas himself as well as Alexander II and Michael Scott, the wizard of the *Lay of the Last Minstrel*. Melrose town, described as Kennaquhair in Scott's *Monastery* and *The Abbot,* is at one corner of what is widely known as the Scott Country, whose boundaries are also delimited by the towns of Galashiels, Selkirk, and Dryburgh, the site of Dryburgh Abbey, where Sir Walter Scott, Earl Haig (commander-in-chief of the British Army during World War I), and members of their families are buried. The ruins of the abbey's cloister are remarkably preserved — far better than those at the ruins of the remaining pair of David I's Border abbeys, Kelso and Jedburgh. Both of these are also worth visiting; at Jedburgh, the house where Queen Mary stayed for a short while can be toured, as can the imposing, 19th-century Jedburgh Castle, which now houses a museum devoted to the penal system of the period. Details: Melrose Tourist Information Center, Priorwood Gardens near Abbey, Roxburghshire TD6, Scotland (phone: 089-682-2555).

SHETLAND ISLANDS, Scotland: Five centuries of Scottish culture have painted little more than a veneer over the deeply rooted Scandinavian character of these hundred-odd islands, which were Danish until they were given away as a dowry to a 15th-century Scottish earl. Their names still read like the pages of a fantasy by Tolkien — Foula, Mousa, Muckle Roe, Noss, and Papa Stour — and their linguistic allegiances are still Nordic. Of a large number of ancient monuments in the Shetlands, perhaps the most important is Jarlshof, occupied for some 3,000 years and now layered with the remains of three prehistoric civilizations that lay buried until a ferocious storm unearthed the site in 1905. Now that it has been finely excavated, visitors can view remains in varying states of preservation: an oval hut dating from the Stone and Early Bronze Age, remains of the larger circular huts and earthen houses from the Early Iron Age, stone wheel houses from the 2nd and 3rd centuries, long houses and a medieval farm complex constructed by two successive groups of Vikings, and a castle built by unpopular 16th-century Stewart earls and sacked a century later. (Sir Walter Scott, sensitive to the romance of this site, set his novel *The Pirate* here, and coined its name, Jarlshof.) The magnificently preserved red sandstone Iron Age broch on the grassy, seal-haunted island of Mousa, currently being considered for designation as a World Heritage Site, is another must, a striking reminder that once every headland on the northern isles was guarded by such an edifice. Standing 43 feet high, this purest surviving example of broch architecture thickens at the bottom to withstand attacks, incorporates a circular courtyard, and has hollow walls pierced by stairways that bind the outer and inner shells together. In addition to Jarlshof and the Mousa broch, there are some 134 other ruins officially classified as being of archaeological importance on the islands, which are accessible by plane and ferry. Details: Shetland Tourist Organisation, Market Cross, Lerwick, Shetland ZE1 0LU, Scotland (phone: 0595-3434).

SKARA BRAE and MAESHOWE, Mainland, Orkney, Scotland: This group of aobut 70 islands across the Pentland Firth from John O'Groats on the Scottish mainland has a dense concentration of prehistoric monuments — an average of about three recorded sites of archaeological note per square mile; those on the large island known as Mainland are particularly notable. Maeshowe (or "greatest mound"), for instance, is Europe's best example of a Stone Age circular chambered cairn, and it has no rival on mainland Britain. Constructed as the tomb of a very important chieftain and measuring over 110 feet across and over 300 feet around, this hollow, 24-foot-high mound of rock and clay is entered through a low stone passageway, which gives access to a vaulted chamber 14 feet square flanked by a trio of burial niches walled and paved in huge single stones embellished in what some authorities believe to be the single richest collection of Runic inscriptions in any one place in the world. The carvings, left by Norsemen who raided the grave in the 12th century, describe how the contents were spirited away by night, hint of a hiding place nearby, and tell of the problems that resulted when two members of a band that had sought refuge here during a storm went crazy. The kind of village where Stone Age men lived can be seen at Skara Brae, which was constructed at about the same time as Maeshowe, lived in for perhaps 6 centuries, and then inexplicably buried with sand for the almost four millennia that followed, until unearthed by another storm around 1850. Most of the pottery, beads, tools, and implements found on the site are now displayed in the National Museum of Antiquities in Edinburgh; but the site as it exists today — a group of small, squared, lane-linked huts clustered around a central courtyard in a field just about 20 feet above sea level — is impressive enough. The flagstone blocks with which the structures were built, the slate shale with which they were paved, the shelves and built-in boxes and cubbyholes, stone beds, drains, and other appurtenances are still remarkably well preserved. Other major sites are nearby: the four remaining Standing Stones of Stenness, a henge dating from about 2300 BC; the great Ring of Brodgar, where more than two dozen stones can be seen inside a ditch on a 2.5-acre site; the Broch of Gurness, Orkney Mainland's best representation of this type of structure, situated amidst a group of other stone buildings of assorted ages; the Onstan Chambered Cairn, dated about 2500 BC; and many more — on this island as well as on the others. Cliffbound Hoy, for instance, boasts two martello towers constructed as defenses against American privateers. The islands are particularly lovely during the twilight nights of late summer, when the sun never quite rests. Not all archaeological sites can be seen at all times, and some are relatively inaccessible, so it's wise to plan a visit well before arriving. For details, contact the Orkney Tourist Board, 6 Broad St., Kirkwall, Orkney Islands KW15 1DH, Scotland (phone: 0856-2856).

CAERNARFON, Gwynedd, Wales: Though little remains of this castle except its walls, it is easy to imagine the grandeur that Edward I planned when he began construction in the late 13th and early 14th centuries. He was building not only a military fortress but also a symbol of his sovereignty over Wales. Accordingly, he had it executed very much in the style of the Romans who had ruled Wales centuries earlier from this site on the Menai Strait, with stonework much like that of the 5th-century Roman wall at Constantinople, the cost of which was immense — the equivalent of nearly $23 million by today's standards. There were shooting galleries both high and low, courtyards and drawbridges, portcullises, arrow loops and spyholes — many of which, or remnants thereof, can still be seen. With the turrets and towers to explore, vaulted chambers to poke around in, walls and lawns to walk upon, a museum to visit, and a film on the castle's history to view, this is understandably a popular destination in Wales. Dr. Samuel Johnson, on visiting the castle 2 centuries ago, remarked that he had not thought such buildings existed, that it surpassed all his ideas. The future Edward VIII was invested here in 1911, as was the present Prince Charles in 1969 — only appropriate since Edward I's son, the first Prince of Wales, was born here. More information about the area is available from the Northern Regional Office, Wales Tourist Board, 77 Conway Rd., Colwyn Bay, Clwyd LL29 7LN, Wales (phone: 0492-531731).

CONWY CASTLE, Conwy, Gwynedd, Wales: Counted among Europe's greatest fortresses when taken together with the town's walls, and once one of its most powerful fortifications, this magnificent piece of medieval architecture, one of 10 castles built by Edward I as his headquarters in his efforts to control the Welsh, must have been all the more striking in its early years when its walls — whitewashed at the time — gleamed brightly from afar. But even now the structure is altogether impressive. Built mainly between 1283 and 1287 after designs by the king's castle engineer, James of St. George, it required the work of some 1,500 men and the expenditure of some £15,000 to complete it. The eight towers, each with walls 15 feet thick, rise to a height of 70 feet; they are not, as they seem, perpendicular to the ground, but instead taper gradually toward the top. The Northwest Tower has a fine view over the river, and the Prison Tower has a concealed dungeon as fearsomely dark and close as the imposing 38-by-125-foot Great Hall just above, which is spacious and airy, with its grand north- and east-facing windows. In the part of the castle known as the Inner Bailey, which lies to the east of the Great Hall, you can view the elegantly detailed Queen Eleanor's Chapel, the best-preserved part of the structure; the name is merely traditional, because the castle wasn't finished during her lifetime. The most important battle fought within the castle's walls took place in 1294, during a rebellion led by Prince Madog ap Llywelyn. Edward I took refuge there and, when trapped without proper food and water by the rising tide of the river, was almost beaten. The castle's subsequent history was marked by a visit of Richard II at the end of the 14th century (he was captured by the Duke of Northumberland and Archbishop Arundel for Henry Bolingbroke, later Henry IV); by occupation by Royalist forces during the 17th century; and by plundering, dismantling, and damage during the 19th century. For more information, contact the Wales Tourist Board's Northern Regional Office (address above).

TINTERN ABBEY, Tintern, Gwent, Wales: On the Welsh side of the border 5 miles north of Chepstow, this most atmospheric and impressive of all the country's ruined abbeys stands in the sheltered lee of wooded hills of a bend in the tranquil river Wye. The beauty and peace of the spot, recorded in poetry by Wordsworth and in watercolors by Turner, is still overwhelming. The Abbey was founded in the 12th century and reached the height of its prosperity in the next 200 years; most of the ruins visible today, including Chapter House, kitchen, refectory, and sacristy, belong to this period. Then, in 1349, the Black Death wiped out most of the monks and lay brothers. The walls of the church still stand, roofless and stretched heavenward, along with four great arches in its center; the windows are huge and exquisitely proportioned, particularly the fine traceried rose window, which takes up most of the supporting east wall and frames the rugged scenery outside. Closed Sunday mornings. Details: South Wales Regional Office, Ty Croeso, 6 Gloucester Pl., Swansea SA1 1TY, West Glamorgan, Wales (phone: 0792-465204 or 02918-251).

For the Experience

Pub Crawling

Everywhere in Britain there are pubs, and in most places, many. London alone has 5,000; in the country, there are so many pubs that during World War II, when road signs were removed, people could give directions in terms of the local watering hole: "Turn left at the *Dog and Duck,* go for half a mile as far as the *King's Arms,* then . . ." Those English villages that have lost their last remaining pub have won some degree of celebrity as a result. There are pubs in the city and in the country, pubs in the theater district, pubs patronized heavily by journalists, pubs with gardens, and pubs where you can listen to music or catch a striptease show.

Yet only a fraction of them have the kind of decor and atmosphere that measure up to most Americans' idea of what British pubs are like. Some do have dark paneling, a long mahogany bar, and an abundance of engraved glass mirrors and gleaming brass fittings, but they're the exception rather than the rule.

Though some of the worst abuses of the recent past — the superabundance of Formica and other plastics, loud jukeboxes, the battery of electronic games that bleep and squeal above the noises of good cheer encouraged by a draft from the pressurized aluminum keg — have begun to disappear in pubs in London and the South, the garden variety British pub generally reflects many of the more obnoxious intrusions of twentieth-century civilization.

Paradoxically, it doesn't seem to matter. Just as an American neighborhood tavern can be entertaining even when the floor is ugly green tile, the bar stools covered with plastic, and the lighting murky, the pub is a center of social life here. It is also becoming a focus of culinary activity — a decided change over earlier years, when "pub grub" meant a sandwich, a mashed-potato-topped ground meat concoction known as cottage pie, or a ploughman's lunch consisting of a hunk of bread and cheese plus pickle. Nowadays, with the burgeoning interest in good food and the proliferation of wine bars, many pubs are setting aside rooms especially for more ambitious sit-down meals, including meats, unusual salads, and homemade desserts.

Before setting off on that most convivial of pleasures, the pub crawl, there are a number of facts a visitor should keep in mind:

Pub crowds vary. British pubs usually attract a mixed crowd of all ages — silver-haired ladies clutching shopping bags and bolting shots of gin; workmen in stained overalls arguing politics and draining pints of beer; young people in preppy clothes and men in bowler hats discussing philosophical ideas or sports over ale; tourists juggling plates of Scotch eggs and pints of lager.

Pub hours differ widely from area to area and occasionally from pub to pub. Most pubs in England, Scotland, and Wales open in the late morning, do a booming business through the lunch hour, shut down for the afternoon, then start serving again at the end of the workday or around the dinner hour; closing is generally around 10:30 or 11 PM, but local variations are legion. Pubs in Scotland, the Isle of Man, the Channel Isles, and the Scilly Isles are licensed from 11 AM to 11 PM, subject only to individual landlord restrictions. Elsewhere in England and Wales, licensing hours are 11 AM to 11 PM Mondays through Saturdays and noon to 3 PM and 7 to 10 PM Sundays — though a certain amount of flexibility exists in pubs that serve food. In some parts of the country, particularly in the islands and in certain corners of Wales, pubs are closed all day on Sundays.

Beer is not the name of the brew. The sheer variety of drafts can perplex newcomers. Britons talk of lagers and of ales and their subtypes rather than "beer." Lager is made from a yeast that sinks to the bottom of the brewing tank during fermentation (rather than rising to the top like the yeast used in traditional ales). It is also activated at a lower temperature, so the product stays clear instead of turning cloudy when cooled. Typically, lagers are also lighter in color and body, fizzier, drier, and taste more of malt than of hops. But there are exceptions, because many lagers are made to taste like ales and vice versa.

Ales fall into several distinct categories. Bitter, usually served on draft, has a good strong brown color, a frothy head, and a taste that tends to be sharp or earthy (owing to a large proportion of hops in the brew). The terms "special" and "best," applied to bitters, refer not to quality but to strength. So-called pale and light ales are the bottled versions of bitter; pale is likely to be the stronger. Mild ale, yet a different brew, is made from a recipe that calls for more sugar and less hops. Served on draft, it is usually sweeter and (except in the Midlands, where the milds look almost like bitter) dark brown to black. Brown ale is like a bottled version of mild. Stouts — brews made from well-roasted, unmalted barley — are all very dark and sometimes sweet; Guinness, Ireland's most famous drink, is thick and rich like all stout, but not at all sweet.

At one time, pubs in Britain served only keg beers, which have been filtered and pasteurized at the brewery and packed under pressure. But because of the "real ale" movement of the past few years, most pubs now also serve brews that are still fermenting when they are delivered. Unlike keg beers, real ales require careful handling, but the taste warrants the effort.

The best guide to pubs is the *Good Beer Guide,* published under the aegis of the active Campaign for Real Ale (CAMRA) and available for $9.10/£5.95 from its offices at 34 Alma Rd., St. Albans, Hertfordshire AL1 3BW, England (published in the US under the title *The Best Pubs of Great Britain,* by Globe Pequot Press, Old Chester Rd., Chester, CT 06412; $9.95). This guide lists over 5,000 pubs that serve the better brews. The annually revised *Good Pub Guide,* published by Consumers' Association and Hodder & Stoughton ($15.25/£9.95), is also recommended.

The following selection, which includes some of the very best, most unusual, and most atmospheric pubs, describes the variety of places travelers will turn up when they prowl farther afield.

MINER'S ARMS INN, Acomb, Northumberland, England: Only 2 miles from Hexham, a busy market town with a beautiful ancient abbey, this cozy 18th-century coaching inn, comfortable if a bit garish in its plushness, has thick stone walls, immense and impressive original oak beams, brass ornaments that suggest antiquity, a garden, and — perhaps best of all — a pleasantly mixed clientele that includes not only locals but also bankers and plastics manufacturers who drive out from 20-mile-distant Newcastle, long-distance hikers heading for the Northumbria National Park, and campers. Steaks are among the dishes available in the restaurant at moderate prices; real ale, imported beers, and vegetarian meals are also on the menu. Phone: 0434-603909.

SARACEN'S HEAD, Bath, Avon, England: The oldest pub in this Georgian city, it looks like an ersatz antique at first. The building, at 42 Broad Street, was completed in 1713, and Charles Dickens stayed here in 1835 when it was still an inn; the display case in the wall has a few items from his time. The beamed ceiling still retains the handsome original plasterwork. Phone: 0225-26518.

BUCKINGHAMSHIRE ARMS, Blickling, Norfolk, England: Blickling Hall, the fine, red brick Jacobean house built for Sir Henry Hobart in the early 17th century, is next door to this inn of the same vintage, and two of its three bedrooms have windows looking out on the handsome structure. Buffet lunches are available except on Sundays, when carved specialties are offered. Phone: 0263-732133.

CORONATION TAP, Bristol, Avon, England: On Saturday nights, this tiny tavern at the end of a cul-de-sac in Bristol's trendy Clifton district bursts at the seams with local students trying to down more than one pint of the pub's famous thick scrumpy, dredged from the bottom of the cider barrels. This is the only pub in the United Kingdom that gets 22-gallon barrels of cider; when emptied, they are added to the decor. In addition to cider, there are English beers and ales, wine, and spirits. Food ranges from tap sandwiches to a full-blown Sunday lunch. Between Sion Pl. and Portland St. Phone: 0272-739617.

THE BULL HOTEL, Burford, Oxfordshire, England: There's history in every nook and cranny of this 14th-century coaching inn on the doorstep of the Cotswolds in one of England's prettiest and most famous High Streets. A log fire roars in the bar in winter. With its bare stone walls and tapestry-covered chairs, the candlelit restaurant has a more elegant coziness. The name recalls a papal bull of 1397 that authorized the building of a rest house for the Priory of Burford. Charles II and Nell Gwyn made the inn their headquarters in 1669. The town is an antiques lover's delight. Phone: 099382-2220.

THREE HORSESHOES, near Cambridge, Cambridgeshire, England: Visitors, academics, university students, and families all patronize this thatched, whitewashed country pub on High Street in the tiny village of Madingly, northwest of Cambridge. They come in winter, when the atmosphere is cozy and warm, and in summer, when dainty elegance prevails among the tables set up on the back lawn. Lunchtime food is a special delight — smoked fish, salads, pâtés, and cold meats. Phone: 0954-210221.

BELL HOTEL, Driffield East, Yorkshire, England: Mr. and Mrs. Riggs's huge white hotel in Market Place was an 18th-century coaching inn popular among wartime officers stationed nearby. Its courtyard is topped by a huge glass dome, and the place more recently has become famous for its buffet lunches, served in the adjacent corn exchange, a venerable environment where the original brickwork coexists happily with baskets of plants and other contemporary decor. Guests line up to have their plates mounded with hot and cold chicken, turkey, or ham, cheeses, and salads. Phone: 0377-46661.

ROYAL OAK, King's Bromley, Burton-on-Trent, Staffordshire, England: The public bar section of this half-timbered erstwhile farmhouse, originally part of a big estate, is basic but congenial. The lounge is wonderfully comfortable, with red carpet, tufted plush seats, and open fires — just the place to while away a long winter's eve. The dining room is equally attractive: The long oak beams there and in the bars — said to have come from early-17th-century sailing ships — impart an Old World look. There's no question that the place really does date from 1610, as local historians assert. The venison and omelets are worth a detour, and the scenery in the surrounding country is exceptionally pretty in places, and highly underrated. Burton-on-Trent is the nearest town of any size. Phone: 0543-472289.

ANGEL, Lavenham, Suffolk, England: Even in a superbly preserved medieval town like Lavenham, where scarcely a dwelling seems less than a few centuries old, this inn on the marketplace overlooking the historic gray-and-white half-timbered guildhall — itself barely changed for hundreds of years — is very old. Dating in part from the 15th century, it was built atop the much older remains of a dormitory for a religious order. There are now two bars — one, the public, caters to the needs of locals; the other, oak-beamed and thickly carpeted, is more attuned to the requirements of the many tourists who flock to Lavenham and, after much rubbernecking around the rural corners of Suffolk, want to put up their feet. Excellent home-cooked meals and snacks are available at midday and in the evening. There are also accommodations. Phone: 0787-247388.

PHILHARMONIC PUB, Liverpool, Merseyside, England: Hands-down Britain's most ornate pub, this one at 36 Hope Street is famous for its men's room — marble lavatories so spectacular that ladies are actually allowed to come in for a look-see when it's unoccupied. The rest of the huge interior consists of several rooms, some divided by carved wooden partitions leading off from a mosaic-decorated central bar, others huge and sumptuous with padded seats, high ceilings, and stained-glass windows. And true Yorkshire bitters are on tap. Phone: 051-709-1163.

AUDLEY, London, England: In London's higher-rent Mayfair district, this large establishment sits on the corner of South Audley Street, only a block from the American Embassy at Grosvenor Square. Its cleanliness makes it a major luncheon favorite, and sitting on one of the stools at the counter is a special treat. The 40-seat restaurant on the first floor serves traditional English fare. The large, recently remodeled bar and cold carvery offer first class sandwiches and, for dessert, a fresh and feisty slab of Stilton. The conversation varies substantially from room to room, and it's fun to move between the two very different groups of customers. The Victorian decor, with its garish ornamentation, provides a very pleasant environment. This is one of the places where you're most likely to run into a friendly accent from home. Phone: 01-499-1843.

DIRTY DICK'S, London, England: When his fiancée was killed on the eve of their wedding day, the Dirty Dick in question, one Nathaniel Bentley, went into seclusion and lived out his life in isolation and ever-increasing squalor in the apartments that now make up the downstairs section of this pub at 202 Bishopsgate. The spiders and bats that used to swing from the walls and ceiling in the downstairs bar as reminders of the weird, Dickensian story have been relegated to a small museum area, and the place is a pleasant enough spot to begin an evening. The area above, rebuilt in 1745, lends itself to other functions. Galleried and spacious, with wood everywhere and sawdust on the floors, it's plain rather than plush (much like the East End surrounding it), and, in its dark and clubby way, is a supremely restful place to quench a thirst after a hectic Sunday morning's bargaining along nearby Petticoat Lane. Phone: 01-283-5888.

EL VINO, London, England: A wine bar rather than a pub, this establishment at 47 Fleet Street deserves special mention as a bastion of City tradition. From its earliest years, for purely chivalrous reasons, women were not allowed to stand at the bar (a High Court action financed by the Equal Opportunities Commission has changed all that). Men must wear collar, tie, and jacket, and women must wear skirts or dresses (never trousers). The magnificently polished Victorian setting makes it almost impossible to imagine a more Dickensian scene. A tony Fleet Street crowd — publishers, editors, feature writers, and a bevy of barristers — savors the varied offerings of wine, both plain and fortified. Phone: 01-353-6786.

GRENADIER, London, England: This is a very special stopping place in a most unlikely location. To get there, it's necessary to ignore a barrier and coachman, forbidding obstacles whose purpose actually is to keep cars, not pedestrians, out of this narrow, mews-style residential street just off Wilton Crescent at 18 Wilton Row, only a block from Belgravia Square. The military moniker derives from the time when this was the Officers' Mess for the Duke of Wellington's soldiers. The exterior is chauvinistically red, white, and blue, featuring a bright sentry box, and access from the north is via narrow Old Barracks Yard. Since it's an ideal place to stop for lunch after a trip to *Harrods* or a boutique browse up Brompton Road, the clientele is unceasingly posh. A tiny bar is at the front, with a rare pewter-topped counter. The two back rooms serve as an intimate candlelit restaurant. The place is reportedly haunted by a ghost who seems to make his presence known especially during September. The resident specter is purported to be a young officer who was caught cheating at cards and was ruthlessly beaten by his fellow officers. But he's apparently a relatively stable spirit and seldom disturbs drinkers or diners. Phone: 01-235-3074.

YE OLDE CHESHIRE CHEESE, London, England: Here's the perfect place to stop and rest during a tour of the nearby Inns of Court, made familiar in those murky scenes on PBS's presentation of Dickens's *Bleak House.* This makes the nip down the narrow alley (beside 145 Fleet Street) to the pub door all the more evocative; it's easy to imagine the London of a century or so ago. Samuel Johnson lived around the corner, and his intimate circle — notably Boswell, Reynolds, and Gibbon — frequented "The Cheese." The character of the pub has remained remarkably intact despite its place on many tourist itineraries. The wooden stairs are narrow and the downstairs bar always several drinkers deep, but somehow the bumping and squeezing past is part of the fun. On a very cold winter's afternoon, a bowl of beef barley soup can be a special savior and the warmth of the roaring fire upstairs a consummate joy. Those interested in unusual beer brands should try a pint of Marston's Pedigree or a mug of Merrie Monk. Phone: 01-353-6170.

SHERLOCK HOLMES, London, England: Forget about Baker Street; this Northumberland Street pub, which Conan Doyle used to frequent when it was called the Northumberland Arms (and which he mentioned in his *Hound of the Baskervilles*), is the nearest most people will ever come to the great man. Drawings and photographs of actors playing Holmes and of scenes from Holmes and all manner of other Holmesiana adorn the downstairs bar; upstairs, on the way to a first-floor restaurant, there's a replica of his Baker Street study, cleverly walled off by glass. The collection of memorabilia was assembled in 1951 by the Sherlock Holmes Society of London for the *Festival of Britain,* and this smart and congenial pub — whose clientele, appropriately enough, includes policemen from nearby Scotland Yard — provides it with an excellent home. Phone: 01-930-2644.

SPANIARDS INN, Hampstead, north of London, England: Perfectly positioned on Spaniards Road between the east and west sides of Hampstead Heath, this establishment attracts Sunday walkers, visitors to nearby Kenwood House, wealthy local residents, and casual passers-by. The building, with its large outdoor garden dotted with wooden tables and chairs, is quite pretty. The labyrinthine interior has low-ceilinged rooms paneled in oak and warmed by open fires. Bar food consists of unexceptional rolls, meat pies, and hot daily specials. Phone: 01-455-3276.

PIKE AND EEL, Needingworth, Cambridgeshire, England: Pubs where fishermen congregate tend to be clubby places, however humble, and ordinary visitors may not feel welcome. This establishment, built of brick in the 16th century and much extended during Oliver Cromwell's time, is an exception — yet there's no mistaking where its loyalties lie. In front, a large garden with lawns and umbrella-shaded tables runs down to the river Ouse, where yachts and cabin cruisers are moored in summer. Inside, glass cases show off stuffed pike and eels (not particularly agreeable to look at but a favorite quarry of nighttime fishermen hereabouts). The flat, windswept, and mysterious fens that surround this low-ceilinged, oak-beamed pub make it all the cozier, and it's pleasant to spend the night in one of the rooms available to overnight lodgers. The restaurant has a fine local reputation, particularly for Dover sole and halibut dishes; bar snacks are also good. There is also a large garden room, seating 85, where bar food and barbecue can be had. Needingworth is not far from St. Ives. Phone: 0480-63336.

ADAM AND EVE, Norwich, Norfolk, England: Dating from 1249, this oldest of the city's pubs, at 17 Bishopsgate, was first used as a brewhouse to which artisans laboring on the nearby cathedral would repair. The ambience is palpable; customers can sit outside on wooden benches or indoors, where low beams and bare tiled floors recall the spit and sawdust of wherryman days. Morning coffee, grills, salads, hot and cold snacks, and a formal Sunday lunch are available. Phone: 0603-667423.

EARLE ARMS, Heydon, Norwich, Norfolk, England: Unpretentious and friendly, this 300-year-old pub has so much character that it has been used as a movie set on several occasions. It's especially pleasant in summer, when visitors can emerge from the darkly subdued interior and take their beer on the village green. The village of Heydon lies at the end of a tiny byroad whose natural quiet is broken only by birds twittering, children laughing, and church bells pealing. Phone: 026387-376.

PLOUGH AND SAIL, near Rochford, Paglesham, Essex, England: This clapboard-walled pub is better known to yachtsmen than to passing motorists. Not far from the town of Rochford, near the Essex marshes and within sniffing distance of the North Sea, it is wonderfully remote. Yet the atmosphere is remarkably lively thanks to the vivacious family of broad-speaking former East Enders who run the place. Summer weekends bring crowds; at other times, things are quieter, and in chilly weather there's always a log fire crackling on the hearth. Phone: 03706-242.

THREE HORSESHOES INN, Powerstock, near Bridport, Dorset, England: Travelers can squeeze into Pat and Diana's "Shoes" (as the locals call it) on a summer's weekend at lunchtime and head straight out through the back door of the structure, which was rebuilt from local stone after a fire in 1906. There, at wooden tables in a garden, they can down crab, lobster, skate, and prawns with a salad and a pint of cool scrumpy with the rolling Dorset countryside in full view. Such fare has recently been drawing crowds from miles around, and four rooms have been converted to guest bedrooms. The view from the front takes in tiny Powerstock's main street, shaded by ancient oaks, where cows walk by at milking time against the backdrop of imposing Eggardon Hill. Phone: 030885-328.

HOLE IN THE WALL, Royal Tunbridge Wells, Kent, England: From the mid-17th century until the early 1970s, this red brick structure, known in Victorian times as the Central Smoking Divan and believed to date back to the Restoration, housed a tobacconist's shop; the snug in the rear was virtually unknown. The establishment that now occupies the premises at 9 High Street is another kind of place altogether, and it has been almost totally transformed. The interior space has been divided into two tiers, one overlooking the other, both done in red flocked wallpaper with comfortable furniture upholstered to match. There's a separate restaurant, but the homemade pies and pasties and assorted other snacks served in the bar are quite tasty. The *Hole in the Wall* is known for its variety of beers; this is a so-called free house — not owned by a brewery — as are most pubs in England. Phone: 0892-26550.

BLACK SWAN, Stratford-upon-Avon, Warwickshire, England: The late Sir Laurence Olivier, Sir John Gielgud, Albert Finney, Peter O'Toole, and Glenda Jackson have all frequented this place at one time or another, and more recently John Hurt, Derek Jacobi, and Helen Mirren have popped by.. The "Dirty Duck," as it's informally known, is very much an actor's hangout — owing not only to its proximity to Stratford's *Royal Shakespeare Theatre* but also to the special attention the management gives its thespian patrons. Although less illustrious visitors may have to try a little harder to order some of the pub food, there's always someone interesting to look at while waiting. The pub also boasts a first class restaurant, specializing in roast duck and oxtail, that stays open for after-theater supper. Phone: 0789-297312.

ROSE AND CROWN, Tewin, Hertfordshire, England: Overlooking the village green, in a part of the Home Counties whose peaceful aspect belies its relative nearness to London (about 25 miles) and its even greater proximity to the new town of Welwyn Garden City, the *Rose and Crown* is a typical country local, with a mixed clientele — deadly serious darts players who monopolize the boards in the public bar, village elders who play cribbage or dominoes, children who frolic out in the garden in summer, and stylish young people who favor the comfortable pile-carpeted lounge. The bar snacks are good, and the warm, candlelit restaurant serves up traditional English food like roast beef, steak-and-kidney pie, and jugged hare. Phone: 043871-7257.

TICKELL ARMS, Whittlesford, Cambridgeshire, England: You can't escape the eagle eye of this pub's owner, Mr. J. H. de la T. Tickell. If your car isn't in line in the parking lot, he will ask you to repark it. No T-shirts are allowed, and if you make the mistake of lighting a cigarette in the main room, you will be asked to extinguish it. Moreover, the inn, which occupies a large blue house with a graveled driveway a mile from the M11 junction 10, has no pub sign. Nonetheless, locals and tourists line up regularly and respectfully for unusual, beautifully presented cold dishes for lunch and dinner, for homemade punch or mulled wine, depending on the season, and for pints of delicious Greene King Abbot Ale. In summer, the outside lawns are crowded with local university students. Phone: 0223-833128 (no calls between 2 and 7 PM).

ROYAL OAK, Winsford, Somerset, England: There are other pubs that claim to be 300 years older than this pretty West Country village inn, adorned outside by hanging flower baskets. However, the fact that it dates from the 14th century (and some parts of it to the 12th century) still ranks it among the nation's oldest. It is certainly one of the most imposing properties in the area, with its whitewashed stone walls, thick thatched roof, and interesting sign — an oak surrounding the head of Charles I. (In English lore, the tree, which supposedly sheltered the king during his flight from Cromwell's troops, is like the bed in which George Washington slept: Almost every community, in search of a claim to fame, has managed to come up with one.) The *Royal Oak,* popular with passing tourists, has two heavily beamed bars — a traditional public, with a dart board, and a comfortable lounge. Good snacks are served, including a fine steak-and-kidney pie. Accommodations are also available. Minehead is the closest good-size town. Phone: 064385-455.

GLOBE INN, Dumfries, Dumfries and Galloway, Scotland: To Scots, the poet Robert Burns is Shakespeare, Tolstoy, Mozart, and Beethoven all rolled into one; and because this pub on a narrow alley near 56 High Street was his "favourite howff," it is very important indeed — even though it was old before he knew it and though only one room of the building where Burns lodged is really part of today's *Globe.* Certainly, it's an exceptionally charming place — and would be even if it weren't possible to see the verses that the poet inscribed in glass with a diamond stylus, sleep in the room where he slept (albeit on rare occasions), and sit in his favorite chair. The *Globe* has as its signpost not a globe but Burns's head. Meals served at lunchtime — soups, roast beef, fish, and sweets — are good and inexpensive. Phone: 0387-52335.

TILTED WIG, Edinburgh, Scotland: This locally famous city pub at 1-2-3 Cumberland Street, in elegant, classically inspired New Town, claims among its distinctions a garden where, in summer, it's possible to sit under umbrellas and order from a waitress; a good selection of beers (real ale among them); and a clientele that, as the name suggests, includes a disproportionate number of lawyers and solicitors, especially at lunchtime. A casual visitor might easily think he had walked in on some private club. The walls are hung with all manner of etchings and engravings on juridical subjects, elegant French wallpaper adorns the ceiling, and there's oak paneling to complete the cozy effect. Haggis is among the assortment of good bar snacks. Phone: 031-556-1824.

OWAIN GLYNDWR, Corwen, Clwyd, Wales: Here's a place with real local character. Frequented by townspeople more often than by tourists, this establishment on the town square occupies a plaster-over-stone building that was partly built in the 13th century, used to be a monastery's outbuilding, and is said to be haunted by the ghost of the 15th-century Welsh freedom fighter Owen Glendower. There are three bars: an unpretentious old-style public bar with a dart board and a jukebox; another, rather plush and cozy with its red carpet, original oak beams, decorative horse brasses, and old saddles; and the third, a small one attached to the restaurant. On tap, a thirsty visitor won't find the aerated (and even gassy), pressurized brews, but instead a good range of real ales. Bar snacks like scampi and steak and chips are provided as well as complete meals. Phone: 0490-2115.

GROES INN, Ty'n-y-Groes, near Conwy, Gwynedd, Wales: Believed by many people to be the oldest pub in Wales, *Groes Inn* is installed in a building that was already old when the pub license was issued in 1573. Whitewashed and pleasantly tree-shaded, with thick walls constructed of locally quarried Conwy stone, which may date from an ice age, the pub is full of charming antique settles — the kind of high-backed wooden bench traditionally used for sitting in front of the fire on a cold night because of the protection it afforded from drafts. Here, the fireplace conceals a locally famous "priest hole," the hideaway for many devout Roman Catholics during the reign of Elizabeth I. The views — looking out over the Conwy valley and distant Snowdon, Wales's highest mountain — are outstanding, and the food is well worth the wait. Phone: 0492-650545.

Rural Retreats

To travelers from abroad, the most striking features of the British countryside are the absence of billboards, the scarcity of motels, and the abundance of homey inns, guesthouses, and country manors turned hotels. The tradition of innkeeping, particularly in England, goes back for centuries, and that's easy enough to see: Wooden stair treads are worn down to concavity by the footsteps of travelers over the ages; walls are half-timbered, ceilings beamed. In northern England, the lodging places tend toward the rickety and quaint; in the South, there is an excellent assortment of charming country-house hotels. In addition, a group known as the Landmark Trust has purchased and restored about 150 buildings of historical importance that have long outlived their original function (the most eccentric is the Pineapple, near Airth, Stirlingshire, in Scotland, built in the 18th century as a fancy summer house for the Earl of Dunmore to celebrate his success in growing hothouse pineapples). These are now available for rent to vacationers, complete with basic comforts, at moderate rents; book well in advance, because, despite infrequent advertising, most properties fill up early. A fully illustrated booklet on the Landmark Trust properties is available for $11 from Mr. and Mrs. Philip Myerly, 248 S. Prospect St., Hagerstown, MD 21740.

As for the food, establishments are in varying states of emergence from the age of soggy sprouts, overcooked fish, meat roasted to a fare-thee-well, and vegetables that would make the army's steam-table offerings look crisp. A whole generation of young chefs trained on the Continent has brought a new look to the nation's menus and such an intense respect for the freshness of ingredients that some masters of the new cuisine don't just go out and buy the best that the local market has to offer, they also work with local farmers to have vegetables planted and grown to their specifications. The undeniably positive by-products are no longer destroyed through overcooking. And unlike some practitioners of the nouvelle cuisine in France, the new chefs here are delightfully straightforward and unpretentious about their presentations.

Some of these special establishments are more noteworthy than others — whether due to their decor, the friendliness of their management (more often than not a whole family), or their setting or food. Here is an assortment of some of the best castle-hotels, inns, country houses, and restaurants the rural region has to offer. Some warrant a stop when you're in the area; a handful of others, perhaps a shade more wonderful on one or more counts, are worth planning a whole holiday around.

WORTH A LONG DETOUR

ELMS, Abberley, near Worcester, Hereford and Worcester, England: Built primarily during the early 18th century after designs by a student of Sir Christopher

Wren, then added to in a neoclassical style during 1927, this grand country house has a magnificent tree-lined drive and gardens as clipped and formal as they come; the scene suggests morning suits and garden party hats, white gloves and flouncy dresses. The interiors are just as elegant, from the sumptuously carpeted oak staircase to the public rooms full of tufted settees and velvet chairs and the fine Library Bar, still adorned with its original mahogany bookcases; the guestrooms boast oil paintings, interesting knick-knacks, spacious bathrooms, antique furnishings (one room is graced by a four-poster bed), and — not the least important — fine views overlooking the surrounding park. Major refurbishment of the bedrooms, restaurant lounges, and bar was completed in the spring of 1989. Despite the luxury of the setting, the *Elms* is never stuffy, and it's easy to spend days on end strolling across the grounds, batting tennis balls on the hotel's courts, and practicing your putting on its green. Details: The Elms Hotel, Abberley, near Worcester WR6 6AT, England (phone: 0299-896666).

EASTWELL MANOR, Ashford, Kent, England: Set in some 3,000 acres of parkland picturesquely speckled with fluffy white sheep, this elegant, rambling stone country house was opened as a hotel just in 1980, and, though the present house was rebuilt in 1926, its history can be traced back to the Norman Conquest. Over the years it has had 20 owners, and Queen Victoria once visited here. (Guests at the manor can see a picture of her, seated in a chair on the property's frozen lake, surrounded by the other members of her skating party.) Purchased in November 1982 by a Canadian family and renovated not long before, the manor has been earning kudos ever since for the lavish use of space and splendid service that remind guests of an earlier, grander age; one visitor called it "the world's best 23-room hotel." Though the rooms are absolutely huge, they are so cleverly decorated with sitting areas, soft colors, and pretty fabrics that they seem positively inviting; all of the bathrooms are vast, and some are sumptuous. Among the public rooms is an oak-paneled bar to lure guests down for drinks before dinner, which is served in a baronial dining room. The menu is English but draws on the best concepts of both classic French and nouvelle cuisine. Vegetables are carefully cooked to retain their natural crispness, and meats are left pink as a matter of policy. You'll find such delicacies as sliced breast of duck laid on a lemon sauce and garnished with glazed raspberries, or salmon steak lightly poached in butter, served on a fresh tomato and dill purée and topped with a sauce of dry vermouth and cream. The chef selects game, lamb, and beef from the Eastwell estate and purchases other ingredients from London and Paris markets. A very extensive wine list, which includes English wines, complements the offerings. Details: Eastwell Manor, Eastwell Park, Ashford, Kent TN25 4HR, England (phone: 0233-635751).

BELL INN, Aston Clinton, Buckinghamshire, England: Once a favorite of Evelyn Waugh, this former coaching post has been welcoming guests since about 1650. But seldom during the past 3 centuries has it looked quite as lovely as it does today, with its cozy bar — the ceiling beamed, the floor paved in flagstones, the air warmed by the fire blazing away on the hearth — and its scattering of antiques. Fresh flowers are a common sight, both in the public rooms and in the guest quarters, which are located in former stables and malt houses ranged around a small, cobbled courtyard. Bath salts, bathroom scales, thick terry robes, refrigerators stocked to quench post-midnight thirsts, and other amenities complete the picture. The setting, on A41 a few miles east of Aylesbury and not far from Heathrow, is not the nation's most pastoral, but when one is cosseted in such fashion, it almost doesn't matter. And the food is good enough to warrant special mention. While there's plenty of traditional English fare such as the famous *Bell Inn* smokies and Dover sole, it's also possible to savor wondrous French specialties such as *canard aux deux cuissons aux cepes des bois* (a pink braised breast and crispy leg of duck with sauerkraut and wild cêpes). Because the restaurant is near Aylesbury, famous as the home of the Aylesbury duck, this fowl is always on the menu. The wine list is especially fine. Details: Bell Inn, Aston Clinton, Buckinghamshire HP22 5HP, England (phone: 0296-630252).

WATERSIDE INN, Bray-on-Thames, Berkshire, England: Multiple Michelin stars are still not all that common in England. Yet this establishment's claim to being one of the only two honorees is just part of the reason to make a detour to the village of Bray, not far from Windsor and 27 miles west of London — even though there are no rooms. Brothers Albert and Michel Roux (French chefs with embassy experience and service for the best private families before they opened London's renowned *Le Gavroche*) chose to open their Thames-side country restaurant in a setting that provides a feast for the eyes before the feast for the palate begins. In spring, enormous red tulips are in bloom all around, flowering cherry trees line the river, and swans circle past almost as though summoned by a magic wand. In summer, apéritifs are served on the terrace and in two delightful summer houses, and the sight of weeping willows and boats on the water may distract a diner — momentarily — from the extraordinary menu. The Roux brothers are ceaselessly inventive. Among their enduring specialties are *tronconnettes de homard* (chunks of lobster in a white port wine sauce); warm oysters served in a puff pastry case, garnished with bean sprouts, raspberry vinegar butter sauce, and fresh raspberries; a medium-rare roast duckling pierced with cloves and served with a honey-flavored sauce; and a Grand Marnier–infused soufflé laid on an orange sauce and garnished with orange segments. The wine list, which counts no fewer than 400 bin numbers, is first rate, and some of the restaurant's personal touches are charming — for example, foie gras tartelettes, gravlax salmon, and haddock quiche served with cocktails. The cost of all this is "rather dear," as the British would say, but less than its equivalent in Paris and well worth it for a memorable occasion. Closed Mondays, Tuesday lunches, Sunday dinners from October through Easter, and for about 6 weeks from December 26 to February 13. No rooms. Details: Waterside Inn, Ferry Rd., Bray-on-Thames, Berkshire SL6 2AT, England (phone: 0628-20691 or -22941).

DORMY HOUSE, Broadway, Worcestershire, England: Built on a Cotswolds escarpment above honey-colored Broadway, *Dormy* began life as a 17th-century farmhouse, and its ancient beams and exposed stone walls confirm the historic pedigree. Open fires, wood paneling, and comfortable cozy-modern bedrooms complete the picture. And the staff, under Ingrid Philip Sorensen, is exceptionally cheery. Details: Dormy House, Willersey Hill, Broadway, Worcestershire WR12 7LF, England (phone: 0386-852711).

LYGON ARMS, Broadway, Hereford and Worcester, England: The *Lygon Arms* isn't nearly as old as some buildings in the Cotswolds, but 1532 seems a respectable enough birth date; that makes it old enough to have frequently welcomed Charles I as a guest and to have harbored Oliver Cromwell on the eve of the Battle of Worcester. And there are indications that the building itself is much older. A stone fireplace set into a 4-foot-thick wall, for instance, appears to have been crafted in the 14th century; and the rear courtyard door dates from the 15th century, the front door from the early 16th. All of the rooms are furnished with antiques of similar vintage, and a few pieces are of such high quality that they are illustrated in *The Dictionary of English Furniture.* The nine rooms in what is called the old wing are a study in Tudor, with beams, charmingly tilted oak floors, and dozens of blue Spode dishes on the fireplace mantels; the Great Chamber — one of the hotel's most famous rooms, for its vaulted timber-crossed ceiling and its massive canopied bed — is number 20. A vigorous refurbishing program has been completed on the entire ground floor of the inn (which once had a distinctly motel atmosphere) and 35 of the 64 bedrooms. Bathrooms have been updated with pressure showers, marble floors, and twin washstands. All this is as might be expected in the inn that is probably Britain's most photographed. What may be a surprise is the quality of the service. For example, a guest who shows a preference for Carlsberg lager on one visit will probably find a Carlsberg waiting when he returns. As for meals, prepared by chef Clive Howe who hails from *Rookery Hall* and the *Dorchester,* they are as elegant as the setting — the Great Hall, with its barrel-vaulted ceiling, great fireplace, and fine wood paneling. The candlelit after-theater suppers — smoked salmon, cold chicken, roast beef, salad, and fresh strawberries in season — can be a joy, as are the Cotswold lamb and game dishes, including venison and wild duck (when available). The wide, mile-long street on which the inn fronts is almost as pretty as the cream-colored stone hotel itself, and Stratford-upon-Avon is just 20 miles away. Details: The Lygon Arms, Broadway, Worcester WR12 7DU, England (phone: 0386-852255).

GIDLEIGH PARK, Chagford, Devon, England: Take over 30 acres of secluded Devon woodlands, add a turn-of-the-century mansion built for consummate comfort and elegance, furnish it in impeccably good taste, and you have *Gidleigh Park.* American owners Paul and Kay Henderson have thought of everything to make guests feel elegantly at home. Each of the 14 rooms is special, but our favorites are Nos. 1, 2, and 3, which overlook the sweeping lawns and rushing brook. Tennis and croquet are popular here, too. A 3-room thatched cottage has recently been built right on the grounds, decorated in the same lovely country-English look as the hotel. As if all this weren't enough, there's superb food: Start with perfect pâté de foie gras or salmon tartare, then move on to sea bass with cucumber on a bed of fried noodles, among other choices. The foregoing, plus a distinguished wine list, have earned the dining room a Michelin star. Details: Chagford, Devon, England (phone: 06473-2367).

THE GREENWAY, Cheltenham, Gloucestershire, England: Proprietor Tony Elliott, who has names like *Savoy* and *Claridges* scattered about his curriculum vitae, runs this recently refurbished and oft-commended old Elizabethan manor, full of antiques and porcelain, flowers and open fires, on the pastoral fringes of Cheltenham. There are 8 rooms in a converted coach house and a dozen more in the main house, where, because Mr. Elliott "has a thing about bumping into one's partner in a pokey bathroom," the lavatory facilities are particularly grand. And in the restaurant, candlelit at dinner, the menu is lively and imaginative. Standing well back from the busy A46 in formal gardens with a further 37 acres of parkland adjacent, the *Greenway* was named for a drovers' road that leads up to the hotel atop the Cotswold escarpment. Details: The Greenway, Shurdington, Cheltenham, Gloucestershire GL51 5UG, England (phone: 0242-862352).

GRAVETYE MANOR, near East Grinstead, West Sussex, England: About halfway between London and Brighton (30 minutes from Gatwick; 60 minutes from Heathrow airports) and about 5 miles from East Grinstead, this ivy-covered Elizabethan manor house, built in 1598 and enlarged in the same style over the centuries, not only has become one of rural England's most impressive hostelries since its conversion to a hotel in 1958, but also has earned an international reputation. In the tranquility of a thousand-acre forest, the gardens were created by *Gravetye*'s most famous owner, the great English horticulturalist William Robinson, who eschewed the popular formalized style in favor of a more natural look. In the years after his death in 1935, the gardens suffered badly, and it was left to the present owners to restore them to their former glory. Whether seen during a stroll along the garden paths or from the mullioned windows, they never cease to give pleasure. Robinson's influence is felt inside as well. The rooms are paneled with the estate's oak, bouquets of flowers he planted brighten the corners of all the rooms, and the 14 guestrooms are named for English trees such as bay, holly, beech, and ash. Many of these rooms have fireplaces; all have thick carpets, soothing decor, and such extras as a fruit basket, a Thermos filled with Gravetye's own chilled spring water, books, a hair dryer, and a special red telephone for emergencies. Touches like these have earned the hotel its membership in the prestigious Relais & Châteaux group. Owner Peter Herbert takes justifiable pride in his wine list, one of the most extensive in the country, and in his menu, which changes with the season. Among the highlights: a velvety chicken liver pâté, *sole de Douvre Victoria* (grilled Dover sole garnished with langoustine, avocado, and tomato), the tenderest

Scotch beef, smoked salmon and venison from the smokehouse on the grounds, and a selection of fresh vegetables from the kitchen garden cooked to crisp perfection. A separate dessert menu lists some 20 sweets (including homemade sorbets and ice creams) as well as savories and cheeses. There are ways to work off a bit of excess: playing croquet on the lawn, fishing in the well-stocked trout pond, or sightseeing in the neighborhood, where there are several other gardens of note. Details: Gravetye Manor, East Grinstead, West Sussex RH19 4LJ, England (phone: 0342-810567).

FLITWICK MANOR, Flitwick, Bedfordshire, England: For most Londoners, who are just a 40-minute car or train ride away from this establishment (whose name is pronounced without the "w"), the meals alone warrant the trip. Seafood, a surprise considering the inland location, comes courtesy of a group known as Somerset's Senders, who comb the coast and supply owner Somerset Moore with the freshest of fish, which are kept alive in the *Flitwick* seawater tanks until called for by the kitchen. Mahogany paneling and a gallery's worth of portraits make the surroundings as attractive as the food. Guests staying in the 15 sumptuous bedrooms of this handsome 17th-century structure will find the breakfasts, brought to the chamber complete with newspapers, equally noteworthy. Honey comes from the manor's beehive, eggs from free-range chickens, tomatoes from the walled kitchen garden, and croissants fresh from the oven; muesli and marmalade are made in-house. A pine chest holds an array of green Wellingtons, the only passport necessary to explore the woodlands all around — the 50 acres of parkland adjoining the house, the bordering Woburn estate, or the many other area footpaths. Details: Flitwick Manor, Flitwick, Bedfordshire MK45 1AE, England (phone: 0525-712242).

COMBE HOUSE, Gittisham, near Honiton, Devon, England: It takes a long time to wend one's way up the winding drive to *Combe House,* a cream-colored Elizabethan mansion that dates back to the 14th century; but it doesn't particularly matter, because the lush emerald parkland that rolls around on all sides, studded with rhododendrons, magnolias, and cedars, is so lovely. The mansion, owned by a descendant of Dr. Johnson's biographer James Boswell, is roomy, elegant, and furnished throughout with antiques, but not too formal. Almost every room has something that catches the eye: for instance, the ornate plaster ceiling and gleaming paneling in the main hall, full of squashy chintz-covered chairs; or the pink dining room's rococo fireplace, attributed to Chippendale, or the bar, hung with old hunting and coaching prints and photographs of the owner's horse-racing triumphs. Most guestrooms are exceptionally large and very quiet. And the food is good, thanks to Cordon Bleu–trained co-owner Therese Boswell and her team of young chefs. The hotel has fishing rights to 1½ miles of the south bank of the river Otter, which produces some good creels of brown trout, and the establishment makes an excellent base for tours of East Devon and for visits to nearby golf courses or to the ocean only 7 miles away. Closed January 8 through February 24. Details: Combe House Hotel, Gittisham, near Honiton, Devon EX14 OAD, England (phone: 0404-42756 or 41938; in the US, 800-548-7768).

LE MANOIR AUX QUAT' SAISONS, Great Milton, Oxfordshire, England: Fifteen minutes from Oxford, this establishment earned two Michelin stars even before it opened in 1984 and is now one of the country's most talked about dining and lodging retreats. Housed in an old, golden-hued, Cotswold stone structure, it has mullioned windows, thick stone walls, and molded cornices that are Tudor to the core. Yet the decor is relaxed and airy, and the 17th- and 18th-century Tudor furniture adds a note of elegance and grace. Some of the bedrooms have half-testered beds and most have fine views of the surrounding 27 acres of gardens. After checking in, guests find fresh flowers, decanters of Madeira, and bowls of exotic fruit in their quarters. In the tranquil pink and peach dining room, the best available ingredients go into every dish (the poultry, fish, cheese, and more come from France), and lightness is the operative word. Diners may sample the *trio de chocolates* or try the fillet of wild, home-smoked salmon with horseradish soufflé and cucumber butter. Closed Mondays and Tuesdays for lunch, and the last week in December through the first 3 weeks of January. Details: Le Manoir aux Quat' Saisons, Church Rd., Great Milton, Oxfordshire OX9 7PD, England (phone: 0844-278881).

HAMBLETON HALL, Hambleton, Leicestershire, England: Set on a peninsula jutting into Rutland Water, this Victorian country house offers lovely views over the lake as well as fishing, tennis, horseback riding, and bicycling. The rooms are a charming, comfortable, eclectic mix — "Fern" is our favorite — and the hospitality and service are warm and genuine. The restaurant, under chef Brian Baker, is one of only a dozen outside London to have earned a Michelin star. Don't miss the hot chocolate pudding. A Relais & Châteaux establishment. Details: Hambleton Hall, Hambleton, Oakham, Leicestershire LE15 8TH, England (phone: 0572-56991).

BOX TREE, Ilkley, West Yorkshire, England: This small restaurant in a 300-year-old cottage may just be the chief industry of the small town of Ilkley, 16 miles northwest of Leeds. The establishment seats only about 50 diners, and the menu is not overly long, but the accomplished cooking, fine service, and opulent setting make dining here a memorable experience. Awarded one Michelin star under owner Eric Kyte, the menus feature excellent beef and lamb, classical and modern French dishes such as coquilles St. Jacques and fricasseed lobster, and irresistible desserts. There's also an admirable wine cellar with some 200 selections, including "native" wines. Given its reputation, it's essential to reserve in advance. Closed Mondays; open on Sundays for lunch. Details: Box Tree, Church St., Ilkley, West Yorkshire LS29 9DR, England (phone: 0943-608484).

ARUNDELL ARMS, Lifton, Devon, England: This former coaching inn covered with Virginia creeper would be pleasant enough by anyone's standards: Log fires blaze away on the hearths downstairs, the floors are laid with locally quarried dark blue slate, the 29 guestrooms are decorated in true English country style, with brightly colored floral chintz fabrics reflecting the beauty of the gardens below, and the culinary offerings of the young French-trained chef (which include an excellent Tamar salmon served with a champagne sauce) are of very high caliber. But it really stands out for its fishing; for half a century now, it has owned the fishing rights on 20 miles of the Tamar, the stream that forms the boundary with Cornwall and ranks as the best of the West Country salmon streams. Some of the smaller streams run knee-deep over pebbly beds, down long riffles of rough white water, sometimes forming deep pools that are especially lovely when dappled with sun and shadow from the leaves of the alder trees whose branches meet overhead. For the past decade or so, the season's salmon take has averaged around 80, and there's an abundance of beautifully colored, wild and wily brown trout — small, but scrappy enough to take a dry or wet fly with a great slash and then fight like tigers. Also impressive is the big run of salmon and sea trout for which the Tamar is famous; the first spring salmon usually have entered *Arundell Arms* waters by mid-May, and the fishing for them, mostly by fly only, runs right through to mid-October. Sea trout fishing, by fly only, runs from late June to early September, and since the best of the sea trout are taken at night, guests usually go out after dinner and fish until midnight, sometimes all night. Details: Arundell Arms Hotel, Lifton, Devon PL16 OAA, England (phone: 0566-84666).

CHILSTON PARK, Maidstone, Kent, England: Except for the occasional sight of a pop star's helicopter on the lawn, this one-of-a-kind hotel is the 17th century incarnate, complete with footmen in tails, maids in mob caps, and 200 candles lit every day at dusk. Set in 250 acres of Kentish Weald countryside just 42 miles from London, *Chilston* is a convenient weekend retreat, with 40 bedrooms and a variety of countryside sports, including clay-pigeon shooting, archery, and lake trout fishing. The hotel is owned by the publishers of *Miller's Price Guide,* the antiques buyer's bible, and consequently is full of marvelous treasures, mostly from their private collection. Details: Chilston Park, Sandway, Maidstone, Kent ME17 2BE, England (phone: 0622-859803).

COTTAGE IN THE WOOD, Malvern Wells, Malvern, Worcestershire, England: Much more than a cottage, this Georgian mansion — rambling but beautifully proportioned — occupies 7 acres of woodlands and enjoys wonderful views over the Severn Valley. The style is very English and very traditional; both in the main building and in the more modern coach house, the rooms are superbly appointed and maintained. Three of the 20 guestrooms have four-posters. The cozy and intimate restaurant is ideal for special meals; English dishes predominate, and the wine list (which includes local English wines) is excellent. Resident proprietors Sue and John Pattin hope to produce wine from their own vines in the future. Malvern Wells is distinct from Great Malvern, the larger, better-known former spa town just to the north, but both places are famous for mineral water, and during a stay, a visitor should be sure to try a bottle of the locally produced Malvern Water — sold in London in the 1780s for a princely shilling. Details: Cottage in the Wood, Holywell Rd., Malvern Wells, Malvern, Worcestershire WR14 4LG, England (phone: 06845-573487).

CHEWTON GLEN, New Milton, Hampshire, England: The New Forest, which William the Conqueror claimed as a royal hunting ground in 1079, was already old when this brick mansion was built on 60 acres of peaceful parkland near its fringes. It must have been an odd contrast at first, but the years have mellowed it, and it now seems almost as old as the forest. Since 1967, managing director Martin Skan has renovated the rooms; built new kitchens; completed a modern wing; converted the coach barn and the stable into suites; added a swimming pool, a tennis court, and a 9-hole golf course; installed a new driveway with a long approach through fields and woods; and adorned the lovely courtyard with an antique fountain. *Chewton Glen* has won an Egon Ronay Hotel of the Year award, a Michelin star, and membership in the exclusive Leading Hotels of the World and Relais & Châteaux associations. The guestrooms — named for characters from *The Children of the New Forest,* whose author, Captain Frederick Marryat, spent some time in the house during the 19th century — are done up with pretty flowered fabrics that are constantly replaced to keep things looking fresh. Color television sets show a feature film every evening, a bottle of sherry is set out to greet arriving guests, and the bathrooms come furnished with fragrant bars of Crabtree & Evelyn soaps and bubble bath. The same perfectionism pervades the hotel's restaurant, the *Marryat Room,* from the fresh bouquets of flowers and the coral and green color scheme to the Villeroy & Boch dinner plates and the exquisite food produced by a young French chef and his staff. Though the raw materials are English, the cooking is nouvelle, with sublime specialties such as *coquilles St.-Jacques au gingembre;* fresh salmon marinated in olive oil, coriander, and lemon juice; *canard aux framboises;* roast rib of Scotch filet stuffed with foie gras, baked in pastry, and served with a Périgordine sauce; and chicken cooked in a mint-flavored cream sauce. The wine list offers nearly 200 selections, ranging from an inexpensive Moselle to a Château Lafite-Rothschild 1952. Travelers who recognize high standards and are irritated by expensive establishments that don't quite measure up will appreciate *Chewton Glen.* Details: Chewton Glen Hotel, New Milton, Hampshire BH25 6QS, England (phone: 0425-275341).

DUCK INN, Pett Bottom, Kent, England: Housed in an unpretentious little 16th-century country cottage (no guestrooms) and patronized by minor royalty and West End stars, this is one of the best-regarded restaurants in southeastern England. Fine French cuisine is painstakingly prepared; the menu changes monthly and features such specialties as pike and Aberdeen Angus (vegetarians catered to on request) and a selection of English fare as well. The place is not easy to find but well worth the effort; it's 3 miles outside Canterbury, near the village of Bridge on the road to Dover. Details: Duck Inn, Pett Bottom, Kent CT4 5PB, England (phone: 0227-830354).

SHARROW BAY, Pooley Bridge, Cumbria, England: For over 4 decades, Francis Coulson and his wonderful staff led by Johnnie Martin have been cooking up some of Great Britain's best food for guests at this lakeshore establishment. A member of the

Relais & Châteaux group, the late-17th-century house has been enlarged over the years with the addition of a quartet of other buildings nearby. A diner might order avocado mousse topped with tiny cooked prawns and unsweetened whipped cream; roast pork loin with fresh rosemary, stuffed with sage and onion dressing and served with apple sauce and cracklings; followed by an egg custard flan and a coffee soufflé served with petits fours. Or end with sticky toffee sponge, almond meringue *gâteau dacquoise* with strawberries, lemon flummery, or any number of other wonderful sweets; the *gâteau Alcazar,* a cake made with almonds and kirsch, is a standout. Judging from the mouthwatering menu, it's not surprising that some people motor up from London, 300 miles away, just to have lunch. The meticulous care that makes every meal such a treat is also accorded the workings of the hotel. Guestrooms are beautifully decorated in the English style, furnished with antiques here and there, and books and parlor games are available for amusement. Thick carpets ensure a quiet more intense than even the country setting alone could provide, and the efficient central heating system keeps the old house comfortably warm when the weather is chilly. Proprietors Francis Coulson and Brian Sack (who joined forces in 1952) try to welcome all their guests personally, which gives the feeling of visiting someone's very elegant country home. There are 30 rooms and suites altogether, including 26 with private bathrooms or showers; about half are in the main house, the others scattered among a cottage and a gatehouse on the grounds, a converted farmhouse a mile away, and a 17th-century cottage in the village of Tirril 4 miles distant. Closed December through February. Details: Sharrow Bay Hotel, Lake Ullswater, Penrith, Cumbria CA10 2LZ, England (phone: 08536-301 or -483).

KING'S HEAD, Richmond, North Yorkshire, England: This 29-room establishment on the edge of the town's impressive cobbled marketplace has hardly changed since the 18th century — at least on the outside. Inside, however, it's plush, warm, and welcoming. The guestrooms are full of 18th-century features — sash windows, elaborate moldings, high ceilings, decorative paneled doors — and are carpeted with red or rich patterns to set off the white or cream walls. The restaurant is comfortable and the service solicitous; the best tables overlook the marketplace. Details: King's Head Hotel, Market Place, Richmond, North Yorkshire DL1O 4HS, England (phone: 0748-850220).

ROTHLEY COURT, Rothley, Leicestershire, England: Straddling several centuries, *Rothley Court,* now a Trusthouse Forte hotel, was built on the site of a Roman villa mentioned in the Domesday Book and has a superbly preserved 13th-century Templars' chapel on the grounds. The 18th-century English philanthropist and statesman William Wilberforce drafted his antislavery treatise in one of the bedrooms, and the 19th-century statesman Baron Macauley was born here. The house was also once home to two Nubian slaves, sent by Lord Kitchener to his sister as gifts. The bedrooms are richly paneled, and two of the "superior" rooms come with a bath that bubbles at the flick of a switch. As for the food, chef David Hamilton prepares both traditional English fare and local specialties. Between the main house and a converted stable, there are in all 36 rooms. Details: Rothley Court, Westfield La., Rothley, Leicestershire LE7 7LG, England (phone: 0533-374141).

GEORGE OF STAMFORD, Stamford, Lincolnshire, England: It is believed that a hostelry in some form has occupied this site for 900 years, but most of the present building was erected by Lord Burghley, high treasurer to Elizabeth I. The gallows sign originally put up to scare away highwaymen still hangs in front of the inn, and the London and York stagecoaches can almost be heard clattering to a stop in the still-preserved cobbled courtyard behind the hotel. The entranceway has stone floors, the ceiling in the bar is beamed, and paneling and rough stone walls are throughout. All 47 rooms have baths and were recently refurbished; some in the front can be a bit noisy because of passing traffic, but many have been double-glazed and are not quite as noisy as they used to be. Good food is available in the restaurant as well as in the bar. Details: The George, 71 St. Martin's, Stamford, Lincolnshire PE9 2LB, England (phone: 0780-55171).

ALVESTON MANOR, Stratford-upon-Avon, Warwickshire, England: Whether or not *A Midsummer Night's Dream* actually was first performed here, as some longtime Stratford residents like to suggest, the *Alveston* fairly oozes the kind of atmosphere most people travel to England to find. From the warm oak-paneled entryway to the fine lounge, it is the sort of place most people feel they could stay in for hours. The atmospheric Manor Bar is remarkable for its attractive paneling and beamed ceiling. Of the 108 guestrooms, those in the main building are the most interesting; those in the new wing tend toward the standard British modern. Best of all, this hostelry is a mere 5-minute walk from the theater. Details: The Alveston Manor, Clopton Bridge, Stratford-upon-Avon, Warwickshire CV37 7HP, England (phone: 0789-204581).

CLIVEDON, Taplow, Buckinghamshire, England: One of England's great country estates, *Clivedon* stands majestically on 400 wooded acres by the river Thames. Long the property of the legendary Astors — and the meeting place of the fabled "Clivedon Set" — it is now managed by Blakeney Hotels (also the proprietors of the *Fenja* hotel in London), who have preserved and classically redecorated the original rooms of the 17th-century mansion, retaining the works of art that reflect the lives of previous owners. New garden rooms were being added as we went to press. The incomparable grounds, which once received the attention of as many as 50 gardeners, include a sweeping pasture, dazzling flower borders, hanging woods, exquisite pavilions, temples, sculptures, 2,000-year-old Roman sarcophagi, and an amphitheater where *Rule Britannia* was first performed in 1740. In addition to beautiful walks, guests enjoy boat trips on the Thames, tennis (on both indoor and outdoor courts), swimming, squash, fishing, horse racing, polo, golf, and rowing. Details: Clivedon, Taplow, Buckinghamshire, England (phone: 06286-5069).

HORSTED PLACE, Uckfield, East Sussex, England: This stately Victorian mansion was built in 1850 and, until recently, was the home of the late Sir Rupert Neville, private secretary to Prince Philip. It has 17 suites, a heated swimming pool, an all-weather tennis court, croquet lawn, and 23 acres of magnificent gardens. Furnished with beautiful antiques, the house is bright and cheery with chintz and exudes comfortable country elegance. Afternoon tea is served in the large, multi-windowed drawing room, and there is an impressive library, complete with fireplace, overlooking the garden. As if all this weren't enough to satisfy the most demanding of guests, the dining room serves remarkable food — not what might be expected in an English hotel, but very French and very fine. The dining room has recently been enlarged to welcome non-residents for lunch and dinner. Only 90 minutes south of London, near Glyndebourne. Details: Horsted Place, Little Horsted, Uckfield, East Sussex TN22 5TS, England (phone: 0825-75581).

MILLER HOWE, Windermere, Cumbria, England: If you tire of looking at the ever-changing light and shade over Lake Windermere in this lovely Wordsworth country hotel, you can play Scrabble, read a book from your private bookshelf, listen to music on the bedroom's cassette player, or just browse through the knickknacks in the room. There is something very personal about the bedrooms here, which may give occupants the feeling that they have borrowed someone else's private domain for a day or two. Guests are permitted to wander into the kitchen and watch the friendly cooks prepare roast loin of lamb with five fresh herbs; pea, pear, and watercress soup; or any number of other goodies that appear on the interesting menu. These eventually wind up on the table in the charmingly autumnal yellow and brown dining room that looks out on a beautiful flagstone terrace and flower-bordered lawns, which in turn slope gently to the lake. The bathrooms here are basically sybaritic. After stepping out of a scented shower, guests will find morning tea waiting in pretty floral pots, along with lemon biscuits to soothe any hunger pangs before the substantial breakfast downstairs. Dinner specialties include loin of Lakeland lamb and smoked salmon and avocado roulade. Details: Miller Howe, Windermere, Cumbria LA23 1EY, England (phone: 09662-2536).

GLENEAGLES, Auchterarder, Perthshire, Scotland: *"Heich abune the heich"* — better than the best — might seem a grandiose claim to make about a hotel. But those who have experienced Britain's finest luxury resort — the Scottish Versailles of hotels — all agree with the decades of hoteliers who have believed the boast, from the early days when a chief point of pride was a private bath with every room, and on through the years, as crowned heads, aristocrats, and millionaires flocked to the establishment. *Gleneagles* recently had a £9-million refurbishing, including upgraded kitchen facilities, a complete country club, and the addition of a new floor, bringing the room total to 242, 20 of which are suites. Most guests rave about the four golf courses. But non-golfers will never be bored: The Gleneagles Mark Phillips Equestrian Centre, run by the husband of Princess Anne, features two covered arenas and instruction in show, jumping, and dressage for everyone from the total novice to those involved in world class competition (Captain Phillips himself is available for instruction by arrangement). The 800-acre grounds also have facilities for fishing, clay-pigeon shooting, croquet, lawn bowling, miniature golf, Ping-Pong, all-weather tennis, squash, dancing, and billiards; plus a sauna and Turkish baths, hairdressing salon, Jacuzzi, swimming pool, and gymnasium. The gardens alone, spotted with bright-colored flowers, are a joy. The high-ceilinged rooms are spacious enough that guests don't trip over each other when room service sets up tea; the windows provide an eyeful of the lonely Scottish hills beyond the gardens; and the service can't be faulted, thanks to a better than one-to-one staff/guest ratio. When pipe bands set up on the velvety lawns, quite a few guests get goose bumps. Details: Gleneagles Hotel, Auchterarder, Perthshire PH3 1NF, Scotland (phone: 0764-62231).

CRAIGENDARROCH HOTEL AND COUNTRY CLUB, Ballater, Royal Deeside, Grampian, Scotland: This pink former mansion of the Kieller jam people sits on a rocky, tree-dotted hillside overlooking the river Dee with the queen's private residence at Balmoral as its distant neighbor. Excluding units in the adjacent time-share development, there are 51 luxurious rooms, plus a health club complex that includes mini-gym, 2 pools, squash courts, Jacuzzi, snooker table, and sauna. There's also a steam room, game room, and a dry ski slope. Chef Bill Gibb aims to serve "the finest cuisine in the Highlands," and as he has been twice voted Scottish Chef of the Year, that is no idle boast. Details: Craigendarroch, Braemar Rd., Ballater, Royal Deeside, Grampian AB3 5XA, Scotland (phone: 03397-55858).

INVERLOCHY CASTLE, near Fort William, Highland, Scotland: When Queen Victoria visited this baronial granite mansion a decade after Lord Abinger built it in 1873, she noted in her diary that she had never seen "a lovelier or more romantic spot." She wasn't the only visitor to express those sentiments. Outside are the terraced gardens, the rhododendron bushes bigger than a child's playhouse, the emerald lawns, and, beyond them, the great mass of Ben Nevis and the Western Highlands rising in the distance; inside, there are enough antiques to do justice to a museum — carved mahogany sideboards, gleaming oak chests, portraits by Sir Benjamin West, as well as wonderful carved paneling, elaborate moldings, and frescoes. Almost everyone who comes for just a night regrets not having planned to stay longer. The 16 guestrooms are spacious and quiet. Dinner consists of regional game and fish, and the wine list is outstanding. Closed November through March. Details: Inverlochy Castle, Torlundy, Fort William, Highland PH33 6SN, Scotland (phone: 0397-2177).

RUFFLETS COUNTRY HOUSE, St. Andrews, Fife, Scotland: The pursuit of excellence has long been the hallmark of this gracious, family-run hotel, to judge from the number of awards it has garnered from the British Tourist Authority, the AA, the

Scottish Tourist Board, and Taste of Scotland. Even head gardener Andrew Duncan has earned high praise for the horticultural beauty of the 10-acre grounds and the vegetable garden, whose produce appears regularly on the table of the hotel restaurant, where Scottish cookery and an innovative approach are the features. And all public rooms overlook the gardens. Details: Rufflets Country House, Strathkinness Low Rd., St. Andrews, Fife KY16 9TX, Scotland (phone: 0334-72594).

SKEABOST HOUSE, Skeabost Bridge, Isle of Skye, Scotland: Built in Victorian times at the southernmost tip of a sea loch, this 27-room hostelry — one of the finest hotels on "the islands" (as Scotland's Inner and Outer Hebrides are widely known) — incorporates all the best in Scottish country hotels, without being exorbitantly expensive. Particularly in the old part of the hotel, the ceilings are high, the furniture old-fashioned or antique, and the armchairs and sofas plush and comfortable; when it's cool, log fires blaze on the hearth. A 9-hole golf course, par 31, has been added. The restaurant is perhaps more functional than might be expected, but a genuine attempt is made to serve interesting local dishes, and at relatively modest prices. Closed November through March. Details: Skeabost House Hotel, Skeabost Bridge, Isle of Skye IV51 9NP, Scotland (phone: 047032-202).

LAKE HOTEL, Llangammarch Wells, Towys, Wales: A truly luxurious country house hidden on on its own 50 acres. Guests step out of a spectacular flower- and antiques-filled drawing room to enjoy a day of trout fishing, bird or badger watching, a set or two of tennis, or an afternoon in the nearby ultra-Victorian spa town of Llandrindod Wells. All that activity should stimulate on appetite, which is fine since guests can eat in one of the best dining rooms in Wales. The local lamb and fish are first-rate, and the variety of herbed rolls (especially the rosemary) and Welsh cheeses are very special. Try to book either the Badger or River suites, each perfectly decorated with small but well-done bathrooms. Details: Llangammarch Wells, Towys LD4 4BS, Wales (phone: 05912-202).

LAKE VYRNWY, Llanwddyn, via Oswestry, Montgomeryshire, Mid-Wales: Perched on the edge of Snowdonia National Park and overlooking Lake Vyrnwy, the views are so dazzling that it takes a real act of will to leave the scenery and take advantage of all the activities this very complete resort has to offer: trap or game shooting, fishing, sailing, ballooning, biking, hiking. Ask to stay in one of the large, lake view rooms — Nos. 1, 5, or 6; these also have extra large bathrooms with spectacular views. Details: Lake Vyrnwy, Llanwddyn, Montgomeryshire SY10 OLY, Mid-Wales (phone: 069-173692).

MAES-Y-NEUADD, Talsarnau, Wales: Pronounced "Mice-er-Nayeth," this establishment run by two families is one of Wales's most charming country-house hotels. The front bedrooms have the best views, overlooking Snowdon and the Troeth Bach estuary. Expect superbly cooked Welsh specialties from the kitchen: lamb in honey, cider, and rosemary; herrings with apple and sage; and Welsh amber pudding. Reservations necessary for non-resident Sunday lunches. Details: Talsarnau, near Harlech, Gwynedd LL476YA Wales (phone: 0766-780200).

PORTMEIRION, Portmeirion, Gwynedd, Wales: The only hotel in the bizarre Italianate village created between 1925 and 1975 by the late and celebrated architect Clough Williams-Ellis, this out-of-the-ordinary, exquisite establishment, the setting for the 1960s television series "The Prisoner" proves its creator's contention that a naturally beautiful site like Portmeirion's could be developed without defiling it. The hotel has a superb view over a river estuary and houses the restaurant and a number of public rooms; the fire of a couple of years ago is now forgotten. Guests stay in rooms there and in a scattering of cottages around the pastel, ornately decorated, and altogether fantastic village; some are set in exotic woodland on a promontory overlooking Cardigan Bay, others atop a hill above it all. The main building, by the estuary, is open year-round; the rest from late March to early November. Details: Portmeirion Hotel,

Box 50, Portmeirion, near Penrhyndeudraeth, Gwynedd LL48 6ER, Wales (phone: 0766-770228).

IF YOU'RE NEARBY

CAVENDISH, Baslow, Derbyshire, England: Set on the Chatsworth estate (described below in *Stately Homes and Great Gardens*), this 18th-century inn restored in 1975 was expanded in 1984 with an extension whose architecture and charm match the original. A renovation has made the kitchen so fine that a dining table for guests' use has been installed along with the fixtures. The rooms are impeccably elegant and splendidly appointed. Details: Cavendish Hotel, Baslow, Derbyshire DE4 1SP, England (phone: 024688-2311).

PRIORY, Bath, Avon, England: This handsome Georgian home built of Bath stone in the Gothic style, now converted to a small hotel, ranks among the best country hotels in England and is an excellent choice for a stay in Bath. Just a short stroll through the park to town, the grounds and public rooms are elegant and tranquil, the staff excellent, the furnishings antique and well kept, the swimming pool in the 2-acre English garden heated, the dining room's cuisine French and highly praised. Each of the 21 guestrooms is different, but each is charming, including 6 beautifully appointed deluxe rooms, and all have private baths or showers. Details: The Priory, Weston Rd., Bath, Avon BA1 2XT, England (phone: 0225-331922).

ROYAL CRESCENT, Bath, Avon, England: Forming the impressive center of the famous Royal Crescent, this elegant and historic Georgian hotel is part of Bath's architectural heritage. With commanding views, it is within walking distance of the Assembly Rooms, the Roman baths, the Pump Room, and the abbey. It has 36 super-deluxe rooms and some extra-special apartments. The Sir Perry Blakeney Suite, for example, has a 17th-century canopied bed, pale blue sofas, an Oriental carpet, and a white-and-gold ceiling of intricate gesso swirls. There are magnificent Georgian public rooms, a good restaurant, and attractive gardens. Details: Royal Crescent Hotel, 16 Royal Crescent, Bath, Avon BA1 2LS, England (phone: 0225-319090).

GARDEN HOUSE, Cambridge, Cambridgeshire, England: The lawn of this modern, luxurious hotel stretches to the edge of the river Cam, and every morning the waiters put out bread for the duck colony that inhabits the peaceful waters. Most of the 117 rooms have balconies overlooking the riverside, and all have private baths and showers. Details: Garden House Hotel, Granta Pl., Mill La., Cambridge, Cambridgeshire CB2 1RT, England (phone: 0223-63421).

THE GRAND, Eastbourne, East Sussex, England: With its white exterior resembling nothing so much as a cake elaborately covered with royal icing, this Victorian hotel is perfectly poised for enjoying the British seaside at its most typical. Outside the hotel are a huge expanse of promenade and shingled beach, quaint shops, and beautifully landscaped gardens; indoors is pure five-star comfort. Guests may book a room with a view as far as the eye can see, and when they tire of watching the waves outside, may make their own in the heated indoor pool. On Fridays or Saturdays, enjoy the weekly dinner-dancing. There are two restaurants. Details: The Grand, King Edward's Parade, Eastbourne, East Sussex BN21 4EQ, England (phone: 0323-412345).

THE SEAFOOD RESTAURANT, Padstow, Cornwall, England: Not only one of the best eating places in all of Cornwall, it also has 8 charming rooms overlooking the harbor, which make a visit to the Cornwall coast especially memorable. Costwolds-born owner Richard Stein displays his considerable culinary talent with the sort of meals found only at the world's finest eating places. The fact that the dining room is full summer and winter suggest that people come a very long way to enjoy very good food; sleeping over just adds the opportunity to enjoy an extra meal. Details: The

Seafood Restaurant, Riverside, Padstow, Cornwall PL28 8BY, England (phone: 0841-532485).

STON EASTON PARK, Ston Easton, Somerset, England: Apart from the ticking clocks, occasional groans from the floorboards, and the restless hush of the river Somer as it cascades through the surrounding landscape laid out by Humphrey Repton, *Ston Easton* trades in the sounds of silence. Within months of opening as a hotel, this Palladian mansion earned Egon Ronay's coveted Hotel of the Year award. And the standards are still high. There are 30 acres of parkland, to which Lucy, the pudgy resident spaniel, likes to act as a guide. Details: Ston Easton Park, Ston Easton, near Bath, Somerset BA3 4DF, England (phone: 076121-631).

THE CASTLE, Taunton, Somerset, England: This erstwhile Norman fortress, now covered with wisteria, has won acclaim from all corners for its peaceful garden and its polished English manner. The 35 bedrooms are especially luxurious; each has its own style (mahogany, walnut, yew, painted bamboo, pickled pine). The fine dining room, which has earned a Michelin star, is the frosting on the cake. Details: Castle Hotel, Castle Green, Taunton, Somerset TA1 1NF, England (phone: 0823-272671).

THE CLOSE, Tetbury, Gloucestershire, England: This former 16th-century wool merchant's home of Cotswold stone offers 15 individually decorated beamed bedrooms fitted out with antiques (3 with four-poster beds); a walled garden with a lily pond; croquet; and a dining room known for its new English cookery and extensive wine list. All rooms have baths or showers. Details: The Close, 8 Long St., Tetbury, Gloucestershire GL8 8AQ, England (phone: 0666-52272).

THE IMPERIAL, Torquay, Devon, England: Built in 1866 to accommodate the resort's winter visitors, this luxurious haven is set on a sheltered clifftop above Torquay harbor in 5 acres of subtropical gardens. Its facilities are so complete that some long-term summer guests never even leave the premises, preferring to lounge around the outdoor pool, pick up barbecue at the grill, shop from the hotel's showcases, and tone up in the hotel's health center. Though such behavior may be a shade extreme, it is totally understandable, particularly to those whose visits coincide with one of the hotel's celebrated Gastronomic Weekends, when a continental chef, usually French, takes over the kitchen with a presentation of ambitious native dishes. Of the 167 rooms, those with the best view look out over Torbay, whose blues and greens, pine-covered cliffs, and Gulf Stream climate have earned it a designation as the English Riviera. Details: The Imperial, Park Hill Rd., Torquay, Devon TQ1 2DG, England (phone: 0803-294301).

ISLAND, Tresco, Isles of Scilly, Cornwall, England: Old and new architecture keep company in this resort hotel on a secluded, car-free island. It has a private beach as well as a heated outdoor pool; fishing, sailing, and rowing can be arranged. All of the 24 rooms and 7 suites have private baths. Visit the Tresco Abbey Garden, about 1¼ miles away, which is world-famous for its sub-tropical vegetation. Hotel closed mid-October through mid-March. Details: Island Hotel, Tresco, Isles of Scilly, Cornwall TR24 0PU, England (phone: 0720-22883).

ALVERTON MANOR, Truro, Cornwall, England: Once an elegant manor house and more recently home to a local order of nuns, its tasteful conversion to the highest rated hotel property in Cornwall contains no hint of the ascetic or monastic life of its former occupants. Not only are its 30 rooms authentically elegant and extremely comfortable, but the kitchen is among the best in western England. A perfect base from which to explore the spectacularly scenic Cornish countryside. Details: Alverton Manor, Tregolls Rd., Truro, Cornwall TR1 1XQ, England (phone: 0872-76633; toll-free from continental US, except New York, 800-322-2403).

BISHOPSTROW HOUSE, Warminster, Wiltshire, England: Most guests come here simply to eat and sleep, so the owner provides the wherewithal for pursuing these activities with consummate style. The moment guests roll up in the driveway of this opulent Georgian establishment on 25 acres of river-crossed lawn and orchard, out pops a concierge, ready to escort arrivals and baggage through the Georgian portico across a carpet as bouncy as a trampoline, past log fires going full throttle, through public rooms scattered with antiques and oil paintings, and, finally, to their home-away-from-home, one of the hotel's calm, elegantly furnished rooms. (Many are deluxe suites with Jacuzzis.) Dinners are equally extraordinary, as exceptional for the setting, a candlelit conservatory, as for the menu, which includes light, French-inspired dishes such as warm salad of pigeon breast in raspberry vinaigrette. Free time between meals and bed can be whiled away on the 25-acre grounds outside, rallying on the tennis courts, fishing on the Wylye River, visiting the temple folly, and making friends with a couple of goats who, bottle-fed at birth, still look upon humans as long-lost mums. There's also an outdoor pool for summer swims and an indoor heated pool for winter exercise. Details: Bishopstrow House, Warminster, Wiltshire BA12 9HH, England (phone: 0985-212312).

WENSLEYDALE HEIFER, West Witton, Leyburn, North Yorkshire: In the heart of James Herriot country, equidistant from the Lake District, the Scottish border, and the North York Moors, and not far from the sparkling river Ure, this picturesque 17th-century coaching inn is full of nice touches like canopy beds, beamed ceilings, and huge old fireplaces that blaze merrily in winter. Accommodations are in the main building and several equally charming adjacent structures. The traditional Yorkshire Sunday lunches are well known. Details: The Wensleydale Heifer, West Witton, near Leyburn, North Yorkshire DL8 4LS, England (phone: 0969-22322).

CULLODEN HOUSE, Inverness, Highland, Scotland: The guestrooms and public rooms of this 18th-century mansion are stuffed with antiques, the dining room was designed by the Scottish master designer Robert Adam, and the former dungeons now house a sauna. All of the 20 rooms have baths and showers. Prince Charles visited here a few years ago; a photograph of him hangs in the hallway below a painting of Bonnie Prince Charlie, who stepped outside one morning in 1746 to fight his last battle. Details: Culloden House, Inverness, Highland IV1 2NZ, Scotland (phone: 0463-790461).

RUTHIN CASTLE, Ruthin, Clwyd, Wales: This hotel occupies a former mansion dating from the 19th century, and some of the public rooms are impressive — for example, the hotel bar in the former library. The establishment is well known for its medieval, Welsh-style banquets. All 58 rooms have baths or showers, and one of the largest has a four-poster bed that has been used by two Princes of Wales. On the extensive grounds are the ruins of the original castle, built in 1282, including the whipping pit, the drowning pool, and the dungeon, all of which bear battle scars from the time of Oliver Cromwell. Details: Ruthin Castle, Ruthin, Clwyd LL15 2NU, Wales (phone: 0824-2-664).

Stately Homes and Great Gardens

Many Britons bemoan their nation's penchant for demolition, and there is a great outcry among preservationists each time Britain's death duties, rising maintenance costs, or a personal financial crisis forces an owner of one of the nation's great stately homes (one that may have been in the family for centuries) to sell out. Over 600 of these structures met the wrecker's ball between the end of World War II and the mid-1970s. Fortunately, however, the number of such unhappy events in England, Scotland, and Wales has dwindled to a fraction of what it was during that period. Whereas approximately 20 per year were destroyed then, only around two or three a year are lost nowadays. And though even that small number may be too many, there are still many fine castles, mansions, and country homes.

These landmarks have been saved by such organizations as the National Trust and the National Trust of Scotland, which have been able to accept great houses and estates in settlement of taxes. The National Heritage Fund sometimes supplies endowments for those homes that the trusts might not be able to take over for want of the monies to maintain them. But the longevity of these stately homes through the centuries also owes to the fact that England, at least, has never been physically invaded, and its society has remained relatively stable through the years. The system of primogeniture, which allowed the eldest son to inherit the whole of a property, also kept estates together. Since the houses were year-round homes and usually not mere refuges from the hot summers of the city, there developed a devotion for ancestral dwelling places akin to that which citizens of other nations extend only to their children. To see these grand homes, standing regally at the end of tree-lined lanes, surrounded by beautiful parks and gardens full of fountains and miniature temples, enormous trees, and fine hedges, is to understand why.

Many of the finest stately homes date back to the very beginning of the great period of English domestic architecture, in the 15th century, when, following the Dissolution of the Monasteries, the estimated one-third of the kingdom that had been cloistral land suddenly became available to the laity. These homes, like others that came later, seldom remained untouched by the fickle hand of fashion, as wealthy landowners strove to keep up with the latest styles. In the 18th century, the symmetrical Palladian style (named for the 16th-century Venetian Andrea Palladio) became the rage, together with the work of designer Robert Adam, who began executing his gracefully articulated designs at Hatchlands, now a National Trust Home in East Clandon, Surrey. In the latter, the ceilings were covered with ornate plasterwork, often painted many colors, and the floors were patterned. But there was a grace and a lightness to it all, and Adam interiors made perfect settings for glittering society in their bright silks and satins. In succeeding years, energetic invention and tireless adaptations of the architectural styles of Italy and France began to appear.

There are so many examples of such houses currently open to the public — sometimes at no charge — in England, Scotland, and Wales, that it would be easy to construct a whole vacation around stately home tours. *Historic Homes of Britain* (21 Pembroke Sq., London W8 6PB, England; phone: 01-937-2402) designs tours for two or more people that may include meals or overnight stays in privately owned historic and stately homes. Tours can be arranged that cater to visitors' special interests — such as gardens, art, or antiques buying — and often feature lectures by specialists in the specific fields.

For the most extensive listing of country houses that are open to visitors, consult the following publications:

The AA 2,000 Places to Visit in Britain available in the US from the British Travel Bookshop, 40 W. 57th St., 3rd Floor, New York, NY 10019; phone: 212-765-0898) gives capsule histories, entrance fees, and hours, which vary wildly and unpredictably from one home to the next.

Castles of England, Scotland, and Wales by Paul Johnson (£12.95, about $21; Weidenfeld & Nicholson).

The Intelligent Traveller's Guide to Historic Britain, by Philip A. Crowl ($19.95; Congdon & Weed). Thorough descriptions. An excellent companion to the above.

The National Trust Guide to England, Wales and Northern Ireland, 3rd edition, edited by Robin Fedden and Rosemary Joekes ($24.95; W. W. Norton). Interesting discussions of the National Trust properties.

Even those who are unimpressed by horticulture are sure to recognize that the English place a high value on their gardens, and not making time for at least one garden stroll during a visit to England is an omission comparable to not partaking of afternoon tea. Although the winter storms of 1988 took their toll (experts say the view from Sir Winston Churchill's window through the beech trees at Chartwell may not be the same for generations), they also presented horticulturists with the opportunity to extend the collections with new plantings and designs.

Generally, English gardens are open several days a week from late March or early April through October. Visitors should check by calling the gardens or inquiring at local tourist offices. A useful folder containing a map and brief descriptions of 150 gardens is available free from the British Tourist Authority, 40 W. 57th St., New York, NY 10019 (phone: 212-581-4700).

A representative selection of stately homes and great gardens follows. Note that admission fees can add up for those who want to see many of the homes, so travelers in England should consider purchasing the Great British Heritage Pass (formerly Open to View ticket) from the *British Travel Bookshop,* 40 W. 57th St., 3rd floor, New York, NY 10019 (phone: 212-765-0898). These passes allow access to all ancient monuments under the wing of the Department of the Environment, every National Trust property, and to more than four dozen other sites.

CHATSWORTH, near Bakewell, Derbyshire, England: Mary, Queen of Scots, stayed at this home on the banks of the river Derwent (now in the Peak District National Park) when she was in the custody of Lord Shrewsbury, the fourth husband of the redoubtable Bess of Hardwick, who began building the place with her second husband, Sir William Cavendish, in 1552. But the quarters in which the unfortunate queen lodged on and off between 1569 and 1584 were rendered unrecognizable in about 1686, when the fourth Earl of Devonshire (a descendant of Sir William's second son, the first earl) spent 2 decades renovating it into one of the finest houses in the nation and among the most beautiful in Europe. The façade is stately, Corinthian-pilastered and strictly classical, and the interiors are insistently baroque, with a splendid ornate silver chandelier; wall coverings of oak, silk, and gilt leather (among other resplendent materials); paintings by Laguerre, Verrio, and Thornhill on the walls and ceilings, and elaborate woodcarvings that for many years passed as the work of Grinling Gibbons (they were actually executed by a local artisan).

Those, together with the *trompe l'oeil* violin painted on an inner door of the State Music Room, may be the most immediately memorable sights in Chatsworth. But the collection of furniture by William Kent, the first English architect to attempt to integrate furniture and architectural ornamentation, is one of the finest that exist. Also on display is a grand collection of works by Hals, Reynolds, Landseer, Lely, Rembrandt, Sargent, and Van Dyck. Travelers have marveled at all of this for centuries, and considering that there are 175 rooms (of which 51 are "very big indeed," according to the Duchess of Devonshire, who lives there), it's not hard to understand the nature of the wonderment, even before a stroll in the 105-acre gardens and the 1,100-acre park, which are no trifles either. A most delightful aspect of a Chatsworth visit, the garden was one of several English preserves formally planted in the 17th century by George London and Henry Wise. It was reconstructed a century later, much to the dismay of 20th-century critics, by the ubiquitous Lancelot "Capability" Brown, who, even in a day of formal architectural styles, espoused naturalistic landscape design. (The gentleman's nickname derived from his habit of referring to the "capabilities" of any tract he had been called upon to improve.)

The Water Garden, which features a great, glittering staircase of water known as the Grand Cascade, retains most of the original design. The Emperor Fountain, a single powerful jet of water capable of shooting 267 feet into the air, is also worth noting. Its designer, Joseph Paxton (1803–65), spent 32 years as Chatsworth's chief gardener; he blessed the estate with greenhouses that were the forerunners of the Great Exhibition of 1851's Crystal Palace, which earned him not only celebrity but also a knighthood. Sadly, the major greenhouses were pulled down long ago, but the garden still illustrates Paxton's prodigious imagination and industry. Details: Comptroller, Chatsworth, Bakewell, Derbyshire DE4 1PP, England (phone: 024-688-2204).

HAMPTON COURT PALACE, East Molesex, Surrey, England: In a stunning location by the Thames in Greater London, this grandiose palace is special among Britain's royal homes. Unlike others that have stood empty as museums, it has been occupied continuously since it was built in 1514 by Cardinal Wolsey, Lord Chancellor of England, who intended to make it the country's largest house, and those who live there today do so with the "grace and favor" of the Queen. Its architecture — including Wolsey's constructions; the modifications made by Henry VIII, its next owner; and additions designed by Christopher Wren for William III in 1689 — represents the very best of England's designers of the 16th and 17th centuries. The equally fine gardens, designed for William and Mary by Henry Wise and George London, comprise a maze and vinery (the Great Vine was planted in 1769). Although part of the outer shell was damaged in a 1986 fire, nearly all of the valuable contents, most notably its tapestries and its outstanding collection of 500 Renaissance paintings, were saved. Hampton Court is probably best known for its associations with Henry VIII. All six of his wives spent time here, and ghosts of two of them, Jane Seymour and Catherine Howard, are said to haunt it still. The gardens are open daily until dusk. Details: Visitor Information, Hampton Court Palace, East Molesex, Surrey KT8 9AU, England (phone: 01-977-8441).

BOUGHTON HOUSE, near Kettering, Northamptonshire, England: In the late 17th century, Englishmen were building grand homes as testimony to their great faith in the future and their increased prosperity — and borrowing architectural styles from the Continent with aplomb. The starting point for the great extension to Boughton House, a prime example of French influence, was Ralph, Earl of Montagu, who served Charles II as ambassador to France beginning in 1669 (and made such a favorable impression there that Louis XIV ordered the Versailles fountains to be played on his every visit). Ralph Montagu laid out new gardens with lakes, fountains, and avenues, and added a château-style front wing. Today, several remodelings beyond its 15th-century beginnings as a monastery, Boughton is an enormous place that boasts a courtyard for every day of the week, a chimney for every week of the year, and a window for every day of the year. The abundance of furniture and porcelain is mostly French, as are the paintings on the ceilings by the Huguenot Louis Cheron, and the floors on a stairway landing and in a state room, made of *parquet de Versailles;* the art collection, which includes paintings by El Greco, Gainsborough, Gheeraerts, Kneller, Lely, and Van Dyck, is particularly impressive.

As for the Earl of Montagu, it has been said that he was "too ambitious and in the end too successful to avoid envy, and too overtly pro-French . . . to be trusted in his own time." After returning from the French court, he became embroiled in the intrigues concerning the succession of Charles II and was forced to live in exile from 1679 to 1685. Snubbed by the Catholic James II upon returning, he repaired to Boughton and began building the great châteaulike addition. His marriage to the wealthy widow Elizabeth Wriothesley, daughter of the Earl of Southampton, facilitated his patronage of the arts and of the Huguenot craftsmen whose works adorn Boughton today. Finally, with Protestants back on the throne, he was made a duke. The property passed through the marriage of his great-granddaughter to the Scottish Duke of Buccleuch, in whose descendants' care Boughton House remains today. Details: Boughton House, Geddington, Kettering, Northamptonshire NN14 1BJ, England (phone: 0536-82248).

HAREWOOD HOUSE AND BIRD GARDEN, near Leeds, West Yorkshire, England: Robert Adam was only in his early thirties when he was invited to begin work on the interiors of Harewood House, designed by the York architect John Carr for one

Edwin Lascelles. The interiors that resulted, full of delicately fluted Ionic columns, beautifully molded plaster ceilings, and classical fireplaces, confirm his great talent (even though his brother joked that he had only "tickled it up so as to dazzle the eyes of the squire"). And despite exterior renovations since then, this remains a stunning house for its fine Chippendale furniture, made after Adam's designs; its collection of paintings by Bellini, El Greco, Gainsborough, Reynolds, Tintoretto, Titian, Turner, and Veronese; and the collections of Sèvres and Chinese porcelain. The grounds were designed by the prolific Capability Brown beginning in 1772, a year after the house was finished; the landscape, meant to look as if it were nature's own, was substantially unchanged, except for the 19th-century addition of the terraces near the house, until 1962, when a furious storm smashed some 20,000 trees. There is also a fine Bird Garden, where rare and endangered species are bred in cooperation with zoos and gardens around the world. The recently refurbished Tropical House and Paradise Garden simulate rain-forest conditions, providing authentic environments for birds, plants, and butterflies. Rain forests are rapidly disappearing, and the purpose of this major development is to illustrate their importance. The estate is currently the home of the seventh Earl of Harewood, whose mother was Mary, Princess Royal, the daughter of George V. Details: Harewood House and Bird Garden, Estate Office, Harewood, Leeds LS17 9LQ, England (phone: 0532-886225).

BEAULIEU ABBEY AND PALACE HOUSE, near Lyndhurst, Hampshire, England: The wars and other extravagances of Henry VIII left the king in less than ideal financial straits, and Parliament was in no hurry to levy new taxes so he could pay his bills. Thus it happened that the Cistercian monastery on the Beaulieu River close to the Solent coastline, for which King John had ceded the lands in 1204, came into the hands of Thomas Wriothesley (you may not believe it, but it's pronounced "Roxley"), who served as secretary of state and lord chancellor to Henry VIII and later became the earl of Southampton. Working with his minister Thomas Cromwell, the king had cajoled Parliament into dissolving the smaller monasteries and confiscating their lands and their fortunes in plate and jewels, tapestries, statuary, and other portable items. Their sale meant an overflowing treasury for Henry, and for England a legacy not only of stark ruins but also of stately homes built on the grounds of former religious houses. The Palace House of Beaulieu Abbey, one of a number of lands granted to Wriothesley at the time of the Dissolution, occupies the former 13th-century cloistral gatehouse; the history of how the 2-story structure has changed through the years is a topic of great interest. Originally converted after the Dissolution in 1538, it was remodeled beginning around 1870, but many of the original Tudor elements — among them the drawing room, the private dining room, the reception hall, and the gables — can still be seen. Scholarly conjecture maintains that Wriothesley's grandson, known for being Shakespeare's patron, was also the Friend described in the sonnets. Palace House is presently the home of Lord Montagu, who in memory of his father, a great pioneer in motoring history, built the world-famous *National Motor Museum* on the property. This museum, one of the best in England, contains over 250 exhibits portraying the history of motoring from 1895 to the present. Details: Palace House, John Montagu Building, Beaulieu, Hampshire S042 7ZN, England (phone: 0590-612345).

CASTLE HOWARD, near Malton, North Yorkshire, England: The socialite Sir John Vanbrugh served in the army, spent 2 years in a French prison on espionage charges, and wrote plays for the theater, such as *The Provoked Wife.* But he is perhaps best known for his work as an architect, and his most famous creation — especially since the television version of Evelyn Waugh's novel *Brideshead Revisited* was filmed here a few years ago — is the palatial home known as Castle Howard. He had met Charles Howard, the third Earl of Carlisle, during his playwriting days, and when the Howard family home was destroyed by fire in 1693, Vanbrugh won the commission. Executed with the help of Nicholas Hawksmoor, who had worked with the great

Christopher Wren, it has been earning paeans from travelers ever since. Horace Walpole, after a visit there two centuries ago, noted that he had expected to see one of the finest places in Yorkshire. "But nobody had informed me that I should at one view see a palace, a town, a fortified city, temples on high places, woods worthy of being each a metropolis of the Druids, vales connected to hills by other woods, the noblest lawn in the world, fenced by half the horizon, and a mausoleum that would tempt one to be buried alive. In short, I have seen gigantic places before but never a sublime one."

Aside from its lovely site on a plateau north of the river Derwent between York and Malton, its sheer immensity is one of its most overwhelming features. Inside the 323-foot-long, cupola-topped south front and the mammoth wings on either side, there are endless rooms and corridors packed with paintings and porcelains, not to mention bronzes, sculptures, gleaming antique furniture, and impressive architectural features such as the multi-windowed dome that lights the vast marble entrance hall. The grounds consist of 1,000 acres that include a splendid, dramatic fountain and formal gardens surrounding the house, the preserve of the Castle Howard peacocks; the broad terrace of grass beyond; and the fine outbuildings meant to add interest to the landscape. Among the latter are the Temple of the Four Winds, which Vanbrugh designed, and Hawksmoor's mausoleum for the Howard family, which inspired Walpole's comment about being buried alive. The elegant stables, designed by the same John Carr of York who worked on Harewood House, now contain tableaux featuring costumes and accessories from a collection of some 18,000 items that span three centuries; the lavish embroideries in silk thread, silver tinsel, and other rich materials call to mind Beatrix Potter's comment that the stitches "looked as if they had been made by little mice." It is not hard to see why the third earl, whose descendants still own and occupy the place, ran out of money before its completion. Details: Castle Howard, York Y06 7BZ, England (phone: 065384-333).

ALTHORP, near Northampton, Northamptonshire, England: This wonderful home had long been known as one of England's greatest country houses at the time the youngest daughter of the present owner, the eighth Earl Spencer, was married to the eldest son of Queen Elizabeth II. The estate was created by John Spencer, who made a fortune through perseverance, hard work, and good business sense, then cemented his family's place in society by alliances with the wealthy. Almost every successive generation has added to its beauty. Robert Spencer bought pictures when he served three successive kings in Paris and Madrid. The first Earl Spencer commissioned a series of portraits from his friend Sir Joshua Reynolds. The house, an early Tudor structure remodeled in the 17th century, was redone in the classical style beginning around 1790 by the architect Henry Holland, who refinished the walls with a grayish-white tile that was popular at the time and added Ionic decorations to the rooms inside on a commission from the second Earl Spencer, a passionate bibliophile whose collections once filled the Long Library, the family's main sitting room. The entire home is filled with great works of art by Gainsborough, Kneller, Lely, Reynolds, Rubens, Sargent, and Van Dyck; fine furniture by Saunier, Vardy, Seddon, and others; china from Sèvres, Chelsea, and Bow; and 18th-century armorial porcelain from China. The high-ceilinged entrance hall, one of the rooms open on guided tours, has been characterized as "the noblest Georgian room in the country." Open September through June, 1 to 5 PM; July through August, 11 AM to 6 PM. Details: The Countess Spencer, Althorp, Northampton NN7 4HG, England (phone: 0604-769368).

BURGHLEY HOUSE, near Stamford, Lincolnshire, England: Queen Elizabeth I last visited this house in the closing years of the 16th century, when its creator and owner, William Cecil Lord Burghley — her secretary of state for four decades and the grandson of an obscure Welshman named Seissylit — was on his deathbed. Its exterior now exhibits the same Italianate columns and the same bristle of domes and clustered chimneys that it did then. Indeed, the design of this assemblage suffers, said one critic, from the loss of the restraints of medieval architectural rules: "Nothing as yet had appeared to take their place, so that the architects, with a number of new processes at their disposal, were at a complete loss as to how best to apply them." But most other visitors to this splendid place, which was built lavishly enough for entertaining a queen and has served as the home of the Cecils and the Exeters for four centuries since, agree that it is not only the nation's largest Elizabethan home but also one of its grandest and most beautiful. A 17th-century remodeling eradicated most of the original Tudor design, but the years since William Cecil's day have also been marked by the acquisition of vast art collections. Together with the second Lord Sunderland of Althorp, the fifth Earl of Exeter ranked among the most discriminating collectors of the Restoration era; few besides Charles I himself, who accumulated nearly 1,400 paintings (most returned to the Continent after a Commonwealth sale), owned as many works of art. Particularly memorable are the magnificent stone staircase and the great hall (both from Tudor days) and the aptly named Heaven Room, where Verrio painted the ceiling and walls with his interpretation of the hereafter. Guided tours are mandatory except on Sunday afternoons. As for the huge park, it was landscaped in the 18th century by Capability Brown. Details: Burghley House, near Stamford, Lincolnshire PE9 3JY, England (phone: 0780-52451).

BLENHEIM PALACE, near Woodstock, Oxfordshire, England: Britons come in droves to see the bedroom where Sir Winston Churchill was born. But that is certainly not all they see in this giant of a house. Built essentially as a monument to England, with funds supplied by Parliament on direction from Queen Anne in gratitude to the Duke of Marlborough for his 1704 victory over the French at Blenheim, the structure was designed by Sir John Vanbrugh with the assistance of Nicholas Hawksmoor, as at Castle Howard. Sarah, Duchess of Marlborough, never wanted anything more than "a clean sweet house and garden be it ever so small"; the battles she had with the architect — while some 1,500 artisans were laboring on the job and the cost of construction climbed toward the final £250,000 — have become legendary. "I made Mr. Vanbrugh my enemy by the constant disputes I had with him to prevent his extravagance," she said at the time. Reportedly, she even refused to let him enter her home after its completion. Whether or not viewers agree with Voltaire's pronouncement that it was "a great mass of stone, unattractive and tasteless," it is impossible to dispute the grandeur of the place. The structure measures 850 feet from end to end, and there are Tuscan colonnades galore, not to mention a vast Corinthian portico, a balustraded roof bristling with statues and towers, and more. From the great state rooms and the library to the saloon, the rooms dwarf mere mortals, and the assemblage brings to mind the rhyme of Alexander Pope: "Thanks sir, cried I, 'tis very fine,/But where d'ye sleep, or where d'ye dine?" The art collections are every bit as dazzling as their setting. The 18th-century gardens, revised in the 1760s by Capability Brown, were restored and expanded by the ninth duke two centuries later. Open daily from mid-March through October. Details: Administrator's Office, Blenheim Palace, Woodstock, Oxfordshire OX7 1PX, England (phone: 0993-811325).

CRATHES CASTLE, Banchory, Grampian, Scotland: In Scotland, the wealthy built not houses but castles, right up until the time of Cromwell. Nonetheless, through the years, the importance of matters of defense in the layout of domestic structures dwindled considerably, and as part of a growing concern with design, erstwhile defensive features were exaggerated and used as decorative elements. Thus Scotland developed an indigenous domestic architecture unique in all of Europe. With Fyvie and Craigievar castles, Crathes Castle offers a prime example of this style. Like them, Crathes is built of stone — the nation had almost no trees until the mid-18th century — in a configuration that is more vertical than horizontal so as to cram the most living space possible under the least amount of roof. And because of the established traffic among Scotland, Scandinavia, and the Benelux countries, it exhibits the national taste for brightly colored designs painted on the ceilings. Crathes Castle is not dreary inside, as a reader of *Macbeth* might surmise, but is surprisingly cheerful, and the procession of gables and turrets is almost as fascinating as the rumor of a female ghost with a child in her arms, or the gardens outdoors, a series of small plantings separated by gigantic yew hedges, which rank among the finest in the country. On the 595-acre estate, there are also some fine trees and 15 miles of nature trails. A visitor center presents exhibitions on the natural history of the area as well as the history of the family that owned the castle, the Burnetts. The newly refurbished restaurant is open daily from 11 AM to 6 PM, Easter through October. Details: The Administrator, Crathes Castle, Banchory, Aberdeenshire AB3 3QJ, Scotland (phone: 033044-525).

ERDDIG HOUSE, near Wrexham, Clwyd, Wales: It's not possible to view these fine old homes without wondering about everyday life — cooking meals, changing sheets, and other such homely chores. Unfortunately, the quarters of the servants to whom these tasks fell are seldom on view. Not so at Erddig. In this 17th-century country home occupied by generations of the Yorke family until a decade ago, though there are numerous stately chambers and an abundance of fine furniture (many pieces with original upholstery), the most riveting area is "downstairs," where some 45 staff members labored. This includes the laundry, where clothing was boiled in copper caldrons, wrung out on rollers, dried on racks, and then ironed; the joiners' shop (still operational), where furniture, fences, and other wooden items were mended; and the new kitchen (detached from the house in the 18th century as a precaution against fire), where three kitchen maids and a cook toiled over the meals. The gallery of staff portraits with clever rhymes penned below and the display of photographs are particularly intriguing. Until 1973, when the National Trust acquired and restored it, the house was in sad disrepair: Philip Yorke III lived in two unheated rooms with no electricity, and he was often seen picking up scraps of paper off the floor. "I wish nothing should be parted with," wrote the first Philip Yorke of Erddig in 1771. Consequently, every bicycle, every automobile, and reams of receipts and letters have been saved; what the master of it all was salvaging from the floor were bits of priceless hand-painted Chinese wallpaper that had peeled off the walls. Details: Erddig, Wrexham, Clwyd, North Wales LL13 0YT (phone: 0978-355314).

PICTON CASTLE, Haverfordwest, Dyfed, Wales: Built ca. 1300 on the site of a Norman fortress 96 miles west of Cardiff, Picton Castle survived three sieges: It was taken by the Welsh hero Owain Glyndwr in 1405; by the Royalists during the Civil War in 1643; and two years later by Cromwell's forces. Now the home of the Philips family, descendants of the medieval owners, it was opened to the public for the first time in 1988. The castle is surrounded by gardens, and its courtyard contains the *Graham Sutherland Gallery,* which houses a famous collection of portraits by this renowned English artist. The main apartments are open at Easter, on May 1 and 29 and August 28 (bank holiday Mondays), and on Sundays and Thursdays from mid-July to mid-September. Details: Picton Castle, Haverfordwest, Pembrokeshire, Dyfed SA62 4AS, Wales (phone: 0437-86326).

Tea Shops and Tea Gardens

That great British institution, afternoon tea, had been given up for lost a few years ago. The cost of the ingredients and the extensive labor required had soared, just as weight watchers had begun to question the healthfulness of the scones and pastries habit that their parents and grandparents had always taken for granted. But like another great British favorite, fish and chips, which for a brief moment was also put down as a thing of the past, afternoon tea has survived and has actually enjoyed a resurgence in popularity. Harried Londoners have given up the rat race, moved to the country, and converted barns and old cottages into quainter-than-quaint tea shops where you can get the kinds of set teas that dreams are made of — those wonderful teas whose passing was so vigorously lamented until just recently.

The reasons for this revival are hard to gauge, but simple economy may be among them. As the prices of full meals climb, tea becomes increasingly attractive to most vacationers, who know that they can get by on nothing more than a full breakfast in their hotel and a relatively inexpensive tea in some country café. Nostalgia, in the form of a stubborn refusal to abandon tradition even in the face of stern realities, may also figure. As an afternoon meal, tea was first served in the late 18th century by the Duchess of Bedford to entertain her guests between the early lunches and late dinners at her house parties. It soon became an integral part of everyday life. A whole industry grew up around the manufacture of teacups and saucers, cake stands, tea forks for the cakes, silver teapots, sugar bowls and tiny silver tongs, linens, and the like. In Victorian days, less aristocratic families developed elaborate teatime rituals around the new meal; at a time when Britons seemingly lived to eat rather than the other way around, it was quite natural to nosh away the otherwise gustatorily empty late-afternoon hours. "Everything stops for tea" became a popular English saying, and the World War I poet Rupert Brooke wrote about it, referring to a tea garden at Grantchester, near Cambridge. (That tea garden still exists, after all these years, in a sun-dappled meadow close to where the undergraduates leave their punts.)

Beginning around the turn of the century, when Miss Cranston established the nation's first tea room in Sauchiehall Street, Glasgow, running tea gardens and tea shops was considered a respectable occupation for spinsters, and the foods served at tea today still reflect their genteel touch. Honey and country preserves, particularly strawberry jam, show up on the tea tables, along with biscuitlike scones. In Devon and Cornwall, thick clotted cream — too stiff for pouring — invariably accompanies the cakes; strawberry teas, a summertime specialty, include a bowl of the luscious red fruit. Visitors to country districts, especially in the midlands and the north of England, will often encounter "farm teas," repasts that include enough salad, ham, fish, and other fairly substantial edibles to allow them to skip the evening meal and still not go to bed with a rumbling stomach.

As served in its most elaborate form at some London hotels, afternoon tea may take a couple of hours to come to the end of the procession of comestibles — thin sandwiches filled with cucumbers, watercress, or smoked salmon, warm scones and delicate pastries, not to mention the good selections of fine China and India brews. A round of the best London teas would take in the following:

Browns Hotel, 19–24 Dover St., W1 (phone: 01-493-6020).
Dacquoise, 20 Thurloe St., SW7 (phone: 01-589-6117).
Grosvenor House, 86–90 Park Lane, W1 (phone: 01-499-6363).
Hyatt Carlton Tower, 2 Cadogan Pl., SW1 (phone: 01-235-5411).
Joe's Café, 126 Draycott Ave., SW3 (phone: 01-225-2217).
Maison Bertaux, 28 Greek St., W1 (phone: 01-437-6007).
Pâtisserie Valerie, 44 Old Compton St., W1 (phone: 01-437-3466).
The Ritz, Piccadilly, W1 (phone: 01-493-8181).
The Savoy, The Strand, WC1 (phone: 01-836-4343).

High teas such as the Scots love so well — still offered in many seaside cafés around Britain — consist of a salad or "something on toast" in addition to the usual spread of buns and cakes, which may include Victoria sponge cakes, gâteaux (cream cakes), rock cakes, fairy cakes, Battenberg and Madeira cakes, buns, scones, flans and egg dishes, savories (meat pies), Bakewell puddings, meringues, cheesecakes, lemon meringue pies, lemon curd tarts, and more. In Scotland, fruitcakes, soda bread, and tea breads (a sort of cake and bread hybrid) show up on the tea table. In Wales, you can expect bacon, fish, pancakes, and bara brith (speckled bread). Many of the food specialties of the south appear most frequently at teatime: brandy snaps doused with fresh cream, custard tarts smoothed with red currant jelly and slathered with more cream, Chelsea buns, and above all, crumpets — wintertime delights that resemble American English muffins, but with holes.

The settings for tea are as varied as the food. In Scotland, with few exceptions, travelers will have to take their chances at big hotels. In Wales, except in a few towns that are more frequented by tourists, café's offer the best teas. In England, tea shops are most numerous in the south and the west; cream teas, originally a West Country specialty, have become equally popular in other areas. Tea lovers may choose to pour their Earl Grey in some unpretentious shop or in the orangery, the dairy, or the stable of one of England's stately homes (especially if the house is owned and run by the National Trust). They can also munch tea cakes on a battlefield and in an old almshouse, a castle, Sally Lunn's original shop, the Pump Room in Bath, and the shop where the lace for Queen Victoria's wedding dress was made (*The Old Lace Shop,* Fore St., Beer, Devon). Or even in a thatched cottage half covered with creepers and rambling roses (*Dunnose Cottage,* Luccombe Chine) on the Isle of Wight, an exceptionally good place for summertime tea seekers. Local tourist offices can generally recommend something good in their area.

WORTH A LONG DETOUR

SHIP'S LIGHTS, near Bridport, Dorset: Eype, a pretty hamlet a mile or so southwest of Bridport and only about a 5-minute walk from the sea, is so tiny that it may come as a surprise to find anything in the way of a tea shop among its handful of little houses. But there it is, in one of those archetypically whitewashed two-story cottages that are scattered so picturesquely along the winding lanes of this part of England. Inside, there's a little parlor for tea when the weather is poor. But the best thing about this establishment is the garden, a glorious flagstone enclosure that in summer fills up with emerald green and scarlet, brilliant yellow and orange, and, next to an old stone wall, there is an old ship's light. Visitors can take tea here and savor scones slathered with clotted cream and jams as sweet and full of fruit as any they'll ever taste; and those who are really hungry can sample some of the establishment's own pastries or fancy cakes and sandwiches — all the tastier for the fresh sea air that comes with the package. Lunch is available in summer. Open Easter through September (phone: 0308-25656).

OLD FIRE ENGINE HOUSE, Ely, Cambridgeshire: Those who have ever been to a first class restaurant, got as far as dessert, and wished they could come back the next day for that will like this well-established restaurant not far from Ely's lovely cathedral, a landmark in this flat, low-lying part of eastern England. Some of the gâteaux, other pastries, and flans served here are worthy of any groaning sweets trolley. Scones are served warm if requested, and there's local honey and homemade shortbread. *The Old Fire Engine House* is a good example of the kind of place best known as a restaurant but also operating, on a more modest and certainly more inexpensive scale, as a tea shop. It's especially handsome, too, with its shady, well-tended garden, large windows and chintz curtains, flagstone floor, and solid wooden furniture. There's even an art gallery, with exhibits that change monthly. 25 St. Marys St. (phone: 0353 662582).

GATEWAY CAKESHOP, Evesham, Worcestershire: With the proliferation of uninspiring snack bars and fast-food chains, it's increasingly difficult to find a pleasant spot for tea in a town; most tea shops are such small operations that rising rents have almost abolished them. But every country market town has its cake shop, and many serve tea on the side. The *Gateway,* in a pretty Tudor townhouse in the oldest part of this historic town, is a good example. Dark and cozy, with plain old-fashioned furniture, ancient oak beams overhead, and round panes of Georgian bottle glass in many of the windows, the establishment is perfect for afternoon tea (and it's for this that the place is locally best known, even though morning coffee and cakes and light lunches are also served). John and James Miller, who do the baking, are famous for their fruit pies and gooey cream-and-liqueur cake. 7 Market Pl. (phone: 0386-2249).

SETTLE, Frome, Somerset: This small establishment is in the most charming part of the oldest corner of this old town, an area of cobbled streets and half-timbered houses. Even from the outside, the *Settle* looks invitingly homey, with its brick walls and black-and-white paintwork. Inside, vases of flowers brighten the windowsills, and pressed wildflowers decorate the menus. An autumnal color scheme — all russets, grays, and golds — makes things even more appealing. Best of all is the immense variety of imaginative yet inexpensive food and beverages: Earl Grey, Somerset cream teas, Chinese and Indian teas, and herbal teas are served along with homemade scones, clotted cream, jams and jellies, and a range of British patisserie, including Sunday cake, a fruitcake traditionally made for the vicar's weekly call, and a luscious chocolate layer cake. The menu also offers English breakfasts of omelettes and toasted cheese muffins; traditional lunches featuring such delights as Granny's old-fashioned cheese puddings, Settle vegetarian bobbins, Priddy Oggies, game casserole, and Elizabethan pork, followed by hedgerow pudding or the specialty, Frome bobbins, a delicious confection of apricots and sultanas steeped in local cider. Cheap St. (phone: 0373-65975).

CLIVEDEN, Taplow, Buckinghamshire, England: One of England's great country estates, *Cliveden* stands majestically on 400 wooded acres by the River Thames. Long the property of the most powerful of the English nobility, it is now managed by Blakeney Hotels, who have preserved and classically redecorated the original rooms of the 17th-century mansion, retaining the works of art that reflect the lives of its previous owners. The incomparable grounds, which once received the attention of as many as 50 gardeners, include a sweeping pasture, dazzling flower borders, hanging woods, exquisite pavilions, temples, sculptures, 2,000-year-old Roman sarcophagi, and an amphitheater where *Rule Britannia* was first performed in 1740. In addition to beautiful walks, guests enjoy boat trips on the Thames, tennis (on both indoor and outdoor courts), swimming, squash, fishing, horse racing, polo, golf, and rowing. Details: Cliveden, Taplow, Buckinghamshire (phone: 06286-5069).

ORIGINAL MAIDS OF HONOUR, Kew Gardens, Surrey: Directly opposite Cumberland Gate at outer London's most famous public garden, the 18th-century Royal Botanic Gardens at Kew, are so busy during the tourist season that it's necessary to go early to enjoy tea in a leisurely fashion, this shop has been serving up Maids of Honour (a tartlike sweet first mentioned in a 15th-century manuscript and said to have been enjoyed by Henry VIII) for over a century. The place is as pretty as ever, partly whitewashed, with a handsome brick and tile roof and broad eaves. The impression of *rus in urbe* is enhanced by the wrought ironwork and Victorian lampposts outside and an old-fashioned interior. Attentive waitresses, helped by a handful of young girls, fuss over orders of pots of tea and toast, scones and fancy cakes, like so many English nannies. Open Tuesdays through Saturdays from 10 AM to 5:30 PM. 288 Kew Rd., Surrey, England (phone: 01-940-2752).

BARN AND PINN COTTAGE, Sidmouth, Devon: Housed not in a barn but in a 15th-century cottage, this pretty stucco establishment looks almost like an antiques and bric-a-brac shop: The walls are hung with old farming implements and pictures by local artists; the shelves of a pretty Welsh cupboard are chock-a-block with old cottage china, vases, miniatures, and assorted other fascinating bygones. Visitors sit at rustic old tables, set with vases of flowers from the garden, and enjoy such fare as homemade cakes and farmhouse cream teas, or a full lunch if desired. Accommodations, with home-cooked evening meals, are sometimes also available. One-night bookings are unavailable during May to September (phone: 0395-513613).

IF YOU'RE NEARBY

OLD ORIGINAL BAKEWELL PUDDING, Bakewell, Derbyshire: Bakewell pudding is said to have been invented here by mistake in 1860, when an original recipe was misunderstood and a cook who had been asked to make a strawberry tart spread a custard mixture on top of the jam instead of stirring the two ingredients together. Mrs. Wilson, a tallow chandler's wife who lived nearby, saw possibilities in making the popular sweet for sale and commenced a business of her own. The house where she made them, a late-17th-century structure owned by the Duke of Rutland until 1921, has become a draw in its own right. There is now an 85-seat restaurant above the shop. On the square (phone: 062981-2193).

OLD LACE SHOP, Beer, Devon: The lace for Queen Victoria's wedding dress was made on these fairly unpretentious premises, now a quaint 17th-century village tea shop noted for its old oak tables and its location in a deep, narrow glen on a small creek that runs out to the sea. Evening meals are available as well as cream teas that feature homemade tea cakes, gâteaux, and plenty of scones still warm from the oven, ready to be slathered with clotted cream and strawberry jam. Fore St. (phone: 0297-22056).

ROSE OF TORRIDGE, Bideford, Devon: Once a hotel (Charles Kingsley wrote part of *Westward Ho!* here), this old-fashioned establishment now serves good cream teas as well as lunches and dinners (no phone).

BANTAM, Chipping Campden, Gloucestershire: An extra-friendly staff serves homemade cakes, buttery shortbread, nutty florentines, and sherry truffles, in addition to salads and hot dishes, in a 300-year-old structure built of honey-colored Cotswold stone, superbly set in the middle of this exquisite and much visited Cotswold village. Hanging baskets of flowers welcome visitors in summer; log fires roar on the hearth come winter. High St. (phone: 0386-840386).

HORSE WITH THE RED UMBRELLA, Dorchester, Dorset: This establishment, in a former theater, offers a very good selection of cakes, pastries, and savories, not to mention the largest selection of fresh cream cakes for miles around, many of them baked by the owners' friends and neighbors. It's a great place to stock up for a picnic. Hot meals are also available from 8 AM to 5 PM. 10 High West St. (phone: 0305-62019).

ANGLER'S REST, Fingle Bridge, near Drewsteignton, Devon: For over 90 years, traditional cream teas — scones, strawberry jam, thick clotted cream, and a pot of perfumed brew — have been served at this delightful family restaurant in the cool green depths of the gorge at Fingle Bridge. Lunch and dinner, as well as bar meals, are also available, and there's a gift shop for those who'd rather spend than ramble the gorge (phone: 0647-21287).

STONE CROSS COTTAGE, Godshill, Isle of Wight: Home-baked scones and cakes, local strawberries and farm cream are served at this thatch-roofed cottage. Local products available include cider, jams, and mustards. Open Easter through October (phone: 0983-840680).

DUNNOSE COTTAGE, Luccombe Chine, Shanklin, Isle of Wight: Tucked away in a thatched cottage half covered with creepers and rambling roses, this bright and sunny tea room serves lovely homemade gâteaux and, on Sundays, a fine hearty roast for lunch and dinner. In fine weather, tea may be taken in the gardens. The proprietors have earned a reputation for their scones and are reputed by some to own the best tea shop on the island (phone: 0983-862585).

BETTY'S, Harrogate, North Yorkshire: In 1988, this was voted the best place in England for tea. Those in the know swear by the Christmas cakes, which *Betty's* ships all over Europe. The shop was founded at the turn of the century by a young Swiss orphan, Frederick Belmont, who arrived in this town by mistake after taking the wrong train. Londoners who choose not to hop on a train and make a similar mistake use the shop's mail order service. 1 Parliament St. (phone: 0423-504073).

ASSEMBLY HOUSE, Norwich, Norfolk: The 18th-century building in whose former banquet hall this restaurant makes its home was once the meeting place for fashionable society, later a dancing academy and a school, and with its fountain playing in the courtyard, is as elegant as can be. No visitor should miss a tea in the ballroom, full of fancy plasterwork and ornate lamps. Theatre St. (phone: 0603-626402).

SUTHERLAND HOUSE, Southwold, Suffolk: In an offbeat little seaside holiday town, this well-established and slightly genteel place, in the former home of a prosperous Elizabethan merchant and still sporting fine plastered ceilings that date from the Armada years, is a good bet for hot meals as well as scones and pastries, all homemade. 56 High St. (phone: 0502-722260).

BAY TREE, Stamford, Lincolnshire: In one of England's loveliest and most historic market towns, this tea room maintains a strong reputation for top-quality gâteaux and lunches in a friendly, relaxed atmosphere. 10 St. Paul's St. (phone: 0780-51219).

COTTAGE TEA SHOP, Tintagel, Cornwall: The homemade pies draw constant crowds to this 500-year-old cottage. Its beamed walls are hung with brass ornaments and prints, and guests are served light lunches or Cornish cream teas, the specialty, on handsome china. There is also seating outside in the garden, and bed-and-breakfast accommodations are available. Bossiney Rd. (phone: 0840-770639).

COFFEE SHOP, Yarm, Cleveland: Quiches, soups, lasagna, chessey prawns, and mushrooms provençal are all available here for lunch, and they're all made on the premises, with no unnatural additives of any sort. The sweets served at afternoon tea include Bakewell tarte, apple pie so full of apples the proprietors say "It will never make us rich," homemade ice cream, hazelnut meringue with raspberries, and Yorkshire curd cake. Guests are served at the back of a family-run gift shop in a Victorian building that most people call genteel and old-fashioned. Old pine church pews and oak chairs provide the seating; high ceilings and big sash windows add another graceful note. 44 High St. (phone: 0642-790011).

Mead and Meat Pies: Historical Banquets

It would be hard to find a more touristy way to pass an evening than by partaking of one of the period banquets held in hotels, castles, and other historic buildings throughout England, Wales, and Scotland. Yet, like a good gothic novel, these entertainments are a painless way to absorb a bit of history; they also afford the opportunity to slurp down a five-course feast in the best Tom Jones fashion — that is, with a knife as the only utensil. Knights and ladies in satins and velvets, jesters, and maybe a king or queen provide entertainment while a Henry VIII, a Queen Bess, a William Shakespeare, or some other figure out of the distant past acts as master of ceremonies.

The festivities usually begin in a foyer, where a bit of bread is served with salt "to ward away evil spirits" and everyone's health is toasted with mead — a heady concoction of fermented honey, apples, and spices, "to be drunk for virility and fertility," as the hosts explain the origins of the word *honeymoon,* "one month, or moon, after a wedding." After the mead has taken effect, the revelry continues in a banquet hall filled with long oak trestle tables set with pewter plates, mugs, and the knives used to shovel in the supper. (Most people find this progressively less difficult as the evening wears on — perhaps thanks to the copious quantities of wine and beer that are poured with each "remove," as a course is called in banqueting parlance.) Serving wenches keep the food coming, and between removes, the singers and jesters and harpists keep guests smiling — or at least try. They actually succeed with some people (and not always the same ones who have swallowed enough wine and beer to put Henry VIII himself under the table). Whether or not you find the entertainers appealing depends on your tolerance for the occasionally forgettable and also on where you go: In the country, the music can be sublime by any standards; city banquet leaders' proclivity for *Oklahoma* and other all-American favorites meant to please the bus groups may instead provoke fury. As for the food, it varies, too. Along with reminders to "belch . . . near no man's face with corrupt fumosity," the menu will list a number of removes in appropriate lingo. There is "Ye Potted Spiced Mete," for example, the making of which is also described, as follows: "Take: Item — Finest Gammons and choicest parts. Boyle them until ye mete so tendre leaves ye bones. Ye whole pounded in a marble mortar to smoothest paste. Strewe over it: Item — Freshly ground Herbes and Spices and Item — Liquor from ye hocks — Then when perfectly mixed, set all into Potting pans." The idea is nice, but the meat may actually taste like nothing more than an American deli's second-best corned beef — and in an urban area, it may not even be that good. Often the distractions of the entertainment and the palate-numbing effects of the wine or beer are a relief; sometimes even the terminally hungry traveler may find himself picking at the plain roast chicken.

On the other hand, it's seldom that something totally inedible is served, and there's usually no shortage of food. Moreover, there are times when guests will toss down the food with the relish of the famous Tudor himself; sometimes they'll find themselves belly-laughing at one of the jester's corny jokes; and sometimes, too, a song will turn out to be so beautiful that it brings tears. The best banquets — a few of which are listed here — may surprise you in just that way.

Some operate nightly, others only on weekends, and still others on a seasonal basis. Reservations are required, and most banquet managers demand a deposit when the booking is made and full payment of the fee — usually from about $15 in more remote areas to about $40 in a city — no later than a month in advance. For listings of other feasts, some from periods other than the medieval, contact the British Tourist Authority.

COOMBE ABBEY, near Coventry, West Midlands, England: Medieval banquets are staged throughout the year in the splendor of a candlelit hall in this ancient abbey. The full evening of entertainment includes songs from the Ladies of the Courte, and there's plenty of mead and wine to consume during the four-course meal, which is presided over by the baron and baroness. Advance bookings are essential. Details: Coombe Abbey, Brinklow Rd., Binley, Coventry, West Midlands CV3 2AB, England (phone: 0203-452406).

BEEFEATER BY THE TOWER OF LONDON, London, England: In the historic vaults of a former ivory warehouse, within cannon shot of the Tower in picturesque St. Katharine's Dock, Henry VIII lords over a crowd that can number 550. Jesters, magicians, sword swallowers, and fighting knights provide entertainment that borders on the vaudevillian; the atmosphere is lively and bawdy, and the setting impressive. The fare includes pâté, leek soup, seafood vol-au-vent, roast chicken, and fruit flan, with unlimited wine and ale throughout. Details: Beefeater by the Tower of London, Ivory House, St. Katharine's Dock, London El, England (phone: 01-408-1001).

COCKNEY CLUB, London, England: Pearly kings and queens, buskers, flower girls, and assorted soloists entertain cabaret-style as guests put away a four-course dinner with unlimited wine and beer. Details: The Cockney Club, 6 Hanover St., London W1R 9HH, England (phone: 01-408-1001).

HWYRNOS, Swansea, West Glamorgan, Wales: The entertainment presented in a historic building in the center of this city in South Wales is not so much a medieval banquet as a Welsh *hwyrnos* (literally "late night"). It's informal, not touristy, and reminiscent of the days before electricity and easy transportation, when rural people used to gather at their neighbor's place to sing along to melodies of the sweet Welsh harp, dance, play games, tell stories, and recite poems. The meal is as hearty as they come, with such fare as roast leg of lamb and the traditional Welsh stew (really a thick soup) known as cawl, followed by a traditional pudding with fresh cream. Inevitably, all the other banquets are attempts to show off the 20th century's idea of life in a previous historical period, but because the Welsh commonly enjoyed just such evenings as this one until very recently, it has an extra bit of authenticity. Open most evenings in summer and at Christmas, several times weekly in spring and fall, and on most weekends in January and February. Details: Hwyrnos, Green Dragon La., Swansea SA1 1DG, Wales (phone: 0792-641437).

RUTHIN CASTLE, Ruthin, Clwyd, Wales: Although history says that Ruthin Castle dates from 1282, when Reginald de Grey enlarged the original wood-and-stone fortress on the site, legend has it that the castle was created by two giants throwing stones at each other from opposite mountaintops. True or not, the castle's subsequent stormy history — with many changes of ownership and an awesome amount of death and destruction that left the castle a near-total ruin more than once — needs no embellishment. Today's offerings are equally awesome, but in a more positive sense, from the wonderful food — among the best in Britain and certainly the best of the banquets — to the entertainment, which features a jester who is actually funny and minstrels (local housewives rather than the usual moonlighting pros) who sing their beautiful Welsh ballads to the accompaniment of harps. The setting — a charmingly pastoral corner of northern Wales, surrounded by rolling hills dotted with peaceful cattle and scattered here and there with quaint old farmhouses and pretty villages — can't be beat. Details: Ruthin Castle, Ruthin, Clywd LL15 2NU, Wales (phone: 08242-3435).

Shopping Spree

No matter where the dollar stands relative to the pound, the lure of shopping in Britain is irresistible. London in particular seems to awaken the dormant consumer in even the most monastic visitor. Sooner or later, he finds himself walking around with a bulging carrier bag, rummaging feverishly through the sale scarves at *Liberty*'s on Regent Street, or shuffling past the bric-a-brac stalls on Portobello Road. Shopping has become such an institution among travelers here that the English word for it has found its way into the other European languages. Oxford Street on a Saturday is the West's most teeming bazaar.

Quality, durability, and what the natives are fond of calling "value for money" are the norm. And the best buys are still those articles in which craftsmanship counts: riding equipment, humidors, umbrellas, china, crystal, fireplace tongs, and other items essential to every well-equipped Victorian household. When it comes to clothing, there are many trendy designers in England today.

WHERE TO SHOP

You can find good buys all over Britain, provided you know where to look.

CHAIN STORES: Some of the great British chain stores are as dedicated to quality as their Bond Street betters. For clothing, *Marks & Spencer* is a prime example of attractive prices and vast selection. The linens and sweaters, especially those in cashmere, lamb's wool, and Shetland wool, are among Britain's best buys. (But get there early before the aisles become impassable with the day's blizzard of buyers.) Also stop at *Boots* for cosmetics, pharmaceuticals, and sundries; *Sainsbury's* for food products; *Habitat* for designer items for the home; *W. H. Smith's* for books and stationery supplies; and *Mothercare* for children's clothes.

POST-CHRISTMAS AND JULY SALES: These British events have the stature of Wimbledon or a royal family christening. Travel agents are now packaging tours to the sales with the promise that participants' savings in discounts will cover the cost of the trip. The winter sale at *Harrods* that begins the first Friday in January is a ritual no devout shopper can afford to miss, and values can be breathtaking. Some stores stay open on *New Year's Day* to accommodate the throngs. But beware of smaller stores that stock their racks with cut-rate merchandise specially acquired for a sale event.

OPEN MARKETS: Never pass up a chance to wander through one of Britain's bustling open markets, a cross section of local life and a glorious experience for all the senses. The stalls are a riot of colors — scarlets and yellows and bright blues. Oranges and tomatoes keep company with spinach and celery and garish crockery. The calls and clatter of startling accents delight the ear. The smells of flowers, cheeses, and fish, one aroma blending with the next, assail the nose.

Bristol, Avon, England – The St. Nicholas markets sell fruits and vegetables, fish, flowers, and even the occasional parakeet Monday through Saturday. Off Baldwin and Corn Sts.

Cambridge, Cambridgeshire, England – There has been a market in Market Square since medieval times. Fruits, vegetables, fish, cheese, fresh flowers, records, books, and inexpensive clothing piled high under brightly colored canopies are available every day but Sunday.

London, England – The Berwick Street market in Soho, W1, has been bustling with fruit-and-vegetable hawkers for over a century now. Never touch the goods or the vendors will get furious. Open Mondays through Saturdays, with an early closing on Thursdays.

The Electric Avenue market in Brixton, SW 9, is chock-a-block with exotic foodstuffs and secondhand clothes. The atmosphere is straight from the West Indies. Open Mondays through Saturdays, a half-day only on Wednesdays.

The Camden Lock Market off Chalk Farm Road, NW1, sells high-quality crafts and bric-a-brac of all descriptions on Saturdays and Sundays.

The Kensington Market, 49–53 Kensington High Street, W8, sells clothing, jewelry, and bric-a-brac from India Mondays through Saturdays.

Petticoat Lane, which radiates from Middlesex Street, E1, overflows with fruits, vegetables, clothes, and crockery. It's mostly rubbish, but the browsing is always fun, and who knows what might turn up? Sunday mornings.

Norwich, Norfolk, England – The 200 striped-canopied stalls in the market square here constitute the largest open-air market in the country. Groceries, clothes, household items, and more are available Mondays through Saturdays.

Oxford, Oxfordshire, England – Built in 1774, this covered market off High Street is a gourmet's paradise where shoppers can pick up game, fresh fish, cheese, baked goods, and vegetables as well as the fixings for a picnic. Open daily except Thursday afternoons and Sundays.

York, North Yorkshire, England – Beautifully situated Newgate Marketplace, the center of local trading since the Middle Ages, sells clothing, bric-a-brac, and foodstuffs from Yorkshire and beyond, Mondays through Saturdays.

Glasgow, Scotland – Glasgow's answer to Petticoat Lane is the Barrows (known in Scotland as "the Barras"), the area on either side of Gallowgate that has been holding forth on Saturdays and Sundays since Victorian times, when people with weekday jobs elsewhere in the community set up stalls to sell whatever they could to bring in extra cash. Today, this square mile of the city, which the BBC called Europe's bargain basement, is packed with stalls — up to a thousand of them, all manned by colorful characters who seem by turns intriguing, exciting, and occasionally ungracious. There are also many convivial pubs in the area.

Cardiff, Wales – Welsh lamb, the fruitcake known as *bara brith,* and a local delicacy called *laverbread* (seaweed) are only a few of the culinary delights on sale in this bustling market, entered by St. Mary Street or the Hayes. Open Mondays through Saturdays.

DEPARTMENT STORES: You'll find some of Europe's greatest department store shopping in Britain. The multitude of stores, the quality of the goods, and the wide price range all make for unparalleled shopping fun.

London, England – For department store shopping, there's no place like London. First, it's the home of *Harrods,* whose motto is *Omnia, Omnibus, Ubique* (Everyone, Everything, Everywhere). This giant among emporiums offers everything from pianos to straight pins. It has a butcher, a bank, a library, a kennel, and whatever it doesn't have it will order. (There is a joke about a man who requested an elephant, only to be asked whether he preferred African or Indian.) The January and July sales are world famous. Brompton Rd., Knightsbridge, SW1 (phone: 01-730-1234).

Peter Jones, where King's Road meets Sloane Square, is a popular emporium that carries just about everything, from washing machines to children's Wellington boots. Sloane Square, SW1 (phone: 01-730-3434).

Harvey Nichols & Co. Ltd., just across from *Harrods,* is a favorite among London's fashion-conscious shoppers. The basement has great "young" clothes and super sales, and there's a café on the third floor. Brompton Rd., Knightsbridge SW1 (phone: 01-235-5000).

Selfridges claims "all the needs of civilized life under one roof." The variety is somewhat smaller than at *Harrods,* but the prices are generally lower. The china and crystal department is extensive and the Miss Selfridge department particularly lively. 400 Oxford St., W1 (phone: 01-629-1234).

Fortnum and Mason, which was founded by a footman and a greengrocer from the 18th-century court of Queen Anne, makes high art of selling fashions, fragrances, fine tableware, clothing, and groceries. Jams and preserves, tea, crocks of Stilton cheese — all sold on the ground floor by salesmen in swallowtail coats — are specialties. Their *St. James* restaurant is popular for lunch and traditional afternoon tea. 181 Piccadilly, W1 (phone: 01-734-8040).

Edinburgh, Scotland – *Jenner's* stands out for its superb stocks of bone china and Scottish crystal. Princes and S. St. David's Sts. (phone: 031-225-2442).

Glasgow, Scotland – Four-tiered, balconied *Fraser's,* a department store of the Victorian vintage, is built around a central court, with a glass-paneled ceiling and a beautiful crystal chandelier. It's a treat, if only for the surroundings. The wares include a good selection of Edinburgh crystal and food delicacies as well as English bone china, clothes, and linens. 21–45 Buchanan St., G1 3HR (phone: 041-221-3880).

SPECIAL SHOPPING STREETS AND DISTRICTS: Endowed with special character and verve, some streets invite shoppers to linger and browse. These areas may be brassy, quaint, or even supremely grand — whatever, these areas offer strollers a real spectacle made up partly of the stores, partly of fellow shoppers. Whether buying or just looking, everyone will find these streets worth a walk.

Bath, Avon, England – The city claims to be the nation's premier shopping center outside London, and most of the major purveyors are represented, including a branch of London's celebrated *Hamleys* (described in "Toys"). Shop displays here are always beautifully executed, and shoppers don't have to walk miles to find what they want, as they do in London.

Brighton, East Sussex, England – Occupying roughly a square mile, the maze of alleyways, byways, and passages known as the Lanes in the Old Town is hard to beat for character. The shops are weighted toward book and antique dealers, but there's no dearth of other stores as well. Entrances off East, North, Ship, and Middle sts.

Another good bet is Western Road, which runs into North Street. Together they offer almost 2 miles of continual shopping in all manner of odd and unusual stores. The North Laine area, between North Street and the railway station, has a multitude of little bric-a-brac and junk shops as well as some unusual specialty shops.

Chester, Cheshire, England – The Rows, an aboveground network of walkways that originated centuries ago, carry everything from antiques to expensive fashions.

London, England – There are so many tempting things to buy on so many streets here that it's hard to point a finger at only a few. But certain streets stand out.

Beauchamp Place (pronounced *beech*-um), a short walk from *Harrods,* off Brompton Road, is a boutique-filled block known for designer clothes and jewelry, trendy shops and shoppers.

New Bond and Old Bond Streets, laid out by Sir Thomas Bond in 1686, would leave even an oil sheik yearning for more of the kinds of luxury items that are specialties at these places. The area was fashionable as early as the Regency days of Beau Brummel and friends; back then, there was an establishment that offered aspiring dandies lessons in tying cravats.

Regent Street, which runs parallel to Bond Street between Oxford and Piccadilly circuses, is as elegant as its shops' façades. It was originally planned as a grand processional between Regent's Park and the Regent's palace, to divide Mayfair from Soho. *Liberty* is just one of its retail landmarks.

Crowded Oxford Street has department stores — *Selfridges, John Lewis* ("never knowingly undersold"), *Debenham's,* and *Marks & Spencer* among others.

The pedestrian streets are special fun. Carnaby Street, which made its name in the sixties, and Rupert Street are lively though tacky. South Molton Street, off Oxford Street, has become a trendy center. Chairs and umbrellas preside over much of the sidewalk in the summer.

Covent Garden, London's longtime vegetable market district, has undergone tremendous redevelopment, and the central market building, which stays open late, concentrates on wares from Britain. The whole area is crammed with trendy boutiques stocked with clothing for men and women, not to mention wine bars, restaurants, discos, and the like.

The Burlington Arcade, a charming covered Regency shopping promenade, is another must. It dates from the early 19th century and is crammed with shops piled elegantly with cashmeres, antiques, and other costly wares. Off Piccadilly near Old Bond St., W1.

Milton Keynes, Bedfordshire, England – Designed on a rectangular grid system around the centrally located Midsummer Boulevard, the ultramodern, half-mile-long, covered shopping center here is stark and functional, like the town itself, relieved only by the occasional potted palm, cactus, and fountain. But all the High Street names are here — and then some. This is a major local tourist destination (although visitors are probably as anxious to see Britain's newest city as they are to devote themselves to serious shopping).

Edinburgh, Scotland – Princes Street, Edinburgh's Fifth Avenue, is the best place in the country to get a good overview of things Scottish, you'll find the *Scotch House, Marks & Spencer, Jenner's,* and *Debenham's,* among other emporiums. Edinburgh Castle and lush, flower-filled gardens flanking the south side make the shopping experience all the more pleasant.

Cardiff, Wales – In addition to the modern St. David's shopping center, there are also a number of covered arcades; among the largest are Morgan and Royal, lined with trendy cafés, bookstores, galleries, and boutiques.

BEST BUYS

Britain may be one of the last holdouts against everything synthetic. Some of the products and shops are of superior quality, which puts them on the road to obsolescence, like the great ocean liners. So shoppers should yield to temptation and shop for the classics — the finest china, the softest cashmere, the sturdiest shoes — while they can still get them. Britain is the perfect place for indulgence.

BAGPIPES: It may take a lifetime to learn to play them, but you'll never forget the day you bought them.

Edinburgh, Scotland – *Hugh Macpherson (Scotland) Ltd.* is a three-generation family business that sells, in addition to bagpipes, Highland costumes handmade by local women. To go with the bagpipes, shoppers might buy a pipe band uniform, order a tartan skirt or a kilt made to measure, or buy Highland and country dance supplies. 17 W. Maitland St. (phone: 031-225-4008).

BASKETS: Traditional English baskets known as "trugs" are the specialty in Herstmonceux, East Sussex. They're shallow and made mainly of bent willow, and they come in seven different styles of varying size at the workshop of *Thomas Smith,* established over 150 years ago. Each one is fully handcrafted, individually finished, and made from locally grown woods — pliable sweet chestnut for the rims and handles and split-resistant willow for the body — to produce a basket that is lightweight and incredibly durable. The wide, shallow flower trugs and the strong, deep fireside log trugs are particularly handsome. *Smith* was the trug manufacturer to Queen Victoria. Hailsham Rd. (phone: 0323-832137).

BOOKS: Don't leave Britain without buying at least one book. Rare and secondhand volumes are available and well priced. Addicted browsers will have to be dragged out of the following haunts:

Cambridge, Cambridgeshire, England – *Heffer's* and *Sherratt & Hughes* are both on Trinity Street — the latter for four centuries now, although under different names during that time (phone: 0223-358351 and 0223-311243, respectively).

G. David is also a Cambridge institution and is now owned by the great-grandson of founder Gustave David. 3 and 16 St. Edward's Passage (phone: 0223-354619).

Edinburgh, Scotland – There's a plethora of wonderful used and antique book stores — explore! One charming shop is Margaret S. Duncan's *Dundas Bookshop,* 23a Dundas St., Edinburgh (phone: 031-556-4591).

London, England – *Foyle's* is the largest general bookstore in the world — and it's enormous. 119 Charing Cross Rd. (phone: 01-437-5660).

Henry Sotheran Ltd., which was founded in York in 1761 and moved to London in 1815, now incorporates *Cavendish Rare Books.* The large stock, handsomely shelved in 100-year-old bookcases, includes books on voyages and travel, Weinrab architectural books, finely bound literature, early English and continental titles, and volumes on maritime history, mountaineering, and polar exploration. A knowledgeable staff is on hand to offer guidance. 2 Sackville St. (phone: 01-439-6151).

The narrow and utterly classic *Hatchard's,* founded in 1797, is London's oldest bookseller — and one of the most civilized. It currently stocks more than 150,000 titles on its four floors. 187 Piccadilly (phone: 01-439-9921).

Robin Greer, a member of the Antiquarian Booksellers Association, specializes in rare books, particularly illustrated children's books, including fairy tales and other tales of wonder. By appointment. 30 Sloane Court West (phone: 01-730-7392).

Maggs Bros. Ltd, A welcoming staff will help you find your way through five floors of antiquarian books on travel, military and naval history, and 17th-century English literature. 50 Berkley Square.

Oxford, Oxfordshire, England – An Aladdin's cave among bookshops, *B.H. Blackwell Ltd.* offers everything from the paperback guidebooks snapped up by tourists to the arcane tomes purchased by undergraduates. It also boasts that its Norrington Room is, perhaps, the largest single room of books in the world. 50 Broad St. (phone: 0865-792792).

Stratford-upon-Avon, Warwickshire, England – The *Shakespeare Centre Bookshop* sells gifts and souvenirs, but the specialty is things Shakespearean, particularly books and other publications on all aspects of his life, times, and works. This is the best place to learn all about Will. 39 Henley St. (phone: 0789-204016).

Hay-on-Wye, Powys, Wales – Hay-on-Wye has become the town of secondhand books. *Richard Booth (Bookseller) Ltd.* on Lion Street (phone: 0497-820322), listed in *The Guinness Book of World Records* as the largest secondhand bookshop on earth, displays about a million books on nearly 11 miles of shelves. A dozen more competitors line the streets. A must for passionate readers.

CHINA: The world's best pottery and porcelain has been produced in England since the 18th century, and many of the factories whose names are synonymous with elegance and quality are in and near the town of Stoke-on-Trent in Staffordshire. Royal Doulton, Spode, Minton, and Wedgwood all originate here. Travelers may visit the factories and the exhibitions; only the most resolute will leave without a souvenir. Contact the British Tourist Authority for its booklet *Fine English Glass and China,* which provides complete information about factory visits.

Derby, Derbyshire, England – Royal Crown Derby porcelain has been "royal" since the days of Queen Victoria. Factory tours are available, and a museum established by the duchess of Devonshire in 1969 is on the premises. 194 Osmaston Rd. (phone: 0332-47051).

London, England – *Thomas Goode and Company* occupies showrooms built in 1845, a half-century after the store first opened, and the lavishly set tables that fill the 13 rooms evoke visions of pheasant, champagne, and brilliant conversation. All the most famous names in china and crystal can be found here under one imposing roof. It's London's best china and glass shop. 19 S. Audley St., W1 (phone: 01-499-2823).

The Reject China Shops offer slightly irregular brand-name china at such reduced prices that they're a bargain even when shipping charges are included. First-quality china, crystal, and gifts from Coalport, Aynsley, and Spode are also available at good prices. 134 Regent St. (phone: 01-434-2502) and 34 Beauchamp Pl. (phone: 01-581-0737) in London; also a branch in Windsor.

Stoke-on-Trent, Staffordshire, England – The following illustrious firms offer tours of their premises. Be sure to call ahead (ask for the tour organizer).

Coalport, Park St., Fenton (phone: 0782-45274). Factory tours (by appointment in advance) provide an opportunity to see the production of figurines, florals, and miniature china cottages. The factory shop has a good selection of slightly imperfect china for sale.

Minton, London Rd., Stoke (phone: 0782-744766). The factory of this company founded in 1793 and patronized by Queen Victoria welcomes visitors. The museum's exhibits date back to the 1790s.

Royal Doulton, Nile St., Burslem (phone: 0782-575454). The *Sir Henry Doulton Gallery* tells the story of the Doulton tradition established by its namesake, who did the work that earned the company the right to call itself "royal." The company's historical figure collection is also on display at the gallery. Visitors to the factory can see the production of tableware, giftware, and figurines, from the automatic platemaking to the hand-painting of limited-edition pieces.

Spode Works, Church St., Stoke (phone: 0782-744011). Bone china was developed on this site in the last years of the 18th century and is still made here by the original processes, which visitors can see while touring the factory. The 2-hour connoisseurs' tour takes visitors through rooms not normally open to the public, including the superb Blue Room. Reservations should be made 2 to 3 weeks in advance.

Wedgwood, Barlaston (phone: 0782-204218). A visitors center offers a craft manufacturing hall, a film, and a new living museum that houses the world's most comprehensive collection of Wedgwood in period settings, such as Josiah Wedgwood's Etruria workshops and the 18th-century London showrooms.

Wedgwood and *Spode* sell seconds, china with slight imperfections, at half the normal retail price. The latter usually has a good selection in the popular Christmas tree pattern. An excellent selection of first-quality goods is also available.

Just outside Stoke-on-Trent in Longton, tour the *John Beswick Studios,* where the Royal Doulton Bunnykins and Brambly Hedge collections as well as a variety of toby jugs and animal figurines are made. Gold St. (phone: 0782-313041.)

CHOCOLATE: The English have long been famous for what's known as confectionery — creams, marzipan, truffles, fudge, and other irresistible sweets. A Mocha Baton, said to be Prince Philip's favorite, can be purchased at *Charbonnel et Walker* in London. This establishment, founded in 1875 and a Royal Warrant holder, "enrobes" its creations' interiors with dark chocolate (bittersweet plain) and white chocolate — nothing so humdrum as milk chocolate. The round white *boîtes blanches* (white boxes) traditionally hold gold-foil-covered chocolates emblazoned with letters and numbers; purchasers make a selection to spell out a message. 28 Old Bond St., W1 (phone: 01-491-0939).

Prestat is a center for the richest of truffles. Brandied cherries, milk, and dark chocolate. 14 Prince's Arcade, W1 (phone: 01-629-4838).

Rococo Chocolates is London's most eccentric candy store. Offerings range from the serious (fresh cream truffles, pralines, and Swiss chocolates made in London) to the sublimely imaginative (for example, sugar engagement rings). A sugar chandelier hangs from the ceiling, and every summer a new artist makes candy creations. Tea served in summer by appointment only. 321 King's Rd., SW3 (phone: 01-352-5857).

CRYSTAL AND GLASS: The manufacture of crystal in England is centered in the west midlands; in Scotland, it's at Penicuik near Edinburgh. But outstanding items can be purchased all over the country.

Bristol, Avon, England – The *City Museum and Art Gallery Shop* stocks among its wares handmade reproductions of the Bristol blue glass for which the town's glassmakers were once famous. Queens Rd., Bristol BS8 1QE (phone: 0272-223571).

Cambridge, Cambridgeshire, England – The *Friar's House* has been descibed as "a collector's treasure house," and it is crammed with fine crystal and porcelain, not to mention a selection of paperweights to delight collectors. Leaflets are sent by request. Benet St., Cambridge CBZ ZQN (phone: 0223-60275).

London, England – *Thomas Goode and Company,* described above in the section on china, also sells the best crystal. 19 S. Audley St., W1 (phone: 01-499-2823).

Newmarket, Suffolk, England – *Barretts,* established in 1782, stocks Waterford, Stuart, Webb, and Edinburgh crystal in addition to David Winter Cottages and a selection of china. 8 Sun Lane, CB8 8EW (phone: 0638-662205).

Stourbridge, West Midlands, England – Many manufacturers of fine crystal offer tours of their premises and sell a good selection of their wares in their factory shops. For tour information or reservations, call ahead and ask for the tour organizer.

Royal Doulton Crystal, by Webb Corbett, Coldbourn La., High St., Amblecote (phone: 0384-440442). On weekday mornings, factory tours are available in which all stages of the manufacture of English full lead crystal are shown. Tours require advanced booking and are mainly for groups of 5 or more.

Stuart and Sons Ltd., the Redhouse Glassworks, Stourbridge (phone: 0384-71161). The *Redhouse Cone Museum* is the historic home of Stuart crystal, and visitors can tour the works to see how modern technology and ancient skills are blended to produce fine crystal.

Tudor Crystal, Junction Rd., Stourbridge (phone: 0384-393325). Visitors may purchase fine Tudor crystal at the shop or take a tour of the factory.

Thomas Webb, King William St. (phone: 0384-392521). Dennis Hall, Thomas Webb's red brick Georgian mansion, houses a museum chock-a-block with crystal, documents, and photographs. After touring the factory, shoppers may want to stop at its shop, which stocks the company's crystal and other products of sister companies — including Denby ware.

Aberbargoed, Mid-Glamorgan, Wales – At *Stuart and Sons Ltd.,* visitors can see every aspect of glassmaking and glass cutting on a tour of the factory — and then purchase the output in the factory shop. Angel La. (phone: 0443-820044).

CURIOSITY SHOPS: England, particularly London, is a wonderful source for eccentric items that elsewhere might never even have been imagined.

Anything Left-Handed offers tools designed specifically for the left-handed person — can openers, over 30 types of scissors, potato peelers, special mugs, pens (including Italic and calligraphy writing sets), knitting guides, corkscrews, bread knives, and boomerangs, among other items. 65 Beak St., London W1 (phone: 01-437-3910).

Naturally British will make you feel as if you've traveled all over the country, even if you never leave London. Its stock includes dolls from Dorset, glass from the Lake District, woolen shirts from Wales, hand-knits from Scotland, and many wooden items such as rocking horses and traditional pub games. 13 New Row, Covent Garden, London WC2 (phone: 01-240-0551).

Norfolk Lavender, England's largest grower of lavender, has plants to suit gardens of all sizes; it's a fragrant marvel, especially in late spring and throughout the summer. On guided tours, scent lovers can learn how lavender oil is extracted, buy some to take home, and top off their visit with a cream tea or a light lunch. The new countryside gift shop features their own lavender gifts and English country gifts. Caley Mill, Heacham, King's Lynn PE31 7JE (phone: 0485-70384).

DESIGN: The best of British craft and design is available at the following London shops:

The Design Centre offers exhibitions of British design and an extensive bookshop of architecture, graphics, and more. 28 Haymarket, SW1 (phone: 01-839-8000).

The Conran Shop, in the magnificently restored Michelin Building on Fulham Road, displays designer furnishings upstairs; downstairs, everything from Oriental treasures to Valentine cards are found. Stop in at the *Oyster Bar,* or book reservations at *Bibendum,* the popular restaurant upstairs. Michelin House, 81 Fulham Rd., SW3 (phone: 01-589-7401).

The General Trading Company has a profusion of serious items with a streak of colorful fun, including shower curtains, mugs, stationery, cookware — and, of course, the ubiquitous Filofax. 144 Sloane St., SW1 (phone: 01-730-0411).

DESIGNER CLOTHING: Britain offers the ultimate in things traditional — and the fantastic. And London is headquarters for all this, never more so than since a young royal named Diana took British fashion under her wing.

The client list at *Bellville Sassoon* reads like a chapter from *Debrett's,* and the Princess of Wales, who chose a saucy sailor dress for her first official picture with the queen, is a loyal customer. The specialty is glamorous evening wear in fabrics and prints specifically designed for the shop. 73 Pavilion Rd., SW1 (phone: 01-235-3087).

Zandra Rhodes, a fearlessly original designer, makes elaborate and intricate garments of hand-printed or hand-embroidered silk chiffon or organza with hand-pleating, ruffles, or other unusual details and extravagant shapes. The prices are even more extravagant. Beaded stoles, beaded sweatshirts, and stockings are also available. 14a Grafton St., W1 (phone: 01-499-6695).

Other London designer showrooms worth visiting are *Katharine Hamnett,* 20 Sloane St., SW1 (phone: 01823-1002); *Jasper Conran,* 49–50 Great Marlborough St., WI (01-437-0386) for women's fashion, 73 New Bond St., W1 (phone: 01-727-0201) for men's fashion; and *Nicole Fahri,* 193 Sloane St., SW1 (phone: 01-235-0877).

FABRICS: The yard goods available in Britain will bring out the seamstress in even the least handy traveler — from luscious woolens in the colors of an Irish landscape to fine lawn reminiscent of an English meadow in springtime. *Laura Ashley* has cloth steeped in the English country look; there are branches in many locations.

In London, the name *Liberty* is synonymous with printed fabrics in cotton, wool, and silk. The scarves and ties are beautiful, and the store's façade — romantic and half timbered — is equally appealing. 210 Regent St., W1 (also on Kings Rd.; phone: 01-734-1234).

FOODSTUFFS AND LIQUOR: Jams and marmalades, blended teas, Stilton cheese, shortbreads, and other edibles for sale throughout Britain make wonderful souvenirs and presents.

London, England – At old-fashioned, wood-paneled *Ferns,* the carved mahogany shelves are crammed with teas, tea caddies, and more, and the drawers are packed with beans of all types. Since many of these are roasted on the premises, you can smell the coffee wares from several doors down. 27 Rathbone Pl., W1 (phone: 01-636-2237).

Fortnum and Mason is the British Empire's most elegant grocery store: The staff wear swallowtail morning coats, and the wine department is noteworthy for its breadth and for the rarity of its selections. 181 Piccadilly, W1 (phone: 01-734-8040).

Harrods is a must, if only for the experience. The gigantic Food Halls, reminiscent of a late-Victorian cathedral, will leave visitors salivating. From poultry to pâtés, plum pudding to pork (the pigs raised to the store butchers' own standards), *Harrods* has it all. The wine selection, one of London's largest, ranges from the insignificant and inexpensive to the superb and very costly. There are also dozens of pure single-malt Scotch whiskies. Brompton Rd., Knightsbridge, SW3 (phone: 01-730-1234).

Justin De Blank sells excellent quality specialty foods, including whole-grain bread baked in century-old ovens on the premises and a wide array of English cheeses, among them Stilton and Shropshire Blue. 42 Elizabeth St., SW1 (phone: 01-730-0605).

Paxton and Whitfield, a pungent paean to cheese housed in a little black-beamed 17th-century building, shows cheeses the way some shops display jewelry. There are cones and cubes large and small, pepper-covered logs of goat cheese, cakes with rinds of gray and tan, huge wheels of snowy Brie, light-gold cheddar, peach-colored Cheshires, deep gold Derbies, and more — all of it superb. Established in 1797, the firm has held the Royal Warrant since 1973. 93 Jermyn St., SW1 (phone: 01-930-0250).

Twinings offers tea — and nothing but — in bags, balls, and bulk. 216 Strand.

Norwich, Norfolk, England – *Colmans* has been milling mustard in this cathedral town for over 160 years. The firm's shop offers unusual varieties not often found elsewhere, along with reproductions of *Colman* posters, tea towels, aprons, and the like. 3 Bridewell Alley, Norwich NR2 1AQ (phone: 0603-627889).

Throughout Scotland – Don't fail to bring home a bottle of Scotch whisky. More than 200 brands are produced here, and although it's not inexpensive, you won't find such a selection at home. Bring home a vacuum-sealed side of salmon, too.

GUNS: London is the source for precision arms. At *Holland and Holland,* gunmaking is high art, and many of the customers choose their weapons with more care than they would choose a home. The curious will want to peek in, if only to inspect the binoculars, the folding earmuffs, and other appurtenances of hunting and shooting and to see the England that used to be — and obviously still is for some. 33 Bruton St., W1 (phone: 01-499-4411).

James Purdey and Sons, royal warrant holders and distinguished gunmakers who have been in business for over a century, have served royalty. Prince Philip and Prince Charles are both supplied from these quiet and dignified premises. Many a sportsman dreams of owning one of the house's beautifully worked metal-and-walnut creations. 57 S. Audley St., London W1 (phone: 01-499-1801).

J.C. Field & Stream features an immaculate and extensive stock of new, rare, and collectible firearms — from antique Purdys to Holland & Holland and W.W. Greener models. 604 Fulham Rd., London SW6 (phone: 01-736-0015).

HANDICRAFTS: Especially in Scotland and Wales, there are hand-wovens, hand-spuns, hand-throwns, and hand-knits galore. The British Tourist Authority publishes *See Britain at Work,* a useful guide to local crafts.

England – Handicrafts centers are scattered throughout the country.

The one in Bristol, the *Bristol Craft Centre,* is typical. At this collection of workshops, a number of jewelers, potters, weavers, leatherworkers, and others offer their wares. 6 Leonard La., beside 31 Corn St., BS1 1EA (phone: 0272-297890).

On Henry Street in Stratford-upon-Avon, just across from Shakespeare's birthplace, there's a "craft cluster" where the products of several craft workers are available.

Scotland – Potters, weavers, and knitters predominate among the artisans who run more than 1,000 crafts workshops here. Jewelers make wonderful pieces using Celtic motifs. For a list of those that welcome visitors, order *See Scotland at Work,* available at no charge from the Scottish Tourist Board.

Travelers not planning a drive around the countryside can visit the *Scottish Craft Centre* (phone: 031-556-8136) in Edinburgh to inspect the selection of handmade glassware, jewelry, woolen goods, and pottery. Acheson House, Canongate.

Wales – The national traditions of weaving, pottery, woodworking, leatherworking, and goldsmithing are still flourishing. The Wales Tourist Board (Brunel House, 2 Fitzalan Rd., Cardiff CF2 1UY; phone: 0222-499909) furnishes information on current goings-on and the whereabouts of craft enterprises open to the public.

Things Welsh in Cardiff offers homey, rural crafts all in one place. Duke St. Arcade, CF1 2AZ (phone: 0222-233445).

Also in Cardiff, *Castle Welsh Crafts & Woollens* sells locally made, traditional Welsh crafts. 1 Castle St. (phone: 0222-343038).

HATS: The traditional cool, damp weather has led to the evolution of a number of distinctive kinds of headgear here. London is home to some of the finest makers.

James Lock and Company, an institution since 1686, is the royal purveyor. The company has fitted a crown for the queen's coronation — and they'll fit a visitor for his first bowler. Bankers, tycoons, politicians, actors, horse owners and trainers have all been hatted here. 6 St. James's St., SW1 (phone: 01-930-5849).

Travelers who fancy a tweed cap or a black topper to protect against the London weather will want to stop at *Bates,* founded by George Bates just after the turn of the century and still in the family. Presiding over the premises — in top hat, of course — is Binks, a huge tabby cat who resided here from 1921–26 and was preserved on his demise by a first class taxidermist. 21A Jermyn St., SW1 (phone: 01-734-2722).

The Hat Shop sells balaclavas, berets, cloches, deerstalkers, fedoras, flying caps, panamas, pillboxes, tam o'shanters, even baseball caps with earflaps, along with hats made by designers and by special request. 58 Neal St., in Covent Garden, WC2 (phone: 01-836-6718).

JEWELRY: Beautiful jewelry is available all over Britain. Nearly every antique shop, for instance, sells jewelry, and more and more craft workers are using silver and gold. In Scotland, shoppers will find Luckenbooth brooches representing two entwined hearts surmounted by a crown, as well as clan brooches, kilt pins, and other treasures set with quartz, amethyst, cairngorm stones, and other semiprecious jewels. Distinctive local pieces are available in three locations:

Castleton, Derbyshire, England – Blue John, the semiprecious yellow and blue decorative stone found in ancient mines of the Peak District, is made into jewelry and sold at the entrances to the mines and in local shops.

London, England – For fine jewelry, silver, and luggage, visit *Asprey & Company* at 165–169 New Bond St., W1 (phone 493-6767); *Mappin & Webb* specializes in fine gold and silver jewelry, 170 Regent St., W1 (phone: 734-5842).

Southwold, Suffolk, England – Amber, a fossilized resin common in Suffolk, is carved or made up into jewelry here. The *Amber Shop* has colors that range from pale opaque yellows to reds and prices from about $6 to $615. Various nuggets are on display in their unworked states along with other pieces made into jewelry; the rarest is a necklet reportedly found in Tutankhamen's tomb. 15 Market Pl. (phone: 0502-723394).

York, North Yorkshire, England – *Preston's of Bolton* calls itself the Diamond Center of the North. Established in 1869, it sells a wide range of watches and jewelry and specializes in diamond rings. St. Mary's Sq., Coppergate (phone: 0904-34315).

St. Andrews, Fife, Scotland – The *Iona Shop* specializes in Celtic jewelry, including handmade pieces in silver studded with burnished Scottish stones. The shop also carries Scottish craft products in hornware and silverplate as well as a line of Art Nouveau–inspired boxes and frames. 7 Bell St. (phone: 0334-73102).

Perth, Tayside, Scotland – Rare freshwater Scottish pearls from mussels in the river Tay are luminous and beautiful with a lovely untouched quality. At *A. and G. Cairncross,* they're used in settings of great delicacy that reflect the mountain stream settings in which they're found. 18 St. John St., (phone: 0738-24367).

Tregaron, Wales – One of only three licenced users of real Welsh gold, the *Craft Design Centre of Wales* produces an exclusive line of Celtic design jewelry. Main Square (phone: 09744-415).

MAPS AND PRINTS: A map of an area just visited makes a fine and eminently packable souvenir, and antique maps are a specialty at many stores. A beautiful print can bring many hours of enjoyment at home — all the better if it's an old one. Again, London offers the widest selection and the highest quality.

Colnaghi is a respected specialist in Old Master prints as well as drawings and paintings, and prices are commensurate with quality. 14 Old Bond St., W1 (phone: 01-491-7408).

Stanford's is the principal destination of map seekers, whether they want a topographic of the mountains they've just walked, a yachting chart for an area they want to cruise, or a road map of the byways just cycled. It may well be, as the proprietors contend, the world's largest map shop. Landsat pictures, world maps, atlases, and globes are all available. 12 Long Acre, WC2 (phone: 01-836-1321).

MENSWEAR: When it comes to clothing, what Paris is to women, London is to men — it has the finest of everything. Herewith, a few of our selections:

Anderson and Sheppard is just one of the city's celebrated made-to-measure tailors. 30 Savile Row, W1 (phone: 01-734-1420).

Gieves and Hawkes, over 200 years old, provides traditional English tailoring at its best, along with "the complete gentleman's wardrobe," from formal dress to the proper attire for hunting and fishing. 1 Savile Row, W1 (phone: 01-434-2001).

Harvie and Hudson offers men's shirts made to order, not to mention a selection of all-silk ties designed and colored to coordinate with the shirts. 77 and 97 Jermyn St., SW1 (phone: 01-839-3578).

Douglas Hayward, one of the most distinctive tailors in London, makes bespoke suits for an exclusive clientele. A boutique stocks knitwear, luggage, and accessories. 95 Mount St., W1 (phone: 01-499-5574).

Turnbull and Asser makes the Rolls-Royce of shirts to order; it provides a shirttail long enough to reach to mid-thigh, so that it stays tucked even after many hours at a desk. Prince Charles is a customer. 71 Jermyn St., SW1 (phone: 01-930-0502).

MUSIC: *Chappell* is London's largest supplier of sheet music, from Bach to rock. It also sells pianos, electronic keyboards, guitars, and metronomes. 50 New Bond St., W1 (phone: 01-491-2777).

PAPER GOODS: England is the source of some of the world's most beautiful stationery.

Bath, Avon, England – Michael and Lula Gibson's tiny *Papyrus* sells books and photograph albums with hand-marbled covers from England and Italy. Lovers of tradition will also find bordered papers, tissue-lined envelopes, gilt-edged cards, and other classic stationery items; and copperplate engravers in the design studio will print stationery, cards, and bookplates. 25 Broad St. (phone: 0225-63418).

London, England – The quality and selection of paper goods are unparalleled here.

Paperchase, a delightful shop, deals in beautiful wrapping paper, unique greeting cards, posters, prints, kites, toys and games, hand-marbled papers, and more. 213 Tottenham Court Rd., W1 (phone: 01-580-8496) and 167 Fulham Rd., SW3 (phone: 01-589-7839).

Smythson of Bond Street has personalized writing paper and visiting cards, sealing waxes, diaries, calendars, and leather-bound pocket notebooks specially designed for wine connoisseurs, golfers, fishermen, gardeners, travelers, etc. Everything is in exquisite taste. The queen patronizes the firm. 54 New Bond St., W1 (phone: 01-629-8558).

PERFUMES: France may be more famous for its scents, but the English have a nose for them as well, and the fragrances are equally subtle and appealing. They make light, inexpensive gifts for men and women alike.

Brighton, East Sussex, England – *Pecksniff's Bespoke Perfumery* has the air of a pharmacy, but the scents are anything but medicinal. Luxurious bath salts, perfumes, soaps, and skin-care products are the staples, and various potpourris are available. 45–46 Meeting House La. (phone: 0273-28904).

London, England – There are some luscious spots in the capital to stock up on the country's most celebrated perfumes.

Floris, for instance, has been blending flower-based perfumes since 1730 when Jermyn Street was a cobbled, unlit byway and the young Spaniard Juan Famenias Floris sailed to England from Minorca. The shop, which holds two Royal Warrants, now sells delicious-smelling powders in boxes and tins, potpourris, toilet waters and perfumes, bath essences and soaps. 89 Jermyn St., SW1 (phone: 01-930-2885).

Penhaligon's Victorian shops offer an extensive range of classical scents, toilet waters, soaps, and bath oils for ladies and gentlemen — along with antique scent bottles and old English silver for the dressing table. They hold Prince Philip's Royal Warrant. 41 Wellington St., WC2, and three other locations (phone: 01-836-2150).

Taylor of London, founded in 1887, offers English floral fragrances not only as perfumes and toilet waters but also as scented sachets, soap, pomanders, and potpourris. Available at finer department stores.

RAINWEAR: The best-quality rainwear in the world is available in London. The umbrellas, particularly, are durable and distinguished. Herewith, the shrines of the rainy day:

Aquascutum, established in 1851, is famous for its tailored raincoats and classic English clothes. 100 Regent St., W1 (phone: 01-734-6090).

Burberry's is home for the superb but expensive men's, women's, and children's raincoats with the omnipresent and often imitated beige and red plaid linings. 18–22 Haymarket, SW1 (phone: 01-930-3343).

James Smith and Sons is Europe's oldest purveyor of umbrellas and one of Great Britain's few specialty shops for umbrella's and walking sticks. Shoppers who don't like anything they see can have the company make something up to their specifications. 53 New Oxford St., WC1 (phone: 01-836-4731).

Swaine, Adeney, Brigg, and Sons is one of the last extant firms to make umbrellas in pure silk. Walking sticks that convert to .410 shotguns are also available, along with riding gear and probably London's largest selection of attaché cases. 185 Piccadilly, W1 (phone: 01-734-4277).

RIDING EQUIPMENT: Horse-mad country that it is, England offers some of the best riding equipment on earth.

London, England – *Gidden's of London,* founded in 1806, sells saddles and other riding equipment to the queen. On three floors, near New Bond St. at 15d Clifford St., W1 (phone: 01-734-2788).

York, North Yorkshire, England – *Ralph Ellerker's,* established in 1795, is dusty, smells of leather and rope, and offers sherry on cold winter mornings in the back room. It's a pleasure just to inhale the scents and to experience the treasury of textures, rough and smooth. Shoppers can buy the famous hand-crafted all-leather Ellerker Dealer Boot, usually worn by market men, Gypsies, and horse traders — but there are also coils of rope, string of all sizes and types, canvas tarpaulin sheets, and many other items, from waterproof suits to leather palms for leather work. Country clothing, boots, and shoes are now part of the stock. 25 Walmgate (phone: 0904-654417).

SHOES: In England there are still places to have a pair of shoes made to order, but patience is required, since the labor can take months. People with time to wait can choose from a seemingly unlimited variety of wonderfully high-quality footgear.

London, England – *John Lobb* will custom-make both men's and women's shoes (for an average of $1,200 a pair) that, with proper care, will likely last longer than the wearer. Still in the family that founded it in 1849, the shop's rich scent of leathers, the superb workmanship, and the opportunity to view Queen Victoria's own lasts make a visit well worthwhile, even if you buy nothing more than a tin of the shop's celebrated shoe cream. 9 St. James's St., SW1 (phone: 01-930-3664).

Church's, over a century old, manufactures footwear with consummate care — and the results are fabulous. 58–59 Burlington Arcade, W1, and 163 New Bond St., W1 (phone: 01-493-8307).

Street, Somerset, England – *Clarks* was founded here 150 years ago and is still going strong. It offers low-priced seconds and a fascinating museum that displays the queer-looking footgear of ages past. 40 High St., BA16 OYA (phone: 0458-43131).

SHEEPSKINS: Warm and nearly indestructible, sheepskin makes up into a winter coat that is close to ideal, and England and Scotland are among the principal sources.

Bungay, Suffolk, England – *Nursey & Sons* keeps on making and selling increasingly lighter and more colorful English sheepskin coats, hats, gloves, rugs, leather jackets, and sheepskin coats. The firm is now nearly 200 years old. Bungay is packed with antiques shops and historical buildings. 12 Upper Olland St., NR35 1BQ (phone: 0986-2821).

York, North Yorkshire – At *Cox,* hats, coats, and rugs are the theme; slippers, gloves, footmuffs, and powder puffs are the variations. 30–32 the Shambles (phone: 0904-624449).

Loch Lomond, Strathclyde, Scotland – The *Antartex Factory Shop,* only about a half hour's drive from Glasgow, offers top-quality sheepskin goods at factory prices. The company, which has supplied sheepskins to British Antarctic expeditions since 1955, has recently broadened its line to include sheepskin accessories, rugs, fashion leathers, and knitwear. Lomond Industrial Estate, Alexandria (phone: 0389-52393).

SPORTING GOODS: The great outdoors figures so strongly in leisure activities here that it's not surprising to find an abundance of excellent equipment for the sportsman's pleasure.

London, England – *Lillywhites* has equipment on a half-dozen floors for some three dozen sports, from cricket (the avocation of its mid-19th-century founder, James Lillywhite) to Ping-Pong to polo. It's the largest store of its kind in the country and has held a Royal Warrant since 1955. Piccadilly Circus, SW1 (phone: 01-930-3181).

TOBACCO: The Englishman's grasp of the world of tobacco is immediately evident at two London shops:

Alfred Dunhill offers the best in precision lighters, pipes, tobacco, and cigars. Claiming to provide almost anything that a man can carry or wear, its offerings include luxury leather accessories, watches, writing instruments, and classically styled casual clothes. The Humidor Room features Havana and other cigars for connoisseurs. The store is redolent with the many fragrances of sweetly scented tobacco. 30 Duke St. (near Piccadilly), St. James, SW1 (phone: 01-499-9566).

James Fox specializes in cigars from around the world, including Havana, and most brands are represented. Another draw for the connoisseur is the use of humidifying rooms, where cigars mature to peak condition. 2 Burlington Gardens, W1 (phone: 01-493-9009).

TOYS: The first stop in London for parents and other doters is *Hamleys,* whose six floors make it one of the world's largest toy shops. There are magicians doing tricks, demonstration models whizzing, dolls walking and talking, teddy bears 6 inches to 6 feet begging to be cuddled, electronic games blipping and bleeping, and trains of every gauge whistling along their tracks. (No fewer than six on the ground floor encircle the escalators and stop at famous London landmarks.) New additions to the ground floor include a coffee shop, sweet shop, and a branch of *Lillywhite's* for children's sports equipment. *Young Hamleys* specializes in playthings for youngsters under 6. Elsewhere there are board games, computers, and a Model Centre that offers scaled-down versions of practically anything. The selection is astonishing, to say the least. 188 Regent St., W1 (phone: 01-734-3161).

Pollock's Toy Museum may have a museum upstairs, but downstairs there are all manner of things to take home, including miniatures, little theaters in the Victorian style to cut out, and teddy bears and reproduction toys from Victorian and Edwardian times. 1 Scala St., W1 (phone: 01-636-3452).

WOOLENS: The tweeds, plaids, and knits of Britain are justly famous, and nearly every shop and department store carries them. Wool is a way of life as well as an attraction for tourists.

Scotland is best known for its subtly patterned and colored Harris tweeds, woven by hand in the Outer Hebrides. Shetland and Fair Isle sweaters are also made here, along with most of the world's best lamb's wool and cashmere pullovers and cardigans. And tartans are a Scottish tradition; there are more than 500 patterns, most of which can be purchased by the yard or stitched up into a kilt (or a "kilted skirt" for women).

St. Helier, Jersey, Channel Islands – There used to be plenty of craftswomen on Jersey who spent their time knitting the island's distinctive navy blue, oiled wool pullovers, and on neighboring Guernsey, women's organizations used to turn out similar models in white as well. Now they only finish by hand what machines have made, and their products come in all colors and can be bought at shops in town. (The cabbage walking sticks that are made and sold here also make unusual mementos.)

London, England – *Scotch House,* founded in 1834, has not only plaids but also lamb's wool, Shetland pullovers, classic cashmeres, and 57 other styles of cashmere, as well as 350 different tartans in pure wool. This may be London's best single source for woolen items. 2 Brompton Rd., Knightsbridge, SW1, and four other locations (phone: 01-581-2151).

Westaway and Westaway has traditional pullovers in cashmere and lamb's wool at particularly good prices. Some are hand-knit, and there's not a synthetic thread in the place. A second shop at 92 Great Russell Street specializes in hand-knits and designer knits, and adjacent premises are devoted entirely to woolens made in the Shetland

Islands. 62–65 Great Russell St., WC1, and 92 Great Russell St., WC1 (phone: 01-405-4479 or 01-405-2128).

Edinburgh, Scotland – Tartans seem to line the streets here.

Kinloch Anderson is the kilt maker for the Royal Family. Kilts and kilted skirts can be purchased either ready-made or made to order in some 400 of the tartans in existence, from the Abercrombie, Black Watch, Bruce, and Culloden patterns to the Urquhart and Wallace. Sporrans, tweed jackets to match the plaids, ties, stockings, garters, and other accessories to complement the outfit are all available. What you can't buy here is the Balmoral tartan; though Kinloch Anderson stocks it exclusively, it is held on behalf of the royal household and is not for sale to the public. 4 Restalrig Dr., Edinburgh EH7 (phone: 0316-520900).

The *James Pringle Woollen Mill* has a comprehensive range of things woolen at mill prices, plus a Clan Tartan Centre that offers an audiovisual presentation covering the complete history of the tartan. 70–74 Bangor Rd., Leith (phone: 031-553-5161).

Pitlochry Knitwear offers excellent prices in Scottish goods, particularly sweaters, kilts, and women's suits. 28 N. Bridge St. and 50 other locations in England, Scotland, and Wales (phone: 03552-43901).

Burberry's Scotch House is the best place in the city for classy, expensive woolens — kilts, sweaters, tweeds, scarves, shawls, and mohairs. 39–41 Princes St. (phone: 031-556-1252).

The Woollen Mill provides a good, inexpensive alternative to *Burberrry's Scotch House.* Outlets are at 453 Lawnmarket (phone: 0312-251525) and 51 High St. (phone: 031-556-9786).

Galashiels and Hawick, Borders, Scotland – Both of these towns are well known for knitwear and woolens. The former is the site of the Scottish College of Textiles, which offers summer courses in techniques. It is also the home of the *Peter Anderson* factory, which offers 750 different tartans as well as factory tours weekdays at 10:30 AM and 2 PM April through October (closed end of July and beginning of August). Nether Mill (phone: 0896-2091).

Nearby shops sell tweeds, mohairs, cashmere items, and knitting yarn.

Hawick, the largest of the Scottish Border towns, has two major weaving mills, *Teviotex* and *Trowmill,* where visitors can see tweeds being made. Some of the most famous knitwear producers also make their home here; they do not have mill shops, but a wide range of local shops stock their goods.

There are also factories in Innerleithen and at Walkerburn, the site of the Scottish *Museum of Woollen Textiles,* a sheep auction mart in Hawick, and annual ram sales at Kelso. Jedburgh, Kelso, Galashiels, and Selkirk also have a good selection of knitwear and tweed shops. *Scotland: Borders Woollen Trail,* a brochure that gives background on the industry and highlights the area mills, museums, and shops, is available from the Scottish Borders Tourist Board, Municipal Buildings, High St., Selkirk TD7 4JX (phone: 0750-20555).

Glasgow, Scotland – *Lawrie's,* established in 1881, has a worldwide reputation for its knowledge of Highland dress in all its nuances. Kilts, skirts, jackets, mohairs, and all manner of accessories and souvenirs are available. 110 Buchanan St. (phone: 041-221-0217).

Inverness, Highland, Scotland – *James Pringle,* which sells possibly the world's best cashmere sweaters, also manufactures cloth and has a factory and shop where you can buy it made up into skirts, sports jackets, and the like and also purchase cashmere, lamb's wool, and Shetland knitwear. Holm Woollen Mills, Dores Rd., IV2 4RB (phone: 0463-223311).

Outer Hebrides, Western Isles, Scotland – The wool cloth bearing the distinctive trademark of Harris tweed, a circle and a Celtic cross, is handwoven by islanders following age-old methods; the yard goods are for sale in shops throughout the islands.

Stornoway, the largest town of the Lewis-Harris landmass, has a mill that sells tweeds at competitive prices. Sweaters knit from Harris wool are available at all the local craft shops. On Eriskay, island women produce distinctively patterned fisherman's sweaters.

St. Andrews, Fife, Scotland – One of the biggest and best outlets for knitted and woven woolens and cashmeres is the *St. Andrews Woollen Mill.* First-quality goods, as well as seconds, discontinued lines, and remnants, are available at its former golf club factory. The Golf Links (phone: 0334-72366).

DIRECTIONS

Southwest England

That the legendary Arthur should spring from this distant corner of England isn't surprising. For here, where the island narrows down to a horny point separating the English Channel from the Atlantic, the boundaries between the natural and supernatural are very indistinct. It doesn't take long to notice it — a constant tug on your imagination; the sense that the low green hills and languorous rivers simmer with an animation barely and only intermittently apparent to human senses. This, after all, is a land where walking sticks sprout into flowering hawthorns, where dancing maidens turn to stone, and where a baby delivered to an old magician on the crest of a fiery wave becomes a warrior, a king, a superhuman mortal who unites and gives identity to the English people. Even today, when modern sensibilities are so ruthlessly rational, there are quite sane folk who claim that fairies dance on the Dorset coast and pixies bedevil Dartmoor travelers.

The land itself conspires to enchant. To the east, Dorset's rich dairyland folds and unfolds in a continuous succession of hills and vales, while Somerset's miles of meadows and orchards are cradled in a basin protected on all sides by hills and the sea. In the heart of Devon, the county occupying the broad square of the peninsula, is Dartmoor, a solitary and taciturn landscape of bare hills bristling with strange winds. Beyond, and to the end of England, lie the neat, stone-walled fields and lanes of Cornwall. But nowhere does the magic seduce as powerfully as where land meets the sea, and the southwest has more miles of coastline than any other part of England. Here are long strands of beach that disappear with the tide, steep coves nearly obscured by their dense foliage, headlands shrouded in mist, and towering black cliffs that meet the crashing sea in an Olympian test of wills.

For all its wildness, though, the southwest is essentially a human landscape. Thousands of years of habitation by man has shaped the countryside as surely and as gradually as the elements. The soft, sculpted shape of the hills is the result of centuries of plowing and grazing, and the high-hedged roads that have carried countless generations from village to village are etched deeply on the land. It's the cluster of thatched cottages covered with roses, the isolated church standing on an open knoll above the sea, that please the eye as much as the grandeur of the setting.

Everywhere are reminders of the successive occupants of the land, from paleolithic drawings in the Mendip caves to a deserted World War II air force base near Bodmin Moor. Bronze Age circles, Iron Age villages, Celtic hill towns, Roman roads, Saxon farms, Norman churches and cathedrals, Tudor coastal fortifications, grand Georgian mansions, and Victorian resorts all combine to make this part of the country a visible record of English history. Some sites, like Stonehenge or the Normans' magnificent cathedrals, are well known, but others, perhaps the most rewarding, are those you come across yourself — an enigmatic formation of stones in the middle of a sheep pasture, or a fanciful church carving done by a nameless artisan of the Middle Ages.

The southwest is hardly an undiscovered paradise. Britons come by the droves to enjoy Cornwall's and Devon's fine beaches and warm weather. But apart from tourism, people make their livings much as they have for centuries, by sheep herding, dairy farming, fishing, and sea trade. There is now a good deal of mining for china clay around St. Austell, but tin mining, which for many hundreds of years brought wealth to Cornwall (or at least to some of its families), is almost a thing of the past. Plymouth and Exeter, both ports, are the only cities of any size that Devon and Cornwall can claim, and although the population in resort towns swells with summer visitors, the rest of the year you'd have to search a bit to find a crowd.

The route suggested here begins in Salisbury and heads west to Sherborne — a Saxon town that arrived in the 20th century with its vitality and charm intact — before plunging south through Dorset's rolling green countryside to Dorchester and following the Dorset coast to Exeter, the gateway to Devon and Cornwall. The route then meanders through Dartmoor, heads back to the coast at the south Devon sea resorts of Torbay and Dartmouth, and rounds the South Hams peninsula to Plymouth. Crossing the river Tamar into Cornwall, the itinerary hugs the coast all the way to the Lizard and Land's End and detours to the Isles of Scilly before turning north. From St. Ives, it climbs up the spectacular west coast of Cornwall, makes a loop through Bodmin Moor, and returns to the coast to stop at Tintagel (the legendary birthplace of Arthur) and Boscastle before continuing along the steep and wooded north coast of Devon to visit such towns as Clovelly and Ilfracombe. Then it passes into the Exmoor Forest and the county of Somerset, cutting across the Somerset levels to the historic town of Glastonbury and the Cheddar Caves.

Take your time through this country. Much of its beauty and charm is to be found down exasperatingly narrow lanes that can't be taken at more than 20 miles an hour or along public footpaths that link village to village. There is also an extensive system of splendid coastal footpaths that even at the height of the tourist season are quiet, private retreats. (The National Trust, which maintains some of these paths, along with scores of historic sites, isn't supported by government funds, as most people think. So don't pass up its contribution boxes without expressing — in cash, that is — your appreciation for the fine job it does.) One last tip: Most towns and villages with tourist attractions have large parking lots near the center of town. Use them and save yourself the aggravation of trying to park on streets built for foot traffic — and possibly a dented fender.

There are so many excellent small hotels in this neck of the woods that you'll be tempted to extend your stay just to sample them all. Most are also well known for their food and open their restaurants to non-residents. These hotels aren't cheap, but they are good value for the money. For a double room with breakfast, expect to pay at least $100 at places we list as expensive; $60 to $100 for those in the moderate range; and under $60 for those listed as inexpensive. Restaurants listed as expensive will charge $55 and up for a meal for two excluding wine; moderate ones will cost between $30 and $55; and the inexpensive ones, less than $30.

SALISBURY: Compared to many, Salisbury is a mere pup of a city. It wasn't until the 13th century that the Church, exasperated by constant quarrels with its military neighbors and tired of the harsh weather it suffered from its exposed position on top of the hill at Old Sarum, decided to move the cathedral to the low-lying meadows beside the river Avon. The very elegant cathedral is crowned by the highest spire (404 feet) and houses the oldest clock (ca. 1386) in the country. Many other buildings in town present fine examples of medieval and Georgian architecture: Mompesson House, built in 1701, retains much of its original plasterwork and paneling (open Saturday through Wednesday afternoons from April through October; admission charge). Part of Malmesbury House dates from the 14th century (open Wednesdays and Thursdays, Easter through September). A colorful market has been held in Salisbury every Tuesday since 1227 and is now held on Saturdays as well.

About 10 miles north, standing silently on the bleak Salisbury Plain, is Stonehenge, a wonder of the world that attracts about three quarters of a million visitors a year (open daily, except Christmas and New Year; admission charge; phone: 09802-3108). The site, about 100 yards in diameter, consists of several earthen banks and barrows (burial mounds); concentric circles of standing stones, some capped in pairs with lintels; and an avenue leading away from the site (originally toward the river Avon). Erected in three stages, beginning in about 2800 BC, some of the stones are aligned with astronomical events (the position of the sun at summer solstice, for example). As a result, it is thought that the site must have had some primitive religious significance. Although the area is surrounded by wire fencing to deter latter-day druids from performing occult rituals, there is none of the usual touristy clutter, and the surrounding rolling, grassy countryside is devoid of 20th-century intrusions. (For more about Stonehenge, see *Ancient Monuments and Ruins,* DIVERSIONS.)

The broad plain north of Salisbury probably contains more prehistoric monuments per square mile than any other part of England. There are literally dozens of other relics left behind by men and women who worked the plain as early as 6,000 years ago. Woodhenge, a few miles to the northeast of Stonehenge, consists of six concentric rings of post holes whose timbers probably supported a circular temple. Durrington Walls, a 30-acre earthwork with a circular structure near the town of Durrington, dates from the same period. Then there are the numerous barrows: long barrows, round barrows, bowl-shaped, disk-shaped, and bell-shaped barrows. The guide, *Stonehenge and Neighboring Monuments* published by English Heritage, shows the location of many of the barrows and temples near Stonehenge.

Closer to town, 2 miles up A345, is Old Sarum, an ancient Briton and Roman camp that became a cathedral and castle town long before Salisbury was even dreamed of. In the 13th century, the bishopric moved to Salisbury and Old Sarum was left to decay, but its castle and cathedral foundations are still standing (open daily, except Christmas and New Year; open afternoons only on Sundays; admission charge).

Salisbury's bustling downtown is full of pubs, and you could hardly go wrong stopping at any for a tasty pub lunch. If you're not deterred by convivial lunchtime crowds, try the *Haunch of Venison,* a venerable old pub in the center of things with a reputation for good food, or the *New Inn,* a cozy 15th-century pub near the cathedral.

CHECKING IN: ***Rose and Crown*** – Right on the bank of the Avon, it's a happy amalgam of half-timbered ancient inn and comfortable modern hotel. Harnham Rd., Harnham, near Salisbury (phone: 0722-27908). Expensive.

White Hart – A city landmark near the cathedral with a Georgian, pillared portico and rooms in traditional style stocked with plenty of comforts. 1 St. John St., Salisbury (phone: 0722-27476). Expensive.

Scotland Lodge – This comfortable 16th-century house in a large garden is within easy reach of Stonehenge and offers a taste of English village life. Serves magnificent breakfasts. Winterbourne Stake, Salisbury (phone: 0980-620943). Moderate.

EATING OUT: *Crustaceans* – A small, pleasant restaurant that is devoted entirely to seafood. Lobster and mussels are among its briny specialties. Dinner only; closed Sundays. 2–4 Ivy St., Salisbury (phone: 0722-333948). Moderate.

Harper's – The place for nouvelle English cuisine, with excellent, home-cooked dishes (chalked up on a blackboard), including old favorites treated in imaginative ways — lamb with apricot and cider sauce, for example — as well as traditional desserts. Closed Sundays from November through April; closed Sundays at lunch the rest of the year. 7 Ox Row, The Market Square, Salisbury (phone: 0722-333118). Moderate.

En Route from Salisbury – A3094 follows the river Avon, but at a safe distance, out of Salisbury to Wilton, passing through the pretty little village of Netherhampton. Wilton was once the capital of King Egbert's Wessex and Kent, and for many years its abbey was Salisbury's ecclesiastical rival. The abbey was dissolved by Henry VIII and the land given to the Earl of Pembroke. The opulent Wilton House that now stands on the abbey grounds was designed by Inigo Jones and contains a superb collection of art and furnishings and enough gilt to blind the eyes (open Tuesdays through Saturdays and Sunday afternoons from April to mid-October; admission charge). Wilton also boasts what is probably the only Italianate basilica in the neighborhood and is the home of Wilton Carpets, which has been producing fine wool carpets since the 17th century (factory tours conducted weekdays year-round). A museum showing the process of carpet production is also open there Mondays through Saturdays, April through October.

Although in this countryside of tidy villages tucked in the folds of green hills it is usually advisable to stick to secondary roads, take the main road, A30, from Wilton to Sherborne. After passing the town of Shaftesbury, one of the wealthiest cities in England until its powerful abbey was destroyed by Henry VIII, there's a stretch of road that affords some of the most scenic driving in the country. To the left, a 15-mile-long escarpment rises dramatically over the gentle rolling pastures of Blackmoor Vale. Objectively, it's not very high, perhaps 400 to 500 feet. But it comes on so suddenly that Thomas Hardy described it as the "green sea of Blackmoor Vale washing up to the foot of the bare chalk uplands." For Hardy enthusiasts, there is an obligatory stop nearby. About 5 miles outside Shaftesbury, turn left onto B3092 for another 5 miles to the pretty, prosperous village of Marnhull, transformed by Hardy into Marlott, the birthplace of the fictional Tess of the d'Urbervilles. Tess Cottage, supposedly the cottage Hardy had in mind when creating the Derbyfields, stands about a mile from the village church. It's a private residence, but can be viewed from the road. Head back to A30 via Fifehead Magdalen — its location above the river Stour is as pretty as its name is melodious.

SHERBORNE: Even before reaching Sherborne, you catch a glimpse of its powerful past. Standing on a knoll to the southeast of town are the ruins of Sherborne Old Castle, a magnificent fortified palace built in the early 12th century by Roger de Caen, Bishop of Sarum and, at his height, second in power only to Henry I. Even the remains are impressive: A grassy moat 30 feet deep encircles the site, and the thick walls and gracefully vaulted hallways catch the late-afternoon sun with a special brilliance (open daily, except Christmas and New Year; admission charge). The castle passed back and forth between the monarchy and the church, and then to Sir Walter Raleigh. Eventually it was razed by Parliamentarian troops during the Civil War. From the southeast corner of the castle keep you can see "new" Sherborne Castle, an Elizabethan house built by

Raleigh after he despaired of ever modernizing Bishop Roger's castle. In the Digby family since 1617, the house contains an impressive collection of paintings, furniture, and porcelain. Sherborne Castle and its grounds, landscaped by Capability Brown, are open Thursdays, weekends, and bank holidays, Easter through September; admission charge.

Like Winchester, Sherborne was a prominent city long before the Normans came. It was chosen as one of two cathedral cities in Wessex in 707, and for the next 400 years the Saxon bishop-warriors consolidated the city's power and prestige. When the Normans moved the see to Sarum in the 11th century, the church became an abbey, and when Henry VIII dissolved the monasteries, the townsfolk bought it for £300 and made it their parish church. Much of the splendid Norman church, built of golden-colored Ham Hill stone, remains, and there's even a door on the west front that dates from the Saxon cathedral.

Sherborne has long since passed into graceful old age. It's a charming town, compact and self-possessed, with an attractive high street. Its main industry is education. There are ten private schools in Sherborne (a town of 9,000 people), and on weekday afternoons the streets are awash with blue-uniformed schoolchildren. The *Three Wishes* restaurant, on Cheap St., does a delicious tea of scones, clotted cream, and jam.

CHECKING IN: ***Eastbury*** – For a taste of seclusion in the town center, try this elegant Georgian townhouse hotel sitting on its own acre of walled garden. It has a large library of antiquarian books, and all bedrooms, newly decorated, are named after English garden flowers. Long St., Sherborne (phone: 0935-813131). Expensive to moderate.

En Route from Sherborne – Quiet, agricultural Dorset is a collection of villages, each prettier than the next, linked together by fields, hills and valleys, rivers, and spring-fed meadows of unparalleled beauty. While you can travel straight down to Dorchester on A37 (pick it up at Yeovil, 5 miles west of Sherborne), you'd be missing the best of this county. This is a route that will take you through a handful of Dorset villages and some of the loveliest countryside. The roads are sometimes little more than cow paths, so don't expect to make good time.

Start at Melbury Osmond, about 6 miles south of Yeovil, just off A37, a village of stone houses jumbled together in some of the greenest hills ever seen. From here there's a public footpath (a little over a mile long) through Melbury Park, a lovely and peaceful private estate, to Evershot, a perfect gem of a village — one street long, one street wide — that looks like Melbury Osmond would if its cottages were laid side by side. (Evershot can also be reached by road.) The cottage just beyond Evershot's parish church is supposedly Hardy's model for the one where Tess rested during her travels.

From Evershot, take an unnumbered road to Minterne Magna, which will follow along the top of Batcombe Hill. It is hard to imagine a more beautiful drive. From the ridge of the escarpment, the land falls away to soft green pastures, hedged fields, and houses and farm buildings built of mellowed Ham Hill stone. This is a human landscape, sculpted by centuries of mankind's careful and continuous husbandry. It's a short stretch of road — perhaps 5 miles — but you'll be tempted to make it last much longer.

When this road runs into A352, turn south and proceed to Cerne Abbas. Once an abbey and market town, Cerne Abbas is now a pretty triangle of pubs, inns, and handsome merchant houses sitting in a little valley among the rolling upland hills of Dorset. One of Cerne's claims to fame is the Cerne Giant, a 180-foot-tall man with prominently exposed genitalia carved into the chalk hillside overlooking the old abbey. There's some disagreement over the identity of the original sculptors, although it's safe to say the giant dates back to at least the Romans.

Drive east, pick up B3143 at Piddletrenthide, and follow the road through the other

Piddle River villages to Puddletown, which for many years also took its name from the river until delicate Victorian tastes demanded the name be changed.

You're in the very heart of Thomas Hardy country now. So many of his fictional characters crisscross this corner of Dorset that there is hardly a village, manor house, farm, or hill that doesn't have literary associations. Hardy himself was born a few miles west of Puddletown (Weatherbury in *Far from the Madding Crowd*) at Higher Bockhampton, on the edge of what he called Edgon Heath, the brooding backdrop for *The Return of the Native.* His cottage is now in the hands of the National Trust and can be visited Easter through October by prior appointment with the occupant (phone: 03056-2366), although the gardens are open daily. A mile or so east of Puddletown is Athelhampton, which Hardy called Athel Hall, a 15th-century Tudor manor house with a remarkably well-preserved dovecote from the same period. Athelhampton is a private home, but is open on Wednesdays, Thursdays, and Sundays from Easter through October, and Sundays through Thursdays in August; admission charge.

CHECKING IN: *Maiden Newton House* – The old stone manor house of the tiny Dorset village of Maiden Newton (which Thomas Hardy called Chalk Newton in *Tess of the D'Urbervilles*) has 12 rooms, mullioned windows, antique furniture, log fires, and 21 acres of parkland. There's a house-party atmosphere with all the guests sitting together for dinner while the owners, Bryan and Elizabeth Ferriss, act as hosts. Elizabeth even does the cooking. Maiden Newton (phone: 0300-20336). Expensive.

Plumber Manor – A small jewel set in 4 acres of gardens in the Dorset countryside southeast of Sherborne. It's best known — and deservedly — for its food, which is elegantly and imaginatively English, but its 12 attractive rooms are easily equal to the food. Closed the last 2 weeks of January and the month of February. Hazelbury Bryan Rd., Sturminster Newton (phone: 0258-72507). Moderate.

Summer Lodge – Everything about this Georgian hotel, another small jewel, speaks of care and thoughtfulness: bouquets of flowers everywhere; homemade shortbread on the tea tray; the quiet, good taste of the decor. The food — traditional English fare cooked with a French feeling for sauces and an oriental respect for vegetables — is excellent. Heated outdoor pool and 10 rooms. Summer La., Evershot (phone: 093583-424). Inexpensive.

EATING OUT: *Le Petit Canard* – Opened in 1988 by the young Canadian chef Geoff Chapman and his English wife, Lin, the restaurant, which is set in a 200-year-old cottage, has offerd fare with French, Oriental, and Canadian influences. The sauces are light, the vegetables crisp, and the meats char-grilled. Closed Sundays. Maiden Newton (phone: 0300-20536). Moderate.

DORCHESTER: Dorchester is Thomas Hardy's town. He lived here, wrote here, and made it live for all the readers who have never set eyes on its ancient cobbled streets or dour stone and brick façades. There's an excellent collection of Hardy material at the *Dorset County Museum* on High West Street (closed Sundays; admission charge) that includes the original manuscript of *The Mayor of Casterbridge* (Hardy's name for Dorchester) and a reconstruction of the author's study. There are also Roman mosaics and other artifacts from when the town was known as Durnovaria. The Roman city boundaries are still visible in the Walks that ring the city center.

There's a relic of even older inhabitants just a mile or so southwest of town. Maiden Castle, an earthen fort believed to be about 4,000 years old, is an astounding piece of work. Sprawling over 120 acres, wave after wave of earth ramparts lap up to an elevated enclosure that could hold 5,000 people. The last occupants of Maiden Castle were forcibly evicted by the vastly superior army of the Romans, who then abandoned the site for Dorchester (open all year).

CHECKING IN: ***Casterbridge*** – This beautifully furnished Georgian guesthouse has no restaurant, but it does have a small bar and a lovely conservatory where tea is served on summer afternoons. Some of the bedrooms are a little on the small side, but this is generously compensated by immense breakfasts. 49 High St., Dorchester (phone: 0305-64043). Inexpensive.

ABBOTSBURY: The straightest route from Dorchester to the seaside village of Abbotsbury also happens to be the most scenic. Head out of Dorchester west on A35. About a mile from town turn left onto an unnumbered road to Winterborne Martinstowe, then follow the signs through Portesham to Abbotsbury, and for the next 6 miles watch the green Dorset hills tumble down to the coast. (Hardy Monument, about midway to the left, commemorates not the novelist but Thomas Masterman Hardy, a captain who served under Admiral Nelson at Trafalgar.) Abbotsbury is an exquisite village of thatch and stone cottages lining a single winding street. All that remains of the 11th-century Benedictine Abbey is the tithe barn, although the abbey has survived, in a manner of speaking, since much of it was used to build many of the village cottages. The Abbotsbury Swannery, a large breeding ground on the edge of the Fleet freshwater lagoon, shelters many species of wild fowl (open daily from May to September; admission charge), while a subtropical garden (open daily from March to October; admission charge) flourishes in a coombe east of the village. Just outside Abbotsbury, southwest on B3157, stop for a lofty look at Chesil Beach, an 18-mile-long, 600-foot-wide stretch of pebble beach that separates the Fleet lagoon from Lyme Bay. The church standing lonely on a hill in the middle distance is St. Catherine's Church, the parish church of Abbotsbury.

En Route from Abbotsbury – Take B3157 along the coast to Bridport, a small market town that was thriving when the *Domesday Book* was written and that has fortunately taken care of its heritage of medieval buildings. Probably the town's greatest event happened in 1651 during the Civil War, when the fugitive Charles II, fleeing Cromwellian troops after the battle of Worcester, came here in disguise hoping to escape by sea. His true identity was uncovered and he was chased out of town, but had he made his escape, it would have been from the little harbor at West Bay, 1½ miles to the south. Bridport's broad sidewalks, originally rope walks, date from a time when local rope manufacturers stretched their famous products along them to dry.

The main A35 winds along the coast to Lyme Regis.

LYME REGIS: Lyme Regis is probably best known for the Cobb, "a long claw of old gray wall that flexes itself against the sea," as the town's most famous citizen, author John Fowles, describes it. (It was from the Cobb that Fowles's heroine, Sarah, the French lieutenant's woman, stared for sad hours at the sea.) Built over 700 years ago to create an artificial harbor, it has probably cost the good folk of Lyme Regis more to repair than it ever generated in trade. Still, the attachment to it is long and unshakable, and today it harbors scores of pleasure craft and lobster boats.

This is the quintessential seaside town — whitewashed and salty, built up the steep hillsides overlooking the harbor. In summer, Lyme Regis is a very popular resort, but at any other time of year, the seagulls make quite a racket. Fossil hunting in the sheer sea cliffs near town is a local sport, but there is also a collection of fossils at the *Lyme Regis Museum* for those who aren't paleontologically prone (open April through October; closed Sunday mornings; admission charge).

CHECKING IN: ***Combe House*** – A slight detour inland from Lyme Regis will take you to this cream-colored Elizabethan mansion run by John Boswell, a descendant of Samuel Johnson's biographer. It's an elegant and roomy hotel, furnished throughout with antiques but retaining an air of informality. It's also equipped for riding, shooting, golf, and trout fishing, and the food is good thanks to Cordon Bleu–trained Therese Boswell. Closed from mid-January through February. Gittisham, near Honiton (phone: 0404-2756). Expensive.

En Route from Lyme Regis – The main road west out of Lyme is A3052. From here, turn left onto B3172 to Seaton, a small fishing town by the mouth of the river Axe catering unashamedly to holidaymakers. Its steep shingle beach is almost overpowered by the great cliffs of Thorncombe Beacon and Golden Cap. The latter is the highest on the south coast, and its views over miles of headland have earned it the distinction of being named an Area of Outstanding Natural Beauty (along with the stretch of coastline from Lyme Regis to Sidmouth). A marked coastal path passing this way is part of the South West Way, one of England's official long-distance footpaths.

The route closest to the coast by car goes through the villages of Vicarage, Branscombe, Weston, and Salcombe Regis. Otherwise, travel westward with more speed on A3052, bearing left at Sidford onto an unnamed road down to Sidmouth. A quiet and distinctly aristocratic resort town where the tiny river Sid meets the sea, this was "discovered" and developed during Georgian times and owes much of its charm to the gracious buildings and crescents of that era. The townspeople have an extraordinary propensity to decorate everything with flowers — even the postboxes wear flowery hats most of the year. Sidmouth offers a popular sailing center, bracing walks along the cliffs, and an International Folk Festival, held the first week in August.

Return to A3052. At Bowd, the junction of A3052 with B3176, a thatched pub with beams, brasses, and log fires serves such good food it sometimes neglects the drinkers (game casseroles and steaks are a particularly good value). Turn left down A376 at Newton Poppleford and pass Otterton Mill, an old, picturesque corn mill still grinding flour with the aid of the river Otter's power. Follow A376 south and west through Budleigh Salterton, a smart little spa town, to Exmouth.

EXMOUTH: Devon's oldest resort, set on the estuary of the river Exe, was popular even before the railway to Exeter began to bring visitors from long distances. The town remains relatively small, although its superb sandy beaches buzz throughout the summer season. A row of elegant 18th-century houses up on The Beacon hill overlooks all this activity, but an even more interesting house, A La Ronde, is just 2 miles up Summer Lane, or A376, north along the Exe toward Lympstone. This extraordinary 16-sided house (open daily from Easter through October; admission charge; phone: 0395-265514) was designed in 1795 by two women who returned from the Continent hoping to combine the grandeur of the Byzantine basilica in Ravenna with the rustic charm of Devon. Whether they succeeded is arguable, but the decoration is remarkable, with ingenious displays of shells, feathers, and seaweeds. A member of the original family still lives here, progressing around the house in pursuit of the sun, breakfasting in the east and taking tea in the west.

Nearby Lympstone provides good views across the Exe estuary to stately Powderham Castle, the seat of the Earls of Devon (open Sundays through Thursdays from late May through September; admission charge), reached by a short passenger ferry trip from Exmouth to Starcross and a drive along A379. On the Lympstone side of the estuary, however, A376 leads north to the M5 motorway — from where roads are well signposted to Exeter.

CHECKING IN: ***Homeleigh Guest House*** – A good, friendly place for bed and breakfast. 132 Exeter Rd., Exmouth (phone: 0395-263491). Inexpensive.

EATING OUT: ***Nookys*** – This beamed restaurant serves English food and specializes in steaks. The Strand, Exmouth (phone: 0395-263086). Inexpensive.

EXETER: In 1282, Isabella de Fortibus, Countess of Devon, in a fit of pique with the citizens of Exeter, built a weir, or dam, across the river Exe below the city in order to deprive it of its access to the sea and the rich trade it brought to Exeter's doorstep. The townsfolk were furious and vowed to undo the countess's work. They did — by building a canal to circumvent the weir (called Countess Wear in its builder's honor) — and even though it took 300 years to accomplish, it's just an indication of Exeter's determination to remain the preeminent city in the region. Exeter is still a thriving commercial center, but it is also a cathedral and university city, a government center, and the gateway to Devon and Cornwall for thousands of vacationers.

At the center of the city sits its grand cathedral, a Norman and Gothic work of great beauty. The cathedral is exceptionally rich in carvings, although you need binoculars to really enjoy the often fanciful creatures carved on the roof bosses. The Minstrels' Gallery on the north side shows an entire angel orchestra and is utterly charming.

Not far from the cathedral is *Mol's Coffee House,* a 16th-century inn, now a gold- and silversmith's shop. Across High Street from the cathedral close is the guildhall, a municipal building built between 1330 and 1593 and in continuous use since then (closed Sundays). North of the guildhall are the ruins of Rougemont Castle, a Norman fortification, and to the south is St. Nicholas Priory, a restored monastic house with a cavernous 11th-century wine cellar that is the envy of all oenophiles (open Tuesdays through Saturdays; admission charge; the castle ruins can be seen anytime). No boating enthusiast should miss the *Maritime Museum* on the Quay. With over 100 vessels from around the world, this is considered to be one of the finest collections extant (open daily; admission charge).

Five miles north of Exeter is Killerton, an 18th-century mansion housing a fascinating collection of costumes displayed in rooms decorated in different periods. Killerton's superb garden, with rhododendrons, azaleas, magnolias, and stately oak and beech trees, is a beautiful spot, and near here, at Killerton Clump, herons nest from March to July. Killerton House, a National Trust property, is open daily from April through October, and the garden is open all year; admission charge.

CHECKING IN: ***Woodhayes*** – A small, peaceful Georgian house set in its own secluded grounds 8 miles northeast of Exeter. Antiques and oil paintings decorate the hotel, and among the refined touches in the half dozen or so bedrooms are novels on the table and bottles of spring water. The restaurant is known for fine English cooking. Closed January. Whimple (phone: 0404-822237). Expensive.

DARTMOOR: Such is its reputation, Dartmoor's name alone evokes a vivid description: treeless brown hills covered with heather and gorse and pockmarked with treacherous boggy pits, a place where shaggy ponies run wild and the black hounds of hell collect the souls of the damned, a spot so godforsaken and bleak that even desperate prisoners prefer the dank gloom of their cells to the inhospitable hills outside. And, in fact, the moors are startlingly severe, especially after the cultivated beauty of most English countryside. The B3212 road from Exeter to Plymouth speeds through this wild landscape, but haste would be a pity, since Dartmoor is far more than the barren, though incontestably beautiful, face it shows the passer-through. More than a dozen rivers rise in the upland moors, and as they make their way to the sea, they carve lush deep wooded valleys. Chagford, a picture-perfect village near the river Teign north of B3212, has for years attracted artists, writers, and fashionable folk, as has Moretonhampstead, the village at the junction of B3212 and A382. Castle Drogo, strategically set on a granite bluff above the Teign northeast of Chagford, may look like a medieval fortress, but it was actually built between 1910 and 1930 by a businessman with the means to indulge a romantic fantasy and make his home his castle. Now a National

Trust property (open daily from April through October; admission charge), it is probably the last private house built on such a scale in Britain.

Scattered throughout Dartmoor are tors, rocky hills as high as 2,000 feet, that offer superb views of the surrounding countryside. One especially accessible tor is Haytor, not far from Widecombe-in-the-Moor, one of the most picturesque villages in England and also, in summer, one of the most crowded. There are also numerous relics from prehistoric times — hill forts, stone circles, and barrows. Grimspound, about 3 miles from Manaton, is a Bronze Age settlement consisting of 24 hut circles and a stone enclosure that was probably used for livestock. And everywhere are the sheep, black-faced and woolly, pursuing scrubby moor grasses up steep hillsides, crowding onto narrow Devon roads through a break in the hedge.

Dartmoor is marvelous hiking country. Much of it is now national park land, so before setting out, stop for maps and advice at the National Park Information Center at Postbridge, which is along the B3212 north of Two Bridges, where the two main Dartmoor roads meet. Although the days when the moors seemed to mysteriously swallow up hapless travelers are gone, it would be foolhardy to misjudge them.

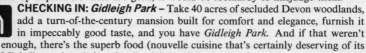

CHECKING IN: ***Gidleigh Park*** – Take 40 acres of secluded Devon woodlands, add a turn-of-the-century mansion built for comfort and elegance, furnish it in impeccably good taste, and you have *Gidleigh Park.* And if that weren't enough, there's the superb food (nouvelle cuisine that's certainly deserving of its Michelin star) and the wine list (distinguished). Chagford (phone: 06473-2367). Expensive.

Teignworthy – This beautiful stone house in a miniscule hamlet near Chagford is an oasis of peace and quiet in the very heart of the national park. Excellent food and wine are guaranteed — it's also one of the best hotels in England in terms of access to footpaths. Frenchbeer (phone: 06473-3355). Expensive.

Holne Chase – At one time a Victorian hunting lodge, it's now a charming retreat with 14 simple rooms overlooking the valley of the river Dart (where salmon fishing can be arranged on a private mile-long stretch) and one self-catering cottage on the grounds. Holne Chase, near Ashburton (phone: 03643-471). Expensive.

En Route from Dartmoor – Leave the area by way of B3357 southeast to Buckfastleigh. Since it was founded in the late 1800s, monks at Buckfast Abbey have prepared Buckfast Tonic Wine (exported all over the world) and also tended one of the largest honey industries in the country. All the products of this hard work are available at the abbey shop (open daily). The abbey church is open daily, except during services, and an exhibition of the site's history is open daily, March through October. Continue, via A364, to Totnes.

TOTNES: The town looks every bit as medieval as its name suggests. Its steep narrow streets curl up and around themselves, and the timbered and slate-shingled buildings that overhang the main street lean and sag like clowns in a Shakespearean comedy. If you climb the narrow passageway to the church and guildhall, a wonderful old building with a columned porch and frightfully low oak doors, you'll peer down onto the roofs of buildings. Totnes Castle, one of the first to be erected by the conquering Normans, stands near the center of town (open daily, March through October; admission charge), and *Totnes Museum,* in one of the Elizabethan merchant houses, has an interesting collection of local costumes and household goods (open April through October; closed Saturdays and Sundays; admission charge).

TORBAY: Take A385 east from Totnes to Paignton. You are now in Torbay, which comprises the large family resort of Torquay, to the north, and the small fishing port of Brixham, to the south, as well as the small seaside resort of Paignton, in the middle. All are on the shores of Tor Bay, and the 22 miles of coastline that join them, commonly referred to as the "English Riviera," wallow in a Gulf Stream climate, which explains the presence of subtropical vegetation. Many of the palm trees in the area were imported from Australia over 150 years ago.

Torquay, centered around its harbor and marina against a backdrop of Devon's green and rolling hills, has a distinct international ambience. A hive of sporting activity by day and illuminated by night, it is a long way from the days when its beaches and coves were a haven for pirates and smugglers. Many of the villas in the older part of town date from the Napoleonic Wars of the early 19th century, when they were built for officers and their families awaiting orders. Torquay later developed into a fashionable winter holiday resort — a spacious, elegant town famous for its health-giving sea breezes and colorful parks and gardens. More recently, large gracious hotels have appeared on the seafront, along with other amenities and trimmings associated with a modern summer resort. Along with the large chain stores, there are prettier specialty shops — for Devon clotted cream, curiosities, bric-a-brac, and such — lining the narrow streets of the Torre area. The best beaches are Ansteys Cove, which involves a short walk through woodland, and Babbacombe Beach, which sits below Babbacombe, a tiny community made up of only a small cluster of houses.

The appeal of Paignton, made popular by the Victorians, has always been its long, safe beaches (Hellicombe is the most northern, bounded at both ends by small, rocky promontories). During the peak holiday season, the resort is alive with carnivals, regattas, and fetes, which culminate in the annual Children's Week in August. Because of the large family clientele, hotels and guesthouses are less sophisticated here than those in Torquay — the smartest overlook Paignton Sands. Brixham, which concentrates on commercial fishing, is less concerned with tourists, but it still manages to attract a number of holidaymakers. (The three — Torquay, Brixham, and Paignton — have successfully marketed themselves as the "English Riviera.") To absorb Brixham's history, roam the narrow, winding streets between its tiers of cottages and thread your way up and down the steep flights of steps connecting them. Brixham is considered the home of trawling — fishing by a net that drags the sea bottom for its catch. In the past, it was noted for its fleet of sailing trawlers, now, motor trawlers can be seen by the hundreds dotted around the main harbor. All the facts are laid out in the *British Fisheries Museum* on the quayside (open daily, except Sundays, October through May; admission charge).

CHECKING IN: ***Imperial*** – The English Riviera's most luxurious hotel occupies a prestigious position overlooking the harbor. The food is so good, special gastronomic weekends are frequently held. Park Hill Rd., Torquay (phone: 0803-294301). Expensive.

Quayside – Six 17th-century cottages have been combined to form this cozy, comfortable, and highly rated hotel. The front bedrooms have views across the inner and outer harbor as does the candlelit restaurant. King St., Brixham (phone: 08045-55751). Moderate.

En Route from Torbay – Drive south to Kingswear and take a ferry across the river Dart to Dartmouth. Part of the way, from Paignton to Kingswear, is covered by the steam trains of the Paignton and Dartmouth Railway, still a working form of transport for those not in a hurry. It leaves from the British Rail station in Paignton from May through September, and during July and August it is especially crowded with holidaymakers exploring the coast.

DARTMOUTH: In 1147, 164 ships sailed from Dartmouth on the Second Crusade. Some 800 years later, a fleet of 485 American ships left Dartmouth's snug harbor on another crusade, this time to the beaches of Normandy. Between the two events, the town grew and prospered, first from the wine trade with Burgundy, later from cod fishing off the coast of Newfoundland, and whenever it could, from piracy and privateering.

It was the Elizabethans who really left their stamp on this thoroughly nautical town on the estuary of the river Dart. The crooked, elaborately decorated half-timbered buildings in the harbor area make Dartmouth look much the way it must have when Sir Walter Raleigh brought his royally sanctioned booty here. Occupying a commanding position above the harbor is the Royal Naval College, Britain's main naval training center since 1905, while right on the town quay is the Royal Avenue Gardens, a charming reminder of the town's present popularity as a resort. Its amusement park entrance, a blue-and-white iron gate strung with colored lights and topped with a crown of lights, fails to suggest the beautifully kept gardens within, where primroses, crocuses, and daffodils bloom as early as March. Just outside town is Dartmouth Castle, one of Henry VIII's many coastal fortifications (open daily; admission charge) and one of the earliest built specifically for the use of guns. Not much is left of its twin across the mouth of the river, Kingswear Castle (now a private residence), which was abandoned when guns became powerful enough to defend the river entrance from one side alone.

EATING OUT: ***Carved Angel*** – The seafood in this bright and airy restaurant on the quay is outstanding, and no one has been known to complain about the other dishes on its imaginatively French menu. Closed Sunday evenings, Mondays, and January. 2 South Embankment, Dartmouth (phone: 08043-2465). Expensive.

En Route from Dartmouth – About 5 miles south on A379 is Slapton Sands, where thousands of American troops were stationed before the invasion of Normandy. In the middle of the 5-mile-long stretch of sand is a monument erected by the US government, thanking the local people for the use of their beach. Nearby a Sherman tank, believed lost at sea but recovered in 1984, stands as a memorial to the Americans who lost their lives when German warships attacked a practice landing fleet. Here and beyond, you are on the South Hams peninsula, which surrounds the river estuary south of Kingsbridge and juts out to Prawle Point, the most southerly point of England outside of Cornwall.

From Kingsbridge, the direct route west to Plymouth is A379, a 21-mile drive, but if you want to explore the area, you'll find its villages are tiny and linked by high-hedged, narrow lanes whose infrequent passing places make them slow going for motorists. A passenger ferry has crossed the Kingsbridge estuary from East Portlemouth to Salcombe for as long as residents can remember, but drivers must take the long way around, via Kingsbridge. The most spectacular stretch of coastline, between Bolt Head and Bolt Tail, begins south of Salcombe and is owned by the National Trust.

CHECKING IN: ***Buckland-Tout-Saints*** – This country house hotel, a superb example of Queen Anne architecture dating back to the late 17th century, stands in secluded parkland about 2½ miles northeast of Kingsbridge. Finely furnished and elegantly run by the Shephard family, it has 13 rooms, all with bath or shower. Goveton (phone: 0548-3055). Expensive.

Burgh Island – A unique sea-tractor transports guests to this Art Deco establishment's 26-acre tidal island off the coast at Bigbury-on-Sea. (At low tide, you can walk to it.) The hotel has been visited by Noel Coward, Agatha Christie, and the *Beatles;* now it offers self-catering suites with a restaurant and shopping facilities nearby. Burgh Island, Bigbury-on-Sea (phone: 0548-81514). Moderate.

EATING OUT: ***Start Bay Inn*** – Situated at one end of Slapton Sands, this thatched pub with log fires and low-beamed ceilings makes a useful lunchtime stopover, specializing in fish (locally caught) and chips. Portions are served medium, large, or jumbo. Torcross (phone: 0548-580553). Inexpensive.

PLYMOUTH: Anyone driving into Plymouth from the east comes across a curious sight — the ruins of a church in the middle of a traffic roundabout. Charles Church was destroyed in the spring of 1941 during a Nazi raid on the city that left over 1,000 people dead, 70,000 homeless, and most of the city center devastated. The shell of the church was left as a memorial to those who lost their lives, and if at first it seems irreverent to surround a memorial with traffic, on second thought it seems entirely appropriate to see it as part of the daily flow of life.

The raid irrevocably changed the face of this vigorous old port, the second largest city in Britain's southwest (Bristol is first). The postwar center is an excellent shopping area that draws people from all over the region, although, unfortunately, it isn't very handsome. A lot of Plymouth, however, was miraculously spared damage. The Barbican, on an indent of the sea called Sutton Harbor, is where rich Elizabethan merchants built their houses and is now a lively spot full of antiques shops, art galleries, restaurants, and pubs. Elizabethan House, on New Street, has fine furnishings from that period (open daily, Easter through September; admission charge). Nearby is Mayflower Steps, a monument commemorating the sailing of the *Mayflower* in 1620 (it set sail from Southampton, but Plymouth was its last port). At the edge of the Barbican is Prysten House, a 15th-century priory that survived both Henry VIII's purge of the monasteries and Hitler's terrible assault. Open Mondays through Saturdays, April through October, other times by appointment; admission charge.

In contrast to the amiable bustle of the Barbican, the face Plymouth shows the sea is a formidable one. The Citadel, a low gray stone fortress built in the late 1600s by Charles II and still used by the military, sits brooding on the high ground above Plymouth Sound. Its strength has never been tested, perhaps because the sight of it alone is enough to deter any would-be invaders. Sharing the commanding position over the sound is Plymouth's famous Hoe, the broad green where Sir Francis Drake leisurely finished his game of bowls before dealing an ignominious defeat to the Spanish Armada. There's a statue of Sir Francis near the bowling green. At the center of the Hoe is another monument, this one to the thousands of sailors, British and Commonwealth, who were killed in the two world wars. It's a moving tribute, especially apt in this city whose namesakes in the far flung reaches of the Empire number no fewer than 40. Close by, the city's new visitor center, Plymouth Dome, opened in 1989 featuring a dramatic exhibition of the city's history from Elizabethan times to World War II. Through satellite and radar facilities, visitors can observe the ships crossing Plymouth Sound. Open daily; admission charge. Before leaving the Hoe, walk to the edge of the seaward side. Built into the rocky cliffs of the headland is a series of steps and platforms that lead down to an open-air bathing pool jutting out into the sound, a surprising retreat hidden away from the city that buzzes above it.

Several historic homes are within striking distance of Plymouth. Just 3½ miles east of the center (between A38 and A379) is Saltram House, a classic Georgian mansion containing Chippendale furniture, portraits by Sir Joshua Reynolds, and interiors by Robert Adam. (The house is open Sundays through Thursdays and some bank holidays from April through October; gardens are open daily all year; admission charge.) About 10 miles north of Plymouth on high ground at Yelverton with a clear view of distant Plymouth Harbor is Buckland Abbey, Sir Francis Drake's home, originally built as a monastery in the 13th century and later turned into a country house. After extensive refurbishment, a new exhibition on its history opened in July 1988 and some nearby outbuildings were opened to the public for the first time. (The home is open daily from Easter through September and Wednesdays and weekends in winter; admission charge).

Across the river Tamar (which forms the border between Cornwall and Devon), about 14 miles from Plymouth and a bit to the north of Buckland Abbey, is Coteheleat Saltash, an especially fine gray granite house, built between 1485 and 1627, in an exquisite setting of wildflowers and meadows on the river bank. Inside are beautiful furnishings, tapestries, needlework, and armor, and there's also a working 18th-century water mill on the grounds (house open daily except Fridays, April through October; gardens open all year; admission charge). Also across the Tamar, 5 miles west of Plymouth via the Torpoint car ferry, is Antony House, a graceful Queen Anne mansion long — and still — the home of the powerful Carew family, although it now, along with the three houses mentioned earlier, belongs to the National Trust (open Tuesdays through Thursdays and some bank holidays, April through October; admission charge).

En Route from Plymouth – As you cross the Tamar on the road bridge to Saltash, look to your left for the Royal Albert Bridge, a railroad bridge completed in 1859 and one of Isambard Kingdom Brunel's engineering masterpieces. Leave Saltash on A38 and join A387 signposted to East and West Looe, two old fishing towns joined by a bridge over the river Looe. Turn left over the bridge, past the 14th-century St. Nicholas Church, to the steep road down to Looe Bay. Beyond the rocks lies St. George's Island, once a Celtic monastery and now a privately owned bird sanctuary. It is possible to walk along the coast path to Polperro from here (a 4-mile walk), but motorists must either return to the church and turn left past the 500-year-old inn, the *Jolly Sailor,* and take the narrow lane — an extremely steep lane worth taking slowly — past Talland Bay to Polperro, or backtrack farther inland and take A387.

Whichever route is chosen, it's wiser in the busy summer period to park outside the village and walk down the hill into town, since Polperro is not much more than a covey of whitewashed cottages spilling down a ravine on the sea, and its streets were made for horse traffic. The tiny harbor, old houses, and narrow alleyways give it the picture book looks of a quintessential Cornish fishing village. In fact, in the peak season it suffers from an excess of picturesqueness and is overwhelmed by tourists, although it somehow retains its charm.

Leave Polperro by driving back along A387 and bearing left along B3359 and left again to Lostwithiel and onto fast A390 into St. Austell. Or proceed west from Polperro, crossing the estuary of the river Fowey aboard the car ferry from Bodinnick. On the other side, Fowey (pronounced *Foy*) clings to a wooded hillside, descending in a maze of twisting, narrow streets. Details of its history are in the *Noah's Ark Museum* in the town's oldest house on Fore Street and in the *Town Hall Museum* of local history in Trafalgar Square. Nearby Menabilly, set in the woods behind Polridmouth Cove, was the home of Daphne du Maurier and the setting for her novel *Rebecca.* From here take B3082 and A390 to St. Austell.

ST. AUSTELL: Clusters of old buildings, still quietly enjoying the life of a medieval village, are harshly offset by a brand new shopping precinct. The traffic-free center has a fine church of Pentewan stone, an Italianate town hall, and a bustling market place. St. Austell, a mile inland from the bay of the same name, has been the headquarters of the English china clay (kaolin) industry since the mid 18th century. The white quarry mountains tend to dominate the skyline all around the town, and if you stand on Black Head, at one end of St. Austell Bay, and look across to Gribbin Head, at the other end, the sea shimmers with the presence of china clay slurry. *Wheal Martyn Museum,* an open-air museum covering the development of the Cornish china clay industry from 1745, is 4 miles north of St. Austell off A391 at Carthew. Set in a restored clay pit, it houses all kinds of extraction and processing machinery. Open daily, April through October.

St. Austell Bay was once one of the greatest pilchard fishing areas in the country, but this important industry declined quite dramatically in the 1890s, when the pilchards simply stopped coming, possibly because they had been overfished. Now only the old pilchard fishing villages (such as Charlestown, with its Charlestown Shipwreck Centre, Porthpean, and Polkerris) remain, while the "seine house" (where fish were salted and pressed for oil) at Polkerris — at one time Cornwall's largest — stands empty.

CHECKING IN/EATING OUT: ***Alverton Manor*** – Once an elegant manor house and more recently home to a local order of nuns, its tasteful conversion to the highest rated hotel property in Cornwall contains no hint of the monastic life of its former occupants. Not only are its 30 rooms authentically elegant and extremely comfortable, but the kitchen is among the best in western England. A perfect base from which to explore the spectacularly scenic Cornish countryside. Details: Alverton Manor, Tregolls Rd., Truro, Cornwall TR1 1XQ, England (phone: 0872-76633; toll-free from continental US, except New York, 800-322-2403). Expensive.

Pier House – A friendly, family-run 12-bedroom hotel overlooking the harbor front in tiny Charlestown. Its restaurant is the best place for sampling locally caught seafood. Harbour Front, Charlestown (phone: 0726-67955). Inexpensive.

En Route from St. Austell – Take A390 southwest and, just beyond the junction with A39, turn left down A3078 to St. Mawes. Alternatively, drive 5 miles south from St. Austell (via B3273) to Mevagissey, a tiny fishing village once famous as a smugglers' hideaway. Today, it's made up of innocent cottages clinging to a hillside around a pretty little harbor. Commercial fishing is still alive here, but with vacationers in mind, the fishermen also rent boats by the hour. A folk museum is housed in an old boatbuilders' workshop. Open daily, Easter through September; admission charge. There is also a model railway museum, a miniature world of almost 50 trains and over 2,000 other models. Open daily, June through October, and Sundays, November through May; admission charge.

ST. MAWES AND FALMOUTH: Its mild climate isn't all that prompts comparisons between St. Mawes and the French Riviera. It has the same easygoing charm and the same air of a perpetual party. Sitting on the tip of a peninsula in a large sheltered bay, St. Mawes is a perfect yachting and fishing town. Add to this stunning coastal walks, secluded beaches, and subtropical gardens where, as one long-time resident says, "there's nothing as *common* as a palm tree"; and it is easy to understand why the mood is so buoyant. Don't look for countrified charm here, although charm certainly exists in this village of whitewashed cottages ranging along the town quay. Do look for good food and gracious hotels, since well-to-do Britons with a yen for the sea and soft climate have made St. Mawes a sophisticated outpost.

Falmouth, a port and also a resort town, is across the Carrick Roads — as the wide estuary of the river Fal is known — from St. Mawes and linked to it by a pedestrian ferry. Sprawling around attractive, wooded rivers and creeks, secluded coves, and subtropical gardens, it is one of the most popular towns on the Cornish Riviera, "discovered" by Sir Walter Raleigh, who recognized its potential as a natural harbor. The deepwater anchorage was once the permanent home of many craft, including the post office's sail and steam packet ships, tea clippers, and windjammers; even now, one of the most modern coast guard services, the Maritime Rescue Coordination Centre, supervises rescues across the Atlantic as far south as Spain. In the older part of town is Custom House Quay, with the great neoclassical Custom House overlooking the King's Pipe, a chimney used to destroy confiscated tobacco, and the *Maritime Museum* (open Sundays through Fridays) includes a small steam tug (open Easter through September). From Falmouth it is possible to take a steamer up the Fal to the ancient high tide port of Truro, Cornwall's cathedral city, or south, down along the coast, then up the Helford River.

Falmouth and St. Mawes share a pair of castles built by Henry VIII. St. Mawes

Castle, its central tower surrounded by three battlemented semicircles, sits on a knoll outside the village of St. Mawes. Unlike Pendennis Castle, its twin at Falmouth, which resisted Parliamentarian troops for 5 months, St. Mawes was never the site of any battles and thus is in near-perfect repair. The view from Pendennis is one of the best — on one side the beaches, on the other, the docks and town. (Both castles are open daily all year; admission charge.)

The gardens that flourish around the Carrick roads are unusually exotic partly because the climate is mild and partly because Falmouth was the first port of call for English ships returning from long voyages, and for hundreds of years sailors brought back plants from the farthest flung reaches of the world. When the English turned their considerable gardening talents to these rare plants, they developed an extraordinary number of subspecies. The church grounds of St. Just-in-Roseland (4 miles outside St. Mawes and linked by coastal and inland footpaths) are a splendid garden where date palms, bamboo, camellias, rhododendrons, azaleas, Chilian fire bushes, and magnolias flourish alongside England's own bluebells, snowdrops, and primroses. North of St. Mawes (4 miles south of Truro at Feock) is Trelissick Garden, a beautifully tended woodland on the river Fal (open daily, March through October; admission charge); 3 miles southwest of Falmouth is Penjerrick Garden (open Wednesdays and Sundays from March through September; admission charge); and 4 miles southwest is Glendurgan Garden, on the Helford River (open Mondays, Wednesdays, and Fridays, March through October; admission charge), each with enough varieties of sub-tropical and indigenous plants to satisfy the most avid gardener.

CHECKING IN: ***Tresanton*** – This lovably overgrown, white vine-covered cottage combines the sophistication and the country charm of St. Mawes in one delightful package. On the coastal road, it has sub-tropical gardens spilling down its hillside toward the bay and a private beach. Sailing and water skiing are possible. All of the 21 bedrooms have private baths; breakfast and dinner are included in the room price, and the food is delicious. Closed mid-November to late March. Lower Castle Rd., St. Mawes (phone: 0326-270544). Moderate to inexpensive.

Rising Sun – It's hard to imagine a quainter, cozier, more gracious hotel than this. The front terrace, which fills with the overflow from its congenial pub in warm weather, faces the town quay, and guests who get a room in the front will fall asleep to the sound of the tide slapping against the harbor wall. Some rooms are even more romantically positioned, in converted fishermen's cottages across the road. From the *Rising Sun*'s justly renowned kitchen comes crème brulée, a creamy caramel-custard confection which to taste once is to yearn for forever. The Square, St. Mawes (phone: 0326-270233). Inexpensive.

THE LIZARD AND WEST PENWITH: It would take a jaded traveler indeed to resist the urge to travel to the ends of the earth, and in England the earth ends most spectacularly at the two tips of a broad stirrup of land called the Lizard and West Penwith. The Lizard, as the Cornish peninsula south of the Helford River is known, terminates in England's southernmost point: Lizard Point. West Penwith, the peninsula farther west, stretches to England's westernmost point: Land's End. Despite the summer crowds that converge on these popular spots, they are, nonetheless, impressive examples of nature's handiwork. The Lizard ends in cliffs of brilliant serpentine — olive green rock veined with red and purple and polished by the sea and wind — while Land's End meets the sea with granite cliffs and a wash of shiny black boulders. Go early in the morning or at sunset to avoid the crowds. Or better yet, park a mile or so away and approach the spots on foot via one of the coastal paths. Note, in passing, that this coast is a notorious shipwrecker: Ferocious seas have slammed many a vessel onto its rocks, and more than one village pub exhibits disaster photos on its walls.

Supposedly, a wreck has been recorded for every eighth of a mile of coastline, and the restless ghosts of dead seamen roam the cliffs because in olden days those washed ashore could not be buried in consecrated ground. Reputedly, earlier Cornishmen caused some of the wrecks by luring ships with misleading lights, and the coast was well known for hosting smugglers (or "fair traders," as they preferred to call themselves).

Just 10 miles from the cliffs of Lizard Point in the northern part of the Lizard peninsula is scenery of a different, but equally pleasing, order — wooded coves leading down to the river Helford. Helford village is a completely charming place on one of these sylvan inlets. The *Shipwrights Inn,* a pretty pub with sunny terraces jutting out over a brook, is a perfect spot to while away a summer evening, especially over a plate of seafood.

On the main road from the Lizard to West Penwith, A394, is Helston, a pleasant market town best known for its Flora Day celebration, when the whole town turns out, flower bedecked and beribboned, to "furry" dance through the streets to a 1,500-year-old processional tune. The date, in early May, is well before the annual influx of vacationers, so the holiday is still mostly an event for townsfolk. On the edge of town, Flambards Theme Park includes a full-size indoor re-creation of a Victorian village. Open daily, Easter through October; admission charge. Also, 3 miles north of Helston on B3297 is the Poldark Mine, an old tin mine that has been converted into an industrial museum (open daily from April through October; admission charge).

Midway between the two peninsulas, and 5 miles northwest of Helston, is Godolphin House, built in the 16th century by one of England's most powerful families, whose fortune came from the rich tin veins in Cornwall (open Thursdays in May and June, Tuesdays and Thursdays from July through September; admission charge). The castle that seems to rise out of the water like a vision as you approach West Penwith is real. It's St. Michael's Mount, once a monastery, later a fortress, and for the last 300 years the home of the St. Aubyn family. It's now owned by the National Trust and can be visited Mondays through Fridays from June through October; Mondays, Wednesdays, and Fridays from November through May; also on Tuesdays in April and May; admission charge.

Penzance, West Penwith's largest town, is a popular resort, warmer year-round than most places in the country and near a broad swath of beach. For that reason, it is crammed with the less appealing aspects of tourism, such as tedious souvenir stores, but the old part of town is attractive, with elegant Regency and Georgian houses and more modest fishermen's cottages. Down quiet Chapel Street (which once bustled with mule trains loaded with copper for ships) stands a remarkable Egyptian house, a whimsical design of the 1820s that is now run by the National Trust as a shop and information center (closed Sundays). At the sea end of the street, opposite the *Admiral Benbow* restaurant, is the *Nautical Museum,* which contains several items salvaged from local wreck diving. The town is laden with memories — Admiral Nelson's victory at the Battle of Trafalgar was first announced at the *Union* hotel as ships were seen racing up the channel, and Gilbert and Sullivan's *The Pirates of Penzance* perpetuates stories of piracy in this area's past.

Penzance is only 10 miles from Land's End, where a new visitors' complex has opened with an information center, 34-room hotel, exhibitions about shipwrecks and Cornwall, craft workshops, and gift shops. Open daily; admission charge (phone: 0736-871501). However, Land's End and the splendor of the Cornish coast are only part of West Penwith's attraction. This westernmost tip of England is an open-air museum of ancient Britons. There are dozens of stone circles (most, for some arcane reason, having 9 or 19 stones), hut circles, and burial mounds. Near Lamorna, south of Penzance, is a fascinating formation called the Pipers and the Merry Maidens — two tall upright stones and a circle of 19 stones. Local legend has it that the village girls were caught dancing on the Sabbath, and they and their musicians were turned to stone as a punishment. Carn Euny, near Crows-an-Wra (Witches' Cross), southwest of Penzance, and Chysauster, northwest of Penzance, are two well-preserved Iron Age villages.

If you want to see the source of much Cornish wealth, head for Pendeen, on the west coast, where you can visit Geevor Mine, a working tin mine that gives guided tours (open daily, April through October; admission charge). Take a look at Cornwall's other mainstay — fishing — just south of Penzance at Newlyn (once a Victorian artists' colony and now the largest fishing port in the southwest; much of the delicious fish eaten in this part of the country comes from here) and at Mousehole, a granity fishing village about 5 miles down the coast. Farther along the coast, at Porthcurno, is *Minack Theatre,* an amphitheater built into the granite cliffs overlooking the sea. The season, which runs from June to September, includes a variety of theater productions — from Gilbert and Sullivan to Maxim Gorki — by different repertory groups. The setting is nothing short of spectacular, but be sure to wear warm clothes.

CHECKING IN: ***Pollurian*** – Set in 12 acres of gardens with a spectacular cliff-top position high above its own sandy beach, this 42-room hotel has been owned and run by the Francis family since the 1940s. Facilities include a heated pool, tennis courts, riding, putting, indoor leisure club, and fishing and sea trips in the hotel's boats. Mullion (phone: 0326-240421). Expensive.

Lamorna Cove – This hotel takes its name from the tranquil wooded cove over which it perches. Although the modern additions don't do justice to the original granite house or the setting, the hotel is very comfortable. Fresh fish, of which there is an unending supply from nearby Newlyn, is a specialty. Lamorna (phone: 0736-731411). Moderate.

ISLES OF SCILLY: The often rough 2½-hour boat passage from Penzance to St. Mary's, the largest of the Isles of Scilly, prompted one wag to describe the islands as a paradise that can only be reached through purgatory. Now, thanks to the 20-minute helicopter flight, you can go straight to heaven, in this case a group of 150-plus islands 30 miles off the Cornish coast. Connected by shallow straits treacherously studded with outcroppings of rock and reef, the islands have a schizophrenic nature. Their northwestern sides are usually bleak, windswept plains of gorse and heather. But the sheltered southern sides support vast fields of flowers — daffodils, jonquils, narcissus, anemones, iris, tulips, and lilies. Flowers are the main business of the 2,000 people who live in the Isles of Scilly: more than 1,000 tons of cut flowers are exported from here every year.

Only five of the islands — St. Mary's, Tresco, St. Martin's, Bryher, and St. Agnes — are inhabited. The rest are home to seals, puffins, gannets, kittiwakes, and other ocean birds. (The rent for the entire island chain in the 15th century was six and eightpence — or 50 puffins.) Their quiet sandy beaches are perfect for picnicking or sunbathing. No wonder former Prime Minister Harold Wilson chose these islands as a refuge from the political hurly-burly of 10 Downing Street.

Travel from St. Mary's to Tresco, Bryher, St. Martin's, or St. Agnes is remarkably easy, as are visits to the outlying rocks to watch colonies of gulls, cormorants, oyster catchers, curlews, and the occasional grey heron, plus seals and, if lucky, playful dolphins. Every morning during the long summer months, the dozen or so ferrymen gather on St. Mary's Hugh Town Quay (known locally as Rat Island, a reference to its earlier residents) to decide on a range of options (depending on the state of the tide and the weather) and then disperse to call on the hotels to inform visitors of where they can go that day. The flotilla of boats leaves at 10 in the morning and again in the afternoon, carrying anywhere from a dozen to 70 people, most of them bound for the 20 or more brilliant beaches that could easily have been lifted from the West Indies yet miraculously manage to remain uncrowded even at the height of summer.

St. Mary's, besides being the largest island in the chain, has the distinction of having what is probably the most inexpensive and quickly constructed castle in Britain — Star Castle, built by Sir Francis Godolphin in 1593 for under £1,000 (about $2,000). The island of Tresco draws the most visitors. The gardens at Tresco Abbey contain a staggering variety of plants — between 3,000 and 4,000 — the lifetime achievement of botanical zealot Augustus Smith, whose descendants still hold the lease on the island (open daily; admission charge). Also on Tresco is the *Valhalla Maritime Museum* (open daily from April through October), which has a fascinating collection of figureheads from shipwrecks, relics of the days when Scilly islanders made their living scavenging from the many ships that went aground on the dangerous reefs in the vicinity. If you stop for a pint of beer at the island's *New Inn,* take a look at the wall chart showing the surrounding savage seas as the graveyard of some 2,000 ships: vessels with salt from Spain, silks from Italy, elephant tusks from Africa, hides from Argentina, cotton from Galveston, and tea from Fuchow. To absorb more of the islands' character, visit Longstone Heritage Centre on St. Mary's, with its garden of Scillonian flora, an exhibition on the history of the daffodil (open Easter through October; admission charge).

CHECKING IN: *St. Martin's* – Opened in 1989, this is the only hotel on St. Martin's (which has just 60 permanent residents). The cottage-style hotel has 24 individually designed rooms, and the setting in the cove by the sea is suberb. There's an indoor pool and sub-tropical gardens. St. Martin's, Isles of Scilly (phone: 0720-22092). Expensive.

ST. IVES: Ferry back to Penzance, from where B3311 slices across West Penwith to St. Ives. Formerly a fishing town, it is now primarily a seaside resort that has retained its old-fangled Cornish looks because as its pilchard industry declined, a small army of potters, painters, and sculptors moved in, setting up studios and galleries along the narrow tangle of cobbled streets. The town was already established as an artists' colony in the 19th century, when such painters as James McNeill Whistler and Walter Sickert set the fashion. In the 20th century, the sculptor Barbara Hepworth spent most of her working life here (the *Barbara Hepworth Museum* in her home on Barnoon Hill is well worth a visit; closed Sundays, except July and August; admission charge) and potter Bernard Leach established one of the most famous potteries in Europe here — students still flock from all over the world to learn their craft from his successors. The *St. Ives Arts Festival* is held annually for 2 weeks beginning the first Saturday in September, but for those in search of sun and sand, there are Porthmeor Beach, with its fine surfing, the smaller Porthgwidden Beach, with its chalets and café, and the long run of Porthminster Beach, with its gentle slope seaward.

En Route from St. Ives – It's best to meander up the rocky north coast of Cornwall. No single road follows the coastline, but there are secondary roads that loop off the main road (A30, which runs about 5 miles inland) to hug the coast for 5 to 10 miles before rejoining it. Newquay, a popular and congested summer resort some 30 miles up the coast from St. Ives, has a fine stretch of beach; in fact, huge Atlantic rollers guarantee the best surfing in Britain. For those still active but uninterested in such sport, there are spectacular cliff walks to be enjoyed, each rocky promontory more interesting than the last. Towan Head, the promontory separating Newquay Bay and Fistral Bay, boasts a small, castellated tower and chapel belonging to a local family, and there are burial mounds at Pentire Point at the other end of Fistral Bay, which prove that prehistoric man thought this a good vantage point, too.

Just past Newquay, take the coast road, B3276, to Bedruthan Steps, near Park Head. Here, the mammoth chunks of the cliff that have tumbled onto the wide strand of beach below are said to be the stepping stones of a Cornish giant, Bedruthan. When the tide is in, Bedruthan's Steps jut out from the white agitation of the sea like bits of black coral strung on a necklace, but when the tide is out, you can explore the rock pools and caverns around them by descending a dramatic cliff staircase. Continue on B3276 another 8 miles to Padstow.

PADSTOW: From June to September, Padstow, with its compact horseshoe of a harbor and pleasant tangle of streets, rings with the holiday fun of summer folk who come to fish, swim, and sail in the waters of the north Cornish coast and the river Camel. But on May 1, before the season gets under way, the town holds its own celebration, the Hobby Horse or, as it is locally known, 'Obby 'Oss, a day when a huge, fierce hobby horse prances through the streets in the midst of singing and dancing villagers. According to one story, the 'Obby 'Oss started when the village women, whose husbands were off fighting the French in one of the numerous wars between the English and their channel neighbors, fashioned an enormous stallion to scare away enemy raiders. However, most think the raucous celebration has its roots in earlier pagan times. Clearly, there is a strain of unrepentant wit — pagan or otherwise — in Padstow: One of the bench ends in the 13th- and 14th-century church shows the devil disguised as a fox, preaching to a flock of geese.

EATING OUT: ***The Seafood Restaurant*** **–** Directly beside the quay stands this light, airy, plant-filled dining find. The tempting menu might offer a seafood salad garnished with violets, with winkles, or lemon sole with scallions and ginger. And if crème brulée ice cream is available, don't hold back. There are 8 bedrooms with private bath; Nos. 5 and 6 on the third floor have big terraces overlooking the docks where the fishing boats tie up. Riverside, Padstow (phone: 0841-532485). Expensive.

En Route from Padstow – A few miles southeast of the town of Bodmin on B3268 is Lanhydrock, a grandiose Tudor house built in the 17th century but almost entirely destroyed by fire and rebuilt according to its original plan in the 1880s (the long gallery remains from the earlier structure). It is set in meticulously tended grounds and rolling parkland, and never were the fruits of the Empire more impressively displayed. The elaborate kitchens — with numerous larders — and lavish baths are especially fascinating insights into that exceedingly wealthy time. The house and gardens are open daily from April through October.

BODMIN MOOR: An Area of Outstanding Natural Beauty north and east of Bodmin, Bodmin Moor reverberates with almost as many legends as the more famous moor in neighboring Devon. Dozmary Pool, a shallow tarn in the center of the moor, is supposedly the pool (one of three) into which Sir Bedivere threw Excalibur, at King Arthur's request. Nearby at Bolventor is *Jamaica Inn,* the scene of Daphne du Maurier's tale of smugglers and pirates. And there are holy wells — at St. Neot on the southern edge, and, on the northern edge, at St. Clether and Altarnun, whose well is reputed to cure madness by the near drowning of the sufferer.

Driving across the bare brown hills broken only by tors, it is easy to see how legends attach themselves to these spots. A few minor roads penetrate the southeast corner of the moor, but to get to Rough Tor (pronounce "Rough" to rhyme with "now") and Brown Willy, the highest points affording the best views, it is necessary to circle the moor and come up behind it at Camelford, on its northwestern edge. From here you can drive to a car park at the foot of Rough Tor and climb up or hike on to Brown Willy, a mile away. Or take the turnoff to the left just before you get to Rough Tor. It leads to an eerie relic of modern times — the ruins of a World War II Royal Air Force base at Davidstow — and could be a scene out of any number of contemporary doomsday stories: abandoned runways, control towers, all the paraphernalia of modern technology left to decay along with the crude barrows and hut circles of ancient Britons.

Then, just to balance the vision of life left by the opulence of Lanhydrock, stop in at the *North Cornwall Museum* at Camelford, which has a reconstruction of a Cornish cottage (open from April through September; closed Sundays; admission charge).

CHECKING IN: ***Arundell Arms*** – This former coaching inn covered with Virginia creeper is well worth a slight detour east of Bodmin Moor (about 4 miles east of Launceston via A30): Log fires blaze away, the floors are laid with dark blue slate, and the culinary offerings are of international standard. The inn offers excellent salmon fishing, since it owns the fishing rights to 20 miles of the river Tamar. Lifton (phone: 0566-84666). Expensive.

NORTH CORNWALL COAST: It would be a Herculean task to find any part of the Cornish coast not worth seeing, but there is a 20-mile stretch of coast north of the river Camel that contains dramatic cliffs, surfing beaches, sand dunes, historic spots, and exquisite villages and is particularly worthwhile.

From Wadebridge, at the mouth of the Camel estuary about 8 miles east of Padstow, take B3314 about 2 miles to the turnoff to Rock. Travel another 3 miles along this unnumbered road (past this not terribly attractive resort town) to a car park at Daymer Bay. The dunes here are marvelous, covered with clumps of coarse grass and just the place to find dog-walkers and families on weekend outings. There is a golf course along the coast, and in the middle of one of the fairways stands St. Enodoc Church, less curious now, even given its fairly odd surroundings, than it was 100 years ago, when it was half buried in sand and the vicar was forced to crawl in through the roof to deliver the sermon; it is hard to imagine who was there to hear it.

Stick to the unnumbered coast road by following signs to Trebetherick, Polzeath (an excellent surfing beach), Pentireglaze, and Port Quin. According to local lore, all the men of Port Quin were lost at sea in one accident, and shortly thereafter, the women mysteriously disappeared as well. The abandoned village — four stone cottages that sit precariously over the water at the end of a steep cove and an old stone barn next to a tumbling stream — is now in the hands of the National Trust and is a lovely, quiet spot.

Just a few miles from Port Quin is Port Isaac, an old corn port and modern-day fishing village that you literally descend into. The streets tumble down to a postage stamp of a beach where visitors pay to leave their cars in summer (the only tidal car park in Britain and hence only for those with an accurate sense of timing). The color-washed houses seem to be piled one on top of the other in the narrow valley — one of the streets is even called Squeezibelly Alley because a mere 18 inches separate one wall from the other. In the very center is The Birdcage, a delightful high, narrow house owned by the National Trust, and right on the harbor wall is the *Golden Lion* pub, a congenial spot from which to watch the tide slowly creep in.

At the end of another steep valley about 10 miles up the coast is Trebarwith Strand, where massive fingers of sculpted black rock, pink-veined and highly polished, lead down to a broad swath of beach that during high tide is completely covered.

From here it is just a mile or so to Tintagel, possibly the most visited spot in Cornwall, although the town itself is rather tacky and unattractive. What draws the year-round crowds is Tintagel Castle, the ruins of a 12th-century dwelling and 6th-century monastery where legend has it that King Arthur (the mythical figure who has fascinated and inspired the English soul for 14 centuries) was born (open daily; admission charge). Even if you don't subscribe to the story, Tintagel is worth a stop. Right on the edge of a rocky promontory, the castle ruins are dramatically beautiful. And if you follow the causeway to the castle and stand on the ramparts looking out to sea, it is hard not to feel a shiver of magic and history come together.

What Tintagel town lacks in charm, Boscastle, just 3 miles on, offers in spades. Boscastle is a cozy village sheltered in a deep valley that is entered from a ridge running along the valley wall. The dark stone buildings and the snug harbor give the village a serious, settled mien, not likely to be altered by the excesses of tourism. And as a conservation area, Boscastle will probably remain that way. The old *Cobweb* pub, though it has lost much of its spooky ambience, is also worth a visit.

CHECKING IN: ***Port Gaverne*** **–** A peaceful restored 17th-century inn tucked into a tiny inlet of the same name, only a few yards from the sea. It's owned by an American, Fred Ross. Closed in February. Near Port Isaac (phone: 0208-880244). Moderate.

Tredethy Country **–** In a spacious 16th-century manor house facing an expansive patchwork of fields, sheep pastures, and woods, this friendly hotel has large, pleasant rooms, a swimming pool and redwood solarium, and 9 acres of grounds in which to wander. Helland Bridge, near Bodmin (phone: 020884-262). Moderate to inexpensive.

Bridge House **–** This 17th-century stone house on Boscastle Harbor offers small attractive rooms, a cheerful ambience, and a most charming location. Bed and breakfast only. Boscastle (phone: 08405-477). Inexpensive.

CLOVELLY: The B3263 from Boscastle leads to the A39 coast road. Unless you want to detour to Bude, continue around Bude Bay and across the Cornwall–Devon border and Hartland Point to Clovelly, 10 miles beyond the border. This delightful village is so quaint, charming, and perfectly picturesque — an unbroken line of shuttered and flower-bedecked cottages down a steep, cobbled street to the harbor — you can't quite believe it isn't contrived, but Clovelly isn't, although it is on the map for every tourist bus coming to the Devon coast. It is probably best to avoid it during the day in July and August, but if you go in the early morning or evening, you'll find simply a beautiful village going about its business. No cars are allowed; visitors and villagers alike have to leave them at a car park at the top of the hill. You might enjoy a stop at *Gladys Friend's* tea room; otherwise, the main activity in Clovelly is strolling down to the quay and making the arduous climb back up; it is steep, so be sure to wear flat shoes.

NORTH DEVON COAST AND EXMOOR FOREST: Continue touring the North Devon coast by following A39 through Bideford to Barnstaple, from where A361 leads north to Ilfracombe, once a port and shipyard, now a popular resort. With its abundance of small hotels with similar sounding names (Golden Sands, Sandy Cove, Cove Haven) and imposing Victorian hotels daringly perched on the city's magnificent cliffs, Ilfracombe has a certain period charm.

Leaving Ilfracombe, take A399 east, a road that for about 8 miles follows a beautiful stretch of coast. Just past Combe Martin, a not very pretty resort town, take an unnumbered road to *Hunter's Inn* and Trentishoe. The variety of landscapes this road covers in a few short miles will make your head spin. First it follows a ridge above gentle green downs dotted with prosperous-looking farms. Then, suddenly, you're on the loneliest coast road in the world: wild moorland, raw against the sea wind, stretches on either side. Press on, for within another mile or so the road runs along the top of a deep, wooded combe. At the bottom of this serene valley lies the door of *Hunter's Inn,* a gabled and Alpinesque inn popular with tourists and a gathering spot for the hunt. The spot is unarguably beautiful and a cool beer on the inn's terrace, in the company of the resident peacocks, is almost mandatory.

Lynmouth, about 5 miles farther, is a pretty resort village encompassed by the sheer cliffs of the Lyn River Valley. It requires steady nerves and reliable brakes to take the direct road from Lynton, a larger town that literally hovers 500 feet above Lynmouth. It is a vertiginous drop, and the three sand-filled offshoots along the road — escape roads for runaway cars — probably see their share of business. Romantic poet Percy Bysshe Shelley lived here for a while, although his cottage no longer exists.

There are two spectacular drives out of Lynmouth. One is along B3223 inland, following the high curving ridge of the East Lyn River valley to Watersmeet, where the East Lyn and the Hoar Oak waters meet. Much of this land is owned by the National Trust, which has marked several nature trails through the dense woods of the valleys. The other drive is along the coast on A39, up Countisbury Hill (as demanding of a car's engine as the road into Lynton was of its brakes). Superlatives only suffice to describe the view. Bracken- and gorse-covered hills break suddenly at black cliffs, and in the distance looms Foreland Point, at 900 feet the tallest cliffs in England.

Porlock, about 12 miles east of Lynmouth on A39 and across the Somerset border, is utterly unlike most southwest sea towns that either cling to the edge of cliffs or shelter in narrow coves. Occupying a broad, sea level plain that opens up in the Exmoor Hills, it's a sweet little place with a sleepy, satisfied air. Porlock Weir, about 2½ miles from town, is a long curving beach of white boulders and pebbles.

Stretching south of this area is Exmoor Forest, a forest in the ancient English sense (meaning land owned by the king and subject to his hunting laws). Anyone expecting dense woods throughout this parcel of hills in northeast Devon and west Somerset is likely to be disappointed, however. In fact, at one time early in the 19th century, a royal commission found only 37 trees in all of Exmoor. There are more trees now, but Exmoor is still more moor and farmland than forest, full of ancient relics, tors, wild red deer, and its famous ponies. Now a 265-square-mile national park, it includes the length of coast from the vicinity of Ilfracombe all the way to Porlock and beyond, but its heart is at Exford, a pretty spot and a good center for fishing, hiking, or horseback riding. Oare, near the Somerset–Devon border, is at the head of Doone Valley, the setting for R. D. Blackmore's story, *Lorna Doone.* Doone Valley and the surrounding area are indeed lovely but, sadly, have been commercialized.

CHECKING IN: ***Simonsbath House*** – In a sheltered valley in the heart of Exmoor, this 17th-century house has 8 pretty bedrooms and a well-regarded menu featuring early English recipes. Simonsbath (phone: 064383-259). Moderate.

Yeoldon House – This rambling Victorian house on the edge of Bideford has been very ably converted to an attractive hotel. The 10 rooms are bright and comfortable, and the English and continental cooking do justice to local produce and fresh fish. Durrant La., Northam, near Bideford (phone: 02372-74400). Moderate.

Heddon's Gate – Perfectly poised close to the sea in the midst of the national park, this 13-room country house has a well-deserved reputation for good food and lodging and is popular with wildlife lovers. Closed from mid-November to Easter. Heddon's Mouth, Parracombe (phone: 05983-313). Inexpensive.

En Route from the North Devon Coast and Exmoor Forest – Around the Somerset town of Dunster (8 miles east of Porlock), the moors give way to soft green meadows backed by even softer hills where clusters of houses linked by ivy-draped walls smugly sit. Dunster itself is a lovely town in a peerless setting, but it is very crowded in summer and is best seen off-season. Dunster Castle, occupying a knoll on the edge of town, has been the home of the Luttrell family for 600 years and was the object of both Royalist and Parliamentarian attacks in the Civil War (open Saturdays through Wednesdays from April through October; the gardens are open daily; admission charge).

Five miles east of Dunster on A39 in a tranquil setting called Flowery Valley is Cleeve Abbey, built by Cistercian monks in the 12th century. It was spared the full wrath of Henry VIII's dissolution of the monasteries, and although the church no longer exists, the gatehouse, refectory, and dormitory are beautifully intact (open daily; admission charge). Continue on A39 another 10 miles or so to Nether Stowey, a village nestling on the eastern slopes of the Quantock Hills, where Samuel Taylor Coleridge wrote *The Rime of the Ancient Mariner.* (For a time William Wordsworth and his sister Dorothy lived about 4 miles away at Holford.) Coleridge's cottage, now owned by the National Trust, opens its parlor doors Tuesdays through Thursdays and Sundays from April through September; admission charge.

The A39 cuts across a broad basin of land between the Quantock and Mendip hills called the Somerset levels, low marshy land reclaimed from the sea over the centuries. Somerton and Glastonbury, about 15 miles inland, were, until the 17th century, islands, and the sea, at high wind and high tide, can still flood these towns. Indeed, it's thought that Somerset takes its name (summer settlers or settlers by the sea lakes) from this region, because during the summer the lagoons would dry up, leaving behind fertile tidal land for grazing. Early inhabitants would drive cattle and sheep down to the plain for the season and then return to the hills when winter brought more flooding.

GLASTONBURY: About 20 miles east of Nether Stowey is Glastonbury, where the strands of early Christianity and English national identity meet and intertwine. Christ himself is said to have built the church that later became the most powerful abbey in the country, and it was to this sacred spot, the fabled Isle of Avalon, that King Arthur and Queen Guinevere were brought to be buried. The long and rich history of Glastonbury and nearby South Cadbury, thought to be Arthur's Camelot, is discussed in *Ancient Monuments and Ruins,* DIVERSIONS.

CHECKING IN: ***George and Pilgrims*** – Many a pilgrim has bedded down for the night at this venerable old hotel, and although it hasn't lost an ounce of the character it has acquired over the years, it has managed to incorporate all the comforts a modern traveler demands. For a real treat, ask for a room with a four-poster bed. 1 High St., Glastonbury (phone: 0458-31146). Moderate.

WELLS: This little town basks on the sunny side of the Mendip Hills about 6 miles up the road from Glastonbury. What makes it a city is its cathedral, an early-English-style church whose elaborately carved west front has been awing visitors for centuries. Inside, of less divine purpose perhaps but of spirited inspiration, is the Wells Clock, an enchanting timepiece made by a Glastonbury monk, Peter Lightfoot, in the 14th century. A carved figure of a man announces the quarter hour by kicking his heels against two bells, and four mounted knights, who charge out and knock each other off their steeds, bring in the hour.

CHEDDAR CAVES: Under the Mendip Hills that tower over the Somerset levels is a labyrinth of caves eaten out of the soft limestone hills by constant flooding. For thousands of years, and until as late as the mid-19th century, many of these caves were inhabited by people. Adventurous spelunkers still explore the underground streams and roads, and thousands of tourists visit the larger caves, Cheddar Caves, near Cheddar, and Wookey Hole, near Wells. Cheddar Gorge, a deep limestone cleft through the Mendips, offers a scenic drive, but is terribly congested in July and August; open daily. The town of Cheddar, home of the most famous English cheese, more recently has become the center of a thriving industry growing strawberries and anemones, which flourish on the sunny sheltered slopes of the Mendips.

From the Cheddar Caves, it's a 30-mile ride to Bristol. (For a complete description of the city, its sights, hotels, and restaurants, see *Bristol,* THE CITIES.)

Southern England

Visitors prepared for a tight little island of narrow, high-hedged roads threaded through a patchwork of tiny fields, orchards, and woods are often surprised by the part of England that lies between the upper reaches of the Thames and the English Channel. Because here, where a subterranean convulsion millions of years ago threw up folds of chalk, limestone, clay, and sand, are some of England's wide open spaces, without a building in sight. There are no mountains or gorges in these lowlands between London and the coasts of West Sussex and Hampshire, yet broad vistas unfold. Expanses of heather sweep the land, purple in late summer, splashed with yellow gorse in spring, plains of grass and corn stretch prairielike to the horizon, and the great whale back of the South Downs — the range of chalkland running parallel to the coast — rolls across the two counties, sheep cropped and sprinkled with wild flowers.

Three times in prehistory this land lay beneath the sea and today it still propels us irresistibly towards the water. The coast of the English Channel, much wider here than at its bottleneck entering the Straits of Dover, is gentler and less dramatic than it is farther east. The chalk, laid down by the broken and powdered shells of primitive crustacea when the land was submerged, does not fling itself against the waves in the white walls seen at Dover and Beachy Head. Instead it approaches the sea down "chines," or ravines, carved through the soft, low hills by time, and there are more stretches of soft sand at the seaside. The only really challenging obstacle between Brighton and Bournemouth are the Needles, those white pinnacles rearing up like icebergs off the most westerly point of the Isle of Wight, where a red-and-white-striped lighthouse warns mariners not to stray too close.

The rivers of Sussex and Hampshire — among them the Ouse, Adur, and Arun, the Test, Stour, and the Avon — do not rush down to the sea but ripple gently, inviting anglers and others to linger on their banks. Between Southampton Water, a tidal estuary into which the Test, Itchen, and Hamble flow, and the old town of Christchurch, on the estuaries of the Avon and the Stour, 90,000 acres of untamed heath, bog, and woodland stretch back into the hinterland. Known as the New Forest, it has been a wildlife preserve for 900 years, since William the Conqueror decreed that any commoners who so much as startled a deer in his hunting ground should have their eyes put out.

Later, great oaks from this forest were felled and carted and rolled to the slipways where men o' war were built, the "hearts of oak" that defended England against invaders and enforced her sovereign rule over a worldwide empire on which "the sun never set." After William I, no invader succeeded in overcoming the English, but the French remained a great threat for centuries. Henry VIII was watching his fleet do battle with them off Southsea when his flagship, the *Mary Rose,* inexplicably went down, and the martello towers that march along the Hampshire coast from Sussex are visual reminders of the fear of Napoleon's fleets.

In 1940, Hitler threatened, but never came. Four years later the whole of the region became one vast military camp, ammunition dump, and aircraft carrier as the Allies, under the supreme command of General Dwight Eisenhower, prepared Operation Overlord, a plan to invade Europe and free it from the Nazi yoke. On June 6, 1944 — D-Day — British and American forces under the command of Field Marshal B. L. Montgomery landed on the beaches of Normandy. Operation Overlord has become part of the history and legend of southern England, along with the battles of centuries past. Museums and galleries enshrine it. There is even an *Overlord Embroidery* to rival the *Bayeux Tapestry,* 41 feet longer than the 11th-century version.

Although London's commuter belt extends into parts of Hampshire and West Sussex, the region is less dominated by the capital than is southeast England. Hundreds of thousands of its inhabitants look to their livelihoods in the new industries that have grown up around the 20th-century cities of Portsmouth, Southampton, and Bournemouth. Tourism is increasingly important. The ancient cities of Arundel, Winchester, and Chichester are easily reached on day trips from London by car or train, as are the seaside resorts of Worthing, Littlehampton, Bognor Regis, and Bournemouth.

Such is the decline of the British Empire and the navy that once ruled the waves, that the harbor of Portsmouth is now more given over to sailing and windsurfing than warships, and there are more day cruisers and motor yachts than merchantmen on Southampton Water. Splendid natural harbors — Chichester, Christchurch, and Poole — abound on this coast, and they are crammed with small boats. Evidently, John Masefield's words "I must down to the seas again, to the lonely sea and the sky. . . . " still strike a chord. It was, after all, in 1851, on the Isle of Wight, a green and pleasant chunk of England adrift a few miles offshore, that the America's Cup (then worth a mere hundred guineas) was born.

Until World War II and for a short time thereafter, the gateway through which most overseas visitors reached southern England was Southampton, which saw the regular arrival and departure of ocean liners loaded with film stars and millionaires. Today the only transatlantic tourists who arrive by sea are the minority who choose *Cunard's Queen Elizabeth 2* in preference to a jumbo jet or *Concorde;* the majority arrive by air at one of London's major airports, Heathrow or Gatwick, both good starting points for a southern England itinerary.

The route outlined here begins at East Grinstead, easily accessible from nearby Gatwick Airport or an hour's drive from Heathrow via the M25 London Orbital Motorway, and proceeds through pleasant countryside to Brighton, just over the border from West Sussex in East Sussex. It then follows the coast west to Arundel (dominated by its castle and cathedral), to Chichester (ancient city of the Saxons and the Romans), and, entering Hampshire, to Portsmouth — known as "Pompey" to sailors, to whom it has been home since the Crusaders built its first dockyards and armories. From Portsmouth, ferries ply regularly to the Isle of Wight, where the route traverses this little bit of England, only 60 miles in circumference, before recrossing the water to Southampton, a major seaport favored by a sheltered position and a double tide. After Southampton, some travelers may want to abandon the *Southern England* route for the *Southwest England* route, which begins at Salisbury, but others will want to continue, heading north to Winchester, capital of England for almost 250 years and the site of a great cathedral. Thereafter, a quick return to London is possible, although this itinerary pushes still farther west into the New Forest, whose glades have witnessed kings and gypsies, smugglers and murderers, heroes and villains, and on to the Dorset resort of Bournemouth, once the belle of the south coast.

Like southeast England, southern England is a magnet for tourists, especially in high summer, so book accommodations well in advance. Expect to pay at least $100 for a double room in those places listed as expensive; from $60 to $100 in the moderate range; and under $60 for the inexpensive. A meal for two, excluding wine, tips, or drinks, will cost about $55 and up in places listed as expensive; $30 to $55 in moderate; and under $30 in inexpensive.

EAST GRINSTEAD: This pleasant country town only 8 miles from Gatwick Airport has expanded as a dormitory for London commuters, but the old High Street, known locally as "the top of the town," has survived the centuries. At its heart is the parish church of St. Swithin, whose great square Norman tower, with a pinnacle at each corner, can be seen for miles over the surrounding countryside (both church and town were built on an outcrop of sandstone, the highest point of the Weald — a band of farm country that separates the North and South Downs). Among the yew trees in the churchyard (approached through an alleyway from one side and a lych gate on the other) are ancient tombstones, including that of Anne Tree, who was "burned in the High Street" as a witch or a heretic in the 1550s.

East Grinstead's name derives from "green stede," or clearing in the forest. The town flourished as an iron-making center until that industry died; it then became merely a staging post on the road from London to Lewes and Brighton. The pub among the half-timbered Tudor buildings on High Street began as the *Newe Inn* and was the *Ounce and Ivy Bush* and the *Cat* before gaining its present name, the *Dorset Arms,* nearly 200 years ago. Now restored, this old coaching inn serves inexpensive traditional and not so traditional dishes in the restaurant upstairs as well as ales and pub grub in the bars below. Nearby is Sackville College, the town's most notable building after the church. An early Jacobean almshouse founded by the second Earl of Dorset in 1609, it is now used as a home for the elderly and can only be visited by prior arrangement.

CHECKING IN: *Copthorne* – This recently refurbished, part 16th-century hotel on a hundred acres of landscaped grounds is only 4 miles from Gatwick Airport. Besides 223 rooms and a restaurant serving international cuisine, it has a croquet lawn and a squash club with sauna, solarium, and gymnasium. A courtesy bus leaves the airport every 15 minutes from 6 AM to midnight. On A264 between Crawley and East Grinstead, at Copthorne (access from the M23 motorway is Exit 10) (phone: 0342-714971). Expensive.

Gravetye Manor – Among the few members of the prestigious Relais & Châteaux association in Great Britain, this ivy-covered, gabled Elizabethan house is set in a thousand acres of forest, with gardens laid out by the English horticulturalist William Robinson, a former owner. Its 14 rooms, paneled in oak from the area, are made inviting with flowers from the garden in season; those with fireplaces, with a cozy log fire. A superb restaurant, well worth a stay in itself, completes the picture. The hotel is midway between East Grinstead and Gatwick Airport (about 5 miles from town), yet peacefully away from the noise of the flight paths. Southwest of East Grinstead via B2110, at West Hoathly (phone: 0342-810567). Expensive.

EATING OUT: ***The Old House*** – In a 16th-century cottage on B2037 (just a mile or two from the *Copthorne* hotel), guests make their selections from a marvelously varied menu amid low, beamed ceilings, log fires, and gleaming brasses. Open for lunch (except Saturdays) and dinner (except Sundays), but avoid weekends, when it is usually fully booked. Effingham Rd., Copthorne, East Grinstead (phone: 0342-712222). Moderate.

En Route from East Grinstead – From the top of the town take A22 south through Forest Row and Ashdown Forest, a remnant of a primeval forest and once a thriving center of the iron industry. Picnic places are signposted and offer panoramic views of this hilly, wooded country. Continue on A22 to Uckfield, then take A26 to Lewes.

Alternatively, fork right at Wych Cross in the heart of Ashdown Forest and take A275 to Lewes. At Birch Grove, just off the road, is the country house (not open to the public) of Lord Stockton, who, as Harold Macmillan, was Prime Minister of Great Britain when he was visited here in 1963 by the young President John F. Kennedy. Lord Stockton died in 1986 and is buried with his wife in the parish churchyard. A few miles farther along A275 is Sheffield Park Garden, owned by the National Trust (open daily except Mondays from April through November). Its hundred acres, laid out in the 18th century by Capability Brown, contain rare trees and shrubs as well as specimen water lilies in five lakes. Half a mile toward Lewes is Sheffield Park Station, terminus of the scenic Bluebell Railway, so called because in early summer the woods flanking it are carpeted with these lovely wild flowers. Bought by a preservation society when British Rail closed the line in 1959, it runs steam locomotives and lovingly restored Victorian coaches (as much in demand by film companies seeking period locations as by visiting tourists) from here to Horsted Keynes. A modestly priced 9-mile trip there and back takes about 40 minutes.

Lewes is a historic East Sussex market town with steep, narrow streets, the ruins of an ancient Norman castle and an equally ancient Cluniac monastery, as well as numerous old houses, including some medieval half-timbered ones, and several interesting museums. (For more on Lewes, see our *Southeast England* route.)

From Lewes, A27 crosses the South Downs to Brighton, passing, at Falmer, the campus of the modern University of Sussex.

BRIGHTON: The popularity of England's most famous resort began in the late 18th century and developed largely during the early 19th century, leaving a wonderful architectural legacy for the modern visitor. Chief among the attractions — the heirloom, you might say — is the Royal Pavilion, the seaside home of the eccentric prince regent who became King George IV. The Royal Pavilion was begun in 1786, then transformed between 1815 and 1821 into the exotic Mogul palace that exists today. Inside, its rooms are crammed with gorgeous chinoiserie and fully furnished in the original grand style. Brighton's seafront — King's Road — is chockablock with fish-and-chip cafés, cotton candy stalls, and amusement arcades, and the Victorian Palace Pier adds to the carnival atmosphere. Another attraction is the Old Town, known as the Lanes, a picturesque area of narrow, brick-paved alleyways full of good tea shops, pubs, and antiques shops. For a full report on the sights, hotels, and restaurants of this seaside resort, see *Brighton,* THE CITIES.

ARUNDEL: From Brighton, A27 hurries west through a not particularly pleasing bit of coast, but the reward for the 20-mile drive is this small, medieval-looking town on the river Arun, spectacularly dominated by its massive castle and an equally large cathedral. The castle (open from April through October daily except Saturdays; admission charge), family seat of the Dukes of Norfolk (nominally the head of England's Catholic church), dates from the 11th century, though most of what is seen today — except for the Norman "keep" — was rebuilt in the 18th and 19th centuries. The picture gallery contains the dukes' collection, including paintings by Van Dyck, Gainsborough, and Reynolds, and on the grounds is the Roman Catholic Fitzalan Chapel, occupying a quarter of the town's 14th-century Anglican parish Church of St. Nicholas. The dual allegiance is explained by the fact that the 15th duke had a wall built to divide chapel from church and they still have separate entrances. The same duke had previously built the imposing, Gothic, Roman Catholic cathedral Church of St. Philip Neri. Around these two monoliths of castle and cathedral are many old houses and small inns, a cheerful Saturday morning market, and *Potter's Museum of Curiosity,* which contains the work of a Victorian taxidermist and naturalist who set animals in nursery rhyme tableaux (open daily from April through October and most days off-season; admission charge). The *Arundel Festival* of the arts takes place in late August.

Less than a mile to the north is the 55-acre Wildfowl Trust, where you can watch a sampling of the world's waterfowl from observation hides. North again, in a 19th-century quarry and limeworks, is the *Chalk Pits Museum* at Amberley (open Wednesdays through Sundays from Easter through October; admission charge). On display in this large outdoor museum of industrial history are the original lime kilns, plus a blacksmith's shop, a locomotive shed, a narrow-gauge railway, and much more.

CHICHESTER: The cathedral city of Chichester is 10 miles from Arundel. The original town was Roman and walled, and the city plan still reflects Roman beginnings in the two long, straight main streets that intersect at right angles at the 16th-century Market Cross. Portions of the walls, both Roman and medieval ones, remain, but Chichester today is predominantly a Georgian market town with many quiet corners and the lovely cathedral at its heart. The cathedral spire, visible from a distance, is a Victorian replacement of one that collapsed over a century ago, but the rest of the cathedral, built between 1091 and 1199, is largely Norman. The 15th-century bell tower is the only example of a detached belfry still surviving in England.

The most attractive buildings of Georgian Chichester are close by on North Street and in an area called the Pallant, a city-within-a-city southeast of Market Cross, while the best of Roman Chichester is 1½ miles west of town. In 1960, workmen laying a water pipe at Fishbourne discovered the remains of a magnificent Roman palace built in AD 70. When fully excavated, it turned out to be the largest Roman palace yet found in Britain. Twelve of the mosaic floors can be seen and there is a museum reflecting the history of the site up to AD 280 (open daily March through November but Sundays only the rest of the year; admission charge). In mid-July, Chichester stages the *Chichester Festivities,* a varied festival of the arts, which includes concerts in the cathedral. Better known is the top-flight *Chichester Festival Theatre* season, four plays running from May through September at a strikingly modern theater in the middle of a 40-acre parkland.

The nearby harbor is one of Britain's prettiest — it's a natural center for sailors with small boats. On its far shores, small resorts such as Bosham, West Itchenor, Emsworth, and Hayling Island are all quietly attractive. Goodwood House, 3 miles north on A286, is the historic home of the dukes of Richmond (open most Sundays and Mondays from May through September and Tuesdays, Wednesdays, and Thursdays in August; admission charge), and the park around it is the site of the racecourse where the "glorious" Goodwood Week of racing takes place at the beginning of August. Six miles north of the city, at Singleton, the Weald and *Downland Open Air Museum,* high on the South Downs, is especially worth a visit. Typical old buildings have been saved from destruction elsewhere in southeast England and transferred here, among them a 14th-century Kentish farmhouse, a 15th-century Wealdian hall house, and others (open daily April through September and Mondays through Saturdays, October through March; admission charge).

CHECKING IN: ***Ship*** – This was originally a private house, built in 1790 for George Murray, one of Nelson's admirals. It is large (36 rooms) and wonderfully old-fashioned in the Georgian manner. In April 1944, General Eisenhower dined here prior to D-Day. North St., Chichester (phone: 0243-782028). Moderate.

Ship Inn – Very small (7 rooms) and friendly, it overlooks the harbor. West Itchenor (phone: 0243-512284). Moderate.

EATING OUT: ***Hole in the Wall*** – This informal pub-restaurant is popular with festival- and theatergoers. 1 St. Martin's St., Chichester (phone: 0243-782555). Inexpensive.

En Route from Chichester – Route A27 continues west to Portsmouth where, after visiting England's naval capital, you can board a car or passenger ferry that will cross Spithead — a body of water no more than 4 miles wide — and deposit you 30 to 45 minutes later at Ryde or Fishbourne on the holiday Isle of Wight. The hovercraft from Southsea, a residential and resort suburb of Portsmouth, makes the trip even faster — in 10 minutes. (Those so inclined can make the trip to the island by ferry or hydrofoil from Southampton or by ferry from Lymington, farther along the coast, crossing the Solent, again a maximum 4 miles wide, to arrive on the island at Cowes or Yarmouth.)

PORTSMOUTH: The city is "Pompey" to the British navy, for whom it has been home and impregnable fortress for centuries. Despite heavy bombing by the Germans in World War II and the new commercial and shopping center that arose from the ruins, Old Portsmouth still survives, an interesting quarter of pubs, fortifications, grey-painted warships, and bustling ferries, with the sounds and smells of the sea on its doorstep. It is best toured on foot, so leave your car at Clarence Pier, from where a short walk northward along the waterfront leads to the King's Bastion and the Long Curtain Battery — all that remains of the medieval ramparts and moat that once surrounded the old town. Continue straight into Broad Street, whose buildings exhibit a colorful mixture of architectural styles; they were once filled with sailors' pubs and brothels, earning the neighborhood the nickname "Spice Island." Henry VIII built the Round Tower beside Broad Street and today military ceremonies dating from the 1840s are regularly reenacted here.

On board Admiral Nelson's flagship *Victory* (open daily; admission charge), in dry dock a mile away in Her Majesty's Dockyard along St. George's Road, you can relive the days of sail and hammocks, rum and the lash, and see the spot on which Nelson fell at the Battle of Trafalgar (1805) to become a hero for all time. Tours are conducted daily by engaging young sailors of today's Royal Navy. A panoramic display of the famous battle is one of the exhibits in the *Royal Naval Museum* (open daily; admission charge), which is housed in one of the 18th-century warehouses next to the dry dock and covers naval history from Nelson's day to the present (it also contains memorabilia of the admiral's beloved Lady Hamilton). Near HMS *Victory* is the Mary Rose Ship Hall and Exhibition. In 1545, King Henry VIII stood on the battlements of his castle at nearby Southsea watching his fleet engage the French. To his and everyone else's astonishment, the *Mary Rose,* the pride of his fleet, suddenly keeled over and sank with the loss of almost all hands. After more than 4 centuries on the seabed, the ship was salvaged in 1982 in a brilliant operation supervised by Prince Charles, himself a naval officer, and the restored hull, plus thousands of items recovered from the ship, are now on view (open daily; admission charge).

Another historic ship, HMS *Warrior,* built in 1860 as the world's first iron-clad warship, is on display in the dockyard (open daily; admission charge), but Portsmouth also has numerous other military and naval attractions elsewhere. At Southsea Castle, on the seafront in the suburb of Southsea, is the new *D-Day Museum* (open daily; admission charge), devoted to the Normandy landings of June 6, 1944, which were planned (using the code name Operation Overlord) at Southwick House in the hills overlooking the naval base. The museum contains a reconstruction of the D-Day operations room, and an adjacent purpose-built gallery houses the *Overlord Embroidery,* commissioned in 1968 and finished after 5 years of painstaking work by 20 needlewomen. It tells the story of the Allied invasion in 34 panels, each 8 feet long, and is 41 feet longer than the *Bayeux Tapestry* recording William the Conqueror's invasion in the opposite direction 9 centuries earlier. Besides the D-Day exhibits, Southsea Castle, which dates from the time of Henry VIII, also contains an older museum of military and naval history (open daily except December 24, 25, and 26; admission charge). The *Royal Marines Museum* at Eastney Barracks, beyond Southsea, presents the history of that corps from the mid-17th century to the present in the original Victorian officers' mess (open daily), while the *Royal Navy Submarine Museum* at Gosport features HMS *Alliance,* a World War II submarine that can be boarded (open daily; admission charge). Gosport is a 4-minute ferry trip across the neck of Portsmouth Harbour (or 13 miles by road).

Charles Dickens was born at Portsmouth in 1812, the son of a dockyard clerk. The modest family home at 393 Old Commercial Road on the north side of town (signposted off A3) is furnished as it might have looked at the time of his birth, although, in fact, the family moved only a few months later. It is open daily March through October (admission charge).

CHECKING IN: *Holiday Inn* – This relative newcomer to ancient "Pompey" offers 170 bedrooms, all with private bathrooms and TV sets, and a convenient harborside location. North Harbour, Portsmouth (phone: 0705-383151). Expensive.

ISLE OF WIGHT: Though it was once part of the mainland, it's a mistake to think of the Isle of Wight as a small (23 by 13 miles) piece of England cast adrift in the channel; it has a flavor of its own, at once pastoral and nautical. The island's northern end is flat, but its steep cliffs to the south are spectacular and draw the majority of visitors. Besides the seaside activity, walking is a major pastime here, and a network of footpaths leads nearly everywhere, including around the circumference of the island. For most visitors, Ryde, one of the major resort towns, is the gateway to the Isle of Wight. On the southeast coast, Sandown, Shanklin, and Ventnor are strictly resorts, busy and particularly sunny ones, and they clearly reflect the Victorian popularity that established and expanded them. Of the three, Ventnor, terraced up to the highest point of the island, is the oldest and perhaps the most interesting. Inland, there are many small villages, doubly remote for their island setting: Godshill has many thatched cottages; Calbourne, too, has thatched cottages and one of the country's finest examples of an early-17th-century water mill, still in working order. Newport, in the center on the river Medina, is the capital, and it's strangely the least hurried town on the island. A mile southwest, Charles I was once held prisoner in Carisbrooke Castle, which is reputedly built on the site of a Roman fort; parts of it date back to the 12th century (open daily except Christmas and New Year; admission charge).

On the north coast, Yarmouth is an ancient town and an important yachting center, but Cowes, divided in two by the Medina, is, as the headquarters of British yachting, internationally famous. It was the Cowes' yacht club, the Royal Yacht Squadron, that in 1851 offered a 100-guinea cup for a race around the island; the trophy, won by the schooner *America* for the *New York City Yacht Club,* has ever after been known as the America's Cup. The highlight of the regatta season is Cowes Week, the first week in August, when ocean racers from all over the world compete in the blue Solent. Cowes is not all ocean yachting, however — there are plenty of facilities for smaller boats. Osborne House, Queen Victoria's palatial Italianate retreat (she used it for over 50 years and died there in 1901), is just outside Cowes. The perfectly preserved state apartments and a museum are open daily April through mid-October; admission charge.

CHECKING IN: ***Farringford*** – A "famous" Isle of Wight property, this once belonged to Alfred Lord Tennyson. In addition to 20 bedrooms, the hotel offers a number of cottages with fully equipped kitchens. Croquet, a 9-hole golf course, and an outdoor pool contribute to the country house atmosphere. Freshwater, Isle of Wight (phone: 0983-752500). Moderate.

Winterbourne – Charles Dickens lived here in 1849 and called it "the prettiest place I ever saw in my life, at home or abroad." Today the 19-room hotel has magnificent sea views, fine cuisine, and an outdoor pool. Closed mid-November to March. Bonchurch, near Ventnor, Isle of Wight (phone: 0983-852535). Moderate.

En Route from the Isle of Wight – Sealink operates frequent car ferries between Fishbourne and Portsmouth and between Yarmouth and Lymington. There is a foot-passenger ferry from Ryde to Portsmouth and hovercraft service between Ryde and Southsea. Car ferries and hydrofoils depart daily year-round from Cowes to Southampton.

SOUTHAMPTON: A fine natural harbor and a famous double tide, which rolls in first from the Solent and 2 hours later from Spithead, made this city at the head of Southampton Water a major seaport. Like Portsmouth, Southampton played an important role in Operation Overlord: The whole area had become one huge tented military camp in the spring of 1944, and the city's main highway, The Avenue, was turned into a camouflaged tunnel down which the invasion force moved to the coast en route to the beaches of Normandy. Because of heavy bombing, Southampton looks largely modern today — the Vickers-Supermarine works at Woolston, which produced the first Spitfire in 1936, was blitzed, and much of the city center was flattened. There are some medieval remains, however, including parts of the ancient walls and the Bargate, now isolated in the middle of a traffic island, but once the landward entrance of the old town.

Southampton was already an important seaport in the Middle Ages, trading with Venice until the early 16th century, but a setback in its fortunes came when the port of Bristol captured the tobacco and sugar trade with the New World — and the black slave trade. Thousands of early American settlers sailed from Bristol, but Southampton has the honor of having waved good-bye to the *Mayflower* in 1620 (and to the *Speedwell,* too, but that ship proved unseaworthy and had to turn back). The Pilgrim Fathers Memorial in the shadow of the old walls near the Royal Pier commemorates the sailing. When the day of the large transatlantic liners dawned, Southampton — its double tide providing round-the-clock access — became Britain's chief port for the Atlantic crossing, bar none. The *Maritime Museum* (closed Mondays), in a 14th-century wool warehouse on nearby Bugle Street overlooking the river Test and Southampton Water, recalls that era with huge models of the steamships *Queen Mary* and *Capetown Castle.* In East Park, a white marble memorial honors the engineers of the ill-fated *Titanic.* Today, the last luxury liner making a scheduled transatlantic run is the *Queen Elizabeth 2,* which in 1986 made its last steam-powered crossing from New York before being refitted with diesel engines. Southampton is *QE2*'s home port as well as an important embarkation point for other large cruise ships.

EATING OUT: ***Pearl Harbour*** – Somehow this Chinese-run upstairs restaurant blends in beautifully with the maritime surroundings. Hot and sour soup, lemon chicken, and paper-wrapped prawns are among the tastiest dishes on the menu. 86A–88A Above Bar St., Southampton (phone: 0703-225248). Inexpensive.

En Route from Southampton – Southwest of the city, the road leads through the New Forest and on to Bournemouth, the end of the *Southern England* route. However, since the cathedral city of Winchester is only 12 miles north of Southampton via A33, don't miss the chance to see it now, returning to the New Forest area after the visit. Another alternative, for those anxious to move along at this point, would be to join the *Southwest England* route, which begins 22 miles northwest of Southampton (via A36) at Salisbury.

WINCHESTER: Here one meets the various people who overran, then settled this part of England: Celts founded the town, Romans took it over, Saxons made it their capital, Danes besieged it, and Normans built the cathedral that presides majestically over it. Although Winchester lost its primacy as the capital of the kingdom when William the Conqueror made it joint capitals with London and had himself crowned in both places, it was not until the 12th century that London began to supercede it.

Sheltered between the green hills of the Hampshire downs and fed by the gentle river Itchen, Winchester takes its physical character primarily from the 18th century — Great Minster Street near the cathedral is a charming example of the graceful architecture that period produced. But it is the harmonious mix of buildings from every era (including low brick structures from the last few decades) and the welcome lack of quaint trappings that give it its air of vitality.

The main tourist area, also the town's business and shopping district, runs along High Street, from the statue of Alfred the Great — the Saxon king who in 871 made this the capital of Wessex — at the east end, to Westgate, at the west end. Westgate, which from the 16th century on was the town's prison (Charles I was among its inmates), is now a small museum (closed Mondays in winter; admission charge). Prisoners' graffiti cover the walls and floors, and among the artifacts on display is the City Coffer, a 16th-century oak and iron-bound casket at least 6 feet long, 4 feet wide, and 3 feet deep, a relic from the days when a city's coffer was something more substantial than the bottom line of an annual report.

Just south of Westgate, and adjacent to the new Crown Court building, is the Great Hall, all that remains of the Norman castle that was a royal residence until destroyed by Oliver Cromwell's Parliamentarians in 1645 and considered to be one of the finest examples of a medieval hall in England. The Great Hall's most famous possession is King Arthur's Round Table although no one claims this great oak table (18 feet in diameter) is *the* legendary table of Arthur's court, since it dates from only the 14th century. But such was the continuing power of Arthur's legend that nearly a thousand years after his death, a shrewd King Henry VIII, wanting to strengthen his family's fairly recent claim to the throne, had the table painted with Arthur seated above a Tudor rose (open daily).

At the center of Winchester, physically and spiritually, stands its magnificent cathedral. The massive transepts are Norman, but the long nave, with its intricate web of fan vaulting, is the work of William of Wykeham, a 14th-century bishop who also founded Winchester College southeast of the cathedral. This, one of the oldest schools in England, retains most of its original 14th- and 15th-century structure (open daily, April through September; Sundays, October through March). The *Wessex* hotel dining room, which faces the cathedral across the green expanse of the close, is a perfect place for afternoon tea. If time permits, take a walk along the Weirs, which follow the Itchen through town, past lovely gardens and the ruins of the bishop's castle (also a victim of the Civil War). Continue on the footpath beside the river for another mile or so and you'll come to the Hospital of St. Cross, an almshouse founded in the early 12th century and still functioning — the Wayfarer's Dole is given out to those who ask for it (closed Sundays; admission charge).

CHECKING IN: ***Lainston House*** **–** This Georgian mansion 2 miles west of Winchester (off A272 to Stockbridge) is surrounded by 60 acres of parkland. Its 32 rooms offer an authentic taste of English country living, while the restaurant serves Swiss-influenced cuisine. Sparsholt (phone: 0962-63588). Expensive.

Southgate **–** Designed by no less an architect than Sir Christopher Wren 5 years after he completed St. Paul's Cathedral in London. The early 18th-century building now has TV sets in all 17 bedrooms and every other modern convenience, plus good food. 14 Southgate St., Winchester (phone: 0962-51243). Inexpensive.

En Route from Winchester – Travelers eager to return to London can easily do so from here — it's only 66 miles away on the M3 motorway. But, for a more leisurely return to the capital, follow A31 across the rolling Hampshire plain. A mile before Alton, off the main road in the village of Chawton, is the house where Jane Austen wrote *Mansfield Park, Emma,* and *Persuasion.* The 2-story red brick building, originally an inn, is furnished with period pieces and things the Austens owned and is open daily from April through October, Wednesdays through Sundays in November, December, and March, and Saturdays and Sundays only in January and February (admission charge). Farther along, in Surrey, is Farnham, a lovely old town of Tudor and Georgian houses. To visit Frensham Great Pond, one of the largest lakes in southern England, and the Devil's Punch bowl, a freak cleft in the landscape caused by spring water, turn south onto A287 at Farnham to join A3. Otherwise, stay on A31, following the ridge known as Hog's Back and swooping down into the ancient town of Guildford (with long distance views of its modern cathedral and university buildings), and proceed to London.

To continue the route from Winchester through the New Forest to Bournemouth, take A3090 south from Winchester, join A31, and stay on it as far as Cadnam. Along the way, you'll pass through Romsey, just outside of which is Broadlands. "One of the finest houses in all England," according to Lord Palmerston, the great Victorian prime minister who lived here himself, it later became the country home of the late Earl Mountbatten of Burma, great-grandson of Queen Victoria and the last Viceroy of India. Queen Elizabeth and Prince Philip, and Prince Charles and the Princess of Wales began their honeymoons in this outstanding example of mid-Georgian architecture that stands elegantly beside the river Test in gardens landscaped by Capability Brown. Inside are notable collections of Van Dyck paintings and Wedgwood porcelain and an exhibition recounting Lord and Lady Mountbatten's eventful lives (open from April through September; closed Mondays, except in August and September and bank holiday Mondays; admission charge).

At Cadnam, leave A31 and proceed south to Lyndhurst, in the midst of the New Forest, which is neither new nor totally a forest (its name goes back to William the Conquerer, who made the area his hunting ground, where a peasant could have his eyes put out for frightening the deer). Much of the 90,000 acres of untamed heath, bog, and woodland is still a wildlife preserve (protected by mounted guards) and two-thirds of it is public domain, its inhabitants enjoying medieval rights such as pannage (the feeding of their pigs on forest acorns), turbary (the right to cut turf), and estover (permission to gather firewood). You are certain to see something of the 2,000 wild horses and ponies that roam the area, and of the deer, but less likely to see the badgers and otters who make their homes here. Watch, too, for rare birds and species of wild flowers. This is walking country par excellence, but there are also many stables and riding schools, since riding and pony trekking are popular pursuits.

At Canterton Glen, northeast of Stoney Cross (off A31 *past* Cadnam), is the Rufus Stone, said to mark the spot where William II, the son of the Conquerer and known as Rufus for his red hair, met his death while hunting in 1100. He was struck in the heart by an arrow shot by Sir Walter Tyrrell, a French nobleman in the hunting party, and to this day the question of whether it was an accident or murder is unresolved. Close by, the village of Minstead (between Cadnam and Lyndhurst) has a 13th-century church with an unusual three-deck pulpit inside, along with "parlour pews" that were reserved for the local gentry (the poor sat under rafters in the "Gypsies gallery"). Sir Arthur Conan Doyle, creator of Sherlock Holmes, is buried in the churchyard. Note the *Trusty Servant* pub at the village crossroads. Its sign, based on a picture at Winchester College, depicts the "perfect" servant as having the body of a pig (suggesting an unfastidious appetite), a locked snout (for discretion), the ears of an ass (patience), and stag's feet (speed), while in its hand are a shovel, a brush, and a fork.

LYNDHURST: The capital of the New Forest is set amid heath and woods, and it's not uncommon to see wild ponies wander through its lanes. The town is the seat of the Verderers' Court, which has administered the forest since 1388. It meets six times a year at Queen's House, whose walls are adorned with stags' heads and whose fireplace has a stirrup iron hanging over it that allegedly belonged to William II. Under Norman law, any dog unable to squeeze through the stirrup was pronounced a danger to the deer in the forest and had its claws cut off. East of Queen's House is the 19th-century parish church, with a fresco of the Ten Virgins painted by the late Lord Leighton and a beautiful pre-Raphaelite east window designed by Burne-Jones. Mrs. Hargreaves, née Alice Liddell, the heroine of *Alice in Wonderland,* lies in the churchyard.

Lyndhurst abounds with pubs, tea rooms, and souvenir shops, all well frequented by tourists. (The New Forest Visitor Centre opened in 1988 and has interesting displays on the history of the area. Open daily; phone: 042128-871501). Since the town is a major crossroads between Southampton and Lymington, Christchurch, and Bournemouth, A35 funnels cars and buses into its narrow main street (where a one-way system operates). Fiercely argued plans for a bypass may yet come to fruition and bring relief, but in the meantime, escape from the noise and fumes of the infernal combustion engine is possible in the acres of open heathland and dense forest that surround the town. The Knightswood Oak, a venerable giant of a tree measuring more than 21 feet around its trunk and thought to be about 600 years old, grows in a peaceful glade to the west of Lyndhurst. To the south is New Park, a 200-acre royal deer park where country fairs and agricultural shows are held in summer.

CHECKING IN: ***Parkhill*** – This 18th-century Georgian manor house is now a 22-room hotel with an outdoor pool and croquet grounds set on 9 acres. A walk from the doorstep takes in stretches of heath and forest of bare oak, golden bracken, and beech. It's a peaceful place, barring the occasional blood-curdling cry of the vixen. All rooms have baths and TV sets; the cuisine is French. Lyndhurst (phone: 042128-2944). Expensive.

Lyndhurst Park – Whitewashed and hung with creeper, it looks out on manicured lawns and has an expensive Art Deco look about it. Besides the landscaped outdoor swimming pool and golf driving nets, it offers a warm welcome within and a traditional but varied menu. High St., Lyndhurst (phone: 042128-2823). Moderate.

Pikes Hill Forest Lodge – Although only a few minutes walk from the town center, the original building — much expanded — was the dower house of King George IV's hunting lodge and it retains an air of seclusion. All 20 rooms have color TV sets, phones, and coffee- and tea-making facilities, and the majority have private bath or shower. The outdoor pool is heated from April through October. Romsey Rd., Lyndhurst (phone: 042128-3677). Moderate.

En Route from Lyndhurst – Take B3056 7 miles southeast to the village of Beaulieu (pronounced *Bew*-lee), set where the Beaulieu River widens into an estuary; midway between Lyndhurst and the village lies Beaulieu Road Station, in reality no more than a halt on the Southampton to Bournemouth railway line. There are usually no passengers except for those coming and going from the *Beaulieu Road* hotel, the local pub, but on five separate days each year, when the New Forest Pony Sales are held, this rather isolated place comes alive with people. The 1-day sales, which take place in April, August, September, October, and November, attract large numbers, especially of Romany traders and excited children looking for their first colt to register with the New Forest Pony Breeding and Cattle Society.

BEAULIEU: From the 13th century to the early 16th century, the main attraction of this village was Beaulieu Abbey, a Cistercian house founded in 1204 by King John. Now visitors come to see the abbey ruins, which survive today, plus Palace House, home of Lord Montagu of Beaulieu and in his family's keeping since 1538, as well as the *National Motor Museum,* on the grounds of the estate. Palace House was originally the gatehouse of the abbey, acquired by the family following the dissolution of the monasteries by Henry VIII, and although the Montagus live here in style with a butler and domestic staff, the house and its gardens are open to the public. The *National Motor Museum,* in a separate building, is one of the most comprehensive of its kind in the world. Begun by Lord Montagu in memory of his father's lifetime interest in the automobile, it tells the story of motoring from 1899 to the present with the help of more than 200 historic vehicles and high-tech showmanship in a display called "Wheels," where the visitor is whirled from one tableau to the next in the style of Disney World. At the other extreme, the abbey cloisters and parts of the chapter house and the monks' dormitory house an exhibition of monastic life.

The Beaulieu estate (phone: 0590-612345) opens at 10 AM every day except Christmas Day, although closing times vary with the season. At holiday times it attracts large crowds, but there is a vast free car park outside the main entrance, about a quarter of a mile from Palace House. One admission fee covers the house and grounds, abbey ruins and monastic life exhibition, and the motor museum; for an extra charge, the grounds can be toured by high level monorail, miniature train, or veteran open-top London bus.

En Route from Beaulieu – Continue southeast to the village of Buckler's Hard, just over 2 miles away. (If you've a penchant for walking, note that a waymarked trail follows the sinuous Beaulieu River from Beaulieu village to Buckler's Hard.) In the early 18th century, the second Duke of Montagu established a town, shipyard, and docks here to receive sugar from his West Indian estates. Although the sugar business fell through, the shipyard's proximity to the great oaks of the New Forest made it an important shipbuilding center, employing 4,000 men who turned out some of the most famous men o' war in British history, including the *Agamemnon,* in which Nelson lost his eye off Corsica, and a good part of the fleet that fought at Trafalgar. A maritime museum (open daily; admission charge) tells the story of the river, the village, and the Adams family who built many of the "hearts of oak" ships; it also displays charts used by Sir Francis Chichester, who in modern times set out from Buckler's Hard on his epic lone voyages across the Atlantic and around the world in *Gypsy Moth* yachts.

Return to Beaulieu and take B3054 6 miles to Lymington. The road crosses one of the largest open spaces in the New Forest, the 5 square miles of Beaulieu Heath. The tumuli, or burial mounds, dotting the landscape were left by a people who lived here 4,000 years ago in the Bronze Age. During World War II, the heath became a military airfield. Today, it is ablaze with purple heather in late summer, ponies and rabbits crop the grass where bombers once landed, and there are clumps of gorse and the occasional willow, birch, and Scots pine. To the northeast, the blazing chimneys of the Fawley petrochemical plant on Southampton Water can be seen, and to the southeast, the green hills of the Isle of Wight.

Lymington became a popular resort with the coming of the railway in the 19th century. Before then some of the local families had become rich from the sale of salt from the salterns along the coast, and the Georgian houses on Lymington's broad main street are their legacy. Today it is a yachtsmen's and fishermen's town and the quay is lined with chandlery stores and fishing tackle shops. Boats can be hired to fish for bass in the Solent or day tickets bought for trout fishing on Lymington River. If you haven't already done so, take the ferry to the Isle of Wight — the crossing from here to Yarmouth is the shortest route to the island. Alternatively, follow A337 west and in 12 miles you'll be in Christchurch.

CHECKING IN: ***Chewton Glen*** – This country house hotel in Georgian style occupies 30 acres of park between Lymington and Christchurch. A member of the Relais & Châteaux association, it's been extensively renovated and expanded since Captain Frederick Marryat, author of *The Children of the New Forest,* spent time here in the 19th century (rooms are named for characters in his book) and is now unashamedly sumptuous. Guests can swim in the heated outdoor pool, play tennis or golf, try their hand at croquet, putting, or billiards, and be wined and dined in a restaurant that lives up to its Michelin star. Christchurch Rd., New Milton (phone: 0425-275341). Expensive.

Rose and Crown – A small 17th-century coaching inn in a New Forest village west of Beaulieu and north of Lymington, it has a cottage garden and comfortable bedrooms. Brockenhurst (phone: 0590-22316). Moderate.

CHRISTCHURCH: Another yachtsmen's and fishermen's haven, this Saxon town was one of Alfred the Great's strongholds against the Danes. It appears as Twynham, "the town between two waters," in the *Domesday Book,* a reference to the fact that the river Stour and the Hampshire Avon entwine here, but its modern name came into being with the town's Priory Church, built from the 12th through the 15th centuries. Originally, the church was to have been built at the top of St. Catherine's Hill. But every night, according to local legend, building materials that had been laboriously carried up the hill during the day were mysteriously transported down again. Eventually, the divine hint was taken and the church built at the foot of the hill. As the work neared completion, an unknown carpenter, who took no pay and ate no food, joined the laborers. Before he disappeared, a roof beam that was found to be a foot short became a perfect fit overnight. The workmen believed that the stranger was Christ, so the building was called Christ's Church and the town renamed in commemoration of the extraordinary events. The largest parish church in England, it has England's two oldest church bells, cast in 1370, ringing out from its square tower and contains a notable reredos carved with the Tree of Jesse.

What was once the town's workhouse on Quay Road is now the *Red House Museum and Art Gallery* (closed Mondays; admission charge), which concentrates on the rural crafts of Hampshire and Dorset, social history, and archaeological finds, including flint tools unearthed at the nearby promontory of Hengistbury Head.

At the same quay where sailing barges used to unload coal and timber, pleasure boats and fishing boats for day trips now ply for hire. At low tide, Christchurch Harbour becomes mud flats, and Stanpit Marsh on its northern shore is a haven for wildfowl, with a nature trail marked across it. While the rivers Stour and Avon offer peace and tranquility for anglers, there are flatfish, mullet, and eels to be caught in the harbor (pending permission from the local angling club), and Mudeford on the north side is a favored spot for fishing from the sea wall, where whelk pots are piled high.

CHECKING IN: ***King's Arms*** – Originally an 18th-century coaching inn, this comfortable, well-run hotel has 32 bedrooms, all of them with private bathrooms, TV sets, and central heating. Castle St., Christchurch (phone: 0202-484117). Moderate.

EATING OUT: ***Splinters*** – This is a good place to taste the local salmon, served *Hollandaise,* or free-range chickens cooked with a variety of sauces and peppers. A well-stocked cellar of 20,000 bottles fortifies the limited menu. 12 Church St., Christchurch (phone: 0202-483454). Expensive.

BOURNEMOUTH: The seaside resort of Bournemouth is only 6 miles west of Christchurch (or rather, central Bournemouth is 6 miles west, because in actual fact, Bournemouth has expanded so far along the coast that it has almost incorporated the older town). A certain Dr. Granville, who recommended its balmy climate and sea air as a cure for invalid Victorians, can be credited with putting Bournemouth on the map in the mid-19th century. Ever since, the resort has struggled to overcome a stodgy bathchair image, and now does its best to live up to its traditional title of Queen of the South Coast, with mild air and glorious clean sands, 2,000 acres of well-tended parks and gardens, West End stars at its shows, symphony concerts, championship tennis courts, golf, riding, water skiing, power boating, fishing, sailing, and more hotels and restaurants than anywhere in England outside London. The Bournemouth International Conference Centre, with its conference and leisure complex and indoor waves, confirms it as a top year-round resort. For a full report on its sights, hotels, and restaurants, see *Bournemouth,* THE CITIES.

En Route from Bournemouth – Salisbury, the starting point of our *Southwest England* route, is 28 miles north of Bournemouth via A338. But if you won't be visiting Wiltshire, Devon, and Cornwall, take A31 out of Bournemouth to the M27 motorway and, above Southampton, join A33, which meets the M3 motorway and will speed you back to London. The distance from Bournemouth to London is 114 miles.

Southeast England

For better or worse, geography conspired to make Kent and East Sussex — the broad heel of land that opens out below London to form the cliff-lined and beach-speckled coast of southeast England — the only welcoming mat England has ever extended to the Continent. It is country suited to landing parties: Kent's rich orchards, hop fields, thatched barns, and high-hedged roads giving way to Sussex's high South Downs, from which one can see for miles in all directions. To the north is the wide estuary of the Thames; to the south, the English Channel; and to the east, where England and France are only some 20 miles apart, the Straits of Dover.

Such an invitation has been hard for European warlords to resist, and for 2,000 years attempts have been made to enter England through the southeast. Some have been successful. The Romans established an administrative center in London, and the Normans conquered all of England after their decisive victory at the Battle of Hastings in 1066, a date no English schoolchild ever forgets. Other attempts have failed. From August to October 1940, Britain stood virtually alone against the full weight of the Nazi war machine as the Battle of Britain raged over Kent. But each of these efforts has left some mark on this extraordinarily rich part of England. Kent, the Garden of England, nurtures as much history as fruit and hops in its fertile countryside.

Much of the southeast is dominated and influenced by London. Hundreds of thousands of those who live in this region commute daily to and from the capital. The region, too, is London's principal playground, and on good summer weekends its beaches and country resorts fill with hosts of fugitives from town. But the countryside and the coast have proved surprisingly tenacious despite their proximity to a city of 8 million inhabitants. Since this area, and especially the northern part of Kent, is Britain's main thoroughfare to Europe and is one of the most densely populated parts of the country, do not expect to find vast tracts of it in virgin condition. But having said that, it is surprising that so much of it is still unspoiled and rarely visited and that it has held on to its history remarkably well.

Along the south shore of the Thames as far as Gravesend, major industries dominate the waterfront before the Kent countryside comes into view and Thameside busyness gives way to the first of several holiday resorts that round the northeast coast of the county. Below the river and the coast, parallel to them, lie the North Downs, a range of low chalkland hills that run east from Surrey to meet the sea spectacularly as the white cliffs of Dover. Impossible to cultivate, they are either forested or left to grazing. Still farther south lies the Weald, the central region of the southeast. The Weald takes its name from the Anglo-Saxon *wold,* meaning "a wood." Throughout the later Middle Ages, the woods of this region were cleared, and the fertile soil turned to agricultural use. The result was a prosperous area of substantial villages and market towns, and to this day it is quite possible to find them still full of 16th- and 17th-century houses and farms, and to sense in them a strong continuity with their isolated past.

Up and over the South Downs that run through Sussex below the Weald, you come to a coast dedicated largely to pleasure. Like the Kent coast, the East Sussex coast abounds with resorts. They are less fashionable now than in their Victorian and Edwardian heydays, but perhaps more attractive for that very reason. In the little ones especially, you will find clear signs of the elegance that transformed these watering places from the fishing villages that they once were.

The major sights of England's southeast — Canterbury, Dover, Hastings and Battle, Eastbourne, and Brighton — can all be visited on day trips from London. Travelers with little time should certainly choose the most appealing destinations and make the journey by car or, even more simply, by train. But more rewarding is a perambulation through the countryside, following the coast as a rough guide, and taking in both the large, obviously popular spots along the beaten path and the smaller, quieter places off of it.

The route outlined here begins in Rochester (familiar to readers of Charles Dickens), then takes the less traveled road to Canterbury through hop-growing country, the town of Faversham, and the old-fashioned seaside resorts of Whitstable and Herne Bay. From Canterbury the route returns to the coast at Sandwich, one of the five Cinque Ports that banded together in the Middle Ages to furnish ships to a previously nonexistent English navy. Next along the coast is the historic port of Deal, and Dover and Hythe, two more of the Cinque Ports, are a short drive farther south. After a detour inland to Ashford (an area rich in old inns, oast houses, and orchards), the route crosses the Romney Marsh — a bleak peninsula once known to smugglers, now livened by a string of tiny, traditional beach towns — on its way to Rye and Winchelsea and to Hastings and Battle, where a new era began for England. Next comes a fork in the road: Either detour into the Kent and Sussex Weald, where the essential character of this part of England can still be felt, or head straight to Eastbourne and the hurly-burly of Brighton. The route then returns to London, taking in the spa town of Royal Tunbridge Wells and several historic houses along the way — such as the jumble of gables and towers that is Knole, or Winston Churchill's country home, Chartwell.

The southeastern region is a very popular vacation spot, so make hotel reservations far in advance. Expect to pay around $75 and up for a double room in those places listed as expensive; from $50 to $75 in the moderate range; and under $45 if listed as inexpensive. A meal for two, excluding wine, tips, or drinks, will cost $50 and up in places listed as expensive; $30 to $45 in those listed as moderate; and under $30, inexpensive.

ROCHESTER: The river Medway forms a natural barrier between London and the channel, neatly dividing Kent in two, making Rochester primarily a bridge town for the river. It can be easily overlooked now that the M2 motorway from London to Dover rushes by it 2 miles upriver, but those who take the turn before the Medway bridge will soon find themselves in the center of the city. The Romans recognized Rochester's strategic importance early and built a bridge (the London to Dover extension of

Watling Street, England's ancient Roman highway, crossed the river here), and after they left, a succession of bridges followed. The Normans, too, saw the importance of the crossing and late in the 11th century began a magnificent castle to defend it. The enormous square keep, 120 feet high with 12-foot-thick walls, was built in the 12th century and is still standing. It is open to adventurous visitors (daily; admission charge) prepared to climb its steep spiral staircases and be rewarded by a marvelous view of the Medway estuary, the North Downs, and, best of all, Rochester Cathedral. Next to the castle, the cathedral is set on a 7th-century foundation, with a plain Norman nave and many features gradually added from the 12th to the 14th century. The Norman doorway at the west entrance, the walled choir, and many of the tombs are noteworthy.

Castle and cathedral share the summit of Boley Hill, the center of the old city and an area that boasts many ancient and interesting buildings. They catch the rare flavor of a Victorian city, a flavor enhanced by their close associations with Charles Dickens, who lived in nearby Chatham as a boy and came back near the end of his life to Gad's Hill, 3 miles west. Many scenes in his novels take place in Rochester and the surrounding countryside, and each year, in late May or early June, the city stages a rich festival in his honor. Dickens's favorite inn, *The Leather Bottle* (in Cobham, 5 miles west), is portrayed in the *Pickwick Papers* and still dispenses food, drink, and atmosphere. The *Royal Victoria and Bull,* on High Street near the bridge and Boley Hill (see *Checking In*), is both the Bull Inn of the same novel and the Blue Boar Inn of *Great Expectations,* and many of the shops around it are readily identifiable as Dickensian settings. The 16th-century Restoration House on Maidstone Road is Miss Havisham's Satis House in *Great Expectations* (not open to the public), and about 6 miles north, in the village of Cooling, there's the original setting of Joe Gargery's forge and the graveyard where Pip first met Magwitch. Both are on the edge of an alluringly bleak marshland. Thinly disguised, Rochester is also the Cloisterham of Dickens's last, unfinished, work, *The Mystery of Edwin Drood.* This strange novel gives a good picture of Victorian Rochester, but much can also be seen in the marvelous Dickens Centre in Eastgate House on High Street (open daily; admission charge). The house itself is Elizabethan and appears in *Edwin Drood* as the Nuns' House. Dickens's Gad's Hill home is not open to the public, but the Swiss chalet in which he wrote has now been moved to the garden of Eastgate House.

CHECKING IN: *Royal Victoria and Bull* – In fact, a 29-room, 400-year-old coach house and, in fiction, the scene of Dickensian revels — the novelist thought it was a "good house" with "nice beds." The food is plain English fare, well cooked and well served. 16–18 High St., Rochester (phone: 0634-46266). Moderate.

En Route from Rochester – Before proceeding to Faversham, you may want to make an 8-mile detour to Maidstone, the bustling agricultural center of Kent, with a long history in the brewing industry. Many old buildings line its streets, several of which have been closed to traffic to preserve these fine examples of early architecture. Near the town's 14th-century Church of All Saints is a medieval building with an Elizabethan front, the Archbishop's Palace. What may have been the palace stable or a tithe barn now houses the *Tyrwhitt Drake Museum of Carriages,* a collection of ornate, horse-drawn vehicles (closed Sundays October through March; admission charge). Chillington Manor, an Elizabethan mansion on St. Faith's Street, is the home of the *Museum and Art Gallery,* which contains the memorabilia of essayist William Hazlitt, a native of Maidstone (closed Sundays; admission charge). Leeds Castle, built in the middle of a lake in the 1200s, is 4 miles east of Maidstone. This former residence of Henry VIII and Lord Culpepper (governor of Virginia, 1680–83) is often the focus of a day trip from London (open daily from April through October, Saturdays and Sundays only in winter; admission charge).

Return to Rochester for Allington Castle, an imposing, moated, 13th-century castle, and the Carmelite retreat, Aylesford Friary, both off A229. The order controls the structures, which are both open daily to visitors in the afternoon (admission charge).

FAVERSHAM: If time is limited or the weather dull, the motorway will whisk you from Rochester to Faversham in half an hour. The old main road (A2), however, winds through Gillingham, then Sittingbourne, where there is a museum of sailing barges at the Dolphin Yard (open Sundays and bank holidays from Easter through October; admission charge), and some Kent countryside that is especially lovely when the apple blossoms are out or the hops are fully grown. Faversham is at the center of hop-growing country, and the conical structures seen frequently in this region, called oasts, are used to dry the hops. Most people bypass the town, a fact that perhaps adds to its attractions for those who do stop. Another Roman site, it received its first charter in 811 and developed afterward into a fine medieval city, not least because it was once a small port on the quiet river Swale, which divides the Isle of Sheppey from the Kent mainland.

The best place to sample Faversham's past is on Preston Street in the Fleur de Lis Heritage Centre, a well-illustrated guide to the town's thousand years of history housed in a converted 15th-century inn (closed Sundays and Thursdays; admission charge). In the marketplace at the center of town, where three of its oldest streets meet, is the guildhall, a 19th-century rebuilding of a 16th-century market hall that is raised on pillars. At the north end of the marketplace is Court Street, with many 17th- and 18th-century houses. Joining it is Market Street where, at No. 12, James II was held prisoner by local fishermen as he tried to escape to the Continent. The many 16th- and 17th-century houses jostling together on West Street, however, make it the loveliest street of all. Faversham Creek, about 3 miles north of town, has medieval warehouses and a delightful pub, the *Coal Exchange Inn,* while the little harbor of Conyer Creek, a few miles west, is a favorite spot for artists and sailors. None of these places is much known except by natives, who understandably have kept them to themselves.

CHECKING IN: ***Ship*** – In an 18th-century coaching house with many Tudor features, it's the perfect place in which to get the feel of this pleasant town. West St., Faversham (phone: 0795-532179). Moderate.

WHITSTABLE AND HERNE BAY: From Faversham, the direct route into Canterbury follows the M2 motorway, but a slower, winding route along the Thames estuary coast leads, after about 10 miles, to the small seaside towns of Whitstable and Herne Bay. Like Faversham and Rochester, these places are usually bypassed by overseas visitors, although they are quite popular with the English holidaymakers who have had the luck to discover their quiet charms. For centuries, Whitstable thrived as a fishing port involved principally in the production of oysters, the famous "Whitstable Natives." But by the 1950s, the Thames had become so polluted that the trade declined almost to nothing. The good news for both environmentalists and gourmets is that the river is now so much cleaner than before that the oysters have returned, and so have the restaurants selling them. (For an especially good one, see *Eating Out.*) The nicest part of the old town still clusters around the old harbor. Here weatherboarded houses perch right on the edge of the shingle beach, and in the narrow streets are a host of small pubs selling local ale and offering a very friendly welcome to the visitor. Another of Whitstable's attractions is the huge number of secondhand or "junk" shops, more per hundred yards than in almost any other town in the southeast. Stroll along High Street from the harbor to the town center to find books, old clothes, antiques, and all sorts of bric-a-brac every few steps of the way. The prices are lower than those in London, so you could pass a profitable day in these shops looking for bargains.

Herne Bay, the small town next to Whitstable, could be the closest thing to a Victorian seaside resort in England. Primarily a retirement town with a predominantly elderly population, it has a general air of sedateness that is very attractive. Like its saltier neighbor, however, it also abounds in friendly pubs and in good secondhand shops. The holiday resorts of Margate, Broadstairs, and Ramsgate lie along the coast beyond Herne Bay, but this route travels south along the pleasant country road leading from Whitstable directly into Canterbury.

EATING OUT: ***Pearson's Oyster Bar*** **–** Don't leave Whitstable without sampling the locally caught seafood at *Pearson's* on the seafront, or the strong local Fremlin's ale. From the restaurant above the bar you can see out over the Thames estuary to the Isle of Sheppey. Sunsets here are so spectacular that the painter Turner used to sketch them for future use. Horsebridge, Whitstable (phone: 0227-272005). Moderate.

CANTERBURY: This is the spiritual center of the Anglican faith and Britain's cathedral city par excellence. It was from Canterbury that St. Augustine converted the English to Christianity, founding both an abbey and a church in AD 602. St. Augustine's Abbey survives in ruins, but the first cathedral was lost to fire and replaced by the massive 11th-century masterpiece that today dominates the red-roofed, still medieval town around it. The murder of Archbishop Thomas à Becket in 1170 and his canonization 2 years later elevated the cathedral to its status as a shrine; ever since Canterbury has been the goal of pilgrims, including Chaucer's group, who, telling tales, wended their way to the scene of Becket's martyrdom. Visitors should allow plenty of time to explore the cathedral — filled with 9 centuries of English history — and the many other ancient buildings nearby. Afterward, explore several inns, such as the 16th-century *White Hart* near Canterbury East Station, the half-timbered *Seven Stars* on Orange Street, or the bow-windowed *Olive Branch* on Burgate Street, all inviting places to stop and rest. For a full report on the city's sights, hotels, and restaurants, see *Canterbury,* THE CITIES.

En Route from Canterbury – Part of Canterbury's prosperity grew from its role as a market center for the many villages and agricultural communities of East Kent, and it still serves the same purpose for the region. If time allows, these small villages are well worth visiting. Particularly nice ones are Chilham, 10 miles to the southwest, which has the magnificent Chilham Castle (open to the public only when Elizabethan banquets are held in the Gothic Hall, although its gardens are open from April to mid-October, and, at various times of the year, jousting and falconry displays are held); Barham, which nestles below the Downs just off the Dover Road, 5 miles southeast of Canterbury; and Westbere, tucked away off the main Margate Road, 3 miles northeast of the city. Westbere has kept its almost medieval character intact, and in the middle of the village is the *Yew Tree,* a delightful inn in a medieval house.

EATING OUT: ***Wife of Bath*** **–** Five miles south of Chilham is Wye, a village that would escape notice altogether if it weren't for this small but very fine restaurant with English and French cuisine. Weekly menus change with the season to ensure as much absolutely fresh food as possible. Closed Sundays and Mondays. Make reservations. 4 Upper Bridge St., Wye (phone: 0233-812540). Expensive.

SANDWICH: The A257 leads due east from Canterbury to the medieval port of Sandwich, one of the original five Cinque Ports (see *En Route from Deal*). As Sandwich's harbor became clogged with silt in the 16th century, the city lost importance and it is now 2 miles from the sea. Sandwich gained lasting fame, however, when the fourth Earl of Sandwich invented the world's most popular and enduring meal. According to legend, the earl was loath to leave the gaming tables to eat and asked that a concoction of bread and meat be made for him. Since he was a dissolute man —

and infamous for having been in charge of the admiralty when Britain lost its North American colony — the story has something of the ring of truth about it. Two inns, the *Bell* and the *King's Arms,* will be glad to provide a sample of this handy bar snack and something with which to wash it down. Richborough Castle, just off A257 a mile and a half outside of Sandwich, was established by the Romans in about AD 43 and added to by the Saxons during the 3rd century (open daily except Christmas and New Year; admission charge). The A258 leads to Deal, about 6 miles south along the coast.

CHECKING IN: ***Fleur de Lis*** – This small (8-bedroom) house is in the center of Sandwich. Its oak-paneled restaurant was converted from the old Corn Exchange. Delf St., Sandwich (phone: 0304-611131). Inexpensive.

DEAL: Deal was an important shipping center through the early 19th century. Under Henry VIII, three castles were erected here: Deal Castle, designed in the shape of a six-petaled rosette (open daily except Christmas and New Year; admission charge); Walmer Castle, more like a four-leaf clover and a mile south of the city (closed Mondays; admission charge); and Sandown Castle, now washed away and nothing more than a pile of stones at the northern end of the seafront. There is a good possibility that Caesar's forces landed along this shore when the Romans invaded Britain, and Henry VIII feared a repeat Roman invasion, this time in the form of a Holy War that the pope might launch against him as the self-proclaimed head of the Church of England. Off the coast of Deal are the Goodwin Sands, a dangerous and complicated series of sandbanks that are exposed at low tide. Lighthouses illuminate the area after dark, but maritime accidents persist even though Deal is no longer the swaggering seaport it once was. Before the coming of steamships, the narrow stretch of shallow water between Goodwin Sands and the shore, popularly known as the Downs and not the safest anchorage, was filled with cargo vessels and men-of-war. The Time Ball Tower on the seafront, a late-18th-century structure, used to give the correct Greenwich time to ships in the Downs (the ball dropped every day at 1 PM). It is now open daily, June through October, except Mondays; admission charge.

CHECKING IN: ***Royal*** – The best features of this comfortable hotel are the balconies of the rooms facing the English Channel. The hotel is decorated with Georgian antiques, and its restaurant serves quite good fresh fish. There are 31 rooms, most with private bath. Beach St., Deal (phone: 0304-375555). Expensive.

En Route from Deal – Traveling south on A258 toward the busy port of Dover, Walmer Castle is only 1 mile from Deal. Built as a fortress by Henry VIII, the castle became the official residence of the Lord Warden of the Cinque Ports in the mid-1700s. This association of seaports began in the 11th century, when five principal ports (Hastings, Romney — now New Romney — Hythe, Dover, and Sandwich) banded together to provide England with a makeshift navy. Later this was formalized by a charter that granted certain privileges in exchange for the pledge of supplying ships and men for the country's defense. Other ports along the southeast foot of England, the part closest to France, became involved in this arrangement during the dangerous period from the 13th to the 16th century. Following the establishment of the Royal Navy, the importance of the association and the post of its highest officer, the lord warden, declined drastically, and though there is still such a title today, it is largely without power. Two of the most prominent lord wardens to live in the castle have been William Pitt the Younger and the first Duke of Wellington. The castle is open to visitors except on Mondays and when the present lord warden is in residence (usually in August). Dover, the Gateway of England, is only 7 miles farther south on A258.

DOVER: The chalky white cliffs of Dover have been a strategic landmark since the early Iron Age, when a settlement was established here. Roman invaders quickly erected a fortress and an octagonal lighthouse, or pharos, and an extension of the ancient Roman roadway called Watling Street ran between Dover and London via Canterbury. The Romans' pharos still stands within the walls of the more recent Dover Castle, an imposing Norman stronghold on the eastern cliffs of the city. Its huge, square keep was built by Henry II in the 1180s around a 240-foot-deep well — the keep had a lead-piped water supply, a surprising amenity for so old a structure. It is easy to spend several hours wandering throughout the towers, gateways, and chambers, outer bailey, inner bailey, and keep of the enormous fortification, and even the underground works, where passages lead into the cliffs, are open to the public daily. On clear days, France is easily visible across the Straits of Dover, roughly 20 miles away, and the view from the battlements of Dover Castle, atop the 400-foot bluff overlooking the city and sea, is magnificent. Dover is one of Britain's main embarkation points for ferries to France (Calais and Boulogne) and Belgium (Oostende and Zeebrugge) and stands to be affected dramatically when the Channel Tunnel linking England and France opens in 1993.

During both world wars, Dover again rose to prominence as a point of departure for troops bound for the Continent and as the goal of planes straggling back from the fighting. The city was pounded by long-range artillery during World War II, and the thick castle walls sheltered the population through the 4-year bombardment.

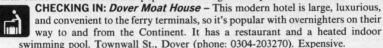

CHECKING IN: ***Dover Moat House*** **–** This modern hotel is large, luxurious, and convenient to the ferry terminals, so it's popular with overnighters on their way to and from the Continent. It has a restaurant and a heated indoor swimming pool. Townwall St., Dover (phone: 0304-203270). Expensive.

En Route from Dover – The famous cliffs extend southwest toward Folkestone, neatly trimming the coastline with a tall white chalk seawall for almost 7 miles. Beyond this point the cliffs fall away, exposing the shore. Stretching westward is a line of defenses constructed in the early 19th century against the threat of an invasion by Napoleon: a series of 74 small coastal fortresses — circular Martello towers — from Folkestone around Beachy Head to Seaford. The towers were reinforced a short distance inland by the Royal Military Canal, dug in the same period, from Hythe to Rye. Additional defenses were erected in 1940 when Hitler massed his forces along the French coast.

Take A20 southwest along the coast from Dover to Folkestone where, if favored with good weather, a stroll on the Leas — a broad, mile-long, grassy walkway on the crest of the cliffs just west of the harbor — is in order. From here the coast of France unfolds in a beautiful panorama 22 miles distant. On the east side of the harbor is the Warren, where a section of the chalk cliff has crumbled and fallen on the beach — a great hunting ground for fossils. Folkestone has a plentiful supply of good, reasonably priced family hotels, many of them on the seafront.

Close by at Cheriton, the official Channel Tunnel Exhibition Centre details the progress of the tunnel being built between England and France. One exhibit shows how the train shuttle system willoperate once the tunnel is completed in 1993, with models of the proposed terminals on both the French and British sides of the tunnel. Maps and other displays tell the story of previous attempts to build this link between the continent and Great Britain — something engineers have dreamed about since the early 19th century. The Centre is open Tuesdays through Sundays; admission charge.

From Folkestone, pick up A259 for the additional 4 miles to Hythe, or, if time permits, detour 16 miles inland by A20 to Ashford, an important market and railway center on the river Stour. When the channel tunnel is built, passengers will board the train on the English side at Ashford; the terminal for cars will be near Folkestone. The town of Ashford itself has little of interest to visitors, but until the whole area turns into an Anglo-French artery, its environs, still a rural backwater, exert a certain appeal. The white cowls of oasts protrude from hop fields and orchards, the latter a breathtaking sight in May when the apple blossoms are out. Inns set in beer gardens are common;

one of the most attractive is the 15th-century *Bell* at Smarden, just west of Ashford on B2077. Its checkered brickwork is overhung with scalloped tiles, and inside patrons sample real ale beneath beams strung with hop bines. Occasionally, as at Little Chart (northwest of Ashford), you will come across a large green known locally as a "forstal," because cattle used to be penned or forestalled on it before being sold at the Ashford market.

CHECKING IN/EATING OUT: ***Eastwell Manor*** – Set in some 3,000 acres of parkland 3 miles north of Ashford, this is an elegant and rambling stone Jacobean country house rebuilt as recently as the 1920s but with a history going back to the Norman Conquest. Its 23 huge bedrooms are positively inviting and some of the bathrooms are downright sumptuous. There's also an oak-paneled bar to lure guests down for drinks before dinner, which is served in a baronial dining room. The menu makes extensive use of local produce as well as more exotic ingredients, and English wines are offered, too. Eastwell Park, Ashford (phone: 0233-635751). Expensive.

HYTHE: Three Martello towers still guard the former Cinque Port of Hythe, although the harbor has long since silted up and the sea receded. There are also fortifications from other periods, including the ruins of a Roman castrum, Stutfall Castle, about 2½ miles west of Hythe along the banks of the Royal Military Canal that bisects the city. Above Stutfall is Lympne Castle (pronounced *Lim*), a home of the archdeacons of Canterbury until the mid-1800s. It incorporates a square 12th-century Norman tower into its otherwise 14th- and 15th-century construction, and though it is not impressively fortresslike, its sweeping views as far as the sea would have satisfied any ancient watchman (open daily May through mid-October and Easter; admission charge). Port Lympne House and Zoo Park, with its herds of rare horses, deer, antelope, gazelle, rhinos, and other beasts, is nearby. Hythe itself is a pleasant seaside town, a mixture of old houses, inns, and antiques shops on narrow streets. The presence of over 1,500 human skulls in the medieval church has never been satisfactorily explained. Hythe is also the place to catch a ride on the Romney, Hythe, and Dymchurch narrow-gauge railway (open daily Easter through September and weekends March through October). Miniature engines hauling real passengers for modest fares puff back and forth along the sea edge of Romney Marsh, the remote, sparsely populated lowland stretching southwest of Hythe.

En Route from Hythe – The A259 leads into Romney Marsh, first following both the coast and the railway as far as New Romney (like Hythe, also a closed port, having lost its harbor in the 13th century), then bearing inland toward the ancient towns of Rye and Winchelsea. If you stopped for the view from Lympne Castle, you will have seen a great deal of this flat, sometimes bleak expanse of low-lying fields and marsh grass full of grazing Romney Marsh sheep and full of memories of the old smuggling days when untaxed (and often illegal) cargoes were unloaded here. In deep winter, the marsh can seem utterly detached from the present century. In summer, however, there are many attractions. The coast is flat, sandy, and ideal for bathing. If watching the English doing all the traditional seaside things holds some appeal, then Dymchurch, St. Mary's Bay, or Littlestone-on-Sea (New Romney's seaside suburb) are the places to go. Dymchurch, a popular weekend resort with a 5-mile beach, lies in the shelter of a 3-mile fortified seawall built by the Romans to prevent the marshes from flooding. The wall has been continuously improved, and the fortifications were added in 1940. Inland, the hamlets and villages of Romney Marsh proper are less frequented than the coastal towns and well worth seeing. These are quiet spots with ancient and historic churches — some of which, at some period in their past, served as caches for smugglers' contraband. Burmarsh, Newchurch, St. Mary in the Marsh, Ivychurch, Snargate, and

Fairfield (all off A259), and Old Romney, Brenzett, and Brookland (on A259) are all typical. After Brookland, A259 crosses the border of Kent and heads into Rye (21 miles from Hythe) in neighboring East Sussex.

CHECKING IN: ***Chantry*** – This friendly half-timbered 8-room hotel is next to fine sandy beaches. Sycamore Gardens, Dymchurch (phone: 0303-873137). Moderate.

Red Tiles – A pleasant country hotel, it sits amid 2 acres of lawns and gardens only half a mile from good beaches. Warren Rd., Littlestone-on-Sea, New Romney (phone: 0679-62155). Moderate.

RYE: Along with Winchelsea, Rye is one of the two "Ancient Towns" added to the original Cinque Ports, though the receding sea and centuries of silt buildup have obstructed its port, limiting traffic to small coastal vessels and fishing boats. Now the harbor is no more than a narrow creek winding its way to town, and Rye, essentially a medieval seaport stranded 2 miles inland, combines the flavor of a large fishing village with that of a remote country settlement. The effect is an alluring one that draws nearly as many visitors as Canterbury. Rye stands on an almost conical sandstone hill, its red roofs piled up to the point of the parish church on top, the whole fairy-tale conception circled by a crumbling 14th-century wall. The town was razed by the French in 1377 and again in 1448, destroying the most historic buildings, but many of the houses erected during the late 15th century still grace the narrow, cobblestone streets. Gabled and half-timbered, Rye is quite simply a lovely town, and it retains the atmosphere of medieval times along with a measure of its former bustling activity.

Both the *Mermaid Inn* (see *Checking In*), rebuilt during the 15th century and rumored to have been a smugglers' rendezvous, and the timbered *Flushing Inn* (15th century) are excellent haunts for travelers. The works of the great clock (ca. 1560) in the 12th-century Church of St. Mary are thought to be among the oldest still functioning in England. Lamb House, a Georgian building on West Street, was the residence of novelist Henry James from 1898 until his death in 1916 (open Wednesday and Saturday afternoons, April through October; admission charge). Fletcher's House, now a tea shop near Lion and Market streets, is thought to be the birthplace of the 16th-century dramatist John Fletcher. The 13th-century Ypres Tower (here pronounced *Why*-pers) was purchased by the de Ypres family in the early 14th century; it is now a museum with exhibitions pertinent to the Cinque Ports and displays of local pottery (open daily from Easter to mid-October; admission charge). Rye specializes in pottery, and it's easy to pick up some good bargains in the many shops and workshops just off the High Street area.

Winchelsea, also added to the Cinque Ports alliance before the changing coastline ruined its harbor, was completely relocated to its present site in 1283 by Edward I. The church, begun soon afterward, is dedicated to St. Thomas à Becket. Parts of William Thackeray's *Denis Duval* are set in these two towns.

CHECKING IN: ***George*** – The tiled façade is a Georgian addition, but behind that is a 400-year-old Tudor inn, with 16 rooms, oak beams and fireplaces. Centrally located. High St., Rye (phone: 0797-222114). Expensive.

Mariners' – The reception and service are exceptionally warm in this lovely 17th-century house, now a 14-room hotel with restaurant. High St., Rye (phone: 0797-223480). Expensive.

Mermaid Inn – When Queen Elizabeth I visited Rye in 1573, she stayed here. Even older than the *George*, this beautifully preserved inn was rebuilt in 1420 and is one of the most charming old hotels in England, now with 30 rooms. Its walls still conceal the priest holes and secret staircase used to avoid arrest in the old days of pirates and smugglers. Mermaid St., Rye (phone: 0797-223065). Moderate.

EATING OUT: ***Flackley Ash*** – This cozy hotel 4 miles from Rye has a well-deserved reputation for its food. It's prepared by owner-chef Clive Bennett, who also holds several "jazz weekends" during the winter. London Rd., Peasmarsh (phone: 0797-21381). Expensive.

HASTINGS (ST. LEONARDS and BATTLE): Nine miles from Rye, A259 meets the coast at Hastings and adjoining St. Leonards. The small town of Battle is 6 miles inland. This area is of immense strategic and psychological importance to England, as becomes clear when its history is reviewed: It was here that the last successful invasion of the British Isles began.

Following the death of Edward the Confessor in January 1066, Harold of Wessex, the son of Edward's adviser, ascended to the throne of England. His claim to the monarchy was weak, however, and Duke William of Normandy felt his own to be more justified, since Edward had been a distant cousin and Harold himself, he said, had previously sworn to support William's right to wear the crown on Edward's death.

It was just a few miles west of Hastings, at Pevensey Bay, that William landed his forces on September 28, 1066.

King Harold and his men were busy fighting his brother Tostig and the invading King of Norway (another claimant to the throne) in the north, and after defeating them at the Battle of Stamford Bridge, Harold and his tired army marched southward. They gathered support en route but it was not until the morning of October 14 that Harold's men, perhaps 10,000 ax- and spear-carrying foot soldiers, formed a shield wall along a ridge just north of Hastings. William's force was composed of a few thousand archers and several thousand mounted knights and armed men. Norman arrows rained on the defenders, and cavalry charges broke on the wall of spears and shields. In the late afternoon William faked a retreat, drawing many of the inexperienced English militiamen from their positions, and decimated them with his cavalry. King Harold and the remainder of his army were soon slaughtered. On the spot where Harold planted the Royal Standard, where he and his closest followers actually died, William the Conquerer erected Battle Abbey. By Christmas, William was crowned King of England in Westminster Abbey.

Hastings today is a popular resort much loved by the British for its wonderful setting between the hilly South Downs and the channel coast. The original Cinque Port city stagnated after the harbor became clogged with silt during the late 12th century, and the 600-year sleep that followed kept the Old Town beautifully intact. This is at the east end of Hastings, which with a substantial fishing fleet retains its traditional raison d'être. The fishermen live here and frequent the *Fishermen's Institute,* a pub on All Saints Street. Narrow streets and age-old houses characterize this area, and two medieval churches survive: the 14th-century St. Clement's and the 15th-century All Saints'. Even the tall, skinny, tarred-wood sheds, or "net shops," built in the 16th century and used to store fishermen's nets, have survived along a part of the beach called the Stade. Near them, the Fishermen's Church is now a museum (open from the end of May through September; closed Fridays). The ruins of Hastings Castle, erected around the time of William's invasion, overlook the 3-mile beach area. The magnificent homes in this section of town reflect the resurgence of Hastings as a resort during the late 18th and 19th centuries when sea bathing became popular among the English. Eventually, the town grew westward to meet St. Leonards, a planned Regency "new" town laid out and developed by architects James and Decimus Burton in the 1830s. By the 1870s, the two had coalesced into one resort, with St. Leonards as its stylish western end. Hastings has all the usual seaside entertainments, and an amusement pier and pavilions plus a model railway add to the gaiety of its beachfront. The most beautiful aspects of the town, however, are natural — St. Clement's Caves (below the castle), once used by smugglers, and the cliffwalks to the east of Hastings.

The nearby small town of Battle, which derives its name from the famous Battle of

Hastings, includes the abbey founded by William the Conquerer. The battle site, from the ridge where Harold formed his lines to the heights of Senlac and Telham on the far side of the valley, where William's forces gathered, is just southwest of the town. The abbey gatehouse is on Market Square, and the ruins of the abbey church (destroyed in about 1540) center on the spot where Harold fell. Those sections of the abbey that survived intact and those added in later years are now used as a school. (The abbey ruins are open Sundays, April through September; admission charge.) The Battle Museum, on High Street, paints a crystal-clear picture of the battle (open daily Easter through September).

CHECKING IN: ***Beauport Park*** – Set off in a beautiful 33-acre park area, this stately Georgian hotel has a formal garden to add to the timeless atmosphere. The service is in keeping with that feeling of another age, and the heated outdoor pool is a bonus during the summer. Battle Rd., Hastings (phone: 0424-51222). Expensive.

George – An old coaching inn, it has modern comforts in its 21 rooms, all of which have private bath or shower (but only one sports a four-poster bed). There is a restaurant serving English and continental cooking, and when it's cold, a log fire burns in the hotel bar. High St., Battle (phone: 04246-4466). Moderate.

En Route from Hastings – If time permits, you may want to leave the sea and salt air behind temporarily and detour inland from Hastings to visit the Weald, the band of fertile farmland that stretches between the North and South Downs as far west as Hampshire. Its unusual name derives from the Anglo-Saxon "wold," or woods, which many centuries ago covered this region.

THE WEALD: Hawkhurst, reached from Hastings via A21, then A229, is not only a typical example of the prosperous market towns and large villages of the Weald but also an excellent base from which to explore the countryside. Hawkhurst grew in association with ancient iron and cloth industries, the wealth of which, together with agriculture, fashioned a village of many substantial, weatherboarded houses. In the early 18th century, the town was also famous as the home of the notorious Hawkhurst Gang of smugglers who terrorized the region — their delinquent faces were well known at the *Mermaid Inn* in Rye.

The countryside around Hawkhurst, spanning the meandering border between East Sussex and Kent, is rich in castles and historic houses. About 9 miles southwest of town (on A265, just outside the town of Burwash) is Bateman's, a 17th-century stone ironmaster's house that became the home of Rudyard Kipling; the study where he wrote some of his best-known books is just as he left it, the windows looking out on one of the Weald's most beautiful valleys (open Saturdays through Wednesdays, April through October; admission charge). Heathfield, a small country town just west of Burwash, has an interesting market on Sunday mornings.

About 6 miles northeast of Hawkhurst (along A229 as far as Sissinghurst) is Sissinghurst Castle. Don't expect to see a castle, however, because this is actually the fragments of a beautiful Tudor house that was rescued from total dereliction by writers Vita Sackville-West and Harold Nicolson — friends of Virginia Woolf and members of the "Bloomsbury Set" — who laid out lovely formal gardens within its red brick walls (open April to mid-October daily except Mondays; admission charge). Bodiam Castle, 3 miles southeast of Hawkhurst (off A229), is most definitely a castle, and its machicolated towers reflected in the still waters of a wide moat make a dramatic first impression. It was built in 1385 against an invasion by the French that never came and has been uninhabited for 300 years, despite which it remains a well preserved and interesting specimen of medieval military architecture (open daily from April through October and closed Sundays the rest of the year; admission charge).

Another moated castle, this one in ruins, is Scotney, about 6 miles northwest of

Hawkhurst and a mile southeast of the village of Lamberhurst (follow A268 out of Hawkhurst, then A21). The attraction here is the romantic garden surrounding the tumbled 14th-century stone walls (the garden is open Wednesdays through Sundays from April to mid-November; the castle, the same days from May through August; admission charge). Two miles west of Lamberhurst (just north of B2169), Bayham Abbey stands in cloistered peace beside the river Teise. Founded in the early 13th century and dissolved in the early 16th century, it has been a picturesque Gothic ruin for centuries (open daily from mid-March to mid-October; admission charge).

CHECKING IN: ***Royal Oak*** – This small, weatherboarded 18th-century inn has 12 rooms. The food is good (the restaurant is open to non-guests Saturday evenings and Sundays at lunch), and accommodations are very reasonable. Rye Rd., Hawkhurst (phone: 05805-2184). Inexpensive.

En Route from the Weald – Bayham Abbey is only 4 miles east of Royal Tunbridge Wells, the health resort that has been extremely popular since the discovery of the "healing powers" of its mineral waters at the beginning of the 17th century. In turn, Royal Tunbridge Wells is only 36 miles from London, and if you decide to cut short this tour of southeast England and return to the capital, you can easily do so by taking A21, which passes just east of town. A slight detour along the way would allow a visit to Knole, a magnificent baronial mansion (open Wednesdays through Sundays April through October) outside the town of Sevenoaks on A225.

The southeast route, however, returns to the coast to visit Eastbourne and Brighton (stopping to see Royal Tunbridge Wells and Sevenoaks at the end of the itinerary). From Hawkhurst, take A229 back to Hastings and from there proceed along the coast 17 miles to Eastbourne. Alternatively, take A265 southwest from Hawkhurst to Hurst Green, then drive south via A21 and A2100 to the junction of A269 in the vicinity of Battle. From here, bear west to the town of Herstmonceux, outside of which is Herstmonceux Castle, a moated red brick fortified mansion built in the 1440s but completely rebuilt in the early 20th century. From 1948 to 1989 it was the home of the Royal Greenwich Observatory (which was forced to leave Greenwich in search of a spot with less pollution and less artificial light blurring the heavens). Crusaders' tombs can be seen in the church opposite, and locally made "trugs," curved garden baskets woven from willow fronds, can be bought in the village. From Herstmonceux, continue west to A22, which heads south to Eastbourne.

EATING OUT: ***Cleavers Lyng*** – Converted from an old cottage, this unpretentious little hotel offers home cooking and especially tasty pies. Church Rd., Herstmonceux (phone: 0323-833131). Inexpensive.

EASTBOURNE: This seaside town, 20 miles west of Hastings on the coastal A259, was developed since the mid-19th century by William Cavendish, the seventh Duke of Devonshire. It was meant to be elegant and has remained so, with a 3-mile long seafront (unbesmirched by shops, which are not allowed), a pier with the colorful Carpet Gardens beside it, and a bandstand distinctively roofed with turquoise-colored tiles. At both ends of the seafront are reminders of Napoleon's plans to invade England in the early 19th century. At the eastern end is the Redoubt, a circular fort built from 1804 to 1812 and now housing a museum of Sussex military memorabilia since the Romans. The Wish Tower, at the western end, is the 73rd of the 74 Martello towers that line the coast beginning at Folkestone; it houses a museum of coastal defense from Napoleonic times to World War II. (Both museums are open daily from Easter through October; admission charge.)

Eastbourne's largely shingle beach (sand is uncovered at low tide) is a relatively sunny one by English standards since Beachy Head, only 3 miles southwest, tends to take the brunt of bad weather and disperse it. This chalk headland is one of the highest points on the Sussex coast, 575 feet above the channel, and the views out to sea or back over the South Downs make it a favorite lookout point. Between Beachy Head and Seaford, several miles west along the coast, the Downs meet the sea in a scalloped white wall of chalk cliffs known as the Seven Sisters. This is a wild and windy nature reserve that can only be explored on foot. In fact, Beachy Head is the Sussex end of the South Downs Way, an official long-distance footpath that stretches 80 miles into Hampshire, and the section between Beachy Head and the Cuckmere Valley — a cliff-top walk across the top of the Seven Sisters — is one of its most beautiful parts. (It's also the only part exclusive to walkers, since the South Downs Way is also the country's only long-distance bridleway, and the rest of it is shared by walkers and horseback riders.)

CHECKING IN: Grand – One of England's most famous hotels, it's a vast Victorian building in a commanding position on the seafront. Extensively modernized, it now includes indoor and outdoor pools, sauna, gymnasium, and putting and snooker facilities. Many of the 164 rooms face the sea. Excellent restaurant. King Edward's Parade, Eastbourne (phone: 0323-412345).

En route from Eastbourne – The coastal road continues west to the large and busy resort of Brighton, another 20 miles or so away. In summer, however, the coastal road is often clogged with traffic, and to avoid it you may want to take the inland route, A27, through Lewes to Brighton, stopping at some notable country houses along the way.

Six miles short of Lewes, down a lane to the left between Firle and Selmeston, is Charleston, the retreat of that Bloomsbury ménage à trois, Vanessa and Clive Bell and Duncan Grant. This 18th-century farmhouse was discovered in 1916 by Vanessa's sister, Virginia Woolf, who told her, "If you lived there, you could make it absolutely divine." The trio who lived there did so by painting everything — tables, chairs, fireplaces, book cases, and bedsteads — according to the inspiration of the moment, and the rooms still echo the conversation and laughter of such guests as Lytton Strachey, T. S. Eliot, E. M. Forster, Bertrand Russell, and John Maynard Keynes. The walled English country garden is filled with mosaics, busts, and sculptures as well as with old-fashioned flowers, fruit trees, and shrubs. Charleston Farmhouse is open Wednesdays, Thursdays, Saturdays, and Sundays from April through October, but since the number of visitors at any one time is limited, it is strongly advised to telephone 0321-83265 in advance for an appointment (admission charge).

Continuing west on A27, in the shadow of Firle Beacon (at 718 feet the highest point of the Downs east of Lewes), a turn to the left a mile or so beyond Charleston leads to the gates of Firle Place, home of the Gage family since the 15th century. The present owner is the seventh Viscount Gage; an earlier member of the family was General Thomas Gage, who, as commander-in-chief of British forces at the outset of the American Revolution, took the blame, unfairly in the view of some historians, for the loss of the colonies. The building underwent alterations around 1730, so although outwardly Georgian, it incorporates a Tudor courtyard house. Great elms and beech trees set off its creamy white stonework and the terraced lawns of its extensive park, while the rooms inside contain a notable collection of European and English Old Master paintings and English and French furniture (open Wednesday, Thursday, and Sunday afternoons from June through September, also on Easter and spring and summer bank holidays; admission charge).

Firle Place is just one of the fine parks taking advantage of the shelter of the steep north-facing slope of the Downs. Still driving westward, a turn to the right off A27 leads to the 16th-century Glynde Place (open Wednesday and Thursday afternoons from June through September; admission charge), and 2 miles farther on is the unique *Glyndebourne Opera House,* which was added to the original partly Tudor Glyndebourne estate in 1934 by John Christie and his wife, the singer Audrey Mildmay. From late May to early August, *Glyndebourne Festival Opera,* one of the social events of the English summer, takes place here (it's a short but sweet opera season). Men in tuxedos and women in long dresses picnic on the lawns before the performances, which are sung by opera stars of international renown (phone for information: 0273-812321).

Monk's House, the home of Leonard and Virginia Woolf from 1919 until his death in 1969, is near the church in the village of Rodmell (a left turn off A27 onto the minor road to Newhaven), 2 miles south of Lewes. She drowned herself in the river Ouse here in 1941 and her ashes are buried in the garden (open Wednesday and Saturday afternoons from April through October; admission charge).

Just south of the A27 is Drusillas Park at Alfriston, a small but extremely interesting zoo, which specializes in preserving rare species. The animals live in attractive landscaped areas and there are well-maintained gardens. Open daily; admission charge.

LEWES: Only 8 miles northeast of Brighton, this is an ancient and still old-fashioned town whose steep and narrow streets are crowded with historical associations. Lewes Castle is in the center of town, its late 11th- to early 12th-century Norman keep in ruins, but its 14th-century barbican, or outer gatehouse, in good condition. The *Barbican House Museum,* in an Elizabethan to 18th-century house nearby, is an archaeological museum with displays from prehistoric through medieval times (castle and museum open daily; admission charge). Anne of Cleves' House on Southover High Street, now a museum of local history, was not her home but was part of her settlement for granting Henry VIII a divorce (open Mondays through Saturdays from mid-February to mid-November, plus Sunday afternoons from April through October; admission charge). Another settlement property was Lewes Priory, or the Priory of St. Pancras, at one time the most important Cluniac house in Britain but an extensive ruin since the Dissolution of the Monasteries in the 16th century. It's best seen from Mountfield Road.

Lewes's most famous resident was probably Thomas Paine, who from 1768 to 1774, just before he emigrated to America, lived at *Bull House* (now a restaurant). The author of *Common Sense,* the influential political pamphlet that pleaded the colonies' case for independence, spent evenings debating at the *White Hart* inn (see *Checking In*), where he repeatedly won the "Headstrong Book," a copy of Homer so named because it was sent in the morning to the most obstinate debater of the night before. Lewes is also known for its own version of Guy Fawkes Day (November 5). While all of Britain celebrates the day with fireworks and the burning of effigies of the man who tried to blow up Parliament in 1605 (an act meant to be the beginning of an uprising of English Catholics), here there are elaborate bonfire ceremonies and a procession to the bridge over the river Ouse, where a blazing tar barrel is hurled into the water. The rites probably pre-date Guy Fawkes and go back to the mid-16th-century reign of Queen Mary, when many Protestants were burned at the stake on School Hill, leaving a legacy of anti-papist feeling.

CHECKING IN: *White Hart* – It was in the wine cellars of this historic coaching inn that many 16th-century "heretics" were held before being burned. It was here, too, that Thomas Paine held the debating club that he later described as the "cradle of American independence." The hotel has 33 comfortable bedrooms and serves excellent ribs of beef and Harvey's real ale. High St., Lewes (phone: 0273-474676). Moderate.

BRIGHTON: England's most famous seaside resort traces its popularity to the late 18th century, when the somewhat eccentric Prince Regent who was to become King George IV began to spend time here. By 1821 he had put the finishing touches — such exotic details as minarets, onion domes, and latticework balconies — on his seaside retreat, the Royal Pavilion that stands in the heart of Brighton today looking less like a stately home than a Mogul palace. (Open daily; admission charge.) The town's King's Road seafront, a holidaymakers' domain of cotton candy, fish and chips, and amusements, endowed with the requisite Victorian Palace Pier, indulges quite another mood. Worth a visit is the Old Town, an area of narrow alleys, tea shops, and pubs known as the Lanes. It's traffic-free and it will give you an idea of what Brighton was like before the fairy godmother touched her magic wand and turned the fishing village of Brighthelmstone first fashionable, then flossy. For a full report on the sights, hotels, and restaurants of this resort, see *Brighton,* THE CITIES.

En Route from Brighton – Return in the direction of London by backtracking through Lewes and taking the quiet B2192 and B2102 northeast, turning north onto A267 at Cross-in-Hand, a village situated high on the Weald. After Five Ashes, A267 curves east on its way to Royal Tunbridge Wells, which can also be reached by turning left onto an unclassified road about half a mile past Five Ashes and continuing to Rotherfield, on the edge of Ashdown Forest. From here, an unclassified road signposted "Eridge" leads to A26, where a right turn will lead to the famous spa.

ROYAL TUNBRIDGE WELLS: This elegant town once rivaled Bath as a health resort. The "healing properties" of its mineral springs were discovered in 1606, and by 1638, the Pantiles, a promenade known for the type of tiles originally used to pave it, had been laid out. Now shaded by lime trees, with colonnaded houses and shops to one side, this is just as popular today as it was in the 18th century, when Richard "Beau" Nash arrived to preside over public entertainments as master of ceremonies and, just as he had previously done for Bath, raise Tunbridge Wells to the heights of fashion. There it remained until the late-18th century, until, that is, sniffing sea air and bathing in saltwater became the socially and physiologically proper thing to do and the smart set transferred its allegiance to the upstart Brighton on the coast. Queen Victoria spent time here as a princess and because of this and other royal visits, the town of Tunbridge Wells — a relatively new town for this region — was permitted by Edward VII to add "Royal" to its name in 1909. A look at the 17th-century church of King Charles the Martyr, near the Pantiles and noted for its plaster ceiling, is on most visitors' agendas. Then, although it is still possible to sample the mineral water from the springs, most prefer tea for two at *Binn's Corner House* or something stronger at the *Hole in the Wall* pub on High Street, formerly a tobacco shop known as the Central Smoking Divan.

CHECKING IN: ***Spa*** – Set on extensive grounds on a hillside with broad views, this 18th-century mansion has 75 rooms, an indoor pool, putting, tennis, and a restaurant with high standards. Mount Ephraim, Tunbridge Wells (phone: 0892-510575). Expensive.

Calverley – Queen Victoria stayed here as a child when this elegant 18th-century mansion was still a private residence. A hotel since 1840, it's set in a delightful garden facing the town's Calverley Park; it has 43 bedrooms (about half of which have baths), antiques throughout, chintz-covered furniture, and a countrified atmosphere. Crescent Rd., Royal Tunbridge Wells (phone: 0892-26455). Moderate.

EATING OUT: ***Cheevers*** – Despite its set-price menu and spartan decor, this is a place where guests can count on eating well. The fare is mostly French, but there are English dishes, too. Open Tuesdays through Saturdays. High Street, Tunbridge Wells (phone: 0892-45524). Expensive.

En Route from Royal Tunbridge Wells – A26 north to A21 is the way back to London. A few short side trips along the way, however, will enable you to visit at least a few of the fine houses in this part of Kent. Penshurst Place, in the village of Penshurst (west of A26, on B2176), was the birthplace in 1554 of the poet, soldier, and statesman, Sir Philip Sidney, and is still the home of his descendant, Viscount de l'Isle. One of the great stately homes of England, it was begun in the 14th century and later enlarged with many additions — which fortunately respect the original Gothic style. The Great

Hall of 1340, in its pristine medieval state, is its most famous feature, while outside there is a lovely walled garden. The noble house (open daily, except Mondays, from April through September; admission charge) is entered through Leicester Square, a miniature version of its better-known namesake in the heart of London.

A few miles farther along (up a small lane off B2027) is Hever Castle, partly built in the 13th century and later the home of the Bullen (or Boleyn) family. Anne Boleyn, who paid with her head for her failure to produce a living male heir for her husband Henry VIII (as well as for adultery), was born here and wooed by Henry here. The moated castle was bought in 1903 by William Waldorf Astor, an American who became a British subject and was later made the first Viscount Astor of Hever. The mock Tudor village around the castle and the wonderful gardens for which the property is particularly noted are the result of Astor's transformation (open daily from mid-March through October; admission charge).

Outside the town of Sevenoaks on A225, deer roam free in the park of Knole, one of the largest private houses in England. This vast mansion was begun in the mid-15th century by an archbishop of Canterbury, then belonged in turn to Henry VIII and Queen Elizabeth I, who gave it to her courtier, the poet Thomas Sackville, whose descendants, the Sackville-West family, have lived here ever since (although Knole has been in the National Trust's keeping since 1946). The writer Vita Sackville-West, member of the Bloomsbury Set and restorer of Sissinghurst Castle, was born and raised at Knole and chronicled both it and her family in *Knole and the Sackvilles,* but it was her friend, Virginia Woolf, who referred to the structure as "a town rather than a house" in her novel *Orlando.* The building sprawls over 3 acres and includes, according to legend, 7 courtyards corresponding to the days of the week, 52 staircases for the weeks, and 365 rooms — one for each day in the year. The state rooms contain a fine collection of portraits, including works by Reynolds and Gainsborough, while the furnishings are virtually as they were in Elizabethan times (open Wednesdays through Sundays, April through October; admission charge).

Six miles east of Sevenoaks, off A25, is Ightham Mote, another moated manor bought by an American, Charles Henry Robinson, a businessman from Portland, Maine. He first stumbled upon this 14th-century gem while touring the leafy lanes of Kent, bought it in the 1950s, and left it to the National Trust in his will (open Mondays, Wednesdays, Thursdays, Fridays, and Sundays from April through October; admission charge).

Another side trip, this time 6 miles west of Sevenoaks on A25, will lead to Westerham, a pretty little town enjoying something of its original peacefulness since much of its through traffic now uses the M25 London Orbital Motorway. *Pitt's Cottage,* a timbered house used as a summer cottage by William Pitt the Younger, stands on the outskirts and now functions as a restaurant. Westerham is best known as the birthplace of General James Wolfe, whose victory over the French at Quebec in 1759 gave England control of Canada. His childhood home, a gabled red brick 17th-century house now called Quebec House, contains portraits and prints and, in the stables, an exhibition about the Battle of Quebec (open from April through October, closed Thursdays and Saturdays; admission charge). A statue of Wolfe, who was mortally wounded during the battle, shares the village green with one of Winston Churchill, whose country home is about 2 miles south of town via B2026.

Churchill bought Chartwell in 1922, entranced by the setting of this Victorian house and by its stunning views across the Weald. The brick wall he built with his own hands around the kitchen garden during his wilderness years in politics in the 1930s, the rose garden where he loved to walk, and the track worn across the carpet of the book-lined study by his endless pacing while dictating to relays of secretaries are as he left them, and the walls of the garden studio are hung with his paintings. The property now belongs to the National Trust, donated by a group of his friends who bought it even before his death so that the home of Britain's foremost 20th-century statesman should belong to the nation. The house, garden, and studio are open Tuesdays, Wednesdays, Thursdays, Saturdays, and Sundays from April through October (Tuesday mornings are for pre-booked groups only); the house is also open Wednesdays, Saturdays, and Sundays in March and November; admission charge; phone: 0732-866368.

Three miles north of Westerham on A233 is Biggin Hill, the airfield from which some of Churchill's "few" took off on the fighter sorties that won the Battle of Britain against desperate odds. A surviving Spitfire and Hurricane stand sentinel at the main gate, and a chapel built on the site of one of the bombed hangars commemorates pilots and ground crew who were killed.

From here, London, about 15 miles away, is reachable by following A233 north to Bromley and picking up A21.

Eastern Midlands

Only an hour's distance from London, it becomes difficult to believe that there are nearly 47 million souls crammed into England. Two hours from the capital, and the visitor can get lost in little country lanes, be the only guest at a medieval inn, the only photographer trying to capture the beauty of a twelfth-century church. It is necessary to leave the main highways, descending from A roads to B roads and even unnumbered roads, to experience such tranquillity, but make the effort and you'll find the England of storybooks, where roses *do* grow at cottage doors even though television aerials sprout from the 500-year-old chimneys. The five shires covered in this itinerary — Cambridgeshire, Leicestershire, Lincolnshire, Northamptonshire, and Nottinghamshire — indulge the traditional fantasy even further, for this is a land of spires, squires, pubs, and hunting horns.

In central England, halfway between London and the cities of York and Birmingham, these five counties make up the eastern part of the Midlands (coinciding roughly with the area English tourist authorities called the "East Midlands," which does not include Cambridgeshire, however, but does include another county, Derbyshire). These shires have provided England with agricultural wealth, and as some landowners become immensely rich in this very fertile part of the country, they patronized architects, artists, and craftsmen who produced wonderful structures and works of art to decorate distinguished buildings. Trade has always been important; indeed, some of the main north-south routes passing through here date back to Roman times. The Romans laid Ermine Street (A1) from London to Lincoln, and the Fosse Way (A46), which sweeps diagonally across England from the channel near Axminster and also leads to Lincoln. The Great North Road, the old coaching road from London to York, was itself a remake of a Roman route.

Because many small towns lay on these main north-south thoroughfares, inns became a feature of the region as early as Saxon times. And once an inn was built, it remained an inn forever. In some, like the *Angel and Royal* in Grantham, royalty held court 7 centuries ago; others found a humbler niche in history: it was a coaching inn in the very ordinary village of Stilton that made the blue-veined cheese of Leicestershire famous. Without busloads of tourists bombarding them, most of the pubs today are comfortable enough for a drink and a sandwich, though some offer more than others. The *Chequered Skipper* at Ashton, near Oundle, is covered in nature conservation posters as enthusiastically as a kid's bedroom. The ancient *Wig and Mitre* in Lincoln stands between the courts and the cathedral, refreshing the servants of both as it has since medieval days.

While the cathedral in Lincoln is one of the most beautiful cathedrals in all of England, a masterpiece in the English Gothic style known as Early English, the region can claim many others of architectural interest. The villages of Northamptonshire especially are known for spectacular churches. A band of limestone arching across England from Dorset in the south to the Wash in the east provided a stone that can be golden or, when mixed with iron, a darker, mahogany hue. The necklace of churches from Stamford down to Thrapston, or from Melton Mowbray in neighboring Leicestershire up to Grantham in Lincolnshire, are separate gems that make an entrancing whole. The tall spires, visible for miles, are often "broach spires," which means that they soar straight up out of the tower, their lines unbroken by a parapet. This same stone was also used in houses as well as churches, so the villages are the equal of those in the Cotswolds. In fact, they are *more* attractive, because tour buses don't line the High Streets, the pubs are not festooned with postcard racks, and local blacksmiths make useful items that work, rather than paltry souvenirs.

The region also boasts a number of large houses — or are they palaces? — that pull in visitors from all over the world. The popularity of the Princess of Wales has made her childhood home, Althorp, near Northampton, a must on everyone's list. Open only 3 days a week a decade ago, it now exposes its treasures daily with excellent guided tours. In the shadow of Stamford, a town that is itself a collection of architectural treasures, is Burghley House, belonging to the Burghley family, Marquesses of Exeter. Vast, palatial, and impressive, it is one of Britain's greatest country homes. Boughton House, home of the Dukes of Buccleuch, and Belton House, former home of the Brownlow family and now in the care of the National Trust, are equally attractive to art lovers and historians.

This is hunt country, too. Hunting deer, especially stags, had always been a royal pastime, enjoyed by King John, for example, in Rockingham Forest, which once stretched across Leicestershire. After the great forests were axed and more and more pasture was turned by the plow, fox hunting replaced deer hunting. In the 18th century, country gentlemen mixed with tenant farmers and village folk in a ritual that was somehow democratic, even though only the aristocracy could afford the huge packs of hounds, stables of horses, and hunt servants all wearing the traditional hunting "pink" (which is, in fact, scarlet). The fox is still common in England, thriving in country areas and making occasional forays into large towns, so the sport continues, centered in towns such as Melton Mowbray and Market Harborough. The Leicestershire countryside around them, a patchwork of fields bordered by brambly hedgerows and small copses, provides a challenge for horses, riders, and hounds, as well as a protective cover for foxes. But this is a winter sport; summer visitors should not expect to see what Oscar Wilde denounced as the "unspeakable in full pursuit of the uneatable," although old prints and long horns decorate every pub and hotel for miles around.

The area has produced some great names and sad stories. Oliver Cromwell was born and educated in Huntingdon, and Samuel Pepys, the diarist, was also a resident. Farther north, Sir Isaac Newton's fertile brain flourished in the peaceful Lincolnshire countryside, producing mathematical principles that were a gigantic step for mankind 300 years ago. Charles Dickens wrote some of his most popular works while staying with friends at Rockingham Castle, and ancestors of George Washington in Thrapston could well have inspired the design of the Stars and Stripes. The less ennobling tales record the execution of Mary, Queen of Scots, at Fotheringhay and the slaughter of the Royalist Army by Cromwell at Naseby, though the tall Eleanor Cross in Geddington is as poignant a memorial as any of a grief-stricken husband for his dead wife.

In order to capture the real country flavor of these shires, a twisting, turning course is necessary. Thus the route described avoids main roads, though fast, straight stretches occur to provide relief from narrow lanes. It begins at Cambridge and "zigs" north, encountering sleepy villages and age-old inns almost immediately on its way to Peterborough, which has a wonderful cathedral. From there, it continues northwest to Stamford and Burghley House, and then "zags" southwest between the rivers Nene and Welland to take in a string of picturesque stone-built villages such as Oundle and Barnwell. Just short of Northampton, and after a visit to Althorp, it circles north again, to Market Harborough and Oakham in old Rutland, at one time the tiniest county in England. Deep into hunt country now, we push on to Melton Mowbray, Margaret Thatcher's home town of Grantham, and Lincoln, the northernmost point of the route and a city whose layers of civilization should put it higher on the visitor's list of priorities. A final about-face south leads to Newark-on-Trent, past Nottingham (see the *Western Midlands* route for information about this city), to Leicester and Coventry. The latter, in the county of West Midlands, is only 18 miles east of Birmingham (see *Birmingham,* THE CITIES), the starting point of our *Western Midlands* route.

Food in the region is straightforward fare, with some traditional goodies such as Melton Mowbray pork pies still surviving. But outstanding cuisine can be found, as in the refurbished *White Hart* hotel in Lincoln, where it is accompanied by luxurious rooms, or at *Hambleton Hall,* on a lake outside Oakham, another example of the best of modern British hotelkeeping. Expect to pay as much as $125 for a double room at those places listed as expensive; from $70 to $125 in the moderate range; and less than $70 if listed as inexpensive. A three-course meal for two, with coffee, taxes, and service, but no wine, will run $75 and up in places listed as expensive; $30 to $75 as moderate; and under $30 as inexpensive.

CAMBRIDGE: For a full report on this city, its sights, restaurants, and hotels, see *Cambridge,* THE CITIES.

En Route from Cambridge – Take A604 northwest and drive 12 miles to St. Ives, turning right onto B1096.

ST. IVES: This small market town on the river Great Ouse was known as Slepe until it was dedicated to St. Ivo in 1050, but the original name lives on at the *Slepe Hall* hotel (see *Checking In*). An imposing statue of Oliver Cromwell in the town center is a reminder that we are entering Cromwell Country. The man who ruled England after the Civil War was born in nearby Huntingdon and spent time in St. Ives; here, in his stylish riding boots and broad-brimmed hat, he looks more like a Royalist than a Puritan as he points accusingly at visitors and their cameras. Russet tiles, pink brick, and half timbering make it a pleasant town, but its main point of architectural interest is in the middle of the river — the Chapel of St. Leger, one of only three medieval bridge chapels still surviving in Britain, sits on the six-arched, 15th-century stone bridge. Built as a place of worship for travelers, it gained some stories in the early 18th century (they were removed in the early 20th century) and was used as a house for a while, as Charles Whynter's painting in St. Ives's *Norris Museum and Library* shows. The museum displays archaeological and more recent finds from the area. Closed Mondays May through September and Sundays and Mondays the rest of the year (phone: 0480-65101).

CHECKING IN: ***Pike and Eel*** – Three miles east of St. Ives, off A1123, this is an attractive local pub dating from the 15th century, when a ferry service operated here. Now lawns run down to a marina and there are 8 simple but comfortable rooms as well as a restaurant to make it a peaceful overnight stop. Overcote Lane, Needingworth (phone: 0480-63336). Inexpensive.

Slepe Hall – A small, old-fashioned, comfortable hotel with no pretentions to greatness. 19 rooms, 9 with private facilities. Ramsey Rd., St. Ives (phone: 0480-63122). Inexpensive.

En Route from St. Ives – Continue in the direction of Huntingdon — 6 miles away whether you follow A1123 west or return to A604 — but take the time to explore some of the delightful Cambridgeshire villages in the vicinity, still amazingly tranquil considering the volume of traffic rumbling close by. The river Great Ouse, lined with cruisers and houseboats, links them all together. Hemingford Grey sits on the bank, clustered around St. James Church and its stump of a tower. A storm blew the steeple down in 1741, burying bits in the mud below, and eight stone balls make up the tower's substitute decoration. Cows drinking from the stream glance occasionally at a 12th-century manor house that is the oldest continuously inhabited house in England. As the home of author Lucy Boston, it is not open to the public but its moat and thick walls can be appreciated from the outside. The twin village of Hemingford Abbots, downstream along the riverside footpath, has its own church, St. Margaret's, built of brown cobbles in the early 14th century. Houghton (pronounced *How*-ton), 2½ miles from St. Ives via A1123, boasts a restored mill on the site of a 10th-century mill. Now owned by the National Trust, the 4-story brick and clapboard building holds much of the original milling machinery. Open daily 2 to 5:30 PM, Saturdays through Wednesdays, May through September; weekends, April through October. Admission charge (phone: 0480-301494). Nearby is the *Three Horseshoes* pub with low beams, an inglenook, and a snug bar serving hearty fare.

Huntingdon is surrounded by a frustrating ring-road system that seems determined to keep visitors out. Follow signs for the town center, park, and walk.

HUNTINGDON: This was once the county town of the tiny county of Huntingdonshire, which was officially swept away in 1974 by 20th-century bureaucracy (monthly publications such as *What's on in Huntingdonshire* show that the locals care little for decisions made in London, however). Originally Godmanchester, on the other bank of the Great Ouse, was more important, since it stood at the intersection of Roman roads such as Ermine Street and the Via Devana. Nevertheless, Huntingdon grew more affluent, leaving Godmanchester behind as a quiet, elegant village with a Chinese bridge and timber-framed houses. When a road bridge was built between the neighboring towns in the 14th century, the construction was noticeably fancier at the wealthier (Huntingdon) end of the bridge.

The town is famous as the birthplace of Oliver Cromwell, who first "saw the light" in a house on the High Street in 1599 and was baptized in All Saint's Church, where his father's tomb can still be seen. Both Cromwell and Samuel Pepys were alumni of the grammar school, which has now become the *Cromwell Museum* (closed Mondays) and contains several good portraits of the Lord Protector. The great man was stocky and rather ugly, with a profusion of facial moles and warts, and always insisted on being portrayed that way. His walking stick, seal, and powder flask are in the museum, as well as the hat which he is reputed to have worn at the Dissolution of the Long Parliament in 1653. Despite Oliver's puritanical leanings, the Cromwells were wealthy landowners, and Hinchingbrooke House, the Tudor house in which they lived from 1538 to 1627, is outside of town on Brampton Road. Cromwell's grandfather, Sir Henry, was important enough to have entertained Queen Elizabeth I here in 1564. The next owners were the Montagu family, Earls of Sandwich — it was the fourth earl who "invented" the world's most famous snack. Now the house that Horace Walpole described as "old, spacious, and irregular" is a school, open for guided afternoon tours on Sundays and bank holiday Mondays April through August (admission charge).

CHECKING IN: ***George*** – A 17th-century inn with 24 comfortable rooms; all have private facilities. Shakespearean plays are performed in the picturesque old courtyard in summer. George St., Huntingdon (phone: 0480-432444). Moderate.

Old Bridge – This Georgian house overlooking the river is the best hotel in town. It maintains tradition by serving English dishes such as roast beef and venison in the large oak-paneled dining room and also serves teas in the garden in summer. The 27 rooms all have private bathrooms, TV sets, and phones. High St., Huntingdon (phone: 0480-52681). Moderate.

En Route from Huntingdon – Pick up A1126, which joins A604, then A1 north. After 8 miles a signpost on the left indicates Stilton, at one time a "pit stop" on the Great North Road. After the visit, continue 6 miles north (A1) and northeast (A15) to Peterborough.

STILTON: Britain's best known cheese is not, and never was, made in the town that gave it its name. Stop outside the *Bell Inn,* easily spotted because of the huge sign. The large arch shows that it was once a coaching inn, with as many as 40 coaches a day stopping to change horses and allow the passengers a bite to eat. According to one of several legends, a certain Mrs. Paulet, a farmer's wife in Wymondham (east of Melton Mowbray in nearby Leicestershire), first made the blue-veined "King of Cheeses" and sent some to her brother-in-law, Cooper Thornhill, at the *Bell.* The inn's customers were so enthusiastic about the cheese that they took it with them to London, calling it "Stilton" after the place where they had first tasted it. By the time Daniel Defoe visited in 1727, the town and the product had become synonymous enough for him to note that he had "passed through Stilton, a town famous for cheese." Even then, however, the cheese was only sold here, not made here, and now that Stilton has become a registered trademark, its production is officially limited to the three shires of Leicester, Derby, and Nottingham, all northwest of Cambridgeshire.

PETERBOROUGH: This a fast-growing city with an industrial past, but its magnificent cathedral, one of the finest examples of Norman architecture anywhere, more than makes up for a dearth of other attractions. Begun in the 12th century on the foundations of a 7th-century monastery, it has an early Gothic, 13th-century west front that immediately arrests the attention, with its three great pointed arches. Inside, the soaring nave is a classic, and its painted wooden ceiling is unique in England: Bishops, saints, and martyrs have adorned the diamond-shaped scenes since about 1220. Note, too, the fan-vaulted retrochoir, a late 15th- to early 16th-century addition. Catherine of Aragon is buried in the church, and so was Mary, Queen of Scots, until her son, James VI of Scotland and James I of England, transferred her remains to Westminster Abbey. Don't miss the painting of the gravedigger who buried them both, one Robert Scarlett, who died in 1594 at the age of 98. It lies to the north of the west door and records the long and worthy duties he had performed: "He had inter'd two queenes within this place and this towne's householders in his live's space . . ."

Outside of Peterborough, 2 miles west (get off the A15 Peterborough bypass at A47 and go into the village of Longthorpe) is Longthorpe Tower, a fortified medieval mansion (open daily from 10 AM to 6 PM, Easter through September; daily, except Mondays, from 10 AM to 4 PM, October to Easter; to confirm hours, phone: 0733-268482). That Robert Thorpe, the great-grandson of a serf, should have acquired enough money and prestige to build a mansion is unusual in itself, but the real interest here is the most complete set of medieval (14th-century) wall paintings in England, discovered, plastered over, by a local farmer in 1945. The murals depict allegorical and biblical scenes such as The Wheel of the Five Senses, over the fireplace; the Nativity, on the north wall; and the Allegory of the Three Living and Three Dead, in a window recess. Despite the interior comfort, the mansion's crenellations reflect the constant fear of attack.

Also in the vicinity of Peterborough is the Nene Valley Stream Railway, a standard gauge steam railway that runs for 7½ miles between its main depot at Wansford, near A1, and Peterborough. The British love their steam trains and here they run continental locomotives and rolling stock along with British trains. The fare is modest and the line is in operation every weekend from April through September, plus Tuesdays, Wednesdays, and Thursdays in June, July, and August (phone: 0789-782854, for information and reservations).

CHECKING IN: ***Peterborough Moat House*** **–** Outside of town, off A15, this modern hotel of nearly 131 rooms is useful in emergencies. Thorpe Wood, Peterborough (phone: 0733-260000). Moderate.

En Route from Peterborough – To reach Burghley House and Stamford, 14 miles away, take A15 in the direction of Sleaford and after 6 miles, in Glinton, make a sharp left turn onto B1443. You'll soon come to Helpston, a pretty village of gray stone houses and the birthplace of the peasant poet, John Clare. Born next to the *Bluebell Inn* in 1793, he became a ploughboy, herdsman, and rural handyman, otherwise unable to hold down a job. After spending the last 23 years of his life in a lunatic asylum, he died in 1864 and was buried at St. Botolph's church on the village green, leaving some memorable lines including the mournful reflection that "If life had a second edition, how I would correct the proofs!"

Farther along, the gray-gold limestone village of Barnack, clustered around the Anglo-Saxon church of St. John the Baptist (to the left of B1443), has its own claim to fame. The "Barnack Hills and Holes" — which make a nice picnic spot — are the extinct quarries that until 4 centuries ago provided the stone for Peterborough and Ely cathedrals and some of the Cambridge colleges. Now the church, two old pubs, and a well-preserved 18th-century windmill make it worth stopping for a stretch of the legs. The church's early 11th-century tower and a fine sculpture of Christ of the same period (in the north aisle) are its highlights. Burghley House is about a mile southeast of Stamford.

BURGHLEY HOUSE: One glance at this magnificent 16th-century mansion with its 240 rooms tells you it was made for show. Indeed, William Cecil, the first Lord Burghley, built it to reflect his position — as Chief Secretary of State, Lord High Treasurer, and Principal Adviser to Queen Elizabeth I. Even she was impressed and visited Burghley about a dozen times, including a final visit when Cecil lay dying in 1598. Later, when King William III first saw the house, he deemed it "too large for a subject."

It took about 30 years to build this classic four-sided Tudor castle, which nevertheless displays numerous influences from the Continent — Italian columns at the front, even a Renaissance, pyramid-shaped obelisk in the courtyard. Because the Burghley family (later Marquesses of Exeter) still lives here, only about half the house is open to visitors; sadly, the great courtyard, an outstanding example of Elizabethan architecture, is off limits, while the exterior of the south and west sides have to be seen from afar. The furniture collection is as good as any in the land, however, and the house boasts one of the finest private collections of Old Masters in the world. Veronese, Cranach, Correggio, Lely, Kneller, Gainsborough, and Lawrence fill every room, seemingly from floor to ceiling, each thankfully numbered for identification.

A guided tour is essential to appreciate the building's art and history. It begins in the oldest part of the house, in the Old Kitchen, where some 260 copper utensils hang from the walls and a huge painting of an ox suggests the size of the beasts that were regularly roasted on the spit. Next, the so-called Roman Staircase leads up to the ornate chapel and affords a glimpse of the courtyard. Queen Elizabeth I worshipped in the chapel, which is dominated by Paul Veronese's altarpiece bought in Venice in 1769 along with the paintings of St. James and St. Augustine hanging in the antechapel. The Almoner's Dish, a gold collection plate used at Queen Anne's coronation, stands on the altar amidst exquisite wood carving usually attributed to Grinling Gibbons. Queen Elizabeth I's bedroom is impressive, since it is largely as the Virgin Queen last saw it, with the original materials covering the canopied four-poster bed and chairs.

The Heaven Room, however, is a real tour de force, perhaps the finest painted room in England. It is covered floor to ceiling with the masterpiece of the Italian painter Antonio Verrio, who also worked at Windsor Castle before moving to Burghley for 12 years. In a wonderful display of perspective and airy, fresh color, cupids rise, gods and goddesses, satyrs, and nymphs tumble down from above, and viewers feel they are floating in the clouds. Surprisingly, Queen Victoria and her retinue took their breakfast here during visits to Burghley house — it's hard to see how the Victorians could have been amused.

The last part of the tour is to the Great Hall, 68 feet long, 30 feet wide, and over 60 feet high, soaring up to a rare double hammer-beam roof. At ground level is the Olympic Gold Medal won by the sixth Marquess of Exeter in the 400-meter hurdles race at the 1928 games. Finally comes the Chinese Orange Court, an 18th-century addition designed by Capability Brown (he also laid out the gardens) and now used as a coffee shop, an essential stop after a grueling tour! Burghley House (phone: 0780-52451) is open to visitors daily from 11 AM to 5 PM Easter through the first week in October; the admission charge includes parking and the house tour. Each September, the grounds are taken over by the world's leading equestrians participating in the Burghley Horse Trials, a 3-day event. Princess Anne won the European Championship here in 1971.

STAMFORD: Once described as "a museum piece from a pre-industrial world" the whole town of Stamford is a conservation area, or landmark district. Built in yellow-gray stone and set peacefully astride the river Welland, it has an overall Georgian look, reminiscent of 17th- and 18th-century prosperity, but it is also a rich fund of medieval treasures including five parish churches, a 12th-century priory, and a 15th-century hospital (open Tuesdays through Sundays from May to September). With 500 buildings recognized as having architectural or historic significance, it is little wonder that Sir Walter Scott judged it "the finest scene between London and Edinburgh."

Brochures describing guided walks through town are distributed by the tourist information center (phone: 0780-55611) in the *Stamford Museum* on Broad Street. Pick one up and stroll through Broad Street's Georgian elegance, then admire the brasses of the Browne family in All Saint's Church (13th- to 15th-century early English with a perpendicular tower and spire), the painted ceiling and timber roof of St. John's (15th-century perpendicular), the 13th-century early English tower and 14th-century decorated spire of St. Mary's, and the 15th-century glass at St. George's. South of the river, view the Cecil family monuments and stained glass in St. Martin's, where the tomb of the first Lord Burghley has the great man stretched out in full armor, a lion at his feet. On the same side of the river is the *George* hotel, at the corner of Station Road and St. Martin's High Street (see *Checking In*). A hostelry since the 10th century, the present building dates from 1597 and still has large paving stones in the floor, sturdy beams, and handsome stonework, as well as a crypt under the cocktail bar. In the 18th and 19th centuries, 20 coaches a day rattled past in each direction from London and York, stopping to change horses in the cobbled courtyard.

The *Stamford Museum* (open daily year-round; closed from 12:30 to 1:30 PM during winter; admission charge) provides a good run-down on the history of the town and also displays a life-size model of Daniel Lambert, a 739-pound unfortunate who died in Stamford in 1809 (at the age of 39) and is buried in St. Martins' churchyard. The model, wearing the only surviving suit of his original clothes, is shown next to the clothing of the American midget Tom Thumb. The *Stamford Brewery Museum,* on All Saints Street (open Wednesdays through Sundays April through September; admission charge), shows how beer was made and what working conditions were like at the turn of the century, with coopers, saddlers, and wheelwrights still displaying their crafts. Visitors to the museum can also have a go at push penny, Stamford's local variation on the British pub game of shove ha'penny. To rest weary bones after a day of sightseeing, stop in at the the *Bull and Swan,* an attractive pub on the High treet, or try the tiny *Bay Tree,* on St. Paul Street, which serves traditional teas.

CHECKING IN: *The George of Stamford* – Recently refurbished, some call it the finest old coaching inn in England. It offers 47 extremely comfortable bedrooms, a walled garden, well-prepared British food in the paneled *York Room* restaurant as well as a good buffet in the almost tropical *Garden Lounge.* The London Room is a quiet sitting room. St. Martin's High St., Stamford (phone: 0780-55171). Moderate.

En Route from Stamford – The 15 miles south from Stamford to Oundle follow country roads and pass through a chain of pretty Northamptonshire villages that parallel anything in the Cotswolds. Leave Stamford on the A43 Kettering road, go through Easton-on-the-Hill, and at Collcyweston, opposite the church, turn left. Turn left again onto A47, and make a sharp right turn soon after for King's Cliffe. Go left again at the church in King's Cliffe, toward Apethorpe, where there is a striking church built between the 13th and 17th centuries. The old stocks and whipping post stand opposite. Then drive on to Fotheringhay, passing through Woodnewton, which has a quaint main street of stone cottages.

FOTHERINGHAY: On February 8, 1587, a plump, 44-year-old woman wearing a reddish wig to hide her greying hair was beheaded in the black-draped Banqueting Hall of Fotheringhay Castle. Thus Mary, Queen of Scots, who had lost her Scottish throne because of her Roman Catholicism (among other considerations) and spent 20 years as a prisoner of the English, finally met her end, convicted of conspiring to assassinate and seize the throne of her cousin, Elizabeth I, who reluctantly signed the death warrant. As the axe fell, it not only extinguished the threat of a Catholic uprising but also provided the plot of a host of now-forgotten romantic novels and plays as well as Donizetti's opera *Maria Stuarda.* The castle itself, at the end of the village, is today nothing but a mound and a fragment of wall enclosed in iron railings — Mary's son, James VI of Scotland and James I of England, who united the two thrones, ordered it destroyed (its stones and a staircase went into the remodeling of the *Talbot* hotel in Oundle). However, Scottish thistles abound in the summer and, as legend would have it, they were planted by Mary just before she lost her head.

Much earlier, in 1483, Richard III had been born in Fotheringhay Castle, one of the strongholds of the Dukes of York. Their family crest, the golden falcon, is repeated at the local pub and atop the tower of St. Mary and All Saints, one of the loveliest Norman churches in England. A cathedral in miniature, it has large but delicate windows that give it an ethereal quality daylight in high summer. Another worthwhile stop is *Fotheringhay Forge* (phone: 08326-323), where proprietor Barry Keightley makes and sells medieval-looking fire baskets and fireside sets with ram- and horse-head handles.

EATING OUT: ***Falcon Inn*** – Everything that a good English pub should be. Feast on ham carved off the bone, thick homemade soups, and walnut fudge! Main St., Fotheringhay (phone: 08326-254). Inexpensive.

En Route from Fotheringhay – Drive on through Tansor, noting its impressive riverside manor house, and turn right at the church to reach Cotterstock and Oundle. Go into Oundle (*Ou* as in *ouch!*) at the roundabout.

OUNDLE: The town sits on a hill above a loop in the river Nene, its steep roofs and dormer windows overlooking streets and alleys of local stone. There is a famous private school here (the British call them public schools), and Catherine Parr, Henry VIII's last wife, died here. The 14th-century church tower is visible for miles around, but it is the *Talbot* hotel (see *Checking In*) that is the main attraction, thanks to William Whitewell's modernization in 1626. He used stones from Fotheringhay Castle, where Mary, Queen of Scots, was executed. The splendid oak staircase down which the sad Scottish queen walked for the last time was also built into the inn, and the outline of a crown in the balustrade is said to be the mark made by her ring as her hand gripped the rail. Her executioner actually stayed at the hotel before performing his bloody deed. Oundle's tourist information center is on the Market Place (phone: 0832-74333).

CHECKING IN: ***The Talbot*** – The character of the old inn has not been lost even though some of the 39 comfortable bedrooms are in a new extension. All rooms have private baths and there is a good restaurant. No one has seen Mary's ghost in recent years, but Whitwell's initials are carved in the gable of a nearby house. New St., Oundle (phone: 0832-73621). Moderate.

En Route from Oundle – Return to the roundabout and take the exit to Ashton. After a half mile, turn left, following the "Ashton Only" sign. If passing through on a Sunday morning in mid-October, be aware that the curious exercise in progress on the village green in front of the *Chequered Skipper* pub is the annual World Conker Championship, held here since 1965. Players take turns swinging their conkers — a horse chestnut strung on a string or a leather lace — at those of their opponents, and the loser is the one whose conker shatters first. The game, played for centuries by English schoolboys, takes little or no skill, as a Mexican tourist proved in 1976 when he turned up by chance, took part, and won! The pub is worth a visit, and not only because it has excellent food. It takes its name from a now-extinct butterfly that once inhabited the nearby woods, 300 of which are encased in glass inside.

Barnwell, one of the most picturesque villages in England, is only 1½ miles from Ashton (return to the road, turn left, and watch for a sign to Barnwell to the right). Really two communities (St. Andrew's and All Saints), divided by a tiny stream, its mellow stone cottages are frequently pictured on calendars. Linking the two banks are small hump-backed bridges, the main one, between the welcoming *Montagu Arms* pub and the general store, being particularly photogenic. On entering the village, the home of the Duke and Duchess of Gloucester (cousins of the queen), a 16th-century manor house next to the pale gray 13th-century castle, can be seen to the right. Neither is open to the public, but a good view of them can be had from the rear of St. Andrew's Church, up a pretty street past a square surrounded by the almshouses. At the other end of the village are the remains of All Saint's Church and, in it, of the Montagu family. Borrow the keys from The Limes, the house next door, to visit the chancel with its poignant red-painted statue of a small boy on an obelisk. Three-year-old Henry Montagu drowned in a pond in 1625, causing his grief-stricken father to commission this work, which stands on two large human feet, dripping with ooze and supporting a gilt cup inscribed "Pour on me the joys of this salvation."

Go back to the entrance to Barnwell; turn left and left again onto A605 toward Kettering. For the next 5 miles lie Wadenhoe, Achurch, Thorpe Waterville, and Titchmarsh — all villages typical of this relatively undiscovered part of Northamptonshire, with typical churches. Thrapston, next, has the added distinction of having Sir John Washington, the uncle of George Washington's great-grandfather, buried in St. James' Church, and his coat of arms bears an uncanny resemblance to the Stars and Stripes. To see for yourself, turn right at the traffic light in Thrapston, turn right on Chancery Lane after a hundred yards, and right again into a car park behind the church. The heraldic shield with its three stars and three stripes is inside, immediately to the left of the interior doors.

Return to the main street and turn right. A mile out of Thrapston, go right at the roundabout, taking A6116 toward Corby. Note the handsome church of Lowick on the left. Shortly after Sudborough, a large sign indicates a right turn onto a single-lane road to Lyveden New Bield, a house begun by Sir Thomas Tresham in 1594, but left an unfinished shell (open daily; admission charge; phone: 08325-358). A brisk walk across a field is needed to reach the house, which Tresham, a faithful Catholic, built according to a floor plan in the shape of a cross and decorated with symbols and texts referring to the Passion.

Continuing on A6116, turn left at Stanion onto A43. After 3 miles, turn left into Geddington, going into the village on West Street. The tiny square by the church is surrounded by stone cottages and distinguished by an Eleanor Cross. When Queen Eleanor of Castile died of a fever in Harby, Nottinghamshire, in 1290, her embalmed body was taken to London. By order of her heartbroken husband, Edward I, each of the 12 overnight resting places of the coffin was subsequently marked by a cross, and Geddington's is one of only three remaining in England. Follow signs past the cross to Boughton House, sheltered behind a high brick wall a bit less than a mile southeast of the village.

BOUGHTON HOUSE: Pronounced *Bow*-ton, as in *cow,* this has been the Northamptonshire home of the Dukes of Buccleuch (pronounced *Buck*-loo) and their Montagu ancestors since 1528. The house is even older than that, however, since it began in 1450 as a monastery. Conversion, alteration, and additions followed, so that by the time Ralph, the first Duke of Montagu and a former ambassador to Paris, added the North Front in the 1690s, a mansion the size of a village was the result. There are no fewer than 7 courtyards, 12 entrances, 52 spindly chimney stacks, and 365 windows, all sheltered by 1¼ acres of Collyweston roof tiles. Called "a vision of Louis XIV's Versailles transported to England" by one writer, its north front does give it the look of a French château. But behind the façade is a very English house that offers good taste more than opulence, with furniture and paintings of quality carefully placed in harmonious, livable context.

The Low Pavilion Ante Room typifies this with Murillo's exquisite *St. John the Baptist,* a French mahogany writing desk inlayed with pewter, brass, and mother-of-pearl (a gift from Louis XIV to Ralph Montagu), eight walnut chairs with their original needlework, and fine bracket clocks from 1700. The Little Hall has El Greco's *Adoration of the Shepherds* facing the window and a most unusual carved stone fireplace that cleverly shows Duke Ralph's family tree back to William the Conqueror. The two pink carpets in the drawing room, as vibrant today as when they were woven 400 years ago — the first made in England — are so precious that they were placed under the coronation thrones of Queen Victoria, King Edward VII, and King George V. Go on to the Morning Room, the Rainbow Room, and then the Audit Room Gallery, 84 feet of family history recorded in portraits that are overhung with the well-preserved green silk banners borne aloft at the wedding of John Montagu back in 1704. Louis Chéron's painted ceilings are the focus of attention (if you crane your neck) in the Egyptian Hall and the Great Hall, although the latter also has an important portrait of Elizabeth I by Gheeraerts hanging next to the fireplace. Boughton House (phone: 0536-82248) is open in August only (daily from 2 to 5 PM), but its extensive grounds are more accessible, open daily except Fridays May through September; admission charge.

En Route from Boughton House – Backtrack through Geddington to A43 and turn left toward Kettering. After half a mile, turn right and go across country to Rothwell. Turn left onto A6 and right after 200 yards to pick up B576 to Lamport. Lamport Hall, a mainly 19th-century building with some worthwhile pictures and furniture, is open to the public on Sundays in summer, plus Wednesday, Thursday, and Friday afternoons from late July through August.

Take A508 to Brixworth, turning right into the village after a couple of miles. All Saints Church, standing proudly on a hill, makes all the fine Norman and medieval churches in the area look modern. Now over 1,300 years old and considered "the finest 7th century building surviving North of the Alps," it is a pecular mixture of Roman tiles, rubble, and stone, with a bulging external stair turret clinging to the side of the tower. Inside, the ring crypt around the apse at the east end is one of only four in the whole of Europe. Pilgrims used this to circle past the church's relic, presumably the throat bone of an early Christian martyr, St. Boniface. The annual *Flower Festival* and *Fete Day* on or near June 5th, the saint's feast day, perpetuates celebrations that are centuries old.

Continue south toward Northampton on A508, past a reservoir on the left. Turn right at the brow of the next hill, following the sign to The Bramptons and Althorp. The famous stately home is well signposted for the remaining 4 miles through country lanes and entered via a long drive through a park.

ALTHORP: The minute Lady Diana Spencer announced her engagement to Prince Charles, the number of visitors to this 16th- to 18th-century mansion, home of Earl (her father) and Countess Spencer, doubled. Since the wedding, visits have continued to increase. Luckily, this is an attraction that has always merited more attention, and it has actually been improved in recent years with refurbishments described by experts as the most extensive to an English country house since World War II (the Spencer family sold off several valuable heirlooms to pay for the renovations). One of Europe's finest private collections of paintings is still intact, however, with superlative examples of Reynolds, Gainesborough, Rubens, Van Dyck, and Lely (not to mention John Wootton's classic 18th-century hunting scenes) adorning the walls of a succession of splendid rooms. The furniture and china collections are also noteworthy for their size and range. The French and English porcelain includes the rare Harlequin Service from Sèvres featuring a different design on each plate.

Because this is still a private house, visitors are guided around in small groups to absorb the cultural wealth of Althorp in an hour or so. The family drawing room has 10,000 books, while the dining room (added a century ago) can seat 22 at the huge table, using just part of a matched set of 54 mahogany chairs made by George Seddon in 1800. The crimson damask on the walls came from a Venetian palace, while the window shutters display an early form of burglar alarm — real bells! King William's room, where William of Orange slept in 1695, is where members of the present Royal Family stay when they come to visit; the bed is the very one used by William, but the large wardrobe has been converted to a 20th-century bathroom. (Lady Di, by the way, may have married a prince to become Princess of Wales, but she herself is descended five times from Charles II — four times out of wedlock — and has reintroduced Stuart blood to the current royal family, which is of a different lineage.)

The highlight of the tour is the 115-foot-long picture gallery, dominated by Van Dyck's *War and Peace,* a double portrait of the Earl of Bristol as war and the Earl of Bedford as peace. Nearby, Kneller's portrait of Sarah, Duchess of Marlborough, shows her holding a lock of her auburn hair — cut off after a quarrel with her husband. Look for the portrait of Charlotte Seymour, Diana's great-great-grandmother. Some say Diana is her double; others say she looks more like her grandmother, Lady Cynthia Hamilton, one portrait of whom is in the library, another in the top gallery.

The outside of the house looks gloomy at first sight, since it is faced with gray tile. This was added by Henry Holland in 1790, covering up the original Elizabethan red brick from the 1660s. In fact, the building has been altered and remodeled several times, but has kept its specious, airy character. End the tour with a visit to the Georgian stable block, now converted into a gift and wine shop. The Spencers, who often drop by, do a roaring trade in quality antiques as well as wines from the earl's own cellars, including some expensive, but competitively priced ports. They also serve excellent teas. Althorp (phone: 0604-769368) is open daily from 1:30 to 5:30 PM year-round and from 11 AM to 6 PM July through September and on public holidays. On Wednesdays, Connoisseurs Day, visitors are treated to a longer tour and additional rooms.

CHECKING IN: *Northampton Moat House* – Part of a chain of competent modern hotels, about 5 miles from Althorp. 137 rooms. Silver St., Northampton (phone: 0604-22441). Moderate.

En Route from Althorp – Exiting by the rear gate, turn right, right again at the church, then left onto A428 to the village of West Haddon. A sharp right turn at the beginning of the village will lead onto B4036 to Market Harborough, 16 miles from Althorp. On the way, after the village of Naseby, a tall stone obelisk standing out on the right marks the spot where, on June 14, 1645, some 20,000 men fought the decisive battle of the English Civil War. Here Cromwell tested his theory that well-drilled and well-paid men led by officers of ability rather than social status would always win the day. His New Model Army outnumbered King Charles' Royalists by two to one and in a mere three hours delivered a crushing defeat despite its inexperience. The village's simple *Battle and Farm Museum* shows how 5,000 Royalists were killed or captured, as well as 200 carriages and all the king's guns confiscated. On entering Market Harborough, which Charles used as his headquarters before the battle, follow signs to the town center, moving toward the church.

MARKET HARBOROUGH: The parish church in the center of this small Leicestershire market town was built in the 14th century and enlarged a century later. Dedicated to St. Dionysius and Perpendicular in style, it has a 161-foot-high decorated broach spire that is visible for miles around. The handsome black-and-white timbered building next to it, dating from 1614, is the Old Grammar School; it perches on carved oak pillars and beams with plenty of room underneath for the traditional butter market — an early example of a shopping mall. Not far away, the river Welland cuts the town in two. During the 19th and early 20th centuries, Harborough was at its apogee as a fox-hunting center. In the winter, followers of the Quorn, Pytchley, and Fernie Hunts would take over hostelries such as the *Angel,* the *Peacock,* and the *Three Swans.* The latter, originally called simply the Swan, boasts a fine and rare example of a wrought-iron inn sign hanging over the High Street. When the name was changed to the *Three Swans* in 1770, two more birds were welded onto the side. The town's tourist information center, in the Pen Lloyd Library on Adam and Eve Street (phone: 0858-62649), can supply information on other sights.

CHECKING IN: ***Three Swans*** **–** This 15th-century coaching inn was upgraded in 1989 to include 20th-century comforts. Two rooms have four-poster beds. High St., Market Harborough (phone: 0858-66644). Moderate.

EATING OUT: ***Freeman's*** **–** The enthusiastic Freeman husband and wife team produce good meals, simply prepared but with subtle sauces: Grilled lamb chops are accompanied by a red currant and rosemary sauce, seafood with a tomato and basil sauce. 4 Roman Way, Market Harborough (phone: 0858-65453). Moderate.

En Route from Market Harborough – Take A427 for Corby and there turn north onto A6003 to Rockingham, 11 miles from Market Harborough. On a fine day, or an Easter Monday, however, opt for a different route to Rockingham — the pretty but complicated one through the little villages northeast to Harborough. In this case, take A6 toward Leicester and after 2 miles turn right onto B6047 toward Melton Mowbray and the Langtons. At the Church Langton village green, turn right for Hallaton. Delightful views open up.

Hallaton and neighboring village, Medbourne, a few miles south, would be worth visiting for their rural prettiness alone, but it's their quaint annual encounter — a bottle-kicking match — that makes them special. At 1 PM on Easter Monday a procession leaves the top of Hallaton to walk to a small hill, the Hare Pie Bank. With the marchers are two locally baked, cut-up hare pies (supposedly a symbolic offering of thanks harking back to a woman saved from a raging bull when a hare popped out of the grass to divert its attention). There is a preliminary hare pie "scrambling" wherein the pie portions are distributed to the crowd, and then the youngsters of the two villages line up for a game much like football, except that two touchdowns win the match, the ball is a "bottle" or rather a small barrel of beer, and the goal lines are the streams outside each village. The *Bewicke Arms,* the *Fox,* and the *Royal Oak* in Hallaton are favored for post-game celebrations, but if you miss the big day, they serve "a good pint" and a snack all year round and the game is explained in Hallaton's simple little *Museum of Village Life.*

To go to Rockingham from Medbourne, turn right onto B664, then left to Drayton. After Drayton, make a sharp right turn through Bringhurst and on to Cottingham. Turn left onto B670 to Rockingham and right onto A6003.

ROCKINGHAM: Even before William the Conquerer built Rockingham Castle in the 11th century, Romans and Saxons had already recognized the strategic importance of its site, an impressive spur overlooking the river Nene. Subsequent Kings were partial to the hunting in nearby Rockingham Forest, and in the early 13th century King John used the castle as a royal hunting lodge. Edward I undertook an extensive rebuilding program in the late 13th century, adding, among other things, the twin drum towers guarding the original Norman gatehouse. By the 15th century, the castle had become derelict, so much so that in the 16th century, Edward Watson, ancestor of the present owners, was able to obtain a lease on the property and turn it into a stately Tudor home. The family bought it the following century, only to see it damaged by Cromwellian forces during the English Civil War. In the 19th century, major renovations took care to emphasize the castle's romantic, medieval appearance.

Charles Dickens, a friend of the Watson family, visited often, put on plays here, and used the castle as the model for Chesney Wold in *Bleak House,* a large part of which was written at Rockingham. More recently it was used in a British television serial about the Civil War. Now a fine display of furniture and armor as well as Charles Dickens mementoes makes it an interesting visit. The castle is open Sundays and Thursdays from 1:30 to 5:30 PM, Easter through September, plus Tuesday afternoons in August; at other times of the year, call 0536-770240 for an appointment; admission charge.

Not much else remains to be seen in Rockingham, but a walk up the wide main street of the village, past the *Sondes Arms* pub and the slate-and-thatched limestone cottages, is like a trip back in history. The view of Corby, a modern steel city over the brow of the hill, brings you back to reality, however!

En Route from Rockingham – Take A6003 north to Oakham, 13 miles away. Uppingham School, a famous private school founded in 1548, dominates the somber ironstone town of Uppingham, about halfway to Oakham, and just before entering Oakham, the road passes Rutland Water, a large, manmade lake.

EATING OUT: ***Lake Isle*** – A small country restaurant in a coverted barber shop. The magnificent list of Burgundies and Bordeaux makes it a pleasure for wine connoisseurs, but the menu is equally good — imaginative soups, roast pork with gooseberry sauce, delicate desserts. 16 High St. E., Uppingham (phone: 0572-822951). Moderate.

OAKHAM: This delightful small town once had greater status as the county town (capital) of Rutland, whose own status as the smallest county of England ended in 1974 when it was merged into neighboring Leicestershire. Oakham Castle (closed Mondays), in the town center, gives an idea of its early importance, even though only the Great Hall remains. Unimpressive outside, this is one of the finest domestic buildings of the 12th century remaining in England, and one of the earliest to be built of stone rather than timber. A collection of 220 horseshoes covers the walls: According to an ancient custom, as lord of the manor, the Earl of Ferrers (meaning blacksmith) may demand this unusual tribute from peers of the realm or royalty on their first visit here. The oldest is from Elizabeth I, while Elizabeth II handed over her horseshoe in 1967.

The old Buttercross, an octagonal market building housing a set of stocks, is nearby on the Market Place. A street market is still held here on Wednesdays and Saturdays. Another private school, Oakham School, founded in 1584, occupies much of the rest of the town center, along with the graceful 14th-century All Saints Church. Not open to the public, but worth a look, are Flore's House (a 14th-century stone merchant's house at 34 High Street) and a thatched cottage on Melton Road, which was the birthplace, in 1619, of Jeffrey Hudson, "the least man in the least county in England." This Rutland dwarf reached a mere 18 inches in height by the time he was 9 and was once served up to Queen Henrietta in a pie! The happy ending is that he became her page and is mentioned in Sir Walter Scott's *Peveril of the Peak.* The *Rutland County Museum* on Catmos Street (open daily except Mondays and winter Sundays) records local history, crafts, and archaeological finds, while the tourist information center is in the public library on Catmos Street (phone: 0572-2918).

Rutland Water, which claims to be the largest manmade lake in Europe, is just east of Oakham. Created in the 1970s, it is 5 miles long, has 24 miles of shoreline, and covers 31,000 acres. It is a well-organized sailing, windsurfing, and fishing center, whose waters produce 60,000 trout a year, many 10 to 12 pounds in weight. Bicycles can be rented to explore the 15 miles of cycle paths that surround the lake; otherwise, take a pleasure cruise on the *Rutland Belle,* which operates daily except Mondays, April through September (phone: 0572-84630). The spire protruding from the water on the eastern side of the lake belongs to Normanton Church, now used as a water museum and accessible by land (open daily April through September and weekends off-season; admission charge).

CHECKING IN: ***Hambleton Hall*** – This luxurious, stylish hotel has a perfect and peaceful setting — it stands just beyond the village of Hambleton on a peninsula jutting into Rutland Water and peers at the lake through trees at the end of a twisting driveway. A one-time Victorian mansion, exquisitely decorated, it still feels like an elegant private house, since it has only 15 bedrooms (all with bath or shower). The bedroom called "Fern" is our particular favorite. The award-winning chef creates such imaginative preparations as a horseradish hollandaise to accompany the roast beef, pigeon pie with wild mushrooms, duck breasts with ginger and honey, and caramelized pears with ginger ice cream served in an almond biscuit basket. The hot chocolate pudding is reason, in itself, to dine here. The wine list is equally outstanding. Hambleton (phone: 0572-56991). Expensive.

Stapleford Park – An English country dream realized in 1988 by Chicagoan-turned-Londoner Bob Payton, who built himself a fortune with his pizza and rib houses in the capital. Payton has re-created an English country squire's domain on 500 acres of rolling countryside. The handsome 16th-century mansion, once the residence of the earls of Harborough, boasts carved woodwork by Grinling Gibbons, as well as "signature" bedrooms designed by the Tiffany, Wedgwood, and Liberty companies, as well as by interior designer Lady Jane Churchill and Linka Ceirach, who created the Duchess of York's wedding dress. The food is traditional English, with occasional American favorites (such as blueberry muffins for breakfast). Outdoors the emphasis is on country pursuits: hunting, carriage driving, clay pigeon shooting, and fishing. No children under 10. Stapleford (pronounced *Stapp*-ul-fird), near Melton Mowbray (phone: 800-223-5581 in US or 057284-522/-229). Expensive.

Whipper-In – This 17th-century coaching inn overlooking the Market Place was recently refurbished with modern comforts, but has retained the oak beams, log fires, and plush red velvet chairs of an authentic old English lodging place. It has 24 rooms with private bath/shower. The char-grilled food is excellent. The Market Place (phone: 0572-56971). Expensive.

En Route from Oakham – West of Oakham, A606 passes through Langham, which real ale fans know as the home of Ruddles Brewery. The cult brew can be sampled at the attractive, old *Noel Arms* pub. Farther along and off to the left is Little Dalby, yet another pretty English village, so small that it has no street names. It's associated with another of the Stilton legends, since local residents claim that it was at Little Dalby Hall in 1720 that the housekeeper, Mrs. Orton, first made the famous blue-veined cheese and sold it to the *Bell Inn* at Stilton. Melton Mowbray, next, is only 11 miles from Oakham. Follow signs to the town center.

MELTON MOWBRAY: The town's market was chartered in 1077, reflecting its situation in rich farming country on the banks of the river Eye. Part of its name comes from the Mowbray family, to whom King Rufus gave Melton in the 11th century and who became so powerful that Richard the Lionhearted, King John, Edward III, Richard III, and Henry VIII were all visitors — the latter to inspect the house on Burton Street, next to the church, that he gave to Anne of Cleves, one of his unfortunate wives. The church, St. Mary's, was begun in the 12th century and finished in the 16th century, and the house, now a restaurant, was built in the 14th century as a residence for priests serving there.

In more recent centuries, royalty came to Melton Mowbray to hunt. In fact, the town is the center of the most famous fox-hunting country in England, and the Market Place marks the traditional meeting point of the territories of three notable hunt clubs: the Belvoir (pronounced *Bee*-vor), Quorn, and Cottesmore hunts. George IV, Edward VII, Edward VIII, and George VI have all cantered across the local countryside, and Prince Charles has followed in their hoofprints.

The rich meadows in the vicinity are also famous for their production of Stilton cheese, which by law must be produced in Leicestershire, Nottinghamshire, or Derbyshire. It was perhaps a farmer's wife in nearby Wymondham who made the first Stilton — at any rate, Melton Mowbray is now considered the center of the industry. The town is also famous for its pork pies and the Melton Hunt Cake, both of which can be bought at *Ye Olde Pork Pie Shoppe* on Nottingham Street, run by a bakery (Dickinson and Morris Limited) that has been making both for more than a hundred years. First recorded in 1831, the unique Melton Mowbray pork pies are "hand-raised," using hot-water crust pastry and no hoop or tin to support them while baking. The filling is chopped (not ground) lean pork, to which a rich stock is added immediately after baking to "jelly" the pie.

The Melton Hunt Cake, "as supplied to Nobility, Clergy and Gentlemen of the Melton Hunt for over 100 years," is a very rich, English-style fruit cake with a liberal measure of Jamaican rum. A solid and portable snack like the pork pie, it has been eaten by huntsmen on horseback — washed down with a glass of sherry or "stirrup cup" — ever since Dickinson and Morris first produced it in 1854. A display of these local delicacies is in the *Melton Carnegie Museum,* Thorpe End (closed Sundays in winter), which also houses Melton Mowbray's tourist information center (phone: 0664-69946).

CHECKING IN: ***George*** **–** An old coaching inn in the heart of town, it has four-poster beds, modern bathrooms, and hearty fare. Not fancy, but it has atmosphere. High St., Melton Mowbray (phone: 0664-62112). Inexpensive.

Harboro **–** On the edge of town, actually on A606 towards Oakham, this is another old inn that is neat, clean, and unpretentious, both in its accommodations and its food. Burton St., Melton Mowbray (phone: 0664-60121). Inexpensive.

En Route from Melton Mowbray – Take B676 east through rolling, open fields. In winter, the bare thorn hedges are characteristic of hunt country. The road jogs through hamlets like Saxby, Garthorpe, Coston, and Stainby, each with a photogenic church, and enters Lincolnshire along the way. Just before Colsterworth, 12 miles from Melton Mowbray, turn left up a small lane to Woolsthorpe Manor. Isaac Newton was born in 1642 in this squat limestone house that is still part of a working farm. He returned in 1665 and 1666 to avoid the Great Plague raging through London and made good use of the surrounding peace and quiet, developing differential calculus and discovering the composition of white light. The gnarled apple tree out front is reputedly the one under which he was sitting when a falling fruit inspired him to "discover" gravity. The house is open Wednesdays through Saturdays, April through October; admission charge.

Return to B676 and go into Colsterworth; turn left at the crossroad and go north to Grantham on A1 followed by B1174, which is well-marked.

GRANTHAM: Because Prime Minister Margaret Thatcher was born here, Grantham has taken to calling itself "the Premier Town." Although not particularly special at first glance, it does have a good ration of history going back to Saxon days. The 283-foot spire of St. Wulfram's parish church is the sixth highest in England and is easily spotted by travelers on the express trains that hurtle up and down the London–Edinburgh line. The 13th-century church dominates the town center and has a 16th-century library of chained books (visits by appointment on Mondays, Thursdays, and Fridays, May through August, from 2 to 4 PM; phone: 0476-61342) as well as St. Wulfram's right arm bone in a room above the North Porch. Isaac Newton went to the nearby King's School and like any normal child carved his initials into the wooden sill of the Old Schoolroom. (The room, with its thick, small-paned windows, is now part of the newer King's School and can be visited by appointment; call 0476-63180). A statue of Newton stands in front of the town hall, and next to it is the *Grantham Museum,* St. Peter's Hill, with a display of his possessions. Grantham's tourist information center is also in the museum (phone: 0476-66444).

Margaret Thatcher's humble beginnings can be traced to North Parade, where she grew up helping her parents weigh groceries in a corner shop that is now the "Premier" restaurant. However, *Catlin's,* at 11 High Street, still thrives, selling Grantham Gingerbread from a 400-year-old building. This local delicacy was invented by mistake in 1740 when William Egglestone stumbled around in the dark on a Sunday morning to bake some surprise cakes for his family and mixed up the wrong ingredients. The *Beehive* pub on Castlegate, down Firkin Street (opposite the *George* hotel), has a most unusual inn sign. Up in a lime tree outside is a real beehive with live bees, a curiosity noted at least 150 years ago in the rhyme, "Grantham, now two rarities are thine, A lofty steeple and a living sign." Another pub, the *Angel and Royal* on High Street (see *Checking In*), has strong claims to being the oldest inn in the kingdom. Built for the Knights Templar, it was requisitioned in 1213 by King John, who held court in the Chambre du Roi (later on, Richard III ordered the death of the treacherous Duke of Buckingham in the same room). The carving of an angel holding a crown set over the 15th-century gateway commemorates the visit of Edward III and Queen Philippa in the 14th century; nevertheless, it was only after a visit of the Prince of Wales in the last century that the title "Royal" was added to the Angel's name.

CHECKING IN: ***Angel and Royal*** – An ancient inn soaked in history, this now has 24 comfortable rooms, all with private baths and such modern touches as color TV sets and telephones. The restaurant and bars, however, retain the stone walls and beamed ceilings of days gone by. High St., Grantham (phone: 0476-65816). Expensive.

George – Mentioned in Dickens's *Nicholas Nickleby* as "one of the best inns in England" and still a busy, family-run hotel. High St., Grantham (phone: 0476-63286). Moderate.

EATING OUT: ***Barkston House*** – This elegant Georgian farmhouse is about 3 miles north of Grantham via A607. A restaurant (with stylish accommodations in 2 bedrooms), it serves excellent food including some old-fashioned British dishes. Try wild duck in cider, rabbit and bacon pie, and the sponge pudding or spotted dick for dessert. Closed Saturdays at lunch and Sunday and Monday evenings. Barkston (phone: 0400-50555). Moderate.

En Route from Grantham – Belvoir Castle is only 8 miles west of Grantham, but this route travels due north to Lincoln and visits the castle on the return trip south. Leave Grantham on A607 toward Leadenham. After Manthorpe, a stone wall on the right announces Belton House, impressively illuminated at night. A particularly fine example of late 17th-century architecture, it is considered by some the "crowning glory of the restoration country house." Built on the proceeds of a successful law practice, the mansion in gray-gold Ancaster stone is beautifully balanced outside, with large windows, a lacy balustrade, and a cupola on top. The interior has several items that were in the 1985 "Treasure Houses in Britain" exhibition in Washington, DC. Furniture and paintings of the 17th and 18th centuries (Reynolds, Lely, Hoppner, and Romney) are matched by Edward Goudge's wonderful plaster ceilings in the Saloon, Little Marble Hall, and Chapel, with Edward Carpenter, a pupil of Grinling Gibbons, proving he was as adept at wood carving as was his teacher. Edward VIII, a friend of the former owners (the Broenlow family), came here during the abdication crisis, and some of the Duchess of Windsor's mementoes are displayed. A thousand acres of landscaped parkland surround the house, which is open Wednesdays through Sundays from 1 to 5 PM April through late October. The gardens open at 11 AM); admission charge (phone: 0476-66116).

Continue on A607 the remaining 22 miles to Lincoln, passing the spires of Fulbeck, Leadenham, and Wellingore and joining A15 for the last 3 miles when Lincoln Cathedral is visible in the hill.

LINCOLN: Tourists too often overlook this city, yet the richness of its history is obvious from the moment you set eyes on its cathedral. Perched high above the surrounding, flat countryside and especially stunning at night when it's usually floodlit, it is a gem of 13th-century architecture and considered one of the finest — if not *the* finest — cathedrals in England. Like Salisbury Cathedral, Lincoln Cathedral (or Lincoln Minster) is essentially early English in design and structure, begun in 1185 after an earthquake destroyed an original Norman cathedral on the spot and largely completely by 1280. The West Front consists of an arcaded screen incorporated the surviving Norman fragments, including an impressive frieze of Old and New Testament scenes. The 271-foot central tower, completed in the 14th century, was once topped with a spire that reached a height of 525 feet (the tallest building in the world at the time), but it was blown down in a gale in 1547. Similarly, the twin spires of the west towers were removed for safety reasons in 1807.

Inside, the nave has few tombs or monuments to detract from the vast, echoing space that is often speckled with color as sunlight streams through the stained glass windows. The 13th-century rose window in the north transept is known as the Dean's Eye, while the Bishop's Eye, from the 14th century, is opposite in the south transept. Notable, too, is the brilliantly sculpted Angel Choir at the east end of the church. Take binoculars to appreciate the 28 angels that accompany the statues of Mary and Christ high up in the spandrels; lower down, the town's symbolic imp can be seen at the foot of one vaulting shaft. Off the northeast transept is the 13th-century cloister and above it is the chapter library designed in the 17th century by Christopher Wren. One of the four copies of the Magna Carta is kept in the library, although it is usually exhibited in North America in the winter months. If possible, try to be in the cathedral at 5:15 PM (Sundays at 3:45 PM), when a choir of 30 men and boys sing Evensong as they have for centuries.

To see the rest of Lincoln requires a good day's worth of walking, best done after a visit to the tourist information center, 9 Castle Hill (phone: 0522-29828 or -512971), for a supply of maps and brochures (or the leaflet detailing the days and hours of walking tours). The city guards a gap in a line of hills and has been important since prehistoric times, when it was called Lindon (Celtic for "hillfort by a pool"). The Romans built it into a thriving town called Lindum Colonia (Lin-coln), and left the West Gate, the remains of the East Gate, and some walls, as well as the 2nd-century Newport Arch, part of the old North Gate. Subsequently, the Anglo-Saxons and Danes maintained its strategic importance: The Danish legacy lingers with streets names ending in "gate," and the Saxon heritage includes the churches of St. Peter-at-Gowts and St. Mary-Le-Wigford, both on the High Street.

But it was the Normans who cleared 166 houses to build the mighty castle (open daily April through October, closed Sundays in winter; admission charge), one of eight known to have been ordered by William the Conquerer himself. Begun in 1068 inside the walls of the Roman city, it is now reduced to its walls of herringbone masonry (with a walkway on top), the entrance gateway, and several towers, including Lucy Tower (actually a shell keep), the Observatory Tower (from which there is a good view of the city), plus a number of 18th- and 19th-century prison and court buildings. The Normans then raised the original cathedral next to the castle, as well as other churches and new suburbs, everywhere substituting stone for Saxon timber. They also left the stone Jews' House (on Steep Hill) with its fine doorway and chimney stack above.

Allowed to tax all wool exports (the Wool Staple), the city thrived in the 12th and 13th centuries. Even the *City and County Museum* (archaeological collections; open daily) is set in a 13th-century building, the Greyfriars Priory, built originally as part of a Franciscan monastery and notable for the oak barrel roof of the upper room. In the 14th century, the Wool Staple was transferred to nearby Boston, and Lincoln began to decline, although the medieval era produced numerous solid timber-framed buildings. Modern Lincoln residents still make time for a drink at the 14th-century *Wig and Mitre* pub on Steep Hill (see *Eating Out*), and they still stop for coffee on the High Bridge where the black and white houses march across the river Witham as they did

400 years ago. The late 15th-, early 16th-century Stonebow gate, with the guildhall above it, is not far from the bridge. The city's recovery began in the 18th century — the Assembly Rooms are typically Georgian, while the 20th century's contribution is the Central Library, with its collection of works relating to Alfred, Lord Tennyson, a local boy.

There are several US links with Lincoln (although no direct connection has been made with Abraham Lincoln). The Pilgrim Fathers and Captain John Smith are shown in the stained glass window in the cathedral's Seamen's Chapel. The formidable Thomas Pownall, born in the Minster Yard, went on to be consecutively Governor of New Jersey, Pennsylvania, and Massachusetts, handing over the reins in New Jersey and Massachusetts to Francis Bernard, who had also lived on the Minster Green. When the first shots in the War of Independence was fired, it was two unknown soldiers from the Tenth Foot, the Lincolnshire Regiment, who died.

CHECKING IN: ***White Hart*** – A fine hotel a few yards from the cathedral, recently refurbished. An inn has been on this site for 600 years, although most of the present building dates to 1722. The 51 bedrooms are luxurious and elegant, antiques grace the reception rooms, and the food in the handsome *King Richard* restaurant is exquisite. Dishes such as warm pigeon breast on wild salad leaves with black currant dressing, guinea fowl Vachell braised with cloves and root vegetables, and spiked filet of halibut with pink peppercorns and red wine grace the menu, while the wine list is innovative and comprehensive, with a dozen English wines. Book a room facing the cathedral or visit the roof garden to admire the illuminated West Front, which seems close enough to touch. Bailgate, Lincoln (phone: 0522-26222). Expensive.

D'Isney Place – This elegant Georgian town house in the shadow of the cathedral is a family-run, 17-room bed-and-breakfast establishment. Luxurious touches, such as four-poster beds and Jacuzzi, pervade. Eastgate, Lincoln (phone: 0522-538881). Moderate.

EATING OUT: ***Harvey's Cathedral*** – Consistent, yet imaginative, their cooking is the reason Adrianne and Bob Harvey can fill this large, smart restaurant at the cathedral entrance. There is a blackboard offering daily specials, a "healthy options" menu for those who want to avoid rich dishes, and a self-service salad bar. But don't imagine this limits the menu — Louisiana shrimp au gratin and crispy cheese duckling are representative of the range, and the wine list is tops. 1 Exchequer Gate, Lincoln (phone: 0522-510333). Moderate.

Wig and Mitre – A 14th-century pub halfway down Lincoln's famous medieval street, this has the unusual attribute of all-day service — food from 8 AM until midnight. Book into the clublike atmosphere of the upstairs dining room with its Victorian settees and armchairs and old pictures of lawyers and churchmen, or join in the jollier downstairs bar. On a fine day, eat on the terrace out back. 29 Steep Hill, Lincoln (phone: 0522-535190). Moderate.

En Route from Lincoln – Take A46 south in the direction of Newark, watching carefully in Swallow Beck for a right turn to Doddington on B1190. Follow the straight road for 7 miles. Doddington Hall, a magnificent example of a late Elizabethan (1600) mansion, sits in the heart of the village near the church, approached through a gabled Tudor gatehouse. The warm red brick building is trimmed with Ancaster stone and shaped like an E with three domed cupolas standing up from the flat roof. The interior is from a later period, because it was refurbished in the 18th century by a local carpenter, who also put in new plaster ceilings. There are good tapestries and fine furniture, as well as portraits of the four families that have lived here (today it is the private home of the Jarvis family). Exhibitions and concerts are set in the 100-foot-long Gallery, while outside, the surrounding walled garden is an explosion of perfumed roses in summer. Doddington Hall (phone: 0522-694308) is open Sundays and Wednesdays from 2 to 6 PM Easter through September; admission charge.

Return to B1190, but after a half mile turn right at the roundabout for Newark on A46 Lincoln Bypass. You'll soon leave Lincolnshire behind and enter Nottinghamshire. Pass *Coddington Air Museum* (stop if you're an aircraft aficionado) and go on into Newark.

NEWARK-ON-TRENT: Often called the "key to the North" because of its strategic position at the crossing of the Roman Fosse Way, the Great North Road, and the river Trent, Newark at one time had a mighty castle. Built between the 12th and 15th centuries, only the Main Gate, West Tower, and a portion of riverside wall still survive. King John died here suddenly in 1216; he would have been borne through the great gate after falling ill at Sleaford in Lincolnshire. The castle, a Royalist stronghold, withstood three sieges by the Parliamentarians before Charles I surrendered in 1646 to end part one of the Civil War; then Cromwell ordered its demolition, an act the townspeople fortunately never fully carried out.

Despite its rich history, visitors often bypass Newark, ignorant of the fact that it contains no fewer than *half* the county's landmark buildings. The 18th-century cobbled Market Square is one of the best in Europe; in it is the handsome Palladian Town Hall (1773), so large that it has a ballroom upstairs and a Butter Market below. Just off the square is St. Mary Magdalene Parish Church, early English to perpendicular in style, with a soaring spire and an impressive collection of silver in the treasury in the crypt. An annual service with distribution of money to the poor takes place here in March thanks to a bequest by Hercules Clay, a prominent citizen of the Civil War era. He moved his family out of his house after a premonition that it was on fire, and almost at once a cannonball hit and ignited the house. Newark also has a number of interesting old inns. The tourist information center is at The Ossington, Beast Market Hill (phone: 0636-78962).

CHECKING IN: *Grange* – A family-run 9-room hotel in a Victorian house, this home-away-from-home has pretty decor and the Edward family's cooking to recommend it. London Rd., Charles Street Corner, Newark (phone: 0636-703399). Moderate.

En Route from Newark-on-Trent – Heading south from Newark (in the direction of Grantham), A6065 soon merges with A1. After about 4 miles, turn left into Long Bennington. Follow the signs right and left for Bottesford, crossing A1. The road winds past abandoned airfields, still marked by hugh wartime hangars, through the hamlet of Normanton. Next is Bottesford, whose residents can claim to have the tallest *village* church spire in the country (113 feet) as well as fine monuments to the first eight Earls of Rutland. The wooden stocks and whipping post by the market cross are supposed to date from Norman times. Follow signs south of Bottesford for Belvoir Castle, which soon appears silhouetted against the sky.

Belvoir Castle, home of the Dukes of Rutland, got its name from the French for "good views." Indeed, this huge brick and stone fortress dominates the Vale of Belvoir as its predecessors have since the days of William the Conquerer. Rebuilt after a fire in 1816, the present building is something of a Gothic fantasy. Several films have been shot here, including *Young Sherlock Holmes,* and the showbiz element is always near. Every weekend the grounds resound with anything from marching bands to demonstrations of medieval jousting, hawking and falconry, archery, and Scottish dancing. Inside, however, there is a fine collection of paintings and furniture, so a tour is worthwhile. After the guard room, entrance hall, and grand staircase up to the ballroom, visitors go through a chilly hall filled with armor and into the 17th/21st *Lancers Museum,* which contains Bill Brittain's bugle, blown for the "Charge of the Light Brigade" on

October 25, 1854. It's a relief to reach the Chinese-style bedroom and dressing room before entering the richly decorated Elizabeth Saloon, the outstanding room in the castle. Matthew Wyatt not only painted the complex mythological ceiling and sculpted his patroness, Elizabeth, fifth duchess of Rutland, in white marble, but also chose the exquisite carpet and gold-trimmed French furniture. After the dining room comes the picture gallery, with a host of great names such as Gainsborough, Poussin, and Holbein. The King's Room, the 150-foot Regent's Gallery, the chapel, kitchen, and cellars make up the finale, a real test of the culture lover's stamina. Belvoir Castle (phone: 0476-870262) is open Tuesday, Wednesday, Thursday, Saturday, and Sunday afternoons (plus bank holiday Mondays) late March through early October, and Sunday afternoons only the rest of October; admission charge.

After the visit, backtrack to Bottesford, turn left onto A52 to Bingham, then left onto A46 for Leicester, 32 miles from Bottesford.

LEICESTER: Although it has played as important a role in English history as any other town, as one of England's ten largest cities, Leicester no longer has any one specific area dense with historic interest. Solid and comfortable, it prides itself on its shopping, which is offered in everything from a large open market to tiny, Victorian pedestrian streets and arcades. The *Jewry Wall Museum and Site,* St. Nicholas Circle, is devoted to archaeology from Roman times to the Middle Ages and is especially notable for its excellent Roman mosaic pavements. Exhibits at the *Newarke Houses Museum,* The Newarke, deal with the social history of Leicestershire since 1500 and include paneled rooms and collections of toys, clocks, and musical instruments. The excellent collection of German expressionist paintings at the *Leicestershire Museum and Art Gallery,* New Walk, are also worth a visit. All the above are open daily. Leicester's tourist information center, 2–6 Martin's Walk (phone: 0533-511300), can provide further information or reserve a place for you on a guided walk about the city.

CHECKING IN: ***Grand*** – Although such a forward-looking town has local links of the *Holiday Inn* and *Post House* chains, this centrally located hotel, with its chandeliers and pillars, is a reminder of Victorian elegance. The 92 rooms are comfortable and the food is competent. Granby St., Leicester (phone: 0533-555599). Inexpensive.

EATING OUT: ***Water Margin*** – A good Chinese restaurant, producing Cantonese-style dishes with fresh seafood. Sunday lunches are excellent. 76 High St., Leicester (phone: 0533-516422). Inexpensive.

En Route from Leicester – Leave on A46 and pick up the M69 motorway to Coventry, 24 miles away and clearly signposted. Coventry is only 18 miles east of Birmingham, starting point of our *Western Midlands* route and itself discussed fully in THE CITIES. Alternatively, those in a hurry to return to London can forego Coventry and speed down M1 for Leicester (107 miles from London).

COVENTRY: The city of Lady Godiva was dramatically transformed on the night of November 14, 1940, when 500 tons of bombs and 30,000 incendiaries aimed at local munitions factories were dropped in a massive German raid that razed most of it to the ground. By the next day, some 50,000 buildings had been damaged or reduced to rubble, including the 14th-century cathedral. The shell of the old cathedral, its sanctuary altar graced with moving crosses — one made of charred timbers, the other of twisted nails — is now a memorial shrine linked to the new cathedral by a porch. Designed by Sir Basil Spence and consecrated in 1962, the new cathedral is theatrical in its use of stained glass windows and lights, but its dominant decoration is the huge *Christ in Glory* tapestry above the altar, designed by painter Graham Sutherland. Jacob

Epstein's bronze of *St. Michael Subduing the Devil* is on the church's outer wall, to the right of the porch.

Lady Godiva was actually Countess Godfygu, wife of Leofric, Earl of Mercia, who established a monastery at Coventry in the 11th century. The good lady tried time and again to persuade her husband to ease the tax burden on the townspeople, and he finally agreed — saying he would do so the day she mounted her horse naked and rode through the marketplace in full view of all. Having told everyone to stay indoors and close the shutters, the courageous Lady Godiva went ahead, her long hair a convenient coverup. Much later, in the 17th century, Peeping Tom became part of the legend: He took a peek and was struck blind. To commemorate these events, an equestrian statue of Lady Godiva and a clock tower with moving figures of both the lady and Peeping Tom now stand in the Broadgate in the center of Coventry.

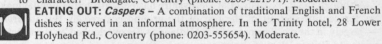

CHECKING IN: ***De Vere*** **–** There are no old-fashioned hotels left in the city; this is large (190 rooms), modern, efficient, business oriented, and located near the cathedral. Cathedral Sq., Coventry (phone: 0203-633733). Moderate.

Leofric **–** Another modern hotel, set in a pedestrian shopping zone — follow the signs to West Orchard car park — and convenient to the cathedral. No pretentions to "character!" Broadgate, Coventry (phone: 0203-221371). Moderate.

EATING OUT: ***Caspers*** **–** A combination of traditional English and French dishes is served in an informal atmosphere. In the Trinity hotel, 28 Lower Holyhead Rd., Coventry (phone: 0203-555654). Moderate.

Western Midlands

The Midlands region of central England is an area of contradiction, its very name evoking images of the "dark satanic mills" of the poet William Blake. Communities like the Black Country and the Potteries spring to mind, industrial zones where blast furnaces once lit the landscape, mining ravaged the hills, and thick grimy coal dust hung in the air, coating houses inside and out. Yet, always just a few miles away is "England's green and pleasant land," in the words of the same poet. Here, too, are the peaceful farmlands eulogized by A. E. Housman in *A Shropshire Lad* and the rugged beauty of the Peak District, England's first national park.

Although the Peak District of Derbyshire has been attracting holidaymakers for centuries, most of the rest of the ground covered by this itinerary — largely in the western part of the Midlands — is overlooked by the average visitor to Britain. Part of the reason may be the sweet and sour nature of the landscape. Even an Englishman might write off Staffordshire and the county of West Midlands (which includes little more than Birmingham and the surrounding area) as industrial and ugly, although they contain surprising rural stretches, not just factories and pitheads. Nottinghamshire has Robin Hood's Sherwood Forest as well as the coal mining community that so influenced D. H. Lawrence. The very birthplace of the Industrial Revolution was in Shropshire, of the peaceful farmlands. Nevertheless, there is much for the visitor in these five counties. Consider them the *real* Britain, where lovely crystal and china is produced in unlovely places like Stourbridge and Stoke-on-Trent, where market towns bustle with activity, where charming villages lie deep in cozy countryside, and where there is plenty of natural beauty.

History, too. Lovers of "industrial archaeology" will certainly be content here, but so will lovers of more distant ages. There are remains of Iron Age forts and also of the Romans, who enjoyed the thermal springs at Buxton and whose Viriconium, outside Wroxeter, near Shrewsbury, was the fourth largest city in Britain. Christianity arrived in the 7th century with St. Chad, missionary to the Anglo-Saxon kingdom of Mercia, and many of the oldest structures on the route are ecclesiastical — Norman abbeys and churches and the medieval cathedral in Lichfield.

Even more is left from Tudor times. Shrewsbury has more than its fair share of black and white half-timbered buildings. Haddon Hall, near Bakewell in Derbyshire, is a fine, well-preserved example of a manor house. Also in Derbyshire is the glorious Hardwick Hall, built by one of the great women of the Elizabethan Age, Bess of Hardwick. One of her husbands, the Earl of Shrewsbury, was gaoler to Mary, Queen of Scots, so the two ladies spent many hours together, working a tapestry that is now displayed at Hardwick Hall.

During the Civil War of the 17th century, Shropshire and Staffordshire aided the Royalist cause, even providing refuge to the defeated Charles II before he fled to France. Then came the Industrial Revolution, which changed the face of the Midlands and the world forever. By 1868 an American consul in Birmingham wrote that "the furnaces roar and glow by night and day, and the great steam hammers thunder . . . and every kind of machinery invented by man are ringing, clicking and whizzing." Thanks to a revival of interest in Britain's industrial heritage, there are now first-rate museums highlighting the achievements of men like Abraham Darby, who discovered how to smelt iron ore with coal, Josiah Wedgwood, who helped to make English china famous around the world, and Thomas Telford, the 19th-century civil engineer who built roads, bridges, and canals.

Important as these men were, however, it was through the labor of ordinary people that industry developed. At Ironbridge Gorge, *Blists Hill Open Air Museum* re-creates the lives of those who went down into the mines, worked the canal boats, and stoked the furnaces. Not everyone worked in industry, of course, and one place to explore the lives of those who didn't is the *Staffordshire County Museum,* devoted to 18th- and 19th-century rural folk. The museum is housed in a wing of Shugborough, a stately home that is not as famous as Chatsworth — among the grandest in Britain and also on this route — but deserves to be better known.

Contrasts of rich and poor, industrial and pastoral are only one of the reasons a tour of the Midlands is so fascinating. It is also an area rich in traditions, where the semipagan ritual of well dressing continues each summer in Derbyshire towns and villages such as Buxton and Eyam. Flowers and leaves pressed into clay form an elaborate natural picture that is used to decorate or "dress" the well, all part of a ceremony giving thanks for water. Another tradition is the brewing of real ale, unfiltered and unpasteurized, so it remains cloudy and tastes distinctly of malt and hops. Like wine, it is "alive" and the taste can vary from day to day, from season to season, and even from the top to the bottom of the barrel. Strike up a conversation about real ale in a local pub and you'll be talking until closing time.

Another attraction of the Midlands, unlike the Cotswolds, is that it is not overcrowded with tourists. Shropshire is surprisingly untraveled, yet it has its own brand of beauty in fertile valleys overlooked by geological uprisings such as the limestone escarpment of Wenlock Edge and the hills of Long Mynd. Derbyshire, of course, is familiar to walkers but seems able to absorb them all in the Peaks — almost half of the county is in the Peak District National Park. The Peaks are not so much mountains (the name probably derives from the Pescaete, a tribe in the area in prehistoric times) as a hilly preamble to the Pennines. The Peaks are of two types: In the north are the Dark Peaks, formed of gritstone — dark rock that juts up from rounded hills covered by gorse and heather. Skylarks sing and goshawks swoop upon their prey — this is open, barren country, with virtually no trees to obscure the view. Just to the south are the White Peaks, undulating country of limestone cut into gentle valleys by rivers like the Derwent and the Wye. In the White Peak area, also known as the Dales, life suddenly seems easier, less exposed to the harshness of rugged wind and weather.

Our tour of the Midlands leaves the Peak District for next to last, beginning in Birmingham and heading west into the Black Country, still an industrial zone although no longer black with smoke. After a visit to Stourbridge, Britain's glassmaking center, and to Ironbridge Gorge, where several impressive museums illustrate the birth of the Industrial Revolution, it continues west to historic Shropshire towns such as Much Wenlock and Shrewsbury before returning due east to the historic Staffordshire town of Lichfield. Turning northwest, and passing the forest of Cannock Chase, this route includes a stately home, Shugborough Hall, then pushes on to Stoke-on-Trent, also known as the Potteries — Britain's chinatown. Scenic Derbyshire follows, as the itinerary continues north to the resort town of Buxton and then loops eastward through the Peak District National Park to the villages of Edale, Castleton, Hathersage, and Bakewell, the Plague Village of Eyam, plus two more stately homes, Haddon Hall and Chatsworth. An Elizabethan mansion, Hardwick Hall, is next, after which we cross into Nottinghamshire and speed down the motorway to Nottingham, the last stop on the itinerary. If so inclined, take the same motorway all the way to London, 135 miles away, after the visit.

Throughout the route there are friendly pubs for lunch or a snack, good restaurants, and comfortable hotels ranging from the simple to the elegant. Expect to pay as much as $125 for a double room at those places listed as expensive; from $70 to $125 in the moderate range; and less than $70 if listed as inexpensive. A three-course meal for two, with coffee, taxes, and service, but no wine, will run $75 and up in places listed as expensive; $30 to $75 in the moderate range; and under $30 if listed as inexpensive.

BIRMINGHAM: For a detailed report on Britain's second largest city, its sights, hotels, and restaurants, see *Birmingham,* THE CITIES.

En Route from Birmingham – The city is a rabbit warren of roads — residents refer fondly to one notorious interchange as "Spaghetti Junction" — so take care when scanning the numerous route signs. The A456 towards Kidderminster leads out of the inner city and through its unattractive outskirts. Turn right onto A491 for Stourbridge, where our itinerary enters the Black Country. Roughly triangular in shape, with apexes at Wolverhampton, Walsall, and Stourbridge, the area takes its name from the black smoke that used to pour from its factory chimneys in the 18th and 19th centuries, when the presence of coal, iron, clay, and limestone made this prime territory for the smelting of iron into steel and the making of everything from locks, keys, and springs to the rolling stock for railways. Today the coal and iron mines are depleted, but the area is still devoted to manufacturing, largely of metal products.

STOURBRIDGE: Rhyming with "hour-bridge," this fairly unattractive town is of interest as the center of Britain's glassmaking industry, a tradition going back some four centuries. The process was refined by "gentlemen glassmakers" of French Huguenot extraction, who fled to England because of religious persecution and began settling here in the early 17th century. By the late 18th century, the landscape was dotted with "glass cones," bottle-shaped structures housing circular furnaces around which teams of glassmakers worked. Bigger and bigger cones were built, but the shape was not stable enough to prevent collapse, so the industry gradually switched to lower, less distinguished-looking, though safer, buildings in the 19th century. The only glass cone remaining in the area (and one of only four left in Britain), is Stourbridge's Redhouse Cone, whose silhouette, rising some 100 feet into the sky, is clearly visible along A491 north of town. Part of the Stuart Crystal manufacturing complex, it is now a museum (open daily) featuring demonstrations of glassmaking as well as an explanation of the art of the engraver, exhibits of old glass, and, of course, a shop.

The Stuart Crystal factory itself is open for guided tours on weekdays, but it's worth calling ahead (phone: 0384-71161) to check the times. Other famous Stourbridge glass manufacturers that organize factory tours include Royal Brierley (phone: 0384-70161), Thomas Webb (phone: 0384-392521), Webb Corbett (phone: 0384-440442), and Tudor Crystal (phone: 0384-393325). Still another attraction in the vicinity is the *Broadfield House Glass Museum,* farther north along A491, at Kingswinford. This tells the whole story of glassmaking, with examples from Roman times right through to contemporary designs, although the focus is on the 19th-century colored glass and the lead crystal for which Stourbridge is famous. The museum is open Tuesday through Sunday afternoons and on Saturday mornings (phone: 0384-273011).

En Route from Stourbridge – Shortly after Kingswinford, A491 becomes A449. Turn left onto B4176 toward Bridgnorth and follow this to a small roundabout by the *Royal Oak* pub; here take the road to Ackleton and continue until it joins A442. After a few hundred yards turn left onto a minor road signposted to Coalport and Broseley. This narrow lane climbs a little hill, then dips down steeply into a valley, the Ironbridge Gorge. At the bottom, turn right and follow the river Severn along to the straggling little town of Ironbridge.

IRONBRIDGE GORGE: The sky of this lovely wooded Shropshire valley was once red from blast furnaces, the air grimy from coal smoke, the ground littered with slag. Peaceful now except for birds' songs, it is considered the birthplace of the Industrial Revolution, because it was here, in 1709, that Abraham Darby first discovered the technique of smelting iron ore with coke. To commemorate, document, and demonstrate the crucial changes wrought by that momentous event, an entire 6-square-mile area has been turned into a remarkable cluster of museums — collectively known as the *Ironbridge Gorge Museum.* The *Museum of the River,* on the left in the town of Ironbridge (and occupying a restored warehouse whose Gothic-style windows look more ecclesiastical than industrial), is the best place to begin. Its various exhibits and audiovisual program serve to introduce the area as a whole as well as present an overview of the other six main museum sites nearby. It's also stocked with pamphlets and books, plus a good selection of gifts such as cast-iron wall plaques and cooking pots.

Pick up a map of the area and walk back down along the river to the Iron Bridge itself, from which the valley takes its name. Pretty though it is, with graceful swirls in a harmonious iron arch, this famous symbol of the Industrial Revolution now looks unremarkable. But when it was cast in 1779 by Darby's grandson, it was the world's first cast-iron bridge, an object of wonderment that people came from all over Europe to see. The remaining museum sights are best reached by car, and even then, it's possible to spend a day "doing" the *Coalport China Museum,* where Coalport china was made until the company moved to Stoke-on-Trent in the late 1920s, the *Jackfield Tile Museum,* where decorative tiles made in the area from the 1850s to the 1960s are on display, and the *Museum of Iron* and the *Old Furnace* — a museum of iron making along with Darby's original furnace.

Leave plenty of time (a couple of hours) for the Blists *Hill Open Air Museum,* however. This re-creation of a 19th-century village, complete with gas lit streets, shops, and pigsties, is a must. Three blast furnaces add authenticity, as does the slag on the hillside, but it is the workers' cottages with their cramped living conditions, the very basic church, the pub, the butcher shop, and the winding machine at the mine — where a man wearing a bowler hat (as badge of authority) worked a 12-hour shift sending men, women, and children 600 feet down to work the coal and iron seams

— that bring the Industrial Revolution down to human terms and illustrate the harsh reality of its everyday life.

The *Ironbridge Gorge Museum* is open from 10 AM to 6 PM year-round (phone: 0952-452166) A gorge "passport" allows admission to all sites.

CHECKING IN: ***Old Vicarage*** **–** This solid, red brick former parsonage was built in 1905 and stands in quiet seclusion in its own grounds at one end of the village of Worfield (take A442 back toward Bridgnorth, then any of three left turns to the village). Victorian antiques, plush yet cozy bedrooms, warm modern bathrooms (complete with bathrobes) all give a homey feel to the hotel, and Peter and Christine Iles, the hosts, are a font of knowledge on local places of interest. Good country cooking in the evening and a proper breakfast. Worfield, off A442 (phone: 07464-497). Moderate.

Park House **–** Two country houses on attractive grounds combine to make a comfortable hotel. It handles a lot of weddings, conferences, and other such functions, so it may be too busy for the leisure traveler; the heated swimming pool, on the other hand, makes it attractive in an area where good hotels are thin on the ground. Park St., Shifnal, 3 miles northeast of Ironbridge on A464 (phone: 0952-460128). Moderate.

En route from Ironbridge Gorge – Continue through Ironbridge, keeping the river and four giant cooling towers to the left. Turn left onto B4378 for Much Wenlock. After crossing the Severn, the road climbs a hill; at the brow, a backwards glance over the shoulder to the right reveals the ruins of the 12th-century Buildwas Abbey. One of many Norman abbeys in England, only the chapter house and a double row of seven arches remain, all open to the heavens. The country lane goes into a narrow valley with hills close upon one another and soon the village of Much Wenlock appears. Turn left into the town center.

MUCH WENLOCK: There is much history in Much Wenlock, a lovely market town where half-timbered houses stand next to Georgian brick. Its charter dates from 1468, although back in the 7th century a nunnery was founded by the King of Mercia for his beloved daughter, Milburga, later recognized as a saint. Destroyed by pillaging Danes, it was refounded in the 11th century by the Earl of Mercia, husband of the famous Lady Godiva. Unfortunately, Wenlock Priory, a center of Cluniac activity in England, suffered ruin again, after the dissolution of the monasteries by Henry VIII. Now green lawns and topiary in the cloister soften the outlines of the limestone chapter house with its interlacing arches. On the lavatorium, a stone trough for hand-washing, carved figures are still visible. The medieval prior's lodge is nearby.

Much Wenlock's 16th-century guildhall houses a tourist information center (open April through September; phone: 0952-727679), with the old Buttermarket next door. Note the iron fetters attached to the whipping post (the second post along from the guildhall), no doubt a center of attraction on market days. Now attention is focused on the stalls of the antiques market inside the Buttermarket every Saturday. Another market, selling homemade goodies such as jams and cakes, plus flowers, fruit, vegetables, knitting, and so on, takes place under the Corn Exchange on High Street on Thursday mornings. If you miss this, stop for lunch or a snack at the 17th-century *Malt House* (there's a gift shop on the ground floor, a restaurant and tearoom above), a few steps away from the Corn Exchange. There are also pubs, including the traditional 16th-century *George and Dragon* (sample the real ale), the *Wheatland Fox,* and the *Talbot.*

At the end of the village is the *Gaskell Arms,* a coaching inn where a local pioneer of physical education, Dr. William Brookes, gave speeches about the Wenlock Games, which he founded in 1850 to combine the Greek ideal of a healthy mind in a healthy body with the British love of sport. Conditions in places such as Ironbridge obviously colored his view that "if there was any class who deserved recreation it was the working class," an unusually enlightened view in Victorian times! The games began with an old English flavor (tilting and medieval costumes), but because the good doctor hoped to revive the ancient Olympics, they gradually took on Greek trappings, with laurel wreaths and medals for the winners. At their height, thousands attended, including, in 1890, Baron Pierre de Coubertin, who founded the modern Olympic Games in 1896. Whether the Wenlock Games added to his zeal or not, they are considered a precursor of the modern Olympic movement, and they continue to be held, on a weekend in late July, on Lenden Field near the secondary school. The little museum across from the Buttermarket has photographs, medals, and other memorabilia from the festivities a hundred years ago.

En route from Much Wenlock – Shrewsbury is only 12 miles away by the direct route (A458), but if it's a nice day and there's time, take the scenic route, approximately a 25-mile drive. In either case, go back to the little roundabout at the end of Wilmore Street in Much Wenlock, turning left to bypass the village. At the intersection opposite the *Gaskell Arms,* turn right onto A458 for Shrewsbury. The scenic route, B4371, is an almost immediate left. The little road climbs up to the top of a ridge from which the views are superb, the land dropping away steeply to the right and more gently to the left. In summer, trees may obscure the panorama, so stop at one of the parking areas to enjoy the Shropshire farmland spread below. After a few miles, Wenlock Edge rises on the left. This escarpment of limestone, covered in a blanket of woods to its green summit, belies its earlier existence, millions of years ago, as a coral reef in a tropical sea. Now it stretches southwest a straight 16 miles, the valley below green with lush meadows.

Cross A49 into Church Stretton, a small town with the Stretton Hills on its eastern side and the Long Mynd (*mynydd* is Welsh for "mountain") running north to south on its western side. Both are very popular areas for walking, and the tourist information center in the town library can supply information on specific trails. (The information center is open summers only; phone: 0694-723133. In other seasons, phone the library: 0694-722535.) One favorite destination is to the 1,500-foot summit of Caer Caradoc, the highest of the Stretton Hills, about 2 miles northeast of town (it was visible on the right as the road into Church Stretton dipped down to A49). As are many hills in the area, Caer Caradoc is topped with the remains of an ancient hillfort, dating from the Iron Age. The fort's double walls protected some 6 acres, surely an impressive camp in those days, and the view that provided its tactical advantage extends over the surrounding countryside in all directions. It's best to have proper hiking boots, however, since the trail to the top is often muddy.

An easier walk out of Church Stretton is up, into, and onto the Long Mynd. The rounded shape of this 6-mile-long line of hills is the result of frosts in the last Ice Age breaking up rocks that are 800 million years old. Springs and streams have cut deep hollows or "batches" in the hillsides, which are covered with bracken and heather. Above, larks sing, although they now have to share the sky with gliders and hang gliders, since gliding is another very popular activity in the vicinity. Much of Long Mynd is owned by the National Trust, so the National Trust Chalet Pavilion in nearby Cardingmill Valley (take the signposted turn left off B4370 in Church Stretton) has plenty of information on the different trails, their condition and difficulty. There is a shop, café, and information center, and from the parking area a walk of about 2 miles leads past Light Spout Waterfall to the top of the Long Mynd.

From Church Stretton, take A49 north to Shrewsbury, passing Caer Caradoc again on the right.

SHREWSBURY: Pronounced *Shroze*-bury, the county town, or capital, of Shropshire is best known for its public (which in Britain means private) school of the same name and for its many half-timbered houses. Charles Dickens would still recognize the view he saw from his rooms at the *Lion* hotel (see *Checking In*) looking "all downhill and slantwise at the crookedest black and white houses, all of many shapes except straight shapes." The dramatic combination of black oak timbers against white plaster left by Tudor times, the more regular lines of Georgian red brick, and later examples of Victorian architecture all contribute immensely to the attractiveness of the town, as does its setting, on a peninsula of rising ground formed by a loop of the river Severn.

No one knows exactly when Shrewsbury was first settled, but it was probably sometime in the 5th century, after the Romans left the nearby settlement of Viriconium (near Wroxeter) and withdrew to Gaul. In Saxon times, the town was already an important outpost against the fierce Celts beyond the Welsh border to the west, and it served the same purpose in Norman times, when William the Conqueror's relative and right-hand man, Roger de Montgomery, built the castle at the neck of the peninsula. The Battle of Shrewsbury, fought in 1403 and described by Shakespeare in *Henry IV: Part I,* underscores the town's continuing strategic importance.

Although some 12th-century portions of the castle survive, what's seen today is mainly the result of a 19th-century rebuilding — the original was demolished after the Civil War for having been a Royalist stronghold. Open daily (closed Sundays in winter), it now contains a small, mainly military museum where Americans may want to search out the colors of the James City Light Infantry, captured by the British at the Battle of Bladensburg during the War of 1812. (After that victory the Red Coats surged into Washington, DC, setting fire to the "President's Palace," later rebuilt and whitewashed to become, of course, the White House.)

From the castle, Castle Street leads up into the old center of Shrewsbury, past the statue of a studious Charles Darwin, who was born just across the river and was a pupil at Shrewsbury School. Turn left into St. Mary's Street to see St. Mary's Church, topped by a spire claimed to be one of the three highest in the country. Inside its 12th-century stone walls are medieval carvings and glorious stained glass windows, including a wonderful 14th-century Jesse window. St. Chad's Church, built some 600 years later, with an unusual round nave and an even more unusual tower, is at the far end of town, overlooking Quarry Park, where on the middle weekend of August the Shrewsbury Flower Show proves that England really is a nation of gardeners. A third important church, the Abbey Church, is across the 18th-century English Bridge, at the eastern entrance to the town (the Welsh Bridge, also 18th century, crosses the Severn on the western side). Largely of the 14th century, the church is all that remains of a monastery founded by Roger de Montgomery in 1083 and contains his final resting place. The other monastic buildings fell victim to Henry VIII's dissolution of the monasteries and to progress, when Thomas Telford (the same engineer who rebuilt the Castle) cut a road straight across the site in 1836.

Shrewsbury's tourist information center (phone: 0743-50761) is in the square, in the center of the peninsula. All around it are narrow streets with such delightful, self-explanatory names as Butcher Row and Fish Street or, less obvious, Dogpole, Wyle Cop, and Grope Lane (light deficient and so narrow that neighbors could shake hands from second-floor windows). Many of the cottages lining the streets were built in the 15th century; in the 16th century, more impressive houses were built with profits from the thriving wool trade. Among these are the elaborately timbered Ireland's Mansion and Owen's Mansion, both on High Street, and the Old Market Hall (where the coat of arms of Elizabeth I is carved over the doorway) in the square. Slightly later is Rowley's Mansion, at the corner of Barker Street and Hill's Lane, surprisingly large for a half-timbered building. Now a museum of local history, it contains Roman relics excavated at Viriconium, including a beautiful silver mirror that has the classical lines of Georgian silver and is amazingly well preserved for its age.

Shrewsbury is particularly bustling on Tuesdays, Wednesdays, Fridays, and Saturdays, market days when people come from miles around to do their shopping. Among the local delicacies they stuff into their baskets are Shrewsbury cakes, a shortbread-type cookie with currants, and fidget (or fitchet) pie, a combination of bacon, onions, and apples rounded off by pastry. Look for simnel cake, a dark, rich, spiced fruitcake originally associated with "Mothering Sunday," the fourth Sunday of Lent, when girls who worked away from their families had some rare time off to return home, taking a simnel cake as a gift. Some say it goes back even further to Roman festivals, since "simila" was their very special, fine white flour. In any case, it now appears at Easter decorated with 11 marzipan balls representing the 12 apostles, Judas excepted.

CHECKING IN: ***Lion*** – It dates from Tudor times and was "modernized" about 200 years ago to become the center of the town's social life. Paganini played his violin in the elegant Adams-style ballroom, Jenny Lind sang here, and Disraeli stayed while campaigning for votes. A George III staircase and huge stone fireplace add to the traditional atmosphere. Underneath it all is a labyrinth of cellars where Catholic mass was whispered in secret during the Reformation. Recently redecorated, the 60 bedrooms (all with bath or shower) are very comfortable and the bar is a pleasant place for a simple lunch. Wyle Cop, Shrewsbury (phone: 0743-53107). Moderate.

Prince Rupert – Named for the Bohemian prince who was a nephew to Charles I and commanded Royalist forces during the Civil War. The hotel incorporates Jones Mansion, his headquarters. This is another good place to stay, though not all the 66 rooms have private baths, so remember to check. Butcher Row, Shrewsbury (phone: 0743-236000). Moderate.

EATING OUT: ***Country Friends*** – This comfortable restaurant is at the end of a 6-mile drive south of Shrewsbury on A49. The building is medieval, with warming fireplaces and sturdy beams, but the food is "New British" in style: Traditional dishes have been rethought for modern tastes and combinations often include fruit, as in the venison with a sauce highlighted by black currant vinegar. The British *can* prepare vegetables well, as you'll see here, but save room for the desserts and particularly the homemade chocolates with the coffee. There are also 3 rooms. Dorrington (phone: 074373-707). Moderate.

Old Police House – The chef is English, the decor Victorian, and the food good — and this really is a converted jail and police station! Castle Court, off Castle St., Shrewsbury (phone: 0743-236200). Moderate.

En Route from Shrewsbury – The road to Lichfield, 36 miles away, is the old Roman Watling Street, straight as a ruler and now the A5 roadway. Atcham, a small village on the banks of the Severn is just 4 miles along. Slow down on approaching the bridge in order to appreciate the *second* bridge, a lovely stone structure with five arches built about 200 years ago. On the left is a grand triumphal arch leading to Attingham Park, a mansion built for the first Lord Berwick in 1785 and now owned by the National Trust. Designed by George Steuart (creator of St. Chad's in Shrewsbury), its interior is notable in that two separate suites of rooms, one for the lord and one for his lady, lie on separate sides of the entrance hall. Also of interest are the unusual picture gallery and fine staircase by John Nash, the glittering collection of Regency silver, and, in Lady Berwick's apartments, a very pretty, very feminine, painted boudoir. Attingham (phone: 074377-203) is open on Saturday, Sunday, Monday, Tuesday, and Wednesday afternoons April through September and on Saturday and Sunday afternoons in October; admission charge.

Soon after Atcham there is a turn on the right signposted "Viriconium" and "Ancient Monument." (Don't worry if you miss it, because there are two other turns, also signposted.) The ruins (open daily for a fee; phone: 074375-330) are worth a side trip, since Viriconium, founded in the 1st century AD and abandoned circa AD 400, was the fourth largest Roman town in Britain, with an area over half that of Londinium. Picture what it must have been like at its height, when the forum was crowded with people and the public bathhouse was in use. The museum at the site helps to fill in the details.

Return to A5 and after a few miles look to the right. The large hump of a hill rising from the surrounding flat farmlands is the Wrekin, a famous landmark. It may not seem impressive compared to the Alps, but in a country where the highest point is just 4,400 feet above sea level, even big hills have significance. In the 4th and 5th centuries BC, the Celts spotted approaching enemies and enjoyed the panoramic view from a fortified settlement on the Wrekin's 1,334-foot summit. The A5 soon joins M54, bypassing Telford, the well-planned and thriving new town named for the civil engineer responsible for so many of Shropshire's bridges, canals, and churches in the early 19th century, as well as for his restoration work on Shrewsbury Castle. At Exit 3, take A41 toward Whitchurch, noting signs for Weston Park. Across to the right is the pretty hamlet of Tong, where Dickens fans may want to look at the distinctive red sandstone Church of St. Bartholomew (it actually looks green) described in *The Old Curiosity Shop* as the church that sheltered poor Little Nell and her grandfather on their journey from London. Inside, the fan-vaulted ceiling of the Golden Chapel and the carved alabaster funerary monuments are a reminder of the skills of craftsmen hundreds of years ago. Among Tong's black and white houses is the *Bell* pub, good for lunch.

Continue on A41 and at the next roundabout take A5 to Weston-under-Lizard. Just before the village is the gatehouse of Weston Park, the home of the Earl and Countess of Bradford, set in beautiful grounds laid out by the famous Capability Brown. Yet this imposing red brick edifice is not the work of a known architect but of Lady Wilbraham, the wife of the owner, who designed it back in 1671 — quite an achievement for anyone with no training in either architecture or building techniques. Inside, the furnishings include works by Van Dyck, Holbein, and Stubbs, as well as tapestries by Aubusson and Gobelins. This is one of an increasing number of stately homes to offer something for children, though what Capability Brown would have thought of the Woodland Adventure Playground hidden away in his artfully "natural" park is hard to fathom! Weston Park (phone: 095276-207) is open on weekends in April, May, and September; daily except Mondays and Fridays in June and most of July; and daily from late July through August; admission charge.

Continue along A5, and after a few miles turn right for Bishops Wood. The oak-lined lane passes the *Royal Oak* pub and soon there is a sharp right turn marked "Boscobel House," with a car park immediately on the left. The 17th-century manor house (open daily; admission charge) is virtually empty (the later addition is private) and known chiefly as the place where Charles II hid in an oak tree to escape Cromwell's forces after Royalist troops were defeated at the Battle of Worcester in 1651, effectively ending the Civil War. The original tree fell prey to souvenir hunters of long ago, but a replacement oak stands a short distance from the farmyard where chickens cluck. The house has secret rooms that also sheltered the monarch before he fled abroad, and about three-quarters of a mile farther down the track (muddy in wet weather) are the remains of the White Ladies Priory, still another of Charles's havens, founded in the 12th century.

Return to A5 and take it straight to Lichfield. (The signs will read: "A5," "Gailey," "Cannock," and eventually "Lichfield.") Just past the Belvide Reservoir the road goes under a canal built, of course, by Thomas Telford. Cross over M6, and remain on A5, signposted first Brownhills, then Tamworth; eventually, after entering Staffordshire, turn left off A5 onto A461 for Lichfield.

LICHFIELD: Besides its fame as Samuel Johnson's birthplace, this attractive town is also known for its cathedral, the only one in England with three spires. Although Lichfield Cathedral is small, the three red sandstone spires — known as the Ladies of the Vale — stand straight up against the sky and are visible from several miles away. Begun in the late 12th century, but mainly 13th- and 14th-century early English and decorated in style, the cathedral succeeds a previous Norman church on the spot, which in turn followed a church consecrated in AD 700 as a shrine for the bones of St. Chad of Mercia. Nothing now is left of either earlier structure, but one relic of the saint's time — a beautifully illuminated manuscript of the gospels of Matthew and Mark known as the "Gospels of St. Chad" — is on view in the Chapter House in the summer months. Similarly, much of the present cathedral is the result of loving restoration (3 centuries' worth), made necessary not only because sandstone is a perishable material but also because the church was fortified by the Royalists during the Civil War and was twice besieged by Parliamentarians. Outside, the 113 statues in row upon row on the west front are almost all reproductions.

Take a stroll in nearby Vicar's Close, a small green surrounded by 14th- and 15th-century cottages, then continue along Dam Street and Quonian's Lane before heading for the pedestrians-only Market Square. There, a statue of Dr. Johnson, wit, writer, and compiler of the *Dictionary of the English Language* (published in 1755), faces the house where his father operated a book shop and where he was born in 1709. Now the Samuel *Johnson Birthplace Museum* (open daily, except holidays and off-season Sundays; admission charge), it contains letters, early editions of his works (including the famous *Dictionary*), and various memorabilia. Have a look at the statue of Johnson's friend and biographer, James Boswell, a few steps away in the Market Square, then adjourn to *The Scales,* an old coaching inn on Market Street. This popular pub offers tasty lunchtime food and real ale, not to mention real pub games like darts, shove-ha'penny, and dominoes. In cold weather the atmosphere inside is cozy; if it is warm and sunny, sit in the pleasant courtyard. Either way, listen to the conversations around you and see if you agree with Dr. Johnson's opinion that the people of Lichfield were "the most sober, decent people in England . . . and spoke the purest English."

CHECKING IN: ***George*** – The 18th-century actor David Garrick, born a few doors away, would have enjoyed the convivial bar and relaxing lounge. The hotel has 39 rooms and an unpretentious restaurant. Bird St., Lichfield (phone: 0543-414822). Moderate.

En Route from Lichfield – Return to the ring road and follow A51 to the unattractive town of Rugeley. From here, if it happens to be the first Monday after the 4th of September, take a side trip to the village of Abbots Bromley (on B5234, reached from Rugeley via the B5013 Uttoxeter road). No one knows for sure whether the annual Horn Dance performed here by a dozen men in Tudor-style clothes dates back to a pagan ritual or, as suggested by the huge reindeer antlers worn by six of the men, a celebration of villagers' hunting rights. The horns, at least, date from about the year 1100.

Otherwise, keep on A51, then bear left at the white-painted *Wolsey Arms* pub onto A513 toward Stafford. Immediately, all is rural again; up the hill to the left is Cannock Chase. Once the hunting preserve of Danish, Saxon, and even Plantagenet kings until ownership was transferred in 1290 to the Bishops of Lichfield, it is now an Area of Outstanding Natural Beauty covering some 26 square miles. The fallow deer that the bishops introduced continue to roam through woodlands of beech, oak, sycamore, and pine, and if you listen carefully, you may hear the yellow hammer singing its distinctive "little bit of bread and no cheese" song backed by drumming woodpeckers. Still on A513, you'll soon come to the edge of Milford. Just before the *Barley Mow Inn* is the entrance to Shugborough Hall, ancestral home of the Earls of Lichfield.

SHUGBOROUGH: This stately home is still lived in by the photographer, Patrick, Earl of Lichfield, cousin to the queen, even though the National Trust now owns and administers the estate. Set in 900 acres of park and farmland, including 18 acres of formal gardens, it has something of interest for everyone, including children. The house itself dates from 1693, although the graceful colonnaded frontage came about later thanks to the good fortune of the first owner's brother, Admiral George Anson, who sailed around the world in the 1740s and was lucky enough to capture a Spanish galleon full of treasure. For those not keen on architecture, furniture, paintings, silver, or the naval memorabilia of the admiral, there are the gorgeous formal gardens, with roses and rhododendrons making their splashes of color, but venture a little farther to find the temples, follies, bridges, and ornamental ponds, some of which were designed by the 18th-century neoclassical revivalist James "Athenian" Stuart.

Also on the grounds — actually in the stable block and domestic buildings — is the *Staffordshire County Museum,* which presents a view of more ordinary life 200 years ago with a working laundry, kitchen, and schoolroom, as well as a (nonfunctioning) brewhouse and a coach house complete with carriages. Antique toys, costumes, guns, and farm equipment are on display, and even the oatcake, a lowly yet staple element of the Staffordshire diet, is given its due. A quarter of a mile from the house and particularly good for children is Shugborough Park Farm, a working museum with rare breeds of farm animals, 19th- and early 20th-century farming implements, and demonstrations of traditional farming methods. Shugborough also has a café that serves home-cooked food, handy for lunch. From Easter to Christmas, the mansion, museum, and farm are open daily; off-season, they are open to groups by appointment only; admission charge. For exact hours, phone 0889-881388.

En Route from Shugborough – Before going on toward Stafford, 6 miles west of Milford, those who "collect" churches may want to search out the rural masterpiece of Sir Christopher Wren at Ingestre, some 4 miles north. A side road off A513 at the entrance to Shugborough leads along the boundary of the estate. Take the right fork at the next junction, go through the hamlet of Tixall, and turn left at a sharp bend in the road, following the sign to Ingestre. The square-towered, 17th-century Church of St. Mary the Virgin has all the hallmarks of Wren's style: classical arches, the contrast of plain white pillars, oaken pews, and an ornate ceiling. Even the beautifully carved pulpit and three-part screen are supposedly the work of Grinling Gibbons. That the two famous names were working in rural Staffordshire is due to the determination of Walter Chetwynd, scion of a local landowning family, who built the church (open during daylight hours in summer; otherwise ask for the key next door).

Return to A513 and take the bypass around Stafford. An ancient market town on the river Sow, it dates back to AD 913 but is now a mish-mash of old and new. During the Civil War, King Charles and his nephew, Prince Rupert, stayed at the *High House* on Greengate Street, and St. Mary's Church around the corner suffered the indignity of having its weathercock blasted as a target while the prince perfected his shooting skills. Inside the church is a bust of Izaak Walton, author of *The Compleat Angler* (1653), who was born in Stafford and baptized at the church's Norman stone baptismal font.

Take A34 north to Stoke-on-Trent, otherwise known as the Potteries, but note that one of the main attractions in the vicinity, the Wedgwood Visitor Centre (see below), is south of town at Barlastan. A sign some 3 miles past Stone and just before Tittensor marks the right turn to Barlastan and Wedgwood.

STOKE-ON-TRENT: Stoke can be confusing, since what is officially known as Stoke-on-Trent is actually six towns — Tunstall, Burslem, Hanley, Fenton, Longton, and Stoke itself — that have managed to hold on to their individuality despite their federation as one city in 1910. To complicate matters further, Arnold Bennett, their most famous son, thought of them in terms of *five* towns. (Why, is not known, but it has been fancifully suggested that he never mentioned Fenton because of a quarrel with a landlady who was a Fenton native.) Their number notwithstanding, the towns are also known as the Potteries, because most of Britain's pottery, from utilitarian earthenware to fine china, has been manufactured here continuously since the 18th century. The area is no longer the "forest of smoking chimneys" that it once was — thanks to the conversion from coal to gas and electricity to fire the ovens and kilns — but it is still no beauty spot. Visitors come to tour the Royal Doulton, Spode, Minton, and other factories (tours usually must be arranged in advance) and to browse through china museums and china shops.

Although potting in the area began as far back as the Neolithic period and continued through Roman and Saxon times, the great leap forward came in the mid 17th century, when trade with China brought about the introduction of tea. The effect on the Potteries was the development of stoneware (harder than porous earthenware) for the pots, caddies, cups, and saucers necessary for the ritual of serving and drinking what would henceforth be the mainstay of British life. The next century saw the rise of the most famous name in English ceramics: Josiah Wedgwood founded his company in 1759 and became synonymous with a particular shade of blue, used as a background to a raised white pattern. Other firms subsequently established themselves. Spode, for instance, has produced its Willow pattern, with only slight variations, since approximately 1780. Although the use of purer clays and the building of canals and later of the railroads allowed an ever-expanding repertoire of elegant tableware to reach growing markets, traditional designs continued. The Toby jug, a mug in the shape of a well-built gentleman in 18th-century frock coat and cocked hat (perhaps a caricature of one Toby Philpott, a renowned drinker in the latter half of the 18th century), is still made and the name is often used for pubs as well.

The Wedgwood Visitor Centre (phone: 0782-204218) at the modern Wedgwood factory at Barlaston (5 miles south of Stoke-on-Trent) is open to visitors daily except Sundays from November through Easter and 2 weeks at Christmas and New Year's; admission charge. Here, a museum traces the development of techniques and decorative styles over the 2 centuries of the company's existence, with a large collection of pieces shown in various period settings. Note the black basalt vase thrown by Josiah Wedgwood himself when he opened his Etruria factory at Stoke in 1769. (The classical-style figures reflected excitement over discoveries at Pompeii and Herculaneum, and the Etruria plant got its name from the mistaken assumption that the discoveries were "Etruscan.") Another early favorite was the cream-colored Queen's Ware, much favored by Queen Charlotte, wife of George III. The center also contains a demonstration hall where potters and painters show their skills and two shops, one selling first-quality pieces and the other less expensive seconds with slight imperfections.

A brochure listing the many other factories in and around Stoke offering tours, museums, or shops can be picked up at the Wedgwood Visitor Centre's helpful information counter. It's difficult to choose among them unless you're partial to a particular manufacturer or are an insatiable shopper — in which case, note that Spode Works, Church St., Stoke (phone: 0782-744011; closed Sundays) is another factory with a seconds shop.

Among the museums not associated with factories, the *Gladstone Pottery Museum,* Uttoxeter Rd., Longton (phone: 0782-311378) is of interest; it features the bottle ovens of a preserved Victorian pottery and also provides demonstrations of pottery making in addition to the usual display of wares (open daily; admission charge). The *Chatterley Whitfield Mining Museum* (phone: 0782-813337), in Tunstall, on the north side of Stoke-on-Trent where the suburbs give way to grazing sheep, provides "demonstrations" of an entirely different sort. An enormous white winding wheel guards the entrance of this formerly active coal mine that once produced the fuel that fired the pottery furnaces. Inside, visitors put on helmets and headlamps, collect a numbered ticket, and descend a short distance underground for a cage ride and a guided tour of the coal face, led by ex-miners. Open daily for a fee, this is an experience to remember, though not for claustrophobics!

CHECKING IN: ***North Stafford*** **–** Mock Jacobean in style and highly regarded locally. A recent facelift, the friendly staff, good potteries flavor (the local product is on display), and the convenient location just opposite the Stoke railway station are all in its favor; 69 rooms with bath. Station Rd., Stoke, Stoke-on-Trent (phone: 0782-744477). Moderate.

En Route from Stoke-on-Trent – The itinerary now leaves Staffordshire's industrial areas behind and makes its way north through glorious countryside. Leaving the *Chatterley Whitfield Mining Museum,* turn left back onto A527, then left again onto B5049. Go straight across the next two small roundabouts and be ready for a sharp left, just before a bridge, to join A53 to Buxton, 24 miles away. After Leek, the landscape opens out, providing welcome relief, and the road roller-coasters along up to the Peak District National Park. Suddenly stone is everywhere, in walls threading their way through meadows, on remote farm cottages, and as big, dramatic jagged rocks on hilltops. A sign proclaims "Derbyshire" (pronounced *Dar*-bee-sher) and the road dips down for 3 miles into Buxton.

BUXTON: This one-time spa town is a favorite base for touring the Peak District, although it is not itself part of the national park. One of the highest towns in England, it is surrounded by protective hills, with the rather cold looking yellow-gray stone of its buildings everywhere softened by trees, bushes, and flowers. The Romans, who discovered the site in AD 79, prized the constant temperature (82F) of the bubbling springs and called their health resort Aquae Arnemetiae, or "The Spa of the Goddess of the Grove." By Tudor times, "taking the cure" was popular, and even poor Mary, Queen of Scots, who suffered from rheumatism, was allowed occasional visits from 1572 to 1580 while in the custody of the Earl of Shrewsbury. (It might have been self-interest on his part since he suffered from gout.) She stayed at Buxton Hall, now the *Old Hall* hotel.

The Buxton of today, however, was created largely in the late 18th century by the fifth Duke of Devonshire, who sought to make it a rival to Bath. The graceful, semicircular Crescent (the town's most elegant building), the Adams-style Assembly Rooms, the broad-domed Great Stables (now the Devonshire Royal Hospital), and the parish church of St. John the Baptist all date from this period. Later, the Victorians added the Pavilion Gardens bedecked with flowers and ornamental lakes, the Pump Room, and the Octagon concert hall. By then the railways had shortened the journey from industrial cities such as Stoke and Manchester, so the huge *Palace* hotel (see *Checking In*) was built above the Crescent to accommodate visitors who prized the fresh air as much as the water.

Today, people who want to sample the waters swim in the warm, spring-fed public swimming pool in the Pavilion Gardens, since the old thermal baths at one end of the Crescent have been turned into a shopping arcade. Farther along in the Crescent is the tourist information center (phone: 0298-5106) and, opposite, a public drinking fountain, also spa fed; the water is tastier than in most spas, but be careful, it comes out steaming! The Pump Room next door now houses the Buxton Micrarium (open daily from late March through early October), a museum where the exhibits — live microscopic specimens — are seen projected onto large TV-style screens. Otherwise, a popular pastime is simply to linger in the 23 acres of the Pavilion Gardens, enjoy the blooms in the restored Conservatory, and watch the river Wye rush by — perhaps with something delicious to flavor the view, like the ginger parkin, ginger slab cakes, Ashbourne gingerbread cookies, or, of course, gingerbread men from *The Gingerbread Shop,* 6

Terrace Rd. The *Buxton Antiques Fair* in May draws a fair number of devotees, and the 3-week *Buxton Festival* of music and the arts, bridging the months of July and August, is a well-known midsummer event.

CHECKING IN: ***Palace*** – Opened in 1870, this is grand in a truly Victorian manner, with a stately staircase, chandeliers, and lofty ceilings. Thanks to recent extensive renovations, however, the 122 bedrooms and bathrooms are prettily decorated and very comfortable, suiting 20th-century tastes. The health spa tradition endures in the new men's and women's gymnasiums, sauna, hydrospa pool, and heated swimming pool. Palace Rd., Buxton (phone: 0298-2001). Moderate.

En Route from Buxton – Edale and Castleton, other Peak District villages, are only a few miles to the northeast. Take A6, which climbs steeply up behind Buxton and then dips down to Chapel-en-le-Frith, and from there take A625 up Rushup Edge. Little sheep farms shelter in deep valleys and moorlands stretch away, smooth except for rocky crags and perhaps a few trees huddled together for comfort. After about 4 miles, a sign for Edale indicates a sharp left turn just before a copse of trees and a car park at the base of a steep hill. This is the back of Mam Tor, or "Mother Hill," known to the locals as Shivering Mountain because the combination of sandstone and shale can become unstable when wet, leading to rock slides. Park in the car park and take the path (a 10-minute or so walk) to the summit, where an Iron Age fort once stood. The view suddenly opens out along the circle of hills and down into a patchwork quilt of brown and green seamed by gray drystone walls: the Vale of Edale.

Back in the car, follow the sign to the village of Edale, on the river Noe. There is not much to the village, but since it is the start of the Pennine Way, the long-distance footpath that ends just over the Scottish border, it's known to walkers all over the country. There is a Peak National Park Information Centre (phone: 0433-70207) and, farther on, *The Old Nag's Head,* a pub catering to hearty appetites; the pub's Hikers' Bar is usually full of groups ready to set off or relaxing after exhilarating exertion. (Note that proper gear is necessary for anything longer than an hour's hike in the area, because even on a fine day a sudden squall can blow over, or mists set in.)

Beyond Edale, the valley road follows the river Noe and then rejoins A625 at Hope, where a right turn leads to Castleton and a left turn to Hathersage.

CHECKING IN/EATING OUT: ***Poachers Arms*** – Comfortable and well-tended, it has 7 large bedrooms and a restaurant serving home cooking. Castleton Rd., Hope (phone: 0433-20380). Inexpensive.

CASTLETON: This village is another popular base for excursions into the Peak District — consult the Peak National Park Information Centre on Castle Street; open daily during summer; weekends during winter (phone: 0433-20679). The town is set in the romantic shadow of Peveril Castle, a ruined Norman construction described by Sir Walter Scott in *Peveril of the Peak.* All along the main street are souvenir shops selling jewelry, bowls, and other items made of "Blue John," a semiprecious stone prized for its striations of brown fading into yellow and pink into a deep purple-blue. Found only in Castleton, the stone was discovered by the Romans and vases made of it even surfaced in the ruins of Pompeii. The Blue John Mine and Cavern west of the village (phone: 0433-20638), which taps 8 of the 14 veins in the vicinity, is open for guided tours daily (admission charge).

The village is also known for its Garland Ceremony, held each year on May 29th, *Oak Apple Day.* The celebration is said to commemorate the restoration of Charles II to the throne (after his narrow escape hiding in an oak tree), but some hold that it goes as far back as pagan times. In any case, a "king" in 17th-century costume is led on horseback along the street to the village church, where the enormous bell shape of flowers that has virtually covered him is removed and put into position on top of the tower, itself covered in oak leaves.

CHECKING IN: ***Castle*** – A comfortable place to stay, just opposite the Peak National Park Information Centre. Recent refurbishment may have dislodged the ghost of a jilted bride whose wedding breakfast at the inn was canceled. There are 10 rooms, all with private shower or bath. Castle St., Castleton (phone: 0433-20578). Moderate.

Ye Olde Nags Head – This 17th-century coaching inn has 8 bedrooms upstairs, 3 with four-poster beds. It's also a good stop for a meal, since it's known for good food and a snug atmosphere, with open fireplaces to take the chill off cold weather. Cross St., Castleton (phone: 0433-20248). Moderate.

HATHERSAGE: Although this pretty little village is only 5 miles (as the crow flies) from the outskirts of the major industrial city of Sheffield, it might as well be 50 miles. Situated on the river Derwent, its origins predate the Norman Conquest and even the Romans, and its name could come from "Heather's Edge." The moors certainly spread out in all directions when viewed from the vantage point of St. Michael's, the 14th-century church on the hill. A few steps from the porch of the church, between two old yew trees, is the 14-foot-long grave of the "friend and lieutenant" of Robin Hood, Little John. It is said that he grew up here, was apprenticed to a nail maker, and died in a nearby cottage (and the legend continues with a well and cave not far away named for Robin Hood). A tall tale perhaps, but the grave, when opened, was found to contain a thigh bone 30 inches long; whoever was buried in it must have been a huge man, particularly for those early times.

St. Michael's is interesting also for the 15th-century brass portraits of a local family, the Eyres. Charlotte Brontë, who stayed at the vicarage during a visit here in 1845, used that name along with a description of the village and the surrounding countryside in *Jane Eyre,* although the name of the village was changed to Morton. Inquire at the vicarage about rubbing the Eyre brasses.

CHECKING IN/EATING OUT: ***George*** – An old coaching inn built in the 16th century. The 18 bedrooms with bath are up-to-date, but the stone walls and beamed ceilings in the bar and restaurant preserve the atmosphere of yore. Main Rd., Hathersage (phone: 0433-50436). Moderate.

Hathersage Inn – A small inn of the Georgian period, it has just short of a dozen rooms with baths. Hearty breakfasts make it a popular spot for visitors, and there is a restaurant, candlelit in the evening. Main Rd., Hathersage (phone: 0433-50259). Moderate.

En Route from Hathersage – Take B6001 south through the wooded valley of the river Derwent. The itinerary now heads into the Dales, and even before Grindleford the landscape begins to change, taking on a gentler aspect. In Grindleford, turn right onto B6521 for Eyam.

EYAM: Pronounced *Ee*-em, this town was ravaged by the Great Plague of 1665–66 and has ever since been known as the Plague Village. Two days after the arrival of a shipment of contaminated cloth from London, the local tailor fell ill and died. Soon, the telltale signs of "swellings and rose-red rash" began to spread, creating panic. In a decision of extraordinary self-sacrifice, the villagers, led by their vicar, cut themselves off from the world to contain the disease. People from the surrounding countryside left food for them by a well nearly a mile away; money left in payment was "disinfected" with vinegar. Now, wooden plaques by the door of cottage after cottage around the church in the old village center record the death toll of families like the Hancocks, seven of whom died in one week. Another of the hundreds of victims was the vicar's wife, Catherine Mompesson, who is buried in the churchyard. (Also in the churchyard is a stone cross, battered and worn by some 1,200 years of weather, but with the pagan and Christian carvings still visible.)

Each year, on the last Sunday in August, a special service in remembrance of the plague is held in nearby Cucklet Dell, where the villagers held their own services during the plague year. Not all ceremonies in Eyam are somber, however, because this is one of several towns in Derbyshire where the tradition of well dressing continues. Here it takes place at the end of August or the beginning of September as part of a week of carnival that's complete with village sports and a whole sheep roasted on a spit set up between the church and manor house.

En Route from Eyam – Take B6521 Bakewell road to A623 and turn left, passing the stone quarry and heading for Calver (pronounced *Car*-ver). Just after the traffic lights, slow down. On the left is the *Derbyshire Craft Centre* (phone: 0433-31231), a small shop full of well-made and well-priced gifts from woolen scarves and jewelry to children's toys, brass, pottery, and glass. The attractive pale wood "eating house" that's part of the center is a good place for a simple lunch or coffee and cake — everything on the menu is homemade. Open daily except during January and February (weekends only).

A few miles farther along is Baslow; take A619 for Bakewell around the roundabout and almost immediately turn right again. The next 12 miles of the route — Baslow-to-Baslow via Bakewell and two of England's most fascinating stately homes — trace a loop through typical White Peak countryside, with the rivers Wye and Derwent cutting deep into the grass-covered limestone hills, softening the landscape and adding charm to already picturesque villages.

BAKEWELL: The town is a popular base for excursions into the southern Peak District, but it is also famous for Bakewell pudding, which dates from 1860 or so when a cook misunderstood a recipe for a jam tart and came up with something that a certain Mrs. Wilson later began selling in a cottage on the square. The *Old Original Bakewell Pudding Shop* still draws queues of tourists, although the "secret recipe" produces a rather ordinary combination of puff pastry and raspberry or strawberry jam. If you want to decide for yourself, the shop is just over the bridge past the tourist information center and Peak National Park Information Centre in the Old Market Hall (phone: 062981-3227). The town's name has no culinary associations but derives instead from the Anglo-Saxon terms "bad" for bath or spring and "quell" for well; the warm springs, here, too, were known as far back as Roman times.

En Route from Bakewell – Take A6 in the direction of Matlock; in 2 miles there are signs for Haddon Hall, the first of the two stately homes in this loop of the itinerary (the car park is on the right, across from the main gate). After the visit, continue to the next stately home, Chatsworth, reached by taking A6 another 2 miles to the pretty stone village of Rowsley and there turning left onto B6012, which passes through a large white gate and into the Chatsworth estate shortly after Beeley.

HADDON HALL: This stately home is sometimes overlooked in favor of its more famous neighbor, Chatsworth, but that is a mistake, since Haddon Hall is a gem of a medieval house. Set on a hill overlooking the peacefully flowing river Wye, it has all the towers, chimneys, gargoyles, and castellations typical of medieval days. Although its ownership dates back to an illegitimate son of William the Conqueror, most of the house was built from the 14th to the 16th centuries, with each generation leaving its mark. The 14th-century banqueting hall has a minstrel's gallery and high-beamed ceilings, the chapel boasts delicate 15th-century murals, and the beautiful late 16th-century Long Gallery has leaded glass windows staggered down both sides of its 110-foot length, creating a surprisingly light room for the Tudor era.

One of Haddon Hall's characters was Sir George Vernon, a 16th-century owner whose nickname was "King of the Peak." A dominating personality, he wanted his daughter, Dorothy, to marry the Earl of Leicester, who held the favor of Queen Elizabeth I. Dorothy refused, however, and while friends and relations were in the Long Gallery celebrating the wedding of her older sister, she quietly stole away to elope with John Manners, son of the Earl of Rutland. Eventually the couple was forgiven; indeed, when Sir George died in 1567, the estate passed to them and is still owned by the Dukes of Rutland. Although it is now their home, it was unoccupied during the 18th and 19th centuries, thus escaping the Georgian and Victorian "improvements" that were the fate of so many of Britain's other grand houses. (The present duke's father restored this one earlier in this century.) Stroll through the fragrant rose gardens, take a good look at the medieval kitchen with its logbox, huge stone fireplace, and meat-salting trough, and pause as the 17th-century clock in the courtyard weakly chimes the hours — it doesn't take much imagination to picture the domestic life of hundreds of years ago. Haddon Hall (phone: 062981-2855) is open Tuesdays through Sundays from Easter through September (but it's closed Sundays as well as Mondays during July and August); admission charge.

CHECKING IN/EATING OUT: ***Peacock*** **–** Built as a manor house in the 17th century and at one time used as the dower house for Haddon Hall, this is now a small hotel with gleaming antiques, warming fireplaces, and quiet gardens stretching to the river Derwent. The 20 rooms all have private bath or shower. The *Peacock* has fishing rights on both the Derwent and the Wye, so the hotel is popular with fishermen. The restaurant has a good reputation and a local following, especially for Sunday lunch. Rowsley (phone: 0629-733518). Moderate.

CHATSWORTH: Severely classical on the outside, splendidly baroque on the inside, Chatsworth is magnificent. It's home to the Duke and Duchess of Devonshire, although ordinary mortals may find it difficult to imagine actually *living* in this virtual palace where earlier in the century more than a hundred people would stay for the Christmas holiday. The first building on the site was the work of Sir William Cavendish, completed after his death in 1557 by his formidable widow, Bess of Hardwick. This structure, however, was slowly demolished and rebuilt from 1686 to 1707 by her descendant, William Cavendish, Lord Devonshire, who was created a duke by William III after the Glorious Revolution of 1688. The building project took up much of the first duke's life, since he became fascinated by architecture, often meddling with the plans and irritating builders by demanding changes. The west frontage is said to be his own design, as is the sanitation system in that wing.

Inside, the eye is almost overwhelmed by detail: ornate wood carving by Samuel Watson, a local artist; painted walls and ceilings by Louis Laguerre and Antonio Verrio, as in the chapel; wrought ironwork by Jean Tijou; and superb illusionist paintings in the Sabine Room by Sir James Thornhill. The second duke was a collector and acquired paintings and furniture that were augmented later by the works of Rembrandt, Velásquez, Inigo Jones, Van Dyck, and others — all part of the inheritance of Charlotte, wife of the fourth duke. It was also the fourth duke who invited Capability Brown to design the 1,100-acre park in 1761. The extensive gardens (105 acres), however, date from Joseph Paxton's three decades as head gardener in the early 19th century. On his first morning, that energetic soul had surveyed the estate and fallen in love with the housekeeper's niece, all by 9 AM!

It is practically impossible to focus on just one or two rooms although the state apartments and the library are particularly impressive and have been attracting visitors since Jane Austen's day. In *Pride and Prejudice,* Elizabeth's tour of Derbyshire includes a visit to Pemberley House, which may very well have been Chatsworth. The view she has of it approaching from Lambton (Bakewell) — "a large, handsome, stone building, standing well on rising ground, and backed by a ridge of high woody hills," with a stream "of some natural importance" in front — is the same and would have been quite as spectacular then as now.

Chatsworth (phone: 024688-2204) is open daily from the end of March through October; admission charge. It is, perhaps, the epitome of the "stately home," but for those with children unimpressed by such grandeur, the grounds also contain the Farmyard (open daily) and Adventure Playground (open Saturdays and Sundays), with play equipment, barnyard animals, and daily milking demonstrations. The Chatsworth tea bar serves food, and visitors are welcome to picnic in the vast park. The little walled village of Edensor (pronounced Ed-*den*-za), just before the northern gate of the park, is an estate village with its own church and, surprise, a post office that serves tea, although not year round.

CHECKING IN: ***Cavendish*** – Set in the Chatsworth Estate and formerly an inn, this is now a luxurious country-house hotel. The Dukes of Devonshire have owned it since 1830, and when it was renamed (Cavendish is the family name of the dukes) and renovated in the 1970s, the duchess herself supervised the decorating — some of the antique furniture and paintings even came from Chatsworth. Views over the estate from the 23 bedrooms are beautiful at any time of year. There's also fly fishing on some 10 miles of the Derwent and Wye, and once you've built up an appetite, the restaurant's award-winning chefs will fill you up with local seasonal produce such as venison, grouse, pheasant, and hare served elegantly on Wedgwood china. Baslow (phone: 024688-2311). Expensive to moderate.

En route from Chatsworth – From Baslow, take A619 to Chesterfield, famous for its crooked spire. Then take A617 southeast to M1, cross it, and follow signs to Hardwick Hall, an elegant National Trust property.

CHECKING IN: ***Chesterfield*** – A good, 62-room, Edwardian-style hotel, opposite the station. All rooms have private bath or shower. Malkin St., Chesterfield (phone: 0246-271141). Moderate.

HARDWICK HALL: Elizabeth, Countess of Shrewsbury, better known as Bess of Hardwick, made a pile of money through four very lucrative marriages, and she plowed all of it into this tall, H-shaped manor house, a wonderful, well preserved remnant of the late Elizabethan era. Hubbie number two had been Sir William Cavendish, from whom she inherited the original Chatsworth; hubbie number four, the Earl of Shrewsbury, threw her out of Chatsworth, so at age 70, the legendary Bess engaged Robert Smythson to design what is a surprisingly modern looking building. Built between 1591 and 1597, it features huge windows ("Hardwick Hall, more glass than wall," said the locals) and other revolutionary design points (i.e., the positioning of the entrance hall at right angles to the façade; family quarters on the second floor and servants' quarters on the ground floor rather than vice versa).

Hardwick Hall is also famous for its contents: 16th- and 17th-century tapestries hanging in the formal rooms, priceless 16th-century embroideries (including needlework executed by Bess and Mary, Queen of Scots), excellent examples of Elizabethan furniture, and contemporary portraits of the Cavendish family, who became the Dukes of Devonshire. The fine formal gardens, which include a walled herb garden, and a country park with rare breeds of domestic animals are a further attraction. But it is Bess herself who is worth reading about — she took on Elizabeth I and, despite being imprisoned in the Tower of London for 3 months for her cheek, she was one of the most powerful women in the land. Hardwick Hall (phone: 0246-850430) is open from April through October on Wednesday, Thursday, Saturday, and Sunday afternoons; admission charge.

En Route from Hardwick Hall – Continuing south on M1 toward Nottingham, fans of D. H. Lawrence may want to take Exit 27 for Eastwood, the dreary mining suburb of Nottingham where the writer was born and grew up (it figures prominently as Bestwood in *Sons and Lovers*). Lawrence's humble birthplace at 8A Victoria Street has been restored to its Victorian appearance and is open daily (phone: 0773-719786; admission charge), while the Breach House at 28 Garden Road (he called it Bottoms in the same novel), the family home from 1887 to 1891, is now a re-creation of the workman's cottage described in *Sons and Lovers* and is open by appointment only (phone: 0773-717581). A walking tour of Lawrence sites in Eastwood would also take in 8 Walker Street, the family home from 1891 to 1904 (he romanticized it as Bleak House), and 97 Lynncroft, where his mother died. Eastwood Library houses the Lawrence Study Room, with a collection of his books and papers. The Eastwood Craft Centre around the corner from the birthplace has small workshops where potters, sculptors, and others make and sell their wares.

NOTTINGHAM: The first name that springs to mind is Robin Hood, battling away against the evil Sheriff of Nottingham. There is still a sheriff, but whether or not there ever was an outlaw who robbed the rich to feed the poor, all that's left of him now is ballad and legend and the statue just outside the walls of the castle. Indeed, most of the main points of interest in this comfortable city are clustered around the castle, which stands on a high rock at the edge of the center. The original fortress on the spot, dating from the time of William the Conquerer, did not survive the English Civil War, but by the late 17th century a new castle — actually more of a ducal residence — had been built to replace it. In the late 19th century, this in turn became the *Nottingham Castle Museum* (phone: 0602-483504), open daily except bank holidays (admission charge on Sundays), exhibiting a good collection of silver, ceramics, and art. Look outside the castle for Mortimer's Hole, one of many subterranean tunnels carved into the soft sandstone on which Nottingham is built. This one, a secret entrance to the castle about a hundred yards long, is thought to have been used in the 14th century by 18-year-old King Edward III when he and a small armed band sneaked in to grab Roger Mortimer, his mother's lover, and avenge his father's death by having Mortimer hanged, drawn, and quartered in London.

Below the Castle, built into the rock, is the famous white-painted *Ye Olde Trip to Jerusalem* pub, yet another claimant to the title of "oldest pub in Britain." Certainly the sand from the rocky ceiling occasionally drops into the beer served here, but locals and visitors alike enjoy the old-world atmosphere. Next door is the delighful row of 17th-century cottages that make up the *Brewhouse Yard Museum* (phone: 0602-483504; open daily), featuring period rooms and other displays that re-create daily life in Nottingham 300 years ago. Across the street in a 15th-century half-timbered building is the Lace Centre (phone: 0602-413539), which houses a collecion of Nottingham's most famous product (it's open daily, and demonstrations of lace making often take place Thursday afternoonsfrom Easter through summer). The excellent *Costume and Textile Museum* is next door (open daily), and a small display about Robin Hood and a collection of arms, uniforms, and rare medals garnered by the Notts and Derby Regiment — otherwise known as the Sherwood Foresters — is in the Castle Gatehouse (open April through September). Recent additions include Lace Hall, High Pavement, in a converted church where lace-making on original machinery is demonstrated, and the Robin Hood Centre, which is a modern "journey through the legend" in carriages à la Epcot Center. There is also a seasonal tourist information center in the Castle Gatehouse, but the year-round City of Nottingham Information Bureau is at 16 Wheeler Gate (phone: 0602-470661).

Elsewhere in this busy but spacious city, there are gardens, parks, and squares to wander through. Wollaton Hall (phone: 0602-281333), a practically awe-inspiring Elizabethan mansion built from 1580 to 1588, is about 2 miles west of the center set in the beautiful grounds of Wollaton Park. It now houses the city's *Natural History Museum* (open daily; admission charge on Sundays and bank holidays), while the 18th-century stable block has become an industrial museum. Newstead Abbey, about 12 miles north of the center (phone: 0623-793557), was built as a priory in the 12th century and converted into a mansion in the 16th century by the ancestors of Lord Byron, who inherited it in 1798. It now contains many of the poet's possessions (it has its own ghost, the Black Friar, seen by Byron himself!) and is open daily from 11:30 AM to 5 PM through September; admission charge.

Besides Lord Byron and D. H. Lawrence, who was born in the suburb of Eastwood (see above), Nottingham has several other famous sons, including George Green, the 19th-century genius who was a pioneer of modern nuclear physics, and William Booth, the founder of the Salvation Army (his house has become a center for the elderly). And then there's Robin Hood. The Tales of Robin Hood theme center on Maid Marian Way, around the corner from the Robin Hood statue outside the castle, is billed as "a flight to adventure" where visitors ride a chairlift to flee from the Sheriff of Nothingham in the medieval city out to Sherwood Forest. It provides 40 minutes of fun. Open daily from 10 AM to 6 PM in summer; 10 AM to 5 PM in winter (phone: 0602-483284). Most of Sherwood Forest, which once stretched from the outskirts of Nottingham north some 19 miles to the village of Edwinstowe and comprised some 100,000 acres, was chopped down for firewood or dug up by coal mining. It's now shrunk to the 450 acres that make up the Sherwood Forest Country Park, just north of Edwinstowe. Here is Robin Hood's legendary meeting place, the Major Oak, still a tree of massive girth, even if it isn't old enough to comply with the legend's demands. The Visitors Centre in Sherwood Forest can provide information on special events such as the *Robin Hood Festival* held during the summer (phone: 0623-823202).

Back in Nottingham there is one vestige of the Middle Ages that has not only survived but thrived. This is the annual *Goose Fair,* which begins at noon on the first Thursday in October and for 3 days thereafter transforms 18 acres of the city into a huge state fair type of celebration. Named for the geese originally sold there, it dates back to the 13th century.

CHECKING IN: ***Albany*** – Modern, central, and efficient, this is the best hotel in town, catering to businessmen and conferences as well as tourists. All 139 rooms have private bath. The *Carvery,* with its "as much as you want" roast beef, pork, lamb, and gammon (similar to ham), is always popular. There are good views from the top floors. St. James's St., Nottingham (phone: 0602-470131). Moderate.

Royal Moat House International – Another modern hotel, convenient to the Royal Centre (the *Theatre Royal* and the *Royal Concert Hall*). Large (201 rooms) and always bustling, a glass arcade with tropical plants links restaurants and bars attractively, and the cocktail bar on the top floor overlooks the city. Wollaton St., Nottingham (phone: 0602-414444). Moderate.

EATING OUT: ***Les Artistes Gourmands*** – About 4½ miles southwest of the city, this is a real French restaurant with flair. The menu ranges from straightforward pork in mustard sauce to salmon with a sauce of passion fruit and local guinea fowl and ducks, and there are good imported French cheeses to match the

French wines. The room is hung with paintings by local artists. 61 Wollaton Rd., Beeston (phone: 0602-228288). Moderate.

Ocean City – Near the university and popular with Chinese students, this spot specializes in Cantonese favorites with some unusual ingredients — steamed eel with crispy pork or sizzling monkfish with chili and black bean sauce. 100 Derby Rd., Notthingham (phone: 0602-475095).

East Anglia

When asked what Norfolk was like, one of Noel Coward's characters simply replied "flat!" The same charge is often leveled at the entire East Anglian region of Britain, which includes Suffolk, Essex, and Cambridgeshire, as well as the county of Norfolk. While the label certainly applies to areas such as the Fens in the western part of East Anglia, it is far too dismissive a description of the remaining parts. With its subtle range of gradients and variety of landscapes — wild and sandy heaths, woodlands, salt marshes, tidal creeks, waterways, and even hills and valleys — East Anglia is never monotonous.

Despite its proximity to London, this fat belly of land that reaches out into the North Sea is surprisingly remote and rural. Few highways bisect it — they could serve as a route to nowhere "farther on." In fact, the majority of its thoroughfares are narrow backroads overgrown with grass and just barely able to accommodate the width of two vehicles. The area is thinly populated, too, although this wasn't always the case. During the 15th century it was the center of a prosperous wool trade and one of Britain's most highly populated regions. The largest city, Norwich, was at one time second in size only to London. Indeed, when the writer Daniel Defoe traveled in East Anglia, he saw "a face of diligence spread over the whole country...thronged with great and spacious market towns, more and larger than any other part of England so far from London." But when the sheep business began to dwindle, shifting farther north to the mills in Yorkshire, people began to drift away. East Anglia was largely unaffected by the Industrial Revolutionary fervor that swept the country in the late 18th to mid-19th centuries and has remained somewhat of an economic backwater ever since.

Today, while driving through the pastoral East Anglian villages, you'll see plenty of testimonials to their former prosperity and importance. Towns that have faded to a fraction of their former size are dominated by churches magnificent both in terms of scale and Gothic richness. It is hard to travel more than a mile or so without seeing at least one — and often several — spiking upwards on the horizon. These churches were built by the wool merchants partly in thanks to God for his help with their commercial success and partly as unholy status symbols. Today, there may be as few as half a dozen red brick cottages in their shadows, and even fewer parishioners for the Sunday morning service.

Most East Anglian villages are found in the classic format of cottages, church, pub, and local manor house, all clustered around a village green where you may see a local cricket or soccer match in progress. Since the cultivation of food crops, particularly potatoes, sugar beets, and other vegetables, is the area's principal industry, the villages are primarily agrarian in nature, hard-working farm communities. They cannot match the bijou villages of Britain's more southerly and westerly belts of countryside in Kent,

Surrey, Sussex, Berkshire, and Hampshire, with their cream tea shops, posh "horse brass pubs," and generally precious airs and graces. But the area is also endowed with an unlikely number of grand houses, ranging from "modest" manor farmhouses to the stately mansions of the aristocracy, such as the Queen's own favorite retreat at Sandringham. Most estates, especially those with fine period furnishings, impressive art collections, and beautiful gardens, open their doors to the public in summer, and many serve tea in as grand a setting as you could ever hope to find.

Our route spans two of the area's four counties: Norfolk and Suffolk, land of the North Folk and the South Folk. These were once two distinct groups of people, kept apart by two rivers and for many centuries left alone by the rest of the country because of the impassable Fens and more southerly bands of dense forest. Even today county chauvinism remains strong, although both "sides" share a similar dialect and a unique vocabulary that includes such unique words as *mardle,* meaning to gossip, *rummun,* meaning a peculiar person, and *squit,* meaning nonsense.

Suffolk is the hillier of the two counties, full of tiny, huddled villages and timber-framed farmhouses, with a coastline indented by finger estuaries and dotted with delightfully old-fashioned seaside resorts. Inland is the leafy, peaceful corner of the country that so inspired the great landscape painter, John Constable. Norfolk has broad, plain-like farmlands and thus far grander horizons. Its coastline, one of the most pristine in Europe, is a moody expanse of salt marshes, tidal creeks, shingle spits, and sandy dunes beloved by sailors ever since Admiral Nelson learned to sail here as a boy. If you can't tour with a hired boat, at least bring binoculars, since flocks of seabirds and waterfowl have chosen its vast acreages as their nesting grounds. Norfolk also has the Broads, a sprawling network of manmade waterways dating from the Middle Ages when peat was cut from the bogs to heat homes and the resulting ditches subsequently flooded. The Broads, too, are best seen from a boat — and soon, before they sink or become silted up, polluted, or commercialized.

The drive outlined below begins not far from Cambridge in Newmarket, Suffolk, and moves east to Bury St. Edmunds before dropping south to wind through wool towns such as Sudbury (a good place to pick up the route for those beginning in London) and Lavenham and dip into the Stour Valley on its way to Ipswich. It hits the Suffolk coast at Aldeburgh, then climbs up the coast into Norfolk. After a visit to the large, rather brash resort of Great Yarmouth, the itinerary turns inland to pass through the Broads, skirting Norwich (covered in detail in THE CITIES). The final leg follows the north coast of Norfolk, visiting such spots as Blakeney, Burnham Overy Staithe, and Brancaster, before culminating at the larger town of King's Lynn.

East Anglia's accommodations range from picturesque village pubs to grand executive hotels in a city such as Norwich. Expect to pay over $100 for a double room in those hotels listed as expensive, from $60 to $100 in moderate, and under $60 in inexpensive. A meal for two excluding wine, drinks, and tips, will run between $55 and $75 in expensive restaurants; $30 to $55 in those listed as moderate, and under $30 in the inexpensive ones.

CAMBRIDGE: The beautiful university city on the Cam is a convenient place to begin a tour of East Anglia; for a detailed report, see *Cambridge,* THE CITIES. From

Cambridge, take A45 northeast to Newmarket, 13 miles away, and then on to Bury St. Edmunds, 14 miles from Newmarket.

NEWMARKET: This town has long been the center of British horseracing. What began as the hobby of King Charles II (his grandfather, James I, built King's House here but was more of a hunting fan) became big business with the establishment of the Royal Stables and the founding of the Jockey Club to set up guidelines for the sport. Now the National Stud, where the kingdom's finest horses are bred, is here, too. Races are held at Newmarket Heath, 1½ miles southwest of town, in April, May, October, and November — the most famous are the One Thousand and Two Thousand Guineas, the Cambridgeshire, and the Cesarewitch. Nearby Devil's Ditch, an enormous 7½-mile embankment built in the 7th century as a boundary marker or a defense wall, is traditionally used by locals for a free "grandstand" view of the races. The National Stud, also near the racecourse, is open to the public for a few hours on racing days, Sundays, and holidays. The galleries of the *National Horseracing Museum,* High St. (phone: 0638-667333), trace the development of British racing — there are also changing exhibitions (open daily, except Mondays, April through early December and daily in August; admission charge).

CHECKING IN/EATING OUT: ***Swynford Paddocks*** – Once the home of Byron's half sister (and lover) Augusta Leigh, it's now a country hotel, 6 miles southwest of Newmarket. The atmosphere is that of a well-appointed private home, with 15 rooms and a good restaurant. Six Mile Bottom (phone: 063870-234). Expensive.

BURY ST. EDMUNDS: The town was named after the last King of East Anglia, who was martyred by Danish invaders (ca. 870). His burial site became a shrine and an abbey founded around it in the 10th century grew to be one of the richest and most powerful in medieval England. Now a ruin, there are only two gate-towers — the Norman Tower and the magnificent 14th-century Abbey Gatehouse — to suggest its former scale. The latter, the town's most distinguished landmark, leads into the attractive Abbey Gardens, which include a rose garden. Very little remains of the abbey church, famous as the spot where the barons conspired to force King John to ratify the Magna Carta. The *Theatre Royal,* Westgate St., is a late-Georgian playhouse designed by William Wilkins, who also did the *National Gallery* in London. It can be toured by visitors when performances are not underway (phone: 0284-755127). The *Market Cross Art Gallery,* on Guildhall St. (off Cornhill St.), also originally a theater, was designed by the well-known Scottish architect, Robert Adam, and is the only one of his buildings in East Anglia (open Tuesdays through Saturdays; admission charge). On display in Queen Anne House, 8 Angel Hill, is the impressive Gershom Parkington Memorial Collection of Clocks and Watches, dating from the 16th century onwards (open daily).

CHECKING IN: ***Angel*** – When Charles Dickens stayed at this creeper-covered hotel, he "had a fine room," now No. 15 and still available but with better plumbing (though the bath still empties to the tune of a sinking ocean liner). Opposite the Abbey Gatehouse, family-owned and run with a warm heart, this is the social hub of town. Angel Hill, Bury St. Edmunds (phone: 0284-753926). Moderate.

Ravenwood Hall – Dating back to Henry VIII's time, this privately owned hotel, with 7 rooms, is set in 7 acres of lawns and woodland. The ornately carved oak structure is decorated with 16th-century wall paintings. The restaurant, formerly a Tudor living hall, has beautiful carved timbers and a huge fireplace. Other facilities include a bar, swimming pool, tennis, and riding. Rougham, Bury St. Edmunds (phone: 0359-70345). Moderate.

En Route from Bury St. Edmunds – Take A134 15 miles south to Long Melford, which is 3 miles north of Sudbury.

LONG MELFORD: The old houses of this beauty of a village 15 miles south of Bury St. Edmunds (take A134) stretch for 3 miles along the main road, hence the "long" in its name. At the core, they expand around a huge village green. Like its neighbors, Long Melford was a thriving wool town during the 15th century, a circumstance that generated enough money to build the great Holy Trinity Church at the top end of the green. Former prosperity is reflected in its ornate flint "flushwork," exquisite stone and wood carvings, and the 100 elegant windows (including one of priceless stained glass) that ignite the interior on the gloomiest winter day.

Melford Hall, now a National Trust property, and Kentwell Hall are Long Melford's two grandest houses. Melford Hall, opposite the church on the other side of the green, was built by William Cordell, a 16th-century statesman important enough to have been visited by Queen Elizabeth I, and eventually sold to the Parker family, one of whose descendants still lives here. Elizabethan and highly turreted, it houses an impressive collection of Chinese porcelain treasures captured from a Spanish galleon by one of the Parker family's famous admirals. Beatrix Potter fans will find a permanent exhibition dedicated to the famous author and her "friends" (open Wednesdays, Thursdays, Saturdays, and Sundays early April through September; admission charge).

Kentwell Hall lies at the end of an avenue of limes north of the village, another red-brick Tudor manor surrounded by a broad moat. It combines a mixture of styles as large parts were gutted by fire in the early 19th century and were subsequently remodeled (major restoration is still in progress). The gardens are especially worth seeing, particularly the walled garden, moated like the house itself (open Thursdays and Sundays April through mid-June and Wednesdays through Sundays mid-July through September; from late June through early July, open to the public on weekends only, because re-creations of Tudor life are staged for school children; admission charge; phone: 0787-310207).

CHECKING IN: ***Bull*** – Built as a wool merchant's house in 1450, this had become, by the middle of the 16th century, a busy coaching inn on the main London to Norwich turnpike. Today you can have lunch, tea, or dinner or stay in one of the 27 rooms surrounded by ancient timbers and antique furniture. Hall St., Long Melford (phone: 0787-78494). Expensive.

EATING OUT: ***Chimneys*** – Sophisticated versions of country fare are the main courses in this beamed village house. For dessert, there are puddings such as vanilla soufflé with a bitter chocolate sauce. Closed Sundays at dinner and on Mondays. Hall St., Long Melford (phone: 0787-79806). Expensive.

SUDBURY: Another town that grew prosperous as a center of the wool trade, Sudbury, 3 miles south of Long Melford on A134, is far larger than its peers, thanks mainly to its commercial importance on the navigable river Stour. It has three Perpendicular churches — St. Gregory's, St. Peter's, and All Saints' — as well as a stock of typical medieval houses, but its most attractive buildings are Georgian, including several three-story weavers' cottages that are recognizable from their wide floor-to-ceiling windows where the looms used to stand. The town's main claim to fame is as the birthplace of one of the greatest British painters, Thomas Gainsborough, whose father, a wool merchant, raised nine children at 46 Sepulchre Street (now Gainsborough Street). Their elegant town house still stands as an art gallery and museum of Gainsborough's life and work (closed Sunday mornings and Mondays; admission charge), much of which featured the local landscape, including the Auberies, an estate 2 miles outside of Sudbury used in the background of his "Mr. and Mrs. Andrews," now hanging in London's *National Gallery.*

En Route from Sudbury – B1115 followed by B1071 lead northeast to Lavenham. The town announces its presence some distance away, the finely tapered tower of St. Peter and St. Paul Church looming larger than a cathedral above the horizon. If its eight bells happen to peal at the time of your arrival the overall impact is overwhelming.

LAVENHAM: Of all the old wool towns, this gem, with over 300 listed buildings, is certainly the best preserved — and the most visited by tourists in summer. It is every foreigner's dream of England and the reality of numerous film makers, since the main street has starred in many a period production. The town looks today as it always has, at least since the 15th and 16th centuries when most of its buildings were constructed. The single most famous of these is the guildhall, a timber-framed Tudor building that is hard to miss in the marketplace. Built in 1529 and now owned by the National Trust, it is home to a local history museum (open daily April through October; admission charge.) Another ancient building, the Priory, has been home to Benedictine monks and wool merchants and now belongs to the Casey family who saved the building from likely ruin and restored it to house an exhibition of paintings and drawings and of photographs illustrating the restoration (open daily; admission charge). The *Angel Hotel,* a very old pub in the marketplace, is popular with locals and visitors alike.

CHECKING IN: ***Swan*** – A 14th-century inn, with most of its timbers twisted and gnarled with age. It has comfortable rooms around a lovely flower-filled courtyard and a separate, heavily beamed restaurant. High St., Lavenham (phone: 0787-247477). Expensive to moderate.

Great House – This hotel and restaurant has 3 large rooms with private baths and separate sitting rooms. The 14th-century building is decorated with antiques and tasteful accessories. There is a candlelit dining room with a blazing fire, along with a paved courtyard where lunch and dinner are served during good weather. Market Place, Lavenham (phone: 0787-247431). Moderate.

En Route from Lavenham – The road to Hadleigh (A1141) is a hilly, rather twisty route. About halfway, off A1141, stands Chelsworth, often bypassed but an absolute delight of old houses, riverside, and graceful trees. Fifteen of its gardens are open to the public on the last Sunday in June.

HADLEIGH: Nestling in the valley of the river Brett, Hadleigh was another important center of the wool and grain trades. The town lies between two bridges — the Iron Bridge, crossed when approaching from the northwest, and the attractive, three-arched Toppesfield Bridge, crossed on the way southeast to Layham. Despite the steady stream of traffic, the town is still fine-looking (although without the timeless air of Lavenham) and has figured in many a painting and photograph of rural Britain. The elegant, lead-covered spire of St. Mary's Church is as it was in the 15th century and its peal of bells still rings out across the valley (the 600-year-old Angelus Bell is inscribed with a worthy sentiment — unfortunately someone forgot to invert the words and they came out of the mold back to front). Inside, in addition to the "ringers' gotch," a jug reserved for the thirsty bellringers' ale, there are two beautiful 15th-century screens and a 14th-century octagonal font with a paneled pedestal and rich tapestry on the bowl. St. Mary's is part of a fine cluster of medieval buildings including the redbrick Deanery Tower and the timber-framed Guildhall, both of the 15th century, while the area between the church and the Guildhall has revealed the foundations of an older Saxon church.

En Route from Hadleigh – Head south on B1070. Just beyond Holton St. Mary turn right onto A12 and then left down B1029 to Dedham.

DEDHAM AND THE STOUR VALLEY: This slice of countryside on the border between Suffolk and Essex counties is known as Dedham Vale, but it's often simply referred to as Constable country. Specifically, the term refers to a collection of villages that line the valley of the river Stour, each one either painted by the great British artist or otherwise linked to his life. "I associate my careless boyhood with all that lies on the banks of the Stour; these things made me a painter, and I am grateful," he once remarked. Prepare to do some walking along the riverside to best appreciate Constable country. The swiftly flowing river, fringed with reeds, winds through silent marshes and gentle farmland, while the wide skies overhead reveal ever-changing cloud patterns, illuminating a landscape of serene beauty.

Begin your explorations with Dedham, an elegant town of Tudor and Georgian shops, houses, and inns that appears frequently on Constable's canvases — indeed, parts of Dedham feel disturbingly familiar, since the painter often indulged in considerable artistic license, changing the location of landmarks (such as Dedham Church) to suit his aesthetic purposes. Dedham's old *Sun Inn* is still in its rightful position, as are the old shop fronts and color-washed cottages with their overhanging stories. On the other side of the river is East Bergholt, where the painter was born in 1776. Although it has suffered somewhat as an object of pilgrimage, it is still a pleasant village of Georgian houses, and its church has an unfinished tower whose bells are enthusiastically rung by hand every Sunday. Constable's home no longer survives, but the cottage attached to the Post Office was his studio, and the graves of his parents and of Willy Lott (see below) are in the churchyard.

Flatford Mill, on the Stour a mile south of East Bergholt, was the subject of a painting of the same name, Constable's first important large canvas (it now hangs in the *Tate Gallery* in London). Follow the road from East Bergholt and park at the mill, taking the footpath down to the bridge over the river. Along the opposite side of the river from the mill is the quiet millpond and Bridge Cottage, instantly recognizable as the setting for "The Hay Wain" (in the *National Gallery*). Bridge Cottage, or Willy Lott's Cottage (the mill-hand who reputedly lived in it for 88 years), has been acquired by the National Trust and now houses an exhibition of Constable's working methods seen through his sketches. Open daily, June through August; Wednesdays through Sundays, April, May, September, and October.

CHECKING IN: *Dedham Vale* – A Victorian mansion, set in spacious grounds by the river Stour. It has 6 rooms and a glass-covered, plant-filled restaurant reminiscent of a greenhouse, the establishment's pride and joy (rotisserie is the specialty). Stratford Rd., Dedham (phone: 0206-322273). Expensive.

Maison Talbooth – Another Victorian house on the banks of the Stour. To say that each of its 10 bathrooms has its own bedroom is a good indication of the grandeur of this country-house hotel, one of Britain's best. Cosseted comfort continues at the breakfast table, but dinners are taken at the *Dedham Vale* hotel (see above) half a mile up the road or at *Le Talbooth* (see below) a quarter of a mile farther on (all under the same ownership). Stratford Rd., Dedham (phone: 0206-322367). Expensive.

EATING OUT: *Le Talbooth* – This 16th-century timber-framed building on the riverbank has been, in its time, a tollhouse, a weaver's cottage, and a tea house. It's now a restaurant, one of the culinary centers of the county, with a classic menu. Gun Hill, Dedham (phone: 0206-323150). Expensive.

En Route from Dedham – Pick up A137 to Ipswich, passing through Brantham, where the altarpiece in the 14th-century church, depicting Christ blessing children, was painted by Constable.

IPSWICH: Its prime location at the head of the river Orwell has made Ipswich, the capital of the county of Suffolk, a busy port since Anglo-Saxon times. The town's history lives in its street names (Westgate and Northgate, for example, are all that remains of the old town wall) and in its medieval churches and merchants' and sea captains' houses. The *Great White Horse Hotel* on Tavern Street, where Charles Dickens stayed, is recognized even today as a setting in his famous novel, *The Pickwick Papers.* The tourist information center, Town Hall, Princes St. (phone: 0473-58070), supplies an excellent *Town Trail Guide* describing walking tours of the city's cobbled streets that will take you past rows of interesting houses.

Two of the most notable buildings in Ipswich are Christchurch Mansion, at Christchurch Park, and the Ancient House, in the Butter Market. Christchurch Mansion (phone: 0473-53246), a 16th-century Tudor town house, has become a museum with a collection of antique furniture, paintings by Constable, Rubens, Reynolds, and Gainsborough, and an outstanding collection of the decorative arts, china, and glass. It's open Mondays through Saturdays from 10 AM to 5 PM and Sundays from 2:30 to 4:30 PM. The Ancient House, now a bookshop, also dates to the 16th century and has an exceptional display of decorative pargeting, or painted plasterwork, on its facade. The *Ipswich Museum,* High Street (phone: 0473-213761), has exhibits on Suffolk geology and natural history, as well as a new Roman Gallery with a reconstructed Roman villa of the type that used to grace the town and a good collection of replicas of the finds at the Sutton Hoo ship burial ground nearby (open Mondays through Saturdays from 10 AM to 5 PM).

CHECKING IN: *Hintlesham Hall* – Behind this imposing 18th-century facade 5 miles southwest of Ipswich is a luxurious country-house hotel whose assets include a handsome library and 10 large antiques-filled bedrooms. A tennis court, farm, orchard, and a lake complete with fountain are all fitted into 18 acres of grounds. Meals are prepared by a chef who has worked both at *Le Gavroche* and London's *Connaught* hotel. Hintlesham (phone: 047387-268). Expensive.

***Marlborough* –** A red brick, 22-room Victorian town house on the far side of Christchurch Park, it is noted for its quiet traditional atmosphere and its thoughtful service, particularly in the black-tie restaurant. 73 Henley Rd., Ipswich (phone: 0473-57677). Expensive.

***Belstead Brook* –** This part Jacobean, creeper-covered manor is about 2 miles southwest of town. Some of the oldest of the 32 rooms still contain their original oak paneling; the 6 garden suites are also antiques furnished, but their age is offset by such ultramodern amenities as whirlpool baths. Belstead Rd., Ipswich (phone: 0473-684241). Moderate.

***Otley House* –** Dinner is taken *en famille* in the candlelit dining room, and there's more than a touch of native Danishness in Lise Hilton's menu. When she's not cooking, Lise is running this part-Tudor, part-Georgian house with her husband. About 8 miles north of Ipswich; closed December through February. Otley (phone: 047339-253). Inexpensive.

WOODBRIDGE: This beautiful boating town is at the head of the long shallow estuary of the river Deban (prnounced *Deeb'n*), only 8 miles from Ipswich via A12 and B1438. It was once prosperous as a commercial port and shipbuilding center, but its boatyards and moorings are now predominantly occupied by pleasure craft, and the town thrives as a center for holidays afloat. Its maritime past resulted in a wealth of historic buildings, from the Elizabethan Shire Hall, now used as a magistrates court, to the Woodbridge Tide Mill, an old weather-boarded mill on the waterfront, restored to working order so that visitors can see just how it harnessed the power of the tide to drive its corn-grinding machinery. It's open most days May through October (admission charge; phone: 03943-2548).

CHECKING IN: *Seckford Hall* – The gabled roof, mullioned windows, beamed ceilings, and huge fireplaces are all authentic — because this country-house hotel about a mile southwest of town is a remarkably well preserved

Tudor mansion. The 24 bedrooms, however, have period furniture. Breakfasts are so huge they'll set you up for a day's walking in the 34 acres of woods and gardens. Off A12, Woodbridge (phone: 0394-385678). Moderate.

En Route from Woodbridge – Follow B1438 a mile to Melton, turn right, and continue about 12 miles along A1152 and B1069 to Snape and then another 5 miles on A1094 to Aldeburgh. Along the way, a couple of miles out of Woodbridge, a sign announces Sutton Hoo, near Rendlesham, where one of the greatest archaeological discoveries in Britain was made in the 1930s. Ancient Saxon Kings were buried in ships, surrounded by all their treasures (a ship burial is described in *Beowulf*), and this was the site chosen by the Saxon Kings of East Anglia for their burial ground. One of several mounds excavated here yielded the remains of an approximately 85-foot-long wooden ship stuffed with priceless 7th-century objects in gold, silver, and iron — coins, jewelry, dishes, spears — as well as a jeweled sword, shield, and helmet (no body was found, leading to the conclusion that this particular king, whoever he was, was buried elsewhere). The spectacular loot is now in the *British Museum,* although the *Ipswich Museum* has a display of replicas. Public access to the site is by weekend guided tour only, April through October (phone: 0394-3397), but you can see quite a lot from the nearby footpath.

EATING OUT: *Old Rectory* – The English cooking in this rambling old house is both adventurous and delicious. Main courses are often left in dishes to help yourself, and the menus are substantial — try Muscovy duck with nut sauce, followed by upside-down ginger cake. The house also offers some accommodations. To reach it, leave B1069 for B1078 a little more than half the way from Woodbridge to Snape. Campsea Ashe (phone: 0728-746524). Moderate to inexpensive.

SNAPE AND ALDEBURGH: Snape is famous for Snape Maltings, a complex of old buildings used to store barley in the 19th century. In the late 1960s, one of the buildings was converted into the magnificent *Maltings Concert Hall,* and now most of the main events of the annual *Aldeburgh Music Festival,* one of Britain's best, are held here. The festival, begun in 1948 by composer Benjamin Britten and tenor Peter Pears, fills the last 2 weeks in June with operas, concerts, lectures, poetry readings, and exhibits, but the concert hall is also in use at the end of August for the Maltings Proms and for various other concerts through the autumn. If you miss all of these, the Maltings complex also contains a public house called *The Plough and Sail,* which originally served the maltsters, whose photos decorate the bar; a crafts shop; an art gallery (mainly contemporary works by East Anglian artists); a country store; and a tea shop. All are open daily from Easter to Christmas. Information on the festival is available by writing the Aldeburgh Foundation, High St., Aldeburgh, Suffolk IP15 5AX (phone: 072885-2935).

Remaining festival events take place in the seaside town of Aldeburgh itself (the name is Old English for Old Borough) as well as in churches and stately homes in the vicinity. Until the festival brought it renown, Aldeburgh was a fisherman's preserve — operagoers might recognize it as the setting of Britten's *Peter Grimes.* A walk through the town is worthwhile: After centuries of erosion, the wide High Street is only a pebble's throw from the shingle beach. In fact, some of medieval Aldeburgh has fallen into the sea. The 16th-century timber-framed Moot Hall (more Old English, meaning "meeting") stands only yards from the shore, continually bearing the brunt of winter gales, but consult the two maps inside and you'll see that it used to stand in the center of town. Stop for a filling game pie or a plate of locally caught seafood at the *Cross Keys Inn* on Crabbe Street, a 16th-century ale house whose old-fashioned atmosphere is enhanced by low ceilings, cozy groups of armchairs, and well-worn settees. By long-standing tradition, it remains open, snubbing the country's restrictive licensing laws, whenever the nearby lifeboat is out on a rescue mission. For milder beverages, look for *Crag Sisters,* also on Crabbe Street, one of the best place in town for afternoon tea.

South of Aldeburgh is Orford Ness, a spit of land some 10 miles long that has diverted the river Alde so progressively south that it doesn't actually meet the sea until Hollesley. The spit is a naturalists' and birdwatchers' paradise, and locals are adamant that there are fossils to be found along the shore.

CHECKING IN: ***Crown*** – Opposite the thatched church in the beautiful village of Westleton, close to Aldeburgh, it has 14 rooms, four-poster beds, and log fires. The restaurant serves a renowned choice of fresh fish. Westleton, Saxmundham (phone: 072873-273). Moderate.

Uplands – A combination of chintz and Georgian elegance is the predominant note in this country house hotel. It has a restaurant overlooking the garden and three family rooms among its 20 bedrooms (not all with private bath). Victoria Rd., Aldeburgh (phone: 072885-2420). Moderate.

Wentworth – With 31 rooms, this highly recommended country house hotel has been owned by the Pritt family since 1920. The hotel, decorated with antiques, has lovely sea views and a sunken terrace. Wentworth Rd., Aldeburgh (phone: 072885-2312). Moderate.

En Route from Snape and Aldeburgh – Take B1122 and hurry through Leiston, an industrial blot on the rural landscape. Bear left here along B1119 and you'll soon see the well-preserved ruin of Framlingham Castle looming unexpectedly into view. Begun in 1190, its construction represented an important advance in castle design for the times, since it was built according to the Saracen method, brought back from the Crusades, employing towers linked by massive curtain walls. The towers carry distinctive dummy chimneys, one of several alterations made in the 16th century by the Howards, then Dukes of Norfolk, who inherited the fortress. It was at Framlingham Castle that Mary Tudor organized her army to oust Lady Jane Grey from the throne, and later, having succeeded, proclaimed herself queen. Nothing much remains inside the walls now except for some picturesque 17th-century almshouses incorporating fragments of the former great hall, but climb a spiral staircase leading up to the battlements for superb views of Suffolk farmland. The castle is open daily from 9:30 AM to 6:30 PM (afternoons only on Sundays, October through March); admission charge.

The town of Framlingham begins at the castle walls — the back gardens of houses on Castle Street finish at the moat, in fact — and centers on a triangular market square. Since it is so tiny, its narrow streets are best explored on foot, particularly Castle and Church streets, and the lovely sequence of Georgian cottages on sweeping Double Street.

Leave Framlingham by heading north to Dennington on B1116. This is the only way you'll be able to look back and see the castle in its full glory: The walls rise high above a 40-foot drop into the valley, a sight to make even the most courageous army pause for thought. Then cut east (via A1120, A12, and an unclassified road) to the coast for Dunwich. The road traverses the ancient farmlands of "High Suffolk" or "The Woodland," a landscape of old copses, hedgerows, and uplands (which may be as "up" as 200 feet) drained by brooks. Nearing the coast they wind down to a heavy clay plateau, marshes, and eventually the sea.

DUNWICH: The main reason for visiting Dunwich is that there's nothing here — most of it has fallen into the sea. Back in the 12th century, this tiny cliff-top village was a walled town enjoying paramount importance as a port, with a thriving shipbuilding and fishing industry, and as a bishop's seat, with nine churches, a hospital, several windmills, a king's palace, and even a mint. The beginning of the end came in the 14th century when unusual storms began to erode the cliffs. Several centuries later, in 1913, the last church fell into the deep. Today only the ruins of a Franciscan priory remain, although some say they have seen the ghosts of former inhabitants on top of the cliffs and others have heard the church bells toll from beneath the sea when a storm approaches. The whole story is chronicled in the tiny Dunwich Museum (open afternoons only: weekends March through October, plus Tuesdays and Thursdays June through September, and daily in August).

CHECKING IN/EATING OUT: ***Ship Inn*** – Simple and cozy and full of seafaring paraphernalia (it was once connected to the old priory but the secret passage has been blocked off). The proprietor will splice you a Dunwich Mainbrace on request, or try a pint of traditional Old Ale. There are 3 rooms for overnighters. Dunwich (phone: 072873-219). Inexpensive.

En Route from Dunwich – There's no direct route to Southwold — you have to drive inland to B1125, turn right and drive to Blythburgh, and after a mile due north on A12, turn right again onto A1095. The grand yet simple 15th-century Holy Trinity Church in Blythburgh is worth a pause. It has a ceiling carved with angels and on its painted roof and carved bench ends are representations of the seven deadly sins.

SOUTHWOLD: Even when it was fashionable as an Edwardian bathing resort, Southwold was discreet, elegant, old-fashioned, and charming. During its years of flourishing trade with the Low Countries, the town absorbed certain foreign characteristics and today English cottages mingle with Dutch-style town houses along the old streets. Other idiosyncracies include seven greens: They mark the sites of houses that burned down in a great fire in 1659 and were never replaced. Among the sights to see, besides the lighthouse on a bracing cliff-top, is St. Edmund's Church, a very fine Perpendicular-style church with a high pitched hammer-beam roof. Southwold Jack, an oak figure who strikes the bell of the church clock on the hour, can be found inside, on time as usual. There is a tiny Dutch-gabled museum with items of local history (open afternoons only in summer) and a Sailor's Reading Room (open to everyone) filled with nautical relics, models, photos, and prints as well as old seafarers reading their daily newspapers and reminiscing. *Sutherland House,* High Street, is an atmospheric place to stop for tea; Adnams "real ale" brewery is also in town, its local deliveries still made by horse-drawn drays.

Walberswick, across the river Blyth from Southwold, was once a prosperous port but is now a sleepy village endowed with an extensive beach and popular with painters and birdwatchers. To reach it by foot, walk a mile and a half along the coast path and cross the river by rowboat — just call the ferryman if he's on the "wrong" side. Otherwise, drive back to Blythburgh and turn left onto B1387.

CHECKING IN: ***Swan*** – Sir Winston Churchill stayed in this ivy-clad Georgian hotel overlooking the market square — he said he enjoyed its "comfortable tranquility." Ask for one of the garden rooms (they're the best) and dine in the fine restaurant, which has a creative menu. Market Place, Southwold (phone: 0502-722186). Moderate.

Crown – The Adnams people who run this hotel are happy to let you taste their brews. An 18th-century coaching inn, it retains much of its original character, with 11 bedrooms; only 400 yards from the beach. Dinners are light, brasserie-style. High St., Southwold (phone: 0502-722275). Moderate to inexpensive.

EATING OUT: ***Mary's*** – Mary Allen and her brigade of helpers serve fish, crab, lobster (caught locally), cod's roe, and sausages smoked on the premises in this tiny dining room surrounded by seafaring odds and ends. Pay a set price for three courses and a wide choice. Open daily except Mondays April through

October and Fridays through Sundays November through March. Manor House, Walberswick (phone: 0502-723243). Inexpensive.

Potter's Wheel – This friendly, family-run establishment offers a set menu, huge dishes of tasty local vegetables, and desserts such as lemon yogurt ice cream with apricot sauce. Village Green, Walberswick (phone: 0502-724468). Inexpensive.

En Route from Southwold – Take B1127 and turn right onto A12 to Great Yarmouth, 24 miles from Southwold. If it's lunchtime, it's worth a detour to Blundeston, where the *Plough Inn* on Market Lane has been brought smartly up to date since Barkis, the carter, was housed here in Dickens' *David Copperfield.*

GREAT YARMOUTH: The fun fairs, amusement arcades, and the constant stream of holidaymakers have all conspired to take their toll on Norfolk's most popular family resort. Nevertheless, it is worth seeing, if only to watch the British at play. There's also an older part of town with relics of Great Yarmouth's heyday as a fishing port. The *Tolhouse Museum,* in a medieval building that was once the town jail, houses local history exhibits (closed Saturdays June through September and weekends October through May), while the *Elizabethan House Museum* hides a largely 16th-century interior including period rooms behind a Georgian facade (same closing days; admission charge). During the summer, there are conducted tours of the town's fortifications, which were originally punctuated by 16 towers and ten gates, and in July and August you can climb 217 steps to the top of the Nelson Monument (closed Saturdays; admission charge). The *Maritime Museum* for East Anglia, on the seafront (open daily except Saturdays June through September and Mondays through Fridays October through March; admission charge), harks back to Yarmouth's herring fishing days — if you still fancy fish after a visit, break new gastronomic ground by sampling a Yarmouth bloater, salted and smoked just enough to retain its plumpness.

Beach lovers can enjoy over 15 unbroken miles of magnificent golden sands backed by waves of grass-covered dunes. Yarmouth is also home to one of the largest open-air marketplaces in England. Traditional seafaring pubs include the *Wrestler's Inn,* Market Place (they claim Lord Nelson stayed here with Lady Hamilton), and the *Dukes Head,* Hall Quay. Great Yarmouth's tourist information center is at 1 South Quay (phone: 0493-846345).

CHECKING IN: *Star* – A member of the Queens Moat House chain, overlooking the river Yare instead of the sea. The building dates from the 16th century, but all 42 bedrooms exude 20th-century modernity. 24 Hall Quay, Great Yarmouth (phone: 0493-842294). Expensive to moderate.

Palm Court – Ask for a room with a sea view in this friendly, medium-size hotel — unless you intend to be too busy in the swimming pool, sauna, or solarium to care. North Drive, Great Yarmouth (phone: 0493-844568). Inexpensive.

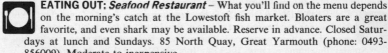

EATING OUT: *Seafood Restaurant* – What you'll find on the menu depends on the morning's catch at the Lowestoft fish market. Bloaters are a great favorite, and even shark may be available. Reserve in advance. Closed Saturdays at lunch and Sundays. 85 North Quay, Great Yarmouth (phone: 0493-856009). Moderate to inexpensive.

En Route from Great Yarmouth – Follow A149. Northwest of Caister-on-Sea (at one time a Roman commercial port), the landscape becomes flat and marshy, dotted with windmills and reminiscent of Dutch polders. You are now in the famous Norfolk Broads, an area of interconnecting waterways that are, surprisingly, manmade. During the Middle Ages, this densely populated region exhausted its woodland fuel supply and had to resort to the peat marshes around the rivers Bure, Yare, and Waveney for an alternative. Wide but not necessarily deep pits were dug to remove the peat, and when the sea began to rise, flooding the digs, they became the shallow "broads" that are today one of the most popular destinations in Europe for a holiday afloat. The natural rivers and artificial cuttings (called "dykes" or "fleets") link up and meander across north Norfolk (the Broads area is roughly triangular, with angles at Lowestoft, Norwich, and Sea Palling), empty into the mud flats of Breydon Water, and eventually meet the sea at Great Yarmouth. Naturally, the best way to explore the 130-some miles of quiet, lock-free, reedy backwaters is by boat. Sailing boats or cruisers can be rented in several Broads towns, such as Acle, Potter Heigham, and Stalham, but particularly in the area's two main boating centers, Wroxham and Horning (see DIVERSIONS for details).

A149 to North Walsham (where you'll turn left onto B1145 to Aylsham) traverses a representative stretch of the distinctive Broads landscape. En route, at Potter Heigham, look for the old bridge that has been the downfall of many a holiday sailor — a favorite pastime for locals is to stand and watch their frantic maneuvering as they try to sail under a bridge with barely any headroom. Alternatively, head for Aylsham directly from Great Yarmouth, going by way of Ranworth (take A47 from Great Yarmouth to Acle, B1140 to South Walsham, and an unclassified road to Ranworth). The view from the tower of the Church of St. Mary in Ranworth is magnificent and inside is one of the best preserved painted rood screens in the country. The Broadland Conservation Centre, a thatched building floating on pontoons on the edge of Ranworth Broad, is a short nature trail through the woods from here.

Beyond Ranworth, the unclassified road continues via Woodbastwick to A1151, which you can take north to A149 for North Walsham, or, from which, at Hoveton, you can take B1354 directly to Aylsham. A further alternative would be to proceed from Ranworth for a visit to Norwich, capital of Norfolk (see *Norwich,* THE CITIES, for a full description of its attractions, hotels, and restaurants). Still another option would be to head for Norwich directly from Great Yarmouth, only 20 miles distant via A47. Aylsham, then, is only 15 miles north of Norwich on A140.

AYLSHAM: Make sure you're here on a Monday to catch its enormous market and auction, the biggest for miles around, just outside town on the Norwich Road. After much haggling, recover in the Queen Anne-style *Black Boy Inn* overlooking the main square, because you'll need every ounce of energy for an afternoon walking around Blickling Hall, a mile and a half to the northwest (on the north side of B1354). Built in the early 17th century, this is one of the finest National Trust properties in the country. Its red brick façade is Jacobean, but the interior was much altered in the 18th century, although the Long Gallery contains a remarkable Jacobean ceiling. The state rooms are full of handsome furnishings, paintings, tapestries, and other works of art of various periods. Outside, the parklands include color-matched herbaceous borders, 300-year-old hedgerows, a mile-long lake, a temple, topiary yews, and even a secret garden. Blickling Hall (phone: 0263-733084) is open daily except Mondays and Thursdays from 1 to 5 PM mid-April through October; admission charge.

CHECKING IN/EATING OUT: ***Buckinghamshire Arms*** **–** Opposite Blickling Hall, which can be seen out of two of this 17th-century inn's three rooms. One room has a four-poster bed. There is an extensive menu, bar snacks, and a Sunday lunchtime carvery. Blickling (phone: 0263-732133). Moderate.

Felmingham Hall **–** An Elizabethan country-house hotel in 60 acres of parkland, it stands close to a stony brook that feeds the river Bure. The dining room is candlelit and warmed by log fires; meals are based on home-grown ingredients (even the bread is home baked). It's about 5 miles from Aylsham, on B1145 between Aylsham and North Walsham. Felmingham (phone: 069269-228). Expensive.

En Route from Aylsham – B1354 and B1149 lead to Holt, a market town whose Georgian houses were built after a fire in 1708 destroyed most of the medieval buildings.

An old coaching inn, *The Feathers,* on the site of the town's cattle market, is a welcome retreat from the perils of the road. Farther north, at Glandford (take B1156), is a unique *Shell Museum* (phone: 0263-740081). Thousands of multi-colored specimens in all shapes and sizes from all over the world — collected by a local traveler, Sir Alfred Jodrell — are on display (open daily except Sundays March through November and Mondays through Thursdays December through February or by appointment; admission charge). Still farther north are Cley-next-the-Sea and Blakeney.

CLEY-NEXT-THE-SEA AND BLAKENEY: Only a mile or so of coast road separates these two towns. Despite its name, Cley (it rhymes with sky) has not been "next the sea" since the 17th century. Walk along the main street, which winds behind the old quay, for a look at its flint-built houses. The village church, largely of the 14th century, is a grandiose building reflecting Cley's former importance as an exporting port of the wool trade, but the town's real landmark is its windmill, a regularly featured "pinup" in local magazines and picture postcards, now converted into a hotel, but open to visitors daily, June through September; admission charge. East of town, between Cley and Salthouse, is Cley Marshes, a nature reserve for migrant birds accessible by permit from the Warden (phone: 0263-740380).

Still another nature reserve is on Blakeney Point, the spit of land that branches away from the Norfolk coastline at Cley. This consists of 1,400 acres of shingle (pebble) beaches, sand dunes capped by marram grass, and flat expanses of mud vacated by each ebb tide. Thousands of birds nest and rear their young on the point, including colonies of common, sandwich, and little terns, plovers, and oyster-catchers. During the summer, the old lifeboat house serves tea and snacks. You can walk to the tip of Blakeney Point from Cley (a tough 3-mile hike), or reach it by taking one of the intimate ferries that ply to and fro from Blakeney, leaving from the quay in front of the *Blakeney Hotel* two or three hours on either side of high tide. Blakeney, in medieval times, was a port of some importance, but the gradual silting up of its creeks has made it accessible only to the ferries and other small craft.

CHECKING IN: ***Blakeney*** – This hotel has grand views and the highest standards of food and comfort. Its restaurant specializes in fish and game, with Holkham venison and Weybourne crab frequently on the menu. There is also an indoor heated pool and a roof that opens on sunny days. The Quay, Blakeney (phone: 0263-740797). Moderate.

Cley Windmill – One of the most photographed windmills in the country was converted into a homey guesthouse in the 1920s but is still open to visitors who can climb to the top of its five floors and view the marshes. It is 166 years old but its sails and brakewheel are still standing. There are 4 bedrooms, 2 with private bath. Open Easter through September. Cley (phone: 0263-740209). Inexpensive.

EATING OUT: ***Gasché's Swiss Restaurant*** – A few miles east of Cley on A149, it offers Swiss hospitality and enormous portions of Franco-Swiss cooking. Lobster, Norfolk duckling, *wiener schnitzel,* and crab are particularly recommended. Closed Mondays. Weybourne (phone: 026370-220). Moderate.

En Route from Cley-next-the-Sea and Blakeney – The road goes through the tiny village of Stiffkey (pronounced Stewkey), which is famous for its cockles, known as Stewkey Blues, and then reaches the resort town of Wells-next-the-sea.

WELLS-NEXT-THE-SEA: A smashing place to enjoy fish and chips, or whelks, for which the Wells' fishermen supply most of the British demand — ships up to 300 tons can be seen unloading their catch. Much of the waterfront has been crassly commercialized, so your time is best spent wandering around the narrow "inland" streets, visiting the several antique dealers, and pausing for a draft of real ale at such pubs as the *Globe, Crown, Buttlands,* and *Edinburgh.* The Wells Centre, in a converted granary, serves light meals and also has exhibitions, a cinema, and a theater running throughout the summer. Or walk along the footpath (paralleling the road on the west side of the harbor) to the old lifeboat house and the magical beach surrounded by dunes beyond.

En Route from Wells-next-the-Sea – Detour inland on B1105 to Little Walsingham, where pilgrims streamed during the Middle Ages to visit the shrine of Our Lady of Walsingham. Built in 1061 to honor the Virgin Mary, it was subsequently destroyed — along with much of the 12th-century Augustinian priory beside it — and later reconstructed by the Church of England. The priory grounds and remains (notably the arch of the east window, gatehouse, crypt, wells, and refectory) are open Wednesdays from 2 to 5 PM in April and on Wednesdays, Saturdays, and Sundays in May, June, July, and September (also open on Mondays and Fridays in August); admission charge. A second shrine, the Roman Catholic Slipper Chapel, is a mile south of the village. The *Black Lion* pub behind the High Street serves lunch and bar snacks.

Five miles farther south at Fakenham, the Pensthorpe Waterfowl Park and Nature Reserve has one of the largest collections of ducks, geese, and swans in the world. A network of attractive paths with several designated vantage points enables visitors to see the birds clearly without disturbing them. Open daily, Easter through October; weekends, November through mid-December; admission charge.

Return to A149 coastal road and continue west to Holkham, where the beach, back by Corsican pines, is a wild expanse of dunes and sand whose strange hills, or "meals" were once spits cut off from the mainland. At Holkham, grandly set in a sprawling park, is Holkham Hall (phone: 0328-710806), an 18th-century mansion originally built for Thomas Coke, the Earl of Leicester and an agriculturalist (potatoes were his specialty). The mansion is enormous and ornate, its interior containing works by Rubens and Gainsborough, plus tapestries, statues, and furnishings. The grounds, laid out by Capability Brown in 1762, include old walled gardens (now a garden center) and an artificial lake inhabited by Canadian geese. Holkham Hall also has an exhibit of several thousand "bygones" — old agricultural and craft tools, cars, carriages — set up in the stable buildings (open Monday, Thursday, and Sunday afternoons June through September as well as Wednesday afternoons in July and August; admission charge).

CHECKING IN: *The Old Rectory* – This manor house in a village south of Little Walsingham is entirely a family affair — Rosamund Scoles running things, her husband doing the odd jobs, her father tending the walled-in gardens, and her mother taking brilliant care of the cooking, which is conservatively English. With just 6 traditionally furnished rooms, it's utterly peaceful and quiet (fitting for Great Snoring). Great Snoring, near Fakenham (phone: 0328-820597). Moderate.

THE BURNHAMS: Burnham Overy Staithe, farther west on A149, is one of several villages beginning with "Burnham." Britain's seafaring hero, Admiral Horation Nelson, was born in the rectory at Burnham Thorpe in 1758. Although the rectory has since been torn down, the restored church has a lectern made of timbers taken from Nelson's flagship, *Victory,* and the *Lord Nelson* pub is full of the admiral's memorabilia. Burnham Market has Georgian houses and old-fashioned stores. The National Trust owns the windmill at Burnham Overy, but it is not open to the public. Burnham Overy Staithe is a beautiful quay and a thriving dinghy sailing center at high tide.

En route from the Burnhams – You're still on A149 when you reach Brancaster, a delightful sailing center, although the salt marshes are exposed at low tide and harbor access is therefore restricted to 2 or 3 hours before and after high tide. The nature reserve at Scolt Head, a 3½-mile shingle spit, attracts many birds, notably red-beaked oyster catchers and several varieties of tern. You can reach it by ferry boat from May through August (they leave from the far end of the dinghy park — check the board opposite the sailing club for times).

At New Hunstanton, A149 drops due south to King's Lynn. Along the way, at Caley Mill, near Heacham, are the lavender fields of Norfolk Lavender, the largest growers and distillers of lavender in Britain. The 100 acres of purple, at their most colorful at harvest time — mid-July through September — are augmented by an herb garden, a shop selling soap, cologne, sachets, and other products, and a tea shop. The grounds are open daily Easter through September and Saturdays and Sundays the rest of the year; no admission charge, but there is a charge for tours, which take place at harvest time and should be arranged in advance (phone: 0485-70384).

Continue on A149 south to King's Lynn, passing a mile from the Queen's country house at Sandringham (turn onto B1140 at Dersingham). Her Majesty's Norfolk estate has a 19th-century Jacobean-style house of brick and stone set on grounds landscaped with lovely gardens and trees. Unless the Queen or another member of the Royal Family is in residence, the house, grounds, and a museum of dolls and cars are open to the public Mondays through Thursdays and Sundays, April through late September (except late July and early August); admission charge. Call 0553-772675 for details of the summer closing and the date of the Sandringham Flower Show, an annual event in late July and a nice time to visit.

Return to A149, and after a mile, an unclassified road leads to Castle Rising, 4 miles north of King's Lynn. Once a port and now deserted by the receding sea, Castle Rising has a ruined shell of a 12th-century Norman castle whose inner keep was at one time the mightiest stronghold in the country. Walk around the grassy ramparts and imagine its proud past (open daily; admission charge). Nearby are nine Jacobean almshouses, with chapel, court, and treasury.

KING'S LYNN: Lynn, as it's colloquially known, lies on the banks of the river Great Ouse close by the Wash, an arm of the North Sea that reaches deep into the East Anglian coastline. People still search the Wash for King John's treasure, lost in 1215 when his entourage miscalculated the tide. The town preserves many medieval buildings that reflect its importance as an international trading center from the 12th to the 15th centuries. Among these is the Guildhall of St. George (1410), the largest surviving medieval guildhall in England and now the theater part of the *Fermoy Arts Centre,* a venue for regular concerts, plays, and art exhibitions, as well as for the annual *King's Lynn Festival* of music and the arts held the last week of July (when not in use as a theater, it's open Mondays through Fridays plus Saturday mornings).

The Tuesday Market Place nearby is the heart of town, especially (and not surprisingly) on a Tuesday morning when the stalls are in full swing. Walk down King Street from here and, after passing the 17th-century Custom House, you'll come to Queen Street, which leads to the Saturday Market Place (where a smaller market is held guess when). Among the buildings clustered around this second market are a second 15th-century guildhall, the Guildhall of the Holy Trinity, which houses a collection of civic plate and regalia, including the King John Cup (open Mondays through Saturdays, June through October; admission charge), and the adjoining 19th-century Town Hall; next to them, in the Gaol House (name only!) is Lynn's tourist information center (phone: 0553-763044). St. Margaret's Church, south of the Saturday Market, contains two of the most elaborate and famous brasses in England. The *Museum of Social History,* King St., displays toys, costumes, and furniture (open Tuesdays through Saturdays; admission charge), while the *Lynn Museum,* Old Market St., has several eclectic exhibits depicting the flora and fauna of the area, archaeological finds, and even flowery Victorian lavatories (open Mondays through Saturdays; admission charge).

CHECKING IN/EATING OUT: ***Congham Hall*** – This Georgian manor house 6 miles northeast of town has only a dozen rooms, but it also has tennis courts, a swimming pool, stabling for visiting horses, and even its own cricket field within its 40 acres. The dining room, which is renowned for its cuisine, features a marathon eight-course menu. Lynn Rd., Grimston (phone: 0485-600250). Expensive.

Duke's Head – Behind the 17th-century façade of this hotel in the town center — Lynn's foremost — are 72 modern rooms. The restaurant exudes Victorian style. Tuesday Market Pl., King's Lynn (phone: 0553-774996). Expensive.

Butterfly – A new, red brick hotel on the outskirts of town just off the ring road, its lounge and restaurant are in light, airy conservatories. Beveridge Way, Hardwick Narrows, King's Lynn (phone: 0553-771707). Moderate.

Yorkshire

In the 18th century, on his famous travels around England, Daniel Defoe reported: "From hense we entered the great county of York, uncertain still which way to begin to take full view of it, for 'tis a county of very great extent." Today, with its administrative marriage to Humberside, its extent would root Defoe to the spot. The historical county of Yorkshire is now the three modern counties of North, West, and South Yorkshire, which together with Humberside encompass over 5,000 square miles, including two national parks — the Yorkshire Dales and North York Moors — and part of a third park, the Peak District. They also include the 1,900-year-old city of York, plenty of villages with cobbled streets, a string of seaside resorts, battle-scarred castles, time-worn abbeys, and sumptuous country houses.

The long shoreline of Yorkshire and Humberside exhibits every kind of coastal scenery and seascape, from high cliffs and rocky headlands to sheltered coves and broad scimitars of sandy beach, from rock pools abandoned by the receding tide to sand dunes capped with marram grass that the sea never molests. There are fishing villages and smugglers' dens, yachtsmen's havens and bird sanctuaries, and, for the family on holiday, several busy resorts, such as Scarborough and Bridlington. Here you'll find modern hotels, all-weather entertainment complexes, and nationwide chain stores, along with all the trappings of the traditional English seaside scene — pail-and-shovel beaches, summer landladies, candy floss (cotton candy), ice-cream parlors, and fish-and-chips shops.

From anywhere along the Yorkshire coast, it's only a short, pretty drive to the North York Moors. This vast, heather-clad wilderness, in full purple bloom in August or cringing beneath heavy, rumbling skies in mid-winter, is ribbed by softer interludes of countryside. The main mass of the moor is a plateau naturally protected from the intrusions of man by the Hambleton Hills and Cleveland Hills to the west, rocky coasts to the east, and by abrupt ridges dropping to valleys on its northern and southern sides. But around the edges are the numerous farms, villages, and market towns of a rich agricultural area, connected by good roads and offering a wide variety of accommodation. Access to the moors is easy, since several roads arrow across the plateau and thread through the beautiful dales, or valleys, that were sculpted by the great glaciers of the Ice Age. Where the roads fail to penetrate, lanes, tracks, and footpaths begin. Here, the pedestrian is king.

The North York Moors were most famously described by the Venerable Bede as "steep and solitary hills where you would rather look for the hiding place of robbers or the lairs of wild animals than the abode of men." Protected as a national park since 1952, they annually attract more visitors than the entire population of London. But apart from obvious peak occasions (Easter and school summer holidays), you won't find the 553-square-mile park spoiled by such invasions, because people have a habit of simply getting lost in the folds until it's time to go home again. If you can manage a stroll or two "over the tops" — across the moors — you'll hardly ever see a soul, barring (baa-ing) the occasional sheep. Their contented stares on the worst of winter days are the most convincing advertisement imaginable for the merits of pure wool!

To the west of York are the rich, green patchwork valleys of the Yorkshire Dales, another national park. Made famous worldwide by James Herriot's series of books on a local veterinarian's life, the dales are peppered with market towns, villages, rows of cottages, and lone farmhouses built of light gray or honey-colored stone, crowned by gray slate roofs and solid as fortresses. This huge upland area covers more than 680 square miles and is incised by rushing rivers, providing a variety of scenery for all kinds of outdoor holiday activities. Bronze Age, Iron Age, and Roman remains abound, including hill forts and "green roads" used by today's hikers en route from dale to dale, while Viking legacies linger in the local dialect and in place names — a "-by" ending means farm, while the very word "dale" comes from "thal," their word for valley.

The whole region, by no means just a pretty face, is full of historic sights and places of interest as well as scenic beauty. In fact, there is so much to see that the itinerary outlined below edits the whole to a densely packed part, concentrating on the eastern side of North Yorkshire (exploring the North York Moors National Park but not the Yorkshire Dales National Park) and dipping into Humberside. The route begins in York, heads northeast to Malton, famous for its agricultural show and its Roman past, then crosses the Wolds Way, a long-distance footpath, and works its way east via Great Driffield to the coast at Bridlington. In Humberside, it takes in the "nose" of Flamborough Head before climbing up the North Yorkshire coastline to Filey, the Victorian spa resort of Scarborough, the little fishing town of Robin Hood's Bay, and Whitby, then makes a U-turn to cross the river Esk. From here it's a steady trek southwest across the North York Moors National Park and along its southern boundary to the market town of Helmsley. The route returns to York after stopping off at Rievaulx to pay respects to the great abbey ruins, detouring to one or two interesting villages in the vicinity, and winding up in Thirsk, James Herriot's hometown.

As for room and board along the way, since northerners in England have always liked comfortably plumped beds and heaps of home cooking, be prepared to find lots of cozy inns rather than gracious hotels and plates of roast beef and Yorkshire pudding, piled high with vegetables and topped with nourishing gravy, rather than delicately presented nouvelle cuisine. It's not the place for picky appetites. Lots of old family-run firms brewing real ale in the traditional manner lie in this neck of the woods, too. One of the strongest of the local brews is Theakston's Old Peculier, a dark, rich beer from Masham, near Ripon, locally nicknamed "lunatic broth." Use it to wash down York ham, Wensleydale cheese, Whitby crabs, Scarborough plaice, Grimsby haddock and kippers, and, of course, the ubiquitous fish cooked in batter with chips.

Expect to pay around $80 and up for a double room with breakfast in places listed as expensive, from $50 to $80 at moderate ones, and less than $50 at inexpensive ones. A meal for two, excluding wine, tips, and drinks, will cost

$50 and up in expensive restaurants, from $25 to $50 in those categorized as moderate, and less than $20 in inexpensive places.

YORK: In the heart of northern England, a 3-hour drive or a 2-hour train trip from London, York is widely considered the best-preserved medieval city in Great Britain. It began, as many old English cities do, as a Roman town, Eboracum, a base for the Roman legions that reinforced and garrisoned Hadrian's Wall against the Picts. Parts of the Roman fortifications remain and even some ghostly legionnaires, who allegedly can be seen marching across the city from time to time. Relics of the next major occupants, the Danes, who called their settlement Jorvik, have been excavated around Coppergate and are displayed in a spectacular exhibition. York entered the Middle Ages with a spate of building, the most magnificent heritage of which is the Minster, the city's cathedral, a towering tracery of cream stone that narrowly escaped complete destruction in the great 1984 fire. After being completely restored by local craftsmen, the south transept, which had been most badly damaged in the fire, was reopened by the Queen in 1988. The whole city can be comfortably explored on foot, from the Shambles (once the butchers' quarter) and Stonegate, two of the best-preserved medieval streets in Europe, to the 3 miles of medieval walls whose crest can be walked for an exciting perspective on ancient history. For a full report on the city's sights, hotels, and restaurants, see *York,* THE CITIES.

En Route from York – Take A64 northeast toward Malton. After 15 miles, turn left and go about 1½ miles to Castle Howard, a stately home that millions of TV viewers will instantly recognize as the setting for the serialization of Evelyn Waugh's novel *Brideshead Revisited.* This imposing baroque mansion, a magnificent showplace, was designed in 1699 by Sir John Vanburgh and is still lived in by descendants of Charles Howard, the third Earl of Carlisle, for whom it was built. Visitors wander through immense rooms filled with marble from Greece and Rome; furniture by Chippendale, Sheraton, and Adam; china from Meissen and Delft; and paintings by Holbein, Van Dyck, Gainsborough, Veronese, Rubens, and Tintoretto. Outside, the 1,000-acre grounds are landscaped with gardens, lakes, fountains, and famous follies such as the Temple of the Four Winds, the Obelisk, and the Pyramid. There's also a mausoleum designed by Nicholas Hawksmoor, where the third earl is buried. The old stable block houses Britain's largest privately owned collection of period costumes. Castle Howard is open daily Easter through October; admission charge includes parking and entry to the house, gardens, and costume collection (phone: 065384-333).

MALTON: A solid, ancient market town (one of the largest livestock centers in England) on the river Derwent, it has dozens of prehistoric burial grounds within a few miles' radius and one of the best small-town agricultural shows in the country, held each July. It was once the Roman station of Derventio, so be sure to see the Roman antiquities in the *Malton Museum,* in the 200-year-old former town hall in the Market Place (open daily May through September and Saturdays October through April; admission charge). Travelers can also follow the path of the old Roman road by taking B1257 west for 7 miles to the pretty village of Hovingham. With its immaculately trimmed lawns, chunky stone cottages, model village green, pub, and hotel, it could almost be described as the perfect village. A mile northeast of Malton is Old Malton, known for its Early English to Perpendicular parish church, part of a former priory.

CHECKING IN: *Talbot* – Originally a hunting lodge, this stone structure was converted to an inn in the 18th century. There are now 23 rooms, and the river Derwent flows past the end of the terraced garden. Yorkersgate, Malton (phone: 0653-694031). Expensive.

Leat House – In a small town just short of a mile east of Malton, it combines the atmosphere of a country house and the convenience of an in-town location. There are 6 bedrooms. Welham Rd., Norton (phone: 0653-692027). Moderate.

EATING OUT: ***Wentworth Arms*** **–** This 18th-century coaching inn, heavily camouflaged by ivy, has a dining room sporting its original stone walls and oak beams — it was once the barn. Town St., Old Malton (phone: 0653-692618). Inexpensive.

En Route from Malton – Take B1248 southeast. At Settrington, just off the route a few miles out of Malton, pick up the Wolds Way. This long-distance footpath runs some 70 miles from the flatlands of the mighty river Humber up and over the range of hills known as the Yorkshire Wolds and down to the coast just above Filey. The landscape is gentle, suitable for the most out-of-practice walker, with only two hardy stretches — the steep banks of Rabbit Warren and Nettle Dale near Millington and the climb up Deep Dale from Wintringham. Details of the walk are available from any local tourist office, or do it yourself with a copy of Robert Ratcliffe's *Wolds Way* ($7.50 from Bernan-Unipub, 4611-F Assembly Dr., Lanham, MD 20706; phone: 301-459-7666).

Turn onto B1253 after North Grimston and pass through Sledmere, a one-road village little bigger than Sledmere House, the Georgian home of the Sykes family, who have been baronets and landowners on the Wolds since the 17th century. A gray, solid-looking building, it sits in grounds landscaped by the famous English gardener Capability Brown (open daily except Mondays and Fridays Easter through October; admission charge). Continue southeast along B1252, an easy, undulating ribbon of road bordered for the most part by long horizons of grass-backed Wolds and fairly empty of traffic, barring the odd precariously overloaded tractor. The stone spire that comes up on the right — looking much like a space-age rocket — is a memorial to Sir Tatton Sykes, baronet of the area in the 19th century, who thus remains a dominating presence for miles around, just as he was in his life. On a clear day the views toward the coasts from up here make you feel on top of the world.

A few miles farther along, branch left onto A166 to Great Driffield. A canal built in the late 18th century to link it with Beverley and Kingston upon Hull led to the town's prosperity and unofficial ranking as the Capital of the Wolds in the early 19th century. Its weekly cattle market is still an important event for farmers in the surrounding area. The town has a complicated one-way system that makes driving confusing, but it's small enough to be pretty, with a plethora of pubs.

Stay on A166 the remaining 12 miles east to Bridlington, detouring briefly at signposts to Burton Agnes Hall. This red-brick Elizabethan manor house has ceilings and overmantels carved in oak, plaster, stone, and alabaster, as well as a superb collection of French impressionist paintings. There's also an unusual donkey treadmill in the paddock, but it's the gardens that are most impressive: Rows of topiary yews shaped like puffballs line the driveway, and the vegetable garden could have come from a Beatrix Potter story. Although descendants of the family who built it still live here, the house and its café are open daily April through October; admission charge.

CHECKING IN/EATING OUT: ***Bell*** **–** Mr. and Mrs. Riggs's 14-room hotel is a traditional English coaching inn dating from 1742, now with a glass-domed courtyard and swimming pool. It's famous for its buffet lunches served in the adjacent old corn exchange, where the original brickwork blends with baskets of plants and modern decor. Line up and have your plate piled high with a choice of 20 salads and traditional dishes prepared in the style of the famous 19th-century English chef, Mrs. Beeten. Market Place, Great Driffield (phone: 0377-46661). Moderate.

Triton Inn **–** Next door to Sledmere House, it lives off its reputation for good-value lunches and dinners. Eight rooms are available. Sledmere (phone: 0377-86644). Inexpensive.

BRIDLINGTON: Besides a dozen miles of beach and safe, clean bathing (in 1982, Bridlington spent £7 million to meet stringent EEC antipollution regulations), the attractions of this seaside resort include a harbor, busy since Roman times, where you can rent a boat, go fishing with an old salt of a skipper, or just take a trip around the bay with a crew singing sea chanteys to the accompaniment of an old-fashioned squeeze-box. If the weather fails, the best place to be is Brid's new leisure center, an indoor entertainment complex containing a swimming pool with a wave machine, plus a sauna, solarium, theater, restaurants, bars, and cafés. Those with a nostalgic hankering for the seaside of their youth can make a beeline for *Topham's* on Cross Street, an ice-cream parlor that still serves a genuine Knickerbocker Glory, a type of ice-cream sundae (layers of different flavors topped with sauce) rarely found in Britain nowadays.

The Old Town, a mile inland, is the site of a medieval priory church and a 14th-century gatehouse, Bayle Gate, also part of the onetime priory and now used as a museum of local history. John Bull's rock factory in Carnaby, about 2 miles inland on A166, is open for guided tours (phone: 0262-678525). Foot-long sticks of rock candy, once synonymous with the British seaside (and now not so common), make fine souvenirs for the folks back home since the name of the resort is traditionally written in color on the end of the stick and through it, like the colored ribbons in a tube of toothpaste. The John Bull factory was the first in the country to open its doors to the public and reveal the secret of putting a name (yours if you like) right through the middle of the stick.

CHECKING IN: *The Expanse* – Up at the northern end of the bay, the resort's best hotel is so close to the waves you can almost hear them crashing on the beach as you eat breakfast. It has 49 unpretentious yet comfortable rooms (most overlooking the bay), a friendly staff, and plenty of fresh seafood on the menu. North Marine Dr., Bridlington (phone: 0262-675347). Expensive to moderate.

Bay Ridge – A small, 14-room, family-run, centrally located hotel close to the harbor. 11–13 Summerfield Rd., Bridlington (phone: 0262-673425). Inexpensive.

EATING OUT: *Blue Lobster* – Mickey Barron, local fisherman and owner of the best seafood restaurant in town, prefers to serve his fish a good deal fancier than the several fish-and-chips shops. If you ask for a straightforward haddock and chips, he'll present you with a bill for $40. Closed Saturdays for lunch and Sundays. West Pier, Lower Harbor area, off South Cliff Rd., Bridlington (phone: 0262-674729). Expensive.

En Route from Bridlington – Proceed north up the Yorkshire Coast via A165 to Filey and Scarborough. Or detour northeast of Bridlington along B1255 to Sewerby Hall and Flamborough Head, then backtrack to A165 and head up the coast. Sewerby Hall, an 18th-century mansion, stands bravely weathering the winds on a particularly exposed stretch of coastline 2 miles from Bridlington, its 50 acres of grounds sweeping down to the cliff edge with superb views back over Bridlington Bay. Inside, the Georgian house has an oak staircase leading to an art gallery and a collection of trophies of the pioneering pilot Amy Johnson. The monkey-puzzle trees (Chile pine) in the formal garden next to the car park were planted in 1847, making them some of the oldest in England. The house is open daily Easter through September, the park daily all year; admission charge.

Continuing east on B1255, you'll come to the village of Flamborough and the chalky white cliffs and chasms of Flamborough Head, which form part of Britain's officially designated Heritage Coast and are home to umpteen squadrons of seabirds. Focus your binoculars on the cliffside at the RSPB (Royal Society for the Protection of Birds) reserve at Bempton and you'll see the only mainland breeding gannets in the entire country nesting in any crevice they can find, together with puffins, gulls, fulmars, kittiwakes, and others. Winter visitors are advised to return in spring along with the majority of birds, which spend the coldest months out in the North Sea.

CHECKING IN: ***Timoneer Country Manor*** – A glamorous building set in parkland close to the sea. There are 10 rooms, each with bath or shower. South Landing, Flamborough (phone: 0262-850219). Moderate.

EATING OUT: ***Royal Dog and Duck*** – A flourishing historic pub with a splendid atmosphere, it's ideal for chatting up the locals and for excellent, inexpensive lunches (fresh lobster or crab salads are especially reasonable from May to September). Tower St., Flamborough (phone: 0262-850206). Inexpensive.

FILEY: Like so many other English seaside resorts, this began as a spa town during the 18th century; by the closing decades of the 19th century, attractive crescents of Victorian guesthouses and hotels had become well established alongside quaint fishermen's cottages. Charlotte Brontë stayed at *Cliff House* on Belle Vue Street, now the *Bronte and Vinery Café* (phone: 0723-514805). The 6 miles of golden sand at Filey Bay, widely considered the best stretch on the Yorkshire coast, are so flat they have been used as a runway for airplanes. Good shelter and safe bathing make it a haven for windsurfers and sailing dinghies.

CHECKING IN: ***White Lodge*** – The best in town, situated on the clifftop above the bay and close to the town center. It has 19 rooms and a sun lounge with fine sea views. The Crescent, Filey (phone: 0723-514771). Moderate.

SCARBOROUGH: The most popular summer resort in northeast England was in the 12th century little more than a castle keep. The ruins of Scarborough Castle still dominate the old town, but in 1622 a canny Yorkshireman saw a way of promoting the virtues of the clear mineral water emerging in a gush at the foot of the South Cliff. The idea caught on but, it was not until Victorian times that Scarborough really took off in popularity. Today's reminders of this spa heritage are an impressive array of excellent clifftop hotels, the most prominent of which are the blockbuster *Grand* (now the domain of a holiday camp operator, however), the *Royal,* and the *Crown.*

Scarborough was also reputedly the first town in England to host nude bathing. In keeping with its family image, there is no longer such daring behavior on either of the two broad beaches that fringe its two bays, North Bay and South Bay (the latter, more sheltered, is the safest for swimming). The two bays are separated by a high headland holding the remains of the Norman castle (open daily; admission charge) and by the fishing harbor nestling below it. The main part of town, which has some excellent shops, stretches inland from the castle headland, effectively split into two distinct halves that present quite a contrast: South Bay, with the newly renovated spa and magnificent conference facilities at its center, has an old-style holiday atmosphere right down to afternoon teas and palm court orchestras, as well as the original old spa (now a theater). North Bay has a livelier, much more modern flavor and is dotted with amusements and theaters. There is, in fact, so much to do indoors that Scarborough now bills itself as a year-round resort. Note that the Scarborough Fair of parsley, sage, rosemary, and thyme fame does not really exist, although an unexceptional *Scarborough International Festival* does take place in June.

CHECKING IN: ***Crown*** – An old, white-painted hotel with Regency origins on the cliffs above South Bay. It has 83 rooms with bath or shower, large public rooms, a small fitness center, and a snooker table. The Esplanade, Scarborough (phone: 0723-373491). Expensive.

Royal – The grand dame of Scarborough's hotels is another South Bay structure of the Regency period. It's a classic of its era, with an amazingly grand foyer, double staircase, chandeliers, columns, and galleries around the upper floors. It has 137 rooms and, in keeping with the times, a basement swimming pool and health center. St. Nicholas St., Scarborough (phone: 0723-364333). Expensive.

EATING OUT: ***Lanterna*** **–** A modest-looking Italian restaurant that hides its light under a bushel. Owners Mr. and Mrs. Arecco produce homemade pasta and desserts and plenty of fresh fish dishes. Closed Sundays and Mondays. 33 Queen St., Scarborough (phone: 0723-363616). Moderate.

En Route from Scarborough – A165 and then A171 lead north from Scarborough to Whitby, entering the North York Moors National Park along the way. Three miles before Whitby, turn right down B1447 to Robin Hood's Bay, a picturesque village on a steep slope. Leave the car in the park at the top and walk down the steps to the cobbled main street. Follow its steep slope down to the sea, past little tea shops, sturdy cottages (with special windows that enable coffins to be removed), narrow alleyways, and the trickles of a stream. The road stops abruptly at the beach, completely covered at high tide, but as the sea withdraws, it leaves an expanse of sand, rock pools, and seaweed, and a tiny promenade, all sheltered by the soft cliffs behind. The village's name comes from a legend that Robin Hood used it as a hide-out when things were too hot for him in Nottinghamshire — supposedly, he even kept a boat here, ready for a quick getaway.

WHITBY: The river Esk flows to the sea at Whitby, cutting the resort in two, with steep cliffs rising from both banks. In the 18th century, it was a shipbuilding center and the home port of whaling fleets; a century later it had become an important herring port. Today, fishing vessels still wait cheek by jowl for the turn of the tide in the busy harbor, while fishermen mend their nets outside cottages that ring the hillsides. The town spawned such famous seamen as Captain Cook, who was an apprentice on coal ships here and went on to explore the South Pacific in locally built ships. A statue of him looking out to sea now stands above the harbor.

Two notable landmarks crown the hill on the southern side of the river, the old part of town. St. Mary's Church, built in the 12th century but much altered in the 17th, is reached by a flight of 199 steps from Church Street. Nearby is Whitby Abbey, founded by St. Hilda in 657 and the scene of an ancient synod in AD 664 that first set the date for Easter. Devastated by Danes in the 9th century and then rebuilt, most of the remains date from the 12th and 13th centuries (open daily; admission charge). Among the monks and nuns cloistered at Whitby was Caedmon, an ignorant 7th-century cowherd who, according to the Venerable Bede, miraculously received poetic powers and became the earliest poet in the English language, the father of English sacred songs. A cross to his memory was placed in St. Mary's churchyard in 1898. The most famous personage connected with Whitby, however, was a vampire from Transylvania — the protagonist of Bram Stoker's mystery thriller, *Dracula* — who operated out of one of the graves in the same churchyard and preyed on the citizenry below. Pleasant dreams.

CHECKING IN: ***Larpool Hall*** **–** A Georgian mansion set in 9 acres of gardens with 11 rooms. The resident owners offer very personal service in relaxing and comfortable surroundings. Larpool La., Whitby (phone: 0947-602737). Moderate.

Old Hall **–** A distinctive, historic building with Jacobean roots but modern comforts. Its 20 rooms are about a mile from the center of Whitby. Open March to October. High St., Ruswarp (phone: 0947-602801). Inexpensive.

EATING OUT: ***Magpie Café*** **–** Tops for fish and chips in Whitby — some even argue in the whole of Yorkshire. Cod, plaice, sole, haddock, crabs, and other local catch are served daytime only (until 6:30 PM). Open daily; closed from November to Easter. 14 Pier Rd., Whitby (phone: 0947-602058). Moderate to inexpensive.

En Route from Whitby – Take A171 in the direction of Guisborough. After about 6 miles, take the small road on your left to Egton and Egton Bridge. East of here, at Grosmont, is the northern terminus of the North Yorkshire Moors Railway — the Moorsrail — which runs restored steam trains 18 miles over Goathland Moor and down lovely Newtondale to Pickering. The line is one of the world's earliest, built by George Stephenson in 1836 (its carriages were horse-drawn at first), and it provides a superb way to see parts of the North York Moors National Park that are inaccessible by road. Trains run from Easter through early November, with daily service from early May through the end of September (phone: 0751-72508 for details). Tickets allow passengers to break the trip en route at Goathland and continue on the next train; a nonstop one-way trip in either direction takes about an hour.

Otherwise, from Egton Bridge, continue south and travel "over the tops" across the moors, past ancient crosses, browsing sheep, pheasant, and the occasional walker, to the village of Rosedale Abbey. Above the village, close to the junction of the Blakey Ridge and Castleton roads, stand two moorland crosses affectionately known as Fat Betty and Ralph's Cross. Together with Margery, a rough-hewn stone a few hundred yards away, they are supposed to commemorate a 13th-century meeting between two nuns — sisters Betty and Margery — and Old Ralph, a faithful servant. But other theories maintain that Fat Betty marks the spot where a farmer's wife fell off the back of a cart on a misty day, unnoticed by her husband, and was never found. Nearby, you can also see Young Ralph, a cross erected in the 17th century with a groove on top where wealthy traders left money for poorer travelers.

CHECKING IN: ***Mallyan Spout*** – A creeper-clad stone building on the fringes of Goathland offering a warm welcome, 20 rooms, open fires, robust meals, and its own health club with sauna, plunge bath (a tiny swimming pool), and solarium. The spout, by the way, is a waterfall that can be reached by following a short riverside path. Goathland (phone: 0947-86206). Moderate.

ROSEDALE ABBEY: A ruined 12th-century Cistercian priory gave its name to this village, which was once the thriving hub of an iron ore industry and home to many miners. Follow the road up the dale (marked "Dale Head only"), park near the village shop, and you'll be able to walk along the track of an old mineral railway and enjoy fantastic views of the dale. Stick to the easily identified path of the railway and return along the far side of the dale (allow 3 hours for a complete circuit).

CHECKING IN/EATING OUT: ***Blacksmith's Arms*** – A white Tudor inn on the edge of a forest about 4 miles south of Rosedale on the road to Cropton. Traditional English country food is served in the dining room or in the bar, where a wealth of brass, copper, and beams recall past duty as a blacksmith's forge and where a cast-iron kitchen range still provides a homey touch. The inn has 12 comfortable bedrooms and its own trout stream. Hartoft End (phone: 07515-331). Moderate.

Milburn Arms – A 14th-century gray stone inn with wooden beams, a fireplace, chintz decor, 14 bedrooms, and a popular 14th-century bar. Its restaurant serves a small selection of well-chosen, expertly cooked dishes using fresh vegetables and other local produce. Rosedale Abbey (phone: 07515-312). Moderate.

En Route from Rosedale Abbey – Following the road southeast toward Pickering, look for a sign to Lastingham (just before a small, humpback bridge) and turn off to your right. Lastingham's old stone houses, stream, and typical village green lie half-hidden in the woods and hollows. The town's beautiful Norman church stands on the site of an older Benedictine monastery whose founding is recorded in the writings of the Venerable Bede; the original crypt survives intact beneath the present church. After Lastingham, the road rises, crosses open moors, and plunges down to Hutton-le-Hole.

HUTTON-LE-HOLE: If the village had been purposely built for the discerning traveler, it couldn't be more picturesque: Lots of cottages of Yorkshire stone sit perfectly poised on the banks of a babbling brook and around a green kept in constant trim by resident sheep. The equally charming *Ryedale Folk Museum* houses a collection of 18th-century farm buildings — barns, stables, cowhouse, hayloft, granary, and wheelshed. Its artifacts are drawn largely from the surrounding area and illustrate the lives of the people who lived here — their farm labors, crafts, pastimes, customs, and superstitions. Ex-curator Bert Frank took a special interest in local witches and the tools of their trade, such as crystal balls and spell charts. The grounds also contain reconstructions of village houses, an Elizabethan glass furnace, a blacksmith's shop, and other buildings. The museum is open daily from April through October; admission charge.

En Route from Hutton-le-Hole – In springtime, before continuing to Kirbymoorside and Helmsley, walk, or drive if you must, north of Hutton-le-Hole into Farndale to see a most stunning display of wild daffodils, more than Wordsworth could ever have laid eyes on in the Lake District. But don't be tempted to pick any, as the area is well patroled by Daffodil Wardens (a highly seasonal occupation).

To reach Kirbymoorside and Helmsley from Hutton-le-Hole, drop south to A170 and proceed west. Kirbymoorside has always had a flourishing market; the tollbooth (or market hall) was built in 1710 with stone from the ancient Neville Castle and is still used on market days. Farther along, Nunnington Hall, a National Trust property located south of A170 between Kirbymoorside and Helmsley, is worth a detour. A lovely manor house on the banks of the river Rye, it dates back to the 16th century, although the fine paneled bedrooms and hall, carved chimneypiece, staircase, tapestries, and china are mostly of the late 17th century. The famous Carlisle Collection of Miniature Rooms, furnished and decorated in the styles of different periods, is now on permanent display in the house. Ten thousand items strong, it includes a William and Mary parlor, a Queen Anne drawing room, a Chippendale library, a Palladian hall, and a greenhouse and aviary. The house is open Tuesday, Wednesday, Thursday, Saturday, and Sunday afternoons May through October and weekend afternoons in April and November; admission charge.

CHECKING IN: ***Ryedale Lodge*** – This former Victorian railway station is now a quiet, small hotel set well back from the nearest road and offering 7 bedrooms. Nunnington (phone: 04395-246). Moderate.

HELMSLEY: Situated at the start of the Cleveland Way, a horseshoe-shaped footpath that extends approximately 100 miles around the rim of the North York Moors National Park and down the Yorkshire coast to Filey, this cobbled market town (Friday is market day) is a popular spot with walkers. It stands in the shadow of its now hag-toothed castle, whose oldest stonework dates from the end of the 12th century (although the extensive earthworks date from shortly after the Norman Conquest). As is the case with virtually all the castles around the moors (and elsewhere in England, too), Helmsley Castle's decay is a result of the English Civil War; in 1644 it withstood a 3-month siege by the Parliamentarian forces of Sir Thomas Fairfax, then finally capitulated and was thereafter partially demolished to render it useless. The castle is open daily; admission charge (phone: 0439-70442).

The ruins of Rievaulx Abbey, 3 miles northwest of Helmsley, are reachable either on foot via a signposted footpath that follows a section of the Cleveland Way, or by driving along B1257, then turning down a tiny signposted lane off to the left. Founded in 1131 by monks from Clairvaux in Burgundy, the abbey quickly became the largest and most splendid Cistercian monastery in England. Housing 140 white-robed monks and 500 lay brothers, it prospered mainly because of the monks' success at sheep farming in the dales. "Everywhere peace, everywhere serenity and a marvellous freedom from the tumult of the world" was how St. Aelred, the third Abbot of Rievaulx, described his surroundings in the 12th century, and little has changed since. Rievaulx's greatest glories are the soaring arches in the church choir and the walls of the adjacent refectory, both masterpieces of early English architecture. Standing in a secluded, deeply wooded valley by the river Rye, still remote from worldly temptations and disturbed only by the cries of rooks and chanting pigeons, they make an inspiring ensemble. Rievaulx is open daily, with a museum that displays findings on the site; admission charge (phone: 04396-228).

Beautiful Rievaulx Terrace, a half-mile of grassy embankment terminating at each end with a temple in classical style, is above the abbey. Added in the 18th century to provide a romantic view of the ruins, it is an excellent example of 18th-century landscaping. Open daily April through October; admission charge.

CHECKING IN: ***Black Swan*** **–** Overlooking the main square and the marketplace, this 400-year-old inn is a tasteful blend of Tudor, Georgian, and modern. It's old enough to be entitled to a ghost, and there is one — a beautiful nun who appears at midnight. In addition to its 38 rooms, the inn has a restaurant with wooden beams, chintz-covered furniture, log fires, and a reputation for good English dishes, including Wensley fowl with port. Market Pl., Helmsley (phone: 0439-70466). Expensive.

Crown **–** Again overlooking the main square, this 16th-century coaching inn has 14 bedrooms and a beamed Jacobean restaurant decorated with antique brass and copper objects. The owners cook traditional country fare. Market Sq., Helmsley (phone: 0439-70297). Moderate.

CHECKING IN/EATING OUT: ***Feversham Arms*** **–** Yorkshire's probably the last place you'd expect to enjoy an excellent paella or an exceptional selection of Rioja wines, but Gonzalo de Aragues, the Spanish owner here, supplies both. Dine in the *Bay* restaurant — shellfish, including paella, and game are often featured — or stick to the snacks in the bar, where visitors can sample 40 different sherries and 20 malt whiskies (not all at once). This old inn has 20 rooms, each with private bath. 1 High St., Helmsley (phone: 0439-70766). Restaurant moderate; rooms expensive.

En Route from Helmsley – Take A170 westward to Sutton Bank escarpment, crossing the Hambleton Hills. (If coming from Rievaulx Abbey, go through Scawton to join A170 and then follow signs to Sutton Bank — or continue along the Cleveland Way footpath from the abbey.) The very edge of the escarpment offers a fine panorama of glacier-formed Gormire Lake, the vales of York and Mowbray, and the distant Yorkshire Dales — a view James Herriot has called the finest in England. There is a North York Moors National Park information center (open daily Easter through October) by the road, with a refreshment bar, picnic area, and an exhibit devoted to the history of the area. Don't be surprised to see a sailplane swish overhead; they are launched from the nearby airfield of the *Yorkshire Gliding Club* and take advantage of the uplift from southwesterly winds blowing against the escarpment. Visitors can book a flight for about $30, including the sailplane, tow, and, of course, an instructor (phone: 0845-597237).

Before proceeding westward to Thirsk, a detour to two interesting villages south of A170 beckons. Descend Sutton Bank on the narrow, rather daunting road to Kilburn. You might want to stop in the small car park to see the famous White Horse carved into the hillside above Kilburn by a 19th-century village teacher and his pupils. Up to 20 people have managed to stand on the horse's eye at the same time — but don't try it, as it would soon wear out. Kilburn itself is remembered mostly because of an ordinary village carpenter whose goal was the "satisfaction of knowing anything I create will outlive me by three hundred years." By the time he died in 1955, Robert Thompson's furniture and carvings in English oak could be seen throughout the world, including Westminster Abbey and York Minster. Today his two grandchildren run the furniture business, and everything produced in the village workshop (where furniture is for sale) still bears the famous wooden mouse trademark.

From Kilburn, drive eastward to Coxwold, a lovely village of a single street, graced by a 15th-century Perpendicular church with an octagonal tower and box pews. "A delicious retreat" was how Laurence Sterne, its famous onetime vicar, described his home. Shandy Hall, the old rambling house where he lived and where he wrote *Tristram Shandy* and *A Sentimental Journey,* is open to the public on summer Wednesday and Sunday afternoons only (admission charge). Newburgh Priory, founded by Augustinians in the 12th century, is just short of a mile southeast of Coxwold (open Wednesdays and Sundays from mid-May through August; admission charge). Byland Abbey, another Cistercian house (open daily; admission charge), is a mile northeast of Coxwold, just outside the hamlet of Wass. Founded in the 12th century, it was moved from its previous address at Old Byland north of A170 in part because of its unsheltered position there and in part because the monks could hear the bells at Rievaulx Abbey — something the inhabitants of neither establishment could endure. Little remains, but the ruins are impressive, especially when silhouetted against a dramatic sky.

Those in a hurry can now backtrack through Coxwold and follow signs to A19 for the return to York. Fans of James Herriot, however, may want to make one final stop at Thirsk, either backtracking through Kilburn and taking A170 west or proceeding to A19 and turning north.

CHECKING IN: ***Forresters Arms*** **–** A comfortable, cozy country inn with 8 bedrooms, next door to Kilburn's "mouseman" furniture maker. Kilburn (phone: 03476-386). Moderate.

THIRSK: Until recently, this market town on the northern flanks of the Vale of York was best known for its Perpendicular parish church. All that changed when a Scottish veterinarian, based in Thirsk but practicing over a very wide area of Yorkshire, wrote *All Creatures Great and Small* and other books describing his lifetime of experience. James Herriot still lives in Thirsk, but the town may not be entirely recognizable as "Darrowby," which the author's says is a composite made up of Thirsk, Richmond, Leyburn, and Middleham (all west of here), plus "a fair chunk" of imagination (and Herriot, too, is a pen name). The town of Thirsk, as it really is, is described in *James Herriot's Yorkshire* (Bantam Books, paperback; $4.50).

CHECKING IN: ***Golden Fleece*** **–** A coaching inn dating from the 17th century, it has 22 rooms and overlooks the cobbled market square. In its heyday, as many as 60 horses were on call in the stables. Market Pl., Thirsk (phone: 0845-23108). Expensive.

Three Tuns **–** Built in 1698 as a dower house, this became a coaching inn in the 1740s to service the Leeds–Edinburgh traffic. After considerable renovation, it reopened as a hotel in the 1970s, with 12 comfortable rooms (8 with bath). Market Pl., Thirsk (phone: 0845-23124). Moderate.

■ **Note:** For travelers interested in mining, the award-winning *Yorkshire Mining Museum* is about 25 miles south of York, near Wakefield on the A642. The museum, which opened in 1988 at a colliery, allows visitors to descend 450 feet underground in a real miners' cage to see how coal is mined and how the techniques have changed over the past 200 years. Open daily; admission charge.

The Cotswolds

Less than 100 miles west of London is the region known as the Cotswolds. It encompasses about 450 square miles of rolling limestone upland of the Cotswold Hills, punctuated by charming, carefully preserved medieval towns and villages built from the honey-colored stone, quarried from the hills, which gives the region its character. The Cotswolds themselves stretch northeast in a curving 60-mile arc from Bath to the vicinity of Stratford-upon-Avon. Along their western edge they form a steep ridge of solid limestone, and their crest is the Thames-Severn watershed. But the overall character of the countryside is tranquil and picturesque, like a rich tapestry. Much of this land is a great, sweeping pasture for the famous Cotswold sheep, with their heavy ringlets of fleece that once upon a time brought wealth to the area.

This is the England of the imagination: rolling hills covered by copses of ancient oak and surviving elm, a landscape scaled to size for country walks and bird-watching. Towns are tied to one another by twisting country lanes that carry a constant commerce of farmers and shepherds, postmen, parsons, and pubgoers. The vista from any hill is as apt to include the square tower of a Norman church as a far field of cropping sheep, and any church is likely to be surrounded by the stone tile or thatched roofs of a tiny village, now no longer populated by farm workers but by retired folk, weekenders, and commuters to the larger towns. Village cemeteries are shaded by yews and village streams guarded by weeping willows. Nothing is very far from anything else, but privacy and protective isolation are accentuated by the quiet and country peace that settles over all. Village names are remnants of an earlier language and a younger England: Wyck Rissington, Upper and Lower Slaughter, Oddington, Guiting Power, Clapton-on-Hill, Bourton-on-the-Water, Moreton-in-Marsh.

The Cotswolds provided a rich agricultural center for the Romans until the 5th century, and the Roman presence is still visible in many places, such as the roads out of Cirencester and the baths in Bath. The Saxons routed the Romans; the Normans routed the Saxons; and they all left their mark. But when the Cotswold sheep began to pay off, it was the wool merchants of the Middle Ages who built the enduring symbols of the area — magnificent churches like the 14th-century one to St. John the Baptist at Cirencester and the 15th-century one at Northleach.

Our route through the Cotswolds is long, lazy, and serpentine. We begin in Oxford and end in Bath, both important and fascinating cities that border the Cotswolds area. In between we savor most of those golden towns that are quintessentially Cotswold in flavor: Northleach, Chedworth, Burford, Bourton-on-the-Water, Stow-on-the-Wold, Moreton-in-Marsh, Chipping Campden, Broadway, Winchcombe, Cheltenham, Cirencester, and Malmesbury.

An eminently English way to see the Cotswolds is to go on shanks' mare and walk all or part of the 100-mile Cotswold Way, a trail that links a series of well-marked and easily negotiated paths that follow the crests of the Cotswold hills from Bath to Chipping Campden in the north. These ancient routes, first used by neolithic travelers 3,000 years ago, were well worn by medieval pilgrims and traders moving from village to village, the same villages that dot the course today. One need not be an accomplished hiker to follow the Way for a distance, and the weak of spirit can take heart from the thought that village and pub are never far apart. The benefits are multiple: immersed in the countryside, you have a walking-pace view of the villages, buildings, cottages, churches, Roman ruins, and barrows — Stone Age burial mounds — that dot the region (the barrow at Belas Knap, between Cheltenham and Winchcombe, is thought to be the most impressive specimen in England). The Way is maintained by the Gloucestershire County Council, which marks its course with large yellow arrows to make hiking easier. Thornhill Press publishes *The Cotswold Way,* an excellent guide by Mark Richards, available throughout the area.

A detailed guidebook, *The Cotswolds and Shakespeare's Country,* is available from the Heart of England Tourist Board Trinity St., Worcester WR1 2PW (phone: 0905-613132).

The area is extremely popular with tourists from all over Britain, as well as visitors from abroad, all wanting to immerse themselves amidst the picturesque villages and gentle countryside. Although the hotels and inns quickly fill up, especially in summer, it is often possible to find last-minute, simple bed-and-breakfast accommodations at farms or private houses. Expect to pay at least $100 for a double room in those places listed as expensive; from $60 to $100 in the moderate range; and under $60 for inexpensive. A meal for two, excluding drinks and tips, will cost about $55 or more in places listed as expensive; $30 to $55 in moderate; and under $30 in inexpensive.

OXFORD: A visit to this beautiful city is the perfect start to a tour of the Cotswolds. For a detailed report on the city, its sights, hotels, and restaurants, see Oxford, THE CITIES.

To begin the Cotswold tour, take A40 west from Oxford to Northleach.

NORTHLEACH: In the 15th century Northleach was one of the busiest wool towns in the Cotswolds. During this period prosperous wool traders built the church of St. Peter and St. Paul, which is designed in the Perpendicular style and constructed of local stone. Note especially how the South Porch is richly decorated with statuary and carved stone. It is perhaps best known, however, for its numerous brasses representing the wool merchants. The church has undergone and survived much recent restoration, including work by Sir Basil Spence, architect of Coventry Cathedral.

Because the river Leach did not provide sufficient power to drive the watermills that were speeding up the manufacturing process in other parts of the region, the wool trade declined after the 16th century and Northleach suffered. But the town came into its own again when stagecoaches began to run between London and Gloucester, and several coaching inns opened their doors to travelers.

Take A429 south from Northleach and follow signs for Chedworth.

CHEDWORTH: This quiet town has a fine Norman church worth a look inside for its carved stone pulpit. About 2 miles outside Chedworth in a pretty, wooded part of the Coln Valley is a partly reconstructed Roman villa. Here you can see some very well preserved examples of Roman mosaic floors and bathhouses. Open Tuesdays through Sundays March through October and Wednesdays through Sundays in November.

BIBURY: This picturesque village, through which the river Coln flows, is one of Britain's most photographed. The avid shutterbug will find yet another perfect composition everywhere he looks: Bibury's partly 13th-century church contains many of the earlier Saxon features as well as some Norman additions. Then there's Arlington Row, a group of early-17th-century stone cottages huddled together on a terraced hillside near the Coln, and Arlington Mill, a former 17th-century corn mill, which houses a country craft museum. Open daily March through October, and weekends November through February.

En Route from Bibury – An interesting side trip would be to Quenington and Fairford; to reach these towns follow an unclassified road toward Coln St. Aldwyne.

At roughly the southernmost extreme of the Cotswolds proper, Quenington, in the Coln Valley, is notable for its well-restored 17th-century buildings, some of which open their gardens to the public in the summer. The best are probably those of Barnsley House, home of Resemary Verey, the gardening writer (open weekdays). The Norman church was built in about 1170 and later restored in 1882 by the architect of Gloucester Cathedral. It's particularly famous for the stone carvings around the north and south doors.

Fairford, a little town perched on the edge of the Cotswolds, boasts a jewel of a parish church — built in the Perpendicular style by 15th-century wool merchants and lit by 28 brilliant stained-glass windows. As was then the custom, the windows were not simply decorative but also educational — they illustrated Bible stories for parishioners who couldn't read.

The English poet and clergyman John Keble was born in Fairford in 1792. He was one of the leaders of the Oxford Movement, which among other things made church services more formal and sought to reduce secular power over the church. Keble College, Oxford, was founded in his memory, partly with money left over from sales of Keble's poetical bestseller, *The Christian Year,* which went into no fewer than 92 editions.

Fairford's main square, the Market Place, is lined with ancient trees and stone houses; there are several inviting old pubs, the best of which are probably *The Bull* and *The George.*

CHECKING IN: ***Swan*** – Crouched low by the river Coln (where you can cast a line for trout), this creeper-covered 17th-century coaching inn has just 24 rooms. On A433 (phone: 028574-204). Expensive.

Bibury Court – Run by the Collier family, this rambling Tudor and Jacobean manor, set in 6 acres of gardens, is furnished in antiques; trout fishing is available. Off A433 (phone: 028574-337). Moderate.

BURFORD: From Bibury, take A433 to Burford. Although on the edge of the Cotswolds, Burford is a typical Cotswold community — its steep main street, stippled with ancient stone houses and shops, rolls down a hill to meet the river Windrush. In the 18th century, Burford was an important coaching stop. Now, in the 20th century, it's an antiquer's delight; Burford is full of antiques shops — some of the most expensive in the country.

A number of Burford's buildings are antiques themselves, notably the almshouses built in 1457; the Grammar School for Boys founded in 1571; the Priory, an Elizabethan house; the Great House, built in 1690; and the Tolsey (or Toll House), now a town museum, open daily Easter through October. The spired church is Perpendicular in style and has an old Norman tower. One of the houses in Sheep Street is known as

"Kit's Quarry," built by Christopher Kempster, who was the master mason commissioned by Christopher Wren to provide stone from local quarries for St. Paul's Cathedral. Tours of Burford take place every Sunday afternoon May through October, conducted by members of the Burford and District Society.

Drive from Burford to Great Barrington, turning left on to an unclassified road just north of the bridge over the Windrush (approximately 4 miles).

THE BARRINGTONS AND WINDRUSH: From the 14th to the 19th century, the quarries of Great Barrington and Little Barrington produced some of the best Cotswold stone. Many of England's more impressive buildings were constructed using the stone, including sections of St. Paul's Cathedral in London and several Oxford colleges.

Great Barrington consists mainly of a double row of cottages partly surrounded by a country estate called Barrington Park. The centerpiece of the estate is a Palladian mansion which dates from 1736–38. Close to the house is a mostly Norman church that underwent complete restoration in 1815.

Little Barrington, across the river Windrush (which meanders rather than rushes), is the prettier of the two villages; it is centered around a triangular green, which was supposedly built over old quarry workings. The pub now called the *Inn for All Seasons* was popular with quarrymen, and it is said that its cellars are on the same level and have access to the quarry's underground passages. Little Barrington's houses are of different shapes, sizes, and periods and present a varied but harmonious composition.

The village of Windrush is also on this side of the river. From the pleasant shaded lane that links it with Little Barrington there are lovely views across to Great Barrington. But the real reason for stopping in Windrush is to visit St. Peter's Church, a Norman building decorated with much fine carving, especially around the south doorway.

CHECKING IN: ***Bay Tree*** – This 16th-century mansion down a quiet side street has retained its cozy, antique and fireplace-lit atmosphere despite recent updating — 16 new rooms in adjacent cottages have been added to the original 24. Sheep St., Burford (phone: 099382-3137). Moderate.

Bull – History is in every nook and cranny of this 14th-century coaching inn on one of England's most famous and prettiest High Streets. There are 14 rooms, peacefully decorated with modern touches, a bar, and a restaurant. High St., Burford (phone: 099382-2220). Moderate.

Lamb Inn – Built of Cotswold stone and dating from the 15th century, this hotel also has a restaurant and a garden. Sheep St. (phone: 099382-3155). Moderate.

BOURTON-ON-THE-WATER: This village is very pretty, with the river Windrush running right through it, crossed by unusual and attractive stone bridges that link rows of shops and small hotels set back behind greenswards where people picnic and children play. Be sure to visit St. Lawrence Church, which has a late-18th-century spire and a 14th-century chancel; it was heavily restored in Victorian times — more successfully than many. Next to the *Old New Inn* on High St. is a famous small-scale model village of Bourton (open daily). Also in town is the Cotswold Perfumery where visitors can sample perfumes manufactured on the premises (open daily). *Note:* Almost too popular, Bourton has allowed itself to become very commercial and is jammed with tourists in the summer.

En Route from Bourton – Stow-on-the-Wold is about 4 miles north via A429; a pleasant detour would be a left turn toward the Slaughters. This lane leads first to Lower Slaughter, named after the Norman De Sclotre family; it's a rather self-consciously pretty village as yet unspoiled by tourist traffic. You may see artists at work on the green banks of the river. Upper Slaughter is on higher ground, as the name suggests, and is reached by winding leafy lanes. This village is more interesting than its sister. The *Lords of the Manor* hotel at Upper Slaughter (see Checking In) was originally the village rectory, and it was enlarged by one incumbent, the Reverend F. E. Witts, also known as the author of the *Diary of a Cotswold Parson.* Upper Slaughter also boasts the oldest and most impressive dovecote in Gloucestershire, dating from the 16th century. Also of note is *The Manor House,* an interesting Elizabethan building that incorporates the remains of a 15th-century priory and has an outstanding Jacobean porch. And so strong is local pride that even some of the council houses (subsidized low-income homes) are roofed in Cotswold stone slates.

CHECKING IN: ***Lords of the Manor*** – If Upper Slaughter didn't have a beautifully preserved 17th-century manor house and surrounding grounds as a hostelry for visitors, it would be necessary to build one. Luckily it was done some 300 years ago, and you need only call for reservations (phone: 0451-20243). Expensive.

STOW-ON-THE-WOLD: This town sits squarely on the Fosse Way, one of the Roman trunk routes that cuts a swathe through southern Britain. (The name is not Roman but Saxon; and the road was used later by Normans as well.) Stow was another important wool market town in medieval times; there were two annual fairs, with merchants dickering over the sale of thousands of sheep. Many hotels, shops, and restaurants sprang up around the famous Market Square designed by the lord of the manor, the Abbot of Evesham, in the 11th century. The *King's Arms,* an old inn on the square (see Checking In), was once a lodging house for household servants of Edward VI, son of Henry VIII; in late March 1646, after what was to be the last battle of the Civil War, Cromwell incarcerated Royalist troops in the church that stands on one corner of the square.

CHECKING IN: ***Fosse Manor*** – This ivy-covered manor house has 21 spacious rooms and a restaurant. Fosse Way, Stow (phone: 0451-30354). Moderate.

King's Arms – A 500-year-old inn that offers simple lodgings and a hearty breakfast. Market Sq., Stow (phone: 0451-30364). Inexpensive.

En Route from Stow-on-the-Wold – It's about a mile to Upper Swell via B4077; Lower Swell lies on A436.

Upper Swell is a charming 18th-century village known for its handsome early-17th-century manor house, arched stone bridge over the river Dikler, and early-19th-century watermill capped with a Welsh slate roof. Stop for a moment at the parish church for a look at its exceptional perpendicular font. Close to the village is the Donnington Brewery, once a corn mill, and now one of the last privately owned breweries. It's been producing beer since about 1865.

A mineral spring was discovered in Lower Swell in 1807, and for a while it was thought that the Swells might develop into another Cheltenham. All that remains of those fine dreams today, however, is a row of curiously decorated and rather exotic houses optimistically known as the "Spa Cottages." Despite this setback, Lower Swell regained its reputation with the success of another kind of watering hole — the *Golden Ball Inn,* which has for many years greeted travelers with food, drink (including Donnington beer), and a warm welcome. Treat yourself to lunch here.

Another sidetrip from Stow-on-the-Wold is in the opposite direction, to Chipping Norton, about 9 miles via A436 and A44.

"Chipping" may be a corruption of "cheapening," meaning "market." Chipping Norton, perched high on a hill near the Evenlode, was a busy market town for centuries. Today its wide streets are no longer filled with medieval wool merchants and its imposing Victorian tweed mill has been closed down. Instead, the market square now bustles with tourists sampling Chipping Norton's many cafés, pubs, restaurants, and hotels. The parish church, built in the perpendicular style by wool merchants in the 14th and 15th centuries, is one of the largest in Oxfordshire and is especially noteworthy for its several fine medieval brasses.

Four miles north of Chipping Norton off A34 are the Rollright Stones, a circle of about 70 stones that date from between 1800 and 500 BC. To one side stand 5 other stones, said to represent a king and his knights. The name of these stones derives, it is believed, from Rollanriht, or "the jurisdiction of Roland the Brave." The name appears in the Domesday Book as Rollandri.

MORETON-IN-MARSH: This town lies on the mainline railway from London, and therefore has a more workaday atmosphere than most other Cotswold communities. It is another old market town that can be fun to explore on foot. Main Street, which follows the route of the Fosse Way, is unusually wide and contains many antique shops. On High Street is the Market Hall, built in Victorian Tudor style in 1887. Note the Curfew Tower on Oxford Street; it dates from the 17th century and its bell was rung daily until the 19th century. About a mile west of town is the Batsford Park Arboretum, with 50 acres of rare trees (open daily, April to October).

CHECKING IN: ***White Hart Royal*** – If you stay here, you will have shared a place with royalty — Charles I spent the night in this half-timbered posting inn in 1644. Cobbles more than 300 years old have been carefully preserved, and old hunting trophies and weapons adorn the Cotswold stone bar. The hotel has 24 rooms and a small timbered dining room. High St. (phone: 0608-50731). Moderate.

En Route from Moreton-in-Marsh – A worthwhile side trip is to Chastleton House; take A44 to the southeast, then turn right onto an unclassified road for Chastleton (approximately 5 miles). Chastleton House was built in 1603 by Walter Jones, a Witney wool merchant who bought the land from one of the Gunpowder Plot conspirators. Jones spent half his fortune improving the house in 1603, and the other half — unfortunately for him — on the Royalist cause during the Civil War. He was a man of taste, as is shown by the richly carved paneling and the furniture. Among the items in the house are Charles I's Bible, which he used on the morning of his execution, valuable tapestries; and rare china. The topiary garden is one of the best in Britain: There are good views of it from the windows of the Long Gallery in the house. The idea of such gardens was imported from the Continent by William of Orange, and although the representation of birds and animals has altered over the years, the layout has remained the same. The house and gardens are open Fridays through Sundays, Easter to September.

From Moreton-in-Marsh, take A44 west for about 6 miles, then turn right onto B4081 for Chipping Campden.

CHIPPING CAMPDEN: This town was restored carefully by the Campden Trust, a group of people mindful of the past; as a result, it is remarkably well preserved. If you can ignore the traffic — mostly visitors looking for somewhere to park — the main street looks just as it did hundreds of years ago. And Chipping Campden's many fine old buildings are a delight. The church, though heavily restored by the Victorians, is one of the best in the Cotswolds. Built in the perpendicular style by the town's wool merchants in the 15th century, it is unusually large and contains several fine brasses. Near the church are almshouses dating to 1612. All along High Street, you'll see many houses built with warm Cotswold stone; also stop at the handsome bow-windowed Grevel House (the former home of a wealthy woolman) on Church Street. Across the way is Woolstapler's Hall, a 14th-century house where wool merchants traded; it's now a museum of the town's history and a tourist information center. The Market Hall, a solid yet graceful structure composed of fourteen stone arches built in 1627, was where the area's farmers sold their dairy products.

CHECKING IN: ***Charingworth Manor*** **–** This fine Tudor manor house with lovely views across the Cotswolds has been painstakingly converted into a luxury accommodation. Service with a personal touch. Ebrington, Chipping Campden (phone: 0386-78219). Moderate.

Noel Arms **–** A pub-like atmosphere prevails at this 14th-century coaching inn — lots of oak beams, armor-hung walls, and a cheering fireplace. Some of the 19 rooms sport four-poster beds. High St., Chipping Campden (phone: 0386-840317). Moderate.

EATING OUT: ***King's Arms*** **–** These two converted 17th- and 18th-century stone houses in Chipping Campden's main square have a total of 14 rooms, a good restaurant serving local fish, game, and (for the most part), home-grown herbs and vegetables, quiet gardens, and a good deal of character. The Square, Chipping Campden (phone: 0386-840256). Moderate.

Bantam Tea Rooms **–** This cozy, traditional tea room is the perfect spot for a cup. High St., Chipping Campden (phone: 0386-840336). Inexpensive.

En Route from Chipping Campden – Take B4081 north to Mickleton, then follow signs for Hidcote Manor Gardens, opposite which are Kiftsgate Court Gardens. (Note that while Hidcote Gardens are open daily except Tuesdays and Fridays, April through October, Kiftsgate Gardens are open Wednesdays, Thursdays, and Sundays, April through September.) Hidcote Manor Gardens are formal, with impressive and varied hedges, rare trees, and shrubs. The gardens were laid out in the first few years of this century by Laurence Johnston, and it was here that he originated the mixed or "harlequin" hedge. There are small individual gardens with pools, rare plants, and gazebos. As the poet Vita Sackville-West said of Major Johnston, "He spilled his cornucopia everywhere." Kiftsgate Court Gardens are steeper, less formal, and, like Hidcote, are enhanced by the presence of an impressive house, Mickleton Manor.

Pick up A46 and proceed south to Broadway.

BROADWAY: Henry James once described Broadway thus: "The place has so much character that it rubs off on the visitor . . . it is delicious to be at Broadway." Many people would agree with James, judging from the traffic and numbers of tourists who throng here to shop for antiques and to stroll among the 17th- and 18th-century golden Cotswold stone houses. (Partly due to heavy tourism and partly just to preserve the old stone — which is highly vulnerable to even the comparatively mild Cotswold weather — there has recently been some renovation and new building. But it has been done well, and stone facing rather than complete razing is the general rule.)

The *Lygon Arms* is probably Broadway's main attraction (see *Checking In*); the hotel's elegance is only exceeded by its history. The main building dates from 1532, though parts of it are more than 600 years old. It was frequented by Charles I and Oliver Cromwell, and rooms named after each have been carefully preserved or restored.

Some of Broadway's other notable structures include Middle Hill, the estate of Sir Thomas Phillips, the eccentric and wealthy book collector; St. Eadburgha's, a Norman church; and Broadway Beacon, an 18th-century, 65-foot-high, stern stone edifice on Broadway Hill, all of which are within Broadway Tower Country Park. You can climb the tower for a view of the countryside, spread your picnic lunch in one of the designated areas, or visit the 150-year-old barn that houses an exhibit on the geology of the hill.

CHECKING IN: ***Lygon Arms*** – Both Charles I and Oliver Cromwell slept in this elegant, 16th-century, ivy-covered inn, now a staple in international hotel rankings and a member of Relais & Châteaux. There are 64 antiques-furnished rooms, 4 with four-poster beds, and an award-winning dining room. High St., Broadway (phone: 0386-852255). Expensive.

EATING OUT: ***Dormy House*** – Built on an escarpment of galloping Cotswolds above the village of Broadway, *Dormy* began life as a 17th-century farmhouse. Ancient beams and exposed stone walls prove the historic pedigree, but open fires, a cheery staff, and French-inspired cuisine provide the contemporary touch. Visitors can stay overnight as there are 50 elegantly furnished rooms. One of the friendliest staffs around. Willersey Hill, Broadway (phone: 0386-852711). Expensive.

En Route from Broadway – Near the western end of Broadway, *before* you reach A46 to Winchcombe, turn left for Snowshill Manor — about 3 miles. The manor house, a fine example of Tudor and Georgian architecture, was part of Catherine Parr's dowry (she was Henry VIII's last wife). The manor is open Wednesdays through Sundays, May to September; weekends April and October. It contains an eclectic collection of antiques and trivia accumulated by Charles Wade, who subsidized his mania with an income from West Indian sugar plantations. He was so devoted to his collection that he actually lived in the adjoining cottage in order to give it more space. Both are open to the public.

Another interesting sidetrip is to the Cotswold Farm Park at Guiting Power, a survival center for rare breeds of British farm animals, including shire horses; Soay and Orkney sheep (the former originally from St. Kilda, a now uninhabited Scottish island far off the mainland in the Atlantic); and examples of the breed of sheep upon which the medieval wool trade depended (the "Cotswold Lions"). To get here, follow the unclassified road from Snowshill toward Bourton-on-the-Water, which joins B4077 directly east of Temple Guiting. The park is just before that junction and open daily, May through September.

You must get back on A46 to drive south to Winchcombe.

WINCHCOMBE: Though it suffers a little from through traffic, not all of Winchcombe is on the main road, and it is a good example of a genuine Cotswold town going about its business as it has done for several hundred years. Before the Norman Conquest this was the capital of Winchcombeshire, and here you will see half-timbering among the stone houses. For example, the *George Inn,* which once provided lodgings for pilgrims visiting nearby Hailes Abbey, has a half-timbered coaching yard. Hailes Abbey was built between 1245 and 1253 and prospered for some 300 years before Henry VIII's Dissolution of the Monasteries, at which time it was razed. (The order to surrender was actually given on Christmas Eve 1539.) Now only the ruins remain; open daily; admission charge. The site is 3 miles northeast of Winchcombe, clearly signed off A46. Winchcombe's 19th-century town hall, which contains the original stocks, now houses the Folk Museum; open daily March through October; admission charge. The parish church is mainly remarkable for the gargoyles that decorate its exterior — at least 40 of them; inside there is an altarcloth believed to have been woven by Catherine of Aragon, Henry VIII's first queen.

Half a mile southeast of the town center, clearly signed, lies Sudeley Castle. Now the private home of Lord and Lady Ashcombe, its interior is quite labyrinthine. The castle has been the home of several of England's queens: Anne Boleyn and Elizabeth I spent time here, and it was the final home and final resting place of Catherine Parr, the only wife to outlive Henry VIII. During the Civil War that affected so much of this now tranquil part of England, Sudeley Castle was extensively damaged, and it was virtually abandoned for nearly 200 years. But with the help of Sir George Gilbert Scott, responsible for, among other things, London's Albert Memorial, the castle was restored. The restoration work went on until the 1930s; tantalizing traces of the original buildings remain, including a few dating to the 15th century, and some very old stained glass. The castle now houses an important collection of art treasures, including works by Constable, Turner, Rubens, and Van Dyck. It is open daily, March through October; admission charge.

From Winchcombe follow A46 to Cheltenham.

CHELTENHAM: Popularly regarded as a genteel place largely inhabited by geriatrics, Cheltenham is more lively than many think. For example, it's practically impossible to find accommodations within a 30-mile radius during Cheltenham Gold Cup Week, a national horse race held every March. (For information, write to Racing Information Bureau, 42 Portman Sq., London W1.) In addition, there is the International Festival of Music in July, and the Festival of Literature in October (for information, write Town Hall Box Office, Imperial Sq., Cheltenham, Gloucestershire; phone: 0242-523690). While here, try the waters that made Cheltenham famous — either at the town hall or the Pittville Pump Room (open Mondays through Saturdays), named after local MP Joseph Pitt, who served in the House of Commons from 1825 to 1830. The medicinal properties of these waters are said to derive from the magnesium and sodium sulphates and the sodium bicarbonate they contain. When your thirst is slaked, visit the Gallery of Fashion in the same building, or stroll to the Gustav Holst Birthplace Museum, a Regency-period house on Clarence Road. Open Mondays through Fridays, noon to 5:30 PM; Saturdays, 11 AM to 5:30 PM; admission charge (phone: 0242-24846). Before you leave Cheltenham, be sure to take a stroll along the famous Promenade, made lovely by its rows of great horse chestnut trees. Along one side are first class shops, similar to those found in the town's Regent Arcade and Montpellier area; along the other side stand beautifully preserved Regency terraced buildings. The town also has many spacious and colorful gardens, the best of which is the Imperial Gardens, adjoining the town hall on Imperial Sq.

The A435 will take you from Cheltenham to Cirencester.

CHECKING IN: ***Hotel de la Bere and Country Club*** – A lovely mock-Tudor mansion (built in this century) with 60 guestrooms and very good sports facilities including tennis, squash, horseback riding, and swimming as well as a sauna and solarium. Southam, 4 miles outside Cheltenham (phone: 0242-37771). Expensive.

Queens – This colonnaded hotel overlooking Imperial Gardens has graced the Promenade since the 19th century. Grand and lofty layouts, with 77 bedrooms, elegantly furnished and beautifully equipped. The Promenade (phone: 0242-514724). Expensive.

EATING OUT: ***Cleeveway House*** – Elegance and charm are the keynotes of this Regency-style restaurant in a delightful 17th-century country house surrounded by neat gardens. Game and fish are the specialties. Open Tuesdays through Saturdays and Monday evenings. Bishops Cleeve, Cheltenham (phone: 024267-2585). Expensive.

Thatchers – Very popular with local people for morning coffee, lunch, or afternoon tea. Cornish cream teas and ice cream sundaes are particularly good. Montpellier St., Cheltenham (phone: 0242-584150). Inexpensive.

CIRENCESTER: Established by the Romans at the junction at which their vital route Fosse Way met five other roads, Cirencester (or Corinium) was a strategic link in their defenses. As a result, Corinium grew to be second in size only to London. In the 6th century it was destroyed by the invading Saxons, so little of the Roman occupation remains in the town itself. However, mosaic floors, sculpture, and pottery recovered from excavations now form the extensive collection of Roman relics in the Corinium Museum on Park St. (open daily, except Mondays in winter). Cotswold Avenue is the site of the ruins of a Roman amphitheater. Periods of English history seem piled one atop another by a profligate hand in Cirencester. The parish church, St. John the Baptist, built by wool merchants in the 14th century, is a fine example of the Perpendicular style. One of the largest churches in England, it is not to be missed for its rich stone carvings, magnificent array of medieval stained glass, and many fine brasses. On Stroud Rd. is Cirencester Park, the 3,000-acre estate of the earl of Bathurst; although the house is not open to the public, the grounds are. Also interesting are the Cirencester Workshops in the center of town. The craft gallery and workshops are open daily except Sundays.

Take A423 from Cirencester to Malmesbury.

CHECKING IN: ***Fleece*** – Outside is a handsome black and white half-timbered façade; inside are Cotswold stone walls, fine open fireplaces, and low-beamed ceilings. Gastronomic festivals are a regular attraction of the hotel restaurant, which specializes in nouvelle cuisine and real ales — try the Three B's Ale, the local brew. Market Pl., Cirencester (phone: 0285-68507). Moderate.

King's Head – Opposite the famous parish church, this 14th-century coaching inn with 70 rooms has been completely modernized without destroying its charm, although the presence of tour parties can sometimes be overwhelming. Market Pl., Cirencester (phone: 0285-3322). Moderate.

MALMESBURY: This pleasant little town high above the Wiltshire Avon is the site of a magnificent Norman abbey with a most unusual history: During the Dissolution under King Henry VIII in the 16th century, the building was sold to a clothier for £1,500. The man promptly brought in his weaving machinery and converted it into a factory. It was not until 1823 that a restoration effort was begun. Despite the many years of decay, the restoration was eminently successful, and today the abbey is considered one of the finest examples of Norman building remaining in Britain. The richly carved south porch and the musicians' gallery are especially impressive.

The town has two special connections with aviation. The first was established at Malmesbury Abbey in the 11th century, when Brother Oliver attempted to defy gravity by leaping from the tower wearing a pair of homemade wings. He survived the leap but was lame ever after. And at Kemble, 6 miles north of Malmesbury, the Royal Air Force aerobatic team, the Red Arrows, practice their aerial formations.

Malmesbury is one of the oldest boroughs in England and a very well planned medieval city; it was already an important town before the Norman invasion. Some medieval remains are still extant, including fragments of walls and ruins of a 12th-century castle that can be seen today at the *Old Bell* hotel. Six bridges lead to the Market Square, at whose center is an impressive octagonal Tudor market cross. There are several lovely 17th- and 18th-century houses built by rich weavers on the adjoining streets. George Washington's ancestors appear to have come from the region, since at least five Washington predecessors are buried in a churchyard in Garsdon, 2 miles east of Malmesbury.

En Route from Malmesbury – Going southwest, there are several noteworthy stops, including Badminton House, off B4040. Another is Dyrham Park, farther south and off A46.

The Badminton estate has been in the same family, the Beauforts, for over 300 years, and is the magnificent setting each April of the Badminton Horse Trials, an international competition. For information, write: Box Office, Badminton Horse Trials, Badminton, Avon, G19 1DF. The house itself is open only on rare occasions during the summer months. (A note of trivia: the game of badminton was invented here by house guests in the 1860s.)

Stop for tea served in the orangery of the elegant, low-lying mansion in Dyrham Park. Afterward, stroll around; the house, built between 1692 and 1704, shows considerable Dutch influence, perhaps because its owner, William Blathwayt, was a representative at the Hague. Open afternoons Saturdays through Wednesdays, April to October, and Thursdays, June through September. Park open daily; admission charge to the mansion.

Follow A46 to Bath.

CHECKING IN: ***Old Bell*** **–** This is a fabulous old inn, a wisteria-clad gabled building on the site of 12th-century Malmesbury Castle. It still retains a medieval spiral staircase, part of the castle wall, and a huge fireplace (recently revealed in all its former glory) in the entrance hall. There are 19 rooms, a garden, a good restaurant, and the charming *Castle Bar.* Abbey Row (phone: 06662-822344). Expensive.

BATH: This city was once one of Europe's greatest spas. Originally founded by the Romans, who in AD 54 built an elaborate system of baths, it was named Aquae Sulis, after Sulis Minerva, a Roman goddess. In succeeding centuries Bath lost and regained its reputation; at one point in the 17th century, it became so popular with royalty and gentry that diarist Samuel Pepys wondered how the water could be sanitary with so many bodies jammed into it. For a detailed report on the city, its sights, hotels, and restaurants, see *Bath,* THE CITIES.

The Lake District

The most efficient bridging of the gap between London and Scotland passes perforce through the western Midlands, an area whose concentration of heavy-duty industrial cities is particularly high and whose interest to visitors is, consequently, supposedly low. Stoke-on-Trent, Sheffield, Manchester, Liverpool — these names reverberate with the crash of the steel mill and the roar of the factory. Well-meaning Londoners will most likely urge you to stay steadfastly to the east, ensuring that you encounter the bucolic pleasures of Cambridge, Lincoln, York, and Durham. Indeed, so splendid are those towns and the country around them that it is hard to argue with such advice unless you are fortified by a familiarity with the less obvious satisfactions to be had in the birthplace of the Industrial Revolution. Or unless bearing east means forgoing forever that crumpled, rumpled, well-watered mountain country known as the Lake District.

Only 30 miles across in any direction, there is a special intensity in the beauty of the Lake District — tarn, mere, beck, and fell, scoured and sculpted by the Ice Age and squeezed into the small county of Cumbria; just an hour or so north of Manchester. It is as though nature were offering a consolation for the sprawling rigors of the industrial belt, much too near-at-hand. No part of England is so universally loved by Britons — for the purity of its clear mountain lakes (meres); its almost vertical fields filled with grazing sheep, each field carefully delineated by painstakingly maintained stone walls; its sharp rocky peaks; and the thousands of tiny lakes (tarns) fed year in and year out by innumerable waterfalls and streams (becks). Its traditional industry has always been hill farming, which gives a steady rhythm to the lakeland year from lambing time onward, but increasingly the area's livelihood is tourism. Since 1951 the Lake District has been a national park, and visitors — hill walkers, rock climbers, historians, artists, ornithologists, and those seeking simply a bit of peace and quiet — number in the millions annually.

What is earth-loving and ancient in the English spirit is drawn irresistibly to the Lake District's uncompromising beauty. Small wonder that J. M. W. Turner, the famous English landscape painter, spent time here sketching it. The Lake District is primarily associated, however, with a group of his contemporaries, poets of the late 18th and early 19th centuries who not only celebrated the beauty of the region in words, but discovered here values to stand against the encroaching horrors of the industrial age. Chief among them was William Wordsworth, who lived here for most of his life, but others are equally well known: Robert Southey, Samuel Taylor Coleridge, and the writers John Ruskin and Thomas De Quincey. Much of what you see and do in the region is associated with the Lake Poets.

One of the most surprising things about the Lake District is how small this famous area really is. You can drive right through it in less than an hour and yet spend a month without ever seeing half of what time and nature have created here. Looking at a map, you see that the principal lakes — Derwentwater, Ullswater, Windermere, wild Wastwater, Buttermere, Crummock Water, Grasmere, and Rydal Water — radiate from the central mass of the Cumbrian Mountains like the spokes of a wheel. A few of them, such as Thirlmere and Haweswater, are reservoirs slaking the thirst and industry of northern cities, but the living lakes are busy with sails and some of them with stately steamers. The distances between these postcard-perfect bodies of water are short, but each of the larger lakes provides a good base for exploring the neighboring area. Allowing time for some hiking as well as exploration of towns and villages, you could easily spend 2 days around each major lake — Windermere, Derwentwater, and Ullswater especially — before moving on.

The route described below begins in the southeastern corner of the Lake District at the town of Kendal, takes the back road to Lake Windermere, and crosses the water on the ferry to Near Sawrey, Hawkshead, and Coniston. The next leg of the trip, north from Windermere, crosses the paths of the Lake Poets. For the last 37 years of his life Wordsworth lived at Rydal Mount, just a few miles from Ambleside. Dove Cottage, the home he had occupied previously, is a few miles farther north, at Grasmere. Thomas De Quincey, author of *Confessions of an English Opium-Eater,* took over the cottage after Wordsworth left for Rydal Mount. The route then proceeds north from Grasmere and passes Thirlmere from where there is easy access to the challenging 3,118-foot mountain peak, Helvellyn. At the end of this leg is Derwentwater — perhaps the most beautiful of all the lakes. Robert Southey made his home here, in the town of Keswick, where he frequently was joined by Percy Bysshe Shelley and Samuel Taylor Coleridge. The twins, Buttermere and Crummock Water, are just a short drive southwest of Keswick, and beyond them, in the northwest corner of the Lake District, is Cockermouth. Wordsworth and his sister Dorothy were both born and raised in Cockermouth, and the family home and nearby fields became part of the joyous imagery of the poetry that introduced this area to readers everywhere. From Cockermouth, two choices present themselves. One possibility is to follow the western boundary of the Lake District, heading south, from where numerous small roads lead into the heart of the mountains and the area's best climbing, a prospect particularly appealing for experienced and properly equipped backpackers and hill walkers. Another is to return to Keswick, drop south off the main road for a visit to the lovely lake of Ullswater, and complete the tour at Penrith, which is conveniently at the northeastern flank of the Lake District at the intersection of several main north-south and east–west routes.

The Lake District offers a wide range of accommodations — from small but comfortable inns to some of the best hotels in the country, and plenty of guesthouses offering bed and breakfast *and* an evening meal for as little as $25 per person. Expect to pay between $70 and $140 for a double in those places listed as expensive; from $45 to $70 in moderate; and under $45 in inexpensive. A meal for two, excluding wine, tips, or drinks, will run about $40 to $55 in places listed as expensive; $30 to $40 in moderate; and under $30 in inexpensive.

KENDAL: Holiday traffic threads constantly through the one-way streets of this old market town, the gateway to the southern part of the Lake District. Because it is busily engaged in the manufacture of shoes, snuff, and Kendal mint cake (after 6 centuries in the wool industry), the town pays less attention to visitors than many another place in Cumbria. Visitors, in turn, in a headlong dash to begin lakeside vacations, often give short shrift to everything but the large shopping center. But the old part of this town on the river Kent is an attractive huddle of slate-roofed buildings separated by small alleyways, yards, and courts, and there are several buildings of particular interest. The ruined Kendal Castle, on a hill east of town, dates back to Norman times and was later the birthplace of Catherine Parr, the last of King Henry VIII's six wives. The 13th-century parish church near the center of town is unusual for its five aisles and its brasses. Abbot Hall, a Georgian house beside the river, is now an art gallery with modern collections and 18th-century period rooms displaying furniture and paintings, including one by Turner and one by the famous portrait artist George Romney, who spent his youth in Kendal. The *Abbot Hall Craft Shop* offers the Lake District's best selection of collectible items such as porcelain, jewelry, carved wood, toys, rugs, leather, and more. Open daily (phone: 0539-22464). The *Museum of Lakeland Life and Industry,* installed in what was once the stables of Abbot Hall, and voted British Museum of the Year in 1986, gives an interesting backward look at the social and economic life of the area. Open daily (phone: 0539-22464). Situated in the middle of Kendal is the *Brewery Arts Centre,* housed in a splendid 15-year-old brewery. A major arts venue, the center presents exhibitions, theater, folk music, jazz, and mime. The restaurant and bar are popular. Open daily (phone: 0539-25133). Also worth checking out is *Webb's Garden Centre* on Bumside Road. This extensive complex includes thousands of plants, a cafè, and gift shop. Open daily (phone: 0539-20068). The *Kendal Museum of Natural History and Archaeology* on Station Road is one of Britain's oldest museums, dating back to 1796. This museum, with its three galleries covering local history from Roman times, Lakeland wildlife, and the *World Wildlife Gallery,* is a must, especially on a rainy day. Open daily (phone: 0539-21374). The tourist information center in Kendal's town hall (phone: 0539-25758) has a mass of leaflets and hotel lists for the southern Lake District.

The main road west out of town climbs a long hill and, after about 2 miles, comes to a large traffic circle. Turn off A591 here and head down B5284 through countryside typical of the edge of the Lake District: neat fields, thick woodland, and a landscape that is all mounds and hummocks building up to the larger hills beyond. The village of Crook is along the way 5 miles from Kendal, and after another 5 miles the route crosses two roads skirting the eastern side of Lake Windermere and comes to a stop at the terminal of the car ferry. Bowness-on-Windermere and Windermere itself are a mile or so north of the terminal.

CHECKING IN: ***Riverside*** – Conveniently located 50 yards from the railway station, this brand new hotel is an impressive addition to Kendal's amenities. All 48 private rooms have a full range of facilities, and there is an excellent restaurant and bar. Stranongate Bridge, Kendal (phone: 0539-724707). Expensive.

Wild Boar – This pleasant country hotel in a converted 17th-century house is a quiet, comfortable staging post. Gardens outside and a beamed bar and fireplaces inside add to its charm. The dining room is highly rated. Crook (phone: 09662-5225). Expensive.

Woolpack – Situated in the center of Kendal, this converted 16th-century inn has immense character and charm, successfully retaining its old world atmosphere. The 53 rooms have a comprehensive range of private facilities. Stricklandgate, Kendal (phone: 0539-23852). Expensive.

Natland Mill Beck Farm – An extremely warm atmosphere at this 17th-century farmhouse with sturdy beams, pine doors, ancient oak cupboards, and 4-foot-thick walls. Kendal (phone: 0539-21122). Inexpensive.

WINDERMERE AND BOWNESS: These adjoining resort areas on Lake Windermere make up one town that is the focal point of tourism in the Lake District. Bowness is the actual port on the water and Windermere is just above Bowness, inland from the lake. Between the two, virtually every recreational activity is available.

It is difficult to actually see Lake Windermere or the surrounding mountains from the town, but a 20-minute walk up Orrest Head hill (to the north of the railroad station) reveals all in a good view of the lake and the hills beyond. Scenic outlooks are a particular attraction of the Windermere countryside and some other notable ones include Queen Adelaide's Hill, an ideal picnic spot between Bowness and the main Ambleside Road; Millerground, a little farther along the same footpath; Biskey Howe, reached from Helm Road, Bowness; and School Knott, which has an easy, winding path to its summit east of Windermere. The information centers at Windermere (phone: 09662-6499) and Bowness (phone: 09662-2895) have details of these and other walks.

Lake Windermere, the largest of the lakes in the district (10½ miles long), has a much softer aspect than most, the happy product of its luxuriantly wooded banks, filled with rhododendrons that burst into flaming color each June. The waterfront of Bowness has been attractively developed with restaurants overlooking the lake, chandleries, and shops. Visitors who fancy a pint in a traditional Lakeland pub should try the *Hole I'th Wall* in Bowness. (The 16th-century pub derives its name from the hole in the wall that was forged to allow the blacksmith working next door to easily get his ale. Throughout the year pleasure cruises operate from the pier nearby along the length of Windermere between Lakeside at its southern end, Bowness, and Waterhead at its northern end (phone: 09662-3360). These services connect with the Lakeside and Haverthwaite Steam Railway, a private line running 3½ miles south of Lakeside through the attractive valley of the river Leven (operates daily May through September; phone: 05395-31594). There are several small islands in the lake, and on one of them, Belle Isle, stands an 18th-century mansion that was the first completely round house built in England. It is one of the more unusual stately homes in the Lake District, and among its contents are portraits by Romney and lake views by the French landscape painter, Philippe de Loutherbourg. Now a conference center, it is closed to the public. The *Windermere Steamboat Museum* just north of Bowness has a wonderful collection of Victorian and Edwardian steam launches, including *Dolly,* the oldest mechanically propelled boat in the world, built in 1850 (open Easter through October; phone: 09662-5565). The museum pieces are afloat and in working order and you may occasionally see them steaming about on the lake. Races are held on the lake on summer weekends, and the biggest, the annual power boat Grand Prix and Record Attempts Week, take place in October. In late summer there is the Windermere Swim, when well-greased long-distance swimmers brave the chill length of the lake. Also worth visiting is the Lake Windermere Aquarium on Glebe Road, which stocks a comprehensive selection of Lakeland fish such as pike, perch, and finch. Open March through October (phone: 09662-4585/2294).

Midway between Windermere and Ambleside off A591 is the Brockhole National Park Centre, a country house set in beautiful gardens and grounds that reach down to the lake. The center (phone: 09662-6601) has a constant program of lectures, films, and exhibitions covering crafts, natural history, farming, industrial archaeology, the ubiquitous Wordsworths, and other aspects of past and present life in the Lake District, and is open daily from 10 AM, late March to early November.

CHECKING IN: ***Belsfield*** – This magnificent Georgian house overlooking Lake Windermere is decorated with an interesting blend of period pieces and modern furnishings. A new wing (in the garden) has been added, making a total of 66 rooms, and there's a ready-made jogging track that winds through 6 acres of grounds. Bowness-on-Windermere (phone: 09662-2448). Expensive.

Miller Howe – Is it the beautiful view of the placid, tree-lined lake that makes this

13-room hotel seem such a bastion of calm, or is it the impeccable service? In either case, there is hardly a better headquarters for touring the area, and the restaurant is excellent, too. Closed mid-December through February. Rayrigg Rd., Windermere (phone: 09662-2536). Expensive.

Old England – Set in a fine old Georgian house in large gardens overlooking Lake Windermere, this luxurious 82-room hotel is a fine base for enjoying Windermere and other local attractions. All rooms have private facilities, and there is an outdoor swimming pool and first class restaurant. Windermere (phone: 09622-2444). Expensive.

Quarry Garth – Built with stone quarried from its beautifully landscaped grounds, this mansion is typical of scores of private summer retreats built in the lakes by wealthy industrialists. Although there are just 11 guestrooms, the place is run with great professionalism. Ambleside Rd., Windermere (phone: 09662-3761). Expensive.

Low Wood – Overlooking Lake Windermere and built around an old stable dating back to 1600, this impressive hotel has just undergone a major £4-million refurbishment. The 98 rooms have a full range of facilities, including private bath. The hotel boasts a brand new international restaurant and a leisure center whose facilities include a swimming pool, muiti-purpose gym, squash courts, solarium, and Jacuzzi. Windermere (phone: 05394-33773). Expensive to moderate.

EATING OUT: ***Burn How*** – Located in secluded gardens in the center of Bowness is this elegant and comfortable restaurant. First class service and exciting English and French food using only fresh produce. Closed January. Bowness-on-Windermere (phone: 09662-6226). Expensive.

Cedar Manor Hotel and Restaurant – Excellent, freshly prepared food is served here in charming surroundings. Local specialties include Herdwick lamb, sugar-baked Cumberland lamb with Cumberland sauce, and a variety of local puddings. Reservations advised. Windermere (phone: 09662-3192). Expensive.

Gilpin Lodge – Just 2 miles from Windermere on the B5284 road is this peaceful country house hotel and restaurant set in 20 acres of woodlands and gardens. Beautifully prepared 5-course meals are accompanied by splendid wines and service. Crook Road, Windermere (phone: 09662-2295). Expensive.

NEAR SAWREY: The ferry to the other side of Lake Windermere deposits travelers on a road leading to the village of Far Sawrey, then on to the village of Near Sawrey, the site of a literary connection more important to children than to adults. This is Hill Top Farm, the home of a Mrs. Heelis, better known as the author Beatrix Potter, whose Peter Rabbit classics, illustrated with drawings and watercolors of the hills and lakes around the village, have been staple reading for generations of youngsters. The quaint 17th-century farmhouse she lived in is open to the public (daily except Fridays April through October); while you are admiring the drawings on display, there may well be some small child searching earnestly through the garden for a glimpse of Peter, Jemima Puddleduck, Tom Kitten, or other old friends. When Mrs. Heelis died in 1943, she left the whole of her property, including 4,000 acres of land, to Britain's National Trust, a bequest that has done much to preserve the surrounding countryside.

HAWKSHEAD: Just beyond the head of Esthwaite Water, a small lake about 2 miles long, the road threads its way through a picturesque row of buildings. This is the quiet little village of Hawkshead, and it offers an introductory course in Lake District life that begins at the 17th-century *Queen's Head Inn* or the *Drunken Duck,* where you can get a pint of ale to fortify you for a stroll through the stone cottages of the town. Start at the Hawkshead Grammar School (open daily), founded in 1585 by native son Edwin Sandys, Archbishop of York, and attended by Wordsworth between 1779 and

1783. He left a lasting impression by carving his name in one of the original desks. While a student, Wordsworth may have lodged at Ann Tyson's cottage, on a lane off Red Lion Square, before moving to Green End Cottage in the hamlet of Colthouse, east of Hawkshead. Years later, he recalled the Esthwaite area where he spent his schooldays as "that belovèd Vale." A new attraction is the *Beatrix Potter Gallery,* which contains a large selection of Beatrix Potter's original drawings and illustrations. Open daily, March through November. Main St. (phone: 09666-355).

EATING OUT: ***Grizedale Lodge*** – Tucked away in an elegant former shooting lodge in the magnificent Grizedale Forest is this fine restaurant, which serves traditional Lakeland and English fare in lovely surroundings. The 5-course dinners are particularly memorable. Grizedale (phone: 09666-532). Expensive.

From Hawkshead, follow the signs over Hawkshead Hill directly to Coniston or detour via a steep byroad that leads to Tarn Hows, a small fir-fringed lake high in the hills that has the best views of the surrounding countryside, especially of Coniston Water to the south and of the mountain called the "Old Man of Coniston," which lords it over the lake.

CONISTON: Approaching from Hawkshead, Coniston is about half a mile around the northwest tip of Coniston Water. It is another charming village with strong artistic associations. A Turner masterpiece, now hanging in the *Tate Gallery* in London, was based on studies done at dawn from the crags above the village. Wordsworth wrote lovingly of the place and Alfred Lord Tennyson spent his honeymoon at Tent Lodge at the head of the lake. John Ruskin, the writer, painter, critic, social reformer, and scientist, moved here in 1871, producing some of his finest work at his home, Brantwood (open daily April through October and Wednesdays through Sundays November through March), on the lake's eastern shore. He is buried in the Coniston churchyard and a *Ruskin Museum* (open daily April through October) is in the village. It was on Coniston Water that Sir Malcolm Campbell set a world water-speed record of 141 mph in his boat *Bluebird* in 1939, and his son, Donald, later set four world records here. The local history section of the *Ruskin Museum* has photographs of the younger Campbell's last (and fatal) attempt, in 1967, to set a new speedboat record on Coniston Water. To explore in less hair-raising style, take the renovated Victorian steam yacht *Gondola,* which tours the lake 4 or 5 times a day from April through November (phone: 05394-41288).

En Route from Coniston – A593 winds north into the junction of the Great Langdale and Little Langdale valleys. A side trip due west from this point follows a narrow road over two high passes in the mountains. The first, Wrynose Pass, is a long but straightforward climb. The second, Hard Knott Pass (at the top of which stands a Roman fort), is reckoned to be the toughest in Britain, a tortuous snake of a road climbing the fellside by hairpin curves and descending in the same style into Eskdale, the valley of the river Esk. The reward of the route is a series of wonderful views, but unless you're ready for some rigorous, adventurous driving, ignore the turnoff and follow the main road to Ambleside, Rydal, and Grasmere. Another alternative would be to take the cutoff to Elterwater, which has an excellent hotel, the *Britannia Inn,* then proceed directly and spectacularly into Grasmere via the narrow road over High Close, dropping steeply into Grasmere down a hill called Red Bank.

AMBLESIDE: Just less than a mile from the north end of Lake Windermere, Ambleside is an excellent touring base for climbers eager to explore lakeland's hills and forests. Wordsworth's famed Scafell Pike (3,210 feet, the highest peak in England) is a considerable hike from Ambleside, but other peaks are more accessible. Be sure to obtain detailed maps of trails and to make proper arrangements before starting any trek. The local information center is in Ambleside's old Court House in Market Square (phone: 05394-32582). A short distance away, up the lane past the *Salutations* hotel (see *Checking In*), is Stockghyll Force, a beautiful waterfall cascading 70 feet to rocks below. St. Mary's Church, erected in 1854 by Sir Gilbert Scott, has a memorial to Wordsworth and a mural of the village's rush-bearing festival, when flowers and rushes are carried through the streets to the church. The festival is thought to descend from a Roman harvest ceremony and is still held yearly on the first Saturday in July. The recently completed *Zesserellis* complex, off Compston Road, has an excellent selection of specialty boutiques, along with a cinema, pizzeria, and arcade. Visitors should also stop at *Adrian Sankey's Workshops* on Rothay Road where guests can watch lead crystal being made into bowls, vases, and other collectibles (open daily; phone: 05394-33039). Waterhead, the northern terminus of the Lake Windermere pleasure cruises (they can also be boarded at Bowness and at Lakeside) is just south of Ambleside on A591. At Waterhead is *Haye's Garden World* whose gardens are housed in an ornate crystal palace. There is also a café, patio lounge, and adventure playground. It's a great place to visit, whatever the weather. Open daily (phone: 05394-33434). Just 2 miles north is Rydal.

CHECKING IN: ***Rothay Manor*** – Near Ambleside at the head of Lake Windermere, this small, elegant hotel has its own croquet lawn. The country house feeling extends to the restaurant with its traditional cuisine. Closed early January through mid-February (phone: 05394-33605). Expensive.

Salutations – Recently refurbished, this 32-room hotel is based in an old 16th-century coaching inn in the center of Ambleside. All rooms have private facilities. The restaurant serves traditional fare. Lake Rd. (phone: 05394-32244). Moderate.

EATING OUT: ***Stampers*** – A small cellar restaurant in an old stamp house, it used to be the workplace of poet William Wordsworth. A wide range of local homemade dishes is served. Fine food and good service support the restaurant's excellent reputation. Reservations advised. Church St. (phone: 05394-32775). Moderate.

Hobsons – Uniquely located beside the mill wheel on the beautiful Langdale Estate is this famous pub where fine beers and ales are served in hospitable Old World surroundings. The food is highly recommended. Langdale Estate, near Ambleside (phone: 09667-302). Inexpensive.

Sheila's Cottage Country Restaurant and Tea Shop – Ideally located in the center of Ambleside is this delightful cottage serving a wide variety of local meat and seafood specialties. Lunch is served beginning at noon, and mouth-watering Cumbrian teas are served from 2:30 PM. Closed Sundays. The Slack, Ambleside (phone: 05394-33079). Inexpensive.

RYDAL: William Wordsworth, with his wife, three children, sister, and sister-in-law, moved to this village in 1813 and lived here until his death 37 years later. His home, Rydal Mount, is an interesting, rambling old house, open to visitors daily, except Tuesdays in winter (phone: 0966-33002). It contains a large collection of memorabilia, including several portraits of his family and friends, and his personal library. His love of nature is reflected in the 4.5-acre garden he grew around Rydal Mount, as attentively cared for today as by the poet himself. Wordsworth drew heavily on the surrounding countryside for inspiration and poetic images, and the mute crags and flowered hillsides around his home appear repeatedly in his work. But the golden daffodils in Dora's Field, a plot of land below the garden, are not the descendants of the golden host he came upon unexpectedly while wandering "lonely as a cloud." The lake referred to in that poem is Ullswater and the poem predates Wordsworth's move to Rydal.

Just a short distance up the road is Nab Cottage, occupied briefly by Thomas De Quincey (1806) and later by Samuel Taylor Coleridge's eldest son, Hartley. The roadway continues to the village of Grasmere along the north bank of Rydal Water, which is one of the smallest lakes in the district and which, together with the river Rothay, links Lake Windermere to Grasmere Lake.

CHECKING IN: ***Belmont Manor*** – Located midway between Ambleside and Windermere, this brand-new country house hotel is built to luxury standards. Each of its 14 rooms has a whirlpool bath and a full range of private facilities. The hotel is situated on beautiful grounds, with a swimming pool. The restaurant, which serves traditional French and English fare, has made a good name for itself in a short amount of time. Windermere (phone: 05394-33316). Expensive.

GRASMERE: The main route north from Rydal Water skirts Grasmere Lake, just a mile long and half as wide and, with an emerald green island in its center, almost too perfect for words. Farther on, off the highway to the right, is Dove Cottage, another of Wordsworth's homes, perhaps the one where his finest work was written. Set in 30 acres of gardens is Rydal Hall. Owned by the Diocese of Carlisle, this Georgian hall is worth a long look. Open daily (phone: 09665-544/-547). Then, at the heart of the Lake District, lies the beautiful and easily accessible village of Grasmere set against a backdrop of high hills. The road winds through town, its path dictated by the haphazard scattering of houses of somber, blue-green lakeland stone.

Wordsworth and his sister Dorothy lived at Dove Cottage from 1799 until 1808. Before their arrival, the house had been a small inn called the *Dove and Olive Branch.* While they lived there, it became a frequent stop for a stream of eminent literary figures such as Coleridge, William Hazlitt, Charles Lamb, and Sir Walter Scott. After Wordsworth married (and fathered three children), he and his family moved, turning the cottage over to their friends Thomas De Quincey and his wife. A new Wordsworth exhibition building, including a fine restaurant, has been constructed in the Dove Cottage complex to replace the former museum, just across the road. It contains manuscripts of letters and poems and a remarkable collection of portraits on loan from the *National Portrait Gallery.* Both the museum and the cottage are open to the public Easter through September. Wordsworth lived in two more houses in Grasmere, first at Allan Bank where Coleridge was his house guest, then at the old rectory, before moving to Rydal Mount where he spent the rest of his life. Now the squat, foursquare walls of the Church of St. Oswald (parts of which may be 13th century) preside over his grave and those of his wife, his sister, and Hartley Coleridge, buried in a corner of the churchyard within earshot of the river Rothay.

Although August is the most crowded month in which to visit the Lake District, it is also the month of the Grasmere Sports, usually held on the third Thursday of the month. Begun in the mid-1800s to encourage Cumberland and Westmorland wrestling, the event now includes other traditional lakeland sports such as fell running and hound trailing. Until Cumberland and Westmorland were combined into Cumbria County (1974), competition between these rivals was intense, and the administrative alteration hasn't changed anything. The wrestling, especially, is a curious sport to watch. Competitors stand chest to chest and grasp one another by locking arms behind each other's back. The aim of this subtle combat is to throw the opponent to the ground and toward this goal the weighty and well-balanced wrestlers may struggle all day while other events take place elsewhere. Fell running or racing, an all-out dash to the top of the nearest mountain and back, is another spectacle at the Grasmere games. The Guides' Race directly up the steep sides of Butter Crags is undertaken by lean, narrow-chested athletes who move with astonishing speed up the fell to the turning point and then bound back down again with the agility of mountain goats. Other events are the hound trail competitions, which reflect the Lake District's importance as a center for fox hunting, done here on foot with packs of hardy hounds that ripple across the fells after their prey. (Caldbeck, in the far north of the Lake District, was the home of the celebrated huntsman John Peel, about whom John Woodcock Graves wrote the song "D'ye ken John Peel?" that practically became the Cumbrian anthem.)

Grasmere, like Ambleside, also has an annual rush-bearing ceremony, held on the Saturday nearest August 5, St. Oswald's Day. If you want to sample the tasty gingerbread that is distributed to the bearers, stop by the *Old Gingerbread Shop* — the local specialty will make a great snack while driving the rest of the route. There are some other distinctive shops in town, among them *English Lakes Perfumes,* offering such fragrances as Grasmere Rose and Keswick Gardenia, and the *Studio,* with the work of W. Heaton Cooper, best known of the Lake District watercolor artists. The sound of industrious clattering comes from the shop of *Chris Reekie,* weaver, who has a nice display of woolen wear, some of it produced on the original loom on which he served his apprenticeship in Scotland.

CHECKING IN: *Michaels Nook* – A charming Victorian country home furnished by the proprietor, Reginald Gifford, with many beautiful antiques. Reservations are necessary for the very fine restaurant. Guests may use the pool, sauna, and solarium at the nearby *Wordsworth* hotel, also owned by Gifford. Grasmere (phone: 09665-496). Expensive.

Red Lion – This old coaching inn is in the center of the village. Grasmere (phone: 09665-456). Expensive.

White Moss House – Originally three separate cottages, owned by Wordsworth's family until the 1930s. The current owners have made this 7-room hotel into a pleasant place to stay. It overlooks Rydal Water, and there's usually a roaring fire to welcome hikers in from the dampness. The dining room serves some uncommon English dishes and reservations are essential. Closed from early November to mid-March. Rydal Water (phone: 09665-295). Expensive.

Swan – Long ago, Wordsworth brought Sir Walter Scott and other friends to enjoy a dram or two at this old coaching inn. Today it's a friendly 36-room hotel with a good restaurant that features vegetarian dishes. Grasmere (phone: 09665-551). Moderate.

EATING OUT: *Rothay Garden* – Beautifully situated overlooking the Riverside Gardens is this internationally renowned restaurant. An interesting choice of 5-course meals is served using seasonal, local fresh meat, fish, game, and vegetables. Reservations advised. Broadgate, Grasmere (phone: 09665-334). Expensive.

En Route from Grasmere – Continuing north on A591, the road climbs Dunmail Raise. Over the summit, Thirlmere comes into view, a long, lifeless-looking lake from which water runs helped only by gravity to the taps and factories of Manchester, 100 miles to the south. In 1876, the lake level was raised artificially by the construction of a 100-foot-high dam intended to meet the needs of the Industrial Revolution in urban Lancashire. The unintended result was one of the earliest environmental battles in Britain and because of it, seeds were sown that eventually brought about the National Trust and, ultimately, the national parks. The village of Wythburn, at the foot of the lake, was lost in the flooding that occurred in the creation of Manchester's reservoir, but the tiny 17th-century chapel at Wythburn was on high enough ground to survive. It's worth a visit and its parking lot is the starting point of a climbing trail to the peak of Helvellyn, the 3,118-foot mountain that rises to the right of A591. Helvellyn offers spectacular views and can be climbed easily from the Thirlmere side. But the climb is more interesting from the east side where long, lateral ridges fall into Patterdale, a village near Ullswater. There are few more exhilarating scrambles in the whole of Britain than along Striding Edge to Helvellyn summit and back to Patterdale via Swirral Edge.

Keswick, 13 miles from Grasmere, is just a few miles beyond the north end of

Thirlmere. You'll get an excellent view of the area from the crest of Castlerigg, and a road on the right leads to the prehistoric Castlerigg Stone Circle.

KESWICK: Sheltered by the towering Skiddaw (3,053 feet), this ancient and prosperous market town sits close to the north shore of Derwentwater, 3 miles long and a mile wide, surrounded by a delightful mixture of bare rock, grassy banks, and forested glens. It is one of the loveliest (some say *the* loveliest) of lakeland's lakes, and there are rowboats and cruising craft that can be rented to explore its variety, troll for trout and pike, or visit some of the many tiny islands that dot its surface. The remains of a 7th-century retreat are on the island of St. Herbert.

Many poets, including Shelley, Southey, Wordsworth, and Coleridge, were drawn to this area and Keswick's *Fitz Park Museum* displays some of their manuscripts, letters, and personal effects (open daily Easter through October). Hugh Walpole, who lived on the shore of Derwentwater and set his powerful "Herries" series of novels in this valley, is also represented in the collection. Wordsworth's memory slips in again at Old Windebrowe, a 16th-century farmhouse lent to the poet and his sister in 1794. The kitchen and parlor are restored to their early condition and an exhibition illustrates the house's links to a number of other leading literary figures. Southey's home, Greta Hall (Coleridge lived in it for 3 years before the Southey family took over), has become Keswick School, and his body lies in the Crosthwaite churchyard. Southey, Wordsworth, and Coleridge all patronized the bar at the *George Hotel,* which claims to be the oldest structure in town. Judging by the crude stone masonry and faded walls, it may well be. Walpole is buried in St. John's churchyard. The *Cumberland Pencil Museum* is a unique attraction that illustrates pencil making. Pencil drawings are also on display, along with the world's largest pencil. Open daily. Southey Hill Works (phone: 07687-73626).

Keswick earns its living from visitors and caters to them with a long list of hotels and boarding houses; the ubiquitous bed-and-breakfast sign is nowhere more evident than here. The information center, in Moot Hall, Market Sq., during the summer (its winter address is Council Offices, Main St.), can advise you on accommodations, walks, and current happenings (phone: 07687-72645).

Two of the best points for viewing Derwentwater and its environs are at Castle Head (529 feet), just south of Keswick, and at Friar's Crag, a rocky headland on the lake. John Ruskin was particularly enamored of the latter, and there is a memorial to him here. Southey favored the view from the hill near Greta Bridge.

CHECKING IN: ***Lodore Swiss*** – Recently refurbished, this hotel lies on the edge of Derwentwater, 3 miles south of Keswick, with glorious views of the lake and Lodore Falls. The building is fairly large (70 rooms) and very grand in appearance. The restaurant features international, including Swiss, dishes. Facilities include indoor and outdoor pools, sauna, massage, tennis, squash, and boat trips on Derwentwater. There is also a beauty shop and a nursery. Closed January through March. Borrowdale (phone: 059684-285). Expensive.

Mary Mount Country House – Also on the shores of Derwentwater and owned by the Englands, this cozy 15-room hotel, with a paneled bar, is set in beautiful woodlands. Guests have access to some of the facilities of the *Lodore Swiss.* Closed in October. Borrowdale (phone: 059684-223). Moderate.

EATING OUT: ***Grenge Country House*** – Set in an elegant hotel is this fine traditional restaurant with a cozy atmosphere and 5-course dinners, served daily. Reservations advised. Manor Brow, Keswick (phone: 07687-72500). Expensive.

Coledale Inn – With lovely mountain views, this friendly family-run inn is located at Braithwaite, just 2 miles from Keswick. Light snacks and full meals of freshly made local dishes are served daily. Braithwaite, near Keswick (phone: 059682-272). Inexpensive.

En Route from Keswick – Drive south on B5289 to the quite beautiful Borrowdale valley. The road runs between the east shore of Derwentwater and high gray cliffs that are immensely popular with climbers. Before the village of Rosthwaite, the Bowder Stone, a huge boulder that tumbled from some nearby height, stands precariously on edge near Castle Crag, a 900-foot-high rock cone that can be climbed without too much effort in under half an hour. Great Gable, a little farther along the route, is a more challenging target — 2,949 feet of tough climbing. It takes about 3 hours to ascend this monster, but the view is well worth the effort: The entire area from Skiddaw to Windermere, and even the Isle of Man are visible from the crest.

Continue on B5289, crossing over Honister Pass, which rises well over 1,000 feet. From the summit there is an impressive view toward Buttermere Lake, with Fleetwith Pike and the steep face of Honister Crag dominating the road. Beyond the pass, the road drops through rough territory before reaching Gatesgarth farm at the foot of the long, winding descent. The farm specializes in raising Herdwick sheep, a tough breed that is able to survive the often harsh conditions of the Lake District fells. They are thought to be either the original native sheep of Britain or to have been introduced by enterprising Norsemen who settled in this region a thousand years ago. (At the well-known Lakeland Sheepskin stores in Bowness, Ambleside, Kendal, and Keswick, you can buy clothing made from Herdwick wool.)

The placid waters of Buttermere come into view as the roadway curves in a giant U, first west and then north. Buttermere's twin, Crummock Water, lies just beyond to the northwest. The flat mile of valley floor separating the two lakes suggests that they were once one, but each now has its own distinct character. In olden days, the village of Loweswater, off the north end of Crummock Water, was the metropolis of these parts and the pretty village of Buttermere lay tucked between the two lakes, nothing more than a huddle of houses and a small click-mill to grind rye and oats. The local balance shifted with the coming of the road across Honister Pass. The Lake Poets discovered and wrote about Buttermere and its charms, Turner painted the lake and Honister Crag, and gradually the number of visitors increased. Today the village has more than one hotel, including the *Fish* hotel, a typical lakeland inn whose name reflects Buttermere's appeal to trout fishermen, particularly in April, May, and September. The village is also another popular base for climbers, and not far from it is Scale Force, a lively waterfall with a drop of over 120 feet, the object of a short, muddy excursion. The easiest access is by crossing the stream between the two lakes and following the path on the far side, but do wear boots or hiking shoes.

A few miles farther north, B5289 intersects B5292; you can either take B5292 east over Whinlatter Pass (not as steep as Honister Pass) toward A66, Keswick, and Penrith, or extend your trip by heading northwest toward Cockermouth.

COCKERMOUTH: An attractive market town with a number of good antique shops, Cockermouth is famous as Wordsworth's birthplace (1770). It is strategically placed at the junction of the Cocker and Derwent rivers and, though its origins date to pre-Roman times, little remains from its earliest period. Even its 12th-century castle was destroyed during the Civil War violence of the mid-1600s. Wordsworth House (open daily except Thursdays April through October) was built in 1745. This house, in which Dorothy and William were born and grew up, is a fairly simple, countrified example of Georgian architecture that has survived intact. The furnishings used by the Wordsworth family, however, are long gone. William's father is buried in the churchyard. Fletcher Christian, leader of the mutiny on the *Bounty,* was born in 1764 at

Moorland Close, a nearby farmhouse. A special place to take children is the *Doll and Toy Museum* where they can play with a huge variety of toys, including dolls, model railways, and remote control racing cars. Open daily, March through October (phone: 0900-85259).

CHECKING IN: ***Pheasant Inn*** – This 16th-century coaching inn, with 20 rooms, huge log fires, and a traditional atmosphere, is on Bassenthwaite Lake near Thornthwaite Forest. Views of the lake are, unfortunately, blocked by a hill. Food in the pub restaurant is simple and English. Bassenthwaite Lake, off A66, near Cockermouth (phone: 059681-234). Moderate.

En Route from Cockermouth – Take A5086 south, explore the western fringe of the Lake District, and leave the area the same way you came in, via Kendal. Or return east through Keswick, detour from the main road onto A5091 to the shore of Ullswater, and leave the district via its northern gateway, Penrith.

If you choose A5086 south, Ennerdale Water, perhaps the least visited of the larger lakes, lies about 10 miles away, on a secondary roadway to the east. A similar turnoff about 10 miles beyond leads to Wastwater, the deepest of the lakes, set among stern and savage-faced mountains in marked contrast to the gentle placement of Windermere. The village of Wasdale Head, a mile beyond the lake, is an excellent climbing center, but these mountains are strictly for experts. Return to the main road (A5086 becomes A595 near Ennerdale Water) and drive to Ravenglass, a port at the mouth of the river Esk about 25 miles from Cockermouth. The Eskdale valley can be explored either by road or on the narrow-gauge, steam-powered *Ravenglass and Eskdale Railway* (narrow is an understatement — 15 inches make it positively skinny), which runs between Ravenglass and Dalegarth Station near the village of Boot year-round, although there's limited service in winter (phone: 06577-226). Just beyond Ravenglass, Muncaster Castle, the seat of the Pennington family for 700 years, overlooks the Esk (open Tuesdays through Sundays Easter through September and bank holidays). Farther on, at Broughton, another secondary road (A593) leads up toward Coniston. Just east of Broughton, A595 bears south along the coast, and A5092 continues east toward A590, A6, the market town of Kendal, and the M6 motorway.

If you choose to visit Ullswater, return to Keswick (either on the main A66 road or on B5292 across Whinlatter Pass). Follow the main road east out of town for 9 miles, then turn south onto A5091, which leads to the second largest of the region's lakes, a lovely winding stretch of water cradled by high fells. The best way to explore Ullswater is to set out on it. Boats are for hire and cruises start at Glenridding pier at the head of the lake, and at its northern end, Pooley Bridge, with a pier to match, is another place to arrange a day's outing. A major attraction near Pooley Bridge is the 18th-century Dalemain Historic House with delightful gardens. There are also two museums and splendid public rooms, as well as a gift shop, restaurant, and adventure playground. Open Sundays through Thursdays (phone: 08536-450). The lake is only 7½ miles long (and an average ½ mile wide) but the distance between the two towns by road is 13 miles, along a stretch of A592 that skirts the northern bank of Ullswater, bypassing Gowbarrow Park. This grassy fell comes alive with daffodils each year and traveling poets can, as Wordsworth did, pause beneath the trees to write about the yellow blooms that may be "fluttering and dancing in the breeze" just as they were when he saw them. On the lake's western shore, the pretty Aira Force waterfall is a pleasant place to stop. A worthwhile diversion from Pooley Bridge is the secondary road along the southern shore of the lake past the *Sharrow Bay Hotel,* which surveys the most scenic views in the district (see *Checking In*); the road leads ultimately to the peaceful valley of Martindale.

Route A592 continues northeast of Ullswater toward Penrith. (South of Glenridding at the opposite end of the lake it heads toward Windermere, crossing the Helvellyn mountain range through Kirkstone Pass, at the summit of which is the *Kirkstone Pass Inn,* one of the highest taverns in England. On the far side of the pass are the Troutbeck Valley, the village of Troutbeck, and the 17th-century Townend House, once the residence of a yeoman's family. The interior, furnishings, and timbered barn remain intact and can be visited daily except Mondays and Saturdays, from April to October.)

CHECKING IN: *Leeming House* – Commanding fine views over Ullswater, this is a gracious, porticoed Georgian country house sitting on 20 acres of landscaped gardens on the northern shore of the lake, not far from the site of the famous daffodils. The 25 rooms all have private baths, and the restaurant is rather grand. Fishing during the summer. Watermillock (phone: 08536-622). Expensive.

Sharrow Bay – Partners Francis Coulson and Brian Sack have spent years making this spot one of the most respected and attractive hotels in the area. This stone country house is on the southern shore of Ullswater, about 2 miles from Pooley Bridge, and rooms in a farmhouse addition are another mile down the road. The restaurant's dinners are a pleasure. Closed December, January, and February. Pooley Bridge (phone: 08536-301). Expensive.

Old Church – About 400 yards of Ullswater lap the front lawn of this 18th-century Georgian country house, with 10 rooms (all with private bath) and a restaurant serving good English fare. Watermillock (phone: 08536-204). Moderate.

PENRITH: This charming town was burned twice during the 14th century by bands of marauding Scots from across the border, but since then it has withstood time and the onslaught of travelers comfortably. Its oldest section grew up around the 13th-century Church of St. Andrew (rebuilt in the 1700s) and the nearby 16th-century schoolhouse. Several conflicting legends surround the presence of the two stone formations on the church grounds, known as Giant's Grave and Giant's Thumb: One version holds that this is the burial place of an ancient king. The ruins of Penrith Castle are now a town park, but two fine 16th-century inns, the *Gloucester Arms* and the *Two Lions,* are still thriving. Close to the town center, near the main railway station, is the *Penrith Steam Museum* which displays steam traction engines (in steam most days), steam models, and working blacksmith's and engineer's shops. Open Mondays through Fridays, Easter through September. Castlegate Foundry (phone: 0768-67466).

CHECKING IN: *North Lakes Gateway* – Conveniently located off junction 40 of the M6 (though not near enough to be affected by the noise of the traffic), this new hotel has 85 rooms, and the facilities include a sauna, swimming pool, Jacuzzi, snooker room, squash courts, and a mini-gym. The restaurant serves a wide range of traditional fare. Ullswater Rd. (phone: 0768-68111). Expensive.

Penrith is at the convergence of several main roads. From here you can take M6 just west of town, pick up A74, and follow A75 into Dumfries to connect with the *Scottish Lowlands* route.

Wales

It doesn't take long to understand why Wales is to many Welshmen a song and an inspiration. It has been so for many centuries. From the earliest times — and Welsh has been written since the 7th century AD — bards have expressed their love of their land. And what an enchanting and enthralling land it is.

Wales is small. So you can get to know quite a lot of it even in a short time. It is just over 8,000 square miles, about half the size of Switzerland, has about 2.8 million people — and about 6 million sheep. It is about 200 miles in length and it takes about 4 hours to travel from north to south in a car in normal conditions. But don't: It would be like bolting down an ambrosial meal.

Wales is special. From its seabird-haunted islets and seal-sentried rocks reaching out into the Irish Sea, to its mountains where Everest teams train, Wales mixes sudden drama with soft stillness. There is a grandeur about it, a sense of stubbornness. It is brightly pastoral, offset here and there with dark smudges of industry.

While Cardiff, the capital, can be reached by the new 125-mph supertrains in less than 2 hours from London, there is a sense in which Wales remains England's unknown neighbor. It is, as it has always been, a mountainous stronghold in the west. The land and the original Celtic people somehow keep their separate character. And a fifth of the people still use the Welsh language, rich in literature and color, older than English, the tongue of the original Britons. It is therefore a great vehicle for legends: Perhaps the legendary King Arthur himself roamed the hills of Wales in noble defiance of the encroaching Saxons.

Indeed, it was the Saxons who gave Wales its name. They called the fiercely defiant people who lived there the *wealas,* meaning "foreigners." The Welsh, however, gave their land a different name: Cymru (pronounced Kum-ree), "the land of brothers." You'll see the word on the signs as you cross the border: "Croeso i Gymru — Welcome to Wales." (Don't be worried that Cymru changes to Gymru. Welsh is a language in which certain initial letters change, depending on the words preceding them.)

Bear in mind, as you travel around, that the story of the language is a considerable part of the story of Wales. It is one of the oldest languages and literatures in Europe. It is flowing and musical. And lovely Welsh first (given) names remain very popular. Females have names like Lowri, Menna, Megan, and Rhiannon. Males are called Idris, Owen, and Rhys. This does not present a problem for the visitor, however — nearly everyone speaks English, albeit with a distinctive lilt.

In the 6th and 7th centuries Wales became a largely Christian country through the work of St. David and his followers. And St. David, the patron saint, is one of the prime figures of Welsh history. Between the 6th and 13th century Wales was divided into kingdoms and princedoms. The rulers sometimes fought among themselves as well as battling the English on the border. But there were exceptions, like the 10th-century King Hywel Dda (Hywel the Good), who framed laws for an orderly way of life. Hywel was not blind to human problems: He was a pioneer supporter of women's equality and decreed that a woman could get a divorce if her husband were impotent and had halitosis!

Under men like Hywel, culture flourished and the *eisteddfod* (pronounced eye-steth-vod), a competitive festival of poetry and song, became part of the Welsh tradition. There are numerous *eisteddfodau* in Wales today, the biggest being the *National Eisteddfod,* which attracts huge crowds. This festival is traditionally a nomadic one, held alternately in north and south Wales. In 1990 it is scheduled to take place in the town of Cwmrumney from August 4 through 11 (phone: 0222-398399). The bardic ceremonies, held on Tuesdays and Thursdays, were invented in the last century to provide pageantry (but no one takes them *too* seriously), and the winning poets are treated like pop stars, feted by crowds, blinking in the TV lights. What other country has, as national hero and king-for-a-day, a poet? The other eisteddfod worth a mention is the *International Eisteddfod,* held every July in a huge field on the boundaries of Llangollen in Clywd, North Wales. Created originally to promote harmony between nations, it now attracts some 30 competing musical teams from all corners of the globe.

During the 12th and 13th centuries the rulers of England sought to bring the troublesome Welsh under their control. The most striking reminders of this period are the great castles that dot the land. There are scores of them, many of them the finest in Europe, majestic residue of war and conquest. They look splendid against their backdrops of coast or mountains and reflect the wild land they were built to defend and subdue. Among the best are the eight built by King Edward I of England to complete and sustain his conquest. Hugely expensive, they brought the King to fiscal crisis. But warrior Edward was determined to defeat Llywelyn, the last native Prince of Wales, and bring the country to heel. Llywelyn's head ended up on a pike in London, and Wales came under English control.

In 1536, during the reign of King Henry VIII, Wales and England were formally joined together and made equal under the law. In the same century the Bible was translated into Welsh, the single most important influence on the language's survival. It made the Welsh a literate people in their own language. And in the 19th century, when Wales embraced the nonconformist form of worship, the Welsh Bible was a keystone of education. During this century the Welsh language has declined in numerical strength. Some fear that it will eventually die out, and there have been many campaigns to strengthen it. Threatened as it is, it nevertheless remains strong and lively in certain respects. It is the domestic language of many people (there are more than a quarter of a million who speak it) and it lives in books, songs, comics, radio, and television.

Much of Wales is rural. It is a farming country. In the mountains you can see the tough little hill farms and hear shepherds whistling for their scruffy, intelligent, black and white dogs. A good Welsh sheepdog is worth hundreds of pounds.

The southeast of the country is heavily industrial (coal mining, steel making, and manufacturing), and this is where most people live. The coal-mining belt stretches from Ebbw Vale in the east to Ammanford in the west, an area known as The Valleys. The narrow and tortuous valleys were once peaceful and wooded gorges, but the coal age changed everything. South Wales became an industrial powerhouse, one of the keys to British economic expansion. A century ago this part of Wales was the most intensively mined area of the world, and during the coal rush thousands of workers poured in from rural Wales, England, Ireland, Italy, Greece, and Spain. They made an exciting mixture, creating a varied and fascinating community, renowned for its spirit, its politics, and its culture. Coal's heyday has passed, but the valley towns, with their neat rows of houses slotted into the steep hillsides and the huge chapels standing guard, remain alluring.

While Welsh coal was warming the world, Welsh slate was roofing it. The great slate quarries and caverns of north Wales were the heart of a big industry. But that industry has shrunk dramatically and vast heaps of slate waste are monuments to an epoch.

Thus Wales is a place of contrasts. You don't have to be there long before you realize how it is weathered by history's storms. Its patches of industrial ugliness are honorable scars. And it has some of the loveliest scenery you are ever likely to see. As for the people, they are proud of their land, aware of its difference, and immensely hospitable. Their accents are distinctive (you will soon tell a South Welshman from a North Welshman) and their humor is delightful.

It is no wonder that Wales intrigues. It has a certain magic about it, an intangible something in the Celtic air.

Our route gives travelers the essential flavor, starting in the southeast and traversing the Brecon Beacons to lovely Carmarthen. It is all dramatic hills, soft pools, rushing waterfalls, and stately rivers. The route heads northwest across old Cardiganshire and to the pleasant and softer land of mid-Wales. Farther on it forges into sublime Snowdonia with its darkly handsome peaks and robust and defiant cottages and farms. It will be hard to resist the temptation to take diversions from the route. Why resist? Off the beaten track are many small pubs, guesthouses, farmhouses, and restaurants where you can get a night's stay and a decent meal for a very reasonable price.

Expect to pay $90 and up for a double room in those places we've listed as expensive; $60 to $90 in the moderate category; and under $60 in the inexpensive range. You'll find that a good majority of the hotels we list in the Welsh countryside are inexpensive — usually small inns with few rooms and delightful surroundings. But even expensive Welsh hotels aren't *too* expensive considering the experience that awaits. No matter where you stay, and even if it's off-season, book your room well in advance. This is especially crucial in summer months when the national music festivals are held throughout the country. Over the last few years, there has been an increase in the number and quality of restaurants in Wales. Witness the *Walnut Tree Inn* near Abergavenny (see below), which won Egon Ronay's Best Restaurant in Britain award in 1987. This recent example notwithstanding, the best (outside Cardiff) are still found in the better hotels, the remainder tending to be small, inexpensive cafés that seem to be caught in a time warp, left behind by the rest of Britain. Expect to pay at least $45 for dinner for two, including wine, at restaurants we list as expensive; $30 to $45, moderate; and under $30 for an inexpensive meal. For further information contact the Wales Tourist Board, Brunel House, Cardiff CF2 1UY (phone: 0222-499909).

MONMOUTH: The Romans saw at once that this site had an important strategic position at the junction of the rivers Monnow and Wye and built a fort here that they called Blestium. There is not much left of the later Norman fortifications except the remarkable bridge and gate house over the Monnow, dating from the 13th century. And, almost nothing remains of the castle where King Henry V was born, probably in 1387. Today, Monmouth is an easygoing market town content with its role. There is an 18th-century shire hall in Agincourt Square with statues of Henry V and Charles Rolls (1877–1910), founder of Rolls-Royce, who grew up nearby. The bottom of the hall is now a cluster of market stalls and parts of the interior, though not original, are interesting and attractive, especially the staircase and dome. Behind the hall is the *Nelson Museum* with some of the sea hero's memorabilia.

The countryside surrounding Monmouth is delightful, particularly the Wye valley. And you can take a meandering side trip to Tintern by driving 7 miles south on the A466 road. The abbey, a lovely 13th- and 14th-century ruin in a tranquil setting beside the river Wye, was founded by a Baron Walter de Clare in 1131. The building fell victim to Henry VIII's Dissolution of the Monasteries in 1539. But though roofless and ruined, it's still romantic and inspiring. William Wordsworth, who wrote the famous poem about the abbey, commented, "No poem of mine was composed under circumstances more pleasant than this."

CHECKING IN: ***King's Head*** – King Charles I of England, beheaded in 1649, is said to have stayed in this handsome place, and there is a fine plaster cast of him to ponder. A bar, a restaurant, and 29 comfortable rooms, each with a private bath. Agincourt Sq., Monmouth (phone: 0600-2177). Moderate.

Stowe Court – Just over the English border, this small 17th-century country house has only 3 double rooms, each with either bath or shower. Book ahead if you'd like a four-course dinner in addition to bed and breakfast. The owners run an antiques shop on the premises and conduct antiques-oriented tours of the Wye Valley, the Forest of Dean, Bath, Bristol, Cheltenham, and Cardiff. St. Briavels, Lydney (phone: 0594-530214). Inexpensive.

En Route from Monmouth – In Gwent, 8 miles on the main A40, is Raglan Castle, built in the 1430s. It's the central feature of the little town and one of the best examples of late medieval castles. One of its oldest sections is the moated, partly destroyed Great Yellow Tower of Gwent. Henry VII lived here as a boy, and Charles I stayed at the castle after his army lost the battle of Naseby in the civil war. Note especially the large hall, the six-sided keep, and the long, surrounding wall.

Six miles south of Raglan, off the A449 road to Newport, is the meadowy little borough of Usk built on the bank of the river from which it derives its name. Taste Usk salmon while you're here; it's justly famous. The history-minded will enjoy the 13th-century Church of St. Mary's and the ruins of the castle dating from the days when barons ruled the border country in the 12th century.

Take A40 west from Raglan to Abergavenny.

ABERGAVENNY: Gateway to the Brecon Beacons National Park, bustling market town, soaked in history, Abergavenny stands beside the river Usk guarded by four mountains: Sugar Loaf, Blorenge, Skirrid, and Little Skirrid. The streets of Abergavenny are lined with Tudor, Georgian, and Victorian buildings, and canny trading takes place in the marketplace, where weatherbeaten farmers sell their sheep, pigs, cattle, and horses. Romans and Normans occupied the site of the town because of its strategic location, and the frontier Braose family made it their base in the battles against the Welsh. Tough William Braose invited Welsh chiefs to a Christmas dinner at Abergavenny castle in 1175 and had them murdered while they supped. The treacherous baron had his comeuppance years later: King John stripped his lands from him in 1207 and William died a beggar in 1211. The castle ruins are worth exploring and from here you can get a great view over the rolling hills. Inside the castle is the *Abergavenny and District Museum.* Abergavenny is a good center for tourists: Hill-walking, fishing, and pony trekking are excellent and you can rent canal cruisers on the west side of town. *Red Line Boats* (Goytre Wharf, Llanover; phone: 0873-880516) has half-day ($30), full-day ($45), and weekly (from $415) rentals. *Road House Holiday Hire* (Main Rd., Gilwern, Gwent; phone: 0873-830240) rents narrowboats — traditional canal boats never more than 6 feet 10 inches wide — on a weekly basis only (about $305 to $600). *Beacon Park Boats* (Llangattock Park House, Crickhowell; phone: 0873-810240) offers half- and full-day rentals and weekly cruises; a 4-berth boat costs from $460 to over $600 a week. There is a tourist information center on Monk Street with an exhibition on Brecon Beacons National Park.

CHECKING IN: ***Angel*** – This handsome old coaching inn, with 29 comfortable rooms and a restaurant, is in the center of town, convenient to the many attractions in the area. Cross St., Abergavenny (phone: 0873-7121). Expensive.

EATING OUT: ***Walnut Tree Inn*** – Advance booking is essential here, especially since it won the Egon Ronay Best Restaurant in Britain award for 1987. Fish dishes, which change daily, predominate, but patrons will also find more elaborate creations, such as guinea fowl with port and truffles. There's an excellent and entertaining wine list. Llandewi Skirrid, 2 miles north of Abergavenny (phone: 0873-2797). Expensive.

En Route from Abergavenny – On A40 toward Brecon is a delightful stretch through the Usk valley, with the Black Mountains to the right and the outriders of the Brecon Beacons to the left. There are pubs and small cottages, and little towns like Crickhowell that welcome fishermen and pony trekkers. Many travelers speak highly of the *Nant-y-ffin Cider Mill* in Crickhowell where you can get hearty homemade food — terrines, pies, cheesecake, and (in season) local salmon. All along this road are interesting narrow lanes turning off into the hills and anyone with the time and inclination to roam is advised to do just that: Turn off and explore. For example, at Llansantffraid you can turn left toward Talybont and drive for 9 miles through forest and hills to Talybont and Taf Fechan reservoirs: This is lovely walking and picnicking country. Another pleasant diversion on the road from Abergavenny to Brecon is to Hay-on-Wye — although you will need the best part of a day to enjoy it. Turn right onto A479 just after Crickhowell, coast through the hills for about 20 miles to Talgarth, and pick up A438 north to B4350 to Hay-on-Wye. Hay is a picturesque little border town, whose main industry is secondhand books; it is absolutely bulging with books, a paradise for bibliophiles, and is reckoned to be the world's largest secondhand bookshop. The *Hay-on-Wye Festival* (about 10 days beginning at the end of May) had its first highly successful run in 1988. It features international writers, local poets, exhibitions, major theatrical events, and the annual Raymond Williams lecture honoring the great border novelist and critic. From here, get back on A438 southwest to Brecon.

BRECON: The district is still called by the old name of Brecknock, as you will see on some maps, while the town of Brecon is known in the Welsh language as *Aber-*

honddu. Its English name is derived from *Brychan,* the vigorous Irish chieftain (sire of 36 children, the story goes) who ruled this region in the 5th century. The Welsh name is taken from the river Honddu which runs into the Usk. Brecon has narrow streets, a cathedral, a busy livestock market, good shops and pubs, and a peaceful air. It's also a convenient home base for exploring Brecon Beacons National Park. The 13th-century cathedral, built first as a fortified priory, overlooks the river Honddu. The town's castle, built by the half-brother of William the Conqueror, was dismantled by the townsfolk during the 17th-century civil war in an attempt to avoid the bloodshed necessary to defend it. The remaining parts of the castle are now in the garden of the *Castle of Brecon* hotel (see *Checking In*).

The *Brecknock Museum,* in the old County Hall in Glamorgan Street, displays interesting examples of Welsh folk art and local crafts, such as the hand-carved wooden "lovespoons" young Welshmen used in bygone days to plight their troth (closed Sundays).

CHECKING IN: ***Castle of Brecon*** – Built of stone and overlooking the River Usk, this hotel adjoins castle ruins. There are 34 bedrooms, 12 more in an annex, and children's facilites, including a babysitting service. Castle St. (phone: 0874-4611).

Miskin Manor – This stone manor house, set on 20 acres of Wye Valley parkland, was glorious in its 1920s heyday (when the then Prince of Wales paid a visit). It deteriorated over the years, but has been restored to its former glory. Miskin, Mid Glamorgan (phone: 0443-224204). Expensive.

Nythfa House – Another Georgian house nicely set on 4 acres, it has 9 guestrooms, squash courts, and a sauna (phone: 0874-4287). Moderate.

Wellington – This old, established centerpiece of Brecon Beacons National Park has 21 comfortable, recently refurbished rooms, a restaurant, and two bars that serve a good variety of beers. The Bulwark (phone: 0874-5225). Moderate.

Bishops Meadow – Most people stay here for the great views of the Beacons. It's a modern motel with 24 rooms, bar, cafeteria, and gas station. On B438, also called Hay Rd. (phone: 0874-2051). Moderate to inexpensive.

George – A small, straightforward place in the center of town, perfect for 1-night stopovers. All 7 rooms come with private baths. Brecon (phone: 0874-3422). Inexpensive.

Landsdowne – In this handsome Georgian building are 12 pleasant rooms and a good restaurant. The Watton (phone: 0874-3321). Inexpensive.

En Route from Brecon – Take A470 south toward Merthyr Tydfil, for grand views of the Beacons' red sandstone peaks. Turn right after Libanus along A4215 to Defynnog and you will soon pick up signs directing you to the Mountain Centre of Brecon Beacons National Park. The park covers 519 square miles, running east to west, in the heart of the mountains of South Wales. The center is out in the wilds and a friendly, informal place where the park's staff is keen to help in your exploration of the mountains. You can use the center as a base for walking, for picnicking, for light meals, or for just sitting and staring (highly recommended). Join up with the A40 trunk road at Sennybridge, a pleasant town, and head west for Trecastle, with its engaging landscape. It used to be an important stop in the old coaching days, and its coaching inns deserve a visit. It is worth pausing here, anyway, to decide on your route to Llandeilo. You can continue on the A40 road, through the village of Halfway, and then go on to Llandovery — in Welsh *Llanymddyfri* ("the church among the waters"). Llandovery is a pleasant town where you can eat well and stay comfortably. It stands by the Tywi (Towy) river, the longest of Welsh rivers and famous for its salmon. The alternative route to Llandeilo needs more careful navigation. From Trecastle, turn left along a little-used country road toward Llanddeusant and thread your way through Twynllanan and up A4069 to Llangadog, a quiet market town. The attractive, quiet village of Bethlehem, off A4069, is also worth a visit.

LLANDEILO: Near this small riverside town are several interesting castles. Dinefwr Castle, described by writer Jan Morris as "the most haunting" castle in Wales, was built in AD 876 by Rhodri the Great, who divided the kingdom of Wales among his three sons so as to strengthen its defenses against invaders. Dinefwr — given to son Cadell — was the stronghold of South Wales. The castle also featured in the wars between the Welsh and the English in medieval times, and was improved by members of the great Rhys family. After the English conquest, Dryslwyn Castle was the center of a Welsh uprising led by Lord Rhys in 1287. It failed, and Lord Rhys was beheaded. Carreg Cennen Castle stands atop a cliff, naturally fortified and a hard nut for those warring medieval chiefs to crack. Dating from about the 13th century, it commands a marvelous view of the Black Mountain. Caerphilly, 8 miles north of Cardiff, is famous as the home of one of Europe's largest castles; the castle's leaning tower (a result of Civil War blasting) features an exhibition recounting the complete history of castle building in Wales.

CHECKING IN: ***Cawdor Arms*** **–** In the center of town with 17 rooms, it's a convenient base for touring West Wales. Rhosmaen St., Llandeilo (phone: 0558-823500). Moderate.

EATING OUT: ***Angel Inn*** **–** This small place is memorable for its home cooking, especially the dessert trolley. Salem (phone: 0558-823394). Inexpensive.

CARMARTHEN: King Arthur's magician, Merlin (Myrddin), was said to have been born hereabouts and that's how this most pleasant of towns got its name. In Welsh it is called *Caerfyrddin,* or "Merlin's City." (The historians tell us that Merlin did not exist, that he lived before Arthur, that he was a mad prophet in Celyddon Wood capable of conversing with animals, that he was based on an Irish poem, or that he was borrowed from the Old Norse.) In ancient times, as now, "Merlin's City" occupied an important and strategic position above the Tywi (Towy) River. The Romans had a base here, as the deteriorated amphitheater testifies, and the ruins of the Norman castle can still be seen. During the early part of the 12th century, monks collected and wrote poems in the *Black Book of Carmarthen,* the oldest known Welsh manuscript, which can be seen in the National Library of Wales in Aberystwyth on the west coast.

Carmarthen is also the administrative hub of the southwestern corner of Wales. Its large covered market draws crowds every Wednesday and Saturday, and behind it the cattle market holds sales each Monday, Wednesday, and Thursday.

In Nott Square stands a monument to Dr. Robert Ferrar, Bishop of St. David's, who was burned at the stake on this site in 1555. Also of interest is the museum housed in what was the Bishop's Palace at Abergwili, on the outskirts of town. Merlin's Oak, formerly on Priory Street, has been moved to the museum's grounds. Legend says that when the oak falls, so will the town; to make sure it does not topple, the townspeople have propped it up with concrete.

An interesting 13-mile side trip from Carmarthen is to Laugharne (pronounced Larn), where the Welsh poet Dylan Thomas (1914–1953) lived and wrote many of his famous works. You can visit his home, called the *Boathouse,* now a Dylan Thomas museum (open daily); *Brown's* hotel, where he drank; and the churchyard where he is buried. Laugharne is reached by driving along A48 to St. Clear's and turning left on A4066. Six miles farther is Pendine with its romantic stretch of sands, on which 1930s heroes smashed world speed records in their roaring cars.

CHECKING IN: ***Ivy Bush Royal*** – With 79 rooms and a sauna, this is certainly one of the best hotels in rural west Wales in terms of atmosphere, design, service, and cuisine. Spilman St., Carmarthen (phone: 0267-235111). Moderate.

Waungron Farm – A comfortable, family-run hotel. Its 14 rooms have four-poster beds and private bath/showers. Good local produce is on the restaurant menu. Waungron Isaf, Whitland, Dyfed (phone: 0994-240682). Inexpensive.

En Route from Carmarthen – For 5 miles, A484 winds through pleasant wooded country to little Cynwyl Elfed with its white- and color-washed cottages, a genuine piece of old Carmarthenshire calm and beauty. Seven miles north of here the road branches northwest to Cenarth, noted for its waterfalls and the last of the coracle men on this stretch of river Teifi. A *coracle* is a little basket-shaped boat made from tarred cloth stretched over a frail wooden frame, and it's been used in Wales for 2,000 years. Coracle fishermen work in pairs, drifting down the river with a net suspended between their boats to catch salmon and sewin, a delicious sea trout. After drifting for a while, the fishermen climb onto the riverbank, hump their coracles onto their backs, and walk back up the river to start all over again. During the 19th century, there were thousands of coracles on Welsh rivers, but laws framed to conserve fish and protect the sport of salmon fishing steadily squeezed the coracle men out. Today there are only about a dozen left, and most are on the rivers Teifi and Tywi around Carmarthen.

If you branch right, on A486, you will soon be in charming Llandysul, with its late Norman church and bridge spanning the river rapids. Here you can pick up A475 to Lampeter. If you have time, pick your way through the lanes and little roads to Llanybydder, a Teifi-side market town with a tradition of weaving. Factories such as the Siwan Woollen Mills (Llansawel Rd.; phone: 0570-480722) welcome visitors. Try to be in town on the last Thursday of any month for the horse fairs, which attract buyers the world over. From Llanybydder it is only 7 miles into Lampeter.

LAMPETER: Lampeter in Welsh is *Llanbedr Pont Steffan.* It's a busy place, where farming folk meet, set in the lush land of the upper Teifi valley. The most famous landmark is St. David's College, part of the University of Wales since 1972. Founded in 1822, it had been a college for training students for ordination in the Episcopalian state church, continued after disestablishment, and was incorporated into the University when it became a liberal arts college. Its buildings are open to visitors.

CHECKING IN: ***Falcondale*** – A historic Victorian country house, set in its own 14-acre parkland grounds, with 20 bedrooms with private bath, a restaurant, 2 bars, and banquet and conference facilities. Activities include fishing, golf, pony trekking, tennis, and clay pigeon shooting (phone: 0570-422910). Moderate.

Black Lion Royal – This hostelry has 14 comfortable rooms, 7 with bath, and a restaurant. High St., Lampeter (phone: 0570-422172). Inexpensive.

En Route from Lampeter – You have a choice of roads to Tregaron: The main A485 is quicker, but B4343 on the eastern side of the Teifi is beautiful. The latter passes through Llanfair Clydogau, where the Romans mined silver, no doubt with the labor of indigenous slaves. The lure of Welsh gold and silver was one reason why the Romans conquered and colonized Britain. The 2,000-year-old gold mines in the hills at Dolaucothi are now open for guided tours. Four miles on is Llanddewi Brefi, where St. David, patron saint of Wales, preached in 519. Stop for a look at the 13th-century church, supposedly built on the spot where David delivered an inspirational sermon.

Tregaron is 3 miles from Llanddewi Brefi. It's a friendly market town with craft workshops and welcoming inns. In the square is a statue of the town's most famous son, Henry Richard (1812–88), who was a member of parliament for Merthyr Tydfil and dubbed the Apostle of Peace for his espousal of international arbitration and founding of the Peace Union, a forerunner of the United Nations. Twm Shon Catti, a 16th-century Robin Hood–like character, rogue, and poet, was born and roamed near here. Just north of the town is the 4-mile-long Bog of Tregaron, said to be the largest peat bog in Britain and now the Cors Tregaron Nature Reserve. Tregaron earns part of its living as a pony-trekking summer holiday center, and the land here is just right for riding: wild and remote. The central agency to contact for information on pony trekking is the Tregaron Pony Trekking Association, Tregaron (phone: 09744-364). It will cost about $18 for a full day of riding.

Not many people know the road from Tregaron to Llanwrtyd Wells (20 miles away; known locally as the Abergweryn Pass), but it is a thrilling journey over a narrow and winding mountain pass. Once in Llanwrtyd, you can pay a visit to the Cambrian Woollen Factory where yarn, spun from locally made wool, is sold. Our main route, however, continues up B4343 to Pontrhydfendigaid and the abbey at Strata Florida, known in Welsh as *Ystrad Fflur,* or "Valley of the Flowers." The abbey, built by Cistercian monks in the 12th and 13th centuries, suffered in the fighting between the Welsh and English in medieval days, and received a final blow when Henry VIII ordered the destruction of monasteries. Although crumbled, it's worth a look. Legend has it that beneath a yew is the grave of Dafydd ap Gwilym, one of the leading medieval poets of Europe, who divided his time between making verse and love.

In this district of old Cardiganshire there were once many lead mines, and the narrow-gauge steam railway, which runs from Devil's Bridge to Aberystwyth on the coast, started life as an ore-carrying line. It's a romantic ride today.

CHECKING IN: ***Lake*** **–** A luxurious country house/hotel on 50 acres, with one of Wales's best dining rooms, and 19 bedrooms with private bath. Activities include golf, tennis, and fishing. Llangammarch Wells (phone: 05912-202). Expensive.

ABERYSTWYTH: A popular seaside resort with both sand and pebble bathing beaches, Aberystwyth is also the seat of the major college for Welsh speakers through the University of Wales and the administrative center for Cardigan Bay. Its lively seafront promenade is lined with hotels and has a bandstand and the ruins of a castle, which stand sentinel on the headland.

History is carefully preserved at the National Library of Wales (Penglais Hill), which houses some of the earliest Welsh manuscripts; and the past is still alive at the station where British Railways' last steam-powered service departs for the spectacular falls at Devil's Bridge, high in the Vale of Rheidol, which according to legend was built by the devil himself. Closer to home, the town's cliff railway carries visitors to the peak of Constitution Hill, where they have a splendid view of the bay and town.

Concerts and evening shows are regular features along the promenade. The *Arts Centre* holds frequent exhibitions and the *University Theatre* presents a summer season of plays. Four miles east of Aberystwyth, off A4120, is the Nanteos Stately Home, a Georgian mansion with an imposing oak staircase, some fine plasterwork, and Italian marble.

CHECKING IN: ***Belle Vue Royal*** **–** This seafront hotel overlooking Cardigan Bay has a large restaurant, 42 comfortable rooms, and an 18-hole golf course nearby where guests can play without charge on weekdays. Marine Terr., Aberystwyth (phone: 0970-617558). Moderate.

Conrah Country House **–** Here's a special blend of historic Welsh country mansion (the original foundation dates from 1753, the present building was rebuilt in 1870) and the comforts of a modern hostelry. There are 13 rooms (most with private bath) set on a secluded site atop a wooded hillside, plus a small heated indoor swimming pool and sauna. The university town of Aberystwyth is only a short distance away. Rhydgaled, Chancery, Aberystwyth (phone: 0970-617941 or 800-221-1074). Moderate.

Marine – On the seafront, it has 35 rooms, 3 bars, a restaurant, and lounges. Marine Terr., Aberystwyth (phone: 0970-612444). Moderate.

Bay – Also facing the sea, this hotel has 32 rooms and a restaurant. Marine Terr., Aberystwyth (phone: 0970-617356). Inexpensive.

University College of Wales – For something different, stay in one of the more than 1,200 rooms when students are away. Write to the Conference Office, Penbryn, Penglais, Aberystwyth SY23 3BY (phone: 0970-3702). Inexpensive.

EATING OUT: ***Julia's*** – There have been many good reports about this pleasant bistro; soups (especially the chilled sort), pâté, and syllabub are specialties. 17 Bridge St., Aberystwyth (phone: 0970-617090). Expensive.

Gannets – Everything on the very reasonable menu is homemade, from the quiche and casseroles to the treacle tart. 7 St. James Sq., Aberystwyth (phone: 0970-617164). Moderate to inexpensive.

Blue Bell Inn – On A44 to Aberystwyth, in Llangurig village by the river Wye, is this attractive 16th-century country inn with good, reasonably priced meals and accommodations (phone: 05515-254). Inexpensive.

DEVIL'S BRIDGE: The devil, disguised as a monk, is said to have built the first bridge over the Mynach River ravine in order to obtain the soul of an old woman who wanted to recover her cow from the other side, but her dog, pursuing the bread she rolled along the newly built bridge, became "the first living thing that crosses the bridge" which the Devil had agreed to be his due. Two modern bridges have been built above the original. It is an attractive spot, and for a small fee you can take the steps down into the gorge and walk the winding paths to admire the river's waterfalls.

CHECKING IN: ***Devil's Bridge*** – Built in 1787 as a hunting lodge, the hotel has an unusual Swiss appearance. There are 22 rooms and a restaurant. Devil's Bridge (phone: 097085-232). Moderate to inexpensive.

Woodlands – This attractive stone house above the gorge at Devil's Bridge has 8 cozy bedrooms as well as a relaxing sitting room with fireplace and a good restaurant. Devil's Bridge (phone: 097085-666). Inexpensive.

En Route from Devil's Bridge – By now you will have decided whether to go to Aberystwyth and the coast. Our route branches inland on A44 from Ponterwyd. On the right you'll see the sweep of the Ystwyth forest and on the left the rolling hills of the Plynlimon range, where the Wye and Severn rivers rise. It is worth penetrating this area on foot if you can. It's wild and haunting, with rushing streams, old caved-in farmhouses, and a few birds circling overhead. The road goes on to Llangurig, which has a handful of inns and shops. A470 forks toward Llanidloes.

LLANIDLOES: The central feature of the town, and you have to drive slowly to negotiate it, is the half-timbered market hall built in 1609. Llanidloes has a long tradition of wool weaving and trade, but the town was not always as calm as it looks today. During the 1830s, the Chartist workmen's reform movement (a political organization popular in Britain then) began to have some impact on Llanidloes's discontented weavers. The Chartists captured and held the town for a few days in 1839. The museum in the market hall has some exhibits devoted to this episode (open June through September).

From Llanidloes, you can take several pleasant side trips into the country lanes of the district. One in particular starts on the eastern edge of the town, on B4518, and leads out to Staylittle and Llanbrynmair. Six miles out from Llanidloes you'll come upon a lovely view over Llyn Clywedog reservoir.

CHECKING IN: ***Severn View Guest House*** – This pleasant inn has a friendly atmosphere and 7 comfortable rooms. China St., Llanidloes (phone: 05512-2207). Inexpensive.

Trewythen Arms – An attractive Georgian house with 12 rooms, 2 bars, and a dining room that offers good country cooking. Great Oak St., Llanidloes (phone: 05512-2214). Inexpensive.

En Route from Llanidloes – Follow A470 along the Severn River northeast and pass through Llandinam. Near the bridge you'll see a statue of the village's most famous son, David Davies, the civil engineer, railroad builder, and developer of coal mining in the Rhondda valleys of South Wales. The town of Caersws above Llandinam is typical of the small settlements in this area, planted in the green and open land. It is worth making an 8-mile diversion here along A492 east to Newtown, a hub of economic growth in this part of rural Wales. Industrial development here is designed to stop the drift of young people out of the countryside into the bigger towns of England. Newtown's past prominence as a weaving industry giant is chronicled at the *Textile Museum* (open Tuesdays through Saturdays, April through October). There is also a museum devoted to Robert Owen (1771–1858), the social philosopher, who was born and buried in Newtown. Owen's many theories finally resulted in an experiment in communal living at New Harmony, Indiana. The museum is open daily except Sundays.

The route from Caersws, slightly northwest of Llandinam, goes through Clatter and Carno (headquarters of the Laura Ashley textile manufacturing empire), Commins Coch, and Cemmas Road along A470. From here you can take a 6-mile side trip down A489 to Machynlleth, a market town with a tall clock tower as its signature, standing on the Dovey (Dyfi) River. The Welsh hero Owain Glyndwr chose Machynlleth to convene a Parliament in 1404. Machynlleth is a busy meeting and trading place, and a good town for strolling.

The main route winds through the Dovey valley by way of A470 to Mallwyd and Dinas Mawddwy, set in alpine countryside.

DINAS MAWDDWY: It looks hard to say, but pluck up some courage and say Deenass Mouth-oo-ee. It's a rather special place. The landscape is singular, with steeply sloped hills, and the soaring peaks of the Arans close by, to the north. The people here were once known for their red hair and independent nature. And 400-odd years ago travelers feared a gang of them known as the Red Brigands. They ambushed and killed a judge in 1555 and for that they were finally hunted down and dispersed. Even today you might see flame-haired people in Dinas Mawddwy. But visitors today need not worry that the spirit of the Red Brigands lives on: Dinas people are as friendly as the little town they inhabit. It is a restful place, with good fishing for salmon and trout or just for walking. The weaving industry has been revived with some success; the Meirion Mill is open to visitors and wools are available for purchase. You can also take a most enjoyable side trip for 15 miles or so along the narrow road to Llanymawddwy and up to Llanuwchllyn, an off-the-beaten-track ride leading to Bala Lake. The largest natural lake in Wales — almost 4 miles long — Bala is the home of the little gwyniad, a fish found nowhere in the world but here. The lake is also a center for sailing, canoeing, and swimming, and the Bala Lake narrow gauge railway runs alongside it (daily April through October). The town, at the lake's eastern end, has plenty of places to eat, drink, and stay. The whole area makes a worthwhile day out from Dinas Mawddwy.

CHECKING IN: ***Pale Hall*** – Originally built in 1874 for a Scottish railway engineer, this country house with its own park was visited by Queen Victoria in 1889. Its present incarnation is a sumptuous hostelry, carefully restored and refurbished to the highest standards. No two of the 17 rooms are alike, and several guest accommodations include a private Jacuzzi and a Victorian or four-poster bed. The hotel also has its own small heated indoor pool, sauna, clay pigeon-shooting facilities on the grounds, nearby sailing, white-water canoeing, and fishing in Lake Bala. There are also excellent golf courses nearby. Llanderfel, Bala (phone: 06783-285 or 800-221-1074). Expensive.

Brigands Inn – A 15th-century coaching inn in the Dovey Valley steeped in history and character, it has roaring fires and 14 cozy rooms. Salmon and sea trout fishing are nearby. Mallwyd, Machynlleth, Powys (phone: 06504-208). Moderate.

Lake Vyrnwy – Perched on the edge of Snowdonia National Park, this hotel in the foothills of the Berwyn Mountains has 30 rooms, all with private bath, and some boast four-poster beds, Jacuzzis, and private sitting rooms. In the years that this hotel has prospered (it has recently completed a total refurbishment) it has served as a haven for travelers seeking tranquility and cozy comfort in the Victorian style. The hotel enjoys exclusive sporting rights to the 24,000 surrounding acres, which provide guests with a unique opportunity to enjoy fly fishing, shooting, tennis, sailing, hiking, ballooning, and birdwatching. Llanwddyn, via Oswestry, Shropshire (phone: 069-173-692 or 800-221-1074). Moderate.

Buckley Pines – The amenities here include 14 comfortable rooms, 5 with private bath; a restaurant; and parking facilities. There's a magnificent view over the Dovey, and fishing. Dinas Mawddwy (phone: 06504-261). Inexpensive.

Plas Coch – This comfortable, centrally located hotel has a restaurant and 10 rooms. High St., Bala (phone: 0678-520309). Moderate.

Red Lion – A bit smaller but just as cozy as the *Buckley,* it has 8 rooms, all sharing a common bath, as well as parking and a restaurant. Dinas Mawddwy (phone: 06504-247). Inexpensive.

White Lion Royal – A large and charming old post house, it's right in the center of town with a good restaurant and 22 rooms. High St., Bala (phone: 0678-520314). Inexpensive.

DOLGELLAU: Pronounced *Doll*-geth-lay, this is the chief town of the old shire of Merioneth, now incorporated into the county of Gwynedd, which also includes Caernarfonshire and the island of Anglesey. Dolgellau is solidly built in dark, local stone and is a sturdy, foursquare town perfectly in tune with its surroundings. It lies under the bulk of Cader Idris mountain (the name means "Idris's Chair") and is an important marketplace for the many small mountain villages in the vicinity. It has ancient origins: The Romans were here, as were Cistercian monks who left Cymer Abbey, founded in 1199. The church, built in 1726, has an interesting barrel roof, and its graveyard has a fascinating mixture of tombstones with Welsh and English inscriptions. The Welsh *er cof* means "in memory." Dolgellau's bridge, built in 1638, is now protected as a historical structure and an old tollhouse also remains.

In the midst of Snowdonia National Park, Dolgellau is naturally an excellent place for touring by foot. Several paths lead up the slopes of Cader Idris ranging from easy walks to hard climbs. Two miles out of town, on the A494 Bala road, there is a turnoff to the left clearly signposted Precipice Walk. This is a scenic walk, not difficult, and takes about 2 hours. Information on all trails winding up to the summit of Cader Idris is available from the park information office at Maentwrog (phone: 0766-770274).

The *Snowdon Sherpa* bus service is an efficient way to get to and around Snowdonia National Park. You catch the bus at designated pick-up points in the area and it drops you off at major walking and hiking paths and trails leading to Mt. Snowdon. A brochure with a map of the bus route is available from the British Tourist Authority or the national park office in Betws-y-Coed.

Gold found at Llanelltyd and nearby Bontddu transformed Dolgellau into a gold rush town for the last part of the 19th century. Traditionally, Welsh gold has been used for royal wedding rings, and you can see some displayed in the little jewelry shop in Dolgellau Square. Although the gold rush days are gone, gold mining is again becoming a lucrative local industry.

CHECKING IN: ***Abergwynant Hall*** **–** This was a holiday home built in 1863 for a Cheshire industrialist. The building still occupies a beautiful site looking out over the Mawddach Estuary and 100 acres of garden and woodland. There are only 3 guest bedrooms, but the decorations are in keeping with the mid-19th-century origins of the house. The restaurant has a well-deserved first class reputation, and special golf and fishing rights are available to guests. Penmaenpool, Gwynedd (phone: 0431-42238 or 800-221-1074). Expensive.

Borthwnog Hall **–** Old deeds reveal that this building was rented by the shoemaker of Dolgellau in 1670 for the sum of one peppercorn, and the present small country house, with 5 guestrooms, is itself over 200 years old. Most rooms offer a spectacular panoramic view that reaches from Cardigan Bay to the Arran Mountains. One of the most unusual features of the hotel is its art gallery, which contains original watercolors, oils, embroidered pictures, sculpture, and pottery. Bontddu (phone: 0341-49271 or 800-221-1074). Moderate.

Ty Isaf **–** Here's the opportunity to live in a traditional Welsh "longhouse" with a long (dating back to at least 1624) and romantic history. With only 3 bedrooms, this old drover's cottage and shoeing station has been lovingly restored and converted into a small, very special house where a maximum of three couples can be accommodated in surprising comfort. The walls are almost 3 feet thick, massive wooden beams cross the ceiling, and, when necessary, a cheerful blaze fills the inglenook fireplace. Each bedroom is furnished with country antiques. Here is an opportunity to enjoy authentic Welsh hospitality. LLanfachreth, Gwynedd (phone: 0341-423261; 0800-26990 for reservations; or 800-221-1074). Moderate.

Dolserau Hall **–** A warm welcome, 13 lovely rooms, and a good restaurant await you. Just outside Dolgellau on the Bala road (phone: 0341-422522). Inexpensive.

Golden Lion Royal **–** The decor ranges from casual to formal, with 28 comfortable rooms furnished with antiques. Lion St., Dolgellau (phone: 0341-422579). Moderate.

Cross Foxes Inn **–** In Snowdonia National Park, with 5 rooms. Dolgellau, at the crossroads of A487 and A470 (phone: 0341-422487). Inexpensive.

George III **–** Gerard Manley Hopkins once wrote a poem telling those "who pine for peace or pleasure" to "taste the treats of Penmaen Pool." And many say he was referring to this 300-year-old hotel and restaurant delightfully situated at the head of the Mawddach estuary. Freshly caught fish is the specialty in summer, and in winter the menu turns to local game. Six of the 13 guestrooms are in a lodge on the grounds, and all have views of the Mawddach estuary and the mountains. Just out of town on A493 in Penmaenpool (phone: 0341-422525). Inexpensive.

Gwernan Lake **–** On the sweeping slopes of Cader Idris, this hotel has 9 simple, attractive rooms. There's also a bar with lakeside view and a restaurant. Cader Idris Rd., Gwernan Lake (phone: 0341-422488). Inexpensive.

En Route from Dolgellau – An English poet once mused that there was only one thing better than going from Dolgellau to Barmouth, and that was going from Barmouth to Dolgellau. This route follows the estuary of the river Mawddach, with its fine scenery. You can go direct by A496, or go to Penmaenpool on A493 and cross the river by the narrow wooden toll bridges. It is a drive worth doing at an easy pace so you can enjoy the grand views.

And just around the corner, so to speak, is jolly little Barmouth, a resort tucked in under the mountainside and edging the waters of the Mawddach estuary. It is a good stopping place with beaches and a variety of sports and entertainment. For a few pence, you can walk across the rail and footbridge that spans the Mawddach. The view is sublime: sands, sea, and mountains. For more active outings, Barmouth has swimming, golf, climbing, fishing, and rough shooting. And, as you would expect in a seaside town like this, there are numerous hotels, guesthouses, and restaurants. It's ideal for those on a modest budget.

The A496 road runs northward to Llanbedr. On the left is the haunting stretch of dunes and marsh known as Morfa Dyffryn and to the right are the rather fearsome mountains called the Rhinogs, said to have been created by God while in a bad temper. Llanbedr is a quiet village and nearby is Mochras Island, or Shell Island, a shingly peninsula famed for the variety of shells on its shores. If you press inland from Llanbedr you will pick up the signs to Cwm Bychan, a remote and peaceful valley.

A few miles north of Llanbedr on A496 is Harlech, one of the romantic names of Wales. Still a small village, Harlech's historic heart and motif is the castle, standing high upon the rocks and defying all who come. It's one of the most photogenic of Welsh castles, and provided the inspiration for "Men of Harlech," one of the best-known traditional Welsh songs. Completed in 1289, the castle was one of the many fortifications built by King Edward I during his campaign to subdue the Welsh in the 13th century. The rebel Owain Glyndwr (freedom fighter for the Welsh) captured it in 1404, but his war of independence came to an end shortly after the castle was stormed and taken by Henry of Monmouth. In 1468, Harlech was the last castle to fall to the Yorkists in the Wars of the Roses. It was also the last castle to hold out on the Royalist side in the 17th-century civil war. Thus, Harlech has its battle scars. Those with no fear of heights can walk all around the castle on its unfenced, 10-foot-thick walls and climb the 143 steps to the top of its gate house. Look toward the sea, half a mile away, and recall that when the castle was built it actually stood on the shore. Since that time, however, the sea has receded. Coleg Harlech, an independent residential college for adult students founded in 1927 by Lloyd George's adviser, Thomas Jones (1870–1955), became a great nursery for writers as staff and students. With many of its graduates going on to university, it is popularly known as "the College of the Second Chance." It makes for an inspirational visit, especially if you attend a dramatic production at *Theatre Ardudwy* on the college grounds.

From here the road winds toward Talsarnau. On your left there is a good view of Tremadog Bay and the glistening Glaslyn estuary. Follow the signs to Penrhyndeudraeth and cross the river by toll bridge. The town's name is a mouthful, it's actually Welsh shorthand for "peninsula with two stretches of sand." A solid and amiable village, it has lots of ships and pubs. But no doubt it is rather overshadowed by Portmeirion, just up the road on A487.

PORTMEIRION: This is an enchanting corner of Wales, a village and hotel created by the distinguished, lovable, and fun-loving architect Sir Clough Williams-Ellis (1883–1978), who dreamed of a village of "beauty without solemnity. Begun in the 1920s, today it is an established, picturesque, and rather Italianate waterside village with views of the mountains, the sea, and the river and accents of rhododendron, shrubs, trees, and flowers. It has been called the Welsh Xanadu. There is a campanile, a dome, a town hall, pools, and statuary. Its character and vistas have made it ideal for film settings. Along with the exquisite *Portmeirion* hotel (see *Checking In*), accommodations are available in 20 self-catering cottages in the village. There is an entrance fee for day visitors.

CHECKING IN: ***Portmeirion*** **–** If the look of this magical place seems familiar, it's because you've probably seen it in the eerie television series, "The Prisoner." The site overlooks Cardigan Bay, and the 14 bedrooms have been returned to their original design and furnishings. Decor in the main hotel includes hand-embroidered white crewel work from Kashmir for the dining room curtains, and antiquities fround in Rajasthan for the main bar. This is ornate Victoriana at is very best, including an outdoor swimming pool and spacious lawns. As close to a fantasy hotel as exists in Wales; perhaps that's why such creative types as Noel Coward, George Bernard Shaw, and Orson Welles spent significant time here. Portmeiron, Gwynedd (phone: 0766-770228 or 800-221-1074). Expensive.

En Route from Portmeirion – Just outside town, on the main road, is the hamlet of Minffordd, where the philosopher Bertrand Russell (1872–1970) lived for some years and where he organized his worldwide campaign against nuclear stockpiles. He loved this part of Wales, and was one of his pleasures in his declining years was to lie in bed and watch the sun go down over Tremadog Bay. A487 leads westward into Porthmadog, often rendered as Portmadoc, which is reached by crossing a causeway for a small toll. The causeway is part of the harbor construction planned by William Madocks in the 1820s, which led to the town's economic success as a port. Madocks also built the town of Tremadog (*tre* means town) nearby, one of the first planned towns in Britain and the birthplace of Lawrence of Arabia. Porthmadog is a busy holiday and business center, a good base for sailing and for exploring the local countryside.

Leaving Porthmadog, take the main road (A487) to Tremadog and turn right onto the Beddgelert road (A498). After 3 miles, turn right to Garreg and Tanybwlch. Incidentally, an interesting and rather spectacular side trip is to Tanybwlch by train, on the narrow-gauge railway from Porthmadog. This is a former slate railway that used to bring the stone down from Blaenau Ffestiniog for shipping from Porthmadog quay. It fell into disrepair, but has been successfully restored. Its gleaming steam engines are an impressive and picturesque sight as they wind through the gorges of Snowdonia. The railroad has been restored and again runs all the way to Blaenau (daily Easter through October). Near the village of Beddgelert, at Sygun, is an old copper mine that was abandoned in the 19th century; now restored, the mine has tours of the workings and rock formations (daily April through October).

Back on the road, join A487 near Maentwrog and from here go through Ffestiniog and pick up A470 north to Blaenau Ffestiniog, 3 miles farther on. Blaenau, one of the great old slate towns, seems to be entirely grayish blue, since buildings, roofs, garden fences, and other items are made from the slate that made Blaenau. The vast slate mines are today a kind of monument to the heyday that straddled the 19th and 20th centuries. Slate is still worked on a smaller scale, and you can visit the enormous caverns hollowed out of the mountains at the Llechwedd Slate Cavern and Deep Mine here. It is worth doing, for slate has a fascinating history, which is related as you explore the underground maze of mines (open daily). We recommend getting there early since there are attractions aboveground as well: the *Slate Heritage Theatre,* which presents a short narrative on slate's importance to Wales; the craft shop where you can see workers carve souvenirs from slate and a gift shop where you can buy them; and a tramway exhibit of the old carriers that transported the slate from the mines. Llechwedd Slate Cavern and Deep Mine is popular so it's a good idea to reserve tickets at least a day ahead (phone: 0766-830306). You can also stop at the Gloddfa Ganol Slate Mine, the world's largest, which is open daily.

The landscape is dramatic in this area and remains so all along A470 north to Betws-y-Coed. It is a noted beauty spot, resting in a narrow valley, and its famous Swallow Falls are close by, to the north, and worth seeing.

BETWS-Y-COED: Pronounce it Bel-*too*-see-Loyd to please those who have gamely suffered the mangling of their town's name (it actually means "Chapel in the

Woods"). Because the town is at a major crossroads with easy access to Snowdonia National Park and Gwydir Forest, there are crowds here during the height of summer, especially on weekends, so a midweek visit then would be more enjoyable. Betws has ancient origins and a very old church with parts dating from the 12th to 16th centuries. Its gray stone buildings are typical of this region. There are a number of craft shops; Welsh woolens are of high quality and Betws has a large selection. The *Anna Davies Welsh Wool Shop* (phone: 06902-292) sells tapestry garments, wools, tweeds, quilts, rugs, pottery, sheepskin, perfume, and knitwear (open daily except Sundays, September through April).

CHECKING IN: *Maes-y-Neuadd* – Whether or not you say the name right, you are certain to enjoy a stay in one of Wales's grandest country house hotels, which was built over the course of 4 centuries — between 1350 and 1720. "Mice-in-Nayeth," as it is pronounced, stands amid gardens overlooking Snowdon and the Troeth Bach estuary. There are 13 bedrooms in this ruggedly constructed (of granite and slate) building, and all are decorated in a very individual style, many furnished with antiques; some boast hand-hewn beams and dormers, while others have high ceilings and elegant Georgian windows. Two couples run the 13-room hotel, and Olive Horsfall, one of the wives, is responsible for cooking the traditional Welsh dishes. Reservations for Sunday lunch are advised. Talsarnau Harlech (phone: 0766-780200 or 800-221-1074). Expensive.

Craig-y-Dderwen – Snuggled in a cluster of trees right on the banks of the river Conwy, the country house hotel has 18 rooms, all with private bath. Reduced charges for all local golf. Betws-y-Coed (phone: 06902-293). Moderate.

Park Hill – With 11 rooms (8 with private bath) high above Conwy Valley and the golf course, this inn is renowned for its cuisine. Facilities include an indoor swimming pool and sauna. Llanrwst Rd., Betws-y-Coed (phone: 06902-540). Moderate.

Royal Oak – Huddled in Snowdonia National Park and set beside the river Llugwy, this 27-room hotel has been completely refurbished but still retains its old-fashioned charm. Six rooms in the back, however, have very modern furniture and built-in stereo equipment. The food is good and the service dependable. Holyhead Rd., Betws-y-Coed (phone: 06902-219). Moderate.

Waterloo – More modern in design than the other hotels mentioned, with 3 bars and 28 rooms, all with private bath. There's also a restaurant for leisurely meals. Betws-y-Coed (phone: 06902-411). Moderate to inexpensive.

Fairy Glen – This 17th-century stone-white house — more of a bed-and-breakfast house than a hotel — is near the entrance of Snowdonia National Park and the Lledr Valley and also overlooks the river Conwy. Some of the 10 rooms have private baths and there is central heating. A bar is available to guests; beef, trout cooked in butter with almonds, and roast duckling are the chef's best for dinner. Dolgellau Rd., Betws-y-Coed (phone: 06902-269). Inexpensive.

EATING OUT: *Plas Bodegroes* – A Georgian country house newly opened as a restaurant with rooms. The owner and chef, Chris Chown, offers fine cuisine based on area freshwater fish and local produce. Pwllheli, Gwynedd (phone: 0758-612363). Expensive.

Maes-y-Neuadd – Comfortable and welcoming, the emphasis at this restaurant is on fresh ingredients, with particularly imaginative use of seafood and lamb, which appears on every menu under a series of beguiling disguises. Take their advice — they know their business.

En Route from Betws-y-Coed – At this point you may choose either of two side trips depending on how much time you have. First, you can make an expedition into deeper Snowdonia (known in Welsh as *Eryri,* "the land of eagles"). Contact Guides (Plas y Brenin, Capel Curig; phone: 06904-214) provides reliable guides through the

Snowdonia area. Or head westward to Capel Curig, Llanberis, Caernarvon, and the Isle of Anglesey.

It is a nice 8-mile drive along A5 from Betws-y-Coed to Capel Curig, and you can circle Mt. Snowdon itself by going 5 miles down to Pen-y-Gwryd and continuing on A4086 to Llyn Peris and Llyn Padarn (two pretty lakes), passing through Llanberis, a Snowdonia town of mountains and quarries. The *Welsh Slate Museum,* near Llanberis, is worth seeing and gives a good insight into the slate industry, once the great industry of this region. The steam trains of the *Llanberis Lake Railway* (1 ft. 11½ in. in gauge) runs alongside Lake Padarn for 2 miles from Padarn Park to Penllyn (daily, April through October). The original railway transported slate from the Dinorwic quarries (the world's largest) to Port Dinorwic on the Menai Strait.

From Llanberis, it's a short trip to Caernarvon and the Isle of Anglesey — a trip worth considering. From Llanberis, take A4086 to Caernarvon.

CAERNARVON: Rendered in Welsh as Caernarfon (there's no *v* in the Welsh language and *f* is pronounced like *v*), the town's magnificence lies in its castle and its setting. Caernarvon Castle is one of Europe's greatest, built in the late 13th and early 14th centuries. Like some other grand castles in Wales, its construction was commanded by King Edward I of England as part of his successful effort to keep the rebellious Welsh in order. From this strategic site on the Menai Strait, beside the river Seiont, the English could control a huge stretch of the Snowdonia wilds.

Although the castle's interior was never fully completed, there are still many turreted towers and narrow passageways to explore. The Queens Tower holds the *Museum of the Royal Welsh Fusiliers* with a collection of regimental memorabilia; the Northeast Tower has an exhibit on the Prince of Wales investiture ceremony (Prince Charles was invested here in 1969); and the Eagle Tower has a display of medieval armor. The latter gets its name from three statuettes of eagles that were once perched on the tower's turrets; today, only one is left guarding it. Caernarvon Castle is open daily; admission charge.

From the castle's ramparts, you can see the town walls. Built at the same time as the castle, the walls still surround the oldest section of the city. Inside the walls are fascinating narrow streets with little pubs and shops. In the main square (Castle Square) there is a statue of David Lloyd George, who rose from humble beginnings in the tiny village of Llanystumdwy, near Criccieth, to become MP for Caernarvon Boroughs, prime minister of Britain, and one of the 20th century's greatest statesmen.

The shopping in Caernarvon includes crafts, and there is a branch of the *Craftcentre Cymru* group that sells tweeds, woolens, pottery, and items made from metal and wood. In addition, there's a market on Saturdays in Castle Square. For sporting activities, Caernarvon boasts two yacht clubs, tennis, and golf facilities, and good river and sea fishing.

Near town is the Roman fort of Segontium, a military center founded in AD 78. Some buildings date only from the 2nd century and some were rebuilt in the 4th century. Although there aren't a great many ruins left to explore, the museum here has interesting exhibits on the history of the Roman takeover of Wales, archaeological finds from the period, and displays on the Roman military system and culture (open daily).

CHECKING IN/EATING OUT: ***Chocolate House*** – There are 7 private studio cottages around the courtyard here, offering full hotel facilities, and the restaurant specializes in chocolate desserts. Activities include flying, photography, and riding. Plas Treflan, Caeathro (phone: 0286-4872). Moderate.

Royal – A modernized coaching inn with 58 rooms and a well-regarded restaurant that uses fresh local produce. North Rd., Caernarvon (phone: 0286-73184). Moderate.

Black Boy Inn – Dating from the 14th century and inside the old walled section of Caernarvon, this 12-room inn has charming wood beams, crooked floors, and low ceilings. Good breakfasts, lunches, and dinners are served in the attractive restaurant, and colorful locals frequent the bar. North Gate St., Caernarvon (phone: 0286-3604). Inexpensive.

ISLE OF ANGLESEY: From Caernarvon, it's about 10 miles along the A487 road to Bangor, where you take a bridge over to the Isle of Anglesey. A lovely stone suspension bridge built in 1826 by Thomas Telford (a Scottish engineer) spans the Menai Strait. The bridge is not only handsome, but a tribute to its designer's skill, since it has no problem coping with the traffic loads of the present century. However, to alleviate congestion, the new Brittania Road Bridge has recently been opened.

These bridges cross over the swirling strait to the island of Anglesey, a corner of Wales that doesn't see many overseas travelers because it's rather off the beaten track. But it repays the trouble. Anglesey is a place for quiet, personal discoveries: a place to wander down narrow side roads and find charming, unspoiled hamlets and pubs.

You can cut diagonally across the island on A5 to Holyhead, a distance of about 20 miles; or northeast to Beaumaris, a 9-mile drive; or, if you have the time, it's very rewarding to drive all the way around the island via A5025 and A4080.

Holyhead and nearby Trearddur Bay bustle with a number of hotels, small restaurants, and pubs. Most likely, the reason for the bustle is the ferry service between here and Dun Laoghaire, Ireland, 3¼ hours away.

The cliff scenery around Holyhead is striking. South Stack, a tiny, rocky island brightened by a lighthouse, is justly famous for its pounding surf, shrieking seabirds, and strong sea breezes.

If you decide to cover the entire coast of Anglesey, there are all sorts of delightful, relaxing places with good beaches: Red Wharf Bay, Moelfre, Amlwch, Bull Bay, Cemaes Bay, and Rhosneigr. Sailing, fishing, walking, swimming, and sunbathing are the order of the day, and you can surf at Rhosneigr.

If you can't travel all the way to Holyhead, you can take the short drive (from the bridge) out to Beaumaris.

BEAUMARIS: The town of Beaumaris (pronounced Bew-marris) proudly harbors the last castle Edward I built in Wales, and many say he saved the best for last. Built at the end of the 13th century, the moated castle guards the entrance to the Menai Strait, and looks particularly fine against a backdrop of sea and mountains. Its beauty, however, is secondary to its strength: It has impenetrable fortifications. The castle was simply a milestone in medieval fortress building. The ingenious design includes two defense walls encircling the castle. The inner wall is square, while the outer wall seems square but actually has bowed sides. This roundedness permitted virtually no corner to go unseen by the castle's keepers. Also interesting is the angle at which the entryways meet the gate houses. Instead of a direct alignment, they're off-center to force a slanted approach by aggressors, making them almost certainly visible to the heavily armed guards. Beaumaris Gaol is also an interesting stop. It has remained virtually unaltered since it was built in 1829. The prison cells, a unique treadwheel, and the condemned prisoner's walk to the scaffold all serve as grim reminders of harsh times. Open June through September.

Back on the main route, from Betws-y-Coed, A470 winds attractively through the Conwy valley north to Llanrwst, a picturesque little market town beside the river with an interesting church and a most striking bridge across the Conwy, built in 1636, thought to have been the work of the noted architect Inigo Jones. From Llanrwst, take A548 and watch, after about 5 miles, for signs pointing to Llansannan on your right. The road winds through wild and spacious country — hills, moors, and river valleys.

From Llansannan, turn southeast onto A544 to Bylchau and look for signs for A543 to Denbigh. It's a lovely run over the moors.

CHECKING IN: ***Bulkeley Arms*** – Overlooking Menal Strait, this fine Victorian establishment offers traditional comforts, including large rooms, high beds (all 42 rooms with private facilities), and a popular bar. Christmas and New Year packages are available. Castle St. (phone: 0248-810415). Moderate.

Henllys Hall – Set on 50 forested acres with superb Snowdonian views, this 19th-century mansion has tennis facilities, a heated outdoor pool, sauna, solarium, Jacuzzi, a good restaurant, and 22 rooms. A former Franciscan monastery site, it also includes 2 cottages, 7 apartments, 2 bungalows, and a farmhouse. Beaumaris (phone: 0248-810412). Moderate.

Ye Old Bulls Head – This establishment has been around since 1472, which makes it something of a historical landmark. Copper ornaments dangling from ceiling beams and snapping fires in the hearths warm up the place and the mood quite a bit. There are 17 pleasant rooms, some with private bath. Castle St., Beaumaris (phone: 0248-810329). Moderate.

DENBIGH: Called *Din*-bych in Welsh, this town looks out over the Vale of Clwyd, the river that gives the county its name. This is true border country, so it has seen its share of battle-axing, swordplay, and the zizz of arrows. The castle, which stands on a hill, was first built by William the Conqueror as part of his effort to annex this region. It was greatly extended and improved during King Edward I's reign, and along with Edward's other castles — Harlech, Beaumaris, Conwy, Caernarvon, and Criccieth — it played a large part in bringing the Welsh under the king's rule in the 13th century. Later, the castle was sold by Queen Elizabeth I to Robert Dudley, her favorite courtier. And it was a focal point of the great civil war in the following century. Action against King Charles's supporters was directed from Denbigh and Sir John Owen, leader of a determined Royalist army, was captured and kept in the castle. It is worth visiting: Note its unusual octagonal towers. The Elizabethan town hall is just one of many interesting corners of Denbigh. The steep streets make for some memorable snapshots. Perhaps Denbigh's most famous son was H. M. Stanley (born John Rolands), the poor local boy who made good; he emigrated to the US, became a newspaper man, explored Africa, and found Dr. Livingstone, he presumed.

CHECKING IN: ***Bryn Morfydd*** – Set on 40 acres, this hotel has 17 comfortable rooms with private bath and great views, tennis court, golf course, and an outdoor heated swimming pool; 3 miles south of Denbigh on A525 in Llanrhaeadr (phone: 074578-280). Moderate.

En Route from Denbigh – Eight miles south on A525 lies Ruthin (pronounced Rithin), a handsome town whose market square is fringed by 16th- and 17th-century houses. It was once a wool trade center, but its history goes much farther back. It was here that Owain Glyndwr started his uprising against English rule in 1400. Glyndwr and his men burned the town but failed to capture the castle. The medieval castle is now a ruin, but the big mansion on the site is a fine 58-room hotel, expensive as Welsh hostelries go, but with good facilities and fine dining. It is called, naturally enough, the *Ruthin Castle,* and you cannot mistake its imposing redstone appearance. The castle offers medieval banquets with ale, mead, roasts and the like done in what is thought to be a medieval style. It makes a jolly evening and you need to go with an empty stomach (phone: 0824-22664).

The route from Ruthin winds across the Vale of Clwyd and across the Clwydian range of mountains by way of A494. But a side trip 15 miles along A525 to A542 to Llangollen is well worth any effort. It stands beside the rushing river Dee, and words simply cannot do it justice. The four-arched bridge across the Dee is traditionally one of the seven wonders of Wales and was built in the 12th century. Later, it was widened. Llangollen is deeply embedded in the history and lore of Wales, and the town is featured in many legends of love, jealousy, rivalry, and blood and thunder. It takes its name from Collen, a saint of the ancient Celtic church. The Valle Crucis Abbey, 2 miles out along the canal, was ruined on Henry VIII's orders when he was stamping out monasteries, but it is still imposing. Any visit to this town must include the home of the "Ladies of Llangollen," two aristocratic Irish women, Eleanor Butler (1739–1829) and Sarah Ponsonby (1755–1831), who settled here in protest against the stifling conformity of the Irish elitist Protestant ascendancy. From 1780 they dominated the life of their haven and shared their happiness with many eminent visitors including Wellington, Burke, Castlereagh, Byron, Shelley, Scott, and Wordsworth. The house, Plas Newydd, is open to visitors.

Nearby, on the Corwen road, is Plas-yn-Ial. This is the ancient seat of the Ial family, whose name, pronounced "Yal," was corrupted to "Yale," and one of whose sons founded the American university. Llangollen is abundantly endowed with pubs, hotels, and cafés, and every July it rings to the sound of music, when the *International Musical Eisteddfod,* founded to bring the world's people together in peace, has the town bulging. People come from all over the world to compete in song and dance and instrument-playing, so that the town is a mass of color and a happy babble of tongues. Evening concerts are given by renowned singers and instrumentalists. Information: Eisteddfod Office, Llangollen, Clwyd, North Wales LL20 8NG (phone: 0978-860236).

Southeast Scottish Lowlands

No traveler should tread the hallowed ground of the Scottish Lowlands without first learning a few rudiments of the history of Presbyterianism. Here's an emergency grab bag of key religious events in Scotland from the sixteenth century to the present as well as brief profiles of the two major players.

John Knox, a brilliant and incendiary preacher fired by the theology of John Calvin, came to St. Giles's Cathedral, Edinburgh, in 1559. Many of the Norman-blooded Scottish nobility, looking to aggrandize themselves as their counterparts in England had done during Henry VIII's dissolution of the monasteries, hopped on Knox's bandwagon to campaign against a corrupt Catholic church and the Catholic Royal House of Stuart. This was the takeoff point for the Protestant Reformation in Scotland. With 15 four-hour sermons a week on the democratization of Christian worship rumbling from his pulpit, Knox soon gathered the rabble to his bosom. His reforms were implemented in every corner of the Lowlands amid the wrecking of church interiors and ravaging of altars. Yet, contrary to generations of popular opinion, Knox was no Puritan; he could enjoy a good belly laugh and freely sanctioned his fellow citizens to drink, dance, and be merry. Social restraints closed in on the Presbyterian faith much later, in the wake of royal persecution from London.

Charles II, successor in 1660 to a disagreeable Cromwellian interlude (which had, however, allowed Presbyterianism to flourish), continued his executed father's bad habit of ramming Episcopacy down Scotland's throat, backed by an obsequious and dissolute Scottish Parliament. Groups of worshipers called Covenanters (because of two written oaths they had signed, some in blood, proclaiming their inalienable anti-Episcopal beliefs) gathered on open hillsides, away from the churches, flouting a parliamentary act. Charles's troops zeroed in for a series of massacres. The Lowlands are full of interesting old churches and Covenanting martyrs' graves.

In 1712 a new act was passed by England's and Scotland's now unified parliaments, which instituted lay patronage. This was a system revoking the right of congregations to choose their own ministers and granting the task instead to each parish's local "laird" (lord or resident aristocrat). Often tyrannical, these hand-picked ministers tightly controlled life in the Lowland towns and villages, banning music, dancing, theatrical performances, and country walks on Sundays. Scotland's national bard, Robert Burns, was one of many who were forced, at the hands of church elders, to appease God's wrath by standing publicly in a wooden dock protractedly confessing to fornication.

With the coming of the Industrial Revolution, economic and social conditions in the Lowlands, especially in Glasgow and Edinburgh, became appalling. In comparison to their working class congregations, men of the cloth were fat cats. In 1843, 450 ministers with sorely tried consciences walked bravely out of their manses, their ministries, and the annual General Assembly of the Church of Scotland to form a new movement, the Free Presbyterian Church. This breach was not healed until 1929, after lay patronage had been abolished within the Kirk (as the established Presbyterian Church was — and still is — called). Attendant upon the tireless and dedicated slum-based social work of the new Free Church was a harsh (but possibly necessary) list of "don'ts" for its followers: no uncleanliness; no laziness; no bankruptcy; no "Sabbath breaking;" no drinking and gambling; no loud, indelicate behavior. As the visitor will quickly discover, these cast-iron virtues are tightly woven into the fabric of Scottish life today, especially on Sundays, when the world stops. The only noticeable shift from the old ways in the last decade — other than a greater availability of intoxicating beverages — has been the Scots' increasing willingness to admit that Christmas is not simply an unnecessarily flamboyant Papish holiday, to be eschewed in favor of New Year. Both holidays are now celebrated for days on end. On January 2, when Americans go back to work, Scots are in bed recovering.

The language spoken by Lowlanders derives from "La'lands," an old form of Norman-infused Anglo-Saxon once known as "Inglis." It's full of dialect words, rolled r's, and unexpected pronunciations: *guid* for "good," *doon* for "down," *fitba* for "football." La'lands is sometimes droll, often pithy, and — with the help of great poets like William Dunbar, Robert Burns, or Hugh MacDiarmid — sweepingly majestic. Dunbar is unfathomable at first sight, like Chaucer, but it's worth reading a bit of Burns or MacDiarmid to get a sense of Lowland Scotland's people, speech, and concept of nationhood.

Have a look also at the English-language Lowland poetry of Sir Walter Scott, who set *Marmion* and *The Lay of the Last Minstrel* among the Border country's rolling, variegated, green and brown brackeny hills. The Borders, Scott's home for many years, are the Lowlands' most intriguing district: It's a moorish land interspersed with lush farms and prosperous mill-spangled towns. Ruined abbeys sit like sad marooned kings above gladed loops in the river Tweed. Picturesque villages dot its valleys. Its folklore is widely known, especially its ballads, from *Thomas the Rhymer and the Queen of Elfland* (on which the English poet John Keats may have based *La Belle Dame Sans Merci*) to narrative poetry that recounts the dramatic cattle-rustling Border raids of the fourteenth, fifteenth, and sixteenth centuries. Under this Scottish version of the chivalric code, knights called "mosstroopers" or "reivers" (raiders) gathered their families and retainers and forayed into each other's territory, burying their differences only when English marauders posed a greater threat. The former British prime minister Sir Alec Douglas-Home is descended from at least two of these families. "The Riding of the Marches," an ancient way of delineating jealously guarded boundries by tracing them in assembled companies on horseback, is ritually practiced on a festival day every summmer by each of the main Border towns — catch one if you can.

Yet literature, high political drama, and ecclesiastical turmoil are not the only features of southeast Scotland's fascinating history. There is in the area an enormous concentration of castles, both ruined and whole. There are aristocratic mansions from every century, with lavish, extensive gardens. There are harbor towns on the coast which have changed very little in a hundred years, supported by a still lively fishing industry; there is the fresh-air-and-countryside, rich Victorian holiday atmosphere of Peeblesshire. And then there is golf — the mainstay of the seaside towns of East Lothian. Eleven mangnificent golf courses dot sandy links from Edinburgh to Dunbar, a great challenge to any golfer used to the manicured parklands of American country clubs. Dune-shaped terrain and winds of changeable direction will affect the game, and golfers may be advised to use a wedge-shaped club. But take heart — some Scottish king probably once played golf in the same place, with a crabbit wooden stick and a ball stuffed with feathers!

The southeast Scottish Lowlands route begins at Edinburgh and runs east along the Firth of Forth to Dunbar, continuing to Berwick-upon-Tweed, where it veers inland to Coldstream and Kelso, and on south to Langholm. From Langholm it circles to the Scott country, and from there to Moffat, sheltered in Tweedsmuir hills. From Moffat the route leads north again to Peebles, Galashiels, and back to Edinburgh. The entire distance is about 330 miles. It should take between 1 and 2 weeks, depending on how many castles, museums, markets, and festivals you stop off to see. There's an exceedingly wide selection.

Be sure to buy the Scottish Tourist Board's kit, *Enjoy Scotland* (about $8), which includes a very detailed touring map and a booklet of 1,001 things to see. Keep scones (biscuits) or sandwiches, bought from bakeries in the towns, in the car for when lunchtime rolls around and you find you're still in the wilds. Don't pass a gas station assuming that there will be another one soon. If traveling from May through September, book hotels in advance.

Tourist kiosks in the towns sell a booklet for hikers and mountain climbers called *Scotland: Hillwalking* (about $4). Ask in the Borders Tourist offices about the Borders Craft Association and opportunities to tour workshops of various Border Crafts such as pottery, candlemaking, woodcarving, and the like; "Scottish Explorer" tickets, giving access to ancient monuments at a fraction of the price it would cost if they were visited individually; and the Borders Woollen Trail of mill factories and shops. A Borders *What's On* guide is published monthly. Taste of Scotland Scheme, Ltd., 33 Melville St., Edinburgh (phone: 031-220-1900) publishes a guide to dining on native fare. Border towns are famous for amusing (and occasionally delicious) individually created types of hard candy. The Royal Commission on the Ancient and Historical Monuments of Scotland has published a very attractive paperback, with photographs, entitled *Exploring Scotland's Heritage, Lothian and the Borders,* by John R. Baldwin (about $10). This is an ideal companion for many of the sights included in this route. Copies are generally available at Edinburgh bookshops, including *Her Majesty's Stationery Office,* 71 Lothian Rd. (phone: 031-228-4181).

The price categories for the hotels listed in this route are: expensive, $95 and up for two for bed and breakfast; moderate, $65 to $95; and inexpensive, $30 to $65. Dinner for two (not including drinks or tip) in a restaurant rated as expensive will run $50 and up; in those rated as moderate, $30 to $50; and in inexpensive, under $30.

EDINBURGH: For a detailed report on the city, its sights, hotels, and restaurants, see *Edinburgh,* THE CITIES.

En Route from Edinburgh – Take A1 east from Edinburgh, as far as Portobello, and then the A199 along the Furth of Forth. In the suburb of Musselburgh, pick up B1348 east and travel 8 miles to Morrison's Haven, site of the 800-year-old Prestongrange coal mine, one of only two former mines open to the public. Operated by the Scottish Mining Museum Trust, the site features a visitor center with exhibitions and an audiovisual display, a massive five-story beam pump dating from 1874, three steam locomotives, a steam navvy (shovel), and a winding engine. (Any of the tour guides can give driving instructions to nearby Lady Victoria Colliery, a mine founded in 1890 and still in operation.) Open Tuesdays through Fridays from 10 AM to 4:30 PM, and Saturdays and Sundays from noon to 5 PM. The first Sunday of every month (April through October) is "Steam Day," when the locomotives operate (phone: 031-663-7519).

Also en route, on A198 before the town of Gullane, are Gosford House, Aberlady Church, and the *Myreton Motor Museum.* Gosford House is a seat of the Earls of Wemyss, built by Robert Adam in 1800 (open Wednesdays, Saturdays, and Sundays from 2 to 5 PM June and July). Aberlady Church, in the village of Aberlady, has part of an 8th-century Celtic cross in the chancel and a fortified 15th-century tower. *Myreton Motor Museum,* displaying vintage cars and cycles, is signposted for its turnoff from A198 just beyond Aberlady. Open from 10 AM to 5 PM.

GULLANE: Despite strong winds in winter, rich Edinburghers maintain a posh surburban existence here. Gullane gets more sun than anywhere else in Scotland. Tourists throng here in late spring and in summer because of its four incomparable golf courses. Muirfield, the finest (a frequent site of the opens), is the home of the Honourable Company of Edinburgh Golfers; in order to play, have your home club secretary send a letter of introduction (include alternate dates of play) to the club at: Muirfield, Gullane, East Lothian EH31 2EG, Scotland (phone: 0620-842123). Play at Muirfield for guests is on Tuesdays, Thursdays, and Friday mornings only and costs $45 a round, $55 for a double. The *Heritage of Golf Museum* shows the game's development from the 15th century to the present and has antique golf clubs for sale. Open by appointment. West Links Rd., Gullane (phone: 08757-277 early mornings or evenings). Gullane also has wide, luxurious sandy beaches.

CHECKING IN: ***Greywalls*** – Gullane's most exclusive place to stay is this lavishly appointed, 23-room golfers' retreat. Next to *Muirfield Golf Course,* Gullane (phone: 0620-842144). Expensive.

EATING OUT: ***La Potinière*** – The French cooking at this small and unassuming restaurant is so good that one of its recipes — *soufflé aux courgettes* — appears in the Good Food Guide's *Second Dinner Party Book.* Reservations are a must. Open daily except Wednesdays and Saturdays for lunch, Saturdays only for dinner; closed October. On the main route through Gullane (phone: 0620-843214). Expensive.

DIRLETON: Continue northeast on A198 to this charming little village. With its spectacular castle and busy yew-encircled bowling green, it is reputedly the prettiest in Scotland. The castle, entered dramatically by a long ramp leading sharply upward to a gate in its stark and stony heights, was built in 1225. Additions were made in the 15th and 17th centuries, but the whole was sacked by Oliver Cromwell's troops in 1650.

It's open Mondays through Saturdays from 9:30 AM to 7 PM in summer, to 4 PM in winter, and Sunday afternoons year-round. The castle shares the borders of the village common with clusters of 17th- and 18th-century cottages. If you feel like taking a walk, trees and springy turf line the lovely Yellowcraig Nature Trail for 2 miles from Dirleton to the sea. Otherwise, continue on A198 to North Berwick.

CHECKING IN/EATING OUT: ***Open Arms*** – A country-style, 7-room hostelry famed for its restaurant, which is included on the Scottish Tourist Board's "Taste-of-Scotland" roster. Decorated in soft pink and lilac, its candlelit tables are graced by such delicacies as salmon, venison, and Cranachan pudding — cream, toasted oatmeal, and rum, topped with fresh berries! On the main route through Dirleton (phone: 0620-85241). Expensive.

NORTH BERWICK: The farming folk who inhabit the surrounding countryside habitually converge on this holiday spot, making the most of its sands, shops, and two fine golf courses. North Berwick has the kind of natural topography that proves God must be British: The middle class beach is divided from the lower class beach by the harbor, and each gives onto its own separate bay. The sun at east coast resorts like this one has a striking, harsh brilliance, unbroken by the soft air and purple-hilled isles that characterize the Atlantic coast to the west. You may offend the natives' old-fashioned priorities if you venture onto the middle class beach without a hat!

A mile or so south of the center of town is North Berwick Law, a grassy once-volcanic rise decked with a whalebone arch, from which to enjoy a magnificent view. Motorboat tours from North Berwick go in summer to the nearby island of Fidra and also to the fascinating Bass Rock, which every Edinburgh schoolchild is whisked off to see by at least one teacher in the course of his or her education. The rock's steep, straight sides make it look much higher than its 350 feet. It's part of a chain of volcanic masses, made of especially hard stone, that withstood glacial pressure in the last Ice Age (the Castle Rock, which Edinburgh Castle sits on, is another). The Bass Rock is inaccessible except at one point, which made it irresistible to hermits in early Christian times; to prison wardens detaining Covenanting ministers at the time of King Charles II; and to soldiers rallying round the flag of the exiled Stuarts who needed a safe fortress during the reign of William of Orange. Today the Bass Rock is "held," as is Fidra, by the keepers of its lighthouse and scores of swirling silvery gannets.

A variety of activities are available in North Berwick: For boat trips, contact Fred Marr, 24 Victoria Rd. (phone: 0620-2838). Mr. Hunter (phone: 0620-3629) or Mr. Small (phone: 0620-3952) will provide sea angling from North Berwick harbor. Peter Hamilton, on West Beach (phone: 0620-4188) takes parties windsurfing, and there is a heated open-air swimming pool on the seafront. Donald and Fiona Fraser operate a weaving studio at 51–53 Forth St., where visitors can buy fabrics and designer clothes. Handmade semiporcelain objects are on sale at *Shape Scrape Ceramics,* The Pottery, Station Hill. The *North Berwick Museum,* on School Road, has a local history and wildlife exhibition. It's open limited hours April through the first week of June; Mondays through Saturdays except lunchtimes and Sundays from 2 to 5 PM the rest of June through the third week of September. The tourist office is on Quality Street (phone: 0620-2197).

EATING OUT: ***Marine*** – A hot and cold smorgasbord lunch — savory pies, lasagna, puddings — is served in a lovely "bar" with enormous bay windows overlooking the sea. Open for dinner as well. North Berwick (phone: 0620-2406). Moderate.

En Route from North Berwick – About 3 miles farther on A198 is Tantallon Castle, on a cliff overlooking the North Sea. An extensive rose-colored ruin that once was a stronghold of the famous Border family named Douglas, it has captured the Scottish popular imagination and worked its way into the native patois. Any feat of the impossible is said to be as hard as to "ding doon" (knock down) Tantallon Castle. Open daily except Sunday mornings during daylight hours only; also closed Wednesday and Thursday mornings in winter.

The village of Whitekirk, also on A198 (which takes a southern course after Tantallon Castle), is worth exploring. In the 15th century, pilgrims from all over Europe drank at Whitekirk's Holy Well, while abiding in stone hostels nearby. The kirk was rebuilt in its original Gothic style after suffragettes burned it down in 1914, presumably because of its association with rack-renting monks (who charged excessive fees to store grain in the tithe barn across the road, also of historic interest).

A 2-mile detour east from Tyninghame along the East Linton road, B1407, leads to Preston Mill and Phantassie Doocot. The mill, with water wheel, was constructed in the 18th century and is still in operation. A "doocot" is a dovecot. This one holds 500 birds and is thought to date from the 16th century, when local lairds kept pigeons to be fattened for their tables, at the expense of their tenants' crops. Open daily except Sunday mornings and lunchtimes April through October; weekends only November through March (phone: 0620-860426).

Just south of the mill and the town of East Linton, pick up the A1 roadway east to Dunbar. If you do not detour to the Preston Mill, continue south on A198 from Tyninghame to the Great North Road, A1 (east), to Dunbar.

DUNBAR: This quiet town, in sailing ship days the only safe port between Edinburgh and the English city of Berwick, is now a golfing and sailing haven for vacationers seeking a rest. But it wasn't always restful. The Earl of Hertford attacked it by land in 1544, during the so-called Rough Wooing by which King Henry VIII tried to force Scotland to bind the young Mary, Queen of Scots, to his son Edward in a treaty of marriage. Years later Mary stayed in Dunbar Castle (today a mere vestige) with her husband and cousin Lord Darnley, and again with her lover Lord Bothwell who carried her off there, fairy-tale style, after the murder of Lord Darnley. The castle was destroyed in 1567, after Mary and Bothwell had fled for their lives. Cromwell laid waste to the town in 1650. Today's harbor — still the home of a small herring fleet — is the more picturesque for the castle ruin. This whole section of Dunbar is very old and was part of the original royal burgh of 1369.

Something very dear to many American visitors had its roots in Dunbar. The building at the north end of High Street is the birthplace of John Muir, the man responsible for the US National Park system. A pioneering geologist, explorer, and naturalist, Muir spent the first 11 years of his life in the top apartment of this building with his family (six brothers and sisters) until emigrating to the US in 1849. The Muir flat is appropriately furnished in the 19th-century style, and one room is reserved for audiovisual presentations of his life and work. Open daily except Wednesdays and Sundays from the end of May through September. For more details contact the tourist information center, in the Town House, also on High St. (phone: 0368-63353), where you can purchase a helpful booklet, *A Walk Round the Old Burgh of Dunbar* by Stephen A. Bunyan. The Town House is a fascinating 17th-century building with a hexagonal tower from which, until recently, a bell rang out at closing time to clear the taverns. It contains Jacobean and Georgian Royal Armorial exhibits and a 16th-century jail.

Other attractions of Dunbar include: the *Lifeboat Museum,* in a harborside shed, staffed by volunteers from the town ladies' Lifeboat Committee (who also organize *Lifeboat Day,* in July, with stalls, bands, and the crowning of a Lifeboat Queen); Lauderdale House, the mansion of an 18th-century merchant and sea captain (which can be viewed from the outside only); Lauderdale Park, with skittles, tetherball, trampolines, and other family-style activities; a small miniature-golf park; an amusement park (also small); tennis courts; and two golf links. The *Dunbar Flower Show* is in early September. The 1,667-acre John Muir Country Park provides a field day for naturalists in love with trees, rocks, plants, butterflies, shells, sea life, birds, and bees. The park ranger (phone: 0620-842637) or the tourist information office have special guidebooks for the park's Clifftop Trail.

Dunbar is the sort of resort where people bring their children and tomorrow is 2 weeks away. It is possible to engage passersby in amiable chats, hearing about eventful winters like the one in 1987, during which the parish church was gutted by fire and subsequently razed, and 100 motorists, trapped in Dunbar by snowdrifts on A1, slept together on the floor of the corn exchange building (the Lothian social work department provided the mattresses).

CHECKING IN: *Battleblent* – Looking somewhat like a small castle with a turreted roof and sitting atop a hill, this recently modernized family-run hostelry features 7 guestrooms, a dining room specializing in seafood, and two bars. One mile east of Dunbar, West Barns (phone: 0368-62234). Inexpensive.

***Bayview* –** The 6 rooms here (sharing one shower!) are graced by sea views and the sparkling *Klownz* dining room, with white walls, white tablecloths, pine chairs, and toy clowns for decoration. Food is British and Italian. 3 Bayswell Rd. (phone: 0368-62778). Inexpensive.

En route from Dunbar – Heading south from Dunbar along A1, before crossing from the East Lothian region into the Borders, a mile north of Cockburnspath, you will pass the entrance to Dunglass Collegiate Church (follow the turnoff sign for Bilsdean), founded in 1450. The nave, choir, transepts, sacristy, and central tower are all still intact. The church was used as a barn after extensive plundering during the Reformation; today it stands empty. The interior stonework is especially arresting. Also at Cockburnspath is the eastern entrance to the Southern Upland Way, a coast-to-coast footpath across the Border hills that takes experienced hikers 15 days.

South of Cockburnspath, bear east off A1 onto A1107. Four miles along A1107 is the signposted approach to the ruins of Fast Castle, an ancient Home stronghold spectacularly poised on a cliff. From the castle, return to A1107, heading south toward Coldingham. At Coldingham is a small 13th-century Benedictine priory. Reformation zealots wrecked most of it, but the choir and sanctuary, with later additions, are now the Coldingham parish church. Legend has it that the stones here glow rose red in a supernatural manner.

The B6438 northeast off A1107 above Coldingham dead-ends at St. Abbs, a tiny storybook fishing village, where strings of whitewashed cottages uncurl down crags to the sea, flanked by clusters of colored boats. If you paint, bring your palette! A small crab and lobster industry survives here, but somehow the setting doesn't seem quite real. You can visit the nearby nature reserve on St. Abbs Head to behold seabirds, wildflowers, and sweeping views.

CHECKING IN: *St. Abbs Haven* – This 7-bedroom paradise on Coldingham Bay has marine panoramas and a sheltered beach. Some rooms with private bath. Approach off B6438 above St. Abbs harbor (phone: 0890-771491). Moderate to inexpensive.

EYEMOUTH: Return to the A1107 and continue south to Eyemouth. Don't be misled by the quaint, old-time atmosphere of the harbor into thinking it's a film set or a ghost town tarted up for tourists: Large trawlers dock here, jammed with herring for the major English cities. Among the clients in the cosy pubs along the quay are packers, truckers, and rosy-cheeked fishermen (and a three-legged marmalade cat called "Tripod," who prowls ye olde *Ship Inn*). The trawlers put out to sea on Sunday and come back Thursday, so Thursday is the town's big night!

Eyemouth is wealthy for a place its size, the modern houses on the outskirts belonging to trawler owners and to executives of a nearby frozen-fish-stick factory.

The *Eyemouth Museum,* in the lovely auld kirk on Market Place, opened in 1981 as a memorial to local fishermen lost in the Great Fishing Disaster of a hundred years before; it has won four tourism awards and is open April through October. Ochre-bright Gunsgreen House, overlooking the harbor pubs, has a romantic history tied to smuggling which the museum colorfully elucidates.

The chief attraction of Eyemouth for tourists is sea angling. Check for details at the auld kirk (phone: 08907-50678). There's a *Herring Queen Festival* in mid-July and *Eyemouth Lifeboat Week* in early August. The western promontory of the bay, because it is so sheltered, has vestiges of various forts, from prehistoric days to the present century.

En Route from Eyemouth – A short detour from the Berwick-bound A1107 to B6355 out of Eyemouth leads to Ayton Castle, where you rejoin the A1. The castle, designed in the 19th century for a governor of the Bank of Scotland, is a huge, flamboyant Scottish baronial type, built of red sandstone (open Sunday afternoons or by appointment; phone: 08907-81212).

BERWICK-UPON-TWEED: South of Burnmouth (on A1) is the city of Berwick — the only town in Britain currently at war with Russia! The town's status on a once-disputed English–Scottish border meant that Queen Victoria and her immediate predecessors were styled rulers "of England, Scotland, Ireland and Our Good Town of Berwick-on-Tweed"; as such, when the Crimean War began in 1854, the town formally declared war on Russia. The style was abolished during the war, so that the town never declared peace.

A medieval walled burgh constructed to withstand invaders' onslaughts, Berwick nonetheless changed hands like a football between warring English and Scots, until it finally became English in 1482. It was in the Berwick Castle Great Hall — now the site of the Berwick railway station — that King Edward I of England announced, in 1292, his choice for King of Scots from among 13 contenders, including Robert the Bruce. He chose the limpid John Balliol, known subsequently to his subjects as "Toom Tabard" ("Empty Coat"). John Balliol's maladministrations cost the two nations the truce that should have left Berwick unharmed. Today the town, despite high unemployment, keeps going, thanks to its small industries, including a woodyard and a Pringle knitwear depot.

Park in the Castlegate car park (where the Berwick tourist information caravan is located). Berwick streets are so ancient a car can hardly move down them, but the town is so full of intriguing nooks and crannies that it's much more fun to walk. Begin by descending from the railway station (it's near the car park) to the river Tweed, through a delightful small wooded garden. A riverside walk affords a splendid view of three bridges of which Berwick's inhabitants are very proud: the old bridge of 1634, with arches decreasing in height from north to south; the Royal Tweed Bridge of 1928, in a modern mode; and the breathtaking Royal Border Bridge, which carries trains between London and Edinburgh. The Royal Border Bridge has 28 celestial arches and was opened by Queen Victoria in 1850; on a grey day, when the Border hills are electrically charged by low-lying clouds, the view upriver beyond this bridge can make beholders feel extremely ethereal.

Around the mouth of the Tweed are ducks, swans, wheeling gulls, and clusters of red-roofed buildings, some newly renovated, others with that rare dereliction that transmits ramshackle charm. Restoration work on houses along the quay walls has drawn artists and craftsmen from other parts of Britain as buyers. All periods of history are represented in old Berwick, in an architectural jumble that is deliciously quaint. The people, too, seem individualistic: Someone with a Slavic name over his door has turned a veritable broom closet into a cheek-to-cheek fast-fooderie, stuffing it with disproportionately massive oak tables and hanging extravagant bunches of dried wildflowers from a roof beam, and an antique bookseller has hastily shunted half his merchandise almost into the street so he can sell oats and lentils to health nuts newly moved to town.

Uphill from all this is Marygate, less old world and more like a typical present-day county town. It's Berwick's main shopping street and houses the old-fashioned offices of the Tweeddale Press Group of local newspapers, as well as the town hall, a striking example of a Georgian public building. The hall has a local history museum, a jail, and a belfry; guided tours are available weekdays at 10:30 AM and 2 PM Easter through September. Year-round there is a high-quality gift shop and a coffee shop with home baking. Open-air market days in Marygate are Wednesdays and Saturdays.

The main tourist sights of Berwick are: the remains of Berwick Castle, on the Tweed at the base of the Royal Border Bridge; the bastioned Walls, built by Elizabeth I, which can be walked along from rampart to rampart looking down onto the city; the Parish Church of 1652, one of only two churches in Britain built under Cromwell, it has a severely Puritan design; and the Vanbrugh-style barracks, now a museum, where troops have been garrisoned since 1721. On Palace Green is the *Wine and Spirit Museum* of the Lindisfarne Liqueur Co. Ltd. (open daily except Sundays Easter through October). You can sample their product and buy Lindisfarne Pottery.

If you're touring with children or need presents for the kids back home, *Border Series* (9 Hide Hill) has a large toy department with outsized electric model trains that chug around a ledge near the ceiling. *Martin's Border Bakery,* in *The Good Food Shop* (7 Marygate) sells beautiful buns. Sit down and try the home baking in the *Scotsgate Tea Room,* also in Marygate (a no-smoking establishment), or at *Popinjay's,* on Hide Hill.

CHECKING IN: ***The King's Arms*** – The tiny lobby of this former coaching inn fans out into two attractive restaurants, a spacious buffet bar, a walled garden café, a snookerama (a pool-like game room), and 36 Cinderella bedrooms. Hide Hill, Berwick-upon-Tweed (phone: 0289-307454). Moderate.

En Route from Berwick – Follow the river Tweed southwest to Coldstream by A698. Halfway along is Norham Castle, an ancient stronghold of the Bishops of Durham which reinforced the fort at Coldstream against Scottish invaders and was of major strategic importance under Kings Edward I and Henry II and III. "The loopholed walls where captives weep" described by Sir Walter Scott in *Marmion* are extant.

CHECKING IN: ***The Tilmouth Park*** – This elegant 13-bedroom salmon-fisher's hotel on 1,500 acres of its own grounds makes guests feel like Victorian aristocrats. Off A698 at Cornhill-on-Tweed (phone: 0890-2255). Expensive to moderate.

COLDSTREAM: The 300-foot Tweed Bridge across the river between England and Scotland was built in 1776, after which it rapidly became notorious for a heavy traffic in eloping couples heading for the Old Marriage House beside its northern entrance. (Scotland has relatively lax marriage laws.) The town is famous too as the starting point of the 1660 march of the Coldstream Guards to London, where they effected the restoration of Charles II. Their original headquarters is on the north side of the main square.

En Route from Coldstream – About 2 miles northwest of Coldstream, on A697, is the Hirsel, Sir Alec Douglas-Home's ancestral home and current residence. The house itself is closed to the public, but the magnificent gardens are open and include rhododendrons, woodlands, and a small lake chockablock with wildfowl. BBC Radio at its most "precious" has been known to fill an idle minute or two with live choruses of Hirsel birdsong. There is now a museum highlighting the estate's history and a crafts center, which holds crafts demonstrations (phone: 0890-2834, -2629). Return to A698 and continue south to Kelso.

KELSO: Site of one of the four Border abbeys of the incomparable Scott country, this small bastion of what could almost be French civilization (its center looks like an enormous *grande place*) is nonetheless the first taste of the netherworld between past and present, legend and reality, which suffuses this part of Scotland. The town, like the abbey, is situated on the rivers Tweed and Teviot. Its five-arched bridge, begun in 1800, was an exact model for the later Waterloo Bridge across the Thames, demolished in 1934. The lamp standards, visible at the bridge's south end, were salvaged and brought here from London after the demolition.

Kelso Abbey, founded in 1128 by King David I (son of the King Malcolm who succeeded Macbeth and ancestor of King Robert the Bruce), was destroyed by the Earl of Hertford in 1545. What remains of it shows a Norman transitional style unique in Scotland. In the largest Kelso car park behind the abbey is *Kelso Pottery,* where you can watch the making and glazing of stoneware and buy some of the products. In late May, gaily costumed local bargemen compete in the Great Tweed Raft Race; *Civic Week,* the third week in July, is full of colorful equestrian pageants; and the mid-September Kelso Ram Sales in Springwood Park provide a fascinating glimpse of Border life. Kelso has a steeplechase racecourse and on the fairgrounds, hosts the Berwickshire, the Buccleuch, and the Jed Forest hunts in "point-to-points" (a horse race with an undefined course — only a start and finish point). There are horse sales in the showground (a different venue from the fairground) as well as Britain's largest dog show. The tourist board office at Turret House, a museum of local history (it's in Abbey Court), has details; it's open April through October (phone: 0573-23464).

Shops of note in Kelso are *Margaret Thompson* (designer knitwear, cashmere, and lambswool), 46 Roxburgh St.; *The Curiosity Shop* (antiques), the Woodmarket; *Inspiration Gift Shop* (clothes, cushions, Liberty scarves), Bridge St. The fishing tackle shops sell visitors' tickets for fishing on the river Tweed, and if you catch a fish, local hotels will buy it from you for about $4 per pound.

En Route from Kelso – Some 2 miles northwest of Kelso, on A6089, is Floors Castle, seat of the Dukes of Roxburgh, said to be the largest inhabited mansion in Britain. It has 365 windows, one for every day in the year. Built by William Adam in 1721, it underwent various additions and remodelings until it became spectacularly grandiose — a kind of fantastic Brobdingnag dollhouse, with its battlements, water spouts, and pepper-pot towers, its amphitheater, and its golden gates. The furniture, porcelain, tapestries, and paintings are all superb. The fine grounds include a holly tree supposedly marking the spot where King James II (of Scotland) was killed in 1460 firing one of his own cannons. An adjoining veranda restaurant serves food from the castle kitchen (open daily except Fridays and Saturdays May through September; closed Saturdays only July and August). Pipe bands perform on certain days in the summer. This was the British location for the film, *Greystoke.*

A 20-mile detour north to Hume Castle, Mellerstain House, and Smailholm Tower is a must (these places are clearly marked on the *Enjoy Scotland* touring map: The route between them from Kelso and back — the B6364, some unnumbered roads, and the B6397 — forms the shape of a fan). Thirteenth-century Hume Castle preceded the Hirsel (see *En Route from Coldstream,* above) as seat of the Earls of Home, but Cromwell destroyed it in 1651. The view from its parapets (these were reconstructed in the 18th century) is glorious. The castle key is available on request at the house called the Smiddy, opposite the castle, in the center of Hume village.

Mellerstain House is, architecturally speaking, an Adam "pie" — begun in 1725 by

William and finished in 1778 by his famous son, Robert. Despite this, it is proportionally perfect. No finer craftsmanship exists anywhere than the plasterwork ceilings inside; Mellerstain is one of the great Georgian houses of Scotland. There are outstanding collections of 18th-century furniture too, and paintings by old masters (open daily except Saturdays May through September). Mellerstain House takes part in an annual Borders springtime rally by presenting an exhibition of its vintage car collection.

Sir Walter Scott used to sit like a medieval princess in the top of Smailholm Tower concocting romantic novels. The best extant example of a 16th-century Border keep, its 57-foot summit overlooks vast expanses of country, both English and Scottish. Strategically placed stone fortresses like Smailholm (into which Border reivers herded women, children, and cattle as enemies approached) had roofs fitted with pans of pitch and peat for kindling; on a clear night it was said to take only two minutes for a chain of danger signals to reach Edinburgh Castle from the English border. Open daily except Sunday mornings, April through September.

Return to A698, continue south to the turnoff for A68 south to Jedburgh.

CHECKING IN: *Sunlaws House* – This appealing Georgian hotel is owned by the Duke of Roxburgh and draws guests who enjoy fishing and shooting. Its 21 rooms contain modern amenities, and its restaurant specializes in local game and in salmon pulled from the river Tweed. Heighton (phone: 0573-5331). Very expensive.

Marlefield Country House – Set in a 12th-century fortified manor, this historic stone buiding is long on character and charm. There are 7 guestrooms and a restaurant featuring international cuisine. Morebattle, south of Kelso (phone: 05734-561/2/3). Expensive to moderate.

Ednam House – Built in 1761 as the abode of a prominent Kelso merchant, this historic, 32-room hotel has an arresting façade as well as its original Italian ceilings. Bridge St., Kelso (phone: 0573-24168/9). Moderate.

Cross Keys – This 25-room, newly renovated old inn has "Taste-of-Scotland" cooking and a charming bar decorated with horse-and-wagon motifs. The Square, Kelso (phone: 0573-23303). Inexpensive.

Queens Head – This family-run old coaching inn is lacking in one or two amenities but compensates with friendliness and architectural fascination. The close-up view of the abbey from the back door is priceless. 24 Bridge St., Kelso (phone: 0573-24636). Inexpensive.

JEDBURGH: Although the priory section of Jedburgh Abbey was leveled during the Rough Wooing, the church is amazingly well preserved. The elegant rose window is nicknamed St. Catherine's Wheel. There was a church here as early as the 9th century, but the abbey dates from 1138, when David I brought Augustinians to Scotland from Beauvais in France. It enjoys a lovely setting above Jed Water, a tributary of the river Teviot, and on some evenings it appears to be made of solid gold (open daily except Sunday mornings).

The great and wise Alexander III, the first king of a truly unified Scotland, was married in Jedburgh in 1285 to his young and beautiful second wife. His love for her seems to have spurred him to foolish and hotheaded passion: It is said that the spectral figure of Death was seen among the dancing guests at the wedding reception in Jedburgh Castle — now the site of the *Jail Museum* — and sure enough, Alexander was killed 6 months later when his horse fell over a cliff as he rode out on a stormy night, against the advice of his aides, from Edinburgh Castle to join his bride in Dunfermline. The museum, in the Castlegate, is as it was in 1823 when erected as an experimental "modern" jail (closed Sunday mornings; phone: 0835-63254).

Jedburgh was once surrounded (for protection) by a series of "bastel houses," one of which, on Queen Street, was a residence of Mary, Queen of Scots. Today it is open to the public (Easter through October) and is fascinating because of the number of portraits it contains of that enigmatic lady, each one looking less like the last. In the unlikely event you are in Jedburgh in mid-February, you can enter the spirit of Mary's troubled times by watching the annual Ba' Game, played in the 16th century with the heads of Jedburgh's slain enemies. The "Uppies" — those born above the mercat (market) cross, and the "Doonies" — those born below, have to get a ball into their goal (the goals are the *Jail Museum* grounds and the Townfoot) by fair means or foul in 2 hours (phone: 0835-63331).

About 1½ miles south of Jedburgh on A68 is Ferniehirst Castle, dating from the 16th-century, the ancestral home of the Kerr family, Marquis of Lothian. The family, which lives there today, opens the castle and its notable collection of 17th-century paintings to the public on Sunday afternoons May through October and Wednesday afternoons in July and August (phone: 0835-62201).

The Friday after the second Saturday in July sees the start of the 3-day *Jethart Callants' Festival,* in which the Riding of the Marches takes the form of mounted ceremonial dashes to historically important places, the Jedburgh flag to the fore. A "callant" is a gallant, or youngblood. Also part of the festival are the Jedburgh Border Games held on the Saturday in Riverside Park from 10 AM to teatime.

At the north entrance to Jedburgh is a complex of mill outlet shops (with its own cafeteria), including *Gleneagles Woollens, The Woollen Mill, The Sheepskin Shop,* and *Jedburgh Kiltmakers. First Impressions,* in Veitch's Close in the Castlegate, has exceptional designer sweaters different from the usual Borders wares. These places are open even on Thursday afternoons, when everything else in town closes. The tourist board office, closed all winter, is at Murray's Green and conducts a "Town Trail" tour to streets of historic interest (phone: 0835-63435, 0835-63688).

The *Woodland Centre,* 3 miles north, is at Harestane's Mill, Monteviot (open daily June through September and Wednesdays and Sundays in April, May, and October). The town has few restaurants and hotels, but coffee and home-baked goodies are available at the *Mercat Café,* in Market Square, and the *Chef's Grill,* 3½ miles south on A68. On sale at *Miller's* (10 High St.) are "Jethart snails," a traditional Jedburgh mint-flavored hard candy of escargotian color and shape, created during the Napoleonic Wars.

CHECKING IN: ***Glenbank Country House*** – A short walk from town, this pretty 7-bedroom Georgian house has home cooking served with tea on the lawn. Castlegate, Jedburgh (phone: 0835-62258). Inexpensive.

En Route from Jedburgh – Retrace A68 north and then head southwest on A698. Halfway to Hawick is charming Denholm, with its 18th-century cottages and expansive village green. John Leyden, a shepherd's son who was a minor poet and friend of Sir Walter Scott, and who left Scotland eventually to become Commissioner of the Calcutta Mint, was born here in 1775. A few miles south of Denholm is Trow Mill, an 18th-century grain mill which became a woolen mill around 1800 and today is completely modernized. The mill has factory tours, its own shop, and free coffee for visitors (no advance notice necessary).

HAWICK: Pronounced *Hoyk,* this largest of the Border burghs, a busy farm market and knitwear and electronics capital, stands at the junction of the Teviot and Slitrig rivers. Its citizens are avid rugby fans, and it has contributed many a famous player to internationally known rugby teams. Its home team, the *Greens,* plays Saturdays at Mansfield Park.

In the leafy shades of the 107-acre municipal Wilton Lodge Park is *Hawick Museum and Art Gallery,* bursting with Border relics (closed Sunday mornings year-round and Saturdays in winter; phone: 0450-73457). The Riding of the Marches is at its zenith in Hawick, where it is called the Common Riding and takes place around the second week in June. It is led by an unmarried callant elected months in advance, the Cornet, who trains his men beforehand in a series of death-defying cavalry charges, culminating in their promotion to the ancient order of mosstroopers. Three days of festivities include the mosstroopers' all-important private performance at breakfast of ancient druidic rites in preparation for the riding; the thrilling equestrian chases that constitute the riding; additional horse races (at which official bets can be placed) on Hawick Moor; athletic matches between top British professionals in Volunteer Park; all-night dinners and dances; and the singing, on the town heights at dawn, of the Hawick battle song "Teribus," which begins in Latin, lurches into Old Norse, and then plunges into Scots. The whole experience is the ultimate in Scottish machismo (if you can stay the course)!

Hawick is picturesque because its rivers rush right through the topographical basin that holds the town center. Mills and markets intermix familially. It's almost possible to swim to the shops adjoining Tower Mill (*Murray Brothers*) and Teviotdale Mills (*Charles Whillans*). For designer cashmeres, try *Valerie Louthan Ltd.,* at 2 Kirk Wynd. Hand-crafted gifts are sold at *Arista Designs,* Victoria Works, Victoria Road; and at the *Teviotdale Design Company,* 14 Buccleuch St. Hawick balls, the local hard candy, are sold at *R. T. Smith,* 16 Commercial Rd.

The Hawick Railway Society sometimes exhibits its model trains; for information, contact the tourist information office in Common Haugh car park (phone: 0450-72547). Nature lovers might like to explore the nearby Craik Forest Walk (take B711, off A7 south of Hawick, to Robertson Church, then follow the side road along the Borthwick Water for 7 miles). Hawick Motte is archaeologically interesting; "mottes" are high cones of earth, artificial in construction, on which sat the timber houses that pre-dated the great stone castles of Norman aristocrats. In the 12th century King William the Lion of Scotland granted Hawick to the Somersetshire Lovels, whose seat Hawick Motte is thought to have been. It's down a side road off A7, inside the town boundaries, on the west side of the river Slitrig.

CHECKING IN: ***Kirklands*** – This 10-room Victorian country house has a striking view across Hawick and the surrounding hills and a reputation for friendliness and elegance. W. Stewart Pl., Hawick (phone: 0450-72263). Moderate to inexpensive.

Mansfield House – Ten bedrooms with views of lush private grounds make this Italian villa-like hostelry an excellent retreat. Weensland Rd., Hawick (phone: 0450-73988). Moderate to inexpensive.

Miss E. Scott's Cottage – This pretty little gingerbread house with two twin bedrooms is near Wilton Lodge Park. In Wilton Dean, on the outskirts of Hawick (phone: 0450-73378). Inexpensive.

En Route from Hawick – *Brook Cottage Workshops,* 5 miles south of Hawick on the B6399, make and sell hand-crafted furniture and smaller gift items; you can watch the whole production process from seasoning the timber to the final finishing. Farther south on B6399 is the historically important Hermitage Castle, miles from anywhere, where Mary, Queen of Scots, dashed on horseback from Jedburgh for a tryst with Bothwell, catching a cold that nearly caused her death. The castle's four towers and connecting walls are in almost perfect condition, powerfully invoking the grim grandeur of 14th-century baronial halls (closed Sunday mornings). The road west along the Hermitage Water joins A7 leading south to Langholm.

LANGHOLM: There is an Old and a New Town here, the latter begun in 1778. Langholm was the birthplace in 1892 of Christopher Murray Grieve, who is famous as the Scottish Nationalist and Marxist poet known as Hugh MacDiarmid. It is in Langholm also that MacDiarmid is buried, despite the furious opposition of the local inhabitants, who were the raw material for some of the poet's most iconoclastic works. His funeral, in 1978, was converged upon by the great bulk of the Scottish literary and left-wing political worlds, while Langholm, apart from one cousin who still lives in the town, boycotted the entire ceremony and its participants. Some honors have since been accorded to the burial site.

En Route from Langholm – Follow B709 and B7009 north to Selkirk. Just outside of Langholm is the *Craigcleuch Scottish Explorers' Museum,* which houses objects brought back from tribal cultures by Scottish explorers in Africa, Asia, and Latin America (open May through September). You can make a literary pilgrimage to the birthplace and grave of James Hogg, "The Ettrick Shepherd." The grave is in Ettrick Kirkyard, a deserted place a mile down the Ettrick Water west of B709; a monument marks the spot. The village of Ettrickbridge, farther north on B7009, is the home of David Steel, until recently the leader of Britain's Liberal Party.

SELKIRK: Halliwell's House, in the main square, is an interesting museum of local history (open daily except Sunday mornings April through October; phone: 0750-20054). Sir Walter Scott was sheriff of Selkirkshire from 1799 to 1832; the courthouse on High Street displays some of his letters. Selkirk's setting is exciting, on a high ridge overlooking the Ettrick and Yarrow River Valley. The mills below the town are architecturally attractive, with clock towers rising symmetrically from their centers and colorful names in bold letters on their sides like "Ettrick and Yarrow Spinners." The weaving process can be watched Mondays through Fridays at Andrew Elliott's, Forest Mill, just north of town on A707.

The *Selkirk Glass* factory and showroom, in the adjacent village of Linglie Mill, allows visitors to watch the making of designer paperweights (closed weekends and Friday afternoons; phone: 0750-20954). The *Wellwood Weavers Shop* on the Galashiels road sells hand-crafted goods, including sweaters, toys, and jewelry. The *Courthouse Coffee Shop* (High St.) is a good place to sit down for a piece of Selkirk bannock, the richest raisin bread in the world. Or buy one whole at *Houston Bakers* (who invented them) across the square.

En Route from Selkirk – A 20-mile circular detour from Selkirk east via A699, A68, A6091, B6360, and A7 takes in Dryburgh Abbey, Melrose Abbey, and Abbotsford House. It is also possible to visit Galashiels at this point, rather than when en route to Edinburgh from Peebles, as advised later. Galashiels is north of Abbotsford on A7 (see the entry for *Galashiels* following *Peebles* below).

On the Tweed near the village of St. Boswell's is majestic Dryburgh Abbey — considered by many to have the most beautiful setting of all. It too was founded during the reign of David I and later ravaged by English raiders. Only the transepts remain of the church, but the cloister is nearly complete. Sir Walter Scott is buried here, as is Earl Haig, Britain's chief World War I general.

Another of David I's now ruined monasteries, Melrose Abbey, graces the central square of the lovely little town of Melrose. Notice that the abbey's exquisite 15th-century traceried stonework features a pig on the roof playing bagpipes. According to one legend the heart of Robert the Bruce is buried in the abbey. According to another, the Eildon Hills, which loom to the southeast, are shaped as they are (two pointed, one shorter and flat-topped) because the devil was so piqued by the dawn chanting of the abbey monks that he thrust three mountains between them and the rising sun, but dropped and broke one mountain in transit. Sir Walter Scott used to gaze across the Tweed at the Eildon Hills from a point above Melrose now known as Scott's View. (It's on B6356 a couple of miles east of Melrose; see the *Enjoy Scotland* touring map.) Dryburgh and Melrose abbeys are open daily except Sunday mornings.

Hikers can take the Eildon Walk with the aid of nature trail leaflets available (free) at the tourist information bureau next to Melrose Abbey (phone: 089-682-2555). The old railway station at Melrose, just off Market Square, has now reopened as a crafts center, shop, and venue for fairs and exhibitions. Priorwood Gardens, beside the abbey, are pleasant — their specialty is flowers suitable for drying (open daily except Sundays April through September and assorted other times except January through March).

Built to Sir Walter Scott's own specifications in 1812–24, his fascinating country home, Abbotsford House, broods in stately somnolence by the Tweed. A trip here gives a vivid picture of Scott's personality. He could carry his starry-eyed antiquarianism to laughable lengths, as when he made off with the door to Edinburgh's just-razed, 15th-century "Heart of Midlothian" (the county jail) and had it installed in a wall at Abbotsford. (He later wrote a not-so-laughable book about the Heart of Midlothian.) There are historic relics he carefully collected, impressive armories, a 9,000-volume library, and the study in which he wrote the Waverley novels in an attempt to reduce a £117,000 debt. The effort eventually killed him; he died here at the age of 61. Open daily except Sunday mornings from the last week in March through October (phone: 0896-2043).

Return to Selkirk (this detour's point of origin) and proceed 3 miles to the west on A708 to find Philiphaugh, the field where the army of the noble Scottish cavalier and poet-soldier, the Marquis of Montrose, lost a key battle to Puritan forces in 1645. Near the Yarrow Water is Bowhill, home of the Dukes of Buccleuch and Queensberry (one dukedom), another of the Borders' ancestral palaces. Bowhill has early-19th-century silk brocades and hand-painted Chinese wallpapers, sumptuous art treasures, lush woods and gardens, an elaborately inventive jungle-playground-type Tarzan complex for kids, and pony trekking. Open afternoons during July only; grounds open every afternoon except Fridays May through August; pony-trekking center open daily from 10 AM (phone: 0750-20732). Adjacent to Bowhill is Newark Castle, a 5-story oblong towerhouse where the "Last Minstrel" recited his "Lay" to the Duchess of Buccleuch. It was a royal hunting seat for the Forest of Ettrick in the Middle Ages. Another 4 miles west along A708 is picturesque Yarrow Kirk, dating from 1640.

Continuing along the Yarrow Water, you reach the wild, godforsaken country over which the merlinhawks fly. These small, ferocious birds are said to embody, by magic, the spirit of Merlin the wizard. Near desolate St. Mary's Loch and its sister lake, the Loch of the Lowes, are two historic inns — the *Gordon Arms* and *Tibbie Shiels* — where Scott met literary friends (both are on the *Enjoy Scotland* touring map, albeit in tiny print). Across the main road from St. Mary's Loch are the remains of Dryhope Tower, which, like Smailholm, is a medieval watchtower, or "peel."

Stay on A708. On the right, about 8 miles before Moffat, is the Grey Mare's Tail, a magnificent 200-foot waterfall formed as the Tail Burn gorge drops from Loch Skeen to meet the Moffat Water (you lose the Yarrow at St. Mary's Loch. The whole area is resplendent with wildflowers. Covenanters used to hide out here. The hollow below the falls is the "Giant's Grave," which figures in Scott's poem *Marmion.* The *Scotland: Hillwalking* booklet gives instructions for climbing to the top of either side of the Tail Burn gorge.

CHECKING IN:

Dryburgh Abbey – This 19th-century house in the baronial mode has all the swagger of the horse-and-hound set that patronizes it. It has 29 rooms and serves elegant afternoon teas, and the restaurant is the last word in traditional Scottish cooking. Some guests choose to park on the other side of the river and cross a footbridge to the hotel, but there's ample parking right outside for travelers with luggage. St. Boswells, on the banks of the Tweed (phone: 0835-22261). Expensive.

Buccleuch Arms – Overlooking the village green of St. Boswells, this hospitable old staging post has recently been renovated to offer 19 luxury bedrooms. On A68, St. Boswells (phone: 0835-22243). Moderate.

Burt's – In addition to full-fledged restaurant meals, this bustling 21-room hostelry provides substantial and delicious bar snacks. Gleaming everywhere under its wooden roofbeams are pieces of copper and brass. Market Sq., Melrose (phone: 0896-822285). Moderate.

Ettrickshaws – The sylvan seclusion and the exceptional food at this 6-bedroom Victorian mansion on the Ettrick Water make these accommodations more costly than is usual for this area. Guests have automatic fishing rights. In the village of Ettrickbridge (phone: 0750-52229). Moderate.

Philipburn House – Families are positively coddled in this modernized old house overlooking the famous battlefield of Philiphaugh. There are 16 rooms, gardens and woodlands, a heated swimming pool, a well-equipped playground, riding and fishing facilities, and real log fires. On A708, 2½ miles west of Selkirk (phone: 0750-20747, -21690). Moderate.

EATING OUT: ***Queenshead*** – Robert Burns once slept in this friendly coaching inn during a stint as an exciseman. Although no lodging is available now, the bar has tasty food including homemade soups. West Port St., Selkirk (phone: 0750-21782). Inexpensive.

MOFFAT: The pride of this town is Colvin Fountain, erected in 1875; the huge bronze ram on top symbolizes the importance of sheep farming in the surrounding districts. For 2 centuries Moffat was a fashionable resort, and among the 18th-century greats who frequented its spa were James Boswell, Robert Burns, and the "fake" folklorist James Macpherson of the Ossianic ballads. Today it's a touring base full of hotels and Italian cafés, but it retains a days-gone-by image and seems unlikely ever to shed its air of pleasant pokiness. The Blacklock family, who have made their now famous Moffat Toffee for generations, maintain a candy shop on High Street.

A good pottery with a retail showroom is the *Moffat Pottery,* Ladyknowe (in the town center beside the telephone exchange). Also at Ladyknowe are the *Moffat Weavers,* who display antique looms as well as demonstrate the art of skirt making. They keep a shop with a wide choice of Scottish products, including their own.

CHECKING IN: ***Auchen Castle*** – This 19th-century great-house-turned-hotel is near Beattock, just south of Moffat. It has 34 bedrooms and is situated in 50 acres of private grounds with a trout loch. A mile north of Beattock on A74 (phone: 0683-3407). Moderate to inexpensive.

Beechwood Country House – A comfortable haven on a Moffat hill, this 8-room home-away-from-home sets a tempting "Taste-of-Scotland" table, including beetroot soup, venison casserole, and the best Orkney cheeses. Restaurant reservations necessary on weekends and for dinner. Closed in January. Harthope Pl., Moffat (phone: 0683-20210). Accommodations, moderate; restaurant, expensive.

En Route from Moffat – Six miles north on A701 is the Devil's Beef Tub, famous in literature and lore. An astonishing feature of Dumfriesshire's natural geography, the Tub's vast, smooth, basinlike recess has a rotund regularity more believable in classical art than in nature. As its name suggests, Border reivers herded pilfered steers into the Devil's Beef Tub to conceal them. If your family name is Armstrong or Douglas, your ancestors were the scourge of this part of Scotland.

Continuing north on A701 to Tweedshaws, the road passes the almost imperceptible source of the river Tweed (a roadsign identifies where), seen in flowing majesty at Berwick, Coldstream, Kelso, St. Boswells, Abbotsford, and Melrose. The route now parallels the Tweed until almost to Galashiels, the last stop before the conclusion of this driving tour. The Tweed River valley boasts some of the finest scenery in the world, especially in very early spring, when snow remains on the hills.

Proceed north on A701 to B712 (east) to visit Tinnis Castle, Dawyck House Gardens, and Stobo Kirk. Tinnis Castle, a ruin, was built in the early 16th century and is now approached on foot by a sheepwalk. Dawyck Gardens, owned by the Royal Botanic Gardens at Edinburgh, consists mostly of rare trees forming a wood in which a pleasant little chapel sits (gardens open daily from 10 AM, April through October). Stobo Kirk, a 12th-century building with additions that were made over the next four centuries, has some particularly fascinating carved tombstones. It's on the west side of the B712 road. From B712 (north), take A72 east to Neidpath Castle.

Neidpath Castle (on A72 just before Peebles) is the next stop; this one is a must. It looms (there is no other word for it) high above the Tweed in a portentous and spectacular fashion. Of 14th-century construction, its walls are 12 feet thick, it is five stories high, and its Great Hall once occupied the entire second floor. It's an interesting example of how such fortresses could be adapted to the more civilized lifestyles prominent in the 17th century; extensive internal renovations tell this tale. After inspecting the pit-prison in its bottom, climb to its parapet. Open Mondays through Saturdays and Sunday afternoons May through the first week in October (phone: 0721-20333 or 08757-201 during winter).

After Neidpath Castle, continue east on A72 to Peebles.

CHECKING IN: ***Crook Inn*** – The panoramic sweep of the moors at this 18th-century coaching inn defies description! There are 8 bedrooms. On A701 about 14 miles north of Moffat, Tweedsmuir (phone: 0899-7272). Moderate to inexpensive.

PEEBLES: Set on a sharp slope beside the meeting of the Eddleston Water with the Tweed, Peebles is the chief town of Peeblesshire (or Tweeddale, as the district used to be called). It is laid out like a Highlands town, with one long, thin street around which everything is focused. A fortified settlement itself in the 16th century, it is an ideal center from which to explore other, much older fortified settlements in the same area. These date from the 1st century and are accessible by traipsing deep into the local hinterlands along old cattle-droving trails. A copy of *Exploring Scotland's Heritage, Lothian and the Borders* will be invaluable here.

The novelist John Buchan, Governor General of Canada 1935 to 1940, is a sort of "cottage industry" of Peeblesshire. He was particularly fond of the area and took as his title Lord Tweedsmuir. Literary tourists use Peebles as a base for visiting sites mentioned in his novels. Nonliterary tourists have a good time sporting, shopping, and soaking up the past.

The *Tweedvale Museum* is on High Street in the Chambers Institution (donated to Peebles in 1859 by William Chambers, the Edinburgh publisher). It displays objects from Peeblesshire's industrial, religious, and domestic heritages and is open weekdays. The *Cornice,* a museum of ornamental plasterwork, such as is found on the ceilings of great houses, is at 31 High Street. Cross Kirk is the remains of a 15th-century Trinitarian priory designed to enshrine an earlier sacred cross and a sculpted stone inscribed to St. Nicholas; for centuries the kirk was a rallying point for St. Nicholas pilgrims. The walls are still standing.

In Hay Lodge Park there are tennis courts, a bowling green, a trim track (for jogging), and boating facilities. There is also a municipal golf course, off Kirkland Street (phone: 0721-20197). *Glentress Mountain Bike Center,* on Venlaw High Rd. (see also *Drummore* inn, under *Checking In*) rents special bicycles on which to explore the local Glentress and Cardrona Forest Trails (phone: 0721-20336, -22934). The tourist board, in the Chambers Institution, has further details (phone: 0721-20138).

Newby Court Centre, down School Brae off High St., is a delight; it's a cluster of shops around a small close that leads downhill to a park by the Tweed. The shops sell Highland wear, jewelry, woodwork, and pottery. *Robert Noble* keeps one of the last mill shops in the Borders specializing in fabrics rather than ready-to-wear (on March St.). *Mrs. Peterson's* (7 High St.) is something of a surprise: It's a continental delicatessen! Plain old lovable Scottish homebaking can meanwhile be taken with tea at the *Sunflower Coffee Shop* (4 The Bridgegate).

CHECKING IN: ***Peebles Hydro*** – A playground of Victorian captains of industry and still famous to the present day, this grand 136-room hotel exudes an air of wealth and celebration. On 30 acres of ground. Innerleithen Rd., Peebles (phone: 0721-20602). Expensive to moderate.

Tontine – This is Peebles' second most famous hotel; it was built in 1808, has 37 well-appointed bedrooms, and is a picturesquely immovable feature of High St. Peebles (phone: 0721-20892). Expensive to moderate.

Cringletie House – Also famous, this private mansion with 16 rooms is opened to guests by the resident owner (a talented interior decorator and cook) from March through December. A 2-acre kitchen garden supplies the highly regarded dining room with fresh vegetables. On A703, 2 miles north of Peebles at Eddleston (phone: 0721-3233). Moderate.

Park – This pleasingly peaceful black-and-white house, with extensions and a turret, has 26 rooms and stunning views of the Cademuir Hills. Innerleithen Rd., Peebles (phone: 0721-20451). Moderate.

Kingsmuir – A captivating hotel on a large green lawn, in the style of a family home of the 1850s, with 10 bedrooms and traditional Scottish cooking. Springhill Rd., Peebles (phone: 0721-20151). Moderate to inexpensive.

Drummore – A guest house in a forest clearing, Mrs. Phillips's little shangri-la has 3 bedrooms and special "mountain bikes" for hire. Venlaw High Rd., Peebles (phone: 0721-20336). Inexpensive.

En Route from Peebles – Two miles east of Peebles on B7062 is Kailzie Gardens, in 17 acres of woodland full of small streams and wild daffodils. There are greenhouses, shrub borders, and a laburnum alley as well as a gift shop, art gallery, and tea room, which are open daily 11 AM to 5:30 PM, from March through October.

At Traquair, where B7062 meets B709, is Traquair House, Scotland's oldest continuously inhabited mansion. Constructed of whitewashed stone during the 10th century, it is four stories high with round turrets. Visitors entering the oldest section are transported back in time, in a way impossible when viewing an abandoned ruin of the same period. The expansiveness of Traquair House and its slight asymmetry derive from extensions built in the 16th and 17th centuries (for the latter of which the then Earl of Traquair rerouted the Tweed!).

The present master of Traquair is Peter Maxwell-Stuart, who is often on hand for a chat and who helps officiate at the yearly *Traquair Fair,* a small performing arts festival held on his grounds the first weekend in August, and at other artistic events. He is a distant descendant of the Stuart kings, who were related to the Earls of Traquair. The Bear Gates at the former main entrance to Traquair House, as guidebooks never tire of telling you, were closed when Bonnie Prince Charlie was defeated at Culloden, and are never to be opened again until a Stuart monarch ascends to the Scottish throne.

Literature about the history of Traquair House is freely available on site and will add to your enjoyment. Also on-site are a working 18th-century brewhouse (sample its ale), four craft workshops, and a tea room and gift shop. Open from 1:30 to 5:30 PM Holy Week (Easter) and May through September; also mornings in July, August, and the first 2 weeks of September (summer opening times vary, so phone ahead: 0896-830323).

Just north of Traquair on B709 is the village of Innerleithen, once a popular spa. Here A72 leads east to Walkerburn, location of *Tweedvale Mills,* makers of Clan Royal woolens. The facilities include a mill shop, a café, and the interesting *Scottish Museum of Woollen Textiles* (open Mondays through Saturdays year-round and Sunday afternoons Easter through Christmas). The name "Walkerburn" (and the surname "Walker") can be traced to "waulking," an early practice during the production of saleable cloth. Maidens would lay out the cloth on the grassy verge of the river, then, to flatten and stretch it, take off their shoes, hoist their skirts, and trample it in a Baccanalian manner!

Next on A72 is Torwoodlee House, 2 miles before Galashiels. It is the home of the Pringle family, who have inhabited this small, elegant Georgian home (with Victorian alterations) since 1783. Open by appointment June through August (phone: 0896-2151).

CHECKING IN: ***Tweed Valley*** – This luxury hotel with fishing, riding, gardens, shops, sauna, and solarium is a 16-bedroom Edwardian country house on its own grounds. Off A72 at Walkerburn (phone: 0896-87636). Moderate to inexpensive.

Thornielee House – A converted farmhouse, this winsome 4-bedroom hostelry in a canny little garden has views across the Tweed Valley that more than make up for the lack of private baths. 3 miles west of Clovenfords on A72 (phone: 0896-85350). Inexpensive.

GALASHIELS: This venerable town's charter was granted in 1599. Situated on the Gala Water, which flows into the Tweed, Galashiels resembles Selkirk and Hawick with its row of quaint mills visible from high above on the roads approaching town. A mill here was the first in Scotland, in 1791, to become a "manufactry," with mechanical spinning jennies turning out yarn.

At the town center is the 17th-century mercat cross and the impressive town hall, built in 1868, the front of which is guarded by the giant bronze statue of a medieval mosstrooper in full armor dashing forward on horseback. The statue is an imaginative memorial to soldiers killed in World Wars I and II. The *Peter Anderson Museum,* opened in 1983, has historical exhibitions including items indispensible to mills of the past, a working water turbine that runs a loom, and informatively captioned early photographs. There are tours of the present factory (four of them daily; admission charge), and its own mill shop sells tartans, tweeds, and knitwear. On Huddersfield St. (open daily except Sundays April through October, and Sunday afternoons June through September).

Old Gala House, on Scott Crescent, is the traditional home of the Pringles and the Scotts, who were known as the "Lairds" of Galashiels because of their knitwear dynasties. Besides the original, centuries-old fixtures and furnishings on display, there's an exhibition showing the history of the house from the perspective of these industrial magnates. Open Sunday afternoons and Mondays, Wednesdays, Thursdays, and Fridays, April through October (phone: 0896-2611).

On A72, on the west outskirts of Galashiels, is the *Andrew Stewart Woollens and Craft Shop. Jackie Lunn* (Channel St.) is an excellent baker; and interesting native candies — such as rose- or violet-flavored chocolate creams, or "soor plooms," which commemorate a surprise attack of Galashiels reivers on English soldiers eating sour plums — are available at *Anne Ruddiman's* (Market St.).

CHECKING IN: ***Kingsknowes*** – A Victorian family house with Scott's Abbotsford within its prospect, this 10-bedroom hotel is just south of Galashiels overlooking the Tweed. Selkirk Rd., Galashiels (phone: 0896-58375). Moderate.

EATING OUT: ***Douglas Hotel Coffee Bar*** – In a converted Victorian drawing room, this cozy eaterie has oak tables and plush velvet seats. This "bar" also serves alcoholic drinks, baked potatoes with a choice of toppings, and coffee, with homemade rolls and shortbreads adorning salads for sale from a glass case. Channel St., Galashiels (phone: 0896-58383). Inexpensive.

En Route from Galasheils – The A7 north leads back to Edinburgh.

SHARING A PINT: At Stow, have a relaxing pint of beer in the *Manor Head House* hotel, whose bar has won three awards, including a "Top 20 UK Pub Caterers" plaque.

Southwest Scottish Lowlands

The Lowlands of southwest Scotland are a myriad of vastly differing locations and traditions: from proud, modern, urban landscapes in Glasgow to isolated but quietly confident Ayrshire towns; from Clydeside ports mourning their former prosperity to remote country towns in Dumfries and Galloway; from coastline visions of Ireland, only a few miles away, to the supreme natural beauty of the Firth of Clyde, where shipping was nurtured that once dominated the north Atlantic.

It was in these Lowlands, in the late eighteenth century, that triumphant Calvinism muted but could not muzzle the poetic genius of Ayrshire's ploughman poet, Robert Burns (1759–96). Here, too, flourished the newer Scottish writers, such as the playwright O. H. Mavor of Glasgow (1888–1951), better known as James Bridie, and novelists Neil Munro (1864–1930), John Buchan (1875–1940), and William McIlvanney (1936–).

From obscure origins among rocky and little-yielding farmlands on the country's west coast, Scotland's national bard, Robert Burns, had a meteoric rise to literary fame. At the age of 25, he was taken into and lionized by the most learned and genteel circles in Edinburgh — at that time the seat of the Scottish Enlightenment. Proficient in Ayrshire dialect and the English versifying conventions of his day, and equally at home writing love poetry or social and political satire, Burns awed audiences across the nation in tavern and parlor alike. The elders of his church at Ayr, however, were signally unawed when his mistress bore him two sets of twins: He was publicly arraigned before the presbytery and constrained to pour out his confession of sins to God and the whole parish congregation. Literary critics see him as a precursor of the romantic movement exemplified by the works of Coleridge and Byron, while the general populace remember him very affectionately for his monumental predisposition to wine, women, and song.

Robert Burns died a young man in Dumfries in 1796, and he lies there now at peace with his more orthodox fellow countrymen. While you will get your fill of "Burns suppers" elsewhere in Scotland in the last days of January, the southwest Lowlands is the place to find them at their most enthusiastic. In many places, indeed, the local Church of Scotland ministers are zealous in celebrating their former reprobate, and if you can get yourself invited to the top table at a Burns "nicht" where several pastors of the kirk are present, a lively evening is assured. Their conversation is usually excellent, and they will extract stories and epigrams from you with one eye on their future sermon-fodder. Stay with the whisky at a Burns supper. The wine is almost invariably bad, being intended for Sassenachs and other related social outcasts, and it is foolish to mix spirits with beer however practiced in the art locals may seem to be. You have a good chance of hearing at least one fine speech of the four or more provided by custom, and with the encouragement of the whisky, you may even render it! These affairs have matured with time. The toast to the "lassies" used to be an unimaginable display of male chauvinism and obscenity, but, since women's liberation, there are now such powerful feminist replies that the more fatuous proponents of the toast are reduced to the level of their own barbs. Or you may be out of luck. There are all too many toasts to the "Immortal Memory" of Burns that sound as if they have been given in reply to the requisite earlier rendition of Burns's poem, "To a Haggis," recited to the pudding made of sheep's stomach that is the culinary mainstay of Burns nichts. (There are particular variations: at a Jewish "Rabbi Burns" supper you will be served kosher haggis, which is excellent, and at a vegetarian Burns celebration you will receive vegetarian haggis, which is not.) In the course of the evening you will hear some very admirable Burns poems and songs, and you are also liable to hear quite extraordinary Victorian sentimentality, but by the time the village music teacher sings "The Star of Rabbie Burns," you will probably be past caring.

The Burns cult has come under a good deal of abuse, especially for the stage-Scotsman image associated with it, but it is hard not to admire a country that reserves its greatest annual celebration for local invocations of a very great poet. Burns's own beliefs in equality and human rights are always in need of remembrance:

For a' that, and a' that,
It's comin yet for a' that,
That Man to Man the warld o'er,
Shall brothers be for a' that.

An American threatened with a demand to read at a Burns supper should respond with Burns's poem about the American Revolution, "Ode for General Washington's Birthday." Fortunately it is in English. Avoid reading Burns in Scots to any audience containing Scots: You do not set your hearers ablaze by setting their teeth on edge.

It is important to realize that, while Burns is the most famous and articulate figure of the Scottish southwest, his work is a remarkable reflection of all its people in his time and ours: their warm if not extraordinary friendliness, their spirit of equality, their fierce devotion to liberty — all attributes of the religion and the region with which Burns maintained a richly seminal love-hate relationship.

But if Burns was a progressive, he was also a great folklorist, preserving — through adaptation into verse — much that would otherwise have been lost. Two hundred years after his death there is still a great concentration of folk memories in the southwest Lowlands, whether in old people's stories of Covenanter and Jacobite times or in artifacts from the past, such as the memorabilia at Culzean Castle, which was General Dwight D. Eisenhower's private headquarters in 1946.

Another great folklorist was Sir Walter Scott. While Scott's career and great house lay in the east, his novel, *Redgauntlet,* was set largely between

Dumfries and points west. Unlike much of his other work, it moves at a cracking pace from the start to culminate in a last, hopeless return of Bonnie Prince Charlie and is notable for including a splendid piece of Covenanter mythology about the Devil and the Covenanters' enemies. Whether the story is primarily folklore or primarily Scott invention, reading it is a great way to discover the hidden folk traditions of the region.

Scotland's southwest Lowlands is a grand place to visit, with endless opportunities for discovery of constantly changing new worlds, in sea and river, mountain, and pasture. It has proved a paradise to many a freshwater fisherman, and it is ideal walking and driving country for people who like to lose themselves in the best of surroundings. The usual warnings apply to the weather, a light raincoat being fairly indispensable even on seemingly cloudless days.

Be aware of what lies hidden from your superficial view; the more effort you make to understand what you find, the more rewarding will be your discovery of the character of Scotland as it quietly deepens under your scrutiny. The country, like its people, has much to tell but is not going to tell all on first acquaintance.

Don't trust your impressions from afar either. Dumfries, the route city nearest the road to England, may seem sizeable enough (with its 30,000 people, it is in a class with Perth and ranks as one of the largest Scottish cities, preceded only by Edinburgh, Dundee, Aberdeen, Kilmarnock, and mighty Glasgow), but it is a quiet city, and growing quieter, as young people move away and old retire here. Major trains bypass it, and its politics are a good-natured and traditional Conservatism, in contrast to the Social and Liberal Democrat country on the southeastern borders, the traditional Labour in South Ayrshire, and the intermittently Scottish Nationalist Galloway. Its charm for the tourist is unshakeable, but it is an unself-conscious charm that knows nothing of ritzy boutiques or of wine bars with nouvelle cuisine.

If you are a thriller enthusiast, remember that all the area from Dumfries to Galloway Forest Park is the location of the lone flight of the hero in perhaps the greatest of all thrillers, John Buchan's *The Thirty-Nine Steps.* The movies of Alfred Hitchcock and his successors will make you think of Forth Road Bridge and a reluctant heroine, but as Buchan wrote it, Richard Hannay was here and he was alone. You may enjoy following the real locations in the book and working out the more obvious antecedents of the imaginary ones; you may still find equivalents of the literary innkeeper, the radical candidate, and the spectacled roadman — but should you find a bald archaeologist he is most unlikely to be a German spymaster.

In any case you have much more distance to cover than Hannay: The driving tour outlined here covers the 250 miles from Glasgow south to Dumfries and back to Paisley; it should be easy to handle in a leisurely week. But take the same precautions as Hannay about carrying sandwiches; and, while cars are more numerous and roads more accustomed to them than he found in 1914, gas stations can still be very scarce, so stock up on fuel. If you run out, you may find yourself having to walk considerably more than 39 steps!

Hotels categorized as expensive cost $95 or more for two for bed and breakfast; those categorized as moderate, $75 to $95; and inexpensive, $55 to

$75. Dinner for two with wine in a restaurant listed as expensive will cost $50 or more; as moderate, $30 to $50; and inexpensive, $30 or less.

GLASGOW: For a detailed report on the city, its sights, hotels, and restaurants, see *Glasgow,* THE CITIES.

RENFREW: West of Glasgow, M8 leads to the urban but peaceful county town of Renfrew. Once the site of Glasgow Airport (the new airport at Abbotsinch, only 3 miles west, serves Britain, Ireland, and Europe), Renfrew is known for its 15 golf courses. This community is proud of its ancient history: Here in 1164 Malcolm IV defeated and killed Somerled, the Norse-Celtic lord of the Isles. Today you may find Hebridean soft voices anywhere in the Clyde valley — reminders that there is still a close relationship between west Glasgow and the islands. Renfrew Castle (of which nothing survives) was given by Malcolm IV to Walter Fitzalan in 1157, along with the office of royal steward, from which the family assumed the name of Stewart and eventually became Kings of Scotland. At Inchinnan, 1 mile west of Renfrew, there are Celtic stones in the churchyard, as well as graves of the medieval crusading Knights Templar. From Renfrew, sightseers can take the only ferry remaining on the upper river Clyde (6:30 AM to 9:30 PM, foot passengers only) for breathtaking views of the area.

CHECKING IN: *Stakis Normandy* – This comfortable, 142-room hotel near the airport offers weary travelers a restaurant, bar, golf course, and large car park. Inchinnan Rd., Renfrew (phone: 041-8864100). Expensive.

***Glynhill* –** A stalwart, 19th-century brownstone building belies the cushy comforts found inside: 80 rooms, private baths, restaurant, and a bar featuring music nights. Outside are pleasant gardens. 169 Paisley Rd., Renfrew (phone: 041-886-5555). Expensive to moderate.

***Dean Park* –** Another large (120 rooms) American-style hotel complex with modern conveniences, bar, and restaurant. Good Scottish fare. 91 Glasgow Rd., Renfrew (phone: 041-8863771). Moderate.

PORT GLASGOW: Continue west on M8, which becomes A8 along the south bank of the river Clyde, to reach Port Glasgow, once the farthest deepwater port up the river. The late 18th-century artificial deepening of the Clyde caused the port to decline, but it then became an important shipbuilding center. James Watt designed the first graving-dock in 1762, and James Wood built the the ship the *Comet* here in 1812. The hills above the port give splendid views across the Clyde to Ben Lomond. Before it was a port, Port Glasgow was the site of the village of Newark. It still is dominated on the east by turreted Newark Castle, famous for its dovecote (closed Sunday mornings).

GREENOCK: Continue westward along A8 to Greenock, the birthplace of James Watt (1736–1819), famous for his discovery of steam power. Watt is memorialized by the monument on Union Street. The Gothic shrine includes a statue by Sir Francis Chantrey and the Watt Scientific Library, and is adjoined by the *McLean Museum and Lecture Hall* and an art gallery (phone: 0475-23741; closed Sundays). Garvel House, formerly the Georgian mansion of a local magistrate, stands at James Watt Dock, and there is a Watt cairn in the cemetery.

Greenock was also the birthplace of Captain William Kidd, who was hanged for piracy in London in 1701. Kidd is famous as a desperate villain played by Charles Laughton and others, but in fact seems to have been a sad figure whose mission as a pirate-catcher strayed over the frontier of lawlessness. He lived for some time in Massachusetts.

During the 17th century Greenock was an important port, especially for the herring trade, from which the town motto originated: "Let herring swim that trade maintain."

Shipbuilding took the place of the herring trade in the 18th century. In World War II, Greenock was the chief naval base for the "Free French" (who opposed France's capitulation to the Nazis). On Lyle Hill, offering a remarkable view overlooking the town, a great granite Cross of Lorraine (the symbol adopted by General Charles de Gaulle) commemorates the French sailors who died in the Battle of the Atlantic. The tourist office is at the Municipal Buildings, 23 Clyde St. (phone: 0475-24400).

CHECKING IN: ***Tontine*** – The biggest (32 rooms) in Greenock, this landmark hotel has recently been sold by its long-time owners, the historic but declining shipbuilders Scott, Lithgow, to a family from nearby Dunoon. The place conveys something of its association with the town's better days. Ardgowan Sq., Greenock (phone: 0475-23316). Moderate to inexpensive.

GOUROCK: To reach Gourock, leave Greenock on A8 and bear right onto the coast road, A770. Gourock runs for about 2 miles, a residential seaside resort and a welcome change from the Glasgow urban environs. There is boating, bathing, and an opportunity to view the lower Clyde in all its beauty. Granny Kempock's stone, a 6-foot grey schist monolith (probably of prehistoric antecedents) on Gourock cliffs overlooking the sea is a reminder that this is occult country. The stone was once employed by fishermen in mysterious rites to ensure good weather (no doubt the rites are no more peculiar by our standards than the television weatherman will seem to our descendants, and probably a good deal more reliable). Granny's weather service also seems to have been connected with ancient fertility rites: Engaged couples would (and still may) circle around it to get "Granny's blessing." Three miles from town southwest on A770 are the ruins of Levan Castle and the 76-foot Cloch lighthouse (1797). The Gourock Tourist Office is at the Municipal Buildings, Shore St. (phone: 0475-39404).

Car ferries from Gourock to Dunoon leave every hour. Inquire at the *Caledonian MacBrayne* ferry company at the pier for information on timetables and fares (phone: 0475-33755). It is a 20-minute crossing, after which you are on your own in Argyllshire (and Campbell country). Other ferries go to the north shore of the Clyde, landing at Kilcreggan (on the somewhat isolated Roseneath peninsula) and Helensburgh (5 miles northwest of which are the bonnie, bonnie banks of Loch Lomond — *don't* take the high road). Caledonian MacBrayne will be glad to supply information about cruises and ferries around the Clyde and from west Highland ports to the Hebrides. Try not to look too appalled at some of the landing times!

CHECKING IN: ***Stakis Gantock*** – An opulent, modern structure, leading the neighborhood hotel status race. It has a leisure center, sauna, jacuzzi, swimming pool, and restaurant. All 101 bedrooms have baths and TV sets. Cloch Rd., Gourock (phone: 0475-34671). Expensive.

WEMYSS BAY: A770 turns sharply south and joins A78 to Wemyss (pronounced *Weems*) Bay, the embarkation point for the car ferry to Rothesay, a sea-licked, hilly town on the Isle of Bute. Excellent views of the Clyde and its sea traffic are to be enjoyed at Wemyss Bay. The 19th-century Castle Wemyss prides itself on being the place where Anthony Trollope wrote part of *Barchester Towers* (not that the book reflects it; in any case he also wrote much of it on railway trains).

LARGS: A78 continues south along the coast and over the border into Ayrshire. Largs is famous as the site of the 1263 battle (commemorated by the "pencil" monument) in which the forces of Haakon IV of Norway were defeated by Alexander III of Scotland, finally ending the 400-year Norse domination of the Hebrides. Every September the *Largs Viking Festival* celebrates the event, with entertainers from Scandinavia pouring in to sing and dance for the locals, and to show that the victors have been forgiven. Brisbane Glen was named to commemorate its having been the birthplace of Sir Thomas Mackdougall-Brisbane (1773–1860), astronomer and Governor of New South Wales, Australia. Largs is an ideal sheltered location for cruising. The National Sports Training Center on Burnside Road offers many indoor and outdoor sporting facilities, with training in water sports on the adjoining Isle of Cumbrae. The island is reached by *Caledonian MacBrayne* ferry, sailing every 15 minutes in summer, and hourly in winter, from 6:45 AM to 8:45 PM, with shorter operating hours on Sundays. The Largs tourist office is on The Promenade (phone: 0475-673765).

ARDROSSAN: Ten miles farther south on A78 is another port, Ardrossan, conceived by Hugh Montgomerie, 12th Earl of Eglinton (1739–1819), who was an army captain against the American rebels and later inspector of Scottish military roads. The harbor was laid out in 1806 based on a plan by the Glasgow mathematician and architect Peter Nicholson (1765–1844). It subsequently became a port for seagoing steamers to Ireland, the Isle of Man, and Arran. (Arran can still be reached from Ardrossan by *Caledonian MacBrayne* ferry; phone: 0475-33755. Stranraer, in southern Galloway, is now the port for Ireland and the Isle of Man. Also see *The Scottish Islands,* DIRECTIONS.) Attractive sand beaches lie south of the port. The 12th-century Ardrossan Castle, which consists of a north tower and two arched cellars, is free and open "at all reasonable times." Its hillside location — above the town overlooking Ardrossan Bay — gives fine prospects of Arran and Ailsa Craig.

SALTCOATS: Saltcoats, just south of Ardrossan on A78, offers the North Ayrshire Museum, which contains domestic and maritime objects from the local life of bygone days (closed Sundays year-round and Mondays and Tuesdays September through April). Local sports, other than water sports, include putting and tennis at South Beach (toward Ardrossan) and at Springvale Place. The name of the community derives from saltworks founded by James V. Twenty-six fossilized tree trunks may be seen in the harbor when the tide is low.

STEVENSTON: A78 curves inland to this very ancient settlement whose prehistoric inhabitants are frequently remembered as their weapons and utensils are unearthed by present-day Stevenstonians. The modern town dates from the mid-13th century or earlier. Today its citizens work principally at the great Imperial Chemical Institute at Ardeer (selected in 1873 by Alfred Nobel for his dynamite factory).

IRVINE: Farther south on A78 along the coast, but still in the same industrial complex, Irvine is the beginning of Burns country. The poet was sent here in 1781 at the age of 22 to learn flax-dressing. The *Burns Lodging and Heckling Shop* is open daily except Sunday (10 Glasgow Vennel; phone: 0294-7505). The *Irvine Burns Club* is most prestigious — possessing the original Kilmarnock edition of Burns's poems — and its headquarters on Eglinton St. are open to the public (phone: 0294-74166). Mary, Queen of Scots, was entertained here in 1563 at Seagate Castle when she made her western tour, and each August there is a "Marymass" celebration, a week of festivities including the Marymass Races, with their thrilling Clydesdale spectacular, and culminating in a procession and the crowning of a local queen. Seagate Castle ruins consist of a tower and huge fireplace. John Galt (1779–1839), author of the remarkable literary classic of local observation, *Annals of the Parish* (1821), was born here, and the town inspired his fictional Ayrshire village. J. B. Dunlop (1840–1921), to whom we owe the pneumatic tire, is another inventor indigenous to the area; he was born at Dreghorn, 2 miles to the east. Irvine had a racecourse, already active in 1806; Scotland's first steeplechases followed here in 1839.

Today, Irvine is a magnet for Ayrshire folk on weekends and holidays. The Magnum is one of the largest indoor sports centers in Europe (open daily; Harbour St.; phone:

0294-78371). The new 150-acre Beach Park features Sea World, where marine life can be viewed in specially designed underwater caverns (open daily; phone: 0294-311414). The *Scottish Maritime Museum* on Gottries Road is open daily from mid-April through mid-October (phone: 0294-78283). There is a 3-day *Harbour Festival* with Highland Games, in late July.

CHECKING IN/EATING OUT: ***Hospitality Inn*** – This ambitious, charming, luxurious 128-room hotel prides itself on its family orientation and its French cuisine. It has two good restaurants: the poolside *Hawaiian Lagoon* (open from 10 AM to 11 PM) and the more formal *Mirage* (conventional lunch and dinner hours), where elegant meals are prepared by one of Scotland's six master chefs. Roseholm, Annick Water, Irvine (phone: 0294-74272). Expensive.

PRESTWICK: To reach Prestwick, site of Scotland's main transatlantic airport, continue south on A78 hugging the coast. The area also has a fine beach and a rather whimsical championship golf course, where the first-ever "Open" was played in 1860. Prestwick Airport was founded in 1935 by the late Duke of Hamilton and Group Captain D. F. McIntyre, the first persons to fly over Everest. It is famous for being fog-free. Bruce's Well and the ruined chapel of St. Ninian commemorate King Robert the Bruce's foundation of a leper hospital here after he discovered that he had the dreaded disease.

CHECKING IN: ***Carlton Toby*** – Travelers deplaning at Prestwick will find the *Carlton Toby,* warmly recommended by locals and others, a short taxi ride from the airport. After having spent hours thousands of feet in the air, one may appreciate its one-level floor plan, of 36 rooms, all with baths and TV sets. 187 Ayr Rd., Prestwick (phone: 0292-76811). Moderate to inexpensive.

AYR: Four miles south of Prestwick, where the river Ayr meets the Firth of Clyde, is a quiet, respectable town that derives much of its current prosperity from the worship and study of its most distinguished reprobate, Robert Burns.

Burns was born in 1759 in the "auld clay biggin" built by his father, now the *Burns Cottage Museum* at Alloway, 2 miles south of Ayr on B7024 (closed Sundays in winter). Also on the site are: the Land O' Burns visitor center, with its audiovisual program, book and crafts shop, cafeteria, and picnic tables (open daily); the Burns monument, a rococo stone folly on a leafy hill; and the 700-year-old Brig O'Doon, the site where the fastest witch in Burns's famous narrative poem, "Tam O' Shanter," caught hold of Tam's mare's tail. Spooky-looking Auld Alloway Kirk, a ruin even in Burns's day, has an empty window through which Tam saw the Devil and his dancers. Burns's father lies in Auld Alloway Kirkyard. The Land O' Burns center has leaflets about a Burns Heritage Trail that can be followed through two counties. A week-long Robert Burns Festival held every June in the Ayrshire district is administered from Alloway and includes music, poetry, exhibitions, dinners, and dances (phone: 0292-43700).

Back in Ayr, the *Tam O' Shanter Museum* on High Street was once a brewery to which Douglas Graham of Shanter (the real-life Tam) supplied the malted grain; it's open daily except Sundays April through September, Sunday afternoons June through August, and afternoons only October through March. Also to be seen in this busy dairy farmers' town are its large harbor; the 13th-century Tower of St. John at Citadel Place; the 15th-century auld brig over the river Ayr; the 16th-century Loudon Hall, house of the hereditary Sheriffs of Ayrshire, in Boat Vennel; and the 17th-century auld kirk where Burns was baptized, just off High Street. Ayr is celebrated, too, for its racetrack on Whitletts Road. and for its panoramic beach viewing the Isle of Arran. Belleisle Park on the south side has a zoo, nature trail, lush gardens, and a championship golf course. The tourist office is at 39 Sandgate, Ayr (phone: 0292-284196).

CHECKING IN/EATING OUT: ***Marine Court*** – After a refurbishment, this seaside hotel now has 30 comfortable rooms and a restaurant with a varied menu. 12 Fairfield Rd., Ayr (phone: 0292-267461). Expensive to moderate.

Belleisle House – Once the property of the Magistrates of Ayr, who evidently saw no reason to stint themselves, this delightful 18-room hotel retains such personal embellishments as engraved fireplaces. (It lends some credence to fellow-Ayrshireman Burns's poetic attacks on the divisions between rich and poor, powerful and lowly.) Elegant traditional dishes are served in one of two dining rooms, one decorated in imitation of Marie Antoinette's music room, the other modeled after her bedroom. Inside Belleisle Park grounds on Doonfoot Rd., Ayr (phone: 0292-42331). Moderate.

Pickwick – One of the best of a seafront string of Victorian villas specializing in pure malt whiskies and Scottish foods. Most of the 15 rooms have baths. 19 Racecourse Rd., Ayr (phone: 0292-260111). Moderate.

En Route from Ayr – Leave Ayr by the coast road, A719. The shoreline here gleams with watery inlets and wild red poppies. South of the cliffs called the Heads of Ayr is the ghostly shell of Dunure Castle, standing like a stony wraith against the sky. Along this route are some of the most beautiful views imaginable, often augmented by extraordinary weather effects creating ethereal lights. One peculiar phenomenon is the Croy Brae, also called "Electric Brae" because when its fantastic properties first became apparent, Ayrshiremen thought the cause could only be electricity. Now they think it's an optical illusion: Switch off the motor and you'll seem to coast uphill. (That, however, is nothing compared to the descent from the brae's other side, where you seem to coast uphill backward!)

CULZEAN CASTLE: About 12 miles south of Ayr (off the coast road) is Scotland's most visited castle, Culzean (pronounced *Koo*-lane), situated within a remarkable 560-acre country park. Designed around an ancient tower of the Kennedy family (the Earls of Cassilis) by Robert Adam in 1777, its turrets flank the Atlantic. General Eisenhower became its chief denizen in 1946, using it as a golfing base on frequent trips to Scotland. Note the drum-shaped drawing rooms in which even the fireplaces are curved (the castle opens at noon during April, September, and October, and at 10 AM, May through August). Ask for the head guide, Mr. McBain, a foremost authority on Culzean's contents and history.

The castle grounds include a walled garden, aviary, swan pond, camellia house, and orangery. There are palm trees everywhere, picnic tables, a seashore trail, and a tea room. Farm buildings also designed by Robert Adam are now a lecture and exhibition theater and are (in summer) the starting point for conducted nature walks. The park grounds are always open; the castle, exhibition theater, and tea room are open April through October only. Go in the morning to avoid the tourist buses that pour in after lunch. For information call the tourist office (phone: 06556-269).

En Route from Culzean Castle – Turnberry Lighthouse, situated on the spot said to be the birthplace of King Robert Bruce in 1274, is near the ninth hole (nicknamed "Bruce's Castle") of the Ailsa championship golf course at the *Turnberry* hotel (see *Checking In,* below). It's best to get there between 2 PM and about an hour before sunset if planning to go inside (phone the lightkeeper in advance: 0655-31225). Just south of Turnberry, A719 becomes A77. Continue south for a view of the regal heights of 1,114-foot Ailsa Craig, an island refuge for Catholics during the Reformation and now a bird sanctuary, rearing out of the sea. Pick up B734 just north of Girvan and follow it to Barr, at the northwest tip of Galloway Forest Park.

CHECKING IN: ***Turnberry*** – Site of the Ailsa championship golf course, this lavish, 120-room, Edwardian resort looks like a landlocked ocean liner. It has a tennis court and indoor swimming pool and offers reduced rates for guests golfing on the Ailsa as well as on the Arran, its other 18-hole golf course. Its acclaimed restaurant specializes in continental cuisine; try the roast lamb, venison in game sauce, or duckling pie. Closed January. Turnberry, south of Culzean, off A719 or A77 (phone: 0655-31000). Very expensive.

Main Court – This hotel — a challenge to the former hegemony of the *Turnberry* resort — overlooks *Turnberry Golf Course* and has 9 rooms and a patio garden. Off the main road, Turnberry (phone: 0655-31457). Expensive to moderate.

GALLOWAY FOREST PARK: A glorious, gargantuan green space, this majestic wilderness's chief fascinations are detailed on the *Enjoy Scotland* touring map, published by the Scottish Tourist Board. Rocky glens and mountain lakes have won it the title, "The Highlands of the Lowlands."

The *Galloway Deer Museum* has a tank full of live trout as well as other exhibitions about indigenous Galloway species (open April through September only). But you don't need a museum to take in the native wildlife: red deer, roe deer, foxes, otters, red squirrels, and wild goats abound on the park's many miles of secluded woodland footpaths, and the wild geese and ducks, pheasants and grouse, falcons, owls, ravens, and golden eagles are an ornithologist's orgy.

Depending on where you exit Galloway Forest Park, pick up A714 (on the southwest of the forest park) or A712 (near the deer museum on the southeast side): both offer routes to Newton Stewart.

NEWTON STEWART: Founded by William Stewart, third son of the Earl of Galloway, the town obtained its charter from Charles II in 1677. Much of its land is reclaimed from the Cree estuary. Smuggling was an early and profitable industry, much more so than later attempts at spinning and carpet making; hand-loom weaving, however, has been a successful local industry. The tourist office is at Dashwood Square (phone: 0671-2431).

CHECKING IN/EATING OUT: ***Kirroughtree*** – A much-awarded hotel with a well-known, excellent restaurant. This luxurious country house has 22 bedrooms, spacious grounds, and lovely gardens. Elegant meals are prepared by a master chef, and there's a good wine cellar. Open March through January. Newton Stewart (phone: 0671-2141). Expensive.

Creebridge House – This white-chimneyed, gabled stone house overlooking its own private lawns and gardens has the romance of a country squire's abode. There are 18 elegant bedrooms, open fires in the public rooms, private salmon and trout fishing for guests, and "Taste of Scotland" home cooking. On the north edge of Newton Stewart (phone: 0671-2121). Moderate.

Bruce – A family-run hotel priding itself on its superb hill views. Personal attention (from owners James and Joanna Wyllie) and interesting cuisine. Closed December. Newton Stewart (phone: 0671-2294). Moderate to inexpensive.

En Route from Newton Stewart – Take A75 southeast from Newton Stewart to the village of Creetown, where the *Gem Rock Museum* on the main road offers a fine collection of rocks, minerals, and semiprecious stones from all over the world (a testament to Galloway's preeminence in stone-building and jewelry-making (open daily). The Mersey Docks and part of the Thames Embankment are made of Creetown granite. John Prince, proprietor of the Creetown Gold & Silversmith Workshop at 98 St. John St., is well worth a visit; he also teaches jewelry and silversmith courses (phone: 067182-396).

From Creetown to Gatehouse-of-Fleet, A75 has delightful views and picnic places. Follow the eastern shore of Wigtown Bay from the Cree River estuary, looking across to the Wigtown peninsula. Carsluith Castle is a roofless, L-shaped, 16th-century structure. Dirk Hatternick's Cave is a voracious crevice in the rocks where pigeonholes were cut to hide the dashing bandit's smuggled brandy. Kirkdale, a wooded glen near the cave, is the entrance to Cairn Holy, a Neolithic graveyard. Cardoness Castle, 6 miles from Carsluith Castle, is a well-preserved 15th-century stronghold with its original staircase.

Gatehouse-of-Fleet is a scenic spot renowned for its archaeological remains and its forest trails leading to lovely little Fleet Bay. Among the ancient sites in the district are: on the northwest outskirts of town, Anworth Church, containing a Dark Ages cross; Palace Yard at Enrick, a medieval moated manor with the foundations of a palace of the Bishops of Galloway destroyed during the Reformation; and a 1st-century Roman fort beside the Water-of-Fleet. Relics of the not-so-distant past are the disused early 19th-century, ivy-covered cotton mill above Fleet Bridge and the soaring 75-foot castellated clock tower in mid-village. Artists of all kinds live in Gatehouse-of-Fleet, as is also true of Kirkcudbright, reached by taking the A755 south from A75.

KIRKCUDBRIGHT: Kirkcudbright (pronounced Ker-*coo*-bree) was used by the late 19th-century Glasgow School of artists as a base from which to create their characteristic "kailyard" (farmyard) scenes of the surrounding countryside. Its flowery lanes, elm-lined streets, and enchanting knots of whitewashed 18th-century cottages appeal no less to today's palettes; all summer the town supports a steady stream of painters, pupils, and patrons. Broughton House on High Street was once the home of A. E. Hornel and contains many of his canvases. Adjacent to the much-photographed picturesque harbor is an exhibition gallery. Dominating the harbor is jagged MacLellan's Castle, built in 1582. The town's impressive mercat (market) cross dates from 1610 and the late 16th- or early 17th-century tollbooth once imprisoned the American naval hero John Paul Jones (1747–92), who was born near here. The *Stewartry Museum* on St. Mary Street houses, among other features of Kirkcudbright history, a John Paul Jones display (open from Easter through October; closed Sundays). The fascinating process of copper-wheel engraving on glass can be viewed at David Gulland's, 6 Barrhill Rd. (phone in advance: 0557-31072). The tourist office is at Harbour Square (phone: 0557-30494).

CHECKING IN: ***Selkirk Arms*** – This charming, historic 16-room, 18th century coaching inn is where Robert Burns wrote the popular *Selkirk Grace.* Some of its paneled walls are inscribed with Burns's verses. Old High St., Kirkcudbright (phone: 0557-30402). Moderate.

EATING OUT: ***Auld Alliance*** – A cheerful, bow-windowed snuggery across from the castle caters to everybody from snackers to three-course gorgers with its Scots-French cuisine. Open from Easter through Halloween. 5 Castle St., Kirkcudbright (phone: 0557-30569). Moderate.

Ingle – The old station building, converted into a family restaurant seating 70, specializes in local seafood: Dover sole, monkfish, queenies (small scallops), and plaice — all caught in the harbor. (The kitchen is where the trains used to come in.) Dinner only. St. Mary's St., Kirkcudbright (phone: 0557-30606). Moderate.

En Route from Kirkcudbright – Take A711 north from Kirkcudbright to rejoin A75. The next major town will be Castle Douglas, an unassuming little place with an idyllic setting on Carlingwark Loch, asprinkle with brightly painted boats. You can rent one and row out. *Galloway Gems,* at 7 Carlingwark St., sells handmade silver jewelry, set with Galloway stones. The tourist office is at Markethill (phone: 0556-2611).

DUMFRIES: A75 north leads to this quaint but sonorous symphony in red sandstone. Although its written history began in 1186, with its legal recognition by King William the Lion, it is in fact much older: Excavations have yielded Bronze Age relics. Here in the gentle dale of the river Nith the visitor will find, as all over the surrounding area of Galloway, hillocked meadows flecked with buttercups, peacefully grazing cattle, and grass as green as any in Ireland. Spring comes earlier to Dumfries and Galloway than elsewhere in Scotland and the climate stays comparatively warm.

In summer Dumfries is populated with students of literature visiting Burns House on Mill Vennel (now called Burns Street), where he died in 1796. His tomb in nearby St. Michael's Churchyard is augmented by an unintentionally humorous sculpture showing him at his plough (Scotland knows him as "the Ploughman Poet") somewhat hampered by Coila, the muse of Scottish poetry, who flings o'er his shoulders a voluminous mantle as cumbersome as a tent. The *Globe Inn,* Burns's "favorite howss" (in a narrow alley off High St.), is exactly as it was in his day, furnishings and all, and is still in the bartending business. The Robert Burns Heritage Centre (Mill Rd.) has an audiovisual show about Burns's life and times and about the Dumfries of his day (phone: 0387-64808).

A saunter through Dumfries will lead to some other not-to-be-missed high spots: Greyfrairs Church on High Street whose monastery (now a supermarket) was the scene in 1306 of the murder by Robert the Bruce of his cousin and heir to the Scottish throne, John "the Red" Comyn; the Burns statue opposite this church; the Mid Steeple of 1707, which is the remains of the central square's old town hall; and Dumfries Academy (Academy St.) where a pupil named J. M. Barrie first conceived the characters Peter Pan and Wendy while exploring the garden of the Moat Brae Nursing Home in the lane behind. The river Nith is spanned by the six-arched Devorguilla's Bridge, a 13th-century gift from Devorguilla Balliol, founder of Balliol College at Oxford (and ancestral cousin-in-law of the Bruce and the Red Comyn). The expansive "caul," or weir, by the bridge is a salmon leap and was once the power supply for the town's many grain mills. The path through the 2-mile wood along the Nith bank is Burns's Walk.

Dumfries has an excellent municipal indoor swimming pool on Greensands by the Nith. *T.C. Farries* (Irongray Rd., Lochside Industrial Estate) is considered by many to be the best bookseller north of Oxford (it's off A76 by New Bridge). The *Burgh Museum* (Observatory Rd.), housed in an 18th-century windmill, has local archaeological and other exhibits and a camera obscura (closed Sundays and Mondays October through March). There's also a folk museum in Old Bridge House (Mill Rd.), adjacent to Devorguilla's Bridge.

The *Theatre Royal* (Shakespeare St.; phone: 0387-54209) bolsters its usual pop-vein fripperies with occasional plays by the likes of Ibsen and Coward. *Gracefield Arts Centre* (28 Edinburgh Rd.; phone: 0387-52895) is a showcase for works by Scottish artists; it also takes part in the *Dumfries and Galloway Arts Festival* every year around the last week in May, providing military, rock, and folk bands, a serious guest orchestra, puppet shows, and exhibitions. *Guid Nychburris* (Good Neighbors) *Week,* in late June, offers concerts, parades, the crowning of a "Queen of the South" (usually a local schoolgirl), the cavalcaded "stobbing and nogging" (tracing out and marking) of Dumfries's boundaries, and the "kirking" (public promenading to church) of a newly elected Cornet, or chief eligible bachelor. The *Dumfries Jazz Festival* takes place in August. The tourist office of Dumfries is on Whitesands (phone: 0387-53862).

Worth a jaunt into the countryside are Shambellie House, at the village of New Abbey, 7 miles south of Dumfries on A710, and the 12th-century Caerlaverock Castle, 9 miles south of Dumfries on B725. Shambellie House, approached through an avenue of tall gracious pines, opened in 1982 for the first time as Scotland's foremost museum of costumes (closed from mid-September to mid-May and on Tuesdays, Wednesdays, and Sunday mornings in season). Caerlaverock Castle is a striking triangular ruin with round turrets and a real moat. For spectacular lighting, see it at sunset. The castle was a prime target in the 14th century for Edward I's wars against Scotland and its weak king, John Balliol (Devorguilla's son, known to his subjects as Toom Tabard, which means "empty coat"). Next to the castle is Caerlaverock National Nature Reserve, on the river Nith estuary and the Solway Firth: Here you can enjoy the exhilarating spectacle of 9,000 barnacle geese in open flight (East Park observation towers open mid-September through April). Also at New Abbey near Shambellie House is Sweetheart Abbey, built in 1273, the last pre-Reformation Cistercian foundation in Scotland and one of the nation's most beautiful. Devorguilla, who established it, is buried here; her husband's heart, encased in an ivory casket, sits in the tomb upon her bosom — hence the abbey's name. The New Abbey Corn Mill (on A710) has been opened as a museum (closed Sunday mornings, Wednesday afternoons, and Thursdays, October through March).

CHECKING IN: ***Cairndale*** – This rose-colored stone inn is what passes in these parts for a *bon viveur's* retreat. Its 60-car parking lot is handy (there are only 45 rooms) and its food — fresh local produce — is excellent. English St., Dumfries (phone: 0387-54111). Expensive..

Hetland Hall – Situated on a hill overlooking the Salway coast, this impressive, gleaming-white, 29-room country house with many chimneys will allow you to play the "local laird" in style. At Carrutherstown, just outside Dumfries (phone: 0387-84201). Moderate.

Station – Owned by one of Dumfriesshire's dairy magnates, this outsized chocolate box with Hansel-and-Gretel portals has 32 rooms, a hearty array of "Taste of Scotland" delights, and two bars offering more than milk. 49 Lovers Walk, Dumfries (phone: 0387-54316). Moderate.

EATING OUT: ***Bruno's*** – Thoughts of salmon and haggis vanish at the flick of a *cannellone* in this ritzy Italian sanctum. The red plush banquettes have at one time or another seated most of the posteriors in Caledonian gourmetdom. Dinner only; closed Tuesdays. 3 Balmoral Rd., Dumfries (phone: 0387-55757). Expensive to moderate.

Casa Toscana – This new and highly acclaimed restaurant features both French and Italian cuisines and is particularly distinguished for its fresh seafood and home-made pasta. Its decor is dominated by a gigantic barrel, set off by 2,000 wine bottles and terra cotta pipes. Dinner only; closed Mondays. Nunbank, Nunholm Rd., Dumfries (phone: 0387-69619). Moderate.

En Route from Dumfries – Take A76 north to Kilmarnock. Lincluden Abbey — 1½ miles outside of Dumfries — was founded by 12th-century Benedictine nuns (later suppressed by the third Earl of Douglas, Archibald the Grim, who changed it to Lincluden College). It survives chiefly in the choir and south transept of its 15th-century church. The stone screen at the choir entry has carvings from the life of Christ, and there is a fine tomb (1430) for Princess Margaret, daughter of King Robert III and wife of Archibald the Loser, the son of Archibald the Grim; ("the Loser" appears in Shakespeare's "Henry IV, Part One"). The carved doorway has the Douglas insignia of the heart (Bruce's, flung into battle against the Saracens by Archibald the Grim's father) and chalices. Garden terraces are about all that remain of the monastic buildings, hardly surprising in an area where patron and predator were often indistinguishable. (The abbey is open Monday through Saturday, and Sunday afternoons, April through September.)

Continue north on A76 to Ellisland, where Burns failed as a farmer in 1788 and wrote "Tam O' Shanter" and "Auld Lang Syne" (which lends for him and maybe you a special applicability to its words, "But we've wandered mony a weary fitt/Sin auld lang syne"). Five miles west is Dunscore, and 6 west of that is Craigenputtock, where Thomas and Jane Welsh Carlyle lived in poverty from 1828 to 1834 (he wrote *Sartor Resartus* here). Dalswinton Loch, east of Ellisland, is where William Symington (1763–1831) made the first ever successful attempt at steam navigation in October 1788 (Burns was a passenger), but he could not maintain financial backing and died in poverty.

Closeburn Castle is north of Ellisland off A76. It closes its doors to tourists, but you will see its 14th-century tower from the road. It is perhaps the oldest inhabited domicile in Scotland. About 3 miles west is Keir, birthplace of the bicycle (1839), whose inventor, Kirkpatrick Macmillan, a native son, made it in a smithy, rode it into Glasgow, and was fined for knocking down a girl. The machine is now in the *Science Museum* in London. Thornhill (north of Closeburn) is a captivating town with trees lining its broad street. A column was erected here in 1714 to the glory of the Douglas Dukes of Queensberry, the second of whom, James (1662–1711) maneuvered in 1708 the extinction of the Scottish Parliament in the union with England and Wales.

Six miles north of Thornhill, take the left fork at Carronbridge to stay with A76. On the left, Drumlanrig Castle (open daily May through August 21, from 11 AM, except Thursdays and Sunday mornings; phone: 0848-30248) is the seat of the Dukes of Buccleuch and Queensberry. It was built in the 17th century for William Douglas, first Duke of Queensberry (1637–95), who is reputed to have spent 1 night only in it on learning its cost. (The comments of his tenantry are unrecorded.) The ruin of the 15th-century castle he occupied instead is just outside Sanquhar, north on A76. Drumlanrig Castle is hosting an *International Festival of Cycling* in 1990 in honor of the 150th anniversary of Kirkpatrick MacMillan's invention. Non-cyclists might well enjoy the castle's paintings by European old masters.

CHECKING IN: ***Buccleuch and Queensberry*** – The name suggests that a night here would cause a guest to see Douglases of all colors, but this is a quiet, unpretentious hotel of 11 bedrooms. Full board, Scottish cuisine. Open year-round. Thornhill (phone: 0848-30215). Moderate.

SANQUHAR: The local post office is Britain's oldest, but the chief historical interest in Sanquhar lies with the extreme Protestant Covenanters (read Sir Walter Scott's *Old Mortality*). An obelisk denotes the site of the mercat cross, where in 1680 and 1685 leaders affixed declarations abjuring allegiance to Charles II and James VII (II of England) respectively: The declarations meant war, to the extent that they and their armed supporters could provide it. The first leader, Richard Cameron, fell in an engagement near Cumnock within a few weeks. His admirers were thenceforth known as the Cameronian sect, and after the Glorious Revolution they founded the Cameronians' Regiment. But meanwhile in 1688 the second declarant, James Renwick, had become the last martyr of the Covenanters, being executed in Edinburgh. The Old Tolbooth in Sanquhar, built in 1735, was restored in 1989 as a museum of local history and is also the site of the Sanquhar tourist office. Their inexpensive publication entitled *Nithsdale Covenanters Trail* gives information about local sites associated with Covenanting.

Very different traditions are commemorated in Eliock Castle (2 miles south of Sanquhar) where James Crichton (1560–82) was born. Crichton debated on scientific questions in 12 languages, disputed theology to its roots, served in the French army, and, despite his excellent swordsmanship, was killed in a brawl in Mantua, Italy. Posthumously this genius became known as "the Admirable Crichton" (characteristically, J. M. Barrie borrowed the title for his play of that name, altering the Renaissance Scottish nobleman of real life to an imaginary shipwrecked butler who proves his leadership).

CHECKING IN: ***Blackaddie House*** – On the banks of the river Nith. Family-operated, this charming haven provides 7 rooms, a children's playground, an adjacent golf course, trout and salmon fishing, and three meals a day. Open year-round. Blackaddie Rd., Sanquhar (phone: 0659-50270). Inexpensive.

En Route from Sanquhar – A76 wanders pleasantly northwest, beside the Nith through Kirkconnel and over the Ayrshire border into New Cumnock. There are people who would travel half the world for the sight of it. It is in two parts (separated by 400 yards): "Bank" on the river Nith, and "Path Head" on the river Afton, which descends from the 2,000-foot Blacklorg Hill. "Flow gently, Sweet Afton, among thy green braes/Flow gently, I'll sing thee a song in thy praise" (Burns). The Tourist Office is at town hall (phone: 0290-38581).

Five miles north is Cumnock, whose spirit is well realized in the statue by Scottish sculptor Benno Schotz at the Council Chamber commemorating the great Scottish socialist and labor leader, James Keir Hardie (1856–1915), a native son who, in the words of the *Dictionary of National Biography,* "did more than any man to create the British political labour movement." This is very much a miners' town. The tourist office is on Glaisnock Street (phone: 0290-23058).

Another 3 miles north is Auchinleck (pronounced Aw-kun-*lek*), where the proprietor of the great house (3 miles west), the Scottish judge Alexander Boswell, Lord Auchinleck (1706–82), found himself in heated argument in 1773 with a difficult English guest introduced by his son and heir, James Boswell (1740–95). Dr. Samuel Johnson (1709–84) is said to have founded this terrible dispute on a disagreement about King Charles (specifically, the retention or removal of his head), but for once it seems to have been a subject James found too embarrassing to record. In any event James Boswell is buried here. There is a museum (phone the curator, Mr. Colin MacDonald, in advance: 0290-21185). The parish church originated in a cell maintained by a holy man of the Celtic Church; it was enlarged in the 12th and 17th centuries.

The road (A76) leads next to Mauchline, where Robert Burns made a bitter enemy of a kirk elder, against whom he wrote "Holy Willie's Prayer," and married, in 1788, Jean Armour, who had previously borne him two sets of twins. Poosie Nansie's hostelry still stands, and you may commune with Holy Willie's ghost in the churchyard, where he is buried. Burns House on Castle Street (open daily except Sunday mornings Easter through November) is where he lived with his wife before removing to Ellisland. His former residence at Mossgiel is 1½ miles to the west. Burns Memorial Tower (pick up the key at the cottage), which contains relics, stands on the north of Mauchline. The town is said to supply the quintessence of Burns, and many of its inhabitants are supposed to be his poetic characters in modern dress. To judge by his career, their relationship with him may be more than literary.

KILMARNOCK: Follow A76 to the town where publisher John Wilson made Burns famous in 1786. The event is commemorated in the 80-foot sandstone tower in Kay Park. Here, too, is the *Burns Museum* abounding in Burns memorabilia, including a large library, which can be visited by appointment only (phone: 0563-26401).

Also in Kilmarnock are: Dean Castle (Dean Rd.), containing a fine collection of European arms and armor as well as early musical instruments (open daily from noon to 5 PM) and the *Dick Institute,* (Elmbank Ave.), with archaeological exhibits, including fossils of international importance (closed Sundays). The tourist office is at 62 Bank St. (phone: 0563-39090). The *Palace Theatre* (Green St.; phone: 0563-23590) was reopened after renovation in 1985, and largely features light entertainment of traditional Scots character; it has a pleasant café for snacks and quick meals. The *Galleon Centre,* Titchfield, is a new leisure and sports complex featuring a swimming pool, ice rink, bowling alley, and the like. Open daily until 11 PM (phone: 0563-24014).

A detour out of Kilmarnock on A71 eastward to Strathaven and Hamilton passes Loudon Hill, site of Wallace and Bruce victories (the latter's turning-point to recovery), and then Drumclog, where there was a Covenanter victory in 1679 over the Royal General Graham of Claverhouse ("Bonnie Dundee"). More constructively, the discoverer of penicillin, Sir Alexander Fleming (1881–1955), born in nearby Darvel, was educated in Kilmarnock.

CHECKING IN: ***Chapeltoun House*** – Small but posh, this is an early 20th-century mansion with a new antique-style cocktail bar that matches the original paneling. There are 6 rooms and wonderful food is produced by the chefs. On A735 through Stewarton, 8 miles north of Kilmarnock (phone: 0560-82696). Expensive.

Howard Park – Sïtuated in a residential area about a a mile from the town center, this 46-bedroom, modern establishment is well supported by its restaurant, which features traditional Scottish cuisine. Exuding both friendliness and efficiency, it makes an admirable base from which to explore Kilmarnock. 136 Glasgow Rd., Kilmarnock (phone: 0563-31211). Moderate.

Foxbar – Modern, spacious 18-bedroom establishment under family management (Catherine and John Stark, sons Derek and Alan). Restaurant and bar. Open year-round. 62 London Rd., Kilmarnock (phone: 0563-25701). Inexpensive.

EATING OUT: ***The Artful Dodger*** – Elegant and expensive restaurant downstairs with French and Italian cooking; inexpensive pizzeria upstairs. 3 St. Marnock Place (phone: 0563-37995).

En Route from Kilmarnock – Take A735 north out of Kilmarnock — it passes through Stewarton, where we encourage a visit to Robert Strang, Handframe Knitters, 68 High St. (phone: 0560-82277). Their cashmere products are impressive, but only a small fragment now of the once-great cottage industry that put Tam O' Shanter bonnets on the (living) skulls of half the world. Continue north through Dunlop, famous for its cheese and for first breeding Ayrshire cows under the auspices of the Dunlop family, magnates from the 13th century until 1858. (General James Dunlop played an important if hopeless part during the final British defeat in the American war of independence.) Join A736 (northeast) and proceed through Barrhead to Paisley.

PAISLEY: The first thing to remember is to make no jokes about the name. Northern Ireland is a tense issue in the west of Scotland. A friendly native may regard the Rev. Dr. Paisely as Messiah, Hitler, or anything in between and may express his opinion in more than words. Much more suitable subjects for conversation can be found in Paisley Abbey, founded in 1163 as part of the European Cluniac Reform movement, destroyed at the orders of Edward I of England (1307), and rebuilt after Bannockburn. Possibly as an omen of the Reformation, the tower collapsed in 1553, wrecking the transept and choir, leaving only the nave as the parish church. Early in this century the abbey was restored. The choir now has a fine stone-vaulted roof. Inside are the tombs of King Robert III and Princess Marjory, daughter of King Robert the Bruce and, by her marriage into the great Stewart family at Paisley, the mother of a great deal of British history. Her effigy supposedly adorns the St. Mirin Chapel. An 11-foot-high ("Barochan") Celtic Cross, also here, is said to date from the 10th century. Open Mondays through Saturdays from 10 AM to 3 PM, closed lunchtimes (phone: 041-889-7654).

The late 19th-century *Paisley Museum and Art Gallery* has a world-famous collection of Paisley shawls, as well as displays on the history of the pattern, the development of weaving techniques, and the social history of a formerly "tight-knit" community. The museum also has exhibits on local and natural history, ceramics, and Scottish painting. Open Mondays through Saturdays from 10 AM to 5 PM. High St. (phone: 041-889-3151).

The town is industrializing but has not lost its individual character. After all, it is the former seat of kings. In 1888 a memorial was placed in the abbey choir "to the members of the Royal House of Stewart who are buried in Paisley Abbey, by their descendant, Queen Victoria." And if her ghost haunts you for insufficient respect, confront her with the ghost of Robert Burns! The tourist office is in the town hall, Abbey Close (phone: 041-8890711).

CHECKING IN/EATING OUT: ***Excelsior*** **–** This highly efficient, friendly establishment with 290 rooms offers full facilities, including sunbeds, game rooms, an à la carte restaurant, and a carvery. Glasgow Airport, Abbotsinch, Paisley (phone: 041-889-0711). Hotel expensive, restaurant moderate, carvery inexpensive.

En Route from Paisley – From Paisley, any of several major roads run east into downtown Glasgow. Or take M8 to A82 north to Inverness (see *Inverness,* THE CITIES, and *Northwest Scottish Highlands,* DIRECTIONS).

Northeast Scottish Highlands

> Here at the World's End, on its last inch of liberty, we have lived unmolested to this day, defended by our remoteness and obscurity . . . there are no other tribes to come; nothing but sea and cliffs and these more deadly Romans, whose arrogance you cannot escape by obedience and self restraint. Robbers of the world . . . if their enemy have wealth, they have greed, if he be poor, they are ambitious . . . To plunder, butcher, steal, these things they misname empire; where they make a desert, they call it peace (*ubi solitudinem faciunt, pacem appellant!*).

These famous words were attributed by the Roman historian Tacitus to Scottish history's first identifiable figure, the Pictish chieftain Calgacus on the eve of his defeat at the hands of Governor Gnaeus Julius Agricola at Mons Graupius, AD 83. Calgacus's speech could hardly have been a more appropriate curtain raiser for his country's history. Internecine warfare, endurance, heroism, treachery, lawlessness, and a fierce spirit of independence are the words that come to mind when contemplating the Scottish past, especially the region encompassed by this northeast Highlands tour route.

The exact location of Calgacus's heroic stand at Mons Graupius is still unidentified, but historians believe it to have been somewhere in the present-day Grampian region. It was from here that the Picts, at the end of the 2nd century AD, swept through the Scottish Lowlands and over Hadrian's Wall to wreak havoc and destruction throughout the Roman province of Britain. This only served to bring vicious retaliation from the formidable emperor, Septimus Severus, in AD 209, and the Picts were saved from extermination only by the timely death of Severus at York in AD 211.

Of the peoples inhabiting Scotland during the Roman occupation of Britain and the subsequent Dark Ages, none retain more interest and mystery than the Picts. The Latin word *picti,* meaning "painted men," was first used in AD 267 to describe the tribes of the north. In actuality, the word was an adaptation of the name by which these tribes already called themselves. They were of Celtic origin but had roots different from the Britons and the Irish. Their language seems to have been closer in form to that of the Gauls than to the Britons' Brythonic, but was distinguishable from both. It differed greatly from Gaelic. The mystery and fascination of the Picts' origins and language remain with us, still unresolved. Northeastern Scotland is strewn with examples of Pictish art, chief of which are stone sculptures of a fine, mature character. The symbols that decorate these fascinating archaeological relics represent status, badges, ownership, religion, hunting, and famous battles.

Perthshire, Angus, and Aberdeenshire are modern names for the area that encompassed the Scottish kingdom of Alban in the 9th, 10th, and 11th centuries. The Kings of Alban merit the same credit as Alfred the Great of England for saving their country from 9th-century Viking invaders. But the greater reason this area and period of Scottish history is of interest to the tourist is that it was the scene for one of William Shakespeare's greatest tragedies — *Macbeth.* Historically, the play derives from events in the time of King Malcolm II (1005–29), whose reign was rife with internal feuds typical of Scottish history. After the death of Malcolm, Macbeth the Mormaer (Earl) of Moray became king by marrying Malcolm's widow, Gruoch, and killing his successor, Duncan, in battle in 1040. Macbeth's reign was one of remarkable contrasts: He and Gruoch were generous benefactors to the shrine of St. Andrew; he went to Rome to see the pope and is said to have scattered "money like seed" there; he was uniquely pious and much more cosmopolitan than any of his predecessors, welcoming Norman refugees who had fallen out of favor with the English king in 1052. Nevertheless, his reign was also very violent, marked by continuous struggle to retain the Scottish crown. He was finally defeated and killed at Lumphanan, just west of Aberdeen, in 1057. His successor, Malcolm III, was then uncontested ruler of Scotland and founder of a long dynasty of Scottish kings. Significantly, however, they all ruled in the shadow of the English — a shadow from which Scotland never fully emerged. Shakespeare, of course, based his version of events on English stories, and his blatant (if ignorant) sacrifice of historical truth is said by superstitious actors to be the origin of the many disasters in productions of *Macbeth;* some will not even mention its name but allude to it as "the Scottish play."

The depths of chaos and lawlessness in northeast Scotland were reached during the reign of Robert III (1390–1406). In the last days of the aged and incompetent Robert II, Forres and Elgin were burned by "wyld wykkyd Heland-men." The wild wicked Highland men were in fact led by Alexander Stewart, Earl of Buchan, who came to be known as the "Wolf of Badenoch." Son of the dying Robert II and brother of the future Robert III, the Wolf demanded what we would now call protection money, then simply termed "black mail." His royal status gave him immunity from the law but might also have exacerbated his banditry. Perhaps if he had been the first-born prince, he might have been the strong king that neither his father nor his brother were able to be.

Similarly, Sir James Graham (1612–50), fifth Earl and later first Marquis of Montrose, is one of the most gallant figures of turbulent Scottish history, admired for his sensationally brilliant military campaign of 1644 (and for his golfing prowess). The year-long campaign had all the ingredients of historical romance and legend and has often been re-created in fiction, most notably by Sir Walter Scott in *A Legend of Montrose.* Although initially with the Covenanter rebels against Charles I, Montrose later joined the king's side in the dispute. His first victory in 1644 was scored at Tippermuir near Perth (on this route). His ragged band of royalists went on to capture and pillage the city of Aberdeen (also on this route), a carnage for which his reputation for gallantry was deservedly stained, comparing uncomfortably with that of the Wolf of Badenoch. After Aberdeen, Montrose led a campaign unmatched in brilliance since the days of William Wallace and Robert Bruce (for more information, see the entry for Stirling). He defeated the Covenanters at Fyvie (about 30 miles northeast of Aberdeen on A947), looted and pillaged Stonehaven (on A92 south of Aberdeen), and won further victories at Auldearn (on A96 a few miles east of Nairn) and Alford (30 miles to the west of Aberdeen on A944). Despite these and other victories, Montrose's military genius proved irrelevant to the outcome of the war, which in fact had been decided almost a year earlier when Charles was defeated by Cromwell at Naseby, England. Futile or not, it was one of the most remarkable campaigns in military history. Montrose went into exile, but on his return to Scotland was hanged, on May 21, 1650, in Edinburgh.

Problems with neighbors to the south have dominated Scottish politics and kept the country on tenderhooks for many centuries: through James VI's inheritance of the English throne from Elizabeth I in 1603; through the Act of Union (uniting the Parliaments) in 1707; through the several rebellions for the exiled Stuart Pretenders; and finally through the modern and still continuing crisis of Scottish identity. This intermittent struggle has helped form the Scottish character. In the 14th century, it served to produce history's first nationalist document embodying the wishes of a country and its people. The Declaration of Arbroath, written in 1320 (an original copy of which is on display in West Register House, Edinburgh), has been compared by historians and commentators with the American Declaration of Independence. It ranks it as one of the world's great assertions in the cause of human freedom.

Northeast Scotland today combines powerful but depopulated landscape with charming seaside resorts and depressed, declining fishing villages. The Highlanders evicted from their crofts in the 18th century were replaced by sheep and their vacant farmland by deer forests for the sport of London-based lairds and their guests. Most recently there has been organized afforestation of the entire region. The oil industry helped some coastal towns to boom, notably Aberdeen, but injured many others such as Dundee and Peterhead. There is evidence of wealth — as at Gordonstoun School near Elgin where the Royal Family sent their sons (and later such film stars as Peter Finch and Sean Connery sent theirs) and at Balmoral Castle, the Royal Family's Scottish country residence, west of Aberdeen — but there is also grinding poverty. The region is at times almost incomprehensibly Scottish in manners and mores and particularly in language. (In Aberdeen, for instance, the word *what* is often pronounced "fit.") The alienation of the people and their sense of having been written off by the British government is reflected by the majority voting Scottish Nationalist.

This tour route covers 250 miles; allow about a week to cover it comfortably. It begins at Stirling, "the Gateway to the Highlands," and follows northwest through Doune, Callander, and Lochearnhead, where it turns eastward through Crieff and Perth to Dundee. From Dundee it swings along the scenic coast through Carnoustie, Arbroath, Montrose, and Stonehaven to the regional capital city of Aberdeen. From Aberdeen it cuts inland through Inverurie, Huntly, Keith, and Elgin to Inverness.

A few points to keep in mind: Because the drive is along "trunk," or main, roads, there should be no difficulty getting petrol (gasoline) or refreshments.

However, for overnight accommodations, book well in advance. Take along a copy of the tourist board's *Enjoy Scotland* road map or the annually updated *AA Big Road Atlas of Britain.* Hotels listed as expensive will cost $95 or more for a double (twin-bedded) room with breakfast, moderate will cost $65 to $95, and inexpensive under $65. All hotels listed contain standard facilities, that is, TV sets and private baths, unless otherwise noted. Dinner for two, including drinks and tip, will cost $50 or more if listed as expensive, $30 to $50 if moderate, and $30 or less if inexpensive. If you intend to treat yourself to a full-scale restaurant dinner or even luncheon, as opposed to a snack, it's sensible to book in advance.

En Route from Glasgow or Edinburgh – Stirling is a short drive north of Scotland's two largest cities. From Glasgow, take A80 to Dennyloanhead, and from there M80 to Stirling. From Edinburgh, take A8 to the junction with M9, which heads northwest to Stirling.

STIRLING: Like Edinburgh, Stirling began on an exalted crag and spread downward; unlike Edinburgh, it failed to develop points of interest outside its ancient zones. Visitors will spend most of their time on Stirling Hill, the site of Stirling Castle, flanked by a handful of aged subsidiary buildings and intriguing ruins. The castle is the most famous in Scottish history, not only for its dramatic 250-foot drop to Stirling Plain and its eye-boggling view, but also for its strategic position, from which it controlled lands to the north during the Middle Ages; for its associations with Robert the Bruce and his predecessor, William Wallace; and for its magnificent Renaissance architecture, lavishly elaborated during its heyday as one of the four royal residences of the Stuart kings. Representations of bacchanalian-looking characters such as Love and Lust on the façade, the work of stonemasons from France employed by Mary of Guise, wife of James V, have been eroded over the centuries but not obliterated. A guidebook available at the castle entrance will increase your knowledge and heighten your enjoyment of the towers built by James III, the fine 15th-century hall, the palace of James V, the parliament hall, and the chapel royal of 1594. Another attraction of the castle is the recently opened *Argylle and Sutherland Highlanders Regimental Museum.* The castle is headquarters of this regiment — one of the most famous in the British Army. The visitor center on the esplanade (Dumbarton Rd.) revives Stirling's past through an imaginative picture gallery and multiscreen show; it also has a bookshop, crafts shop, and tea garden. Closed Sunday mornings October through March. Joint admission charge to castle (phone: 0786-50000) and center (phone: 0786-62517).

Mar's Wark, beside the castle, was built in about 1570 by the first Earl of Mar, Regent of Scotland, and was the home of his descendants until 1715, when the sixth earl had to flee the country after leading a major, but unsuccessful, Jacobite rebellion. The building became a barracks, then a workhouse (hence its name). Bonnie Prince Charlie's army sacked and ruined it in 1746, but some of its exquisitie embellishments remain. Also by the castle are: the still-used Church of the Holy Rude, dating from 1414, where John Knox preached the sermon when James VI, aged 13 months, was crowned (open weekdays May through September and Sundays for 11 AM service); the guildhall, south of the church, founded in 1639 by the then dean of the guild for the support of 12 "decayed Guild Breithers"; and the impressive 17th-century town house, Argyll's Lodging, now a youth hostel but once the residence of Sir William Alexander of Menstrie, the founder of Nova Scotia. An exhibition displaying the coats of arms of 107 Nova Scotian baronetcies is at 16th-century Menstrie Castle, Sir William's birthplace 5 miles to the east on A91 (open May through September by arrangement with National Trust for Scotland; phone the Perth office: 0738-31296). Cambuskenneth

Abbey, on the river Forth a mile northeast of Stirling, was founded in the 12th century by the Scottish King David I, and was the scene in 1326 of King Robert the Bruce's first formal parliament. The church and conventual buildings are rubble, but a detached 67-foot, 13th-century bell tower survives intact.

The Scottish Wars of Independence, which took place around the turn of the 13th century, were distinguished for the valor not only of the aristocrat King Robert the Bruce ("Robert de Brus" in his native Norman tongue) but also of William Wallace, the People's Hero, who drove back an English army in 1297 at the Battle of Stirling Bridge, a mile north of the castle. Wallace's control over Scotland was short-lived — he was defeated at Falkirk in 1298 by a massive avenging force, imprisoned in London, and hacked limb from limb in 1305 — but his memory is sacred in Scottish hearts. The grandly towering Wallace Monument near the site of his triumph (off Hillfoots Rd., 1½ miles north-northeast of town) is a famous landmark, erected in 1861. Inside, the Stirling District Council offers an audiovisual historical crash course. Views are heavenly from its 220-foot top. Closed November through January and Wednesdays and Thursdays in February, March, and October (phone: 0786-72140).

Bannockburn, off M80 just south of Stirling, is a must. Beside the Battlefield is the *Bannockburn Heritage Centre,* which includes a film theater where the full story of the Wars of Independence can be viewed (open daily April through October; phone: 0786-812664) and a brand new Heritage Exhibition detailing the fascinating history of Scottish kings, called "The Kingdom of Scots". Bruce was not eager to fight the English at the time and place now so famous for his victory, but his hand had been forced by his brother, who made a deal in 1313 with the Governor of Stirling Castle — in English hands since soon after the defeat of Wallace — securing the castle's return to Scotland if the English did not relieve it by St. John the Baptist's Day (Midsummer Day) of the following year (the Bruces had the castle under siege). On Midsummer Day, 1314, 20,000 English troops, commanded by King Edward II himself, marched on the castle. Bruce's tactics were brilliant: He let the English come within 2 hair-raising miles of the target and then attacked — on the only piece of ground on Edward's route north where his mere 5,500 spearmen could hope to hold out — at first light, before the King's cavalry could see to charge. Finding themselves cut off to the left and right by unexpected and treacherous marshes, Edward's stalwarts fell back in confusion and flight. A magnificent 20-foot equestrian statue of Robert the Bruce in shining armor, unveiled by Queen Elizabeth II on the battle's 650th anniversary, stands today on the spot reputed to have been the Scottish royal headquarters during the fighting.

Also to be seen in Stirling are: its old mercat cross (market cross) and its 18th-century tollbooth on Broad Street; the bastion, or jail, within the original fortified town wall, just inside the Port Street entrance to the Thistle Shopping Centre; the 15th-century Auld Brig still used by pedestrians at Stirling Bridge (north of city center off A9); and the *Smith Art Gallery and Museum* on Dumbarton Road, housing, among other treasures, objects from early local history (open year-round, call for opening hours; phone: 0786-71917). The *MacRobert Arts Centre,* one of Scotland's foremost music, film, and theater venues, is on the grounds of Stirling University off A9, 2 miles north of town (phone: 0786-61081). During the *Stirling District Festival,* held around the first 2 weeks of August, the center hosts Scottish dancing and other events. Another important event is the *Stirling Tartan Week,* held the second week of July. It includes Tartan exhibitions, pipeband championships, *ceildhes,* dancing, tartan banquets, and beating of the retreat, from the Castle Esplanade. The Stirling Tourist Office is on Dumbarton Road (phone: 0786-75019).

CHECKING IN: ***Stakis Dunblane Hydro*** **–** Set in a 60-acre park, this is the largest hotel in the area and a holiday center in itself. Along with 224 well-equipped rooms and a restaurant serving traditional Scottish cuisine, the hotel has a heated indoor swimming pool, tennis courts, sports hall, Jacuzzi, and more. Seven miles north of Stirling in Dunblane (phone: 0786-822551). Expensive.

Golden Lion – Having recently been renovated — and so once again worthy of its immaculate historic pedigree — this 76-room hotel is decidedly the best of Stirling's center-city choices. Robert Burns, the Royal Family, Billy Graham, and a host of film stars have all been guests. 8 King St., Stirling (phone: 0786-75351). Moderate.

Royal – Robert Louis Stevenson stayed in this impressive 32-room mansion house as a boy, when his family visited the nearby spa. Henderson St., in Bridge of Allan, 4 miles north of Stirling (phone: 0786-832284). Moderate.

Granada Lodge – A new and comfortable custom-built hotel on the outskirts of Stirling, all 60 rooms have modern conveniences including tea- and coffee-making facilities. At Pirnhall Roundabout, where M9 meets M90 (phone: 0786-815033). Inexpensive.

King's Gate – This pleasant, down-to-earth, individualistic 16-room establishment is uniquely decorated; its walls are ornamented with zebra skins brought from East Africa by the proprietors. The food is good and inexpensive. 5 King St., Stirling (phone: 0786-73944). Inexpensive.

Castle – Built in 1472 as a school for the children of Scottish noblemen — and reputedly where James VI of Scotland (later James I of England) was taught — this attractive, historic building is now a hospitable 6-room hotel. The restaurant offers Scottish fare, and there's also a bar and beer garden. Castle Wynd, Stirling (phone: 0786-72290). Inexpensive.

EATING OUT: *Cross Keys Inn* – Dinner at this little English pub with a restaurant and 3 rooms is worth the 10-mile run from town. In Kippen village, via A811 west of Stirling (phone: 078687-293). Inexpensive.

En Route from Stirling – Take A84 northwest to Doune.

DOUNE: The dark fastnesses of 14th-century Doune Castle, ancestral seat of the Earls of Moray, have lasted unscathed. Not so some of its owners: the "Bonnie Earl" of Moray, who was the "Queen's love" in the famous murder ballad (actually he was her nephew; the queen was Mary, Queen of Scots), was killed by the Earl of Huntly in a clan feud in 1592. Doune Castle is beautifully set in a wooden clearing at the junction of the Teith and Ardoch rivers, approached just south of Doune village by a side road off A84 (open year-round; phone: 0786-841072). *Monty Python's Flying Circus* filmed *The Holy Grail* here.

Doune village has a 16th-century bridge, built originally by James IV's tailor to spite a ferryman who had refused him passage. A mile north of the village is the *Doune Motor Museum,* exhibiting the present Earl of Moray's collection of 40 vintage cars, including the second oldest Rolls-Royce in the world (open April through October). Nearby on the A84 is the magnificent Blair Drummond Safari and Leisure Park. Attractions include a comprehensive selection of animals, picnic sights, boat trips, a pet farm, an adventure playground, shops, and a restaurant. It makes for an ideal family outing. Open daily from 10 AM to 4:30 PM, from mid-March to late October (phone: 0786-841456).

CALLANDER: The A84 continues northwest to Callander. A very long street with mountains to either side, this bustling gateway to Sir Walter Scott's beloved Trossachs, the "bristly country," just misses being a typical Highland town — the Teith flows through it too complacently for that, and its fields are too prosperously green. In former times it was a cattle drovers' stop.

CHECKING IN: *Cromlix House* – This lovely mansion set on 500 acres has recently been converted to a hotel. All 14 rooms have private baths, and some have sitting rooms. Shooting, riding, tennis, and fishing for brown trout are some of the activities here. This is also the perfect headquarters for golfers since many of Scotland's finest courses are within an easy drive. (Edinburgh and Glasgow are less than an hour away as well.) Dunblane (phone: 0786-822125). Expensive.

Roman Camp – Lawns sweeping down to the river Teith and lordly old-world hospitality are the keynotes here. There are 11 guestrooms, and the excellent traditional dishes include beef, salmon, and venison. Open year-round. Off Main St., Callander (phone: 0877-30003). Expensive.

Dalgair House – A distinguished, family-run town house, with 9 recently refurbished rooms, traditional Scottish home cooking, and a wide selection of wines and whiskies. 113–115 Main St., Callander (phone: 0877-30283). Moderate.

Lubnaig – Formerly a private residence, now a family-owned and -run haven with 10 rooms, located just north of central Callander. The gables and compact little bay windows are gracious rather than grand, and the grounds are spacious. Open Easter through October. At Leny Feus (phone: 0877-30376). Inexpensive.

En Route from Callander – The A84 leads north through the Pass of Leny, noted for its waterfall, dwarfed oaks, and wild primroses. Four miles north of town, 2,875-foot Ben Ledi (Hill of God), overlooking Loch Lubnaig, is an easily manageable, highly rewarding 3½-hour climb on foot. The A84 skirts the edge of the lake to the picturesque hamlet of Strathyre, once a crofting settlement. Rob Roy's grave is along an unnamed side road turning west 2 miles farther north. The fabled outlaw lies in a setting of seraphic peace in the Macgregor family plot in Balquhidder Churchyard, beneath the lovely Braes of Balquhidder at the head of Loch Voil. The church itself contains an 8th-century carved tombstone and some old Gaelic bibles.

Farther north on A84 lies Lochearnhead.

LOCHEARNHEAD: Famous throughout Scotland for its water-skiing facilities, this resort town on the west shore of Loch Earn is also an excellent spot for boating. The Lochearnhead Water Sports Centre (phone: 05673-330) beside the lake on A85 (east of town), will cater to your sporting needs. In July, Lochearnhead hosts the Balquhidder–Lochearnhead–Strathyre Highland Games.

CHECKING IN: ***Clachan Cottage*** – This row of 250-year-old white cottages — with 23 rooms — winks at Loch Earn with its prettily lamplit windows. On A85 along the loch's north shore (phone: 05673-247). Inexpensive.

Kingshouse – Once the hunting lodge of the "Bonnie Earl" of Moray and Stewart kings, this small, white edifice with 7 rooms has recently been renovated in traditional, elegant style, with chandeliers and an Adam style fireplace in the lounge. The bar attracts "shepherds and gamekeepers". The hotel can arrange shooting, hunting, and fishing trips with local estates. On A84, 2 miles north of Strathyre (phone: 08774-646). Inexpensive.

En Route from Lochearnhead – East on A85, along the northern shore of Loch Earn, there will be lovely views of the loch, including 2 fairytale mansions owned by local aristocrats on the south shore. At the east end of the loch is the picturesque village of St. Fillans, offering fishing, sailing, hiking, and mountaineering. Also in St. Fillans is the Lochearn Sailing and Watersports Centre (phone: 0764-2292). Continue east on A85 along the river Earn to the pleasant holiday resort of Comrie where the river converges with the Lednoch and the Ruchill waters. Comrie is known as "Earthquake Village" because of the frequency of minor tremors in the immediate area. These (usually mere rattlers of crockery) occur because Comrie lies precisely on the Highland fault. If interested in tracing your family's tartan, stop off at the *Scottish Tartans Museum* on Drummond Street in Comrie (open April through October; phone: 0764-70779), where a detailed history of the tartan and Highland dress is presented.

The next route city, Crieff, lies east of Comrie on A85. Glenturret Whisky Distillery, which rivals the Strathisla Distillery as the oldest in Scotland, is on the approach to Crieff. Glenturret has a heritage center and restaurant (open weekdays from 9:30 AM to 4:30 PM March through December and Saturdays from 10 AM to 4 PM, April through October; phone: 0764-2424).

CRIEFF: Situated at the foot of the Grampian Hills, Crieff opens the way to the Highlands. Its perch on the Knock of Crieff (911 feet), overlooking the river Earn, offers splendid views of the surrounding area. It has picturesque steep streets, attractive parks, and excellent golf and fishing facilities nearby — there are over 20 golf courses in a 20-mile radius. The town was founded in the 17th century, but every building was razed to the ground by the Jacobites in 1716 (in revenge for the numerous hangings of Highlanders over the years on Gallows Hill). It was rebuilt, thanks largely to the Duke of Perth, after 1731. The tollbooth dates from that time. Bonnie Prince Charlie stayed here at the site of the present Drummond Arms on his way to disaster at Culloden in 1746. Other attractions in and around town include: Ardoch Roman Camp (10 miles south of Crieff on A822), one of the largest Roman stations in Britain, going back to the 2nd century; Stuart Strathearn Crystal Factory and Showroom, Muthill Rd. (open year-round; phone: 0764-4004); and, opposite the factory, Crieff Visitors' Centre, which includes a restaurant and a pottery workshop showing the manufacture of Perthshire paperweights (phone: 0764-4014). (Stuart Strathearn crystal, pottery, and paperweights are for sale at both the factory and the visitors' center.) The Crieff Tourist Information Office, recently moved from James Square to the Old Town Hall (phone: 0764-2578), is open year-round. They also can provide information on local nature trails and walks.

Drummond Castle is 3 miles south of Crieff on A8022. Overlooking small Strathearn Loch, the castle consists of a 15th-century keep with a 17th-century extension and a late Victorian mansion. Its formal gardens are in the shape of St. Andrew's Cross. In the 15th century, it was the scene of treacherous Scottish politics when Margaret, the daughter of the keep's builder, Sir John Drummond, was evidently poisoned by Scottish nobles who wished to prevent her marriage to James IV. (The King subsequently married Margaret Tudor and established the Stuart claim to the English throne.) The lovelorn James and, later, his hapless and equally lovelorn granddaughter, Mary, Queen of Scots, were frequent visitors to Drummond Castle. Open from 2 to 6 PM daily May through August and Wednesdays and Sundays in September (phone: 076481-257).

CHECKING IN: ***Cultoquhey House*** – A 10-bedroom old country house hotel known for its friendly atmosphere. Its justly celebrated restaurant features traditional Scottish cooking. Crieff (phone: 0764-3253). Expensive to moderate.

Crieff Hydro – With 200 rooms, by far the biggest hotel in the area, it has a swimming pool, golf course, squash courts, sauna, and solarium. It is an ideal base from which to explore the surrounding area, especially if there are children along. Crieff (phone: 0764-2401). Moderate.

Murraypark – There are 14 rooms at this secluded, friendly, old-fashioned hotel. Its restaurant is a local favorite, favoring traditional Scottish and French cooking, and was recently designated a "Taste of Scotland" winner. Connaught Terrace, Crieff (phone: 0764-3731). Moderate.

Drummond Arms – Built 160 years ago on the site of the hostelry where Bonnie Prince Charlie stayed on his way to Culloden, this pleasant, 36-room family-style hotel overlooking Crieff Earn is comfortable and convenient. James Sq., Crieff (phone: 0764-2151). Inexpensive.

En Route from Crieff – Continue east along A85 through the southern portion of Glen Almond, passing through the village of Fowlis Wester, the site of an intesting

Pictish stone — a 12-foot-high red sandstone slab, now eroded but with a glyphic picture of someone, possibly Jonah, being swallowed. At the village of Methven (5 miles west of Perth) is 17th-century Methven Castle, on the site of an earlier building that had been the residence of the widowed Margaret Tudor, queen to James IV. The castle is one of the last fortified houses built in Scotland. Continue to Perth.

PERTH: For a detailed report on the city, its sights, hotels, and restaurants, see *Perth,* THE CITIES.

En Route from Perth – Continuing east on A85, cross the river Tay and turn right around Kinnoull Hill, crossing the flat land known as Carse of Gowrie. At the village of Rossie Priory are Pictish sculptured stones. Approaching Dundee, look sharp for directions, which are sometimes very clear, sometimes very invisible; both entering and leaving the city it is perilously easy to drive as much as 20 minutes out of the way, especially at night. Keep on A85 past Queen's College of the University of St. Andrews, heading along the Nethergate into the city.

DUNDEE: Scotland's fourth largest city, with a population of 202,000, Dundee owes its fame to its commercial interests — the jute industry, jam and fruit cake production (it was a Dundonian who invented marmalade), the whaling industry, and journalism. Because the city suffered more than any other the devastation and looting of Scotland's turbulent past, it has only one building of any antiquity, and that dates from the 15th century — St. Mary's Tower (Old Steeple), Kirk Style, Nethergate. The tower is not only of historical interest, but affords a splendid view over the city center. It is open by appointment (phone the Dundee District Council during working hours: 0382-23141). Other buildings of historical interest are the *McManus Galleries* (containing both art and historical exhibits) in Albert Square (closed Sundays), the high school on Reform Street, and the remains of the Wishart Arch at Old Cowgate. These buidings are all within a 10-minute walk.

The city's tourist board (whose information center is at 4 City Square; phone: 0382-27723) has dubbed Dundee "City of Discovery" (after Antarctic explorer Captain Robert Falcon Scott's ship). What will be discovered here are friendly and helpful people, among other things (listed below), and magnificent views. The view from St. Mary's Tower is enjoyable, but that from the top of Dundee Law, an old volcano of 572 feet, has been compared to Italy's Bay of Naples. Dundee's 2-mile-long Tay Rail Bridge, one of the largest in Europe, also provides a point for sensational viewing — the river Tay estuary during a "good" sunrise or sunset is magic. The rail bridge in itself does not provide the spectacle offered by the Forth Road Bridge, but it is an extraordinary feat of engineering. (This site was the scene of a tragedy when in 1879 a hurricane caused the previous bridge to collapse and a trainload of people to plunge to their deaths. Legend has it that a ghost train crosses the Tay Rail Bridge every year on the night of December 28, the anniversary of the accident.)

Dundee dates from Roman times, and there are many old Roman camp sites in the surrounding area. The so-called "first King of the Scots," Kenneth MacAlpin, used the city as his base when he set out to defeat the Picts in AD 834. The most poignant feature of the city's history is the number of times it has been sacked. In 1296 Edward I of England pillaged Dundee and sacrilegiously burned the Sacred Church of St. Mary. The English returned during the reign of their Richard II, in 1385, burning and looting. They tried a new approach in 1547, sailing up the Tay, as part of Henry VIII's "Rough Wooing" of the infant Queen Mary on behalf of his son Edward. During the civil wars of the mid-17th century, Dundee was plundered by the Royalists under Montrose and then by the Cromwellian troops of General George Monck. It took over a century to recover from this last episode, and as a result Dundee lost its place as the second wealthiest of Scotland's burghs.

The city became an important fishing center in the 19th century, when whaling was a formidable industry and the courageous if destructive ships made their way from here to the coasts of Greenland. (Readers of Sherlock Holmes may remember that "Black Peter" in the story of that name was captain of the *Sea Unicorn* of Dundee in 1883; Arthur Conan Doyle had been the doctor on a Greenland whaler in 1880.) Appropriately, the jute industry boomed in these years as well. From 1800 to 1850, the population nearly quadrupled, as Dundee became the second most desirable Scottish destination for Irish immigrants (Glasgow was the first). It was also a center for shipbuilding; the city's most famous product was the R.R.S. *Discovery,* built in 1901 and used by Captain Robert Falcon Scott (1868–1912) in his Antarctic expedition of 1901–04. You can see the *Discovery* at Victoria Dock (for further information, phone: 0382-201175). Dundee's naval links are also celebrated in its ownership of the oldest warship afloat — H.M.S. *Unicorn.* Launched in 1824 and now berthed at Victoria Dock, this 46-gun frigate has been recently restored as a floating museum; for a clear indication of the appalling conditions Britain's "Jolly Jack Tars" endured during the days of sail, the *Unicorn* is well worth a visit (open daily April through mid-October; phone: 0382-200900).

Dundee houses the publishing empire of D.C. Thomson, a company famous for juvenile fare of sufficient ingenuity and diversity to make it a British literary counterpart of Walt Disney. Many of its comic characters have justly become household words throughout the British Isles: Their ethos varies between 20th-century conservatism and impassioned 19th-century radicalism. Thomson's adult fodder caters to a much less intellectual market. Its severely parochial *Sunday Post* is the world's largest-selling Sunday newspaper.

Dundee is well served by its attractive parks, the most outstanding of which is Camperdown Park, where there is every conceivable form of recreation (playgrounds, restaurants, and so on), and a restaging of the naval battle of Camperdown (1797), fought against Revolutionary France's Dutch allies. The Grecian mansion within the park's grounds houses a golf museum and a display of Georgian furniture. A recently expanded *Wildlife Centre* features a comprehensive variety of indigenous species; phone: 0382-623555).

The city has recently rebuilt its *Repertory Theater* in Tay Square (box office phone: 0382-23530). The theater features a variety of productions, with some imaginative casting and direction, varying from comedies and musicals to modern classics. Eating facilities here are excellent, and the auditorium is admirably conceived: spacious, comfortable, and affords fine visual involvement with the stage. The *Caird Hall* is a major venue for rock and classical concerts, including the world famous Scottish National Orchestra (phone: 0382-23141, ext. 4288). Dundee has a wide selection of art galleries and museums, notably: the *McManus Galleries* on Albert Square (open Mondays through Saturdays from 10 AM to 5 PM; phone: 0382-23141), in a fine Victorian Gothic building with many Victorian Scottish paintings and local history displays; the *Barrack Street Museum* (open Mondays through Saturdays from 10 AM to 5 PM; phone: 0382-23141); Dundee Printmakers Workshop on Seagate (open daily; phone: 0382-26331); and the Mills Observatory on Glamis Road in Balgay Park (open varying hours Mondays through Saturdays; phone: 0382-67138). A very recent development is the annual *City Festival,* from June 1–August 7. The celebration includes a water festival, a jazz festival, a folk festival, children's week, fireworks, a horticultural show, parades and floats, and highland games.

Dundee has conducted a major campaign to attract more visitors in recent years. The City Square off High Street has just been completely renovated with 2 new fountains, re-paved grounds, and new benches, as well as sandblasting the surrounding buildings, all making for a much more pleasant city center. Another important development is the *Wellgate Shopping Centre.* Located between Victoria Road and Panmure Street, it is the largest of its kind in the region. All major stores are represented. The city fathers — to their credit — have invested substantial sums of money to provide indoor leisure and sports centers (phone: 0382-23141). The newest is the *Swimming and Leisure Centre* at Earl Grey Place. Facilities include a swimming pool (of course) and a crèche for use during one's swim, a flume, a fitness center, and table tennis (phone: 0382-203888).

East of Dundee on A930 is the seaside resort and residential suburb of Broughty Ferry, a quaint and traditional fishing village with a long sandy beach. Apart from excellent sailing and fishing, the town's most notable draw is *Broughty Castle Museum,* a reconstructed 16th-century fort now hosting natural history (including whaling) collections. Open daily except Fridays and Sundays from 10 AM to 1 PM and from 2 to 5 PM year-round and Sunday afternoons July through September (phone: 0382-76121).

CHECKING IN: *Old Mansion House* – Situated outside Dundee at Auchterhouse, this hotel is a must for lovers of Old World tradition. A 16th-century house set in 11 acres of park, it contains only 6 rooms. Facilities include a heated outdoor pool, a grass tennis court, and a squash court. Excellent restaurant (see *Eating Out*). Dundee (phone: 082626-366). Expensive.

Stakis Earl Grey – Dundee's newest hotel, with 104 rooms, offers luxurious facilities including sauna, jacuzzi, heated swimming pool, and first class banqueting and conference facilities. Earl Grey Place, Dundee (phone: 0382-29271). Expensive.

Swallow – Prides itself particularly on the Swallow Leisure Club, which includes a swimming club, spa pool, solarium, and a fitness room with the latest equipment. The hotel has 110 rooms, all facilities. Kingsway West, Invergowrie, off the Perth road (phone: 0382-641122). Expensive.

Invercarse – A comfortable establishment of 40 rooms set in its own grounds, this hostelry has the ambience of a country house with the facilities of a first class hotel. 371 Perth Road, Dundee (phone: 0382-69231). Expensive to moderate.

Queen's – This centrally located hotel was built in 1878 in the imposing Victorian Gothic style. It combines elegantly laid-out public rooms with 30 recently refurbished rooms. Much in demand by conference delegates (some of whom tell very funny stories that reflect well on the good nature of the management). 160 Nethergate, Dundee (phone: 0382-22515). Expensive to moderate.

Angus Thistle – This centrally located, recently refurbished hotel has 58 rooms (with all amenities from hair dryers to videos), several private suites with whirlpools, and conference and banqueting facilities. It also has much more personality than is suggested by its formidable exterior. Excellent restaurant (see *Eating Out*). 101 Marketgate, Dundee (phone: 0382-26874). Moderate.

Tay – Dundee's longest established hotel (whose ghosts probably could tell a few stories that might spawn some startling revisions of the history books). It has 87 rooms and, on Fridays, the added attraction of a nightclub. Whitehall Crescent, Dundee (phone: 0382-21641). Moderate.

Ballinard House – There are splendid views of the River Tay in this 19th century country house hotel. It has 32 rooms, all with modern conveniences, and magnificent gardens. 26 Claypotts Rd., Broughty Ferry, Dundee (phone: 0382-739555). Inexpensive.

Dunella – In Broughty Ferry, with peace and tranquillity in abundance (as distinct from the business-oriented, conference-style central Dundee hotels). The building is an old house with a large garden. 76 Strathern Rd., West Ferry (phone: 0382-74156). Inexpensive.

EATING OUT: ***Angus Steak Bar*** – This carvery of local renown is in the *Angus Thistle* hotel (see *Checking In*). Angus steaks are served efficiently, agreeably, and eminently digestably — with a very decent choice of red wines. 101 Marketgait, Dundee (phone: 0382-26874). Expensive to moderate.

Old Mansion House – This award-winning restaurant in the *Old Mansion House* hotel (see *Checking In*) is, in the view of some hardened perennial pilgrims to Dundee, the best of the lot, and by anyone's estimate has an excellent choice of Scottish cuisine. Dundee (phone: 082626-366). Expensive.

L'Auberge – In the nearby resort suburb, which means seclusion and comfort and, in this instance, first class French cuisine as well. 594 Brook St., Broughty Ferry (phone: 0382-730890). Expensive to moderate.

Jahangir – Dundee's most upmarket Indian restaurant features a wide variety of exotic food superbly prepared. 1 Session St., Dundee (phone: 0382-202022). Moderate.

Raffles Café – A fine reputation for its fresh products in Scottish cuisine. 18 Perth Rd., Dundee (phone: 0382-26344). Moderate to inexpensive.

En Route from Dundee – For an interesting, day-long detour from the main route, leave Dundee by A929 north and bear northwest at Todhills onto A928, which leads to Glamis (the *i* is silent). Fairy-tale Glamis Castle was the towering, turreted, historic home of the Lyon family, Earls of Strathmore and Kinghorne. It claims association with the Macbeth story and also has its own legend of a monster. The castle and grounds offer many attractions, including a tea room, shops, formal garden, nature trail, and picnic area (open daily from 12:30 to 5 PM, May through mid-October; phone: 030784-242). In Glamis village is the *Angus Folk Museum,* a treasure for folklore enthusiasts (open from noon to 5 PM May through September; phone: 030784-288). The museum staff will direct you to the garden of the manse nearby where there is a sculptured Pictish stone. You can continue north on A928 to Kirriemuir, the birthplace of Sir James Matthew Barrie (1860–1937) — author of the plays *Peter Pan, Dear Brutus, Mary Rose, The Admirable Crichton,* and *What Every Woman Knows* where there is a museum of his memorabilia (open daily except Sunday mornings from 11 AM to 5:30 PM May through September; phone: 0575-72646).

The main tour route leads out of Dundee by A930 east to Carnoustie, famous above all else for its championship golf course, which frequently hosts the British Open. There are three excellent golf clubs — local hotels will help with membership arrangements — and several fine sporting goods shops. The town overlooks a lovely bay with sandy beach, popular in summer with sailors and surfers.

CHECKING IN: ***Carlogie House*** – A 10-minute walk from the championship golf course, this 11-room hotel welcomes the public for bar snacks and full meals. Comfortable and reliable. Carlogie Rd., Carnoustie (phone: 0241-53185). Moderate to inexpensive.

Brax – Another hotel that overlooks the famous course and earns its living from the golf trade. With 6 rooms, it is a good value. 11 Links Parade, Carnoustie (phone: 0241-53032). Inexpensive.

Glencoe – Directly opposite and overlooking the championship golf course's first tee and 18th green, this well-regarded hotel with 11 rooms is ideal for the golfing fanatic (unless his or her name is Campbell). 8 Links Parade, Carnoustie (phone: 0241-53273). Inexpensive.

ARBROATH: Take A930 north out of Carnoustie and turn east at Muirdrum onto A92. The next town on the route, Arbroath, is famous for its "Arbroath Smokies" (believed to have been invented at Auchmithie, 3 miles away), a smoked haddock that is a favorite dish among Scots. It is possible to obtain this admirable fish from the supplier to the Royal Family, no less, R. R. Spink and Sons, Seagate, Arbroath. Moreover, Mr. Spink (or son) will give you a fine selection of recipes.

The fascinating *Signal Tower Museum* is housed in the Bell Rock lighthouse, built in 1813 by Robert Stevenson (1772–1850), grandfather of the writer R. L. Stevenson. It stands on the south shore of the harbor (open Mondays through Saturdays year-round and Sunday afternoons in July and August; phone: 0241-75598). The harbor itself is lively, its fishing dating back at least to medieval times. The afternoon fish market merits a visit (open weekdays). While in the vicinity, don't miss the opportunity to see the imposing ruins of Arbroath Abbey, founded in 1178 and famous as the scene of the authorship of the Declaration of Arbroath in 1320. This document, probably composed by Bernard of Linton, Abbot of Arbroath and Chancellor of Scotland, compares in importance in Scottish history to the American Declaration of Independence. The tourist information center at Marketgate (phone: 0241-72609 or -76680) can give additional information on this and other sites in Arbroath, as well as directions for walks along the scenic coastline.

CHECKING IN: ***Letham Grange*** – A 20-room Victorian mansion on its own grounds, this is the leading hotel in the area. Facilities include a private golf course and a curling rink. The hotel can arrange clay pigeon and other shooting, horseback riding, hunting, and fishing. However, advance booking is required for these activities. Letham Grange, Colliston, near Arbroath (phone: 0241-89373). Expensive.

Seaforth – A fine 21-room hotel operating its own Tay estuary cruises and a popular restaurant (see *Eating Out*). Facilities include a swimming pool, sauna, solarium, Jacuzzi, snooker, and golf course. Dundee Rd., Arbroath (phone: 0241-72232). Expensive.

Windmill – Traditional, old-fashioned, 15-room hotel built in 1824. A pleasant stay with the accent on comfort and good nature. Millgate Loan, Arbroath (phone: 0241-72278). Inexpensive.

EATING OUT: ***Meadowbank Inn*** – The *Carriage Room* restaurant serves rich Scottish meals of very high quality, specializing in fresh viands and vegetables of its own produce, priding itself on its own bread. Also an excellent stopping-off place for coffee and snacks, with a real flavor of the locality. Montrose Rd., Arbroath (phone: 0241-75755). Expensive.

Idvies – In an old country house, a fine, traditional, and elegant restaurant which has been granted the "Taste of Scotland" award. Worth the 8-mile drive north of town to Letham (phone: 030781-787). Moderate.

Seaforth – In the hotel of the same name (see *Checking In*), this locally popular restaurant has recently augmented its traditional Scottish cuisine to emphasize seafood, particularly priding itself on its lobsters. Dundee Rd., Arbroath (phone: 0241-72232). Moderate.

SHARING A PINT: The *Old Brew House* and *Smugglers Tavern,* both on the harbor, are the best bets for traditional pubs in the community.

MONTROSE: Leaving Arbroath north along the coast on A92 to Montrose, there are excellent views of lovely Lunan Bay, a favorite spot for windsurfers despite the rocks at either end. Montrose is set on the river South Esk; when crossing it, observe the tidal basin and its bird sanctuary — it is an ornithologist's paradise. Montrose was an important fishing port in the 17th and 18th centuries; it still is the center of the east coast salmon fishing industry. By permission of the Earl of Southesk, the river is still fished locally with much enthusiasm. A popular holiday resort, the town has a distinctively Flemish layout, deriving from trade links with the Netherlands. We recommend a stroll around the town center to take in the fine old buildings. A particular attraction is the *Montrose Museum and Art Gallery* on Panmure Place, which has many fascinating exhibits, including three Pictish stones, the sword of the great poet-general, the Marquis of Montrose (see the introduction), a collection of silver, and a maritime gallery (open Mondays through Saturdays year-round, Sunday afternoons in July and August, and weekday afternoons November through March; phone: 0674-73232). Montrose is now a minor base for the offshore oil industry.

CHECKING IN: ***Park*** – With spacious lounges, well appointed bedrooms, excellent food, and pleasant service, this hotel is an ideal base from which to pursue fishing, wildlife watching, and walking among the lovely Angus hills and glens. The bar from time to time acts as a social center for some of the local gentlemen farmers, businessmen, and fishermen. 59 rooms. John St., Montrose (phone: 0674-73415). Moderate.

Links – Another very pleasant hotel with good service and food, comfortable layout, and 20 smart rooms. A good base from which to pursue boat trips, walks, fishing, and sightseeing. Mid-Links, Montrose (phone: 0674-72288). Moderate to inexpensive.

EATING OUT: ***Corner House Hotel*** – The high teas at this hotel would satisfy the most gluttonous appetites, and in fact are its main attraction. Menu includes delicious mixed grills, beautiful homemade scones, cakes, and the like. 131–133 High Street, Montrose (phone: 0674-73126). Inexpensive.

En Route from Montrose – For a quick (perhaps 2-hour) detour to Brechin, take A935 west from Montrose. A royal burgh since 1641, Brechin has a long history; some of its buildings date from the 10th, 11th, and 12th centuries. In 1303, its castle held out for 3 weeks against Edward I's besieging army, surrendering only after Governor Sir Thomas Maule was killed. The town itself saw a ritualized clan slaughter between the Douglases and the Gordons in 1452. Steam railway enthusiasts will be delighted by a trip on the nearby Caledonian steam railway. For details, contact the Brechin Tourist Information Office on St. Ninian's Place (phone: 03562-3050). Nearing Forfar, 6 miles from Brechin off B9134, is the village of Aberlemno where there are four Pictish sculptured stones, certainly worth a few minutes drive.

A92 departs Montrose north along the rugged Kincardine coast, passing through St. Cyrus, the site of a national nature reserve noted for its great variety of plant life. Further north is the fishing village of Gourdon, the only place in Britain that still uses the old-fashioned line method of fishing for haddock; travelers can buy fresh fish direct from the filleting sheds. At Inverbervie, A92 overlooks the lovely Bervie Bay, popular for sailing. Just south of Stonehaven stands the imposing and bleak ruin of Dunnottar Castle, situated on a vast isolated rock. (If the weather is at all damp, walk with great circumspection to the door or you may lose your balance and dignity.) Dunnottar is famous as the stronghold where the Scottish crown jewels were taken for protection in 1651; they were then smuggled out under the eyes of the besieging Cromwellian forces and buried under nearby Kinneff church floor until the restoration of Charles II in 1660. It is said that 167 Covenanters were imprisoned in a single dungeon here in 1685; the stone recording the names of those who died may be found in Dunnottar churchyard. Follow A92 into Stonehaven.

STONEHAVEN: Stonehaven is an ideal seaside resort, with outdoor heated swimming pool, sea fishing, sailing, golf, and other family attractions. It is also a good place to be when the weather turns wet. The leisure center, open since 1985, has an indoor pool and provides a variety of other indoor activities as well (phone: 0569-63162). Among the town's other attractions are a seabirds' nesting sanctuary run by the Royal Society for the Protection of Birds and the Foulsheugh Wildlife and Seabird Colony. The tourist office on the square (phone: 0569-62806) can give details on this and other walks. The Stonehaven harbor, which used to be important as a fishing center, is now host to pleasure yachts, for which it is ideally suited. The oldest building in town — the tollbooth at the harbor — houses the Stonehaven museum and its collection of local artifacts (open daily except Wednesday and Sunday mornings June through September; phone: 0779-77778).

CHECKING IN: ***Commodore*** – A modern hotel with 40 bedrooms, it has a well-stocked wine cellar and an excellent restaurant. Situated across from the historic fishing village of Cowie, only a 10-minute walk from Stonehaven harbor. Cowie Park, Stonehaven (phone: 0569-62936). Moderate.

Heugh – Small (5-room) but highly regarded establishment in a baronial mansion with turrets. Westfield Rd., Stonehaven (phone: 0569-62379). Moderate.

Marine – The main attraction of this 8-room hotel is its unique location overlooking the harbor. Shorehead, Stonehaven (phone: 0569-62155). Moderate to inexpensive.

Royal – A pleasant, 36-room hotel with fine service and traditional cuisine. Market Sq., Stonehaven (phone: 0569-62979). Inexpensive.

En Route from Stonehaven – Continue north on A92, a beautiful drive along the Aberdeenshire coastline. On the way is Muchalls Castle, dating from 1619, a well-preserved, L-shaped fortalice with handsome plasterwork ceilings, a splendid fireplace, a secret staircase, a nearby smuggler's cave, and an extraordinary view of the North Sea (open Tuesday and Sunday afternoons May through September). Approaching Aberdeen, A92 bears left and A956 forks to the right along the coastline. Both roads lead into Aberdeen.

ABERDEEN: For a detailed report on the city, its sights, hotels, and restaurants, see *Aberdeen,* THE CITIES.

En Route from Aberdeen – You could spend a summer in northeast Scotland and not cover it adequately, for there are literally scores of castles, amusements, and parks in this area. The leaflet/folder, *Scotland's North-East — What to See and Where to Go,* available at any tourist information office free of charge, provides a comprehensive list of tourist attractions — good luck!

A trip on the Northern Belle railway is strongly recommended. It's a splendid way to see a large section of this country in style in only one day. Departing from Aberdeen, the train takes a 128-mile run through the magnificent castle country of northeast Scotland to Dufftown, then continues back to Aberdeen, with stops at a "Loch Park" for lunch and at a restored working mill in Auchindechy. The carriages are luxuriously appointed; the food is excellent. The railway operates from July to September only; it departs Aberdeen at 10:25 AM and returns at 6 PM. For details, contact *Grampian Rail Tours Ltd.,* Aberdeen Station, Aberdeen (phone: 03586-89513). *Note:* At press time, the future of this operation was in doubt due to a conflict between the operators and British Railways. Be sure to call in advance.

On leaving Aberdeen, take the road to Inverurie, A96 (northwest), passing the airport at Dyce; A96 follows the river Don as far as Inverurie.

INVERURIE: This ancient royal burgh is one of the most interesting areas in Britain for archaeological remains and prehistoric sites. The booklet, *Early Grampian,* available at the tourist information office in the town hall (phone: 0467-20600), is a good guide to these. The *Carnegie Museum,* in the town hall (open Saturdays and weekday afternoons except Wednesdays; phone 0779-77778), has a display of local archaeological relics. A few miles south of Inverurie off B993 is Castle Fraser (open daily from 2 to 6 PM May through September; phone: 03303-463), a splendid tower house, one of the finest 17th-century castles in the northeast.

Inverurie has had a lively history. On the site of the present Barra Castle just outside of town (off B9170), Robert Bruce defeated John Comyn, third Earl of Buchan (with whom he was at blood-feud for the murder of Comyn's cousin John "the Red" Comyn), on Christmas Eve, 1307. The castle itself, one of Scotland's most unusual and attractive, may be visited by written appointment only (contact Dr. and Mrs. Bogdan, Barra Castle, Inverurie). In 1411, the bloody battle of Harlaw was fought between the citizens of Aberdeenshire and the Lord of the Isles 2 miles northwest of Inverurie. Known as "Red" Harlaw, the battle is commemorated by a monument on the B9001 road, erected in 1911. North of Inverurie, off B9001, is the Loanhead stone circle, a Bronze Age monument, and standing at the roadside on A96 is a granite Pictish stone, the Brandsbutt Stone.

CHECKING IN: ***Pittodrie House*** – Situated in an old country house, this 12-room hotel has a good reputation locally. Food and service are excellent. Staff can arrange fishing and shooting trips. At Pitcapel, near Inverurie (phone: 04676-444). Expensive.

Strathburn – A new hotel with 15 well-appointed rooms, pleasant atmosphere, and modern decor. Burghmuir Dr., Inverurie (phone: 0467-24422). Moderate.

Thainstone House – Charming hotel of 9 rooms in a very old country house. Service and facilities are excellent. Inverurie (phone: 0467-21643). Moderate.

Westhall House – This 12-bedroom hotel is situated in a 16th-century keep, and has the character of a medieval castle. Good service and food. Westhall Estates, Oyne (phone: 04645-225). Moderate to inexpensive.

Gordon Arms – Centrally located, this old and established 11-room hotel frequented by local residents offers a high standard of comfort and fine Scottish food. Salmon fishing and golf are available locally. Market Place, Inverurie (phone: 0467-20314). Inexpensive.

HUNTLY: Continue northwest on A96. For so small a town, Huntly has had an eventful history. Situated on a defensive site between the rivers Deveron and Bogie, it has been fortified since 11th- and 12th-century Norman times and was the power base of the Gordon clan in the 14th century. It contains many fine buildings. A free guide to the Huntly architectural trail is available from the tourist information center at the square (phone: 0466-2255). The town's most famous attraction is the magnificent ruin at Huntly Castle. The original fortress was destroyed by Archibald Douglas, Earl of Moray, in 1452; the present structure dates from 1454. The castle began its decline in the mid-17th century when the second Marquess of Huntly was beheaded for supporting Charles I; it now has monument status and is open daily except Sunday mornings. Leith Hall, also dating from the 17th century, is 7 miles southwest of Huntly (take A97 to B9002; it contains some fine 18th-century furniture, portraiture, and military memorabilia (open daily from 2 to 6 PM May through September; phone: 04643-216). The Glendronach Whisky Distillery — which still malts its own barley and was the setting for part of the televised historical drama, *King's Royal* — is at Forgue, 10 miles northeast of Huntly (take A97 to B9001); visits by appointment (phone: 046682-202).

CHECKING IN: ***Battlehill*** – Highly recommended 5-bedroom hotel in a Victorian house. Battlehill, Huntly (phone: 0466-2734). Inexpensive.

Castle – Family-run, with 24 rooms in a 220-year-old mansion that was formerly the residence of the Dukes of Gordon. Offers splendid views. Good traditional Scottish food and a friendly atmosphere. (phone: 0466-2696). Inexpensive.

KEITH: Situated where the main Aberdeen–Inverurie road and railway cross the river Isla (continuing northwest on A96), Keith owes its present configuration to the 18th-century fashion for planned towns, but its existence dates from AD 700 when Saint Maelrubha of Applecross converted the local population to Christianity. Scotland's first post-Reformation saint, St. John Ogilvie, is believed to have been born in 1580 just outside Keith. (He was hanged in Glasgow in 1615 for refusing to take an anti-Catholic oath of loyalty to the Crown.) Today's town dates from 1750, when it was laid out by the Earl of Findlater (also an Ogilvy). The Auld Brig o' Keith, built in 1609, is a favorite subject of artists; the new bridge was built in 1770. Keith is a lovely town with three parallel streets bisected by narrow lanes. Among its charms are: the Strathisla Whisky Distillery, established in 1786, one of the oldest distilleries in Scotland (open weekdays from mid-May to mid-September; phone: 05422-7471); and Eggs and Co., producers of exquisitely decorated duck and goose eggs, located 5½ miles east of Keith on A95 — visitors can watch the process and buy samples (phone: 05425-695).

En Route from Keith – The village of Fochabers, on A96 northwest toward Elgin, offers an unusual opportunity for food shopping. Baxters Speyside Co. — specializing in top-quality traditional Scottish recipes, such as soups, preserves, and sauces — has opened a visitors center 1 mile west of Fochabers on A96. The original shop has been re-created, with an audiovisual display, a Victorian kitchen, a tea room, and George Baxter's cellar, where you can buy produce available nowhere else. It is a fine emporium, and it compels admiration as a brilliant advertising gimmick (open weekdays from 10 AM to 4 PM April through October). Another interesting venue in Fochabers is the *Fochabers Folk Museum,* Pringle Church, High Street, with its extensive and impressive collection of horse-drawn vehicles, agricultural implements, and costumes (open daily year-round; phone: 0343-820362).

ELGIN: Elgin can convey a haunting, medieval feeling. The third largest town in the area, with a population of 20,000, it was created a royal burgh by Alexander II, who reigned from 1198 to 1249. Its original street plan is very well preserved, and several of its buildings have great historical interest. To appreciate the old-world aura, take a walk along the old cobbled marketplace at Plainstones. Elgin Cathedral, founded in 1224, reflects the town's turbulent past: It was burned to the ground in 1390 by the Wolf of Badenoch and stripped of its lead in 1573 as a pious activity of the Reformation; its Great Tower collapsed in 1711. In restoration since 1825, the cathedral is a magnificent ruin well worth exploration (open year-round). *Elgin Museum,* begun in 1836, contains a notable archaeological collection including Pictish stones and an internationally renowned collecton of fossils (phone for opening times: 0343-3675). A recent addition to Elgin's attractions is the *Moray Motor Museum,* Bridge Street, with a fine collection of vintage cars (open daily 10 AM to 5 PM, April through October). Also, check out the Old Mills Visitor Centre, on Old Mills Road, where there is a meal and water mill that has been restored to full working order, plus a craft center and picnic area. Open June through September (phone for hours: 0343-45121).

North of Elgin, off B9012, is another ruined castle, the motte (moat)-and-bailey at Duffus (open at all times). Pluscarden Priory, 6½ miles south of Elgin, is a 13th-century abbey founded by Alexander II in 1230. It has been restored by Benedictine monks who took up residence in 1948 and who welcome travelers, including tourists, seeking religious retreat and contemplation (open year-round; phone: 034389-257). Just 2½ miles north of Elgin are the massive ruins of Spynie Castle, the residence of the Bishops of Moray, the exterior of which can be viewed year-round; a project is underway to make the ruins safe for exploration. In Burghead, northwest of Elgin off B9013, are a number of Pictish stones.

CHECKING IN/EATING OUT: ***Mansion House*** – The charm of the past is preserved here in a peaceful wooded setting by the river. The hotel, an imposing mansion of 20 recently renovated rooms, has up-to-date comfort and all imaginable facilities including a pool, gym, sauna, Jacuzzi, and excellent Scottish food. The Haugh, Elgin (phone: 0343-48811). Expensive.

Eight Acres – This modern 57-room hotel on its own landscaped grounds on the western approaches to Elgin provides an ideal base for exploring the many attractions of the Moray area. In addition to a distinguished restaurant, it has a swimming pool, squash court, sauna, solarium, and snooker hall. Morriston Rd., Elgin (phone: 0343-3077). Moderate.

Park House – A delightful Georgian building in the west end of town near most of Elgin's amenities and historic sites. Small — just 6 rooms — but with splendid service and food. South St., Elgin (phone: 0343-7695). Moderate.

FORRES: A96 west leads into Forres. If you were bewitched by Elgin, Forres will increase the sensation. The town is famous as the setting for the opening scenes of *Macbeth.* (OK, so how do we *know* Shakespeare never saw it?) The "blasted heath" where Banquo and Macbeth met the witches is said to be at Hardmuir, 6 miles west of town. (Banquo lived several centuries after Macbeth, but what use are witches — or playwrights — if they let such details impede them?) Forres retains its medieval street plan, so that visitors actually get some sense of how the place might have looked to the real Macbeth.

The focal point of town is the tollbooth (built in 1838) and the adjoining mercat cross of 1842, fashioned after the Scott Monument in Edinburgh. The town is considerably enhanced by its extensive parks, such as Grant Park, which has a beautiful flower display in summer — so beautiful that it regularly wins the annual "Britain in Bloom" contest. A recent acquisition is the Dallas Ohu Visitor Centre. This is a former whisky distillery where visitors can see in detail how whisky is produced. Open daily April through September, except Sunday mornings (phone: 0309-76548).

One of the most interesting features of the town is the Sueno Stone, a wonderous example of Pictish sculpture that has been compared to an Assyrian relief. Standing 20 feet tall, the stone depicts living creatures, warriors, and symbols. It is thought to date from the 9th century and to commemorate a great victory over the Viking raiders. The tourist information center (in the *Falconer Museum,* Tolbooth St.; phone: 0309-72938) can give more details on this and other Forres sites. The stone is a mile northeast of town.

The area has several other attractions: Brodie Castle, 3½ miles west on A96 has been the residence of the Brodie family since 1160; it contains a fine collection of furniture and paintings, and its beautiful gardens are renowned for their display of daffodils; it has an adventure playground and a shop (open daily except Sunday mornings April through September; phone: 03094-371). Darnaway Castle in the Findhorn Valley, 3 miles west of Forres was the seat of the Earls of Moray; Mary, Queen of Scots, held court here in 1564, and the castle is famed for its splendid 15th-century hammer beam roof, as well as for its fine collection of Stuart portraits (tours from Darnaway Farm Visitor Center June through August; phone: 03094-469). Nearby are the Culbin Sands, where the entire barony of Culbin was engulfed by a sandstorm in 1694; the Sands are now famous for their variety of rare fauna. Another popular beauty spot, ideal for picnics, is Randolph's Leap (7 miles southwest of Forres; take A940 south to B9007) named for the Earl of Moray, who drove displaced landowners across the gap. Incidentally, not all the magic here is black: King David I (also a saint) founded Kinloss Abbey, 3 miles north of Forres off B9011, as a Cistercian retreat when he was led to its site by a dove; the Reformation turned it into a quarry.

CHECKING IN: ***Parkmount House*** – Situated in a quiet, secluded area of Forres is this 6-room family hotel specializing in high-quality home cooking, traditional comfort, and attractive surroundings — very much an example of Scottish hospitality at its best. Midway between *Muiryshade Golf Course* and the town center, St. Leonard's Rd., Forres (phone: 0309-73312). Inexpensive.

NAIRN: A96 continues to Nairn, passing through Auldearn, site of one of Montrose's victories. Nairn is an attractive holiday resort on the coast overlooking the Moray Firth, known (to the English) as "the Brighton of the North," a Shangri-La for golfers, with two excellent courses, Newtown Golf Course to the west and Nairn Dunbar to the east. The Brighton comparison stems from the Victorian urban planning, particularly on the west side of town. The *Nairn Literary Institute Museum* is a 150-year-old institution admired for its varied ethnographic, folk life, and natural history exhibits (opening hours are limited; at the Viewfield House on King St.; no phone). The tourist information office is at 62 King Street (phone: 0667-52753). Just 3 miles south of Nairn off A939 stands Rait Castle, where in 1424 the Mackintoshes slaughtered the Comyns. Balblair, on the eastern outskirts of Nairn, is where Prince William Augustus ("the Butcher"), Duke of Cumberland (1721–65), son of George II, camped with his army on their way to defeat his cousin Bonnie Prince Charlie and to massacre Charles's unfortunate followers at Culloden in 1746. Five miles south of town on B9090 is Cawdor Castle (for information, see "Special Places," in *Inverness,* THE CITIES).

CHECKING IN: ***Clifton*** – Renowned for its excellent dining, this 16-room hotel is situated in a lovely building in the Victorian (and exclusive) west end of Nairn. Its restaurant is excellent, specializing in local produce from oysters, salmon, and venison to garden-fresh vegetables and eggs from home-raised chickens. Pigeon, beef, and seafood dishes are especially fine. Good wine list. Viewfield St., Nairn (phone: 0667-53119). Expensive to moderate.

Golf View – In a lovely old mansion overlooking the Moray Firth, this famous hotel with its 50 rooms abounds in facilities for families, from in-house movies to outdoor swimming pool. Seabank Rd., Nairn (phone: 0667-52301). Expensive to moderate.

Newton – Another famous old-style baronial hotel with 44 rooms. Staff here are naturally proud of it having been the home-away-from-home of such luminaries as Charlie Chaplin, Larry Hagman, and Harold Macmillan. Inverness Rd., Nairn (phone: 0667-53144). Expensive to moderate.

En Route from Nairn – Drive directly to Inverness via A96 southwest. For information on Culloden Battlefield and other sights west of Nairn see "Special Places,' *Inverness,* THE CITIES.

Northwest Scottish Highlands

The northwest Highlands of Scotland: The very words evoke romantic visions of hill and glen, bagpipe and drum, purple heather and curling mist. But behind the picture-postcard Highlands seen by every visitor from Queen Victoria to Pope John Paul II is a real highlands that, though scenically among the most glorious places on earth, was for centuries a land of harsh living conditions, brutal internecine clan warfare, and rank exploitation by aristocratic power. It is a kind of divine wilderness suffering from depopulation even today.

That, however, only makes it more attractive to travelers, who can still escape to paradise for 2 or 3 weeks in the Highlands, away from the grime and confusion of modern city life. Just driving through the mountains, with their ancient Gaelic names (Beinn Eildeach, Beinn Eighe, Sgurr Dubh) and their plethora of interlinking waterways, is a soul-stirring experience. Even better is getting out and walking — hillwalking, as it's called (it's really mountain climbing), is one of the great Scots pastimes — or just stroll down the glens and look up! Climbers should have a compass, warm clothes, and the right sort of boots since the hills have everything underfoot from bogs to "scree" (loose slate rubble). And beware of hidden treacheries: A hike to a seemingly low peak from a warm sunlit valley could lead into snow, thick fog, and a loss of direction. Every year people die on Scottish mountains from lack of knowledge, equipment, and judgment.

Historically, where the Lowlands came under English, French, Norman, and Scandinavian influence, the west Highlands were dominated by the Irish, so that true Highlanders, those with Celtic blood, are very like their cousins in the Emerald Isle (always excepting Dublin). They are socially conservative, community conscious, and hostile to cosmopolitan ideas; they are courteously hospitable and as a rule no longer speak Gaelic, but an English of old-fashioned phrasing. While Lowlanders got on with the business of urbanization, farming, trading, and general money making in the seventeenth and eighteenth centuries, Highlanders remained cut off, nomadic, warlike, and idealistic. Loyalty to clan chiefs held good almost to a man. Cattle rustling, raiding, and feuds were rife. A Highlander's home, a bleakly appointed thatch-roofed stone cottage called a "black house," contained only one room — with a smoky fire on an earthen floor in its middle and wooden shelves for beds — and one stable, joined to family quarters by a large and gaping doorway.

Religion in the Highlands was, as the historian and essayist T.B. Macaulay put it, "a rude mixture of Popery and paganism." But after the Glorious

Revolution of 1688–89 (by which the Roman Catholic James II was deposed from the British throne in favor of Protestants William and Mary), Episcopalianism and Presbyterianism both began to penetrate behind the Plaid Curtain. The powerful clan Campbell, Dukes of Argyll, became Presbyterians and others followed, especially during the late eighteenth century, when Episcopalianism in its turn declined. For 3 centuries since 1700 a series of schisms rocked Presbyterian Highland Scotland, throwing up movements faster than people could count them and leaving large parts of the west Highlands today under the rod of the archaic sect, the "Wee Frees." A Wee Free Sabbath makes an ordinary Lowland Sunday look like a chapter in the life of Sodom and Gomorrah, so if you're anywhere west of Inverness on the Day of Rest, don't try to buy anything, including gasoline. Nor is it a bad idea to walk funereally, wear black, and make sure the proprietor of your chosen hotel sees you in church.

Not only religious but social shakeups in the Highlands occurred on a massive scale. The late eighteenth and early nineteenth centuries saw the Clearances, the cruelly inhuman spectacle of landowners driving tenants from their homes in order to replace them with sheep, financially a more profitable venture. Thousands of Highlanders teemed south into Glasgow's slums (and points more distant), never to return. Next came the era of the deer park, when a coterie of London-based aristocrats, the 7% of the Scottish population who owned 84% of the land, evicted another wave of Highlanders in order to create holiday playgrounds in the shape of private shooting and fishing preserves. Queen Victoria's love affair with her Highland castle at Balmoral inadvertently provided these plunderers with a fashionable impetus. Now the Highlands are undergoing another change: The Highlands and Islands Development Board, seeking to lure tourists and to take advantage of the North Sea oil boom that began in the early 1970s, has aided new wealth in parts of the Highlands but has increased the isolation of other parts, especially where fishing has suffered from oil operations or railway lines have been cut.

Customs and preoccupations that would long ago have vanished in less remote districts continue in the Highlands and form no small part of Scotland's tourist delights. Apart from obvious examples such as kilt wearing, bagpiping, and the drinking of pure malt whiskies tasting of smoked peat (*never* water them!), there are Highland games (contests of strength featuring such marathon events as "tossing the caber" — a full-grown debranched tree); the National Mod (Scotland's peripatetic annual orgy of Gaeldom in which Gaelic singers and reciters compete for prizes — the Scottish *Eisteddfod*) and other folk and musical happenings; and "Nessie-Watching" (a sport begun by St. Columba of Iona, the 6th-century Christianizer of Scotland, who sighted a prehistoric monster in Loch Ness's mysterious deep).

Battlefields, too, are a big draw, not only for tourists but for a number of Scots. Culloden Moor, near Inverness, is thus a focal point. Here Jacobitism, primarily a Highland movement seeking to restore the Stuart descendants of King James VI and I to the British throne, met a dire end in 1746 at the hands of the Duke of Cumberland, second son of the Hanoverian King George II. Whole clans were wiped out under the inadequate generalship of "Bonnie" Prince Charles Edward Stuart, the Jacobite royal heir, who fled in defeat to

France from whence he had come. All signs of Highland culture, including the kilt and the Gaelic language, were proscribed for a long time afterward, and the Culloden legend swelled the characteristic ethereal glooms of Celtic composers and poets in both Scotland and Ireland for generations.

The northwest Highlands route begins at Inverness, crosses the Black Isle to the north, and, after a swing west through Strathpeffer, follows A9 along Scotland's coast to the old town of Wick. From Wick the route takes in Thurso, then bends west, winding south at Durness into the ethereally haggard fastnesses of the world-famous mountainy Scottish west coast. A series of sea lochs are now encountered as the route continues south through Lochinver and Ullapool, returning from Ullapool directly to Inverness. The full distance is 365 miles: Allow at least a week.

As with the other Scottish tour routes, book hotels in advance from May through September; keep sandwiches in your car and be opportunistic about petrol pumps (gas stations), which are harder to find than Brigadoon! Remote areas have paved cattle tracks as roads — if you meet a vehicle head-on you'll have to back into one of the lay-bys provided at several-hundred-yard intervals. An alternative to traveling by car is a Travelpass, which, for a flat fee, provides 7 or 14 days' unlimited travel through the Highlands and Scottish islands by train, bus, and ferry. For more information contact *Hi-Line* (Highlands and Islands Booking Information Service), Bridgend Rd., Dingwall (phone: 0349-63434) or *BritRail Travel International,* 630 Third Ave., New York, NY 10017 (phone: 212-599-5400). Carry the Scottish Tourist Board's *Enjoy Scotland* road map, which shows information centers, picnic tables, and woodland and nature trails in abundance. Also helpful are the Scottish Tourist Board's publications *Walks and Trails* (about $4) and *Hillwalking* (about $3.50).

Hotels listed as expensive will charge $85 and up for bed and breakfast for two; moderate ones, from $45 to $85; and inexpensive ones, less than $45. A meal for two, excluding wine and tip, in an expensive restaurant will cost $40 or more; in a moderate one, $25 to $40; in an inexpensive one, less than $25.

Many Highland hotels have reduced-rate 3-, 5-, or 7-day package deals, offering dinner as well as bed and breakfast, plus advice on and/or access to local sports facilities.

INVERNESS: For a complete report on the city, its sights, hotels, and restaurants, see *Inverness,* THE CITIES.

En Route from Inverness – Follow A9 north across the recently constructed Kessock Bridge over the Beauly Firth to Black Isle. At the village of Tore's crossroads, take the new A835 northwest to Maryburgh, then west to Contin; from Contin, A834 northeast leads to Strathpeffer.

STRATHPEFFER: Strathpeffer was founded in the 18th century as a spa. English dandies and their dames, as well as foreign royals, came here to sample springs of sulphur and chalybeate. The old pump room was reopened in 1960, so visitors today can take its healing waters, too. The town's population of 1,000 is housed almost entirely in a delicious-looking collection of gingerbread hotels and confectionary cottages; even the old railway station, which is now a crafts shop, looks like a piece of wedding cake (open daily April through September, and evenings for audiovisual displays only). The Strathpeffer *Museum of Dolls, Toys and Victoriana* — at Spa Cottage on the square, is the private collection of Mrs. Angela Kellie, who lives in the cottage. (Mrs. Kellie receives visitors Mondays through Fridays from Easter to mid-October; also Monday and Thursday nights in summer.) Also at Strathpeffer is the Pictish Eagle Stone, displaying two etched symbols — a horseshoe and two eagles — that have mystified archaeologists. Was this a marriage stone? Some say it commemorates a 15th-century victory of the clan Munro over the clan MacDonald (which would make it non-Pictish or pseudo-Pictish). The various legends associated with the Eagle Stone can be teased out of Strathpeffer's hotel bartenders.

Strathpeffer's public gardens, beside the square, have putting and bowling greens and a dance pavilion. The 18-hole golf course is a 15-minute walk away. There is salmon fishing in the Conon and Blackwater rivers (permits can be obtained from local hotels). The tourist information office on the square (phone: 0997-21415) will give advice on short hikes from Strathpeffer to places of interest in the surrounding area. Strathpeffer Highland Games are held on the grounds of the 17th-century Castle Leod, seat of the Earls of Cromarty, on the first Saturday in August. The town presents *Victorian Special Events* for 4 days in mid-June, and Saturdays June through September there is a pipe band and Highland dancing in the square at 8:30 PM.

CHECKING IN: ***Ben Wyvis*** – A small Victorian palace, 110 rooms on 6 acres of landscaped gardens, with an imposing view of Ben Wyvis. Open March through November. On A834 north of Strathpeffer (phone: 0997-21323). Moderate.

Coul House – A secluded 20-room country mansion surrounded by fields and forests. "Taste-of-Scotland" cooking and real log fires. Open year-round. On A834 southwest of Strathpeffer, Contin (phone: 0997-21487). Moderate.

Craigendarroch Lodge – In a country setting with its own trout and salmon fishing. The table at this 13-room hostelry is renowned for fresh produce. On A834 southwest of Strathpeffer, Contin (phone: 0997-21265). Moderate.

Highland – An original 134-room, Victorian luxury-lagoon opposite Strathpeffer's Spa Pavilion. Open March through December. Follow the signpost off A834, Strathpeffer (phone: 0997-21457). Moderate.

Holly Lodge – A hilltop hotel on its own grounds, a cheerful, multiwindowed Victorian stone building with 7 bedrooms. Overlooking Strathpeffer Sq., Golf Course Rd., Strathpeffer (phone: 0997-21254). Moderate.

Richmond – Resident proprietors of this cozy, 14-room Victorian stone family house cater to all needs, including the locals', with its bar suppers. In Strathpeffer village, Golf Course Rd., Strathpeffer (phone: 0997-21300). Inexpensive.

Kilvannie Manor – A winsomely renovated former parish church and manor house that has 8 bedrooms (no private baths), warm hospitality, and home-cooked meals. One mile north of Strathpeffer on A834, Fodderty (phone: 0997-21389). Inexpensive.

DINGWALL: Situated on the Cromarty Firth (6 miles east of Strathpeffer on A834), the ancient Norse burgh of Dingwall is a complete contrast to Strathpeffer. A down-to-earth farm market town not particularly aware of tourists, Dingwall has a furniture factory, a foam rubber factory, a "champion haggis maker" (haggis is a traditional pudding made of sheep's stomach), and a railway junction. Rape, a tall yellow crop used in the making of margarine, is grown in surrounding fields and shipped from here. Two spires — on the parish church and the town house (1730) — give flat-landed Dingwall a momentary jolt of grandeur.

Here, it is said, Macbeth was born; and here commences the Dingwall–Kyle of Lochalsh train trip which was featured in the BBC-TV series, "Great Railway Journeys of the World" (for details, phone *Hi-Line:* 0349-63434). Inside the town house (or town hall) on High Street is a local history museum (open May through September), including memorabilia of Dingwall's own "Fighting Mac," General Sir Hector MacDonald (1853–1903). Mac rose from the ranks by distinguishing himself in the fighting in 1895 at Omdurman (East Africa) avenging General Gordon at Khartoum 10 years before. An impressive memorial to this gritty soldier sits on Mitchell Hill (to obtain the key to its tower, phone: 0349-62391). The parish church is distinguished by an obelisk in its parking lot, a small replica of a 50-foot-high original, marking the would-be burial place of George Mackenzie, first Earl of Cromarty (1630–1714). He arranged instead to be buried "3 ft. 6 in. to the S. thereof," in unmarked ground, in order to foil his wife, who had announced her intention of dancing on his grave!

Dingwall has tennis courts and a boating park at Pefferside Park; these facilities are administered by the Sports Centre, Tulloch Ave. (phone: 0349-64226). The *Highland Traditional Music Festival* convenes in Dingwall the third week in June; the Dingwall Highland Games are held in early to mid-July; and the Highland Whippet Derby invigorates the town around July's end.

En Route from Dingwall – Take A862 northeast to A9, which stretches along the Cromarty Firth. On the right across the firth continues the verdant Black Isle, with its wild ducks and the whitewashed crofters' cottages. The whole Strathpeffer–Dingwall–Black Isle area is full of walks and trails (consult the *Walks and Trails* booklet).

At Evanton, reached by a short detour off A9 onto B817, is the Fyrish Monument, or "Indian Temple," erected by General Sir Hector Munro (1726–1805), a latter-day member of the warlike clan Munro, on a site high above town on Knock Fyrish. Begun in 1782 and modeled on the gates to Seringapatam, India, which the British captured in 1799, its construction gave work to the impoverished unemployed in the area. A mile's walk from Evanton up Black Rock Ravine reveals a startling 110-foot chasm only 15 feet wide, through which plunges the river Glass.

Return to A9 from Evanton, proceeding northeast to Alness. This market town — on the river Averon, crossed by an attractive old bridge — serves the local industries, including agriculture, forestry, saw-milling, and distilling. From here A9 zigs past Nigg Bay's North Sea Oil installations and loops westward to Tain on the Dornoch Firth.

CHECKING IN: *Novar Arms* – This old coaching inn within Evanton village has 10 bedrooms. Staff can arrange a program of hillwalking and deerstalking for guests. On the main road, Evanton (phone: 0349-830210). Moderate to inexpensive.

TAIN: A royal burgh since Macbeth's time, Tain is steeped in history. It was the birthplace of St. Duthoc, a leading light of 11th-century Celtic Christianity, in whose honor the impressive St. Duthus Chapel (now a ruin) and Collegiate Church (renowned for its stained glass) were built. In Castle Brae is the *Tain Museum* (open Mondays through Saturdays Easter through September), which contains historical documents, photographs, and relics of the clan Ross. William, Earl of Ross, captured Robert Bruce's wife and daughters, who sought asylum in St. Duthus Church, in 1306 and handed them over to Edward I of England. On a main corner of the town is the 16th-century tollbooth, in perfect condition with a curfew bell in its turreted top that still rings. ("Tolbooths" were entry points for medieval walled towns.) Refugees were imprisoned here during the Clearances. Tain's medieval mercat (market) cross has been restored and stands before the tollbooth. King James IV came to St. Duthus Church on pilgrimage every year for 20 years (James V did it once, barefoot).

Today the town's busy traffic — almost entirely pedestrian — reflects the prosperity of the lush surrounding farmlands and the activity generated by the Royal Air Force base nearby. Quaint and colorful, High Street is a jumble of blue-gabled buildings that huddle narrowly together against long winters of cruel North Sea winds, obviating the passage of cars. Tain's location on the Dornoch Firth gives it a beautiful golden strand of beach, on which is a fine golf course. There is an air of civic pride about Tain, from the picture in the *Royal* hotel lobby of the Queen Mother in the company of a past lord provost in his ermine stole, to the "900 Roses" Garden planted on the 900th anniversary of the town's charter.

Visitors less than royalty will probably go unnoticed by the local residents — there is no tourist office in Tain. Literature published in Inverness lists facilities for fishing, sea angling, windsurfing, and pony trekking. There is a boating pond and the Morangie Forest Walk from Tain quarry, where visitors can see deer, blue hares, wildcats, and herons. The High Street bakery, *Strachan's* (which also has a small, very unpretentious restaurant), is excellent.

CHECKING IN: ***Mansfield*** – A baronial-style mansion with downy green lawns, this has 18 bedrooms, and a tower that looks like a gigantic, ornate chess piece. Scotsburn Rd., Tain (phone: 0862-2052). Moderate.

Royal – Smack at the head of the High Street, where (in a less idiosyncratic town) the city hall would normally be, this turreted 25-room wonder is graciously cozy rather than glamorous. High St., Tain (phone: 0862-2013). Moderate.

En Route from Tain – The Glen Morangie Distillery, purveyors of a satiny malt whisky, is just outside Tain on A9. If you telephone in advance, they will give you a guided tour and a wee dram (phone: 0862-2043).

Now commences a scenically ravishing skirt round the Dornoch Firth. There used to be a ferry service across the firth to Dornoch village, but those days are gone. Plans to build a road bridge across the old ferry route have received planning permission, but the Scottish Office has roused Ross-shire fury by scotching plans for a similar rail bridge, leaving trains to wind north to Wick through the Rorschach test of a route seen on the map. The road goes through Redfern Forest and fields with farmhouses that would delight an expert in vernacular architecture.

At Bonar Bridge (northwest of Tain on A9), on the firth's innermost point at the mouth of the river Shin, motorists can glimpse the ludicrously sumptuous Carbisdale Castle 5 miles upriver. Known locally as the "Castle of Spite," it was built around 1900 by a former dowager Duchess of Sutherland, who, following (perhaps) in the footsteps of the first Earl of Cromarty at Dingwall, foiled her ex-husband by choosing the Ross-shire border for the site of her castle, forcing the duke to pass within view of it (and her!) every time he entered his own county. Today Carbisdale is a youth hostel, where guests — who are required in all British hostels to do a household chore before leaving the premises — may elect to dust the 6-foot marble statues of naked nymphs in the entrance hall.

DORNOCH: From Bonar Bridge, A9 begins moving east along the northern shore of the firth. From A9, the A949 detours southeast to Dornoch — widely known for its golf course, which is so challenging that, were it not for its remote location, it would be on the Open Championship rota (with Muirfield, St. Andrews, Turnberry, Troon, and so on). After playing here, five-time British Open champion Tom Watson said, "This is the most fun I've ever had playing golf." Call the pro shop for details; to be safe, book in advance with the secretary of the club: Mr. A. Kinnear, *Royal Dornoch Golf Club,* Golf Road, Dornoch (phone: 0862-810219).

Dornoch is the county town of Sutherland, receiving its royal charter in 1628. Its beach, known countrywide as "Dornoch Sands," is a sparkling slice of paradise with a view across open seas into blue oblivion. (It is only somewhat cluttered on one side by a colony of small trailers.) In winter Dornoch is as sleepy as a dormouse, but in summer it is suddenly jolted awake by an onslaught of sportsmen, holiday-making families, and the skirling *Dornoch Pipe Band,* which at intervals blasts away in the large central square. Near the end of July is the annual Sutherland County Show; at the beginning of August, the Dornoch Highland Games.

The Craft Centre, in an old jail with its own historical exhibition, is on the central square: Visitors can have a cup of coffee here and watch weavers at work (open April through September). There are more craft workshops at Station Square, a short walk up Station Road. One of the best is Treecraft Woodwork, where they display boomerangs made for export to Australia! The homemade ice cream at *Luigi's,* on Castle St., is delectable.

Dornoch's cathedral (now the parish church) is another highlight of the town. Sixteen Earls of Sutherland (Gordons) are buried here. The cathedral, small in size, was founded in 1224 as the seat of the Bishops of Caithness. It has been restored three times but still has fine original stonework. The Bishop's Palace, across the road, is now a hotel (see *Checking In,* below).

CHECKING IN: ***Dornoch Castle*** – The oldest part of this glorious 20-room phenomenon, on Dornoch's main thoroughfare, was the medieval residence of the Bishops of Caithness. The dining room is famous for Scottish dishes. Views from the rooms are of a delightful sheltered formal garden, as well as the Dornoch Firth. Open mid-April through October. Castle St., Dornoch (phone: 0862-810216). Expensive.

Royal Golf – This is actually *on* the golf course, and it is where the professional golfers stay. A Victorian country house with some modern additions. There are 35 bedrooms, not all of which have private facilities. Open April through October. Grange Rd., Dornoch (phone: 0862-810283). Expensive.

Dornoch – A gigantic, Strathpeffer-style, 110-room resort hotel overlooking the golf course. With all 35 of the tourist board-listed amenities of the other *Dornoch* hotels, plus live music. Open April through October. On the Dornoch Sands (phone: 0862-810351). Moderate.

Burghfield House – An architectural hodgepodge with a castellated tower, this highly respectable hostelry run by long-established residents has 46 bedrooms and 5 acres of lovely gardens. Open April through October. Overlooks the town above Station Rd., Dornoch (phone: 0862-810212). Moderate to inexpensive.

Evelix Farm – For sheer atmosphere, this original Jacobean farmhouse, in the countryside outside Dornoch on the river Evelix, cannot be beat. Commended by the tourist board despite its mere 3 bedrooms (without private baths). Open April through October. On A9 west of Dornoch, Evelix (phone: 0862-810271). Inexpensive.

Trevose Guest House – Next to the tourist office on the central square, this sweet, old-fashioned, former private dwelling with 5 bedrooms allows guests to feel as if they *live* in Dornoch. Central Sq., Dornoch (phone: 0862-810269). Inexpensive.

En Route from Dornoch – Take the unmarked coast road north and rejoin A9 to cross Loch Fleet, passing Skelbo Farm, a Norse settlement of about AD 850, and the remains of Skelbo Castle, which overlook Loch Fleet. At this castle in 1290 King Edward I's heralds learned from Norse messengers that the 7-year-old Maid of Norway, nominal Queen of Scotland and fiancée of Edward's son, was dead. So ended Edward's hopes for the peaceful union of the English and Scots crowns. West of Skelbo Farm and out of view is Skibo Castle, to which the Scottish-born American steel baron Andrew Carnegie (1835–1919) retired.

The Loch Fleet Causeway (A9) leads to Golspie, the estate village of Dunrobin Castle, seat of the Dukes of Sutherland. A giant statue of George Granville Leveson-Gower, first Duke of Sutherland (1758–1833), towers to the left as you enter the town:

He was the infamous "improver," who masterminded the bulk of the Clearances on the estate.

GOLSPIE: There is an 18-hole golf course here, a long sandy beach, and opportunities for sea angling. The duke's private railway station, name-plated "Dunrobin Castle," rather than "Golspie," is adorable. St. Andrew's Church in the town center is an interesting 17th-century design, with a canopied pulpit, wood carving, and paneling. On the main road through Golspie, there is a crafts center opposite the old coaching inn, the *Sutherland Arms* hotel. The Golspie Sheep Dog Trials are in August. There is a very nice picnic area at Big Burn Waterfall; follow the path just behind the *Sutherland Arms* hotel.

CHECKING IN: ***Golf Links*** – A pleasant old country house with its own gardens near the sea, this quiet 8-room haven arranges golfing packages on the Royal Dornoch, Golspie, and Brora courses. On the links. Church St., Golspie (phone: 04083-3408). Moderate.

DUNROBIN CASTLE: Set on a natural plateau above the sea a mile north of Golspie, the original castle is medieval, antedating the dukedom by about 400 years (when the Gordons were mere Earls of Sutherland). Finally finished in 1921, after many extensions and one fire, today's version looks like an enormous French château, unusual in Scotland. The extensive formal gardens are modeled on those at Versailles. The magnificent interiors include priceless furniture and paintings. Grounds include a small museum in the park and a tea room with "Taste-of-Scotland" home baking. Open daily except Sunday mornings June through mid-September (phone: 04083-3177).

En Route from Dunrobin Castle – A9 now rollercoasts northeast for about 60 miles along the Sutherland coastline to Wick. The views, particularly on a blazing sunny day, are breathtaking as the road winds and switches, dips and climbs. The 20th-century fades as you gaze to the left on steeply rising green vastnesses, broken only by ancient stone dykes and oblivious sheep, and to the right on the emerald sea. The road passes through the village of Brora, which has sea angling, small craft launchings, and an annual *Golf Week* (usually in May); through Helmsdale, where the last wolf was killed in Scotland about 1700 (a stone south of Helmsdale marks the spot, at Loth); and through tiny Berriedale, Dunbeath, Latheron, and Lybster. The Helmsdale Tourist Office (on A9) has details on how to pan for gold (yes, really) in the adjacent Strath of Kildonan (phone: 04312-640).

On the coast to the right before Berriedale are the ruins of Badbea village, where Clearance victims had to be tied to stakes to prevent their being blown over the cliffs, and the remains of Ousdale Broch (a broch is a circular Iron-Age castle with galleries in the thickness of its walls). Langwell House at Berriedale is the Caithness estate of the Dukes of Portland; open only on certain days (the garden center, open daily, has details; phone: 05935-237). The castle at Dunbeath (not open to the public) goes back to the early 15th century; also at Dunbeath is the Dunbeath Preservation Trust, with local natural history displays (open daily, including Sundays, May through September). Toremore, north of Dunbeath, is the site of the *Lhaidhay Croft Museum* (in a typical croft of the mid-19th century), open daily year-round.

The Clan Gunn Heritage Centre, just north of Latheron, is open daily except Sundays June through September. Lybster, a short detour east off A9 (follow the signpost), is a popular spot for vacationers; it has a famous hotel (the *Portland Arms* — see *Checking In,* below), facilities for sea angling, and the charming Rumster Nature Trail. It was founded in the late 18th century by a patron who wished to see an ideal fishermen's and farmers' village. A mile farther north off A9 is Watten Road, leading to Camster Cairns, thought by many to be one of the most impressive prehistoric burial chambers in Europe.

Just before Wick is the Kyleburn Candy Factory, makers of hard candy and "tablet" (sugary fudge). It has factory tours and a tea room and is open weekdays from 10 AM to 4 PM (phone: 05932-353).

CHECKING IN: ***Links*** – This genial, spacious, 2-story beach hotel with 22 bedrooms is the host each May of Brora Golf Week. On the beach, Brora (phone: 0408-21225). Expensive.

Royal Marine – Another festive holiday hotel, with 11 bedrooms, on the village harbor. Indoor sports facilities include a swimming pool, curling rink, and snooker room. It also has its own boat on Loch Brora. Harbour Rd., Brora (phone: 0408-21252). Expensive.

Navidale House – Originally built as a hunting lodge for the Dukes of Sutherland, this cozy 16-room inn on the edge of a high cliff is rapidly gaining fame for its "Taste-of-Scotland" dining room. (Do the salmon leap right from the sea to the frying pan?) Closed November and December. Cliff Rd., Helmsdale (phone: 0431-2258). Moderate.

Portland Arms – This early 19th-century coaching inn was built for the new Parliamentary Road linking Wick with points south. It has 19 bedrooms; staff can arrange hunting, shooting, and fishing. On the main road through Lybster (phone: 0593-2208). Moderate.

WICK: A Norse settlement, then a royal burgh, and today the county town of Caithness, Wick, on either side of the river Wick, is a rough-and-ready, otherworldly sort of place, as if it were still a 19th-century frontier outpost. Its narrow, crooked High Street is full of rugged individualists in rubber boots who never heard of tourists. Its fishing industry has declined in recent times, leaving its complex of piers and old harbors in a state of partial abandonment, but as the market town for Caithness's neighboring farmlands and the focal point for trade with the more gentrified Orkneys and Shetlands, it throbs apace.

Historically Wick has been under the thumb of the Sinclair clan, Earls of Caithness, since the 15th century. The Sinclair Castle ruin is north of town near Noss Head Lighthouse, on a cliff next to another ruin, Castle Girnigoe. A modern descendant of the Sinclairs founded the Caithness Glass Factory on Harrowhill, which exports goods to all parts of the world and has branches at Perth and Oban; visitors can watch the glass-blowing process and buy samples on weekdays (phone: 0955-2286).

Other sights at Wick are: the *Wick Heritage Museum,* Bank Row, where there is a prize-winning herring industry display (open daily except Sundays June through September); the Castle of Old Wick, dating back to Norse times, on the coast south of town; and St. Fergus Gallery in Wick Library, where local crafts are exhibited and sold (open daily except Sundays). The tourist office is on Whitechapel Road (phone: 0955-2145). The Caithness Highland Gathering and Games are held in Wick in early July.

A tip for wealthy adventurers: Mr. W. J. Banks — if you can find him midst the sea of floor-to-ceiling longjohns and anoraks in his High Street general clothing store of the same name — has been known to toss a coin to determine the price of a hand-knitted Aran sweater.

CHECKING IN: ***Ladbroke Mercury Motor Inn*** – A 48-room, centrally located, somewhat faceless but reliable chain hotel. Modest rooms; good bar. Address notwithstanding, it is separated from the river Wick by a supermarket parking lot. Riverside, Wick (phone: 0955-3344). Expensive.

THURSO: Take A882 directly from Wick northwest to Thurso. A complete contrast to Wick, Thurso is a quiet, even stately, town. It has fine examples of Georgian architecture along the river Thurso and on Thurso Bay, and its central square, a large fenced-in green space, is dominated by an elegant church of 1833, with an illuminated clock tower. The name "Thurso" means "Thor's River." The town is kept alive by a small fishing industry and the nearby Dounreay nuclear power station (see *En Route from Thurso,* below).

Chief sights in Thurso are: the *Thurso Folk Museum,* in the town hall, with exhibits of objects from local agricultural and domestic life, including a Pictish stone (open daily except Sundays June through September); St. Peter's Church, a medieval edifice with 17th-century additions, now in ruins but with an impressive surviving south-gable window, by the harbor; Pennyland Farm, birthplace of the Victorian philanthropist and founder of the Boys' Brigade, Sir William Smith (1854–1914), who sought to provide discipline-with-fellowship for working class youths; and Swanson Gallery, in Thurso Library, which has traveling crafts exhibitions, including some items for sale. Rotterdam Street is a center for buying toys.

Just outside Thurso are: Harald's Tower, the 19th-century Sinclair clan mausoleum, above the grave of a noble ancestor slain in a battle nearby; an 18-hole golf course; and dainty Scrabster harbor, departure point of boats to Orkney and home of the *Thurso Yacht Club.* Thurso also hosts the National and International Surfing Championships, but because of the reefs, beginners should stick to the beach. Sea angling is offered here as well. The tourist office, with further details, is in the Riverside Car Park (phone: 0847-62371).

CHECKING IN: ***Pentland*** – A modern hotel on one of Thurso's main streets. There are 56 bedrooms here and a spacious, plush restaurant and bar. Princes St., Thurso (phone: 0847-63202). Moderate to inexpensive.

Park – Another modern hotel, a flat white box with 16 bedrooms, on a green tablecloth of a lawn. On the edge of Thurso at Oldfield (phone: 0847-63251). Inexpensive.

En Route from Thurso – Take A836 west. On the coast near Forss is Crosskirk, site of the 12th-century St. Mary's Chapel; its rudely constructed low doors give some idea of the height of human beings in north Scotland in medieval days. Farther on is Dounreay Nuclear Power Development Establishment, Europe's only fast-breeder nuclear power station; it has an exhibition for tourists on nuclear power, with guided tours of the reactor for those over 12 years of age (exhibition and tours available daily May through September). Dounreay sits on the edge of a sweeping canvas of isolated brackeny moors, dotted and dashed with lone farms and stone dykes.

Don't miss *Strathnaver Museum* (closed Sundays and Mondays), with its presentation of the story of the Clearances, at Bettyhill, a tiny village set up to make a fishing life for Clearances' victims. There is a nature reserve just past Bettyhill at Invernaver, with seabirds and Alpine plants; and the Borgie Nature Trail is an interesting walk. For details, call the tourist information center at Bettyhill (phone: 06412-342).

Farther west on A836 is the town of Tongue, dominated by Castle Varrich, a ruined 14th-century Mackay stronghold, and Tongue Church, where the "Laird's Loft" is of interest. Cross the Kyle of Tongue by the causeway, which gives good views of the flat land at the head of the loch and the hills beyond. At this point, A836 has become A838. Continue west, passing views of Ben Loyal and Ben Hope (to climb these, consult *Scottish Hillwalking*), rounding Loch Eriboll and fetching up at far-flung Durness.

CHECKING IN: ***Forss House*** – This mysterious-looking, stone country house with 7 bedrooms and high multichimneyed gables, enshrouded by pines, overlooks the river Forss. With open log fires, it is definitely the place for a romantic interlude. Forss (phone: 0847-86201). Moderate.

DURNESS: Durness is famous for Smoo Cave, a limestone cavity in a cove in the seacliff wall, with three chambers hollowed out by the pouring and retreating sea. One of the chambers can safely be entered by land. Up a small road to Balnakeil Sands is Balnakeil Craft Village, where 12 independently owned small handicraft businesses sell wares such as pottery, jewelry, tapestry, and candles, in a former Ministry of Defense early warning station. The sands of Sango Bay are popular with strollers. Visit Durness Old Church, an early 17th-century ruin, and take the passenger ferry (offered only in summer) and minibus to the Cape Wrath Lighthouse, past Britain's highest cliffs at Clo Mor (920 feet).

En Route from Durness – Follow A838 about 20 miles south to Laxford Bridge, then pick up A894 southwest to Scourie on the Sutherland west coast. A possible scenic detour is to Tarbet, north of Scourie, where local boatmen run trips across the sound to Handa Island Nature Reserve, which harbors numerous species of seabirds, including auks (open April through mid-September). Beyond Scourie, peaks begin to appear on all sides. Continue south, crossing Loch a Chairn Bhain, to Kylesku, then west on B869 past Shangri-la lagoons and heaven-scented hills to the tiny port of Lochinver.

CHECKING IN: *Eddrachilles* – Facing the sunset on the islet-studded junction of two bays, this whitewashed country house with 10 bedrooms and no neighbors is a pure golden idyll. Open March through October. Badcall Bay, Scourie (phone: 0971-2080). Moderate.

Scourie – A popular hotel for trout and salmon fishermen, this larger, more modern establishment in Scourie village itself has 21 bedrooms and its own vegetable garden. Open March through October. Scourie (phone: 0971-2396). Moderate.

LOCHINVER: Around this small commercial fishing port lies some of Scotland's most spectacular scenery. Quinag, Suilven, Cul Mor, and Stac Pollaidh are favorite mountain climbs (see *Scotland Hillwalking*). Baddidarroch, just west of Lochinver, boasts the Highland Stoneware showroom and workshops, open Mondays through Saturdays. Their stoneware is hand-painted.

CHECKING IN/EATING OUT: *Inver Lodge* – This glossy hotel built in 1987 has 20 rooms, a fishing school, a very good restaurant specializing in country fare, especially fresh fish, and a heavenly view. Open May through October. Lochinver (phone: 05714-496). Expensive.

En Route from Lochinver – The A837 runs east along Loch Assynt, brooded over by the three-story ruin of Ardvreck Castle, a seat of the MacLeods through the 15th century. The Royalist poet-general, the Marquis of Montrose, was imprisoned here before his execution at Edinburgh in 1650. At the south tip of Loch Assynt is the hamlet of Inchnadamph, to which geologists and botanists flock to examine limestone caves. Bones of late Pleistocene animals have been found here as well as traces of early man.

At Ledmore Junction, leave A837 to take A835 southwest, a magnificent, deserted road that offers glimpses of the sea as it buckets through sharply rising, blue craggy hills. On the left about 12 miles before Ullapool is Knockan Cliff, which has a car park, an eye-boggling view, a cliff-top nature trail, and a tourist information center (open weekdays May through September; phone: 085484-256). On the right is the exciting, tractless expanse of Inverpolly Nature Reserve, with miles of uninhabited bog, moorland, woodland, cliffs, and summits. A "Motor Trail" runs through it back to Lochinver. Continue south on A835 to Ullapool.

ULLAPOOL: Sweeping down into town from the Inverpolly vastnesses, visitors may think they have stumbled into paradise. Here is a model 18th-century fishing village — all the cottages match! — in a sheltered inlet, on the shores of mountain-hemmed Loch Broom. Designed and built by the British Fishery Society in 1788, Ullapool still has a colorful pier, where the Stornoway Ferry docks, oilskin-clad fishermen arrive with their catch, and boatloads of vacationers depart for a day on the deep. The air is kept soft by the neighboring Gulf Stream; the prevailing wind is westerly, bathing the area with passing gentle rains and scenting the air with the smell of salt and fish. The townspeople here have certainly heard of tourists; they will lay out everything for you.

There are opportunities in Ullapool for sailing, canoeing, sea angling, deep-sea diving, and loch and river fishing. There is a pony-trekking center at the Captain's Cabin souvenir shop on Quay St. (phone: 0854-2356). Cruises — to the nearby Summer Isles, to the bird-haunted islands of Loch Broom, and to Gruinard Bay — are run by *Islander Cruisers* (Eilean Donan Guest House, 14 Market St.; phone: 0854-2264) and by *Mackenzie Marine* (The Pier, Shore St.; phone: 0854-2008). No Sunday sailing. The tourist office is also on Shore Street (phone: 0854-2135).

The *Ullapool Museum* (on Quay St.) focuses on local history (open Mondays through Saturdays April through October). Good shopping can be had on Shore Street at the *West Highland Woolen Co.*

A pleasant excursion from Ullapool is a trip to Achiltibuie, on the southern shore of Inverpolly Nature Reserve. The *Summer Isles* hotel (see *Checking In,* below) runs much shorter boat trips than those at Ullapool to the Summer Isles. Also at the hotel is the Hydroponicum, a set of hi-tech, soil-less growing houses; tours of the vegetables are conducted April through October. A mile or two north is the *Achiltibuie Smokehouse,* where visitors can watch the curing of meat, fish, and game in summer, and buy the resulting products.

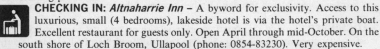

CHECKING IN: ***Altnaharrie Inn*** **–** A byword for exclusivity. Access to this luxurious, small (4 bedrooms), lakeside hotel is via the hotel's private boat. Excellent restaurant for guests only. Open April through mid-October. On the south shore of Loch Broom, Ullapool (phone: 0854-83230). Very expensive.

Royal **–** This 52-room, sparkling white, 2-story resort hotel by Loch Broom prides itself on being open year-round. North shore of the loch, Garve Rd., Ullapool (phone: 0854-2181). Expensive to moderate.

Summer Isles **–** As the name suggests, this old-fashioned, 12-room hotel by the sea has a timeless view of the isles. Its distinguished dining room is famous for fresh seafood and for fresh-picked vegetables from its Hydroponicum. Guests are supplied permits to fish among the hill lochs. Open April through October. Twenty-five miles north of Ullapool on A835, Achiltibuie (phone: 085482-282). Expensive to moderate.

Ceilidh Place **–** A lovely whitewashed row of cottages with 15 bedrooms and an adjacent clubhouse with 11 additional bedrooms. Not all have private baths. Nightly ceilidhs (Scottish jam sessions). 14 W. Argyll St., Ullapool (phone: 0854-2103). Moderate.

Four Seasons **–** This 16-room modern hotel of no architectural pretension is run by a friendly family of excellent seafood cooks. Garve Rd., Ullapool (phone: 0854-2905). Moderate.

EATING OUT: ***Morefield Motel*** **–** The owners of this unusual establishment are members of the Shellfish Wholesalers of Great Britain and own one of the local fishing fleets. Patrons can eat inexpensively at the bar, or for moderate cost in the candlelit restaurant. On A835 just north of Ullapool (phone: 0854-2161).

En Route from Ullapool – Drive south on A835. At Corrieshalloch Gorge the river Broom drops a noisily spectacular 150 feet over the Falls of Measach on its way to Loch Broom. The gorge itself, in a thick wood, is 200 feet deep. The National Trust for Scotland has bought the gorge and established a viewing platform for the falls (only two people at a time may stand on it), along with a Reichenbach-style bridge (six people at a time). A signpost marks the way to the gorge and a roadside parking lot.

From this point, travelers can quickly get back to Inverness and "civilization" via A835, which joins A832 just north of Garve. Continue on A832 through Contin and the Tore roundabout, then pick up A9 to Inverness.

Alternatively, for an additional 3 to 4 days in the northwest Highlands, the drive can be extended from Ullapool to Kyle of Lochalsh, Invershiel, Invergarry, and Fort Augustus, returning to Inverness along the famous Loch Ness. This adds another 200 to 250 miles to the tour, depending on the number of side trips taken along the spectacular coastline or to hidden inland lochs. Refer to the *Enjoy Scotland* road map.

Scottish Islands

Scotland has 787 islands, including uninhabited stone dollops like Ailsa Craig and the Bass Rock (see the *Lowlands* routes). These vary in size, topography, history, climate, racial mix, and ethos. Of the ones included here, however — Orkney and Shetland plus the Hebridean Arran, Skye, Harris, and Lewis — there are common denominators. All have a remote otherworldliness, a sense of infinite time; all but Arran reflect antiquity both in archaeological riches and in the natives' ardent stubborn tribalisms; all have vivid, unusual flora and fauna, colonies of seals, seabirds, and wildlife; all possess multicolored skies and magic, luminous air. All are sparsely populated. Winds can be incredible (a gale is recorded at the Butt of Lewis one day in every six) and on Shetland, Orkney, Harris, and Lewis there are almost no trees. Skye, Orkney, Arran, and Harris have fantastic gnomic rock formations, whipped perhaps from briny deeps by the gnarled wand of some primeval wizard. All but Arran and Orkney live by fishing and crofting, and all but Orkney and Shetland show a dangerous dependence on Highlands and Islands Development Board projects, and on tourism. So far tourists continue to roll in.

And not just tourists! Drawn to the Islands are artists, craftsmen, poets, scholars, and dreamers, who set up shop in deserted thatched-roofed cottages and hag peat, write books, throw pots, and weave caftans. You'll have access to the wares of this entrepreneurial yeomanry as well as to Shetland sweaters and Harris tweeds. Don't miss reading the *West Highland Free Press,* a radical weekly published Thursdays by immigrant intellectuals. Hugh MacDiarmid, the greatest Scottish poet of the 20th century, lived for a time in Shetland; the composer Peter Maxwell Davies finds inspiration in the sounds around his Orkney home; Sorley Maclean, chief among contemporary bards of the Gaelic tongue, dwells in Skye. In addition to works by giants like these you should try a page or two by Orkney's favorite sons, George Mackay Brown and Eric Linklater, and the Outer Hebrides's Compton Mackenzie (his novel *Whisky Galore* is especially delicious).

Two centuries of Viking invasions, from 800 to 1000, left all the islands under Norse control, linked with the also-vanquished city of Dublin and Isle of Man. In the Hebrides, Scottish Gaelic leadership gradually reemerged though the Gaelic Lordship of the Isles was not absorbed into the Scottish crown until the reign of James IV. But Orkney and Shetland continued under Scandinavian occupation through the end of the Middle Ages. Their inhabitants today are still primarily Nordic; they keep up special friendship societies with Iceland and the Faroes, and surnames — a break from Scandinavian custom — have existed in Shetland only for the last 100 years. Orcadians and Shetlanders are a down-to-earth, straightforward people — Celtic Twilights and such mystiques have no place among them. Until recently they spoke Norn, a Viking dialect that has fostered a pleasing singsong quality in their

English. Shetland fisherfolk employ many "haaf" words from Norn even now (there's a handy selection of 10 different nouns for "wind" and 19 for "sea").

The Western Isles preserve both the Highland culture now lost on the mainland (Gaelic is still spoken in parts of Harris, Lewis, and Skye) and the old Presbyterianism gone from the Lowlands. Many guesthouse owners eschew cooking, watching TV, etc., on the Sabbath, so mind when you wash your socks. A duality of the public and private man exists in the Hebrides, epitomized by areas that vote themselves dry before dotting the moors with illegal makeshift drinking *bothans* ("cabins"). The satiric tradition of the ancient Gaelic bards — in which verses were thought to wield witch-doctor-style curses — may have reinforced in Hebrideans their unquenchable love of invective; their mellifluous lilts promise Paradise but shoot wide of the mark, delivering the sentiments of hexmen in accents of angels.

Despite drawbacks like high prices, frequent wet weather, summer midges, and occasional roadside views of gargantuan rubbish dumps, the Scottish Islands are unsurpassed as holiday spots. Their romance is legendary. It's said there are peat fires in Hebridean houses alight continuously for over a hundred years, and that you can spy faeries in Skye's unearthly kaleidoscopes of sunbeams, mists, and rainbows. In Orkney and Shetland, where the land is so flat it scarcely breaks the sky's endless embrace, the moon, stars, and aurora borealis are dazzling. Fiddling and dancing swell all the village halls. Even the food tastes different; for example "bere bannocks" are made from a grain grown only in Orkney, and lamb in Harris and Lewis has a special sweetness caused by the heather in the sheepfeed. Best of all are the island people, who welcome you into their lives unquestioningly.

Airports in Lewis, Skye, Orkney, and Shetland are a thrill to set down at because of the comprehensive overviews you get of famous landscapes. Rentable cars get snapped up fast, so make sure you book yours before touchdown. Or, for a flat fee, you can buy a *Travelpass,* providing 7 days' or 13 days' unlimited travel through the Scottish Islands and Highlands by train, bus, and ferry. For more information contact *Hi-Line,* Bridgend, Dingwall, Ross-shire (phone: 0349-63434) or *Britrail Travel International,* 630 Third Ave., New York, NY 10017 (phone: 212-599-5400). Sea and air links are detailed below for each island individually under the name of the island. So are addresses of main tourist offices, where you should go for additional sightseeing advice. Hotels listed as expensive will charge about $90 and up for bed and breakfast for two; moderate ones, from $60 to $90; and inexpensive ones, under $60. A meal for two in an expensive restaurant will cost $45 or more; in a moderate one, $30 to $45; in an inexpensive one, less than $30.

ARRAN

Just 14 miles off Ayrshire's shore, Arran has nine charming villages, no towns, and only three roads, one of which skirts in a circle a ravishing 60-mile coastline. A schizophrenic terrain, full of craggy Highland hills in the north but lush lowland farms and winsome little resorts in the south, makes the island a miniature Scotland. Arran's climate is comparatively dry and warm (here and there palm trees kiss the breeze) and every summer families arrive for idyllic low-key holidays. Jukeboxes, casinos, and chromium-fronted fish and chip shops are rare; 2-year-olds on beaches with buckets and spades are prolific.

The chief villages, all by the sea, are Whiting Bay, Lamlash, Corrie, Lochranza, and Brodick. From Whiting Bay you can walk inland to the beautiful 140-foot Glenashdale Falls. Lamlash was a naval base till World War I and is now an educational and administrative center. Corrie with its adorably dinky harbor is the prettiest hamlet on Arran, while northerly Lochranza, dwarfed by a semicircle of most of Arran's spectacular over-2,000-foot peaks, is dramatically stark. Brodick is the island's main port and biggest tourist haunt; it's guarded by the soaring presence of Mt. Goatfell and has an entrancing *cladach* (old fishing wharf).

Brodick Castle and Gardens are owned by the National Trust for Scotland, which also owns 7,000 acres nearby, including the lovely Glen Rosa. The castle is an ancestral seat of the Dukes of Hamilton and contains fine silver, porcelain, pictures, and trophies. The Duchess of Montrose founded its opulent rhododendron garden in 1923 and its formal garden dates from 1710 (1½ miles north of Brodick Pier; open afternoons May through September, plus Monday, Wednesday, and Saturday afternoons in April and the first half of October). Lochranza Castle in Lochranza is a picturesque 16th-century ruin with two square towers (the key is with the custodian at his house, Croft Bank). Lochranza is only one of three places on Arran visited by Robert the Bruce — the others are King's Cross by Whiting Bay, where he embarked for the mainland in 1307 on the slow boat to Scottish independence, and King's Cave, 2 miles north of Blackwaterfoot on the west coast (you have to walk it), a possible site of the legendary spider incident.

Isle of Arran Heritage Museum, in an 18th-century croft on Brodick's northern edge, includes a smithy who occasionally demonstrates the art of horseshoeing; it's open Mondays through Saturdays, May through September (phone: 0770-2636). Near Kilmory village on the south coast are the Neolithic Kilmory Cairns, while the Standing Stones of Machrie Moor, a complex of six 15-foot Bronze Age megalithic circles, rise skyward on Moss Farm Road just south of westerly Machrie Bay; try to see them at sunset. Folklore maintains they supported the giant Fingal's cooking pot.

Details of fishing, sailing, deep-sea diving, golf, swimming, pony trekking, hiking, and hill-walking are available from the Tourist Information Centre on Brodick Pier (phone: 0770-2401). The center also issues a comprehensive guide to Arran's crafts shops. Boat trips to Holy Island across Lamlash Bay (Wednesdays and Thursdays, Easter through October) give you a gander at a 12th-century fort, St. Molios's Well (St. Molios was an Irish missionary), and a pleasant nature reserve. You can buy locally produced mustard at the Arran Mustard factory shop in Lamlash (phone: 07706-606).

Festivals are Arran's long suit: there's a *Music Festival* (in February/March), a *Sea Angling Festival* (in May), the *Goatfell Race* (May) and *Fiddlers' Rally* (June), a steady stream of assorted small festivals at Brodick Castle all summer long, the *Brodick Sheepdog Trials* (June), the *Heather Queen Gala* (in July), the *Arran Riding Club Horse Show* (July or August), *Lamlash Laughabout Week* (July), *Whiting Bay Fun Week* (July), the *Lam-*

lash Horticultural and Agricultural Shows (in August), the *Corrie Capers,* with family events like puppet and dog shows (August), and the *Brodick Highland Games* (August).

Several car ferries go daily from Ardrossan on the mainland to Brodick; space should be reserved on summer weekends. During the tourist season, there's a route (about ten sailings a day) from Claonaig on Kintyre to Lochranza. For further information, contact *Caledonian MacBrayne Ltd.,* Ferry Terminal, Gourock, Scotland (phone: 0475-34531). Ask about their special deals called Hebridean Drive-Away, Island Hopscotch, and Car Rover Tickets; these could save you money.

CHECKING IN: ***Anchrannie Country House*** – Set in its own country park, this secluded, sumptuously elegant hotel has an undeniably holiday flair, with 12 bedrooms, antique-style furniture, and a tea room in a conservatory. Brodick (phone: 0770-2234). Expensive.

Lagg – The setting here is lovely, with gardens, a secluded beach, and a river full of salmon. There are 15 rooms. Regional specialties, including fresh salmon and venison, are served in the restaurant. Closed November through March. On the south end of Arran at Lagg (phone: 077087-255). Moderate.

Glenisle – Opened in December 1986, the motto of this 17-room, family-run establishment is, "We treat people as we would expect to be treated ourselves." A wide choice of Scottish/European–style food is served in a traditional dining room (with open hearth fire). It has earned a good reputation in a short time. Closed in November. Lamlash (phone: 07706-258). Moderate to inexpensive.

Kingsley – Real beer in the bar makes this modest 27-room seafront affair a worthy bet. Closed November through February. Brodick (phone: 0770-2226). Inexpensive.

EATING OUT: ***Carraig Mhor Eating House*** – A popular bayside restaurant with a homey air, converted from a dwelling. Seafood at lunch, full dinners at night. Lamlash (phone: 07706-453). Expensive to moderate.

Nags Inn – A former coach house, with an inventive menu. On A841 at the south end of Whiting Bay (phone: 07707-283). Inexpensive.

SKYE

Skye is a large island with six peninsulas, a coastline of sparkling sea lochs, and countless fabulous panoramas. Traditionally it has belonged to the clans Macdonald and Macleod. Set very close to the most isolated parts of the West Highlands (herdsmen used to swim cattle across the narrow strait of Kyle Rhea from Skye to the mainland at low tide), it has a population of only 7,000.

On Skye's south shore are the legendary, oft-climbed Cuillins, a high mountain range whose tops Sorley Maclean described rhapsodically as "exact and serrated blue ramparts." In some lights they look black — like the teeth of a black saw blade. Their strange shape is the result of basalt dykes seeping into a hard underlayer of gabbro. Just west of the Cuillins is the lovely lochside campsite Glen Brittle; northeast is Glen Sligachan, whose inn was visited in 1773 by James Boswell and Samuel Johnson (see *Checking In*). Bonnie Prince Charlie had popularized Skye by fleeing to it after Culloden in company with Flora Macdonald, a brave Skye native, disguised as Flora's maid; Boswell and Johnson met Flora 27 years later and wrote a tribute to her, enshrined today on a Celtic cross in Kilmuir Churchyard near the island's north tip.

Oak, birch, willow, and hazel grace most of Sleat, Skye's southernmost peninsula. The Aird of Sleat, below the village of Ardvasar, is barren, but its view across Sleat Sound to Mallaig is a wow! Lava flows and landslips have caused the phantasmagoric moss-dappled marvels on the basaltic northern peninsula of Trotternish, including the Old Man of Storr, a 160-foot obelisk well over 2,000 feet above the sea (a 3-to-4-hour climb from your car); the Kilt Rock; and the weird, pinnacled Quirang. Don't miss traveling the small corkscrew road from the Quirang to the Trotternish west coast.

Give equal time to castles and villages: Knock Castle on Sleat, with a vista across Knock Bay to the mainland territory of Knoydart, is a ruined Macdonald stronghold; so is Dunscaith Castle at blissful Tokavaig on Sleat's opposite side, and Duntulm Castle near the tip of Trotternish. Castle Moil ("The Roofless Castle"), a welcoming beacon for voyagers by ferry to the Skye pier at Kyleakin, was a keep of the Mackinnon clan. Armadale Castle, north of Ardvasar, was a 19th-century Gothic mansion and family seat of the Macdonald chiefs, Lords of the Isles; nowadays, in summer it's a clan Donald museum, congenial tea room, and bookshop loaded with stuff about Skye (phone: 04714-227). Dunvegan Castle, on northwesterly Loch Dunvegan, is the island's only remaining stately home, the 700-year-old abode of the Macleods (open Easter through mid-October; phone: 047022-206). Villages to see are Portree, Skye's harbor and capital, where you can shop and mail postcards (have a bun from *Mackenzie's Bakery* in the main square, too); Stein, a dreamy shell of an 18th-century fishing settlement on the Vaternish peninsula beside lavish fields of sweet wild orchids; Carbost, fermenting ground of the incomparable Talisker whisky, on a forgotten corner of the Minginish peninsula; and Broadford and Elgol, at opposite ends of the majestic A881 past the Red Hills and Mt. Blaven on the island's lower wing. Beautiful Elgol, from which Bonnie Prince Charlie left Scotland forever, has boat trips across Loch Scavaig into Loch Coruisk, a favorite subject of Romantic painters, hemmed in like a mighty well by the Cuillins. For more information contact the boatman Mr. MacKinnon, 1 Glasnakille (phone: 04716-242).

The *Skye Museum of Island Life* near Kilmuir Churchyard is one of three folk museums on Skye (open Easter through October); another is the Skye Black House on Loch Dunvegan (open Easter through September). Glendale, not far from the Black House, has a tempting lineup of crafts shops. There's a permanent display on the history of the bagpipes at Boreraig, also on Loch Dunvegan (open Easter through September).

Tourist Board offices in Broadford, open May through November (phone: 04712-361) and Meall House, Portree, open year-round (phone: 0478-2137), have information about climbing and hiking, swimming, fishing, golf, pony trekking, bird-watching, sailing, cruising, and dinghy excursions. En route to the neighboring island of Raasay you can see seals, porpoises, and (with luck) bottle-nosed whales. The Portree Highland Games and Dunvegan Piping Competition both take place in August.

Ferries leave the mainland for Skye from Mallaig (in summer), from near Glenelg (in summer), and from Kyle of Lochalsh. Details from Caledonian

MacBrayne (except for the Glenelg run, owned by M. A. Mackenzie; phone: 059-982-224). *Loganair* operates flights from Glasgow to Broadford (phone for details: 041-889-3181, or call Glasgow Airport at 041-887-1111).

CHECKING IN: ***Kinloch Lodge*** – This is the lovely home of Lord and Lady Macdonald (who will immediately insist that you call them Godfrey and Claire). From the 10 cheery, individually decorated guestrooms to the excellent homecooked meals to the relaxed conversation with other guests before a crackling fire, a stay here is supremely pleasant. Closed in February. Sleat, Isle Ornsay (phone: 04713-333). Expensive.

Sconser Lodge – A 16-room, gabled hunting lodge, featuring a steak bar, a private boat for guests, and sweeping views. At Sconser, on A850 north of Broadford (phone: 047852-333). Expensive.

Rosedale – The only hotel in Portree situated on the waterfront. The building is an amalgamation of three fishermen's houses dating from the 1830s. It makes an attractive setting for a visit. There are 23 rooms, each with a private bath. Portree (phone: 0478-2531). Expensive to moderate.

Coolin Hills – Situated on its own grounds and overlooking Portree Bay, this old Victorian mansion used to be a hunting lodge of the Macdonald clan. All its 26 rooms have the facilities of a first class hotel. Closed October through April. Portree (phone: 0478-2003). Moderate.

Eilean Iarmain – Unique in its Gaelic-ness — there's a Gaelic-speaking staff, and Gaelic menus — this 13-room hotel, owned and run by an Edinburgh banker who has also established on Skye a thriving Gaelic college, proffers the local whisky, *Té Bheag.* The food is excellent. Isle Ornsay (phone: 04713-332). Moderate.

Skeabost House – Built in Victorian times, and beautifully set at the southernmost tip of a sea loch, this 27-room hostelry is one of the finest on Scotland's islands. The furniture is antique, log fires blaze on the hearth, and the restaurant serves interesting local dishes. Closed November through March. Skeabost Bridge (phone: 047032-202). Moderate.

Sligachan – Travelers, aristocrats, painters, anglers, and climbers have been packing out this famous 23-room landmark for over 200 years. A fascinating logbook documenting first ascents of the Cuillins is on show. Closed November through February. Junction of A850 and A863 at Glen Sligachan (phone: 047852-204). Moderate.

Broadford – Also in business over 200 years, the dining room at this serviceable old 28-room favorite exhibits a 4-foot Drambuie bottle honoring a past chef who invented the stuff for the Bonnie Prince. Broadford (phone: 04712-205). Moderate to inexpensive.

Stein Inn – Right by Loch Bay, this quaint and beckoning 6-room edifice at the outer edge of civilization is one of the most romantic hostelries on Skye. Stein, on the Waternish peninsula (phone: 047083-208). Inexpensive.

EATING OUT: ***Glenview Inn*** – This traditional Scottish-French restaurant has won the "Taste of Scotland" award for its cuisine. On the Staffin road (A855), 13 miles north of Portree (phone: 047062-248). Expensive.

Three Chimneys – Scallops, crab, salmon, and trout are specialties at this white-washed cottage restaurant decorated with propped-up wagon wheels. Colbost, beside the *Black House Museum* (phone: 047081-258). Expensive to moderate.

Three Rowans – Also a candlemaker's shop, this inviting hilltop dining-cum-tea room has a native Skye cook and three aged rowans outside to ward off evil (planted in the days when rowan trees had magic powers). Kildonan, near Edinbane on the Portree-Dunvegan road (phone: 047082-286). Inexpensive.

HARRIS

So unspoiled and deserted is Harris, 40 miles off Scotland's northwest coast, that the Scottish Tourist Board lists only one Harris entry in its booklet *1001 Things to See in Scotland.* That entry is St. Clement's Church, a cruciform building dating from about 1500 (restored in 1873) at Rodel on the island's southern tip. The exquisite carved stonework behind a Macleod chief's tomb shows the Twelve Apostles, a stag hunt, and an angel and devil weighing souls of the dead. Rodel itself is a tiny hamlet with clean-looking cottages and a pond ringed by slopes of mushrooms and wild blue irises. The key to St. Clement's Church is at the *Rodel* hotel.

North Harris is full of mountains, eight of which exceed 2,000 feet; according to geologists these peaks are so old they antedate the separation of the continental land mass from Britain and Ireland and make parvenus of the Alps. Also on Harris are gleaming beaches, green seas, and, on lucky days, a still, clear air bright with the songs of birds. There are ranging moors with no roads; the whole atmosphere is primitive; the only real village — a one-streeter — is Tarbert. On the east coast are rocky shores verdant with "lazy beds," thin half-arable plots once tilled by crofters driven off richer lands in the west. The west coast has the almost Mediterranean sands of Luskentyre and Hushinish.

Your Harris survival kit should contain ordnance maps, sandwiches, dubbined boots, midge repellent, whisky, binoculars, and your own angling equipment if you fish (fishing tackle is hard to come by on Harris). Bathing suits will be useful only if you like swimming in temperatures not usually above 55F.

Tarbert is a picturebook townlet with general stores, a harbor, and a vast public vegetable patch full of strutting roosters. The Harris tourist office is in Tarbert (phone: 0859-2011). Harris Tweed jackets for sale dangle from hangers on the outer walls of brightly painted corrugated-iron Tarbert sheds (you can also buy Harris Tweeds in Stornoway, or by the yard — about $6 per yard — from the weavers themselves in Drinishader on the coast farther south). Hard-wearing, made from the wool of Harris sheep, this world-famous fabric was, until recently, hand-spun, hand-dyed, and handwoven on antiquated looms producing only an old-fashioned, narrow cloth length. Today, a Miss Campbell of Plockropool (the village above Drinishader) is the only Harris native who still spins and dyes by hand, though handweaving continues apace.

Toe Head, the outermost point of the small peninsula northwest of Rodel (served by a sand track), is a wilderness full of golden eagles, sheep, and the distinctive and beautiful *machair,* a beach grass vibrant with a species of pale wildflower found only on Hebridean dunes. The trail from B887 past Mt. Uisgnaval More to Loch Voshimid, about 12 miles round-trip on foot, is in some weathers very eerie: it's the setting for J. M. Barrie's play *Mary Rose,* about a mysterious, mist-enshrouded, disappearing maid. *An Clachan,* at Leverburgh on A859, northwest of Rodel, is Harris's main center for local crafts (phone: 085982-370).

Ferries dock at Tarbert from Skye's port of Uig. Details from *Caledonian MacBrayne Ltd.,* Ferry Terminal, Gourock, Scotland (phone: 0475-34531).

CHECKING IN: ***Scarista House*** – Once a manse, this delightful 7-room hotel, near Scarista beach, still has a fine library that's open to residents. Although there's no bar, liquor can be served at the table. Closed November through March. 15 miles southwest of Tarbert on the A859 (phone: 085985-238). Expensive.

Harris – This faithful 24-room standby lacks the refinement of *Scarista House* but is a reasonable (and more accessible) eatery, drinkery, and sleepery. Tarbert (phone: 0859-2154). Moderate to inexpensive.

Ardvourlie Castle – Indescribably romantic, this 4-room gabled house is set on a deserted moor with portentous mountains looming over it. No private baths. At Ardvourlie, north of Tarvert on Loch Seaforth (phone: 0859-2307). Inexpensive.

Rodel – Unchanged since the 17th century (there are fascinating antiques everywhere including, in the boudoirs, wee wooden washbasins), this former great house has passed from an aristocratic family to Jock McCallum, host extraordinaire and distiller of Royal Household, the smooth-as-silk house whisky. Jock recently handed the business down to his son, who closed it for modernization and expects to reopen this year. The pub is open, however. Check before you visit. Rodel (phone: 0859-82210). Inexpensive.

LEWIS

Lewis adjoins Harris, making the combined island 95 miles in length. Lewis is the upper partner. It consists of marshy peat bogs and a coastline dappled with 25 beaches.

Its center is Stornoway, the only actual town in the Outer Isles. Stornoway has a charming landlocked harbor with a large, tame colony of inquisitive gray seals — you can watch them from the pier along with the nostalgic spectacle of colorful homeward-bound fishing boats. Churches are everywhere, as befits a locale so Sabbath-conscious you can't even buy cigarettes from a machine on Sundays; neither shall ye drink in hotels ye aren't staying at. There's a pleasant square with an attractive town hall and a huddle of gracious houses on a hill. The *Stornoway Gazette,* with news of local events, comes out on Thursdays. Key shops are *Loch Erisort Woollens* on Cromwell St., and *Lewis Crofters* (for outdoor gear), on Island Rd.

The A858 west from Stornoway has Lewis's main attractions including the Standing Stones of Callanish, an elaborate setting of megaliths, unique in Scotland, running Stonehenge a close second; Dun Carloway Broch, a well-preserved 30-foot Iron Age tower; the *Shawbost Museum* and Mill illustrating old Lewis folkways (open April through November; closed Sundays); and the Black House Village, a clachan, or adjoining series of traditional thatched-roofed huts, now operated as a tourism gimmick — these were inhabited till 1960! Lews Castle Gardens on the west side of Stornoway harbor are worth a visit; so is St. Moluag's, a restored 12th-century Episcopal church with regular Sunday services at the village of Eoropie, near the Butt of Lewis, the island's north tip (apply to the general store in the village for the key). On the Eye Peninsula to Stornoway's east is Ui Chapel, a picturesque ruin of a former priory in the burying ground of the Lewis Mcleod chiefs. *An Lanntair,* the Western Isles' first permanent art gallery, is on the second floor of Stornoway Town Hall. It has changing exhibitions in both English and Gaelic. Open Mondays through Saturdays. No admission charge (phone: 0851-3307).

The Lewis tourist office is at 4 South Beach St., Stornoway (phone: 0851-3088); here you can get advice on sailing, fishing, golf, hiking (the remote western parish of Uig is a good place), and bird-watching (Tiumpan Head on the Eye Peninsula has a burgeoning rabble of petrels and kittiwakes). The tourist office has a leaflet detailing Hebridean crafts and craftshops: consider buying a handmade set of Lewis Chessmen, modeled on four ancient sets discovered under Uig sands in 1831. Scandinavian in design, carved from walrus tusks and stained red on one side, the originals are thought to have been buried in the 12th century by a shepherd after he murdered a merchant sailor whose ship, carrying the chessmen, ran aground. Museums in London and Edinburgh have the originals today.

Sea-angling competitions are a highlight of Stornoway summers, with the Western Isles and the Highlands and Islands Open Boat Championships in July or August.

Ferries to Stornoway are from Ullapool on the northwest Scottish mainland: for further information contact Caledonian MacBrayne (don't forget you can drive right into Lewis from Harris). British Airways flies to Stornoway from Glasgow and Inverness.

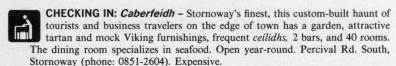

CHECKING IN: ***Caberfeidh*** – Stornoway's finest, this custom-built haunt of tourists and business travelers on the edge of town has a garden, attractive tartan and mock Viking furnishings, frequent *ceilidhs,* 2 bars, and 40 rooms. The dining room specializes in seafood. Open year-round. Percival Rd. South, Stornoway (phone: 0851-2604). Expensive.

Seaforth – A 56-room downtown establishment with a nightly movie, disco, and cabaret. Open year-round. James St., Stornoway (phone: 0851-2740). Expensive.

Crown – Hospitality is an important feature of this fine hotel overlooking the harbor and the pier. Each of the 15 rooms has a private bath. Open year-round. Castle St., Stornoway (phone: 0851-3734). Moderate.

County – A warm welcome is assured in this centrally located, family-run hotel with traditional pine-paneled interior design and 11 rooms. Open year-round. Francis St., Stornoway (phone: 0851-3250). Moderate to inexpensive.

ORKNEY

Orkney comprises about 70 islands, some 29 of which are inhabited. Throughout the whole cluster lie chambered cairns, traces of 78 brochs, rings of standing stones, and vestiges of prehistoric villages. Many are extensive survivals, making Orkney the archaeological treasure house of Great Britain.

Several pre-Pictish peoples lived on Orkney, then Picts, then Vikings. Strangely none of the races they conquered are mentioned by the Vikings in their remarkable medieval epic and folk history, the *Orkneyinga Saga,* a product of Orkney's Golden Age. A fine long literary tradition of which the *Saga* is part stretches even to America: Washington Irving's father was an Orkney sailor and James Russell Lowell's forebears included two Orcadian clans.

More sunshine bathes Orkney (and Shetland) than almost anywhere else in Britain, and there are bright-hued farmhouses, green fields, primroses, violets, golden sands, and clifftop sea-pinks. Fulmars, cormorants, Manx shearwaters, petrels, gulls, kittiwakes, guillemots, puffins, and gannets abound. On country strolls watch out for bulls. Hotels should be booked several months in advance; so far Orkney seems oblivious to the lucrative potential of tourism, and accommodations are few.

Orkney's two centers of civilization are Stromness and Kirkwall on the largest island, the so-called Mainland. Stromness, in the west (Kirkwall is in the east), is a small 18th-century port that hasn't changed since its founding; it's full of charm and has a main street that snakes along the sea. The *Pier Arts Centre* on Victoria St. in Stromness contains an internationally famous display of works by Ben Nicolson and Barbara Hepworth (closed Sundays except in June, July, and August, and Mondays); the *Stromness Museum,* 52 Alfred St., has a curio collection that derives from local history; closed Thursday afternoons except during July and August; also closed Sundays and during February. *Stromness Books and Prints* on Graham Place is well worth a browse (limited hours).

Kirkwall is Orkney's capital, site of St. Magnus Cathedral, Orkney's pride. The cathedral is an impressive 12th-century pink sandstone Norman building still in use, the burial place of St. Magnus, Orkney's patron saint. Take it easy in Kirkwall's ancient streets, which wind narrowly and look illusively like pedestrian precincts — till cars belt down them full throttle! A thriving stone-built town with crow-stepped gabled houses and magnificently old-fashioned shops painted berry and peach, Kirkwall also encompasses Earl Patrick's Palace, the imposing remains of an accomplished piece of Renaissance architecture belonging originally to a wicked Stewart earl, a nephew of Mary Queen of Scots; the Bishop's Palace, a 13th-century ruin with an ascendable 16th-century round tower; Tankerness House, a 16th-century merchant-laird's mansion and museum — sometimes with guest exhibitions — of 4,000 years of Orkney life (closed Sundays, except Sunday afternoons, May through September); the Highland Park Distillery, which has recently opened a visitors' center, gives tours of its nearly 200-year-old special processes (and free sips of its whisky), Mondays through Fridays, Easter through September, and at 2:30 PM on Tuesdays, Wednesdays, and Thursdays in March and October; *Robert Towers's Workshop* at Rosegarth, St. Ola (phone: 0856-3521), a manufacturer of traditional Orcadian tall-backed, straw-weave chairs. Behind Kirkwall on Wideford Hill the view is a superb pastiche of bays and islets.

In a knot in mid-Mainland near the Harray and Stenness lochs are three venerable marvels: Maeshowe, the Standing Stones of Stenness, and the Ring of Brodgar. Maeshowe, the finest chambered cairn in western Europe, was constructed around 1800 BC, and is entered on hands and knees by a narrow downward-sloping tunnel. Viking marauders wrote the runic inscriptions in the cells. In midwinter, dusk's last shaft of sunlight strikes one of the dark entombing walls, as it has done for untold centuries, a deeply moving sight with a mystic suggestion of resurrection. The Standing Stones of Stenness — four are still upright — are part of a circle of 3000 BC; the Ring of Brodgar, 340 feet in diameter, boasts 36 stones of its original 60. Also on the Mainland are: Skara Brae, a neolithic complex with a paved courtyard, covered passages, and 10 one-room houses full of "built-in" stone furniture (life here came to an end when a sandstorm blanketed all, sometime after 4500 BC); Gurness Broch, over 10 feet high, surrounded by stone huts and inhabited well into Viking times; Click Mill, the only operative example of old-style horizontal-wheeled Orkney water power (wear rubber boots, it's in a bog); *Corrigall Farm Museum* showing old Orkney folkways (open April through September); and Birsay, a quaint village with another ruined palace of the Stewart earls. Opposite Birsay is the Brough of Birsay, an adorable island and beachcombers' delight accessible only at low tide, where you'll find the remains of a Romanesque church and of Pictish and Nordic settlements.

Hoy, Orkney's most romantic island, is famous for its strange offshore rock formation, the Old Man of Hoy, a supreme test for rockclimbers. Hoy has hills, gaunt high cliffs, and wild unpopulated valleys. There's only one road, along the east coast, passing the martello towers built in 1812 against attack by American ships. Attainable by tramping inland is panoramic Ward Hill, Orkney's highest point at 1,565 feet, near the site of a supposedly haunted *neolithic* sepulcher called the Dwarfie Stone — this overlooks the beautiful half-deserted hamlet of Rackwick, Peter Maxwell Davies's home. If you go to Hoy, take a picnic; there's almost nowhere to buy food.

The island of South Ronaldsay is another good place to go, completely different from Hoy; you can drive to it from near Kirkwall via the island-hopping Churchill Causeway, erected in 1939-40 to protect the adjacent waterway of Scapa Flow, then a naval base. En route at the island of Lamb Holm is the ornate Italian Chapel, built from a mere Nissen hut by Italian World War II prisoners and affectionately preserved to this day by admiring Orcadians. It was in Scapa Flow in 1916 that Lord Kitchener's ship, the *Hampshire,* was blown up with him on board, and there 3 years later that the German Fleet of World War I heroically scuttled itself. Hoxa Head, the entrance to Scapa Flow, is a fascinating surreal jumble of half-sunk hulks and wartime concrete barriers. A brisk trade in boat hire and deep-sea-diving equipment rental has sprung up around this maritime graveyard; ask at the tourist offices for more information. Also on South Ronaldsay is St. Margaret's Hope, an idyllic coastal settlement popular with artists and craftsmen, an excellent place to shop for handmade goods. The *Wireless Museum,* exhibiting wartime communications, is open April through September.

Other islands are alluring, too: northerly Westray has Noltland Castle, a prepossessing 16th-century relic; Wyre near the Mainland has 12th-century Cobbie Row's Castle, the earliest authenticated castle in Scotland (it's mentioned in the *Orkneyinga Saga*), and nearby St. Mary's Chapel of the same date; ruin-rich Rousay, the "Egypt of the North" beyond Wyre, has bicycles for hire and boat trips to Egilsay, another island, where St. Magnus was murdered (there's part of a fine medieval church on Egilsay). Sanday, well north of the Mainland near Westray, is seal country, a place full of beaches to take kids and has sales in *The Wool Hall* (in the evenings) of goods made by the Sanday Knitters, a women's cooperative. The goods can also be seen and purchased by appointment (phone: 08575-367).

Tourist Board offices in Broad St., Kirkwall (phone: 0856-2856) and the Ferry Terminal Building, Stromness (phone: 0856-850716) have data on the rest of Orkney's islands and archaeology and on interesting natural features you can explore — most of the latter have intriguing names (Yesnaby Cliffs, Brinkie's Brae, St. John's Head, the Gloup of Deerness, the Barrel of Butter). Also available are tips on fishing, golf, deep-sea diving, crafts (potters are plentiful), walks, sailing, swimming, bird-watching, and island-to-island travel. Many British seafowl nest in Orkney (the season is May-July); their favorite places include the deserted islands of Copinsay and Eynhallow, the Mainland cliffs at Marwick, and the bird reserve on Westray at Noup Head. Local events are published Thursdays in the *Orcadian.*

Twice a winter Kirkwall's annual Ba' Games are played (they're just like the Jedburgh ones — see the *Southeast Lowlands* route). Other orgies are the internationally important *St. Magnus Festival of the Arts* in June; Kirkwall's County Show, a major agricultural fair in August; the *Orkney Folk Festival* in late May; and *Stromness Shopping Week* in July, when all Orkney comes to Stromness for 7 days of fêtes, dances, and general merriment.

A 2-hour car-ferry route links Stromness with Scrabster, near Thurso on the Scottish mainland. For details: P&O Ferries Terminal, Pierhead, Stromness (phone: 0856-850655); or P&O Ferries Terminal, Jamieson's Quay, Aberdeen (phone: 0224-572615). As well as regular services, including an 8-hour Aberdeen-to-Stromness crossing every Saturday, *P&O* offers special motorists' package tours. A new ferry company — *Orkney Ferries PLC* — runs a 45-minute crossing from Gills Bay, north of Wick on the Scottish mainland, to South Ronaldsay. For more details contact the Orkney terminal (phone: 0856-83343). British Airways flies every day but Sunday from Aberdeen and from Inverness to Kirkwall; details of other flights, including inter-island Orcadian puddle-jumps, are at Kirkwall Airport (phone: 0856-2421). Summer coach tours of major Orkney sights are organized by James Peace, Junction Rd., Kirkwall (phone: 0856-2866). Since opening in 1982, a new tour company called *Go Orkney* has been wowing visitors and locals alike with its upbeat style (6 Old Scapa Rd.; phone: Kirkwall 0856-4260).

CHECKING IN: ***Balfour Castle*** – The Zawadski family welcomes paying guests in their late-19th-century fantasy mansion. All the trimmings of Victorian romanticism are here — dark paneling, a huge staircase, big rooms with gold-etched period floral wallpapers, intriguing outbuildings, and an island setting. They also run boat trips. A real find. On Shapinsay across Shapinsay Sound from the Orkney mainland (phone: 0856-71282). Expensive.

Foveran – A comfortable, modern 8-room affair near Kirkwall, famous for its cuisine. Closed in November. St. Ola, overlooking Scapa Flow (phone: 0856-2389). Inexpensive.

EATING OUT: ***Hamnavoe*** – An extensive variety of international cuisine can be found at this spot. It has already found its way into various good food guides. Closed Thursdays and during January. 35 Graham Pl., Stromness (phone: 0856-850606). Expensive to moderate.

Creel – An award-winning establishment (the BTA's Best Scottish Restaurant for 1986), the dining room here overlooks the harbor and the open coal fire provides a cozy, intimate atmosphere. Serving dinner only, a wide choice of seafood, roasts, and venison is on the menu. Closed Mondays and Tuesdays and during January. St. Margaret's Hope, south of Kirkwall (phone: 0856-83311). Moderate.

Binnacle – You guessed it, the theme here is nautical. This restaurant, in the *Commodore* motel, serves a good selection of locally caught seafood and produce. Its steaks are notable, too. Open year-round. St. Mary's on Holm, south of Kirkwall (phone: 0856-78319). Moderate to inexpensive.

SHETLAND

"Ultima Thule" sounds like the name of a fashionable debutante, but in fact it's what the Romans called Shetland. Nothing lies between Shetland and the Arctic Circle. Lerwick, Shetland's capital, is much farther from Edinburgh than Edinburgh is from London; it's breached even from Kirkwall by a distance of over 60 miles. The famous north Shetland outpost, the Muckle Flugga Lighthouse, a remarkable feat of engineering poised on faces of sheer, almost vertical rock, is Britain's last window on the world (alas, it's not open to the public, but you get a good view of it from the coast).

Shetland's 100 islands (only 3 are of any size) are chilly even in summer. Winters are very dark but May, June, and July nights are aglow with the "simmer dim," a beautiful horizontal twilight lasting several hours, the next thing to a midnight sun — everything under its luminous rays looks phosphorescent. There are no rivers on Shetland, but sparkling streamlets, lily-bright lochans, and bays jeweled with waving sea-pinks. The sea is inescapable, for you can always see or hear it; Lerwick rises right out of it as if in a fairy tale — houses, stone steps, ramp-shaped flagstone alleys, and all; nets and fishing boats are everywhere and the raucous cry of seabirds splits the air (300 bird species nest in Shetland, lining up colony by colony on rock cliff shelves in a surreal cross between a supermarket and an aviary).

Traditionally it's said that an Orcadian is a farmer with a boat, whereas a Shetlander is a fisherman with a croft. This is still true, but North Sea oil has given Shetland an added dimension: coffers are bulging, Portakabin villages full of roustabouts have sprung up overnight, and there are symptoms of boomtown-ism like prostitution and black-marketeering. Sullom Voe, a waterway along the north Mainland (as in Orkney, the chief island is called the Mainland) serves a massive oil terminal covering a whole neck of land from sea to sea; helicopters carrying shiftmen whiz back and forth between offshore sites and Sumburgh Airport; tourists must battle riggers for rooms in Shetland's precious few hotels (reservations are vital). But around all this, life on the islands goes on as it has for generations, with great tracts of land given over to grazing the special small sheep that provide the wool for Shetlanders' famous sweaters.

Vikings dominated Shetland as long as 13 centuries ago, though other settlers were on the scene 1,000 years before that, as you'll see on the Mainland's south tip at Jarlshof, a fascinating sunken city with overlayers from three prehistoric civilizations. Orkney's archaeological treasures are older, but it's Shetland that clings to primitive forms: Shetland ponies are still reared on common landholdings, and Lerwick is in a way another Jarlshof with its arrow-thin streets, enclosing wharves, and snuggling clusters of stone homes and warehouses. Commercial Street, Lerwick's main thoroughfare, is anything but a boulevard — yet it has its own glamour.

In pre-Victorian days when half the fishing fleet of Holland put in at Shetland after sailing the North Sea, Lerwick was a smugglers' nest and an almost European city. Explore Shetland's history at the Shetland Museum, Lower Hillhead, Lerwick (closed Sundays). Other Lerwick attractions are Fort Charlotte, built in 1665 to protect the Sound of Bressay from the Dutch; the Lerwick Town Hall, a Scots-baronial building with stained-glass windows and a climbable tower; and Clickhimin Broch, an ancient 17-foot stronghold within the remains of an Iron Age stone fort. *The Shetland Workshop Gallery,* 4-6 Burns La., Lerwick, has native crafts for sale: sealskin handbags, silver and polished stone jewelry, sweaters, and Shetland shawls (the last, though large, warm, and sturdy, are so fine they can be drawn through a wedding ring).

Yell and Unst are the next biggest islands after the Mainland; they continue north from the Mainland in that order and are easily accessible. On Unst is Mu Ness Castle, constructed from rubble in the 16th century with an amazing eye for architectural detail. The prettiest Shetland islands are Bressay, Whalsay, Noss, Fetlar, Foula, the Out Skerries and Muckle Roe. Foula, 30 miles west of the Mainland, is the most isolated and therefore perhaps most exciting — it's served twice a week by a regular passenger line (no cars) and by *Loganair* (ask at the airstrip at Tingwall; phone: 0595-84246). But close your eyes, touch your map, and go where your finger falls! The islands are *all* pretty and there's no place you can't get by hiring a boatman, unless the weather's too rough — ask at the Lerwick tourist office, Market Cross (phone: 3434), or in outlying coastal pubs.

The tiny seal-haunted island of Mousa opposite Sandwick on the east Mainland (7 miles south of Lerwick) holds Mousa Broch, a princely 40 feet high, some say the best broch in Britain. To get ferried across (a 15-minute ride), phone Tom Jamieson at 09505-367. St. Ninian's Isle, not an island but a small south Mainland peninsula, is famous for white sands and the priceless 5th-century silver plate unearthed there on a Dark Age church site in 1958. Other Mainland must-sees are the *Croft Museum* of 19th-century Shetland life on the A970 at South Voe (open May through September; closed Mondays); the Ness of Burgi, an Iron Age defensive stone structure near the southern town of Sumburgh; and Stanleydale, a neolithic heel-shaped edifice containing an oval chamber, at the western hamlet of Walls. Ruined Scalloway Castle, a building dating from 1600 in a flamboyant corbel-turreted medieval style, overlooks Scalloway, the unbelievably picturesque west coast Mainland fishing village that once was Shetland's capital (the castle belonged at that time to the wicked Stewart earls prominent also in Orkney).

Geological wonders of Shetland, visitable by boat, include "Orkneymen's caves," narrow of entrance but inside grand like cathedrals (the best is the stalactited Cave of Bressay, and there are lots along the coast of the island of Papa Stour); the sea-filled, once natural-bridged Holes of Scrada on the Mainland's northwesterly Esha Ness peninsula (you view these on foot); the Grind of the Navir, also at Esha Ness, where waves have ripped off huge cubic rock hunks and carried them 180 feet; and the Bressay Giant's Leg (his other leg is said to be in Orkney and his body above you somewhere midway).

The Shetland tourist office (the one in Lerwick) has information on fishing, golf, deep-sea diving, hiking, crafts, and bird-watching. Unst is a good place to see Icelandic owls. Fetlar is now a 1,400-acre Statutory Bird Reserve; other ornithological havens are the islands of Foula, Noss, and Haaf Gruney, the Pool of Virkie on the Mainland's south tip, and Hermaness on Unst opposite the Muckle Flugga Lighthouse.

"Up Helly Aa," a dramatic boat-burning ceremony celebrating the return of the sun, dates from pagan times and is still performed in Shetland every January using traditional Viking costumes and boats; the *Viking International Festival* at Lerwick in September is a major sea-angling competition; a *Shetland Folk Festival* in late April or early May gives full rein to Shetland fiddlers, a breed admired and envied by all of musical Scotland; and the *Lerwick Midsummer Carnival* in mid-June features a parade of floats and dancing in the streets. The *Shetland Times,* published Fridays, has news of other events.

P&O Ferries runs an overnight route from Aberdeen directly to Lerwick, weekdays; on weekends it makes a stop at Orkney. Details from P&O. Flights into Shetland are frequent; *British Airways* goes from the major Scottish airports (there are at least four flights every weekday from Aberdeen alone) and from Kirkwall, and *Loganair* zooms direct daily to a small landing strip at Tingwall from Edinburgh.

CHECKING IN: ***Shetland*** – Situated directly opposite the ferry docks is Shetland's largest hotel, with 64 rooms. It contains all the facilities of a modern hotel, including a swimming pool, fitness center, solarium, and sauna. Open year-round. Lerwick (phone: 0595-5515). Expensive.

Busta House – This hotel's specialty is traditional Scottish food, but its location — in a splendid 400-year-old country house overlooking the picturesque Busta Voe fjord and harbor — is also special. It has the full range of private facilities in its 21 rooms. Open year-round. Brae (phone: 0806-22506). Moderate.

Grand – Recently modernized, this historic old building stands at the center of Lerwick. The 20 rooms contain private facilities. The hotel has a nightclub and a beauty salon. Open year-round. Lerwick (phone: 0595-2826). Moderate.

Queen's – This property has two things in common with the *Grand:* a central location and its phone number (the latter similarity seems to cause no problems). *Queen's* is an old-fashioned, comfortably appointed hotel. The sea washes against the building on two sides. Most of its 26 rooms overlook the Island of Bressay and have the full range of private facilities. Open year-round. Lerwick (phone: 0595-2826). Moderate.

St. Magnus – Another fine example of Shetland's many picturesque hotels. Built of pine and spruce in a traditional Scandinavian clapboard style, it overlooks St. Magnus Bay on one side and West Beach Bay on the other. Its 26 rooms all have private bath. The hotel's restaurant has won several awards for its outstanding Scottish cuisine. Open year-round. Hillswick (phone: 0806-23372). Moderate.

Sumburgh – Conveniently located near Sumburgh airport, this hotel is next to two sandy beaches and boasts its own birdwatching sanctuary. The 24 rooms all have standard private facilities, and the dining room specializes in seafood. Open year-round. Sumburgh (phone: 0950-60201). Moderate.

Baltasound – A 10-room hybrid that is, on the whole, more modern extension than grand old Victorian abode. There's a big bar with attractive local posters. Open year-round. Baltasound, Unst (phone: 095781-334). Inexpensive.

Westings – Another contemporary hostelry based on an old building but with a distinctly Scandinavian appeal, it has 6 rooms and a large new bar. The service is friendly, the food good, and the proprietors organize pony treks. Open year-round. Wormadale, near Whiteness, Mainland (phone: 059584-242). Inexpensive.

EATING OUT: *Burrastow House* – Set amid scenic beauty in a renovated building dating back to 1759, this excellent inn has a distinguished reputation for its traditional British cuisine: game, roasts, seafood, and vegetarian dishes. Open year-round. Walls (phone: 059571-307). Moderate.

Channel Islands

Geographically the Channel Islands, lying as little as 8 miles off the coastline of Normandy and Brittany, are close to France. But historically the islands — Jersey, Guernsey, Alderney, Sark, Herm, Jethou, and a smattering of islets — have been connected with the British Crown for more than a thousand years. They were part of the Duchy of Normandy when William the Conqueror invaded England in 1066 and became its king, and they remained part of Britain when Normandy was subsequently reunited with the rest of France.

This heritage has given the Channel Islands a curiously mixed identity — they are a sort of halfway house between England and France stuck out in the English Channel. Partly self-governing, and with a hodgepodge of English and French laws, they retain French as their official language yet universally speak English. They issue their own banknotes, coinage, and stamps, yet British currency is accepted. The food is French, but habits and manners are English.

The Channel Islands attract upward of 2 million tourists every year. Their popularity is partly due to the feeling of being "abroad" that the blend of cultures gives to both British and French visitors, partly due to their enviable sunshine record (about 100 miles south of the English mainland, they get the best of the weather), and partly because no two of the islands are the same and so offer visitors the opportunity to have one or several kinds of holiday. Jersey, the most southerly of the islands and also the largest (although it only measures 9 by 5 miles), has a reputation as a "swinging" holiday resort with a wide choice of hotels, restaurants, and entertainments. Quieter, centrally situated Guernsey, the other main island has turned from agriculture to tourism as its principal livelihood. And on the smaller islands there is little to do except eat, sleep, walk, and admire some stunning seascapes and cliff scenery.

The islanders have been molded both by history and by the surroundings in which they live. Calm, unhurried, contemplative, yet with a sharp sense of humor, they also have remarkably sophisticated taste when it comes to food and wine — the development of smart restaurants on wealthy Jersey or Guernsey may be due to the close proximity of France.

They couple this with an enthusiasm for their own dialect — a Norman-French patois that differs from island to island and can still be heard in the countryside and markets — and with an equal enthusiasm for their ancient traditions, the most famous of which is a legal oddity dating from the Norman period and known as the *Clameur de Haro.* There's no need to call an attorney if you feel that you are being legally wronged in Jersey or Guernsey — you just drop to your knees and shout: *"Haro! Haro! Haro! à l'aide, mon Prince, on me fait tort."* ("Help, my Prince, they are wronging me.") This has the same effect as a court injunction, but nowadays it is only used in cases of interference with real property. The penalties for ridiculing or abusing this ancient law are heavy.

Other island oddities include the ormer, a rubbery-fleshed shellfish related to the abalone but unique to the Channel Islands, which has a particularly attractive mother-of-pearl-like shell; and giant cabbages with stalks so long that walking sticks can be made from them. More practically, for souvenir hunters, there are the heavy-knit oiled wool sweaters known as "jerseys" and "guernseys," which have given their names to knitwear all over the world.

In recent years, Jersey and Guernsey have both made strenuous attempts to extend their tourist seasons. Both offer discounted, inclusive winter holidays at major hotels, and provide entertainment that often comes up to London standards. This trend is likely to continue because, as the islanders optimistically point out, the climate is similar to that of Bermuda and thus offers an escape from British winters.

Prospective visitors should also note, however, that because the islands are exposed to the Atlantic, the sea is colder than you might expect, and swimming is comfortable only between late May and late September. The islands are also subject to occasional dense sea mists that can disrupt air traffic. Such disadvantages, however, are easily outweighed by the exceptionally clean air.

Jersey has led the way in introducing new attractions such as a spring festival and an annual *Good Food Festival,* which encourages island restaurants to submit their culinary delights to be judged by both French and English gourmets. But the most popular carnival on both Jersey and Guernsey dates back to the 1902 coronation, the annual Battle of Flowers. This colorful and picturesque event, involving processions of floats decorated with flowers as well as other, less formal, celebrations, takes place in August and is the high spot of any visit.

Hotel prices throughout the Channel Islands range from $100 per person in places noted as expensive, to $50 to $80, moderate. Lodging costing less than $50 is considered inexpensive. An expensive dinner for two, without wine, drinks, or tips, begins at $55. A moderately priced meal will be in the $30 to $50 range, and anything below $25 is inexpensive.

JERSEY

Jersey, the largest of the Channel Islands, got its name from the Normans, who called it Gersey ("the grassy isle"). Between World War I and World War II it earned the nickname "honeymoon isle" because it had become so popular with newlyweds from the mainland. (Traditionally, March was the most popular time for honeymooning because couples who married at the end of the fiscal year could claim full tax allowances for the preceding year. Now, however, honeymooning is a year-round activity, and newlyweds even get a small gift from the local tourism department!)

It was during the interwar period that Jersey became less of an isolated farming community and more of a modern holiday resort. Initially, the main attractions then were the big, safe, sandy beaches, and the inexpensive accommodations. Today the beaches are unchanged, but now the island also boasts a sparkling nightlife as well as many fine shops, hotels, and restaurants. The tiny land area also offers some glorious woodland walks, exceedingly narrow but navigable roads bordered with brilliant blue and pink hydrangea, and lots of quiet countryside, particularly in the north, where grazing Jersey cattle and historic castles make interesting sightseeing.

The island's capital is the south coast port of St. Helier, which contains about half of Jersey's population. Built around the rather ugly — though recently improved — harbor, it is divided by a massive rock on which stands the Napoleonic Fort Regent — now converted into a comprehensive, all-weather entertainment, leisure, and sports complex complemented by a new marina frequented by visiting yachts. The town itself is a maze of narrow streets, some of them for pedestrians only and many having French names, with a big range of shops specializing in tax-free luxury goods.

Another plus for St. Helier is its location on one of Jersey's best beaches, St. Aubin's Bay. Elizabeth Castle is here, too, built on rocks in the 16th century and named after Queen Elizabeth I by Sir Walter Raleigh when he was governor of the island. On summer nights the castle is dramatically floodlit, and at low tide can be reached on foot by causeway; boats service the area at other times.

Five miles out of St. Helier on the east coast at Gorey there is another fine castle, Mont Orgueil. Built to defend Jersey against attacks by neighboring France, during the 13th to the 15th century, it is beautifully preserved and floodlit. Below the castle is the tiny fishing village of Gorey. It's worth exploring, if for nothing else than the popular, reasonably priced pub lunches.

After exploring the east coast, head for the north coast of the island, which is composed mostly of cliffs, hiding many small, sheltered beaches and tiny harbors. Walking here is a must, since there are fine views of the other islands as well as of France.

In contrast to the east coast, the west coast of the rectangular island consists almost entirely of St. Ouen's Bay, backed by sand dunes. Winter seas here, rolling in from the Atlantic, can be awesome. During the summer St. Ouen's is a popular beach so large that it's never crowded.

In addition to St. Aubin's Bay, the south coast has the island's most attractive bay, St. Brelade's, which has good recreational facilities as well as miles of sand. The nearby sheltered Portelet Bay is also popular. Those who tire of the beach will find an interesting little structure hidden beside St. Brelade's Church called the Fishermen's Chapel; it is an ancient monastic chapel with some parts of the structure dating back to the 6th century. It also has some recently discovered 14th-century murals on the walls (seen at their best in damp weather).

Visits are free to the island's chapels, old Norman churches, and more modern churches (the "glass church," at Millbrook, is lavishly decorated with glass by the Parisian artist René Lalique). But even the island's organized excursions are relatively inexpensive, and three of them are particularly worthwhile.

The first of these is *St. Peter's Bunker,* in the center of the island. This museum, housed in a 7-room German bunker, provides fascinating insight into the German occupation of the Channel Islands during World War II and shows how both occupiers and occupied lived during the war years. Open mid-March through October.

Far more ancient history is found at La Hougue Bie, one of Jersey's two best-preserved neolithic tombs. Visitors to the site, at Grouville, can creep down the 33-foot-long tunnel entrance to the tomb itself, where the temperature remains constant whatever the weather. The tomb is covered by a 40-foot-high mound on which two medieval chapels were constructed under a single roof. There are other historical displays on the grounds as well. Open Tuesdays through Sundays April through October.

Finally, one of Europe's most interesting zoos is on the grounds of Les Augrés Manor in the northeast of the island. Jersey Zoo is not the typical zoo dedicated to the display of animals or to entertainment, but to the preservation and rearing of some of the world's rarest and endangered species. Watch for the families of lowland gorillas, orangutans, Tibetan white-eared pheasants, and Egyptian bare-faced ibis.

Jersey has direct airline links with most British airports, and there are daily services to and from London — Heathrow, Stansted, and Gatwick — only 45 minutes away. There is also air transportation from France. British Channel Island Ferries has service from Poole to both Jersey and Guernsey (phone: 0202-681155). A number of firms specialize in inclusive holidays to the Channel Islands from Britain; these include *Preston Travel* (phone: 01-349-0311) and *Modernline Travel* (phone: 0534-35511).

CHECKING IN: ***L'Horizon*** – Nestled in St. Brelade's Bay, considered one of Europe's finest beaches, this 104-room hotel has its own indoor pool, solarium, and sauna. St. Brelade's Bay (phone: 0534-43101). Expensive.

Longueville Manor – A magnificently restored and elegantly furnished 34-room manor house, set on 15 acres. There is also a heated outdoor pool, riding stables, and a first-rate dining room. A member of the Relais & Châteaux Association. St. Helier (phone: 0534-25501). Expensive.

Water's Edge – At the bottom of a steep hill, beside the sea on the north coast, this handsome 51-room hotel is well away from the crowds and has a swimming pool. Bouley Bay (phone: 0534-62777). Moderate.

EATING OUT: ***Victoria's*** – A mock-Victorian restaurant in one of Jersey's period hotels, the *Grand,* overlooking the seafront, serving French nouvelle cuisine. Esplanade, St. Helier (phone: 0534-72255). Expensive.

La Capannina – Much favored by residents, this place specializes in Italian dishes. Halkett Pl., St. Helier (phone: 0534-34602). Moderate.

Granite Corner – Only 24 diners can be accommodated in this small building looking out over Rozel Harbour. Chef Jean-Luc Robin is a true master. Rozel Harbour, Trinity (phone: 0534-63590). Moderate.

GUERNSEY

The second largest of the Channel Islands, Guernsey is roughly triangular; its 5-mile-long east coast contains its two towns: the industrial port of St. Sampson, and the island's capital of St. Peter Port. The latter is a pretty town, built on a hillside overlooking the large harbor and the smaller islands of Sark, Herm, and Jethou. Like the other islands, Guernsey enjoys tax advantages, which makes shopping in the narrow, winding streets of St. Peter Port doubly appealing.

St. Peter Port is dominated by the town church, a granite building known as "the Cathedral of the Channel Islands," and by the medieval fortress of Castle Cornet, which overlooks the harbor. Castle Cornet saw action in the English Civil War, when the Royalist governor held it throughout a 9-year siege against a predominantly Cromwellian populace (the castle finally fell to the Parliamentary forces in 1651).

In addition to the castle and the church, St. Peter Port's most interesting building is Hauteville House, the 19th-century home of the French writer Victor Hugo who lived in exile in Guernsey from 1855 to 1870; it now belongs to the City of Paris, and is furnished and maintained just as it was in the eccentric Hugo's day. Hugo chose the house because of its fine views of the French coast. Open Mondays through Saturdays April through September.

With beaches on all three of its coasts, Guernsey can provide a sheltered bay whatever the direction of the wind. In good weather, the big, sandy beaches of the west coast are the best, particularly Cobo and Vazon, although swimmers should beware of the strong currents in places marked with danger flags. Children will like Portelet, a little harbor forming a tiny beach of its own within Rocquaine Bay. Lihou, a tiny islet, is offshore, as are the dangerous rocks of the Hanois, marked with a tall lighthouse.

There are several lovely walks along the picturesque south coast, which has a number of rocky headlands, towering cliffs, and good, sandy beaches — of these, Moulin Huet, Petit Bôt, Petit Port, and Saints Bay are the most popular. Visitors can stroll down to the beach along wooded paths beside streams known as "douits."

Although it's the beaches and cliffs that draw tourists, this is still predominantly a horticultural island, and much of the interior is given over to greenhouses in which early tomatoes and flowers are cultivated.

Many of the islanders' houses are notable for having "kitchen stones" sticking out from their chimneys. Guernsey was at one time a superstitious island, and legend says that passing witches will not curse a house if they can stop and warm themselves by the chimney.

Some of the parish churches on the island are Norman in origin. The sloping aisle of one of these, St. Pierre du Bois (St. Peter-in-the-Wood), has lead to a popular local joke that any bridegroom leaving the church after a wedding is already going downhill. Outside St. Martin's Church stands Guernsey's most famous resident, a prehistoric stone figure known as La Grandmère de Chimquiere or, more simply, La Grandmère. Locals do not pass La Grandmère without saying good morning to her.

Excursions on Guernsey are varied, and a circular coach tour of the island is interesting. You can get anywhere on the bus services radiating from St. Peter Port. But do not miss seeing the grim German Underground Hospital, a relic of the World War II occupation (open daily April through October and Sundays and Thursdays in November), or the shell-dotted Little Chapel at Les Vauxbelets, an 18-by-10-foot model of Our Lady of Lourdes shrine in France — big enough only for a priest and a congregation of two.

Guernsey has direct airline links with most British airports, and there are daily services to and from London (Heathrow, Stansted, and Gatwick) and Southampton. The islands' own Aurigny Airlines (based at Alderney Airport on Alderney island) provides a regular inter-island service as well as connections to Southampton and France. *British Channel Island Ferries* operates car ferries between Poole and Guernsey. *Condor* operates hydrofoil services between Weymouth and Guernsey (2 hours, 10 minutes). For package tours to Guernsey, contact the firms listed for Jersey.

CHECKING IN: ***La Frégate*** **–** Set on a hill above the harbor, this restored 18th-century manor house has a good restaurant (French, natch) and 13 modern rooms, most of which overlook the sea and the other Channel Islands. Les Cotils, St. Peter Port (phone: 0481-24624). Expensive.

Novotel **–** Guernsey's newest hotel, opened in 1988, overlooks Grand Havre Bay. Facilities include a heated outdoor pool (padded pool for toddlers), game room, and restaurant (open 6 AM to midnight). Les Dicqs, Vale (phone: 0481-48400). Expensive.

Old Government House **–** Once the town's principal hotel, it is still striving to retain that position by combining old-fashioned courtesy with 68 modern rooms and a pool. Ann's Pl., St. Peter Port (phone: 0481-24921). Expensive.

St. Pierre Park **–** Fast becoming the island's best, this smoothly run modern hotel has 133 rooms, tennis courts, 9-hole golf course designed by Tony Jacklin, swimming pool, sauna, solarium, and a host of other facilities. It's popular with business travelers as well as tourists. St. Peter Port (phone: 0481-28282). Expensive.

Le Chalet **–** A mile outside St. Peter Port, above a sheltered but stony beach, the 47-room *Le Chalet* offers a peaceful atmosphere, fine sea views, and a good restaurant. Closed in winter. Fermain Bay (phone: 0481-35716). Moderate.

Les Douvres **–** This restored 18th-century manor house on the south coast is within easy reach of St. Peter Port. There are 20 guestrooms and a heated swimming pool. St. Martins (phone: 0481-38731). Moderate.

Havel Court **–** A small, select, 12-room hotel in the quiet southern quarter of St. Peter Port, it has spectacular views over Havelet Bay, Castle Cornet, and the neighboring islands of Herm, Jethou, and Sark (phone: 0481-710110). Moderate.

EATING OUT: ***Le Nautique*** **–** A delightful harborside restaurant offering a wide choice of fish (taken live from their own tanks) and special meat dishes in season (phone: 0481-21714). Expensive.

Steak and Stilton **–** A popular seafront lunch spot, it's also nice in the evenings. The menu combines local fish dishes with those suggested by its name. Esplanade, St. Peter Port (phone: 0481-23080). Moderate.

ALDERNEY

Besides being the most northerly and the most barren of the Channel Islands, Alderney is often ignored by tourists. It's only about 3½ miles long and 1½ miles wide, and although it has a massive breakwater built as part of a Napoleonic military harbor, the port itself is a tiny one. Most of the population of only 1,700 live in or around the centrally situated town of St. Anne.

Hotel accommodation is usually available in all but the peak months, but can be expensive for what you get. For diversion there is sailing, windsurfing, tennis, squash, or simply walking alongside or swimming in one of the safe and sandy south coast bays. It's also possible to take a scenic steam locomotive ride on the Channel Island's only working railway between the two broad beaches of Braye and Longy.

Aurigny Airlines provides several flights a day from and to Southampton, and has frequent interisland flights from Guernsey and Jersey. There are also flights and a summer hydrofoil service to France, 8 miles away. The Condor hydrofoil operates between Alderney and Guernsey.

CHECKING IN/EATING OUT: ***Belle Vue*** – One of the largest hotels on the island, this family-run stopping place and restaurant is located close to the small town of St.Anne (phone: 048182-2844). Moderate.

Inchalla – Located on secluded grounds on the edge of St. Anne, the hotel offers a relaxed and informal atmosphere. The restaurant is renowned for its food and wines; a traditional roast luncheon is offered on Sundays (phone: 048182-3220). Moderate.

Moorings – Overlooking the sea and sandy beach of Braye Bay, the hotel offers bedrooms with TV sets and tea- and coffee-making facilities. Live jazz is performed at the bar most Sunday evenings. Restaurant. Open year-round (phone: 048182-2421). Moderate.

SARK

An unspoiled atmosphere and an extraordinary individuality are the hallmarks of the feudal island of Sark — a rocky plateau of an island 9 miles off the coast of Guernsey. Its constitution dates back to Elizabethan times, and it still has a hereditary ruler, called the Seigneur, who today is Mr. Michael Beaumont, son of the famous Dame of Sark and her American husband. Cars, divorce, adoption, and income tax are banned on the island, and the Seigneur retains such ancient feudal rights as that of being the only person on Sark who may keep pigeons (a rule designed to protect seed corn).

Sark is, in fact, the smallest state in Europe, which no doubt adds to its attraction for visitors. Several small bays and coves are good for swimming and sunbathing; Grande Grave is one of the most popular. There is no actual town and most tourists travel around by horse-drawn carriage (expensive) or hired bicycle (inexpensive) and visit tiny Creux Harbour; the 16th-century Seigneurie with its walled gardens; the two-man prison, Sark's only other noteworthy building; and the precipitous path known as La Coupée, where only 10 feet of soft rock and clay stops Sark from dividing itself into two islands.

There is a frequent ferry service from Guernsey, weather permitting, and summer excursions also run from Jersey.

CHECKING IN/EATING OUT: ***Aval du Creux*** – A family-run hotel, it is a favorite rendezvous for islanders and continental yachtsmen. Facilities include a heated pool and gardens floodlit at night. Closed during winter (phone: 048183-2036). Moderate.

Stocks – As one of the oldest established hotels on Sark, it has many links to the island's history. Facilities include a restaurant, swimming pool, comfortable lounge, and library with log-burning fires on chilly spring and autumn evenings. Closed during winter (phone: 048183-2001). Moderate.

HERM

The attractive little island of Herm, 3 miles off Guernsey's capital of St. Peter Port, belongs to Major Peter Wood, an ex-Army officer who leases and farms it. Roughly 1½ miles long and ½ mile wide, it is a Channel Island in miniature, with cliffs on its northern tip and long, sandy beaches to the south.

It's a very popular destination for day-trippers from Guernsey, but some visitors like to stay overnight because of the island's solitude. A pub, some shops, and the island's only hotel cluster around the harbor, and footpaths lead from there to the common, the beaches (Belvoir Bay, on the east coast, is the best), and the farm. Shell Beach, also on the east coast, is the most famous beach in the Channel Islands: Instead of sand, it is made up of millions of tiny shells washed up by the Gulf Stream — many of them originating in the Gulf of Mexico.

A frequent launch service operates from St. Peter Port, Guernsey, in summer; winter visitors are met by arrangement.

CHECKING IN: ***White House*** – An unpretentious yet comfortable hotel (the only one on the island), offering an unexpectedly high standard of service for so small an island. Several of its 32 rooms feature superb views and were so much in demand that 20 more were added in 3 cottages on the grounds. Self-catering cottages and family campsites are also available here. Closed November through April (phone: 0481-22159). Moderate.

JETHOU

This island, once the home of the English writer Sir Compton Mackenzie, is privately owned and cannot be visited.

INDEX

Index